CONVAIR B-36 PEACEMAKER
PILOT'S FLIGHT OPERATING INSTRUCTIONS

REVISION NOTICE

LATEST REVISED PAGES SUPERSEDE THE SAME PAGES OF PREVIOUS DATE

Insert revised pages into basic publication. Destroy superseded pages.

This publication replaces Safety of Flight Supplement T. O. 1B-36D(II)-1K. Supplements C, D, E, and F remain active as well as any new ones issued subsequent to K.

This handbook is incomplete without Confidential Supplement T. O. 1B-36D(II)-1A.

Commanders are responsible for bringing this technical publication to the attention of all Air Force personnel cleared for operation of affected aircraft.

PUBLISHED UNDER THE AUTHORITY OF THE SECRETARY OF THE AIR FORCE AND CHIEF OF THE BUREAU OF AERONAUTICS

©2010 Periscope Film LLC
All Rights Reserved
ISBN #978-1-935327-87-5   1-935327-87-9

T. O. 1B-36D(II)-1

FLIGHT HANDBOOK

USAF SERIES
B-36D-II
AIRCRAFT

Featherweight — Configuration II

REVISION NOTICE

LATEST REVISED PAGES SUPERSEDE THE SAME PAGES OF PREVIOUS DATE

Insert revised pages into basic publication. Destroy superseded pages.

This publication replaces Safety of Flight Supplement T. O. 1B-36D(II)-1K. Supplements C, D, E, and F remain active as well as any new ones issued subsequent to K.

This handbook is incomplete without Confidential Supplement T. O. 1B-36D(II)-1A.

Commanders are responsible for bringing this technical publication to the attention of all Air Force personnel cleared for operation of affected aircraft.

PUBLISHED UNDER THE AUTHORITY OF THE SECRETARY OF THE AIR FORCE AND CHIEF OF THE BUREAU OF AERONAUTICS

8 APRIL 1955
REVISED 18 MAY 1956

T.O. 1B-36D(II)-1

Reproduction for nonmilitary use of the information or illustrations contained in this publication is not permitted without specific approval of the issuing service (BuAer or USAF). The policy for use of Classified Publications is established for the Air Force in AFR 205-1 and for the Navy in Navy Regulations, Article 1509.

LIST OF REVISED PAGES ISSUED

INSERT LATEST REVISED PAGES. DESTROY SUPERSEDED PAGES.

NOTE: The portion of the text affected by the current revision is indicated by a vertical line in the outer margins of the page.

Page No.	Date of Latest Revision	Page No.	Date of Latest Revision	Page No.	Date of Latest Revision
*23	18 May 1956	295	13 January 1956	510	13 January 1956
*24	18 May 1956	302	13 January 1956	511	13 January 1956
*26	18 May 1956	303	13 January 1956	512	13 January 1956
*29	18 May 1956	304	13 January 1956	513	13 January 1956
*34	18 May 1956	305	13 January 1956	556	28 October 1955
*34A	18 May 1956	*349	18 May 1956	557	28 October 1955
*34B	18 May 1956	*350	18 May 1956	558	28 October 1955
*36	18 May 1956	*385	18 May 1956	559	28 October 1955
*58	18 May 1956	*386	18 May 1956	560	28 October 1955
*61	18 May 1956	*419	18 May 1956	561	28 October 1955
*77	18 May 1956	*420	18 May 1956	562	28 October 1955
*78	18 May 1956	*421	18 May 1956	563	28 October 1955
80	13 January 1956	430	13 January 1956	566	28 October 1955
80A	13 January 1956	448	13 January 1956	567	28 October 1955
80B	13 January 1956	449	13 January 1956	568	28 October 1955
*81	18 May 1956	454	13 January 1956	569	28 October 1955
83	13 January 1956	455	13 January 1956	570	28 October 1955
*91	18 May 1956	456	13 January 1956	571	28 October 1955
*92	18 May 1956	*458	18 May 1956	572	28 October 1955
*93	18 May 1956	*476	18 May 1956	*573	18 May 1956
*95	18 May 1956	479	13 January 1956	574	13 January 1956
*98	18 May 1956	480	13 January 1956	*575	18 May 1956
*107	18 May 1956	481	13 January 1956	749	13 January 1956
116	28 October 1955	482	13 January 1956	754A	13 January 1956
117	13 January 1956	483	13 January 1956	754B	13 January 1956
118	28 October 1955	484	13 January 1956	755	13 January 1956
*128	18 May 1956	485	13 January 1956	*756	18 May 1956
*129	18 May 1956	486	13 January 1956	*757	18 May 1956
135	13 January 1956	487	13 January 1956	*758	18 May 1956
136	13 January 1956	488	13 January 1956	*759	18 May 1956
139	13 January 1956	489	13 January 1956	*760	18 May 1956
144	13 January 1956	490	13 January 1956	*760A	18 May 1956
151	13 January 1956	491	13 January 1956	*760B	18 May 1956
*157	18 May 1956	492	13 January 1956	*769	18 May 1956
*158	18 May 1956	493	13 January 1956	*770	18 May 1956
171	13 January 1956	494	13 January 1956	*771	18 May 1956
*178	18 May 1956	495	13 January 1956	772	13 January 1956
186	13 January 1956	496	13 January 1956	*773	18 May 1956
186A	13 January 1956	497	13 January 1956	774	13 January 1956
186B	13 January 1956	498	13 January 1956	*776	18 May 1956
187	13 January 1956	499	13 January 1956	*777	18 May 1956
191	13 January 1956	500	13 January 1956	778	13 January 1956
192	13 January 1956	501	13 January 1956	*779	18 May 1956
192A	13 January 1956	502	13 January 1956	*780	18 May 1956
192B	13 January 1956	503	13 January 1956	*781	18 May 1956
*241	18 May 1956	504	13 January 1956	*782	18 May 1956
*273	18 May 1956	505	13 January 1956	783	13 January 1956
*274	18 May 1956	506	13 January 1956	*784	18 May 1956
*274A	18 May 1956	507	13 January 1956	*785	18 May 1956
*274B	18 May 1956	508	13 January 1956	*786	18 May 1956
*287	18 May 1956	509	13 January 1956	*787	18 May 1956
				*788	18 May 1956

* The asterisk indicates pages revised, added, or deleted by the current revision.

ADDITIONAL COPIES OF THIS PUBLICATION MAY BE OBTAINED AS FOLLOWS:

USAF ACTIVITIES.—In accordance with Technical Order No. 00-5-2.
NAVY ACTIVITIES.—Submit request to nearest supply point listed below, using form NavAer-140; NASD, Philadelphia, Pa.; NAS, Alameda, Calif.; NAS, Jacksonville, Fla.; NAS, Norfolk, Va.; NAS, San Diego, Calif.; NAS, Seattle, Wash.; ASD, NSC, Guam.
For listing of available material and details of distribution see Naval Aeronautics Publications Index NavAer 00-500.

A3 USAF

Revised 18 May 1956

This handbook contains all the information necessary for safe and efficient operation of the B-36 series airplanes. The instructions do not teach basic flight principles but provide you with a general knowledge of the airplane, its flight characteristics, and specific normal and emergency operating procedures. Your flying experience is recognized, and elementary instructions are avoided.

The only source of current, technically accurate operating instructions is your Flight Handbook. Instructions in the handbook are based on the technical knowledge of the aircraft manufacturer and the Air Force, as well as on the experience of the using commands. This handbook has no similarity to your old -1 Technical Order. Here your specific problems have been considered - - - - current and accurate information is presented to you in an attractive and usable form. Not all Flight Handbooks have been prepared in accordance with the new requirements, but you can easily tell the new from the old. New type handbooks have a full page cover illustration; old type books have only a small "spot" illustration.

Each flight crew member *except those attached to an administrative base* is entitled to a personal copy of the flight handbook while he is stationed at a given base. Do not let any one tell you differently! *Air Force Regulation 5-13*, issued in 1953, specifically makes this provision.

You will be surprised at how well the Technical Order distribution system will work if you do your part. Order your required quantity of handbooks before they are needed instead of waiting until the need arises. If you order them early, the Air Force will print enough to cover your requirements. If you delay you will probably be kept waiting a long time when you order, because sufficient copies may not have been originally printed to cover your request. It sometimes takes a discouragingly long time to get new printing.

The Technical Order system is very easy to cope with.

Technical Order 00-5-2 explains in a very few pages the easy means by which you can set the automatic machinery in motion. Actually, all you have to do is register your required quantities on the *Publications Requirements Table, T.O. 0-3-1;* then all revisions, reissues, and supplements will be automatically forwarded to you in the same quantities. Talk to your base supply officer — he should know all about the system since it is his job to fulfill your technical order requests. Each base must develop a system of feeding the handbooks and related data to their flight crew members so that no one will be using an obsolete book.

One more thing - - - we admit it takes a long time to revise the Flight Handbook. And, since the time lag is excessive for safety of flight information, a new program has been put into effect to get such information to you in a hurry. This is done by means of Safety of Flight Supplements which use the same number as your flight handbook except for the addition of a suffix letter. Supplements covering loss of life will get to you in 48 hours; those concerning serious damage to equipment will make it in ten days. And what do you have to do to get these supplements? Absolutely nothing! If you have ordered your Flight Handbook on the Publications Requirements Table, you will automatically receive all supplements pertaining to your aircraft. (Additional information regarding these supplements can be obtained from Technical Order 00-5-1E.)

Just as it is necessary to have a thorough knowledge of the airplane in order to operate it efficiently, so must you understand the arrangement of this handbook in order to benefit from it fully. A list of the sections and type of information contained in each is given here to aid you in using your handbook.

Your comments and questions regarding any phase of the Flight Handbook program are invited. They should be directed to the Wright Air Development Center, Attn: WCSOH.

SECTION I, DESCRIPTION—A detailed description of the airplane and all its systems and controls which contribute to the physical act of flying the airplane. Also, this section includes all the emergency equipment that is not part of an auxiliary system. This section is reserved solely for descriptive material and, therefore, does not contain any operating procedures.

SECTION II, NORMAL PROCEDURES—A section containing the procedures to be accomplished from the time the airplane is approached by the flight crew until it is left parked on the ramp after accomplishing one complete flight under normal conditions.

SECTION III, EMERGENCY PROCEDURES—Specific instructions to be followed by the crew under all emergency conditions (except those connected with the auxiliary equipment) that could reasonably be expected to be encountered.

SECTION IV, DESCRIPTION AND OPERATION OF AUXILIARY EQUIPMENT—A section including the description, normal operation, and emergency operation of all equipment not directly contributing to flight, such as armament, radio, oxygen, etc.

SECTION V, OPERATING LIMITATIONS—A section covering all airplane and engine operating limitations that must be observed during normal operation.

SECTION VI, FLIGHT CHARACTERISTICS—A section describing the flight characteristics of the airplane.

SECTION VII, SYSTEMS OPERATION—A discussion of the operation of the various airplane systems under all conditions of airplane operation.

SECTION VIII, CREW DUTIES—An amplified check list covering a discussion of the primary and alternate functions of each crew member.

SECTION IX, ALL WEATHER OPERATION—A supplement to Section II providing additional instructions for turbulent air and instrument flying; and for cold weather, desert, and tropical operation.

APPENDIX I, PERFORMANCE DATA—A section containing operating data essential to flight planning.

AIRPLANE GROUP NUMBER CODE.
Airplanes having a particular control or system in common have been assigned group numbers to avoid breaking the continuity of the text with the listing of airplane serial numbers. The groups with the airplanes they include and the items that are peculiar to each group are listed as follows:

GROUP 1 — Disc type brakes with one hydraulic accumulator—Airplanes USAF Serial No. 44-92030 through 44-92087 and 44-92098.

GROUP 2 — Airplanes which have undergone latest modification. (These modifications will be processed on all airplanes eventually.)

GROUP 3 — Expander tube brakes with two hydraulic accumulators — Airplane USAF Serial No. 49-2648 and subsequent.

GROUP 4 — Dual indicating instruments—Airplanes USAF Serial No. 44-92026 through 44-92087.

GROUP 5 — Single indicating instruments—Airplane USAF Serial No. 44-92095 and subsequent.

Table of Contents

		Page
SECTION I	DESCRIPTION	1
SECTION II	NORMAL PROCEDURES	87
SECTION III	EMERGENCY PROCEDURES	175
SECTION IV	DESCRIPTION & OPERATION OF AUXILIARY EQUIPMENT	219
SECTION V	OPERATING LIMITATIONS	283
SECTION VI	FLIGHT CHARACTERISTICS	301
SECTION VII	SYSTEMS OPERATION	309
SECTION VIII	CREW DUTIES	381
SECTION IX	ALL WEATHER OPERATION	433

Section I
Description

T.O. 1B-36D(II)-1

THE B-36D-II AIRPLANE

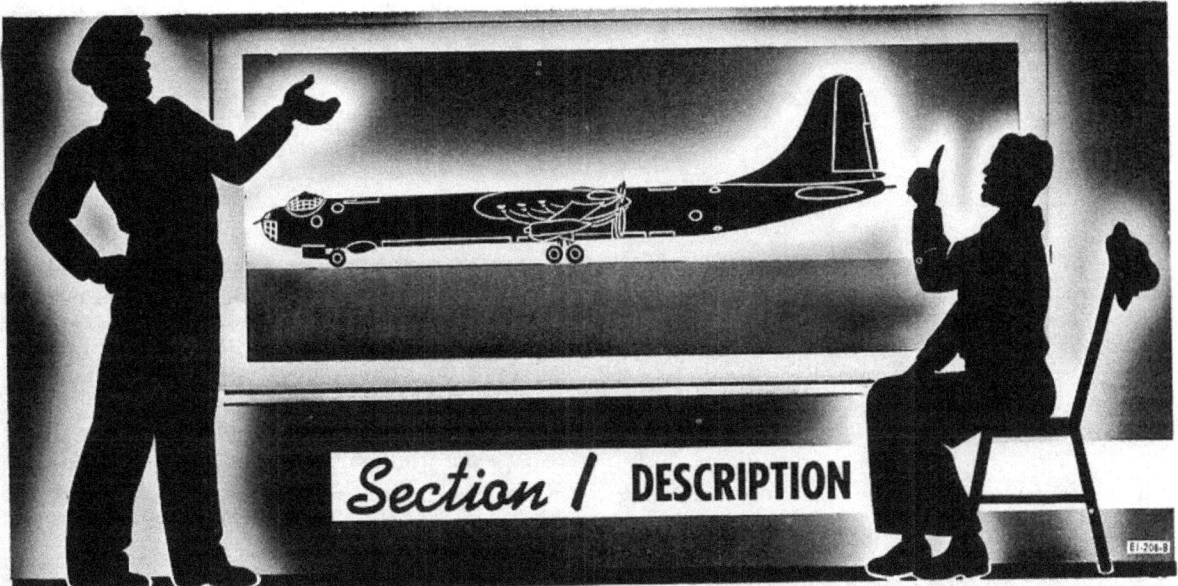

Section I DESCRIPTION

THE AIRPLANE.

The B-36D-II is a long-range, high altitude, heavy, bombardment airplane built by Convair, a Division of General Dynamics Corporation, Fort Worth, Texas. Its tactical mission is the destruction of land and naval objectives by bombing. Six Pratt and Whitney R4360-41 reciprocating engines drive pusher-type Curtiss propellers which can be synchronized in normal or reverse pitch. Additional power is provided by four General Electric J47 jet engines. The control surfaces consist of servo-tab-operated ailerons, elevators, and rudder. The flap system consists of three pairs of flaps. Four a-c alternators, driven by four of the reciprocating engines through constant-speed drives, furnish the power to operate the airplane's electrical equipment. A portion of the a-c power is rectified to provide d-c power and electrical control. The landing gear, the brakes, the bomb bay doors, and the nose wheel steering system are hydraulically operated. The crew compartments are pressurized, heated, and ventilated, and are provided with an oxygen system. Compartment heating; enclosure and blister defrosting; and wing and tail anti-icing are accomplished by heated air. Heat for the air is obtained through the use of heat exchangers installed in the reciprocating engine exhaust systems. Offensive armament consists of four bomb bays which are designed to carry 500-, 1000-, 2000-, 4000-, 12,000-, 22,000-, and 43,000-pound bombs. In addition 100-, 115-, 125-, 250-, 325-, and 350-pound bombs can be carried at the 500-pound stations. Defensive armament consists of eight remotely controlled gun turrets, each containing two 20-millimeter guns. The nose and tail turrets are nonretractable. All other turrets retract into turret bays which are faired with the fuselage by turret doors.

DESIGN GROSS WEIGHT.

The design gross weight is approximately 357,500 pounds.

FLIGHT CREW.

The normal flight crew consists of 15 men as follows:

FORWARD CABIN
- Aircraft Commander
- Pilot
- Copilot (Left Forward Gunner)
- First Engineer
- Second Engineer
- Navigator
- Radar Observer
- Observer (Nose Gunner)
- First Radio Operator (ECM Operator)
- Second Radio Operator (Right Forward Gunner)

AFT CABIN
- Upper Aft Gunner (Right)
- Upper Aft Gunner (Left)
- Lower Aft Gunner (Right)
- Lower Aft Gunner (Left)
- Tail Gunner

Airplane Dimensions

Approximate overall dimensions are as follows:

- Length .... 162 feet, 2 inches
- Wing Span .... 230 feet
- Height (to top of fin) . 46 feet, 10 inches
- Wing Area .... 4772 square feet

Section I
Description

T.O. 1B-36D(II)-1

RECIPROCATING ENGINES.

The airplane is primarily powered by six pusher-type, Pratt and Whitney, R4360-41 Wasp Major engines. Each engine has 28 cylinders which are arranged helically in seven four-row banks around the crankshaft which rotates counterclockwise as viewed from aft of the wing. Each engine is equipped with a water injection system which permits the horsepower rating to increase from 3250 (dry) to 3500. A torquemeter system for each engine measures the torque transmitted by the crankshaft to the propeller. This measurement is used to determine the actual power output of the engine. Carburetor and engine cooling air enters each nacelle at the wing leading edge. The flow of engine cooling air is augmented by an engine-driven fan. Controls are provided for varying the temperature of carburetor air and two turbosuperchargers maintain the required carburetor inlet pressure for each engine during high altitude operation. The cylinders of each engine are fired by a seven-magneto, high tension ignition system which is automatically pressurized for operation at high altitudes. A two-position controllable spark advance system permits efficient engine operation with certain power settings.

THROTTLE CONTROLS.

A set of throttle levers (14, figure 1-14) on the pilots' pedestal is mechanically interconnected with a set of throttle levers (16, figure 1-21) at the engineer's table. A lock lever (13, figure 1-14) on the pilots' pedestal will lock the throttle levers in any desired position. This lock can be overridden by the engineer.

A warning horn provides an indication of an unsafe condition of the throttle levers with respect to the position of the flaps or landing gear. The horn will sound when all six reciprocating engine throttle levers are

Main Differences TABLE

MODEL	DESIGN G.W. (LBS)	PRESSURIZED CREW COMPARTMENTS	CREW	ENGINEER'S STATION	RECIP. ENGINES	WING FUEL TANKS	GUN TURRETS	BOMB BAYS	BOMBING SYSTEM
B-36D	357,500	2	15	SINGLE	R4360-41	8	8	4	K( ) & UNIVERSAL
B-36D-II	357,500	2	15	SINGLE	R4360-41	8	8	4	K( ) & UNIVERSAL
B-36D-III	357,500	2	13	SINGLE	R4360-41	8	1	4	K( ) & UNIVERSAL
B-36F	357,500	2	15	SINGLE	R4360-53	8	8	4	K( ) & UNIVERSAL
B-36F-II	357,500	2	15	SINGLE	R4360-53	8	8	4	K( ) & UNIVERSAL
B-36F-III	357,500	2	13	SINGLE	R4360-53	8	1	4	K( ) & UNIVERSAL
B-36H	357,500	2	15	DUAL	R4360-53	8	8	4	K( ) & UNIVERSAL
B-36H-II	357,500	2	15	DUAL	R4360-53	8	8	4	K( ) & UNIVERSAL
B-36H-III	357,500	2	13	DUAL	R4360-53	8	1	4	K( ) & UNIVERSAL
B-36J	410,000	2	13	DUAL	R4360-53	10	1	4	K( ) & UNIVERSAL
RB-36D & E	357,500	3	22	SINGLE	R4360-41	8	8	2	CONV. & UNIVERSAL
RB-36D & E-II	357,500	3	22	SINGLE	R4360-41	8	8	2	CONV. & UNIVERSAL
RB-36D & E-III	357,500	3	19	SINGLE	R4360-41	8	1	2	CONV. & UNIVERSAL
RB-36F	357,500	3	22	SINGLE	R4360-53	8	8	2	CONV. & UNIVERSAL
RB-36F-II	357,500	3	22	SINGLE	R4360-53	8	8	2	CONV. & UNIVERSAL
RB-36F-III	357,500	3	19	SINGLE	R4360-53	8	1	2	CONV. & UNIVERSAL
RB-36H	357,500	3	22	DUAL	R4360-53	8	8	2	CONV. & UNIVERSAL
RB-36H-II	357,500	3	22	DUAL	R4360-53	8	8	2	CONV. & UNIVERSAL
RB-36H-III	357,500	3	19	DUAL	R4360-53	8	1	2	CONV. & UNIVERSAL

Figure 1-1.

advanced for take-off and the flaps are not extended at least 20 degrees (±4 degrees). The horn will also sound when the landing gear is up and locked and any throttle lever is retarded below minimum cruise. See "Landing Gear Warning Horn" and "Flap Warning Horn" of this section.

MIXTURE CONTROLS.

Two methods are available for controlling the mixture. Normally, control is accomplished electronically through the use of a set of control levers (13, figure 1-21) located on the flight engineer's table. Each lever is geared to a potentiometer which is located beneath the lever. Movement of the lever will move the potentiometer to originate a signal which is sent through an amplifier to an a-c actuator in the nacelle. The actuator positions the mixture control valve of the carburetor in response to the signal. In the event this method becomes inoperative, the mixture can be controlled by a set of override switches (7, figure 1-21) located on the engineer's table. These switches are connected directly to the mixture control actuators in the nacelles through an electrical circuit and provide emergency means of positioning the control valves. Both the normal and the override method of mixture control use 115-volt a-c power. No mixture controls are provided for the pilots.

Mixture Control Selector Switches.

Six two-position switches (8, figure 1-21), one for each engine, are provided to select the method of controlling the mixture. When these switches are placed in the LEVER position, the mixture control levers are effective for mixture control. When the switches are placed in the SWITCH position, the mixture control override switches become the means of controlling the mixture.

Mixture Control Levers.

Six mixture control levers (13, figure 1-21) are located on the engineer's table for normal control of the mixture. The positions on the control quadrant are IDLE CUT-OFF, NORMAL, and RICH. The NORMAL position, which is used for all normal operation, is a rich setting and the range between NORMAL and IDLE CUT-OFF provides manual lean settings. The range between NORMAL and RICH provides a mixture too rich for normal engine operation; however, settings in this range can be used effectively under certain operating conditions. (Refer to "Cooling," Section VII.) Six normal mixture indicator lamps (6, figure 1-21) are provided and will glow when the mixture controls are set for normal mixture. The control quadrant is graduated with index marks for reference in positioning the control levers.

WARNING

On some airplanes the IDLE CUT-OFF position on the mixture control quadrant is *away* from the operator. On other airplanes the IDLE CUT-OFF position is *toward* the operator. Therefore, the engineer must carefully check the arrangement of the mixture control quadrant of the airplane he is going to fly and become thoroughly familiar with mixture control lever positions.

CAUTION

Should an output tube of the electronic mixture control system fail while the selector switch is in the LEVER position, the mixture can be expected to go to the idle cut-off or rich position, depending on which tube fails.

Mixture Control Override Switches.

Six mixture control override switches (7, figure 1-21), located on the engineer's table, are provided for controlling the mixture in the event the normal mixture controls become inoperative. Each switch has a spring-loaded IDLE CUT-OFF position, a spring loaded AUTO-RICH position, and a neutral center position. No NORMAL position is provided, but a normal setting can be obtained by jiggling the switches between IDLE CUT-OFF and AUTO-RICH until the normal mixture indicator lamps light.

CARBURETOR AIR TEMPERATURE CONTROL.

Temperature control of carburetor air is accomplished by varying the volume of cooling air passing through the intercooler. This operation is accomplished through the use of intercooler shutters, which are controlled electrically from the engineer's station. Induction air may be heated before it enters the carburetor by diverting heated engine cooling air through the turbosuperchargers (figure 1-6) by means of the carburetor preheat switches.

Three dual indicating carburetor air temperature gages (23, figure 1-17) are located on the flight engineer's main instrument panel of group 4 airplanes. Six single indicating carburetor air temperature gages (13, figure 1-16) are located on the same panel of group 5 airplanes.

Intercooler Shutter Switches.

The six three-position intercooler shutter switches (1, figure 1-22) are on the flight engineer's auxiliary control panel. Each switch has a spring-loaded OPEN position, a spring-loaded CLOSE position, and a neutral OFF position. When a switch is held in the OPEN or CLOSE position, a 28-volt d-c control circuit energizes relays to supply 115-volt alternating current to the intercooler shutter actuators to obtain the desired

Section I
Description

carburetor air temperature. The switches can be placed simultaneously in the OPEN position by means of a gang bar.

> **Note**
> On some airplanes the left intercooler shutter closes automatically when a shift from dual to single turbo is accomplished.

Carburetor Preheat Switches.

Three carburetor preheat switches (32, figure 1-20) are ganged together on the engineer's control panel. A 28-volt d-c control circuit supplies 115-volt alternating current to the carburetor preheat actuators. Placing the switches in the ON position closes valves in the turbo air inlet ducts and opens valves in the carburetor preheat ducts. This permits heated engine cooling air, which is obained from the engine bay, to circulate through the turbos.

> **CAUTION**
> When the preheat valves open, the cabin pressure wing shutoff valves automatically close to prevent the possibility of carbon monoxide contamination of the cabin air.

Carburetor Air Filter Switch.

Provisions have been made for the installation of carburetor air filters. When these filters are installed, they are controlled by an ON-OFF switch-type circuit breaker on the engineer's table. Placing the switch in the ON position closes off ram air to the turbosuperchargers and draws air from the underside of the nacelle through the carburetor air filter. In the ON position the switch closes a 28-volt d-c control circuit which in turn supplies 115-volt a-c power to the carburetor air filter actuators.

TURBO SYSTEM.

Each reciprocating engine has two exhaust-driven turbosuperchargers which are used to maintain a constant carburetor inlet pressure up to 35,000 feet. The right turbo for each engine also provides pressurized air for the cabins. (See figure 4-6.)

Turbo Controls.

Engine Supercharger Switches. Six two-position switches (12, figure 1-20), located on the engineer's control panel, are provided to select dual or single turbo operation. Placing the switch in R.H. ONLY

GENERAL ARRANGEMENT *Diagram*

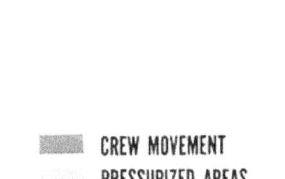

CREW MOVEMENT
PRESSURIZED AREAS

Figure 1-2. (Sheet 1)

will apply 115-volt a-c power to a turbo selector valve to divert all exhaust gases through the right turbo. On some airplanes, placing the switch in R. H. ONLY positions the turbo selector valve and also closes the intercooler shutters on the left side of the induction system to reduce drag. Dual operation is provided when the switch is in the BOTH position.

Turbo Boost Selector. An electronic turbo regulator system is used to control the boost of the turbos and is regulated from a master control panel on the engineer's table. This panel contains a turbo boost selector lever (4, figure 1-21) and six calibration potentiometer knobs (5, figure 1-21). The knobs are used to make small individual adjustments of manifold pressures during flight to compensate for small differences in engine or turbo performances. Moving the knobs counterclockwise reduces manifold pressure. Once the system is calibrated, the engineer can control the boost of all engines simultaneously by operating the turbo boost selector lever. The lever has travel graduations from zero to ten. Normally, position 7 is used for take-off and contains a detent to hold the lever in that position. The lever can be forced past the detent toward position 10 to obtain additional boost. A turbo boost selector lever (22, figure 1-14) is also provided for the pilots and is mechanically interconnected to the engineer's lever. This lever is located on the pilots' pedestal. The regulator system operates on 115-volt alternating current.

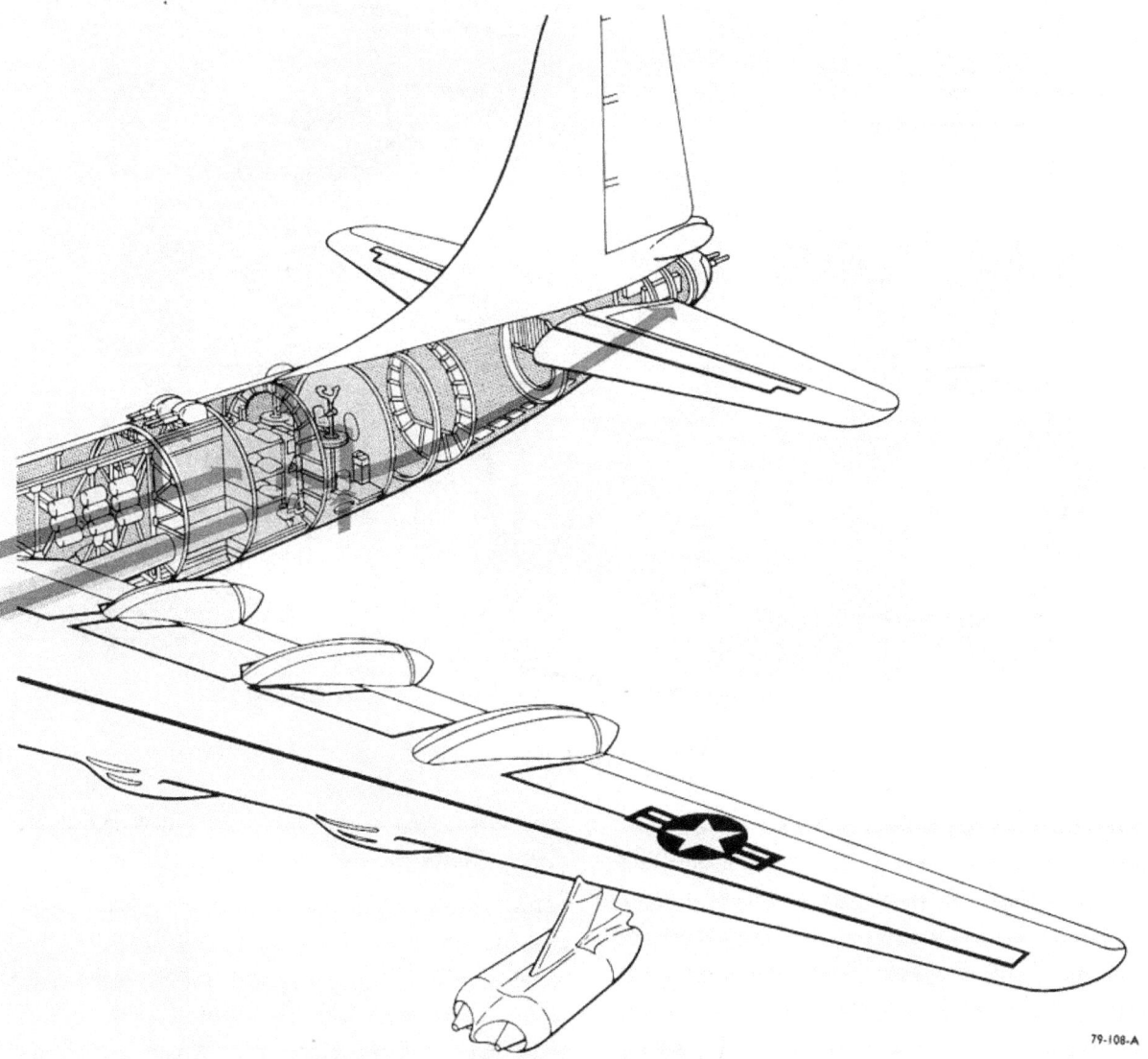

Figure 1-2. (Sheet 2)

Section I
Description

T.O. 1B-36D(II)-1

FORWARD CABIN *Arrangement*

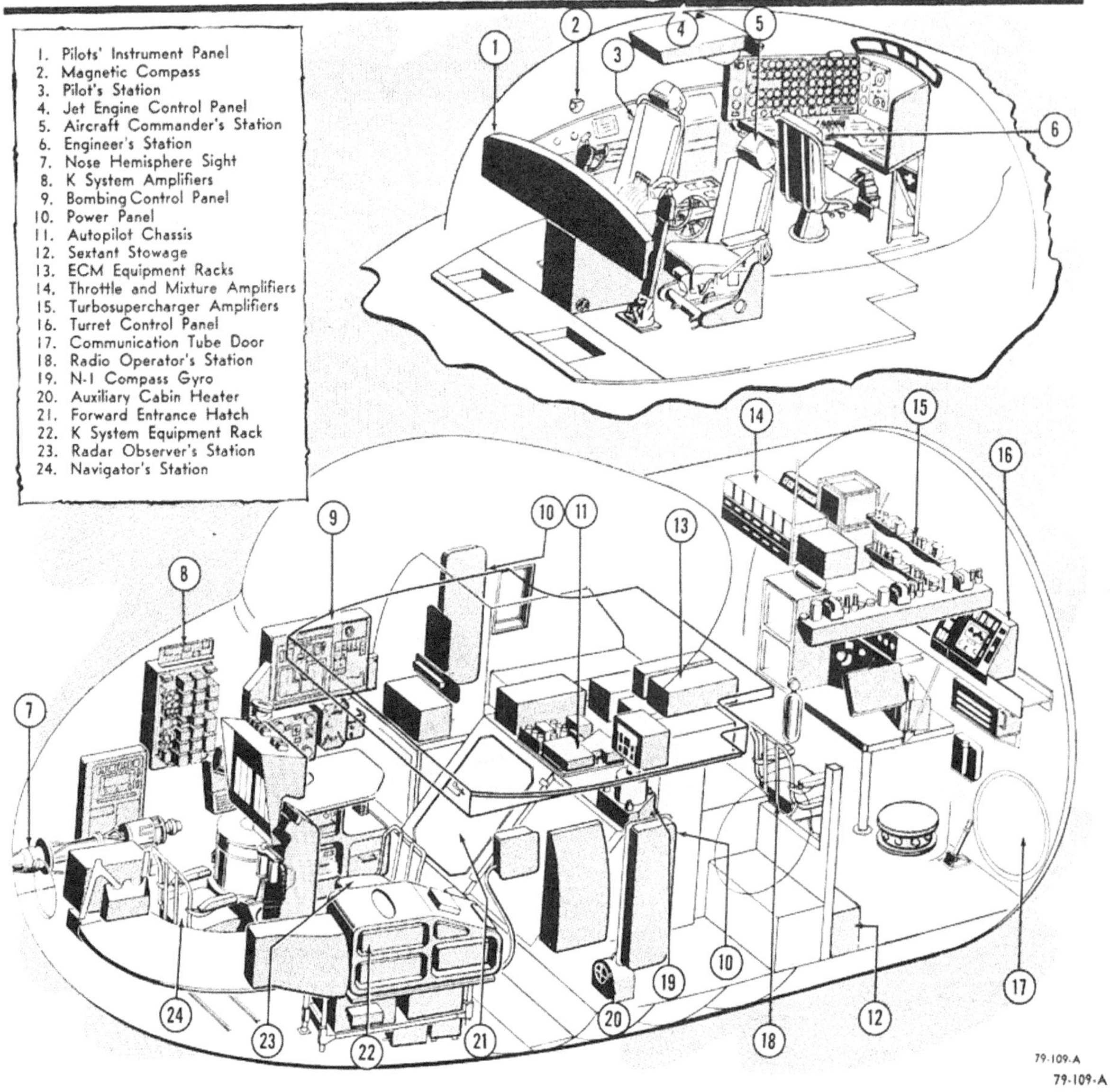

1. Pilots' Instrument Panel
2. Magnetic Compass
3. Pilot's Station
4. Jet Engine Control Panel
5. Aircraft Commander's Station
6. Engineer's Station
7. Nose Hemisphere Sight
8. K System Amplifiers
9. Bombing Control Panel
10. Power Panel
11. Autopilot Chassis
12. Sextant Stowage
13. ECM Equipment Racks
14. Throttle and Mixture Amplifiers
15. Turbosupercharger Amplifiers
16. Turret Control Panel
17. Communication Tube Door
18. Radio Operator's Station
19. N-1 Compass Gyro
20. Auxiliary Cabin Heater
21. Forward Entrance Hatch
22. K System Equipment Rack
23. Radar Observer's Station
24. Navigator's Station

Figure 1-3.

Turbo Control Change-Over Switches. Six two-position switches (21, figure 1-21) marked MAN and AUTO are located on the engineer's table of group 2 airplanes. When the switches are in AUTO the turbo electronic regulator systems control the waste gates. Placing the switches in MAN energizes one phase winding of the waste gate motor from a transformer which is energized by 115-volt alternating current. This sets up the motor for waste gate positioning through use of the override switches.

Turbo Control Override Switches. Six override switches (21, figure 1-21) are located on the engineer's table of group 2 airplanes. Each switch has a spring-loaded OPEN position which opens the turbo waste gates, a spring-loaded CLOSE position which closes the turbo waste gates, and a neutral OFF posi-

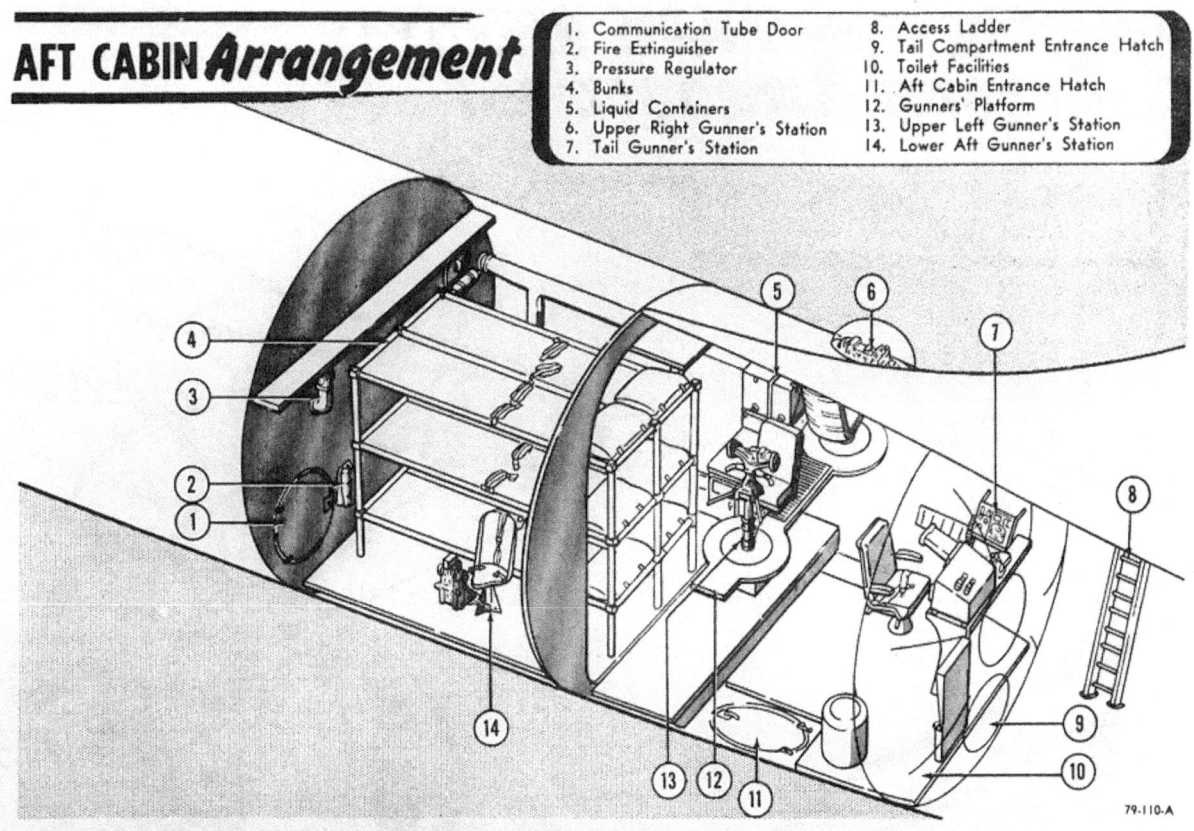

Figure 1-4.

tion. With a turbo change-over switch in the MAN position, the respective turbo override switch can be used to open or close the turbo waste gates. When the override switch is placed in the OPEN or CLOSE position 230-volt current is taken from a transformer to energize the unenergized waste gate motor windings for actuating the waste gate to the desired position. The transformer has an input of 115-volt alternating current. The switches can also be utilized during emergency electrical operation. (See "Obtaining Emergency Electrical Power," Section III.)

Turbo Control Vernier Switch. On group 2 airplanes, a switch-type circuit breaker (21, figure 1-21) located on the engineer's table provides 28-volt d-c power to the turbo override relays for incremental operation of the waste gates when the turbo control override system is in use. When this switch is ON, each actuation of an override switch will operate the corresponding waste gate motor for approximately 0.05 second. With the vernier switch OFF and an override switch held in OPEN or CLOSE, the waste gate motor will operate until the override switch is released or until the waste gates reach their travel limit.

Turbo Tachometers.

Six turbo tachometers (25, figure 1-16) are provided on the engineers' main instrument panel. Each tachometer indicates the rpm of the right turbo for the respective engine.

Note

The speed of the left turbo is normally equal to right turbo speed since a governor controls both turbos.

WATER INJECTION SYSTEM.

Each reciprocating engine is equipped with a water injection system for permitting the development of additional power during take-off. The systems are of

RECIPROCATING ENGINE NACELLE
General Arrangement

1. ANTI-ICING DUCT
2. ENGINE COOLING AIR DUCT
3. ANTI-ICING AIR DUMP VALVE
4. TURBO OIL TANK
5. ENGINE MOUNT
6. Y-DUCT
7. CARBURETOR AIR SCOOP
8. WATER TANK
9. R4360-41 ENGINE
10. PROP SPINNER
11. ENGINE COOLING AIR PLUG
12. INTERCOOLER SHUTTER (2)
13. PRIMARY HEAT EXCHANGER (2)
14. EXHAUST EXIT DUCT
15. INTERCOOLER (2)
16. TURBOSUPERCHARGER (2)
17. CARBURETOR PREHEAT DUCT
18. AIR INDUCTION DUCT
19. OIL COOLER ARMOR PLATE
20. AIR INLETS

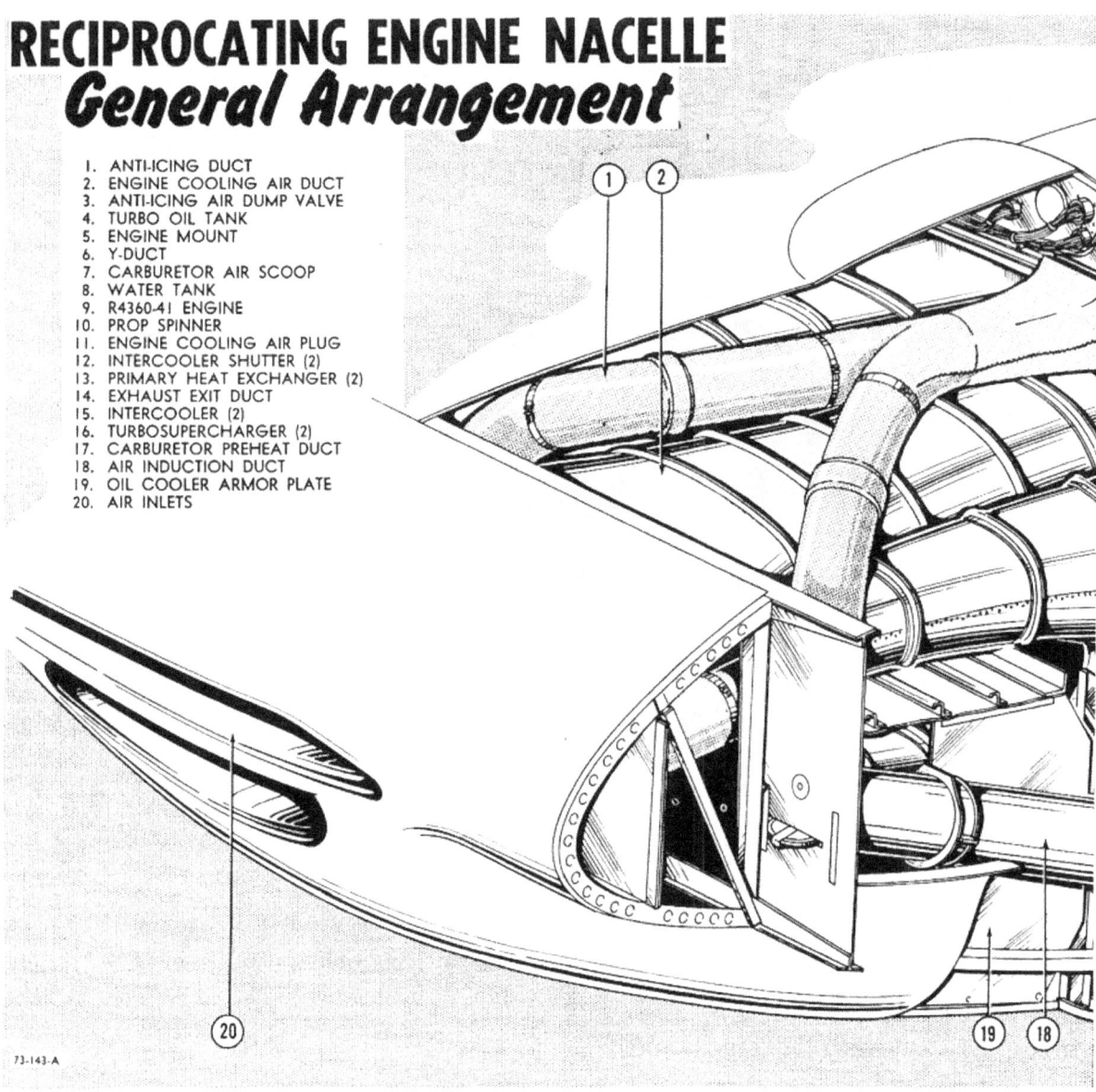

Figure 1-5. (Sheet 1)

the nonhesitating type and include a nine-gallon water tank, a booster pump, and a water regulator. A 28-volt d-c circuit controls 208-volt alternating current for pump power. The regulator controls the flow of water as it is injected into the blower case to be mixed with fuel and air before entering the intake manifold. On airplanes not in group 2, when the booster pumps are operating, the regulators automatically meter water to the engine when a manifold pressure of 53.5 inches is attained. The systems operate continuously for approximately five minutes, after which the water supply is depleted and the booster pumps automatically stop. On group 2 airplanes, water is injected into the engines by the actuation of the water injection control switches. This permits the use of water at any power setting. However, at manifold pressures less than 50 inches, water has little net effect upon the power output of the engines.

Water Injection Switches.

These six on-off switches (10, figure 1-20) are located on the engineer's main control panel. When the switches

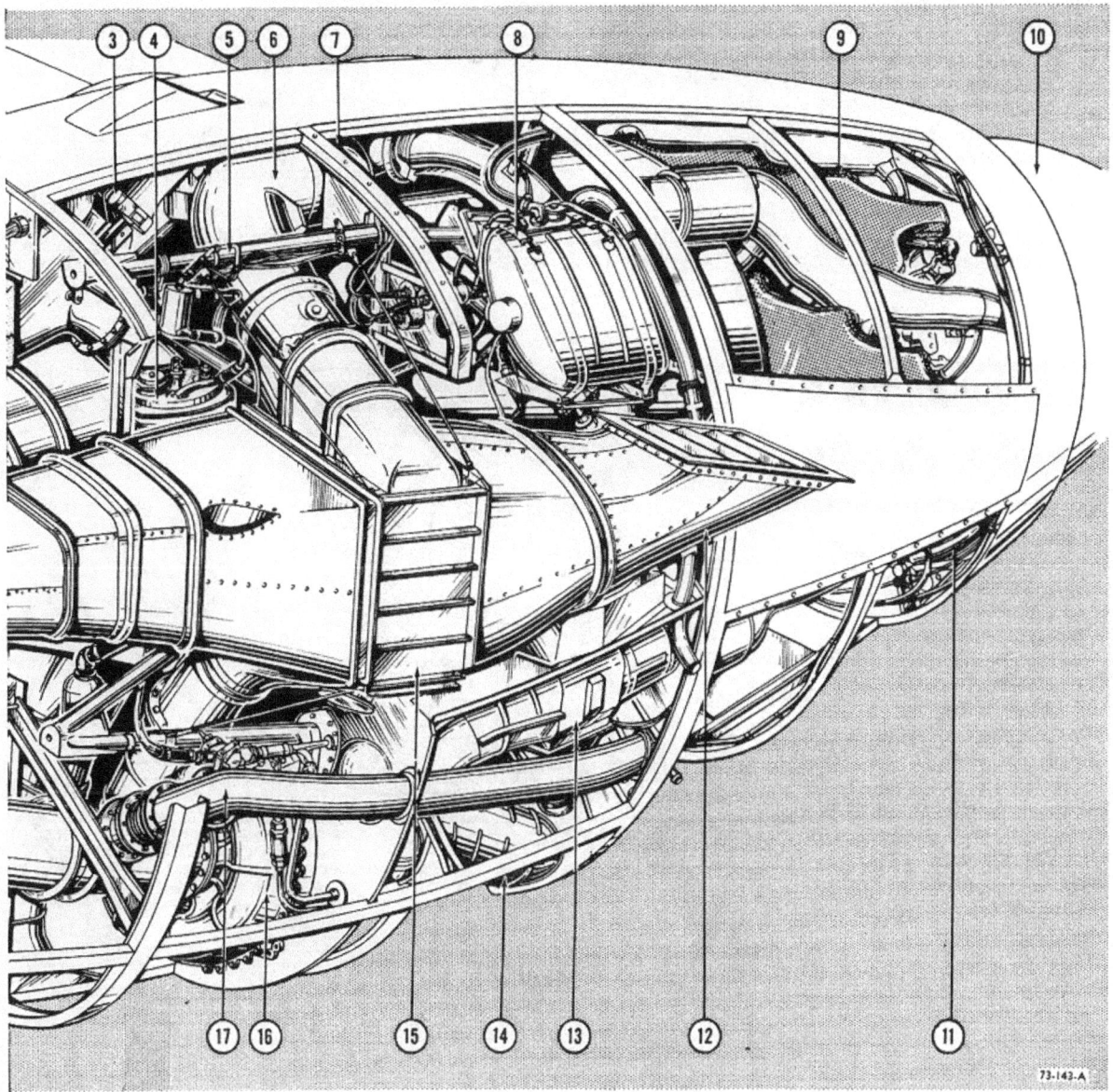

Figure 1-5. (Sheet 2)

on airplanes not in group 2 are placed ON, the booster pumps are started and an electrical circuit it set up to solenoid valves in the water regulators. The valves will then open, when 53.5 inches manifold pressure is attained, permitting water to enter the engines. Placing the switches OFF renders the systems inoperative. On group 2 airplanes, the switches are a direct means of injecting water into the engines. When the switches are placed ON, the pumps are started and water enters the regulator to be metered to the engines. The pumps on this group of airplanes continue to operate after the five-minute water supply is depleted. They are stopped only by moving the switches to OFF.

CAUTION

On group 2 airplanes if a water pressure pump is operating and no water pressure is indicated on the gage, the water supply is depleted and the control switch should be turned OFF. The pump should not be allowed to operate for more than 2 minutes without water, since water is required to cool the pump motor.

Section I
Description

Water Pressure Gages.

There are three dual indicating water pressure gages (16, figure 1-17) on the engineer's main instrument panel of group 4 airplanes, and six single indicating water pressure gages (4, figure 1-16) on the same panel of group 5 airplanes, which indicate psi pressure in the water injection system.

Note

With the control switches OFF, normal indication of the gages is approximately 10 psi. This reading indicates metered fuel pressure.

ENGINE COOLING SYSTEM.

Engine cooling air is introduced into the nacelle through a cooling air tunnel. Air is taken from the tunnel for cooling the turbosuperchargers, the exhaust system, the propeller mechanism, and various electrically driven actuators. The flow of the remainder of cooling air is routed over the engine and is controlled by a ring-shaped air plug. Six switches on the flight engineer's auxiliary control panel are provided to control the air plugs in maintaining the proper cylinder

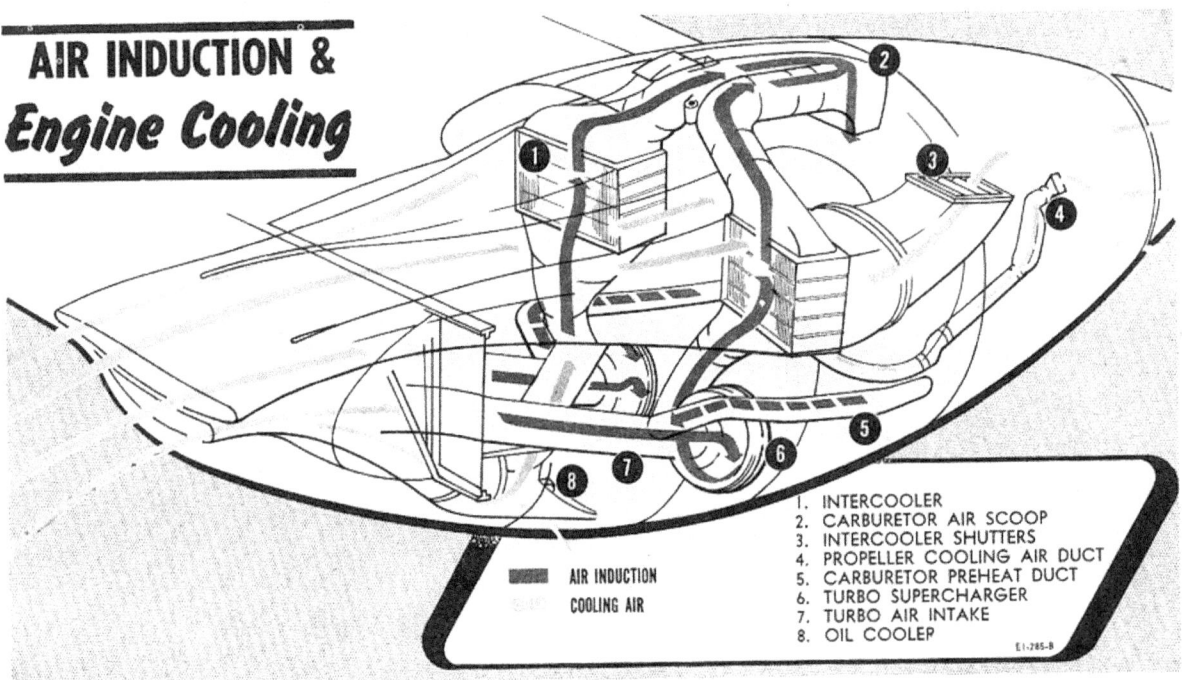

1. INTERCOOLER
2. CARBURETOR AIR SCOOP
3. INTERCOOLER SHUTTERS
4. PROPELLER COOLING AIR DUCT
5. CARBURETOR PREHEAT DUCT
6. TURBO SUPERCHARGER
7. TURBO AIR INTAKE
8. OIL COOLER

AIR INDUCTION
COOLING AIR

Figure 1-6.

EXHAUST & ANTI-ICING Air Flow

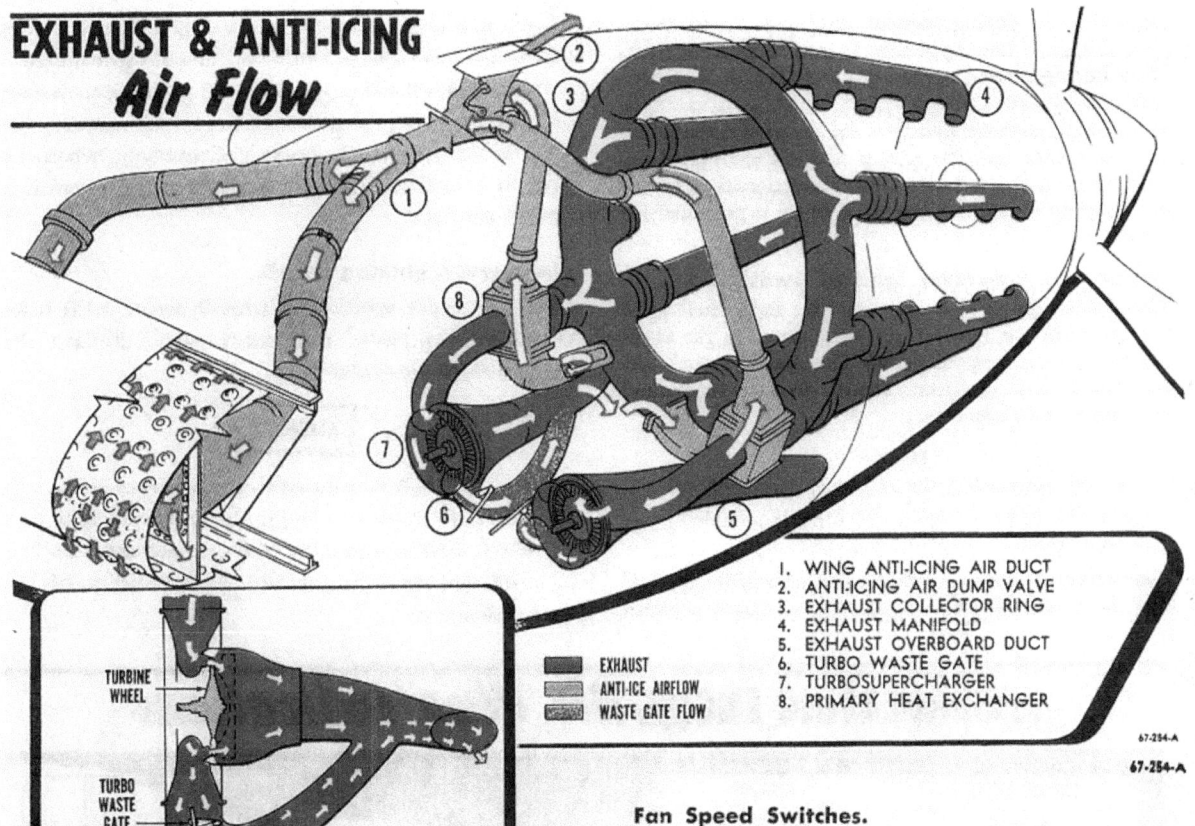

1. WING ANTI-ICING AIR DUCT
2. ANTI-ICING AIR DUMP VALVE
3. EXHAUST COLLECTOR RING
4. EXHAUST MANIFOLD
5. EXHAUST OVERBOARD DUCT
6. TURBO WASTE GATE
7. TURBOSUPERCHARGER
8. PRIMARY HEAT EXCHANGER

■ EXHAUST
■ ANTI-ICE AIRFLOW
■ WASTE GATE FLOW

Figure 1-7.

head temperature. The position of the air plugs can be determined from the gunners' stations by observing the positions of the diamond-shaped markers painted on the air plugs. (See figure 1-8.) A two-speed engine-driven fan is installed in the air tunnel of each engine to increase the rate of cooling air flow.

Air Plug Switches.

Six three-position switches (4, figure 1-22), located on the flight engineer's auxiliary control panel, control the engine air plugs. Each switch has a spring-loaded OPEN position, a spring-loaded CLOSE position, and a neutral center position marked OFF. The air plug is controlled by holding the switch in either the OPEN or CLOSE position to obtain the desired cylinder head temperature. The switches are provided with a gang bar for simultaneous operation in the OPEN position. A 28-volt d-c circuit controls 208-volt alternating current, which operates the air plug actuator motor.

Fan Speed Switches.

Six two-position switches (14, figure 1-20), marked LOW RPM and HIGH RPM, control the speed of the engine cooling fans. The fan speed control actuators use 115-volt alternating current. For additional information on fan speed control see "Cooling Fan Control," Section II.

IGNITION SYSTEM.

Ignition for each engine is furnished by seven double magnetos—one for each bank of cylinders. Each of the double magnetos has a right and left system which supplies the electrical impulses to the right and left spark plug of each cylinder at the proper time of the engine cycle.

Note

The right spark plug is on the intake side of the cylinder and the left spark plug is on the exhaust side of the cylinder.

The engineer can set the spark to occur at either 20 degrees or 30 degrees before the piston reaches top-dead-center of the compression stroke by means of a set of spark advance switches. The 20-degree setting is used for normal operation. The spark advance setting of 30 degrees is used for certain cruise control

Section I
Description

T.O. 1B-36D(II)-1

configurations during manual leaning for greater engine efficiency (see Appendix 1) and to prevent backfiring during certain operating conditions at high altitude (see "Power Collapse," Section VII). In addition to the spark advance switches, the ignition controls include a master ignition switch and six individual engine ignition switches. An emergency ignition switch for stopping all engines simultaneously is provided for the pilots.

Master and Individual Ignition Switches.

The master ignition switch and the individual ignition switches (19, figure 1-20) are located on the flight engineer's main control panel. The master switch sets up 28-volt d-c ignition circuits to the individual switches when pushed in.

Note

In an emergency the engineer can stop all engines simultaneously by pulling the master switch.

The individual ignition switches have positions marked OFF, L, R, and BOTH. The unmarked detent between L and R is another BOTH position. The L and R positions are used in checking the left and right magneto systems. When the switch is in the L position, the left magneto system is grounded and the right magneto system is the one being checked. Conversely, when the switch is in the R position, the left magneto system is being checked.

Emergency Ignition Switch.

The emergency ignition switch (29, figure 1-13) is located on the pilots' instrument panel. Pulling the switch stops all engines.

CAUTION

This switch is to be used in emergency situations only. When testing the emergency ignition circuit, actuation of the switch must be instantaneous to prevent the possibility of backfiring.

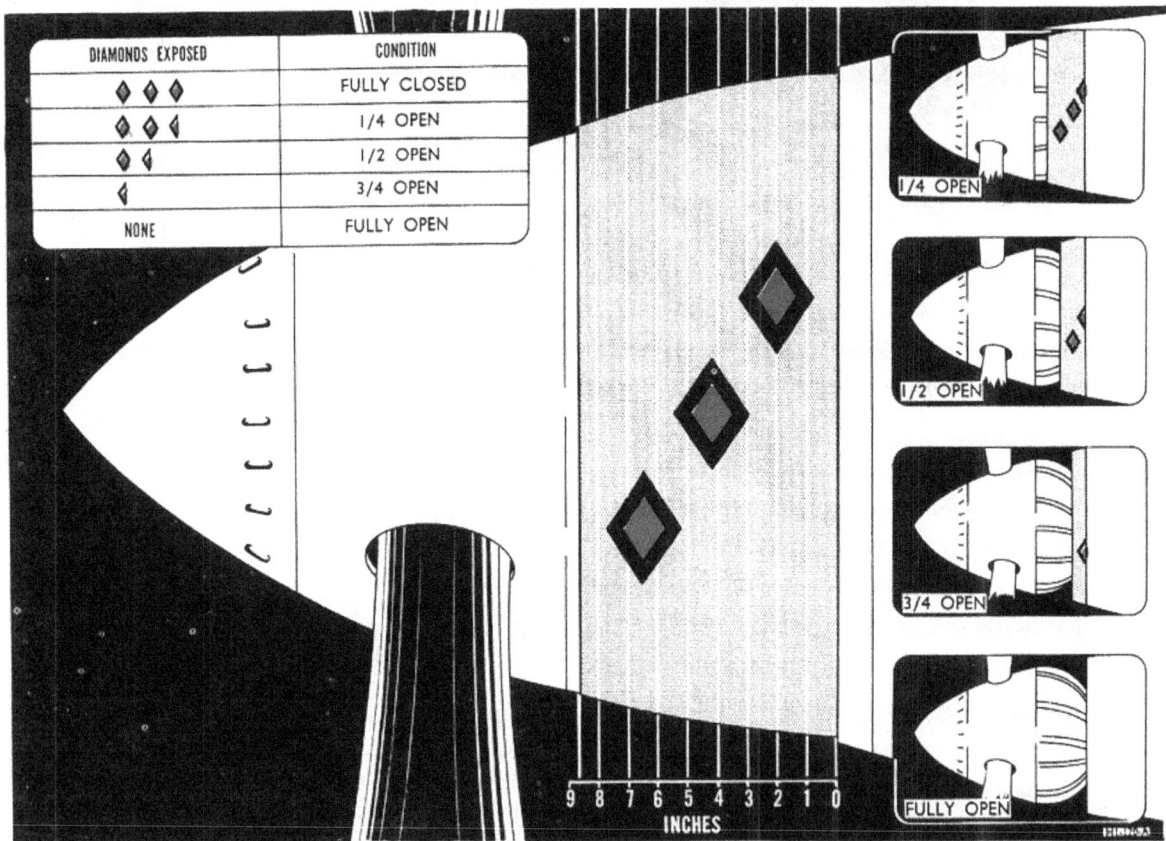

Figure 1-8.

Spark Advance Switches.

The six spark advance switches (9, figure 1-21) are located on the engineer's table and have positions marked ADVANCE and RETARD. When a switch is placed in the ADVANCE position, a 28-volt d-c circuit is completed to a solenoid and the spark is advanced from the normal setting of 20 degrees to a setting of 30 degrees. Placing the switch in the RETARD position returns the spark to the normal 20-degree setting.

PRIMING SYSTEM.

Each reciprocating engine is equipped with a separate priming system to assist in starting whenever necessary. Priming is controlled by a solenoid-operated valve on the carburetor which allows fuel under booster pump pressure to pass into the blower case of the engine.

Engine Primer Switches.

The six priming systems are controlled by three three-position switches (17, figure 1-20) located on the engineer's control panel. The switches are marked OFF in the center position with engine numbers above and below. When a primer switch is held in an engine position, a 28-volt d-c circuit is completed to a primer solenoid and fuel is injected directly into the blower case of the corresponding engine.

STARTING SYSTEM.

A heavy duty direct-cranking starter is mounted on the lower side of each reciprocating engine accessory case for cranking the engine. The starter cranks the engine through a planetary gear system, a dry-disc friction clutch, and a cranking jaw which engages the engine cranking jaw. The starter jaw automatically disengages when the engine starts. Engine damage due to hydraulic lock is minimized by the friction clutch which is preset to slip at approximately 400-foot pounds of torque.

Engine Starter Switches.

The six direct-cranking starters are controlled by three three-position switches (18, figure 1-20). The switches are marked OFF in the center position with engine numbers above and below. Holding a starter switch in an engine position engages the starter and cranks the corresponding engine. A 28-volt d-c control circuit controls 208-volt alternating current which is applied to the engine starter.

PROPELLER SYSTEM.

The airplane is equipped with six Curtiss constant-speed, full-feathering, reversible propellers. The propellers are 19 feet in diameter and have three hollow steel blades installed in a two-piece steel hub. The propellers of some airplanes have round-tipped blades. Other airplanes have propellers equipped with square-tipped blades. These blades have a thinner airfoil section which provides greater efficiency at higher speeds and altitudes than the blades with round tips. The control system of both propeller models is identical and is similar to that used on previous models of synchronizer-equipped propellers except that synchronization is possible in the reverse range.

PITCH CHANGE SYSTEM.

Pitch change is accomplished mechanically by power taken directly from propeller shaft rotation. Clutch engagement for operation of the pitch changing mechanism is accomplished hydraulically. The hydraulic power is controlled by small solenoid valves. A small electric motor drives the blades in the last of the feathering and the beginning of the unfeathering cycles when the engine is operating below 450 rpm and is unable to furnish sufficient power to operate the pitch changing mechanism.

Note

Pitch change during feathering and reversing is 45 degrees per second. Pitch change during normal operation is 2-1/2 degrees per second.

NORMAL PROPELLER CONTROLS AND INDICATORS.

Control of the propeller speed is conventional, but synchronization is accomplished by making the speed of all engines compare with the speed of an electrically driven master motor. A propeller alternator on each engine supplies an electrical indication of engine speed to a contactor assembly on the master motor. If the engine speed does not coincide with that of the master motor, corrective impulses are transmitted to the pitch changing mechanism until the engine is operating at master motor rpm. All engines operate at master motor rpm when their respective selector switches are placed in the AUTOMATIC OPERATION position and their throttles are advanced sufficiently for the engine to attain master motor rpm. Because of a protective relay in the master motor, if a master motor failure occurs the propeller will remain at the pitch in effect when failure occurred. Pitch changes will then be accomplished by moving the selector switches to the INC. RPM or the DEC. RPM positions.

Propeller Selector Switches.

Six conventional propeller selector switches (4, figure 1-9) having four positions—AUTOMATIC OPERATION, DEC. RMP, INC. RPM, and FIXED PITCH— are provided on the engineer's table and operate on 28-volt d-c power.

Master Motor Control Lever.

(See 18, figure 1-14 and 1, figure 1-9.) Two control levers are provided to control the speed of the master motor. The lever located on the engineer's table is mechanically interconnected to the one on the pilots' pedestal. As well as controlling master motor rpm, these levers control the supply of 28-volt d-c power to

Engineer's PROPELLER CONTROL PANEL

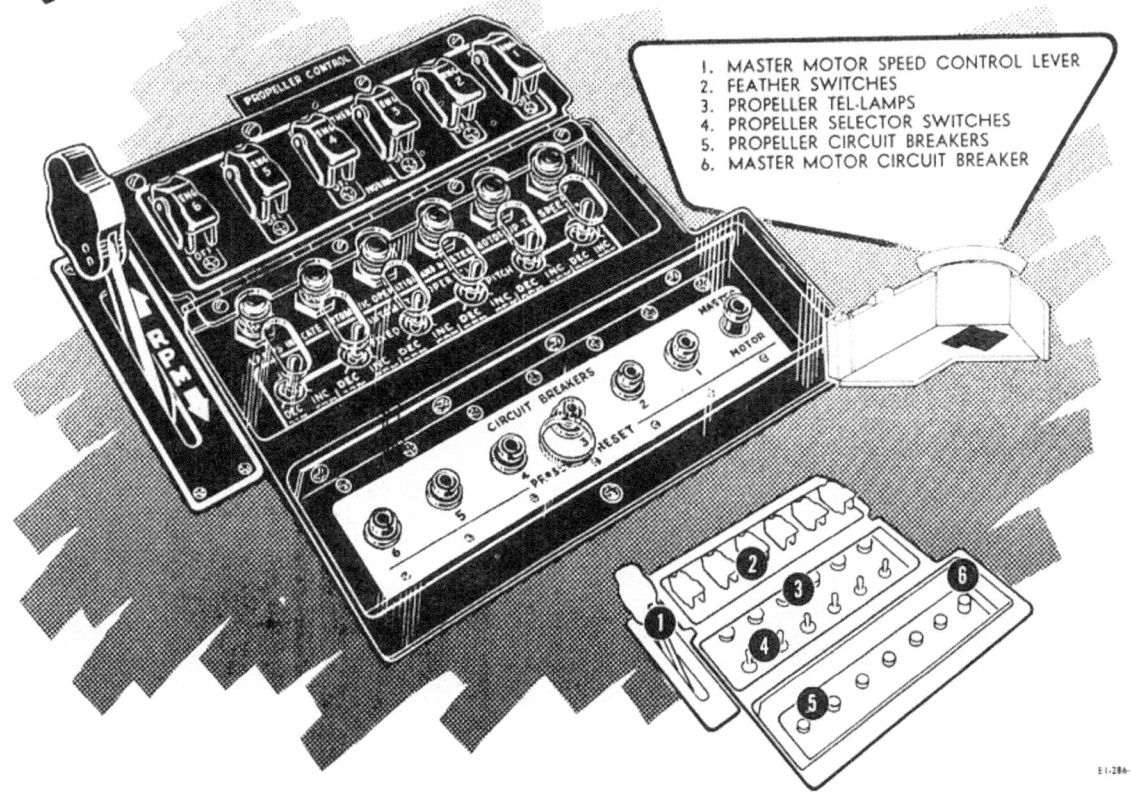

Figure 1-9.

operate the master motor through a micro switch which is set to cut out below 1250 rpm.

Master Tachometers.

(See 7, figure 1-13 and 3, figure 1-16.) The master tachometers indicate master motor rpm. It should be noted that master motor rpm will not always coincide with engine rpm, since the master motor may be operating at any selected rpm during ground operations, even when the engines are not running.

Propeller Tel-Lamps

Six push-to-test tel-lamps (3, figure 1-9) are provided to indicate proper operation of the synchronization system. When the propeller selector switches are placed in the AUTOMATIC OPERATION position and the master motor is on-speed, the tel-lamps will light. If the master motor fails, all lamps will go out. Each lamp will go out when its corresponding selector switch is moved out of the AUTOMATIC OPERATION position.

PROPELLER REVERSE PITCH CONTROLS AND INDICATORS.

Reverse Selector Switches.

Three propeller reverse selector switches (10, figure 1-14) marked READY and SAFE are located on the pilots' pedestal. These switches are used to select symmetrical pairs of propellers to be reversed by setting up a 28-volt d-c circuit to the reverse pitch switch. The propellers are returned from reverse by placing the switches in the SAFE position.

Although it is possible to reverse the propellers in the air, this action is prohibited.

Reverse Pitch Switch.

A push-button type reverse pitch switch (19, figure 1-14), located on the pilots' pedestal, completes a 28-volt d-c circuit which reverses the symmetrical pairs of propellers selected by the reverse selector switches.

AIRCRAFT COMMANDER'S Station

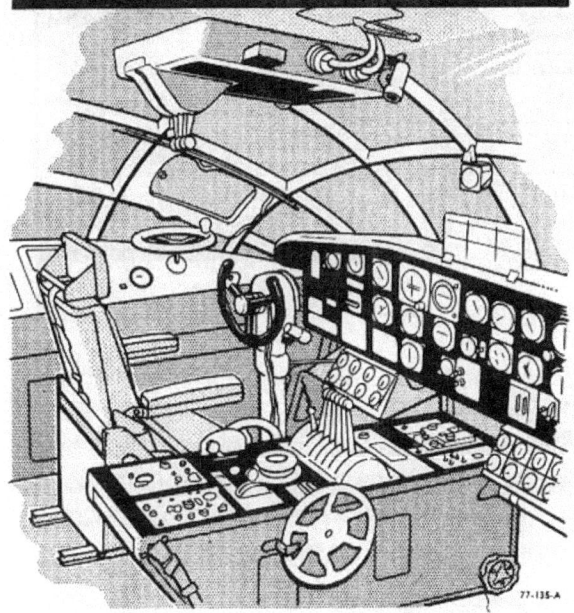

Note

When one pair of propellers is in reverse pitch, the remaining pairs can be reversed by placing their reverse selector switches in the READY position.

WARNING

If an engine is shut down (propeller feathered) the propeller of the symmetrical engine cannot be reversed unless the feather switch of the inoperative engine is returned to NORMAL. However, this would create an unsafe condition during reversing after landing in that an unbalanced power would be present.

Propeller Reverse Warning Lamps.

Six red warning lamps (40, figure 1-13) are located on the pilots' instrument panel. When any propeller is in reverse pitch, the corresponding red lamp will be lighted. The lamp will go out when the propeller is returned to normal pitch.

Note

The lamp lights when the propeller blades reach a positive pitch angle of 10.5 degrees going into reverse. Conversely, coming out of reverse, the lamps will go out at the 10.5-degree positive pitch angle.

Propeller Normal Pitch Indicator Lamps.

Six green lamps (2, figure 1-16) are located on the flight engineer's main instrument panel. These lamps indicate when the propellers are in normal pitch. When any propeller is in reverse pitch, the respective lamp will not burn.

Note

The lamp lights when the propeller blades reach a positive pitch angle of 10.5 degrees coming out of reverse. Going into reverse, the lamps will go out at the 10.5-degree positive pitch angle.

PROPELLER FEATHER CONTROLS.

Six two-position switches (2, figure 1-9), marked FEATHER and NORMAL, are located on the engineer's table. The switches are guarded in the NORMAL position.

WARNING

If the individual circuit breaker is out or defective, the propeller cannot be feathered nor the blade angle changed.

PILOT'S Station

Oil Tank Capacities
APPROXIMATE GALLONS

TANK	NO.	TOTAL VOLUME (NOTE 1)	EXPANSION SPACE (NOTE 2)	MAXIMUM CAPACITY (NOTE 3)	NORMAL LOADING (NOTE 4)
INBOARD	2	241	41	200	150
CENTER	2	248	48	200	150
OUTBOARD	2	262	62	200	150

NOTES:
1. Total volume is the total amount of internal space of each tank in gallons and is NOT to be interpreted as any oil loading capacity.
2. Expansion space cannot be used for additional oil because of the location of the filler neck.
3. 200 gallons is the maximum amount of oil that can be put into the tank.
4. The maximum normal loading is 150 gallons for each tank because of the following reasons:
   A. Oil in excess of 150 gallons will vent overboard.
   B. At high altitude, oil vented overboard will congeal, break loose, and damage the airplane.
   C. 150 gallons of oil per tank is all that is needed for normal engine operation.

Figure 1-10.

RECIPROCATING ENGINE OIL SYSTEM.

Each reciprocating engine has an independent oil system which includes a tank, a shutoff valve, a means of oil dilution, and a cooling system. (See figure 1-12.) The capacity of each tank is given in figure 1-10.

An oil shutoff valve is located in the supply line between each tank and engine. A set of six switches at the engineer's station provide 115-volt a-c power for operation of the valves. To aid in oil scavenging and to prevent excessive loss of oil at altitude, the engine oil tank is pressurized for high altitude operation. The oil tanks are pressurized by air taken from the cabin pressurization system and by the normal pressure input from the engine-driven scavenge pump. An aneroid-type valve, which incorporates a relief valve, is installed in the tank vent lines to maintain a 2.75 psi differential between the ambient and oil tank pressure above approximately 20,000 feet. This pressurization is necessary to insure an adequate supply of oil to the engine oil pump and to minimize oil foaming. To obtain proper engine lubrication when low ground temperatures are experienced, the engineer can dilute the oil by injecting fuel into the oil supply line. (Refer to "Oil Dilution," Section IX for additional information.)

Electrical heating elements are provided for the tank vent lines and hoppers. For detailed information see "Oil Tank Vent Heaters" and "Oil Tank Hopper Heaters" in Section IV. Refer to figure 1-48 for servicing information.

OIL SYSTEM CONTROLS.
Oil Shutoff Valve Switches.

The engineer has six two-position switches (11, figure 1-20) on his main control panel for operating the oil shutoff valves. The switches have positions marked OPEN and CLOSE and are guarded in the OPEN position. With the exception of the valve for engine No. 6, the shutoff valves are accessible from the wing crawlways and can be operated manually.

Oil Dilution Switches.

There are six oil dilution switches (33, figure 1-20) on the engineer's main control panel. Each switch has two spring-loaded ON positions and a neutral OFF. One ON position is provided for using the switches individually. The other ON position permits gang bar operation for simultaneous dilution of the oil for all engines. When a switch is placed ON, a 28-volt d-c circuit is completed to an oil dilution solenoid allowing fuel to be discharged into the engine oil inlet line.

OIL SYSTEM INDICATORS.
Oil Temperature Gages.

Oil temperature gages (8, figure 1-16) are located on the engineer's main instrument panel and indicate, in centigrade, reciprocating engine oil temperatures. The temperature indicating system is energized by 24-volt d-c power.

Oil Pressure Gages.

Oil pressure gages (11, figure 1-16), located on the engineer's main instrument panel, indicate the nose oil pressure of the reciprocating engines. Each oil pressure indicating system is energized by 26-volt a-c power from the related engine power panel.

RECIPROCATING ENGINE OIL SYSTEM Schematic

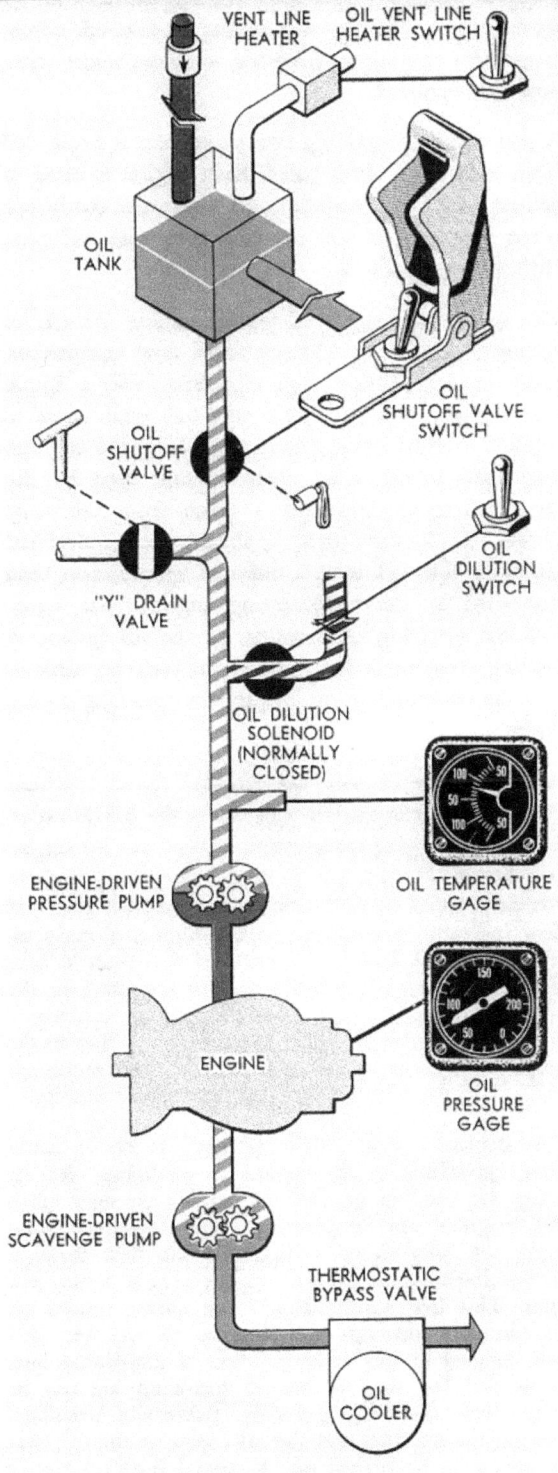

Figure 1-11.

Oil Quantity Gages.

There are six single-indicating oil quantity gages (5, figure 1-16 and 8, figure 1-17) located on the engineer's main instrument panel. The gages indicate oil quantity in US gallons. The oil quantity indicating system is energized by 28-volt d-c power from the engineer's circuit breaker panel.

OIL COOLING.

Oil cooling is completely automatic for some airplanes. Thermostatically controlled valves regulate the flow of oil and cooling air through the oil cooler to keep the temperature within the desired operating range. On group 2 airplanes an oil cooler door override system is installed to provide a means of overriding the automatic control when oil temperature drops below or exceeds the normal operating temperature. Two methods of routing the cooling air through the cooler are provided to insure proper operating temperatures in both ground and flight operations. On the ground, air is drawn through the oil cooler by the engine-driven fan. During flight ram air independent of the fan passes through the oil cooler. Two doors in the air inlet ducts control the routing of the oil cooling air. The door actuators operate on 115-volt alternating current and are energized through a switch actuated by the movement of the left main gear oleo strut during take-off and landing. (See figure 1-12.)

Oil Cooler Door Mode Selector Switches (Group 2 Airplanes).

Six switch-type circuit breakers (20, figure 1-16) marked AUTO and MANUAL are located on the engineer's main instrument panel. When the switches are in AUTO, the automatic control circuit operates the oil cooler doors. When the switches are in MANUAL position, the automatic circuit is cut out and 28-volt direct current is fed to a manual control circuit. This sets up the manual control circuit for operation by means of the manual override switches.

RECIPROCATING ENGINE
Oil Cooling

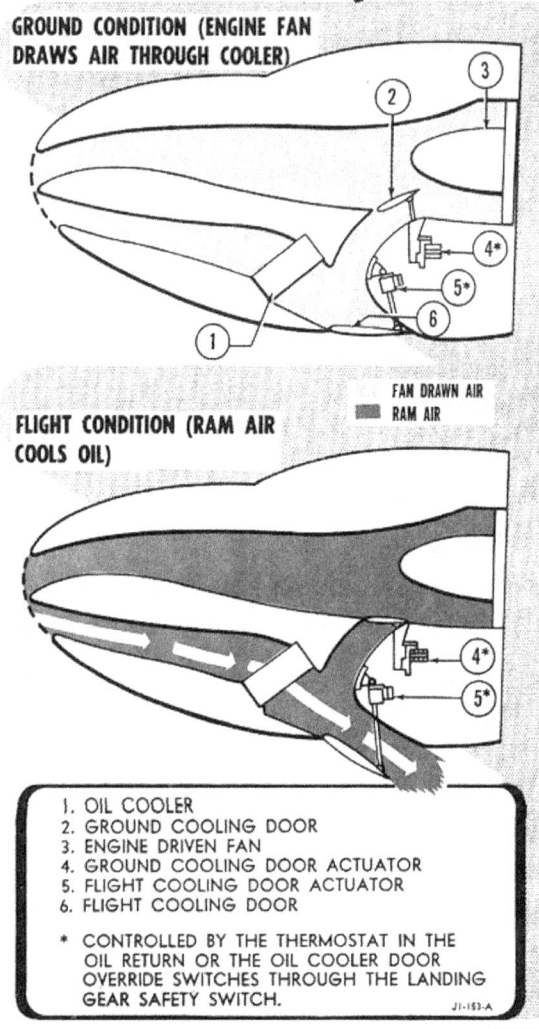

Figure 1-12.

Oil Cooler Door Override Switches (Group 2 Airplanes).

Six three-position switches (20, figure 1-16) located at the engineer's station are provided for direct control of the oil cooler doors. Each switch has spring-loaded OPEN and CLOSE positions and a neutral OFF position. When an oil cooler door mode selector switch is in MANUAL, the related oil cooler doors is operated by holding the corresponding override switch in OPEN or CLOSE. Intermediate positions of the door can be obtained by jiggling the switch. The override circuit provides 115-volt a-c power to the flight cooling door actuator during flight or the ground cooling door actuator during ground operations.

JET ENGINES.

In addition to the six reciprocating engines, the airplane is equipped with four General Electric J47-19 jet engines to provide extra power for take-off, climb, target area operation, and other instances where extra power is required.

A pod nacelle containing two jet engines is suspended from each wing outer panel. Each engine is rated to deliver 5200 thrust pounds at sea level static conditions when operating at 100 per cent rpm with tail pipe temperature at 690°C.

The main components of the jet engine include an accessory section, a 12-stage axial flow compressor, eight can-type combustion chambers, and a single stage turbine. A tail cone and tail pipe serve to conduct the hot exhaust gases away from the engines. Fuel used is the same grade as that used by the reciprocating engines and is taken from the same system. Oil for each jet is supplied from an individual oil tank. The oil is of a different specification than that used by the reciprocating engines. See figure 1-48 for servicing information on the oil system. A heating element is incorporated in each oil tank to heat the oil while the engines are not operating during flight.

All jet engine controls are grouped on an overhead panel which is located directly above the pilots' pedestal. All jet engine instruments, except the jet engine fuel flow indicators, are grouped below the pilots' instrument panel on each side of the pedestal. The fuel flow indicators are located on the engineers' main instrument panel. Each jet is controlled by a throttle lever which acts through a fuel regulator mounted on the engine accessory section. The regulator controls a fuel control valve to meter the amount of fuel to the engine called for by the throttle lever after automatically compensating for engine rpm and air density.

The airplane can fly with or without the jets in operation, according to the conditions of flight. Jet air plugs are used to shut off the engine air flow when the engines are inoperative. When the air plug doors are fully closed, enough air will flow through to windmill the engines at approximately 5 per cent rpm. This low windmilling speed allows heated oil to circulate through the engines so the oil will not congeal at low temperatures. If additional heat is needed for the oil, heated anti-icing air can be taken from the wing anti-icing system and circulated around the oil lines and the oil cooler or the oil tank heaters may be turned on. A special ignition circuit which by-passes the starters is provided to start the jet engines in flight.

Pilots' INSTRUMENT PANEL

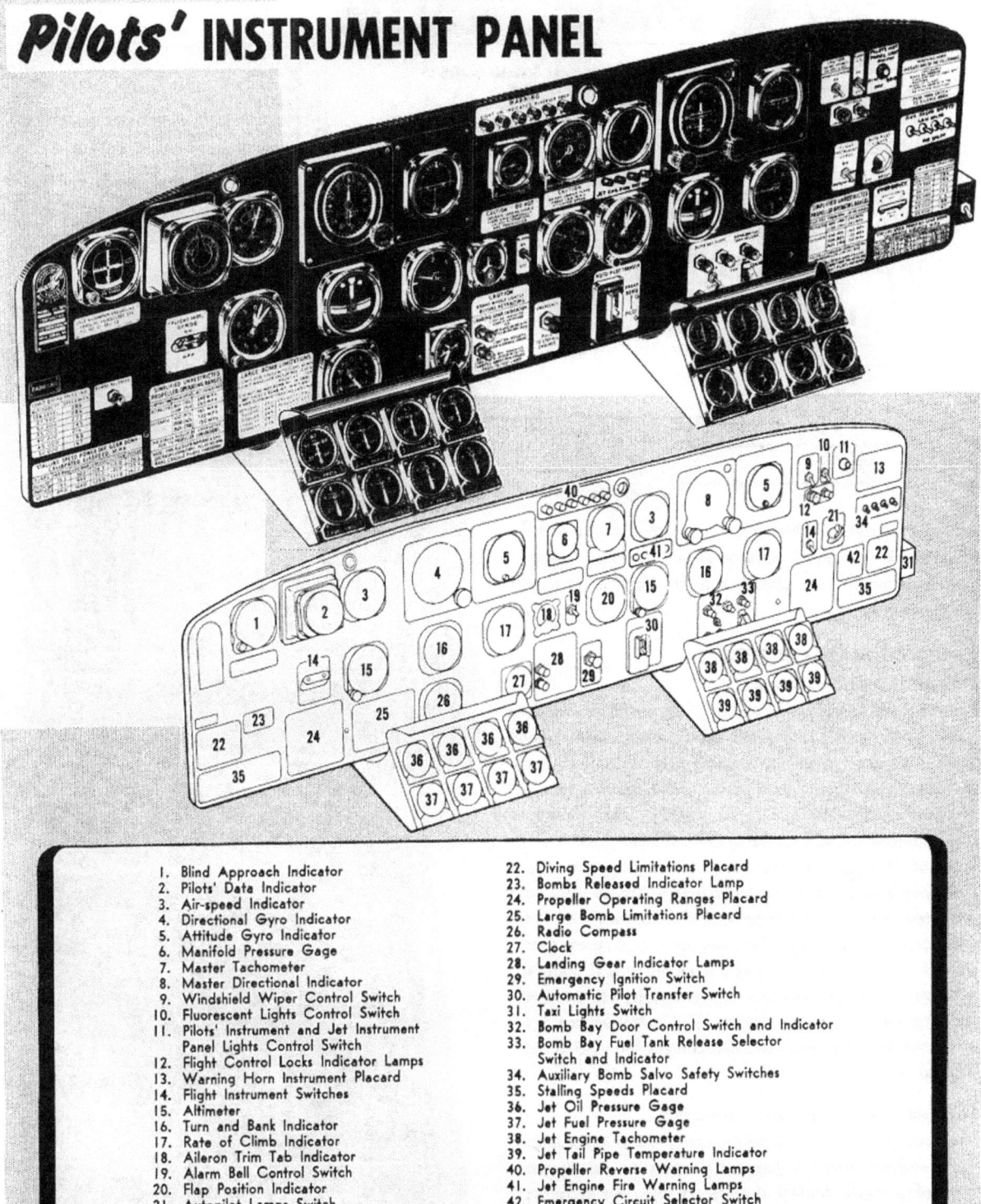

1. Blind Approach Indicator
2. Pilots' Data Indicator
3. Air-speed Indicator
4. Directional Gyro Indicator
5. Attitude Gyro Indicator
6. Manifold Pressure Gage
7. Master Tachometer
8. Master Directional Indicator
9. Windshield Wiper Control Switch
10. Fluorescent Lights Control Switch
11. Pilots' Instrument and Jet Instrument Panel Lights Control Switch
12. Flight Control Locks Indicator Lamps
13. Warning Horn Instrument Placard
14. Flight Instrument Switches
15. Altimeter
16. Turn and Bank Indicator
17. Rate of Climb Indicator
18. Aileron Trim Tab Indicator
19. Alarm Bell Control Switch
20. Flap Position Indicator
21. Autopilot Lamps Switch
22. Diving Speed Limitations Placard
23. Bombs Released Indicator Lamp
24. Propeller Operating Ranges Placard
25. Large Bomb Limitations Placard
26. Radio Compass
27. Clock
28. Landing Gear Indicator Lamps
29. Emergency Ignition Switch
30. Automatic Pilot Transfer Switch
31. Taxi Lights Switch
32. Bomb Bay Door Control Switch and Indicator
33. Bomb Bay Fuel Tank Release Selector Switch and Indicator
34. Auxiliary Bomb Salvo Safety Switches
35. Stalling Speeds Placard
36. Jet Oil Pressure Gage
37. Jet Fuel Pressure Gage
38. Jet Engine Tachometer
39. Jet Tail Pipe Temperature Indicator
40. Propeller Reverse Warning Lamps
41. Jet Engine Fire Warning Lamps
42. Emergency Circuit Selector Switch

Figure 1-13.

Section I
Description

T.O. 1B-36D(II)-1

Pilots' PEDESTAL

1. Navigation Light Selector Switch
2. Master Code Controls
3. Autopilot Control Panel
4. Nose Wheel Steering Switch
5. Landing Gear And Brake Pump Switch
6. Landing Light Extend And Retract Switches
7. Landing Light Filament Switch
8. Navigation Light Switches
9. Formation Light Switch
10. Code Flashing Selector Switch
11. Propeller Reverse Selector Switches
12. Flap Control Switches
13. Throttle Lock Lever
14. Throttle Levers
15. Elevator Trim Tab Control Wheels
16. Warning Horn Shutoff Switch
17. Rudder Trim Tab Control Knob
18. Parking Brake Switch
19. Master Motor Speed Control Lever
20. Propeller Reverse Pitch Switch
21. Aileron Trim Tab Control Switch
22. Turbo Boost Selector Lever
23. Command Radio Control Panel
24. Liaison Radio Control Panel
25. Radio Range Receiver Control Panel
26. Radio Compass Control Panel
27. Instrument Approach Control Panel
28. Bomb Salvo Switch
29. Special Interphone Switch (Some Airplanes)

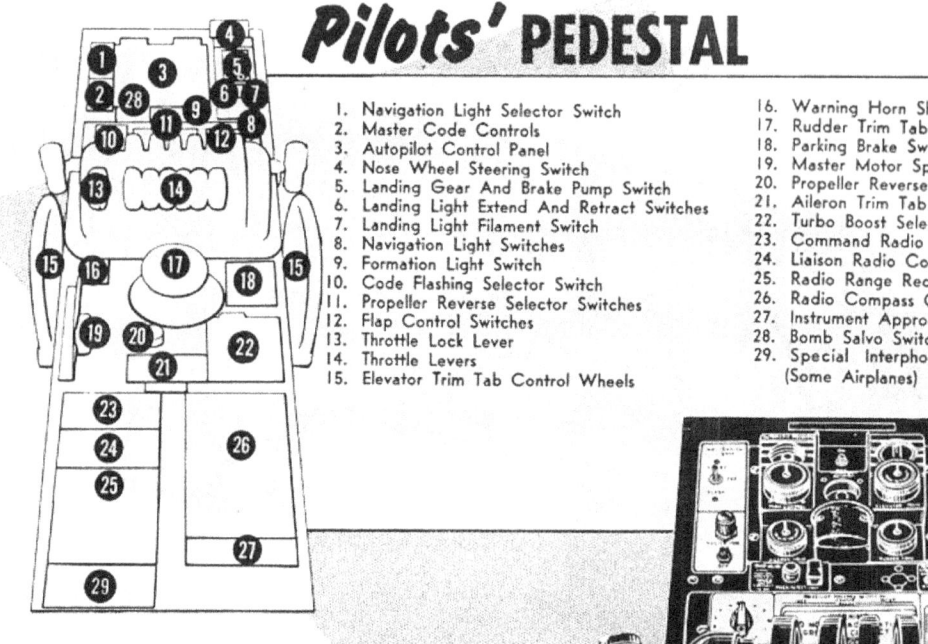

An inlet air screen between the air plug doors and the inlet guide vanes of each engine prevents engine damage from foreign objects which might otherwise enter the compressor.

FUEL REGULATOR CONTROLS.

Throttle Control Levers.

Four throttle levers (1, figure 1-23) and a friction lock lever (2, figure 1-23) are located on the pilots' overhead jet control panel. The lock lever will lock the throttles in any desired position. The throttle lever positions are CLOSE, IDLE, and OPEN. Throttle control employs an electronic system similar to the reciprocating engine mixture control. Movement of a lever originates a 115-volt a-c signal which ultimately positions the fuel regulator and the stopcock of the corresponding engine. The stopcock acts as a fuel shutoff valve when the throttle is closed and functions as a fuel metering valve for engine starting before the fuel regulator becomes effective. The initial movement of a lever also completes the related ignition circuit for ground starting.

Throttle Control Selector Switches.

Four two-position switches (22, figure 1-23), located on the overhead control panel are used to select the type of throttle control desired. When the switches are in the LEVER position, the throttle levers provide throttle control. When the switches are placed in the SWITCH position, throttle control with a set of override switches is effective.

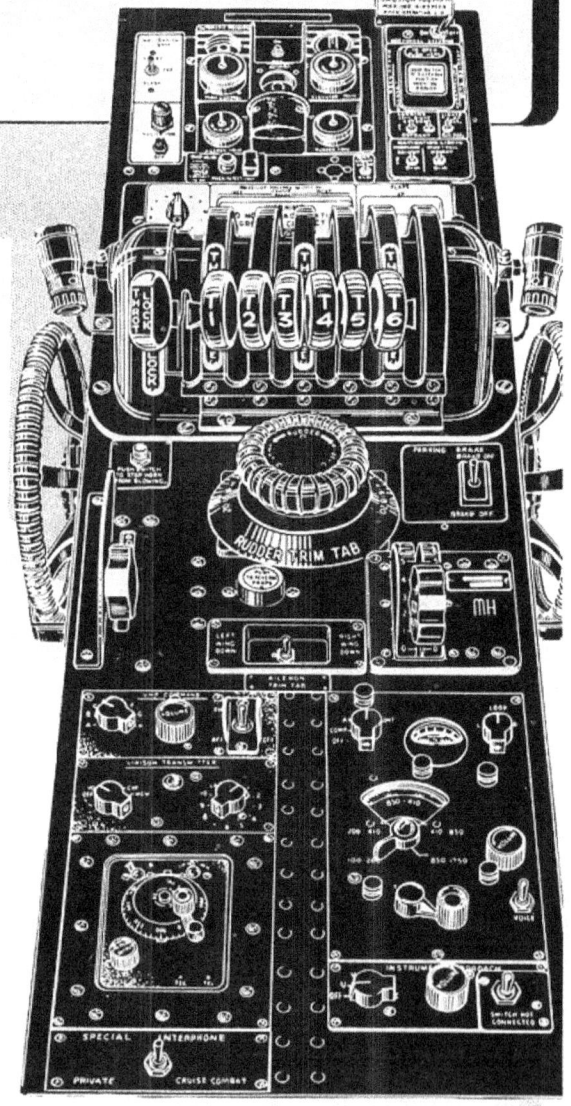

Figure 1-14.

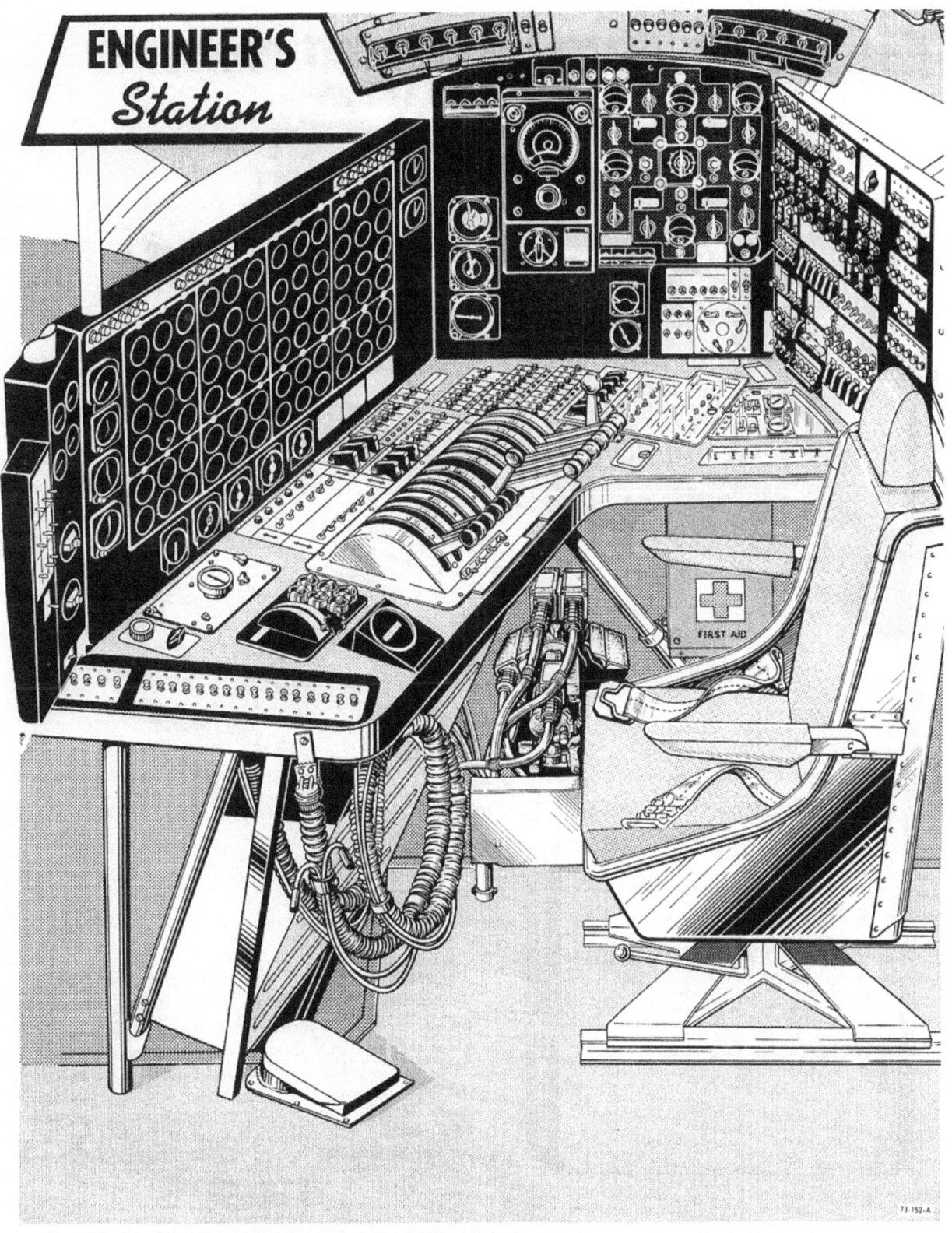

Figure 1-15.

Section I
Description

T.O. 1B-36D(II)-1

Engineer's MAIN INSTRUMENT PANEL
(GROUP 5 AIRPLANES)

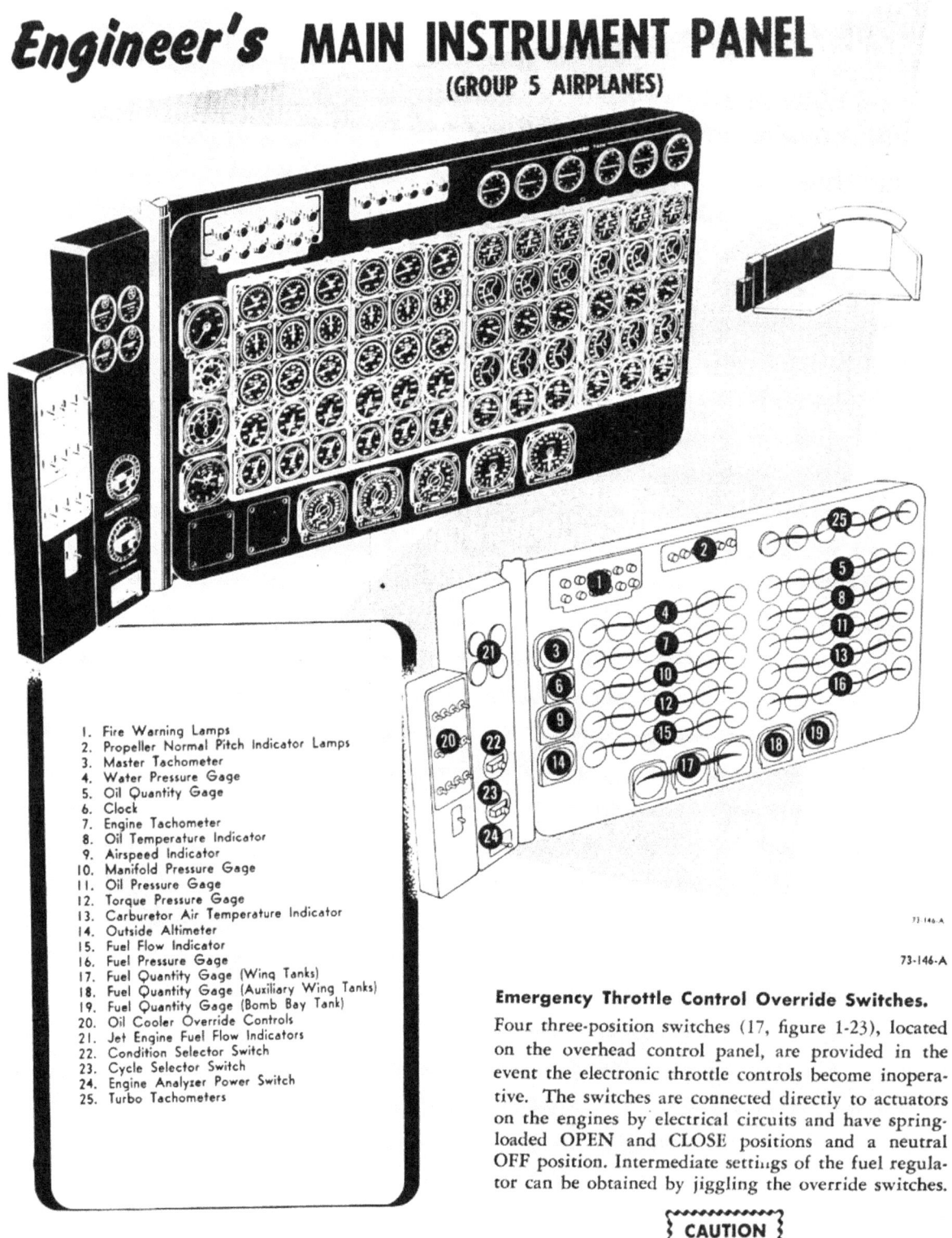

1. Fire Warning Lamps
2. Propeller Normal Pitch Indicator Lamps
3. Master Tachometer
4. Water Pressure Gage
5. Oil Quantity Gage
6. Clock
7. Engine Tachometer
8. Oil Temperature Indicator
9. Airspeed Indicator
10. Manifold Pressure Gage
11. Oil Pressure Gage
12. Torque Pressure Gage
13. Carburetor Air Temperature Indicator
14. Outside Altimeter
15. Fuel Flow Indicator
16. Fuel Pressure Gage
17. Fuel Quantity Gage (Wing Tanks)
18. Fuel Quantity Gage (Auxiliary Wing Tanks)
19. Fuel Quantity Gage (Bomb Bay Tank)
20. Oil Cooler Override Controls
21. Jet Engine Fuel Flow Indicators
22. Condition Selector Switch
23. Cycle Selector Switch
24. Engine Analyzer Power Switch
25. Turbo Tachometers

Figure 1-16.

Emergency Throttle Control Override Switches.

Four three-position switches (17, figure 1-23), located on the overhead control panel, are provided in the event the electronic throttle controls become inoperative. The switches are connected directly to actuators on the engines by electrical circuits and have spring-loaded OPEN and CLOSE positions and a neutral OFF position. Intermediate settings of the fuel regulator can be obtained by jiggling the override switches.

CAUTION

Throttle control is very sensitive when using the emergency throttle override switches.

Engineer's MAIN INSTRUMENT PANEL
(GROUP 4 AIRPLANES)

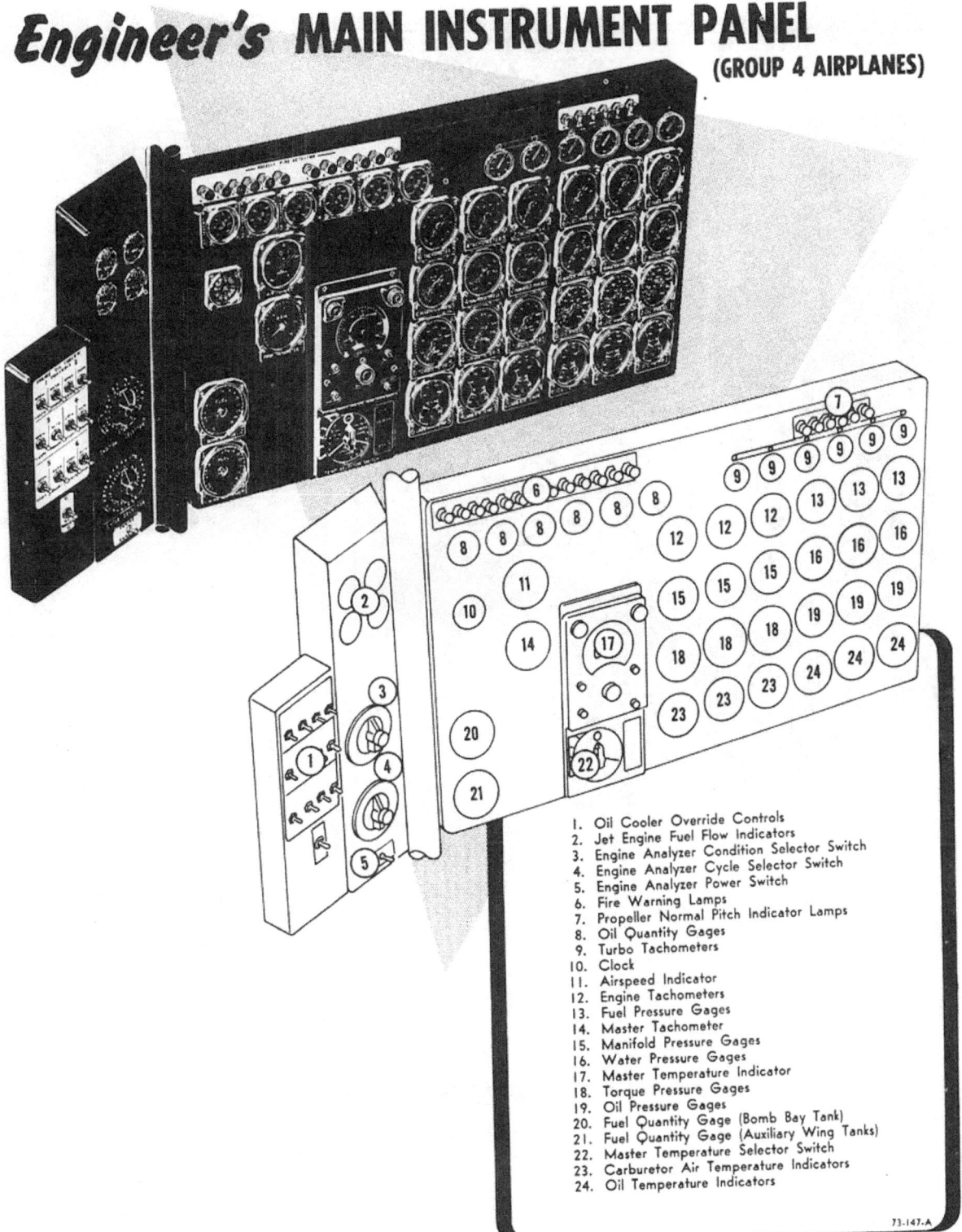

1. Oil Cooler Override Controls
2. Jet Engine Fuel Flow Indicators
3. Engine Analyzer Condition Selector Switch
4. Engine Analyzer Cycle Selector Switch
5. Engine Analyzer Power Switch
6. Fire Warning Lamps
7. Propeller Normal Pitch Indicator Lamps
8. Oil Quantity Gages
9. Turbo Tachometers
10. Clock
11. Airspeed Indicator
12. Engine Tachometers
13. Fuel Pressure Gages
14. Master Tachometer
15. Manifold Pressure Gages
16. Water Pressure Gages
17. Master Temperature Indicator
18. Torque Pressure Gages
19. Oil Pressure Gages
20. Fuel Quantity Gage (Bomb Bay Tank)
21. Fuel Quantity Gage (Auxiliary Wing Tanks)
22. Master Temperature Selector Switch
23. Carburetor Air Temperature Indicators
24. Oil Temperature Indicators

Figure 1-17.

Section I
Description

T.O. 1B-36D(II)-1

Engineer's AUXILIARY INSTRUMENT PANEL
(GROUP 5 AIRPLANES)

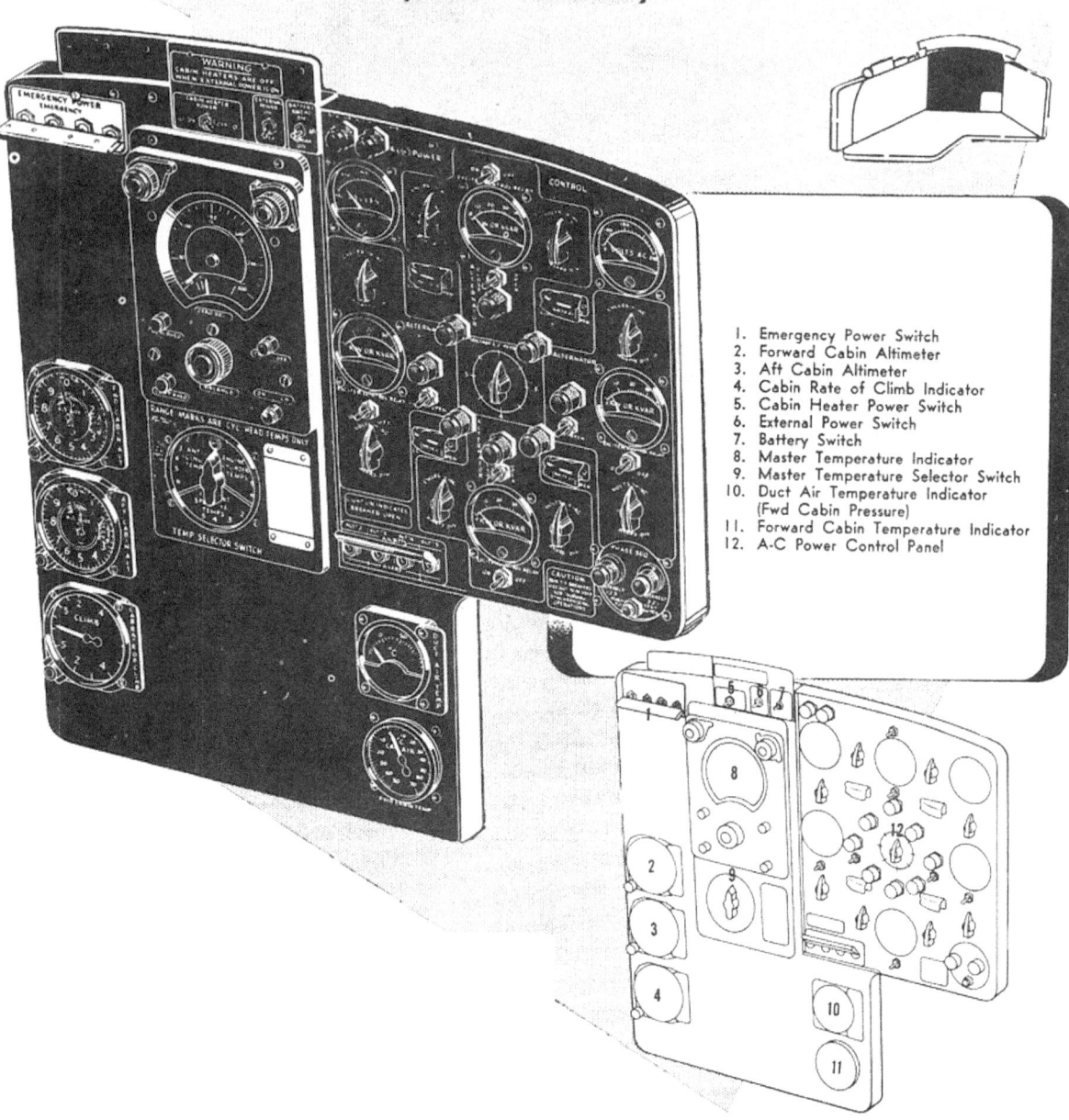

1. Emergency Power Switch
2. Forward Cabin Altimeter
3. Aft Cabin Altimeter
4. Cabin Rate of Climb Indicator
5. Cabin Heater Power Switch
6. External Power Switch
7. Battery Switch
8. Master Temperature Indicator
9. Master Temperature Selector Switch
10. Duct Air Temperature Indicator (Fwd Cabin Pressure)
11. Forward Cabin Temperature Indicator
12. A-C Power Control Panel

Figure 1-18.

AIR INTAKE CONTROL.

The air intake of each jet engine is controlled by an air plug which is made-up of eight leaf-type doors and are operated by an actuator mounted in the nose cone. During jet engine operation the plugs must always be open. When the jets are shut down, the plugs

Revised 18 May 1956

Engineer's AUXILIARY INSTRUMENT PANEL
(GROUP 4 AIRPLANES)

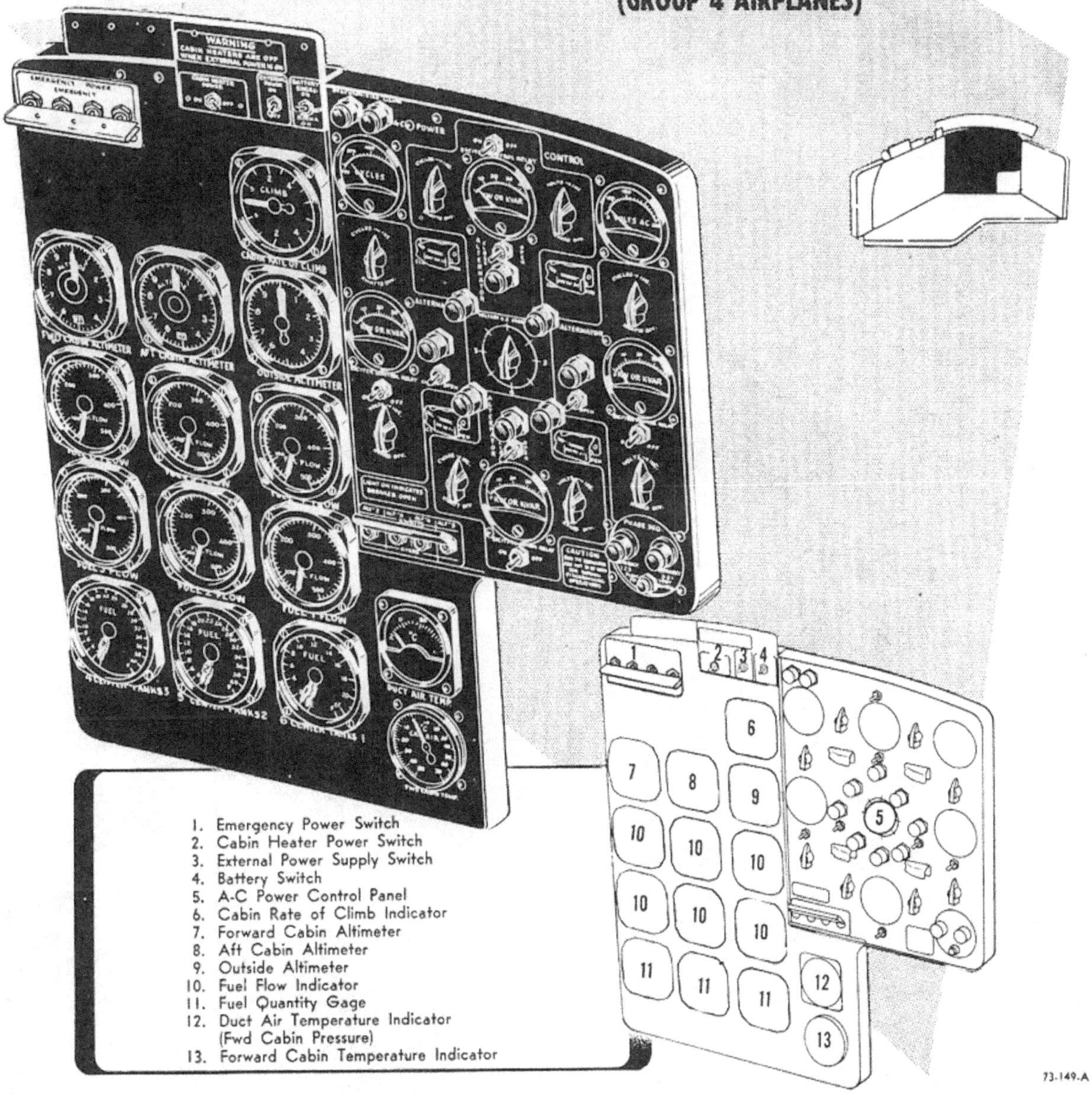

1. Emergency Power Switch
2. Cabin Heater Power Switch
3. External Power Supply Switch
4. Battery Switch
5. A-C Power Control Panel
6. Cabin Rate of Climb Indicator
7. Forward Cabin Altimeter
8. Aft Cabin Altimeter
9. Outside Altimeter
10. Fuel Flow Indicator
11. Fuel Quantity Gage
12. Duct Air Temperature Indicator
    (Fwd Cabin Pressure)
13. Forward Cabin Temperature Indicator

Figure 1-19.

should be closed to prevent excessive windmilling, minimize drag, and keep foreign objects from entering the air intake.

Note

When the plugs are fully closed, the engine will windmill at approximately 5 per cent rpm to maintain oil circulation.

Jet Air Plug Switches.

Four three-position switches (23, figure 1-23), located on the pilots' overhead jet control panel, provide control for the electrically operated engine air plugs. The switches have full-on positions marked OPEN and CLOSE and a neutral OFF position. The switches receive 28-volt direct current from a single circuit breaker to close relays which supply 115-volt a-c

Engineer's MAIN CONTROL PANEL

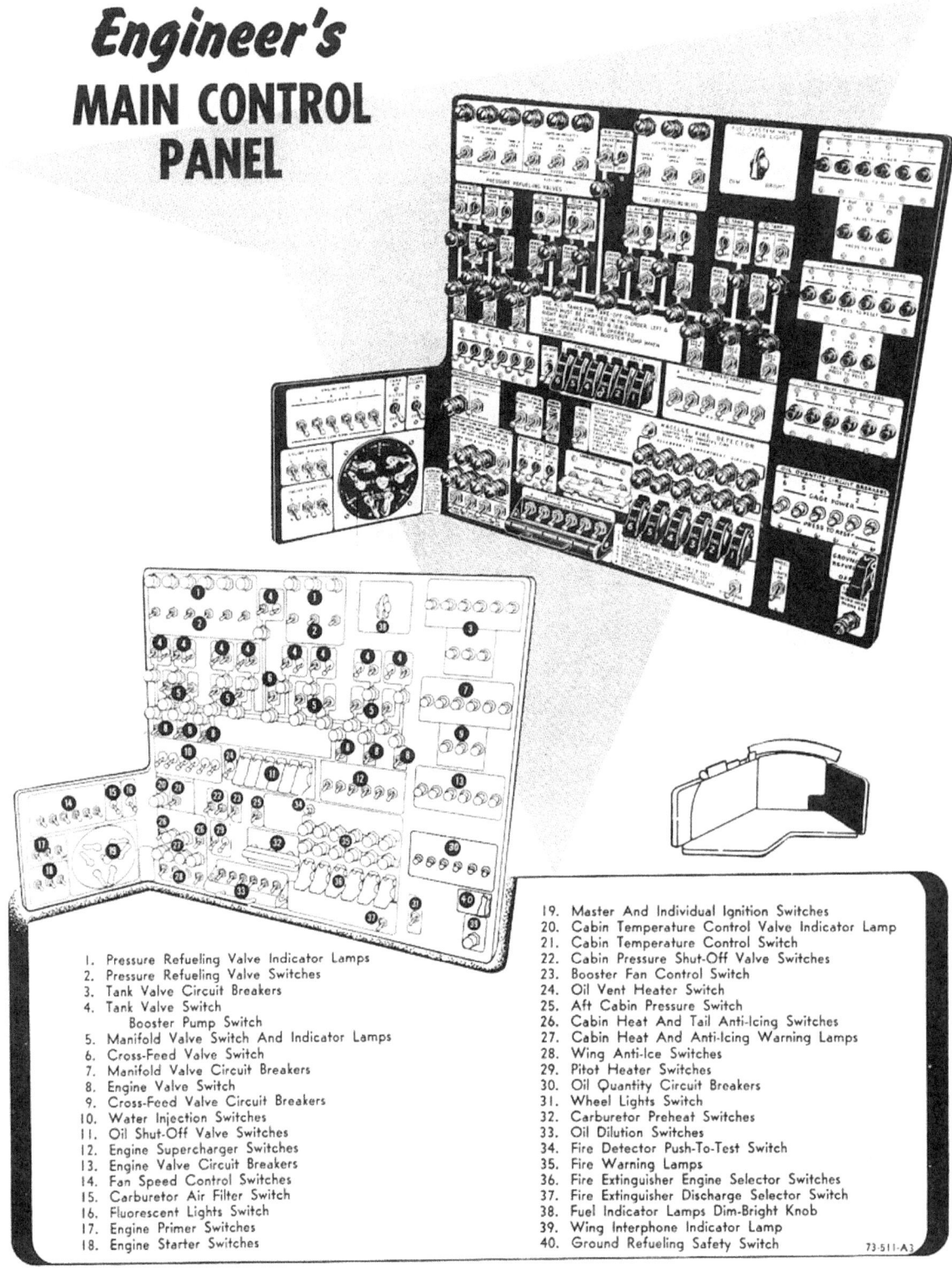

1. Pressure Refueling Valve Indicator Lamps
2. Pressure Refueling Valve Switches
3. Tank Valve Circuit Breakers
4. Tank Valve Switch
   Booster Pump Switch
5. Manifold Valve Switch And Indicator Lamps
6. Cross-Feed Valve Switch
7. Manifold Valve Circuit Breakers
8. Engine Valve Switch
9. Cross-Feed Valve Circuit Breakers
10. Water Injection Switches
11. Oil Shut-Off Valve Switches
12. Engine Supercharger Switches
13. Engine Valve Circuit Breakers
14. Fan Speed Control Switches
15. Carburetor Air Filter Switch
16. Fluorescent Lights Switch
17. Engine Primer Switches
18. Engine Starter Switches
19. Master And Individual Ignition Switches
20. Cabin Temperature Control Valve Indicator Lamp
21. Cabin Temperature Control Switch
22. Cabin Pressure Shut-Off Valve Switches
23. Booster Fan Control Switch
24. Oil Vent Heater Switch
25. Aft Cabin Pressure Switch
26. Cabin Heat And Tail Anti-Icing Switches
27. Cabin Heat And Anti-Icing Warning Lamps
28. Wing Anti-Ice Switches
29. Pitot Heater Switches
30. Oil Quantity Circuit Breakers
31. Wheel Lights Switch
32. Carburetor Preheat Switches
33. Oil Dilution Switches
34. Fire Detector Push-To-Test Switch
35. Fire Warning Lamps
36. Fire Extinguisher Engine Selector Switches
37. Fire Extinguisher Discharge Selector Switch
38. Fuel Indicator Lamps Dim-Bright Knob
39. Wing Interphone Indicator Lamp
40. Ground Refueling Safety Switch

Figure 1-20.

Engineer's TABLE

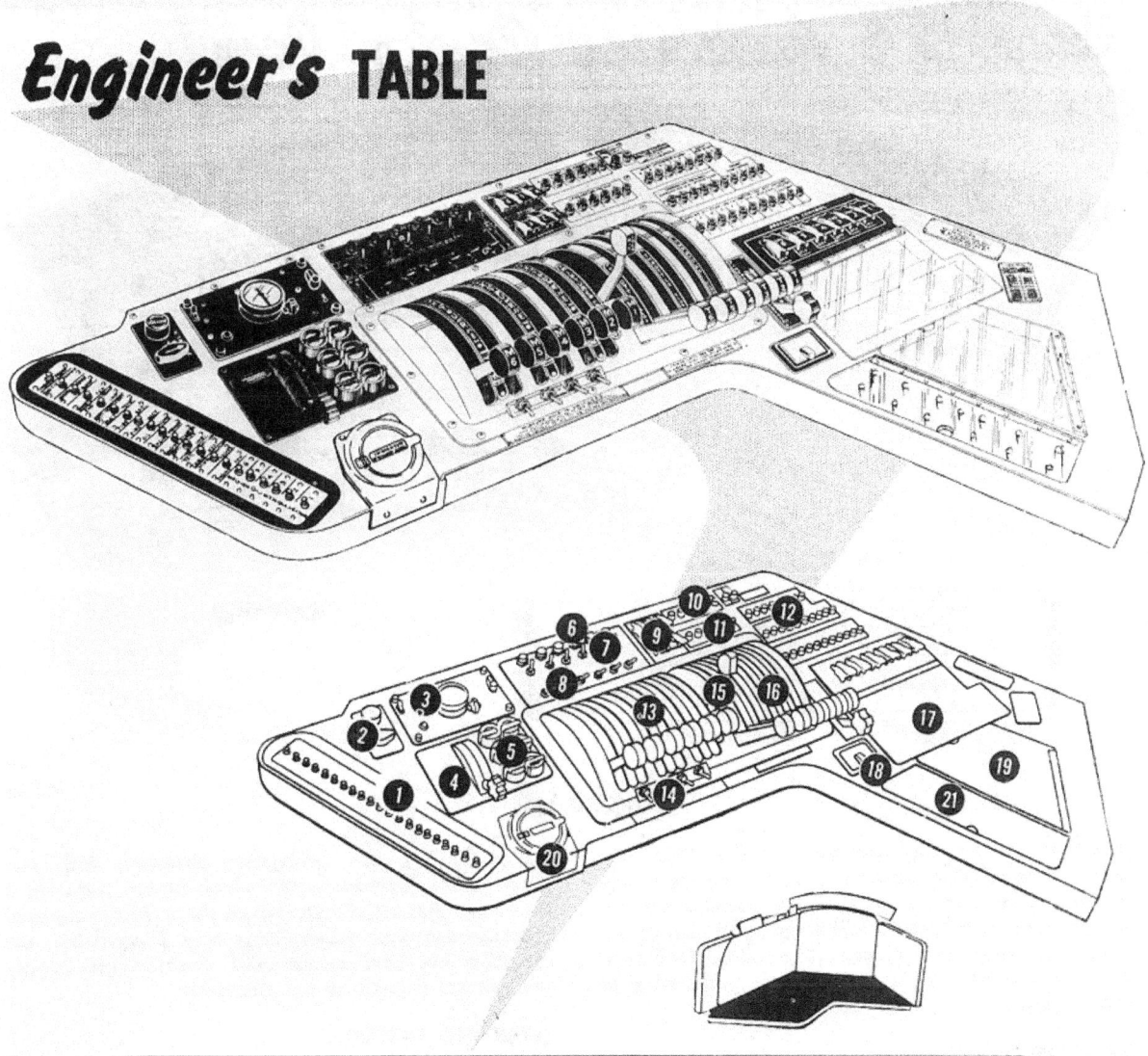

1. Circuit Breakers
   Interphone
   Bus Tie Breaker Control
   Emergency Brake Pump
   Booster Fan
   Engine Temperature Indicator
   Anti-Ice Duct Temperature
   Fire Extinguisher
   Fire Detector
   Oil Dilution
   Engine Primer
   Engine Starter
   Wing Anti-Ice
   Tail Anti-Ice
   Wing Shut-Off Valves
   Engine Fan
   Engine Oil Shut-Off Valve (6)
2. Interphone Control Panel
3. Oxygen Control Panel
4. Turbo Boost Selector Lever
5. Turbo Calibration Potentiometer Knobs
6. Normal Mixture Indicator Lamps
7. Mixture Control Override Switches
8. Mixture Control Selector Switches
9. Spark Advance Switches
10. Engine Fuel Mixture Circuit Breakers
11. Carburetor Preheat Circuit Breakers
12. Circuit Breakers
    Cabin Duct Temperature
    Prop Pitch Indicator
    Engine Supercharger Selector (6)
    Engine Spark Advance (6)
    Carburetor Air Temperature Indicator (6)
    Engine Oil Temperature Indicator (6)
    Fuel Tank Level Indicator (5)
13. Mixture Control Levers
14. Alternator Breaker Hold-In Switches
15. Mixture Control Lock Lever
16. Throttle Levers
17. Propeller Control Panel
18. Ash Receiver
19. Hydraulic Control Panel
20. Engine Analyzer Indicator
21. Turbo Override Control Panel

Figure 1-21.

ENGINEER'S Auxiliary Control Panel

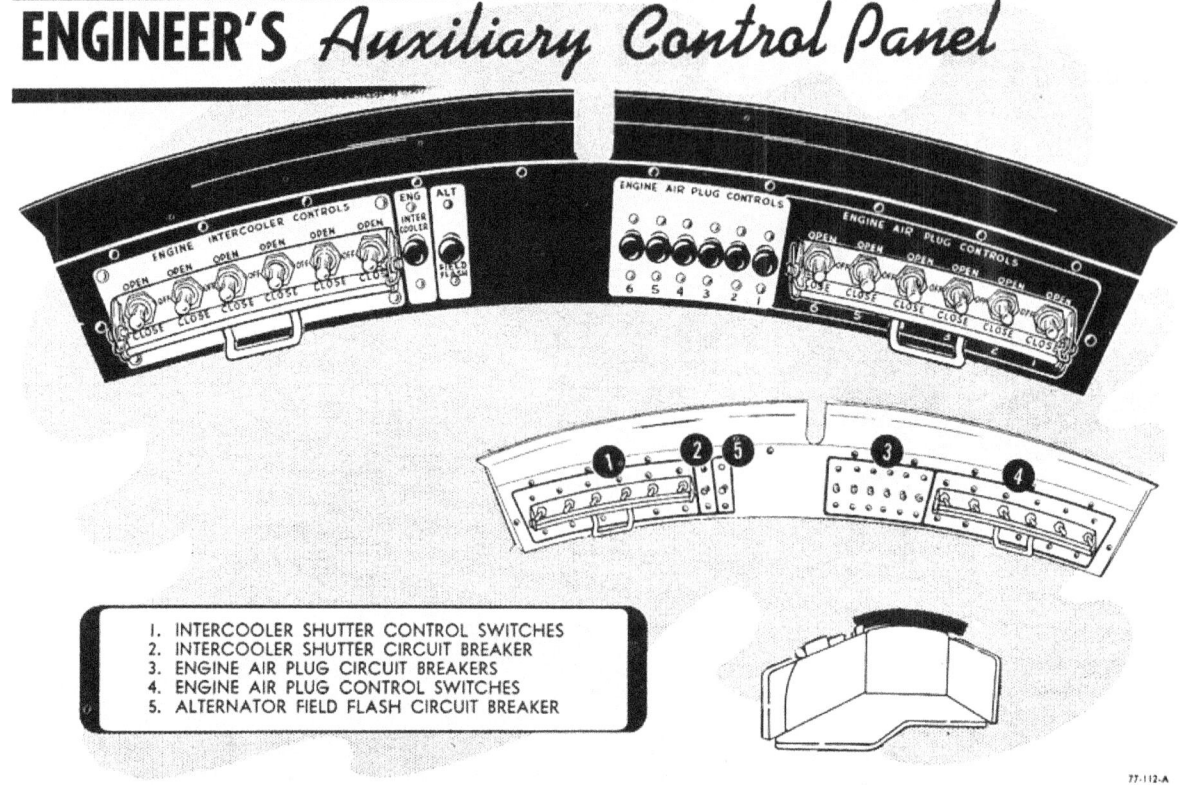

1. INTERCOOLER SHUTTER CONTROL SWITCHES
2. INTERCOOLER SHUTTER CIRCUIT BREAKER
3. ENGINE AIR PLUG CIRCUIT BREAKERS
4. ENGINE AIR PLUG CONTROL SWITCHES
5. ALTERNATOR FIELD FLASH CIRCUIT BREAKER

Figure 1-22.

power to the air plug actuators. In the event of a short in one air plug control circuit, placing the switch of the defective circuit in the OFF position and resetting the circuit breaker will allow continued operation of the other three circuits. The neutral OFF position can also be used for intermediate positioning of the air plugs.

IGNITION SYSTEM.

Ignition start switches supply electrical energy to ignition electrodes which are mounted in combustion chambers No. 3 and 7 of each jet engine. Complete combustion is carried out by flame propagation between the chambers through the crossfire tubes. Ignition is used only for starting as combustion in the chambers is self-sustaining once it has been started, except when flame-out conditions occur.

Ignition Start Switches.

Four three-position switches (16, figure 1-23), located on the overhead control panel, are provided for starting the engines during flight. Each switch has a neutral OFF position, a NORMAL position, and a spring-loaded ALT position. With the switches in the NORMAL position, ignition occurs when the starter switches are held ON and the throttle levers are advanced from the CLOSE position. This pre-

vents flooding the combustion chambers with raw fuel before ignition occurs which would result in a hot start. For aerial starts where the starter is not used because sufficient windmilling rpm is available, the switches are held in the ALT position and supply a-c current directly to the electrodes.

STARTING SYSTEM.

Each jet engine is equipped with an a-c starting system containing a starter switch and a starter. The starter is used for ground starts only, as the jet engine is windmilled for aerial starts. After the engine fires during ground starts, the starter is used to aid engine acceleration up to 20 to 25 per cent rpm to prevent excessive tail pipe temperatures and possible compressor stall.

Engine Starter Switches.

Four spring-loaded switches (15, figure 1-23), located on the overhead control panel, are provided for ground starting only. When the switches are held ON, 28-volt direct current closes relays to supply 208-volt a-c power to the starters. Closing the switches also sets up the ignition circuits. When the switches are released, the starters are de-energized and the ignition is cut off.

PILOTS' Jet Control Panel

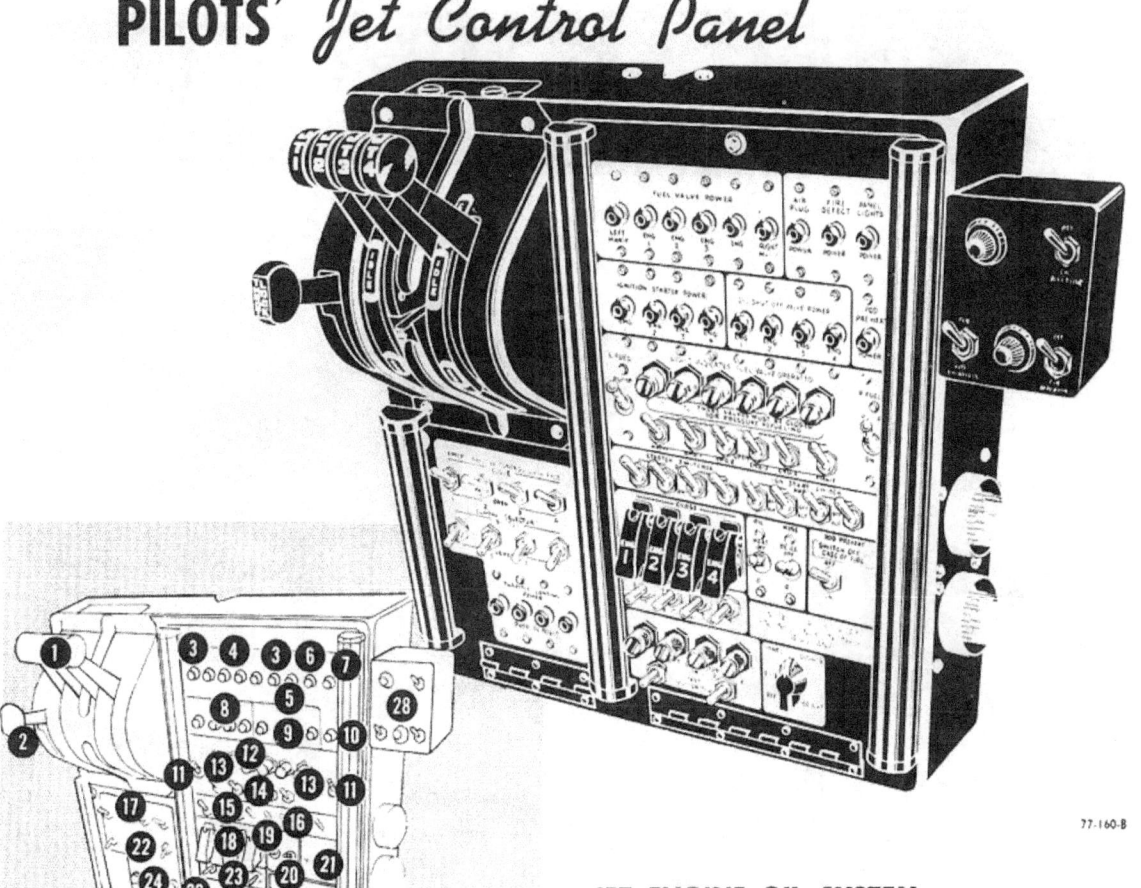

1. Throttle
2. Throttle Lock Lever
3. Manifold Fuel Valve Circuit Breakers
4. Engine Fuel Valve Circuit Breakers
5. Air Plug Circuit Breaker
6. Fire Detection Circuit Breaker
7. Control Panel Lights Circuit Breaker
8. Ignition Circuit Breakers
9. Oil Shutoff Valve Circuit Breakers
10. Pod Preheat Circuit Breaker
11. Booster Pump Switches
12. Fuel Valve Indicator Lamps
13. Manifold Valve Switches
14. Engine Valve Switches
15. Engine Starter Switches
16. Ignition Start Switches
17. Throttle Control Override Switches
18. Oil Shutoff Valve Switches
19. Oil Heater Switch
20. Nose De-Ice Control Switch
21. Pod Preheat Control Switch
22. Throttle Control Selector Switches
23. Air Plug Switches
24. Throttle Control Circuit Breakers
25. Panel Lights Control Switch
26. Fire Warning Lamps
27. Fire Detection Switches
28. Automatic Approach and Altitude Control Panel

Figure 1-23.

JET ENGINE OIL SYSTEM.

Each jet engine has an independent oil system consisting principally of a 20-gallon supply tank, lines, pressure and scavenge pumps, a filter, an oil cooler, and an oil tank heater. The tanks, installed in the wing above the jets, will hold 13 gallons of oil with the remaining 7-gallon space reserved for oil foaming. The oil flows from the tank to a gear-driven combination pressure and scavenge pump mounted on the accessory section and is pumped to the lubrication points and to the fuel regulator. A filter mounted on the compressor case filters the oil passing through the line from the pressure pump to the aft bearings. A scavenge pump in the mid-frame returns the oil in the aft section through the cooler to the tank. The cooler is mounted on the compressor casing and uses fuel as a cooling medium. The oil cooling is fully automatic with a thermostatically controlled by-pass and relief valve regulating the flow of oil through the cooler. Lubricating oil pumped to the forward section of the engine is scavenged and returned to the supply tank by the scavenge side of the combination pressure and scavenge pump. This oil is not cooled, as temperatures are not high in the section it lubricates. Strainers within the accessory section gear case clean the oil of any large foreign

FUEL SYSTEM Schematic

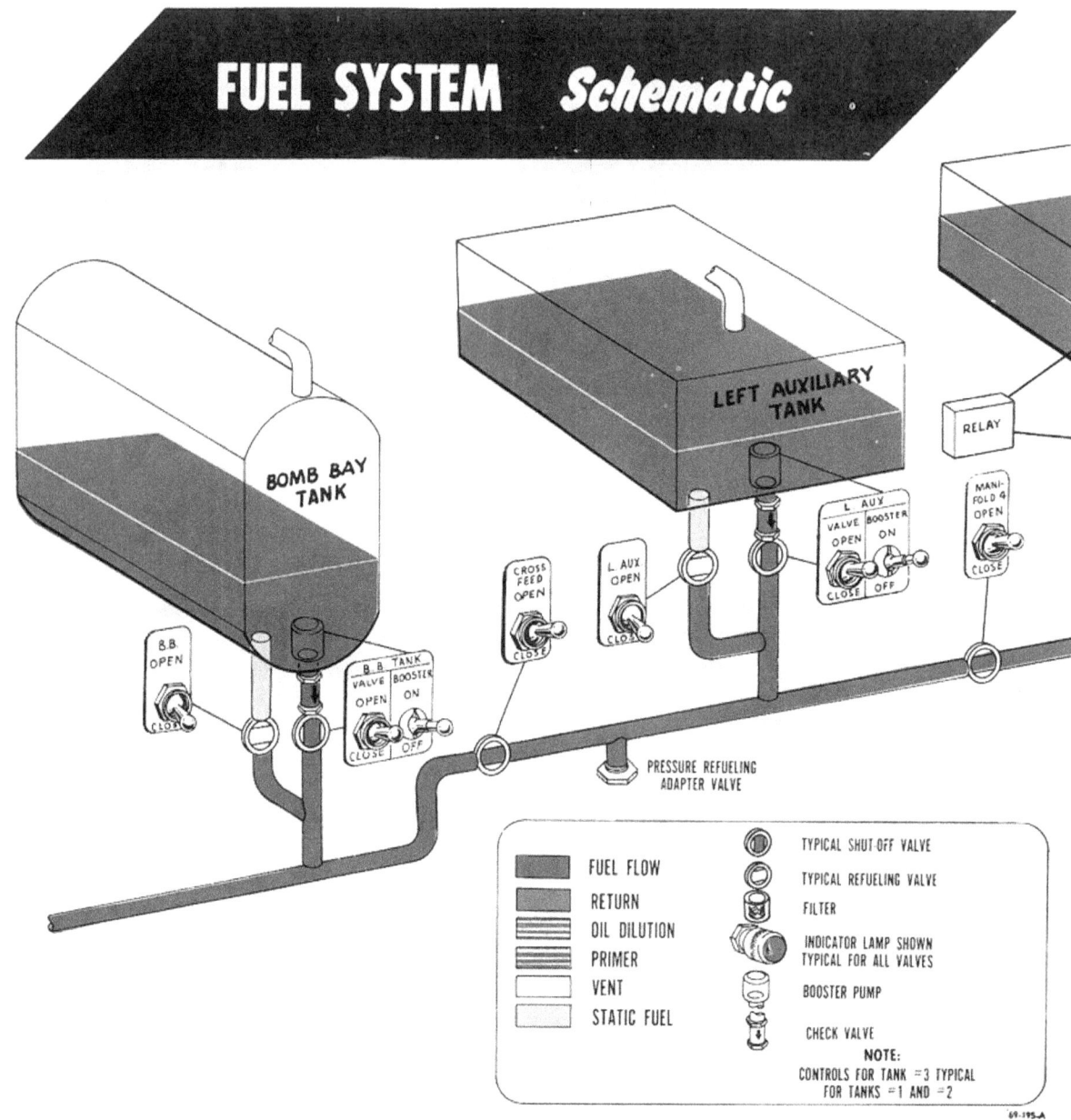

Figure 1-24. (Sheet 1)

particles. A combination filter and orifice, filters and meters the oil supply to the fuel regulator. Some airplanes have cell-type tanks which are pressurized to prevent their collapse. This is accomplished by means of a pressure relief valve located in the oil tank vent line which maintains a 2.75 psi differential between the ambient and the oil tank pressure. Other airplanes are equipped with metal tanks which do not require pressurization. Refer to figure 1-48 for servicing information.

CONTROLS AND INDICATORS.

Oil Shutoff Valve Switches.

Four ON-OFF switches (18, figure 1-23), located on the pilots' overhead control panel, are provided to control the oil shutoff valves. The valves operate on 115-volt a-c power.

Oil Pressure Gages.

Four oil pressure gages (36, figure 1-13), one for each jet engine, are located on the pilot's jet instrument panel.

T.O. 1B-36D(II)-1

Section I
Description

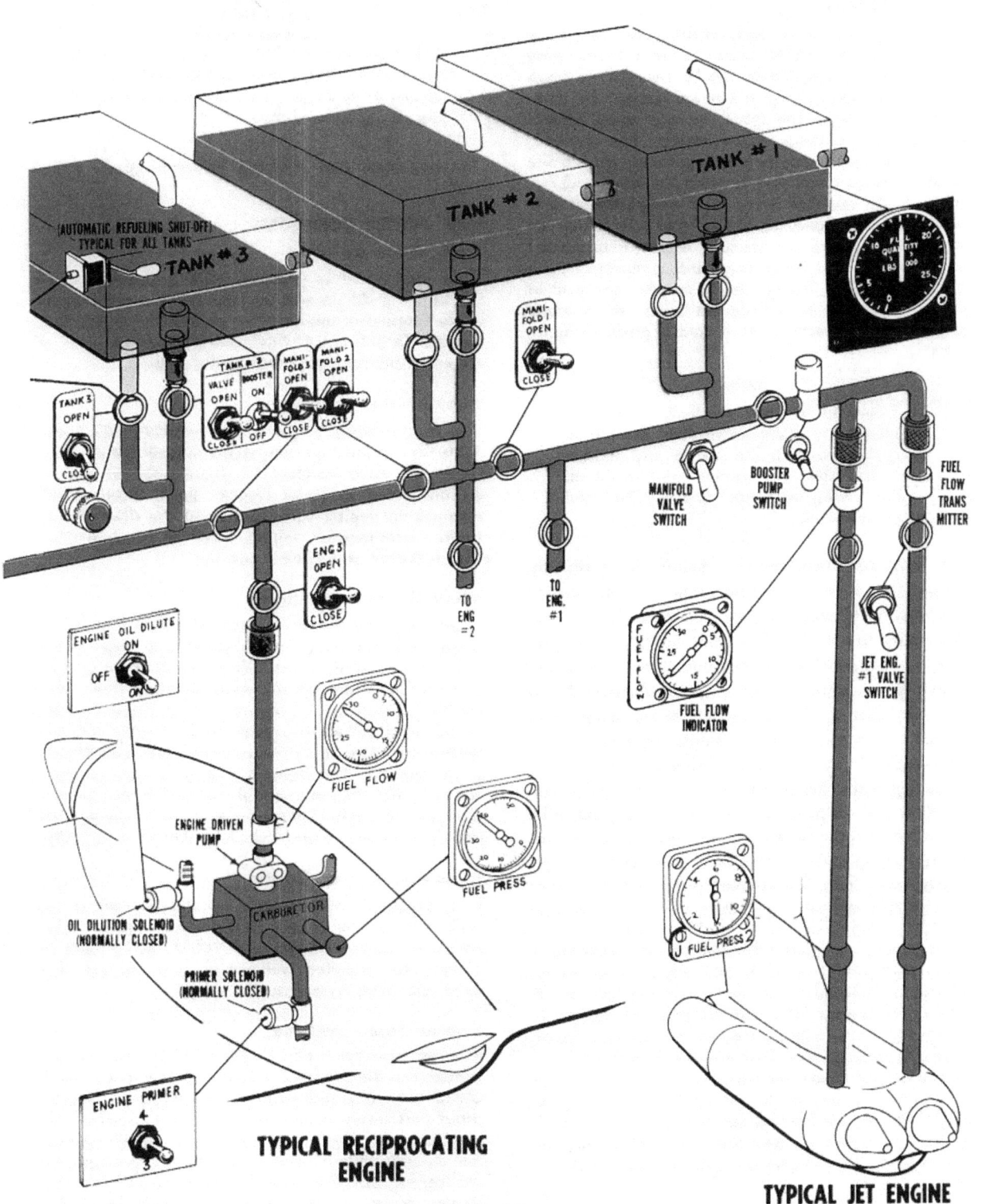

Figure 1-24. (Sheet 2)

Section I
Description

T.O. 1B-36D(II)-1

FUEL SYSTEM.

Fuel is supplied to the reciprocating and the jet engines from six main wing tanks and two auxiliary wing tanks. An additional tank can be installed in bomb bay 3. The main wing tanks are formed by compartments between the front and rear spars inboard of each reciprocating engine nacelle. The auxiliary wing tanks are formed by a compartment on each side of the fuselage center line between the front and rear spars. Each auxiliary wing tank compartment contains four interconnected bladder-type cells which are nonself-sealing and are made of rubber impregnated nylon fabric. The bomb bay tank is equipped with quick disconnect fittings so it can be dropped in flight. It is supported within the bomb bay by bomb shackles. The capacity of each tank is given in figure 1-25.

Note

The capacity of each auxiliary wing tank varies from airplane to airplane because of small differences in the size of the bladder-type cells. For the sake of uniformity all auxiliary wing tanks are rated at 4788.5 gallons usable fuel.

All tanks are interconnected, making it possible to supply fuel from any combination of tanks to any combination of engines. Each fuel tank has an inlet and outlet line with a fuel valve in each. The inlet line is a provision for single point pressure refueling which is accomplished from a special adapter valve in the left side of the fuselage between bomb bays 2 and 3. The outlet line connects the tanks to the main manifold fuel line which interconnects all of the wing fuel tanks. From this main manifold, fuel is supplied to the reciprocating and the jet engines. Fuel vapor which forms in the carburetor and the jet engine booster pump tanks is returned to the tanks through vapor return lines. The amount of fuel returned varies considerably and could possibly amount to 150 gallons for all six engines during a long flight. For fuel system arrangement, see figure 1-24. Fuel flow is controlled by tank, manifold, cross-feed, and engine fuel valves. Normally these valves are electrically operated by 28-volt direct current. With the exception of the engine valves for the jet engines, the valves can be positioned manually during flight. Fuel pressure is provided by an engine-driven pump on each engine and a booster pump in each tank. An additional booster pump is installed in the fuel line leading to each pair of jet engines. The booster pumps operate on 208-volt alternating current. For fuel system management, see Section VII.

Fuel conforming to Specification **MIL-F-5572** (AN-F-48), grade 115/145, is used. **Grade 100/130** may be used as an alternate fuel.

CAUTION

When an alternate fuel is used, engine limitations differ from those established for the recommended fuel grade. Refer to Section V for all operating limits.

For additional fuel servicing information, see figure 1-48.

FUEL SYSTEM CONTROLS.

Tank Valve Switches.

Each tank valve is provided with a control switch (4, figure 1-20) located on the main control panel at the engineer's station. The switches have positions marked OPEN and CLOSE, and are used to open or close the fuel supply lines from the tanks.

Engine Valve Switches.

Six reciprocating engine valve switches (8, figure 1-20) are located on the main control panel. Four jet engine valve switches (14, figure 1-23) are located on the pilots' overhead control panel. Each switch operates an engine valve to control the flow of fuel to its corresponding engine. Each of these switches has an OPEN and CLOSE position.

Manifold Valve Switches.

Eight manifold valve switches (5, figure 1-20) are located on the main control panel and each switch controls a manifold valve. These manifold valves control fuel flow through the main manifold line. Two additional switches (13, figure 1-23) are located on the pilots' overhead control panel. Each of these switches operates a valve which controls the flow to each pair of jet engines. The electrical circuits of these switches are such that they must be in the OPEN position before the jet engine booster pumps will operate. All manifold valve switches are marked OPEN and CLOSE.

Cross-Feed Valve Switch.

One cross-feed valve switch (6, figure 1-20) is located on the engineer's main control panel. The switch is marked OPEN and CLOSE, and is used to operate the cross-feed valve which controls fuel flow from one wing system to the other.

Booster Pump Switches.

Nine switch-type circuit breakers (4, figure 1-20) are located on the engineer's main control panel. Each switch controls a fuel tank booster pump. Two additional switch-type circuit breakers (11, figure 1-23), located on the pilots' overhead control panel, operate the booster pumps for the jet engines provided the jet engine manifold valve switches are OPEN. The booster pump switch positions are ON and OFF. Each switch controls 28-volt d-c power to a relay which controls 208-volt a-c power to the related booster pump motor.

Fuel Indicator Lamps Dim-Bright Knob.

This rheostat knob (38, figure 1-20), located on the engineer's main control panel, controls the brilliance of the fuel valve indicator lamps on the fuel control panel except those for the pressure refueling valves.

FUEL INDICATORS.

Reciprocating Engine Fuel Flow Indicators.

Six fuel flow indicators (10, figure 1-19) are located on the engineer's auxiliary instrument panel of group 4 airplanes. Each indicator is electrically connected to its respective flowmeter transmitter, which is located in the fuel line upstream from the engine-driven pump on each reciprocating engine. The indicators register fuel flow in gallons and pounds per hour. Six fuel flow indicators (12, figure 1-14) for the reciprocating engines are located on the engineer's main instrument panel of group 5 airplanes and indicate fuel flow in pounds per hour. There are no indicators to register fuel flow to the jet engines. The system is energized from a transformer which receives 115-volt alternating current from the engineer's power panel.

Jet Engine Fuel Flow Indicators.

Four fuel flow indicators (21, figure 1-16) are located on the engineer's main instrument panel. Each indicator is connected to its related flowmeter transmitter which is located in the fuel line between the filter and the engine shutoff valve. The indicators register flow in pounds per hour.

Fuel Pressure Gages.

Three dual indicating fuel pressure gages (7, figure 1-17) for the reciprocating engines are located on the engineer's main instrument panel of group 4 airplanes. Six single indicating fuel pressure gages, (15, figure 1-16) for the reciprocating engines are located on the engineer's main instrument panel of group 5 airplanes. Four gages (37, figure 1-13) for the jet engines are mounted on the pilot's jet instrument panel. Power for the jet fuel pressure indicating system is

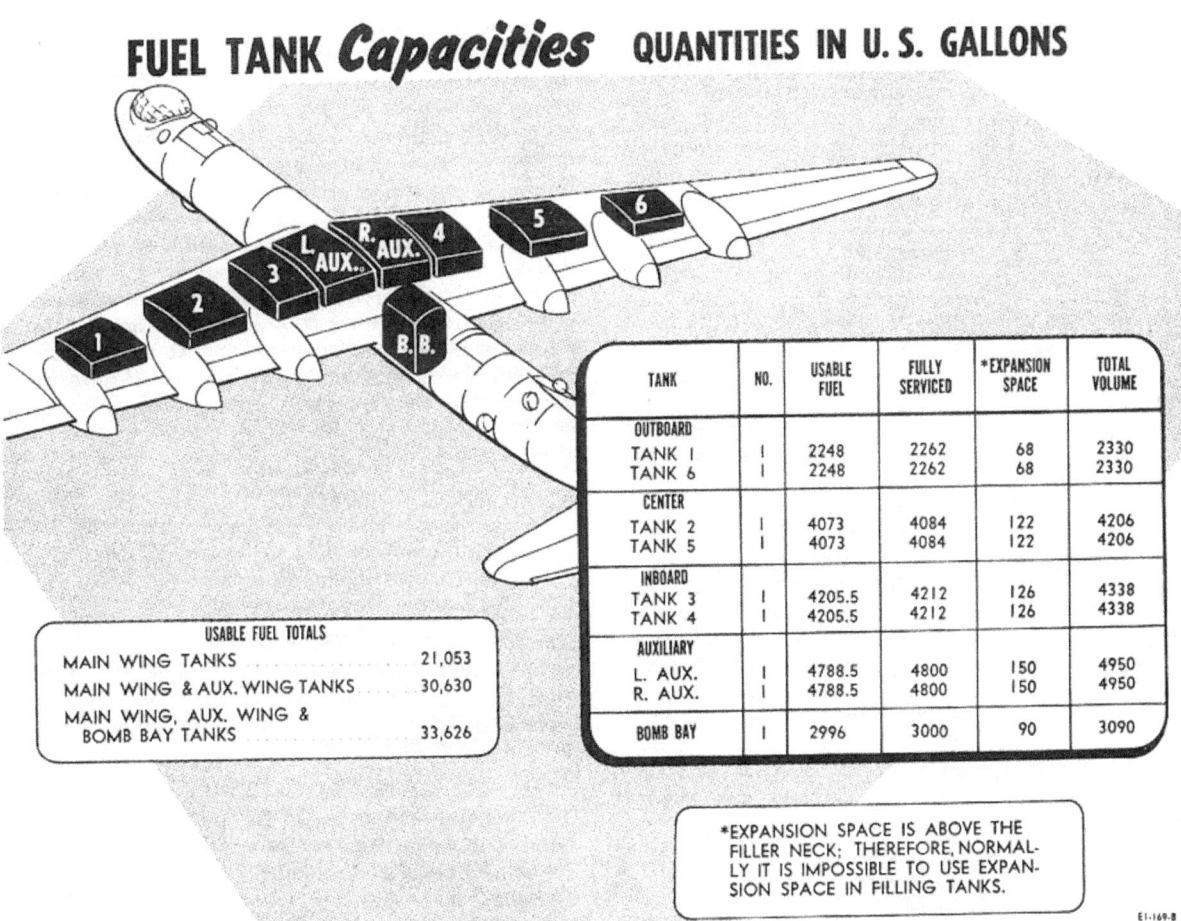

FUEL TANK Capacities QUANTITIES IN U.S. GALLONS

TANK	NO.	USABLE FUEL	FULLY SERVICED	*EXPANSION SPACE	TOTAL VOLUME
OUTBOARD					
TANK 1	1	2248	2262	68	2330
TANK 6	1	2248	2262	68	2330
CENTER					
TANK 2	1	4073	4084	122	4206
TANK 5	1	4073	4084	122	4206
INBOARD					
TANK 3	1	4205.5	4212	126	4338
TANK 4	1	4205.5	4212	126	4338
AUXILIARY					
L. AUX.	1	4788.5	4800	150	4950
R. AUX.	1	4788.5	4800	150	4950
BOMB BAY	1	2996	3000	90	3090

USABLE FUEL TOTALS	
MAIN WING TANKS	21,053
MAIN WING & AUX. WING TANKS	30,630
MAIN WING, AUX. WING & BOMB BAY TANKS	33,626

*EXPANSION SPACE IS ABOVE THE FILLER NECK; THEREFORE, NORMALLY IT IS IMPOSSIBLE TO USE EXPANSION SPACE IN FILLING TANKS.

Figure 1-25.

Section I
Description

received from a transformer which has an input of 115-volt alternating current from the jet pod power panel.

Fuel Quantity Gages.

For group 4 airplanes, three dual indicating fuel quantity gages (11, figure 1-19) for the main wing tanks are located on the engineer's auxiliary instrument panel and a dual indicating gage (21, figure 1-17) for the auxiliary wing tanks is located on the engineer's main instrument panel. A single indicating instrument (20, figure 1-17) for the bomb bay tank is also located on the engineer's main instrument panel. For group 5 airplanes, three dual indicating fuel quantity gages (17, figure 1-16) for the main wing tanks and a dual indicating gage (18, figure 1-16) for the auxiliary wing tanks are located on the engineer's main instrument panel. A single indicating gage (19, figure 1-16) for the bomb bay tank is located on the flight engineer's main instrument panel. The gages operate on 28-volt direct current from the engineer's circuit breaker panel.

Fuel Valve Indicator Lamps.

Fuel valve indicator lamps (5, figure 1-20 and 12, figure 1-23) are located on the engineer's main control panel and the pilots' overhead jet control panel. The lamps represent fuel control valves and burn continuously when the power is on and the valve gates are in either extreme position. At the beginning of valve gate travel, the corresponding lamp goes out; normally relighting of the lamp indicates successful operation of the valve.

> **CAUTION**
>
> The light indicates motor travel and will give an erroneous indication if the motor is disconnected from the valve.

The specific position of a control valve gate is indicated by the position of the corresponding switch only.

PRESSURE REFUELING CONTROLS.

Pressure Refueling Valve Switches.

Nine pressure refueling valve switches (2, figure 1-20), one for each wing tank and the bomb bay tank, are on the engineer's main control panel. Each switch has OPEN and CLOSE positions and controls the fuel valve in the inlet line of each tank. During pressure refueling, the valves automatically close when their tanks are within 25 to 75 gallons of being full; then, the valves cannot be opened electrically until 150 to 300 gallons of fuel are used. In this condition, the switches must first be placed CLOSE and then OPEN to obtain successful operation.

> **CAUTION**
>
> During pressure refueling, someone should be stationed at the main control panel to observe the fuel level indicators and the refueling valve indicator lights. The refueling valves must be closed if they fail to operate automatically. Failure of a valve to operate is determined when the valve indicator light does not light and the fuel quantity gage pointer moves past the point at which the tank is full.

Note

Approximately one second is required for a refueling valve to travel from one extreme position to the other after the valve actuator has been energized.

Pressure Refueling Valve Indicator Lamps.

An indicator lamp (1, figure 1-20) for each pressure refueling valve glows when its corresponding valve is fully closed. Each lamp is dark when its valve partly or fully opens.

> **CAUTION**
>
> The light indicates motor travel and will give erroneous indication if the motor is disconnected from the valve.

Ground Refueling Safety Switch.

An on-off switch (40, figure 1-20) is located on the engineer's main control panel to eliminate the possibility of fire due to sparks caused by inadvertent equipment operation or equipment malfunction during single point refueling operations. This switch is normally guarded in the OFF position. Place the switch in the ON position isolates all a-c and d-c power from the forward cabin external power source except the power required to accomplish single point refueling. Power is supplied only to the fuel quantity gage and tank refueling valve control circuits. Moving the switch to the OFF position returns all circuits to normal.

> **CAUTION**
>
> This switch isolates electrical equipment from electrical power applied to the forward cabin external power receptacle only.

EMERGENCY FUEL CONTROLS.

The fuel valves operate manually in the event of electrical failure. (See figure 3-12.) The valves for the auxiliary wing tanks and the bomb bay tank are accessible from the bomb bay. The jet engine fuel valves are not accessible in flight.

BOMB BAY TANK RELEASE CONTROLS.

The bomb bay fuel tank can be jettisoned by a bomb bay tank release selector switch on the pilots' instrument panel and the salvo switches at the pilots' and the radar-observer's stations. Refer to "Emergency Release Controls," Section IV for information on the bomb salvo switches.

Bomb Bay Tank Release Selector Switch.

This two-position switch (33, figure 1-13), marked NO SALVO and CAN SALVO, is provided on the pilots' instrument panel to either set up or de-energize a 28-volt d-c bomb bay tank salvo circuit. When the switch is in the NO SALVO position, the bomb bay fuel tank can not be salvoed. When it is in the CAN SALVO position, the tank will release upon actuation of any one of the bomb salvo switches. Also, when the switch is in this position, a green indicator lamp (33, figure 1-13) adjacent to the switch glows, indicating the fuel tank can be salvoed. An indicator lamp is also on the bombing control panel.

ELECTRICAL SYSTEM.

A 3-phase, 400-cycle, a-c electrical system is employed because it permits a considerable weight saving in required wire gages, actuators, and generators. Alternating and direct currents are supplied the airplane through a primary and secondary power distribution network. The primary network is a 208/115-volt, 3-phase, 400-cycle, alternating-current power system (figure 1-26) supplied by four engine-driven alternators. The secondary network is a direct-current power system (figure 1-29) supplied by transformer-rectifier units fed from the alternating-current system. The alternating-current system supplies 400-cycle a-c power to the electronic-controlled turrets, heavy-duty motors, high speed actuators, lighting circuits, flight control equipment, and radio and radar equipment. The 28-volt direct-current system supplies power to such vital equipment as the bomb release system, radio and radar sets, propeller reverse and feathering control, fuel valves, and alarm bells.

A-C POWER DISTRIBUTION

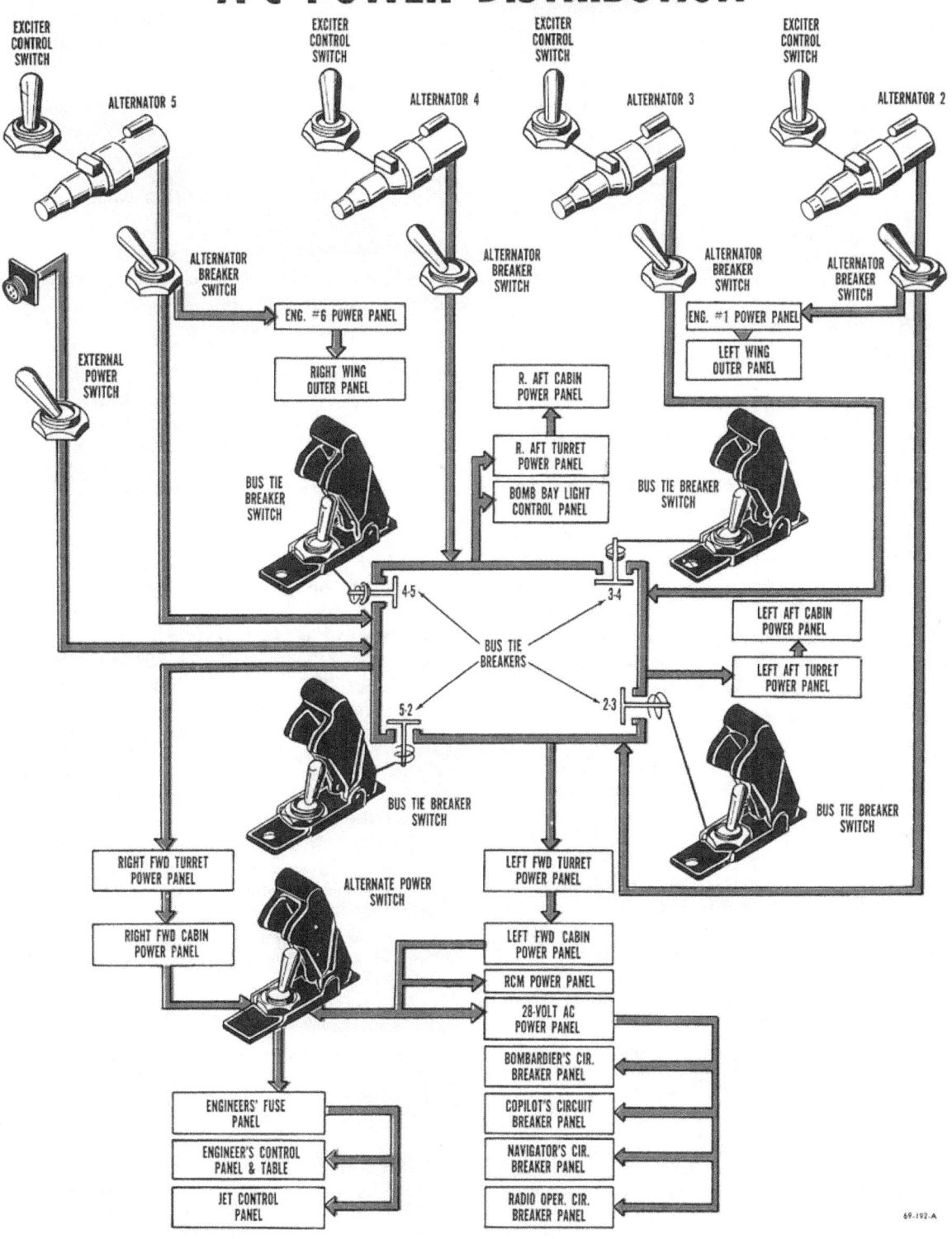

Figure 1-26.

Section I
Description

T.O. 1B-36D(II)-1

The electrical system employs fuses and circuit breakers to protect the electrical system from faults automatically. Multicircuit feeders of three or four wires per phase are incorporated in the power distribution system. A multicircuit feeder will provide continued service after one of its conductors has been broken, causing an open circuit. To furnish the necessary protection against faults or shorts occurring on a feeder section, fuses are located on each end of the conductors. Should a conductor break and the two loose ends cause a short circuit, the fuses at each end will clear, isolating the fault and permitting continued operation of the feeder section through the remaining conductors. Any one of the four alternators supplies sufficient electrical power for emergency operations provided all unnecessary equipment is turned off.

EXTERNAL POWER SOURCE.

When the airplane is on the ground, electric power is obtained from a B-10 portable power cart on which is mounted an alternator driven by a gasoline engine. During normal operation, the cart is connected to the airplane through a six-prong external power receptacle located on the under side of the fuselage below the wing. The power cart supplies 208-volt, 3-phase, 400-cycle, alternating current, part of which energizes the airplane's transformer-rectifier units and furnishes 28-volt direct current. When the portable power cart is connected to the airplane, it is imperative that the 3-phase power supplied has the same phase sequence as the alternators installed in the airplane. The direction of rotation of a 3-phase electric motor is entirely dependent on the phase sequence of its power supply. If two of the three power lines to a motor are interchanged, resulting in reversed phase sequence, the direction of motor rotation reverses, nullifying limit switches and causing damage to aircraft and equipment. Therefore, if the power leads from the cart are interchanged so that the phase sequence of the power output is incorrect, motors on the airplane will run in the wrong direction when energized from the portable power cart. To prevent this error, indicator lamps for determining phase sequence are provided.

> **CAUTION**
>
> Serious damage will result to certain types of motors and equipment on the airplane if they are operated in the wrong direction.

For ground operation of the K-( ) bombing system and the single-point refueling system, a forward cabin external power receptacle is located in the nose wheel well. On some airplanes a switch which isolates power applied to this receptacle from all electrical equipment except the fuel quantity gages and the refueling valves is located on the engineer's main control panel. Isolating the power from all but these two systems reduces the possibility of sparks which could cause a fire during single-point refueling.

External Power Supply Switch.

This two-position ON-OFF switch (7, figure 1-18), when in the ON position, completes the circuit from the portable power cart to the airplane's electrical system and breaks the circuits to all cabin heaters. The switch is on the engineer's auxiliary instrument panel.

Phase Sequence Lamp Test Switch.

A push-to-test switch (15, figure 1-27) adjacent to the phase sequence lamps tests their operation.

Phase Sequence Lamps.

Two lamps (14, figure 1-27) on the engineer's auxiliary instrument panel indicate phase sequence. If phase sequence of the cart is correct, the lamp marked CORRECT 1, 2, 3 will light. If it is incorrect, the lamp marked INCORRECT 3, 2, 1 will light.

> **Note**
>
> If both lamps light, the indication of the brightest lamp should be followed.

ALTERNATING-CURRENT SYSTEM.

The a-c power supply consists of four 40-kva, 208/115-volt, 3-phase, neutral grounded, 400-cycle alternators. One alternator each is installed on engines No. 2, 3, 4, and 5. Each alternator feeds into the main power panels in the fuselage, from where the power is distributed to the various electrical loads in the airplane. In the event of complete loss of a-c power, the reciprocating engine instruments will react as follows:

1. The fuel, oil, water, and manifold pressure gages, the fuel flow indicators; and the torquemeters will fail but will remain in the approximate positions they were in when the failure took place.

2. The master temperature indicator (airplanes not in group 2) and engine tachometers will continue to operate.

3. The fuel and oil quantity gages will continue to operate on battery.

4. The carburetor air and oil temperature gages will operate on battery power if required. The master tachometer will operate when the master motor is in use.

Alternator Controls and Indicators.

Power output of any alternator is possible only when its field is excited by direct current supplied by a generator built into the alternator. This d-c flow

ENGINEER'S A-C Power Control Panel

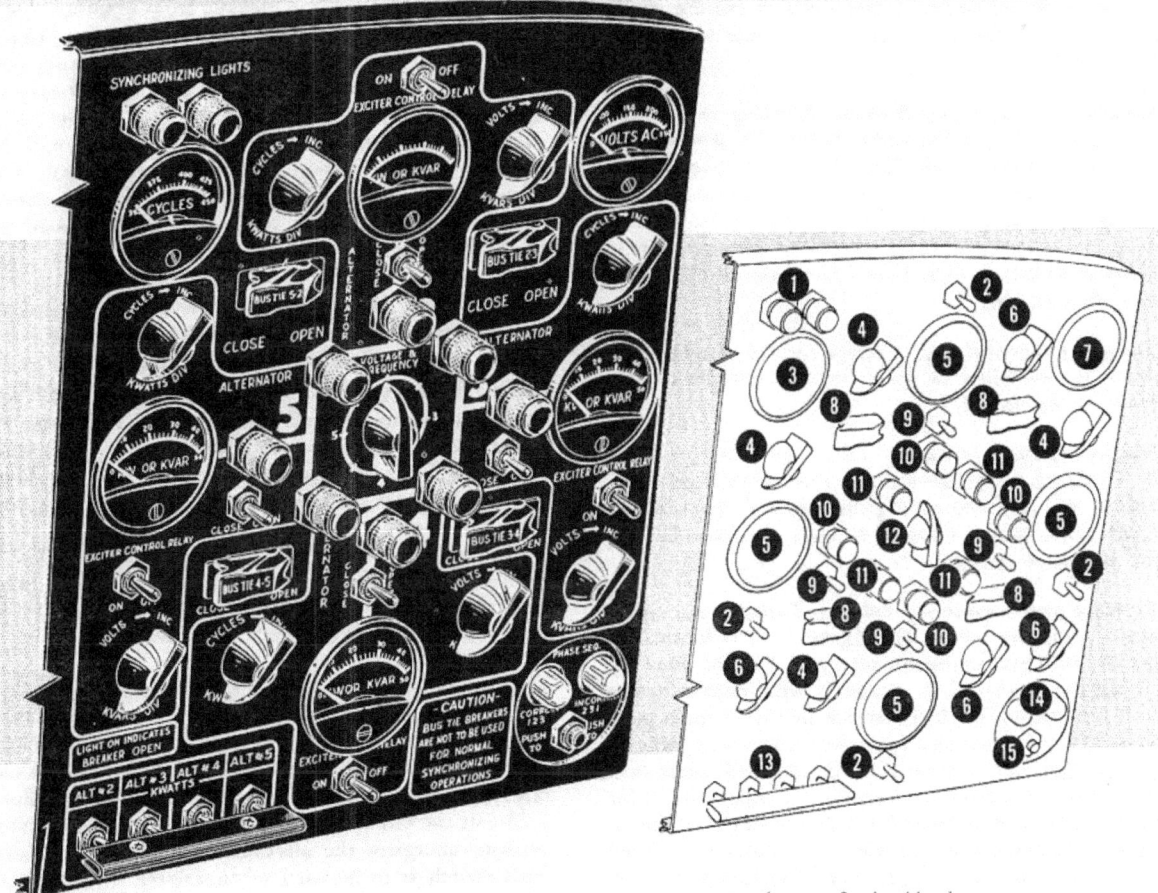

1. Alternator Synchronizing Lamps
2. Exciter Control Relay Switch
3. Frequency Meter
4. Frequency Control Knob
5. Kilowatt-Kilovar Meter
6. Voltage Control Knob
7. Voltmeter
8. Bus Tie Breaker
9. Alternator Breaker Control Switch
10. Alternator Breaker Indicator Lamp
11. Bus Tie Breaker Indicator Lamp
12. Voltage And Frequency Selector Switch
13. Kilowatt-Kilovar Selector Switches
14. Phase Sequence Lamps
15. Phase Sequence Lamps Test Switch

Figure 1-27.

is controlled by a three-position, spring-loaded, on-off exciter control relay switch (2, figure 1-27). Voltage output of the alternator is controlled by regulating the voltage of the exciter field. The real load output is measured in kilowatts. The real load output is accompanied by a reactive current during inductive load output; this reactive current is measured in kilovars.

One of the most important devices in the a-c power supply system is the unit used to drive the alternator at a constant speed throughout the range of various engine speeds. Alternator frequency varies with alternator speed; therefore, in order to generate a constant frequency, which is necessary for correct operation of much of the electrical equipment as well as being a prerequisite to parallel operation of alternators, a reliable constant-speed source is required. The constant-speed drive used is a mechanical-hydro-electric governor and drive unit. The drive unit, a variable ratio hydraulic transmission, delivers power to the alternator at a speed which is held constant through controlling action applied to the drive by the governor equipment.

Parallel operation (more than one alternator supplying a common bus) is desirable, since it will give greater stability to the electrical system; and in the event one alternator is inoperative, the entire power supply will not be cut off. (See "The Alternator," Section VII.) One kilowatt-kilovar meter (5, figure 1-27) is supplied for each alternator to indicate its power output. Although it is desirable that the three

Section I
Description

alternators divide the load as much as possible, the free-wheeling feature of the constant-speed drive permits alternator motoring for periods up to 5 minutes without damage to the drive. (See "Alternator Motoring," Section III.)

Exciter Control Relay Switch. Holding this switch (2, figure 1-27) momentarily in the ON position excites the alternator. Holding the switch momentarily in the OFF position de-excites the alternator and discontinues its output. The OFF position is also used to flash the alternator field when the alternator field flashing switch is ON. (See "Alternator Field Flashing," Section III.)

Voltage Control Knob. Voltage control of each alternator is controlled by its associated voltage control knob (6, figure 1-27).

Frequency Control Knob. This knob (4, figure 1-27) is connected to the governor control circuit and provides a means of controlling the speed of the constant-speed drive, which directly controls the frequency of the alternator output.

Voltage and Frequency Selector Switch. An eight-position selector switch (12, figure 1-27) is located on the engineer's main instrument panel. Four of these positions are marked 2, 3, 4, and 5, with respect to the four alternators. With the switch in any of these positions, the voltmeter and frequency meter will indicate the voltage and frequency of the selected alternator. Also, the kilowatt-kilovar meter (5, figure 1-27) for each alternator will indicate the power output of the selected alternator when its alternator breaker is closed and electric power is being used. The four unmarked positions are connected to the four main bus bars. The position between 2 and 3 is connected to bus 201, the position between 3 and 4 to bus 301; the position between 4 and 5 to bus 401, and the position between 5 and 2 to bus 501. With the switch in any of these positions, the voltmeter and frequency meter will indicate the voltage and frequency of the current on the selected bus, provided the bus tie-breakers are open. If the bus tie-breakers are closed, any of these four positions will give the voltage and frequency of the current on the connected bus bars.

Alternator Breaker Switch. Each alternator is connected to the power distribution network by an alternator breaker. A three-position switch (9, figure 1-27) spring-loaded in the OPEN and CLOSE positions controls the breaker which is a d-c operated solenoid. Individual alternator breaker idnicator lamps (10, figure 1-27) are located adjacent to each alternator breaker switch. These red lamps glow when the breaker is in the OPEN position. In the event an alternator breaker of a particular alternator is closed and the mixture control lever of that engine is moved to the IDLE CUT-OFF position, the breaker will automatically be opened.

Alternator Breaker Hold-In Switches. A hold-in switch (14, figure 1-21) for each alternator is provided to prevent the alternator breaker from opening when the corresponding mixture control lever is moved to the IDLE CUT-OFF position. The switches are used during normal engine shutdown when it is necessary to keep the alternator breaker of the last engine being shut down closed so that electrical power will be available to properly position the mixture control. The switches each have a spring-loaded HOLD IN position and a full-on NORMAL position and are located on the flight engineer's table.

Kilowatt and Kilovar Selector Switches. A bank of four kilowatt-kilovar selector switches (13, figure 1-27) is used to determine the power output of the alternators. These switches, which are ganged together, are used to select the desired reading by placing them in either the KWATTS or KVARS position. Indicators (5, figure 1-27) are provided for use with the kilowatt-kilovar selector switches. During parallel operation the division of real load is indicated by these meters when the selector switches are in the KWATTS position. When the switches are in the KVARS position, the meters register the reactive current measured in vars being put out by each alternator.

Alternator Field Flashing Circuit Breaker. A circuit breaker (5, figure 1-22) is provided at the engineer's station to flash the alternator exciter field. When this switch is placed in the ON position and the exciter control relay switch is held in the OFF position, a 28-volt d-c circuit, stepped down through a 25-ohm resistor, energizes the alternator exciter field circuit. This switch is to be used when exciter field reversal is encountered (as indicated by extreme fluctuation of the voltage) or when an alternator fails to excite.

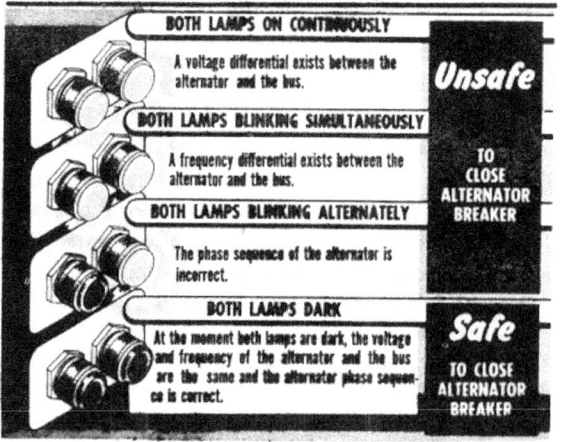

Figure 1-28.

DIRECT—CURRENT POWER DISTRIBUTION

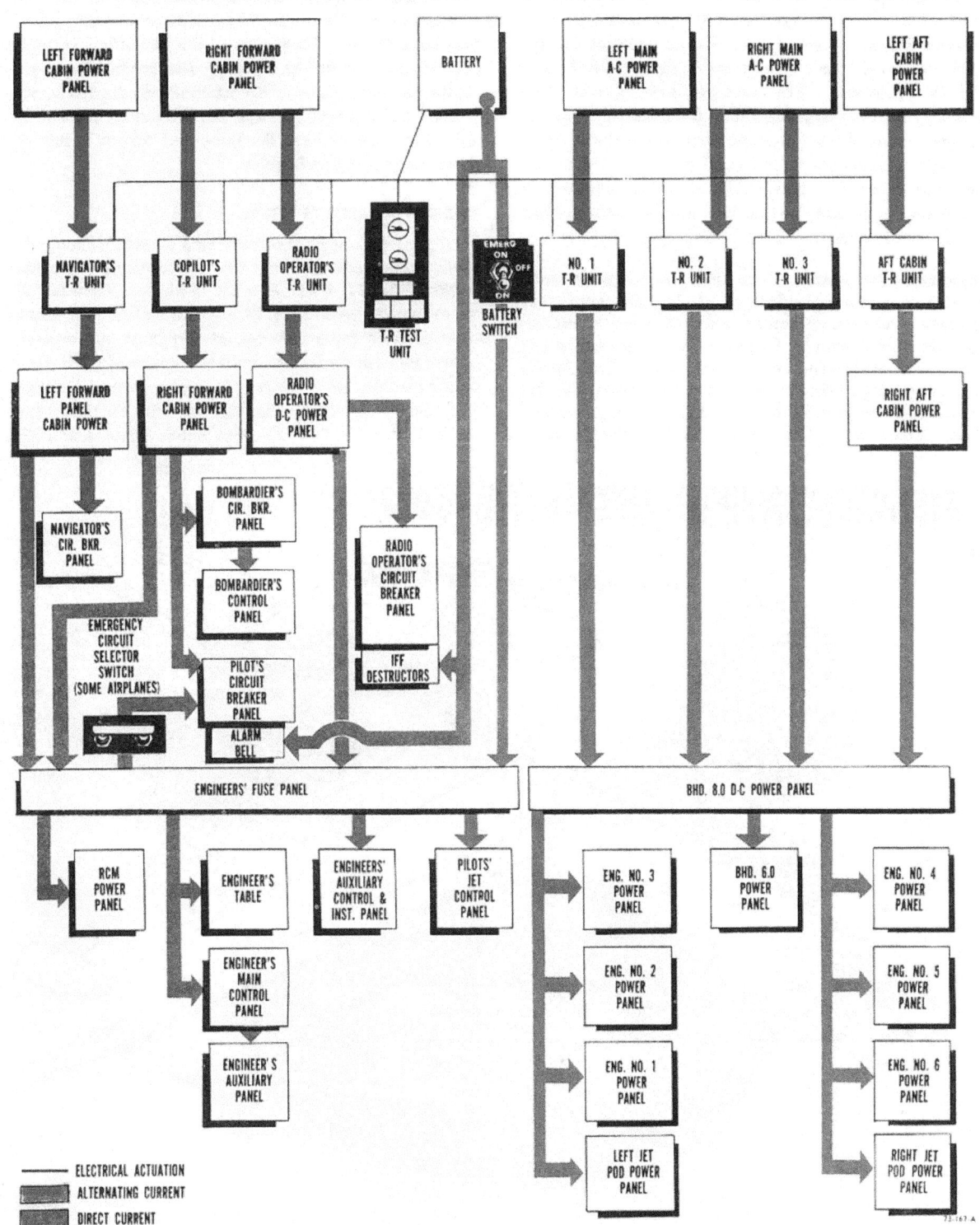

Figure 1-29.

Section I
Description

Bus Controls and Indicators. When in parallel operation, the individual alternators are all interconnected to a common bus. This bus is divisible by means of tie breakers. The tie breakers are controlled by four three-position bus tie-breaker control switches (8, figure 1-27) which are spring-loaded in the OPEN and CLOSE positions. The switches have guards that identify the bus segments they interconnect. The arrangement of the main a-c power bus and the individual bus tie-breakers is illustrated in figure 1-26. A red indicator lamp (11, figure 1-27) is located adjacent to each bus tie-breaker switch and blows when the bus tie-breaker is open.

Synchronizer Lamps. The synchronization controls and indicators are provided to equalize the output and frequency of each alternator so that they may be put in parallel. Two lamps (1, figure 1-27) on the engineer's panel and used to synchronize alternators. These lamps are connected so that by means of the voltage and frequency selector switch each lamp is placed between one phase of the power bus and the corresponding phase of the alternator to be paralleled with the bus. Therefore, the lamps will light when a difference exists between the frequency of the power bus and the frequency of the alternator. If the alternator voltage does not have the same frequency as the power bus voltage, the lamps will flicker. During the period that both lamps are dark, there is no difference in the frequency between the power bus and the alternator, indicating that the polarities are the same and that it is safe to close the alternator breaker.

DIRECT-CURRENT SYSTEM.

The d-c power system consists of a 24-volt, 17 ampere-hour storage battery and seven transformer rectifier units. The t-r units convert 3-phase, 208-volt, alternating current into 28-volt direct current. Each unit is rated for a continuous output of 50 amperes. The units are located as follows: one under the navigator's table, one behind the radar observer's control panel, one under the radio operator's table, and three in No. 3 bomb bay. (See figure 1-30.) The addi-

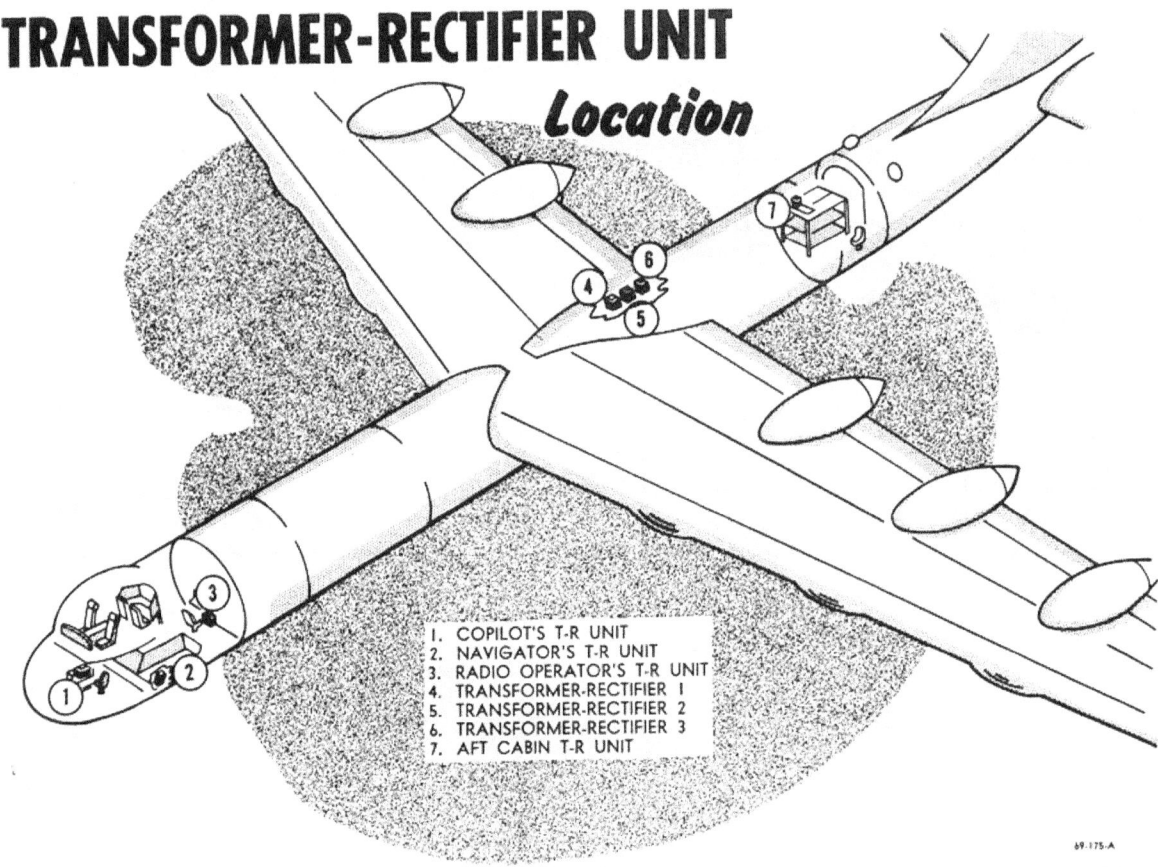

Figure 1-30.

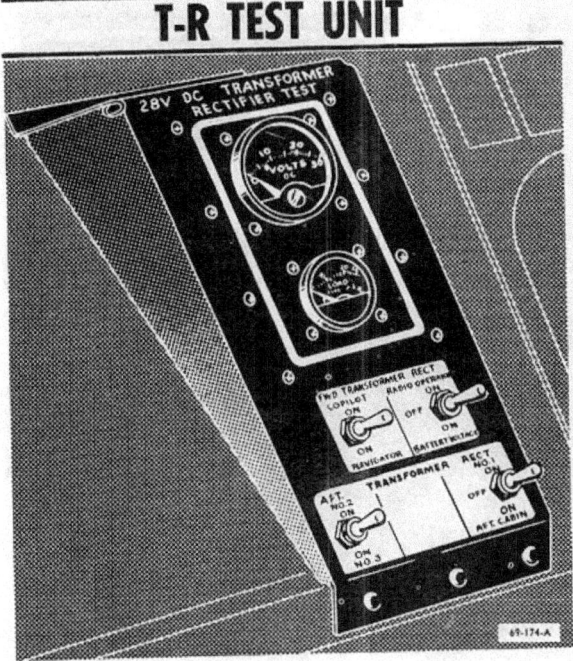

Figure 1-31.

tional unit in group 2 airplanes is installed on bulkhead 10.0 in the aft cabin. The units are connected through fuses to the a-c system and operate in parallel to deliver direct current when power is on the a-c bus. The total load of the system is automatically shared by the units.

The battery is located in the aft end of the nose wheel well. The battery is connected through a relay which is controlled by a battery switch at the engineer's station. Power for the relay is received directly from the battery.

Note

A direct circuit from the battery supplies continuous power to the alarm bell control switch on the pilots' instrument panel and to the destructor unit of the AN/APX-6 identification set at the radio operator's station. This feature permits operation of these units regardless of the position of the battery switch.

On airplanes not in group 2, the battery relay is controlled exclusively by the battery switch. On airplanes in group 2, the battery relay is controlled by the battery switch but is normally grounded by a relay which receives 115-volt a-c power from the engineer's fuse panel. Thus, whenever a-c power to the fuse panel is disrupted, the battery relay will open to prevent excessive drainage of battery power due to nonessential equipment being connected to the d-c bus.

Repositioning the battery switch will provide a d-c ground to close the battery relay.

If a complete loss of a-c power is encountered, it is recommended that battery power be conserved as much as conditions will allow so that systems requiring dc, such as the propeller reverse pitch and feathering systems, can be operated in the event of an emergency. Refer to Section III for emergency electrical power operation.

Battery Switch.

This switch (10, figure 1-19) is located on the engineer's auxiliary instrument panel. On airplanes not in group 2, this switch has two positions marked ON and OFF, and controls the battery relay which connects the battery to the d-c power distribution system. On airplanes in group 2, this switch has three positions marked EMER ON, OFF, and NORM ON. When the switch is in NORM ON, the battery relay is grounded by an a-c relay when a-c power is is on the airplane. When a loss of a-c power occurs, placing the switch in EMER ON will provide a d-c ground for the battery relay. A lamp, located on the cable guard opposite the forward escape hatch, is lit whenevr the a-c relay is closed and goes out when the relay opens.

Transformer-Rectifier Test Unit Panel.

A transformer-rectifier test unit panel (figure 1-31), installed on the radio operator's equipment shelf, is provided to check the voltage and amperage output of the transformer-rectifier units. It is also used to check the voltage of the battery. The unit consists of selector switch or switches, a voltmeter, and an ammeter.

Transformer-Rectifier Test Unit Selector Switch (Airplanes not in Group 2). A selector switch having eight positions—RADIO OPER, CO-PILOT, BOMBARD, BATTERY VOLTAGE, AFT, CENTER, FWD, and OFF—is provided to select the t-r unit to be tested. Placing the switch in the RADIO OPER, CO-PILOT, or BOMBARD position selects the t-r unit to be tested in the forward cabin. Placing the switch in the AFT, CENTER, or FWD position selects the t-r unit to be tested in the bomb bay. The BATTERY VOLTAGE position is provided to check the voltage of the battery.

Transformer-Rectifier Test Unit Selector Switches (Group 2 Airplanes). Four three-position switches are provided to select the t-r unit to be tested. Each switch has two springloaded ON positions and a neutral OFF position. The switches marked CO-PILOT—NAVIGATOR and RADIO OPERATOR—BATTERY VOLTAGE select the t-r units in the forward cabin or the battery. The switches marked No. 2—No. 3 and No. 1—AFT CABIN select the t-r units in the bomb bay and the aft cabin. Placing a switch ON tests the voltage and the load output of the t-r unit selected or the battery voltage as indicated by the switch position.

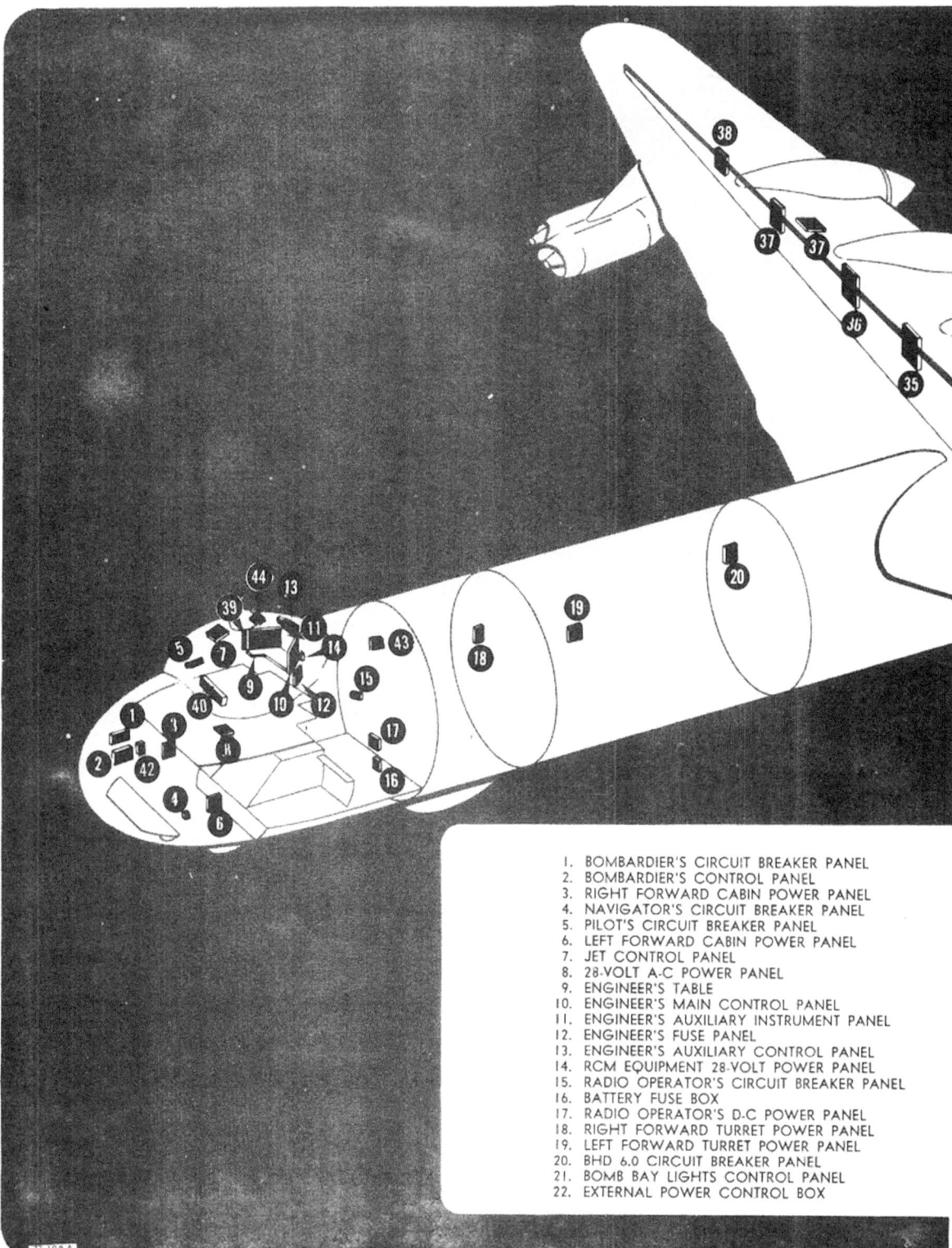

Figure 1-32. (Sheet 1) Fuse and Circuit Breaker Panel Location

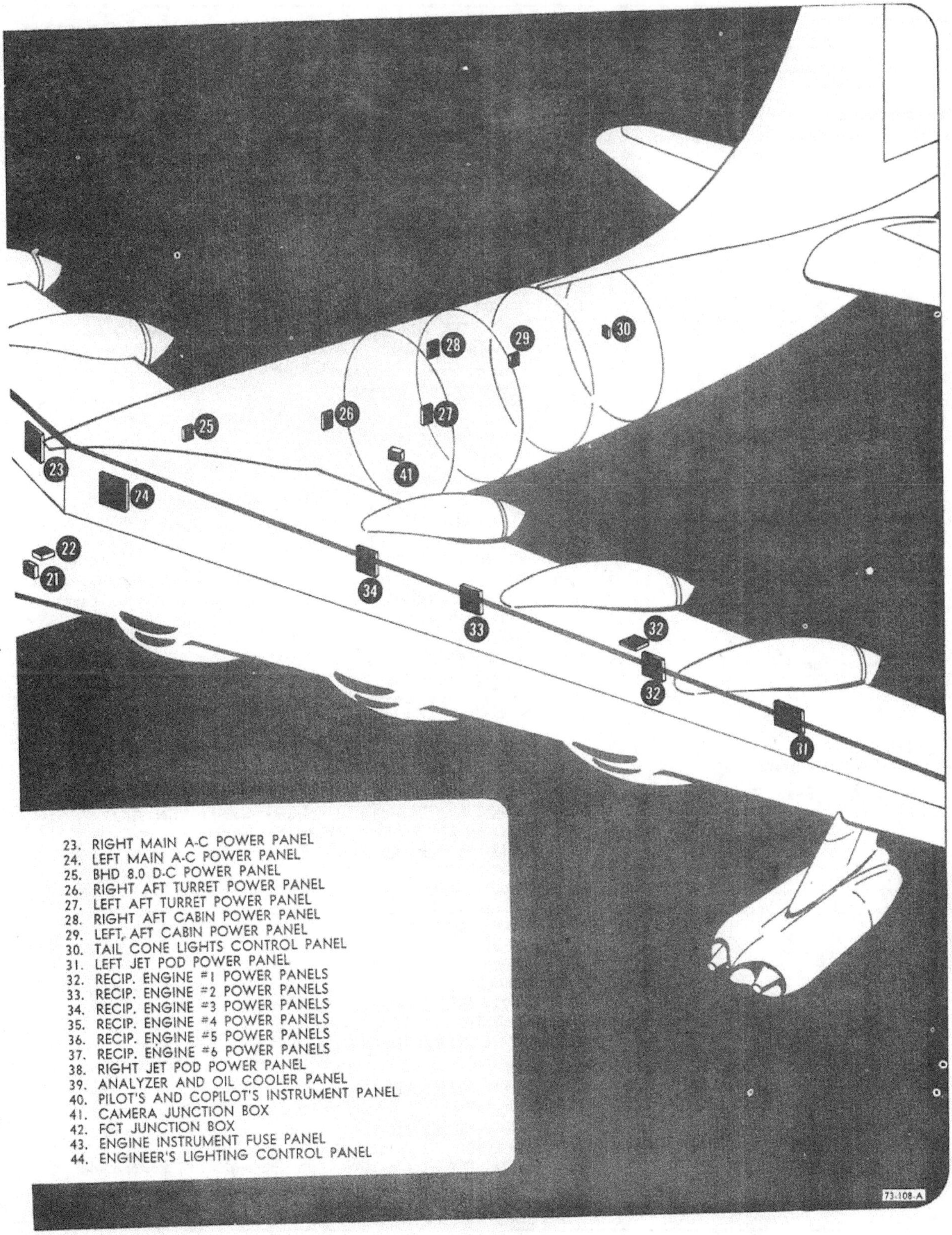

T.O. 1B-36D(II)-1

Section I
Description

23. RIGHT MAIN A-C POWER PANEL
24. LEFT MAIN A-C POWER PANEL
25. BHD 8.0 D-C POWER PANEL
26. RIGHT AFT TURRET POWER PANEL
27. LEFT AFT TURRET POWER PANEL
28. RIGHT AFT CABIN POWER PANEL
29. LEFT AFT CABIN POWER PANEL
30. TAIL CONE LIGHTS CONTROL PANEL
31. LEFT JET POD POWER PANEL
32. RECIP. ENGINE #1 POWER PANELS
33. RECIP. ENGINE #2 POWER PANELS
34. RECIP. ENGINE #3 POWER PANELS
35. RECIP. ENGINE #4 POWER PANELS
36. RECIP. ENGINE #5 POWER PANELS
37. RECIP. ENGINE #6 POWER PANELS
38. RIGHT JET POD POWER PANEL
39. ANALYZER AND OIL COOLER PANEL
40. PILOT'S AND COPILOT'S INSTRUMENT PANEL
41. CAMERA JUNCTION BOX
42. FCT JUNCTION BOX
43. ENGINE INSTRUMENT FUSE PANEL
44. ENGINEER'S LIGHTING CONTROL PANEL

Figure 1-32. (Sheet 2) Fuse and Circuit Breaker Panel Location

Section I
Description

T.O. 1B-36D(II)-1

AC SYSTEM FEEDER FUSES

LOCATION	QUAN-TITY	SIZE (AMPERES)	DECAL NOMENCLATURE	CONNECTED TO
Engineer's Fuse Panel (Some Airplanes)	2	30	"ENGINEER'S PANEL"	Engineer's Table
	3	30	"ENGR'S PANEL POWER INPUT"	Engineer's Fuse Panel A-C Power Switch
	1	20	"MASTER TURBO"	Turbosupercharger Regulator Control
	3	30	"ENGR'S PANEL POWER INPUT"	Engineer's Fuse Panel A-C Power Switch
	1	30	"ENGR'S PANEL"	Engineer's Table
	1	30	"JET PANEL"	Jet Control Panel
	1	10	"CYL HD TEMP IND"	Engine Instrument Fuse Panel
	1	10	"INST PWR NORMAL"	Engine Instrument Fuse Panel
	1	10	"INST PWR ALT"	Engine Instrument Fuse Panel
	1	20	"MASTER TURBO"	Turbosupercharger Regulator Controls
Left Aft Cabin Power Panel	9	30	"WIRE SERIES 450-451-452"	Left Aft Turret Power Panel
Left Aft Turret Power Panel	12	40	"WIRE SERIES 400-401-402-403"	Left Main A-C Power Panel
	9	30	"WIRE SERIES 450-451-452"	Left Aft Cabin Power Panel
Left Forward Cabin Power Panel	3	30	"ENGR'S ALT POWER"	Engineer's Fuse Panel A-C Power Switch
	3	20	"LH TRANS RECT UNIT"	Navigator's Transformer-Rectifier
	2	40	"RCM POWER PANEL"	RCM Equipment 28 Volt Power Panel
	12	40	"WIRE SERIES 307-308-309-329"	Left Forward Turret Power Panel
	1	20	"28 V TRANS"	28 Volt A-C Power Panel
Left Forward Turret Power Panel	12	40	"WIRE SERIES 300-301-302-303"	Left Main A-C Power Panel
	12	40	"WIRE SERIES 307-308-309-329"	Left Forward Cabin Power Panel
Left Jet Pod Power Panel	9	60	"WIRE SERIES 124-125-126"	Recip. Engine #2 Power Panel
Left Main A-C Power Panel	3	20	"BOMB BAY TRANSF RECT UNIT"	Transformer-Rectifier #1
	12	60	"WIRE SERIES 110-111-112-113"	Recip. Engine #2 Power Panel
	12	60	"WIRE SERIES 140-141-142-143"	Recip. Engine #3 Power Panel
	12	40	"WIRE SERIES 300-301-302-303"	Left Forward Turret Power Panel
	12	40	"WIRE SERIES 400-401-402-403"	Left Aft Turret Power Panel
	12	40	"WIRE SERIES 420-421-422-423"	Right Main A-C Power Panel
	12	40	"WIRE SERIES 430-431-432-433"	Right Main A-C Power Panel
Recip. Engine #1 Power Panel	12	60	"WIRE SERIES 116-117-118-119"	Recip. Engine #2 Power Panel
Recip. Engine #2 Power Panel	12	60	"WIRE SERIES 110-111-112-113"	Left Main A-C Power Panel
	12	30	"WIRE SERIES 116-117-118-119"	Recip. Engine #1 Power Panel
	9	60	"WIRE SERIES 124-125-126"	Left Jet Pod Power Panel

Figure 1-33. (Sheet 1) Fuse and Circuit Breaker List

AC SYSTEM FEEDER FUSES (Continued)

LOCATION	QUAN-TITY	SIZE (AMPERES)	DECAL NOMENCLATURE	CONNECTED TO
Recip. Engine #3 Power Panel	12	60	"WIRE SERIES 140-141-142-143"	Left Main A-C Power Panel
Recip. Engine #4 Power Panel	12	60	"WIRE SERIES 240-241-242-243"	Right Main A-C Power Panel
Recip. Engine #5 Power Panel	12	60	"WIRE SERIES 210-211-212-213"	Right Main A-C Power Panel
	12	30	"WIRE SERIES 216-217-218-219"	Recip. Engine #6 Power Panel
	9	60	"WIRE SERIES 224-225-226"	Right Jet Pod Power Panel
Recip. Engine #6 Power Panel	12	30	"WIRE SERIES 216-217-218-219"	Recip. Engine #5 Power Panel
Right Aft Cabin Power Panel	9	30	"WIRE SERIES 440-441-442"	Right Aft Turret Power Panel
Right Aft Turret Power Panel	12	40	"WIRE SERIES 410-411-412-413"	Right Main A-C Power Panel
	9	30	"WIRE SERIES 440-441-442"	Right Aft Cabin Power Panel
Right Forward Cabin Power Panel	3	20	"BLKHD 4.0 TRANS RECT UNIT"	Radio Operator's Transformer-Rectifier
	3	30	"ENGR'S FUSE PANEL"	Engineer's Fuse Panel A-C Power Switch
	3	20	"RH TRANS RECT UNIT"	Copilot's Transformer-Rectifier
	12	40	"WIRE SERIES 317-318-319-339"	Right Forward Turret Power Panel
Right Forward Turret Power Panel	12	40	"WIRE SERIES 310-311-312-313"	Right Main A-C Power Panel
	12	40	"WIRE SERIES 317-318-319-339"	Right Forward Cabin Power Panel
Right Jet Pod Power Panel	9	60	"WIRE SERIES 224-225-226"	Recip. Engine #5 Power Panel
Right Main A-C Power Panel	3	20	"BOMB BAY TRANSF RECT CENTER"	Transformer-Rectifier #2
	3	20	"BOMB BAY TRANSF RECT AFT"	Transformer-Rectifier #3
	12	60	"WIRE SERIES 210-211-212-213"	Recip. Engine #5 Power Panel
	12	60	"WIRE SERIES 240-241-242-243"	Recip. Engine #4 Power Panel
	12	40	"WIRE SERIES 310-311-312-313"	Right Forward Turret Power Panel
	12	40	"WIRE SERIES 410-411-412-413"	Right Aft Turret Power Panel
	12	40	"WIRE SERIES 420-421-422-423"	Left Main A-C Power Panel
	12	40	"WIRE SERIES 430-431-432-433"	Left Main A-C Power Panel
	12	40	"WIRE SERIES 475-476-477-478"	External Power Control Box
	1	20	"28V TRANSF"	Bomb Bay Lights Control Panel
28 Volt A-C Power Panel	1	30	"BOMBARDIER'S PANEL"	Bombardier's Circuit Breaker Panel
	3	20	"COPILOT'S PANEL"	Copilot's Circuit Breaker Panel
	1	30	"NAVIG'S PANEL"	Navigator's Circuit Breaker Panel
	1	30	"RADIO OPER'S PANEL"	Radio Operator's Circuit Breaker Panel

Figure 1-33. (Sheet 2) Fuse and Circuit Breaker List

DC SYSTEM FEEDER FUSES

LOCATION	QUAN-TITY	SIZE (AMPERES)	DECAL NOMENCLATURE	CONNECTED TO
Battery Fuse Box	1	30	"ALARM BELL"	Copilot's Circuit Breaker Panel
	3	40	"ENGINEER'S PANEL"	Engineer's Fuse Panel
	2	30	"SCR695 DETONATOR"	Radio Operator's Circuit Breaker Panel
Bhd. 6.0 D-C Power Panel	3	50	"50 AMP FUSE"	Bhd. 8.0 D-C Power Panel
Bhd. 8.0 D-C Power Panel	3	50	"AFT CABIN"	Right Aft Cabin Power Panel
	3	40	"AFT TRANSF RECT"	Transformer-Rectifier #3
	3	50	"BLKHD 6.0 CIRCUIT BREAKER PANEL"	Bhd. 6.0 D-C Power Panel
	3	40	"CENTER TRANSF RECT"	Transformer-Rectifier #2
	3	30	"FWD CABIN"	Engineer's Fuse Panel
	3	40	"FWD TRANSF RECT"	Transformer-Rectifier #1
	3	20	"LEFT WING"	Recip. Engine #1, 2 & 3, AND Left Jet Pod Power Panels
	3	20	"RIGHT WING"	Recip. Engines #4, 5 & 6, AND Right Jet Pod Power Panels
Engineer's Fuse Panel	3	40	"BATTERY"	Battery Fuse Box
	3	30	"BOMB BAY"	Bhd. 8.0 D-C Power Panel
	3	30	"L.H. FWD PANEL"	Left Forward Cabin Power Panel
	3	30	"RADIO OPER'S PANEL"	Radio Operator's D-C Power Panel
	3	30	"R.H. FWD PANEL"	Right Forward Cabin Power Panel
Left Forward Cabin Power Panel	3	30	"ENGR'S PANEL"	Engineer's Fuse Panel
	3	40	"LH TRANS RECT UNIT"	Navigator's Transformer-Rectifier
	3	30	"NAVIG PANEL"	Navigator's Circuit Breaker Panel
	3	30	"RH POWER PANEL"	Right Forward Cabin Power Panel
Left Jet Pod Power Panel	3	10	"28V DC POWER"	Bhd. 8.0 D-C Power Panel
Radio Operator's D-C Power Panel	3	40	"BLKHD 4.0 CONVR'T"	Radio Operator's Transformer-Rectifier
	3	30	"ENGR'S PANEL"	Engineer's Fuse Panel
	3	30	"RADIO OPER'S PANEL"	Radio Operator's Circuit Breaker Panel
Recip. Engine #1 Power Panel	3	10	"28V DC POWER"	Bhd. 8.0 D-C Power Panel
Recip. Engine #2 Power Panel	3	10	"28V DC POWER"	Bhd. 8.0 D-C Power Panel
Recip. Engine #3 Power Panel	3	10	"28V DC POWER"	Bhd. 8.0 D-C Power Panel
Recip. Engine #4 Power Panel	3	10	"28V DC POWER"	Bhd. 8.0 D-C Power Panel
Recip. Engine #5 Power Panel	3	10	"28V DC POWER"	Bhd. 8.0 D-C Power Panel
Recip. Engine #6 Power Panel	3	10	"28V DC POWER"	Bhd. 8.0 D-C Power Panel
Right Aft Cabin Power Panel	3	50	"BHD 8.0 DC POWER PANEL"	Bhd. 8.0 D-C Power Panel
Right Forward Cabin Power Panel	3	30	"BOMB'S CIRCUIT BREAKER PANEL"	Bombardier's Circuit Breaker Panel
	3	30	"COPILOT'S CIRCUIT BREAKER PANEL"	Copilot's Circuit Breaker Panel
	3	30	"ENGR'S PANEL"	Engineer's Fuse Panel
	3	30	"LH POWER PANEL"	Left Forward Cabin Power Panel
	3	40	"RH TRANS RECT UNIT"	Copilot's Transformer-Rectifier
Right Jet Pod Power Panel	3	10	"28V DC POWER"	Bhd. 8.0 D-C Power Panel

Figure 1-33. (Sheet 3) Fuse and Circuit Breaker List

AC SYSTEM EQUIPMENT FUSES AND CIRCUIT BREAKERS

*Push-Pull Type Circuit Breaker
†Switch Type Circuit Breaker

The words "Power" and "Control," in parenthesis, are used in conjunction with certain "Equipment or Circuit" designations in both the AC and DC Equipment Fuse and Circuit Breaker lists. The word "Power" is used to indicate an electrical circuit which is completed through a relay. "Control" indicates an energizing circuit for a relay. For each power circuit, or groups of similar power circuits, there is a corresponding control circuit. For example, in the a-c system you will find:

    Aileron Trim Tab (Power):
        Left
        Right

The corresponding control circuit appears in the d-c system as:

    Aileron Trim Tab (Control),
        Left and Right

Normally, a-c power has d-c control. However, some equipment has d-c power with d-c control. Any equipment or circuit designation which does not contain either of the specified words, indicates a power circuit without a controlling relay.

EQUIPMENT OR CIRCUIT	LOCATION (PANEL NO.)	QUANTITY	SIZE (AMPERES)	DECAL NOMENCLATURE
Aileron Trim Tab (Power):				
Left	32	3	10	"AILERON TRIM TAB"
Right	37	3	10	"AILERON TRIM TAB"
Air Plug (Power):				
Jet Engine 1	31	1	10	"#1 AIR SHUT OFF DOORS"
Jet Engine 2	31	1	10	"#2 AIR SHUT OFF DOORS"
Jet Engine 3	38	1	10	"#3 AIR SHUT OFF DOORS"
Jet Engine 4	38	1	10	"#4 AIR SHUT OFF DOORS"
Recip. Engine 1	32	3	10	"ENGINE AIR PLUG"
Recip. Engine 2	33	3	10	"ENGINE AIR PLUG"
Recip. Engine 3	34	3	10	"ENGINE AIR PLUG"
Recip. Engine 4	35	3	10	"ENGINE AIR PLUG"
Recip. Engine 5	36	3	10	"ENGINE AIR PLUG"
Recip. Engine 6	37	3	10	"ENGINE AIR PLUG"
Alternating Current Phase Sequence Indicator Lamps	22	3	10	"EXTERNAL POWER PHASE SEQUENCE INDICATOR FUSE"
Anti-Icing:				
Jet Pod Heaters (Power):				
Left	31	3	30	"NOSE DOORS DE-ICE"
Right	38	3	30	"NOSE DOORS DE-ICE"
Tail, AND Cabin Air Temperature Control Valve	9	1	*5	"ANTI-ICE TAIL AND CABIN HEAT"
Wing Anti-Icing Control Valve	9	1	*5	"ANTI-ICE WING IND."
Autopilot (Power), E6	3	1	10	"AUTO PILOT"
Bomb Station Indicator Lights	3	1	10	"BOMB ST. IND. LTS."
Brake Pump	See: "Hydraulic Pump (Power), Brake"			
Cabin Air Temperature Control Valve	See: "Anti-Icing, Tail, AND Cabin Air Temperature Control Valve"			
Cabin Pressurization	See: "Pressure Shut Off Valves, Aft Cabin AND Wing"			
Camera Door (Power) (Airplanes Not in Group 2)	27	3	10	"CAMERA DOOR MOTOR"
Camera Door Power (Group 2 Airplanes)	29	1	10	"CAM DR. MOTOR"
Carburetor Air Filters (Power):				
Recip. Engines 1, 2, & 3	34	1	10	"CARB. AIR FLTR."
Recip. Engines 4, 5, & 6	35	1	10	"CARB. AIR FLTR."

Figure 1-33. (Sheet 4) Fuse and Circuit Breaker List

AC SYSTEM EQUIPMENT FUSES AND CIRCUIT BREAKERS (Continued)

EQUIPMENT OR CIRCUIT	LOCATION (PANEL NO.)	QUANTITY	SIZE (AMPERES)	DECAL NOMENCLATURE
Carburetor Air Preheat (Power):				
Recip. Engine 1	32	1	10	"CARB. PREHEAT"
Recip. Engine 2	33	1	10	"CARB. PREHEAT"
Recip. Engine 3	34	1	10	"CARB. PREHEAT"
Recip. Engine 4	35	1	10	"CARB. PREHEAT"
Recip. Engine 5	36	1	10	"CARB. PREHEAT"
Recip. Engine 6	37	1	10	"CARB. PREHEAT"
Compass, Radio AN/ARN-7	4	1	* 5	"RADIO COMPASS 28V AC"
Compass, Radio-AN/ARN-7	6	1	10	"RADIO COMPASS"
Compass, Slaved Gyro Magnetic	6	3	10	"GYROSYN COMPASS"
Compass, Radio AN/ARN-14	6	1	10	"COMPASS C-1 AMPLIFIER"
Control Surface Locks (Power)	23	3	10	"CONT. SURF. LOCK R.H. AIL. L.H. AIL. TAIL"
Engine Analyzer Power Supply	39	1	† 5	"ENGINE ANALYZER"
Engine Analyzer Relay Box:				
Left	33	1	10	"ENG. ANALYZER"
Right	36	1	10	"ENG. ANALYZER"
Fan:				
Cabin Air Booster (Power)	23	6	40	"CABIN PRES. BOOST. FAN"
Forward Cabin Ventilating	6	3	10	"CABIN VENT. FAN"
Fans, Engine Cooling — Recip. Engines 1, 2, 3, 4, 5, & 6	9	1	* 5	"ENGINE FAN"
Flap (Power):				
Center, Left	33	3	20	"CENTER FLAPS"
Center, Right	36	3	20	"CENTER FLAPS"
Inboard, Left	34	3	20	"INBOARD FLAPS"
Inboard, Right	35	3	20	"INBOARD FLAPS"
Outboard, Left	32	3	20	"OUTBOARD FLAPS"
Outboard, Right	37	3	20	"OUTBOARD FLAPS"
Fuel:				
Pump (Power), Booster:				
Auxiliary Tank, Left	24	3	10	"LEFT WING AUX. BOOST PUMP"
Auxiliary Tank, Right	23	3	10	"RIGHT WING AUXIL. BOOST PUMP"
Bomb Bay Tank	27	3	10	"BB #3 FUEL BOOST PUMP"
Jet Engines 1 & 2	31	3	10	"FUEL PUMP"
Jet Engines 3 & 4	38	3	10	"FUEL PUMP"
Wing Tank 1	33	3	10	"FUEL BOOSTER PUMP"
Wing Tank 2	34	3	10	"FUEL BOOSTER PUMP"
Wing Tank 3	34	3	10	"FUEL BOOSTER PUMP"
Wing Tank 4	35	3	10	"FUEL BOOSTER PUMP"
Wing Tank 5	35	3	10	"FUEL BOOSTER PUMP"
Wing Tank 6	36	3	10	"FUEL BOOSTER PUMP"
Mixture — Recip. Engines 1 2, 3, 4, 5, & 6	9	6	* 5	"ENGINE FUEL MIXTURE 1, 2, 3, 4, 5, & 6"
Gyro Indicator:				
Type C-5, Navigator's	3	3	10	"PILOTS GYRO HORIZON"
Type E-1, Copilot's	6	3	10	"NAVIG DIRECTIONAL GYRO"
Gyro Indicators, Type B-1 AND E-1 — Pilot's	6	3	10	"PILOTS GYRO HORIZON"
Heater, Pitot Tube: (Some Airplanes)				
Left	10	1	† 5	"PITOT TUBE HEATER L.H."
Right	10	1	† 5	"PITOT TUBE HEATER R.H."
Heater (Power), Auxiliary Cabin:				
Aft Cabin, Left	29	3	30	"CABIN HEAT"
Aft Cabin, Right	28	3	30	"CABIN HEAT"

Figure 1-33. (Sheet 5) Fuse and Circuit Breaker List

AC SYSTEM EQUIPMENT FUSES AND CIRCUIT BREAKERS (Continued)

EQUIPMENT OR CIRCUIT	LOCATION (PANEL NO.)	QUANTITY	SIZE (AMPERES)	DECAL NOMENCLATURE
Heater (Power) Continued				
Bombardier's	6	3	30	"CABIN HEAT"
Radio Operator's	3	3	30	"RADIO OPERATOR'S COMPT."
Heater (Power), Oil:				
Jet Engine 1	31	1	10	"OIL CELL HEATER #1"
Jet Engine 2	31	1	10	"OIL CELL HEATER #2"
Jet Engine 3	38	1	10	"OIL CELL HEATER #3"
Jet Engine 4	38	1	10	"OIL CELL HEATER #4"
Heater (Power), Oil Vent Line:				
Recip. Engine 1	32	1	10	"OIL VENT HEAT"
Recip. Engine 2	33	1	10	"OIL VENT HEAT"
Recip. Engine 3	34	1	10	"OIL VENT HEAT"
Recip. Engine 4	35	1	10	"OIL VENT HEAT"
Recip. Engine 5	36	1	10	"OIL VENT HEAT"
Recip. Engine 6	37	1	10	"OIL VENT HEAT"
Hot Cup Receptacle:				
Aft Cabin	28	1	20	"HOT CUPS"
Forward Cabin and Liquid Container	3	1	10	"BEV TANK"
Hydraulic Pump (Power):				
Brake	24	6	60	"BRAKE PUMP"
#1	23	6	60	"HYDRO PUMP MOTOR"
#2	24	6	60	"HYDRO PUMP MOTOR #2"
Ignition (Power): (J47-19 Engines)				
Jet Engine 1	31	1	10	"#1 IGN."
Jet Engine 2	31	1	10	"#2 IGN."
Jet Engine 3	38	1	10	"#3 IGN."
Jet Engine 4	38	1	10	"#4 IGN."
Intercooler (Power):				
Close:				
Recip. Engine 1	32	1	10	"INTR COOL CLOSE"
Recip. Engine 2	33	1	10	"INTR COOL CLOSE"
Recip. Engine 3	34	1	10	"INTR COOL CLOSE"
Recip. Engine 4	35	1	10	"INTR COOL CLOSE"
Recip. Engine 5	36	1	10	"INTR COOL CLOSE"
Recip. Engine 6	37	1	10	"INTR COOL CLOSE"
Open:				
Recip. Engine 1	32	1	10	"INTR COOL OPEN"
Recip. Engine 2	33	1	10	"INTR COOL OPEN"
Recip. Engine 3	34	1	10	"INTR COOL OPEN"
Recip. Engine 4	35	1	10	"INTR COOL OPEN"
Recip. Engine 5	36	1	10	"INTR COOL OPEN"
Recip. Engine 6	37	1	10	"INTR COOL OPEN"
Instruments, Reciprocating Engine: (Some Airplanes)				
Cylinder Head Temperature Amplifiers	43	6	1	"ENGINE CHT AMPLIFIER 1, 2, 3, 4, 5 & 6"
Selsyn	43	6	5	"ENGINE SELSYN INSTRUMENTS 1, 2, 3, 4, 5 & 6"
Instruments, Turbo Jet Engine	31	2	1	"FUEL PRESS TRANS NO. 1 & NO. 2 JET"
	31	2	1	"OIL PRESS TRANS NO. 1 & NO. 2 JET"
	31	2	1	"FUEL PRESS & OIL PRESS IND. NO. 1 & NO. 2 JET"

Figure 1-33. (Sheet 6) Fuse and Circuit Breaker List

Section I
Description

T.O. 1B-36D(II)-1

AC SYSTEM EQUIPMENT FUSES AND CIRCUIT BREAKERS (Continued)

EQUIPMENT OR CIRCUIT	LOCATION (PANEL NO.)	QUAN-TITY	SIZE (AMPERES)	DECAL NOMENCLATURE
Instruments, Turbo Jet Engine (Continued)				
	31	2	1	"JET FUEL FLOW ENG NO. 1 & NO. 2"
	38	2	1	"FUEL PRESS TRANS NO. 3 & NO. 4 JET"
	38	2	1	"OIL PRESS TRANS NO. 3 & NO. 4 JET"
	38	2	1	"FUEL PRESS & OIL PRESS IND. NO. 3 & NO. 4 JET"
	38	2	1	"JET FUEL FLOW ENG. NO. 3 & NO. 4"
Panel Vibrator	3	1	1(	"JET INST VIB"
Instruments, Autosyn Jet (Some Airplanes)				
Jet Engine 1	31	1	10	"NO. 1 AUT. TRANS"
Jet Engine 2	31	1	10	"NO. 2 AUT. TRANS"
Jet Engine 3	38	1	10	"NO. 3 AUT. TRANS"
Jet Engine 4	38	1	10	"NO. 4 AUT. TRANS"
Instruments, Autosyn Recip. Eng. (Some Airplanes)				
Recip. Engine 1	32	1	10	"ATOSN. TRANS"
Recip. Engine 2	33	1	10	"ATOSN. TRANS"
Recip. Engine 3	34	1	10	"ATOSN. TRANS"
Recip. Engine 4	35	1	10	"ATOSN. TRANS"
Recip. Engine 5	36	1	10	"ATOSN. TRANS"
Recip. Engine 6	37	1	10	"ATOSN. TRANS"
Instrument, Hydraulic Pressure Indicator (Some Airplanes)	23	1	10	"HYD PRESS"
K-1 Bombing System:				
Amplifier — Computer, Type A-2	6	1	10	"K-1 SYS. REG."
Amplifier — Computer, Type A-2	6	1	30	"K-1 SYS. UNREG."
Filter, F-67/APS-23	6	1	20	"BOMB'G RADAR"
Relay, Aft Heater Junction Box	3	3	30	"K-1 SYS. HEATERS"
Relay, Forward Heater Junction Box	6	3	30	"K-1 SYS. HEATERS"
Transformer, Forward Heater Junction Box	6	3	10	"K-1 SYS. GYROS"
Lights, Navigation Wing Tip (Red & Green) Rudder (White)	8	1	10	"WING TIP LIGHTS"
Lights, Pilot's & Copilot's Cockpit				
Inter-Aircraft Signal Instrument Panel Jet Instrument Panel	5	1	* 5	"COCKPIT"
B-16 Magnetic Compass	44	1	5	"FLOOD LIGHTS"
C-4 Cockpit	8	1	10	"ENGR'S DOME LIGHTS"
Lights, Engineer's Lighting Control Panel				
Red	44	1	5	"RED LIGHTS"
White	44	1	5	"WHITE LIGHTS"
Auxiliary Panel				
Red	44	1	5	"RED LIGHTS"
White	44	1	5	"WHITE LIGHTS"
Dome (L & R)	8	1	10	"ENGR'S DOME LIGHTS"
Lights, Hatch Dome	5	1	* 5	"COCKPIT"

Figure 1-33. (Sheet 7) Fuse and Circuit Breaker List

AC SYSTEM EQUIPMENT FUSES AND CIRCUIT BREAKERS (Continued)

EQUIPMENT OR CIRCUIT	LOCATION (PANEL NO.)	QUAN-TITY	SIZE (AMPERES)	DECAL NOMENCLATURE
Lights, Navigator's				
Fluorescent				
Cockpit	4	1	* 5	"FLUORESCENT LIGHTS"
Table	4	1	* 5	"TABLE LIGHTS"
Lights, Bombardier's				
Cockpit				
Dome (R & W)				
Fluorescent	1	1	* 5	"FLUOR LIGHTS"
Table				
Cockpit				
Fluorescent	1	1	* 5	"TABLE LIGHT"
Lights, Radio Operator's				
Sub-flight Deck C-4	15	1	* 5	"SUB FLT DECK LT"
Dome	15	1	* 5	"DOME LIGHT"
Cockpit	15	1	* 5	"COCKPIT LIGHT"
Lights, Flight Deck Flood				
Engineer's				
Pilot's				
Copilot's	8	1	10	"FLT DK FLOOD LIGHTS COND"
Landing Light Filament (Power)				
Left	8	1	30	"L.H. LANDING LIGHT"
Right	8	1	30	"R.H. LANDING LIGHT"
Lights, Bomb Bay & Turret (Power)				
Fwd Turret Bay				
Fwd Turret Passageway				
R. Fwd Turret Power Panel				
L. Fwd Turret Power Panel				
Dome Sta 7.0				
Bomb Bay #1				
Bomb Bay #2	21	1	†15	"BOMB BAY LIGHTS 1 & 2"
Aft Turret Bay				
Aft Turret Passageway				
R. Aft Turret Power Panel				
L. Aft Turret Power Panel				
Bomb Bay #3				
Bomb Bay #4				
Alternate Flap Sw Panel				
R. Main Power Panel				
L. Main Power Panel	21	1	†15	"BOMB BAY LIGHTS 3 & 4"
Lights, Formation				
Right Wing				
Left Wing				
Bomb Bay	5	1	* 5	"LIGHTS FORM"
Lights, Landing Gear Wheel Well				
Nose				
Left MLG				
Right MLG	10	1	† 5	"WHEEL LIGHTS"
Lights, Aft Cabin & Tail Cone				
Dome				
Communication Tube	28	1	* 5	"DOME LIGHTS"
Fwd L & R Scanner				
Tail Gunner	28	1	* 5	"COCKPIT LIGHTS"
Tail Cone Dome				
Tail Turret Dome	30	1	† 5	"TAIL CONE LIGHTS"
Meters, Voltage AND Frequency, Watt AND Var. AND Phase Sequence Lamps from:				
Alternator 2	33	3	10	"AC INST"
Alternator 3	34	3	10	"AC INST"

Figure 1-33. (Sheet 8) Fuse and Circuit Breaker List

Section I
Description

T.O. 1B-36D(II)-1

AC SYSTEM EQUIPMENT FUSES AND CIRCUIT BREAKERS (Continued)

EQUIPMENT OR CIRCUIT	LOCATION (PANEL NO.)	QUANTITY	SIZE (AMPERES)	DECAL NOMENCLATURE
Meters, Voltage AND Frequency, Watt AND Var. AND Phase Sequence Lamps from: (Continued)				
Alternator 4	35	3	10	"AC INST"
Alternator 5	36	3	10	"AC INST"

NOTE

The above fuses are in the circuits which lead from each alternator to the positions marked "2," "3," "4," and "5" of the Voltage and Frequency Selector Switch. THESE CIRCUITS ARE ALSO THE SOURCE OF EMERGENCY POWER, when the selector switch is positioned for any alternator which will excite, and when the Emergency Power Switch is in the "EMERGENCY" position.

EQUIPMENT OR CIRCUIT	LOCATION (PANEL NO.)	QUANTITY	SIZE (AMPERES)	DECAL NOMENCLATURE
Meters, Voltage AND Frequency from:				
Bus 201	24	2	10	"AC INST"
Bus 301	24	2	10	"AC INST"
Bus 401	23	2	10	"AC INST"
Bus 501	23	2	10	"AC INST"
Oil Cooler Manual Override (Power) (Some Airplanes)	39	1	* 5	"OIL COOLER CONT."
Oil Cooler (Power):				
Recip. Engine 1	32	1	10	"ENG. OIL COOL"
Recip. Engine 2	33	1	10	"ENG. OIL COOL"
Recip. Engine 3	34	1	10	"ENG. OIL COOL"
Recip. Engine 4	35	1	10	"ENG. OIL COOL"
Recip. Engine 5	36	1	10	"ENG. OIL COOL"
Recip. Engine 6	37	1	10	"ENG. OIL COOL"
Oil Shut Off Valves — Jet Engines 1, 2, 3, & 4 (Some Airplanes)	7	4	* 5	"OIL SHUT OFF VALVE POWER ENG. 1, 2, 3, & 4"
Oil Shut Off Valves — Recip. Engines 1, 2, 3, & 4 (Some Airplanes)	9	6	* 5	"ENGINE OIL SHUT OFF VALVES 1, 2, 3, 4, 5, & 6"
Oven, B-4 AND Liquid Container, Aft	28	1	20	"BEV. TANKS & OVEN"
Oven, B-4 AND Hot Cups, Aft	28	2	10	"HOT CUPS & OVEN"
Preheat, Jet Pod	7	1	* 5	"POD PREHEAT POWER"
Pressure Shut Off Valves, Aft Cabin AND Wing	9	1	* 5	"WING SHUT OFF VALVES"

NOTE

Either one of the following groups of RCM equipment may be installed in the aircraft.

EQUIPMENT OR CIRCUIT	LOCATION (PANEL NO.)	QUANTITY	SIZE (AMPERES)	DECAL NOMENCLATURE
Radar Countermeasures Equipment, Group I:				
AN/ALA-2, or				
AN/APA-38	14	1	10	"RACK POSIT. #5A"
AN/APR-4	14	1	10	"RACK POSIT. #2"
AN/APT-4 — Rack Position 4	14	1	20	"RACK POSIT. #4"
AN/APT-4 — Rack Position 5	14	1	20	"RACK POSIT. #5"
Radar Countermeasures Equipment, Group II:				
AN/ALA-2, or				
AN/ALA-38	14	1	10	"RACK POSIT. #5A"
AN/APR-4	14	1	10	"RACK POSIT. #2"
AN/APT-1	14	1	20	"RACK POSIT. #4"
AN/APT-5A	14	1	10	"RACK POSIT. #1"
AN/ARQ-8	14	1	20	"RACK POSIT. #5"
Radar Set:				
AN/APG-32	28	1	20	"APG-3"

Figure 1-33. (Sheet 9) Fuse and Circuit Breaker List

AC SYSTEM EQUIPMENT FUSES AND CIRCUIT BREAKERS (Continued)

EQUIPMENT OR CIRCUIT	LOCATION (PANEL NO.)	QUANTITY	SIZE (AMPERES)	DECAL NOMENCLATURE
Radar Set (Continued)				
AN/APN-9A — Loran	6	1	10	"LORAN RECVR"
AN/APX-6	6	1	10	"APX-6 I.F.F."
Radar Set Pressurization:				
AN/APG-32	28	1	10	"APG-3 PUMP"
AN/APQ-31	3	1	10	"RADAR PRESS PUMP"
Spark Advance — Recip. Engines 1, 2, 3, 4, 5, & 6	9	6	* 5	"ENGINE SPARK ADVANCE 1, 2, 3, 4, 5, & 6"
Special Bombing System (Airplanes With Special Bombing in BB 1 & 4)				
Heater Trans (BB 1)	19	1	10	"SPECIAL BOMBING BB 1"
Heater Trans (BB 4)	27	1	10	"SPECIAL BOMBING BB 4"
Trans FCT Junct Box (BB 1 & 4)	3	1	10	"SPECIAL BOMBING"
(Airplanes With Special Bombing in BB 1 & 4)				
Heater Trans (BB 1 & 2)	19	2	10	"SPECIAL BOMBING BB 1 & 2"
Heater Trans (BB 3 & 4)	27	2	10	"SPECIAL BOMBING BB 3 & 4"
Transformer FCT Junction Box (BB 1, 2, 3, 4)	3	2	10	"SPECIAL BOMBING"
Transformer	42	4	5	
Starter (Power) — Jet Engines 1, 2, 3, & 4 (Connected Direct to Bus Bar — No Fuses)				
Starter (Power):				
Recip. Engine 1	32	3	60	"STARTER"
Recip. Engine 2	33	3	60	"STARTER"
Recip. Engine 3	34	3	60	"STARTER"
Recip. Engine 4	35	3	60	"STARTER"
Recip. Engine 5	36	3	60	"STARTER"
Recip. Engine 6	37	3	60	"STARTER"
Throttle — Jet Engines 1, 2, 3, & 4	7	4	* 5	"THROTTLE CONTROL POWER 1, 2, 3, & 4"
Turbo Boost Override	9	1	5	"OVERRIDE"
Turbosupercharger Regulator — Recip. Engines 1, 2, 3, 4, 5, & 6	12	6	10	"ENGINE 1, 2, 3, 4, 5, & 6 TURBO"
Turbosupercharger Selection — Recip. Engines 1, 2, 3, 4, 5, & 6	9	6	* 5	"ENGINE SUPERCHARGER SELECTION 1, 2, 3, 4, 5, & 6"
Turret Computer Heater, AND Thyratron Energizing (Control):				
Aft Lower, Left	27	1	10	"LOW LH TURRET"
Aft Lower, Right	26	1	10	"LOW RH TURRET"
Aft Upper, Left	27	1	10	"UP LH TURRET"
Aft Upper, Right	26	1	10	"UP RH TURRET"
Forward, Left	19	1	10	"UPPER LH TURRET"
Forward, Right	18	1	10	"UPPER RH TURRET"
Nose	3	1	10	"NOSE TUR"
Tail	28	1	10	"TAIL TUR"
Turret Desiccator, Nose	3	3	10	"NOSE TURRET DESICCATOR"
Turret Door:				
Aft Lower	27	3	10	"LOWER TURRET DOOR MOTOR"
Aft Upper	26	3	10	"UPPER TURRET DOOR MOTOR"
Forward, Left	19	3	10	"UPPER LH TURRET DOOR MOTOR"
Forward, Right	18	3	10	"UPPER RH TURRET DOOR MOTOR"
Turret (Power):				
Aft Lower, Left	27	3	50	"LOWER LH TURRET"

Figure 1-33. (Sheet 10) Fuse and Circuit Breaker List

Section I
Description

T.O. 1B-36D(II)-1

AC SYSTEM EQUIPMENT FUSES AND CIRCUIT BREAKERS (Continued)

EQUIPMENT OR CIRCUIT	LOCATION (PANEL NO.)	QUANTITY	SIZE (AMPERES)	DECAL NOMENCLATURE
Turret (Power): (Continued)				
Aft Lower, Right	26	3	50	"LOWER RH TURRET"
Aft Upper, Left	27	3	50	"UPPER LH TURRET"
Aft Upper, Right	26	3	50	"UPPER RH TURRET"
Forward, Left	19	3	50	"UPPER LH TURRET"
Forward, Right	18	3	50	"UPPER RH TURRET"
Nose	3	3	40	"NOSE TURRET"
Tail	28	3	40	"TAIL TURRET POWER"
Voltage Regulator:				
Alternator 2	33	3	10	"AC PWR. EQUIP."
Alternator 3	34	3	10	"AC PWR. EQUIP."
Alternator 4	35	3	10	"AC PWR. EQUIP."
Alternator 5	36	3	10	"AC PWR. EQUIP."
Water Injection (Power):				
Recip. Engine 1	32	3	10	"WATER INJECTION PUMP"
Recip. Engine 2	33	3	10	"WATER INJECTION PUMP"
Recip. Engine 3	34	3	10	"WATER INJECTION PUMP"
Recip. Engine 4	35	3	10	"WATER INJECTION PUMP"
Recip. Engine 5	36	3	10	"WATER INJECTION PUMP"
Recip. Engine 6	37	3	10	"WATER INJECTION PUMP"
Windshield Wiper (Power), Pilots'	3	3	10	"PILOTS WINDSHIELD WIPER"

DC SYSTEM EQUIPMENT FUSES AND CIRCUIT BREAKERS

EQUIPMENT OR CIRCUIT	LOCATION (PANEL NO.)	QUANTITY	SIZE (AMPERES)	DECAL NOMENCLATURE
Aileron Trim Tab (Control), Left AND Right	5	1	* 5	"TABS AILERON"
Aileron Trim Tab Position Indicator:				
Left	32	1	10	"AIL. TAB"
Right	37	1	10	"AILERON TRIM TAB"
Air Plug (Control):				
Jet Engines 1, 2, 3, & 4	7	1	* 5	"AIR PLUG POWER"
Recip. Engines 1, 2, 3, 4, 5, & 6	13	6	* 5	"ENGINES AIR PLUG CONTROLS 1, 2, 3, 4, 5, & 6"
Alarm Bell	5	1	* 5	"ALARM BELL"
Alternator:				
Exciter Relay 2	33	1	10	"ALT. CONT."
Exciter Relay 3	34	1	10	"ALT. CONT."
Exciter Relay 4	35	1	10	"ALT. CONT."
Exciter Relay 5	36	1	10	"ALT. CONT."
Fielding Flashing	13	1	* 5	"ALT FIELD FLASH"
Anti-Icing:				
Air Temperature Warning Lamps	9	1	* 5	"ANTI-ICE HEAT DUCT TEMP."
Jet Pod Heaters (Control), AND Thermal Valves (Control)	7	1	† 5	"NOSE DE-ICE"
Jet Pod Thermal Valves (Power), Left	31	1	10	"POD DE-ICE"
Jet Pod Thermal Valves (Power), Right	38	1	10	"POD DE-ICE"
Autopilot (Control), E-6	5	1	*10	"AUTO PILOT"
Bomb Bay Doors (Control):				
Bombardier's	1	1	* 5	"BOMB BAY DOOR"
Pilots'	5	1	* 5	"BOMB DOORS"
Bomb Master Switch	2	1	†25	"MASTER POWER"

Figure 1-33. (Sheet 11) Fuse and Circuit Breaker List

DC SYSTEM EQUIPMENT FUSES AND CIRCUIT BREAKERS (Continued)

EQUIPMENT OR CIRCUIT	LOCATION (PANEL NO.)	QUANTITY	SIZE (AMPERES)	DECAL NOMENCLATURE
Bomb Nose Arming (Control) — Bomb Bays 1, 2, 3, & 4	1	1	* 5	"NOSE FUSING"
Bomb Nose Arming (Power):				
Bomb Bay 1	20	1	†25	"BOMB NOSE FUSING B.B. 1"
Bomb Bay 2	20	1	†20	"BOMB NOSE FUSING B.B. 2"
Bomb Bay 3	25	1	†20	"BOMB NOSE FUSING B.B. 3"
Bomb Bay 4	25	1	†25	"BOMB NOSE FUSING B.B. 4"
Bomb Rack Compressor, Pneumatic: (Some Airplanes)				
Bomb Bay 1	20	1	†25	"PNEUMATIC BOMB RACK COMP."
Bomb Bay 4	25	1	†25	"PNEUMATIC BOMB RACK RIGHT COMP."
Bomb Rack Junction Box, Pneumatic Bomb Bay 2 & 3 (Some Airplanes)				
Bomb Bay 1 & 2	20	2	†25	"PNEUMATIC BOMB RACK JUNCT BOX BB 1 & 2"
Bomb Bay 3 & 4	20	1	†25	"SPECIAL SYSTEM BB 3 & 4 SALVO"
Bomb Rack Selector:				
Bomb Bay 2	20	1	† 5	"B.B. 2 RACK SELECTOR"
Bomb Bay 3	25	1	† 5	"RACK SELECTOR B.B. 3"
Bomb Bays 1 & 4	25	1	† 5	"RACK SELECTOR B.B. 1 & 4"
Bomb Release Switch	1	1	*10	"BOMB RELEASE"
Bomb Release Intervalometer	1	1	* 5	"INTER HEATER"
Bomb Salvo (Control) — Bomb Bays 1, 2, 3, & 4:				
Bombardier's	1	1	*10	"BOMB SALVO"
Pilots'	5	1	*10	"BOMB SALVO"
Bomb Salvo (Power):				
Bomb Bay 1	20	1	†25	"BOMB SALVO B.B. 1"
Bomb Bay 2	20	1	†25	"BOMB SALVO B.B. 2"
Bomb Bay 3	25	1	†25	"BOMB SALVO B.B. 3"
Bomb Bay 4	25	1	†25	"BOMB SALVO B.B. 4"
Bomb Scoring Tone Relay	1	1	* 5	"BOMB SCORING TONE"
Brake Pump	See: "Hydraulic Pump (Controls), Brake"			
Bus Tie-Breakers	9	1	* 5	"BUS TIE BREAKERS CONTROL"
Cabin Air Duct Temperature Indicator	9	1	* 5	"CABIN DUCT TEMP."
Camera (Airplanes not in Group 2)				
Bomb Impulse	1	1	* 5	"CAMERA BOMB IMPULSE"
Door	41	1	† 5	"CAMERA DOOR"
Heater	41	1	†10	"POWER HEATER"
Vacuum	41	1	†10	"VACUUM PUMP"
Camera Operation Indication	41	1	† 5	"OPERAT'N INDIC."
Control Panel Power	25	1	†25	"CAMERA"
Camera (Group 2 Airplanes)				
Bomb Impulse (Normal)	1	1	* 5	"CAMERA BOMB IMPULSE—NORMAL"
Bomb Impulse (Salvo)	1	1	* 5	"CAMERA BOMB IMPULSE—SALVO"
Camera Power	2	1	*10	"CAMERA POWER"
Door	2	1	* 5	"DOOR"
Initiation	2	1	* 5	"CAMERA INITIATION"
Intervalometer	2	1	* 5	"INTERVALOMETER"
Vacuum	2	1	*10	"VACUUM SYSTEM"

Figure 1-33. (Sheet 12) Fuse and Circuit Breaker List

Section I
Description

DC SYSTEM EQUIPMENT FUSES AND CIRCUIT BREAKERS (Continued)

EQUIPMENT OR CIRCUIT	LOCATION (PANEL NO.)	QUAN-TITY	SIZE (AMPERES)	DECAL NOMENCLATURE
Camera Initiation, O-15	1	1	*10	"RADAR CAMERA"
Carburetor Air Filter (Control) — Recip. Engines 1, 2, 3, 4, 5, & 6	10	1	† 5	"CARB. AIR FILTER"
Carburetor Air Preheat (Control) — Recip. Engines 1, 2, 3, 4, 5, & 6	9	6	* 5	"CARBURETOR PREHEAT 1, 2, 3, 4, 5 & 6"
Carburetor Air Temperature Indicators — Recip. Engines 1, 2, 3, 4, 5, & 6	9	6	* 5	"TEMPERATURE INDICATORS CARBURETOR AIR 1, 2, 3, 4, 5, & 6"
Chaff Dispenser				
Left	28	1	*15	"CHAFF DISPENSER LH"
Right	28	1	*15	"CHAFF DISPENSER RH"
Compass, Radio — AN/ARN-7	4	1	* 5	"RADIO COMPASS"
Compass, N1 Gyro Magnetic	5	1	* 5	"HIGH LATITUDE COMPASS"
Control Surface Locks (Control)	5	1	* 5	"CONTROL SURFACE LOCKS"
Fan, Air Circulating:				
Copilot's	3	1	20	"CO-PILOTS FAN"
Pilot's	6	1	20	"PILOTS FAN"
Fan (Control), Cabin Air Booster	9	1	* 5	"BOOST FAN"
Fire Detection:				
Recip. Engine 1	32	1	10	"FIRE DETECT"
Recip. Engine 2	33	1	10	"FIRE DETECT"
Recip. Engine 3	34	1	10	"FIRE DETECT"
Recip. Engine 4	35	1	10	"FIRE DETECT"
Recip. Engine 5	36	1	10	"FIRE DETECT"
Recip. Engine 6	37	1	10	"FIRE DETECT"
Fire Detection AND Test — Jet Engines 1, 2, 3, & 4	7	1	* 5	"FIRE DETECT POWER"
Fire Detection Test — Recip. Engines 1, 2, 3, 4, 5, & 6	9	1	*10	"FIRE DETECT"
Fire Extinguisher	9	1	*15	"FIRE EXT."
Flaps (Control), Alternate	25	1	† 5	"ALTER. FLAP CONTROL"
Flaps (Control), Normal:				
Center	5	1	* 5	"FLAPS CENTER"
Inboard	5	1	* 5	"FLAPS INB'D."
Outboard	5	1	* 5	"FLAPS OUTB'D."
Flaps Position Indicator	5	1	* 5	"FLAP POSITION IND."
Flaps Position Transmitters, Center, Inboard, AND Outboard	25	1	† 5	"FLAP TRANS"
Fuel:				
Gage, Quantity:				
Bomb Bay Tank	9	1	* 5	"FUEL TANK LEVEL INDICATORS BOMB BAY"
Auxiliary Tanks, Left AND Right	9	1	* 5	"FUEL TANK LEVEL INDICATORS L. & R. AUX."
Wing Tanks, 1 & 6	9	1	* 5	"FUEL TANK LEVEL INDICATORS 1 & 6"
Wing Tanks, 2 & 5	9	1	* 5	"FUEL TANK LEVEL INDICATORS 2 & 5"
Wing Tanks, 3 & 4	9	1	* 5	"FUEL TANK LEVEL INDICATORS 3 & 4"
Pump (Control), Booster:				
Bomb Bay Tank	10	1	÷ 5	"BB TANK BOOSTER"
Jet Engines 1 & 2	7	1	÷ 5	"L. FUEL PUMP"
Jet Engines 3 & 4	7	1	÷ 5	"R. FUEL PUMP"

Figure 1-33. (Sheet 13) Fuse and Circuit Breaker List

T.O. 1B-36D(II)-1

Section I
Description

DC SYSTEM EQUIPMENT FUSES AND CIRCUIT BREAKERS (Continued)

EQUIPMENT OR CIRCUIT	LOCATION (PANEL NO.)	QUAN-TITY	SIZE (AMPERES)	DECAL NOMENCLATURE
Fuel (Continued)				
Pumps (Control), Booster:				
Auxiliary Tanks, Left & Right	10	2	† 5	"TANKS L. & R. AUX. BOOSTER"
Wing Tanks 1, 2, 3, 4, 5, & 6	10	6	† 5	"TANKS 1, 2, 3, 4, 5, & 6 BOOSTER"
Tanks, Bomb Bay:	10	1	* 5	"BB TANK VALVE POWER"
Valve				
Valve, Pressure Refueling				
Tanks, Auxiliary — Left AND Right:	10	2	* 5	"L. & R. AUX. TANK VALVE POWER"
Valves (2)				
Valves, Pressure Refueling (2)				
Tanks, Wing — 1, 2, 3, 4, 5, & 6	10	6	* 5	"1, 2, 3, 4, 5, & 6 TANK VALVE POWER"
1. Heaters (Control), Purging (6)				
2. Transmitters, Quantity (6)				
3. Valves (6)				
4. Valves, Pressure Refueling (6)				
Valve:				
Cross-Feed	10	1	* 5	"CROSS FEED MANIFOLD VALVE POWER"
Manifold — Jet Pod, Left	7	1	* 5	"FUEL VALVE POWER LEFT MANIFOLD"
Manifold — Jet Pod, Right	7	1	* 5	"FUEL VALVE POWER RIGHT MANIFOLD"
Jet Engines 1, 2, 3, & 4	7	4	* 5	"FUEL VALVE POWER ENG. 1, 2, 3, & 4"
Manifold — 1, 2, 3, 4, 5, 6, 7, & 8	10	8	* 5	"FUEL MANIFOLD VALVE POWER 1, 2, 3, 4, 5, 6, 7, & 8"
Recip. Engines 1, 2, 3, 4, 5, & 6 AND Oil Cooler (Control — Flight Cooling — Recip. Engines 1, 2, 3, 4, 5, & 6	10	6	* 5	"ENGINE VALVE POWER 1, 2, 3, 4, 5, & 6"
Gyro Indicator, Pilot's	6	1	10	"PILOT'S GYRO HORIZON"
Heaters (Control), Auxiliary Cabin	11	1	† 5	"CABIN HEATER POWER"
Heaters (Control), Oil — Jet Engines 1, 2, 3, & 4	7	1	† 5	"OIL HEAT"
Heaters (Control), Oil Vent Line — Recip. Engines 1, 2, 3, 4, 5, & 6	10	1	† 5	"OIL VENT HEAT"
Heater, Pitot Tube (Some Airplanes)				
Left	10	1	† 5	"PITOT TUBE HEATER LH"
Right	10	1	† 5	"PITOT TUBE HEATER RH"
Hydraulic Fluid Temperature (Control)	9	1	† 5	"HYD. PUMP FLUID TEMP."
Hydraulic Pump (Control):				
Brake	5	1	* 5	"BRAKE PUMP"
Brake — Emergency	9	1	* 5	"EMERG. BRAKE PUMP"
#2 — Emergency	9	1	† 5	"HYD. PUMP OVERRIDE"
Hydraulic Pump (Controls):				
#1	See:	1. "Bomb Bay Doors (Control), Bombardier's"		
		2. "Bomb Bay Doors (Control), Pilots'"		
		3. "Hydraulic Fluid Temperature (Control)"		
		4. "Landing Gear Extension AND Retraction (Control)"		
		5. "Landing Gear Steering (Control), Nose"		
#2	See:	1. "Hydraulic Pump (Control), #2 — Emergency"		
		2. "Landing Gear Extension AND Retraction (Control)"		
IFI Accessory Equipment (Airplanes with Special Bombing Equipment in BB 1 & 4)				

Figure 1-33. (Sheet 14) Fuse and Circuit Breaker List)

57

Section I
Description

DC SYSTEM EQUIPMENT FUSES AND CIRCUIT BREAKERS (Continued)

EQUIPMENT OR CIRCUIT	LOCATION (PANEL NO.)	QUANTITY	SIZE (AMPERES)	DECAL NOMENCLATURE
IFI Accessory Equipment (Continued)				
Suit Heater Receptacle and Test Receptacle	25	1	†25	"BB TEST RECP HEAT SUIT"
Suit Heater Receptacle & Test Receptacle	20	1	†25	"H-I EQUIPMENT TEST RECP HEAT SUIT"
Test Receptacle				
BB 1		1	†25	"TEST RECEPTACLE"
BB 4		1	†25	"TEST RECEPTACLE"
Panel Lights				
BB 1		1	† 5	"WORK LIGHT"
BB 4		1	† 5	"WORK LIGHT"
(Airplanes with Special Bombing Equipment in BB 1, 2, 3 & 4)				
Suit Heater Receptacle & Test Receptacle (BB 3 & 4)	25	2	†25	"BB-4 HEAT SUIT & IFI EQUIP TEST REC HEAT SUIT"
Suit Heater Receptacle & Test Receptacle (BB 1 & 2)	20	2	†25	"HI & IFI EQUIPMENT TEST REC HEAT SUIT"
Test Receptacle				
BB 1		1	†25	"TEST RECEPTACLE"
BB 2		1	†25	"TEST RECEPTACLE"
BB 3		1	†25	"TEST RECEPTACLE"
BB 4		1	†25	"TEST RECEPTACLE"
Panel Light				
BB 1		1	† 5	"WORK LIGHT"
BB 2		1	† 5	"WORK LIGHT"
BB 3		1	† 5	"WORK LIGHT"
BB 4		1	† 5	"WORK LIGHT"
IFI Heater (Some Airplanes)	25	1	†15	"IFI POWER"
IFI Power (Some Airplanes)	25	1	†25	"IFI HEATER"
Ignition Booster (Power)				
Recip. Engine 1	32	1	10	"IGN BOOST"
Recip. Engine 2	33	1	10	"IGN BOOST"
Recip. Engine 3	34	1	10	"IGN BOOST"
Recip. Engine 4	35	1	10	"IGN BOOST"
Recip. Engine 5	36	1	10	"IGN BOOST"
Recip. Engine 6	37	1	10	"IGN BOOST"
Ignition (Control) Recip. Engs. 1, 2, 3, 4, 5, & 6	9	1	*20	"IGNITION"
Ignition (Control), AND Starter (Control), AND Starter Engaging (Control) — Jet Engines 1, 2, 3, & 4	7	4	* 5	"IGNITION STARTER POWER ENG. 1, 2, 3, & 4"
Instrument Approach System — Glide Path AND Localizer Receivers (Some Airplanes)	1	1	*10	"INST. APPROACH"
Intercoolers Close AND Open (Control) — Recip. Engines 1, 2, 3, 4, 5, & 6	13	1	* 5	"ENG. INTERCOOLER"
Interphone:				
Amplifier, Mixer:				
Copilot's	5	1	* 5	"COMBAT INTERPHONE"
Pilot's	5	1	* 5	"PILOT INTERPHONE"
Radio Operator's	15	1	* 5	"MIXER AMP"
Amplifier — Normal Channel	15	1	* 5	"INTERPHONE"
Amplifier — Private Channel (Through Audio Input Relays "A" & "C")	9	1	* 5	"INTERPHONE"
K-1 Bombing System:				
Amplifier — Computer, Type A-2	6	1	30	"K-1 SYSTEM"

Figure 1-33. (Sheet 15) Fuse and Circuit Breaker List

DC SYSTEM EQUIPMENT FUSES AND CIRCUIT BREAKERS (Continued)

EQUIPMENT OR CIRCUIT	LOCATION (PANEL NO.)	QUAN- TITY	SIZE (AMPERES)	DECAL NOMENCLATURE
K-1 Bombing System: (Continued)				
Filter, F-67/APS-23	6	1	30	"BOMB'G RADAR"
Landing Gear Extension AND Retraction (Control), AND Oil Cooler (Control) — Ground Cooling — Recip. Engines 1, 2, 3, 4, 5, & 6	5	1	* 5	"LANDING GEAR CONTROL"
Landing Gear Steering (Control), Nose	5	1	* 5	"LANDING GEAR NOSE STEER"
Lights, Jet Switch Panel				
Panel Lights (Red)				
Periscope Sextant				
Auto Pilot	7	1	* 5	"PANEL LIGHTS"
Inter-Aircraft Signal				
Nose Gunner Lamp Recp.	3	1	10	"ALDIS RECP."
Navigator Lamp Recp.	6	1	10	"ALDIS RECP."
R. Fwd Gunner Lamp Recp.				
L. Fwd Gunner Lamp Recp.	17	1	10	"ALDIS RECP."
R. Upper Aft Gunner Lamp Recp.				
L. Upper Aft Gunner Lamp Recp.	28	1	*10	"UPPER ALDIS LAMP RECP."
R. Lower Aft Gunner Lamp Recp.				
L. Lower Aft Gunner Lamp Recp.	28	1	*10	"LOWER ALDIS LAMP RECP."
Landing-Extension AND Retraction, and Filament (Control)	5	1	* 5	"LANDING LIGHTS CONTROL"
Taxi Lights (Some Airplanes)				
Left (Power)	31	1	30	"TAXI LIGHT"
Right (Power)	38	1	30	"TAXI LIGHT"
Left & Right (Control)	40	1	† 5	"TAXI LIGHT"
Landing Gear Wheel Well	10	1	† 5	"WHEEL LIGHTS"
Navigation, Tail (Yellow)	See: "Lights (Control), Navigation — Wing (Red AND Green) AND Tail (White), AND Lights, Navigation — Tail (Yellow)"			
Wing Internal	25	1	†10	"WING TE LIGHTS"
Lights (Control), Navigation — Wing (Red AND Green) AND Tail (White), AND Lights, Navigation — Tail (Yellow)	5	1	* 5	"LIGHTS NAVIGATION WING & TAIL"
Lights (Control): Bomb Bay & Turret	28	1	* 5	"TURRET & BB LIGHTS"
1. Dome, Aft Turret Bay				
2. Dome, Aft Turret Passageway				
3. Dome, Bomb Bay 3				
4. Dome, Bomb Bay 4				
5. Dome, Main A-C Power Panels				
6. Instrument, Flap Control Panel				
Lights (Control):	15	1	* 5	"LIGHTS TURRET BB 1 & 2"
1. Dome, Bomb Bay 1				
2. Dome, Bomb Bay 2				
3. Dome, Forward Turret Bay				
4. Dome, Forward Turret Passageway				
5. Dome, Station 7.0				
6. Instrument, Forward Turret Power Panels				
Lights (Control) — (Alternate Control Circuit for the Two Preceding Groups)	25	1	* 5	"TURRET & BB LIGHTS"
Marker Beacon Set, AN/ARN-12	15	1	* 5	"MARKER BEACON"
Marker Beacon Test Lamp	5	1	* 5	"ARN-12 LAMP TEST"
Master Temperature Indicator (Some Airplanes)	9	1	* 5	"ENG TEMP IND"

Figure 1-33. (Sheet 16) Fuse and Circuit Breaker List

Section I
Description

T.O. 1B-36D(II)-1

DC SYSTEM EQUIPMENT FUSES AND CIRCUIT BREAKERS (Continued)

EQUIPMENT OR CIRCUIT	LOCATION (PANEL NO.)	QUANTITY	SIZE (AMPERES)	DECAL NOMENCLATURE
Oil Cooler (Control) — Flight Cooling — Recip. Engines 1, 2, 3, 4, 5, & 6	See: "Fuel Valves — Recip. Engines 1, 2, 3, 4, 5, & 6, AND Oil Cooler (Control) — Flight Cooling — Recip. Engines 1, 2, 3, 4, 5, & 6"			
Oil Cooler (Control) — Ground Cooling — Recip. Engines 1, 2, 3, 4, 5, & 6	See: "Landing Gear Extension AND Retraction (Control), AND Oil Cooler (Control) — Ground Cooling — Recip. Engines 1, 2, 3, 4, 5, & 6"			
Oil Cooler Manual Override (Control) (Some Airplanes)	39	6	† 5	"ENG OIL COOLER CONTROL"
Oil Dilution — Recip. Engines 1, 2, 3, 4, 5, & 6	9	1	*15	"OIL DILUTE"
Oil Quantity Gages — Recip. Engines 1, 2, 3, 4, 5, & 6	9	6	* 5	"OIL QUANTITY GAGE POWER 1, 2, 3, 4, 5, & 6"
Oil Shut Off Valve, Jet Engines 1, 2, 3 & 4 (On Airplanes Equipped with D.C. Actuators)	7	4	* 5	"OIL SHUT OFF VALVE POWER ENG. 1, 2, 3 & 4"
Oil Temperature Indicators — Recip. Engines 1, 2, 3, 4, 5, & 6	9	6	* 5	"TEMPERATURE INDICATORS ENGINE OIL 1, 2, 3, 4, 5, & 6"
Parking Brake Control (Some Airplanes)	5	1	* 5	"PARK BRAKE"
Primers — Recip. Engines 1, 2, 3, 4, 5, & 6	9	1	* 5	"ENGINE PRIMER"
Propellers Feathering, Reversing, AND Pitch Changing — Recip. 1, 2, 3, 4, 5, & 6	9	6	*15	"PROPELLER CONTROL 1, 2, 3, 4, 5, & 6"
Propeller Master Motor	9	1	*10	"PROPELLER CONTROL MASTER MOTOR"
Propeller Pitch Indicator Lamps, Engineer's AND Pilot's	9	1	* 5	"PROP PITCH IND"

NOTE

Either of the following groups of RCM equipment may be installed in the aircraft.

Radar Countermeasures Equipment, Group I:				
AN/APR-4	16	1	* 5	"RACK POSIT. #2"
AN/APT-4 — Rack Position #1	16	1	*10	"RACK POSIT. #1"
AN/APT-4 — Rack Position #4	16	1	*10	"RACK POSIT. #4"
AN/APT-4 — Rack Position #5	16	1	*10	"RACK POSIT. #5"
Radar Countermeasures Equipment, Group II:				
AN/APR-4	16	1	* 5	"RACK POSIT. #2"
AN/APT-1	16	1	*10	"RACK POSIT. #4"
AN/APT-5A	16	1	* 5	"RACK POSIT. #1"
AN/ARQ-8	16	1	*10	"RACK POSIT. #5"
Radar Set:				
AN/APG-32	28	1	*15	"TAIL RADAR POWER"
AN/APN-9A — Loran	4	1	* 5	"LORAN"
AN/APX-6	15	1	* 5	"IDENT. REC'R"
AN/APX-6 Detonator	15	1	*10	"IDENT. DETONT'R."
Radio Range Receiver, BC-453 (Some Airplanes)	5	1	* 5	"RANGE RECEIVER"
Radio Set:				
AN/ARC-3 — Command	17	1	30	"COMMAND AN/ARC-3"
AN/ARC-8 — Liaison (Dynamotor)	17	3	20	"LIAISON RADIO DYN"
AN/ARC-8 — Liaison (Receiver)	15	1	* 5	"LIAISON REC'R"

Figure 1-33. (Sheet 17) Fuse and Circuit Breaker List

DC SYSTEM EQUIPMENT FUSES AND CIRCUIT BREAKERS (Continued)

EQUIPMENT OR CIRCUIT	LOCATION (PANEL NO.)	QUAN- TITY	SIZE (AMPERES)	DECAL NOMENCLATURE
Radio Set: (Continued)				
AN/ARN-14 (Some Airplanes)				
Glide Path Rec	1	1	*5	"GLIDE PATH RECVR"
Test Receptacle	28	1	*5	"ARN-14 TEST RECP."
Receiver	28	1	*10	"ARN-14 NAV. RECVR"
AN/ARC-27				
Set Control	15	1	*10	"COMMAND RADIO"
Receiver-Transmitter	28	1	*25	"ARC-27 RECVR"
Special Bombing System (Airplanes with Special Bombing Equipment in BB 1 & 4)				
Arming & Release (Power)	2	1	*25	
Release & Heater (Control)	2	2	*5	
T-35	42	2	*15 or *35	"T-35"
T-19	42	2	*15 or *35	"IFC"
T-18	42	2	*15 or *25	"IFM"
Test	42	2	*20	"TEST"
FCT Junction Box (DC Feeder)	12	3	60	"AUX BOMB RACK TEST EQUIP"
(Airplanes With Special Bombing Equipment in BB 1, 2, 3 & 4)				
Arming & Release (Power)	2	1	*25	
Release & Heater (Control)	2	4	*5	
T-35	42	4	*15 or *35	"T-35"
T-19	42	4	*15 or *35	"IFC"
T-18	42	4	*15 or *25	"IFM"
Test	42	4	*20	"TEST"
FCT Junction Box (DC Feeder)	12	3	60	"AUX BOMB RACK TEST EQUIP"
Starters (Control) — Jet Engines 1, 2, 3, & 4	See: "Ignition (Control), AND Starter (Control), AND Starter Engaging (Control) — Jet Engines 1, 2, 3, & 4"			
Starters (Control) — Recip. Engines 1, 2, 3, 4, 5, & 6	9	1	*5	"ENGINE STARTER"
Starter Engaging (Control) — Jet Engines 1, 2, 3, & 4	See: "Ignition (Control), AND Starter (Control), AND Starter Engaging (Control) — Jet Engines 1, 2, 3, & 4"			
Starter Engaging (Power):				
Jet Engine 1	31	1	10	"#1 STARTER ENGAGING"
Jet Engine 2	31	1	10	"#2 STARTER ENGAGING"
Jet Engine 3	38	1	10	"#3 STARTER ENGAGING"
Jet Engine 4	38	1	10	"#4 STARTER ENGAGING"
Test Power Terminal:				
Recip. Engine 1	32	1	10	"TEST POWER"
Recip. Engine 2	33	1	10	"TEST POWER"
Recip. Engine 3	34	1	10	"TEST POWER"
Recip. Engine 4	35	1	10	"TEST POWER"
Recip. Engine 5	36	1	10	"TEST POWER"
Recip. Engine 6	37	1	10	"TEST POWER"
Turbo Boost Regulator Control (Some Airplanes)	9	1	†5	"VERNIER"
Turn AND Bank Indicator				
Copilot's	5	1	*5	"TURN & BANK IND. COPILOT"
Pilot's	5	1	*5	"TURN & BANK IND. PILOT"
Turret Interlocking Relay	25	1	†5	"TURRET DOOR IN'LOCK"
Turret Sight Test Receptacle:				
Aft	28	1	*10	"28V DC RECP."
Forward	17	1	20	"GUNSIGHT CHECKER"
Water Injection (Control) — Recip. Engines 1, 2, 3, 4, 5, & 6	10	6	†5	"ENGINE WATER INJECTION 1, 2, 3, 4, 5, & 6"
Windshield Wiper (Control), Pilots'	5	1	*5	"WINDSHIELD WIPER"

Figure 1-33. (Sheet 18) Fuse and Circuit Breaker List

Revised 18 May 1956

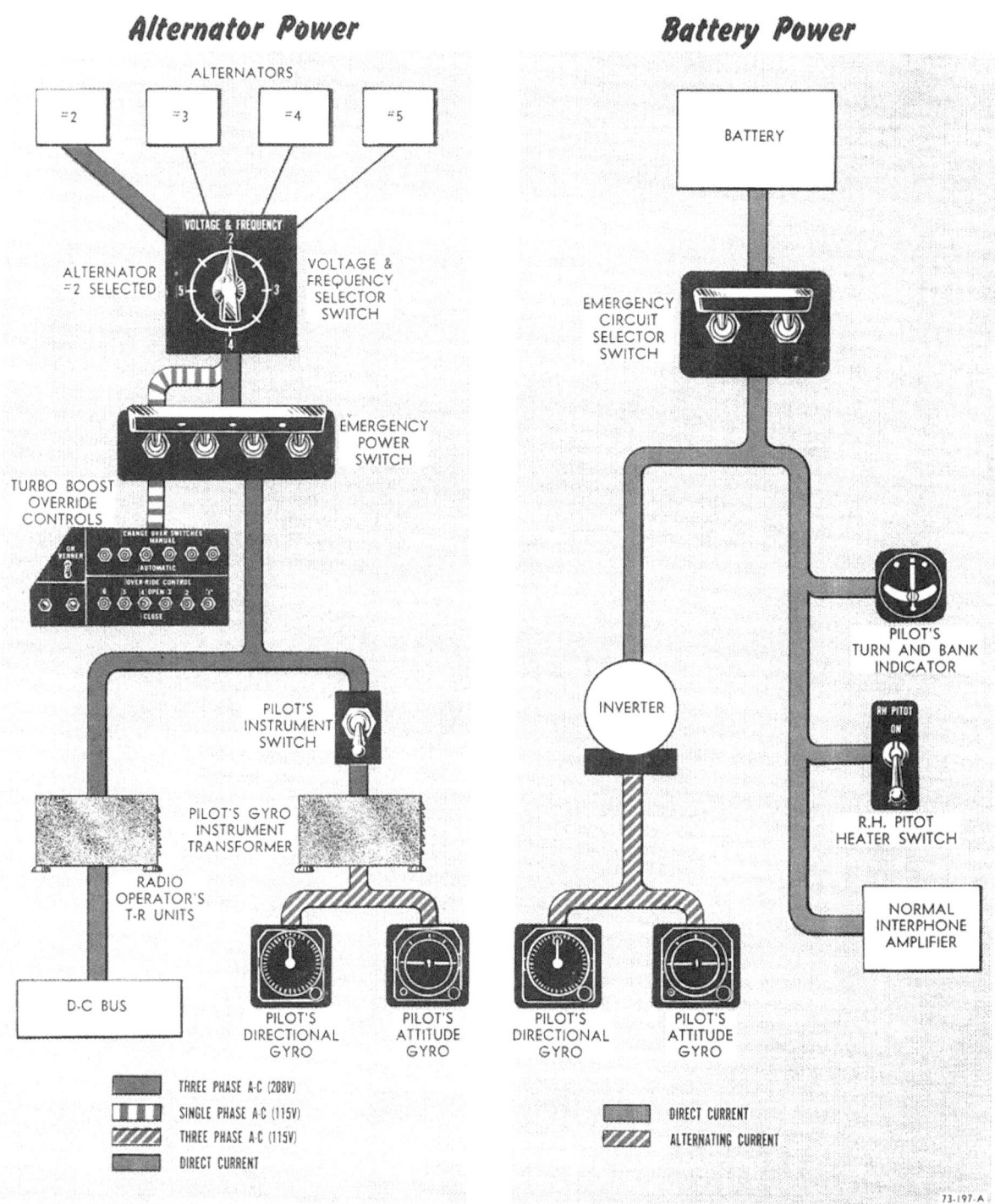

Figure 1-34.

Transformer-Rectifier Test Unit Voltmeter. Voltage output of the unit being tested is indicated by the voltmeter.

Transformer-Rectifier Test Unit Ammeter. This meter is provided to indicate the amperage output load of the unit being tested. A reading of 1.0 on the meter indicates 100 per cent (50 amperes) output.

EMERGENCY ELECTRICAL SYSTEM.

In the event all alternators "jump" off the line, an emergency circuit is provided to restore enough power to operate essential electrical equipment. The emergency circuit begins at the terminals of each alternator and goes through the voltage and frequency selector switch to an emergency power switch. By use of the emergency switch, a-c power is fed to the pilot's flight instrument switch and the radio operator's transformer-rectifier; in group 2 airplanes power is also fed to the turbo boost override controls. The d-c output of the t-r can be used to close the alternator breaker when attempting to get an alternator back on the line or, if such attempts fail, to operate essential d-c equipment. (See figure 1-34.)

Airplanes in group 2 are equipped with an additional emergency circuit. This circuit starts at the battery and by-passes the battery relay to feed power directly to an emergency circuit selector switch on the pilots' instrument panel. This switch connects battery power to an inverter which is installed on the flight deck just forward of the pilots' pedestal. The inverter receives battery power from the copilot's circuit breaker panel and supplies a-c power to the pilot's directional and vertical gyros. When inverter operation is selected, the pilot's turn and bank indicator, the right hand pitot heater, and the normal interphone amplifier are disconnected from the d-c bus and are connected directly to the battery.

WARNING

Do not permit the d-c load to exceed 1.0 (50 amperes) as indicated on the load meter of the transformer-rectifier test unit, when selected to the RADIO OPER position. An overload can damage the t-r unit or blow out the a-c fuses at the respective engine distributing panels with a resulting loss of all emergency power.

Emergency Power Control.

On airplanes in group 2, the emergency power control (1, figure 1-18) consists of four two-position switches ganged together on the engineer's auxiliary instrument panel. Airplanes not in group 2 have only three switches. Placing the switches in EMERGENCY completes the emergency power circuit; moving the switches to NORMAL breaks the circuit. During normal

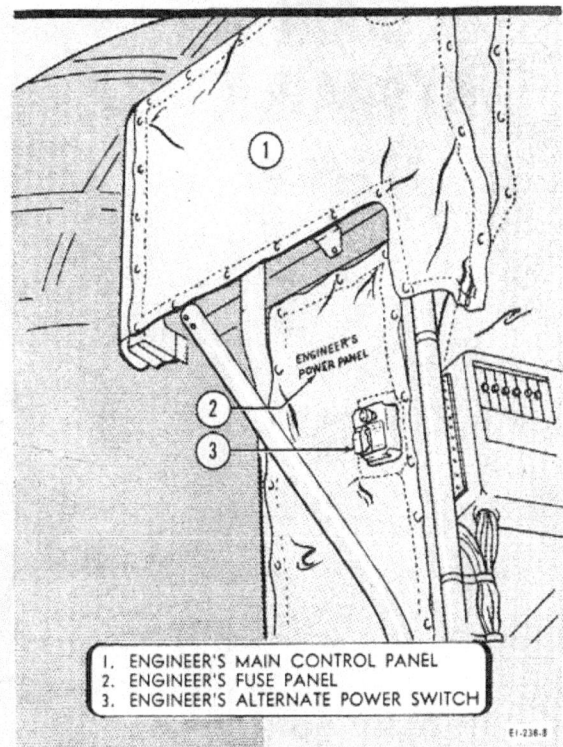

1. ENGINEER'S MAIN CONTROL PANEL
2. ENGINEER'S FUSE PANEL
3. ENGINEER'S ALTERNATE POWER SWITCH

Figure 1-35.

operation the switches should always be in the NORMAL position.

ALTERNATE SOURCE OF A-C POWER TO ENGINEER'S FUSE PANEL.

A two-position switch (figure 1-35), is located on the engineer's fuse panel. This switch has positions marked NORMAL and ALTERNATE and is used to select one of two sources of a-c power for the engineer's fuse panel. This switch is wired in the NORMAL position, and power is supplied from the right forward cabin panel. The ALTERNATE position provides power from the left forward cabin power panel. Adjacent to this switch is a lamp which indicates when power from either source is being supplied to the engineer's fuse panel.

Emergency Circuit Selector Switch (Group 2 Airplanes).

This switch (42, figure 1-13) consists of two switches ganged together on the pilot's instrument panel. The switch has two positions marked NORMAL and EMERGENCY. When all a-c power is lost, placing the switch in EMERGENCY will connect 28-volt d-c power directly from the battery to the inverter which supplies a-c power for operation of the pilot's directional and vertical gyros. The EMERGENCY position

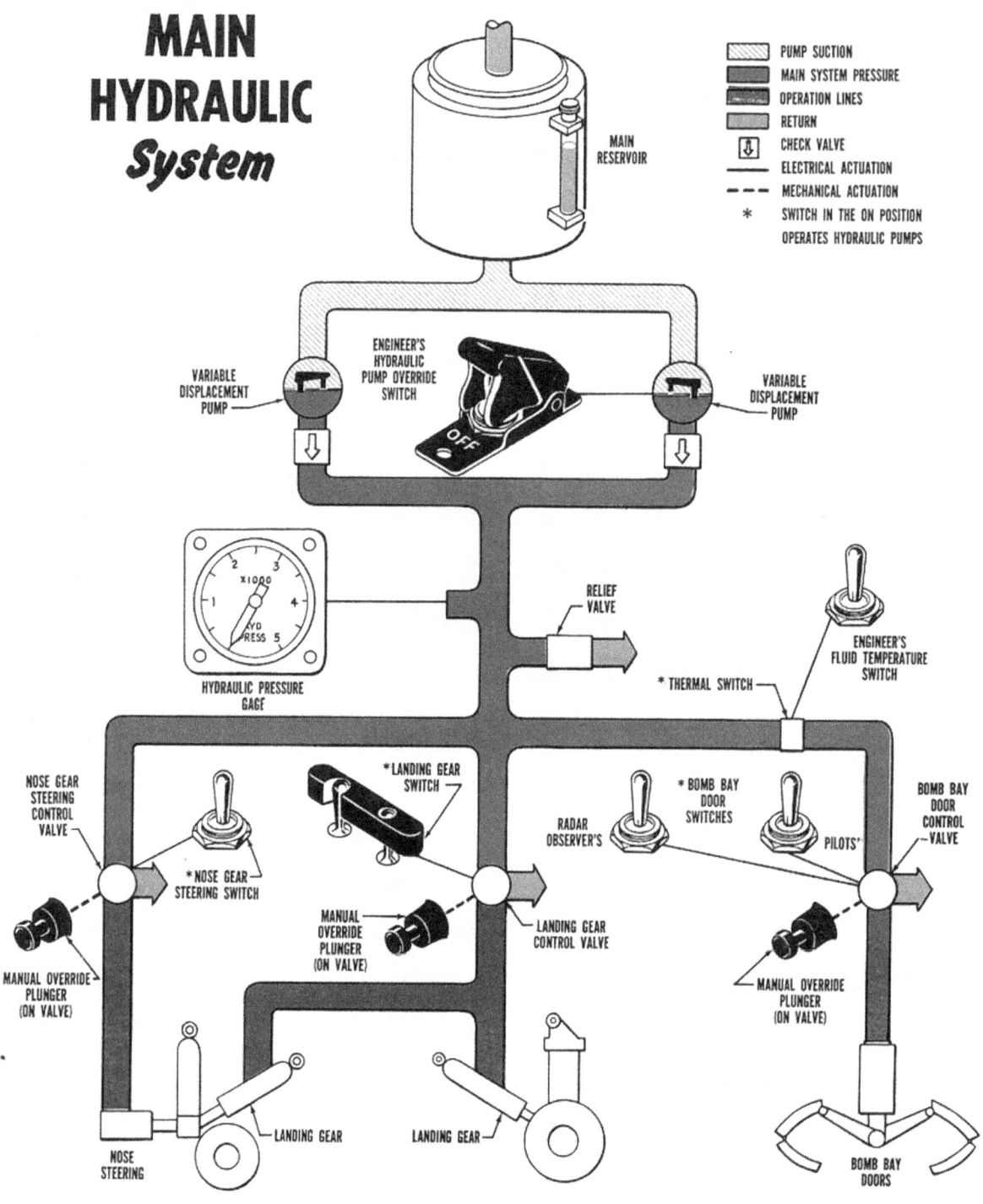

Figure 1-36.

ENGINEER'S Hydraulic Control Panel

1. HYDRAULIC FLUID TEMPERATURE CONTROL SWITCH
2. HYDRAULIC PUMP OVERRIDE SWITCH
3. BOMB BAY DOOR, NOSE WHEEL STEERING AND LANDING GEAR HYDRAULIC PRESSURE GAGE
4. BRAKE PUMP PRESSURE OVERRIDE SWITCH
5. LOW BRAKE PRESSURE WARNING LAMP
6. BRAKE HYDRAULIC PRESSURE GAGE

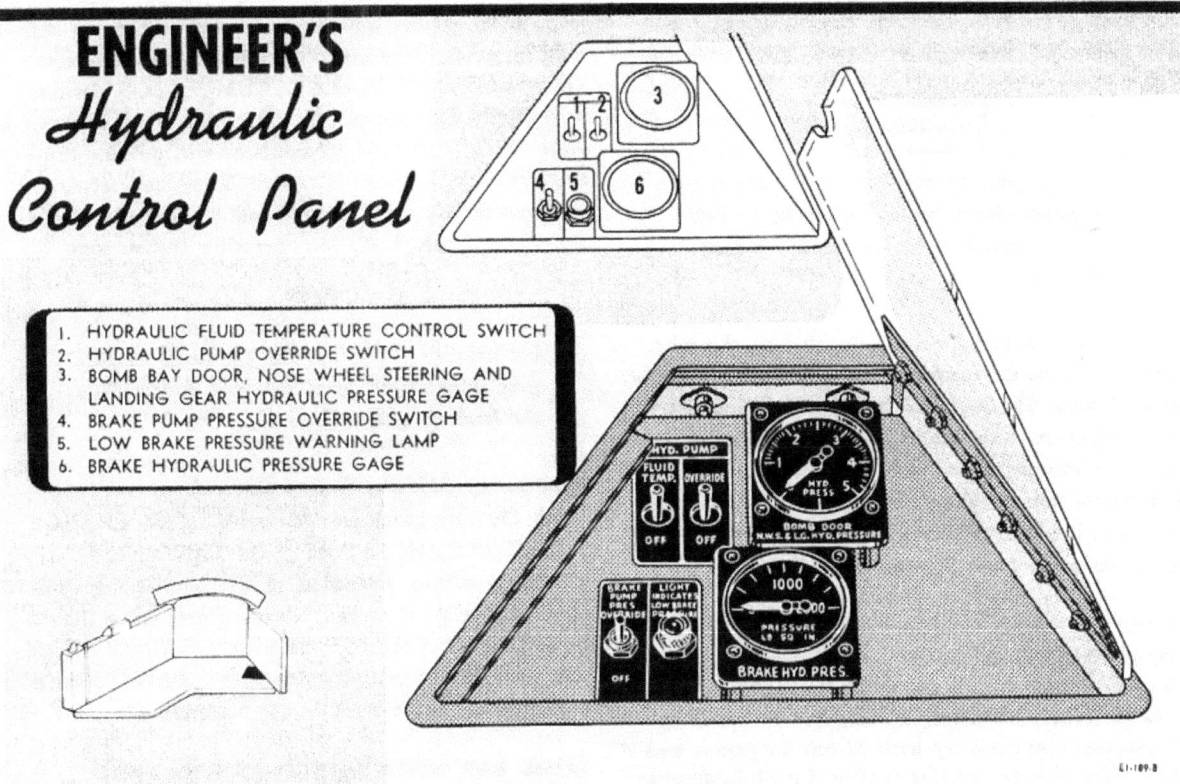

Figure 1-37.

also disconnects the pilot's turn and bank indicator, the right hand pitot heater, and the normal interphone amplifier from the d-c bus and connects these units to the emergency circuit.

HYDRAULIC SYSTEM.

The hydraulic system is composed of four independent systems: a main system, a brake system, and two emergency systems. Each system has its own reservoir and selector valve. Main system pressure is supplied by two electrically-driven pumps. Hand pumps provide pressure for the emergency systems. The main system operates the landing gear, bomb bay doors, and nose wheel steering. Pressure from one emergency system can be used to extend the landing gear or to charge the brake system accumulators.

The other emergency system can be used to open or close the bomb bay doors.

Note

Normally, brake pressure is supplied by an independent hydraulic system. For detailed information, refer to "Brake System" of this section.

MAIN HYDRAULIC SYSTEM.

The main hydraulic system supplies fluid pressure for landing gear, nose wheel steering, and bomb bay door operation. The system consists of a reservoir, two electrically-driven hydraulic pumps, and a main selector valve.

The main system reservoir, located on the wing front spar inside the fuselage, is provided with a sight level gage and filler neck. Fluid can be added during flight, provided the main reservoir pressurization line is disconnected. For servicing information, refer to figure 1-48.

The main hydraulic system pumps operate whenever the associated control switch for landing gear operation, nose wheel steering, or bomb bay door operation is actuated.

Note

For information concerning these switches, refer to "Landing Gear Switch" and "Steering Switch" of this section and "Bomb Bay Door Switch" of Section IV.

Both pumps operate for landing gear retraction and bomb bay door operation. Only one pump operates during landing gear extension and nose wheel steering. The pumps operate on 208-volt a-c power received through relays which are controlled by 28-volt direct current and deliver approximately 3100 psi fluid pressure to the system. The pumps stop operation through the action of limit switches after the bomb bay doors open or close or after the closing of the canoe doors upon completion of a landing gear operation cycle.

> **CAUTION**
>
> To prevent overheating of the hydraulic pump motor, limit pump operation to one retract or extend cycle in each 5-minute period.

The main system selector valve, located on the wing front spar inside the fuselage, is controlled by 28-volt direct current. The valve controls fluid pressure from the main pumps to the landing gear, nose wheel steering, and bomb bay door mechanisms. In the event of an electrical control failure, the valve for the selected system can be operated manually as directed in "Manual Operation of Main Selector Valve," Section III.

Hydraulic Pump Override Switch.

This on-off switch (2, figure 1-37) is used to control one pump motor during emergency manual operation of the main selector valve. Placing the switch in the ON position closes a relay with 28-volt d-c power and routes 208-volt ac to energize the No. 2 main hydraulic pump motor.

Hydraulic Fluid Temperature Switch.

This switch (1, figure 1-37) at the engineer's station is used to set up a temperature control circuit for bomb bay door system hydraulic fluid. (Refer to "Hydraulic Fluid Temperature Control," Section IV.)

Hydraulic Pressure Gage.

A pressure gage (6, figure 1-37), at the flight engineer's station indicates the hydraulic pressure for the landing gear, bomb bay door, and nose wheel steering operation.

LANDING GEAR AND BRAKE EMERGENCY HYDRAULIC SYSTEM.

This system consists of a reservoir, a hand pump, and a selector valve, (figure 1-45). Since the system serves for emergency operation of both landing gear and brakes, the selector valve is provided so that fluid pressure can be directed to the proper system. The emergency system hydraulic lines are separate from the main system. Shuttle valves are installed between the normal and emergency hydraulic lines so that pressure from either side can close the other line, directing fluid pressure into the actuating units. With the selector valve in LANDING GEAR DOWN position, hand pump operation extends and locks the landing gear. Hand pump operation with the selector valve in CHARGE BRAKE ACCUMULATOR position will supply fluid pressure to charge the brake accumulator. A fully charged accumulator will provide three full brake applications. Refer to "Emergency Hydraulic Landing Gear Extension" and "Emergency Brake Pressure," Section III, for operating instructions.

Note

When the emergency hydraulic system is used for landing gear extension, the main landing gear wheel well doors will not retract after the landing gear is lowered.

Emergency Selector Valve Control.

With the emergency selector valve in the CHARGE BRAKE ACCUMULATOR or the LANDING GEAR DOWN position, operation of the hand pump produces the selected action. Normally the valve should be left in the CHARGE BRAKE ACCUMULATOR position. This permits any pressures caused by thermal expansion to be relieved in the accumulators.

BOMB BAY DOOR EMERGENCY HYDRAULIC SYSTEM.

The bomb bay door emergency hydraulic system has a separate reservoir, hand pump, selector valve, and hydraulic lines. The emergency lines are connected to the bomb bay door main actuating units through shuttle valves similar to the landing gear emergency system. For operation of this system, refer to "Operation of Bomb Bay Door Emergency Hydraulic System," Section IV.

FLIGHT CONTROL SYSTEM.

The movement of the ailerons, elevators, and rudder in response to their controls is conventional; however, the method of moving the main surfaces is unique. The controls are mechanically linked to flying servo tabs. When a control is moved to deflect a tab in one direction, the air load on the displaced tab causes the main surface to be deflected in the opposite direction. Though an extra step is involved between the control movement and the main surface movement, response time is less than one-tenth of a second.

To provide control feel to the pilot, a spring-loaded piston in each main surface compresses when the related tab is deflected. In addition, the piston spring operates the tab to produce a damping effect when

CONTROL SURFACE Deflections

Surface		
Aileron	Up 20°	Down 20°
Aileron Servo Tabs	Up 25°	Down 25°
Elevator	Up 25°	Down 20°
Elevator Servo Tabs	Up 20°	Down 20°
Elevator Trim Tabs	Up 24°	Down 12°
Flaps	Up 0°	Down 30°
Rudder	Left 16°	Right 16°
Rudder Servo Tabs	Left 14°	Right 14°
Rudder Trim Tab	Left 20°	Right 20°

Figure 1-38.

the main surface is deflected by turbulence. The tab counteracts the movement of the main surface and restores the surface to its original position. These pistons also provide for movement of the main surfaces when the airplane is on the ground and there are no air loads on the surfaces. When a tab is moved, the piston spring compresses until the spring load is sufficient to overcome the friction at the main surface pivot points; then the main surface moves.

The rudder and elevators lock simultaneously by means of hydraulic locks. The locks are electrically controlled and lock the surfaces at whatever position they are in. A bleed orifice allows hydraulic locking pressure to bleed from one side of the piston to the other. Control surfaces deflect to either full position while locked. Six flaps are on the wing trailing edge. They are electrically controlled and actuated and are synchronized in symmetrical pairs by an electro-mechanical system.

The table in figure 1-38 shows the maximum deflection of all control surfaces. The reference point for these deflections is the chord plane of the surface.

SURFACE CONTROLS.

Control Columns and Rudder Pedals.

The aircraft commander's and pilot's stations are each provided with a control column and a set of rudder pedals. Operation of the columns and pedals is conventional.

Aileron Trim Tab Switch.

The aileron tab acts as a trim tab as well as a servo tab. A spring-loaded switch (21, figure 1-14), located on the pilots' pedestal, supplies 28-volt direct current to relays which supply 208-volt a-c power to the trim tab actuators. The switch positions are LEFT WING DOWN, RIGHT WING DOWN, and neutral OFF.

Aileron Trim Indicator.

An indicator (18, figure 1-13), on the pilots' instrument panel, shows the degree of aileron trim. The indicator operates on 28-volt direct current in response to a signal from potentiometers on the trim tab actuators.

Elevator Trim Tab Control Wheels and Indicators.

The elevator trim tabs are set by a pair of dual-operating control wheels (15, figure 1-14) on the pilots' pedestal. A rotable dial on the hub of each wheel indicates the trim condition of the tabs.

Rudder Trim Tab Control Knob and Indicator.

Rudder trim is set by a control knob (17, figure 1-14) located on the pilots' pedestal. A rotable dial around the base of the knob indicates the trim setting of the rudder trim tab.

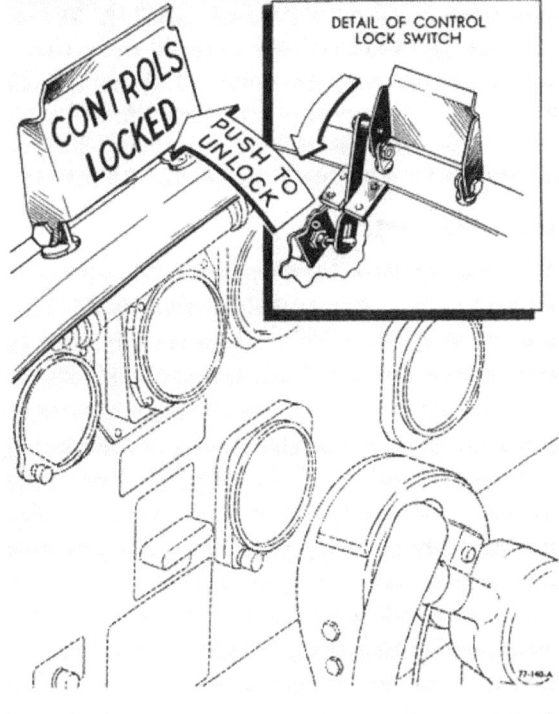

Figure 1-39.

Section I
Description

T.O. 1B-36D(II)-1

CONTROL SURFACE LOCKS.

The rudder and elevators are hydraulically locked in the position they are in when the locks are engaged.

Note

The aileron control locks have been rendered inoperative.

The locks prevent any sudden movement of the surfaces, but allow the surfaces to creep under load; therefore, locked controls will not restrict small movements of the control columns or rudder pedals. A safety switch, actuated by the movement of the right main oleo strut, automatically unlocks the controls as soon as the weight of the airplane is removed from the gear. Indicator lamps show when the surfaces are locked or unlocked.

Control Lock Switch.

The flight control lock switch (figure 1-39) is actuated by a yellow flag on the pilot's coaming. Raising the flag to its vertical CONTROLS LOCKED position locks all control surfaces. The switch supplies 28-volt direct current to relays which permit the flow of 115-volt a-c power to the control lock actuators.

Control Lock Indicators.

A red indicator lamp (12, figure 1-13) burns continuously when any one of the controls is locked. The red indicator light will go out the instant all lock actuators *start* their unlocking movement. With all controls unlocked on the ground, a green indicator lamp (12, figure 1-13) burns continuously. When the main gear is unlocked for retraction, the green lamp will go out.

WING FLAP SYSTEM.

The wing flap system consists of six slotted flaps which are mechanically and electrically synchronized in symmetrical pairs. Normally, all flaps are controlled by three ganged switches. These switches supply 28-volt direct current to close relays which supply 208-volt a-c power to the flap speed control relays. A synchronizer is connected to each pair of flaps by cables and keeps these flaps within 2 degrees of each other by operating the speed control relay. Whenever a flap gets more than 2 degrees ahead of its symmetrical flap, the speed control relay will place the lead flap motor in low speed until the lagging flap is again in synchronization at which time they will both operate at high speed. If the flaps become misaligned by 3 degrees, the normal flap control for the unsynchronized pair becomes inoperative. Emergency controls are provided for adjusting each flap individually if the normal control system fails.

Note

When one pair of flaps is inoperative because of misalignment, normal operation of the remaining pairs is unaffected.

Normal Controls.

Flap Switch. This switch (12, figure 1-14) is actually three switches ganged together and is located on the pilots' pedestal. The switch has spring-loaded UP and DOWN positions and a center OFF position.

CAUTION

If it is necessary to operate the flaps for more than two cycles on the ground, allow the actuators to cool for approximately 15 minutes between cycles.

Indicators.

Flap Position Indicator. This indicator (20, figure 1-13) is located on the pilots' instrument panel and consists of three separate indicators. Each individual indicator reflects the position of one pair of flaps as transmitted from the associated flap synchronizer.

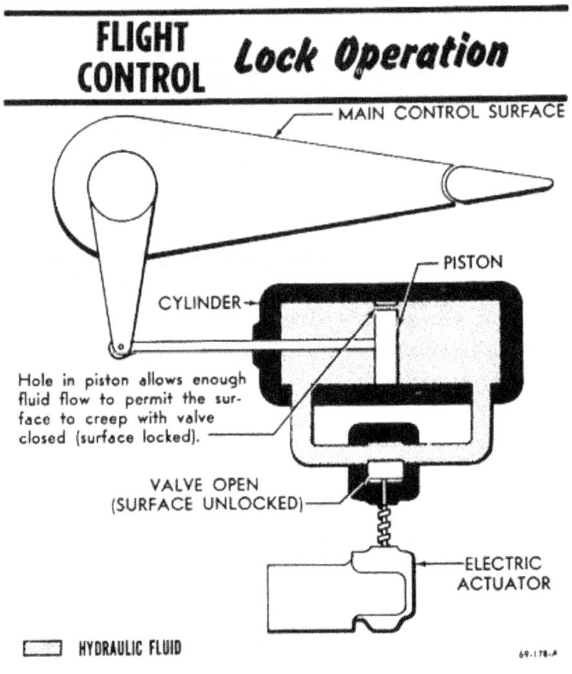

FLIGHT CONTROL Lock Operation

- MAIN CONTROL SURFACE
- PISTON
- CYLINDER
- Hole in piston allows enough fluid flow to permit the surface to creep with valve closed (surface locked).
- VALVE OPEN (SURFACE UNLOCKED)
- ELECTRIC ACTUATOR
- HYDRAULIC FLUID

69-178-A

Figure 1-40.

68

Warning Horn. A warning horn, which is also used for landing gear warning, is provided for the flap system. The horn is electrically connected to the synchronizers and the throttles and indicates an unsafe condition of the flaps with respect to throttle position. If all throttles are advanced to take-off power and the flaps are not extended at least 20 degrees (± 4 degrees) the horn will sound. No silencing button is provided for this circuit; therefore, the throttles must be retarded or the flaps extended to shut off the horn.

Emergency Controls.

An emergency flap control panel is located on the right side of the fuselage near the wing crawlway hatch. A separate 28-volt d-c source (bulkhead 8.0 power panel) is provided for this emergency panel. Three master selector switches are mounted at the top of the emergency panel, and six individual flap switches are grouped by pairs below the master switches. The individual switches supply 28-volt direct current to close the relays for the flap actuator motors.

Emergency Flap Switches. Each of these six switches has spring-loaded UP and DOWN positions and a center OFF position. Holding either of the switches in the UP or DOWN position and then holding the corresponding flap master selector switch in the ALTERNATE position will move the flap in the desired direction.

Flap Master Selector Switches. These switches are used to complete the emergency circuit for the system that has been "set up" by the individual emergency flap switches. Each master switch is marked NORMAL and ALTERNATE, and is spring-loaded to return to NORMAL when released. These switches operate the slow speed relays.

Note

When a flap is adjusted to the same position as its symmetrical flap, the synchronizing system (if operative) will maintain synchronization; therefore, any further actuation of either individual selector switch and the master selector switch for that pair will result in movement of both flaps. However, the flap which is individually selected will be operated at slow speed while the flap which is not selected by the individual switch will follow with a jerky motion at fast travel.

LANDING GEAR SYSTEM.

The airplane has a tricycle landing gear consisting of two four-wheel main gears and a two-wheel nose gear. The nose and main gear and the main gear wheel well doors are hydraulically operated. The other fairings are mechanically operated by the movement of the gear.

The main landing gear is designed so a single oleo strut on each main gear cushions the taxiing, take-off, and landing shocks. Each set of dual wheels in the tandem arrangement is attached to the bottom of the main column by a separate axle beam which permits it to pivot up and down independent of the other set. These separate axles will permit one set of duals to pass over an obstacle approximately 16 inches high while the other set remains in contact with the runway. To permit even distribution of loads, the sets of duals in tandem are linked together through an equalizer which pivots on the main column; the aft set of duals is linked to the aft end of the equalizer by the oleo strut and the forward set is linked to the forward end by a fixed link. This system transfers the shocks taken by either set of duals to the oleo strut.

Hydraulic pressure for landing gear operation is furnished by the main hydraulic system pumps. The pumps supply fluid under pressure to the main selector valve where the fluid is directed to either the extension or retraction mechanism. The landing gear is normally operated by a single switch located on the pilots' pedestal. In the event the normal system fails, emergency controls are provided for gear operation. These include a means of manually positioning the main selector valve for retraction or extension of the gear, an emergency hydraulic landing gear extension system, and a method of manually releasing the gear for a free fall extension.

A safety switch, actuated by the oleo strut on the left main gear, prevents gear retraction while the airplane is on the ground. Ground safety locks are provided in the flyaway tool kit. When installed they prevent unlatching of the gear.

NORMAL CONTROLS.

Landing Gear Switch.

The landing gear switch (5, figure 1-14) is located on the pilots' pedestal and has positions marked EXTEND and RETRACT on either side of a center OFF position. When the switch is moved from OFF to RETRACT, both main system hydraulic pumps are started and the main selector valve is positioned to retract the landing gear. When moved from OFF to EXTEND, the switch starts one hydraulic pump and positions the selector valve for landing gear extension.

Note

When the landing gear control switch is moved to EXTEND, a gang bar automatically turns on a brake pump control switch to prevent landing with low brake pressure. Refer to "Brake Pump Switch" of this section.

MAIN LANDING GEAR *Arrangement*

1. OLEO STRUT
2. FILLER PLUG
3. EQUALIZER ASSEMBLY
4. FAIRING
5. POSITIONING JACK
6. AIR VALVE
7. MAIN COLUMN
8. OUTBOARD TRUSS TUBE
9. INBOARD TRUSS TUBE
10. PIVOT SHAFT
11. MAIN DRAG STRUT
12. AUXILIARY DRAG STRUT
13. MAIN ACTUATING CYLINDER
14. AUXILIARY ACTUATING CYLINDER
15. LATCH LINK ROD
16. INDICATOR FLAG
17. LATCH LINK PIN
18. LATCH
19. SIDE BRACE
20. HYDRAULIC SNUBBER
21. FIXED LINK

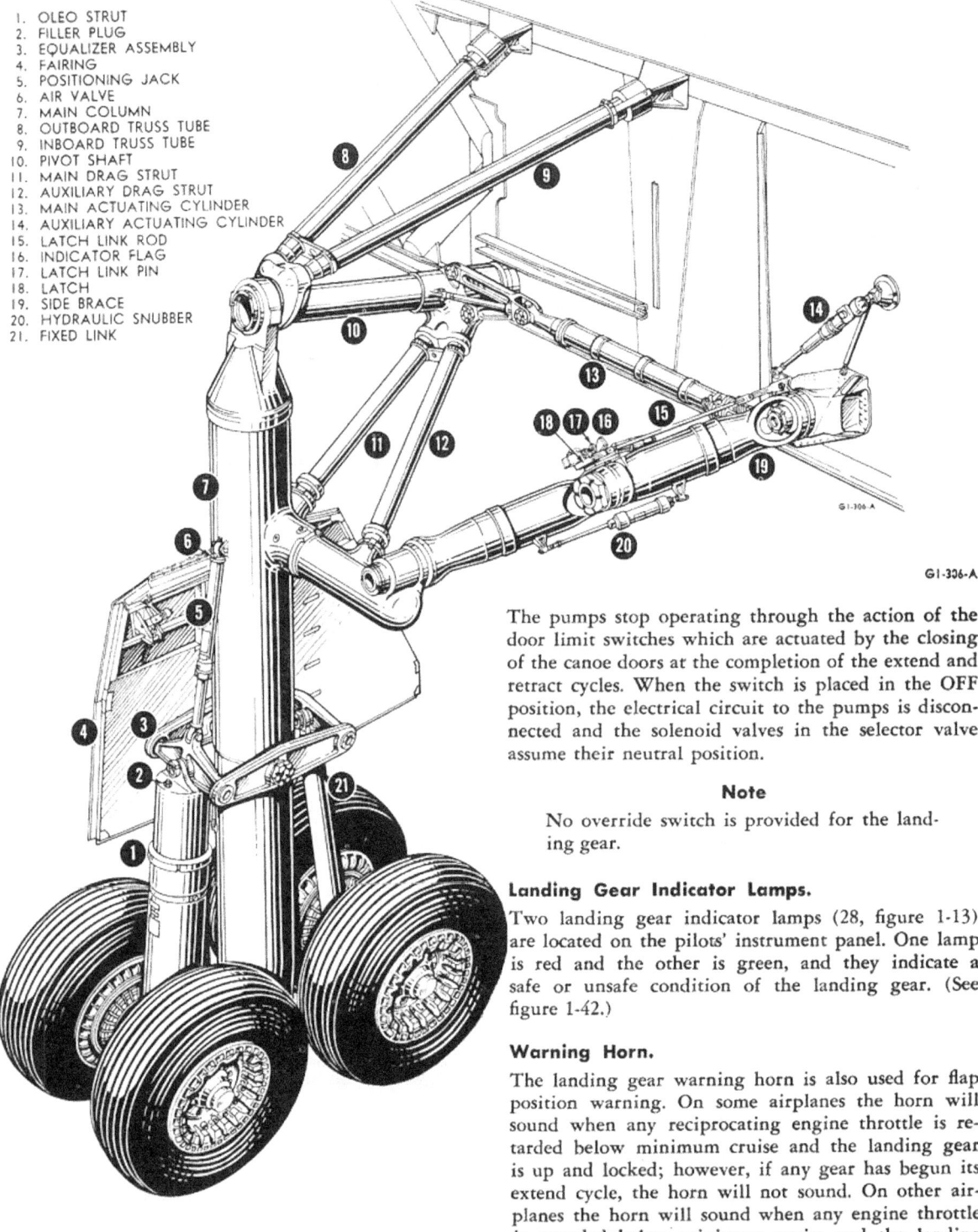

The pumps stop operating through the action of the door limit switches which are actuated by the closing of the canoe doors at the completion of the extend and retract cycles. When the switch is placed in the OFF position, the electrical circuit to the pumps is disconnected and the solenoid valves in the selector valve assume their neutral position.

Note

No override switch is provided for the landing gear.

Landing Gear Indicator Lamps.

Two landing gear indicator lamps (28, figure 1-13) are located on the pilots' instrument panel. One lamp is red and the other is green, and they indicate a safe or unsafe condition of the landing gear. (See figure 1-42.)

Warning Horn.

The landing gear warning horn is also used for flap position warning. On some airplanes the horn will sound when any reciprocating engine throttle is retarded below minimum cruise and the landing gear is up and locked; however, if any gear has begun its extend cycle, the horn will not sound. On other airplanes the horn will sound when any engine throttle is retarded below minimum cruise and the landing gear is *not* down and locked with both main wheel

Figure 1-41.

LANDING GEAR POSITION *Indications*

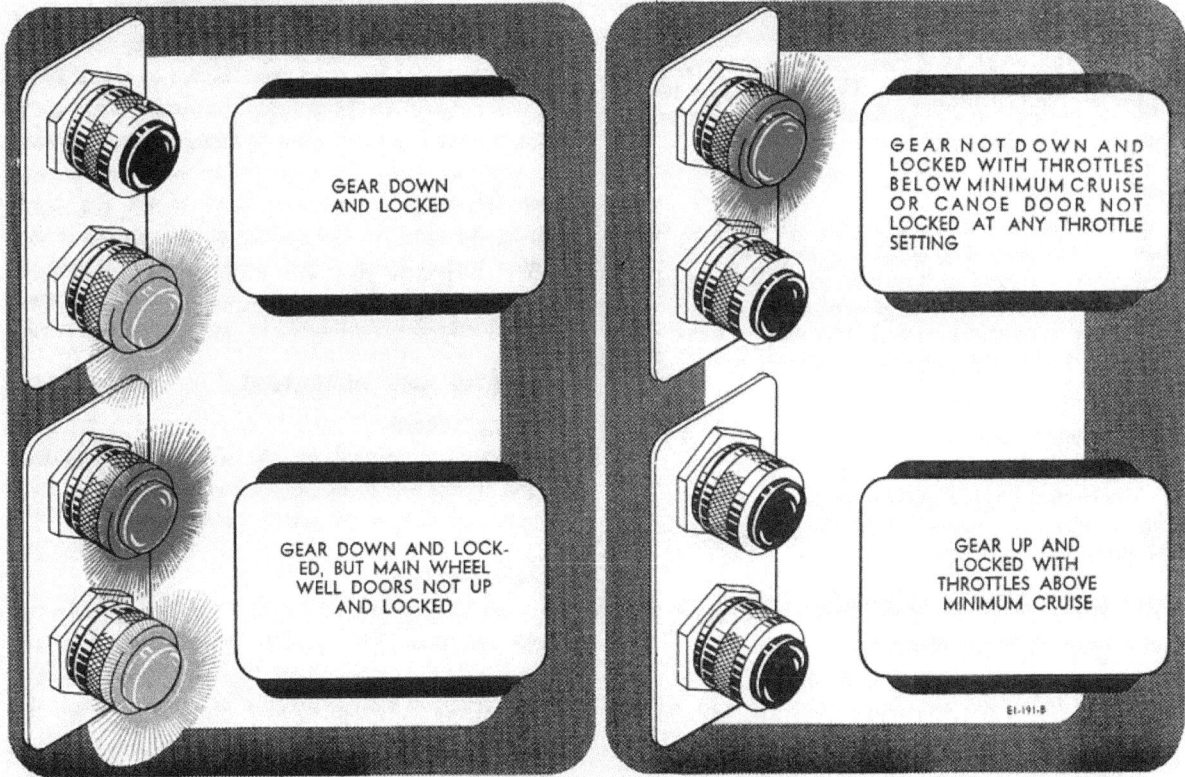

Figure 1-42.

well doors up and locked. The warning horn is located on the pilots' pedestal and may be shut off with a switch (16, figure 1-14) located on the pilots' pedestal. The sounding of the horn must be stopped each time a single reciprocating engine throttle lever is retarded below minimum cruise.

Note

The landing gear warning and the flap position warning are connected to the horn through separate circuits.

MANUAL SELECTOR CONTROLS.

The main selector valve (figure 3-14) can be operated manually in conjunction with the hydraulic pump override switch to extend or retract the landing gear. A DOWN plunger and an UP plunger are provided on the valve body. When a plunger is depressed, hydraulic pressure is directed to accomplish the selected action. Plungers are also provided for operating the bomb bay doors and nose wheel steering.

MAIN GEAR MANUAL EXTENSION CONTROL.

The main gear may be released manually for a free fall extension through the use of manual controls (figure 3-15) located in each main gear wheel well.

The main gear is locked in both the UP and DOWN positions by a side brace. The side brace pivots on each end, and has a latch-secured breaking point in the center. The breaking point is slightly off-center from the ends, making it possible for the weight of the landing gear to hold the side brace in its locked position. During normal extension the side brace is unlatched and pulled off center by linkage connected to the side brace unlatching jack. During manual extension the hoist accomplishes the same actuation. (Refer to "Manual Extension of Main Landing Gear," Section III.)

Main Gear Door Release Handle.

One of these T-handles is located at the outboard edge of each main gear wheel door. When turned, the handle will unlatch the door for a free fall extension.

WARNING

The handle is attached to the door and will fall when the door is unlatched.

Section I
Description

Latch Link Pin.

This pin is painted red and is in the side brace unlatching linkage. Normally this linkage is operated by a hydraulic unlatching jack; however, during manual extension the unlatching linkage is disconnected by pulling out the latch link pin. This prevents the possibility of pressure in the hydraulic system interfering with manual unlatching.

Manual Hoist.

A manual hoist is located above the side brace of each main landing gear. The hoist is operated by a ratchet handle and is rigged with a cable which is attached to a hoist hook. To unlatch and raise the side brace the hoist hook is engaged with a latch release lever and the hoist is operated until the side brace is unlocked and raised.

Latch Release Lever.

A latch release lever is located on the side brace latching mechanism of each main gear. The lever has a fitting to which the manual hoist hook is engaged for unlocking the side brace.

NOSE GEAR MANUAL EXTENSION CONTROLS.

Nose Gear Release Handle.

This release handle (figure 3-18) is located on the floor near the radio operator's station, and when pulled will unlock and allow a free fall extension of the nose gear. (Refer to "Manual Extension of Nose Landing Gear," Section III.)

Nose Landing Gear Emergency Latch Hook.

This latch hook (figure 3-18) stowed on the side of the food locker, is used to operate the latch after an emergency manual extension of the nose gear has been effected.

NOSE WHEEL STEERING SYSTEM.

Nose steering is accomplished by a cable-controlled hydraulic system. (See figure 1-45.) The main components of the system are a steering switch, a 28-volt d-c control circuit, a steering wheel, a directional valve, an actuating cylinder, and control cables. Hydraulic fluid for steering operation is supplied by the main hydraulic system, and pressure is provided by one of the main system pumps. Movement of the steering wheel directs the pressure into the geared actuator which turns the nose wheel. Nose steering hydraulic pressure is indicated on the main hydraulic system pressure gage. A safety switch installed on the nose gear scissors renders the steering system inoperative when the nose gear is off the ground.

Note

A safety switch on the left main landing gear also prevents steering when the main gear is off the ground.

When the nose gear leaves the ground and the nose gear strut extends, centering cams are engaged to keep the nose wheel straight during retraction. Upon landing, the cams disengage when the weight of the airplane compresses the strut three inches or more. If the nose gear strut has been heavily charged with air to support a high gross weight at take-off, the weight of the airplane at landing may not be sufficient to compress the strut the required three inches for disengaging the cams. In this condition, the nose gear will remain locked in its center position. Before landing, the strut must be depressurized by the nose gear strut pressure release valve located in the forward turret bay.

CONTROLS AND INDICATORS.

Steering Wheel.

This wheel is located on the aircraft commander's fairing to the left of the aircraft commander's control column and directs the action of the nose gear.

Steering Switch.

This ON-OFF switch (4, figure 1-14) is located on the pilots' pedestal. This switch energizes one of the main hydraulic system pump motors and actuates the main hydraulic system selector valve to provide the

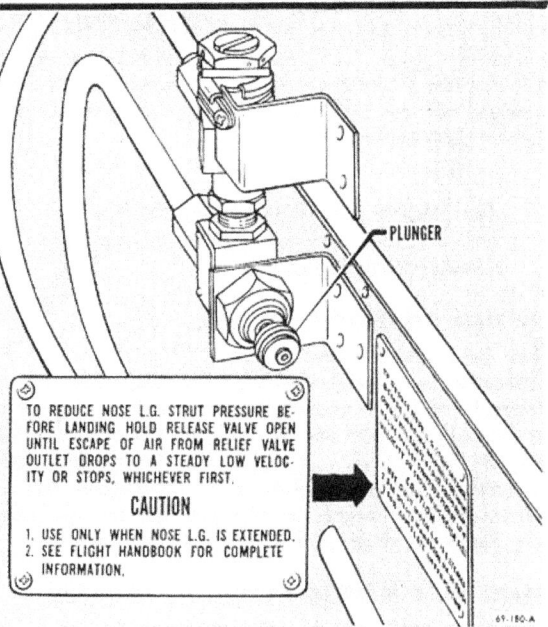

Figure 1-43.

Nose Strut Pressure Release Valve.

The manually operated pressure release valve is provided to reduce the pressure in the nose gear strut in flight. (Refer to "Nose Gear Strut Depressurization," Section VII.) The valve is located just aft and to the right of the forward catwalk entrance hatch and is operated by means of a spring-loaded plunger on the valve body. (See figure 1-43.) When the plunger is held in, pressure will be bled from the strut. When strut pressure has dropped to a value which will permit steering, a relief valve automatically closes. This prevents depressurization below the amount necessary to sustain the weight of the airplane.

CAUTION

The relief valve is set to shut off the escape of air at a pressure occurring when the weight of the airplane is NOT on the nose gear. Therefore, to prevent damage to the strut, the nose gear pressure release valve must not be used for depressurizing when the airplane is on the ground. Also, to prevent the loss of hydraulic fluid, do not depressurize while the nose gear is retracted.

Note

Depressurization should be accomplished during approach after the landing gear is extended.

Nose Wheel Steering Indicator.

An indicator is provided adjacent to the nose steering wheel to indicate the direction and degree of deflection of the nose wheel from its center position.

BRAKE SYSTEM.

Each wheel of the main gear on the B-36 is equipped with a hydraulically operated brake. The normal brake system is an independent hydraulic system. (See figure 1-45.)

Note

Emergency brake pressure is provided by an emergency system which is also used for landing gear extension. See "Landing Gear and Brake Emergency Hydraulic System" of this section.

The brake hydraulic system consists of the main brake system and the slave brake system. The main system is the power source for the brakes, and the slave system controls the power source through a brake control valve. The slave brake system extends from the flight deck controls to the main brake system which is located in the bomb bay directly between the

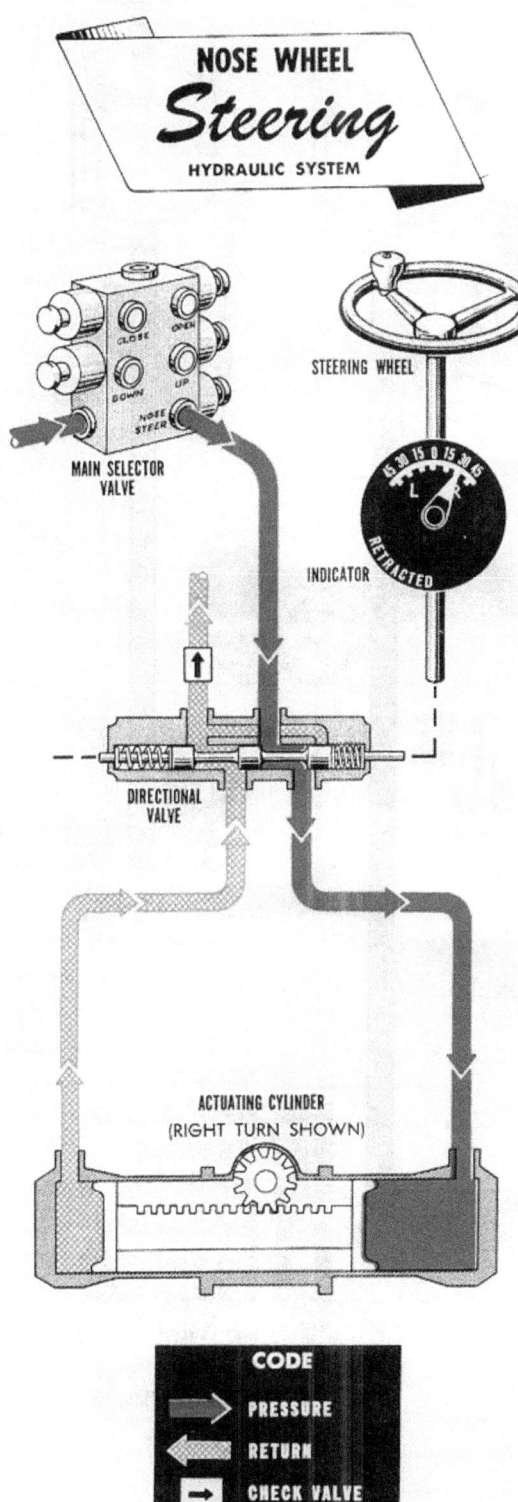

Figure 1-44.

Section I
Description

T.O. 1B-36D(II)-1

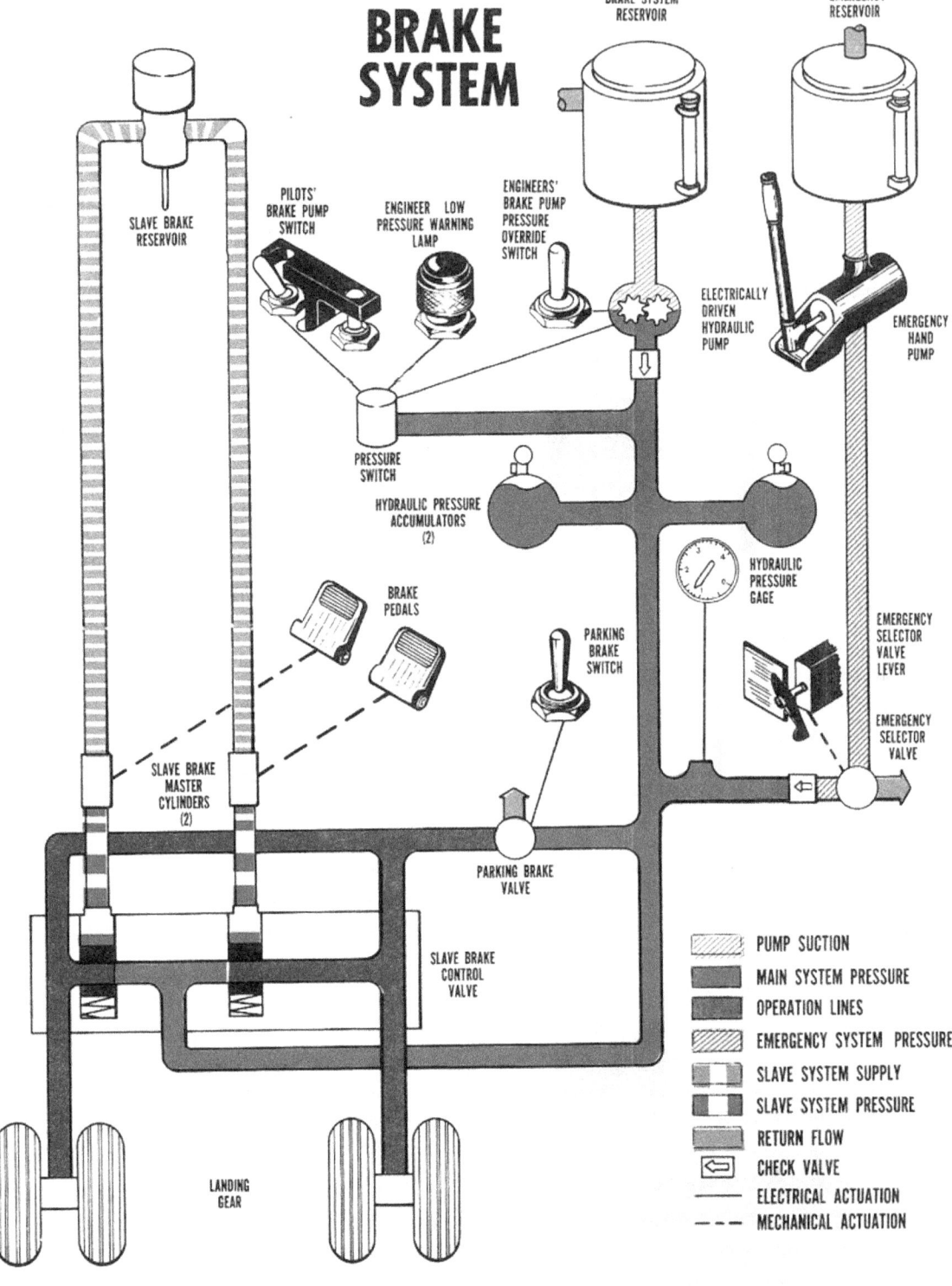

Figure 1-45.

two main landing gears. Since the slave system operates on low pressure as compared with the high pressure main system, considerable weight saving is realized and the possibilities of leakage in the main system lines are reduced by the use of long low-pressure lines and comparatively short high-pressure lines. The slave brake system consists of two pressure reservoirs, a master slave cylinder mechanically connected to each brake pedal, and a slave cylinder which is located in the control valve. When a brake pedal is depressed, the pressure is transmitted from the master slave cylinder to the brake control valve. The brake control valve is positioned by this pressure, allowing main system pressure to pass through the valve to the brakes. The main brake system consists of a reservoir, a pump, two accumulators, and a brake control valve. The accumulators store pressure for the main system, and accumulator pressure is maintained by the 208-volt a-c motor-driven pump. Normal system pressure is from 1125 to 1500 psi. Pump motor power is controlled by a 28-volt d-c circuit through the brake pump switch on the pilots' pedestal. A pressure switch installed in the control circuit holds the circuit open when accumulator pressure is from 1450 to 1500 psi. The pressure switch will close the circuit to start pump operation when the accumulator pressure drops to 1125 to 1225 psi. In the event of a malfunction in the control circuit, the pump can be operated by the pump pressure override switch, located on the engineer's table. The pressure switch also has a set of contacts which control power to the low brake pressure warning light. These contacts close when the pressure decreases from 25 to 100 psi below the pressure where the pump power contacts close. The light contacts will open, turning off the light when the pressure increases to within ±100 psi of the pressure where the pump power contacts open.

Note
Group 1 airplanes are equipped with disc-type brakes utilizing a system pressure of from 850 to 1025 psi; and have only one accumulator installed in the brake system.

BRAKE CONTROLS AND INDICATORS.

Brake Pump Switch.
This switch (5, figure 1-14) controls the normal operation of the brake pump motor. To prevent landing with low brake pressure, a gang bar will move the brake pump switch to the ON position when the landing gear control switch is placed in the EXTEND position. In flight, however, the switch must be moved to the OFF position to minimize pump wear, as the gang bar control is not effective when the landing gear control switch is moved to RETRACT.

Parking Brake Lever (Some Airplanes).
The parking brake lever is located on the pilots' pedestal and controls the parking brake valve for applying accumulator pressure to the brakes.

CAUTION
On those airplanes equipped with a brake line gage fuse the *parking brakes* are inoperative when the fuse is blown. Pressure is available for foot brakes although no pressure is indicated on the gage.

Parking Brake Switch (Some Airplanes).
The parking brake switch (1, figure 1-9), with positions BRAKE ON and BRAKE OFF, is located on the pilots' pedestal and electrically controls the parking brake valve for applying accumulator pressure to the brakes.

Brake Pump Pressure Override Switch.
This spring-loaded switch (4, figure 1-37) is provided to energize the brake pump motor in the event the normal brake pump control circuit fails. If the brake pressure gage or warning lamp indicates low brake pressure when the brake pump switch is ON, system pressure can be brought within operating range by holding the override switch in the ON position.

CAUTION
Since the brake pump will operate continuously when the override switch is held ON, the switch must be released when the pressure is within operating range.

Pressure Gage.
Hydraulic pressure for the brake system is indicated on the hydraulic pressure gage (6, figure 1-37) located on the flight engineer's table. A gage is also located beneath each accumulator.

Low Pressure Warning Lamp.
A low pressure warning lamp (5, figure 1-37) is located adjacent to the brake hydraulic pressure gage and gives a warning when brake pressure falls below normal.

INSTRUMENTS.
Reciprocating engine instruments are located at the engineer's station. In addition, a master tachometer and manifold pressure gage are provided for the pilots. The pilots' manifold pressure gage is for No. 4 engine only.

Fuel pressure, water pressure, oil pressure, torque pressure, manifold pressure, and fuel flow indications are supplied by autosyn transmitters. The transmitters and indicators operate on current fed from transformers which step down 115-volt alternating current.

Autosyn-type reciprocating engine instruments on airplanes not in group 2, operate on current fed from a transformer in the wing adjacent to each nacelle. Group 2 airplanes are equipped with the regular type of autosyn instruments and a more sensitive type. Both types operate on current supplied by a single transformer on bulkhead 4.0 adjacent to the radio operator's station. A two-position switch marked NORMAL and ALTERNATE is located on the instrument fuse panel. This switch permits transferring to an alternate transformer, also adjacent to the radio operator's station, in case the one being used fails. The fuse panel is located on the upper right side of the radio operator's station.

On airplanes not in group 2, anti-icing air, cylinder head, and constant-speed drive oil temperature readings are obtained from a battery-operated master temperature indicator located at the engineer's station. Airplanes in group 2 have six cylinder head temperature gages and five anti-icing air temperature gages, all located at the engineer's station.

Note

Because the constant-speed drive will not overheat with oil in accordance with Specification MIL-L-6387, an oil temperature indication is not provided on group 2 airplanes.

The jet engine instruments are located at the pilots' station. The instruments include an oil pressure gage, an engine tachometer, a fuel pressure gage, and a tail pipe temperature indicator for each engine, are located at the pilots' station. The jet engine fuel flow indicators are at the engineer's station. The instruments are fed from transformers on the jet pod power panels.

All gyroscopic instruments are electrically powered. Control switches are provided for turning off the directional gyro at the navigator's station and the gyro horizon and vertical and directional gyros at the pilots' station. Airplanes in group 2 have a pair of ganged switches on the navigator's instrument panel for turning off the N-1 high latitude compass.

TORQUEMETER INDICATORS.

Torquemeters are located on the engineer's main instrument panel. Dual indicating instruments (18, figure 1-17) are provided in all group 4 airplanes; group 5 airplanes are equipped with single indicating instruments (12, figure 1-16). These torquemeters provide a convenient and accurate bhp determination based on easily measured quantities. For further information refer to "Torquemeter," Section VII.

PITOT STATIC SYSTEM.

The airplane contains two pitot static systems. Each system consists of a pitot head, two static ports, pitot static instruments, and necessary drains. Pitot heads are located on each lower side of the forward position of the fuselage, and static pressure ports are located just forward of bomb bay No. 1 on each side of the airplane for each system. One system, with the pitot head on the right side of the airplane, contains the engineer's altimeter and airspeed indicator, and the pilot's rate-of-climb indicator, altimeter, and air-speed indicator. The other system, with pitot head on the left side of the airplane, contains the aircraft commander's rate-of-climb, altimeter, and air-speed indicators, the navigator's true air-speed indicator and altimeter, the radar observer's true air-speed indicator, and the altitude control unit.

Air-Speed Indicators.

Conventional air-speed indicators are provided for the aircraft commander and the engineer. True air-speed indicators are located at the navigator's and radar observer's stations. The pilot is provided with a maximum allowable air-speed indicator which has two pointers. The red pointer indicates the limit dive speed in mph or the limiting Mach number whichever is lower. These limiting air speeds are indicated by the red line in figure 6-3. The other pointer is a conventional air-speed indicator and a window in the instrument shows the Mach setting. The pointers should not be permitted to cross each other, as it would be an indication of operation in excess of safe speeds.

OUTSIDE AIR THERMOMETERS.

Three direct-reading type C13B outside air thermometers are mounted in the airplane. One is located on the flight deck above the engineer, one is located above the aircraft commander's station and the other is located on the left side of the observer's enclosure. These instruments give direct readings of the outside air temperature in degrees centigrade.

MASTER TEMPERATURE INDICATOR (Airplanes not in Group 2).

A flashlight battery-operated potentiometer-type temperature indicator (17, figure 1-17) is located on the engineer's main instrument panel in group 4 airplanes. In group 5 airplanes, this instrument (9, figure 1-18) is mounted on the engineer's auxiliary instrument panel. This instrument is used to obtain temperature readings from cylinder heads, anti-icing air ducts, and alternator constant-speed drive oil.

Master Temperature Indicator Selector Switch.

This switch is used to select the particular engine for which the cylinder head, anti-icing air, or constant-speed drive oil temperature is to be determined.

Master Temperature Indicator Switch.

This ON-OFF switch controls the power from the flashlight batteries.

Check Switch.

This two-position switch, marked CH and ON, places the galvanometer in the check circuit.

Compensating Rheostat Knob.

This rheostat marked COMP RHEO. adjusts compensating current when the check switch is in the CH position.

Balance Knob.

The balance knob is used to zero the galvanometer pointer when the check switch is in the ON position.

Slide Wire Rheostat Knob.

This rheostat, marked SL. W. RHEO., is turned clockwise when the galvanometer cannot be zeroed with the balance knob. Normally, it is adjusted to remain as far counterclockwise as possible while still maintaining full scale balancing with the balance knob.

Galvanometer Pointer.

When the check switch is placed in the CH position, the galvanometer pointer functions as a milliammeter and measures the amount of compensating current required to obtain an accurate temperature indication on the potentiometer. When the check switch is in the ON position, the galvanometer mechanism is in series with the thermocouple circuit and serves as a galvanometer.

Main Indicator Pointer.

This pointer acts as a direct reading temperature gage.

Battery Receptacles.

The master temperature indicator receives power from flashlight batteries installed in receptacles in the upper corners of the instrument. Two spare batteries are stored in a container in back of the indicator.

CYLINDER HEAD TEMPERATURE INDICATORS (Group 2 Airplanes).

Group 2 airplanes are equipped with six cylinder head temperature gages calibrated in degrees centigrade and located at the engineer's station. On some of these airplanes the gages indicate the temperature of cylinder D-5 of each engine. This indicating system operates on 28-volt direct current. On other airplanes the gages indicate the temperature of cylinders D1 and D6 of each engine. Selection of a cylinder for a temperature reading is made by means of a rotary selector switch marked D1 or D6. These indicating systems operate on 115-volt alternating current.

FLIGHT INSTRUMENT SWITCHES.

A pair of ON-OFF switches (14, figure 1-13) is located on the left side of the pilots' instrument panel and one three-position switch (14, figure 1-13) is on the right side. When the pair of ganged switches on the left side of the panel is placed in the ON position, the aircraft commander's attitude gyro is energized from a transformer which has an input of 208-volt, three-phase, a-c power. When the single switch on the right side of the panel is placed in the ON position the pilots' attitude and directional gyros are energized from a transformer which has an input of 208-volt, three-phase, a-c power. Placing the pair of switches or the single switch in the OFF position disconnects the related instrument from electrical power.

Note

Both turn and bank indicator needles operate automatically on 28-volt dc through the pilot's circuit breaker panel. Fundamental flight instruments (needle, ball, and air-speed) should therefore be available during emergency power operation as long as battery power exists.

The single switch on the right side of the panel connects the directional gyro and the pilot's gyro horizon with 208-volt ac. When this switch is ON the power comes through the right forward cabin power panel; when the EMERGENCY position is used, power comes through the engineer's auxiliary instrument panel. Both instruments can be disconnected by the OFF position when they are not in use.

ATTITUDE GYRO INDICATOR.

Some airplanes are equipped with A-1 (or A-2) attitude gyros. Other airplanes have J-8 indicators. These instruments (5, figure 1-13) operate on 115-volt, 3-phase, a-c power and they provide visual indications of the pitch and roll attitude of the airplane. The gyro of these instruments is enclosed in a sphere, a portion of which is visible through the opening in the face of the instrument. On the J-8 indicator, a flag marked OFF appears at the top of the instrument when the power is off. When the instrument is turned on, the OFF flag disappears. On the A-1 or the A-2 indicator,

Revised 18 May 1956

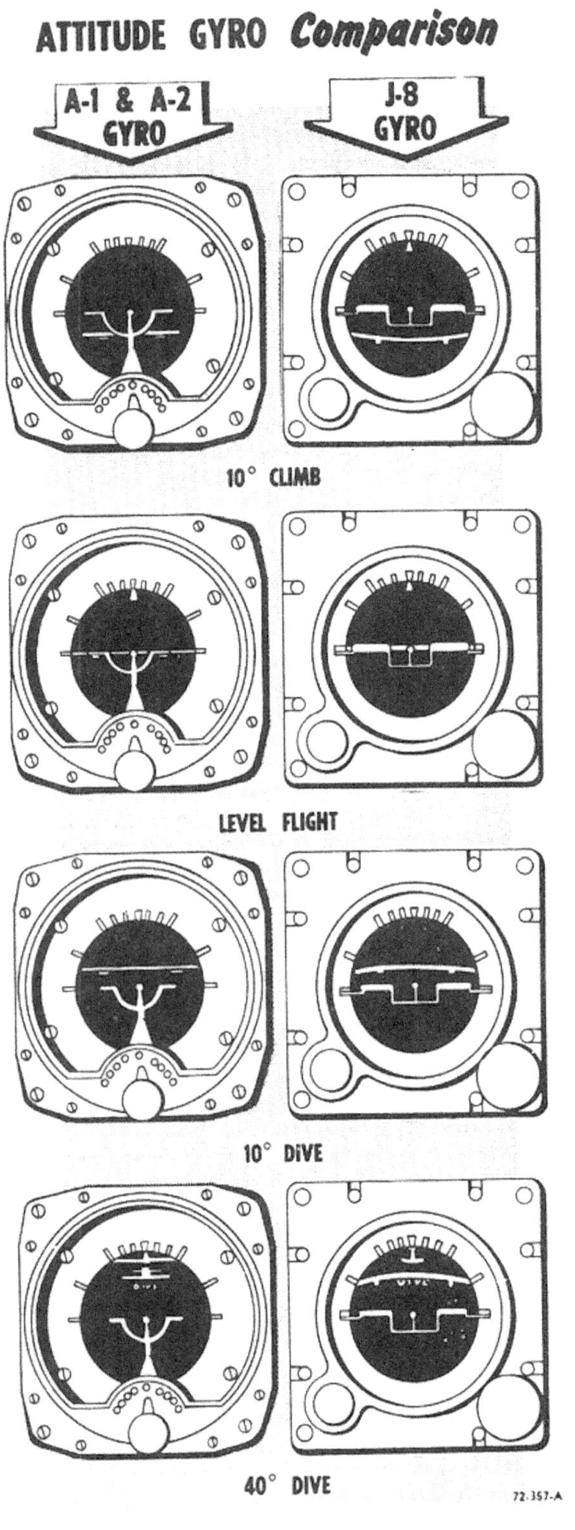

ATTITUDE GYRO *Comparison*

A-1 & A-2 GYRO | **J-8 GYRO**

10° CLIMB

LEVEL FLIGHT

10° DIVE

40° DIVE

Figure 1-46.

OFF flag disappears. On the A-1 or the A-2 indicator, a blinker light in a small opening of the sphere flashes about 66 times per minute to indicate power is being supplied to the unit and that the gyro is up to speed. The indications of these two types of instruments may be confusing since the presentation of pitch differs.

1. On the A-1 and A-2 instruments, a horizon bar presents a conventional pitch indication—the miniature airplane appearing above the horizon bar in a climb and below the horizon bar in a dive. However, a climb or dive exceeding 27 degrees of pitch, the horizon bar stops at the bottom or top of the instrument case and the sphere then becomes the reference.

2. On the J-8 indicator, the pitch attitude of the aircraft is indicated within a range of about 25 degrees climb or dive by displacement of the horizon bar with respect to the adjustable attitude bar. When the aircraft exceeds approximately 25 degrees in pitch, the horizon bar is held in the extreme position and the sphere becomes the reference. As the pitch angle increases, the word DIVE or CLIMB appears on the sphere at the top or the bottom (respectively) of the dial. When the DIVE or CLIMB indication intersects the attitude bar, approximately 60 degrees of pitch has been reached.

CAUTION

Allow sufficient time for the gyros to come up to speed and erect before relying on their indications. For A-1 or A-2 gyros, 8 to 13 minutes is required. For J-8 gyros about 15 minutes wait is necessary.

JET ENGINE INSTRUMENTS.

Tail Pipe Temperature Indicators.

Four tail pipe temperature indicators (39, figure 1-13), one for each jet engine, are located on the pilot's jet instrument panel.

Engine Tachometers.

Four engine tachometers (38, figure 1-13), one for each jet engine, are located on the pilot's jet instrument panel.

Revised 18 May 1956

ENGINE ANALYZER.

Ignition Analysis.

The engine analyzer is designed to detect, locate, and identify abnormalities in the operation of the reciprocating engines. It performs these functions by presenting patterns on the screen of a cathode ray tube, of voltages across the primary circuits of the magnetos. By use of the analyzer, the engineer can keep the reciprocating engines under constant surveillance during flight and thereby determine the severity of any engine malfunctions and make the required adjustments. He can also detect and analyze troubles peculiar to high altitude which could not be normally discovered during ground checks. Any decision on the feathering of an engine as a result of analyzer observations should include consideration of normal engine instrument indications. The engine analyzer checks the performance of the magneto coils, condensers, and breaker points; it checks magneto timing, breaker point synchronization, and spark advance; it checks the operation of the spark plugs and distributors; and it checks the condition of the spark plug leads and ignition harnesses. During normal operation, an ignition system establishes a characteristic pattern and any malfunction in the system will alter this pattern. Since malfunction patterns are also characteristic of the malfunction, they serve to identify the specific nature of the trouble.

The basic components of the engine analyzer consist of a synchronizing generator for each engine, a condition selector switch, a cycle switch, two relay boxes, a power supply-amplifier, and an indicator. The analyzer control panel is located adjacent to the engineer's main instrument panel and the indicator is flush mounted in his table. (See figure 1-15.)

Note

Resistors are provided in analyzer electrical circuits to automatically isolate the analyzer system from the engine, so that a malfunction in the analyzer will not interfere with engine operation.

Cylinder Vibration Analysis (Some Airplanes).

In addition to the ignition analysis provisions, some airplanes have provisions for analyzing cylinder vibration. This is accomplished by presenting patterns on the indicator scope of voltages generated in vibration pickups by cylinder vibration. By inspecting these vibration patterns, the engineer can analyze the performance of the valves, pistons, wrist pins, and many other engine parts; he can also detect the presence of detonation. In addition to the other analyzer components, airplanes in this group have two pickup selector switches mounted on the analyzer control panel, and a vibration pickup unit mounted on each engine cylinder.

Controls.

Condition Selector Switch. A condition selector switch located on the engine analyzer control panel is used to select the particular engine to be analyzed and the type of analysis; ignition (left, right, or both magnetos), or engine rpm synchronization. In some airplanes is it also used to select vibration analysis and the engine to be analyzed. The condition selector switch consists of a fixed index ring surrounding a switch dial. The index ring is divided into three general sectors which are engraved as follows:

1. The first sector is marked SYN, 2, 3, 4, 5, and 6, for selecting any of these engines to check their rpm synchronization with the rpm of engine No. 1.

2. The second sector, marked 1, 2, 3, 4, 5, and 6, is used for selecting an engine. The inner radius of this sector has designations L, B, and R opposite each engine number for selecting left, both, or right magnetos when making an ignition analysis. On some airplanes this sector is used for selecting a particular engine for either vibration or ignition analysis. For vibration analysis the switch dial may be indexed to either L, B, or R within the engine sector.

3. The third sector, marked PULL BUTTON FOR VIBRATION, is not used except for this notation which refers to the push-pull knob centrally located on the switch dial. This knob must be pushed IN to select ignition analysis. The pull out position is inoperative except in some airplanes, where the pulled out position selects vibration and the pushed in position selects ignition analysis.

Pickup Selector Switches (Some Airplanes). Airplanes in this group have two pickup selector switches. One for engines 1, 2, and 3, and the other for engines 4, 5, and 6, are used to select a specific cylinder for vibration analysis. These switches each have a fixed index ring engraved with cylinder designations which are arranged in the firing order of an engine. A switch dial with a single index line moves relative to these designations to select the cylinder to be checked. They are not involved in ignition analysis.

Cycle Selector Switch. The cycle selector switch located on the analyzer control panel is marked as follows:

1. A fixed index ring is inscribed with symbols corresponding to cylinder designations of an engine.

2. A dial, with an index line labeled IGN, is divided into four quadrants representing the four strokes of a reciprocating engine. Around the periphery of the dial at specific points are designations EC, IO, IC, and EO which are abbreviations for valve operations occurring during the engine cycle. For ignition analysis, only the IGN index line is used.

3. A push-pull knob, located in the center of the switch dial, selects a fast sweep when pushed IN, and a slow sweep when pulled OUT. To select a cylinder for ignition analysis, place the IGN index line opposite the cylinder designation. If the push-pull knob is OUT for a slow sweep, all four ignition patterns for one magneto will appear. The pattern of the selected cylinder will appear first in the series followed by the others in the order of firing of that magneto. If the knob is pushed IN for a fast sweep, only the significant oscillatory portion of a single ignition pattern will appear. This pattern is expanded at the expense of eliminating some of the trailing portion of the pattern including the section at which the breaker points close.

On some airplanes, the cycle switch is used in conjunction with the other switches to set up the analyzer for vibration analysis. When performing vibration analysis, the cycle switch is used to select the specific point of the engine cycle at which the horizontal time sweep across the scope is to be initiated. Positioning one of the designations, such as EC (exhaust valve closing), of the dial adjacent to a cylinder number on the fixed ring will cause that engine event to appear first in a slow sweep pattern. Exact alignment of the dial with a cylinder designation is not necessary; instead, the detent nearest to alignment which does not split a given pattern should be used. A slow sweep pattern covers all vibration-producing events in the selected cylinder for 720 degrees of crankshaft rotation. A fast sweep shows a horizontally expanded pattern of vibration events for a selected 80 degrees of crankshaft rotation.

Note

The cylinder selected on the cycle switch must correspond to the cylinder selected on the pickup selector or an inaccurate pattern will be shown.

Engine Analyzer Power Switch. This ON-OFF switch-type circuit breaker located on the analyzer control panel is used to turn the system ON and OFF.

Indicators.

Engine Analyzer Indicator. The engine analyzer indicator consists of a three-inch cathode ray tube mounted in the engineer's table.

EMERGENCY EQUIPMENT.

RECIPROCATING ENGINE FIRE EXTINGUISHER SYSTEM.

An electrically operated, two-shot fire extinguisher system (figure 1-47) is provided for combating reciprocating engine fires. The system is controlled by 28-volt direct current and uses either methyl bromide or bromochloromethane as the extinguishing agent. The extinguishing agent is stored in four metal containers, two in each main gear wheel well; and each pair or bank of containers constitutes a discharge.

All of the controls for the system are located at the engineer's station. The bank of containers to be discharged is determined by the position of a discharge selector switch. Six engine selector switches are provided to discharge the containers and direct the discharge to the proper engine. Since the supply lines extend to engines No. 1 and 6, directional valves are provided for diverting the discharge to engines No. 2, 3, 4, and 5. Normally, the supply line to the left wing is open; therefore, when engine No. 4, 5, or 6 is selected, a directional valve opens the line to the right wing and closes the line to the left wing.

Note

The four engine directional valves and the wing directional valve are spring-loaded and are first positioned electrically then held in that position by the force of the discharge. For this reason, an engine selector switch should be held for approximately 5 seconds to assure pressure at the valves.

A relay is provided to delay the discharge of extinguishing agent for approximately one-tenth of a second to give the directional valves sufficient time to complete their operation.

Note

The jet engines are not equipped with an extinguisher system.

Discharge Selector Switch.

The discharge selector switch (37, figure 1-20) marked DISCHARGE 1 and DISCHARGE 2 permits the selection of either of the two banks of extinguishing agent containers for discharge.

Reciprocating Engine Selector Switches.

Six reciprocating engine selector switches (36, figure 1-20) are located on the engineer's control panel. The switches are used to discharge the selected containers and, at the same time, to position the directional valves to direct the flow of extinguishing agent to the proper reciprocating engine.

RECIPROCATING ENGINE FIRE EXTINGUISHER
System

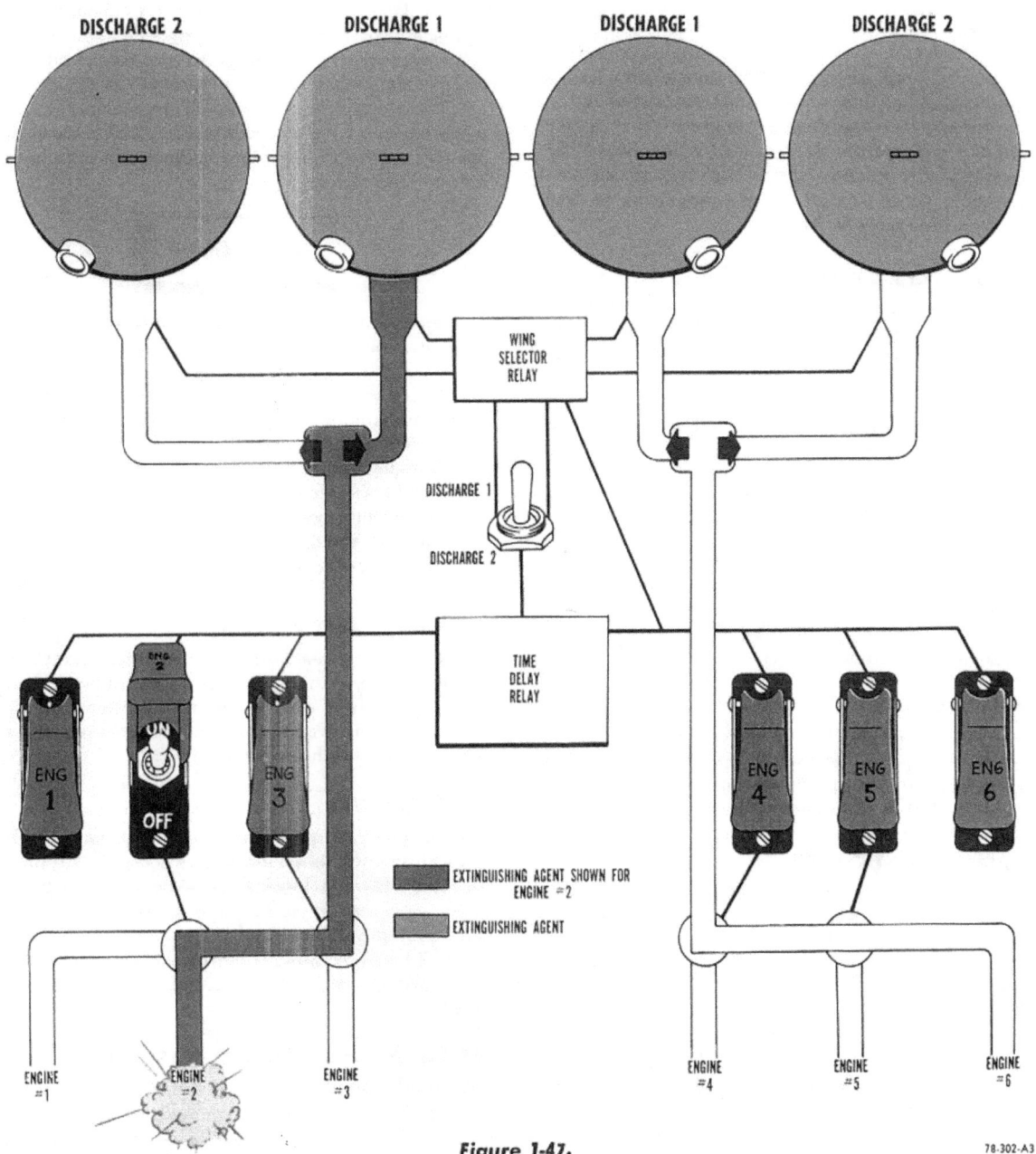

Figure 1-47.

that the system is not in perfect condition, but not necessarily that it is completely inoperative.

Airplanes with a cable-type detector system have six warning lamps, one for each nacelle, located on the engineer's main instrument panel. A push-to-test switch, provided adjacent to the lamps, is used to check the continuity of all six detector circuits simultaneously.

JET ENGINE FIRE DETECTOR SYSTEM.

The fire detector system on each jet engine consists of ten cartridge-type detector units strategically located in potential fire zones. The units are calibrated to close electrical contacts when subjected to a predetermined temperature. In event of a fire, when this temperature is reached, the 28-volt d-c circuit to a warning lamp on the jet control panel will be completed and the lamp will light.

Jet Engine Fire Detection Switches.

Two two-position switches (27, figure 1-23), one for each pair of jet engines, are located on the pilots' overhead control panel. When the switches are in the ON position, the fire detector circuits to the jet nacelles are set up. Placing the switches in the TEST position checks the continuity of the circuits from the nacelles to the warning lamps.

Jet Engine Fire Warning Lamps.

Four fire warning lamps (26, figure 1-23), one for each jet engine, are located on the pilots' overhead jet control panel. The lamps give a visual indication of jet engine fires. On group 2 airplanes an additional set of jet engine fire warning lamps (41, figure 1-13) is located on the pilots' instrument panel.

ALARM BELLS.

An alarm bell is located in each crew compartment. The bells are controlled by an ON-OFF switch (19, figure 1-13) on the pilots' instrument panel and use 28-volt d-c power from the airplane's battery.

PARACHUTE STATIC LINES.

Parachute static lines are located forward of the forward hatch in the forward cabin and forward of the entrance hatch in the aft cabin.

EMERGENCY ESCAPE ROPES (GROUP 2 AIRPLANES).

Emergency escape ropes are located in the crew compartments of group 2 airplanes to provide a means for emergency escape of personnel to the ground after crash landings. A rope is located at the left forward escape hatch in the forward compartment and at the right and left lower sighting stations and near the entrance hatch in the aft cabin.

SURVIVAL SUITS.

Hooks are provided at each crew station for the stowage of survival suits.

LIFE RAFTS.

No emergency sea equipment is provided. When the mission requires such equipment, life rafts will be issued to the crew.

HAND FIRE EXTINGUISHERS.

The airplane is equipped with four hand fire extinguishers. In the forward cabin one type 4-TB extinguisher is left of the engineer's station and one type A-20 is right of the ECM equipment. In the aft cabin a 4-TB extinguisher is mounted on the left side, and a type A-20 on the right side. The A-20 extinguishers are charged with bromochloromethane and can be used on any type of fire.

WARNING

Repeated or prolonged exposure to high concentrations of bromochloromethane (CB) or decomposition products should be avoided. CB is a narcotic agent of moderate intensity but of prolonged duration. It is considered to be less toxic than carbon tetrachloride, methyl bromide, or the usual products of combustion. It is safer to use than previous fire extinguishing agents; however, normal precautions should be taken including the use of oxygen when available.

HAND AXES AND KNIVES.

Provisions have been made for installing a panel containing a hand axe and a knife in each crew compartment. One panel can be installed above the food locker in the forward cabin and one above the catwalk entrance hatch in the aft cabin.

FIRST AID KITS.

The airplane is equipped with seven first aid kits. In the forward cabin the kits are located as follows: one near the food locker, one above the navigator's table, one near the left escape hatch, one near the ECM equipment racks, and one under the engineer's table. The aft cabin contains two kits, one under the sighting platform and one on the forward bulkhead.

BATTLE SPLINT AND BLOOD PLASMA KITS.

In the forward cabin a battle splint kit and a blood plasma kit are located near the left escape hatch. In the aft cabin a similar set of kits is on the aft end of the bunks in airplanes not in group 2 and under the sighting platform in airplanes in group 2.

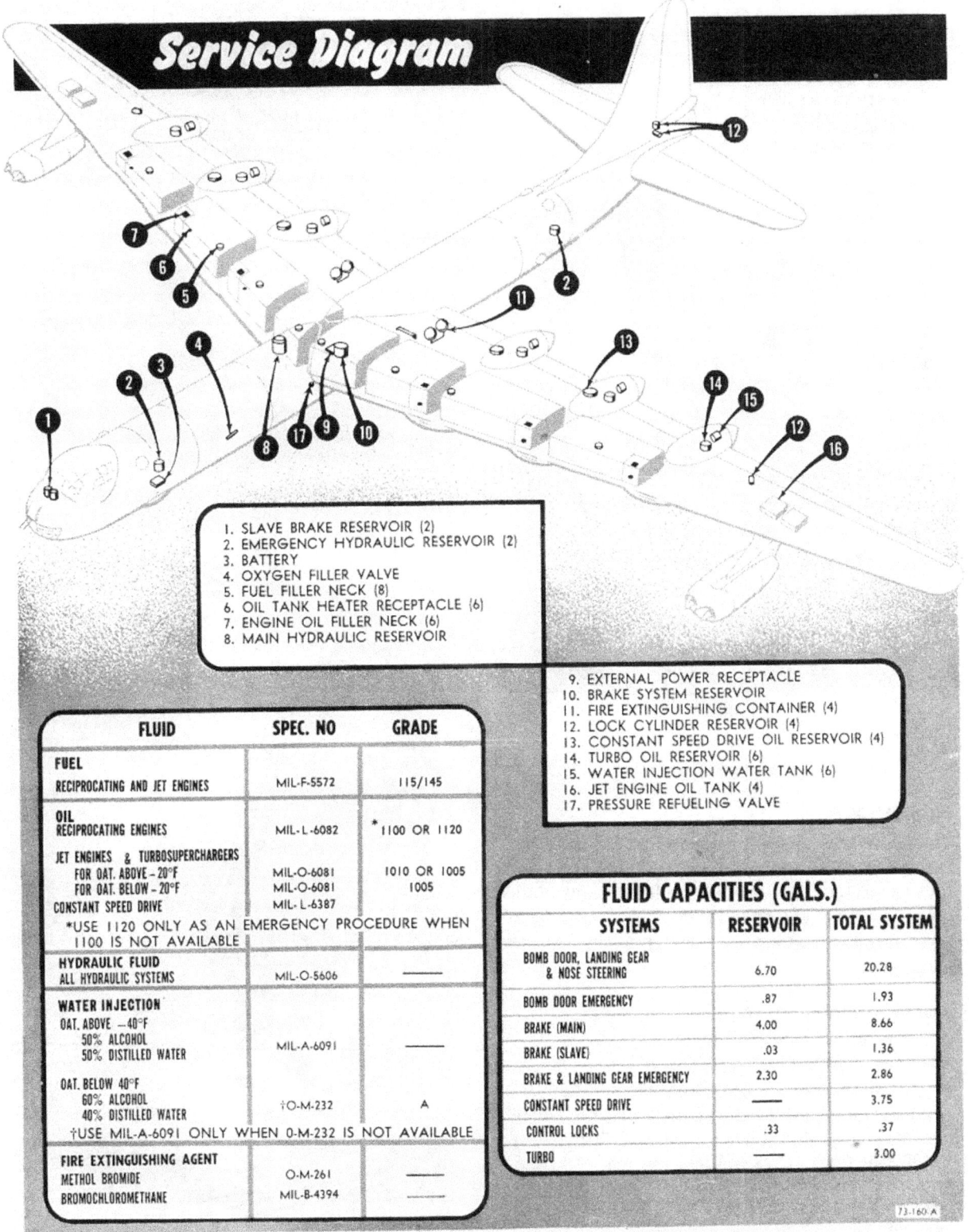

Figure 1-48.

Section I
Description

T.O. 1B-36D(II)-1

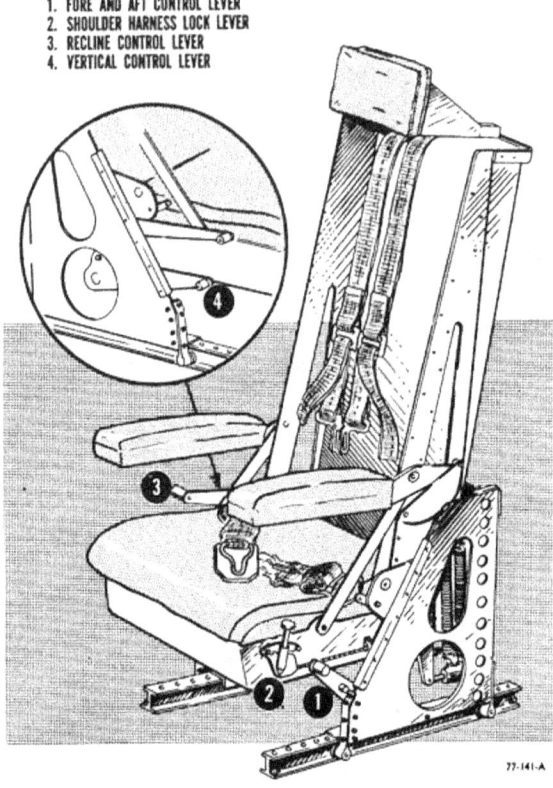

Figure 1-49.

3 g's is encountered. When the reel is locked in this manner, it will remain locked until the control handle is moved to the LOCKED and then returned to the UNLOCKED position. When the control is in the LOCKED position, the reel harness cable is manually locked so that the pilot is prevented from bending forward. The LOCKED position is used only when a crash landing is anticipated. This position provides an added safety precaution over and above that of the automatic safety lock.

ENGINEER'S SEAT.

A swivel-type seat mounted on a fixed conical base is provided for the engineer. The seat can be rotated approximately 60 degrees to the right and 110 degrees to the left. Adjustments can also be made fore and aft and vertically. Fore-and-aft movement is controlled by a knob located on the right side of the seat support. A pedal, located on the forward side of the support, controls vertical movement. The seat is equipped with a folding arm rest and a safety belt.

On group 2 airplanes a swivel-type seat (figure 1-50), which has fore-and-aft and vertical adjustments, is pro-

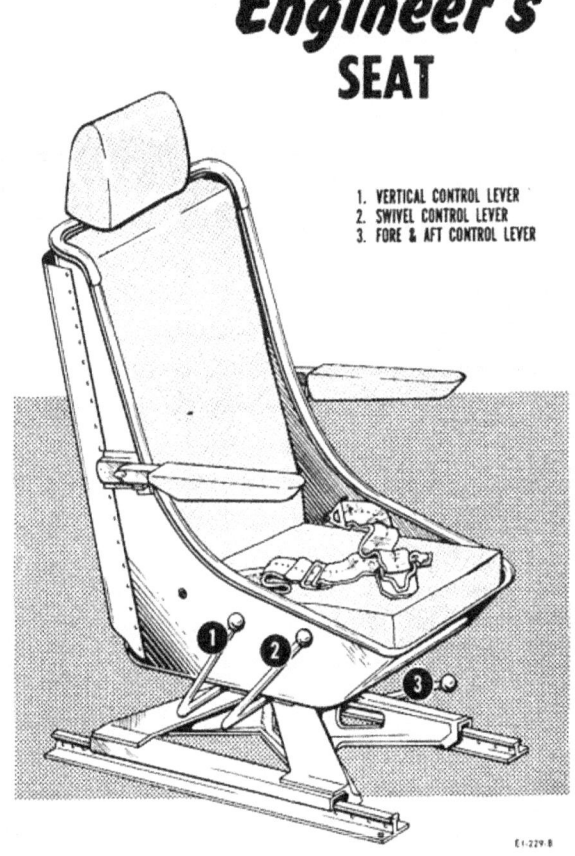

Figure 1-50.

PILOTS' SEATS.

The pilots' seats (figure 1-49) have fore-and-aft, vertical, and angular adjustments and arm rests which retract to permit easy movement into and out of the seats. They are also equipped with inertia reel lock-type shoulder harnesses for the protection of the occupants.

Shoulder Harness Control.

A two-position LOCKED-UNLOCKED shoulder harness inertia real lock control is located on the left side of the pilots' seats. A latch is provided for positively retaining the control handle at either position of the quadrant. By pressing down on the top of the control handle, the latch is released and the control handle may then be moved freely from one position to another. When the control is in the UNLOCKED position, the reel harness cable will extend to allow the pilot to lean forward; however, the reel harness cable will automatically lock when an impact force of 2 to

vided for the engineer. Vertical and swivel movements are controlled by two levers on the right side of the seat support. A lever on the left side of the support controls fore-and-aft movement. The seat is equipped with folding arm rests and a safety belt. No shoulder harness is provided.

AUXILIARY EQUIPMENT.

Information concerning the following equipment and systems is given in Section IV.

1. Heating and Anti-Icing System.
2. Pressurization System.
3. Cabin Ventilating Equipment.
4. Auxiliary Cabin Heaters.
5. Jet Pod Heating and Anti-Icing System.
6. Pitot Tube Heaters.
7. Oil System Heaters.
8. Communication and Associated Electronic Equipment.
9. Lighting System.
10. Oxygen System.
11. Autopilot.
12. Navigation Equipment.
13. Gunnery Equipment.
14. Bombing Equipment.
15. Photographic Equipment.
16. Miscellaneous Equipment.

Section I
Description

T.O. 1B-36D(II)-1

Section II
NORMAL PROCEDURES

INTRODUCTION.

In general, the purpose of this section is to establish a proper sequence of events and to set forth those procedures and techniques which must be performed in a prescribed manner during a complete flight under normal conditions. The scope has been expanded to include as much training information and normal operating procedures as practical. The sequence begins when the flight is conceived and does not end until the crew has completed their postflight duties. This provides a comprehensive picture of the requirements of a typical mission.

The arrangement of the data presented in this section has been devised by experienced personnel. It reflects the best information obtainable from all available sources including the using tactical organizations. It is only natural to expect that, from time to time, new and revised procedures will be necessary due to modifications of the systems and the development of new techniques. Revisions will be published from time to time to cover these changes.

To prevent undue complication of this section it will only include normal operating procedures applicable to the aircraft commander, pilot, copilot, first engineer, and second engineer. Procedures for other crew members will be dealt with only so far as co-ordination requires to properly execute a particular function. For the specific duties of other crew members see Section VIII, "Crew Duties." For emergency procedures refer to Section III, "Emergency Procedures." Other sections in this publication will deal with various aspects of the aircraft and equipment from the standpoint of basic operation and peculiarities characteristic of the equipment under various conditions. If information is desired on any particular phase of operation not covered in this section, reference to the other sections should provide the answer. If any question should arise that is not covered in this handbook, check with the standardization board. They will help you evaluate the situation and submit recommended changes to this publication through the proper channels.

The phases of operation covered in this section will follow a normal sequence as though you were actually planning and flying the mission. The sequence recommended is based upon the experience of tactical organizations in actual operation and constitutes the best compromise to reduce mission failures, crew fatigue, and maintenance to an acceptable minimum. Certain local considerations may require that the exact sequence be varied to meet the situation. However, the amplified procedures and techniques described herein are mandatory to provide a complete check and must be performed in the prescribed manner.

A unique innovation in normal operating procedures of the complex B-36 might be called a dual preflight run-up system. The first preflight run-up is called a "Preflight Operational Equipment Check" and is designed to check equipment aboard the aircraft from the safety standpoint as well as reasonably assuring its successful operation during any phase of the mission. This is a *complete* check of all operational equipment and normally is accomplished as early as possible within a 24-hour period; however, it may be accomplished up to and including 72 hours prior to estimated take-off time. The second preflight run-up occurs just prior to the actual take-off and is known as a minimum safety check. Experienced B-36 units have found that this system, coupled with good maintenance, has reduced

Section II
Normal Procedures

their mission failure rate from very excessive to almost negligible. It has also reduced the ground time required on the reciprocating engines, although an unqualified inspection of the dual run-up system would not make this fact apparent. The times shown in figure 2-1 represent the amount of time that is generally required to perform each phase or event.

GENERAL MISSION PLANNING.

The mission may be conceived at any level of command. Each lower level of command must do a certain amount of planning upon receipt of the operations order. However, the final details of any mission plan and the execution of the individual mission is always up to the individual crew. The exact requirements for mission planning are set forth in Air Force, major command, and local directives with which the crew should be familiar. Receipt of an operations order dictates a multitude of tasks that must be performed by the combat crew as a team with time being a limiting factor. The crew should be assembled by the aircraft commander and notified of the impending flight. At this time the crew learns which aircraft is to be flown and approximately what is to be accomplished on the mission. Since time is a limiting factor and crew fatigue must be held to a minimum prior to a lengthy mission, a logical sequence of events must take place to make sure that everything required is accomplished with absolute efficiency. The responsibility for insuring efficient team work is the aircraft commander's. Through co-ordination with the engineering section, it should be determined when the assigned aircraft will be ready

Typical TIME SCHEDULE

PHASE OR EVENT	AVERAGE ELAPSED TIME
GENERAL MISSION PLANNING	2:00
PREFLIGHT OPERATIONAL EQUIPMENT CHECK	5:00
DETAILED MISSION PLANNING	3:00
FORMAL BRIEFING	0:45
CREW INSPECTION	0:25
VISUAL PREFLIGHT INSPECTION	1:00
FINAL CREW BRIEFING	0:10
BOARDING AIRCRAFT	0:05
STATION TIME	0:10
STARTING RECIPROCATING ENGINES	0:05
COMPLETE ENGINE RUN-UP	0:25
TAXI	0:10
STARTING JET ENGINES	0:00 (INCLUDED IN OVER-ALL TIME)
CLEARANCE, LINE-UP, TAKE-OFF CONFIGURATION, SET POWER	0:05

Figure 2-1.

for preflight. If there is to be some delay, notify the crew so that they may continue with the next phase, "Detailed Mission Planning" while standing by for the "Preflight Operational Equipment Check." As soon as each component system is declared ready, see that those crew members concerned proceed directly to the aircraft to perform their portion of the "Preflight Operational Equipment Check." This will allow maintenance maximum time to correct any discrepancies noted during this check and assures the crew that their aircraft is prepared to perform the anticipated mission before they proceed with other time-consuming requirements.

PREFLIGHT OPERATIONAL EQUIPMENT CHECK.

This preflight check is designed to be a thorough, comprehensive, and complete check of each crew member's operational equipment. This check constitutes the first of two preflight run-ups for all crew members. Many items not directly affecting safety of flight, but promoting successful accomplishment of the mission, need not be rechecked during the second preflight run-up just prior to take-off, unless a recheck is dictated by inclement weather conditions, additional repairs after the preflight operational check, or an unusual delay before take-off. This operational equipment check is amplified and aligned in such a manner that all crew members except the engineers can use their standard and preflight check lists to accomplish this complete check. A "Standard Check List" for the engineer is provided to insure that a complete, comprehensive preflight is accomplished as required for an "Operational Preflight Equipment Check." It can also be used to replace both run-ups and still provide a complete check in event only one run-up is desired due to the nature of the mission such as aircraft ferry flights, maintenance test flights, or due to the time factor. The pilots will accomplish a visual inspection in accordance with the visual preflight as outlined in this section.

The aircraft commander should co-ordinate his mission planning with all sections concerned and order the necessary equipment for accomplishment of the mission. It is impractical for other crew members to safely accomplish their respective preflights during the reciprocating engine preflight. This will necessitate the aircraft commander's scheduling crew members to accomplish their individual preflights as soon as their respective component systems are declared in commission. The following time allocations are recommended; however, they may be modified as required by experience and local conditions:

1. Observers, photographers, and radio ECM operators (simultaneously) 2 hrs.

2. Pilots and engineers (simultaneously) 2 hrs.

3. Gunners (actual gunnery) 3 days.
(camera gunnery) 2 hrs.

Each crew member will accomplish his respective preflight as outlined in his handbook and/or other handbooks governing the operation of this aircraft. A preflight check list will be utilized at all times to insure the accomplishment of every item.

On completion of his preflight the crew member should immediately notify his aircraft commander and record any discrepancy in the Form 781 (Form 1). Auxiliary equipment to be checked includes all operational systems that are to be utilized during the forthcoming mission and items pertaining to safety of flight. *Wing flaps, hydraulic system, gunnery system, jet engine starter operation, and any other equipment demanding high electrical loads will not be operated during the radar preflight operational equipment check.*

In addition to an operational check of normal and special equipment, this preflight includes a complete reciprocating engine run-up. The jet engines should only be run to make sure that known deficiencies have been cleared since the preceding flight. All newly installed, jet equipment must be thoroughly checked. Since this preflight is an operational check of all equipment, it should be accomplished as soon as possible. The necessity of the aircraft commander and pilots to accomplish the "Visual Preflight Inspection" twice is to insure that the aircraft is ready for engine run-up (cowling, stands, etc.) and also to check all systems for operation. There will of necessity be some duplication of effort with this system; however, those preflight procedures which are duplicated are necessary to insure the best interests of flying safety.

Before deciding where the aircraft is to be parked for run-up, check the wind direction and velocity. If practical, the aircraft should be headed directly into the wind for several reasons. Considerable difficulty may be experienced in moving the rudder in strong cross winds. Tail winds can cause excessive or erratic tail pipe temperatures during jet engine starting and operation. A direct head wind provides maximum ground cooling and even propeller loading during engine run-up and single magneto check. Wind velocity affects the idle speed setting of the reciprocating engines. Other considerations also affect the choice of a proper parking spot for run-ups. Park the aircraft on a clean, hard surface to prevent pick-up and throwing of gravel and debris by the jet intakes or propeller blast. Avoid tailing the aircraft toward other aircraft, buildings, close taxi strips, or runways to prevent damage from propeller or jet engine blast and to allow the run-up to progress as rapidly as possible without interruptions.

Section II
Normal Procedures

T.O. 1B-36D(II)-1

If possible, maintain a minimum of 250 feet frontal clearance during the run-up.

Note

Before boarding the aircraft, the engineers will check the following:

1. Contact the crew chief and determine what maintenance has been performed, and that the bomb bay and wing crawlway inspection has been completed (fuse panels, fuel leaks, etc.) as outlined in present maintenance regulations.

2. Proper status of the aircraft as reflected in Form 781 (Form 1).

3. Bomb bay doors open and safety locks installed. If the bomb bay doors are closed, they will be pumped open and safety locks will be installed prior to starting the auxiliary power unit.

4. Make certain that the ground observer who will operate the ground interphone understands proper ground reporting procedures on engine starts, control checks, propeller checks, etc.

5. Insure that the auxiliary power unit is as far upwind from the aircraft as the electrical cord will permit.

CAUTION

Before the APU is plugged in, make certain that the external power switch is OFF.

The aircraft commander, pilot, and engineers proceed to their stations with their headsets and microphones and the pilot will read the check list to the aircraft commander, who will complete the checks. In the same manner, the second engineer will assist the first engineer. Co-ordination items between the aircraft commander and the first engineer are indicated on the check list and must be checked as indicated in the amplified check list.

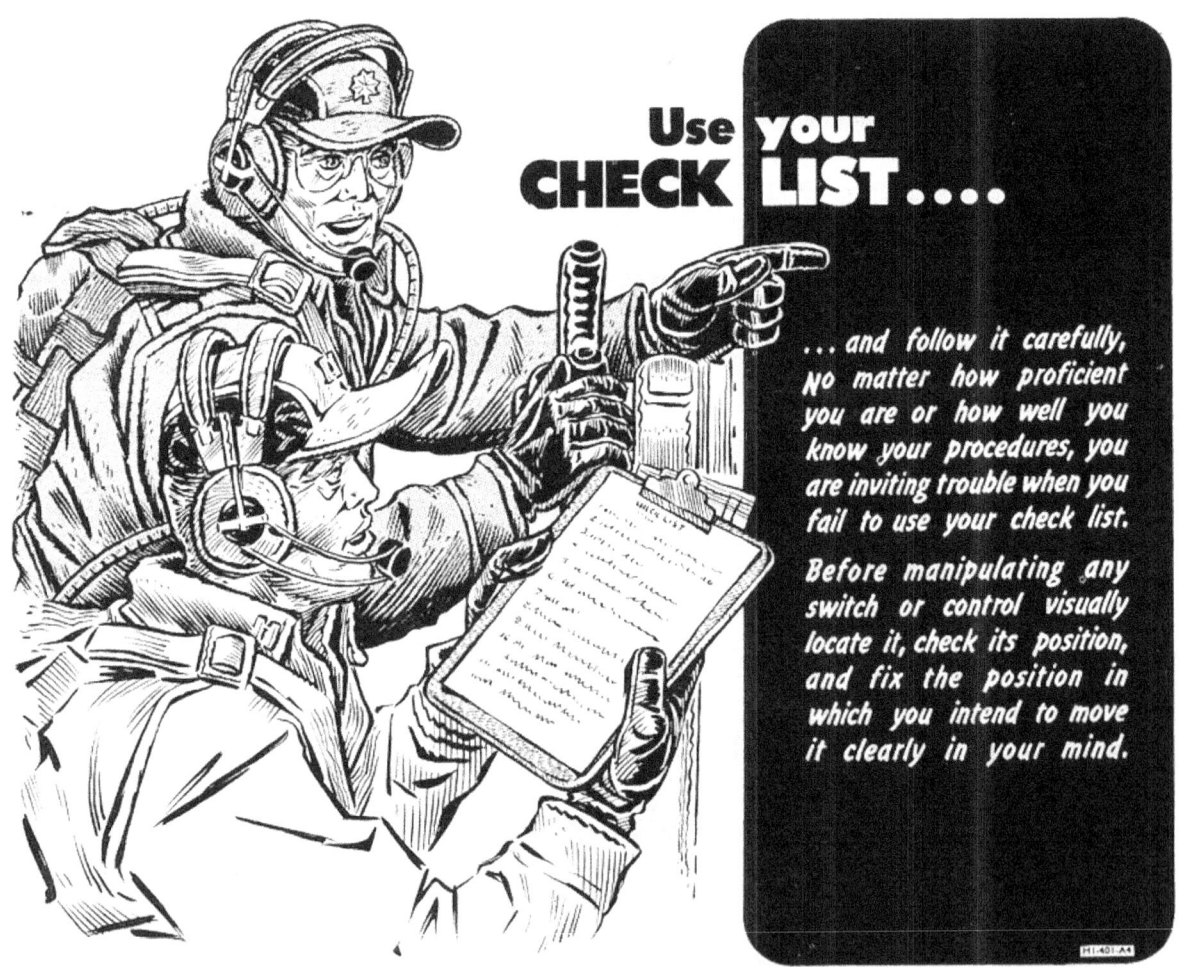

Use your CHECK LIST....

...and follow it carefully, no matter how proficient you are or how well you know your procedures, you are inviting trouble when you fail to use your check list.

Before manipulating any switch or control visually locate it, check its position, and fix the position in which you intend to move it clearly in your mind.

B-36D-II PILOTS' STANDARD CHECK LIST

BEFORE STARTING ENGINES

1. Landing Gear Control Switch .... EXTEND
2. Visual Inspection—Forms 781 (Form I), F, and Loading List .... COMPLETED
3. Pitot Covers and Ground Locks .... REMOVED
4. Nose Wheel Scissors .... CONNECTED
5. Personal Equipment .... CHECK IN PLACE
6. Seats and Pedals .... ADJUSTED
7. All Circuit Breakers (Except Bomb Bay Door and Bomb Salvo) .... IN
8. All Indicator Lamps .... PUSH TO TEST
*9. Tower Call .... COMPLETED
10. Propeller Reverse Selector Switches .... SAFE, LIGHTS OUT
11. Flight Instrument Switches .... ON
*12. Nose Steering and Brakes .... CHECKED AND SET
13. Bomb Bay Door Locks .... REMOVED
14. Fire Equipment .... IN PLACE
15. Emergency Ignition Switch .... IN
*16. Receive Engineer's Report and Notify Engineer, "BRAKES SET, FIRE GUARD STANDING BY, START ENGINES."

STARTING RECIPROCATING ENGINES

A/C Observes Engineer's Reciprocating Engine Starts and Handles Throttles On Idling Engines. Maintain Approximately 1100 RPM.

DURING ENGINE WARM-UP

1. Bomb Bay Door and Salvo Circuit Breakers .... IN
2. Bomb Bay and Camera Doors .... CLOSED
3. Flaps and Indicators .... CHECKED
*4. Propeller Reverse Check, Idle Rpm .... COMPLETED (IF REQUIRED)

ENGINE RUN-UP

1. Parking Brake Control .... ON
2. Propeller Reverse Selector Switches .... SAFE (LIGHTS OUT)
3. Nose Wheel Steering Switch .... OFF
4. Pilot's Manifold Pressure Gage .... CHECKED
5. Master Tachometer .... CHECKED
*6. Propeller Reverse Check .... COMPLETED

TAXIING

1. Nose Wheel Steering Switch .... ON
2. Engineer's Taxi Configuration .... CHECKED
3. Receive Ground Man's Report "NOSE WHEEL DOORS FULL OPEN, ALL STATIC WIRES REMOVED, WHEEL CHOCKS REMOVED, EXTERNAL POWER UNIT CLEARED, DISCONNECTING."
4. Interphone, Alarm Bell Check .... COMPLETED
5. Call Control Tower .... TAXI INSTRUCTIONS
6. Inboard Propeller Reverse Selector Switch .... READY
7. Taxiing .... ANNOUNCE "TAXIING" OVER INTERPHONE

STARTING JET ENGINES (GROUND)

1. Notify Engineer .... SET UP JET START CONFIGURATION
2. All Circuit Breakers .... IN
3. Fire Detection Test Switches .... TEST AND RELEASE
4. Throttle Selector Switches .... LEVER
5. Throttles .... CLOSED
6. Pod Preheat Switch .... OFF
7. Nose De-Ice Switch .... OFF
8. Oil Heater Switch .... AS REQUIRED
9. Oil Shutoff Valve Switches .... OPEN
10. Danger Area Clear and Fire Equipment Standing By
11. Jet Air Plug Switches .... OPEN
12. Jet Manifold Valve Switches (L and R) .... OPEN
13. Booster Pump Switches (L and R) .... ON
14. All Ignition Start Switches .... NORMAL
15. (Deleted)
16. J-1 Engine Fuel Valve .... OPEN
17. J-1 Fuel and Oil Pressure Gages .... NOTE READING
18. Notify Aft Gunner .... STARTING J-1
19. J-1 Starter Switch .... HOLD ON
20. J-1 Throttle .... OPEN AT 6 PER CENT RPM TO OBTAIN 25 to 30 PSI FUEL PRESSURE

CAUTION

WHEN IGNITION OCCURS ADJUST THROTTLE TO MAINTAIN A CONSTANT TAIL PIPE TEMPERATURE. DO NOT EXCEED 690°C TPT.

21. J-1 Oil Pressure .... REPORT INDICATION ON INTERPHONE
22. J-1 Starter Switch .... RELEASE AT 20 PER CENT RPM
23. J-1 Throttle .... ADJUST TO MAINTAIN IDLE RPM
24. J-2, J-3, J-4—Repeat Steps 15 thru 23
25. All Ignition Start Switches .... OFF

BEFORE TAKE-OFF

1. Landing Lights .... AS REQUIRED
2. Flaps and Indicator .... SET AT 20° AND CHECKED
3. Trim Tabs .... SET
4. Abort Procedure and Take-Off and Landing Data .... BRIEFED AND REVIEWED
5. Safety Belts and Safety Harnesses .... FASTENED
6. Salvo Safety Switches .... AS REQUIRED
*7. Engineer's Take-Off Configuration—ENGINEER READS— Take-Off Configuration Completed; Standing by for Propeller Reverse Safety Check and Take-Off Power."
8. Tower Clearance .... RECEIVED

NOTE

THE FOLLOWING STEPS MUST BE ACCOMPLISHED AFTER THE AIRCRAFT IS ALIGNED WITH THE RUNWAY.

9. Parking Brake Control .... ON
10. Propeller Reverse Selector Switches .... SAFE, LIGHTS OUT
11. Pitot Heat .... AS REQUIRED
12. All Compartments .... ENTRANCE LADDERS, WINDOWS, AND HATCHES, READY FOR TAKE-OFF.
13. Gyros .... SET AND UNCAGED
14. Nose Wheel Steering Switch .... ON
15. Surface Controls .... UNLOCKED AND CHECKED
16. Read Pilots' Take-Off Configuration: "Controls—UNLOCKED; Flight Instrument Switches—ON; Flaps—20 DEGREES; Trim Tabs ____DEGREES (UP OR DOWN); Autopilot—OFF; Nose Steering—ON; Propellers—SAFE, LIGHTS OUT."

TAKE-OFF

1. Parking Brakes .... RELEASED
*2. Set Take-Off Power .... JETS TAKE-OFF RPM

* PILOT-ENGINEER CO-ORDINATION ITEM

Figure 2-2. (Sheet 1)

Revised 18 May 1956

Section II
Normal Procedures

T.O. 1B-36D(II)-1

B-36D-II PILOTS' STANDARD CHECK LIST (Cont'd)

AFTER TAKE-OFF

1. Foot Brakes .... APPLY TO STOP WHEEL ROTATION
2. Nose Steering Switch .... OFF
*3. Landing Gear Control Switch .... RETRACT
4. Landing Lights .... RETRACTED & OFF
5. Flap Switch .... UP

INITIAL CLIMB

*1. Power Condition No. 2 .... JETS 96 PER CENT RPM
*2. Landing Gear and Brake Pump Switch   OFF WHEN PRESSURE
                                                             IS RELIEVED
3. Hold Best Climb IAS .... REFERENCE TAKE-OFF AND
                                                      LANDING DATA CARD
4. Bomb Bay Area .... CHECKED

STOPPING JET ENGINES (GROUND-AIR)

1. Throttles .... IDLE THREE MINUTES, THEN CLOSE
2. Booster Pumps .... OFF
2A. (Air) Jet Air Plugs .... CLOSED AT OR BELOW
                                                 100°C TPT AND 30 PER CENT RPM
3. Engine Fuel Valves .... CLOSED BELOW 10 PER CENT RPM
4. Nose De-Ice .... AS REQUIRED
5. Pod Preheat .... AS REQUIRED
6. Oil Heater Switch .... AS REQUIRED
7. Oil Shutoff Valves .... ALWAYS OPEN DURING FLIGHT
8. Throttle Circuit Breakers .... OUT
9. (Ground) Jet Air Plugs .... CLOSE AFTER 30 MINUTES
9A. (Air) Jet Air Plugs .... ADJUST TO WINDMILL 5 TO 7
                                                            PER CENT RPM

STARTING JET ENGINES (AIR)

*1. Notify Engineer .... SET UP JET START CONFIGURATION
2. All Circuit Breakers .... IN
3. Fire Detection Test Switches .... TEST AND RELEASE
4. Throttle Selector Switches .... LEVER
5. Throttles .... CLOSED
6. Pod Preheat Switch .... AS REQUIRED
7. Nose De-Ice Switch .... AS REQUIRED
8. Oil Heater Switch .... AS REQUIRED
9. Oil Shutoff Valve Switches .... OPEN
10. Jet Air Plug Switches .... OPEN
11. Jet Manifold Valve Switches (L and R) .... OPEN
12. Booster Pump Switches (L and R) .... ON
13. (Deleted)
14. J-1 Engine Fuel Valve .... OPEN
15. J-1 Fuel and Oil Pressure Gages .... NOTE READING
16. Notify Aft Gunner .... STARTING J-1
17. J-1 Ignition Start Switch .... HOLD IN ALT
18. J-1 Throttle   OPEN TO OBTAIN 16 to 20 PSI FUEL PRES-
                          SURE (10 to 15 PSI ABOVE 40,000 FT)
19. J-1 Oil Pressure .... REPORT INDICATION ON
                                                             INTERPHONE
20. J-1 Ignition Switch .... RELEASE AT IDLE
21. J-1 Throttle .... ADJUST TO MAINTAIN IDLE RPM
22. J-4, J-3, J-2 .... REPEAT STEPS 13 thru 21

BEFORE LANDING

1. Notify Crew .... "PREPARE TO LAND."
2. Bomb Bay Area .... CHECKED
3. Autopilot .... OFF
4. Jet Air Plugs .... OPEN
5. Jet Engines .... AS REQUIRED
*6. Engineer's Landing Configuration .... ENGINEER READS—
   "Before Landing Check List Complete, Standing by for RPM,
   Landing Gear and Brake Check, Gross Weight _____."

7. Stalling Speeds and Take-Off and Landing Data .. CHECKED &
                                                                 REVIEWED
8. Master Tachometer .... 2550 RPM
9. Landing Gear Control Switch .... EXTEND
   a. Receive Aft Gunners' Visual Report, "Gear Down and
      Locked."
   *b. Receive Engineer's Report, "Hydraulic Pressure Relieved."
   c. Receive Radio Operator's Visual Report, "Nose Gear Down
      and Locked."
   d. Landing Gear Lights .... CHECKED GREEN
   e. Nose Wheel Steering Indicator .... ZERO
10. Parking Brake Control .... OFF
*11. Left and Right Brakes .... CHECKED
12. Nose Gear Strut .... BLED IF REQUIRED
13. Nose Steering Switch .... ON
14. Pilot—Recheck Gear Down and Locked, Autopilot Off, Nose
    Wheel Steering Switch On and report to A/C, "Gear Down and
    Locked, Landing Configuration Complete."
15. Flaps .... 10 DEGREES

BASE LEG

1. Flaps .... 20 DEGREES
2. Jet Air Plugs .... CLOSE
3. Landing Lights (If Required) .... EXTENDED AND CHECKED

FINAL APPROACH

At High Gross Weights, High Field Elevation, and in Emergencies
2700 RPM and No. 7 TBS Setting May Be Used.

1. Flaps .... 30 DEGREES

LANDING

1. Propeller Reverse Selector Switches .. READY ON MAIN GEAR
                                                             CONTACT
2. Propeller Reverse Pitch Switch   DEPRESS ON A/C's COMMAND
3. Control Surfaces .... LOCKED AT APPROXIMATELY 50 MPH
4. Propeller Reverse Selector Switches .... SAFE
5. Flaps .... RETRACTED
6. Jet Oil Shutoff Valve Switches .... CLOSED AT ZERO
                                                              PER CENT RPM

POSTFLIGHT ENGINE RUN-UP

1. Parking Brake Control .... ON
2. Propeller Reverse Selector Switches .... SAFE (LIGHTS OUT)
3. Nose Wheel Steering Switch .... OFF
4. Notify Engineer, "Start Postflight Engine Run-up."

STOPPING RECIPROCATING ENGINES

1. Parking Brake Control .... ON
2. Propeller Reverse Selector Switches .... SAFE (LIGHTS OUT)
3. Nose Wheel Steering Switch .... OFF
4. Flight Instrument Switches .... OFF
5. Contact Engineer, "Ready To Stop Engines."
6. Radio Equipment .... OFF

BEFORE LEAVING AIRCRAFT

1. All Control Switches .... PROPERLY POSITIONED
2. Wheel Chocks .... IN PLACE
3. Parking Brake Control .... OFF AFTER WHEELS
                                                          ARE CHOCKED
4. Postflight Visual Inspection .... COMPLETED

* PILOT-ENGINEER CO-ORDINATION ITEM

Figure 2-2. (Sheet 2)

T.O. 1B-36D(II)-1

Section II
Normal Procedures

B-36D-II ENGINEERS' STANDARD CHECK LIST

BEFORE STARTING ENGINES

1. Required Forms .... ABOARD AND CHECKED
2. All Circuit Breakers and Control Switches .... PROPERLY POSITIONED
2A. Ground Refueling Safety Switch (Some Airplanes) ..... OFF
3. Emergency Power Switch .... NORMAL
4. Cabin Heater Power Switch .... OFF
5. External Power Supply Switch .... OFF
6. Battery Switch .... ON
7. Alternator Panel Configuration .... CHECKED
8. External Power .... PLUGGED IN
9. Correct A-C Phase Sequence Lamps .... LIGHTED
*10. External Power Supply Switch .... ON
11. Master Ignition Switch .... PULL OFF
12. Liquid Lock Check (With Ignition Switches OFF) .. COMPLETED
13. Mixture Control Check .... COMPLETED
14. Throttle Lever and Flap Warning Horn Check .... COMPLETED
15. Fuel Panel Configuration .... CHECKED
16. Intercoolers and Air Plugs .... AS REQUIRED
17. Oil Cooler Door Manual Operation (Some Airplanes) CHECKED
18. Water Injection Switches .... OFF
19. Oil Vent Heater Switch .... AS REQUIRED
20. Oil Shutoff Valve Switch Guards .... DOWN
21. Engine Supercharger Switches .... BOTH
22. Cabin Temperature Control Switch ... FULL DECREASE UNTIL LAMP LIGHTS
23. Cabin Pressure Wing Shutoff Valve Switches .... OFF
24. Cabin Booster Fan Switch .... AS REQUIRED
25. Aft Cabin Pressure Switch .... ON
26. Wing, Cabin Heat and Tail Anti-Ice Switches ...... OFF
27. Pitot Heat Switches .... OFF
28. Carburetor Preheat Switches .... OFF
29. Nacelle Fire Detector and Extinguisher .... CHECKED
30. Wheel Well Lights Switch .... AS REQUIRED
31. Turbo Override Control Panel (Group 2 Airplanes) . CHECKED
*32. Hydraulic Control Panel .... CHECKED
33. Propeller Control Panel .... CHECKED
34. Fan Speed Control Switches .... LOW RPM
35. Carburetor Air Filter Switch .... AS REQUIRED
36. Panel Lights .... AS REQUIRED
37. Spark Advance Switches ...... RETARD (GUARDS DOWN)
38. Turbo Boost Selector .... ZERO
39. Turbo Calibration Knobs .... INDEXED TO THE FULLY COUNTERCLOCKWISE POSITION
40. Engine Analyzer Power Switch .... OFF
41. Master Temperature Indicator .... ON AND COMPENSATED
42. Instrument Check .... NORMAL
43. Master Ignition Switch .... ON
*44. Report to A/C, "Check List Completed, Ready to Start Engines."

STARTING RECIPROCATING ENGINES

1. Engine Analyzer Power Switch .... ON
2. Fuel Tank Valve Switches .... OPEN
3. Booster Pumps of Tanks Being Used .... ON
4. Voltage and Frequency Selector Switch ..... NO. 4 POSITION
5. Throttle Levers .... AS REQUIRED
6. Inform Ground Observer, "Ready to Start Engines, Clear No. 4."
7. Engine No. 4 Starter Switch .... ON
8. Engine No. 4 Ignition Switch .... BOTH
9. Engine No. 4 Primer Switch .... AS REQUIRED
10. No. 4 Mixture Control Lever .... NORMAL
11. Report, "Alternator Normal, Oil and Fuel Pressure Normal."
12. Repeat Steps 4 thru 11 for Starting Engines 5, 6, 3, 2 and 1.

DURING ENGINE WARM-UP
(PREFLIGHT OPERATIONAL EQUIPMENT CHECK)

1. Ignition Switch Check .... IDLE RPM
2. Engine-Driven Fuel Pumps .... CHECK
3. Heat and Anti-Icing Check .... COMPLETED
4. Alternator Checks .... COMPLETED
5. Engine Oil-In Temperature .... MINIMUM 40°C
*6. Propeller Reverse Check, Idle Rpm .... COMPLETED (IF REQUIRED)

ENGINE RUN-UP
(PREFLIGHT OPERATIONAL EQUIPMENT CHECK)

1. Inflight Oil Cooling Doors .... CHECKED
*2. Propeller Control System .... CHECKED
3. Cabin Pressure Wing Shutoff Valve and Carburetor Preheat Checks .... COMPLETED
4. Barometric Pressure Checks .... COMPLETED
5. Ignition System Check .... COMPLETED
6. Full Power No Boost Checks .... COMPLETED
7. Turbo Override and Single Turbo Check .... COMPLETED
8. Full Power With Boost Checks .... COMPLETED

DURING ENGINE WARM-UP
(DAY OF FLIGHT)

2. Engine-Driven Fuel Pumps .... CHECK
4d. Alternators on Line .... MINIMUM OF TWO
5. Engine Oil-In Temperature .... MINIMUM 40°C
6. Propeller Reverse Check, Idle RPM .... COMPLETED (IF REQUIRED)

ENGINE RUN-UP
(DAY OF FLIGHT)

*2. Propeller Control System .... CHECKED
5. Ignition System Check .... COMPLETED
6. Full Power No Boost Checks .... COMPLETED
8. Full Power With Boost Checks .... COMPLETED

TAXIING

1. Taxi Configuration, "Alternators on the Line and Paralleled, Brake and Nose Steering Pressure Normal, Ready to Taxi."

STARTING JET ENGINES (GROUND-AIR)

*1. Jet Start Configuration .... CHECKED AND REPORT "Standing By For Jet Engine Start."

BEFORE TAKE-OFF

1. Engine Supercharger Switches .... BOTH
2. Fuel Panel Checked .... BOOSTER PUMPS ON
3. Oil Vent Heater Switch ..... ON, IF 0°C OAT IS ANTICIPATED
4. Carburetor Preheat Switches .... OFF
5. Cabin Pressure Wing Shutoff Valve Switches .... OFF
6. Cabin Booster Fans Control Switch .... AS REQUIRED
7. Pitot Heater Switches .... AS REQUIRED
8. Wing and Cabin Heat and Tail Anti-Icing Switches ... OFF
9. Engine Fan Speed Switches .... LOW RPM
10. Three Alternators Paralleled on the Line, One Excited and Standing By.
11. Air Plugs and Intercoolers .... AS REQUIRED
12. Cabin Heater Power Switch .... OFF

* PILOT-ENGINEER CO-ORDINATION ITEM

Figure 2-3. (Sheet 1)

Section II
Normal Procedures

T.O. 1B-36D(II)-1

B-36D-II ENGINEERS' STANDARD CHECK LIST (Cont'd)

BEFORE TAKE-OFF (Cont'd)

13. Temperatures .... CHECKED AND WITHIN LIMITS
14. Mixture Control Selector Switches .... LEVER
15. Mixture Control Levers .... NORMAL
16. Spark Advance Switches .... RETARD (GUARDS DOWN)
17. Propeller Selector Switches .... AUTOMATIC OPERATION
    (TEL-LAMPS LIGHTED)
18. Propeller Normal Pitch Indicator Lamps .... LIGHTED
19. Brake Pressure and Nose Steering Pressure .... NORMAL
20. Turbo Control Change-Over Switches (Group 2 Airplanes) AUTO
21. Turbo Control Vernier Switch (Group 2 Airplanes) .... OFF
22. Hydraulic Fluid Temperature Control Switch .... OFF
23. Oil Cooler Door Mode Selector Switches .... AUTO
24. Safety Belt .... FASTENED
*25. Engineer's Take-Off Configuration .... ENGINEER READS—
    "Take-Off Configuration Completed, Standing by for Propeller Reverse Safety Check and Take-Off Power."

TAKE-OFF

*1. Propeller Reverse Safety Check and Set Take-Off Power Corrected for Humidity.
2. Report, "Power Stabilized," Prior to Nose-Up Speed.

AFTER TAKE-OFF

*1. Observe Main Hydraulic Pressure Normal
2. Report, "Main Hydraulic Pressure Relieved," After Gear Retraction is Completed.

INITIAL CLIMB

*1. Power Condition No. 2 .... UPON PILOT'S REQUEST
2. Turbo Boost Selector .... REDUCE M.P.
3. Water Injection Switches .... OFF
4. Reduce Power to Predicted Climb Schedule.
5. Torque, Fuel Flow, CHT, CAT. and M.P. .... WITHIN LIMITS
6. Anti-Icing Duct Temperatures .... INCREASE AS REQUIRED

CRUISE

For Specific Cruise Data See Appendix 1 and Amplified Check List.

BEFORE CLIMB (HIGH POWER OPERATION, AFTER A MANUAL LEAN SPARK ADVANCE CRUISE)

1. Air Plugs and Intercoolers .... OPEN
2. Spark Advance Switches .... RETARD
3. Mixture Controls .... NORMAL (LIGHTS ON)
4. Engine Supercharger Switches .... BOTH
5. Desired Power .... SET
6. Anti-Icing Duct Temperatures .... INCREASE AS REQUIRED

BEFORE LANDING

1. In-Flight Engine Checks .... COMPLETED, IF DESIRED
2. Engine Supercharger Switches .... BOTH
3. Fuel Panel Checked .... BOOSTER PUMPS ON
4. Oil Vent Heater Switch .... AS REQUIRED
5. Carburetor Preheat Switches .... AS REQUIRED
6. Cabin Pressure Wing Shutoff Valve Switches .... OFF
7. Booster Fan Switch .... AS REQUIRED
8. Pitot Heater Switches .... AS REQUIRED
9. Wing and Cabin Heat and Tail Anti-Icing Switches .... OFF
10. Engine Fan Speed Switches .... LOW RPM

11. Electrical System .... CHECKED
12. Air Plugs and Intercoolers .... AS REQUIRED
13. Cabin Heater Power Switch .... OFF
14. Temperatures .... CHECKED AND WITHIN LIMITS
15. Mixture Control Selector Switches .... LEVER
16. Mixture Control Levers .... NORMAL
17. TBS .... ZERO, CALIBRATION KNOBS INDEXED
18. Spark Advance Switches .... RETARD (GUARDS DOWN)
19. Propeller Selector Switches .... AUTOMATIC OPERATION
    (TEL-LIGHTS LIGHTED)
20. Propeller Normal Pitch Indicator Lamps .... LIGHTED
21. Turbo Control Change-Over Switches (Group 2 Airplanes) AUTO
22. Turbo Control Vernier Switch (Group 2 Airplanes) .... OFF
*23. Engineer's Landing Configuration .... ENGINEER READS—
    "Before Landing Check List Complete, Standing by for RPM, Landing Gear, and Brake Check, Gross Weight _____."
24. Master Tachometer .... 2550 RPM
25. Report, "Hydraulic Pressure Relieved."
*26. Observe Brake Check and Report, "Pressure Normal."

LANDING

1. Brake and Nose Steering Pressure .... NORMAL AFTER NOSE
    WHEEL CONTACTS GROUND
2. RPM and M.P. .... CHECKED

TAXIING

1. Alternators (Minimum of Two on the Line) .... PARALLELED
2. Brake and Nose Steering Pressure .... NORMAL

POSTFLIGHT ENGINE RUN-UP

1. All Propeller Normal Pitch Indicator Lamps .... LIGHTED
2. Master Tachometer .... 2700 RPM
3. Parking Brakes .... SET, PRESSURE NORMAL
4. Nose Steering Pressure .... ZERO
5. Announce over Interphone, "Ready for Postflight."
6. Engine Run-Up .... COMPLETED
7. Repeat Step 6 for Remaining Symmetrical Engines.
8. Shut down engine 1 & 6 after checking that CHT's are 180°C or below.
9. Report to A/C, "Postflight Run Complete, Ready to Taxi."
10. Repeat steps 1 thru 4 and step 8 before shutting down remaining engines.

STOPPING RECIPROCATING ENGINES

1. Air Plug Switches .... OPEN
2. Master Motor Speed Control Lever .... FULL DECREASE
3. Propeller Selector Switches .... FIXED PITCH
4. Booster Pump Switches .... OFF
5. Alternator Control Checks .... COMPLETED
6. Engine Analyzer Power Switch .... OFF
7. Idle Speed and Mixture Checks .... COMPLETED
8. Fuel Tank Valve Switches .... CLOSE
9. Cross-Feed, Manifold, and Engine Valve Switches .... OPEN
10. Individual Ignition Switches .... OFF
11. Master Ignition Switch .... PULL OFF
12. Intercooler Shutter Switches .... CLOSE
13. Static Propeller Feather Check .... COMPLETED
14. Oil Cooler Door Mode Selector Switches .... MANUAL
15. Battery Switch .... OFF
16. Master Temperature Indicator .... OFF

BEFORE LEAVING AIRCRAFT

1. Fuel Dip Stick Readings .... AS REQUIRED
2. Forms and Reports .... COMPLETED

* PILOT-ENGINEER CO-ORDINATION ITEM

Figure 2-3. (Sheet 2)

Proceed with the applicable entries of the pilots' and engineer's checks lists as amplified below:

BEFORE STARTING ENGINES.

1. Landing Gear Control Switch—EXTEND. The landing gear control switch should be in the EXTEND position for all ground operations. With the switch in this position, a gang bar arrangement holds the brake pump switch ON.

2. Visual inspection; Form 781 (Form 1), F, and Loading List—Completed.

Before flight the visual inspections, loading lists, and Forms 781 and F must be complete. Visual inspection should be completed to the aircraft commander's satisfaction. Discrepancies noted in the Form 781 which have been corrected should be particularly checked to insure that those items of equipment are in proper working order.

The Form F which was filled out by the engineer must be thoroughly checked for accuracy and signed by the aircraft commander. Take-off and landing data will be computed by the engineer and reviewed by the aircraft commander and the pilot prior to take-off. This information will be given to the pilot by the engineer on a take-off and landing data card. The original copy Form F must be filed with Operations. Loading list must be checked to insure that the name, rank, serial number, and organization of every person on the flight is on the loading list. One copy of the loading list must be filed with the aircraft clearance at base operations.

3. Pitot Covers and Ground Locks—Removed. The external control locks and the pitot head covers will be removed during the "Preflight Operational Equipment Check." The pitot head covers will be replaced after the pitot heat check is completed.

On the day of flight the aircraft commander will personally check just before he enters the aircraft to see that all locks (main landing gear, nose gear, and external control locks) have been removed and that the pitot covers have been removed.

4. Nose Wheel Scissors—Connected. The aircraft commander will also check just before he enters the aircraft to insure that the nose wheel scissors have been connected. The nose wheel scissors will be disconnected only when it is necessary to move the aircraft by use of a tug or towing equipment.

The aircraft should be in proper taxi position when the crew boards the aircraft so that it is unnecessary

1. Required Forms—Aboard and Checked. Check the AF Form 781 (Form 1) before any preflight or flight operations. Before flight, complete the Form F, and check the Flight Log initiated with proper headings, correct gross weight and fuel load in pounds, and predicted take-off and climb power settings indicated. Check other required forms aboard such as engineers' reports, prediction forms, or test flight reports as required by local directives.

2. All Circuit Breakers and Control Switches—Properly positioned. To make certain control circuits are connected to their respective power source and to prevent inadvertent operation of systems when power is applied to the aircraft.

2A. Ground Refueling Safety Switch (Some Airplanes) —OFF (Guard Down). To insure that power will be available to the forward cabin when the external power supply is connected to the aircraft.

3. Emergency Power Switch—NORMAL. To insure that the normal power distribution system is not partially blocked out; for example, one phase to the radio operator's t-r unit would be blocked out when the bus selector switch is in the bus position except when fed by an excited alternator which has been selected by

4. Cabin Heater Power Switch—OFF. The circuit is automatically de-energized when the external power is ON. However, the switch will be OFF before engine starting to prevent overload of the a-c system after external power is turned off and the engine alternator is placed on the line.

5. External Power Supply Switch—OFF. To prevent inadvertent connection of the external power supply to the bus before correct phase sequence has been established and the alternator breakers checked open.

6. Battery Switch—ON. To energize the d-c bus system, providing power for the interphone indicator lamp and control circuits.

Note

On airplanes equipped with an inverter, the battery switch must be placed in EMER ON to energize the d-c bus when no a-c power is on the airplane. After alternating current is on the airplane, place the switch in NORM ON.

7. Alternator Panel Configuration—Checked.

a. Frequency Control Knobs—Full Decrease.

BEFORE STARTING ENGINES (Cont'd)

to have the nose wheel scissors disconnected for any further towing operations.

5. Personal Equipment—Checked in place. (Not to be accomplished during "Preflight Operational Equipment Check.") Oxygen equipment, headset, and mike should be in place and plugged in. Other equipment necessary for the immediate flight should be readily available at each station. All other personal equipment should be in the A-3 bag and properly stowed.

6. Seats and Pedals—Adjusted. Make certain that the seat and rudder pedals are in proper position for the most efficient use of brakes and rudder.

7. All Circuit Breakers (Except Bomb Bay Door and Bomb Salvo)—In. To make sure that various indicator lamps, instruments, and control circuits are connected to the electrical power distribution systems, including the jet panel.

8. All Indicator Lamps—Push to test. To see that the indicator lamps are not burned out.

b. Bus Tie-Breaker Switches—CLOSE.

c. Alternator Breaker Switches—OPEN.

Note

The following check need only be performed following periodic inspections and whenever maintenance on the system has been performed.

Note

Any discrepancies noted during this check must be corrected.

d. Frequency Control Knobs—Full Decrease. This is the normal position for these controls when the alternators are not operating. It provides a safety precaution against constant-speed drive surging and overspeeding during engine start.

e. Bus Tie-Breaker Switches—CLOSE. Check the action of these breakers by raising the switch guards and open each breaker. Lamp on indicates breaker is open. Close each breaker and place switch guards down. Lamp out indicates breaker closed. All breakers closed insures that a-c power is feeding all four bus systems. Push-to-test any lamps that do not appear to be operating to make sure lamp is not burned out.

f. Mixture Control Levers—Move out of IDLE CUT-OFF position. It will be necessary to move the mixture control levers from the IDLE CUT-OFF position on the alternator-equipped engines, because a microswitch behind each mixture control lever of these engines keeps the exciter relay control circuit broken.

g. Exciter Control Relay Switches—ON. Exciting the alternators prior to engine start allows the operator to see that the alternator control circuits are functioning normally as each engine is started by watching the voltage and frequency indications.

h. Alternator Breaker Switches—OPEN (lamps lighted). To insure that alternator breakers are open prior to placing the external power switch ON, thus placing a-c power on the bus system. The open position prevents motorizing of the engine-driven alternators and subsequent excessive loads on the auxiliary power unit.

BEFORE STARTING ENGINES (Cont'd)

> **CAUTION**
>
> Never close the alternator breakers while external power is ON.

i. All Alternator Breaker Switches—CLOSE (lamps out).

j. All Alternator Exciter Control Relay Switches—Momentarily OFF. Observe that the alternator breaker lamps are lighted. If an alternator breaker lamp does not light, check alternator d-c fuse at the respective engine power distribution panel.

> **CAUTION**
>
> Do not attempt to start alternator-equipped engines until this condition is corrected.

k. All Alternator Exciter Control Relay Switches—ON.

l. All Alternator Breaker Switches—CLOSE (lamps out).

m. All Alternator Breaker Hold-In Switches—Hold in. Return each mixture control lever of the alternator-equipped engine to IDLE CUT-OFF. See that the alternator breaker lamps are still out. Then move the mixture control lever for alternator-equipped engines out of IDLE CUT-OFF and release the hold-in switches.

See that the alternator breaker lamps are still out. Move each mixture control lever slowly towards IDLE CUT-OFF and observe the position of the mixture control lever when the respective alternator breaker lamp lights.

Note

Maladjustment of the microswitch and the travel of the mixture control lever towards the manual lean range will open the alternator breaker.

8. External Power—Plugged In.

The ground observer can either close the APU circuit breaker or plug in the external power, depending upon type of power unit involved. You also know he is standing by on interphone to make any adjustments to power found necessary by aircraft instrumentation.

9. Correct A-C Phase Sequence Lamp—Lighted. To insure that external power is in correct phase (1, 2, 3) with the aircraft wiring system. Push to test to insure that the lamps are operating and to positively assure proper phase sequence. If *incorrect phase* external

Section II
Normal Procedures

BEFORE STARTING ENGINES (Cont'd)

9. Tower Call—Completed.

Contact the control tower and request fire equipment. Receive OAT. and dew point and inform engineer. If instrument conditions are to be encountered immediately after take-off, have radio navigational equipment tuned to appropriate facilities. Either the aircraft commander or pilot will monitor interphone at all times.

10. Propeller Reverse Selector Switches—SAFE. Lights out. This will prevent inadvertent operation in reverse pitch. The red propeller reverse warning lamps indicate when the propellers are in reverse pitch. The lamps should go out when the propeller reverse selector switches are in the SAFE position.

11. Flight Instrument Switches—ON. These switches are provided so that the flight instruments may be spared hours of ground operation during maintenance of the airplane. These switches must be ON approximately fifteen minutes before take-off so that the gyros can stabilize and so that flight instrument operation can be checked. During the preflight operational equipment check, place the pilot's flight instrument switch to EMERGENCY until the emergency electrical power system check has been completed. While the switch is in this position, check for proper operation of instruments.

Note

On airplanes equipped with an inverter, place the emergency circuit selector switch to EMERGENCY and check that the pilot's directional and attitude gyros continue to operate. This indicates proper operation of the inverter. After checking, immediately return the switch to NORMAL to conserve battery power.

power were placed on the aircraft a-c power distribution system, it would cause all three phase motors to operate in reverse, nullifying limit switches on electrical actuators and resulting in immediate damage to aircraft structure and equipment.

10. External Power Supply Switch—ON. Check bus voltage (208V) and frequency (405 cycles ± 5). Have the ground observer adjust if necessary.

11. Master Ignition Switch—Pull off.

12. Liquid Lock Check (with ignition switches OFF)—Completed. Perform a liquid lock check at this time with the ignition switches OFF. Pull propellers through 15 blades with starters. Sequence 4, 5, 6, 3, 2, 1.

CAUTION

Energize starter continuously for 15 blades. Maintain contact with observer for reports of propeller movement. A minimum of eight blades is required to avoid possible damage from hydraulic lock; however, a total of 15 blades is necessary to provide adequate lubrication to the reduction pinion bearings during engine starting.

13. Mixture Control Check—Completed.

a. Mixture Control Levers—Move from IDLE CUT-OFF to RICH and note that the indicator lamps light and go out as the mixture control travels through NORMAL.

b. Move mixture control levers back to NORMAL—Lights on.

c. Selector Switches—SWITCH.

d. Override Switches—Hold to RICH and note that the indicator lamps go dark as mixture control travels toward RICH.

e. Override Switches—Hold to IDLE CUT-OFF and note that the indicator lamps light and go out as mixture control travels through NORMAL.

f. Selector Switches—LEVER, and note that the indicator lamps light as mixture control travels to NORMAL.

g. Mixture Control Levers—IDLE CUT-OFF and note that indicator lamps go dark as mixture control moves to IDLE CUT-OFF.

Note

Normally it will be necessary to check only the normal mixture control system on the day of flight.

BEFORE STARTING ENGINES (Cont'd)

14. Throttle Lever and Flap Warning Horn Check—Completed. Move the throttle levers to the full open position. Observe closely for binding to insure freedom of movement thru entire range of travel. When all six levers are full open, check sounding of the flap warning horn. Check individual throttles for cutting out of warning horn. Return throttles to closed position and check for proper cushioning at extreme limits of throttle lever movement.

15. Fuel Panel Configuration—Checked.

   a. Pressure Refueling Valve Switches—CLOSE. These valves should always be closed except when fuel is being transferred. Normally closed, these valves prevent inadvertent fuel transfer.

> **CAUTION**
>
> Inadvertent transfer of fuel may result in fuel tank overflow if pressure refueling valve switches are left OPEN and a malfunction exists which would prevent automatic closing of the valve. Open valves would also cause abnormally low fuel pressures during checks and operation.

   b. Fuel Booster Pumps—OFF. Always OFF except when fuel is to be used from tank and respective tank valve is open.

   c. Fuel Tank Valves—CLOSE. Normal position when fuel is not being used or transferred and engines are not running.

   d. Engine Fuel, Manifold, and Cross-Feed Valves—OPEN. These valves are open at all times except when checking valve operation or during fuel system emergencies. In the OPEN position these valves permit any fuel tank to feed any engine plus allowing for temperature expansion of fuel in the long manifold system.

   e. Fuel System Operation Check.

> **Note**
>
> The following check should be made during the "Preflight Operational Equipment Check" to assure that all valves and booster pumps in the fuel system perform their designated functions. It should only be necessary to perform one complete check prior to any flight to prevent wear from added operation of these components, but additional checks may be made any time it is deemed advisable and in any case where a recheck is dictated by repair or replacement of equipment.

BEFORE STARTING ENGINES (Cont'd)

(1) Fuel Pressure—Zero.

(2) Engine Valves—CLOSE.

(3) No. 1 Tank Valve—OPEN

(4) No. 1 Tank Booster Pump—ON (observe zero pressure on all engines).

(5) All Engines Valves—OPEN. Check for 10 to 14 psi fuel pressure on all engines.

(6) No. 1 Manifold Valve—CLOSE.

(7) R. Auxiliary Pressure Refueling Valve—OPEN to drop pressure to zero on all engines; except No. 1; then CLOSE.

(8) No. 2 Manifold Valve CLOSE, No. 1 Manifold Valve OPEN. Note pressure on No. 2 Engine.

(9) Continue closing and opening manifold and cross-feed valves, noting fuel pressure on engines across the panel.

(10) No. 1 Tank Booster Pump—OFF.

(11) No. 1 Tank Valve—CLOSE.

(12) No. 1 Tank Refueling Valve—OPEN. Note pressure zero, then CLOSE.

(13) Cross-Feed Valve—CLOSE.

(14) No. 1 and 6 Tank Booster Pumps—ON. Note zero pressure.

(15) No. 1 and 6 Tank Valves—OPEN. Note 10 to 14 psi fuel pressure on all pressure.

(16) No. 1 and 6 Tank Booster Pumps—OFF. Note that fuel pressure remains steady.

(17) No. 1 and 6 Tank Refueling Valves—OPEN to drop fuel pressure to zero; then CLOSE.

(18) Repeat above check on each remaining symmetrical pair of tanks.

(19) Cross-Feed Valve—OPEN.

(20) No. 6 Booster Pump On and check for 10 to 14 psi fuel pressure on all engines.

(21) No. 6 Tank Booster Pump—OFF.

16. Intercoolers and Air Plugs—As Required. Normal position for all ground and high power operation is full open. However, the desired position should be dictated by good reasoning after due consideration of such factors as weather, accelerated warm-up, etc. A complete cycle of operation of these controls may be performed at this time or during the engineers' preflight inspection. A check of the left intercooler shutters may also be made at this time. This check is made by placing the turbo selector switches in R. H. only and noting that the left intercooler shutters close and

BEFORE STARTING ENGINES (Cont'd)

then by returning the turbo selector switches to BOTH and open the left intercooler shutters. It should not be necessary to check cycle of operation more than once prior to any flight. This will prevent undue wear on actuators and linkage.

17. Oil Cooler Door Manual Operation (some airplanes)—Checked—Auto. It should not be necessary to check cycle of operation more than once prior to any flight. Check manual operation as follows:

   a. Engine Fuel Valves—OPEN.

   b. Request the pilot, "Pull landing gear control circuit breaker." Ask the ground observer to inform you of inflight oil cooler door operation.

   c. Oil Cooler Door Mode Selector Switches—MANUAL. This sets up manual override operation. It may not be possible to operate all switches at one time due to overloading the circuit breaker.

   d. Oil Cooler Door Override Switches OPEN. Fully open all inflight cooling doors to check the control circuits and door actuators.

   e. Oil Cooler Door Override Switches—CLOSE: Close all inflight cooling doors, check the control circuits and door actuators. Close doors approximately half way.

   f. Oil Cooler Door Mode Selector Switches—AUTO. Inflight oil cooler doors should close. AUTO is the normal position for these switches and provides automatic oil cooling.

   g. Request the pilot "Close the landing gear control circuit breaker." This provides normal ground cooling for the oil system.

   h. Engine Fuel Valves—CLOSE.

18. Water Injection Switches—OFF. To prevent operation of water injection pumps.

19. Oil Vent Heater Switch—As Required. To prevent vapors from congealing, freezing, and consequently plugging the engine oil tank vent lines. This switch should be placed in the ON position for ground and flight operations when the ambient air temperature is at 0°C (32°F) and below.

20. Oil Shutoff Valve Switch Guards—DOWN. This is the normal position for these controls to prevent starvation of oil to engine when started.

21. Engine Supercharger Switches—BOTH. Normal position for all ground operation to prevent abnormal manifold pressure during run-up.

BEFORE STARTING ENGINES (Cont'd)

22. Cabin Temperature Control Switch—FULL DECREASE until lamp lights.

23. Cabin Pressure Wing Shutoff Valve Switches—OFF. This closes the wing shutoff valve and is the normal position for these valves prior to engine start. This also prevents drainage of manifold pressure during full power checks.

24. Cabin Booster Fan Switch—As Required.

25. Aft Cabin Pressure Switch—ON. Sets up aft cabin for pressurization. There is no reason for this valve to be closed except when it is desired to depressurize the aft cabin during flight or to check cabin air flow.

26. Wing, Cabin Heat and Tail Anti-Ice Switches—OFF. (Push to test warning lamps.) The cabin heat and tail anti-ice switches must be held in the OFF position for approximately 8 seconds. This opens the engine dump valves and prevents heating the leading edges of wings and empennage during engine run-up. If leading edges are heated over 50°C above OAT during ground operation, damage such as permanent wrinkling of the leading edges will probably result.

27. Pitot Heat Switches—OFF. This is the normal position for these switches except during operational checks or when icing is anticipated during flight. Leaving pitot heat switches ON on the ground will burn out the heater elements.

28. Carburetor Preheat Switches—OFF. These switches should be OFF at all times except when checking system or when icing is anticipated. If left ON, excessive carburetor temperatures will be experienced during run-up and control of cabin pressure wing shutoff valves will be lost, since these valves automatically close when carburetor preheat is ON.

29. Nacelle Fire Detector and Extinguisher—Checked.

   a. Fire Extinguisher Engine Selector Switches—OFF (guards down). To prevent accidental discharge of the fire extinguisher system.

   b. Fire Detector Push-to-Test Switch—Push to test circuit. This tests the complete warning circuit for continuity and normal operation from a rapid rate heat rise. If any one lamp does not light within 10 seconds, the circuit is defective and must be checked.

30. Wheel Well Lights Switch—As required. This switch should be OFF except during gear operation at night, when a crew member is in the wing, or when a crew member is checking the nose gear latch. It controls lamps that shine upon the landing gear release mechanism.

BEFORE STARTING ENGINES (Cont'd)

12. Nose Steering and Brakes—Checked and set. This check must be made in co-ordination with the engineer. It includes a check of the nose steering system, a brake check, and setting of the parking brake prior to engine start.

a. Steering Control Switch—ON, and check for normal pressure.

CAUTION

Do not apply steering pressure to the nose wheel while the aircraft is static. This would cause undue stress and strain on nose gear components and scrubbing abrasions of the tires.

b. Steering Control Switch—OFF.

c. Landing Gear and Brake Pump Switch—Neutral and OFF. The brake check will be made with the brake pump switch OFF and the parking brake control OFF.

Note

Steps c, e, and f need be performed on the preflight operational equipment check only. On the day of flight a check of the automatic system is adequate, with the engineer noting pressure drop and build-up as the left and right brakes are depressed.

31. Turbo Override Control Panel—Checked (group 2 airplanes).

a. Turbo Change-Over Switches—AUTO. In this position the TBS is effective for controlling the turbo waste gates.

b. Turbo Control Vernier Switch—OFF.

32. Hydraulic Control Panel—Checked. It should not be necessary to perform a complete hydraulic control panel check more than once prior to any flight; however, nose steering pressure and automatic operation of the brake pump must be checked on the day of flight.

a. Hydraulic Fluid Temperature Control Switch—As Required. Use to keep bomb bay door fluid temperatures between —18°C (0°F) and 38°C (100°F) to insure proper operation of the bomb bay door system. Turn ON when ambient air temperature is below —18°C (0°F) if bomb bay door operation is anticipated.

b. Hydraulic Pump Override Switch—OFF. Turn ON momentarily (approx 1/4 sec.) and then OFF. Observe surge of main system hydraulic pressure and electrical load. Main system hydraulic pressure should return to zero with override switch OFF. The above check with the override switch assures that the override circuit and relay and No. 2 hydro pump and motor are operational.

c. Report nose steering pressure on pilot's request.

d. Brake System Check—Completed. Contact pilot and announce "Ready for brake check." Report pressures during check.

BEFORE STARTING ENGINES (Cont'd)

d. Announce, "Left brake," and firmly depress left brake pedal and release. Then announce, "Right brake," and firmly depress right brake pedal and release. The engineer will check for pressure drop.

e. Depress and release both brake pedals until brake pressure drops to air charge in accumulator.

e. As pilot depresses and releases brake pedals, report remaining pressure, "———psi."

Note

Steps e through i need be performed on the preflight operational equipment check only. On the day of flight a check of the automatic system is adequate. After the pilot depresses the left and right brakes, the engineer will report, "Pressure drop OK, pressure normal."

f. Have ground observer report accumulator preload pressure. Accumulator pressure should be approximately 300 psi (group 7 airplanes), 450 psi (group 8 airplanes).

g. Brake Pump Pressure Override Switch—Hold ON until pressure is 500 to 600 psi; then release and announce, "———psi with override."

f. Landing Gear and Brake Pump Switch—EXTEND and ON.

h. Observe low brake pressure warning lamp lighted and then pressure build-up until lamp goes out. Observe continued build-up of pressure to normal. Report, "Brake pressure normal."

g. Parking Brake Control—ON. Announce, "Parking brake set."

i. Observe and announce, "Pressure down, building up, normal."

Brake pedals should be fully extended. Normal pressure on the brake pedals should not cause any depression.

If the brake pedals move spongily, the slave brake system must be bled and rechecked.

On airplanes which have a brake gage line fuse, if pressure does not force the foot pedals out, the fuse is probably blown. If this has happened, hold the aircraft with the foot brakes, have the radio operator or the second engineer place the emergency hydraulic selector valve in the CHARGE BRAKE ACCUMULATOR position, and operate the hand pump four or five strokes. This will reset the brake fuse and the parking brakes should operate normally. The aircraft must be completely stopped for normal parking brake setting because of the instantaneous locking action of the system. The foot brakes will be used to hold the airplane when releasing the parking brake. Rapid successive movement of the parking brakes on airplanes which have a brake gage line fuse will cause the fuse to move and drop the brake pressure, rendering the parking brakes inoperative. If this condition exists place the emergency selector valve in the

33. Propeller Control Panel—Checked.

a. Propeller Feather Switches—NORMAL (guards down). To prevent accidental feathering of propeller. All normal circuits pass through each propeller feather switch.

b. Propeller Circuit Breakers—In. Connects all propeller controls to d-c power distribution.

c. Propeller Selector Switches—AUTOMATIC OPERATION. Sets up system for eventual run-up and for a check on the protective relay tel-lamps as master motor speed is increased.

d. Master Motor Speed Control Lever—2700 rpm, full INCREASE rpm position. This step checks automatic increase rpm controls and the master motor protective relay circuit as indicated by the tel-lamps. The tel-lamps should go out during any rapid change of the master motor speed control lever and come on again as the master motor begins governing at this new setting. This indicates that the master motor protective relay is breaking the ground of each contactor, thus preventing undesired rpm changes in event of a master motor failure. Any time the tel-lamps are out (provided the bulbs are good), the automatic control circuit is disrupted and the propellers assume a fixed

BEFORE STARTING ENGINES (Cont'd)

CHARGE BRAKE ACCUMULATOR position and operate the hand pump four or five strokes. This action will position the fuse to give the proper pressure. The emergency selector valve should be allowed to remain in the CHARGE BRAKE ACCUMULATOR position at all times except during emergency hydraulic extension of the landing gear.

13. Bomb Bay Door Locks—Removed. Bomb bay door locks should be removed at this point so that the doors can be closed after engine start. The locks have been left on up to this point so ground crew personnel could safely observe any fuel leaks in the bomb bays and to make the interior of the bomb bays readily accessible to fire fighting equipment in the event of a fire in the bomb bays.

14. Fire Equipment—In Place. A fire truck or an officially authorized equivalent will be in place accessible to the engine being started before attempting to start engines.

15. Emergency Ignition Switch—IN. When the engineer has completed his check list up to placing his master ignition switch ON, he will request the aircraft commander to push in the emergency ignition switch.

pitch position until the system is again in balance and the tel-lamps come back on.

e. Propeller Tel-Lamps—Lighted. Tel-lamps indicate that contactors are properly grounded through the master motor protective relay and that control panel is set up for automatic operation.

34. Fan Speed Control Switches—LOW RPM. Normal position for all ground operation except when checking engine cooling fan. The LOW RPM position, being normal, prevents low torque readings during run-up and prevents damage to fan, cooling tunnel, accessory case, and shear couplings during full power checks.

35. Carburetor Air Filter Switch—As Required. Used only under extreme dust conditions. The switch is inoperative and filters are not installed on most airplanes under normal conditions.

36. Panel Lights—As Required. Check the operation of panel and overhead lights.

37. Spark Advance Switches—RETARD (guards down). This places engine ignition timing in retard position (20 degrees BTC), which is normal for all ground and high power operation except when checking ADVANCE position during engine run-up for proper operation.

38. Turbo Boost Selector—ZERO. Waste gates should be full open to prevent damage due to afterfire during starting and excessive back pressure and overheating during run-up.

39. Turbo Calibration Knobs—Indexed to the fully counterclockwise position. This prevents staggered indications and probable excessive manifold pressures when setting TBS for full take-off power.

40. Engine Analyzer Power Switch—OFF.

41. Master Temperature Indicator (Some Airplanes) —ON and compensated. Adjust master temperature indicator as follows:

a. Selector Switch—Select any engine.

b. Control Switch—ON.

c. Adjust slide wire rheostat to obtain full scale deflection with balance knob.

d. Turn Check Switch to CH position.

e. Adjust Comp. Rheo. Knob until galvanometer needle is directly over CH line.

Section II
Normal Procedures

T.O. 1B-36D(II)-1

BEFORE STARTING ENGINES (Cont'd)

f. Turn check switch to the ON position.

g. Move selector switch through all positions checking for open circuits and ambient temperature indications. Leave selector switch on first engine to be started (normally No. 4 engine).

42. Instrument Check—Normal. This can be accomplished while manipulating air plugs and intercooler. See that all temperature indicators check against ambient air. On aircraft that have a cylinder head temperature selector switch, make sure that all positions are checked. Check rpm, torque, fuel flow indicators and turbo tachometers for zero reading, and fuel, oil, and water pressures normal. Have second engineer observe static M.P. for future use during check field barometric pressure.

43. Master Ignition Switch—ON.

16. Receive engineer's report and notify engineer, "Brakes set, fire guard standing by, start engines."

44. Report to aircraft commander, "Check list completed, master ignition in, ready to start engines."

STARTING RECIPROCATING ENGINES.

The minimum team required for engine operation during the Operational Preflight Equipment Check shall consist of the aircraft commander, the pilot, one engineer, two aft cabin gunners, a qualified crew member, and a qualified ground observer. During darkness or under conditions of poor visibility, an additional qualified crew member will be present.

During engine starting, the ground observer shall be in constant communication with the engineer. The other crew members will be stationed as follows: the pilots in their seats, the two gunners at their stations, and the qualified crew member standing by on interphone at the emergency brake pump. The engineer shall announce what he is going to do at all times during engine operation so that the other crew members will be able to anticipate their activities when co-ordination is required.

During darkness or under conditions of poor visibility, the additional crew member will be stationed in the airplane at the nose wheel well entrance hatch. He will be equipped with a headset, a microphone and an Aldis lamp and will observe through the entrance hatch for any movement of the aircraft prior to and during engine run-up. If at any time communication from this observer is broken or aircraft movement is reported, engine run-up shall cease.

The pilot and the aft gunners will maintain visual contact with reference points immediately adjacent to the aircraft and will notify the aircraft commander of any movement of the aircraft. If necessary, the pilot will use a landing light and the gunners will use the main gear wheel well lights for illumination of the reference points. Ground fire equipment of adequate capacity to combat any anticipated fire should be properly manned and standing by. See "Reciprocating Engine Fire on the Ground," Section III, for instructions on combating engine fires. As each of the engines is turned over, any observation of abnormal operation must be reported to the engineer immediately. The engine starting sequence is 4, 5, 6, 3, 2, 1. The aircraft commander will observe the engineer's procedure during reciprocating engine starts. The aircraft commander can assist the engineer during starts by handling the throttle of each engine to maintain specified idling speeds after the engineer has it started.

1. Engine Analyzer Power Switch—ON. This allows the analyzer time to warm up for monitoring the ignition system during starting.

2. Fuel Tank Valve Switches—OPEN. Use a minimum of two tanks containing fuel.

3. Booster Pumps of Tanks Being Used—ON. To provide positive fuel pressure (10 to 14 psi) to engine-driven fuel pump and fuel under pressure to primer. The primer is effectively inoperative without pressure.

4. Voltage and Frequency Selector Switch—No. 4 position. See that bus voltage provided by external power source is within limits by moving the selector switch to the bus position. Then move it to the No. 4 position. This will allow you to observe voltage and frequency of engine being started.

5. Throttle Levers—As Required. If it becomes necessary to restart a relatively "hot" engine, a more open throttle setting may be required.

6. Inform ground observer, "Ready to start engines, clear No. 4."

7. Engine No. 4 Starter Switch—ON. Energize starter continuously for eight blades. Maintain contact with observer for reports of propeller movement. This procedure is followed to minimize the possibility of damage in the event of a liquid (hydraulic) lock.

Note

Eight blades are necessary to provide an adequate liquid lock check.

8. No. 4 Engine Ignition Switch—BOTH after eight blades of propeller rotation.

9. Engine No. 4 Primer Switch—As Required.

10. No. 4 Mixture Control Lever—NORMAL.

CAUTION

Maximum continuous cranking time is *one minute*—then allow the starter to cool a minimum of *three* minutes.

1. As the engineer starts other engines, control the throttles of the engines that have been started to maintain the recommended idle speed (1000 to 1200 rpm).

11. Report, "Alternator normal, oil and fuel pressure normal."

CAUTION

If oil pressure does not register 25 psi within 30 seconds, the engine will be shut down and the cause investigated.

STARTING RECIPROCATING ENGINES (Cont'd)

Note

Minimum oil pressure at ground idle speed after oil has reached operating temperature is 25 psi.

Adjust voltage to 208 volts and check frequency for normal indication to allow control circuits to stabilize. Move the voltage and frequency selector switch to the number of the next alternator-equipped engine to be started.

Note

The frequency will increase with the temperature of the control circuit resistor.

Do not move the frequency control knob beyond the mechanical stop during ground operation. If the mechanical limit is exceeded overspeeding may occur.

CAUTION

a. If excitation of the alternator is not immediately apparent, the field will be flashed. If flashing the field fails to excite the alternator, shut down the engine. With no meter indication, malfunctions which might cause alternator damage would not be evident.

b. Alternators must be excited and properly governed before advancing the throttles above 1400 rpm. This is necessary so that the alternators can be checked when the engines are run up. If the frequency of any alternator increases with an increase in engine rpm and cannot be adjusted, then the affected engine must be shut down and the constant-speed drive unit checked. Otherwise an overspeed condition may be reached, causing the units to disintegrate and cause a serious fire.

12. Repeat steps 4 through 11 for starting engines 5, 6, 3, 2, and 1. Since No. 1 and No. 6 engines are not alternator-equipped, references to alternators in the starting procedure should be disregarded.

Note

If the engine stops running with the mixture control in NORMAL, the lever should be returned to the IDLE CUT-OFF position. After the starter has been allowed to cool, the starting procedure may be repeated.

RECIPROCATING ENGINE GROUND OPERATION.

During darkness and under conditions of poor visibility, a designated crew member, equipped with headset, microphone, and Aldis lamp, will be stationed inside the aircraft in direct communication with the aircraft commander and engineer and will observe through the nose wheel entrance hatch for any movement of the aircraft prior to and during engine run-up. At any time that communication is broken or aircraft movement reported, engine run-up will cease. The aft gunners, by illumination from the wheel well lights, will maintain visual contact with a reference point immediately adjacent to the aircraft, and notify the aircraft commander of any movement of the aircraft. The pilot, using a landing light if necessary, will maintain visual contact with a reference point immediately adjacent to the aircraft, and will notify the aircraft commander of any movement of the aircraft.

The ground operation of each engine must be held to an absolute minimum. During idling, an attempt should be made to maintain cylinder head temperatures between 170° to 220°C by use of the air plugs. This will minimize the possibility of spark plug fouling. Normally, high idle speed will not be used to keep cylinder head temperature high. However, if these temperatures cannot be maintained with the air plugs, it may be necessary to use higher idle speeds provided oil temperatures are within limits. Engines shall be run only when it is necessary to perform the required checks. An engine should be shut down, when possible, if running unnecessarily during a prolonged check of another engine. Spark plug fouling occurs very rapidly during ground idling, particularly if the idle mixture setting is too rich. This type fouling can be minimized by using the following procedures:

When it is necessary to run an engine on the ground for an extended time and lead fouling is suspected, it may be run up to 2200 rpm, 37 inches manifold pressure, for a one-minute period every 15 minutes. This procedure will act to clear away the fouling deposits in their early stages.

If the above procedure does not clear the fouling, the following procedure may be used as an alternate method.

1. Operate the engine at 2000 rpm and bring the cylinder head temperatures to 200° to 220°C.

2. Increase to take-off power with water on and hold for 30 seconds.

3. At the end of 30 seconds operate for 1 minute at dry take-off power and then repeat wet take-off power for 30 seconds.

4. Reduce manifold pressure to 55 inches, turn water injection switches OFF, and reduce rpm to idle.

Note

If the above procedure does not clear the fouling, the spark plugs must be changed.

The normal operating range of the turbosupercharger tachometers is above the range obtainable during engine ground operation. Therefore, no ground checks of the turbo tachometers are recommended. However, a low rpm indication will occur during power checks with boost and water. Failure to obtain such an indication may be indicative of a malfunction and should be investigated before flight.

CAUTION

If the fuel pressure drops below the operating limits during ground operation but the engine continues to operate normally, shut down *immediately,* investigate the cause, and take corrective action.

DURING ENGINE WARM-UP.

All reciprocating engines have now been started and are operating at idle speed. Do not exceed 1400 rpm until the engine oil-in temperature reaches 40°C. Make all ground operations with the mixture controls in the NORMAL position. The engine analyzer may be used to perform the following checks:

1. Slow sweep check of all magnetos and spark plugs.

2. Ignition grounding system.

3. Breaker point synchronizer.

4. Fast sweep of ignition check pattern at magneto check power.

The following procedures call for an ignition switch check, engine-driven fuel pump check, heat and anti-icing check, and alternator checks. To reduce engine ground test time, these checks can be made on all six engines at once.

Normally, it should be necessary to perform the ignition switch check once prior to any flight provided the engine analyzer is used to determine condition of ignition system prior to the ignition system checks. Normally it will be made after engine start of the initial complete reciprocating engine run-up during the "Preflight Operational Equipment Check." *If the engine analyzer is inoperative, it is imperative that an ignition switch check be made after each engine start.*

While the engineer makes the ignition switch check, the aircraft commander should maintain idle rpm on the engines the engineer is not working on. Proceed with the checks as follows:

1. Ignition Switch Check—Idle Rpm.

a. Individual Ignition Switches—L, Detent, R, Detent, L, BOTH. Check for a slight drop in rpm and torque pressure in the L and R positions and for a return to the original settings in the Detent and BOTH positions. Make this check starting with engine No. 1 and continuing with engines 2, 3, 4, 5, and 6. Use your right hand to move the ignition switch from BOTH to L and then to the Detent position between L and R; then switch from the Detent position to R and finally back to BOTH.

Note

If a cutout occurs with the switch in either L or R position, check the ignition system before further operation.

The L position of the ignition switches grounds out the left (exhaust side) bank of spark plugs and checks the right (intake side) bank and vice versa.

CAUTION

Never leave the ignition switches in the Detent position between L and R. If they are left in this position and the pilots' emergency ignition switch or the engineer's master ignition switch is pulled out (off), the ignition relays will chatter, causing severe backfiring.

Do not investigate the OFF position with the individual ignition switches.

b. Master Ignition Switch—Momentarily OFF. Move the emergency ignition switch momentarily OFF. Place your hands over this push-pull type switch so that you can get a positive and straight "out-in" action without any side force.

CAUTION

Do not allow the switch to be cut (off) for more than a split second. If the switch remains OFF too long, *do not turn it back on* for severe backfire will occur on all engines.

2. Engine-Driven Fuel Pumps—Check. Turn all booster pumps OFF and check fuel pressures to see that they remain within limits. Erratic fuel pressure readings indicate a faulty engine-driven fuel pump or other defects which must be investigated before flight. When this check has been completed, turn booster pumps of tanks being used ON.

DURING ENGINE WARM-UP (Cont'd)

3. Heat and Anti-Icing Check—Completed.

Note

This check need only be performed following periodic inspections and whenever maintenance on the system has been performed.

On airplanes that have a master temperature indicator, use master temperature selector switch to check wing and tail anti-icing temperatures. Zero the highest indication and turn ON all cabin heat and tail and wing anti-icing switches until temperature rise is noted; then turn OFF. Move the temperature selector switch through the anti-icing positions. A galvanometer needle deflection left to zero indicates a temperature rise. On airplanes that have individual indicators turn all cabin heat and tail and wing anti-ice switches to ON until a temperature rise occurs; then turn to OFF.

CAUTION

Do not allow temperatures to exceed 50°C above ambient air temperature.

Check a little later to see that temperatures have receded to normal, indicating that the engine dump valves have operated through one complete cycle and are in the open position.

4. Alternator Checks—Completed. No constant-speed drive oil warm-up is required. Proceed with the following check:

  a. Voltage and Frequency Range—Checked.

Note

Alternator control circuits will normally take approximately 5 minutes to warm up in normal ambient temperature ranges.

(1) Voltage and frequency selector switch to desired alternator.

(2) Voltage Control Knob—Check voltage range. The voltage range should be at least 195 to 215 volts by adjustment of the engineer's voltage control knob. Reset voltage to 208 volts.

(3) Frequency Control Knob—Check frequency range. The maximum frequency should be 440 (± 5) cycles. DO NOT go above 445 cycles. If the limit 440 (± 5) cycles is not obtained, adjustment should be made to the frequency control rheostat located in the governor control "J" box on the respective engine distribution panel. On some airplanes, the frequency control rheostats are located in the lower left side of the

Section II
Normal Procedures

T.O. 1B-36D(II)-1

DURING ENGINE WARM-UP (Cont'd)

forward cabin between the radio and observers' compartment. While adjustments are being made, the engineer's frequency control knob will be turned to full decrease to preclude the possibility of the constant-speed drive going into underdrive. After the adjustment is made, the minimum indication with the engineer's knob in the FULL DECREASE position will be approximately 375 cycles, depending upon the constant-speed drive and control circuit temperatures. Reset frequency to 405 cycles.

(4) Repeat the above steps on alternator-equipped engines.

h. Emergency Power—Checked.

Note

This check need only be performed following periodic inspections and whenever maintenance on the system has been performed.

The alternator will be checked by using the emergency method of restoring normal electrical power. The in-flight procedure is given in Section III, "Emergency Procedures." This ground check will vary slightly. Proceed as follows:

(1) Reduce a-c and d-c electrical loads to a minimum and request all crew members to turn off all unneccessary electrical loads.

(2) De-excite all alternators.

(3) External Power Switch—OFF.

(4) Battery Switch—OFF.

(5) Turn the voltage and frequency selector switch to No. 3 alternator.

(6) Move the emergency power switch to EMERGENCY and momentarily hold the respective exciter control relay switch ON.

Pilot's Flight Instrument Switch—EMERGENCY and check instruments for proper operation. When check is completed, place the switch in the ON position.

(7) Request the pilot to move his flight instrument switch to EMERGENCY and to check that his flight instruments are functioning properly.

CAUTION

With the t-r test unit selector switch in RADIO OPER position, a crew member on interphone should observe the load on the unit during the check of the first alternator. Do not permit the d-c load to exceed 1.0 (50 amperes) as indicated on the test unit. An overload can damage the t-r unit or blow out the a-c instrument fuses at the engine

DURING ENGINE WARM-UP (Cont'd)

distribution panel with a resulting loss of all emergency power. The voltage output of the transformer-rectifier should be 24 to 28 volts. It is the characteristic of the t-r unit that as the load is increased its output voltage decreases. A d-c overload on the radio operator's t-r unit may occur when power is suddenly applied through the emergency circuit, causing the voltage to be low for a short time.

(8) Repeat steps 4b (5) thru 4b (6) for 4, 5, and 2 alternator-equipped engines.

(9) Close the alternator breaker switch of No. 2 alternator.

Note

If you find that the alternator functions normally on the line, return the emergency power switch to NORMAL and readjust voltage and frequency.

(10) Request pilot to place his flight instrument switch back to ON.

(11) Battery Switch—ON.
  c. Alternate Power Check—Checked.

(1) No. 2 Alternator Breaker Switch—Momentarily CLOSE, lamp out. All other alternators off the line.

(2) Bus Tie-Breaker Control Switches 5-2 and 3-4 —Momentarily OPEN, lamps on. Observe a loss of electrical power on the panel as indicated by the normal mixture indicator lamps going out or by the engine analyzer.

(3) Alternate Power Switch—ALT, observe the return of panel electrical power by the lighting of the mixture indicator lamps or by the engine analyzer.

(4) Bus Tie-Breaker Control Switches 5-2 and 3-4 —Momentarily CLOSE, lamps out.

(5) Alternate Power Switch—NORM.

(6) Parallel remaining alternators as required.
  d. Alternators On Line—Minimum of two.

(1) Voltage and Frequency Selector Switch—No. 4 position.

(2) No. 4 Voltage and Frequency—Adjust to 208 volts and 405 cycles.

(3) Voltage and Frequency Selector Switch—Bus Position (Detent between 4 and 5).

(4) External Power Supply Switch—OFF. Watch bus voltage and frequency drop-off.

(5) No. 4 Alternator Breaker Switch—CLOSE.

Section II
Normal Procedures

T.O. 1B-36D(II)-1

DURING ENGINE WARM-UP (Cont'd)

Watch bus voltage and frequency build-up. Adjust frequency if necessary.

(6) Voltage and Frequency Selector Switch—No. 5 position.

(7) No. 5 Voltage and Frequency—Adjust to 208 volts and 405 cycles. Make fine adjustment on frequency until alternator synchronizing lamps blink at slowest rate possible.

(8) No. 5 Alternator Breaker Switch—CLOSE. (When alternator synchronizing lamps are out.) The synchronizing lamps indicate three things. First, when both lamps are blinking simultaneously, they indicate correct phase sequence. Second, alternately blinking lamps indicate a crossed phase sequence; very serious damage will result if two alternators with opposing phase sequences are paralleled. It would amount to a direct short of the total output of both units. Third, the lamps indicate when two alternators of correct phase sequence are in or out of step. Lamps out indicate "in step" and lamps on indicate "out of step."

(9) Adjust the kilowatt and kilovar load division as indicated on the kilowatt-kilovar meters. These meters read kilowatts when the kilowatt-kilovar selector switches are in the KWATTS position. Use the frequency control knobs to divide the kilowatt load. Move the kilowatt-kilovar selector switches to the KVAR position and use the voltage control knobs to divide the kilovar load.

(10) Repeat steps (6) thru (9) to parallel No. 3 and No. 2 alternators.

(11) Voltage and Frequency Selector Switch—Detent position between any two alternator positions. This will allow you to read bus voltage on the voltmeter. Selections of any alternate position enables you to read individual frequency and voltage of alternators on stand-by.

(12) Instruct ground crew to unplug the external power supply if the aircraft is to be taxied. When it is unplugged, the Correct-Incorrect phase sequence lamps will go out.

1. Bomb Bay Door and Salvo Circuit Breakers—In. Check that both the radar observer's and pilots' salvo circuit breakers are pushed in.

2. Bomb Bay and Camera Doors—Closed. Closing the camera doors as soon as possible will eliminate the possibility of the window being splattered with mud, snow, or slush during taxi and engine run-up. Bomb bay doors will be closed before taxiing to prevent anything from being blown into the bomb bays by the propeller blast.

3. Flaps and Indicators—Checked. Fully extend the flaps and have the ground observer report their position. Check the flap indicators for 30-degrees. Fully raise the flaps and check ground observer's report with indicators. If it is necessary to operate flap actuators for more than two cycles on the ground, allow the actuators to cool for approximately ten minutes between cycles.

Note

This check should be made on the preflight operational equipment check only.

4. Propeller Reverse Check, Idle Rpm—Completed (if required). If it is necessary to move the aircraft to a run-up area, a propeller reverse check must be made before taxiing to assure a means of stopping the aircraft in the event of brake failure. This check may be made at idle rpm.

5. Engine Oil-In Temperature—Minimum 40°C. Check all engine temperature in limits, paying particular attention to oil-in temperatures prior to advancing throttles for engine run-up. CHT must be above 120°C before exceeding 1400 rpm.

6. Propeller Reverse Check, Idle Rpm—Completed (if required). Observe that propeller pitch indicator lights go out during check.

TAXIING.

If it is necessary to move the aircraft to a run-up area, taxiing will be accomplished in accordance with the instructions given in "Taxiing" of this section.

ENGINE RUN-UP.

The operational preflight procedures call for propeller checks, ignition system checks, and power checks. Power checks include full power no boost and full power with boost. A complete check will be accomplished on the following systems after a periodic inspection or whenever maintenance on the system has been performed: inflight oil cooling doors, cabin pressure wing shutoff valve and carburetor preheat checks, and turbo override and single turbo checks. After power checks are completed on any engine it should be shut down as soon as its cylinder head temperature cools to 180°C, provided take-off is not to follow and provided it is not needed for taxiing or for jet engine starting or operation. Run-up procedures are as follows:

1. Parking Brake Control—ON. The aircraft commander will set the parking brakes and both he and the pilot will stand by on the foot brakes in case the aircraft creeps forward during engine run-up or in case of parking brake failure.

2. Propeller Reverse Selector Switches—SAFE (lights out). When the aircraft commander has the aircraft in position for engine run-up he should announce over interphone, "Nose steering switch off, all propeller reverse selector switches safe, parking brakes set, ready for engine run-up." As each item is announced, the aircraft commander should check each one by putting his hand on the item being checked. The propeller reverse selector switches have a gang bar to move all three switches to the READY position, but in order to place them in the SAFE position, each of the three switches must be moved individually.

Note

Pull the pilot's landing gear control circuit breaker upon the engineer's request. Close the circuit breaker as soon as the engineer requests it.

3. Nose Wheel Steering Switch—OFF. This switch must be in the OFF position during all ground operation—except when you are taxiing—to eliminate unnecessary hydraulic pump operation.

1. Inflight Oil Cooling Doors—Checked.

Note

On airplanes equipped with manual override controls, this check need only be performed following periodic inspections and whenever maintenance on the system has been performed.

Request the pilot, "Pull landing gear control circuit breaker." Ask the ground observer to let you know when all inflight oil cooling doors are open. Keep a close watch on oil temperatures during this check. While the oil temperature is increasing you can continue with your other checks. The doors will be visibly open at approximately 86°C oil-in temperature. Ask the pilot, "Close the landing gear circuit breakers,"

ENGINE RUN-UP (Cont'd)

4. Pilots' Manifold Pressure Gage—Checked.
This is a check to insure that the instrument is functioning normally by cross checking the indication on the engineers' No. 4 engine manifold pressure gage with the pilots' manifold pressure gage. The pilots' manifold pressure gage gives an indication of No. 4 engine only and is used as master indicator for the pilots' observation.

5. Master Tachometer—Checked. Cross check the pilots' master tachometer setting with the setting on the engineers' master tachometer during all propeller automatic checks. This check should be made when the engineer sets 1700 rpm with the propeller master motor. When this check is complete, stand by for a propeller reverse check.

6. Propeller Reverse Check—Completed, lights out. The propeller reverse check will be made at the same time as the engineer's propeller control system check. The engineer will notify the aircraft commander when he has 1700 rpm set and ready to check propeller reversing.

Propellers will be checked in symmetrical pairs (inboards, centers, outboards) in that order. This will minimize flutter of the aileron tabs.

a. After the engineer reports that engines are ready for propeller reverse check, place the inboard reverse selector switch in READY.

b. Announce over the microphone, "Reversing inboards." This alerts the engineer. Then depress the propeller reverse pitch switch, thereby energizing the circuit and reversing the selected pair of propellers. After the circuit has been energized, it is not necessary to depress the reverse pitch switch again as long as one pair of propellers remain reversed. As each pair of propellers is reversed, check to see that the corresponding red propeller reverse warning lamps light.

c. Announce, "Reversing centers," and place the center reverse selector switch in READY. Check corresponding red propeller reverse warning lamps.

d. Announce, "Reversing outboards," and place the outboard reverse selector switch in READY. Check corresponding red propeller reverse warning lamps.

> **CAUTION**
>
> Do not allow outboard propellers to remain in reverse pitch longer than 5 seconds because of possible aileron damage due to aileron flutter.

as soon as the ground observer reports or as soon as the oil-in temperature reaches 98°C.

2. Propeller Control System—Checked.
This is to provide a complete operational check of the automatic, reversing, manual increase and decrease, and feather control circuits.

a. Throttle Levers — Set to obtain approximately 1900 rpm.

b. Master Motor Speed Control Lever—Decrease until master tachometer indicates 1700 rpm. The rpm of all engines should decrease until the engine tachometers indicate 1700 ($\pm$ 120) rpm.

This step checks automatic decrease rpm controls and resets propeller low limit blade angle limit switches.

c. Advise aircraft commander, "Ready for propeller reverse check."

d. Observe propeller reversing in symmetrical pairs. Note for definite increase in engine rpm and then the decrease back to the original rpm. This is a definite indication that the propellers are governing in reverse. Also note that normal pitch lamps go dark.

e. After propellers are reversed, report to aircraft commander, "Propellers reversed, lights out."

ENGINE RUN-UP (Cont'd)

e. The propellers will be brought out of reverse in symmetrical pairs (outboards, centers, and inboards) in that order. Move outboard reverse selector switch to SAFE and announce, "Outboards safe, lights out."

f. Move center reverse selector switch to SAFE and announce, "Inboards safe, lights out."

g. Move inboard reverse selector switch to SAFE and announce, "Inboards safe, lights out."

h. Receive engineer's report, "Propellers normal, lights on," after reverse check.

f. As propellers return from reverse, obtain definite increase in engine rpm and then decrease back to the original rpm. Also note that normal pitch lamps light.

g. After propellers return to normal pitch report to aircraft commander, "Propellers normal, lights on."

h. No. 1 and 6 Propeller Selector Switches—DEC. RPM until engine speed drops to 1400 rpm, then INC. RPM until engine speed reaches 1500 rpm. Finally, place selector switches in AUTOMATIC OPERATION. Engine speed should return to original rpm. Repeat this procedure on remaining engines, working inboard on symmetrical pairs—i.e., 2 and 5, 3 and 4. Rpm's quoted are approximate. You are looking for direction of control primarily and not for specific rpm. However, when switches are released, pitch change must stop and rpm should not overshoot over 100 rpm unless the propeller selector switches are sticking. Anticipate instrument lag, power build-up, and power drop; release the switches about 50 to 100 rpm shy of the value you are shooting for. All engine rpm's should return to their original value after this check.

i. Momentary Feather Check—Completed. Perform check in this order: Engines 1, 2, 3, 4, 5, and 6. All engines should return to their original rpm after this check. Raise the propeller feather switch guard. Place your fingers behind the switch guard, actuate the switch with your thumb, and immediately slap the guard down with your fingers. Shoot for a 100-rpm drop-off and automatic return to the original rpm. This checks the fast rate feather operation.

> **CAUTION**
>
> Do not leave the propeller feather switch in FEATHER longer than 1/4 of a second, or the propellers will go into full feather.
>
> Stand by on the mixture control levers and, in the event of a malfunction, move to IDLE CUT-OFF immediately to lessen the possibility of a fire.

j. Master Motor—2700 rpm.

ENGINE RUN-UP (Cont'd)

Note

If you are proceeding with the cabin pressure wing shutoff valve and carburetor preheat checks, the master motor should remain at 1700 rpm.

3. Cabin Pressure Wing Shutoff Valve and Carburetor Preheat Checks (all six engines at one time)— Completed.

Note

These checks need only be performed following periodic inspections and whenever maintenance on the system has been performed.

a. Aft Cabin Pressure Shutoff Valve Switch—OFF.

b. Turbo Boost Selector Lever—10 position.

c. Throttle Levers—Adjust to obtain 35 inches M.P.

d. Cabin Pressure Wing Shutoff Valve Switches—L. WING ON and R. WING ON.

e. Carburetor Preheat Switches—ON and check the following:

   (1) Ceasing of cabin pressure air flow into the cabin.

   (2) M. P. drop of 2 to 4 inches.

   (3) Rapid increase in carburetor air temperature.

Do not allow CAT. to exceed 43°C.

f. Carburetor Preheat Switches—OFF and check the following:

   (1) Resumption of cabin pressure air flow into the cabin.

   (2) Rise in M. P.

   (3) Decrease in carburetor air temperature.

g. Aft Cabin Pressure Shutoff Valve Switch—ON.

h. Cabin pressure wing shutoff switches—L. WING OFF and note decrease in air flow; then R. WING OFF and note further decrease in air flow.

i. Turbo Booster Selector Lever—ZERO.

j. Throttles—Idle.

k. Master Motor—2700 rpm.

4. Barometric Pressure Checks—Completed. Set throttles to manifold pressure values observed by second engineer prior to engine start. Observe the rpm, torque, and fuel flow of all engines while you are making this check in order to insure a positive check of return from the high fan drive and spark advance

ENGINE RUN-UP (Cont'd)

checks before proceeding to higher powers. Proceed with the following checks:

a. Engine Cooling Fan Speed Check.

Fan Speed Control Switches—HIGH RPM and check torque pressure and rpm drop (approximately 100 rpm). Normal torque pressure drop is 10 to 20 psi.

Fan Speed Control Switches—LOW RPM and check torque pressure and rpm return to normal. After return to normal, check the anti-icing temperature again to see that the dump valves are open and temperatures have receded. On aircraft that have a master temperature indicator, return the selector switch to the number of the engine with highest CHT. Torque pressure and rpm should now be stabilized, so proceed with the next check.

b. Spark Advance Check.

Spark Advance Switches—ADVANCE and check for a definite rise in torque pressure up to 6 psi and an rpm increase of 25 to 50.

Note

If a definite rise in torque pressure is not noted, either a malfunction of the spark advance system or improper spark timing exists. A torque pressure rise in excess of 6 psi may be indicative of an engine out of time. Although an engine slightly out of time will operate satisfactorily, engine efficiency (maximum economy) will be affected.

Spark Advance Switches—RETARD and check for a drop in torque pressure to normal.

Note

In the event that the torque indicating system does not determine proper spark advance operation, use the engine analyzer as follows:

(1) Index the cycle selector switch to D1 cylinder and select the desired engine on the condition selector switch.

(2) Mark the scope at the normal firing event with a soft pencil.

(3) Move the spark advance switch to ADVANCE. The scope pattern will shift to the left approximately 5/16 inch in a proper spark advance operation.

(4) Return the spark advance switch to RETARD. If proper operation occurs, the pattern will shift back to its original position.

ENGINE RUN-UP (Cont'd)

> **CAUTION**
>
> Spark must be retarded before going to higher power. If in doubt of spark position, make a single ignition check. If the spark is still advanced, the rpm drop will be negligible.

Note

Note oil, carburetor air, and cylinder head temperatures before proceeding with the next check.

5. Ignition System Check—Completed. This check should be performed first on engines 1 and 6, recording rpm drop, then retarding throttles to idle; second, engines 2 and 5, recording rpm drop, then retarding throttles to idle; and third, engines 3 and 4, recording rpm drop, then retarding throttles to idle. Keep your left hand on the throttle of the engine being checked so that it may be retarded in the event of "cutting-out" of the engine due to a faulty ignition system or inadvertent turning off of the ignition switch. If either occurs, retard the throttle immediately, move the mixture to IDLE CUT-OFF, and allow the engine to stop. Clear the engine and restart.

Use your right hand to manipulate the ignition switches. Normal engine drop-off when operating on one magneto is 35 to 75 rpm; maximum permissible is 100 rpm. Normal torque drop is 10 to 15 psi.

> **CAUTION**
>
> Drop-offs *lower* or *higher* than these indications must be corrected prior to take-off.

Note

When altitudes above 34,000 feet are anticipated, maximum rpm drop-off is 60.

Use the following procedure to check individual engines in the recommended sequence:

 a. No. 1 Ignition Switch—L and note rpm drop-off.

 b. No. 1 Ignition Switch—To detent between L and R and note rpm return to normal.

 c. No. 1 Ignition Switch—R and note rpm drop-off.

 d. No. 1 Ignition Switch—Detent L, and back to BOTH and note rpm return to normal. Do not switch from R back to BOTH too rapidly or the ignition relays will chatter causing violent backfiring.

 e. Repeat steps a thru d on remaining engines in the recommended sequence. When the above procedure is completed on the last symmetrical pair of engines,

ENGINE RUN-UP (Cont'd)

the first pair that was checked will be cool enough to continue with the next check.

6. Full Power No Boost Checks—Completed. These checks may be performed on one engine at a time or in symmetrical pairs as conditions, time, or engine temperatures permit. Use the following procedure to check engines:

   a. Intercooler Shutter Switches—OPEN.

   b. Advance throttle lever (or levers) of coolest engine to full open and check for proper acceleration. Allow this full throttle no boost power to stabilize for approximately 30 seconds. Observe rpm, M.P., torque, and fuel flow. If manifold pressure varies more than 3 inches between engines with a corresponding variation in torque reading (11 psi), the engine is not operating correctly or the propeller low pitch stop setting is incorrect. However, if the manifold pressure spread is greater than 3 inches and the torque pressure is greater than 11 psi, there is a malfunction in the system which must be corrected prior to flight.

7. Turbo Override and Single Turbo Check—Completed.

Note

This check need only be performed following periodic inspections and whenever maintenance on the system has been performed.

Note

Do not operate the turbo override system on more than two engines at a time. The turbo waste gate has a fast rate of travel when the vernier switch is OFF.

   a. Turbo Control Change-Over Switches—MANUAL, on the engines being checked.

   b. Turbo Control Vernier Switch—ON.

   c. Turbo Control Override Switches—Jiggle in the CLOSE position until a rise of 3 to 5 inches M.P. is obtained.

   d. Turbo Vernier Switch—OFF.

   e. Turbo Control Override Switches—Momentarily hold in the OPEN position until a drop of 1 to 2 inches M. P. is obtained.

   f. Turbo Control Change-Over Switches—AUTOMATIC and check that M. P. returns to the original value.

   g. Engine Supercharger Switches—R. H. ONLY. Check manifold pressure rise (approximately 6 inches).

   h. Engine Supercharger Switches—BOTH and check M. P. drop to original value.

ENGINE RUN-UP (Cont'd)

 i. Intercooler Shutter Switches—OPEN. Check positions with gunners or ground observer.

Note

If engine temperatures permit, continue on to next check. If not, retard throttles to allow engines to cool and repeat steps 6a thru 7i on remaining engines.

8. Full Power With Boost Checks—Completed.

 a. Turbo Boost Selector—Advance smoothly to position 7. To avoid sudden overboost of engines, always exercise due caution when moving turbosupercharger controls or when moving throttles of an engine if turbosupercharger controls are set.

 b. Turbo Calibration Knobs — Trim M. P. to 55 inches.

 c. Water Injection Switches—ON and note decrease in fuel flow and an increase in water pressure to 23 to 27 psi on aircraft with electrical derichment and 30 to 36 psi on aircraft with hydraulic derichment.

Note

If there is not a proper rise in water pressure, the water injection switches must be turned OFF immediately.

 d. Turbo Calibration Knobs—Trim to 60 inches M. P. and note rpm, torque, and fuel flow.

Note

If desired, full take-off power may be set up in lieu of the 60-inch check.

 e. Water Injection Switches—OFF and note rise in fuel flow. To prevent flooding the engines when reducing power, water injection must be turned OFF before reaching 55 inches M. P.

 f. Turbo Boost Selector—Zero and not M. P. drop.
 g. Throttle Levers—Retard to Idle.
 h. Repeat steps 6a thru 8g on remaining engines.

Note

After all reciprocating engines have been checked and trimmed to 60 inches M.P. with water injection ON, check that the index marks on the knobs are in the same relative position with each other. If the index mark of an individual knob is not in the relative position of the index marks of the other knobs, that engine must be checked for turbo system malfunction or induction system leaks. Upon completion of the check, re-align the index mark on each knob with the index mark on its housing without disturbing the screw driver adjustment.

TAXIING.

> **CAUTION**
>
> When any malfunction of the hydraulic system or related electrical circuits is indicated during taxiing, e.g., if the canoe doors creep open during taxiing and do not return to and remain in the closed position with the landing gear control switch in the EXTEND position, the aircraft must be brought to a smooth stop as soon as possible. *Do not* stop the aircraft suddenly since doing so would cause the aircraft to rock and, in the event that the nose gear is unlocked, this rocking action could cause the nose gear to retract. After the aircraft is stopped, install the landing gear down locks and investigate and correct the malfunction prior to further taxiing.

1. Nose Wheel Steering Switch—ON. This switch energizes the main hydraulic system pump motor and actuates the main hydraulic system selector valve to provide pressure for nose wheel steering. This pressure is indicated on the engineer's hydraulic pressure gage and is indicated only when the airplane is on the ground.

2. Engineer's Taxi Configuration—Checked. Check the pressure in the brake system and nose wheel steering hydraulic system. These readings are obtained from the engineer. Never release the parking brake before checking for normal brake pressure. Never start to taxi until the engineer tells you he is prepared. Request, "Engineer's taxi configuration," over interphone.

3. Receive Ground Man's Report—"Nose wheel doors full open, all static wires removed, wheel chocks removed, external power unit cleared, disconnecting." After all checks are completed on the "During Engine Warm-up" check list and the engineer is ready to taxi, have the ground observer check to be certain that all obstructions have been removed and that the aircraft is clear. Before the aircraft commander clears the ground observer off interphone, the ground observer will give his report. He will then pass the ground communications cord into the forward compartment, come forward, and signal to the aircraft commander that he is clear to taxi.

1. Taxi configuration. "Alternators on the line and paralleled, brake and nose steering pressure normal, ready to taxi."

   a. A minimum of two alternators must be on the line and in parallel.

   b. Note and report brake and steering pressures at frequent intervals during all taxi operations in congested areas and prior to turns.

   Note

   It is permissible to taxi with the master motor set at 2000 rpm.

Section II
Normal Procedures

T.O. 1B-36D(II)-1

Minimum TURNING RADIUS

MINIMUM WIDTH OF RUNWAY—300 FT.;
MINIMUM DISTANCE FOR TURNING AND
LINING UP WITH RUNWAY—400 FT.

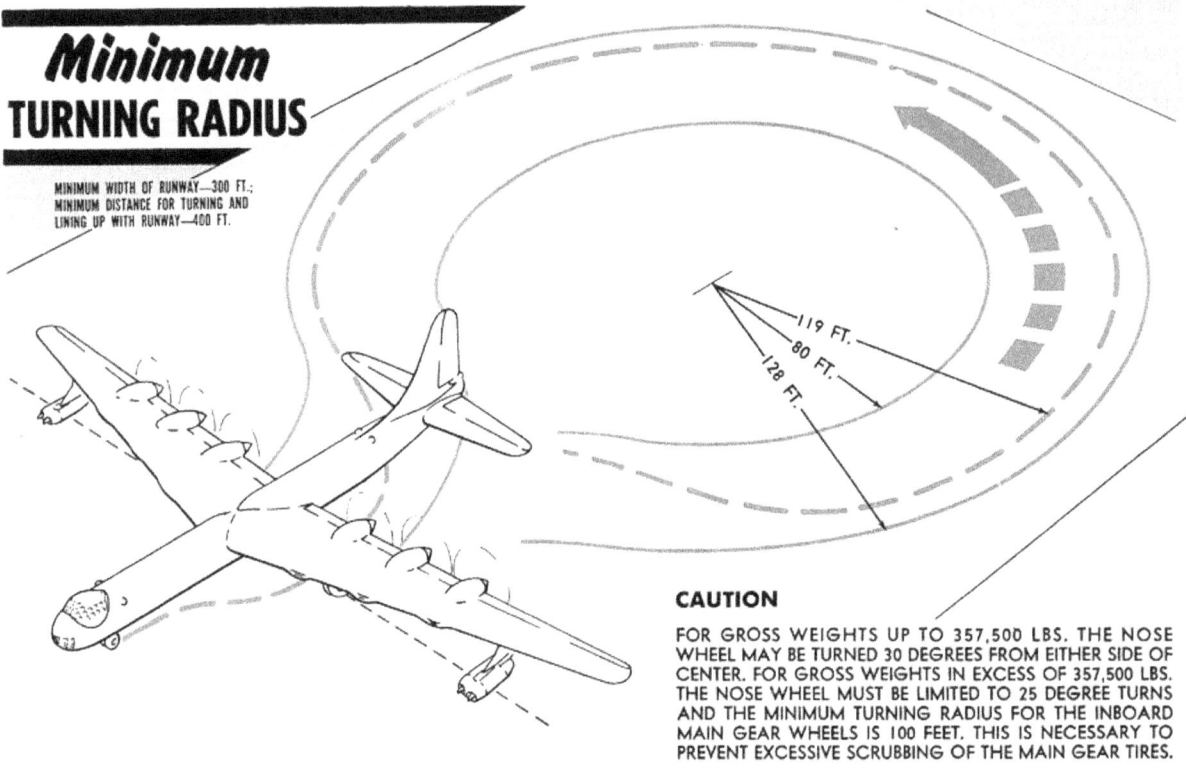

CAUTION

FOR GROSS WEIGHTS UP TO 357,500 LBS. THE NOSE WHEEL MAY BE TURNED 30 DEGREES FROM EITHER SIDE OF CENTER. FOR GROSS WEIGHTS IN EXCESS OF 357,500 LBS. THE NOSE WHEEL MUST BE LIMITED TO 25 DEGREE TURNS AND THE MINIMUM TURNING RADIUS FOR THE INBOARD MAIN GEAR WHEELS IS 100 FEET. THIS IS NECESSARY TO PREVENT EXCESSIVE SCRUBBING OF THE MAIN GEAR TIRES.

Figure 2-4.

TAXIING (Cont'd)

4. Interphone and Alarm Bell Check—Completed. The aircraft commander will announce on private interphone, "Crew, this is Aircraft Commander. All crew members switch to normal interphone for interphone and alarm bell check." The aircraft commander will then ring the alarm bell. All compartment commanders will report. "Normal interphone and alarm bell loud and clear, ready to taxi." This check will be made by compartments, progressing from tail to nose.

5. Call Control Tower—Taxi instructions. While the aircraft commander is clearing with the ground observer, the pilot will contact the control tower and receive taxi instructions and clearance to taxi.

6. Inboard Propeller Reverse Selector Switch—READY. Propeller reverse thrust will be used to aid in controlling taxi speed. This reduces the use of brakes and increases their usefulness. Continuous cycling of the propellers will not be used; slight adjust-

TAXIING (Cont'd)

ments of throttle to control the forward speed will be used instead. For normal taxi operation, No. 3 and 4 propellers will be used in reverse pitch. When taxiing with tail winds or when taxiing down slopes, it may be necessary to have two pairs of propellers in reverse. The aircraft commander will move the inboard propeller reverse selector switch to READY and stand by to reverse.

Note

Outboard propellers should not be reversed during normal taxiing except in an emergency. Reversing outboard propeller below 40 mph IAS results in sudden aileron movement which could cause aileron damage.

7. "Taxiing." Announce "Taxiing" over the interphone. Allow the aircraft to roll forward from its parked position and check braking action before pushing the reverse pitch switch to reverse the inboard propellers. This will eliminate the necessity for additional power on the center and outboard engines in order to get the aircraft in motion.

Note

There will be a gunner in each blister on interphone during all taxi operations. At night the forward and aft gunners will be equipped with Aldis lamps.

The control surfaces must be locked at all times during taxiing. The B-36 has a normal nose-down attitude while on the ground. Don't let this attitude bother you, you'll become accustomed to it. Directional control while taxiing is accomplished hydraulically through the use of the steering wheel.

CAUTION

In order to minimize drag loads on the main gear, steer with the nose gear and avoid steering with the brakes; avoid braking over ice-spotted surfaces as much as possible; minimize the sudden application of brakes while taxiing, especially at low speeds and when the brakes are cold; and reduce taxiing as much as feasible.

Jet air plugs should be closed during taxi operations. This will expose the jet engines to a minimum amount of foreign material while propellers are in reverse.

Section II
Normal Procedures

T.O. 1B-36D(II)-1

TAXIING (Cont'd)

> **CAUTION**
>
> If the jet engines have been running, the thirty minute cooling period with jet air plugs open will apply.

This airplane is the largest that you have yet encountered, and several new techniques must be learned before becoming adjusted to its size. One of these is the procedure used to make turns. Because of the make-up of the main gear "skate," the aircraft must be turned with caution to prevent skidding of tires. The airplane must be in motion before executing turns; use the largest turning radius possible and limit taxi speed to approximately 12 mph while turning in order to minimize tire wear and landing gear stress. Make alternate right and left turns, when practical, to equalize tire wear. Make a visual check of all gyros during taxiing. The minimum turning radius recommended for the nose gear is 119-feet for gross weights up to 357,500 pounds. The pivot point is about two-thirds from the outboard engine toward the wingtip. It must be remembered that you are about 50 feet in front of your main gear so that when lining up with the runway you must over turn and then bring the nose wheel back to the center line. A runway width of 300 feet is adequate for executing normal turns. After making a turn allow a short roll and stop with the nose wheel in line with the fuselage center line, thereby reducing nose wheel stresses at the start of take-off. Aircraft clearances are especially important during taxiing. The B-36's wing span of 230 feet will in many cases overlap on both sides of the taxi strip. Along taxi strips be careful to avoid damaging obstacles such as boundary lights, vehicles, etc. Use particular care at night; all crew members must be alert to avoid any obstructions. Use your taxi and landing lights and have your gunners observe for obstructions while taxiing. (For aircraft equipped with blisters at the lower aft sighting stations, the gunners will use Aldis lamps.) Partial retraction and extension of landing lights will throw some light in the desired direction when trying to see obstructions on the sides of the taxi strips. When in doubt about aircraft clearance, send out crew members with flashlights to act as "wing walkers." A tip is to use shadows cast by the aircraft to judge aircraft clearance while taxiing. Remember, be safety-conscious while taxiing as well as when flying.

> **CAUTION**
>
> The aircraft should not be taxied without brakes except in an extreme emergency.

STARTING JET ENGINES.

Jet engines are considered to be supplementary power for the B-36. They provide an ease of operation never before experienced in heavy gross weight take-offs and high altitude performance of a basically reciprocating engine-powered aircraft. Due to their relatively high specific fuel consumption, the jet engines should not be used unwisely.

Unlike the complex reciprocating engines, your jet engines are mechanically simple. Although a preflight run-up of the jets cannot be omitted, they need not be run during the "Preflight Operational Equipment Check" except to ground-check a new installation or to clear previous discrepancies. Ordinarily, if your jet engines were satisfactory on the last flight and the required visual inspections reveal nothing of any consequence, they may be started immediately prior to take-off with a power check constituting the preflight run-up.

Consult the maintenance records and the crew chief to find out which jet engines, if any, must be checked. Let your engineer know before engine start whether or not any jet engines are to be run so that he may arrange his run-up accordingly.

Once the engineer starts his reciprocating engine run-up, it will be necessary for him to utilize the interphone and the ground observer if ground time is to be held to a minimum. Therefore, the best time to start the jet engines is probably after the engineer has finished his power checks and has shut down No. 1 and No. 6 engines. After the jets are started and are idling satisfactorily, all but two alternator-equipped engines which have their alternators on the line may be shut down.

Record the starting times, temperature of each hot start, and the number of minutes at each power setting. The "Time Today" and "Hot Starts" are recorded in the Form 781 (Form 1), along with other noted discrepancies. The number of minutes at each power setting affects fuel consumption and should be given to your engineer.

By the time you have taxied into position for reciprocating engine run-up, the control tower should have dispatched a fire truck to the area so that you can start your jet engines.

Before starting jet engines, make certain that the danger areas, as shown in figure 2-5, are clear of personnel and ground equipment. When a jet engine instrument is read during starting or during changes of power and rpm, the instrument panel may be vibrated to get accurate readings from the instruments.

Cautions To Observe During Jet Engine Starting.

Throttle Sensitivity. The throttles are very sensitive to throttle lever movement; therefore, extreme care must be used when operating the throttle levers.

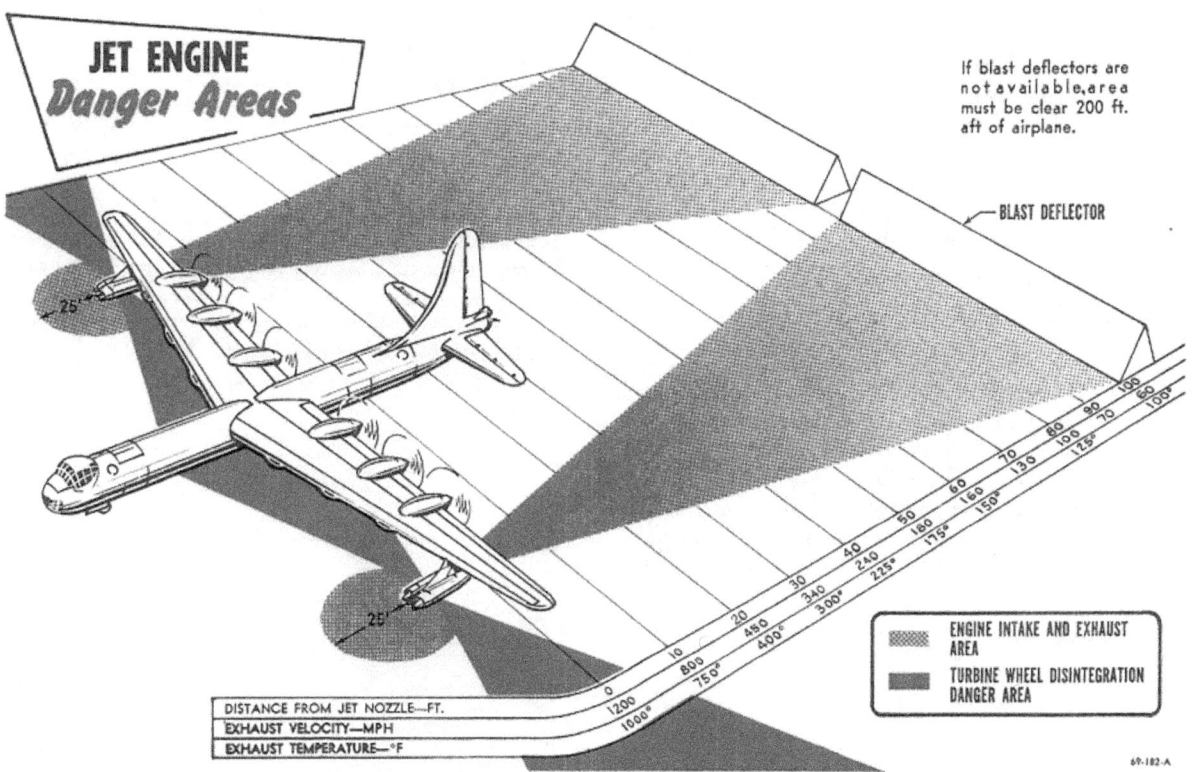

Figure 2-5.

Section II
Normal Procedures

T.O. 1B-36D(II)-1

Hot Starts. For information on hot starts, refer to "Jet Engines," Section V.

Failure to Start. If the engine fails to start before 11 per cent rpm is reached, close the throttle, close the engine fuel valve, and release the starter switch. Allow 3 minutes for fuel to drain from the combustion chambers before attempting another start.

Engine Starter Limitations. Operation of the engine starter is limited to three starting attempts of 45 seconds duration each. If more than three attempts are required, allow the starter to cool one hour. Do not attempt a start until the engine has come to a complete stop.

In the event false starts are experienced, operation of the starter is limited to two false starts of 20 seconds duration each and one actual start during a 30-minute period. If necessary this cycle may be repeated immediately; however, after the second cycle a one-hour cooling period will be required before any further attempt is made to start the engine.

Accelerations and Decelerations. The engine should accelerate from 50 to 100 per cent rpm in approximately 12 seconds. When 100 per cent rpm is obtained, the high rpm stop should prevent overspeeding. If time permits, accelerations and decelerations should be slow in order to prevent unnecessary wear and tear on the engine. If time does not permit, then rapid throttle movements can be accomplished and the fuel regulator will control the acceleration rate. The exhaust temperature during rapid acceleration may climb momentarily to a value over 690°C but not over maximum allowable for take-off and acceleration.

Starting Procedure.

The jet engines are simple to start and easy to operate, but always use your check list and complete it in the following sequence:

1. Notify engineer, "Set up jet start configuration."

2. All Circuit Breakers—IN. Push in all circuit breakers on the pilots' jet control panel. Don't forget the throttle circuit breakers.

3. Fire Detection Test Switches—TEST and release. This will test the continuity of the fire detection circuits from the jet pods to the lamps.

4. Throttle Selector Switches—Lever.

5. Throttles—Closed.

6. Pod Preheat Switch—OFF.

7. Nose De-ice Switch—OFF.

8. Oil Heater Switch—As required. Turn this switch ON to heat the jet engine oil if the ambient air temperature is below 5°C (41°F).

9. Oil Shutoff Valve Switches—OPEN.

10. Danger area clear and fire equipment standing by. Clear the starting area of personnel and equipment.

1. Jet Start Configuration—Checked and report, "Standing by for jet engine start."

 a. At least two alternators paralleled on the line (three on the line and one excited and standing by recommended).

 b. Engines with alternators, which are on the line, operating above 1200 rpm for heavy electrical loads to minimize wear on the constant-speed drives.

 c. Two tank valve switches OPEN and two booster pump switches ON in each wing.

STARTING JET ENGINES (Cont'd)

If the jet engines cannot be started in the parking position, have the aft gunners clear the danger area and have a fire truck proceed to the starting position.

11. Air Plug Switches—OPEN. Check doors visually. The aircraft commander will make a visual check of J-1 and J-2 while the pilot is visually checking J-3 and J-4 to see if the doors are open.

12. Manifold Valve Switches (L and R)—OPEN.

13. Booster Pump Switches (L and R)—ON. No pressure will be indicated on the fuel pressure gage until the throttles are advanced to open the stopcock.

14. Ignition Start Switches—NORMAL.

15. (Deleted.)

16. J-1 Engine Fuel Valve—OPEN.

17. J-1 Fuel and Oil pressure Gages—Note reading.

18. Notify ground observers or aft gunner—"Starting J-1." If a ground observer is present he will move to a position where the engine being started can be seen and will report any unusual conditions.

19. J-1 Starter Switch—Hold ON until the engine attains 20 per cent rpm.

20. J-1 Throttle—OPEN at 6 per cent rpm to obtain 25 to 30 psi fuel pressure. Move the throttles slowly to prevent overshooting due to the lag in the pressure indication. Maintain 25 to 30 psi during initial acceleration to avoid excessive temperatures in the tail pipe and around the shroud ring and shroud ring binding which are caused by higher fuel pressures.

Although the engines will probably start at 6 to 11 per cent rpm, the starter switch should be held ON to aid engine acceleration until 20 per cent rpm has been reached. This reduces the possibility of excessive tail pipe temperatures during the initial acceleration period. During a normal start, combustion will occur immediately after fuel pressure is indicated.

21. J-1 Oil Pressure—Report indication on interphone. This precludes the possibility of operating an engine with no oil pressure and also permits the crew member keeping the jet engine log to maintain an accurate record of operating time.

22. J-1 Starter Switch—Release at 20 per cent rpm.

23. J-1 Throttle—Adjust to maintain idle rpm (25 to 30 per cent) keeping the tail pipe temperature below maximum allowable used for normal flight operation.

24. J-2, J-3, and J-4—Repeat steps 15 thru 23.

25. All Ignition Start Switches—OFF.

Section II
Normal Procedures

T.O. 1B-36D(II)-1

STOPPING JET ENGINES (GROUND).

The pilots will stop the jet engines as follows:

STOPPING RECIPROCATING ENGINES.

The engineer will stop the reciprocating engines as follows:

Note

Jet engines must be stopped prior to shutting down the last two alternator-equipped reciprocating engines.

1. Throttles—Idle for 3 minutes; then CLOSE. The 3-minute idle period will stabilize temperatures throughout the engines, preventing malfunctions due to differential expansion and contraction on engine parts. Remember that the tail pipe temperature indicator takes the temperature at the tail pipe only.

Note

If shroud rub is being experienced during jet engine shutdowns, the following procedure is recommended: Slowly retard the throttle to approximately 70 per cent rpm and hold this setting for one to three minutes. Then, close the throttle rapidly to the full-closed position. When the throttle is fully closed, combustion will cease immediately and the exhaust temperature will drop rapidly. The engine will coast to a stop. This short holding period at 70 per cent also permits the engine to properly scavenge the oil system.

2. Jet Booster Pump Switches—OFF.

3. Engine Fuel Valves—CLOSE below 10 per cent rpm.

4. Nose de-ice Switch—OFF.

5. Pod Preheat Switch—OFF.

6. Oil Heater Switch—OFF.

7. Oil Shutoff Valve Switches—CLOSE after engines stop rotating.

8. Throttle Circuit Breakers—OUT.

9. Jet Air Plug Switches—CLOSE, after thirty minutes.

Jet air plugs should remain open for approximately thirty minutes after stopping jet engines to allow sufficient circulation of air through the engine to dissipate the residual heat. It will be necessary to vary this procedure as weather conditions dictate. The advisability of leaving the airplugs open during blow-

1. Air Plug Switches—OPEN until air plugs are fully open. This will allow the engines to cool to 190°C before shutdown, and will allow heat to dissipate after shutdown.

2. Master Motor Speed Control Lever—Full DECREASE.

3. Propeller Selector Switches—FIXED PITCH.

4. Booster Pump Switches—OFF.

5. Alternator Controls—Positioned.

  a. Voltage and Frequency Selector Switch—To position of alternator-equipped engine to be shut down.

  b. Alternator Breaker—OPEN. Observe that the alternator breaker lamp lights.

  c. Frequency Control Knob—Full Decrease.

  d. Repeat the above steps on alternator-equipped engines, one at a time, until only one alternator is left. After completing the above steps on the last alternator, re-establish electrical power by reclosing the alternator breaker or by placing the external power switch ON if an auxiliary power unit is available. If the correct phase sequence lamp is on, the APU is plugged in and standing by.

STOPPING ENGINES (Cont'd)

ing snow, sand, etc. must be carefully considered by the aircraft commander. If these conditions exist, air plugs will not be closed above 100°C tail pipe temperature and zero per cent rpm.

Note

Gunners will observe jet engines for residual fire during all jet engine shutdowns and immediately report any fire.

DURING RECIPROCATING ENGINE SHUTDOWN.

The aircraft commander will accomplish the following during reciprocating engine shutdown:

1. Parking Brake Control—ON.
2. Propeller Reverse Selector Switches—SAFE (lights out).
3. Nose Wheel Steering Switch—OFF.
4. Flight Instrument Switches—OFF.
5. Contact engineer, "Ready to stop engines."

CAUTION

Aircraft commander, engineer, and the lower aft gunners will remain on interphone. The pilot will have radio tuned to tower frequency until the last propeller has stopped turning.

6. Radio Equipment—OFF.

6. Engine Analyzer Power Switch—OFF.
7. Perform idle speed and mixture check as engines are shut down as follows:

   a. Check to see that cylinder head temperature is at 190°C or below.

   b. Throttle Lever—Advance to 1700 to 1800 rpm and allow engine to operate at this rpm for approximately 10 seconds for scavenging purposes. Then return to idle and allow rpm to stabilize.

   c. Idle Speed—Checked. Should be set for 1100 rpm with throttles fully retarded, approximately 160°C (±10°) CHT, no wind condition, and average barometric pressure for seasonal conditions at the base at which your aircraft is primarily stationed. Allow a 30-rpm variation for each 10 mph effective head wind.

   d. Mixture Control Lever—IDLE CUT-OFF. When the mixture control is moved *slowly* to IDLE CUT-OFF, check the idle mixture setting for a minimum 5-rpm rise and a maximum 10-rpm rise as indicated on the respective engine tachometer. Record the readings that do not fall within these limits so proper settings may be made at the earliest possible convenience. A minimum 5-rpm rise when leaning the mixture assures that the idle mixture is not too lean while the 10-rpm maximum rise prevents idling in the "too rich" range.

Note

When making the idle speed and mixture check on the last alternator-equipped engine, the hold-in switch must be actuated until the engine drops to 1000 rpm. Release the hold-in switch as soon as the engine drops below 1000 rpm and observe that the alternator breaker lamp comes on, indicating that the alternator breaker has opened.

CAUTION

Do not hold the alternator on the line until the engine stops. This will reduce the stress imposed on the constant speed drive input shaft since the peak load on the shaft occurs as the engine speed drops below 1000 rpm.

8. Fuel Tank Valve Switches—CLOSE.
9. Cross-Feed, Manifold, and Engine Valve Switches—OPEN.

Note

Allowing these valves to remain open will prevent fuel expansion damage to the main manifold line.

Section II
Normal Procedures

T.O. 1B-36D(II)-1

STOPPING ENGINES (Cont'd)

10. Individual Ignition Switches—OFF after propellers have stopped.

11. Master Ignition Switch—Pull Off.

12. Intercooler Shutter Switches—Close, until intercooler shutters are fully closed.

13. Static Propeller Feather Check—Completed.

Note

The static feather check is required only after engine shutdown following completion of the "Preflight Operational Equipment Check."

   a. Contact ground observer on interphone—"Ready for static feather check."

   b. Propeller Selector Switches—FIXED PITCH.

   c. All propeller feather switches FEATHER position for 30 seconds then return to NORMAL position (feather switch guards down).

Note

If longer than 30 seconds is required to feather any propeller (i.e., cold weather operation), wait at least two minutes before attempting to complete the feather operation. Allow feather motors to cool a minimum of two minutes between feather and unfeather operation. Allow a minimum of five minutes before attempting to complete another cycle if a recheck is required.

   d. The second engineer or a qualified observer will report all blade angles in the approximate feather position. Any propeller that will not reach the feather position on this check will not feather in the air and must be repaired or changed prior to flight.

   e. Propeller Selector Switch—INC RPM. Hold in INC RPM until normal low pitch position is reached.

   f. The second engineer or a qualified observer will report all blade angles returning to normal low pitch position.

14. Oil Cooler Door Mode Selector Switches — MANUAL.

15. Battery Switch—OFF.

16. Master Temperature Indicator—OFF.

Note

Thirty minutes after engine shutdown, have the propellers pulled through 10 blades with the starters. Energize the starter continuously for 10 blades.

DETAILED MISSION PLANNING.

Mandatory requirements for detailed mission planning are set forth in Air Force, major command, and local directives. The purpose here is to maintain a proper sequence of events and to remind the aircraft commander that a study of the proper directives and a common sense application of the principles involved will promote better teamwork in developing good flight planning techniques.

Note

Normally the basic Form F is completed during this planning phase; however, alterations will probably have to be made after the visual preflight inspection.

FORMAL BRIEFING.

As in "Detailed Mission Planning," the requirements for a formal briefing are set forth in other directives with which you must be familiar. Again, it is mentioned here to maintain proper sequence of events, to provide ready information as to the aircraft commander's responsibilities pertaining specifically to the B-36 aircraft, and to provide helpful suggestions or hints based on principles derived from experience gained in managing the B-36 combat crew. For aircraft commander's responsibilities see "Crew Duties," Section VIII.

CREW INSPECTION.

The time for crew inspection shall be established during formal briefing. Normally, the crew will report to the airplane for this inspection.

Note

During inclement weather, the inspection may be accomplished under any available shelter. After such an inspection, all equipment should be packed in A-3 bags, transported to the airplanes, and loaded aboard before "Final Crew Briefing."

In addition to the personal equipment required, each crew member will wear identification tags on each flight. The information on these tags must be kept current. All crew members will wear tags on a chain around their necks. Crew formation for crew inspection should be standardized so that all crew members know exactly what is expected of them. The crew will form on the left side of the aircraft and will lay out their personal equipment as shown in figure 2-6. Then the aircraft commander will accomplish the inspection as follows:

1. Give command, "Fall in," and call the roll.

2. Give commands, "Right face," "At ease," and "Inspect parachutes." Each crew member shall check the parachute of the man in front of him. The aircraft commander's parachute shall be checked by the pilot. After checking the parachutes of the men in front of them, the crew members standing next to last in each line shall turn around and check the parachute of the man on the end of each line. As each crew member completes his part of the parachute check, he shall assume the "at ease" position.

Note

If both chest-type and back-type parachutes are used, each crew member must check his own chest pack in addition to checking the back pack as indicated in the preceding paragraph.

3. Give commands, "Attention," "Left face," and "At ease." Check each crew member's displayed equipment for completeness and condition. Spot check any crew member's equipment as desired. Each crew member will come to attention as the aircraft commander approaches to inspect his equipment.

4. Read discrepancies which are pertinent to your mission as noted in Form 781 (Form 1).

5. Have the navigator give the crew a time "hack."

6. Designate specific crew members for command of the nose, radio, and aft compartments. Each of these men will command his compartment under all conditions. He will be responsible for the execution of all normal and emergency instructions affecting his compartment, and will subsequently notify the aircraft commander.

7. Give the crew any special instructions not previously covered and order any special checks necessary on preflight. Also, answer any questions the crew may have. Assign oxygen stations to extra crew members and passengers.

8. Announce the time for the final crew briefing.

9. Give commands, "Attention" and "Dismissed."

BOARDING AIRCRAFT.

All equipment will be loaded and stowed before "Final Crew Briefing" time. Each crew member will make a preflight check of his oxygen station and mask in accordance with the procedure described in "Oxygen System," Section IV. In checking his interphone, each crew member will use his oxygen mask mike and helmet, and check the normal interphone for side tone. He will then plug in his normal headset and switch to PVT INTER, checking this interphone channel in the same manner as the normal interphone check.

Compartment commanders will insure that all regulators in the compartment have been checked and that

Section II
Normal Procedures

T.O. 1B-36D(II)-1

CREW *Inspection* . . . . .

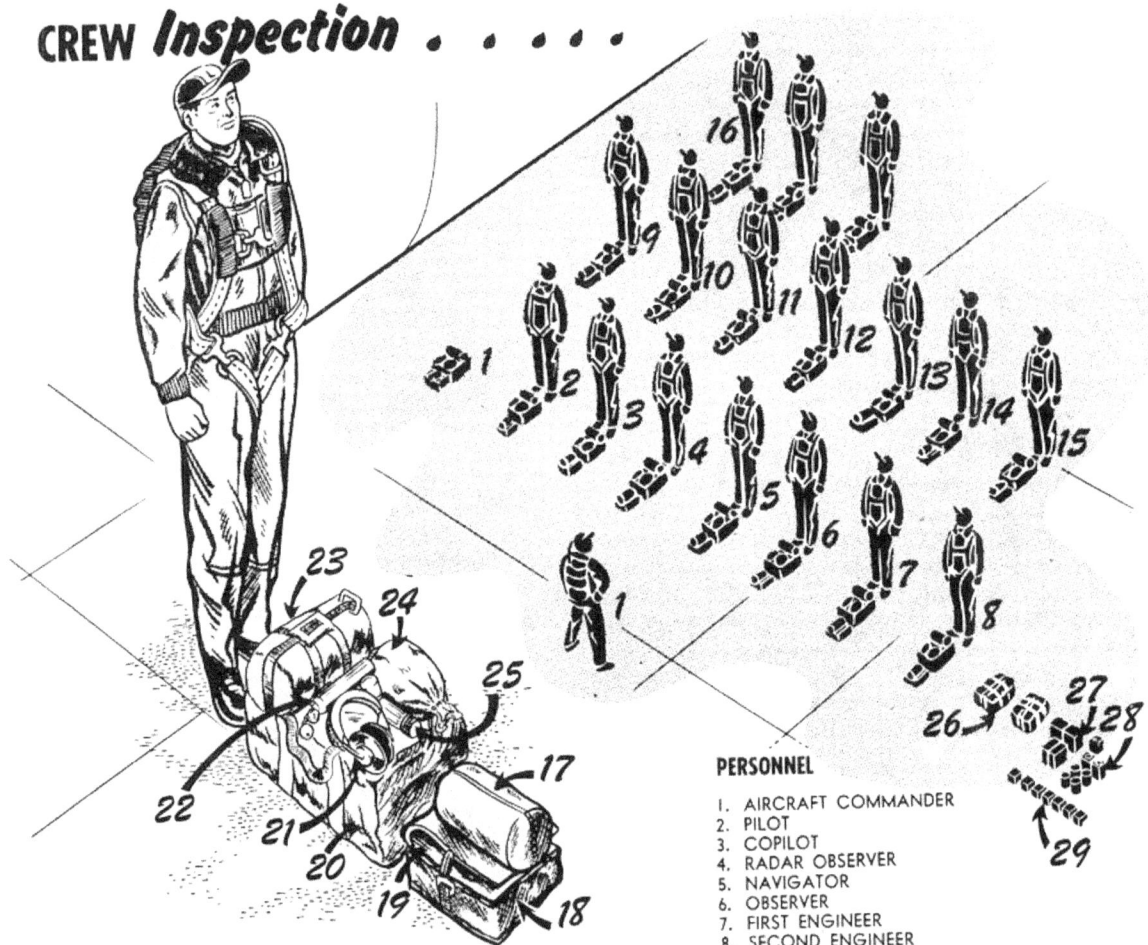

a uniform, full oxygen supply is provided. In addition each will check that all regulators are in OFF, NORMAL.

Note

Before boarding the aircraft, the second engineer will check that the bomb bay doors are open with safety locks installed and that the auxiliary power unit has been started and is operating properly. If the bomb bay doors are closed, they will be pumped open and safety locks will be installed prior to starting the auxiliary power unit.

AIRCRAFT VISUAL PREFLIGHT INSPECTION.

HOW TO MAKE A GOOD PREFLIGHT.

The aircraft commander is responsible for performance of preflight inspections; however, the complexity of the aircraft and the detailed check lists make it necessary for the aircraft commander to delegate some of

PERSONNEL

1. AIRCRAFT COMMANDER
2. PILOT
3. COPILOT
4. RADAR OBSERVER
5. NAVIGATOR
6. OBSERVER
7. FIRST ENGINEER
8. SECOND ENGINEER
9. FIRST RADIO OPERATOR
10. SECOND RADIO OPERATOR
11. UPPER AFT GUNNER (RIGHT)
12. UPPER AFT GUNNER (LEFT)
13. LOWER AFT GUNNER (RIGHT)
14. LOWER AFT GUNNER (LEFT)
15. TAIL GUNNER
16. PASSENGERS

PERSONAL EQUIPMENT

17. ANTI-EXPOSURE SUIT
18. ONE-MAN LIFE RAFT
19. MAE WEST
20. A-3 BAG
21. HEADSET AND MICROPHONE
22. BAIL-OUT BOTTLE
23. CHEST-TYPE PARACHUTE
24. OXYGEN MASK AND HELMET
25. FLASHLIGHT

MISCELLANEOUS EQUIPMENT

26. EXTRA PARACHUTES, OXYGEN MASKS, AND BAIL-OUT BOTTLES (ATTACHED TO PARACHUTES)
27. FOOD AND BEVERAGE CONTAINERS
28. ALDIS LAMPS
29. FIRST AID KITS

79.115-A

Figure 2-6.

Aircraft Commander's Visual Preflight Inspection

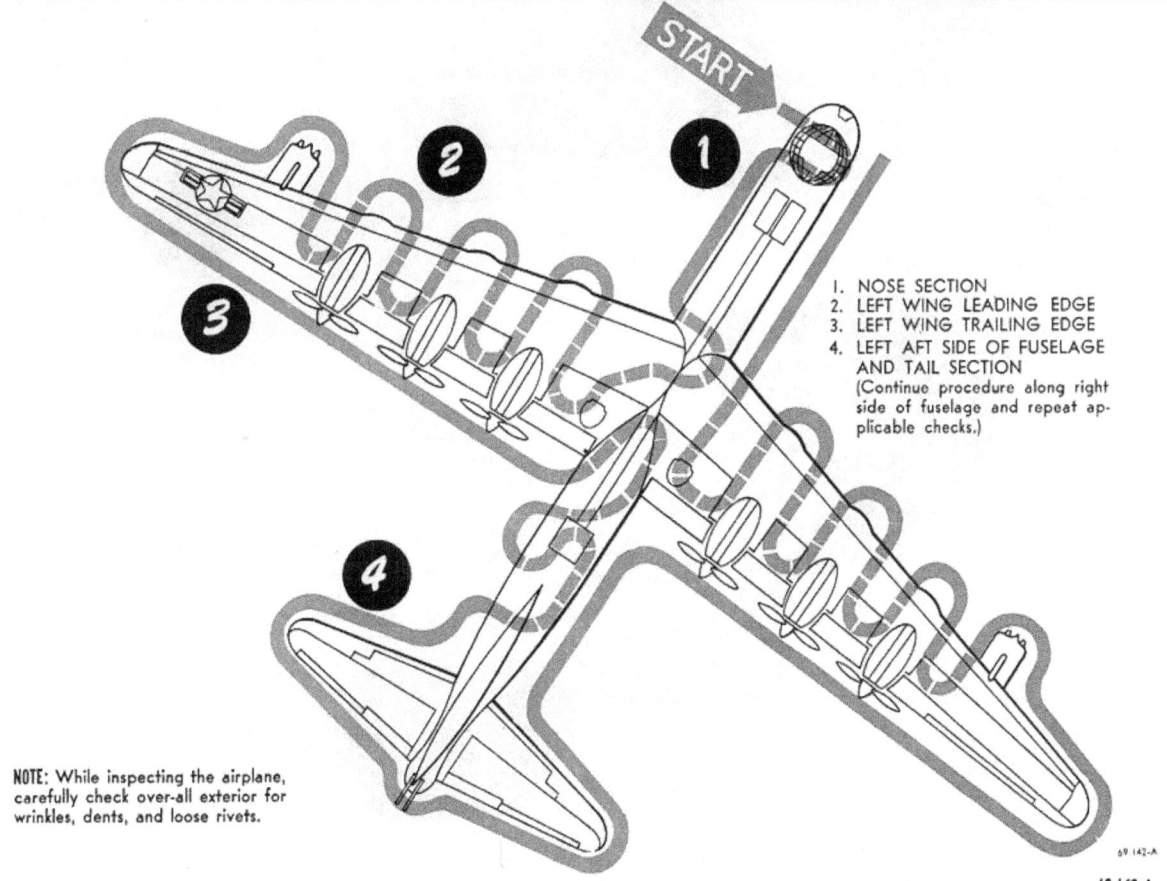

Figure 2-7. (Sheet 1)

these preflight duties to the pilot and copilot as well as to other crew members. Being a teamwork airplane, close co-ordination and wise planning are required to effect a good preflight in a minimum amount of time. A good aircraft commander guards against fatiguing himself or his crew before starting on the mission. At the same time, he does not make a sketchy preflight inspection and risk an aircraft accident. Plan wisely and delegate responsibility.

A good aircraft commander will make the checks listed in figure 2-7 carefully and completely. Omit nothing. Follow the route shown in this figure. As your training and familiarization with the airplane progress, you will be able to speed up this inspection so that it does not hold up your preparation for flight, but still accomplishes its purpose. It is the aircraft commander's responsibility to see that the inspection is actually made and not just signed off on the AF Form 781 (Form 1).

Normally about two hours before take-off, it is necessary to complete all phases of the aircraft preflight and final crew briefing. This time will vary with the crew experience. In order to accomplish the preflight inspection in minimum time, it is well to delegate certain duties to the pilot and copilot. As aircraft commander you are personally responsible for the entire preflight inspection, but that does not mean you will accomplish the entire inspection yourself. Delegate the responsibility of certain portions of the aircraft preflight inspection to each pilot.

Have your pilots accompany you on preflight inspections until they become thoroughly familiar with inspection procedures and can be relied upon to make an inspection by themselves. Then you will be able to divide the aircraft up in sections, having one pilot inspect the top of the wings and the other pilot inspect one side of the aircraft while you inspect the other

Section II
Normal Procedures

T.O. 1B-36D(II)-1

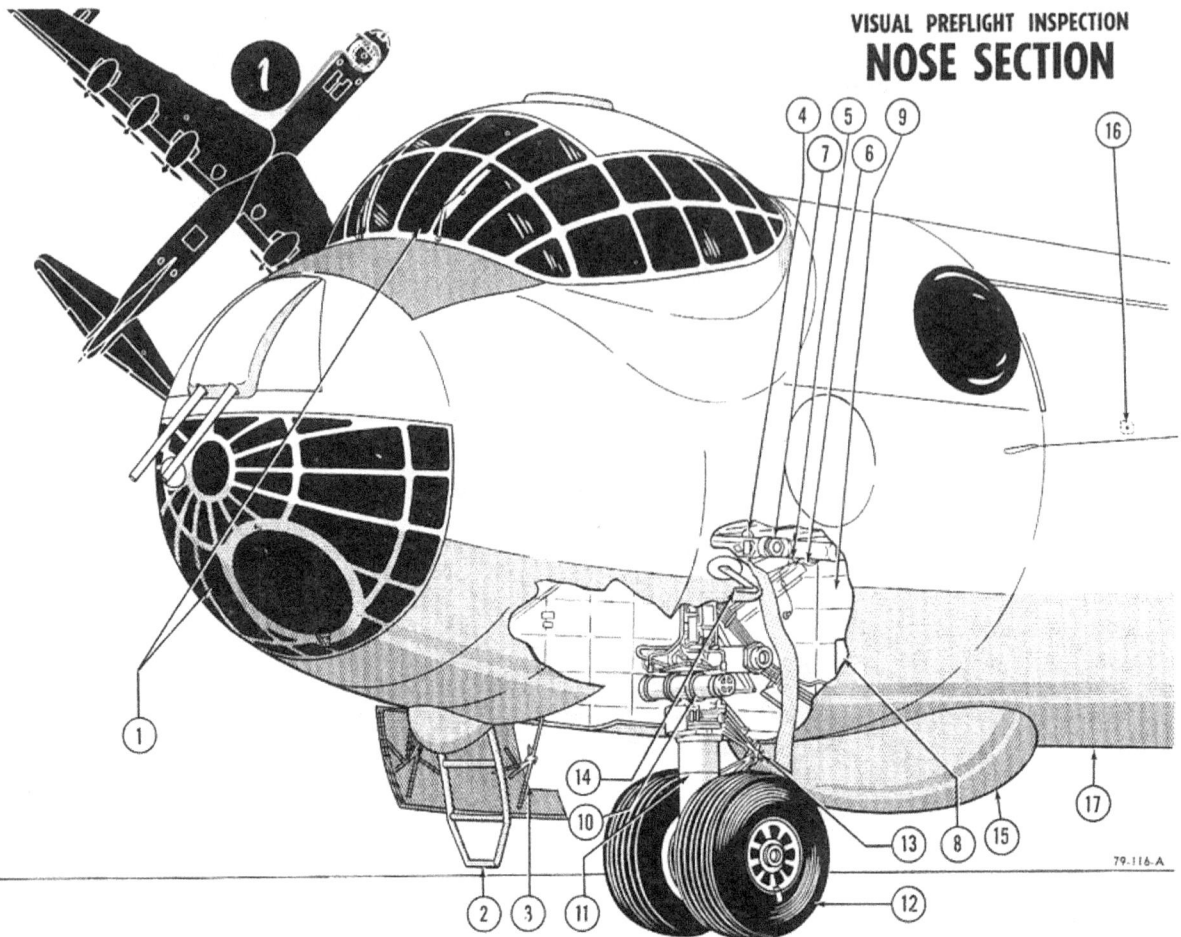

VISUAL PREFLIGHT INSPECTION
NOSE SECTION

1. Nose glass and pilots' windshield for cracks and cleanliness.
2. Condition of nose entrance ladder, linkage, and stowage provisions.
3. Condition of nose wheel well doors, linkage, and pick-up arm.
4. Nose gear ground safety lock in place.
5. Nose gear latch mechanism and latch release link and pin in place.
6. Emergency release cables and pulleys for proper rigging.
7. Nose gear latch spot light for proper operation and security at mounting.
8. Battery for mounting, connections, and signs of corrosion in general area of battery.
9. Nose wheel area for hydraulic leaks.
10. Nose steering unit and equipment, including cable system and nose steering safety switch.
11. Oleo strut for cleanliness, proper inflation (3 inches plus or minus 1/4 inch), and general condition.
12. Tires and wheels for general condition, cuts, blisters, proper inflation, slippage, and wear. Security of co-axial retaining plate and pick-up arm roller.
13. Nose gear scissors for condition (up and connected).
14. Pitot mast covers removed and tube clear.
15. Radar dome for cracks.
16. Static port clear.
17. Fuselage for cracks, blister for cleanliness and cracks.

Figure 2-7. (Sheet 2)

side. This will expedite the inspection and reduce the individual time and effort expended to accomplish a full preflight.

The aircraft commander, pilot, and copilot will inspect and check the aircraft as outlined in the following preflight check lists.

Aircraft Commander.

1. Oxygen supply and equipment checked in accordance with existing oxygen preflight procedure. Check normal interphone using helmet and oxygen mask, verifying side tone.

Note

During the preflight operational equipment check, only the station regulator need be checked, oxygen masks are not required.

2. Check private interphone with regular headset, verifying side tone.

3. Assist pilot in checking control surfaces.

4. Check all lights at aircraft commander's station.

5. Visual preflight of aircraft as shown in figure 2-6.

6. Stow personal equipment.

7. Place jet air plugs switches in CLOSE.

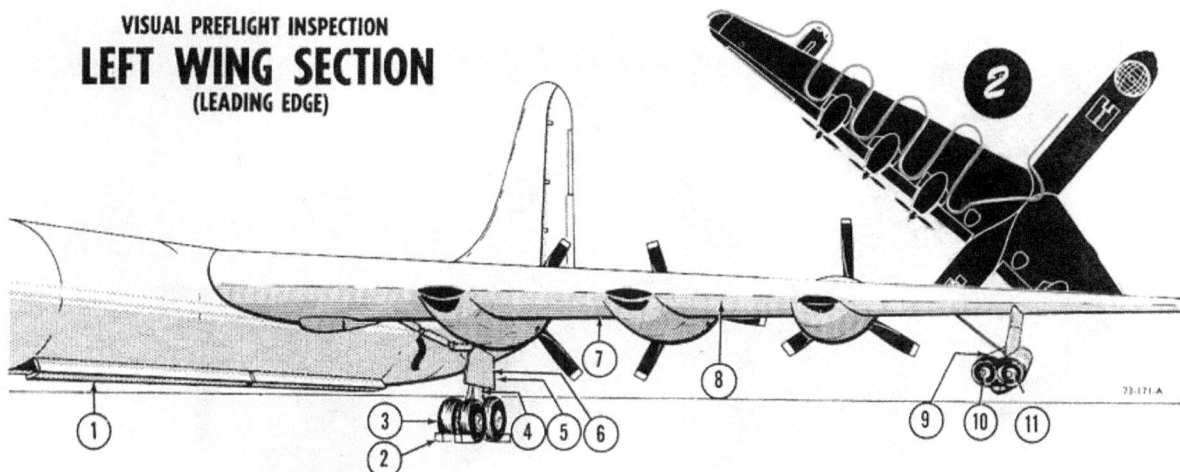

VISUAL PREFLIGHT INSPECTION
LEFT WING SECTION
(LEADING EDGE)

1. Forward bomb bay and wing center section area for hydraulic and fuel leaks and for general condition.
2. M.L.G. safety lock and wheel chocks in place.
3. Inspect tires and wheels for general condition, cuts, blisters, proper inflation, slippage and wear.
4. Left main wheels hydraulic brake lines, gear struts, and positioning jacks for leaks and safety switch for condition and mounting.
5. Oleo struts for cleanliness and proper inflation (3½ inches plus or minus ¼ inch.)
6. Condition of equalizer assembly, wheel fairing, and main column.
7. Underside of wing for loose rivets, cowling, inspection plates, open vents, fuel leaks, oil leaks, and cracks.
8. Leading edge for excessive dents and warping.
9. Jet engines 1 and 2 for loose cowling and general condition.
10. Jet engines starter cooling inlet plugs removed.
11. Jet air plugs open. Intakes for foreign material.

Figure 2-7. (Sheet 3)

8. Conduct final crew briefing and receive preflight report.

9. Final check of aircraft (down locks, pitot covers, control locks, wing access panels, and nose scissors).

Pilot.

1. Oxygen supply and equipment checked in accordance with existing oxygen preflight. Check normal interphone using helmet and oxygen mask, verifying side tone.

Note

During the preflight operational equipment check, only the station regulator need be checked, oxygen masks are not required.

2. Check private interphone with regular headset, verifying side tone.
3. All circuit breakers in.
4. Check parking brake pressure on engineers' auxiliary panel and set parking brakes.
5. Surface Controls and Trim Tabs—Checked. Before unlocking the controls, check for wind velocity and directions, and if possible, head the aircraft into the wind. Considerable difficulty may be experienced in moving the rudder and elevator in strong cross winds.

Under these conditions it will be necessary to head the airplane into the wind before a rudder movement check can be made. In the event ramp congestion prevents moving the aircraft into the wind, this check will be made when the aircraft is lined up into the wind prior to take-off.

Note

When the control lock switch is placed in the unlocked position, the red indicator lamp will go out the instant all lock actuators start their unlocking movement. If the green light does not come on after a slight delay, one or more control lock actuators are probably inoperative in the intermediate position. Even though the green light indicates controls unlocked, a complete freedom of movement check must be accomplished. When controls fail to unlock, check the appropriate control lock fuse in the right main power panel.

A ground observer will check proper movement of the control surfaces and tab. The controls should be checked in the following order; elevators, rudder, and ailerons. To expedite this check it is recommended that the trim control be moved in the same direction as the control surface and that the surfaces, servo tabs,

Section II
Normal Procedures

T.O. 1B-36D(II)-1

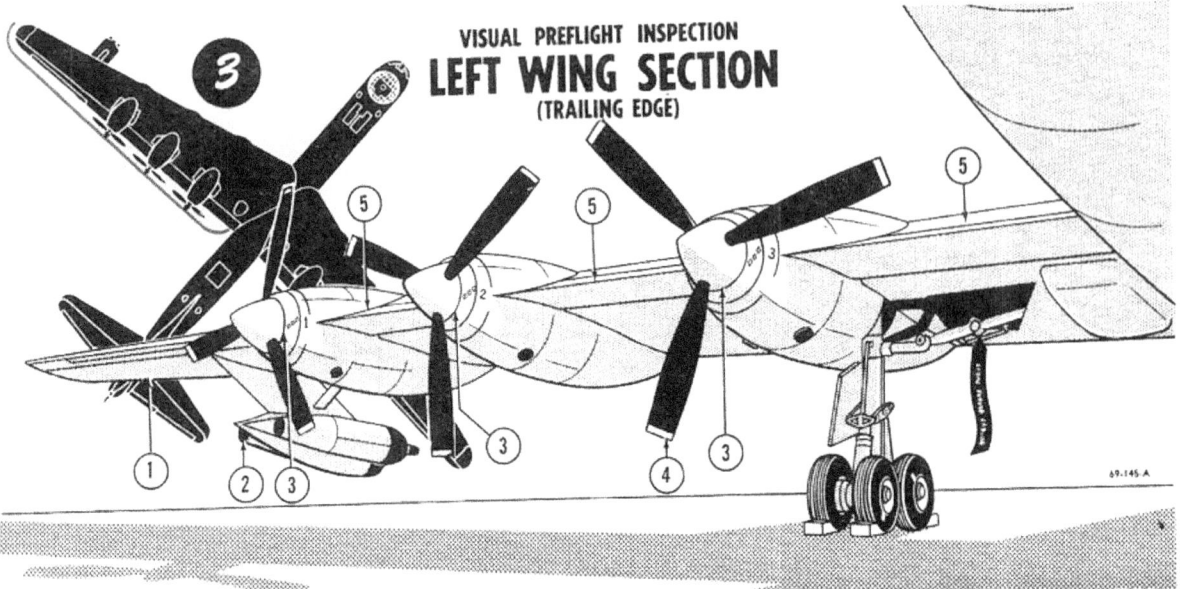

1. Wing tips, ailerons, and trim tabs for general condition. Aileron ground locks removed.
2. Jet tail section for general condition.
3. Air plugs and propeller after bodies for general condition.
4. Propeller blades and spinners for general condition and oil leaks.
5. Flaps for general condition.

Figure 2-7. (Sheet 4)

and trim tabs be checked simultaneously. For example, elevator trim full nose-up and control column full back gives elevator surface up with servo and trim tab down. Aileron trim tabs are checked by operating trim tab control switch in each direction and observing proper movement of control wheel and correct indication on the indicator. It should be remembered that aileron trim tabs are electrically operated and that a few minutes cooling period should be allowed to cool the electric motor. After this check set trim tabs to neutral.

6. Surface Controls—Locked. After the surface control check is completed, the lock will be engaged. A red lamp will burn for controls in the locked position and a green lamp will burn for controls in the unlocked position. If neither green nor red lamp burns, the condition can be caused from the lamps being burned out.

7. Turn autopilot ON.

8. Check instrument panel and flight deck lights and see that spare bulbs are available.

9. Autopilot—Checked and OFF.

   a. Turn autopilot on.

   b. Pilot's turn control in detent.

   c. Slaved gyro magnetic compass annunciator cleared.

   d. Engage the autopilot when the green lamps come on. If only one green lamp burns, the other lamp is merely burned out and will not hinder operation of the autopilot.

CAUTION

Do not engage the autopilot with heavy preload on the controls due to high winds. This will result in clutch slippage with consequent overheating and burning out.

   e. Turn each trim knob (aileron, rudder, and elevator) and check control movement for proper direction.

   f. Turn pilot's turn control and check control movement for proper direction.

   g. Turn slaved gyro magnetic compass push-to-set pointer knob and check control movement for proper direction. Controls should move to make a turn in a direction opposite to that in which the pointer moved. Only a slight movement is necessary to produce control movement.

   h. In turn, disengage the aileron, the rudder, and the elevator trim knobs. The green lamps should blink when any one surface is disengaged, and normal manual control should be obtained in that axis.

   i. Re-engage the autopilot and depress each autopilot release switch to ascertain proper operation. Then check for freedom of movement of the controls.

   j. Turn the autopilot off.

Section II
Normal Procedures

VISUAL PREFLIGHT INSPECTION
LEFT AFT SIDE OF FUSELAGE & TAIL SECTION

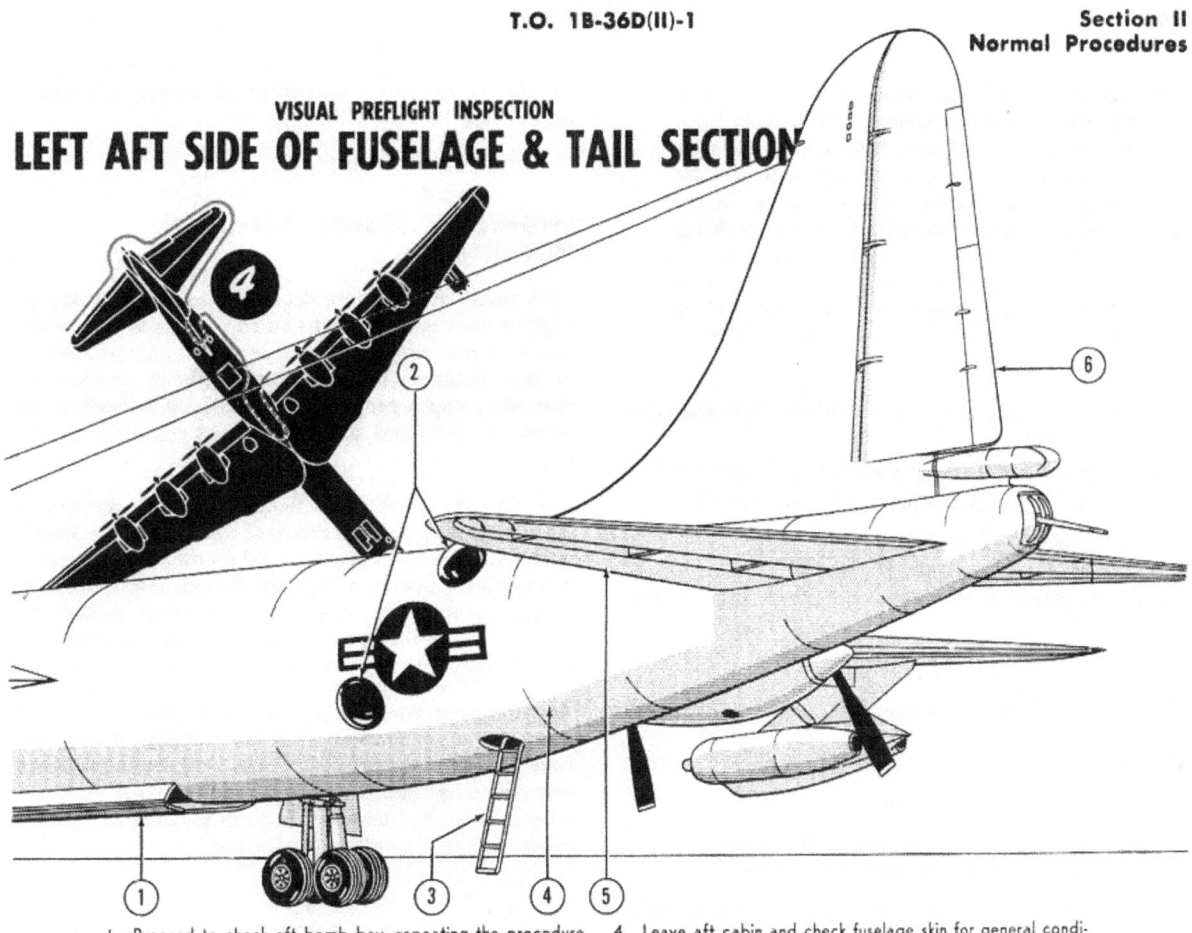

1. Proceed to check aft bomb bay, repeating the procedure followed for forward bomb bays. If a bomb bay tank is installed, check for leaks and general condition.
2. Sighting blisters for cleanliness and cracks.
3. Enter the aft cabin through the aft entrance hatch and check for cleanliness, stowage of equipment, and general condition.
4. Leave aft cabin and check fuselage skin for general condition.
5. Horizontal and vertical stabilizers for general condition. Rudder ground locks removed.
6. Rudder, elevator and tabs for general condition.

Figure 2-7. (Sheet 5)

10. Turn on landing, taxi formation, and position lights.

 a. Landing and taxi lights OFF after ground check.

 b. Formation and fuselage light will be checked by the copilot while he is inspecting the top of the wing.

 c. Position lights will be visually checked in FLASH and STEADY position. (This can be accomplished during jet engine pressure check.)

11. Check pitot covers removed by ground observer and turn pitot heater switch ON.

 a. Turn pitot heater switch OFF after being checked by ground observer.

12. Jet Engine Fuel System Pressure Check.

 a. Jet Air Plug Switches—OPEN.
 b. Throttle Selector Switches—LEVER.
 c. Throttle Levers—Closed.
 d. All Circuit Breakers—In.
 e. Jet Manifold Valve Switches (L and R)—OPEN.
 f. All Jet Engine Fuel Valve Switches—OPEN.
 g. Fuel Booster Pump Switches—ON.

Note

This jet panel configuration will be maintained for a minimum of 2 but no more than 5 minutes. This procedure allows an adequate fuel pressure check of the entire jet engine fuel system down to the jet engine fuel stopcock. On engines equipped with a check valve in the by-pass line between the fuel pump and the flow divider, leakage from the aft drain system is not normal and an engine start must not be attempted until the source of difficulty is located and corrected. On engines not equipped with a check valve in the by-pass line, slow dripping from the aft drain system is normal because of the bleed by-pass. However, if the dripping appears to be excessive, disconnect the line between the aft drain and the combustion chamber drain manifold. If it is determined that fuel is leaking from the combustion chamber, an engine start must not be attempted until the source of difficulty is located and corrected. If fuel is leaking from the forward drain and it is determined to be from the flow divider, an engine start may safely be attempted provided the leak is not in excess of approximately 90cc per minute (steady flow).

    h. Obtain ground observer's report—Fuel Pressure Check—Normal.

    i. Jet Fuel Booster Pump Switches (L & R)—OFF.

    j. All Jet Engine Fuel Valve Switches—CLOSE.

    k. Jet Throttle Circuit Breakers—OUT.

    l. Jet Air Plug Switches—CLOSE.

13. Check pilots' night flying curtain stowage in the forward cabin.

14. Notify aircraft commander of aircraft discrepancies.

15. Stow personal equipment.

Copilot.

Note

If a copilot is not assigned to the crew, the pilot will perform the following steps.

1. Oxygen supply and equipment check in accordance with existing oxygen preflight procedure.

2. Proceed to the left and right outer wing panels and check the following:

    a. Distribution panel for security and condition.

    b. Fuel and oil lines for condition, installation, and leaks.

    c. Fuel and oil valves for mechanical hook up.

    d. Jet booster pump tank for installation and leaks.

    e. All structure for condition and security.

    f. Aileron control linkage and aileron lock for security.

3. Proceed to tail cone and check the following:

    a. Tail cone lights ON to check operation and OFF when tail cone inspection is complete.

    b. Tail anti-icing ducts for general condition.

    c. Remote interphone jackbox plugs connected.

    d. Visually inspect the condition of the elevator, rudder control system, and rudder casting.

    e. Check the condition and servicing of the rudder and elevator control locks, making sure that cylinders have been properly filled.

    f. Check the mounting and linkage of the autopilot servos.

    g. Security of loose equipment.

    h. Tail cone section for breaks, cracks, and general condition.

4. Notify aircraft commander of aircraft discrepancies.

5. Stow personal equipment.

ENGINEERS' VISUAL PREFLIGHT INSPECTION.

This inspection will be accomplished on the day of flight with a minimum of two engineers. Although the first engineer will be assisted in the inspection, this in no way relieves him of the responsibility of insuring that every step is properly completed. He is expected to know the B-36 and to determine its condition before flight.

The procedure contained herein comprises an inspection route (figure 2-8) arranged in a sequence which will allow greatest efficiency. The procedure results in a thorough inspection. Various factors may force it to be modified slightly. Additional items may be inspected as warranted by local conditions and requirements; but all items must be performed.

Actually your preflight inspection begins as you and the second engineer approach the aircraft. You should have immediately noticed if any obvious maintenance was still in progress and if adequate stands, auxiliary power units, lighting, towing equipment, fire equipment, etc., are standing by for use.

Note

Insure that the wing access panels between the outboard and center engines on left and right wings have been removed in order to provide an escape route in the event of fires occurring during the wing crawlway inspection. Also check to see that the inboard jet access panels are removed.

Recheck the status of the aircraft with the crew chief as reflected by AF Form 781 (Form 1). Pay particular attention to the corrective action taken on all discrepancies noted by the crew during the preflight operational equipment check.

The AF Form 781 should indicate that the daily inspection has been completed, the amount of fuel, oil, and water injection fluid serviced, and the totals of fuel and oil by location.

Stand by for crew inspection. Upon completion of this crew inspection both engineers will proceed with their preflight inspection.

Note

In order to prevent an abort or late take-off, any discrepancies discovered during the preflight inspection will be reported to the crew chief immediately so that corrective action may be started as soon as possible.

FIRST ENGINEER.

Engineer's Station.

1. Required Forms—Aboard and Checked.
2. All Circuit Breakers and Control Switches—Properly Positioned.
3. Emergency Power Switch—NORMAL.
4. Cabin Heater Power Switch—OFF.
5. External Power Supply Switch—OFF.
6. Battery Switch—ON.
7. Alternator Panel Configuration—Checked.
8. External Power—Plugged In.
9. Correct A-C Phase Sequence Lamp—Lighted.
10. External Power Supply Switch—ON.
11. Master Ignition Switch—Pull Off.
12. Liquid Lock Check (with ignition switches OFF) —Completed.
13. Mixture Control Check—Completed.
14. Throttle Lever and Flap Warning Horn Check—Completed.
15. Fuel Panel Configuration—Checked.
16. Intercooler and Air Plugs—As Required.

Note

If an operational preflight was not performed, a static propeller feather check will be performed at this time. See "Stopping Reciprocating Engines" for amplification.

17. Instrument Check—Normal.
18. Altimeter—Check and set at 29.92.
19. Panel Lights—Check.
20. Wheel Well Lights Switch—ON.
21. Nacelle Fire Detection Circuit—Push to test.
22. Wing, Cabin Heat and Tail Anti-ice Switches—Full Decrease.
23. Minimum of two tank valves OPEN and booster pumps ON (one in each wing to provide system pressure).
24. Oil Cooler Door Mode Selector Switches—AUTO.
25. Oxygen supply and equipment check in accordance with existing oxygen preflight procedure. Check normal interphone using helmet and oxygen mask, verifying side tone.
26. Engineer's Fuse Panel—Check for security of fuses.
27. Alternate A-C Power Switch—NORMAL, lamp lighted.

Radio Operator's Compartment.

1. Emergency dump valve pedal reset in untripped position and valve closed (manual modulating knob full clockwise).
2. Visually inspect condition of normally accessible control cables and pulleys.
3. T-R Test Unit—Check voltage and load output of each t-r unit and the battery.

CAUTION

Operate only one selector switch at a time to prevent burning out of the ammeter.

4. Turbo, jet throttle, and mixture control amplifiers. Check wiring, mounting, and presence of spares.
5. Inspect autosyn instrument amplifier, transformers, and fuse panel for condition, wiring, mounting, and presence of spare fuses.

Forward and Aft Bomb Bays.

1. Bomb bay lights switch ON.
2. Check general condition and security of the following:
   a. A-C and d-c fuse panels.
   b. Bomb bay for cracks, breaks, etc.
   c. Heat and pressurization ducting.
   d. Loose equipment.
3. Connect interphone at station 6.1.
4. Inspect main hydraulic panel.
5. Check aileron cross-over cables, pulleys, and autopilot servo for interference and condition.
6. Inspect emergency flap switches.
7. Connect interphone at station 7.1.
8. Inspect bomb bay 3 fuel tank quick-disconnects.
9. Inspect auxiliary spar (station 8.0) for evidence of failure.
10. Inspect transformer-rectifier units (fans operating).
11. Wing crawlway and interphone switches—ON.

Inside Right Wing.

1. Inspect the following items for general condition, security connections, routing, etc.
   a. Accessible portions of the fuel manifold lines, valves, and tanks.
   b. Wheel well and wing crawlway lights.
   c. Throttles and flap synchronizer cables for general condition.
   d. Fuel level transmitters for proper mounting and wiring.
   e. Fuel tank vent lines and vapor return lines.
   f. Pressurization ducting and flow limiters.
   g. Accessible wing bracing.
   h. Accessible wiring.
2. Fire extinguisher agent cylinders, valves, and pressure. Auxiliary spar forging for cracks.
3. Inspect condition of all hinges, levers, and actuating linkages for landing gear fairings, doors, and sequence valves.

Section II
Normal Procedures

T.O. 1B-36D(II)-1

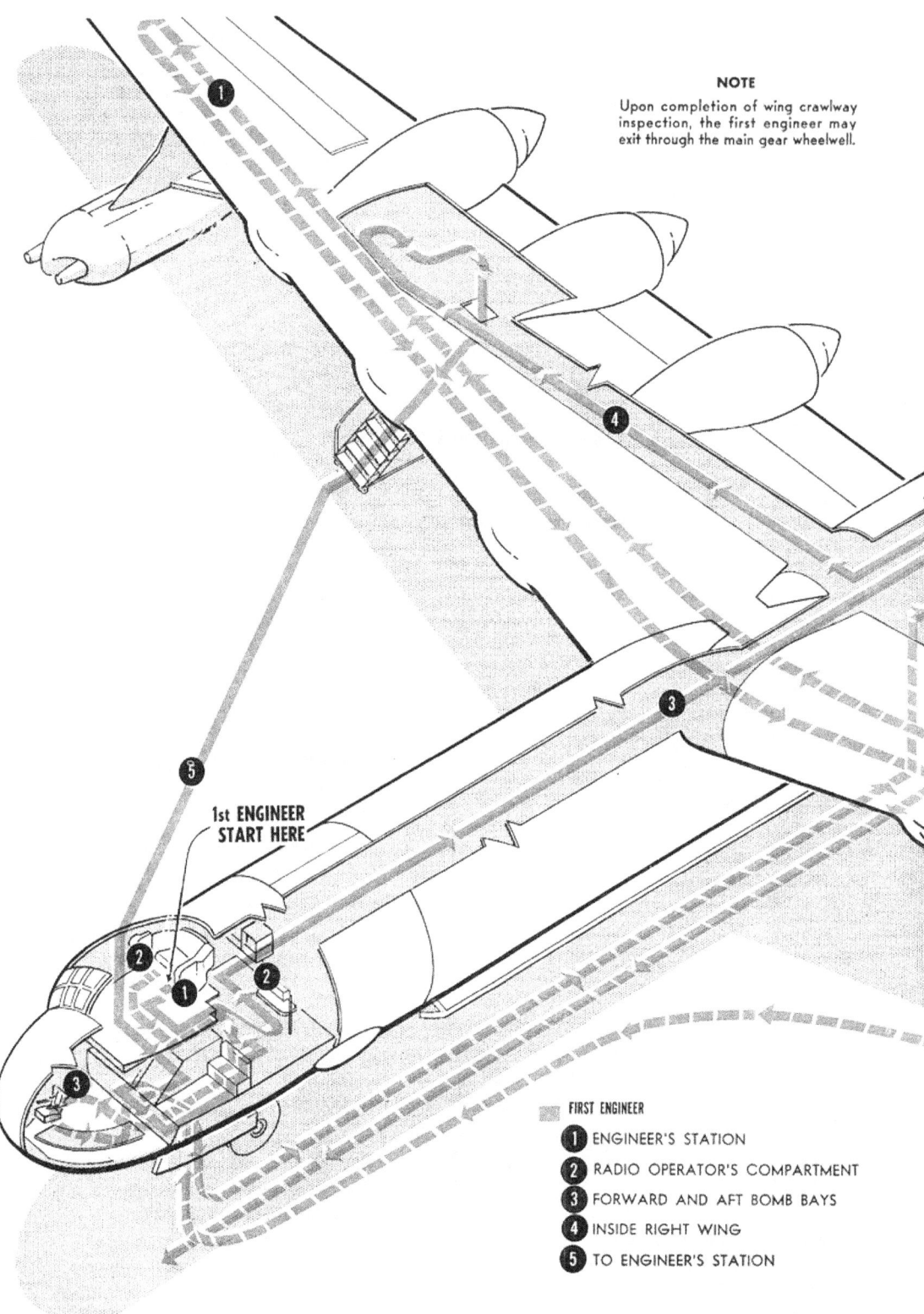

Figure 2-8. (Sheet 1)

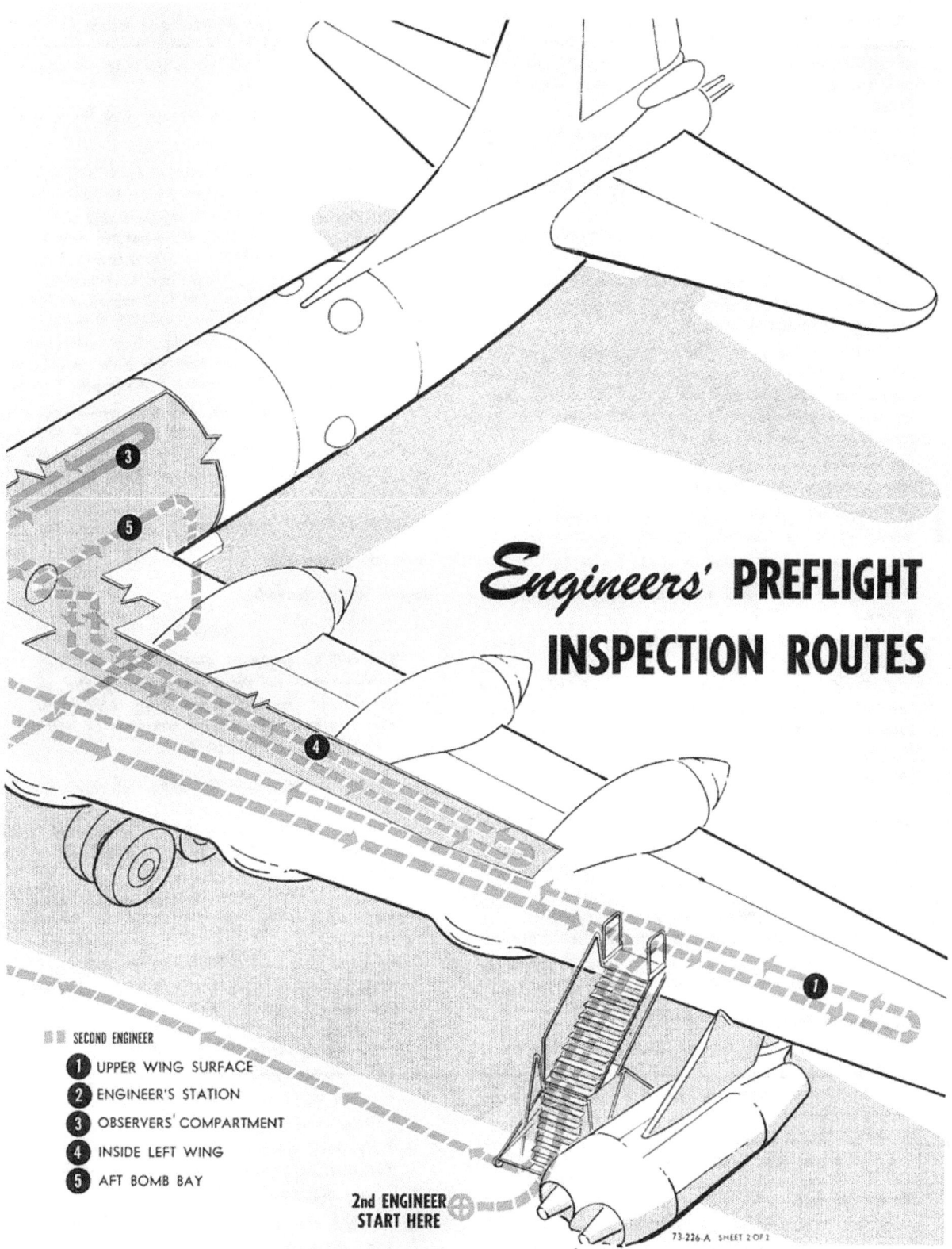

Figure 2-8. (Sheet 2)

Section II
Normal Procedures

4. Inspect the latch mechanism and main gear wheel well door limit switches for proper condition, security of mounting, proper electrical connections, and corrosion or binding of the micro-switch actuating mechanism.

5. Make the following inspection of the main landing gear manual extension controls:

   a. Cable wound correctly on large drum approximately 2 turns.

   b. Hoist hook and spring properly stowed, rachet handle for security.

6. Check the main landing gear hydraulic actuating mechanism, lines, and connections for security, condition, and evidence of leakage.

7. Check the main side brace for general condition of the latching mechanism, proper connecting and alignment of latch release arm at both ends, and security and condition of hydraulic snubber. See that the ground safety lock is in place.

8. Landing gear pivot shaft attachments for fuel leaks, security, and condition.

9. On airplanes not equipped with nacelle fire curtains inspect the following at each engine nacelle:

   a. Alternator and turbo oil tanks for leaks.

   b. K-truss cutout and accessible engine mounts for cracks.

   c. Accessible ducting for alignment, cracks, breaks, connections, etc.

   d. Check tank-to-engine oil lines and connections for leaks, oil thermostats for proper operation, and manual crank stowed on engine oil shutoff valves.

10. Inspect each engine power distribution panel for the following:

   a. Check the A, B, C phase power-on indicator lamps and proper installation of the active and spare fuses. Check bottom of the panel for cleanliness.

   b. Check the 28-volt d-c power lamp and the alternator control fuses.

   c. Check the relays for security of mounting.

   d. Visually inspect the mounting of the alternator control units.

11. Check wing crawlway lights off.

Engineers' Station.

1. Fuel Panel Configuration—Booster pumps OFF.

2. Note fuel quantity as indicated on tank gages and check this later with quantities dip sticked by second engineer.

3. If no one is using external power, turn OFF the external power and battery switches.

Miscellaneous.

1. Check status of all last minute repairs with the crew chief and insure that wing access panels have been replaced.

2. Complete or revise Form F and return to the aircraft commander, who will check it for accuracy and sign. It is your responsibility to see that the aircraft is properly loaded and balanced.

3. Complete or revise the take-off and landing data card.

Obtain the take-off and the anticipated landing gross weights and CG locations. Also check to ascertain that the required amounts of fuel, ammunition and bombs have been loaded. Loading information can be obtained from the "Handbook of Weights and Balance," T.O. 1-1B-40. Refer to "Operating Limitations," Section V for operational weight limitations. Check the basic weight of your aircraft carefully. Remember, it probably has undergone modification affecting its weight. Be absolutely sure that the basic weight you are using applies to the airplane you are going to fly.

4. Check the results of the preflight inspection with your second engineer. You and the second engineer will then meet with the aircraft commander and go over all discrepancies noted. Enter them in Form 781 (Form 1).

5. Stow personal equipment.

SECOND ENGINEER.

Upper Wing Surface.

Note

The second engineer may delegate the electrical-gunner to assist him during the inspection of the top of the wing. This in no way alleviates the second engineer of being responsible for this check.

1. Proceed to the top of the wing and check the following:

   a. Check fuel level, using the dip stick, and record the amount in each tank. Record temperature of fuel if required.

   b. Check oil level, using dip stick, and record the amount in each tank.

Note

After the above checks, it is essential that all fuel and oil caps be checked for security.

2. Check for condition of the following:
   a. Loose rivets and fasteners.
   b. Control surfaces and aileron curtains.
   c. Fairings and cowlings.
   d. Propellers, spinners and intercooler shutters.
   e. All anti-icing ducts and accessible valves.
   f. Turret doors.
   g. Hatches and general condition of fuselage.
   h. Formation and fuselage lights.
   i. Tail surfaces.

LEFT MAIN A-C POWER PANEL

1. BUS 301
2. BUS 201
3. LEADS TO BUS TIE BREAKER 5-2
4. LEADS TO BUS TIE BREAKER 4-5
5. SPARE FUSES
6. FUSES
7. LEADS TO LEFT FORWARD TURRET POWER PANEL
8. LEADS TO LEFT AFT TURRET POWER PANEL
9. BUS TIE BREAKER 2-3
10. BUS TIE BREAKER 3-4

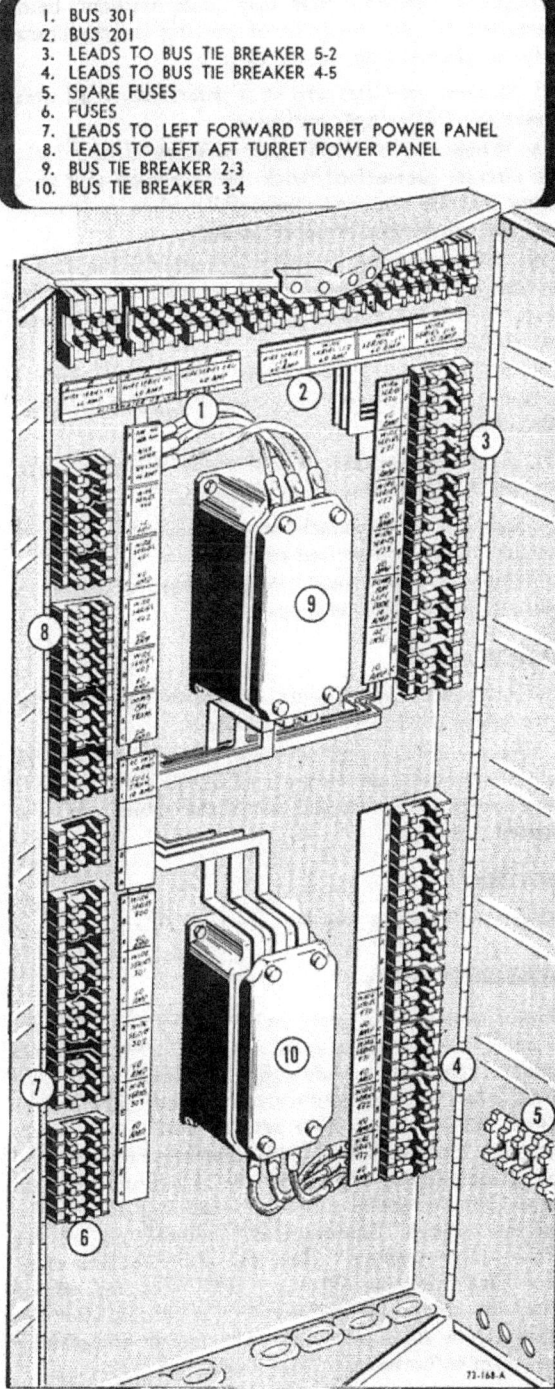

Figure 2-9.

Engineer's Station.

1. Oxygen supply and equipment check in accordance with existing oxygen preflight procedure. Check normal interphone using helmet and oxygen mask, verifying side tone.

2. Check private interphone with regular headset.

Observer's Compartment.

1. Remove sufficient overhead upholstery (under flight deck) to visually inspect control column and brake pedal rigging. Depress the plunger on the slave brake reservoirs. If these plungers can be pushed full in, the reservoirs are fully serviced. If the plungers extend over 3/4 inch when depressed, the slave brake system should be bled of all air and reservoirs reserviced. Also check the master cylinders.

Inside Left Wing.

1. The second engineer will perform the same check inside the left wing as the first engineer performs inside the right wing.

Aft Bomb Bay.

1. Wing crawlway lights OFF.

2. Inspect a-c power panels.

3. Inspect auxiliary spar (station 8.0) for evidence of failure.

4. Inspect heat and pressurization ducting, accessible cables, and general condition.

5. Check oxygen bottles for condition and security.

Miscellaneous.

1. Report to the first engineer the results of your preflight inspection and submit to him the quantities of fuel and oil loaded.

2. Standby with the first engineer to assist in completing or revising the Form F and to report the results of your preflight inspection to the aircraft commander.

3. Stow personal equipment.

FINAL CREW BRIEFING.

When all crew members have completed their preflight, have stowed their equipment, and the aircraft commander is satisfied that a thorough preflight inspection has been completed, he will conduct an informal final crew briefing.

1. Call the roll, and have each crew member give preflight report. Any discrepancies will be reported.

2. Check Form 781 (Form 1) to see that specialized equipment has been signed off after preflight.

3. Brief crew on emergency signals and procedures and on oxygen, interphone, and parachute discipline. If passengers are aboard, make sure they know emergency signals; positions for take-off, landing and crash

Section II
Normal Procedures

landing; oxygen outlets; primary and secondary exits for bailout and ditching; and proper operation of their parachute, bail-out bottle, oxygen equipment, etc.

4. State time interval at which aft cabin gunners are to render visual engine check during the flight. During daylight, it will be every hour; during night, high altitude cruise, weather, and high power, it will be every 30 minutes. In addition, during the visual engine check, the right gunner will give the aft cabin altimeter reading to the engineer during pressure flight.

WARNING

The aft lower left and right scanning stations must be manned at all times during flight.

5. Designate an observer in the nose to aid in clearing the aircraft during flight at night, in periods of restricted visibility, and when flying through congested control areas.

6. The N-1 compass heading will be cross-checked with the magnetic heading every 30 minutes.

7. Cover route, altitudes to be flown, weather, and duration of flight. If information has not changed since formal briefing, it is unnecessary to cover it again at this point.

8. Announce station time, start engine time, and take-off time.

9. Answer any questions crew may have.

10. Have ground locks removed before boarding aircraft.

11. Crew members board the aircraft. All crew members will go on interphone and stand by as soon as they board the aircraft.

RULES TO BE ENFORCED ON EACH FLIGHT.

SMOKING.

1. No smoking during ground operation, take-off, and landing.

2. No smoking at any time gas fumes are detected.

3. No smoking except in crew compartments.

4. Make sure all cigarettes are completely out before throwing away.

5. Do not attempt to throw a lighted cigarette from the airplane.

6. No smoking while wearing helmet with oxygen mask attached.

WARNING

Keep lighted cigarettes away from oxygen masks at all times that masks are connected to the airplane's supply system.

PARACHUTES.

Parachutes will be worn at all times by crew members while they are occupying the aircraft commander's, pilot's, engineer's, and gunners' positions. This is considered necessary so that these key crew members may devote complete attention to coping with an emergency situation that may arise without being distracted by the necessity of putting on parachutes prior to abandoning the aircraft.

1. All crew members will wear parachutes at all times under the following conditions:

   a. When above 25,000 feet pressure altitude with the aircraft pressurized, with the exception that parachute may be removed temporarily when it is necessary for proper performance of duty.

   b. During take-off, landing, formation flying, fighter passes, gunnery practice, when emergency conditions exist, when gas fumes are detected, or any time danger is imminent.

   c. While occupying positions when the aircraft is pressurized and there is imminent danger of explosive decompression.

2. At all other times parachutes need not be worn, but will be kept close by at all times.

3. Stow an extra parachute with bail-out bottle attached in each pressurized compartment.

4. Make sure all parachutes have been properly inspected and packed before take-off.

SAFETY BELTS.

1. One pilot, the engineer, and blister gunners will have safety belts fastened at all times.

2. Above 25,000 feet altitude aircraft commander, pilot, engineer, and gunners at blister positions will have safety belts fastened when the cabins are pressurized.

OXYGEN.

(Refer to "Oxygen System," Section IV.)

STATION TIME.

Station time is designated by the aircraft commander to make sure that each crew member knows the exact time he should be at his assigned station aboard the aircraft ready for engine start, taxi, and take-off. The pilots and engineers have several duties to perform between "Station Time" and "Starting Engines" and should be allowed approximately 15 minutes between these times to make sure the remaining schedule is not interrupted. "Station Time" immediately follows "Final Crew Briefing." Since the pilot and first engineer have the most duties to perform before engine start, they should be first to enter the aircraft after dismissal from final briefing. The aircraft commander will want to be last for several reasons:

1. *To see that all personnel and equipment are aboard.*

2. To make a last visual check to see that gear-down locks, pitot covers, and control locks are removed and that the wing access panels are secured and the nose gear scissors are connected.

3. To see that the area is clear of obstructions and adequate fire equipment is available preparatory to engine start.

The aircraft commander, pilot, and engineers will recheck and complete applicable items of the "Before Starting Engines" check list and stand by for starting engines.

STARTING RECIPROCATING ENGINES.

The reciprocating engines will be started in accordance with the instructions given under "Preflight Operational Equipment Check, Starting Reciprocating Engines" of this section. An effort should be made to start the engines as close to take-off time as the situation and the experience of the crew permits in order to conserve fuel and engine life.

DURING ENGINE WARM-UP.

If a complete "Preflight Operational Equipment Check" was accomplished, the only checks that must be made during this engine warm-up are listed below:

1. Engine-Driven Fuel Pumps.

2. Alternators Paralleled (three on the line, one standing by).

3. Engine Oil-In Temperatures—Minimum 40°C.

4. Propeller Reverse Check—As Required.

ENGINE RUN-UP.

If a complete "Preflight Operational Equipment Check" was accomplished, the only checks that must be made during this engine run-up are listed as follows:

1. Propeller Control System.

2. Ignition System Checks—Completed.

3. Full Power No Boost Checks.

4. Full Power with Boost Checks.

STARTING JET ENGINES.

Start the jet engines in accordance with the instructions given under "Preflight Operational Equipment Check, Starting Jet Engines" of this section. All four jets should be started as close to take-off as remaining time will allow to conserve fuel and engine life.

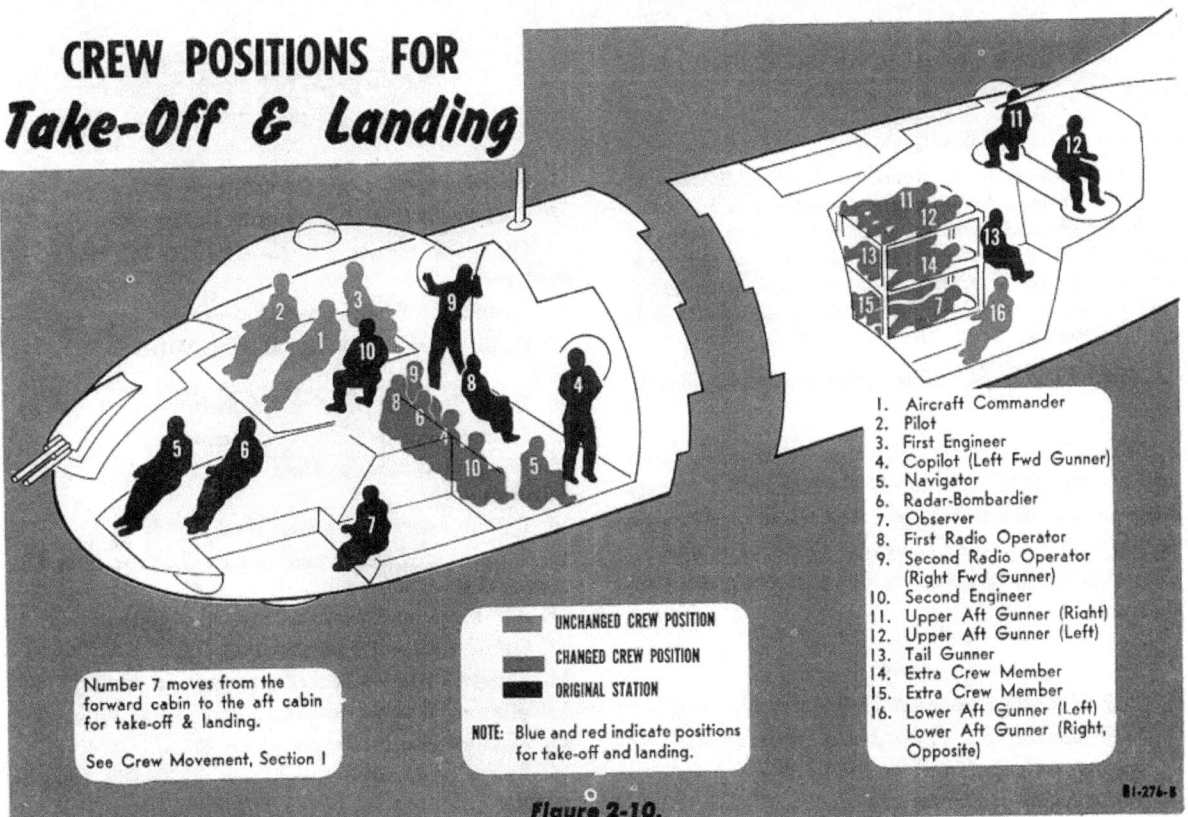

Figure 2-10.

Section II
Normal Procedures

T.O. 1B-36D(II)-1

BEFORE TAKE-OFF.

Before and during take-off your perspective will differ from that experienced on other airplanes. Your flight deck is higher, the wing is approximately 40 feet aft, and the reciprocating engines are pusher type. Therefore, you will not have the customary reference to the wings and engines. However, with a few flights you will develop the proper perspective.

When the aircraft is taxied into position for take-off, the aircraft commander will align the nose wheel on the center marker for the runway and make certain the nose wheel indicator reads zero before setting the parking brakes.

The engineer will give basic take-off information to the aircraft commander on the take-off and landing data card. The aircraft commander will study this information and pass the card to the pilot. The pilot will then call off the pertinent data prior to and during take-off.

While the engineer is completing his final engine checks, the aircraft commander and the pilot will be going through the "Before Take-Off" check list.

CAUTION

Use your check list and follow it carefully. No matter how proficient you are or how well you know your procedures, you are inviting trouble when you fail to use your check list.

Note

Tests indicate that approximately 5 seconds less time is required to operate the elevator trim tab control wheel from one extreme position to the other when the operator's inboard arm rest is in the up position. At a speed of 135 mph this 5 seconds represents 990 feet of travel which could mean the difference between a successful maneuver and a crash during take-off or landing.

The aircraft commander will have the jet engines started at this point and will keep them in stand-by until the engineer is ready to set take-off power on the reciprocating engines. While the engineer sets take-off power, the pilot will advance all jet engines to take-off rpm.

Note

All reciprocating and jet engines will be operating for take-off.

1. Landing Lights—As Required. Landing lights will normally be used for all night take-offs. Under conditions of restricted visibility, such as haze, fog, snow, or rain, and when the aircraft commander is of the opinion that the use of landing lights is a hindrance rather than an aid to visibility, use of the landing lights is not mandatory.

2. Flaps and Indicators—Set at 20 degrees and checked.

3. Trim Tabs—Set. Set trim tabs for take-off, using 30 per cent MAC as neutral elevator; set 1 degree elevator trim for each 1 per cent variation from 30 per cent MAC. If nose is heavy (30 per cent minus), trim nose up; if tail is heavy (30 per cent plus), trim nose down.

Note

To facilitate movement of the elevator trim tab control, the inboard arm rests on the pilots' seats should be in the up position for all take-offs and landings.

1. Engine Supercharger Switches—BOTH.
2. Fuel Panel Checked—Booster pumps ON.
3. Oil Vent Heater Switch—ON, if 0°C OAT. is anticipated.
4. Carburetor Preheat Switches—OFF.
5. Cabin Pressure Wing Shutoff Valve Switches—OFF.
6. Cabin Booster Fan Control Switch—As Required.
7. Pitot Heater Switches—As Required.
8. Wing and Cabin Heat and Tail Anti-Icing Switches—OFF.
9. Engine Fan Speed Switches—LOW RPM.
10. Three Alternators Paralleled on the Line, One Excited and Standing By.
11. Air Plugs and Intercoolers—As Required.
12. Cabin Heater Power Switch—OFF.
13. Temperatures—Checked and within limits.
14. Mixture Control Selector Switches—LEVER.
15. Mixture Control Levers—NORMAL.
16. Spark Advance Switches—RETARD (guards down).

BEFORE TAKE-OFF (Cont'd)

4. Abort Procedure and Take-Off and Landing Data—Briefed and Reviewed. The aircraft commander will review the abort procedure and take-off and landing data with the pilot and engineers.

5. Safety Belts and Safety Harnesses—Fastened. Crew members will be in their take-off positions. Safety belts and shoulder harnesses will be fastened and inertia reel lock controls UNLOCKED.

6. Salvo Safety Switches—As Required. Have salvo circuits set for salvo if heavily loaded for take-off.

7. Engineer's Take-Off Configuration—Engineer reads, "Take-off configuration completed, standing by for propeller reverse safety check and take-off power."

8. Tower Clearance—Received.

Note

The following steps must be accomplished after the aircraft is aligned with the runway.

9. Parking Brake Control—ON.

10. Propeller Reverse Selector Switches—SAFE (lights out). Observe that all propeller reverse warning lights are out, indicating all propellers are in normal pitch.

11. Pitot Heat—As Required.

12. All Compartments—Entrance ladders, windows, and hatches, ready for take-off. The compartment commanders are responsible to check that all crew members have assumed their take-off position (figure 2-10), and that all ladders are up, all windows and hatches are closed, all defroster nozzles are removed, and all equipment is properly stowed. After this check is completed, the compartment commanders will report to the aircraft commander, "Ready for take-off."

13. Gyros—Set and Uncaged. Observe the indications of the directional gyro, vertical gyros, turn and bank indicators, and slaved gyro magnetic compass or the N-1 high latitude compass. Set the directional gyro with the magnetic compass.

The accuracy of the turn and bank indicators should have been checked during taxiing. When setting the compass, attempt to remove the white dot or white cross from the small window at the upper right corner of the compass.

17. Propeller Selector Switches—AUTOMATIC OPERATION (Tel-Lamps Lighted).

18. Propeller Normal Pitch Indicator Lamps—Lighted.

19. Brake Pressure and Nose Steering Pressure—NORMAL.

20. Turbo Control Change-Over Switches (Group 2 Airplanes)—AUTO.

21. Turbo Control Vernier Switch (Group 2 Airplanes)—OFF.

22. Hydraulic Fluid Temperature Control Switch—OFF.

23. Oil Cooler Door Mode Selector Switch—AUTO.

24. Safety Belt—Fastened.

25. Engineer's Take-Off Configuration—Engineer reads, "Take-off configuration completed, standing by for propeller reverse safety check and take-off power."

Section II
Normal Procedures

T.O. 1B-36D(II)-1

BEFORE TAKE-OFF (Cont'd)

14. Nose Wheel Steering Switch—ON. This will turn on one hydraulic pump and circulate fluid through the system at approximately 600 psi.

15. Surface Controls—Unlocked and Checked. Check the control lock indicator lamps; the green lamp should be on and the red lamp out. If the green lamp is out and the red lamp is on, check the toggle switch which is actuated by the flag on the pilots' instrument panel. This switch may not have been actuated by the flag. Check controls for freedom of movement at full throw.

16. Read pilot's take-off configuration. This will insure that all checks made by the aircraft commander before take-off are completed. The pilot should recheck each item when he calls it off as follows: "Controls—Unlocked; Flight Instrument Switches—ON; Flaps—20 degrees; Trim Tabs—____ degrees (up or down); Autopilot—OFF; Nose Steering—ON; Propellers—SAFE, Lights Out."

The aircraft commander will be sure the jet booster pumps are on, all jet manifold and engine valves are open, pod preheat and nose de-ice switches are off, and the jet engine oil tank heater switch is as required. It will take about 30 seconds to read and visually check the entire take-off configuration.

TAKE-OFF.

Note

If high carburetor air temperatures were encountered during ground run-up, use the procedures outlined in "Take-Off, Hot Weather Procedures," Section IX.

1. Parking Brakes—Released. The aircraft commander and pilot will hold the aircraft with foot brakes while setting take-off power.

2. Set take-off power—Jets take-off rpm. When the aircraft commander has completed his take-off configuration (including take-off clearance from tower) he will instruct the pilot to advance the jets to take-off

1. Propeller reverse safety check and set take-off power. Advance throttles to 35 inches M. P. on all engines, decrease master motor to 2000 rpm to insure that prop limit switches are against low blade stops,

TAKE-OFF (Cont'd)

rpm and the engineer to advance his throttles at the same time to make propeller reverse check and set take-off power.

> **CAUTION**
>
> In order to minimize drag loads on the main landing gear, the time interval for the full power checks prior to releasing the brakes should be held to a minimum.

When the foot brakes are released, directional control will be maintained by use of nose steering until the rudder becomes effective at 50 to 60 mph. As soon as power has been stabilized during take-off roll, the engineer will report this fact to the aircraft commander.

The pilot should keep his hand on the jet throttles during the take-off run in order to handle immediately any jet emergency on take-off. Start applying elevator pressure at approximately 10 mph below nose-up speed. When an air speed of approximately 5 mph below nose-up speed has been attained, apply and maintain 50 to 75 pounds pull on the elevator control wheel. If control wheel pull is maintained until nose-up speed is attained, the airplane will begin to move to the take-off attitude.

As take-off air speed is approached, the 50 to 75 pound pull requirement of the control wheel will subside and, at the instant of take-off "get-away," the force required will be reduced to approximately zero.

As the airplane emerges from ground effect to climb, a normal tendency of the airplane to nose up will be experienced. This tendency must be countered by elevator "push force" and retrimming of the elevator trim tabs.

Initiate landing gear retraction as soon as the airplane is positively air-borne.

Retraction and extension of the landing gear induces a mild change in longitudinal trim of the airplane. The sweepback of the wing causes flap movement to exercise a great effect on longitudinal trim. The resultant effect of flap movement can be reduced by operating the flaps in increments of 5 degrees.

increase master motor to 2700 rpm, and recheck to insure that 35 inches are on all engines. If any propeller is in reverse, rpm on that engine will be approximately ·300 higher than rpm of engines with propellers in normal pitch. Set TBS7, advance throttle to 55 inches M. P., water injection on, set take-off power corrected for humidity. Report to aircraft commander, "Power set, propellers normal, ready for take-off."

2. Report, "Power stabilized," prior to nose-up speed.

AFTER TAKE-OFF.

1. Foot Brakes—Apply to stop wheel rotation. If the wheels are allowed to spin during gear retraction, unnecessary loads will be imposed on the retraction mechanism because of the gyro effect of the spinning wheels. The tires could also be damaged if the wheels were allowed to rotate in the wheel wells.

2. Nose Steering Switch—OFF.

3. Landing Gear Control Switch—RETRACT. The aircraft commander will give the order, "Gear up," over the interphone in addition to a visual order for gear up to the pilot. During retraction the gunners will report, "Left door coming open, right door coming open"; and after gear retraction, "Left door closed, right door closed." If the gear retraction sequence is not normal, or if the gear positioning jacks are not functioning properly, the gunners will report the discrepancy to the aircraft commander. It will take approximately 50 seconds to retract the gear.

Note

When the red landing gear indicator light remains on after gear retraction, a visual check should be made of the canoe door latches for proper engagement.

4. Landing Lights—Retracted and OFF.

5. Flap Switch—UP. At the verbal order from the aircraft commander on interphone, the pilot will begin to retract the flaps. Retraction should be accomplished in 5-degree increments to allow the pilot to trim the airplane as the flaps are raised.

Flap retraction should not begin until 130 mph IAS or 125 per cent of stalling speed, whichever is higher, has been obtained. (See "Flap Retraction Speeds," figure 6-6.) Since drag with the gear and flaps down is excessive, if it is practical the landing gear should be retracted immediately and retraction of the flaps begun at 130 mph, even though the gear is not completely retracted. At least two alternators on the line is a requirement for simultaneous operation of the gear and flaps. Do not fully retract the flaps until 140 mph IAS or 125 per cent of stalling speed, whichever is higher, has been reached.

1. Observe main hydraulic pressure normal.

2. Report, "Main hydraulic pressure relieved," after gear retraction is completed.

AFTER TAKE-OFF (Cont'd)

The aft gunners should report the action of the flaps as they are raised to be sure that all flaps operate in unison. If either the inboard or outboard flaps fail to rise, the attitude of the airplane will be affected. If the inboard flaps fail, the aircraft will have a tendency to nose up; if the outboard flaps fail, the tendency will be to nose down. With any pair of flaps fully extended, the stalling speed is reduced approximately 6 mph. To operate one pair of flaps, open the circuit breakers for the other two pairs and operate the flap control switch. In the event the normal flap controls fail, use the alternate flap controls as described in "Wing Flaps," Section III.

CAUTION

Flaps must not be extended during flight except for take-off, landing, and emergencies. Propeller vibratory stresses encountered are increased with flaps extended.

INITIAL CLIMB.

1. Power Condition No. 2—Jets 96 per cent rpm. After gear and flaps are up and a minimum of 500 feet above terrain has been reached. Unless some abnormality arises this should serve as a notification to the pilot and engineer that you consider the aircraft safely air-borne and that power may be reduced as predicted for the flight. At the aircraft commander's discretion, each take-off is usually predicted to last from 3 to 5 minutes. At the end of the predicted period the pilot will reduce power on the jet engine to planned climb schedule.

2. Landing Gear and Brake Pump Switch—OFF when pressure is relieved. This is an added precaution against inadvertent operation of hydraulic motors and subsequent loss of system operation.

3. Hold Best Climb IAS—(Reference Take-off and Landing Data Card). Climb performance has been tested and charted for all normal operation. Request the climb speed for your configuration from the engineer. Climb speed varies with power and altitude for long range climb. It also varies with gross weight for normal rated climb when maximum rate of climb is desired. The initial indicated air speed will drop off approximately 3 mph for each 5000 feet of altitude

1. Power Condition No. 2—Upon pilot's request.
2. Turbo Boost Selector—Reduce M. P.
3. Water Injection Switches—OFF. Use individual switches to cut off one water injection pump at a time.

Note fuel flow increase, water pressure decrease to static value, and slight torque pressure drop-off.

Note

All ADI fluid may be expended during climb, if desired.

4. Reduce power to predicted climb schedule.

WARNING

During flight, do not move more than one mixture control lever at a time. This precludes the possibility of inadvertently moving all mixture levers to IDLE CUT-OFF and consequently, losing power on all reciprocating engines.

INITIAL CLIMB (Cont'd)

up to 35,000 feet and slightly more thereafter. Hold the correct air speed during climb—then performances should equal the engineer's and navigator's prediction. Charted climb air speed values result in stable operation under all weather conditions and the best compromise between power available from jet and reciprocating engines. This results in the best rate of climb consistent with efficient operation. If the jet engines are not be used after level-off, they should be reduced to idle speed, preparatory to shutdown, the instant planned altitude is reached.

As the planned level-off altitude is attained, the aircraft may be climbed 200 to 500 feet above cruising altitude prior to reducing power unless instrument flight rules dictate leveling off at the exact altitude. This small amount of altitude will allow a cushion for the pilot to trim the aircraft while the engineer is stabilizing reciprocating power. Regardless of level-off technique, the engineer has sufficient power available from the reciprocating engines, at less cost in fuel consumption to complete this maneuver.

4. Bomb Bay Area—Checked. A designated crew member will inspect the bomb bay area for fuel fumes and fuel and hydraulic leaks. Upon completion of the check, the crew member will report to the aircraft commander.

5. Torque, Fuel Flow, CHT, CAT. and M. P.—Within limits. Manually adjust controls to obtain specifications desired. Specified fuel flow for climb is indicated in the "Fuel Consumption" curves of the appendix.

Note

Engine fuel flow meters should be calibrated.

Torque varies with altitude due to engine cooling fans absorption of bhp. During any climb power setting, engine overheating can be combatted by opening intercoolers and air plugs to lower CAT. and CHT; by enriching fuel flows; by reducing bmep; and by increasing air speed.

Note

Normally the alternator frequency will decrease during an extended climb and increase during descent because OAT. affects the resistance of the control circuit. So you must remember to adjust alternator frequency to compensate for these variations.

6. Anti-icing Duct Temperatures—Increase as required.

STOPPING JET ENGINES (AIR).

After climb when the flight plan calls for shutting down the jet engines, the pilot will shut down jet engines as follows:

1. Throttles—Idle three minutes and then close. This procedure is followed in order to let temperatures throughout the jet engine stabilize. Because of the close tolerances involved and the fact that metals with different expansion and contraction factors were used in manufacturing the various parts of the engines and

STOPPING JET ENGINES (AIR) (Cont'd)

shroud ring, binding can result unless temperatures are stabilized. Remember that the tail pipe temperature indicator shows the temperature of the tail pipe only.

2. Booster Pumps—OFF.

2A. Air Plugs—Closed at or below 100°C tail pipe temperature and 30 per cent rpm. Check the fuel pressure and see that it reads zero before closing the air plugs. Watch tail pipe temperatures as the air plugs are closing; if temperatures rise sharply, open the air plugs on the affected jet immediately. Tail pipe temperature rise is an indication that the jet is still running. Attempt to shut off the affected jet by using the switch position of the throttle. If the jet still continues to run, close the engine fuel valve.

3. Engine Fuel Valves—Closed below 10 per cent rpm.

Note

Immediately after shutdown, position the air plugs to allow the engine to windmill at 10 to 12 per cent rpm for a period of 10 minutes. After the 10-minute period, adjust the air plugs to maintain a windmilling rpm of 5 to 7 per cent.

4. Nose de-ice—As Required.

5. Pod Preheat—As required. Since pod preheat must be off when wing anti-icing is being used, in order to give adequate heat for wing anti-icing, preheating the jet pod must be handled with care when flying in icing conditions. Keep wing anti-icing heat on until the wings are free of ice, turn on pod preheat long enough to free the strut of ice, start the jets, and then turn pod preheat off and route the heat back to the wing.

6. Oil Heater Switch—As required. (Leave on at 15,000 feet and above or when OAT. is 5°C (41°F) or below.

7. Oil Shutoff Valves—Always open during flight.

8. Throttle Circuit Breakers—Out, to prevent unnecessary operation of jet throttle amplifiers and inadvertent opening of the throttles.

9A. Air Plugs—Adjust to windmill 5 to 7 per cent rpm.

CRUISE NO. 1 (LOW ALTITUDE-HEAVY GROSS WEIGHT).

Cruising at any altitude calls for real cruise control. The responsibility for cruise control rests heavily on the engineer. By working closely with his aircraft commander and navigator, the engineer must base his operations on calculations derived from a series of performance charts and curves. In addition he must develop operational techniques such as *manual adjustment* and *manual leaning,* and *dual* and *single* turbo operation. While maintaining a reasonable balance of the many operational variables and techniques involved, he must develop, in co-ordination with his aircraft commander and the navigation team, definite procedures in conjunction with the *Long Range Cruise* problem to compromise with other problems such as navigation, bombing, gunnery, etc.

Cruise No. 1 is the initial leg of the normal mission after take-off at maximum gross weight. At this time the long range air speed is, of necessity, relatively fast. The combination of gross weight, air speed, and altitude demands power settings which are above the manual leaning range. With perfect carburetion, operation would simply be in NORMAL mixture setting, but reasonable manufacturing tolerances do not allow such simplicity. To correct for this variable it is necessary to manually adjust the mixture controls until a specified fuel flow is obtained. These specified fuel flows are furnished the aircraft manufacturer by the engine manufacturer and in turn are plotted on engine fuel consumption curves, which are found in the appendix along with other operational data. For further information on manual adjustment, refer to "Mixture Control," Section VII.

Proper manual adjusting calls for accurate instrumentation; however, it must be noted by the operator that when operating below rated power, manually adjusted power settings are just slightly richer than best power. Investigate and observe the fuel flow at which best power is obtained. Common sense application of these observations will serve as a check of instrument calibration when compared with the average engine and will prevent marginal operation which might be detrimental to engine life.

After two or three cruises at this altitude, your gross weight and air-speed requirements will decrease to such a point that subsequent operation will phase into the manual leaning power range. Manual leaning procedures are given in Section VII, "Manual Leaning." Study these procedures carefully, for manual leaning is the "heart" of the overall operation of the B-36. It is one procedure that must be precise. Study the entire Section VII, "Reciprocating Engines" carefully, for it contains valuable information which will assist you in understanding various operational techniques and procedures.

BEFORE CLIMB OR HIGH POWER OPERATION.

Normally the first leg of the mission is accomplished with the jet engines off and the initial high reciprocating engine powers phased into lean operation. On some long initial cruises, it may become necessary to resort to single turbo operation if low rpm's in manual lean are attempted. You must anticipate the end of this leg, for several important steps must be taken before establishing a climb to a higher altitude. The engineer should know whether jet engines will be required for additional power, and will inform the aircraft commander of the required power configuration including the indicated air speeds to be maintained during the climb. In addition, the engineer and aircraft commander should allow themselves sufficient time to perform the items included in the following check lists when co-ordinating with the other crew members and establishing a time at which the climb should start.

STARTING JET ENGINES (AIR).

Note
Prior to starting jet engines, nose and cowl lips must be free of ice accumulation.

1. Notify engineer, "Set up jet start configuration."
2. All Circuit Breakers—In. To connect control and actuator circuits to their respective power sources.

1. Jet Start Configuration—Checked and, "Standing by for jet engine start." To insure positive fuel pressure to support reciprocating and jet engine operation,

STARTING JET ENGINES (AIR) (Cont'd)

3. Fire Detector Test Switches—TEST and release. This action checks the continuity of the detector system. Failure of any lamp to light within a reasonable length of time, or any light that flickers indicates a detector system malfunction and any later indications may not be reliable.

4. Throttle Selector Switches—LEVER.

5. Throttles—Closed.

6. Pod Preheat Switch—As required. ON when icing is anticipated or 10 minutes prior to jet engine start when OAT. is —30°C (—22°F) or colder. When jets are inoperative, pod preheat will not be effective unless the engineer's wing anti-icing switches are ON. Pod preheat should be turned off any time there is suspicion of fire so that fire may not enter the wing area.

7. Nose de-ice Switch—As Required. ON only to prevent ice forming on the jet air plugs.

8. Oil Heater Switch—As required. To maintain jet engine oil temperature when the ambient air temperature is below 5°C (41°F).

9. Oil Shutoff Valve Switches—OPEN. Always open during normal flight.

10. Air Plugs—OPEN (check doors visually). The aircraft commander and pilots will visually check their respective sides to see that air plugs are opening. The jet engines should start windmilling as the air plugs open. Approximately 185 mph IAS should result in a windmill speed of about 15 per cent rpm at any altitude. After air plugs have opened and the initial rpm build-up has stabilized, the desired starting speed may be controlled by varying the indicated air speed.

11. Manifold Valve Switches (L & R)—OPEN.

12. Booster Pump Switches (L & R)—ON.

13. (Deleted.)

14. J-1 Engine Fuel Valve—OPEN.

15. J-1 Fuel and Oil Pressure Gages—Note Reading. Notice where these pressure instruments zero so that you can tell when a pressure indication is obtained as rpm increases and the throttles are opened for a start.

16. Notify Lower Left Gunner—"Starting J-1." The gunners should be able to detect and report any unusual leaks or fire noted. With experience they will let you know when combustion occurs by observing the heat waves.

two tank valves and two booster pumps should be on in each wing.

BEFORE CLIMB (HIGH POWER OPERATION, AFTER A MANUAL LEAN SPARK ADVANCE CRUISE).

A tremendous amount of reciprocating engine damage can result if you fail to properly prepare the engine for high power operation. A good engineer should always remember the following items which must be checked, but even the best are prone to forget or overlook an item under certain conditions of stress or fatigue. By actually using the following check list, any oversight will be avoided and the transition from low to high power operational configurations will be successful.

1. Air Plugs and Intercoolers—OPEN. To prevent engine overheating during subsequent operation at higher bmep and increased fuel-air ratio.

STARTING JET ENGINES (AIR) (Cont'd)

17. J-1 Ignition Switch—Hold in ALT. This operation sets up the spark action which will ignite a combustible mixture as the proper fuel-air ratio is obtained when opening the throttle. Do not release the ignition switch until idle rpm for your specific altitude is stabilized.

18. J-1 Throttle—Open throttle to obtain 16 to 20 psi fuel pressure for normal altitude starts and 10 to 15 psi fuel pressure for starts at 40,000 feet or above. Ignition is primarily indicated by a sharp increase in tail pipe temperature. A successful start at any altitude is dependent on the correct fuel-air ratio; consequently, at high altitudes less fuel must be used because of the rarified air. As fuel pressure indication is received, the throttle should be retarded to obtain the desired fuel pressure mentioned above. In some instances this will necessitate retarding the throttle almost to the CLOSE position. Since low fuel pressure of this kind cannot easily be read, the tail pipe temperature indicator and tachometer can be used as reliable references. The tail pipe temperature should be increased very gradually from 100°C as engine speed increases toward idle rpm. For altitudes of 30,000 to 40,000 feet, the tail pipe temperature should not exceed 350°C for start and idle. Throttle technique is very important and at high altitude the throttle must be advanced gradually and slowly allowing enough time for per cent rpm to increase to the corresponding throttle position. It may at times become necessary to retard the throttle slightly if it is noted that the tail pipe temperature is rapidly increasing, if the tail pipe temperature is above the aforementioned value, or if a false start condition is evident. Use of the starter is not required for an air start.

> **CAUTION**
>
> Do not exceed maximum allowable tail pipe temperature when starting or during acceleration or operation.

Note

If combustion does not occur within 30 seconds after fuel pressure is available, discontinue this starting attempt and allow the excess fuel in the engine to drain. Close the

2. Spark Advance Switches—RETARD.

Note

See Section VII, "Spark Selection," for the specific procedure for return from manual lean spark advance operation to retard spark.

3. Mixture Control—NORMAL (Lights On). To provide an adequate fuel flow for any condition until the desired power is set.

4. Engine Supercharger Switches—BOTH. Dual turbo and high power operation go hand in hand. Use of single turbo in conjunction with a dual turbo power setting will result in overheating, turbo overspeeding, and, if allowed to continue at high bmep, severe engine damage. Abnormally high CAT. is a prime indication of an engine stuck in single turbo in flight when setting up a dual turbo power setting. See "Supercharging," Section VII, for further information on use of single and dual turbo and shifting procedures. If a malfunction of the system forces single turbo operation on one or more engines, they may be safely operated at sufficiently reduced powers to prevent excessive CAT.

5. Desired Power—SET. Procedure for setting powers, after observing the above steps, is normal.

6. Anti-icing Duct Temperatures—Increase as required. It is important that the anti-icing duct temperatures be increased prior to climb to higher altitudes. Doing this will prevent enclosure and blister icing during the climb, thereby eliminating the need to defrost after reaching the scheduled altitude. In some cases it may be feasible to increase the duct temperatures to the maximum limits. This will depend, of course, upon the conditions which are anticipated to be encountered at the higher altitudes.

STARTING JET ENGINES (AIR) (Cont'd)

throttle and place the ignition switch OFF. After allowing approximately one minute for draining, the starting attempt may be repeated.

19. J-1 Oil Pressure—Report indication on interphone. The oil pressure should increase with rpm. If a positive increase has not been observed by the time a start has been effected, the engine should be shut down to prevent damage from lack of lubrication.

20. J-1 Ignition Switch—Release at idle. When idle rpm for your specific altitude is stabilized, flame propagation should be complete and selfsustaining. Release the ignition switch, which is spring-loaded, to the OFF position.

21. J-1 Throttle—Adjust to maintain idle rpm. Allow the initial engines started to idle while starting subsequent engines. This aids in preventing a more asymmetrical power condition while starting the corresponding symmetrical jet engine.

22. J-4, J-2, J-3—Repeat steps 13 through 21. As for a ground start, begin the start procedure with the engines which have accumulated the least time. However, subsequent starts will be from side to side in order to maintain the best balanced power condition. In order to even up the logged time when operating only two jets, you may operate any combination of jet engines provided one on each wing is used. One or two engines may be started at any time to offset loss of reciprocating engines if sufficient fuel remains or safety is a factor.

Simultaneous Starts.

The simultaneous air starting of two jet engines can be accomplished at altitudes of 30,000 feet and below. Jets should be started in symmetrical pairs. The normal starting procedure and check list will be used with the following:

1. The aircraft commander will simultaneously place the appropriate ignition start switches in the ALT position with his right hand.

2. He will simultaneously open both throttles normally with his left hand. Individual adjustments to control tail pipe temperatures during combustion will be made.

3. After combustion both throttles will be cautiously advanced to idle rpm and the ignition switches will be released. Both throttles will continue to be advanced together until the desired jet power setting is reached, before the remaining pair of jet engines is started.

The above procedure is useful during formation climbs and is also desirable from a standpoint of fuel economy.

Section II
Normal Procedures

CLIMB TO HIGH ALTITUDE.

Crew co-ordination is very important during climb to altitude, particularly co-ordination between the aircraft commander, the engineer, and the gunners. The gunners must keep check of reciprocating engine air plug settings, evidences of over-heating, oil leaking, or any other sign of malfunction of the airplane. The engineer must be aware of all malfunctions as indicated by the engine instruments and reported by the gunners so as to effectively control the engines at peak efficiency during the climb. The aircraft commander must fly the correct air speed, maintaining the rate of climb steady for the given air speed, and retrim the airplane frequently to obtain best climb performance.

The engineer will maintain a close surveillance on the engine instruments and keep the air plugs adjusted to maximum allowable cylinder head temperatures, thereby obtaining minimum drag. The air plug is a direct control over cooling air flow and can be considered a throttle to the cooling passages. When the combination of air speed and fan results in an excess of air being pumped over that required to maintain satisfactory temperatures, considerable drag is eliminated by restricting the passage and, consequently, the weight of air being pumped.

The entire crew must be well trained, properly disciplined and prepared to operate as a co-ordinated team if safety and efficiency are to be obtained at high altitudes. The B-36 has been operated consistently at extreme altitudes where the greatest strain is placed upon both the airplane and the individual. How well it will perform for you depends upon all the preparation, training, checking, and planning thus far—plus an alert ability to anticipate the requirements that will provide an ease of operation with a reasonable margin of safety. Any time operation is to be above 25,000 feet altitude, each crew member should have some specific task to perform that will aid the operation. All crew members should be notified and prepared for altitude operation before the climb begins until after the descent below critical altitude. The engineer's log should be up-to-date and the climb and initial cruise powers and air speeds should have already been entered in appropriate columns for ready reference and information to the aircraft commander and navigator when requested. Last minute preparations for pressurization, heating, and anti-icing should be considered. Any equipment needed must be accessible to your oxygen station.

The navigation team should be prepared to keep the pilot informed of correct headings to fly and to make frequent position reports.

You will normally use the jet engines for long range climb above 25,000 feet altitude. (See Appendix I for recommended climb power for various gross weights and altitudes.) The fuel consumed for a given climb increment for normal rated power is about equal to the fuel consumed using the recommended long range climb power, but a greater distance is covered since the time and average speed are greater.

CREW SAFETY AT ALTITUDE.

Crew safety at altitude is extremely important. The aircraft commander should be on guard at all times while flying at high altitude in seeing that his crew is doing the right thing at the right time. One of the most important aspects of altitude flying is oxygen discipline. Refer to "Oxygen System," Section IV.

HIGH ALTITUDE CRUISE.

Cruise at high altitude is normally defined in two categories: Cruise No. 2, which is cruising at high altitude with the jet engines operating, and Cruise No. 3, which is cruising at high altitude without the use of jet engines. Again the main factor is manual leaning, and the engineer must concern himself with the many problems that will confront him during these operations.

As cruise control extends the range of the airplane, so does it amplify the duties and responsibilities of the engineer. Complete proficiency in the use of the charts and curves will be attained only by understanding them and working with them. Conscientious study of the pages to follow and of Appendix I is essential.

Obviously, the term cruise control cannot be applied exclusively to any single operation. Actually, it consists of five interrelated operational steps as follows:

1. Preflight planning.
2. Inflight operations.
3. Inflight replanning.
4. Operations after failure of one or more engines.
5. Postflight analysis.

These steps are founded on a series of performance curves and charts. Since these charts and the use of them are basic to the other operations, they will be discussed first. However, before considering the charts and curves at length, let's have a brief explanation of "Drag Factors," and "Air Speed Versus Gross Weight and Altitudes," since doing so will make certain features of the charts and curves more readily understandable.

DRAG FACTORS.

Unnecessary drag is a very detrimental factor in planning proper cruise control. It can be caused by improper trimming of the airplane or by improper settings of air plugs or cooling doors.

To combat improper trim of the aircraft, it is recommended that a definite schedule of trimming be set up. For instance, if the engineer is on a 2-hour power schedule, the aircraft should be retrimmed every hour on the elevator axis. In all cases of power changes the aircraft should be retrimmed to conform with the new air speed, and it should also be retrimmed after all fuel transfers and changes in cg of the aircraft.

A second cause of drag to be reckoned with is the settings of the air plugs and cooling doors. From their fully open to fully closed positions the air plugs on all six engines can vary the air speed as much as six mph EAS and the intercoolers as much as four mph EAS. Open doors and hatches also cause drag. Keep them closed. When an air speed is given, it should be maintained as closely as possible to get maximum cooling of the engine with air plugs and cooling doors shut down as far as possible so as to maintain the engine temperatures within limits. The opening of these doors and plugs will reduce air speed considerably by increasing the drag.

AIR SPEED VERSUS GROSS WEIGHT AND ALTITUDE.

Air speed versus gross weight and altitude is the basis for the development of the nautical mile per pound charts which determine long-range cruising plans. In the nautical mile per pound charts a recommended EAS is obtained for a given weight and altitude. Through proper power setting and proper trimming of the airplane, the engineer and pilot maintain these recommended air speeds.

Since long-range flying is based on cruise control, it is necessary to see the effect of gross weight and altitude in air speed. Air speed is the starting point for the engineer in setting proper power, while the pilot must maintain level flight through correct trimming of the aircraft. The final goal, nautical miles per pound, can then be attained.

Level-off for cruising altitude should be made from an altitude of 200 to 500 feet above cruising altitude. The engineer should set up cruise power commensurate with aircraft weight and altitude, less the extra 200 to 500 feet, to help establish cruising air speed and trim the aircraft cruising straight and level. Efficient cruising requires maintaining a recommended air speed which can be obtained from the "Specific Range Curves." Maintain the desired air speed by use of the elevators and vary power settings slightly to maintain altitude. Do not allow air speed to drop; if it is impossible to maintain altitude with a given air speed, check trim and then add power as necessary.

SYSTEMS OPERATION.

Operation of the various systems during flight is given in Section VII, "Systems Operation."

FLIGHT CHARACTERISTICS.

Refer to Section VI, "Flight Characteristics," for the characteristics of the aircraft during flight.

DESCENT FROM HIGH ALTITUDE.

After cruising at high altitudes, the next phase will be to descend to a medium altitude. For information concerning descents, refer to "Normal Descent" of this section.

CRUISE NO. 4 (MEDIUM ALTITUDE-LOW GROSS WEIGHT).

Cruising at a medium altitude at low gross weight on the last leg of the journey home is known as Cruise No. 4. Again the engineer concerns himself with manual leaning.

DESCENT.

NORMAL DESCENT.

Descent in every case should be governed by the air speed and propeller limitation specified in "Operating Limitations," Section V. Air speed is the more critical limit because undetected flutter could cause structural failure. Propeller vibration, however, usually means a sharp reduction in blade life rather than an immediate failure.

Descents should always be made at long-range air speed. Most long-range flights are made with the airplane on automatic pilot, and the rate of descent will be approximately 300 feet per minute. When necessary, power reduction will be made in accordance with the bmep power schedule of the Appendix in order to maintain efficient and economical engine operation.

> **CAUTION**
>
> Do not collapse reciprocating engines except for emergency descent. This procedure is discussed in Section III.

Under no-wind conditions, approximately 2.2 nautical miles of range can be gained for every 1000 feet of altitude. For example, descent from 25,000 feet to sea level will add about 55 miles to the range. However, this is a small factor compared with the magnitude of winds at altitude. Consequently, wind conditions must be given primary consideration in making a descent. If there is a strong head wind at a high altitude and a tail wind is predicted for a lower altitude, obviously descent should be made to the lower altitude to take advantage of the tail wind. On the other hand, if the winds at all altitudes are the same but the nautical miles per gallon at the higher cruising altitude is greater than that which would be obtained at the lower altitude, the high altitude should be maintained since the airplane is already at altitude.

Another factor entering into the descent picture is crew fatigue. If there is only a slight difference in nautical miles per gallon obtainable at high and low altitude, the decision would probably be made to remain at the higher altitude so as to reduce the time required to complete the mission.

RAPID DESCENT.

When head winds are encountered, it is best to descend rapidly through the regions of high adverse winds and cruise at altitudes where wind conditions are more favorable. Regardless of these factors, however, you should in no case descend below the altitude you will have to maintain for the remainder of the flight because of topographic conditions.

Rapid descent like normal descent should also be governed by the air speed and propeller limits specified in Section V. In this case, however, power settings are reduced to minimum values required to prevent excessive wear and stress from reverse bearing loads. The absolute minimum setting is 1550 rpm and 15.5 inches

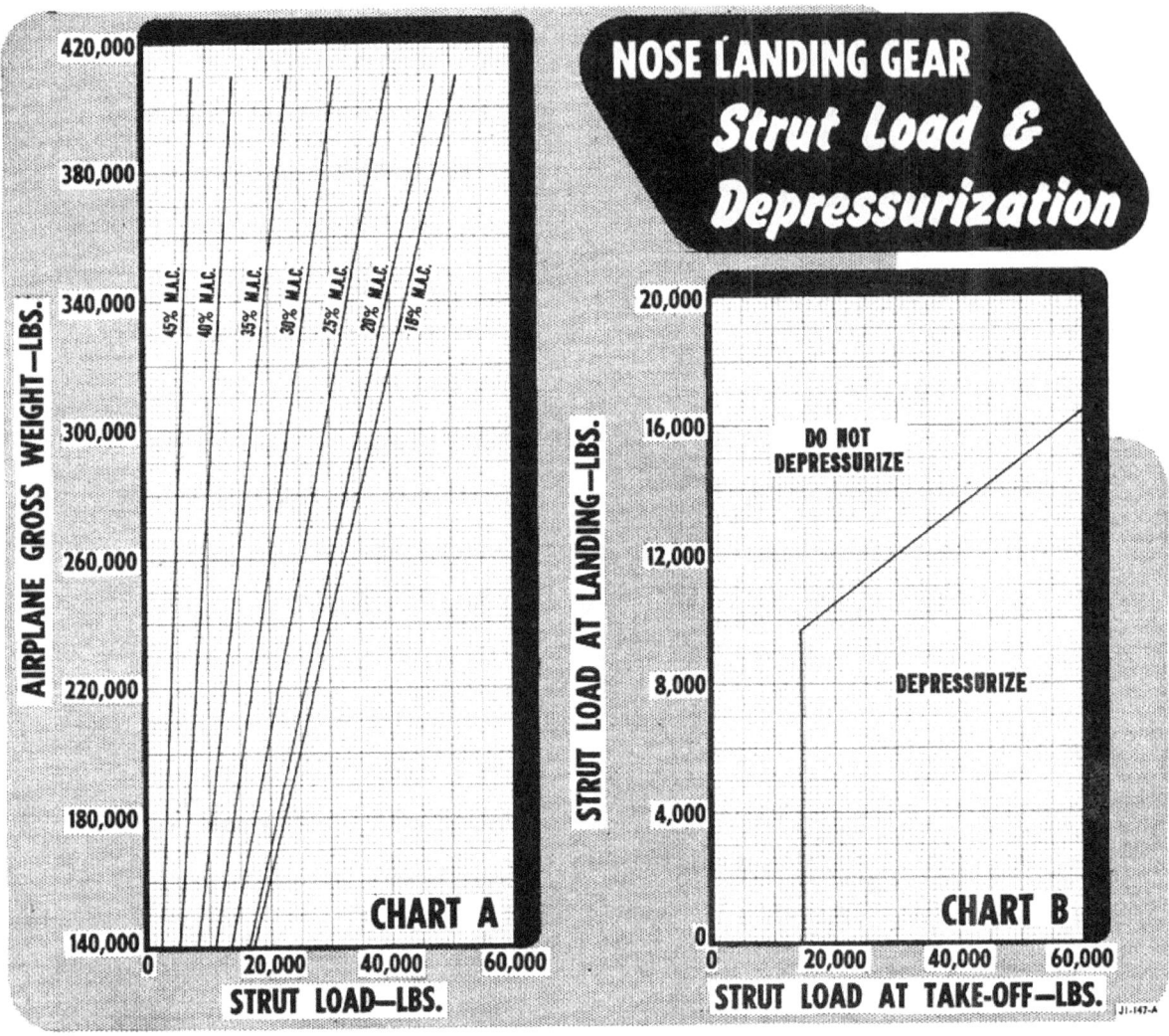

Figure 2-11.

M.P. Settings above this minimum should be computed on the basis of 1 inch M.P. for each 100 rpm increase.

> CAUTION
>
> Manifold pressures below these minimum values will be limited to 30 seconds or less. Gas pressure is needed inside the cylinder to prevent stress and wear caused by windmilling.

NORMAL LANDING.

This airplane is not difficult to land after you've made a few landings to adjust yourself to its landing attitude. This adjustment is necessary because your station is so far forward of the wing; and, with the nose-up condition of a normal landing, you are about 40 to 50 feet in the air. Since this airplane has such a large wing span, you must realize that somewhat less control response can be expected at the slower air speeds encountered during final approach. However, if you use good judgment and apply the knowledge gained from landing other airplanes, you can land this airplane without difficulty.

Note

Tests indicate that approximately 5 seconds less time is required to operate the elevator trim tab control wheel from one extreme position to the other when the operator's inboard arm rest is in the up position. This time saving could mean the difference between a successful maneuver and a crash during landing.

NOSE GEAR STRUT DEPRESSURIZATION.

The requirements for depressurization of the nose strut are based on the relationship of nose strut loads at take-off and landing. This relationship can be obtained from the charts in figure 2-11 to determine whether depressurization of the nose gear strut is necessary. The charts are used in the following manner:

1. Using Chart A, determine the strut load at take-off by finding the point of intersection of the lines representing take-off gross weight and cg location. From this point, follow the vertical line to the bottom of the chart and read the strut load.

2. To determine the strut load at landing, repeat step 1, using landing gross weight and cg location.

3. Using Chart B, follow the lines representing the strut loads at landing and at take-off until they intersect. The area in which the lines intersect will indicate whether or not depressurization is required.

TRAFFIC PATTERN.

Because of the high stability of the airplane, considerable longitudinal retrimming will be necessary when executing steep turns. This trimming must be accomplished during the entry and exit periods of the turns to maintain constant air speed and nominal elevator control forces.

The traffic pattern should be entered by flying upwind parallel to the landing runway at traffic altitudes. This will give you an opportunity to observe airdrome traffic and space your aircraft in the traffic pattern accordingly. The downwind leg is approximately two or three miles out from the landing runway at 1500 feet above the terrain. A 500-foot descent should be made on the base leg so that the turn on the final approach is accomplished at 1000 feet. Before turning on the base leg, the "Before Landing" check list should be complete and the landing configuration should be received from the engineer. This will permit a correct approach speed with a 500-foot per minute descent on the final leg.

A minimum air speed of 150 mph IAS should be maintained on the downwind leg during normal landings. The landing gear should not be extended until you are halfway through the downwind leg or when opposite the end of the landing runway. When the gear is extended and checked, the flaps should be lowered to 10 degrees. The minimum air speed for the downwind leg will be maintained for the base leg, and the flaps will be extended to 20 degrees. On the final approach, air speed should be maintained at a minimum of 135 per cent of stalling speed. Do not exceed 145 per cent of stalling speed. The flaps should also be lowered to 30 degrees.

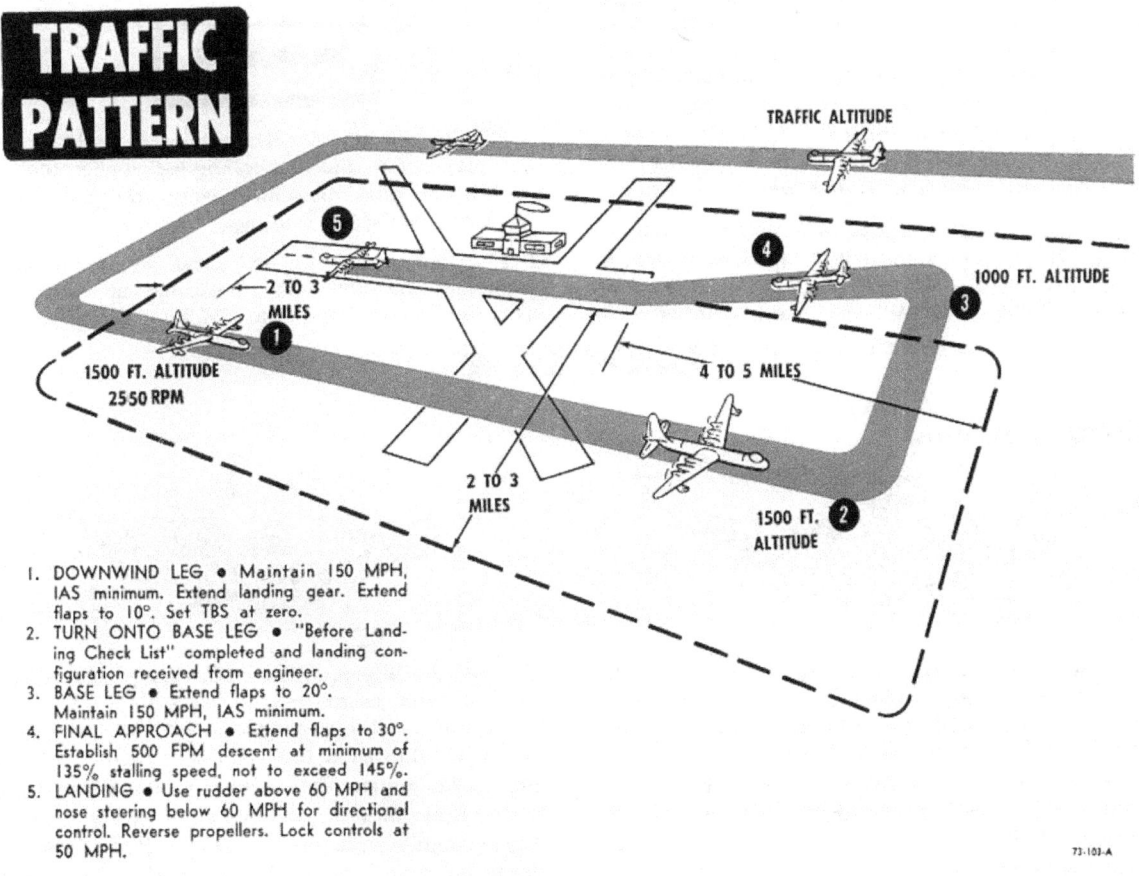

1. DOWNWIND LEG • Maintain 150 MPH, IAS minimum. Extend landing gear. Extend flaps to 10°. Set TBS at zero.
2. TURN ONTO BASE LEG • "Before Landing Check List" completed and landing configuration received from engineer.
3. BASE LEG • Extend flaps to 20°. Maintain 150 MPH, IAS minimum.
4. FINAL APPROACH • Extend flaps to 30°. Establish 500 FPM descent at minimum of 135% stalling speed, not to exceed 145%.
5. LANDING • Use rudder above 60 MPH and nose steering below 60 MPH for directional control. Reverse propellers. Lock controls at 50 MPH.

Figure 2-12.

When the flaps are lowered, the airplane tends to nose up and gain altitude. Therefore, when the flaps are lowered, anticipate this change in attitude and roll in enough nose-down elevator trim to counteract this tendency. Each successive lowering of the flaps on the base and final legs will require further down-elevator trim.

When the aircraft is at an average landing weight of about 200,000 to 230,000 pounds, a power setting of about 30 inches M. P. should maintain sufficient air speed and altitude on the downwind leg. When the gear is lowered and flaps set at 10 degrees, an increase in power to about 37 inches M. P. is necessary to maintain correct air speed and altitude.

Control effectiveness versus air speed is very important during the final approach while trying to maintain a constant IAS. Excessive aileron movement, cross trim, improper throttle settings, or overcontrolling tend to increase stall characteristics and decrease control effectiveness, with a resultant loss of air speed. On the final approach, keep the wings as level as possible. For directional control, minimize the use of aileron control. During cross-wind landings, employ rudder control rather than aileron control to correct for drift. Aileron control sluggishness is evident at low approach speeds and can cause wing wallow if inadvertent aileron overcontrol is used. Because of this condition and the low clearance of pods and outboard propellers from the runway (5-foot clearance between outboard propeller tips and the ground and 5-foot, 8-inch clearance between the pods and the ground), *it is imperative to maintain wings level during flare-out and landing.*

The aircraft should be landed in a slightly nose-high attitude at as high a touchdown speed as practical. In no case should full stall landings be attempted. Flare-out should be started from an altitude of 60 to 70 feet. Keep airspeed well above stalling speed during the round out. When landing with an aft cg location, it must be remembered that during the flare-out the tail will drop more rapidly than with forward cg location. When the main gear is on the runway, the pilot will ready the propellers on the order of the aircraft commander. The nose should be eased down on the runway and directional control maintained with the rudder. Rudder control is effective down to speeds of 60 mph. Propellers will be reversed on the command of the aircraft commander who will apply the necessary power with the throttles to slow down the airplane. This application of power should not exceed 30 inches M. P. unless there is an emergency. The pilot will hold forward pressure to keep the nose wheel firmly on the runway. After the air speed has dropped to 50 mph IAS, the aircraft commander should lock the controls with his right hand and use nose wheel steering with his left hand. If nose steering is inoperative, differential power with the propellers in reverse pitch can be used to maintain directional control. Caution should be taken not to use the nose steering to make any large corrections until the airplane has slowed considerably. Severe oscillations or buffeting of the nose section will occur if you use overcontrol of the nose wheel steering on fast ground rolls.

WARNING

Flight crew will not be stationed in the lower nose section during landing because of the likelihood of personnel being trapped in event of a crash landing.

The aircraft commander will stand by on the interphone and the pilot will be on command radio with the mixer selector switch at INTER.

BEFORE LANDING.

1. Notify Crew—"Prepare to land." The safety belts and shoulder harnesses fastened and inertia reel lock controls UNLOCKED. The landing check should be started 8 to 10 minutes before landing.
2. Bomb Bay Area—Checked. A designated crew member will inspect the bomb bay area for fuel and hydraulic leaks.
3. Autopilot—Off.
4. Jet Air Plug Switches—OPEN. Although the 5

1. In-Flight Engine Checks—Completed, if desired. The following checks may be made prior to landing as conditions and time permit. In no way should these checks be allowed to interfere with normal landing procedures. Engine checks which are not accomplished at this time must be accomplished during the postflight engine checks on the ground. If the following checks are completed during flight they need not be re-checked on the ground.

BEFORE LANDING (Cont'd)

to 7 per cent windmilling rpm experienced in flight with the jet air plugs closed will scavenge most of the jet oil, a certain amount will tend to collect in the engine. To scavenge all of the oil, it is necessary to open the air plugs to increase windmilling rpm when entering the landing pattern.

5. Jet Engines—As required. If landing at heavy gross weights, start the required number of jet engines at this time.

Note

The following analyzer checks can be accomplished in accordance with local procedure. Standard analyzer check procedure will be included when available.

a. Slow sweep 14 patterns for each magneto.
b. Magneto synchronization check.
c. Magneto dwell check.

2. Engine Supercharger Switches—BOTH.
3. Fuel Panel Checked—Booster pumps ON.
4. Oil Vent Heater Switch—As required.
5. Carburetor Preheat Switches—As required.
6. Cabin Pressure Shutoff Valve Switches—OFF.
7. Booster Fan Switch—As required.
8. Pitot Heater Switches—As required.
9. Wing and Cabin Heat and Tail Anti-Icing Switches—OFF.
10. Engine Fan Speeds Switches—LOW RPM.
11. Electrical System—Checked.
12. Air Plugs and Intercoolers—As required.
13. Cabin Heater Power Switch—OFF.
14. Temperatures—Checked and within limits.
15. Mixure Control Selector Switches—LEVER.
16. Mixture Control Levers—NORMAL.
17. Turbo Boost Selector Lever—ZERO, calibration knobs indexed.
18. Spark Advance Switches—RETARD (guards down).
19. Propeller Selector Switches—AUTOMATIC OPERATION, Tel-Lamps Lighted.
20. Propeller Normal Pitch Indicator Lamps—Lighted.
21. Turbo Control Change-Over Switches (Group 2 Airplanes)—AUTO.
22. Turbo Control Vernier Switch (Group 2 Airplanes)—OFF.
23. Engineer's Landing Configuration — Engineer reads—"Before Landing Check List Complete, Standing by for RPM, Landing Gear, and Brake Check, Gross Weight_____."
24. Master Tachometer—2550 rpm. At high gross weights, high field elevations, or in emergencies, 2700 rpm and 7 TBS setting may be used.

6. Engineer's Landing Configuration — Engineer reads—"Before Landing Check List Complete, Standing by for RPM, Landing Gear, and Brake Check, Gross Weight_____."

7. Stalling Speeds and Take-off and Landing Data—Checked and reviewed. A check of the placard on your instrument panel will give you the stalling speeds at various flap settings for the landing gross weight. Also, review the take-off and landing data with the pilot.

BEFORE LANDING (Cont'd)

8. Master Tachometer—2550 rpm.

9. Landing Gear Control Switch—EXTEND. The gang bar arrangement will turn the brake pump switch ON. The pilot will report on the interphone "Gear coming down," and will place the landing gear and brake pump switches in EXTEND and ON, respectively. The aft gunners will watch gear operation through the complete cycle and will report on interphone as follows: "Left door coming open, right door coming open. Left gear down and locked, right gear down and locked. Left door fully closed, right door fully closed." The pilot will observe the landing gear indicator lamps and note whether the warning horn is sounding; also he will receive the engineer's report that main hydraulic system pressure is relieved. The radio operator will check the nose gear through the inspection window and will report, "Nose gear down and locked." Complete extension of the gear normally takes approximately 45 seconds. After receiving the pilot's report that the gear is down and locked, the aircraft commander will check to see that the red landing gear indicator lamp is out and the green lamp is lighted. As an additional check to determine whether the landing gear is fully extended, he will retard at least one reciprocating engine throttle and check that landing gear warning horn does not sound.

25. Report, "Hydraulic Pressure Relieved."

The indicated air speed must not exceed 188 mph during landing gear extension. A visual check of the landing gear by the aft gunners and radio operator is very important. The green indicator lamp is operated by the main and nose gear limit switches and is not a positive check. The aft gunners check of the flags on the main gear side braces and the radio operator's check of the nose gear, together with the hydraulic pressure relief noted by the engineer, is a positive check. After receiving the radio operator's and gunners reports that the landing gear is down and locked, check that the nose wheel steering indicator is at zero.

10. Parking Brake Control—OFF. The parking brakes can be set accidently by personnel moving about on the flight deck.

11. Left and Right Brakes—Checked. After the gear is down and locked, check the brakes. The pilot will depress the foot pedals one at a time, and the engineer will report a drop in brake pressure as each pedal is operated. After both pedals are operated and the pressure has returned to normal, the engineer will report the fact on interphone.

26. Observe brake check and report, "Pressure normal."

12. Nose Gear Strut—Bled, if required. See figure 2-11 to determine whether depressurization is necessary.

BEFORE LANDING (Cont'd)

13. Nose Steering Switch—ON. No steering pressure will be indicated until the nose strut is compressed below 10 inches after landing.

14. Pilot rechecks gear down and locked, autopilot off, nose wheel steering switch ON, and reports to aircraft commander, "Gear down and locked, landing configuration complete."

15. Flaps—10 degrees.

BASE LEG.

1. Flaps—20 degrees.

2. Jet Air Plug Switches—CLOSE.

3. Landing Lights (if required)—Extended and checked.

FINAL APPROACH.

1. Flaps—30 degrees.

Maintain a minimum of 135 per cent of stalling speed or a minimum of 120 mph IAS, whichever is higher. Do not exceed 145 per cent of stalling speed. Lift with 30-degree flap setting is sufficient to allow a very steep landing approach with power off; however, normal approach is made with power on to prevent overcooling of the engines.

The aircraft commander will be advised by the pilot whenever the air speed falls below final approach speed or whenever a visual and altimeter cross-check indicates the aircraft to be dangerously low to the ground or other obstructions. The pilot will continuously monitor the air-speed, altimeter, and rate-of-climb indicators and will maintain a visual check of the ground or obstructions when possible. This will insure the immediate recognition of a dangerous condition for relay to the aircraft commander.

Note

The pilot will call out each 5 mph change in IAS and each 100-foot change in altitude, except during GCA and instrument letdowns.

WARNING

Extreme caution must be observed when in close proximity to the ground as only a small angle of bank can be executed before propellers or pods contact the runway.

LANDING.

PILOTS

1. Propeller Reverse Selector Switches—READY, on main gear contact. The pilot will place these switches in READY at the order of the aircraft commander.

> **CAUTION**
>
> Do not ready the propellers until ground contact has been made.

2. Propeller Reverse Pitch Switch—Depressed on aircraft commander's command. The pilot will actuate this switch at the order of the aircraft commander after the nose wheel has contacted the runway. When the pilot actuates the switch, the aircraft commander will increase the throttles to the desired power. With the propellers in reverse during normal landings, 30 inches M.P. is maximum; however, in emergencies full power application is acceptable. The pilot will stand by on the controls and will hold them in neutral while reversing with the exception of holding forward pressure on the elevators. The effect of reverse thrust from the propellers is greater at high speeds; thus, it is desirable to use reverse thrust as soon as possible after landing.

3. Control Surfaces—Locked at approximately 50 mph. On normal landing the flight controls should not be locked until forward speed reaches approximately 50 mph. This will permit the use of the rudder for directional control for as long as it is effective. Since gusty winds can cause serious rudder damage when the airplane's speed is less than 50 mph, the controls must be locked at approximately 50 mph on all landings. If more than 30 inches M. P. is needed after reverse pitch, controls must be locked at all speeds.

4. Propeller Reverse Selector Switches—SAFE. The aircraft commander will return the desired pairs of propellers to the normal position after the landing. The engines should be reduced to idle before returning the reverse selector switches to SAFE.

> **CAUTION**
>
> If the outboard propellers are not needed for emergency stopping, they must be placed in normal pitch before reaching 40 mph to prevent aileron flutter and possible damage.

5. Flaps—Retracted.

ENGINEERS

1. Brake and Nose Steering Pressure—Normal after nose wheel contacts ground.

2. RPM and Manifold Pressure—Checked. After propellers are reversed, the engineer will normally stabilize power. Do not exceed 30 inches M.P. except in an emergency. This in no way means that the engineer will restrict additional power application required by the aircraft commander to maintain directional control.

LANDING (Cont'd)

6. Jet Oil Shutoff Valve Switches—CLOSE, at zero per cent rpm. These valves should be closed at zero per cent rpm to trap all of the oil in the tanks. If this is not done and the oil tanks are filled before the next flight, the excess oil trapped in the engine will be forced out the vent lines on the next jet start. When closing the valves, be sure the associated circuit breakers are pushed in.

Note

One of the symmetrical pairs of reciprocating engines will be stopped on command of the aircraft commander after landing has been completed, after the airplane has been turned off the active runway, and after the engines have been checked for proper operation.

HEAVY GROSS WEIGHT LANDINGS.

With the forward cg location of the B-36 at high gross weights, very large up-elevator deflections are required when flying at low air speeds in the landing condition near the ground. This is caused by the great amount of static stability possessed by the aircraft when in a forward cg condition combined with the nullifying effect of the ground on the down wash air load over the tail. This requires additional up-elevator deflection to produce the total tail-down load needed to balance the pitching moments of the aircraft.

The following piloting techniques are recommended for landings with gross weights of approximately 283,-000 pounds or more:

1. Start two jet engines on the downwind leg and have them operating at 90 per cent rpm.

2. Conduct the final approach portion of the landing as flat as practicable with power on, maintaining a minimum of 135 per cent stalling speed. Do not exceed 145 per cent stalling speed. Adjust reciprocating engine power to maintain these speeds.

3. Allow the power to remain on until the aircraft actually touches the runway. As soon as the main gear wheels are on the runway, cut power and apply additional up-elevator control force to counter the rapidly increasing nose-down moment of the aircraft which occurs when power is cut. This will minimize the impact of the nose wheel when the aircraft pitches forward.

4. When the nose wheel contacts the runway, reverse the propellers immediately. In the event of a minimum run landing, keep power on and reverse the propeller as soon as the main gear wheels touch the runway. No difficulty will be experienced in getting the nose wheel down. In fact, the nose will still go down rapidly unless additional up-elevator is employed.

MINIMUM-RUN LANDINGS.

Use the same procedure as that used in normal landing with the following exceptions: Reverse the propellers after the main landing gear touches the ground and before the nose wheel touches the ground. When reversing the propellers with the nose still in the air, the nose must not be at too high a deck angle and must be held steady since there is a slight tendency to nose up. When a maximum of 30 inches M.P. is used, reduce master motor speed to 2000 rpm. This will give a more effective reverse thrust.

CAUTION

Since the airplane has a very responsive brake system and is equipped with four-wheel main gears, extra care must be used to avoid skidding the rear wheels. Gunners should be alert for such observations and should notify the aircraft commander.

CROSS-WIND LANDINGS.

Cross-wind landings will be avoided if at all possible. If, at any point during final approach, lateral corrections of an appreciable magnitude are required, an immediate go-around will be executed in order to avoid having a wing drop while near the ground. Avoid dropping one wing to correct for a cross-wind. The recommended procedure for making a cross-wind approach and landing is to head into the wind (crab) just enough to keep a straight ground path and hold the wing level. Take out the crab with the rudder after flare-out and before touch-down, being careful not to inadvertently drop a wing. Put nose gear down as soon as possible after touch-down and apply forward pressure on the control column.

GO-AROUND.

The decision for go-around should be made before descending to 500 feet, if possible. The sooner the decision to go-around is made, the better the chances are for success. When weighing the possibilities for go-around in terms of altitude, air speed, gross weight, aircraft configuration, wind conditions, runway facilities, and visibility, the aircraft commander should always consider the advantages of a controlled crash landing over an unsuccessful go-around. This is especially true if aircraft performance is critical or altitude (500 feet or less) is marginal.

In the event a go-around becomes necessary, proceed as follows:

1. The aircraft commander will announce over interphone, "Go-around, flaps 20 degrees."

2. The pilot will raise the flaps from full down position to 20 degrees on aircraft commander's command.

CAUTION

Drag with full flaps is excessive. Raise the flaps to 20 degrees as quickly as possible when the decision to go around has been made. Do *not* raise flaps past 20 degrees until a safe IAS has been obtained. Flaps should not be completely retracted before reaching 140 mph IAS or 125 per cent of stalling speed (whichever is greater).

WARNING

A safe IAS must be maintained in a go-around; therefore, continue on the same approach angle until safe flying speed has been reached.

3. The aircraft commander will adjust power as required, co-ordinating reciprocating engine and jet engine power with the pilot.

4. Landing Gear Switch—RETRACT. The aircraft commander will give the order, "Gear up."

Note

A landing gear check will be made in accordance with the procedure in "Take-Off" of this section.

1. Smoothly increase M. P. to 55 inches. If additional power is required, increase master motor cautiously to 2700 rpm and manifold pressure as required.

CAUTION

To avoid overspeeding propellers when increasing power in a go-around, advance the throttles to full open before advancing the turbo boost selector to 7 position.

GO-AROUND (Cont'd)

WARNING

The landing gear will not be retracted until it is certain that the touch-down will not be made. Remember that the aircraft will continue to settle for a short period after full power has been applied.

TAXIING AFTER LANDING.

For taxiing instructions after landing, refer to "Taxiing" of this section. When taxiing after landing and after postflight engine checks, one symmetrical pair of engines may be shut down.

POSTFLIGHT ENGINE RUN-UP.

The postflight engine run-up will be performed by the pilots and engineer as follows:

CAUTION

Make sure wheels are chocked if engine run-up is performed in a congested area.

1. Parking Brake Control—ON.
2. Propeller Reverse Selector Switches—SAFE (lights out).
3. Nose Wheel Steering Switch—OFF.
4. Notify engineer, "Start postflight engine run-up."

1. All Propeller Pitch Indicator Lamps—Lighted.
2. Master Tachometer—2700 rpm.
3. Parking Brakes—Set, pressure normal.
4. Nose Steering Pressure—ZERO.
5. Announce over interphone, "Ready for postflight."
6. Engine Run-up—Completed.
   a. Idle speed and mixture—Check.

Note

Refer to "Stopping Reciprocating Engines, Preflight Operational Equipment Check."

POSTFLIGHT ENGINE RUN-UP (Cont'd)

 b. Set throttles 1 and 6 to field barometric pressure.

 c. Note and record rpm, M. P., torque, and fuel flow.

 d. Perform single ignition check.

 e. Throttle lever—Closed.

7. Repeat step 6 for remaining symmetrical engines.

8. Check that cylinder head temperatures are 180°C or below. Shut down engines 1 and 6 in accordance with "Stopping Reciprocating Engines" of this section.

9. Report to aircraft commander, "Postflight run complete, ready to taxi."

10. Repeat steps 1 through 4 and step 8 before shutting down remaining engines.

CAUTION

If an engine has been shut down in flight then unfeathered for emergency use, that engine should be carefully watched during engine shutdown on the ground. This is necessary because loss of ram air and an accumulation of oil or fuel around the engine and exhaust system creates a fire hazard. A check of that engine should be made before leaving the aircraft.

STOPPING RECIPROCATING ENGINES.

The engineer will stop engines in accordance with the instructions given in "Preflight Operational Equipment Check, Stopping Reciprocating Engines." The aircraft commander will accomplish the following during engine shutdown.

1. Parking Brake Control—ON.

2. Propeller Reverse Selector Switches—SAFE (lights out).

3. Nose Wheel Steering Switch—OFF.

4. Flight Instrument Switches—OFF.

5. Contact engineer, "Ready to stop engines."

STOPPING RECIPROCATING ENGINES (Cont'd)

> **CAUTION**
>
> Aircraft commander, engineer, and the lower aft gunners will remain on interphone. The pilot will have radio tuned to tower frequency until the last propeller has stopped turning.

6. Radio Equipment—OFF.

BEFORE LEAVING AIRCRAFT.

Check and accomplish the following before leaving the aircraft:

1. All Control Switches—Properly positioned. Check that the navigation, fuselage, cabin, compass, fluorescent, and all other miscellaneous lights are off. Pull the following circuit breakers on the pilot's circuit breaker panel; slaved gyro magnetic compass or N-1 compass, bomb salvo, bomb bay doors, aircraft commander's and pilot's turn and bank indicators. Check that all oxygen regulators are off.

2. Wheel Chocks—In Place.

3. Parking Brake Control—OFF after wheels are chocked.

4. Postflight Visual Inspection—Completed.

   a. The aircraft commander will state time for postflight crew inspection and will give crew permission to exit the aircraft.

   b. Ground locks installed.

   c. Unload the aircraft.

   d. A rapid visual inspection of the exterior should be made by the aircraft commander.

   e. Crew will fall in at the left side of the nose in two ranks.

1. Fuel Dip Stick Readings—As required (or the best available method of determining fuel remaining).

2. Forms and Reports—Completed. Co-ordinate with maintenance and operations.

Section II
Normal Procedures

BEFORE LEAVING AIRCRAFT (Cont'd)

f. Roll call and aircraft discrepancies for entry in Form 781 (Form 1).

g. Collect all reports, logs, etc.

h. Dismiss crew.

Note

The postflight visual inspection will normally be conducted after each flight; however, weather, crew fatigue, and other intangible factors may sometimes necessitate a modification.

Section III
EMERGENCY PROCEDURES

Survival in an emergency requires the fully coordinated effort of each crew member. A well trained crew will know what to do and, if properly disciplined, will react with efficiency. Since procedure drills are the nearest approach to reality, they should be conducted at every opportunity so that the crew will be familiar with each procedure and will learn to accomplish it in a minimum of time. If time and circumstances permit, planning for an impending bailout or forced landing will increase the chances for survival. The chances of survival depend critically on communication equipment; water, food and medical supplies; and crew discipline.

Note

In case of any emergency, the aircraft commander will be notified over interphone on the CALL channel.

Emergency signals are given on the alarm bells and are as follows:

1. Prepare to bail out—Three short rings.
2. Bail-out—One long ring.
3. Prepare to ditch or crash land—Six short rings.
4. Ditching or crash landing—One long ring.

Note

If possible the crew should be warned and acknowledgement received by interphone.

ENGINE FAILURE.

In the event it becomes necessary to shut down two or more engines, the mission will be aborted and the aircraft will be landed at the nearest SAC base, returned to the home base, or landed at the nearest suitable air base, whichever is considered most practicable from a safety of flight standpoint in the opinion of the aircraft commander. At the discretion of the aircraft commander, if the aircraft is in the immediate vicinity of the target on a unit simulated combat mission, the bomb run may be completed prior to aborting the mission.

WARNING

If an engine fire is experienced, the mission will be aborted immediately.

FLIGHT CHARACTERISTICS WITH PARTIAL POWER.

The airplane is not difficult to maneuver under conditions where some engines are inoperative. The ease of maneuverability results from the free-floating characteristic of the servo-operated control surfaces and the positive means of trimming the airplane. Remember too, that in case of critical power failure, the jet engines are there to supplement the remaining power.

It is important to be familiar with the appendix which gives rate of climb versus air speed for various flap and gear positions with engines inoperative. Do not be apprehensive about turns into dead engines. However, it should be remembered that with asymmetrical power, the drag of the inoperative engine and the thrust of the opposite engine combine to form a powerful turning effect. Any resulting turn increases the lift of the faster moving wing, causing a roll into the dead engine. Normal aileron correction tends to bring up the low wing but at the same time adds adverse yaw into the inoperative engine. With speed reduction the drag of the inoperative engine decreases, but the thrust of the opposite engine (at constant power setting) increases. As speed is decreased, both ailerons and rudder become less effective. Above the safety speeds listed in figure 3-2, full control of the airplane can be maintained with high asymmetrical power. When cruising on four or five engines, all engines should be kept operating at the same power setting. At low speeds, however, it is necessary to adjust to more symmetrical power conditions in order to maintain directional control. When it is necessary to apply power when in an asymmetrical power configuration, it must be remembered that power must be applied on symmetrical engines first. The charts shown in figure 3-2 represent the best available information until such time as the stall and lateral control tests are completed.

Section III
Emergency Procedures

T.O. 1B-36D(II)-1

Reciprocating Engine SHUTDOWN IN FLIGHT

Step 1

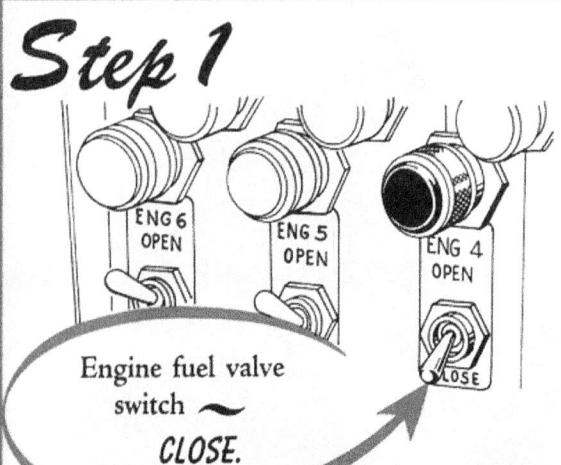

Engine fuel valve switch — *CLOSE.*

WARNING

Do not, without forethought, close other fuel valves or shut off fuel booster pumps, since other engines may be dependent on their position or operation.

CAUTION

Do not close oil shutoff valves unless engine is being feathered because of fire.

Step 2

Mixture control lever *IDLE CUT-OFF* alternator-breaker indicator lamp lighted

WARNING

On some airplanes the IDLE CUT-OFF position is away from the engineer. On other airplanes IDLE CUT-OFF is toward the engineer.

Step 3

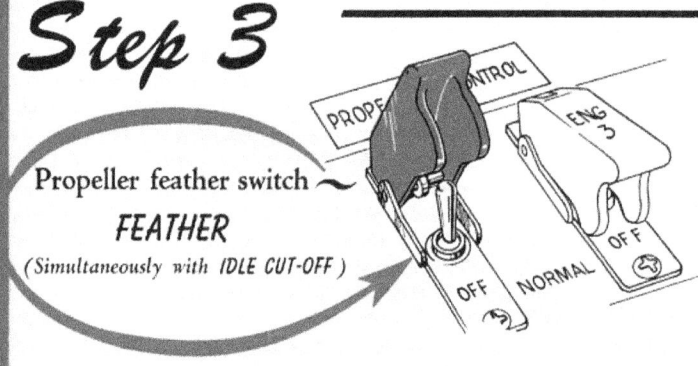

Propeller feather switch — *FEATHER* (Simultaneously with *IDLE CUT-OFF*)

NOTE

Because of an aerodynamic characteristic slight windmilling in reverse will occur on completion of the feathering cycle of propeller No. 1, 2, or 3. To remedy this condition, place the propeller selector switch of the affected propeller in FIXED PITCH, return the feather switch to NORMAL, and then jiggle the selector switch in the INC. RPM position until the windmilling has ceased. Leave the selector switch in FIXED PITCH position. If the propeller is inadvertently moved through the feather position and begins to windmill in the normal direction, actuate the feather switch and repeat the above procedure. When a propeller is feathered, the lower aft scanners will report to the engineer, "Propeller feathered and stopped." Report any rotation of the propeller after it is feathered.

CAUTION

Do not allow a propeller to windmill in reverse, because the engine may be damaged because of inadequate lubrication. If an engine is subjected to reverse windmilling for an appreciable length of time, it should be thoroughly checked after the flight.

Figure 3-1. (Sheet 1)

T.O. 1B-36D(II)-1

**Section III
Emergency Procedures**

Step 4

Intercooler and airplug control switches ~

Hold in **CLOSE** *position until intercoolers and air plug are fully closed.*

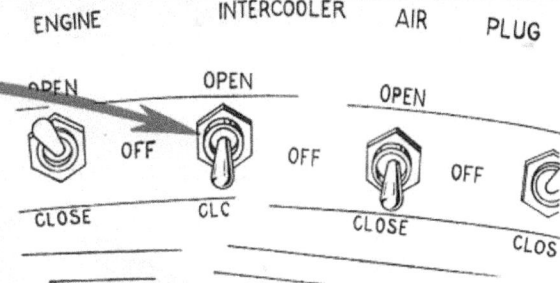

Step 5

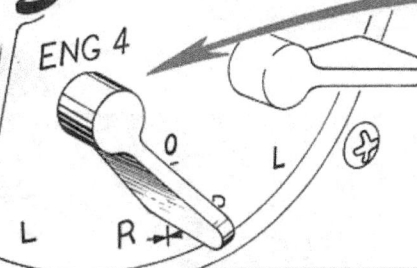

Ignition switch ~ *OFF*

after emergency is over.

Note

The following steps may be accomplished at anytime after the emergency.

Step 6

Propeller selector switch ~ **FIXED PITCH.**

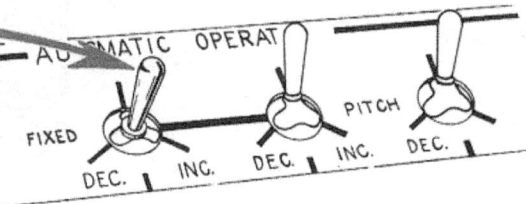

Step 7

Note
Turn the voltage and frequency selector switch to the number of the feathered engine if it is alternator-equipped and check for zero readings on the frequency meter and the voltmeter.

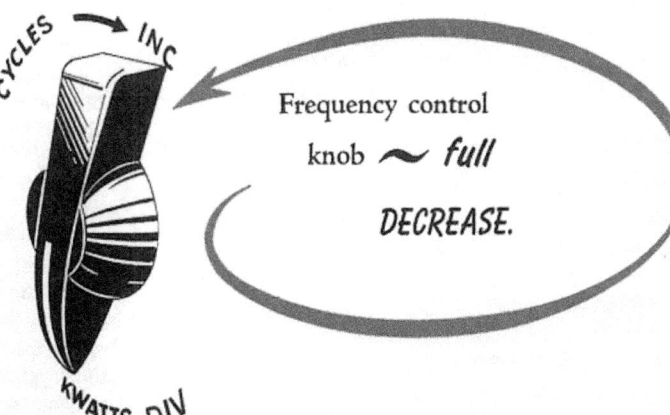

Frequency control knob ~ *full* **DECREASE.**

Figure 3-1. (Sheet 2)

177

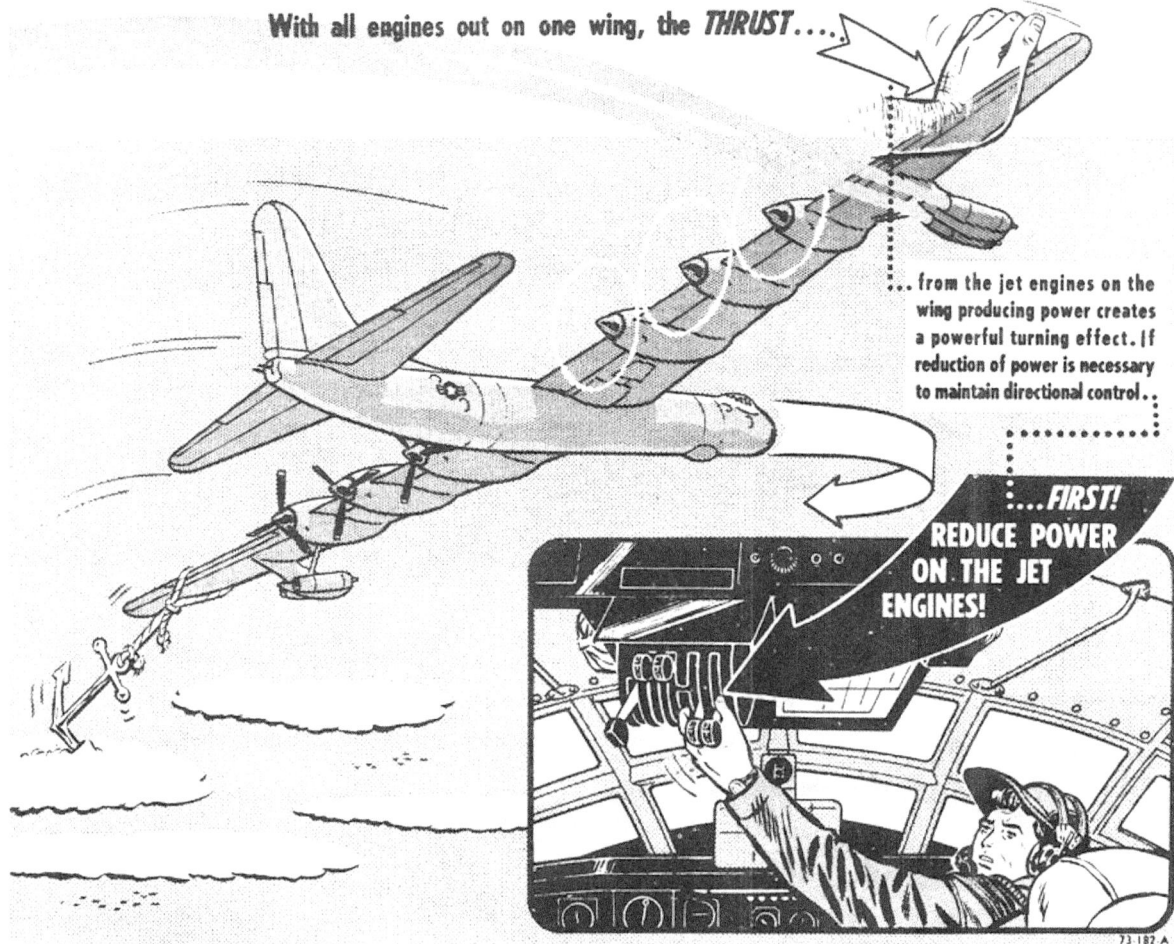

With all engines out on one wing, the THRUST.... from the jet engines on the wing producing power creates a powerful turning effect. If reduction of power is necessary to maintain directional control.. ....FIRST! REDUCE POWER ON THE JET ENGINES!

OIL DILUTION AFTER ENGINE SHUTDOWN.

After engine shutdown, if the engine is operable, the following procedures will be used:

1. Oil shutoff valve—Check OPEN.

2. Immediately after feathering, windmill the engine 50 to 100 rpm and allow the engine to cool to an oil temperature of 30° to 40°C.

3. Windmill engine to 800 rpm.

4. Engine fuel valve—Check OPEN.

5. Use normal oil dilution procedure. Refer to the oil dilution table, "Oil Dilution," Section IX.

FUEL PRESSURE DROP—ENGINE OPERATING NORMALLY.

If an engine's fuel pressure drops below the operating limits but the engine continues to operate normally, proceed as follows:

1. During ground operation:

a. Stop the airplane.

b. Shut down the engine immediately.

c. Investigate the cause and correct the trouble before flight.

2. During flight—Attempt to determine the source of trouble, such as primer leakage, oil dilution solenoid valve leakage, engine driven fuel pump by-pass valve leakage, clogged pressure line, instrument failure, or fuel line leakage. After determining the source of trouble, proceed with one of the following courses of action:

a. Shut down the affected engine immediately if it is not needed to sustain flight.

b. If the fuel pressure drop was not caused by a fuel leak, continue normal operation of the engine.

c. If the exact source of trouble cannot be established and the engine is required to sustain flight, keep the affected engine in operation at or above cruising speed. Maintain a close watch for indications of fire. Prior to reducing power for entrance into the landing pattern, shut down the affected engine.

MINIMUM IAS (MPH) FOR ZERO YAW
FULL RUDDER DEFLECTION

RED FIGURES ARE INDICATED AIR SPEEDS (MPH).
(ALL ENGINES AT TAKE-OFF POWER)

CONFIGURATION	77°F (OAT.) SEA LEVEL		104°F (OAT.) SEA LEVEL		NACA DAY SEA LEVEL		NACA DAY 3000'		NACA DAY 6000'		NACA DAY 9000'	
	300,000 LBS	370,000 LBS	300,000 LBS	370,000 LBS	300,000 LBS	370,000 LBS	300,000 LBS	370,000 LBS	300,000 LBS	370,000 LBS	300,000 LBS	370,000 LBS
6 RECIP ENG +3 JETS	105	99*	104	99*	106	100*	97*	97*	93*	93*	88*	88*
+2 JETS	146	148	143	146	146	149	141	144	135	139	130	131
5 RECIP ENG +4 JETS	118	112*	106	110*	119	113*	118	112*	115	109*	103	108*
+3 JETS	147	150	145	148	149	151	147	150	144	146	143	146
+2 JETS	174	175	172	173	175	176	172	173	168	169	163	165
4 RECIP ENG +4 JETS	140	143	139	142	142	145	141	144	140	143	137	141
+3 JETS	163	164	161	163	166	168	165	166	162	164	161	163
+2 JETS	185	186	183	184	190	191	187	188	182	183	181	182
3 RECIP ENG +4 JETS	150	152	148	151	152	155	152	154	146	149	145	148

Speeds quoted are for the most asymmetric configuration, i.e., inoperative engines are those most outboard on one side.
*AIRPLANE IN GROUND ATTITUDE WHEN CG IS APPROXIMATELY 22% MAC FOR 370,000 LBS OR 26% MAC FOR 300,000 LBS
TAKE-OFF CONFIGURATION

Figure 3-2.

WARNING

Unless the added power is essential to effect a safe landing, do not reduce airspeed until the affected engine is shut down. Engine shutdown is necessary since a fuel leak may exist. Such a leak may not be evident during cruise due to the cooling and dispersing effect of the airflow over the engine. However, when power is reduced, the reduced cooling and dispersing effect may cause the fuel leak to ignite.

PROPELLER UNFEATHERING DURING FLIGHT.

CAUTION

If a propeller has been feathered for 5 minutes or more in low temperatures requiring oil dilution as given in Section IX, "Oil Dilution," and the oil was not diluted at engine shutdown, do NOT unfeather. Also, due to the existence of a potential fire hazard, no attempt will be made to restart a reciprocating engine that has been feathered due to a malfunction, unless the aircraft commander deems it necessary to use that engine because of power loss of other engines.

1. Mixture control lever—IDLE CUT-OFF.
2. Throttle lever—Approximately 1/4 open.

Note

Above 30,000 feet a more open throttle will be required to initiate an engine start.

3. Engine oil shutoff valve switch—OPEN.
4. Engine fuel valve switch—OPEN.
5. Fuel pressure—10 to 14 psi.
6. Propeller selector switch—FIXED PITCH.
7. Propeller feather switch—NORMAL (guard down).
8. Propeller selector switch—INC. RPM until engine rpm is 10 to 50.

CAUTION

If rpm does not increase when the propeller selector switch is engaged, hydraulic lock is indicated; therefore, discontinue starting procedure and refeather.

Section III
Emergency Procedures

9. Propeller selector switch—Hold in INC. RPM until engine turns over 600 to 800 rpm; then return to FIXED PITCH.

> **CAUTION**
>
> Check for an indication of oil pressure and alternator excitation. If there is no oil pressure indication within 30 seconds, refeather the engine.

10. Ignition switch—ON.
11. Mixture control—NORMAL.

Note

The torquemeter will indicate a successful engine start. When the mixture is brought to NORMAL, if the torque oil has congealed in the line to the autosyn transmitter, a power surge and a normal rise in CHT indicates a successful start. To accomplish a successful engine start at altitude, it may be necessary to increase rpm.

12. Propeller selector switch—INC. RPM, until 1400 rpm; then return to FIXED PITCH.
13. Throttle lever—Advance until M.P. is approximately 25 inches.
14. Propeller selector switch—As required to maintain 1400 rpm during throttle advance.

> **CAUTION**
>
> Warm up the engine at 1400 rpm and 25 inches M.P. until engine oil temperature reaches 40°C.

15. Propeller selector switch—INC. RPM, until rpm nearly matches rpm of the other engines.
16. Propeller selector switch—AUTOMATIC OPERATION.
17. Throttle lever—Advance as required for power setting.
18. Alternator—Parallel on bus. (Engines No. 2, 3, 4, or 5.)

ABORTING TAKE-OFF.

The aircraft commander is charged with the responsibility of making the decision on whether to abort a take-off. There will not be time to make a delayed decision. No one can tell you what to do in these situations; however, you can equip yourself with knowledge on which to base your decision by knowing your REFUSAL SPEED, your STOPPING DISTANCE WITH BRAKES ONLY, and your STOPPING DISTANCE WITH BRAKES AND REVERSE PROPS. Then if you have sufficient runway left when the decision is made to abort the take-off, you will know what to do.

If the aircraft commander should decide to abort a take-off after take-off power has been established, he should notify the crew by announcing over the interphone, "Aborting take-off." Immediately following this announcement, the crew members concerned will comply with the following procedure:

1. Engineer—Turn water injection switches OFF.
2. Pilot—Shut down jet engines and place propeller reverse selector switches in READY.
3. Aircraft Commander—Power as required.

Note

Propellers may be reversed at full take-off power; however, slight overspeeding of engines will occur.

4. Pilot—Depress reverse pitch switch upon command of aircraft commander.
5. Pilot—Check jet engine rpm and close all jet engine fuel valves if jets are still running.
6. Aircraft Commander—Use maximum brakes but avoid skidding.
7. Pilot—Hold forward pressure on control column, after nose gear is on the runway, to insure nose steering.
8. Aircraft Commander—Lock controls, if possible, below 50 mph.

Note

Prior to each take-off the aircraft commander will personally brief the pilot and engineers on the above "aborting take-off" procedure.

ENGINE FAILURE DURING TAKE-OFF.

In the event of engine failure on take-off, accomplish these steps:

1. Obtain directional control by using rudder with a minimum of aileron.
2. Pick up at least minimum control air speed before attempting to climb. (See figure 3-2.)
3. Raise the landing gear immediately, if practical, and start retracting the flaps at 125 per cent of stalling speed, even though the gear is not completely up. (See figure 6-6.)
4. If emergency power is being used, reduce this power as soon as possible.
5. Determine which engine or engines have failed and whether or not they are delivering enough power to carry themselves; if they are not, feather their propellers and make a normal landing approach.

> **CAUTION**
>
> Failure of an output tube of the electronic mixture control system may cause the mixture control to be driven to the IDLE CUT-

OFF position. If there is evidence of such a failure as shown by complete loss of power with a sharp decrease in fuel flow and torque, with fuel pressure normal, retard throttle to prevent power surge and back firing and use the mixture control override switch to reset the mixture. If power is not restored, then feather the propeller.

Note

If sufficient power is not available to execute the landing pattern, prepare to crash land straight ahead. Refer to "Crash Landings" of this section.

WARNING

Never attempt a turn before directional control is obtained and a safe flying speed is reached.

TURBO BOOST CONTROL (Group 2 Airplanes).

When the normal turbo controls fail, proceed as follows:

.. Control manifold pressure within limits by use of the throttles.
2. Turbo vernier control switch—OFF.
3. Turbo control change-over switch—MAN.
4. Turbo override control switch—Move toward OPEN or CLOSE to attain the approximate manifold pressure desired.
5. Turbo vernier control switch—ON.
6. Turbo override control switch—Jiggle OPEN or CLOSE to trim to the desired manifold pressure.

Note

With the vernier switch ON, each actuation of the override switch will operate the waste gate for approximately 0.05 of a second. Therefore, when adjusting the manifold pressure, the override switch must be jiggled.

The turbo override system can be operated during emergency power operation to open the waste gates. (See "Obtaining Emergency Electrical Power" of this section.) However, there will be no indication from critical engine instruments such as manifold pressure, CHT, CAT., torque pressure, or fuel flow gages. Therefore, there can be no assurance of obtaining the proper power setting.

Note

If overboost occurs during take-off and the take-off manifold pressure is exceeded by more than 10 inches for a period of 15 seconds, the engine must be changed before the next flight. If the take-off manifold pressure is exceeded by not more than 10 inches for a period of 15 seconds, the engine must be inspected prior to the next flight.

OIL SPEWING.

Oil spewing at altitudes of approximately 37,000 feet and above is caused by insufficient crankcase scavenging. This condition can become a serious problem. A dangerous amount of oil may be lost, making it necessary to feather engines to prevent seizing. Also, oil spewing from the breather vent congeals on the wing trailing edge and is thrown into the propellers by the slipstream, damaging the propellers and the fuselage. If conditions allow, attempt to stop oil spewing by reducing rpm. If this does not alleviate the condition, reduce altitude. (For further information, refer to "Oil Spewing" of Section VII.)

PARTIAL POWER TAKE-OFF.

This procedure should be used when some engines are inoperative and the airplane must be flown from a base where repair facilities are inadequate.

Note

If symmetrical engines are inoperative, use the normal take-off procedure. See Appendix I for take-off performance.

CAUTION

This procedure does not apply in the event of engine failure on take-off or reduced power take-off.

Study the applicable portion of the "Take-Off and Distance Curve" in the appendix. Prepare the airplane by closing the air plug doors of the inoperative jets and sealing the air intakes of the inoperative reciprocating engines, but do not seal any exhaust or air outlets. One point to consider in this type of take-off is the unbalanced thrust created by asymmetrical power. With full take-off power, full opposite rudder will not be sufficient to counteract the yaw at low speeds. Therefore, with all operative engines idling and the airplane restrained with the foot brakes, the take-off should be accomplished as follows:

1. Apply full take-off power to the symmetrical engines.
2. Release the foot brakes.

Note

If an outboard engine is inoperative, rudder trim should be set to approximately 8 degrees. If a center is inoperative, set 5 degrees. If an inboard is inoperative set 3 degrees.

Section III
Emergency Procedures

T.O. 1B-36D(II)-1

3. As the airplane accelerates and the rudder becomes more effective, slowly apply power to the remaining engines and compensate with rudder.

> **CAUTION**
>
> At no time should full power be applied to a strong side engine until all engines inboard from it are operating at full power.

4. When all operative engines are at full power, reduce rudder deflection to maintain zero yaw.

5. Use rudder trim and hold the nose wheel on the ground as long as possible to aid in maintaining directional control.

6. As soon as take-off air speed is reached, make a rapid pull-off followed by level flight to accelerate to a safe climbing speed; retract the landing gear as soon as the airplane is postively airborne.

> **WARNING**
>
> Remember that minimum safe climb speed is 120 per cent of stalling speed. See figure 3-2 for minimum yaw.

PARTIAL POWER LANDING.

It may sometimes be necessary to land with two or more engines inoperative; however, with careful planning there is seldom cause for alarm. When operating with asymmetric reciprocating engines inoperative, the resulting conditions of unbalanced thrust and lift greatly affect directional control at low air speeds with high powers on the remaining engines. For the critical air speeds below which effective control cannot be maintained with a given asymmetrical power configuration, refer to figure 3-2. There are many factors that must be considered in attempting a partial power landing. The aircraft commander must know the condition of critical systems needed for landing. He should weigh these factors and determine the subsequent action. After alerting the crew to prepare for a possible crash landing, proceed as follows:

1. Make sure that the cg location is within proper limits for landing.

2. Based on expected landing gross weight, determine whether jet engine thrust is required to replace the loss of the reciprocating engines.

3. If the jet engines are to be used, they should be operated at the required per cent rpm (figure 3-3), maintaining pattern speeds and final approach glide angle by retarding the reciprocating engine throttles.

4. The jets should be started as early as practical prior to entering the traffic pattern, based on estimated power requirements, fuel reserve, etc. (For starting procedure see "Starting Jet Engines in Flight," Section II.)

5. During the landing approach, maintain a safe air speed of 135 per cent of stalling speed. Do not exceed 145 per cent of stalling speed.

6. If altitude and power conditions are critical, leave the gear up as long as practical before entering the final approach, thereby eliminating the need for high engine power to overcome landing gear drag. Care must be used to insure that gear is fully down and locked prior to turning on final approach. Normal gear extension requires approximately 45 seconds.

7. Adjust power on operating engines to maintain the desired approach speed.

8. Adjust directional trim with the rudder trim tabs during final approach.

9. Position flaps at 20 degrees until there is no possibility of undershooting; then extend full flaps.

10. Just prior to touchdown, if conditions permit,

Jet Engine REQUIREMENTS
(PARTIAL POWER LANDING)

5 RECIPROCATING ENGINES

GROSS WEIGHT – POUNDS		JET POWER REQUIREMENTS	
FROM	TO	JETS	% RPM
—	236,000	None	—
236,000	288,000	2	90
288,000	303,000	2	96
303,000	313,000	2	100
313,000	331,000	4	90
331,000	362,000	4	96

4 RECIPROCATING ENGINES

GROSS WEIGHT – POUNDS		JET POWER REQUIREMENTS	
FROM	TO	JETS	% RPM
—	187,000	None	—
187,000	240,000	2	90
240,000	253,000	2	96
253,000	262,000	2	100
262,000	294,000	4	90
294,000	322,000	4	96
322,000	340,000	4	100

3 RECIPROCATING ENGINES

GROSS WEIGHT – POUNDS		JET POWER REQUIREMENTS	
FROM	TO	JETS	%RPM
—	192,000	2	90
192,000	208,000	2	100
208,000	236,000	4	90
236,000	264,000	4	96
264,000	275,000	4	100

> **NOTE**
>
> When landing gross weight is 283,000 pounds or over and all six reciprocating engines are operative, two jet engines will be run at 90% rpm to insure sufficient power in the event of reciprocating engine failure during landing.

Figure 3-3.

fully retard throttles on live reciprocating engines and simultaneously neutralize the rudder trim controls. Do not reduce jet power until a safe landing is assured; however, slight reductions may be necessary to maintain correct final approach air speeds even after reciprocating engines have been fully retarded.

> **CAUTION**
>
> Jet engines do not provide as rapid acceleration of the aircraft as do reciprocating engines; therefore, required jet engine power changes must be anticipated earlier.

11. After the airplane contacts the runway, place the propeller reverse selector switches in the READY position in preparation for thrust reversal.

12. Shut down the jet engines and reverse the propellers simultaneously.

PROPELLER FAILURE.

RUNAWAY PROPELLER (OVERSPEEDNG ENGINE).

Failure of the propeller snychronizing system may result in a runaway propeller. When such a failure occurs, the engine may exceed allowable limits. Attempt to reduce rpm as follows:

1. Engineer—Hold the propeller selector switch in the DEC. RPM position.

2. Engineer—Maintain M.P. within limits simultaneously with step 1.

3. If the above procedure does not reduce rpm, use momentary feather to control rpm.

> **CAUTION**
>
> When using momentary feather, remember that pitch change is 45 degrees per second.

4. Engineer—If this procedure does not reduce rpm, feather propeller on order from aircraft commander.

Note

If the propeller will not feather, engine overspeeding can be reduced by decreasing air speed and/or altitude.

> **CAUTION**
>
> All conditions of overspeeding should be noted on Form 781 (Form 1). If engine rpm was between 3100 and 3300 rpm, the engine must be inspected before the next flight. If the engine speed exceeded 3300 rpm, the engine must be changed.

EMERGENCY PITCH SETTING BEFORE LANDING.

When a landing is to be made in fixed pitch because of synchronizer failure, set the propeller blades and turbos to insure full power in the event of a go-around. This is done at traffic altitude before entering the final approach by using the following procedure:

1. Aircraft Commander—Maintain 135 per cent of stalling speed or 145 mph IAS whichever is greater, based on gear down and flaps 20 degrees while the engineer performs the following steps:

2. Engineer—Propeller Selector Switches—Increase all engines to approximately 2200 rpm then return to fixed pitch. This will provide the aircraft commander with sufficient power to maintain IAS and altitude.

3. Engineer—Turbo Calibration Trim Knobs—Full Decrease.

4. Engineer—TBS-7.

Note

Accomplish the remaining steps, one engine at a time symmetrically or on symmetrical engines No. 1 and 6, 2 and 5, and 3 and 4, respectively. The aircraft commander can use remaining throttles to maintain the required airspeed. It is important that a constant airspeed and altitude be maintained while the engineer is setting this power to assure adequate and balanced power for go-around.

5. Engineer—Throttle Lever—Full Open.

6. Engineer—Turbo Calibration Knob—Increase to 55 inches M.P. maintaining 2550 rpm with propeller selector switch (normal rated power).

Note

The values desired are 2550 rpm and 55 inches M.P. which is adequate power for normal landing weights. At any rate, more power should be used only in an emergency since maximum dry engine power would be exceeded. When stabilized at 2550 rpm and 55 inches M.P., retard the throttle to the average power of the other engines and proceed with the next engine.

7. Aircraft Commander—Gear and flaps will be lowered at same time as in normal landing procedure.

> **CAUTION**
>
> In the event a go-around is necessary, advance throttle levers to full open *slowly* and *smoothly* to avoid over-speeding the propellers.

**Section III
Emergency Procedures**

T.O. 1B-36D(II)-1

DIAGNOSING *Smoke & Fire* . . . .

• • RECIPROCATING ENGINE FIRE IN FLIGHT

Engine abnormalities are often difficult to diagnose either rapidly or accurately while in flight; however, from indications of the engine instruments coupled with information from the scanners in the aft cabin, fairly effective action can be taken in a minimum time. Engine malfunctions are often indicated by smoke or fire. Torching exhaust stacks are observed sometimes when the engine is operating on excessively rich mixtures. In some instances flame may extend through the air plug opening and the propeller. Effective leaning of the mixture will stop this condition almost immediately.

	PROBABLE CAUSE	CORRECTIVE ACTION
THIN BLACK SMOKE FROM EXHAUST 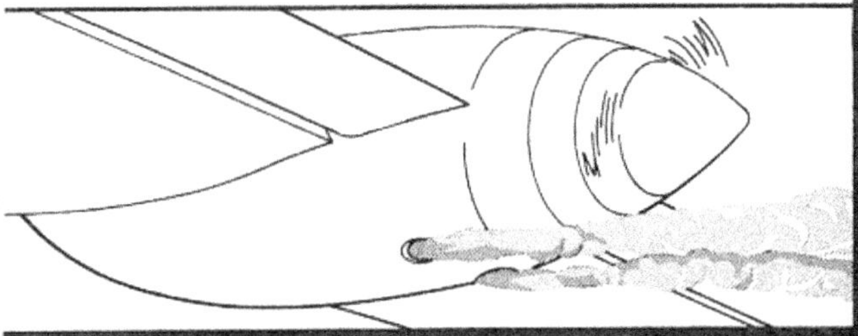	RICH MIXTURE AT HIGH POWER	NONE
	RICH MIXTURES AT HIGH RPM AND LOW MANIFOLD PRESSURE	ADJUST POWER SETTING
	LEAKY PRIMER	NONE
PUFFS OF BLACK SMOKE FROM EXHAUST 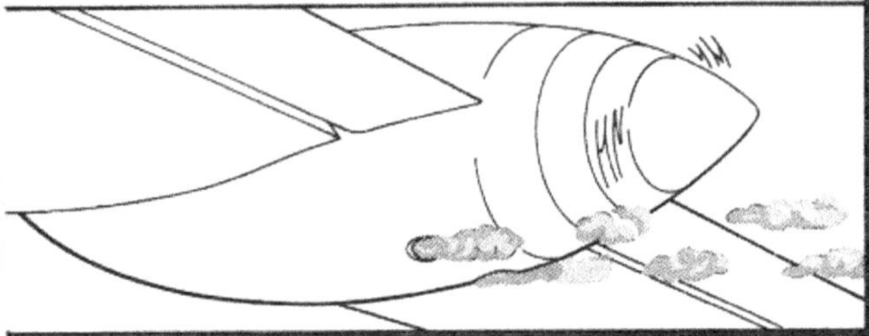	DETONATION	CHECK FUEL PRESSURE. CHECK MIXTURE CONTROL SETTING RICHEN MIXTURE. REDUCE MANIFOLD PRESSURE. REDUCE CYLINDER HEAD TEMPERATURE.
	CYLINDER MALFUNCTION	REDUCE POWER. WATCH FOR FIRE.
	FOULED SPARK PLUGS	INCREASE CYLINDER HEAD TEMPERATURE TO LIMIT.
THIN BLUISH WHITE SMOKE FROM EXHAUST 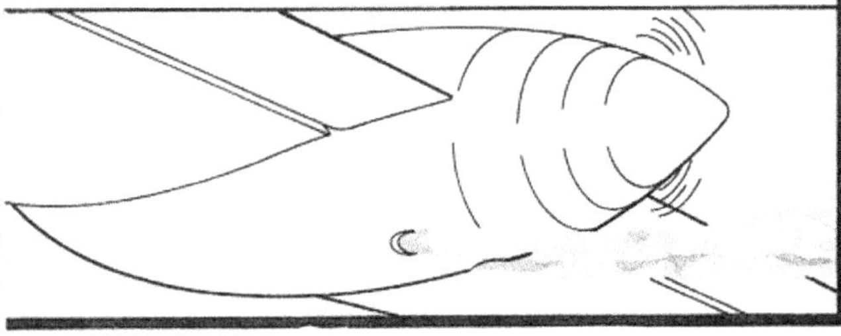	INTERNAL FAILURE— RINGS	CHECK OIL PRESSURE. CHECK OIL QUANTITY.
	IMPELLER SEAL OR TURBO SEAL OIL LEAKAGE	

Figure 3-4. (Sheet 1)

T.O. 1B-36D(II)-1

Section III
Emergency Procedures

Illustration	PROBABLE CAUSE	CORRECTIVE ACTION
WHITE SMOKE FROM AIR PLUG OPENING 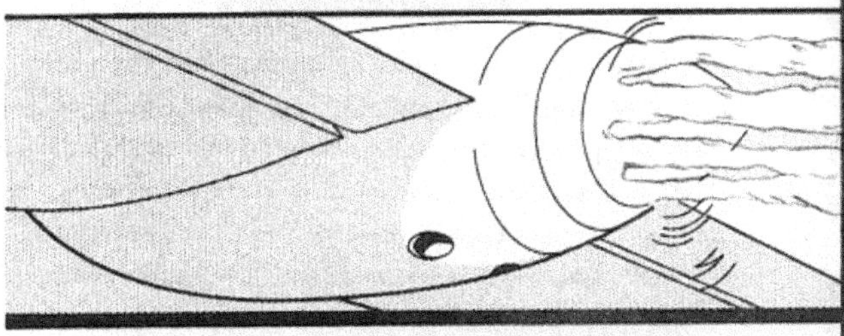	EXHAUST SYSTEM FAILURE	CUT OFF FUEL. FEATHER PROPELLER. WATCH FOR FIRE.
BLACK SMOKE FROM LOUVERS, BLUISH WHITE SMOKE FROM LOUVERS OR OIL COOLER DOOR. 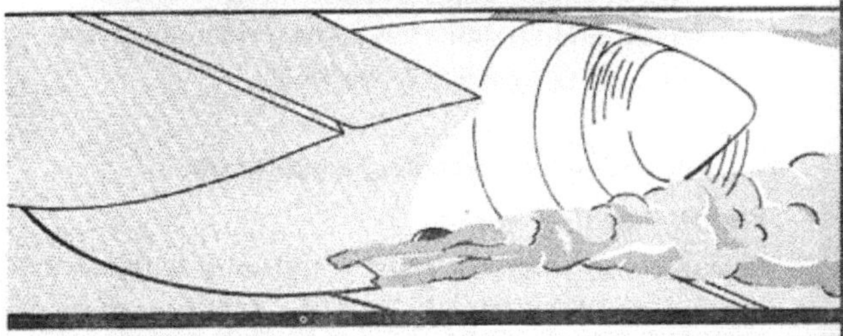	FUEL LINE AFIRE	CUT OFF FUEL. FEATHER PROPELLER. USE FIRE PROCEDURE.
	OIL LEAK	CHECK OIL PRESSURE. CHECK OIL QUANTITY. WATCH FOR FIRE.
DENSE BLACK SMOKE AND FLAME FROM AIR PLUG OPENING. FIRE MAY IMMEDIATELY BURN THROUGH UPPER COWLING OF NACELLE. 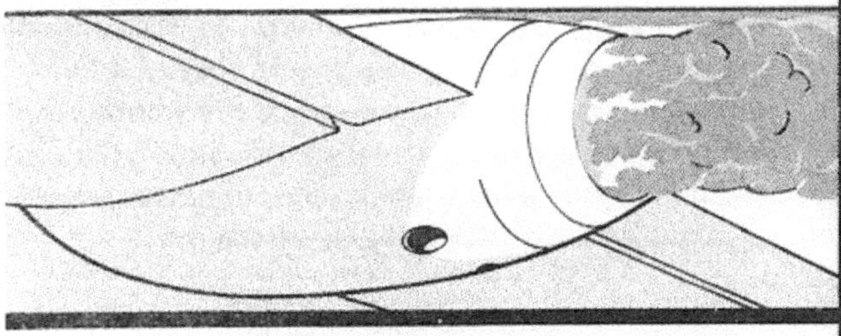	BROKEN FUEL LINE OR ACCESSORY SECTION FIRE	CUT OFF FUEL. FEATHER PROPELLER. USE FIRE PROCEDURE.
THIN BLUISH WHITE SMOKE FROM AIR PLUG OPENING 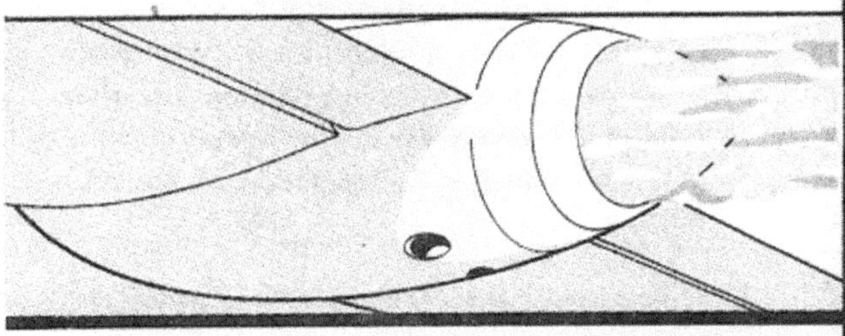	OIL LEAK	CHECK OIL PRESSURE. CHECK OIL QUANTITY. WATCH FOR FIRE.
PUFFS OF BLUISH WHITE SMOKE FROM AIR PLUG OPENING 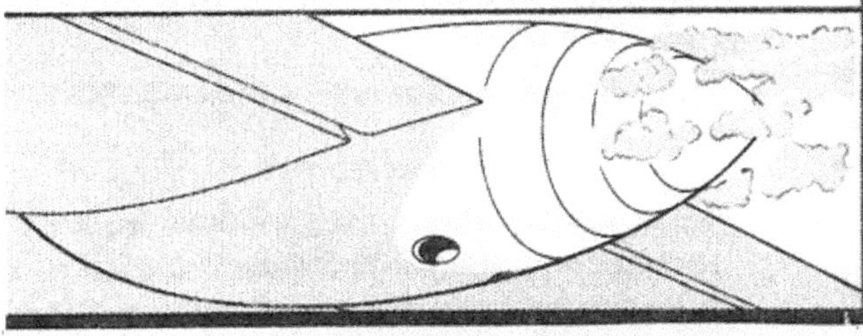	OIL LEAK	CHECK OIL PRESSURE. CHECK OIL QUANTITY. WATCH FOR INTERNAL ENGINE FAILURE. WATCH FOR FIRE.

Figure 3-4. (Sheet 2)

Section III
Emergency Procedures

FIRE.

JET ENGINE FIRE ON THE GROUND.

In event of a jet engine ground fire, the pilot must call the tower and position his controls as follows:

1. All throttles—CLOSE.
2. Both manifold fuel switches—CLOSE.
3. All engine fuel valve switches—CLOSE.
4. All fuel booster pump switches—OFF.
5. All oil shutoff valve switches—CLOSE.
6. Pod preheat switch—OFF.

CAUTION

In the event fuel is burning on the ground, move the airplane upwind.

RECIPROCATING ENGINE FIRE ON THE GROUND.

If your aft gunners report a flaming exhaust stack, the fire is probably a torching turbo and may be put out by increasing the throttle momentarily. For other fires on the ground immediately warn the crew, signal to fire truck and the ground crew for portable equipment, and notify the control tower. Meanwhile the engineer should carry out this procedure:

CAUTION

If the jet engines are operating, shut them down.

1. All engine fuel and oil shutoff valve switches—CLOSE.
2. All alternator breaker hold-in switches—Hold in.

Note

This step is applicable only when the alternators are furnishing electrical power to the airplane.

3. All mixture control levers—IDLE CUT-OFF.

Note

There are instances where the fire will burn itself out after the fuel has been shut off; therefore, before proceeding to the next step check to see whether the fire is out.

4. Proper engine fire extinguisher selector switch—Hold ON for at least five seconds as soon as the engine stops.
5. Fire extinguisher discharge selector switch—Place in the reserve position—Discharge if fire is still burning.
6. All ignition switches—OFF.
7. External power and battery switches—OFF.

WARNING

Repeated or prolonged exposure to high concentrations of bromochloromethane (CB) or decomposition products should be avoided. CB is a narcotic agent of moderate intensity but of prolonged duration. It is considered to be less toxic than carbon tetrachloride, methyl bromide, or the usual products of combustion. It is safer to use than previous fire extinguishing agents; however, normal precautions should be taken including the use of oxygen when available.

INFLIGHT FIRE FIGHTING PROCEDURES.

Reciprocating Engines.

When a crew member spots a fire he will place his interphone selector switch in the CALL position and report "Flame" or "Smoke," whichever is applicable, "From No._____engine." The crew member will further identify the location of the flame or the type and location of the smoke. The engineer will use this information in conjunction with his fire warning lamp indicators to determine the exact location of the fire and he will immediately inform the aircraft commander of the extent of the emergency condition.

Note

It is possible to isolate engine or wing fires through the use of fuel shutoff valves. To accomplish this the engineer must take into consideration his fuel configuration—then determine the valves that can be shut off without jeopardizing the operation of other engines.

1. Affected engine's fuel shutoff switch—CLOSE.
2. Mixture control lever—IDLE CUT-OFF.
3. Propeller feather switch—FEATHER, simultaneously with idle cut-off.
4. Affected engine's oil shutoff switch—CLOSE.

Note

There are cases when the fire will burn itself out after the engine is feathered and the fuel is cut off. Therefore, before continuing with the fire fighting procedure, check to see whether the fire is extinguished.

5. Proper fire extinguisher engine selector switch—Hold ON for at least five seconds as soon as engine stops.

6. Air plug and intercooler switches—OPEN.

7. Proper cabin pressure wing shutoff valve switch—OFF. Use pressure from unaffected wing.

8. Proper cabin heat and tail anti-ice control switch—OFF, if fire is in engine No. 3 or No. 4.

9. Proper wing anti-ice control switch—OFF, if fire is in engine No. 1, 2, 5, or 6.

10. Fire extinguisher discharge selector switch—Place in reverse position and repeat step 5 if necessary.

11. After the emergency is over, the proper ignition switch may be turned OFF.

12. Do not restart engine.

Analysis of Fire Warning Lamp Indication. When a reciprocating engine fire warning lamp lights, the engineer will take action to determine the cause of the indication. This action is necessary to prevent inadvertent shutdown of a good engine due to a false indication.

If a fire warning lamp lights during flight, the engineer will hold his interphone selector switch in CALL and request the applicable lower aft gunners to check for flame, smoke, or any other abnormality. If flame or smoke is reported, follow the instructions described under "Inflight Fire Fighting Procedures" of this section. If the gunner reports, "No smoke or flame," position the controls of the affected engine as follows to determine the cause of the warning indication.

1. Position the air plug fully OPEN to dissipate nacelle heat and check the resultant drop in CHT.

Note

If the warning lamp goes out, normal operation of the engine can be continued. If the lamp remains lighted, proceed with step 2.

2. Temporarily reduce power on the affected engine to check for an exhaust system failure.

3. If the lamp remains lighted after power is reduced, shut down the engine.

Note

If the lamp remains lighted after the engine is shut down, the fire detector system is probably faulty. In this case, unfeather the engine and resume normal operation.

4. If the lamp goes out after power is reduced, shut down the engine unless it is needed to maintain safety of flight in which case it may be operated at reduced power.

Jet Engines.

In the event of a jet engine fire in flight, the pilot will position the jet engine controls as follows:

1. Throttle—CLOSE.

2. Proper engine fuel valve switch—CLOSE.

3. Proper oil shutoff valve switch—CLOSE (OPEN, after fire is extinguished).

4. Pod preheat switch—OFF.

5. Nose de-ice switch—OFF.

Note

If fire is not extinguished, repeat steps 1 through 3 on remaining jet engine in affected pod and proceed with steps 6 and 7.

6. Proper manifold fuel valve switch—CLOSE.

7. Proper fuel booster pump switch—OFF.

WING FIRE.

A wing fire involving fuel and oil tanks may be difficult to identify, because the smoke and flames will probably emerge from the engine nacelle. A wing fire will, therefore, probably be reported as an engine fire by the aft cabin gunners and should be fought as such until all the extinguishing agent is exhausted. The engineer will turn off the anti-icing system and stop the flow of cabin pressurizing air from the wing on fire. Check that the other wing is furnishing pressurization. After the fire is out, a reasonable length of time must be allowed for the fumes to dissipate before investigating the damage via the wing crawlway.

FUSELAGE FIRE.

Reduce the draft by shutting off pressurized or ventilating air. Isolate the fire by use of valves and doors. Know the locations and limitations of the hand fire extinguishers.

1. Crew—Don oxygen masks and goggles and set diluter lever of oxygen regulator to 100% OXYGEN. On A-14 regulator, set dial according to altitude. On D-1 regulator, push emergency toggle lever to left or right.

2. Crew—Locate cause of fire.

3. Crew—If it is an electrical fire, isolate the circuit.

4. Crew—If the fire is caused by fluid leak, stop the fluid flow.

5. Engineer—Affected cabin pressure control—OFF, if necessary.

6. Engineer—Cabin pressure wing shutoff valve switches—OFF, if necessary.

7. Crew—Aft cabin manual pressure shutoff valve—CLOSED, if necessary.

8. Crew—Use hand fire extinguishers.

WARNING

Do not increase ventilation until the flames are extinguished. Use oxygen masks for protection against fumes.

9. Crew—Open dump valves, doors, or hatches as required *after* the fire is out.

ELECTRICAL FIRE.

Fuses and circuit breakers protect most of the electrical circuits and tend to isolate an electrical fire. However, there are cases where fuses of high capacity will permit a short sufficient to cause a fire. In such instances use A-20 fire extinguisher and attempt to isolate the circuit containing the short.

WARNING

Repeated or prolonged exposure to high concentrations of bromochloromethane (CB) or decomposition products should be avoided. CB is a narcotic agent of moderate intensity but of prolonged duration. It is considered to be less toxic than carbon tetrachloride, methyl bromide, or the usual products of combustion. It is safer to use than previous fire extinguishing agents; however, normal precautions should be taken including the use of oxygen when available.

SMOKE ELIMINATION.

To eliminate smoke and toxic fumes from the cabins, use the procedures in the following paragraphs:

UNPRESSURIZED FLIGHT.

Forward Cabin.

1. Open the nose turret disposal door.
2. Open the left forward escape hatch.

3. Partially open the aircraft commander's and pilot's clear vision panels.

4. Partially remove the right forward blister.

Note

The smoke and fumes should be completely eliminated in approximately 1 minute and 15 seconds after the fire is extinguished. Most of the smoke will dissipate through the clear vision panel openings.

CAUTION

If the clear vision panels are opened while a fire is still burning in the observer's compartment, flames may be drawn up to the flight deck.

Aft Cabin.

1. Open the catwalk entrance hatch.
2. Open the tail cone access door.
3. Open the cabin entrance hatch.

Note

The aft cabin should be entirely clear of smoke and fumes in approximately 3 minutes. Most of the smoke will dissipate through the cabin entrance hatch.

PRESSURIZED FLIGHT.

If a fire occurs during pressurized flight, the airplane must first be depressurized; then the cabins can be cleared of smoke as indicated in the preceding paragraph. During depressurization approximately 50 per cent of the smoke and fumes will be eliminated before the exits and hatches are opened.

EMERGENCY DESCENT.

Emergency descent should be used only when circumstances call for maximum rate of letdown. Engine wear and propeller vibration must be tolerated under these conditions, but air-speed limits should be observed to avoid immediate structural failure.

Throttles on six engines should be fully retarded, the auxiliary cabin heater switch OFF, engine speed 2300 rpm above 40,000 feet and 2550 rpm below 40,000 feet, and maximum allowable IAS (figure 5-3) maintained for maximum drag. The degree of emergency will be the governing factor, but engines No. 3 and 4 can be maintained at sufficient power to provide pressure and heat.

Section III
Emergency Procedures

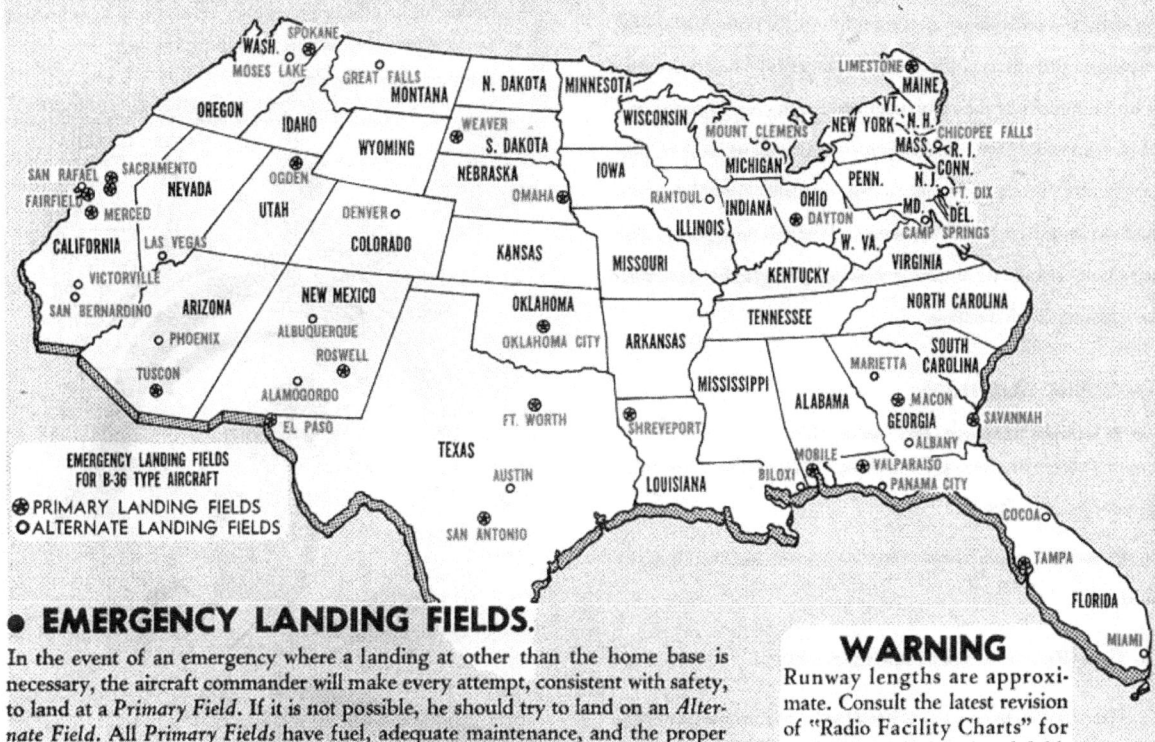

● EMERGENCY LANDING FIELDS.

In the event of an emergency where a landing at other than the home base is necessary, the aircraft commander will make every attempt, consistent with safety, to land at a *Primary Field*. If it is not possible, he should try to land on an *Alternate Field*. All *Primary Fields* have fuel, adequate maintenance, and the proper type of runway for B-36 operation. All *Alternate Fields* are adequate for limited B-36 operation only. They cannot refuel or perform major maintenance on B-36 type aircraft, and the runways are not stressed for continuous B-36 operation.

WARNING

Runway lengths are approximate. Consult the latest revision of "Radio Facility Charts" for correct runway lengths of fields listed below.

PRIMARY FIELDS

Location	Base	Longest Runway
Alabama, Mobile	Brookley AFB	8800
Arizona, Tucson	Davis Monthan AFB	7900
California, Fairfield	Travis AFB	8100
California, Merced	Castle AFB	7000
California, Sacramento	Mather AFB	7500
California, Sacramento	McClellan AFB	7000
Florida, Tampa	MacDill AFB	10,000
Florida, Valparaiso	Eglin AFB	8000
Georgia, Macon	Robins AFB	7000
Georgia, Savannah	Hunter AFB	10,500
Louisiana, Shreveport	Barksdale AFB	10,000
Maine, Limestone	Loring AFB	10,000
Nebraska, Omaha	Offutt AFB	6100
New Mexico, Roswell	Walker AFB	8500
Ohio, Dayton	Wright-Patterson AFB/Patterson	8000
Oklahoma, Oklahoma City	Tinker AFB	7800
South Dakota, Weaver	Ellsworth AFB	10,500
Texas, Fort Worth	Carswell AFB	8200
Texas, El Paso	Biggs AFB	9500
Texas, San Antonio	Kelly AFB	6700
Utah, Ogden	Hill AFB	7500
Washington, Spokane	Fairchild AFB	10,500

ALTERNATE FIELDS

Location	Base	Longest Runway
Arizona, Chandler	Williams AFB	6100
California, San Bernardino	Norton AFB	7600
California, San Rafael	Hamilton AFB	6200
California, Victorville	George AFB	9500
Colorado, Denver	Lowry AFB	8300
Florida, Cocoa	Patrick AFB	10,000
Florida, Miami	Miami International	9400
Florida, Panama City	Tyndall AFB	8000
Georgia, Albany	Turner AFB	9200
Georgia, Marietta	Dobbins AFB	7500
Illinois, Rantoul	Chanute AFB	6300
Maryland, Camp Springs	Andrews AFB	5500
Massachusetts, Chicopee Falls	Westover AFB	7300
Michigan, Mt. Clemens	Selfridge AFB	8200
Mississippi, Biloxi	Keesler AFB	6500
Montana, Great Falls	Great Falls AFB	9500
Nevada, Las Vegas	Nellis AFB	6800
New Jersey, Fort Dix	McGuire AFB	8200
New Mexico, Alamogordo	Holloman AFB	8400
New Mexico, Albuquerque	Kirtland AFB	10,200
Texas, Austin	Bergstrom AFB	8000
Washington, Moses Lake	Larson AFB	10,000

Figure 3-5.

Section III
Emergency Procedures

T.O. 1B-36D(II)-1

● FORCED LANDINGS

Successful forced landings depend on the crew's familiarity with the proper procedures. One crew member will be designated for the command of each compartment during emergencies and will be responsible for reporting the compartment clear of personnel before leaving. Frequent dry-run drills should be conducted so that the crew will be prepared for this emergency. The instructions contained in the following paragraphs deal with crash landing and ditching.

● ● CRASH LANDINGS.

● ● ● Crash Landing On Take-Off.

In case of an impending crash landing immediately after take-off, proceed as follows:

1. Pilot—Warn crew to brace for the impact and land straight ahead.

2. Crew—Remain in crash landing positions.

3. After the impact and decelerations, the lower aft gunners will proceed as follows.

WARNING

It is the aircraft commander's responsibility to see that the following escape procedures are regularly rehearsed. The importance of regular escape drills cannot be over-emphasized.

   a. Undo safety belt.

   b. Stand up.

   c. Swing outboard arm rest into an upward position.

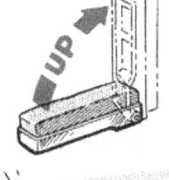

TIME IS IMPORTANT

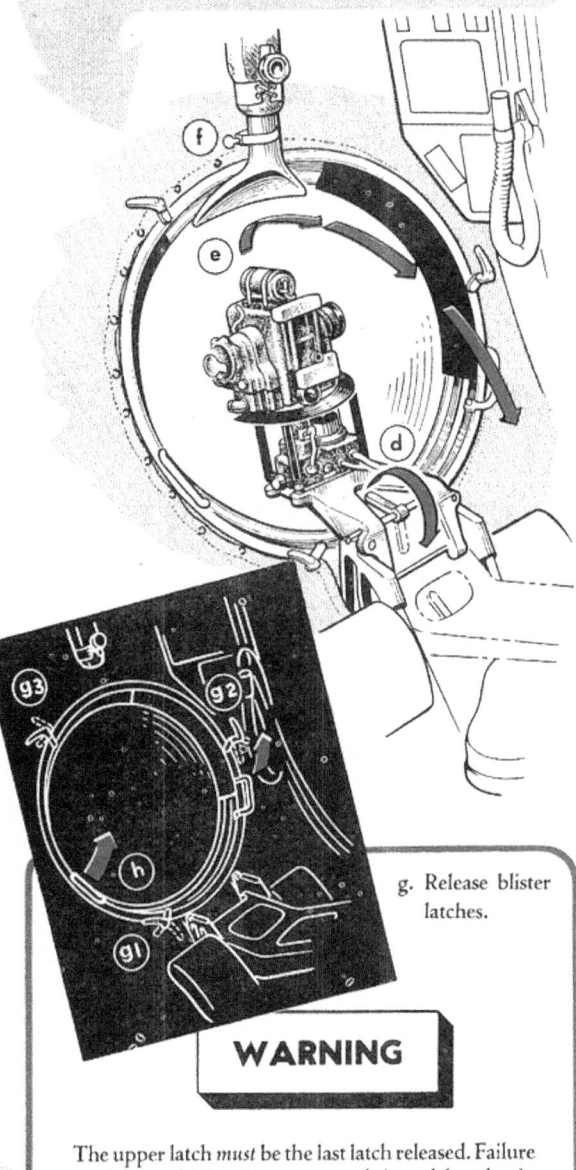

d. Swing sight mount emergency release handle inboard.
e. Pivot sight inboard, up, and out of blister.
f. Remove defroster duct.

g. Release blister latches.

WARNING

The upper latch *must* be the last latch released. Failure to observe this caution may result in a delayed exit, for there is danger that the latch may fall back into place or that the blister may fall out and strike the crewmen.

h. Grasp blister handles and pull blister inboard and upward. (Pivot blister about the aft edge to clear the gunner's control panel.)

Figure 3-6. (Sheet 1)

j. Stow blister, release escape rope, and make exit.

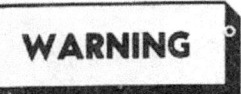

When the blister is removed, be sure that it is stowed clear of the exit so as not to hamper exit of those who must follow you.

4. The tail gunner and crew members on the right bunk exit through the right blister port; those on the left bunk exit through the left blister port.

NOTE

If escape through the two lower aft sighting blisters is impossible, follow procedure in step 5 and exit through the upper aft sighting blister ports.

5. The upper aft sighting blisters are alternate escape exits. To escape through these blister ports proceed as follows:

a. Position gunner's seat on the forward side of the left sight (aft side of right sight).

b. Position yourself to the aft side of the left sight (forward side of right sight).

c. Unlock sighting station azimuth lock.

d. Rotate sighting station head into a forward firing position. This is necessary in order for sight to clear blister frame.

e. Swing sight mount emergency release handle upward and outboard.

f. Pivot sight down.

g. Remove defroster nozzle.

h. Release blister latches.

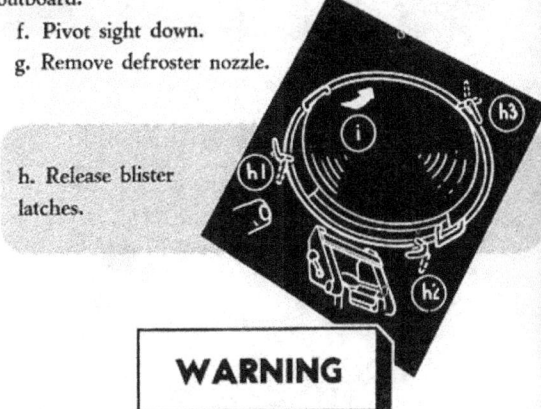

The upper latch *must* be the last latch released. Failure to observe this caution may result in a delayed exit for there is danger that the latch may fall back into place or that the blister may fall out and strike the crewman.

i. Grasp blister handles and remove blister.

WARNING

When blister is removed be sure that it is stowed clear of the exit and that it is not dropped on crewmen behind you.

j. Stow blister, release escape rope if provided, and make exit.

6. The pilots and engineers exit through their hatches in the canopy.

7. All personnel in the radio operator's compartment must use the left escape hatch if possible; however, if jamming prevents removal of this hatch, use the right and left blister ports.

Figure 3-6. (Sheet 2)

Controlled Crash Landing.

When it is possible, the decision to crash land should be made early enough to allow the crew time for adequate preparation. These general instructions must be remembered in case of a crash landing:

1. If control of the landing gear position is retained by the aircraft commander and an airfield is not available for landing, land the aircraft with the gear retracted on the smoothest possible terrain. If an airfield is available, normal wheels-down landing should be accomplished. If the gear cannot be extended, make the landing on terrain as smooth and hard as possible, preferably an airfield runway if available.

2. If it is possible, crash land near a road, a telephone line, or a small settlement to assure quick communication and immediate medical aid.

3. The crew will take the positions used for ditching (figure 3-9).

Miscellaneous Emergency Equipment

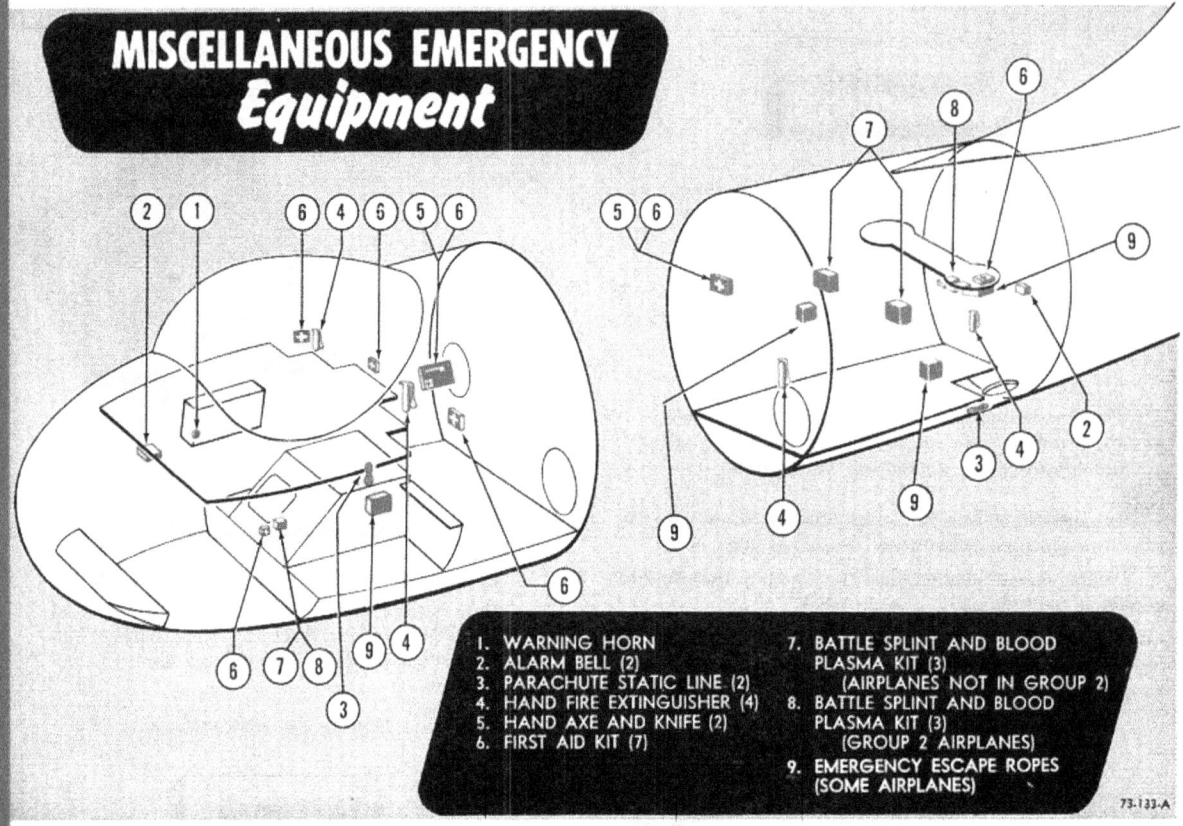

1. WARNING HORN
2. ALARM BELL (2)
3. PARACHUTE STATIC LINE (2)
4. HAND FIRE EXTINGUISHER (4)
5. HAND AXE AND KNIFE (2)
6. FIRST AID KIT (7)
7. BATTLE SPLINT AND BLOOD PLASMA KIT (3) (AIRPLANES NOT IN GROUP 2)
8. BATTLE SPLINT AND BLOOD PLASMA KIT (3) (GROUP 2 AIRPLANES)
9. EMERGENCY ESCAPE ROPES (SOME AIRPLANES)

Figure 3-7.

4. The crew must brace for the impact and remain braced until the airplane has come to rest. The forces generated during deceleration are enough to cause serious injury to any unprepared crew member.

Before Approach. When the decision to crash land is made, warn the crew by interphone and by six short rings of the alarm bells. The crew must immediately make the following preparations:

1. Pilot—Salvo all bombs and bomb bay tanks over an unpopulated area if possible.

2. Pilot—Bomb bay door switches—CLOSE.

3. Radio Operator—Transmit course, altitude, ground speed, and position; and turn IFF to EMERGENCY.

4. Navigator—Remove left forward escape hatch and stow in nose of airplane.

5. Forward Gunners—Open forward turret bay doors and point guns aft.

Note

Opening the turret doors will interfere with the source of airspeed indication.

WARNING

If turret doors fail to open, notify aircraft commander.

6. Aircraft Commander—If turret doors fail to open, direct crew members to assume crash landing positions in the radio compartment. The second engineer will remain on the flight deck.

7. Crew—Jettison all loose equipment and items which might fly loose on impact.

WARNING

Do not jettison the hand axes, because they may be needed to cut through the fuselage.

8. To prevent jamming, leave all emergency hatches open, but leave bomb bay doors closed.

Crash Landing EXITS & ENTRANCES

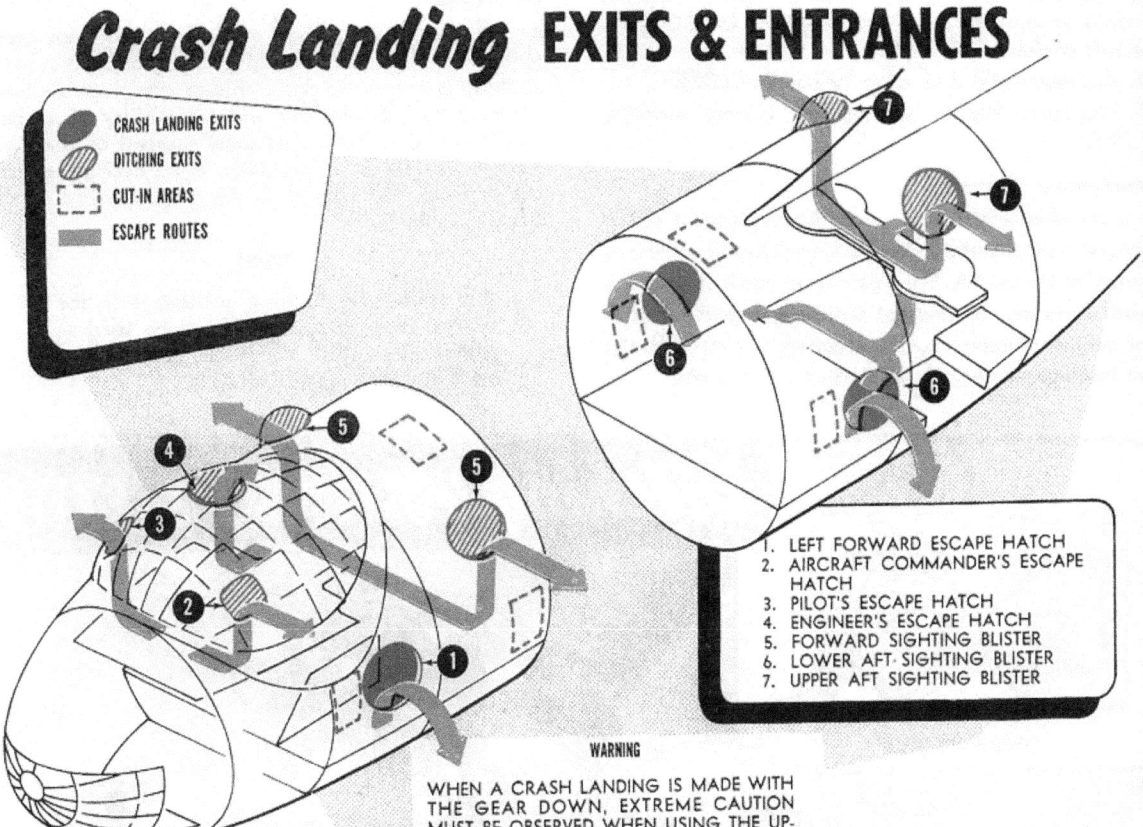

Figure 3-8.

9. Crew—Release the three locking clamps on respective blisters and pull inside the fuselage. Blisters must be placed in the nose of the airplane.

10. Crew—Assume crash landing positions.

11. All crew members will remove parachute and flak suits and use for padding. Don flak helmets and loosen neckties.

12. Compartment Commander—Report to aircraft commander when his compartment is ready for crash landing. Crew members in the turret bay will report to the aircraft commander when they are ready for crash landing.

13. Aircraft Commander—Give crew members not essential to crash landing permission to bail out.

14. Aircraft Commander—If practical, circle the landing area until the remaining fuel supply is 500 gallons in each wing.

15. Aircraft Commander—If the landing is to be made on a known airfield, notify the tower to clear traffic and have crash equipment standing by.

Approach and Contact. Begin the approach far enough from the landing area to allow the remaining crew members time to make last minute preparations. The pilot and the engineer must accomplish the following:

1. Engineer—Obtain a fuel configuration in each wing of one tank feeding three engines and close the fuel cross-feed valve and the necessary manifold valves.

2. Aircraft Commander—Fully extend the flaps and maintain a very flat approach.

3. Aircraft Commander—By one long ring of the alarm bell and by interphone warn the crew to prepare for the impact.

4. Pilots—Tighten safety belts and shoulder harnesses and lock inertia reel lock controls.

CAUTION

The pilots are prevented from bending forward when the inertia reel is locked; therefore, all switches not readily accessible must be "cut" before moving the control to the LOCKED position.

Section III
Emergency Procedures

T.O. 1B-36D(II)-1

5. Engineer—All alternator breaker hold-in switches—Hold in; mixture control lever—IDLE CUT-OFF on aircraft commander's request.

6. Engineer—All fuel valve switches—CLOSE.

7. Engineer—Engine ignition and battery switches—OFF.

Emergency Entrance.

If it becomes necessary to enter the airplane to rescue trapped crew members, use the emergency entrances as shown in figure 3-8. The left escape hatch in the forward cabin can be released from the outside if it is not jammed. Otherwise, it is necessary to chop through the fuselage at one of the marked cut-in areas.

DITCHING.

At the present time B-36 type aircraft do not carry permanently installed ditching equipment; however, ditching is considered preferable to over water bail-out when water temperatures and availability of surface vessels would indicate that mass survival of the crew members would be improbable. Final decision to bail out or ditch the aircraft is the responsibility of the aircraft commander.

Note

The following ditching procedure is for a 15-man crew and is meant to be used as a guide only until adequate provisions are made for ditching the aircraft.

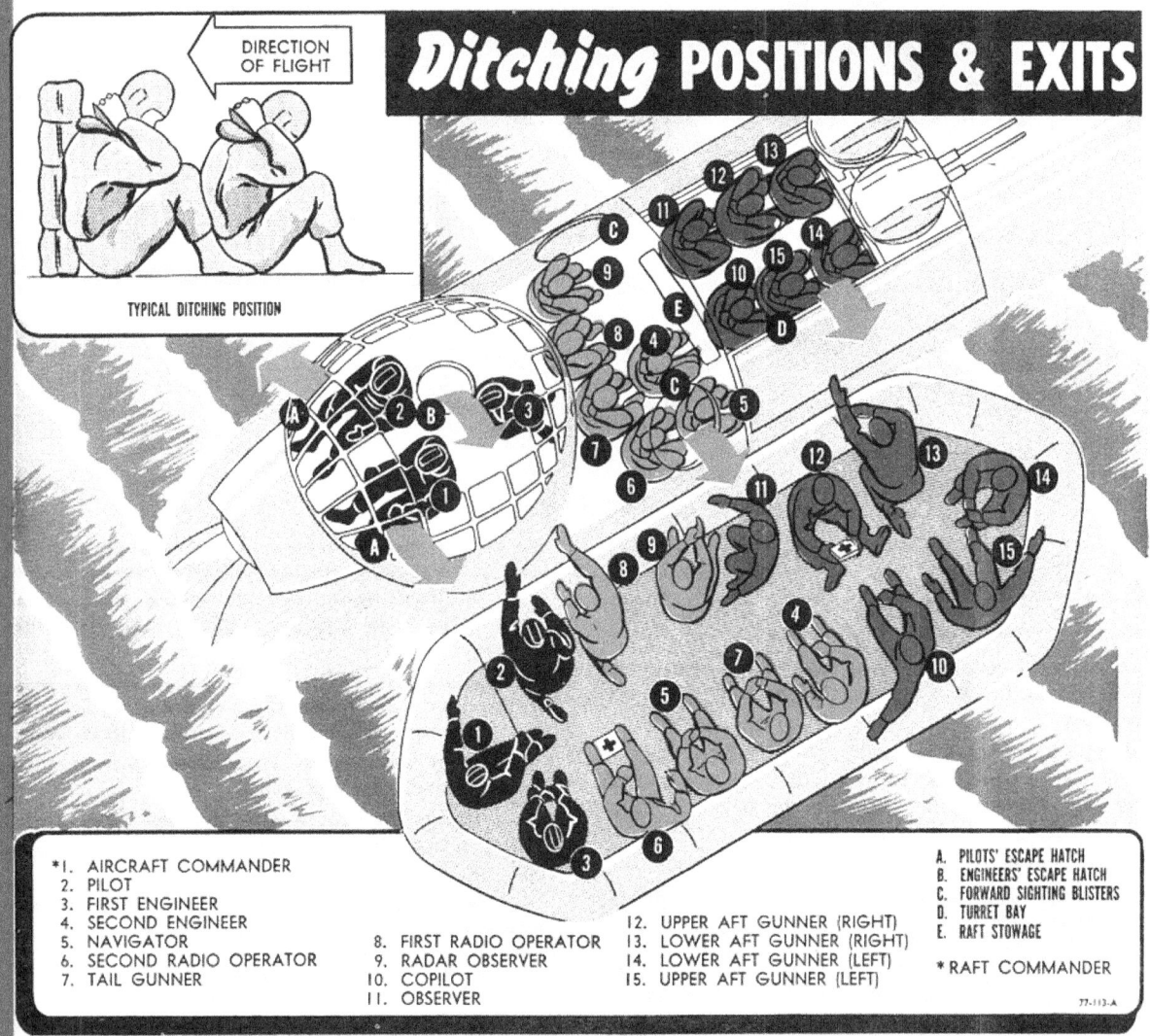

Figure 3-9.

Ditching drills should be performed until each crew member is thoroughly familiar with the procedure and the specific duties for which he is responsible. Make an equipment check before each overwater flight. Kits should be complete and crew life vests, survival suits, and life rafts should be in good condition.

Preparation For Overwater Flight.

Spare emergency equipment for crew members using the turret bay positions for ditching shall be stowed in the bay to eliminate any hindrance in assuming positions. A long interphone cord should also be provided for communication with these crew members.

One type F-2A 20-man life raft should be stowed in the forward turret bay.

A static line 30 feet in length should be provided for the raft to prevent its drifting free from the airplane after ditching. The static line must be attached to the raft in a manner that will cause the discharge of the inflating bottle when the line is pulled.

WARNING

The 30-foot static line must be cut after the life raft is loaded and the crew members are aboard to prevent the sinking airplane from pulling the raft under.

CAUTION

Be careful to prevent entanglement of the static line which might result in inflation of the life raft before its ejection.

A Gibson Girl radio should be stowed on the floor of the radio operator's compartment. Two static lines and a G-8 aerial delivery-type parachute shall be provided for the radio. The static lines serve the same purpose as the one provided for the life raft.

Before Approach.

When ditching becomes imperative, give the crew warning over the interphone and also by six short rings of the alarm bells. Crew members not actively engaged in controlling the airplane should jettison loose equipment and any objects which might fly loose on impact. When jettisoning is completed, crew members must assume the positions shown in figure 3-9 for ditching.

CAUTION

Make sure the forward turrets are extended and the guns pointed aft before removing the gun sights. The guns must be stowed aft to provide clearance for the men using the turret bay for exit.

WARNING

If turret doors fail to open, notify the aircraft commander. Aircraft commander will then direct crew members to assume crash landing positions in the radio compartment. The second engineer will remain on the flight deck.

All crew members should remove their flak suits and parachutes. The one-man rafts should be removed from the parachutes and stowed for later use. The crew must don R-1 anti-exposure suits, flak helmets, emergency kits, lift vests, and gloves. Neckties should be loosened. Crew members using the turret bay for ditching will enter through the catwalk entrance hatch, into the forward bomb bay, and up the ladder just aft of the turret bay. The life raft in the turret bay must be placed vertically against the forward wall of the turret bay so that it will cushion the shock of the impact for the crew members.

Note

One man in the upper forward turret bay is required to have his headset plugged into the interphone jackbox located at the right side of the forward bulkhead in bomb bay No. 1. Since the channels which the jackboxes are on vary between airplanes (either NORMAL or PRIVATE), *check* and *know* which channel the bomb bay interphone of your airplane is on prior to flight.

All crew members except the aircraft commander and the pilot shall sit facing aft with their hands clasped behind their heads to prevent snapping their necks on impact. They should use their parachutes and all available padding for their backs. The crew members in the turret bay should sit in three-man tandems, with the back men braced against the life raft. All blisters, pilots' windows, and the engineer's escape hatch must be removed and the blisters stowed prior to impact. After the impact each man must take his one-man life raft when he leaves the airplane.

Crew Responsibilities.

When a decision is made to ditch the airplane, each crew member must follow the procedures established in the following paragraphs:

Aircraft Commander.

1. Duties before impact:

a. Warn pilot—"Prepare for ditching in .... minutes."

b. Give 6 short rings on the alarm bells.

c. Order pilot—"Open emergency exits and jettison loose equipment." Open canopy windows and jettison if possible.

Section III
Emergency Procedures

d. Fasten saftey belt and shoulder harness.

e. Radio other craft of your distress, giving position and time. Have the radio operator broadcast a position report and turn the IFF switch to EMERGENCY.

f. Order pilot—"Stations for ditching. Impact in ... minutes." Have pilot obtain weight from engineer and figure the stalling speed.

g. About five seconds before impact, give order, "Brace for impact." Have the pilot give one long ring on the alarm bell.

h. Instruct engineer to complete ditching configuration.

i. Just before impact have pilot pull emergency ignition switch.

2. Ditching Position:

a. Lower seat and push rearward. Brace feet on rudder pedals with knees flexed and hands on control wheel after locking inertia reel.

> **CAUTION**
>
> The pilots are prevented from bending forward when the inertia reel is locked; therefore, all switches not readily accessible must be "cut" before moving the control to the LOCKED position.

3. Duties after impact:

a. Check to see that the crew is clear, and exit through the left canopy window.

b. Take command of the 20-man raft. Supervise removal of injured crew members and the securing of emergency equipment, food, and water aboard the rafts. When all crew members have boarded the raft, direct the observer to cut the raft static line. Guide the raft a safe distance from the airplane.

Pilot.

1. Duties before impact:

a. Relay the aircraft commander's instructions to the crew. Receive acknowledgements and notify the aircraft commander, "Crew notified."

b. Open the canopy window; jettison if possible.

c. Fasten shoulder harness and safety belt.

d. Stand by on interphone to relay aircraft commander's orders to crew. Check progress of crew in jettisoning equipment. A minimum of one minute before impact, order radio operator to clamp down key and assume ditching position. Relay command, "Brace for impact." Send one long ring on the alarm bell.

e. Pull emergency ignition switch just before impact.

2. Ditching position:

a. Lower seat and push rearward. Brace feet on rudder pedal stand with knees flexed, left hand on left knee, and right hand braced against the right window frame after locking inertia reel.

> **CAUTION**
>
> The pilots are prevented from bending forward when the inertia reel is locked; therefore, all switches not readily accessible must be "cut" before moving the control to the LOCKED position.

3. Duties after impact:

a. Throw out one-man life raft, exit through the right window, and proceed to 20-man raft.

b. Assist aircraft commander in supervising removal of injured crew members and emergency equipment.

First Engineer.

1. Duties before impact:

a. Acknowledge ditching order.

b. If ditching is necessary because of insufficient fuel, estimate the remaining time aloft and inform aircraft commander and the navigator.

c. Fasten safety belt.

d. On command, open the engineer's escape hatch and pass it to the nose compartment. If possible, obtain a fuel configuration in each wing of the most outboard tank feeding three engines and close the cross-feed valve and the necessary manifold valves.

e. On aircraft commander's command, "Complete ditching configuration"; CLOSE the tank valves; all hold-in switches—IN; mixture control levers—IDLE CUT-OFF; master ignition switch—OFF; battery switches—OFF.

2. Ditching position:

a. In the engineer's seat facing aft with hands clasped behind head to prevent snapping the neck on impact.

3. Duties after impact:

a. Take all necessary equipment and exit through the engineer's escape hatch to 20-man raft.

b. Assist injured crew members and aid in stowing equipment aboard raft.

Navigator.

1. Duties before impact:

a. Acknowledge ditching order.

b. Through coordination with the aircraft commander and the engineer calculate the course, altitude, ground speed, and position of ditching. Give this information and an accurate Loran line to the radio operator so that he may broadcast a position report.

c. Inform aircraft commander of surface wind speed and direction.

d. Destroy classified documents and material and aid in jettisoning all loose equipment. Gather essential maps and navigation equipment (including octant if possible) into water-tight bags or tuck into clothing.

2. Ditching position:

a. Seated on left side of radio compartment floor, facing aft, with back to second radio operator. Use all available padding, and clasp hands behind head to prevent snapping neck on impact.

3. Duties after impact:

a. Assist in ejecting emergency equipment from left blister.

b. Take navigational equipment and proceed to the 20-man raft.

c. Assist injured crew members and aid in stowing equipment aboard the raft.

Second Radio-ECM Operator.

1. Duties before impact:

a. Acknowledge ditching order.

b. Assist radio operator in jettisoning all unnecessary equipment.

c. Secure first aid kit to arm.

d. Destroy all classified documents.

e. Fire all ammunition from right forward turret. Leave turret doors open and guns pointed aft.

WARNING

If turret doors fail to open, notify the aircraft commander. The aircraft commander will then direct crew members to assume crash landing positions in the radio compartment. The second engineer will remain on the flight deck.

f. Remove the upper right blister and pass it to the nose section.

2. Ditching position:

a. Between navigator and tail gunner, facing aft, on left side of radio compartment. Use all available padding, and clasp hands behind head to prevent snapping neck on impact.

3. Duties after impact:

a. Assist in ejecting emergency equipment from left blister.

b. Take CRC-7 VHF transmitter-receiver and water jug, and proceed to 20-man raft.

Tail Gunner.

1. Duties before impact:

a. Acknowledge ditching order.

b. Destroy all secret equipment.

c. Remove all food and liquid containers and put in A-3 bag.

d. Proceed through communication tube to forward ditching position with first aid kit secured to arm.

2. Ditching position:

a. Seated on floor in radio compartment between first and second radio operators, facing aft. Use all available padding, and clasp hands behind head to prevent snapping neck on impact.

3. Duties after impact:

a. Assist in ejecting emergency equipment through left blister.

b. Take A-3 bag containing food, and board the 20-man raft.

First Radio-ECM Operator.

1. Duties before impact:

a. Acknowledge ditching order.

b. Set IFF switch on EMERGENCY, if installed.

c. Transmit position, course, altitude, and ground speed as received from navigator. Relay fix or bearings and estimated time and positon of ditching.

d. Jettison radio operator's chair.

e. Remain on interphone.

f. On command of pilot, screw down transmitter key.

2. Ditching position:

a. Seated on floor in radio compartment between tail gunner and radar observer, facing aft. Use all available padding, and clasp hands behind head to prevent snapping neck on impact.

3. Duties after impact:

a. Proceed to 20-man raft through left blister with Gibson Girl radio.

b. Assist injured crew members and aid in stowing equipment aboard raft.

Second Engineer.

1. Duties before impact:

a. Acknowledge ditching order.

b. Assist first engineer.

c. Assist in jettisoning loose equipment.

2. Ditching position:

a. Seated in radio compartment, facing aft, with back to tail gunner's knees. Use all available padding, and clasp hands behind head to prevent snapping neck.

3. Duties after impact:

a. Take emergency equipment and food, and proceed through engineer's escape hatch to 20-man life raft.

b. Assist in loading equipment aboard raft.

c. Assist injured crew members.

Section III
Emergency Procedures

Radar Observer.

1. Duties before impact:

   a. Acknowledge ditching order.

   b. Salvo bombs on command of aircraft commander. Do not salvo bomb bay fuel tank if empty. Close the bomb bay doors.

   c. Take first aid kit from nose compartment and secure it to arm.

   d. Take navigation equipment to ditching position.

2. Ditching position:

   a. Seated on right side of radio compartment next to first radio operator, facing aft. Use all available padding, and clasp hands behind head to prevent snapping neck on impact.

3. Duties after impact:

   a. Take emergency equipment and water jug and exit through left blister to 20-man raft.

   b. Assist in loading equipment aboard raft and assist injured crew members.

Copilot.

1. Duties before impact:

   a. Acknowledge ditching order on interphone. If not on interphone relay acknowledgment through someone else.

   b. Fire all ammunition from left upper forward turret. Leave turret doors open with guns stowed aft. Remove left blister and pass it to the nose section. Remove sight and jettison.

   Note

   Prior to removing sight, turn all power off.

   c. Proceed directly to forward turret bay and connect the interphone cord to the jack box in the forward bomb bay for contact with other compartments.

2. Ditching position:

   a. Sitting against forward bulkhead on left side of forward turret bay. Use parachute and 20-man raft for padding.

3. Duties after impact:

   a. Assist in lowering the life raft into the water.

   b. Proceed from turret bay to the 20-man raft.

   c. Assist injured crew members and aid in stowing equipment in raft.

Observer (Nose Gunner).

1. Duties before impact:

   a. Acknowledge ditching order.

   b. Proceed directly to forward turret bay with ground communication cord.

2. Ditching position:

   a. Sitting against forward bulkhead on right side of forward turret bay. Use 20-man raft for padding.

3. Duties after impact:

   a. Assist in lowering the life raft into the water.

   b. Proceed across the turret bay to the 20-man raft.

   c. Cut the raft static line on aircraft commander's command.

Left and Right Aft Gunners.

1. Duties before impact:

   a. Acknowledge ditching order.

   b. Secure first aid kits to arms.

   c. Take water jugs to ditching positions.

   d. Proceed through the tunnel to the radio compartment and then through catwalk entrance to forward upper turret bay ditching positions.

2. Ditching positions:

   a. Left gunners on left side and right gunners on right side of turret bay, seated facing aft. Use all available padding, and clasp hands behind head to prevent snapping neck on impact.

3. Duties after impact:

   a. Assist in lowering 20-man raft into the water.

   b. Take water jugs, food, and emergency equipment and proceed to 20-man raft.

   c. Assist in loading equipment aboard raft.

Approach and Contact.

It is believed that ditching the airplane with 30-degree flaps while maintaining 9 degree nose-high attitude at a low air speed will result in the most satisfactory procedure. This must be accomplished while power is still available in order to maintain the lowest possible rate of descent. The landing gear should be up and the bomb bay doors closed. Head the airplane parallel to uniform waves or swells. If the sea is irregular and confused, make the ditching into the wind. Aim for contact along the swell crest or just after the crest has passed.

BAIL-OUT.

If over uninhabited territory, all bail-outs should be made so that the crew will land in the same vicinity. If over water and surface vessels are below, the airplane should be headed so that crew members will drift onto the course of the vessel. A slow turn may be executed or two bail-out runs made, if necessary, to place the men close together. See figure 3-10 for emergency exits. Procedure varies according to conditions. If circumstances permit, descend to at least 10,000 feet and minimize forward speed. Over-water or polar bail-outs should be made with as much of the survival equipment as possible. When alerting the crew, it is advisable to remind them of their survival equipment. How to attach all survival equipment to the parachute should be stressed at practice drills. Successful bail-outs result chiefly from the intuitive action

Bail-Out ROUTES & EXITS

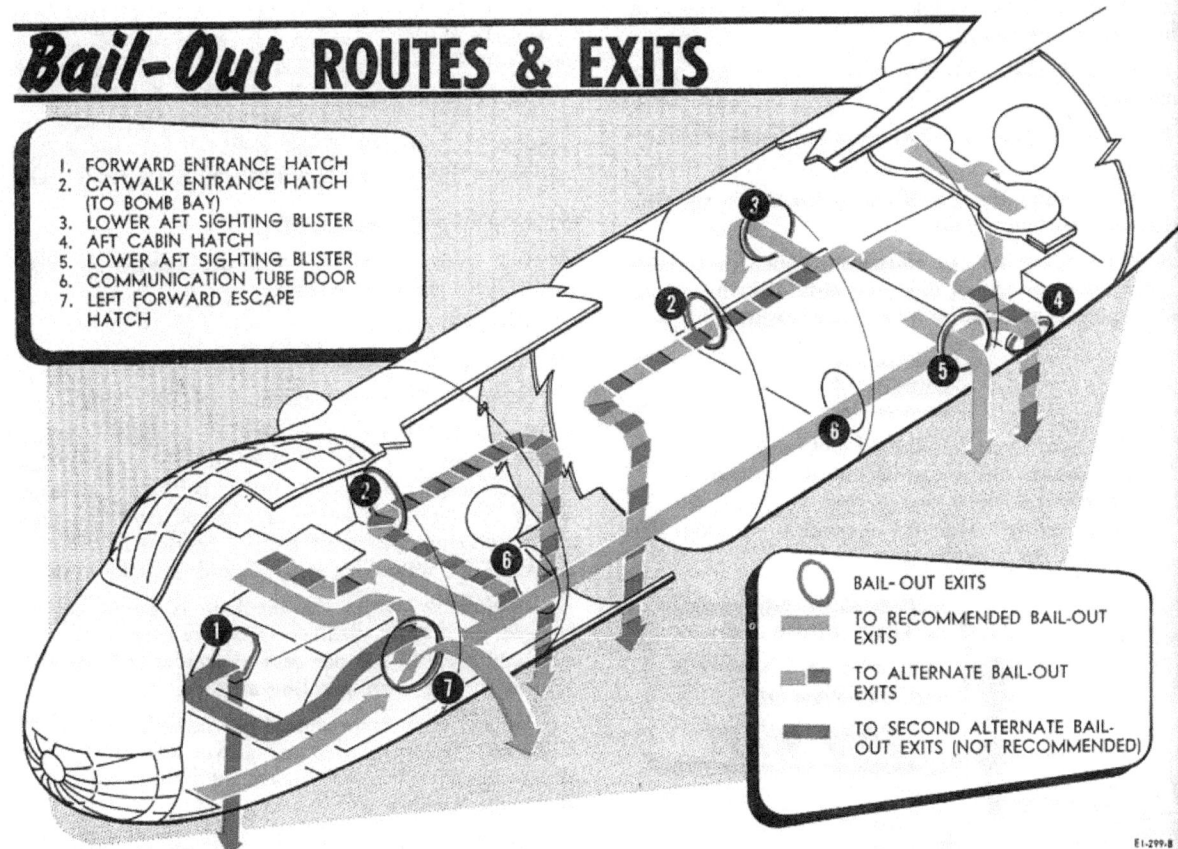

1. FORWARD ENTRANCE HATCH
2. CATWALK ENTRANCE HATCH (TO BOMB BAY)
3. LOWER AFT SIGHTING BLISTER
4. AFT CABIN HATCH
5. LOWER AFT SIGHTING BLISTER
6. COMMUNICATION TUBE DOOR
7. LEFT FORWARD ESCAPE HATCH

○ BAIL-OUT EXITS
▬ TO RECOMMENDED BAIL-OUT EXITS
▬ ▬ TO ALTERNATE BAIL-OUT EXITS
▬ TO SECOND ALTERNATE BAIL-OUT EXITS (NOT RECOMMENDED)

Figure 3-10.

taken by the crew members under circumstances frequently unfavorable for clear thinking and logic. It is strongly recommended that frequent and thorough drills be performed at the aircraft to instill conditioned habits and to insure smoothness of performance of each man's duties.

When bailing out, it is essential to remember a few elementary points concerning the parachute.

1. If the bail-out is made at night, it is advisable to place your right hand very close to the ripcord since you must rely on feel alone.

2. If the bail-out is during daylight hours, place your right hand near the ripcord. When you are ready to open your chute, look to see where the handle is rather than depending upon feel.

3. Keep your legs together and your body straight with the elbows close in and the left hand holding the oxygen mask tight to the face.

4. If feasible, the best body position for you to attain at the time of opening is feet toward the ground with the back and chest style parachutes.

5. During an emergency jump, do not waste too much time attaining a particular body position. Delay long enough to be certain you have cleared the aircraft, then pull the ripcord.

Steps given below apply to standard unpressurized bail-out procedure:

1. Aircraft Commander—Perform the following:

   a. Direct pilot to give "prepare to bail out" emergency signal: three short rings on the alarm bells, amplified by interphone warning.

   b. Ascertain that crew members have completed special and general duties as outlined below.

   c. Check parachute, bail-out bottle, goggles, gloves, and helmet with mask. Secure E-1 kit or dinghy to the parachute harness after leaving the seat. If over water, wear a Mae West under the chute.

2. Pilot—Actuate salvo switch to open bomb bay doors and salvo if not over populated area.

3. Radio Operator—Transmit course, altitude, ground speed, and estimated position of bail-out as received from the navigator; turn IFF switch to EMERGENCY.

Section III
Emergency Procedures

4. **Observer**—Remove left escape hatch and place it in the nose compartment.

5. **Navigator**—Compute position report for radio operator.

6. **Crew**—If time permits, destroy classified equipment.

7. **Aft Cabin Gunners**—Remove lower aft sighting blisters. (See figure 3-6.)

8. **Pilot**—Give bail-out emergency signal on aircraft commander's direction: one long sustained ring on the alarm bells, amplified by interphone warning.

CAUTION

The No. 3 engine should not be feathered to position the propeller for bail-out unless sufficient altitude and power of other engines remain to enable successful abandonment of the aircraft.

All compartment commanders will report to the aircraft commander, "Compartment Clear." After determining that all crew members have bailed out, the aircraft commander will be free to abandon the aircraft after putting it on autopilot with a heading that will avoid populated areas.

To bail out of the recommended exit in the forward or aft cabin, the crew members sit at the escape hatch in a tight ball and roll out of the exit. This procedure will eliminate the possibility of being caught on the edge of the hatch.

Note

If time and condition permit, as many crew members as possible should bail out of the aft compartment since it is considered the safest.

When using the forward bomb bay for bail-out, crew members should sit at the forward right side of the bay and roll out head first. Interphone contact between the bomb bay and the aircraft commander must be established before the bomb bay is used for bail-out. Personnel using the wheel well for bail-out should climb down the entrance ladder and jump from there.

HIGH ALTITUDE BAIL-OUT.

During high altitude bail-out the jumper is faced with three major problems:

1. Lack of oxygen.
2. Low temperatures.
3. High shock during opening of parachute.

If it becomes necessary to bail out at high altitude, every attempt should be made to ride the airplane down to at least 30,000 feet before bail-out is attempted. If bail-out is necessary at extreme altitudes, refer to "Emergency Depressurization," Section IV. During descent, the following steps should be taken:

1. If possible while the airplane is being depressurized, each crew member should remain at his station and breathe 100 per cent oxygen at the required setting for the corresponding altitude.

2. Helmet chin straps should be cinched, mask straps tightened, flying clothes and gloves secured, goggles put in place, and oxygen mask disconnect secured to parachute harness.

3. Bail-out bottles should be fastened to parachutes just above the accessory ring and connected to oxygen masks with oxygen hose under parachute harnesses.

4. Portable oxygen bottles should be used by crew members opening the emergency exits.

WARNING

Each crew member using a portable oxygen bottle will be closely watched by another crew member. At the first sign of anoxia, he will be returned to the ship's system and replaced by another man.

When the alarm bell rings and the interphone command is received for bail-out, each crew member should proceed as follows:

1. Take several deep breaths from the airplane's oxygen system.

2. Pull out the safety pin, actuate the bail-out bottles, and disconnect from the aircraft's oxygen system.

3. Go quickly to the designated escape hatch.

4. Place right hand near ripcord but not on it.

5. With the left hand holding mask to the face and with chin on chest, bail out.

Free Fall. (See figure 3-11.)

Remember, the average useful consciousness is about 15 seconds at 40,000 feet without oxygen. After clearing the airplane, straighten the body and keep the knees flexed and the elbows at the sides. The right hand should remain near the rip cord and the left hand on the mask as during bail-out. If the ground is visible, pull the rip cord to open the chute between 10,000 and 5000 feet (approximately two minutes after bail-out from 40,000 feet). At night or in weather conditions where the terrain is not visible, attempt to free fall for one minute before pulling the rip cord if bail-out is made from above 35,000 feet. When the parachute has opened, readjust and tighten the oxygen mask.

Note

Some parachute assemblies are equipped with an automatic ripcord release. The release is preset by the parachute rigger for a time delay of 5 seconds and an altitude of 5000 feet above the highest terrain on the projected flight path. If you have a parachute with an automatic release, pull the arming knob (red ball on the left side of the harness just above the leg strap fastener) at the instant of bail-out. The automatic release will then release the parachute at the preset altitude. The automatic release does not interfere with the manual operation of the rip cord.

VELOCITY OF DESCENT FROM 50,000 FT.
FREE FALL AND WITH PARACHUTE

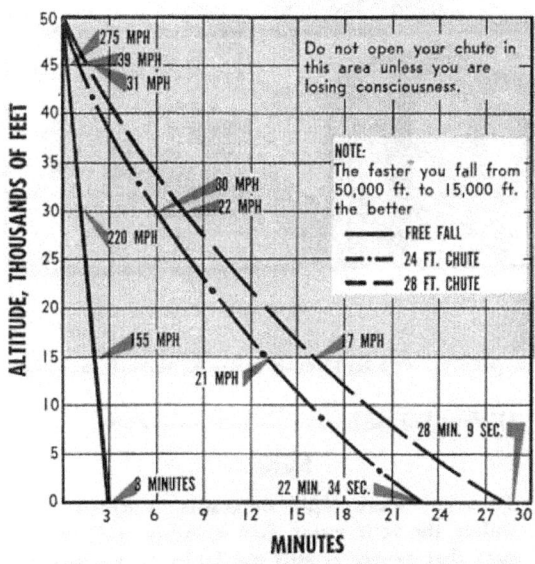

Figure 3-11.

OVERWATER BAIL-OUT.

Normally, on over-water flights a Mae West will be worn under the parachute harness. If time permits (there is no fire aboard or other emergency demanding immediate bail-out) put on all of your overwater survival equipment. Over your regular flying clothes put on the following items in the following order:

1. Emergency survival vest buttoned tight. (Either C-1 vest or E-1 kit, not both.)

2. Rubberized anti-exposure suit, with air squeezed out of lower extremities and fitted snugly around face.

Note

Do not put suit on unless water temperature is approximately 52°F or below.

3. Mae West.

4. Parachute. Attach your one-man dinghy to the parachute harness making sure that the dinghy lanyard is under the harness and attached to the "D" ring of the Mae West.

All compartment commanders will report to the aircraft commander.

POLAR BAIL-OUT.

Since most of the polar flights are over desolate, frozen country, the E-1 kit has been designed to fasten to your parachute harness in the same manner as the dinghy. For bail-out over remote areas, and when time permits, the following items should be put on over your regular flying clothes in the order listed:

1. Emergency survival vest buttoned tight. (Either C-1 vest or E-1 kit, not both.)

2. Rubberized anti-exposure suit fitted snugly around the face, if there is the slightest chance of landing in water.

3. Parachute. Fasten the E-1 kit to your parachute harness. Because of the weight and bulk of the kit, it can be attached most easily by sitting on it and then snapping to the harness.

FUEL AND OIL SYSTEMS.

ENGINE-DRIVEN FUEL PUMP FAILURE.

The loss of an engine-driven fuel pump will result in a sharp decrease in fuel pressure and a loss in torque pressure. If this occurs, determine whether or not the engine is delivering enough power to carry itself; if not, feather the propeller. Additional power may be obtained by use of the engine primer in an emergency.

MANUAL OPERATION OF FUEL AND OIL VALVES.

If electrical failure or unit malfunction should prevent normal operation of the fuel and oil shutoff valves, they can be operated manually. (See figure 3-12.) The jet engine fuel and oil shutoff valves and

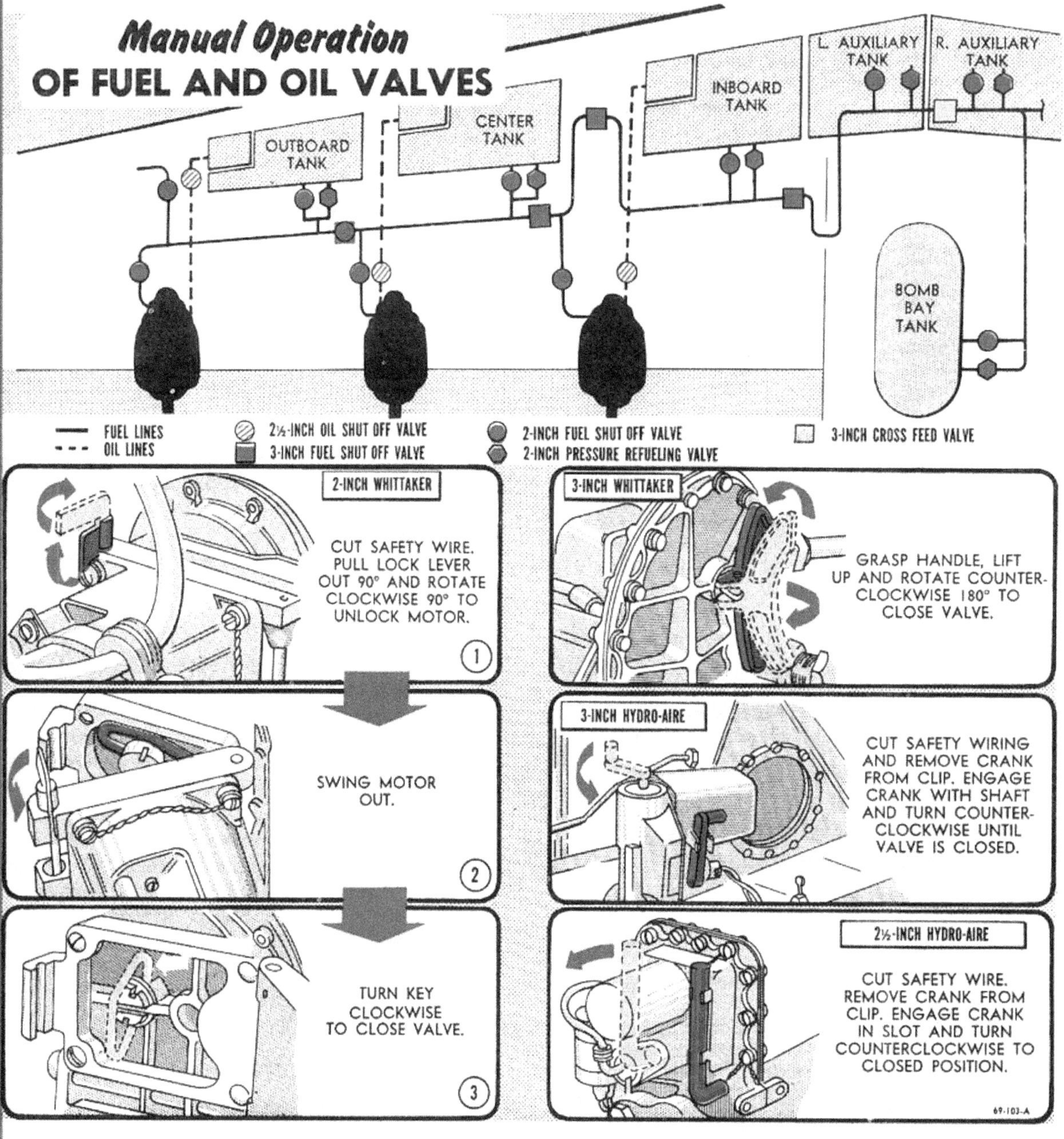

Section III
Emergency Procedures

T.O. 1B-36D(II)-1

Manual Operation
OF FUEL AND OIL VALVES

— FUEL LINES
--- OIL LINES

◎ 2½-INCH OIL SHUT OFF VALVE
■ 3-INCH FUEL SHUT OFF VALVE

● 2-INCH FUEL SHUT OFF VALVE
● 2-INCH PRESSURE REFUELING VALVE

□ 3-INCH CROSS FEED VALVE

2-INCH WHITTAKER — ① CUT SAFETY WIRE. PULL LOCK LEVER OUT 90° AND ROTATE CLOCKWISE 90° TO UNLOCK MOTOR.

② SWING MOTOR OUT.

③ TURN KEY CLOCKWISE TO CLOSE VALVE.

3-INCH WHITTAKER — GRASP HANDLE, LIFT UP AND ROTATE COUNTERCLOCKWISE 180° TO CLOSE VALVE.

3-INCH HYDRO-AIRE — CUT SAFETY WIRING AND REMOVE CRANK FROM CLIP. ENGAGE CRANK WITH SHAFT AND TURN COUNTERCLOCKWISE UNTIL VALVE IS CLOSED.

2½-INCH HYDRO-AIRE — CUT SAFETY WIRE. REMOVE CRANK FROM CLIP. ENGAGE CRANK IN SLOT AND TURN COUNTERCLOCKWISE TO CLOSED POSITION.

Figure 3-12.

the oil shutoff valve for reciprocating engine No. 6 are inaccessible during flight. The cross-feed valve and the bomb bay tank valves are accessible from the catwalk. The other valves are accessible from the wing crawlway.

ELECTRICAL SYSTEM.

EXCESSIVE ELECTRICAL LOADS.

At the first indication of an unusual or excessive electrical load for which no correction is immediately evident, perform the following steps as rapidly as possible:

1. All four bus tie-breaker switches—OPEN.

Note

To allow more rapid diagnosis, completely isolate the four buses. Bus isolation will insure that power is still available on normal buses. A faulted bus will be indicated by a high kilowatt reading. Any load division malfunction will be eliminated by bus isolation.

See Section VII, "Chart For Electrical System Troubling Shooting" for probable causes and remedies.

2. Immediately de-excite any alternator that is carrying too much load, (kwatt or kvar), or that is fluctuating over 10 cycles or volts.

> **CAUTION**
>
> If it becomes necessary to de-excite No. 5 alternator (which feeds bus 501), the engineer's fuse panel a-c power switch must be placed in the ALTERNATE position. (Check indicator light.)

3. Check the frequency and voltage control and stability of remaining isolated buses.

4. Reduce all electrical loads to a practical minimum until diagnosis is complete.

5. Connect adjacent operative bus to the dead bus and note for excessive loads or fluctuations. If the dead bus is clear of fault, allow the bus to remain energized. If excessive loads or fluctuations are noted, isolate immediately and do not restore power to the affected bus.

6. Place the selector switch between the two buses to be connected. When the synchronizing lamps are dark, close the bus tie-breakers.

> **CAUTION**
>
> Restore only essential electrical loads to prevent overloading remaining alternators.

7. If check as stated in step 5 reveals a faulted bus, that bus and its alternator must be left isolated and must not be used until the fault is cleared.

ALTERNATE SOURCE OF A-C POWER FOR THE ENGINEER'S FUSE PANEL.

Should it be determined that a-c power for the engineer's fuse panel has been disrupted, as indicated by the lack of power for such critical items as mixture controls, spark advance, turbosuperchargers, anti-icing, cabin pressure, etc., check the indicator lamp on the engineer's fuse panel to see whether power is being supplied to that panel. If the lamp is not burning, place the fuse panel a-c power switch in the ALTERNATE position. If there is still no indication of power, check the feeder fuses in the left and right cabin power panels.

EMERGENCY ELECTRICAL POWER OPERATION.

Restoring Normal Electrical Power.

If a complete loss of normal alternator power occurs, the following operating procedure will be followed:

1. All bus tie-breakers OPEN.

2. De-excite only the alternators indicating abnormal readings.

3. Recheck to insure that the alternator breaker indicating lamps of previously parallel alternators are lighted.

4. Reduce a-c and d-c electrical loads to a minimum. Notify all crew members that the battery switch is going to be turned OFF, rendering the interphone inoperative; then turn the battery switch OFF.

> **CAUTION**
>
> If the battery switch is left ON, the d-c load requirements will drain battery power which should be conserved for operation of essential equipment.

5. Turn the voltage and frequency selector switch to any alternator which is excited or will excite.

6. Re-excite this alternator as follows:

   a. Place the emergency power control in the EMERGENCY position.

   b. Momentarily hold the exciter control switch ON.

   c. Adjust voltage and frequency to normal.

   d. If voltage and frequency cannot be adjusted, momentarily hold the exciter control switch in the OFF position and proceed to another alternator.

7. If voltage and frequency can be adjusted to normal, connect the alternator to its respective bus by holding the alternator breaker switch in the CLOSE position until the indicator lamp goes out.

> **CAUTION**
>
> The kilowatt-kilovar meter should be observed closely while connecting the alternator to the respective bus to assure that an overload condition does not exist. If the kilowatt-kilovar meter indicates that the overload condition exists, the bus is faulted and cannot be used until the fault is cleared. In this case, the alternator should be removed from the line immediately and care exercised to keep the faulted bus disconnected from the rest of the electrical system.

8. Return the emergency power control to NORMAL.

> **CAUTION**
>
> Do not leave alternator selector switch in any bus position with an alternator on the line while switches are in EMERGENCY.

9. After the above procedure is accomplished for each alternator, parallel all working alternators using the bus tie-breakers. Use normal paralleling procedures except connect the voltage and frequency selector

Section III
Emergency Procedures

switch between the two buses to be paralleled. When the alternator synchronizing lamps are dark, close the bus tie-breaker switch connecting these two buses.

10. Battery switch ON.

Obtaining Emergency Electrical Power (Group 2 Airplanes).

When a-c power to the engineer's fuse panel is disrupted, the battery will automatically be disconnected from the d-c bus. Reconnect the battery to the bus by placing the battery switch in EMER ON.

CAUTION

Reduce d-c load requirements to a minimum before connecting the battery. This will conserve battery power for the operation of essential equipment.

If all a-c power is lost, place the emergency circuit selector switch in EMERGENCY to obtain power for operation of the pilots' directional and attitude gyros.

Note

Power for the gyros is available from the inverter regardless of the position of the battery switch. Direct current for the pilots' turn and bank indicator, the right hand pitot heater, and the normal interphone amplifier is also provided by this circuit.

Obtaining Emergency Electrical Power.

Note

On group 2 airplanes, an additional emergency power circuit is provided. This additional circuit can be utilized (refer to "Obtaining Emergency Electrical Power, Group 2 Airplanes" of this section) while emergency power is being obtained by the procedure described in this paragraph.

If attempts to get an alternator back on the line fail and there is an alternator capable of being excited, enough a-c and d-c power can be obtained to operate all d-c units, the pilot's attitude and directional gyros and, if installed, the turbo override controls. Proceed as follows:

1. Position the voltage and frequency selector switch to any alternator which will excite or which appears to be in underdrive.

Note

An underdrive condition may be verified by increasing or decreasing engine speed and noting that the frequency is proportional to engine rpm.

2. Place the emergency power control in the EMERGENCY position.

3. Momentarily hold the exciter control relay switch ON.

4. Place the pilot's flight instrument switch in the EMERGENCY position.

5. Restore only essential d-c loads.

WARNING

Do not permit the d-c load to exceed 1.0 (50 amperes) as indicated on the loadmeter of the transformer-rectifier test unit, when selected to the RADIO OPERATOR position. An overload can damage the t-r unit with a resulting loss of emergency power. In this event, the radio operator's t-r unit can be replaced with another t-r unit even during pressurized flight.

RELEASING THE CONSTANT-SPEED DRIVE FROM UNDERDRIVE.

If the constant-speed drive goes into underdrive, proceed as follows:

CAUTION

If the alternator overspeeds and does not go into underdrive, feather the engine immediately to avoid alternator disintegration.

1. Open the alternator breaker.

CAUTION

Prolonged motoring of the alternator may damage the override clutch in the drive.

2. Shut down the engine.

Note

When the engine is feathered, the overspeed control will automatically reset itself.

3. Turn the frequency control knob fully counterclockwise to avoid overspeeding of the drive when the engine is restarted.

4. Start the engine and advance the throttle to obtain 1150 to 1200 rpm. This will hold alternator speed within safe limits in the event the cause of overspeeding still exists.

5. If frequency control is normal and the cause of overspeed no longer exists or if the overspeed control puts the alternator in underdrive again, resume normal operation of the engine.

Note

If the alternator stays in underdrive, full rated alternator power may be obtained by increasing engine rpm to approximately 2800 to obtain a minimum of 360 cycles.

ALTERNATOR MOTORING.

The free-wheeling element in the constant-speed drive permits motoring of the alternator, for short periods of time, as indicated by low or negative kilowatt indications; however, if the alternator has motored continuously for approximately 5 minutes and attempts at adjusting the alternator have failed, OPEN the affected alternator breaker.

> **CAUTION**
>
> Do not feather the affected engine. This action is not necessary since opening the alternator breaker protects the electrical system and the shear section of the constant-speed drive protects the engine in the event that the motoring was caused by internal drive failure.

ALTERNATOR FIELD FLASHING.

Extreme fluctuations of voltage during alternator excitation may be the result of improper voltage regulation caused by reversed alternator exciter field polarity. If this condition exists, flash the alternator field in the following manner:

1. Isolate the affected alternator by placing the alternator breaker switch in the OPEN position. Check to see that the alternator breaker indicator lamp is lighted.
2. Check that the alternator field flashing circuit breaker is engaged.
3. De-excite the alternator and flash the field by momentarily holding the exciter control relay switch in the OFF position.
4. The alternator field is now flashed, and the alternator is ready for excitation.
5. If the extreme fluctuations continue when the alternator is excited, flash the field again.
6. If the malfunction persists, repeated use of the flashing circuit is not recommended.

EMERGENCY FLIGHT PROCEDURE IN THE EVENT OF A COMPLETE FAILURE OF A-C POWER.

A complete failure of all four alternators to the extent that not even one could be excited through the emergency electrical system or by use of the battery constitutes an extreme emergency. The battery switch must be placed in the OFF position immediately and only be turned to the ON position when an engine rpm change is desired. All electrical switches throughout the aircraft must be placed to the OFF or neutral position in order to conserve the battery.

This type of electrical failure would most probably occur during a cruise condition; but regardless of when it occurs, every precaution must be taken by the aircraft commander and the engineer to control the engines so as not to cause engine failures before a successful landing is accomplished.

If cruise is required before reaching a landing field, and the electrical failure occurred when cruise power was set, leave the engine controls as they were when the electrical failure occurred. The engineer would have no indication of the engine power since all autosyn instruments (torque pressure, manifold pressure, CHT, CAT., and fuel flow) would be inoperative.

Note

For airplanes in Group 2, refer to "Engine Instrument Trouble Shooting," Section VII.

Air speed would be the best indication of the power settings of the engines. If the air speed is excessive, retard the throttles. If the air speed is too low, increase the engine rpm gradually by intermittent use of the battery and propeller selector switches. Because the waste gates should remain where they were at the time of the electrical failure, engine power may be varied by gradual changes in engine rpm and throttle settings.

If a descent of several thousand feet is to be made and a relatively low engine rpm was set at the time of electrical failure, the rpm must be increased occasionally by intermittent use of the battery and the propeller selector switches in the descent. This is due to the more dense air at lower altitudes which would tend to automatically decrease the engine rpm (approximately 50 rpm decrease for each 1000-foot descent). Continue to hold the desired rpm throughout the descent by intermittent use of the battery and propeller selector switches at 5000-foot increments and control air speed by use of the throttles. As the aircraft approaches the landing pattern altitude, *gradually increase* the rpm to 2550 and continue to adjust the throttles to maintain the desired air speed. This procedure will prevent exceeding the engine limitations to destructive values even if the waste gates are closed more than they normally would be. Extreme care must be exercised when increasing the engine rpm since the manifold pressure is dependent upon the waste gate position. As the rpm is increased, RETARD the throttle at the same time and cross reference cylinder head temperature. A safe landing can be accomplished even if the engines were in advanced spark and manual lean at the time of the complete electrical failure. By constant surveillance of air speed and adjustment of the throttles, the engines would be operating at a reasonably low bmep which would "cushion" the manual lean and spark advance settings.

The aircraft commander will order the landing gear extended by use of the emergency hand pump and selector valve in the radio compartment.

Section III
Emergency Procedures

T.O. 1B-36D(II)-1

> **CAUTION**
>
> The emergency reservoir must be reserviced after the landing gear is extended. If this method of extension is unsuccessful the aircraft commander will order a mechanical drop of the landing gear. The aircraft commander will accomplish the landing without the aid of the wing flaps and a "go-around" should not be attempted due to the high engine power requirements with these adverse conditions.

Reverse propellers may be used after touch-down by use of the battery and reverse pitch switches. A crew member will be standing by at the emergency hand pump in the radio compartment with the selector to the CHARGE BRAKE ACCUMULATOR position. The aircraft commander must use steady pressure on the brake pedals to conserve brake accumulator pressure. After the aircraft has stopped the engineer will shut down all engines by CLOSING all engine fuel valves and then turning the battery switch OFF. The aircraft commander will then set the parking brakes.

Note

The parking brakes can be set after the battery switch is turned off.

A-C POWER DISTRIBUTION TO CRITICAL EQUIPMENT.

The following table shows the power distribution from each main a-c bus to various equipment whose operation is considered essential for safety of flight.

BUS 201 (AC)

PANELS FED BY BUS 201

Engine No. 2 Power Panel
Engine No. 1 Power Panel
Left Pod Power Panel
Left Fwd Turret Power Panel
Left Fwd Cabin Power Panel
DECM Power Panel
28V A-C Power Panel

Bombardier's Circuit Breaker Panel
Copilot's Circuit Breaker Panel
Navigator's Circuit Breaker Panel
Radio Operator's Circuit Breaker Panel
Engineer's Fuse Panel
Engineer's Control Panel & Table
Jet Control Panel

EQUIPMENT FED BY ABOVE PANELS

‡Air Plugs, Jet
‡Aileron Trim Tab, L Wing
‡Air Plugs, Recip Eng Nos. 1 & 2
*Anti-icing, Cabin Heating and Tail
‡Anti-icing, Jet Nos. 1 & 2
*Anti-icing, Wing
‡Carb Preheat, Recip Eng Nos. 1 & 3
*Fan Speed
‡Fuel Booster Pump, Jet, L Wing
‡Fuel Booster Pump, L Outbd Wing Tank
‡Fuel Booster Pump, L Aux Tank
‡Flaps, L Outbd & L Center
‡Gyro Horizon Indicator, Pilots'
‡Ignition, Jet Nos. 1 & 2
 Instruments, Jet Nos. 1 & 2
*Instruments, Recip Eng Nos. 1, 2, 3, 4, 5 & 6
 (Some Airplanes)
 Instruments, Recip Eng Nos. 1 & 2 (Some Airplanes)
‡Intercooler Control, Recip Eng Nos. 1 & 2

†‡Hydraulic Pump No. 1, Main
 Mixture Control
‡Oil Cooler Control, Recip Eng Nos. 1 & 2
*‡Oil Cooler Override, Recip Eng Nos. 1, 2, 3, 4, 5 & 6
*Oil Valves, Jet (Some Airplanes)
*Oil Valves, Recip Eng Nos. 1, 2, 3, 4, 5 & 6
*Pitot Heaters (Some Airplanes)
*Spark Advance (Some Airplanes)
*Throttle, Jet
 Transformer Rectifier, Navigator's
*‡Turbo Override Control
*Turbo Regulator Control
*Turbo Select, Recip Eng Nos. 1, 2, 3, 4, 5 & 6
 Vertical Gyro, Pilot's
‡Water Injection, Recip Eng Nos. 1 & 2
 28V A-C Power System, Fwd Cabin
 Flight Cabin Interior Lights
 Flight Deck Flood Lights
‡Landing Lights

---

*Alternate power source through Engineer's Alternate Power Switch
‡Equipment requiring A-C and D-C power for operation
†On airplanes USAF Nos. 44-92095, 44-92096, 44-92098 only

BUS 301 (AC)

PANELS FED BY BUS 301

Engine No. 3 Power Panel
Left Aft Turret Power Panel
Left Aft Cabin Power Panel

EQUIPMENT FED BY ABOVE PANELS

‡Air Plug, Recip Eng No. 3
‡Carb Preheat, Recip Eng No. 3
‡Flap, L Inbd
‡Fuel Booster Pump, L Center Wing Tank
‡Fuel Booster Pump, L Inbd Wing Tank
◻‡Hydraulic Brake Pump
▲‡Hydraulic Pump No. 1, Main

Instruments, Recip Eng No. 3 (Some Airplanes)
‡Intercooler Control, Recip Eng No. 3
‡Oil Cooler Control, Recip Eng No. 3
Transformer Rectifier, Aft Cabin
Transformer Rectifier No. 1, Bomb Bay
‡Water Injection, Recip Eng No. 3

BUS 401 (AC)

PANELS FED BY BUS 401

Engine No. 4 Power Panel
Bomb Bay Lighting Control Panel
Right Aft Turret Power Panel
Right Aft Cabin Power Panel

EQUIPMENT FED BY ABOVE PANELS

‡Air Plug, Recip Eng No. 4
‡Carb Preheat, Recip Eng No. 4
‡Flap, Right Inbd
‡Fuel Booster Pump, R Inbd Wing Tank
‡Fuel Booster Pump, Right Center Wing Tank
Hydraulic Pressure Indicator

Instruments, Recip Eng No. 4
‡Intercooler Control, Recip Eng No. 4
Transformer Rectifier No. 3, Bomb Bay
‡Water Injection, Recip Eng No. 4
26V A-C Power System, Aft Cabin
‡Oil Cooler Control, Recip Eng No. 4

BUS 501 (AC)

PANELS FED BY BUS 501

Engine No. 5 Power Panel
Engine No. 6 Power Panel
Right Pod Power Panel
Right Fwd Turret Power Panel
Right Fwd Cabin Power Panel
Engineer's Fuse Panel
Engineer's Control Panel & Table
Jet Control Panel

EQUIPMENT FED BY ABOVE PANELS

‡Aileron Trim Tab, R Wing
‡Air Plugs, Recip Eng Nos. 5 & 6
‡Air Plugs, Jet Nos. 3 & 4
Anti-icing, Cabin Heating & Tail
‡Anti-icing, Jet Nos. 3 & 4
Anti-icing, Wing
‡Carb Preheat, Recip Eng Nos. 5 & 6
Directional Gyro, Copilot's
Fan Speed
‡Flaps, R Outbd & R Center
‡Fuel Booster Pump, Jet, R Wing
‡Fuel Booster Pump, R Wing Aux
‡Fuel Booster Pump, R Outbd Wing Tank
⊛‡Hydraulic Brake Pump
‡Hydraulic Pump No. 2, Main
‡Ignition, Jet Nos. 3 & 4
Instruments, Jet Nos. 3 & 4
Instruments, Recip Eng Nos. 1, 2, 3, 4, 5 & 6
(Some Airplanes)
Instruments, Recip Eng Nos. 5 & 6 (Some Airplanes)

‡Intercoolers, Recip Eng Nos. 5 & 6
Lighting, Engineer's Instrument Panel
Lighting, Pilot's & Copilot's Instrument Panel
Mixture Control
‡Oil Cooler Control, Recip Eng Nos. 5 & 6
‡Oil Cooler Override, Recip Eng Nos. 1, 2, 3, 4, 5 & 6
Oil Valves, Jet (Some Airplanes)
Oil Valves, Recip Eng Nos. 1, 2, 3, 4, 5 & 6
Pitot Heaters (Some Airplanes)
Spark Advance (Some Airplanes)
Throttle, Turbo Jet Nos. 1, 2, 3, & 4
Tranformer Rectifier No. 2, Bomb Bay
Transformer Rectifier, Copilot's
Transformer Rectifier, Radio Operator's
‡Turbo Override Control
Turbo Regulator Control
Vertical Gyro, Copilot's
‡Water Injection, Recip Eng Nos. 5 & 6

* Alternate power source through Engineer's Alternate Power Switch
‡Equipment requiring A-C and D-C power for operation
†On airplanes USAF Nos. 44-92095, 44-92096, 44-92098 only
▲On all airplanes except (†) airplanes
◻On airplanes USAF No. 49-2647 and subsequent
⊛On airplanes prior to USAF No. 49-2647

Section III
Emergency Procedures

WING FLAPS.

At any time a pair of flaps fails to extend or retract normally it will be necessary for someone to operate the emergency switches on the alternate flap control panel near the right wing crawlway entrance. The following steps should be accomplished to raise or lower the flaps in an emergency:

1. Plug in a headset at the alternate flap control panel to establish interphone contact with the pilots and gunners.

Note

In some airplanes it will be necessary to turn the wing crawlway lights and interphone switches to the ON position to utilize this jackbox.

2. Hold the proper alternate flap control selector switch in the UP or DOWN position, depending on the flap movement desired.

3. With the aft cabin gunners checking flap position, hold the proper master flap control selector switch in the spring-loaded ALTERNATE position.

4. If the synchronizing system is completely inoperative, proper flap positioning will depend on the judgment of the gunners.

5. For landing, set flaps at 20 degrees and land in this configuration.

WARNING

Do not lower flaps to 30 degrees since flaps cannot be raised quickly in the event of go-around.

If the synchronizing system is operative and you move the lagging flap approximately two and one-half degrees past the position of the symmetrical good flap, the gunner will notice that the good flap will follow with a jumping motion. To keep the flap settings at the required deflection, the gunner must inform you to release the switch at the first movement of the good flap. At this point, both flaps will be equal in deflection.

Note

If the emergency flap control system is inoperative, check alternate flap panel circuit breaker switch at bulkhead 8.0 d-c power panel then check the fuses at the respective engine power panel of each flap. If the fuses are blown, replace them and attempt the emergency switches again before trying the normal system. If the emergency system works, do not use the normal system until maintenance can be accomplished. For further information, refer to "Emergency Operation of Electrical Equipment," Section VII.

EMERGENCY LANDING GEAR OPERATION.

If the landing gear fails to respond to the positioning of the landing gear control switch, three emergency methods are provided to effect landing gear operation. Emergency gear extension procedures should be attempted in the order listed, except when the main hydraulic reservoir is empty; in this case the first procedure should be omitted. These methods are as follows:

1. Manual Operation of Main Selector Valve.
2. Emergency Hydraulic Landing Gear Extension.
3. Manual Extension of Main and Nose Landing Gear.

Note

Gear retraction can be accomplished by the first method only. Extension can be accomplished by any of the three methods.

To determine the probable cause of normal control failure, proceed as follows:

1. Place the landing gear control switch in EXTEND or RETRACT as required.

Note

If no hydraulic pressure is indicated, the landing gear extend or retract relays may be inoperative.

2. Hold the hydraulic pump override switch ON.

Note

a. If there is no hydraulic pressure, check the main hydraulic reservoir fluid level and the main hydro pump fuses in the main a-c power panel.

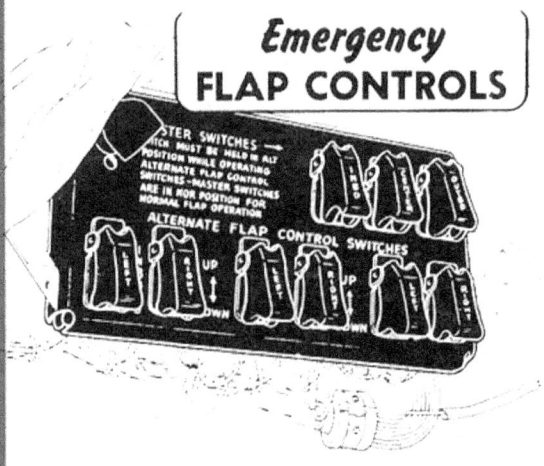

Figure 3-13.

b. If pressure is indicated, but the gear does not operate, a faulty electrical circuit to the selector valve may be the source of trouble.

3. Turn the landing gear control switch OFF and release the hydraulic pump override switch to OFF.

CAUTION

Do not operate the main hydraulic pumps more than two out of every ten minutes at maximum pressure since sustained operation will damage the pump motors.

Note

For further information, refer to "Emergency Operation of Electrical Equipment," Section VII.

MANUAL OPERATION OF MAIN SELECTOR VALVE.

1. Landing gear control switch—OFF.
2. Landing gear control circuit breaker—Pull out.

CAUTION

The preceding steps should be accomplished to prevent inadvertent operation of the gear.

3. Main selector valve—Push in and hold the UP or DOWN landing gear plunger, as desired.

CAUTION

The crew member operating the selector valve must be in interphone contact with the aircraft commander, engineer, and gunners, and must notify the engineer when he has positioned the valve plunger.

4. Hydraulic pump override switch—Hold ON until lower aft cabin gunners report, "Door open, gear coming down, door closed"; then turn OFF.

CAUTION

To prevent pump motor damage, limit the operation of the main hydraulic pumps to two minutes out of every ten minutes at maximum pressure.

Note

At any time normal gear sequence stops, the gunners will immediately report this condition over interphone.

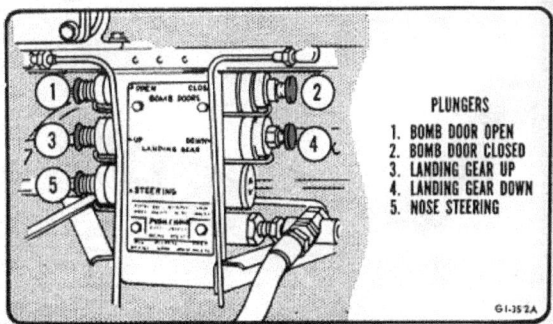

Figure 3-14.

5. Main selector valve—Release plunger when notified that gear action has been completed.

WARNING

To be sure the gear is down and locked, the aft gunners should visually check the position of the pink flourescent flag (figure 3-15) on each main gear side brace. The flags will not be visible when the gear is down and locked. Gunners will also notice a snapping motion of the latch link rod as it goes into the locked position.

6. Landing gear control circuit breaker—IN and check gear position indicator lights.

Section III
Emergency Procedures

7. Nose gear—Checked visually down and locked by the radio operator.

EMERGENCY HYDRAULIC EXTENSION.

If the main hydraulic pumps fail to operate in response to the landing gear control switch or the pump override switch, use the following procedure to extend the landing gear:

1. Landing gear control switch—OFF.
2. Landing gear control circuit breaker—Pull out.

CAUTION

The preceding steps will prevent inadvertent operation of the gear. The crew member pumping the gear down must establish interphone contact with the aircraft commander and the gunners.

3. Emergency selector valve—Position at EXTEND LANDING GEAR.

WARNING

Make sure that the emergency selector valve is held in the detent position during landing gear extension to prevent rupture of the hydraulic lines.

4. Hand pump—Operate until the gear is down and locked. Pump vigorously for the first 10 cycles to position the shuttle valve. The nose gear usually extends first, the main gear doors open, and then the main gear extends.

Note

The main gear doors will remain down since they cannot be retracted by hand pump operation.

Figure 3-15.

Landing Gear & Brake
EMERGENCY HYDRAULIC CONTROLS

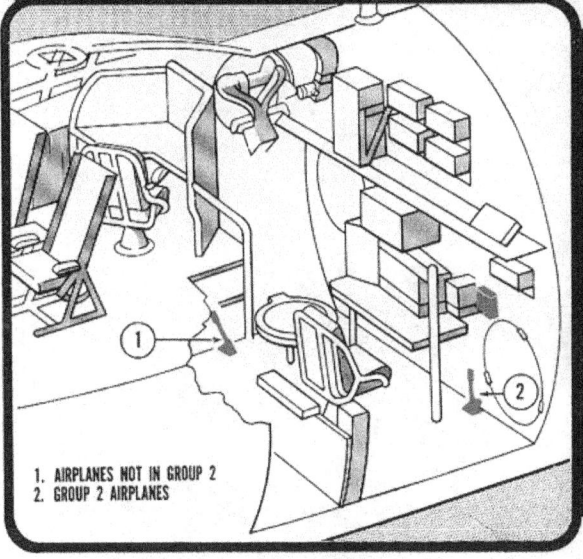
1. AIRPLANES NOT IN GROUP 2
2. GROUP 2 AIRPLANES

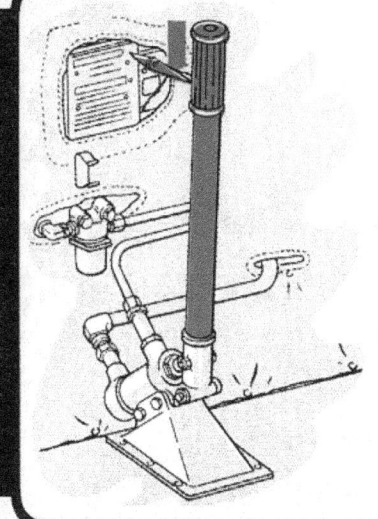

MOVE LEVER UP FOR BRAKE PRESSURE OR DOWN TO EXTEND LANDING GEAR

PUMP HANDLE TO BUILD UP PRESSURE

Figure 3-16.

WARNING

If the green landing gear indicator light does not come on when the landing gear control circuit breaker is pushed in, make a visual check at the wing crawlway entrances to be sure the gear is down and locked.

5. Emergency selector valve lever—Return to the CHARGE BRAKE ACCUMULATOR position.

CAUTION

The emergency selector valve must be placed in the CHARGE BRAKE ACCUMULATOR position before operating the normal brake hydraulic system. Otherwise, fluid will be transferred into the emergency reservoir if the emergency brake check valve between the emergency selector valve and the hydraulic gage line is leaking. If fluid begins to overflow in the emergency reservoir during gear extension, the emergency selector valve must be placed in EXTEND LANDING GEAR to prevent further loss of fluid.

WARNING

If the normal gear system is operated after an emergency extension of the gear, the landing gear control switch must first be moved to EXTEND to position shuttle valves properly and close canoe doors. Because the landing gear doors remain down after a hand-pump extension of the gear, the gear and the doors might retract simultaneously if the landing gear control switch was moved to RETRACT first.

CAUTION

If during hand pump extension of the gear, the landing gear control switch is inadvertently moved to RETRACT, a hydraulic lock will be created between the nose gear emergency extension line and the emergency hand pump. To overcome this condition, momentarily place the landing gear control switch in EXTEND. This action will reposition a shuttle valve in the nose gear emergency line and remove the hydraulic lock. There will be no loss of hydraulic fluid and the resulting pressure will be normal.

6. Reservice emergency hydraulic reservoir prior to landing, if necessary.

Section III
Emergency Procedures

T.O. 1B-36D(II)-1

1. HOIST
2. HOIST HOOK
3. CRAWLWAY
4. REAR SPAR
5. DOOR DIRECTIONAL VALVE
6. LATCH
7. DOOR RELEASE HANDLE
8. STATIONARY STRUCTURE

Manual Extension
MAIN LANDING GEAR

Before attempting a manual extension of the main gear, the landing gear control switch must be OFF and its circuit breaker pulled. Two crew members will proceed to the wing crawlway entrance hatch. One will plug into the interphone system at the hatch. The other will gain access to the manual extension controls shown above via the wing crawlway and extend the gear as follows:

WARNING

No parachute will be worn in the wing crawlway at any time.

Step 1

Assume a position on the wing crawlway from where it will be possible to reach the red latch link pin. Remove this pin and allow the latch link rod to drop free of the latch. This prevents the possibility of pressure in the hydraulic system interfering with manual unlatching and also eliminates the hazard of someone operating the gear while you are working in the wheel well.

Note

A complete inspection of manual extension equipment will be made before extending the gear.

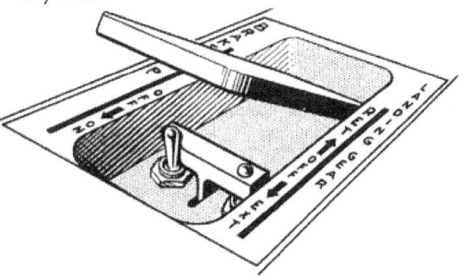

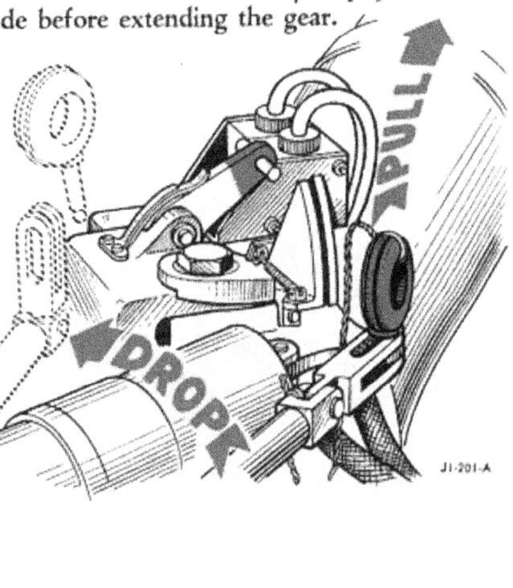

Figure 3-17. (Sheet 1)

T.O. 1B-36D(II)-1

Section III
Emergency Procedures

Step 2

Assume a position on the wheel well stationary structure and remove the safety wire or strap from the main wheel well door release handle. Turn the handle clockwise until the door is unlatched and falls open.

HANDLE GOES WITH THE DOOR —— DO NOT HOLD ONTO IT

If the door does not extend completely, a hydraulic lock is indicated between the main selector valve and the door jack. Relieve this lock by disconnecting the rod from the valve handle and pushing the handle down.

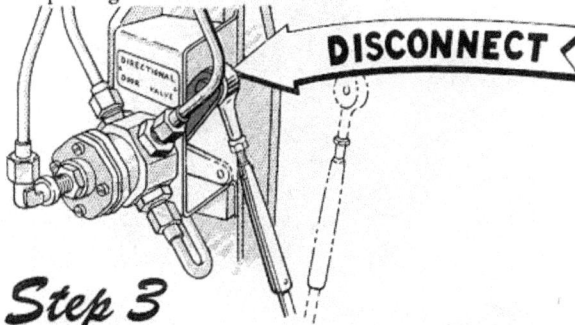

DISCONNECT

Step 3

From a position on the wheel well stationary structure, unstow the hoist hook.

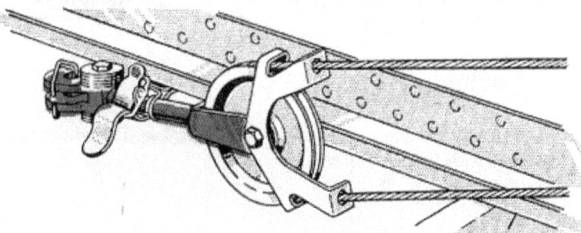

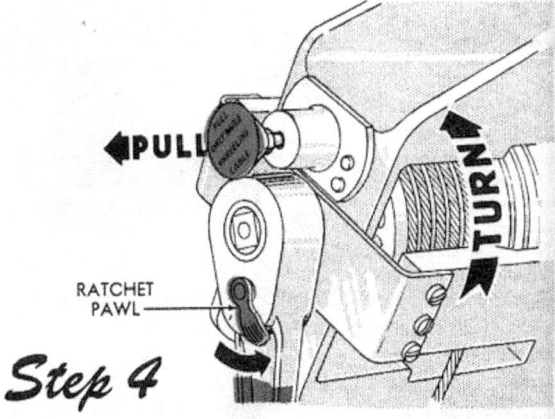

◀ PULL   TURN ▶

RATCHET PAWL

Step 4

If the hoist hook does not reach the latch release lever, the hoist lock pin located above the ratchet handle on the cable drum must be disengaged from the drum to extend the cable. The hoist lock pin is disengaged by pulling out and holding its spring loaded button. The ratchet handle pawl must then be set to allow unreeling of the cable (counterclockwise turning of the drum). The cable extends by unwinding from the large drum and winding onto the small drum. Releasing the button will re-engage the hoist lock pin with the cable drum.

Step 5

Engage the hoist hook with the pins on the latch release lever and hold it there making sure that the spring release on the hoist hook is behind the pins. This will insure positive release of the hook when cable tension is relieved after the side brace is raised. Also, when engaging the hoist hook, make sure that the cables are not crossed.

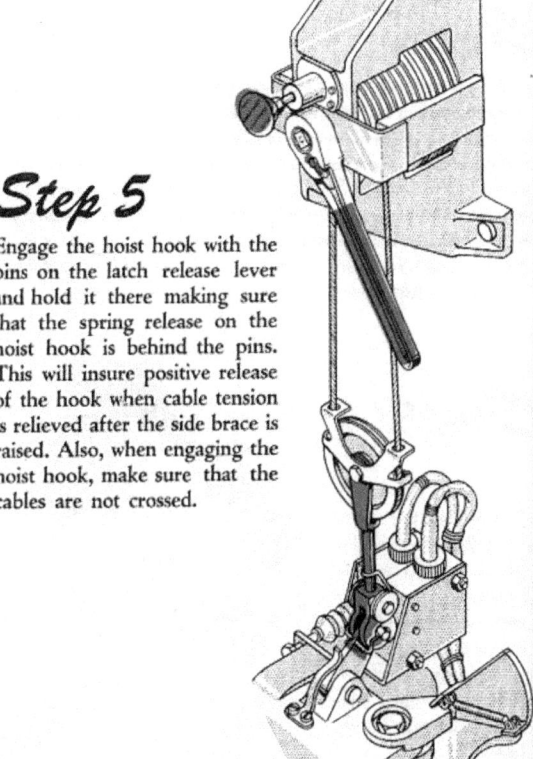

Figure 3-17. (Sheet 2)

Step 6

Engage the hoist lock pin by releasing the button. Reverse the ratchet handle pawl so that operation of the ratchet will wind the cable onto the large drum (force being applied to the ratchet handle in the clockwise direction).

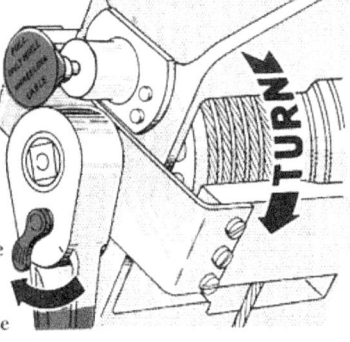

Step 7

Tighten the cable by a clockwise movement of the ratchet handle while holding the hoist hook on the latch release lever until the cable slack is taken up. When the hoist lock pin is engaged, the only movement that can be made is in the clockwise direction (cable unwinding onto the large drum).

Step 8

For the right main gear, lying on the catwalk facing aft, *push* the ratchet handle for clockwise movement of the drum. For the left main gear, lying on the catwalk facing aft, *pull* the ratchet handle for clockwise movement of the drum. Continue applying force to the ratchet handle in the clockwise direction to apply tension to the cable, and turning the handle in the counterclockwise direction to obtain a new "bite" on the drum. This ratcheting is necessary because of the limited space and leverage when in a prone position.

Step 9

When the latch release lever unlatches the side brace, and the side brace begins to rise, cable tension will be relieved and the hook should spring free. If the hook remains engaged, disengage it by hand.

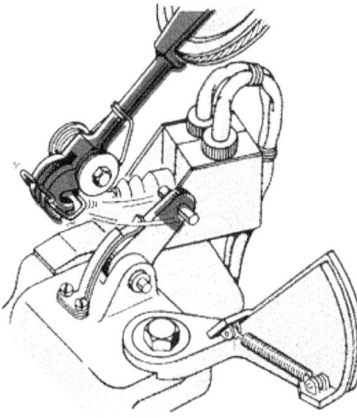

Step 10

The gear will fall away under its own weight and should lock after extension. If it does not lock in the down position a slight kicking of the latch link bracket should engage the lock.
Note: If the latch cannot be engaged install the ground safety lock.

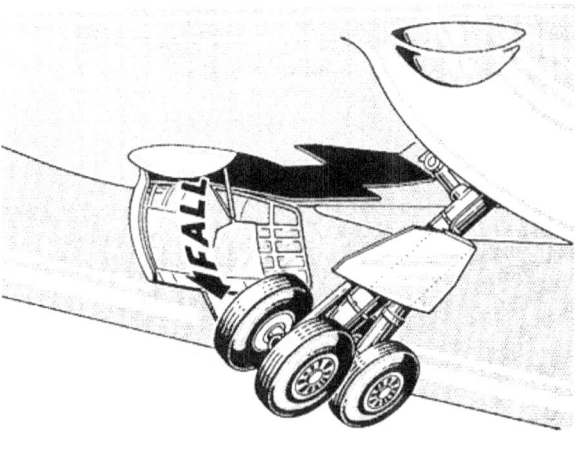

Step 11

Check the position of the pink flag on the landing gear side brace. If the gear is down and locked, the flag will not be visible.

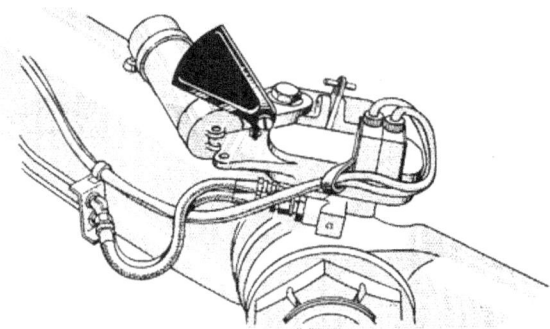

Step 12

Push in pilot's landing gear circuit breaker and check landing gear indicator lamps.

Step 13

Leave the landing gear switch OFF and place the brake pump switch ON.

Figure 3-17. (Sheet 3)

EMERGENCY RETRACTION OF NOSE LANDING GEAR.

In the event the nose gear fails to retract with the main landing gear, determine whether the emergency release pin is in place by looking through the inspection window in the floor of the radio operator's compartment. If the pin is not in place, the nose gear latch will not unlock. When this occurs, the nose gear can be retracted by either of two methods.

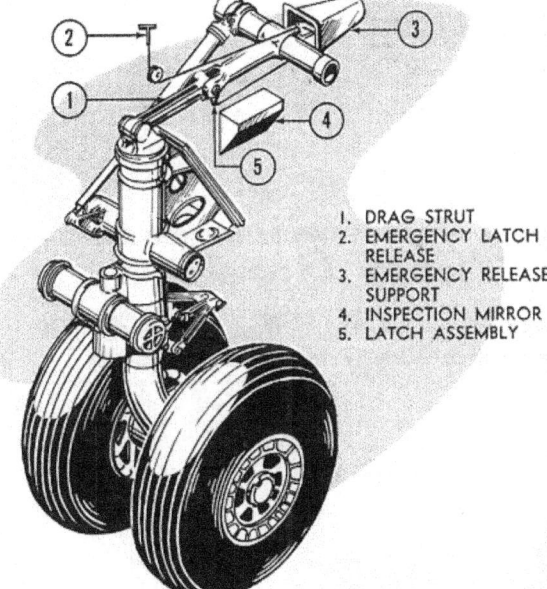

1. DRAG STRUT
2. EMERGENCY LATCH RELEASE
3. EMERGENCY RELEASE SUPPORT
4. INSPECTION MIRROR
5. LATCH ASSEMBLY

Method 1

If the emergency release pin is still available but not in place, use the following procedure:

1 Aircraft Commander – Instruct that all radar equipment be turned OFF.

2 Pilot – Place the landing gear control switch off, check for zero hydraulic pressure, and pull the landing gear circuit breaker.

3 Crew member–Enter the radar equipment bay beneath the forward turrets and, using the access hole in the forward bulkhead, insert the release pin through the latch assembly beneath the forward end of the latch release rod.

4 Crew member–To connect the unlocking arm it may be necessary to rotate the unlocking arm collar slightly. *Do not attempt to adjust the rod length.*

5 Pilot – After crew member is clear, push in circuit breaker and retract the nose gear in the normal manner.

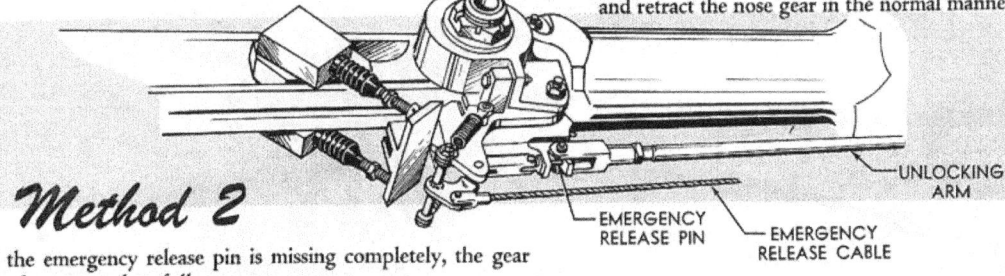

UNLOCKING ARM
EMERGENCY RELEASE PIN
EMERGENCY RELEASE CABLE

Method 2

If the emergency release pin is missing completely, the gear can be retracted as follows:

1 Pilot–Place the landing gear control switch OFF, check for zero hydraulic pressure, and pull the landing gear circuit breaker.

2 Crew member–Apply a steady pull of approximately 150 pounds on the nose gear release handle. The latch will open and the cable will pull through the floor another two or three inches. Check the position of the latch by looking through the inspection window.

3 Crew member–While holding the cable tight, inform pilot to push in circuit breaker and place the landing gear control switch in RETRACT. When the gear begins to retract, release the handle; the gear should then lock in the retracted position.

4 Crew member–Make sure that the release cable is properly seated over the pulleys; this is essential because the nose gear must be extended manually when the above method is used for retraction.

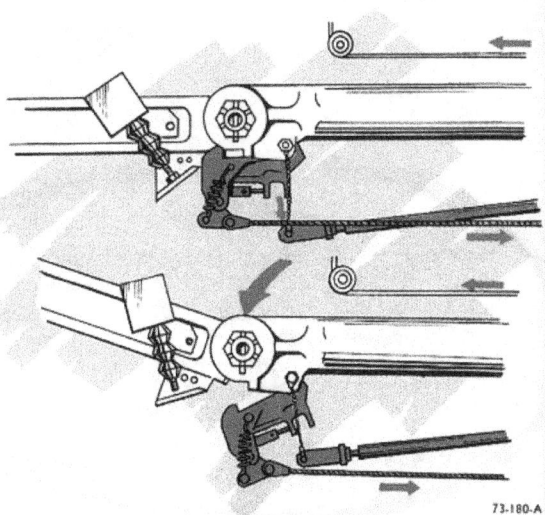

Figure 3-18.

Section III
Emergency Procedures

T.O. 1B-36D(II)-1

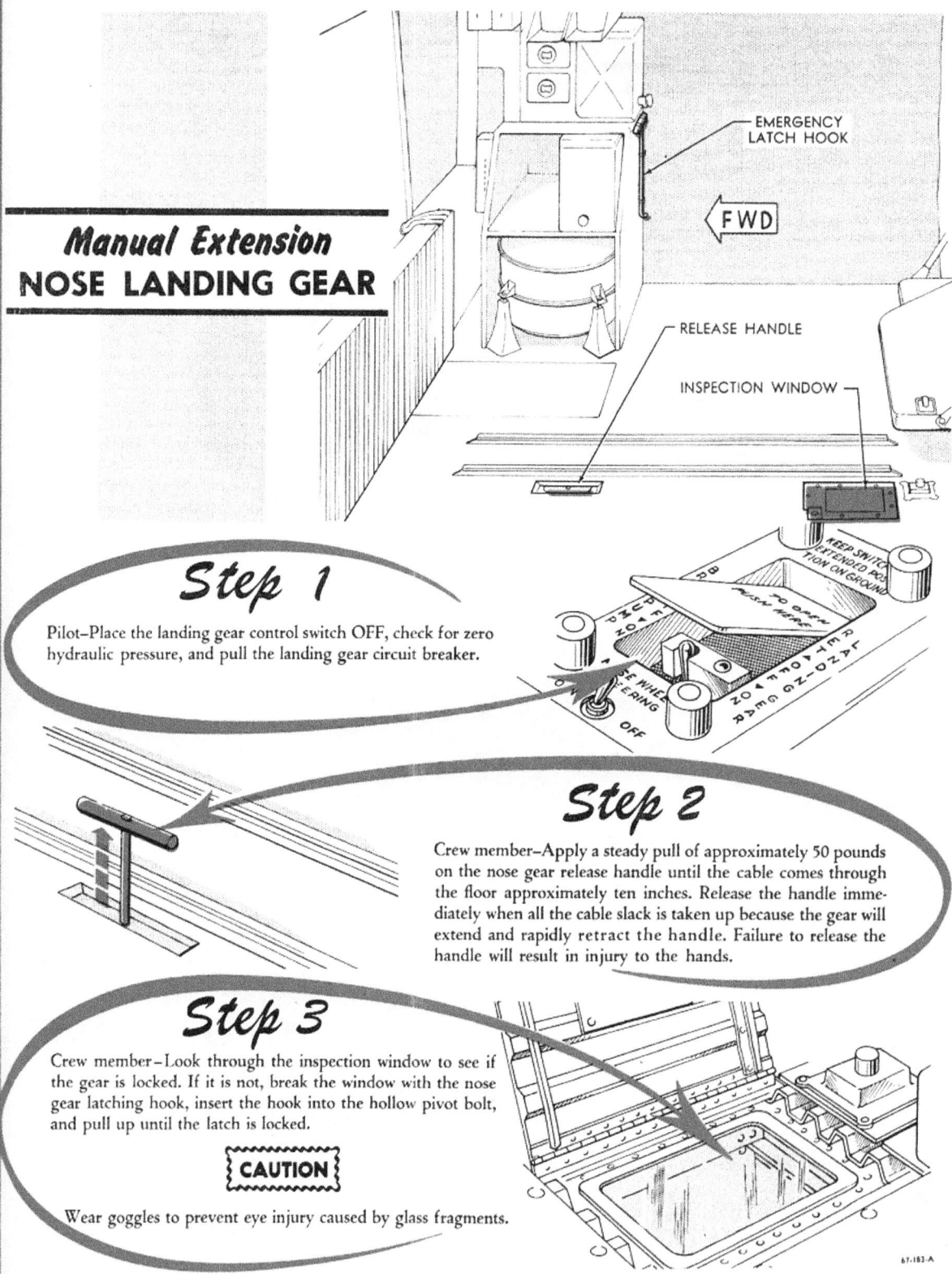

Manual Extension
NOSE LANDING GEAR

Step 1
Pilot—Place the landing gear control switch OFF, check for zero hydraulic pressure, and pull the landing gear circuit breaker.

Step 2
Crew member—Apply a steady pull of approximately 50 pounds on the nose gear release handle until the cable comes through the floor approximately ten inches. Release the handle immediately when all the cable slack is taken up because the gear will extend and rapidly retract the handle. Failure to release the handle will result in injury to the hands.

Step 3
Crew member—Look through the inspection window to see if the gear is locked. If it is not, break the window with the nose gear latching hook, insert the hook into the hollow pivot bolt, and pull up until the latch is locked.

{ CAUTION }

Wear goggles to prevent eye injury caused by glass fragments.

Figure 3-19.

EMERGENCY STOPPING.

USE OF BRAKES AND PROPELLERS.

For normal stopping of the aircraft, reverse pitch of the six reciprocating engines is sufficient to slow down or stop the aircraft with little or no brake action required. However, for emergency stopping you are concerned only with stopping the aircraft in as short a space as possible without going off the runway. Therefore all normal restrictions on use of brakes and props will not apply. To increase the effects of reverse thrust, reduce rpm to 2000 with the master motor as power is applied.

You will not be concerned with burning out a set of brakes or exceeding prop restrictions in reverse. Your main concern is to save the crew and the aircraft. The brakes have an independent hydraulic system which keeps pressure available in two accumulators. The accumulators are kept automatically charged by an a-c motor-driven pump; however, if the automatic operation fails the engineer has an override switch to maintain the necessary pressure in the accumulators. If neither of these systems are available, an emergency hand pump method is available.

CAUTION

With the brake system off, a fully charged accumulator will furnish enough pressure for three brake applications. In order to obtain the most effective braking action with a minimum of three applications available, keep the brake pedals depressed as long as the action is required.

The normal operating limits of 30 inches M.P. for use in reverse pitch may be exceeded if necessary for emergency stopping. When this limitation is exceeded, the controls must be LOCKED to prevent damage to the control surfaces.

CAUTION

If the brakes are not available during landing, landing roll, or while taxiing, the aircraft will be stopped on the runway or taxi strip by using reverse pitch for braking action. Hold the aircraft stationary by using either reverse or forward action of the propellers. If the cause is from a broken hydraulic line, the brake pump circuit breaker will be pulled to prevent fluid from being pumped overboard. *Do not* shut down engines until chocks or other objects have been placed under the main gear to prevent the aircraft from rolling after the engines have been stopped. Stop engines at low rpm regardless of propeller pitch position. The aircraft will be towed to the parking apron. If the active runway has to be cleared, the aircraft may be taxied off the runway with extreme caution and stopped not less than 100 feet from the active runway and then towed to the parking apron.

EMERGENCY BRAKE PRESSURE.

If the pilots' brake pump switch is on, the brake low pressure warning lamp is lighted, and a pressure gage check indicates low brake pressure, proceed as follows:

1. Pilot—Brake pump switch—ON.

2. Engineer—Brake pump pressure override switch—ON; hold until pressure is within range.

Note

Should step 2 fail to produce pressure, perform the following steps:

3. Crew—Emergency selector valve—CHARGE BRAKES.

CAUTION

Be sure that the emergency selector valve is held in the detent during charging or the hydraulic lines may rupture.

4. Crew—Operate hand pump until pressure is within normal range.

Note

Fully charged accumulators will supply brake pressure for three full brake applications.

To obtain maximum efficiency from fully charged accumulator, apply the brakes moderately and hold them using differential braking as required.

CAUTION

Do not fully release the brake pedals. If you do, the efficiency of the brake system will be decreased.

Section III
Emergency Procedures

T.O. 1B-36D(II)-1

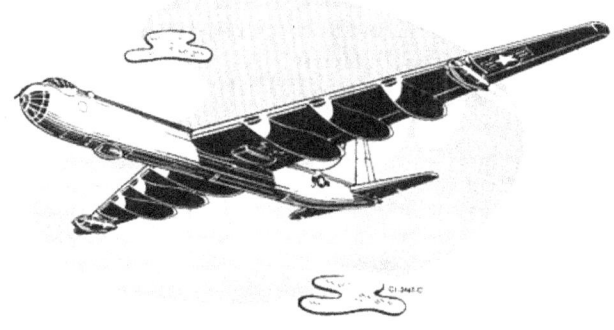

Section IV
DESCRIPTION & OPERATION OF AUXILIARY EQUIPMENT

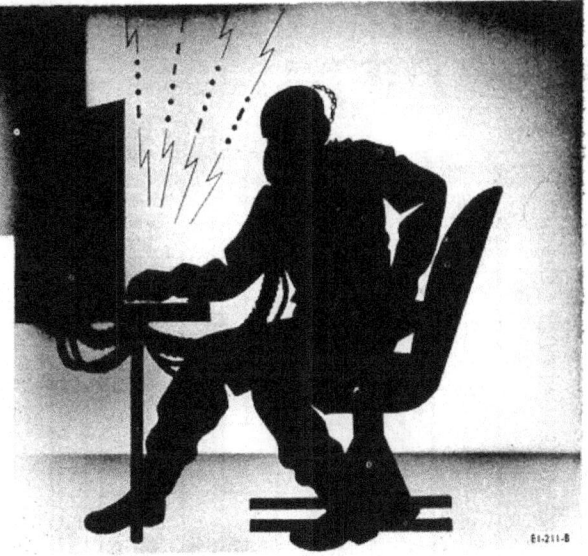

HEAT AND ANTI-ICING SYSTEM.

Heated air for wing and tail anti-icing and for heating pressurized air is obtained by ducting ram air from the nacelle cooling air tunnel through the two primary exhaust gas heat exchangers in each nacelle. The heated air from engines 1, 2, 5, and 6 is used for wing anti-icing. Engines 3 and 4 provide the air which is used as required in the secondary heat exchanger to heat the pressurized air for cabin heating. The air from engines 3 and 4 is also used to provide tail anti-icing. A duct system routes the air from the nacelles to the leading edges of the wing and tail. Flow is controlled by electrically operated valves located in the duct system. These valves are controlled from the engineer's station and operate on 115-volt a-c power. See figure 4-6 for system arrangement.

Note

During operation of the anti-icing system, the leading edge of the wing and tail surfaces may "oilcan." The "oilcanning" is a normal occurrence and will not have any damaging effects.

HEATING AND ANTI-ICING CONTROLS.

Cabin Heat and Tail Anti-Icing Switches (Cabin Air Supply From Turbos).

For operating the modulating dump valves in the inboard nacelles there are two three-position switches (26, figure 1-20) on the engineer's control panel. These switches are spring-loaded to the neutral position and enable you to regulate the amount of heated air going to the tail for anti-icing or to supply the secondary heat exchanger for cabin heat. When the switches are held ON, the valves are positioned for full cabin heat and tail anti-icing; when they are held OFF, the valves are positioned for full dump.

Cabin Temperature Control Switch.

This three-position switch (21, figure 1-20) controls a modulating valve which regulates the amount of heated air passing through the secondary heat exchanger on its way to the tail for anti-icing. When the switch is held in the INCREASE position, the tail anti-icing air is routed through the secondary heat exchanger to heat the cabin air. In the DECREASE position, the tail anti-icing air by-passes the secondary heat exchanger and no heat is supplied to the cabins other than that provided by the heat of compression of the pressurized air from the turbos. An indicator lamp (20, figure 1-20) glows when the valve has reached either of its extreme travel limits.

Wing Anti-Icing Switches.

Four three-position switches (28, figure 1-20) are located on the engineer's control panel to control the dump valves for engines 1, 2, 5, and 6. These switches have operating positions marked ON and OFF and a neutral center position which is not marked. Placing the switches in the ON position actuates the valves in a direction which permits heated air to enter the anti-icing ducts. With the switches in the OFF position, the valves are actuated in the opposite direction to route the heated air overboard. The valves may be stopped at any intermediate position by returning the switches to the neutral center position. In this manner the anti-icing air temperature is controlled by regulating the volume of heated air which enters the system.

INDICATORS.

Duct Air Temperature Gage.

The temperature of air entering the forward cabin through the pressure duct is read from a gage (12, figure 1-19) at the engineer's station. Temperature indications are supplied by a temperature bulb located in the pressure duct.

219

Section IV
Auxiliary Equipment

T.O. 1B-36D(II)-1

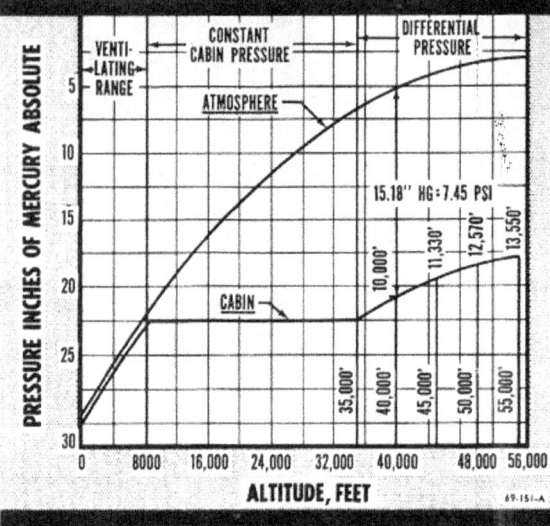

Figure 4-1.

Cabin Heat and Anti-Icing Air Maximum Temperature Warning Lamps.

Cabin heat and anti-icing temperature warning lamps (27, figure 1-20) are located at the engineer's station. The thermal switches which relay temperature indications to the warning lamps are located as follows: one thermal switch in the anti-icing duct downstream from each nacelle dump valve, and two fire detector thermal switches in the heating ducts between the dump valve and the primary heat exchanger. When the thermal switch downstream from the dump valve is subjected to temperatures in the range of 210° to 221°C for the tail air and 171 to 182°C for the wing air, the corresponding warning lamp will light. The lamp will also light when the corresponding fire detector thermal switches are subjected to temperatures in excess of 425°C.

> **CAUTION**
>
> For two or three minutes after turning the system on, you may get erroneous indications from the maximum temperature warning lamps of the wing and tail anti-icing system. This false reading is caused by the time lapse required for the internal temperature of the thermal switches to stabilize.

Master Temperature Indicator (Airplanes not in Group 2).

Temperature sensing devices located downstream of the dump valves in each nacelle heat anti-icing duct are connected to the master indicator (17, figure 1-17 and 8, figure 1-18). For a description of the indicator see "Master Temperature Indicator," Section I.

> **CAUTION**
>
> An anti-icing temperature of 70°C or over when the anti-icing is not being used indicates that a dump valve is leaking excessively and should be replaced.

Wing and Tail Anti-Icing Air Temperature Gages (Group 2 Airplanes).

Five anti-icing air temperature gages are located on the engineer's auxiliary instrument panel. Four of the gages indicate temperature in the wing ducts and one, the temperature in the tail anti-icing duct.

> **Note**
>
> The tail anti-icing temperature indication for airplanes in group 2 is taken as the air enters the tail and is lower than that for airplanes not in group 2, where the indication is taken as the air enters the fuselage.

Cabin Temperature Control Valve Indicator Lamp.

This lamp (20, figure 1-20) glows when the valve has reached either of its extreme travel limits.

PRESSURIZATION SYSTEM.

The forward and aft cabins and the interconnecting communication tube are pressurized by a controllable system which utilizes air from the right turbosupercharger in each nacelle. Pressure regulators are located in each cabin to maintain cabin pressure automatically. The pressure regulators are set to allow an unpressurized condition from sea level to 8000 feet, to permit a constant pressure altitude of 8000 feet from 8000 to 35,000 feet, and to hold a constant differential pressure of 7.45 psi above 35,000 feet. (See figure 4-1.) In pressurized flight, either cabin can be depressurized while maintaining pressure in the other. A booster fan is provided to draw ambient air into the duct system when an auxiliary source of ventilating and pressurizing air is required. See figure 4-6 for system arrangement.

> **CAUTION**
>
> Cabin pressurization is not available when carburetor preheat is used. Some pressurization and cabin heat can be made available at low altitudes by turning on the cabin

booster fan. However, as altitude is increased the efficiency of the booster fan will be reduced at an increased rate. Above 12,000 feet the booster fan operates at such low efficiency that cabin pressure can decrease to the extent that some airplane equipment becomes inoperative. Normal cabin pressurization will be available above 12,000 feet in most cases however, since carburetor preheat is seldom required above this altitude because of the heat provided by turbo boost. Above 12,000 feet altitude carburetor preheat should be used only as an emergency measure.

NORMAL CONTROLS.

Cabin Pressure Shutoff Valve Switches.

The flow of pressurized air from the nacelles to the fuselage is controlled by two three-position switches (22, figure 1-20) located on the engineer's control panel. These switches operate two modulating shutoff valves which control the flow of pressurized air from each wing system by connecting 115-volt a-c power to the valve actuators. The switches have a neutral off position and positions marked ON and OFF.

Note

The cabin pressure shutoff valves are automatically turned off when the carburetor preheat system is turned on. In this condition the cabin booster fan should be turned on.

Aft Cabin Pressure Switch.

The flow of pressure air to the aft cabin is controlled by a two-position switch (25, figure 1-20) located on the engineer's control panel. This switch completes 115-volt a-c circuit to the aft cabin pressure shutoff valve for valve operation.

CABIN AIR BOOSTER FAN.

A two-speed booster fan is located in the ventilating air duct and supplies air independent of the turbos to the cabins. The fan is operated on LOW when it is used to ventilate the cabins during ground operation and flight altitudes up to 8000 feet. For pressurized flight above 8000 feet it is operated in the HIGH position to furnish additional boost to the cabins for more positive pressurization and heating. The fan can also be used in conjunction with the secondary heat exchanger to supply heated air to the cabins independent of the cabin pressure system in unpressurized flight.

CABIN AIR BOOSTER FAN CONTROL SWITCH.

A three-position switch (23, figure 1-20) located on the engineers' auxiliary control and instrument panel, controls the action of the booster fan. This switch has positions marked HIGH ABOVE 8000 FEET, BELOW 8000 FEET LOW, and OFF. The low speed position is used for ventilating the cabins during ground operation and at altitudes up to 8000 feet. This position can also be used in conjunction with the secondary heat exchanger for cabin heat during unpressurized flight. The high speed position can be used at altitudes above 8000 feet to create additional boost for more positive heating and pressurization. Each switch position completes a 28-volt d-c circuit to the respective fan speed control relay which connects 208-volt 3-phase alternating current to the fan motor.

CAUTION

Never run the fan at high speed at altitudes below 8000 feet except for a few seconds to check its operation. The greater air resistance to the fan blades at altitudes below 8000 feet will cause the motor to burn out.

INDICATORS.

Cabin Altimeters.

Two altimeters located at the engineer's station, one for the forward cabin (7, figure 1-19) and one for the aft cabin (8, figure 1-19) indicate the pressure altitude for each cabin. Some airplanes have an additional cabin altimeter located at the tail gunner's station for the convenience of the aft cabin personnel.

Note

The engineer's aft cabin altimeter static port is located in the forward end of the communication tube. Any condition causing loss of pressurization in the communication tube will cause the aft cabin altimeter to read incorrectly.

EMERGENCY CONTROLS.

Manual Shutoff Valves.

In the event of failure of the electrical pressurization shutoff valves, which are controlled by the cabin pressure shutoff valve switches, manual shutoff valves are provided in each cabin. The extreme positions of the valve handles are OPEN and CLOSED. The forward shutoff valve (3, figure 4-2) is located in the pressure duct inlet just forward of the aft bulkhead in the forward cabin. The valve (4, figure 4-3) in the aft cabin is located in the pressure duct inlet near the forward bulkhead.

Forward Cabin Dump Valve.

The forward cabin dump valve (2, figure 4-2) located under the flight deck step, has a foot-operated dump pedal provided on the valve body. This valve can be used to decrease the pressure in all cabins simultaneously, provided the communication tube doors are open. Release of the pressurized air is obtained by depressing the quick-release pedal on the valve body.

Section IV
Auxiliary Equipment

The dump valve hand knob (1, figure 4-2) located on the floor near the engineers' station can be used to control the pressure in the forward cabin manually.

Note

To reset the valve after using the pedal for depressurizing, the knob must be rotated counterclockwise several times and pulled up until the release pedal locks in its untripped position. Then the knob must be turned clockwise until the valve is closed.

Pressure Relief and Dump Valves.

To supplement the forward cabin dump valve in cabin depressurization, the forward and aft cabins are equipped with pressure relief and dump valves (4, figure 4-2 and 2, figure 4-3). The normal function of these valves is to automatically relieve excess cabin pressure; however, each valve is equipped with a handle for emergency depressurization. By cutting the safety wire and moving the handle from NORMAL to DUMP, the valve is opened to release cabin pressure.

Vacuum Relief Valves.

A vacuum relief valve is provided in each crew compartment (5, figure 4-2 and 3, figure 4-3). The strap on the valve is pulled for emergency depressurization.

Pressure Regulator Control.

In the event of a pressure regulator failure which would allow the escape of pressurized air, a manual shutoff valve on the side of the regulator (6, figure 4-2 and 1, figure 4-3) can be used to close off its air exit provisions; the forward cabin dump valve hand knob can be used to modulate air pressure.

CABIN HEATING, DEFROSTING, AND ENCLOSURE ANTI-ICING.

After heated air is ducted into the cabins, it can be regulated by manual controls. These controls consist of selector valves, restrictor dampers, and various types of outlets. (See figures 4-4 and 4-5.) The defroster outlets, which are nonadjustable, provide heating as well as defrosting. Adjustable heating outlets provide heated air when defrosting is not required.

CONTROLS.

Heat and Anti-Ice Selector Valve.

This valve (5, figure 4-4) is in the heating duct in the right forward side of the radio operator's compartment. Double ducting runs from the valve forward into the flight compartment. One section carries air to

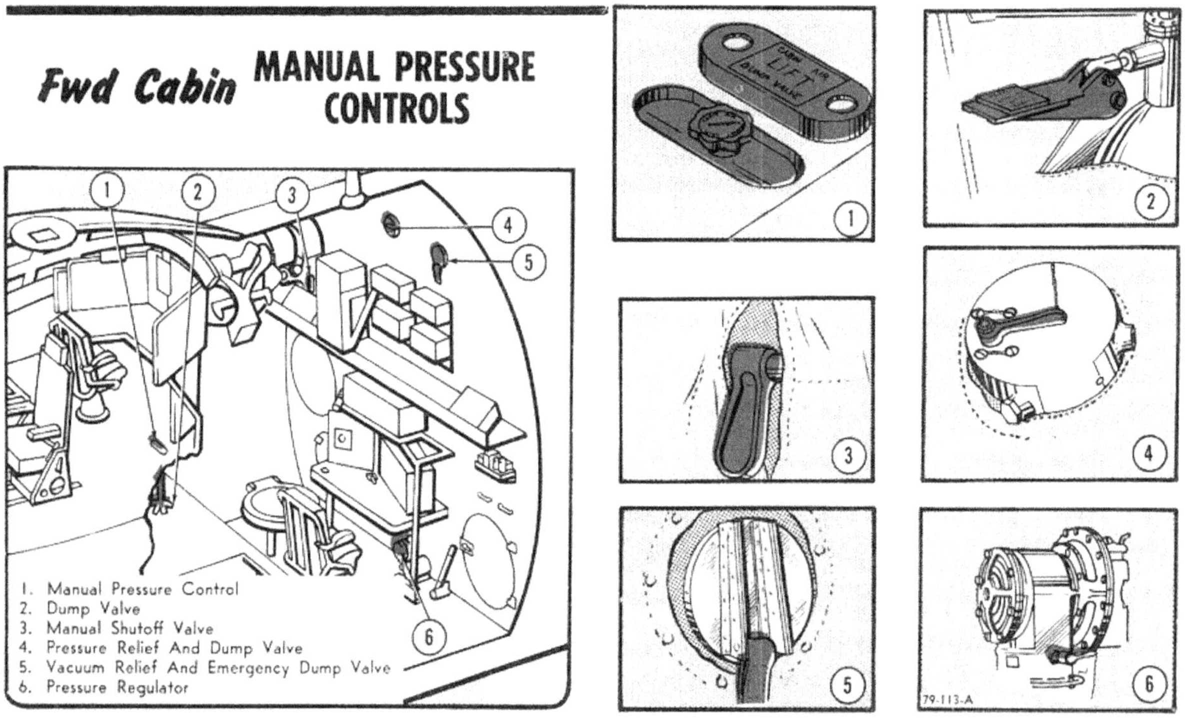

Fwd Cabin MANUAL PRESSURE CONTROLS

1. Manual Pressure Control
2. Dump Valve
3. Manual Shutoff Valve
4. Pressure Relief And Dump Valve
5. Vacuum Relief And Emergency Dump Valve
6. Pressure Regulator

Figure 4-2.

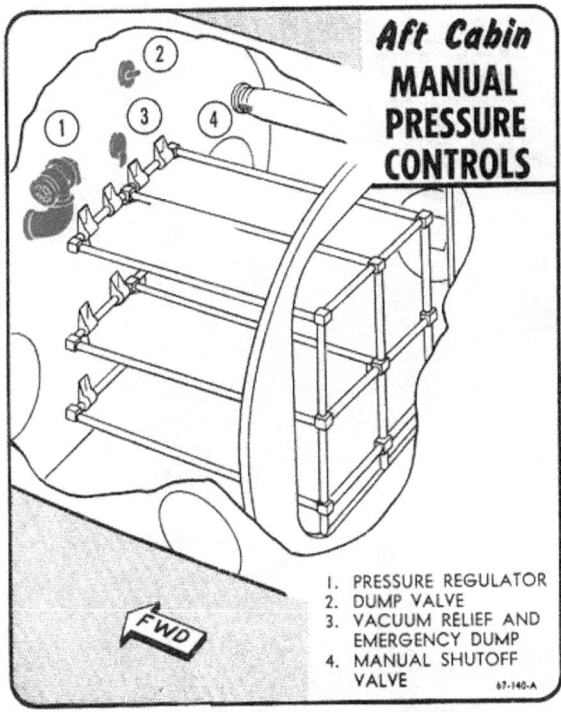

Figure 4-3.

enclosure defrosting and anti-icing outlets; the other carries it to heating outlets. The valve control knob can be moved to the HEAT position when cabin heating alone is required or the ANTI-ICE position if both heating and defrosting are required.

> **CAUTION**
>
> Place the selector valve in its center position to prevent excessive pressure in the forward cabin ducts at high altitude in an unpressurized high airflow condition.

Pilot-Bombardier Selector Valve.

This valve (3, figure 4-4) is located forward and to the right of the pilot's rudder pedals. This knob has positions marked PILOT and BOMB'R. The PILOT position is used to route the flow of heated air for the pilot's enclosure defrosting outlet. The BOMB'R position directs the heated air to the bombardier-gunner selector valve.

Bombardier-Gunner Selector Valve.

This valve (2, figure 4-4) is located over the radar observer's station. The control knob has positions marked BOMB, BOTH, and GUN. The BOMB position is used to route the heated air to the optical flat and to the defrosting duct on the left side of the nose enclosure. The GUN position is used to route the air to the nose gunner's scanning window and to the defrosting duct on the right side of the nose enclosure. The BOTH position allows heated air to flow to both locations simultaneously.

Restrictor Dampers.

Restrictor dampers (figures 4-4 and 4-5) are installed in heating ducts leading to the following locations in the forward cabin: defrosting nozzles at the sighting blisters, heating outlets in the radio operator's compartment, pilots' heating outlets, and radar observer's heating outlet. A restrictor damper is also in the duct to the right forward heating outlet in the aft cabin. The dampers are used to regulate the flow of heating air to the various outlets noted.

Heating Outlets.

Seven outlets are in the heating ducts—four (figure 4-4) in the forward and three (5, figure 4-5) in the aft cabin. In the forward cabin an outlet is at the aircraft commander's station, the pilot's station, the right side of the radio operator's compartment, and the nose gunner's station. In the aft cabin, heating outlets are just aft of each lower sighting blister and in the right forward side of the cabin near the catwalk entrance. Each outlet has five manually controlled positions which provide five flow patterns.

Defrosting Nozzles.

Defrosting nozzles (figure 4-4 and 4, figure 4-5) are at sighting stations, the engineer's clear vision window, each side of the nose enclosure, and the nose gunner's scanning window. These nonadjustable units provide heating as well as defrosting.

OPERATION OF CABIN HEATING, ANTI-ICING, AND PRESSURIZATION SYSTEMS.

CREW RESPONSIBILITY.

Obtaining optimum cabin heating and defrosting requires the cooperative effort of every crew member. They are responsible for the duties listed in the following paragraphs.

Aircraft Commander and Pilot.

Before flight the aircraft commander will assure himself that a periodic check of the cabin pressure duct system has been made with the cabin pressure test machine. From the results of the test he will determine what the capabilities of his system will be.

Engineer.

The engineer is responsible for the control of his valves and will maintain optimum duct temperatures and air flow. To achieve this he will receive reports from other crew members as to the results of his configuration. If a crew member becomes uncomfort-

Section IV
Auxiliary Equipment

T.O. 1B-36D(II)-1

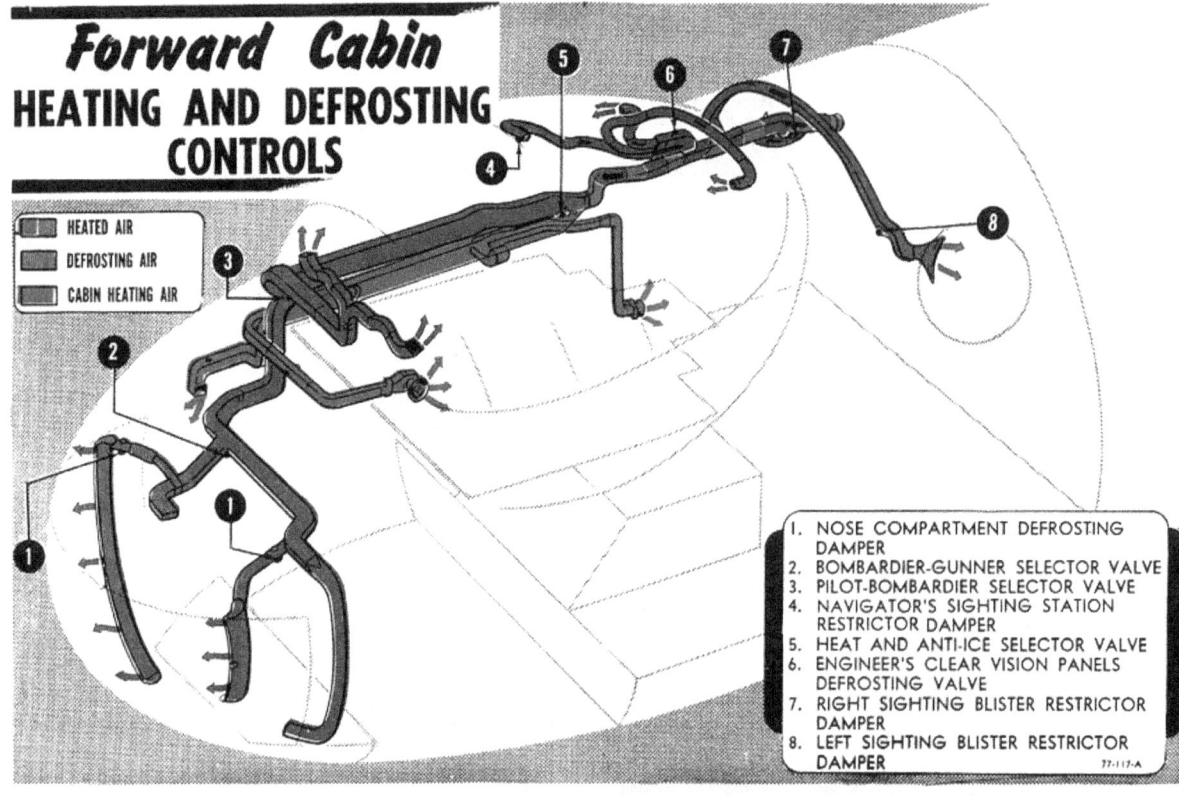

Forward Cabin HEATING AND DEFROSTING CONTROLS

- HEATED AIR
- DEFROSTING AIR
- CABIN HEATING AIR

1. NOSE COMPARTMENT DEFROSTING DAMPER
2. BOMBARDIER-GUNNER SELECTOR VALVE
3. PILOT-BOMBARDIER SELECTOR VALVE
4. NAVIGATOR'S SIGHTING STATION RESTRICTOR DAMPER
5. HEAT AND ANTI-ICE SELECTOR VALVE
6. ENGINEER'S CLEAR VISION PANELS DEFROSTING VALVE
7. RIGHT SIGHTING BLISTER RESTRICTOR DAMPER
8. LEFT SIGHTING BLISTER RESTRICTOR DAMPER

Figure 4-4.

able because of the temperature, it is the engineer's responsibility to correct the condition as nearly as possible.

Radar Observer.

The pilot will control the pilot-bombardier valve. The radar observer will control the bombardier-gunner valve, the radial radar observer enclosure defrosting valve, and the auxiliary cabin heater.

Note

For airplanes having radar observer enclosure defrosting, the pilot-bombardier valve is normally placed about the 3/4 position toward BOMBARDIER CONTROL.

Radio Operator.

The radio operator will set the two sighting blister valves, the heat anti-ice valve, and the engineer's clear vision double pane valve. He will also control the auxiliary cabin heater.

Note

If trouble is encountered in obtaining enough heat for defrosting, place the heat anti-ice valve in the full ANTI-ICE position.

Aft Cabin.

The compartment commander in the aft cabin will have the duty of obtaining optimum valve settings, through cooperation with other crew members, for defrosting and for the operation of the auxiliary cabin heaters. He will also keep the engineer informed as to the cabin temperature and the condtition of the sighting blisters.

Note

If defrosting of the sighting blisters becomes critical, completely shut off the heating outlets, allowing all air to flow from the blister defroster nozzles.

NORMAL OPERATION.

Cabin Heating and Defrosting.

To obtain heat for the forward and aft cabins use the following procedure:

1. Place the aft cabin pressure switch in the ON position.

2. Check to determine that the forward and aft cabin manual shutoff valves are open.

3. Place the left and right cabin pressure wing shut-off valve switches in the ON position.

> **CAUTION**
>
> If the carburetor preheat is being used, the wing shutoff valves cannot be opened. In this condition the cabin booster fan should be turned on to supply some heat. However, heat will be reduced as altitude is increased.

4. Hold the cabin temperature control switch in the DECREASE position until the lamp lights.

5. Place the cabin heat and tail anti-ice control switches in the ON position.

Note

These dump valves may be modulated if necessary to prevent exceeding a temperature of 215°C as read on the flight engineer's master temperature indicator.

6. Jiggle the cabin temperature control switch in the INCREASE position until the temperature of the air is suitable for cabin heating.

> **CAUTION**
>
> Do not exceed 105°C as read on the flight engineer's duct air temperature indicator.

Note

As an alternate method for controlling the cabin air temperature, hold the cabin temperature control switch in the INCREASE position until the lamp lights. Then jiggle the cabin heat and tail anti-ice switches in the DECREASE position until the desired cabin air temperature is obtained. During icing conditions the procedure as outlined in steps 4, 5, and 6 should be used to insure maximum air flow for anti-icing the tail.

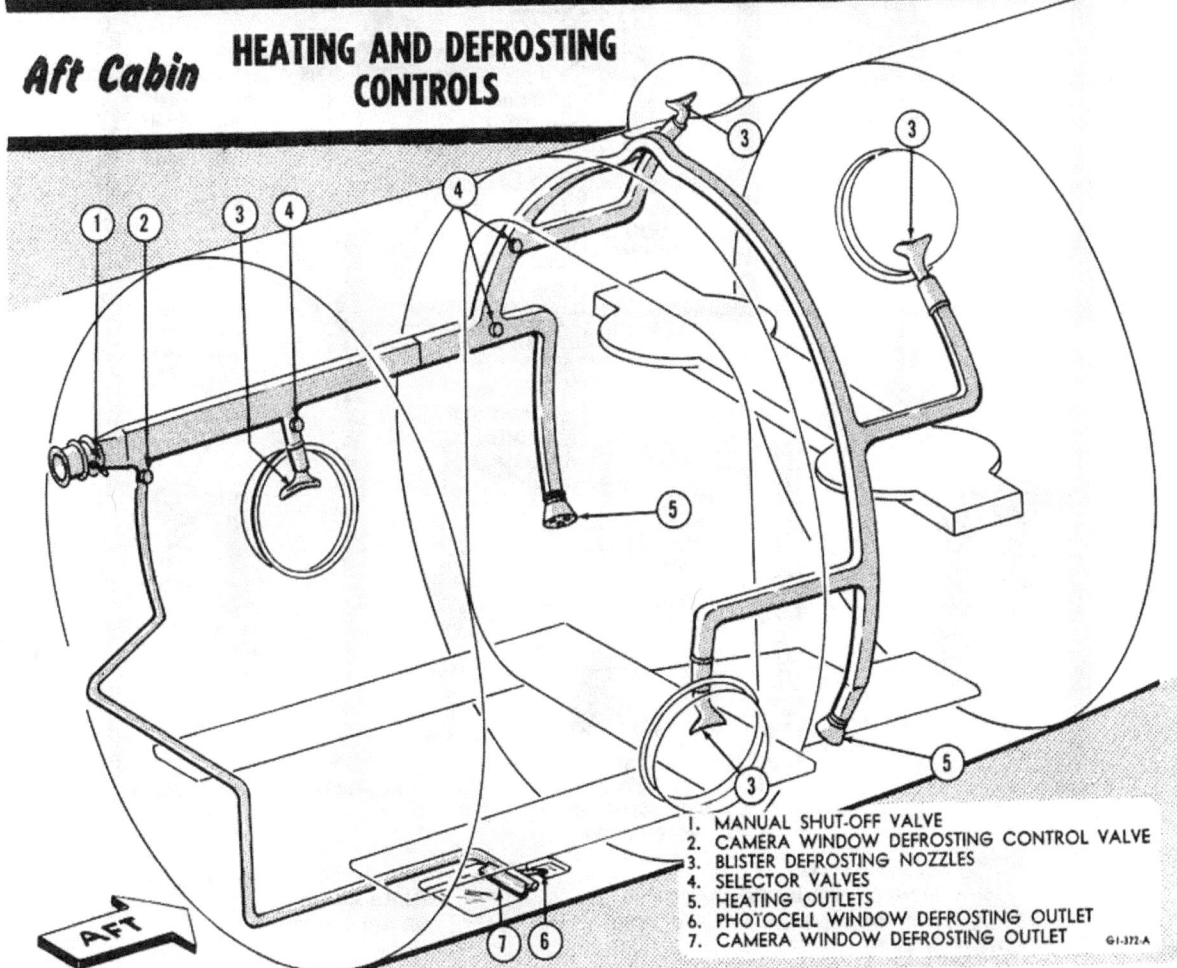

1. MANUAL SHUT-OFF VALVE
2. CAMERA WINDOW DEFROSTING CONTROL VALVE
3. BLISTER DEFROSTING NOZZLES
4. SELECTOR VALVES
5. HEATING OUTLETS
6. PHOTOCELL WINDOW DEFROSTING OUTLET
7. CAMERA WINDOW DEFROSTING OUTLET

Figure 4-5.

Section IV
Auxiliary Equipment

T.O. 1B-36D(II)-1

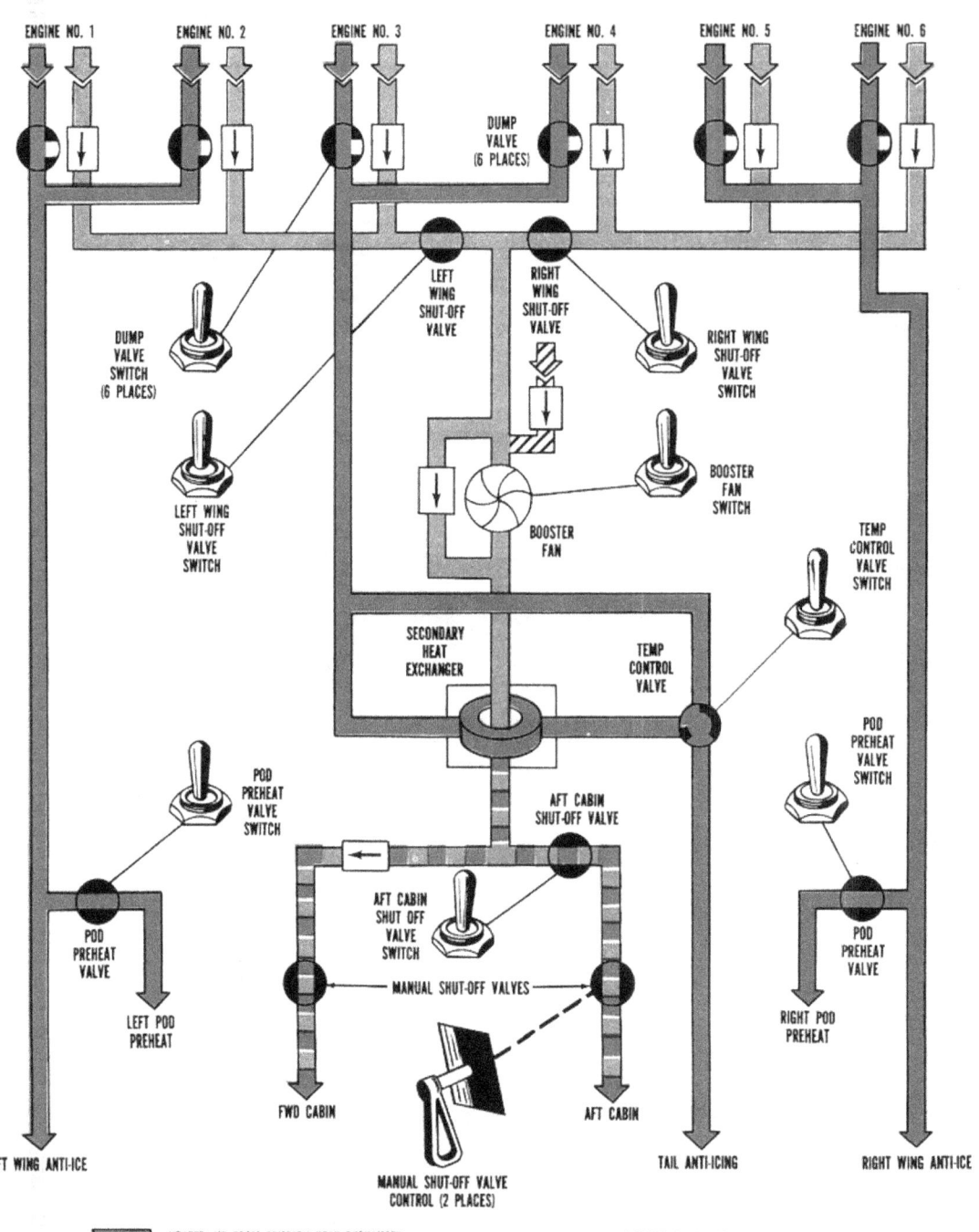

Figure 4-6.

7. In the forward cabin perform the following:

a. Place the right sighting blister defrosting restrictor valve in the 1/2 OPEN position.

b. Place the left sighting blister defrosting restrictor valve in the full OPEN position.

c. For those airplanes equipped with a defrosting system for the flight engineer's two clear vision panes, restrict the flow to the amount required for vision.

d. Place the heat anti-ice valve located behind the flight engineer's panel in full ANTI-ICE position, thus diverting all of the air from the heating outlets to the pilots' and observers' enclosure for defrosting purposes.

e. Place the pilot-bombardier enclosure defrosting control located near the pilot's rudder pedals 3/4 from PILOT toward BOMB.

f. In the observers' compartment place the bombardier-gunner selector valve on BOTH.

g. In those airplanes having defrosting nozzles for the side radial panes on the observers' enclosure, adjust the selector valves in the ducts for optimum defrosting.

h. As a refinement to the above system, provided acceptable defrosting is obtained, the valve listed under step d above may be moved slightly off the ANTI-ICE position toward HEAT. After this has been done, the restrictor valves in the ducts to the radio operator's compartment, the observers' compartment, and the pilot's station should be adjusted, as well as the heating outlets to these stations and to the copilot's station.

i. Adjust the blister defrosting restrictor valves to the minimum flow position for acceptable defrosting.

8. In the aft cabin the restrictor and selector valves should be adjusted so that optimum blister defrosting and cabin heating are obtained. Generally this will require restricting or closing the heating outlets to obtain acceptable defrosting of the blisters. It may be necessary to restrict the flow to the right sighting blisters to force air to the left sighting blisters.

9. Turn the auxiliary cabin heater switches to LOW or HIGH as required.

CAUTION

Do not turn the heaters on if the pressure altitude of the cabin exceeds 12,000 feet, because the cooling air supplied by the heater fan would be insufficient to cool the fan motor, causing rotor seizure.

10. Turn on cabin booster fan.

Enclosure Anti-Icing.

For optimum enclosure anti-icing under severe icing conditions, it will be necessary to obtain maximum flow of heated air to the pilots' and observers' enclosures. Maximum flow is accomplished as follows:

1. Place the heat anti-ice selector control knob in the ANTI-ICE position.

2. Place both cabin pressure wing shutoff valve switches in the ON position.

3. Restrict flow to the aft cabin to that required for pressurization.

4. Obtain high manifold pressure by placing the engine supercharger switches on BOTH. (See "Shifting Turbos," Section VII.) Also advance the turbo boost selector lever as near to position 10 as conditions permit.

5. Hold the cabin heat and tail anti-icing control switches in the OFF position.

Note

If tail anti-icing temperatures are too high, jiggle the cabin heat and tail anti-icing control switches to obtain proper temperatures.

6. Hold the cabin temperature control switch in the INCREASE position until the indicator lamp lights.

CAUTION

To forestall damage to the enclosure panes, the duct temperature must not be allowed to exceed 105°C.

7. Close or restrict the flow to the forward cabin sighting blisters.

8. Turn on the cabin booster fan.

9. Adjust the flow between the observers' and pilots' enclosures as required.

When frosting or icing of a certain enclosure becomes critical, such as the pilots' enclosure during landing, it may be necessary to direct the entire flow of heated air to that area by adjusting the selector provided in the heating ducts for these stations. When the entire supply of heating air is being used for defrosting purposes, the auxiliary cabin heaters can be used for cabin heating if required.

Under certain atmospheric conditions, moisture will form between the inner and outer panes of the enclosures. This condition can be alleviated by obtaining a maximum flow of heating air to the enclosure as described in the preceding paragraphs. The pilots' ventilating fans, located on each outboard frame of the rudder pedal, can be used to obtain a more uniform and lower temperature on the flight deck, since they tend to replace the hot air with cooler air from the lower portion of the cabin.

Cabin Pressurization.

The pressurization system is put in operation by placing the cabin pressure shutoff valve switches ON. The aft pressure switch must be ON for aft cabin pressurization.

EMERGENCY OPERATION.

Anti-Icing System Overheating.

When any of the warning lamps indicate an excessive temperature, check this temperature immediately and govern any subsequent action on the basis of the master temperature indicator rather than the warning lamps. If an excessive temperature is indicated, proceed as follows:

1. Engineer—Proper wing or cabin heat and tail anti-ice switch—Momentarily OFF, routing some of the heated air overboard, until the temperature is within limits.

2. Engineer—Reduce power of the engine in the nacelle indicated. Opening the air plugs will also aid in diminishing heat.

WARNING

If none of the above efforts reduce the excessive temperature satisfactorily, position the proper wing or tail anti-ice switch to OFF for full dump. Observe the warning lamp; if it still burns, a temperature in excess of 425°C between one of the heat exchangers and the dump valve in the affected nacelle is indicated. The only known cause of this condition is a ruptured heat exchanger which permits exhaust gases to enter the anti-icing duct. If this condition exists, alert the gunners, because a fire may be imminent and engine shutdown may be necessary.

3. Pilot—If climbing, increase the air speed without increasing power.

Cabin Pressure Control.

If a pressure regulator fails, shut off the unit and let the other regulator control the pressure air exit for both compartments. If a single regulator proves insufficient, the engineer must assist the single regulator by manual operation of the manual pressure control. In case of aft cabin shutoff valve failure, shut off the pressure by closing the manual shutoff valve in the compartment.

EMERGENCY DEPRESSURIZATION.

If it becomes necessary to depressurize the cabins so that escape hatches can be opened in an emergency, all crew members must go on 100 per cent oxygen and the airplane must be depressurized as soon as possible. The engineer must cut off cabin air flow, and the compartment commander of each cabin must see that all dump valves are opened. In the aft cabin the strap on the vacuum relief valve should be pulled and held open to speed depressurization. If the dump valves do not do the job, use the hand axes and cut through the fuselage along the stringers. The stringers will act as barriers to any objects being sucked out of the airplane.

WARNING

Do not attempt to break the sighting blisters to depressurize the cabins.

VENTILATION EQUIPMENT.

The cabin air can be circulated for ventilation by means of eight electrically operated fans. The main source of ventilation is provided by the cabin air booster fan, which can be used to pull outside air through the pressurizing ducts into the forward and aft cabins. (Refer to "Cabin Air Booster Fan" of this section.) Two circulating fans are located at the pilots' station to aid in ventilating the flight compartment. The fans of the four auxiliary cabin heaters can be used independently of the heating elements to provide additional air circulation in the cabins. (Refer to "Auxiliary Cabin Heaters" of this section.)

PILOTS' AIR CIRCULATING FANS.

The pilots' two air circulating fans are installed on the outboard frames of the rudder pedals. The fans are adjustable and are operated by an ON-OFF switch located on each mounting bracket.

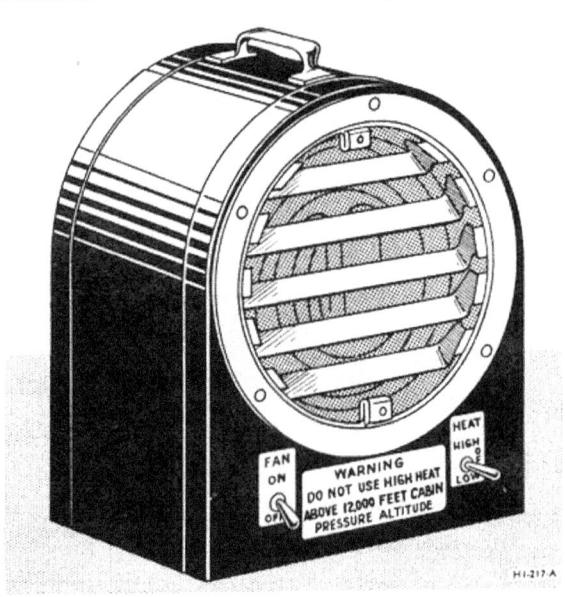

Figure 4-7.

T.O. 1B-36D(II)-1

Section IV
Auxiliary Equipment

OBTAINING CABIN VENTILATION ON GROUND.

For ventilation during ground operations, accomplish the following:

1. Open the communication tube doors.
2. Turn the cabin heat and tail anti-icing control switches OFF.
3. Place the cabin air booster fan switch in the low speed position and control the air flow with the selector valves and restrictor dampers.
4. Utilize the pilots' air circulating fans and the auxiliary cabin heater fans for ventilating local areas.

OBTAINING CABIN VENTILATION IN FLIGHT.

For ventilation during flight, perform the following steps:

1. Turn the cabin pressure shutoff valve switches—OFF.
2. Turn the cabin heat and tail anti-icing switches—OFF.
3. Turn the aft cabin presure switch—ON.
4. Place the cabin air booster fan switch in the low speed position and control the air flow with the selector valves and restrictor dampers.
5. Utilize the pilots' air circulating fans and the auxiliary cabin heater fans for ventilating local areas.
6. Open the communication tube doors.
7. If a small quantity of heat is desired, perform the preceding steps, with one exception: Place the cabin pressure shutoff valve switches ON. In this manner the heat of compression can be utilized, eliminating use of the tail anti-icing system to obtain cabin heat.

AUXILIARY CABIN HEATERS.

In addition to the regular cabin heating system, four portable cabin heaters are stowed in the airplane. (See figure 4-7.) One is located under the flight deck step in the forward cabin, and one is on the radio operator's floor just below the catwalk entrance hatch. In the aft cabin a heater is stowed at the forward bulkhead and the other is at the aft bulkhead. Each heater is comprised of a heating element and a motor-driven fan which operate on 208-volt, 3-phase alternating current. Each heater is equipped with an electric cord of sufficient length to allow the heater to be moved about the cabin.

CONTROLS.

Heater Control Switch.

Each heater is controlled by a three-position switch marked HIGH, LOW, and OFF. The HIGH and LOW positions are provided to control the output of the heating element. The heater power circuit is provided with power from the fan control circuit; therefore, the fan switch must be ON before the heater will operate.

Fan Control Switch.

When cabin heating is not required, the fan of each heater may be operated independently to provide additional air circulation. Independent operation is made possible by a fan control switch located on each unit. This on-off switch controls the fan motor and applies power to the heater control switch.

Cabin Heater Power Switch.

This two-position switch (2, figure 1-19) located on the engineer's auxiliary instrument panel, is used to shut off all auxiliary cabin heaters. During engine starting or when a partial loss of alternator power occurs, this

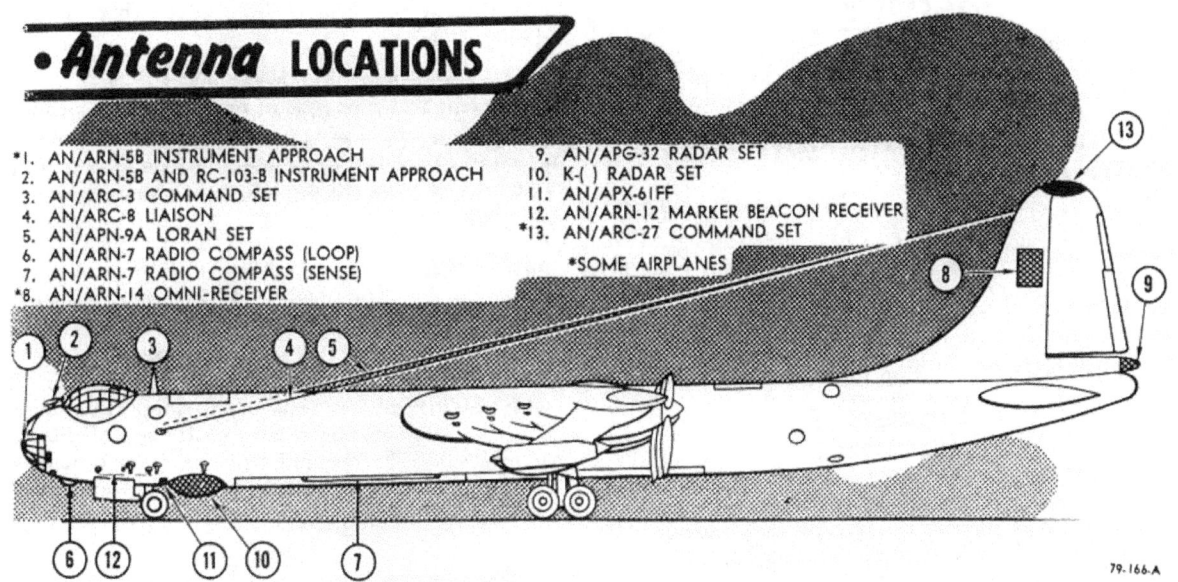

Figure 4-8.

RADIO OPERATOR'S Station

1. AN/APS-54 Radar Warning Panel
2. Lighting Control Panel
3. Portable Oxygen Bottle
4. Oxygen Controls
5. Turret & Bomb Bay Lights Switch
6. Sub Flight Deck Light Switch
7. Dome Light Switch
8. Communication Tube Light Switch
9. Auxiliary Cabin Heater
10. Clock
11. Liaison Monitoring Switch
12. AN/ARC-27 Control Box
13. Liaison Transmitter
14. AN/ARA-3 Control Box
15. Interphone Control Panel
16. Circuit Breaker Panel
17. Liaison Receiver
18. Transmitter Key
19. Pressure Regulator
20. Microphone Switch
21. Nose Gear Latch Observation Window

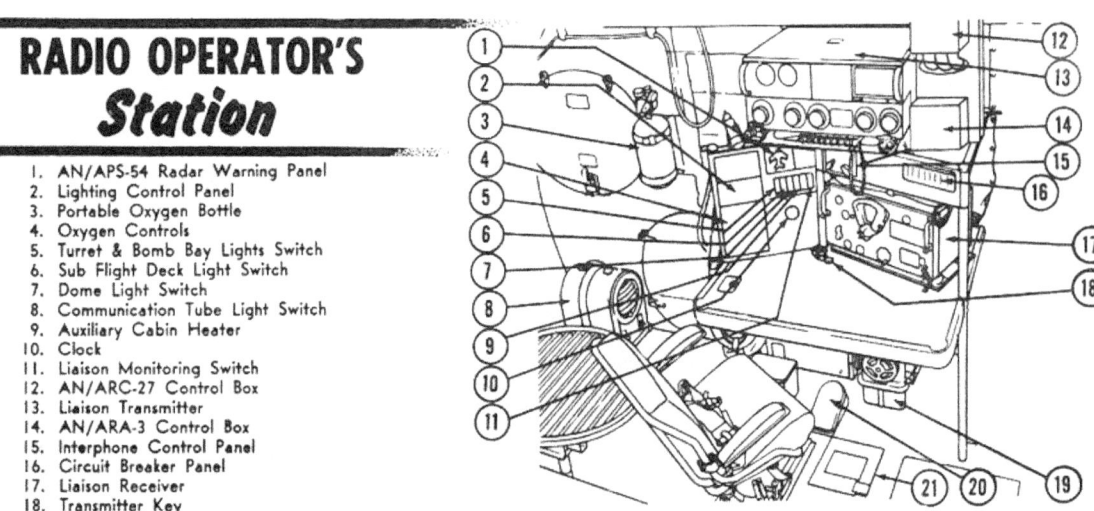

Figure 4-9. (Sheet 1)

switch should be placed in the OFF position. With either of these conditions existent there is a possibility of overloading the a-c system because of the high power requirements of the heaters.

Note

When external power is on the airplane, the heater power circuit is automatically de-energized, regardless of the position of heater power switch.

CAUTION

Crew members must be sure that the heaters are free of obstruction at all times in order to avoid inadvertent operation of the heaters.

JET POD HEATING AND ANTI-ICING SYSTEM.

The jet pod heating and anti-icing system employs three independent sources of heat and is designed to perform the following functions: to prevent icing of the nacelle and the strut leading edges, to prevent the formation of ice on the nose cones and air plugs, and to provide heat for the jet oil system prior to starting the engines during flight.

CAUTION

There are no provisions for internal anti-icing of the jet engine. Internal icing is indicated by an increase in tail pipe temperature which can be alleviated by reducing the rpm.

JET NACELLE AND STRUT ANTI-ICING.

For nacelle and strut anti-icing when the jet engines are operating, hot air is bled through a port at the 12th stage of each compressor and is controlled by a valve, which operates in conjunction with the nose cone and air plug anti-icing facilities. A portion of the heated air is ducted to the nacelle leading edge where it flows aft between the inner and outer skins and exits from the nacelle through louvers in the cowling forward of the fire wall. The remainder of the air is used for anti-icing of the strut leading edge and is ducted through the double skin passages of the leading edge to the top of the strut. The air then flows aft to the strut trailing edge where it exits through louvers.

NOSE CONE AND AIR PLUG ANTI-ICING.

The air plug and nose cone of each engine are provided with electrical heating elements to prevent the formation of ice on these sections. The system should be turned on in icing conditions when the engines are operating.

PREHEATING.

Wing anti-icing air is used to provide heat for the jet engine oil system prior to starting the engines during flight. The flow of this air is controlled by a valve located in the duct which conveys the air from the wing leading edge to each jet pod. A portion of this air is used for heating the oil cooler and oil lines in each nacelle. The remainder of the air is ducted into the strut to heat the lines which lead from the oil tank to the engines.

Note

The wing anti-icing system must be in operation before jet pod preheating can be accomplished.

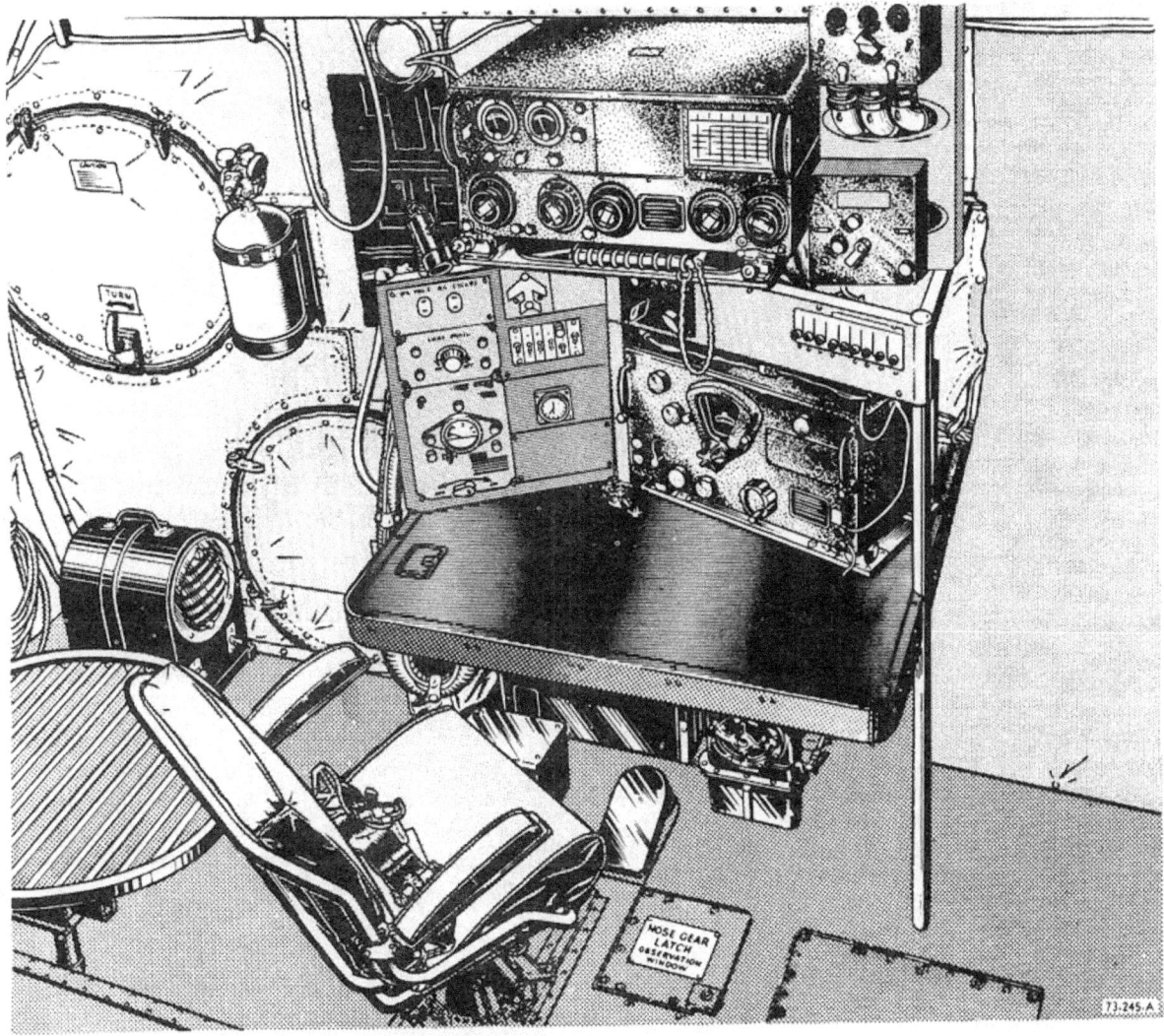

Figure 4-9. (Sheet 2)

CONTROLS.

Nose De-Ice Control Switch.

This on-off switch-type circuit breaker (20, figure 1-23) located on the jet control panel, controls the nose cone and air plug heating elements and the internal anti-icing valve for nacelle and strut anti-icing. When this switch is placed ON, 28-volt direct current energizes a relay which connects 208-volt a-c power to electrical heating elements of the nose cone and air plug doors. Also, 28-volt direct current opens a valve which permits heated air from the engine compressor to be routed into the pod nacelle and strut for anti-icing.

Pod Preheat Control Switch.

This on-off switch (21, figure 1-23) operates a valve in the duct leading from each wing leading edge to the jet nacelles and their strut. When the switch is placed ON, 115-volt alternating current is routed to the pod preheat valve actuators which opens the valves. Wing anti-icing air is then routed to the nacelles and struts for pod preheating, provided the wing anti-icing system is in operation.

WARNING

In the event of a jet engine fire, this switch must be placed in the OFF position to prevent fire from passing through the duct to the interior of strut and wing.

Note

When the wing anti-icing system is being used during severe icing conditions, the pod preheat control switch must be in the OFF position to obtain maximum heat for wing anti-icing.

Section IV
Auxiliary Equipment

T.O. 1B-36D(II)-1

PITOT TUBE HEATERS.

Pitot tube heat is controlled by two ON-OFF switches (29, figure 1-20) located on the flight engineer's control panel. When the switches are in the ON position 28-volt d-c power is routed to the heaters.

OIL HEATERS.

OIL TANK VENT LINE HEATERS.

Each reciprocating engine oil tank vent line is equipped with a heating element to prevent vapors from congealing, freezing, and consequently plugging the vent lines. The heaters are controlled by a single switch (24, figure 1-20) located on the engineer's control panel. The switch positions are ON and OFF. When the switch is in the ON position, 28-volt direct current is routed to a relay which in turn energizes the heater element circuit with 115-volt alternating current. This switch should be placed in the ON position for ground and flight operations when the ambient air temperature is at 0°C (32°F) and below.

OIL TANK HOPPER HEATERS.

Electrical heating elements for each oil hopper and outlet line are provided for preheating the reciprocating engine oil prior to starting. The heating elements require a power output of 5250 watts and operate on 115 volts—either alternating or direct current. Because the portable power cart of the airplane does not have sufficient output, the power must be supplied by ground facilities. An oil tank heater receptacle (figure 1-48) for plugging in the external power source is located beneath each oil tank. Access to the receptacles is gained through panels on the lower surface of the wing. Time required for the oil to become properly heated is approximately one minute for each degree below 0°F.

JET ENGINE OIL HEATERS.

The jet engine oil tanks are equipped with 28-volt d-c controlled, 115-volt a-c actuated heating elements for maintaining the oil temperature above an operating minimum. A thermal switch located in each tank closes when the oil temperature drops to approximately 4°C (40°F) and reopens at approximately 2 degrees above its closing temperature. If the jet engine oil heater switch is turned ON, the oil is heated automatically when the thermal switch closes. For additional information regarding the heating of jet engine oil, refer to "Jet Pod Heating and Anti-Icing System," of this section.

Jet Engine Oil Heater Switch.

A two-position switch-type circuit breaker (19, figure 1-23) located on the pilots' overhead jet control panel controls the action of both oil heaters. When it is in the ON position, 115 volt a-c power is supplied to each heating element.

COMMUNICATION AND ASSOCIATED ELECTRONIC EQUIPMENT.

The communication and associated electronic equipment consists of radio and interphone equipment to provide airplane-to-airplane communication, airplane-to-ground communication, and intraplane communication between crew members; navigation sets for guidance and blind landing; and radar sets for identification, long range navigation, radar defense, radar bombing, and tail turret control. Equipment is provided on each wing and on the rudder and elevators to discharge static electricity. For antenna arrangement see figure 4-8. A functional breakdown of the equipment is listed in figure 4-10.

COMBAT INTERPHONE SYSTEM.

The interphone system provides communication between all crew stations. In addition, remote interphone jackboxes are located in the wing crawlways between the nacelles, in the tail section, in the bomb bays, and outside under the fuselage between No. 2 and No. 3 bomb bays. The basic interphone system is conventional. The system, however, has been modified to include a private interphone channel; a call circuit; and provisions for either the aircraft commander or pilot, or both, to mix command radio, radio compass, interphone, marker beacon, and localizer audio signals into one output. To start the interphone amplifier, turn on the airplane's main power supply. Make sure the ON-OFF switch on the amplifier is in the ON position.

Note

Normally this switch is safety-wired in the ON position.

Private Interphone Channel.

The private interphone channel employs a private interphone amplifier and can be used in the event of normal interphone channel failure. Two variations of the private interphone channel are used. On airplanes not included in group 2, a special interphone switch (1, figure 4-16) on the pilots' pedestal provides primary control of the private interphone channel. When this switch is in the normal CRUISE COMBAT position and the private interphone channel is in use, communication between all crew stations is available. Placing the switch in the PRIVATE position removes all crew stations from the channel except those for the aircraft commander, pilot, navigator, and radar observer. Thus a private communication channel is available for close coordination between these stations and the remainder of the crew can still use the normal interphone system.

COMMUNICATION AND ASSOCIATED ELECTRONIC EQUIPMENT

	TYPE	DESIGNATION	USE	PRIMARY OPERATOR	RANGE	LOCATION
COMMUNICATION EQUIPMENT	INTERPHONE	USAF COMBAT	CREW COMMUNICATION	CREW		ALL CREW STATIONS
	COMMAND RADIO	AN/ARC-3	PLANE-TO-PLANE OR PLANE-TO-GROUND COMMUNICATION	AIRCRAFT COMMANDER AND PILOT	30 MILES AT 1000 FEET	PILOTS' STATION
	COMMAND RADIO	AN/ARC-27	PLANE-TO-PLANE OR PLANE-TO-GROUND COMMUNICATION	AIRCRAFT COMMANDER AND PILOT	30 MILES AT 1000 FEET	PILOTS' STATION
	LIAISON RADIO	AN/ARC-8	CODE OR VOICE TRANSMISSION AND RECEPTION	RADIO OPERATOR	5000 MILES HIGH FREQUENCY	RADIO OPERATOR'S STATION
	RADIO SET (WALKIE-TALKIE)	AN/CRC-7	EMERGENCY USE	CREW	15 MILES AT 2000 FEET	
NAVIGATION EQUIPMENT	INSTRUMENT APPROACH (GLIDE PATH)	AN/ARN-5( )	VERTICAL PATH INDICATOR DURING INSTRUMENT LANDINGS	AIRCRAFT COMMANDER AND PILOT	LOCAL	PILOTS' STATION
	RADIO COMPASS	AN/ARN-7( )	RECEPTION OF CODE OR VOICE SIGNALS, DIRECTION BEARING, AND HOMING	AIRCRAFT COMMANDER AND NAVIGATOR	200 MILES	PILOTS' AND NAVIGATOR'S STATION
	MARKER BEACON SET	AN/ARN-12 OR RC-193-A	TO OBTAIN FIX ON NAVIGATION BEAM		LOCAL	
	OMNI-DIRECTIONAL RECEIVER	AN/ARN-14	POSITION FINDING, HOMING, AND INDICATION OF LATERAL ALIGNMENT FOR INSTRUMENT APPROACH	AIRCRAFT COMMANDER AND PILOT	200 MILES AT 40,000 FEET	PILOTS' STATION
	LORAN SET	AN/APN-9( )	LONG RANGE NAVIGATION	NAVIGATOR	570-1600 MILES	NAVIGATOR'S STATION
RADAR EQUIPMENT	IDENTIFICATION SET	AN/APX-6	IDENTIFICATION	RADIO OPERATOR		RADIO OPERATOR'S STATION
	RADAR SET	AN/APQ-31	HIGH ALTITUDE BOMBING AND NAVIGATION AID	RADAR OBSERVER	200 MILES	RADAR OBSERVER'S STATION
	AUTOMATIC GUN LAYING	AN/APG-32	TO CONTROL THE TAIL TURRET	TAIL GUNNER		TAIL GUNNER'S STATION
ECM EQUIPMENT (SOME AIRPLANES)	RADAR COUNTER-MEASURE	AN/APT-4	TO JAM RADAR SIGNALS	RADIO OPERATOR		RADIO OPERATOR'S STATION
	RADAR COUNTER-MEASURE	AN/APT-5A	TO JAM RADAR SIGNALS	RADIO OPERATOR		RADIO OPERATOR'S STATION
	RADAR COUNTER-MEASURE	AN/APR-4	TO DETECT AND MEASURE FREQUENCY OF RADIO AND RADAR SIGNALS	RADIO OPERATOR		RADIO OPERATOR'S STATION
	RADAR COUNTER-MEASURE	AN/APT-1	TO JAM RADAR SIGNALS	RADIO OPERATOR		RADIO OPERATOR'S STATION
	RADAR COUNTER-MEASURE	AN/ARQ-8	TO DETECT AND MEASURE FREQUENCY OF RADIO AND RADAR SIGNALS	RADIO OPERATOR		RADIO OPERATOR'S STATION
	PANORAMIC ADAPTER	AN/APA-38	TO PROVIDE VISUAL INDICATION OF RECEIVED RADIO AND RADAR SIGNALS	RADIO OPERATOR		RADIO OPERATOR'S STATION

Figure 4-10.

Section IV
Auxiliary Equipment

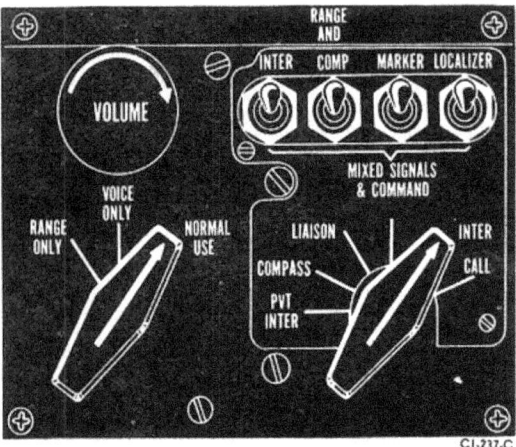

Figure 4-11. Pilots' Interphone Panel

On airplanes in group 2, interphone contact with the wing, bomb bay, and external audio outlets must be made by using the private interphone channel. On airplanes not in group 2, these outlets are on the normal interphone channel.

When it is desired to restrict the private interphone channel to any of the four designated stations on airplanes not in group 2, the aircraft commander or the pilot perform the following steps:

1. Place the special interphone switch in the PRIVATE position.
2. Hold the selector switch on the interphone control panel in the spring-loaded CALL position.
3. Direct the crew members with whom communication is desired to place their selector switches in the PVT. INTER position.
4. Release the selector switch, place it in the PVT. INTER position, and continue the conversation on the private interphone channel.

On group 2 airplanes the special interphone switch for the private interphone channel has not been incorporated, thereby eliminating the restrictions on the private interphone channel use except those imposed by crew discipline. Use of the special interphone switch in the PRIVATE position prevents communication between aft cabin crew members and the flight deck if the normal interphone channel becomes inoperative.

When use of the private interphone channel is desired, the following steps must be performed:

1. Hold the selector switch on the interphone control panel in the spring-loaded CALL position and speak into the microphone, directing the crew members with whom communication is desired to place their selector switches in the PVT. INTER position.

Note
This also places all panels in direct communication with all audio outlet stations.

Note
The call position will be inoperative if the private interphone circuit breaker is pulled.

2. Release the selector switch, place it in the PVT. INTER position, and continue the conversation on the private interphone channel.

Emergency Interphone Operation.
(Excluding Group 2 Airplanes)

When it is apparent that the normal interphone system has become inoperative, the crew member first noticing the deficiency will alert the rest of the crew to switch to PVT. INTER. The special interphone switch on the pilots' pedestal must be in the CRUISE COMBAT position at all times, except in instances when close coordination is required between the five crew members on the private circuit. Three amplifiers are provided; one for the normal, private, and special interphone systems. In case of amplifier failure, any one of the three amplifiers can be interchanged.

Emergency Interphone Operation.
(Group 2 Airplanes)

When it is apparent that the normal interphone system has become inoperative, the crew member first noticing the deficiency will alert the other crew members to switch to PVT. INTER.

Note
The call circuit operates through the normal interphone amplifier only.

Wing Interphone Control Switch.

An on-off wing interphone control switch is provided at each wing crawlway entrance hatch. This switch is used to isolate the wing interphone channel from the basic interphone channel so that, in the event a nacelle fire short circuits the wing interphone channel, the basic interphone channel will remain operative. Each switch is mechanically ganged to a wing crawlway light switch.

CAUTION
When the wing interphone channel is not in use, the wing interphone control switch must be in the OFF position to prevent failure of the private interphone channel in event of a short circuit in the interphone wiring.

On group 2 airplanes an indicator lamp (39, figure 1-20) on the flight engineer's panel lights when one or both of the wing interphone control switches are on.

Call Circuit.

A call circuit is provided to enable a crew member at any crew station to interrupt the reception of the other stations provided the normal interphone channel is operative. When the call circuit is selected by holding a selector switch in the spring-loaded CALL position, all other interphone controls are switched from any facility being used to the output of the normal interphone amplifier.

T.O. 1B-36D(II)-1

Section IV
Auxiliary Equipment

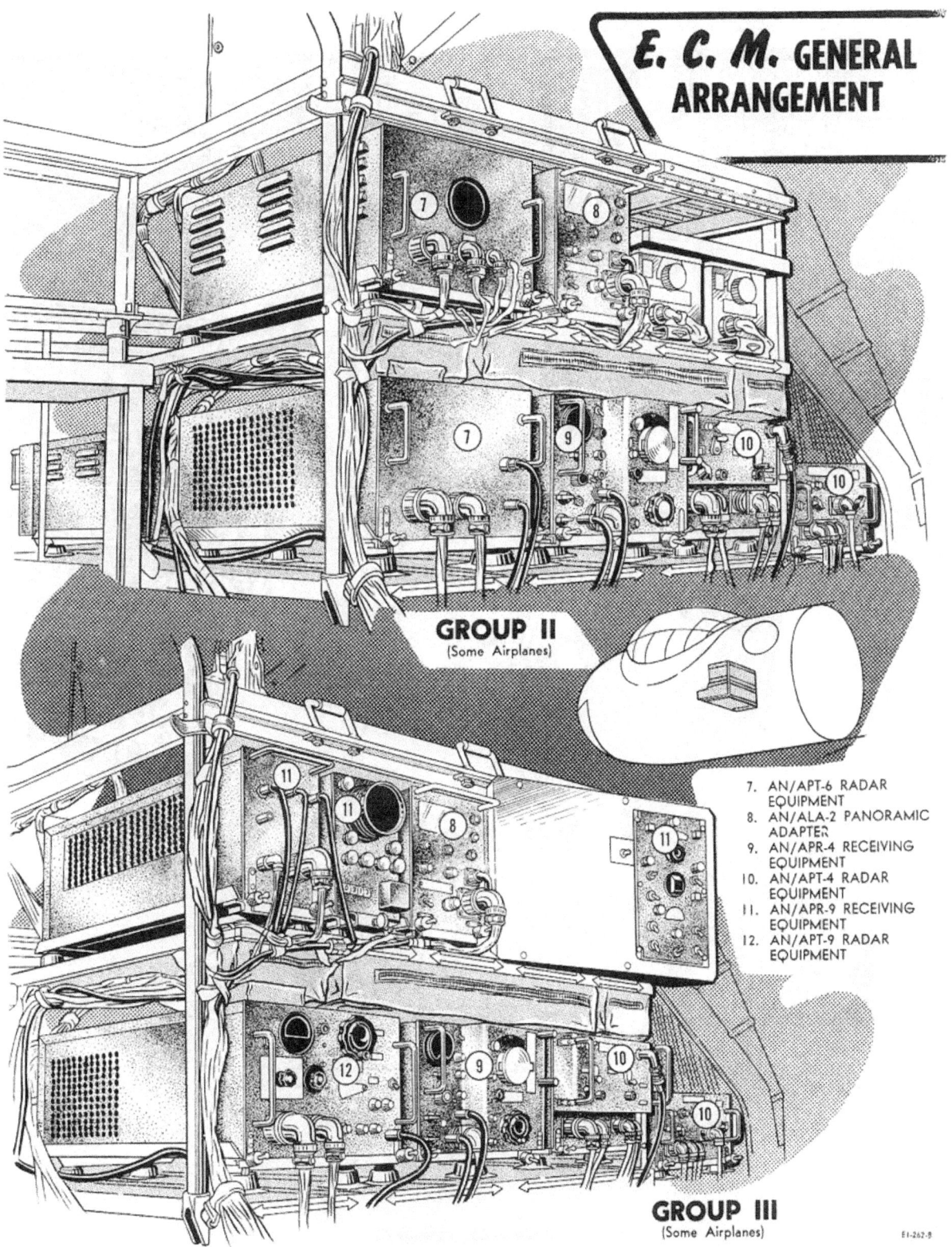

E. C. M. GENERAL ARRANGEMENT

GROUP II
(Some Airplanes)

GROUP III
(Some Airplanes)

7. AN/APT-6 RADAR EQUIPMENT
8. AN/ALA-2 PANORAMIC ADAPTER
9. AN/APR-4 RECEIVING EQUIPMENT
10. AN/APT-4 RADAR EQUIPMENT
11. AN/APR-9 RECEIVING EQUIPMENT
12. AN/APT-9 RADAR EQUIPMENT

Figure 4-12.

Section IV
Auxiliary Equipment

T.O. 1B-36D(II)-1

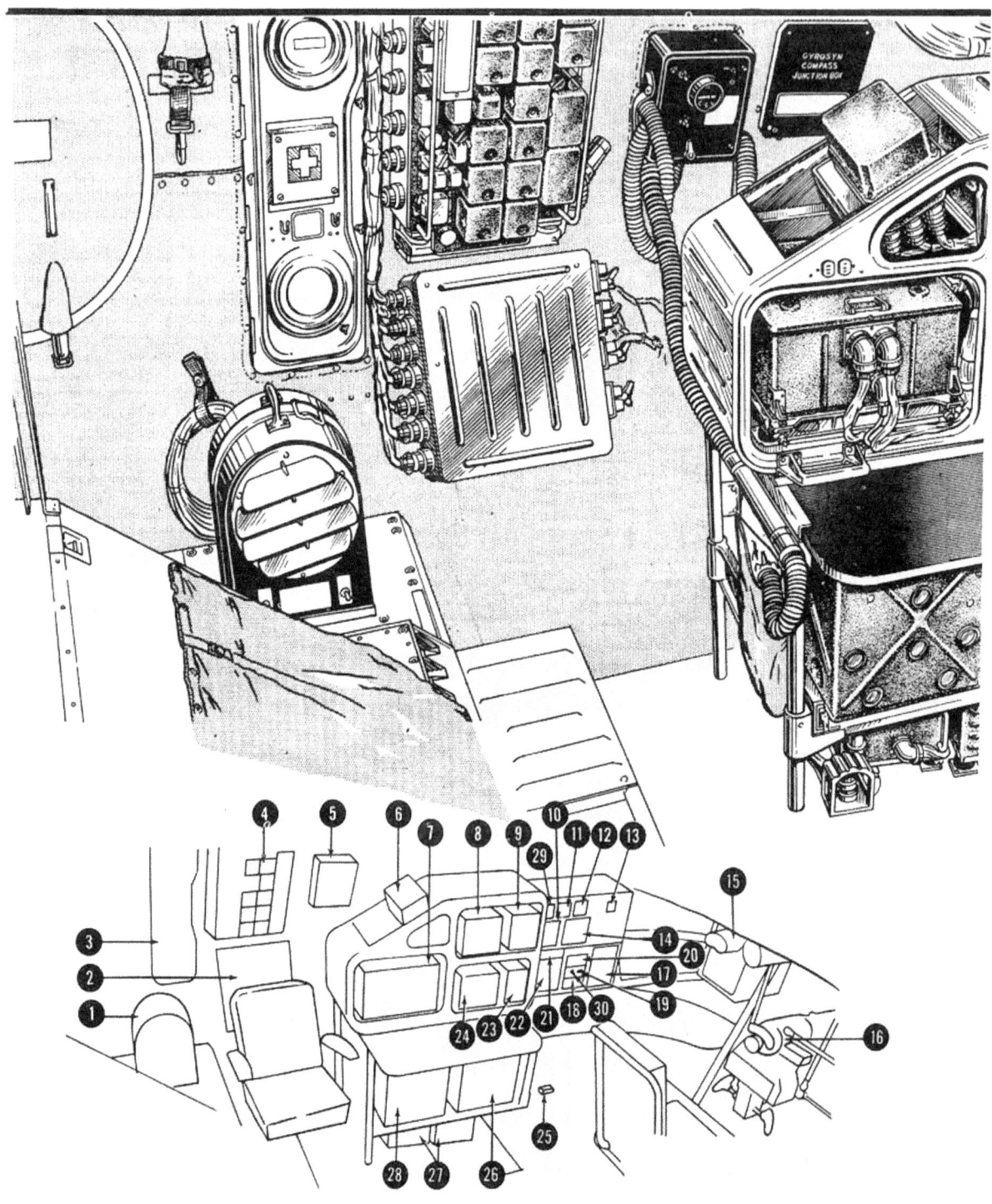

Figure 4-13. (Sheet 1)

Section IV
Auxiliary Equipment

Navigator's STATION

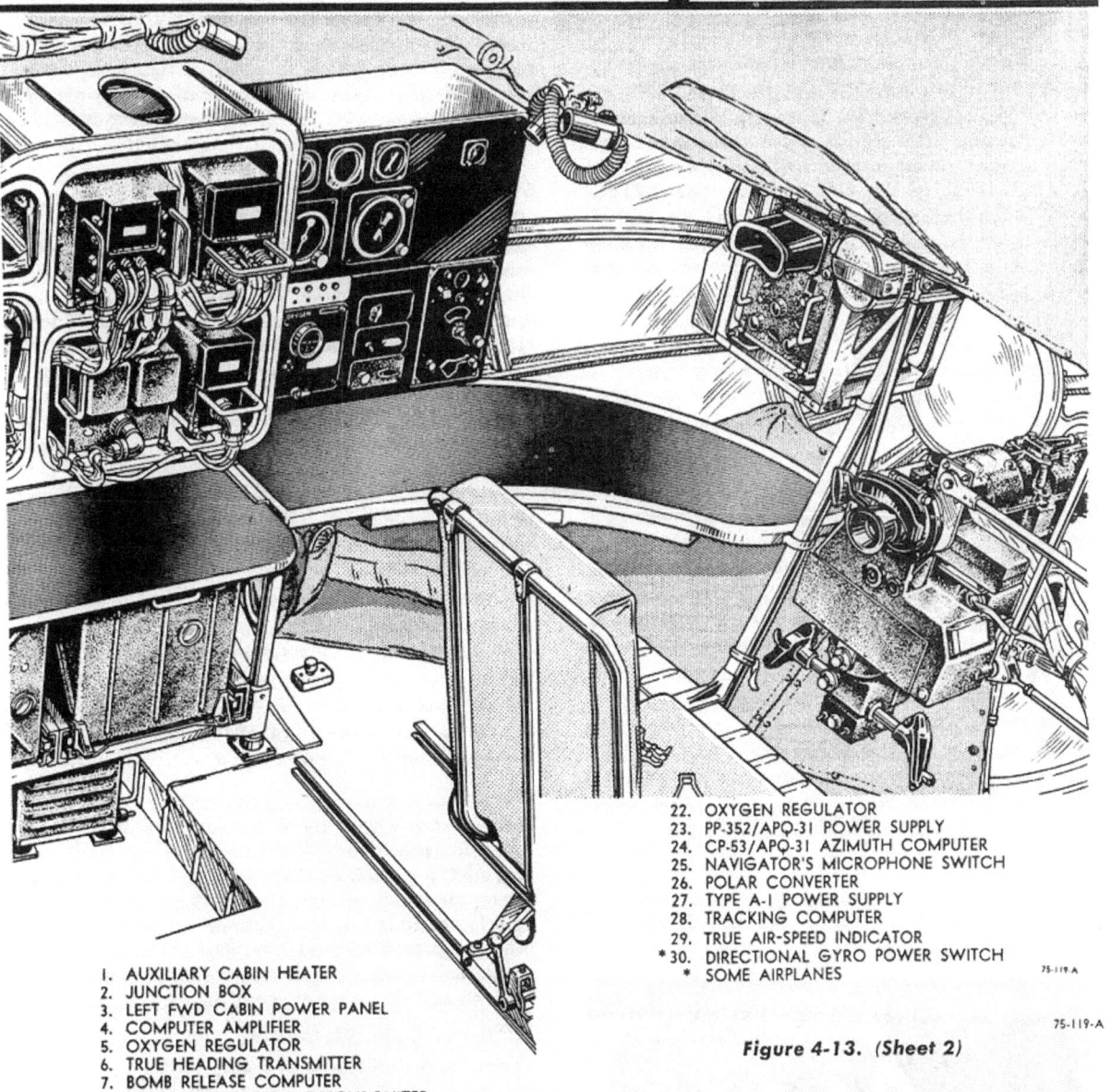

1. AUXILIARY CABIN HEATER
2. JUNCTION BOX
3. LEFT FWD CABIN POWER PANEL
4. COMPUTER AMPLIFIER
5. OXYGEN REGULATOR
6. TRUE HEADING TRANSMITTER
7. BOMB RELEASE COMPUTER
8. SN-57/APQ-31 RADAR SYNCHRONIZER
9. PP-353/APQ-31 POWER SUPPLY
*10. DIRECTIONAL GYRO INDICATOR
11. ALTIMETER
12. ARN-14 MAGNETIC INDICATOR
13. CLOCK
14. N-1 COMPASS MASTER INDICATOR
15. AN/APN-9 LORAN RECEIVER INDICATOR
16. NOSE SIGHT
17. RADIO COMPASS CONTROL PANEL
18. INTERPHONE CONTROL PANEL
19. N-1 COMPASS POWER SWITCH
20. NAVIGATOR'S LIGHT SWITCH
21. CIRCUIT BREAKERS
22. OXYGEN REGULATOR
23. PP-352/APQ-31 POWER SUPPLY
24. CP-53/APQ-31 AZIMUTH COMPUTER
25. NAVIGATOR'S MICROPHONE SWITCH
26. POLAR CONVERTER
27. TYPE A-1 POWER SUPPLY
28. TRACKING COMPUTER
29. TRUE AIR-SPEED INDICATOR
*30. DIRECTIONAL GYRO POWER SWITCH
 * SOME AIRPLANES

Figure 4-13. (Sheet 2)

Mixed Signals and Command.

This feature of the interphone system is provided for the aircraft commander and pilot only. (See figure 4-11.) It allows either or both of them to mix any combination of radio compass, interphone, marker beacon, and localizer audio signals with command radio signals, affording close coordination for take-off or landing operation. To use the mixed signals and command feature, proceed as follows:

1. Place the selector switch on the interphone control panel in the MIXED SIGNALS & COMMAND po-

237

sition. The command radio signals will be received in the headset, provided the set is in operation and its volume is properly adjusted.

2. Adjust the volume control on the interphone control panel for the desired output level.

3. To transmit on the command radio set, close the microphone switch and speak into the microphone.

4. To receive signals from other sets in conjunction with command radio signals, place any combination of the toggle switches marked INTER-COMP-MARKER-LOCALIZER in the ON position. The INTER switch is for the interphone channel, and the COMP switch is for the radio compass channel. The MARKER switch is for the marker beacon channel, and the LOCALIZER switch is for the localizer channel.

Note

These four channels are operative only when their switches are on and the interphone selector switch is set at MIXED SIGNALS & COMMAND.

Mixed Signals and Liaison.

This facility is provided for the radio operator only and is utilized as follows:

1. Place the selector switch on the interphone control panel in the MIXED SIGNALS & LIAISON position. The liaison radio signals will be received in the headset, provided the set is in operation and its volume is properly adjusted.

2. Adjust the volume control on the interphone panel to the desired output volume.

3. To transmit on the liaison radio set, close the microphone switch and speak into the microphone. The VOICE-CW-MCW switch on the liaison transmitter must be in the VOICE position.

Note

Other crew members can hear the liaison set by placing their selector switches in the LIAISON position.

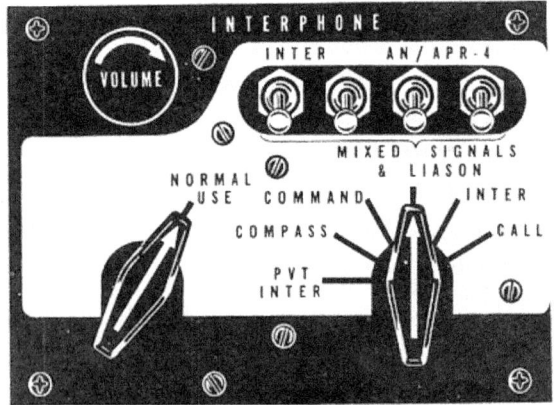

Figure 4-14. Radio Operator's Interphone Panel

Radio Operator's Interphone Control Panel.

This panel is a modified pilots' interphone control panel. Its operation is conventional except that it permits the radio operator to receive AN/APR-4 audio signals. To receive these signals, place the second switch from the right in the gang of four switches in the up position. (The three adjacent switches are inoperative.) Then place the selector switch on MIXED SIGNALS & LIAISON.

COMMAND RADIO EQUIPMENT.

All airplanes are equipped with the AN/ARC-3 command radio set for plane-to-plane or plane-to-ground communication. The set operates in the VHF range. On airplanes in Group 2 the UHF AN/ARC-27 set is also installed. On airplanes equipped with both sets, both receivers may be operated at the same time to permit reception on all channels. Transmission on a desired set is controlled by the pilots' command radio selector switch. If both sets are operated when a signal is received which does not disclose its type of command set or frequency range, the pilots must determine which set is receiving the signal before they can transmit on the correct command set. To determine which operating set is receiving an undisclosed signal, proceed as follows:

1. Vary the volume on one set. If the audio level remains unchanged, the set with the original volume setting is receiving the signal and must be used for transmission.

2. If the receiving set cannot be determined by varying the volume, transmit on first one set and then the other until contact is made.

Pilots' Command Radio Selector Switch.

This switch (7, figure 4-16), marked ARC-3 and ARC-27, permits the pilots to transmit on either the AN/ARC-3 or AN/ARC-27 command radios, depending on the switch setting. The pilots may receive radio signals on either set, regardless of the selector switch position, providing their interphone selector switches are placed in the MIXED SIGNALS & COMMAND position and the sets are turned on.

Command Radio AN/ARC-3.

Operation of this equipment is accomplished from the control panel (2, figure 4-16) on the pilots' pedestal. Operate as follows:

1. Place the selector switch on the interphone control panel to MIXED SIGNALS & COMMAND.

2. Place the command radio selector switch in the ARC-3 position (group 2 airplanes).

3. Place the ON-OFF switch on the command set control unit to the ON position and turn the channel selector switch to any one of the positions designated A through H on the control unit. This action applies power to the unit, which then automatically tunes itself to the channel selected.

4. To stop the equipment, place the ON-OFF switch in the OFF position.

Command Radio Set AN/ARC-27 (Group 2 Airplanes).

Operation of this equipment can be accomplished from either the pilots' (5, figure 4-16) or the radio operator's position, depending on the setting of the control panel at the radio operator's station (figure 4-15). For operation from the control on the pilots' pedestal, the radio operator's control panel is adjusted as follows:

1. Place the LOCAL-REMOTE switch in REMOTE position.

2. Place the TONE-VOICE switch in VOICE position.

With these adjustments made, operate from the control panel on the pilots' pedestal as follows:

1. Place the selector switch on either the aircraft commander or pilot's interphone control panel in MIXED SIGNALS & COMMAND position.

2. Place the command radio selector switch in the ARC-27 position.

3. Turn on the command radio set by operating the OFF—T/R — T/R + G REC—ADF switch to the T/R position.

Note

Allow at least one minute warm-up time before attempting transmission.

4. With the switch in T/R position, the equipment is ready for transmission and reception on any of eighteen preset frequencies and the guard frequency depending on the setting of the channel selector switch. Operate the channel selector to the desired preset channel.

5. Turn the OFF — T/R — T/R + G REC — ADF switch to the T/R + G REC position, making reception possible on both the main and guard channel frequencies. For transmission on the guard channel frequency, the OFF — T/R — T/R + G REC — ADF switch must be in the T/R position and the channel selector switch in G position.

6. Tone or modulated continuous wave operation for an emergency signal or to aid direction finding equipment is accomplished from the radio operator's control panel.

a. Place the TONE-VOICE switch in the TONE position.

b. Place the power switch in the ON position.

c. Place the LOCAL-REMOTE switch in the LOCAL position.

d. Place the radio operator's GUARD, BOTH, COMD T/R switch in the BOTH or COMD T/R position.

e. Adjust the local channel selector switch as needed.

f. To turn the equipment off from the radio operator's control panel, place the LOCAL-REMOTE switch in LOCAL and the power switch in the OFF position.

7. To turn the equipment off, place the OFF — T/R — T/R + G REC — ADF switch in the OFF position.

LIAISON RADIO SET AN/ARC-8.

Control of transmitting equipment is accomplished from the radio operator's table. (See figure 4-9.) The equipment is started by placing the LOCAL-REMOTE switch to the LOCAL position and setting the emission switch to VOICE. A remote control panel (4, figure 4-16) is located on the pilots' pedestal for use by the aircraft commander or pilot. Control of this panel is attained when the radio operator places the LOCAL-REMOTE switch to REMOTE. A green light on the pilots' remote control panel will indicate that the transmitter is ready for remote control. To stop the transmitter, place the EMISSION switch in the OFF position.

RADIO RANGE RECEIVER BC-453-B (Airplanes not in Group 2).

Operation of this equipment is accomplished from a remote control panel on the pilots' pedestal. The receiver is started by placing the CW-OFF-MCW switch on the control panel in either the CW or MCW position. To turn the equipment off, place the CW-OFF-MCW switch in the OFF position.

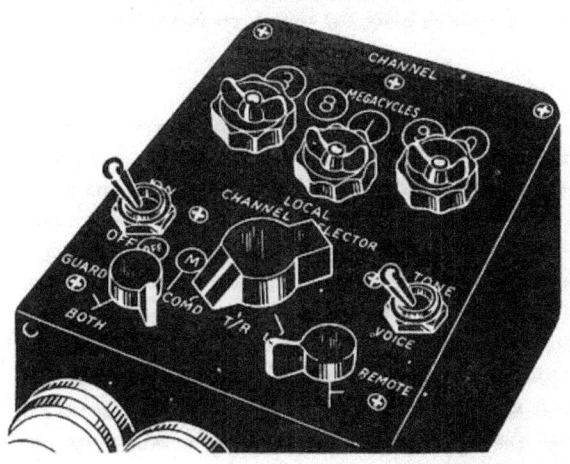

Figure 4-15.

Section IV
Auxiliary Equipment

T.O. 1B-36D(II)-1

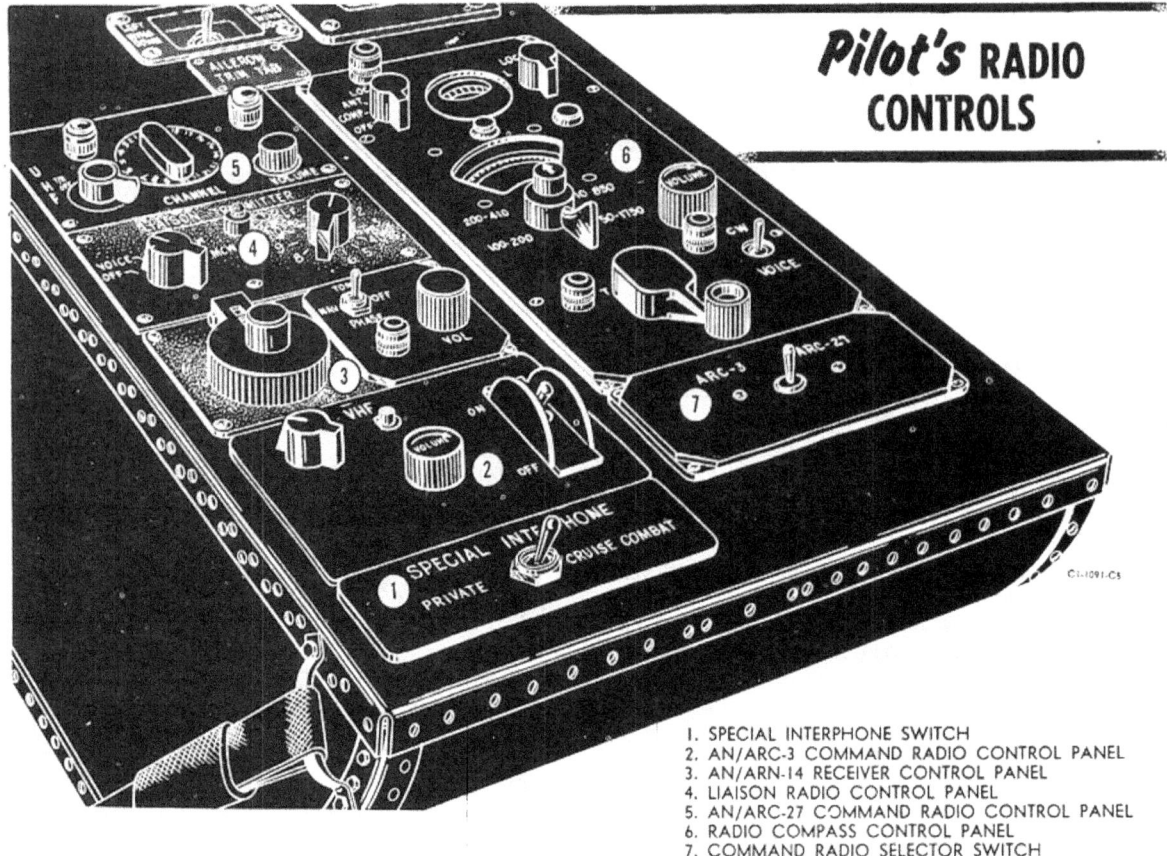

1. SPECIAL INTERPHONE SWITCH
2. AN/ARC-3 COMMAND RADIO CONTROL PANEL
3. AN/ARN-14 RECEIVER CONTROL PANEL
4. LIAISON RADIO CONTROL PANEL
5. AN/ARC-27 COMMAND RADIO CONTROL PANEL
6. RADIO COMPASS CONTROL PANEL
7. COMMAND RADIO SELECTOR SWITCH

Figure 4-16. Pilots' Radio Controls

RADIO SET AN/CRC-7 ("WALKIE-TALKIE").

This set is stowed on the left side of the radio operator's compartment adjacent to the food locker and is provided for emergency use. To start the unit, remove the lock pin from the three switch keys marked TONE, TRAN, and REC and press the desired key. To stop the set, release the keys.

INSTRUMENT APPROACH EQUIPMENT.

The instrument approach equipment of airplanes not in group 2 consists of AN/ARN-5A and RC-103-A receivers, a control panel on the pilots' pedestal, and an indicator (1, figure 1-13) on the pilots' instrument panel. About 20 minutes before approaching the runway, turn the selector switch to the appropriate channel and allow the receivers to warm up. Visual indication of the signals received by both receivers is transposed onto the pilot's indicator.

Airplanes in group 2 obtain glide path signals from AN/ARN-5B receiver and obtain localizer signals from the AN/ARN-14 receiver. These signals provide visual reference on the course indicator located on the pilots' instrument panel. For instrument approach operation, set the switch on the AN/ARN-14 control panel (3, figure 4-15) to the TONE position. To stop the equipment place the switch on NAV OFF.

Radio Compass AN/ARN-7( ).

This equipment is used by the pilot and navigator; each has a control panel and an indicator. The pilots' control panel (6, figure 4-16) is located on the pilots' pedestal and the navigator's control panel (17, figure 4-13) is located above the navigator's instrument panel. On airplanes not in group 2, one radio compass indicator is located on the navigator's instrument panel, and one is located on the pilot's instrument panel. On group 2 airplanes the radio compass indication is read on the front pointers of the radio magnetic indicators for the AN/ARN-14 receivers. One radio magnetic indicator is located on the pilots' instrument panel and one is located on the navigator's instrument panel.

To start the radio compass equipment, momentarily hold the function switch on the control panel in the spring-loaded CONT position and move the function switch to the COMP or ANT position. To stop the equipment, turn the function switch to OFF.

Note

On group 2 airplanes the radio compass will not give visual indications unless the N-1 high latitude compass or the AN/ARN-14 receiver is operating.

MARKER BEACON SET AN/ARN-12 OR RC-193A.

Some airplanes are equipped with the RC-193A set, while other airplanes have the AN/ARN-12 set. The operation of this equipment is automatic when the aircraft's d-c power is on and its circuit breaker is closed. Marker beacon signals are indicated by a lamp at the corner of the instrument approach indicator on the pilot's instrument panel. To receive signals aurally the interphone control panel marker switch must be on MARKER and the selector switch must be on MIXED SIGNALS & COMMAND.

Radio Receiver AN/ARN-14 (Group 2 Airplanes).

This radio navigational aid consists of a receiver, a course indicator, two radio magnetic indicators, and a bearing converter indicator.

Note

The bearing converter indicator is located in the aft cabin and is for test and adjustment purposes only.

The course indicator and one magnetic indicator are located on the pilots' instrument panel. The other magnetic indicator is located on the navigator's instrument panel. The course indicator provides the facilities for an instrument approach indicator, a magnetic heading indicator, a course selector, and a marker beacon indicator. The radio magnetic indicators consist of a rotating compass card that indicates the magnetic heading as detected by the N-1 high latitude compass, a number 1 pointer actuated by the radio compass, and a number 2 pointer actuated by the AN/ARN-14 receiver.

Note

Oscillation of the number 2 pointer will occur when engines are operating at speeds between 1550 and 1800 rpm. This erratic action is due to propeller modulation and is not cause for concern.

To turn on the AN/ARN-14 receiver, place the switch on the AN/ARN-14 control panel in the TONE or ON position. To stop the operation, place the switch in the OFF position.

LORAN SET AN/APN-9

The receiver-indicator (15, figure 4-13) of this set is installed on the navigator's table. A control panel incorporated on the front of the receiver-indicator in conjunction with a detachable visor provides all of the manual controls. To start the set, proceed as follows:

1. Set the AMPLITUDE BALANCE control at its center position.
2. Turn the FINE DELAY control to its center position of rotation.
3. Set the DRIFT control at its center position of rotation.
4. Turn the RECEIVER GAIN control clockwise until the STATION rate identification (pilot light) illuminates. Wait at least five minutes to allow the equipment to warm up. The set is now ready for operation. (See figure 4-17 for calibration information.)
5. To stop the equipment, turn the RECEIVER GAIN control to POWER OFF and check to see the pilot light is not illuminated. Also check to see that the pattern on the indicator screen has disappeared.

IDENTIFICATION SET AN/APX-6.

Provisions have been made for the installation of an AN/APX-6 identification set at the radio operator's station.

Operation.

To operate the identification set AN/APX-6, proceed as follows:

CAUTION

Before take-off, insert three destructors in the face of AN/APX-6 IFF transpondor located beneath the step under the left escape hatch. Remove all three destructors immediately after landing, and insert dummy plugs.

1. Master control in OFF position.
2. Set receiver frequency counter to correct frequency channel.
3. Turn low frequency counter to same channel.
4. Set transmitter frequency counter to transmitting channel.
5. Rotate master control to NORM position (full sensitivity and maximum performance) or to STDY or LOW as required.
6. Set the mode 2 switch to I/P or required position.
7. Set the mode 3 switch to OUT or required position.
8. For emergency operation, press the dial stop, and rotate master control to EMERGENCY position.
9. An impact switch to fire the detonators and destroy the IFF system is incorporated in the system as a security measure. However, the detonators may be fired manually by a destructor switch on the IFF control panel. To manually fire destructors, lift destructor guard by breaking safety wire and place toggle switch in the ON position.

Section IV
Auxiliary Equipment

T.O. 1B-36D(II)-1

AN/APN-9 LORAN CALIBRATION Chart

FUNCT	STN	PRR	SCOPE PATTERN	REMARKS	ADJ	CRSE	FINE
5	0	L OR H		ADJUST FOR DISTINCT PICTURE	FOCUS		
5	0	L OR H		ADJUST TO OPERATOR'S DESIRE	BRILL		
1	0	L OR H		ADJUST ALTERNATELY FOR LENGTH & POSITION	SL. SWP. H. CENT. & AMPL.		
2	0	L OR H		ADJUST ALTERNATELY FOR LENGTH & POSITION	FA. SWP. H. CENT. & AMPL.		
2	0	L OR H		ADJUST TO CENTER VERTICALLY	VERTICAL CENTER		
5	0	L OR H		ADJUST 1000 MS MKRS 1/8"- 1/4" ABOVE 100 MS MKRS	MARKER AMPL.		
5	0	L OR H		ADJUST UNTIL CROSS HAIR BARELY TOUCHES 10 MS MARKERS ON UPPER TRACE	CROSS HAIR		
4	0	H		5 (1000 SPACES) BETWEEN (5000 MKRS)	C		
4	0	H		3 (5000 MS MARKERS)	D		
4	0	L		4 (5000 MS MARKERS)	E		
5	0	H		4 (10 MS MKRS) BETWEEN (50 MS MKRS)	A		
5	0	H		9 (100 MS MKRS) BETWEEN (1000 MS MKRS)	B		
5	0	H		COUNT 8 SPACES FROM CROSS HAIR ON LEFT TO FIRST STN RATE ON RIGHT (BTM TRACE)	B		
5	1	H		COUNT 7 SPACES FROM CROSS HAIR TO STN RATE MARKER	B		
5	2	H		COUNT 6	2		
5	3	H		COUNT 5	2		
5	4	H		COUNT 4	4		
5	5	H		COUNT 3	4		
5	6	H		COUNT 2	F G		
5	7	H		COUNT 1	F G		
5	4	H	MOVE L-R SWITCH TO RIGHT, STN RATE MARKER SHOULD JUMP TWO SPACES LEFT.		B R-L		
4	0	H		MARKER READS BETWEEN 11,000 & 11,500	5 HOLE RIGHT SIDE	C.C.W.	C.W.
4	0	H		MARKER JUST OFF SCREEN. RECHECK PREVIOUS STEP	2 HOLE RIGHT SIDE	C.W.	C.W.
4	0	L		MARKER READS BETWEEN 13,500 & 14,000	4 HOLE RIGHT SIDE	C.C.W.	C.W.
4	0	L		MARKER JUST OFF SCREEN. RECHECK PREVIOUS STEP	3 HOLE RIGHT SIDE	C.W.	C.C.W.
5	0	H	ROTATE FINE DELAY C.W. TO C.C.W. & COUNT HUNDREDS; READ NO LESS THAN 700 NOR MORE THAN 1500		1 HOLE RIGHT SIDE	SET ON 5000	C.W. & C.C.W.

Figure 4-17.

> **CAUTION**
>
> The destructor switch should be operated only when AN/APX-6 equipment is in danger of falling into enemy hands.

10. To turn off equipment, rotate master switch to the OFF position.

RADAR SET AN/APQ-31.

For information on the AN/APQ-31 radar set refer to "K-( ) Bombing Navigation System," Section VIII.

RADAR PRESSURIZATION.

A 115-volt, a-c, motor-driven pressure pump located in the lower section of the forward cabin provides pressurized air for the radio frequency unit, the radio frequency line (wave guide), and the modulating unit of the AN/APQ-31 radar set. The pressure pump draws cabin air through a dehydrator to remove all moisture and then pressurizes it before it is routed to the units. The system incorporates a pressure pump switch, a pressure gage, an indicator lamp, and a pressure drain valve located on the radar-bombardier's K-( ) control panel. The system is controlled by the pressure pump switch which has three positions—AUTOMATIC ON, OFF, and MANUAL ON. When the switch is in the AUTOMATIC ON position, operation of the pump is controlled automatically by the action of a pressure switch. The indicator lamp lights when the pump is in operation.

> **CAUTION**
>
> If the pressure begins to exceed its specified limits, as indicated on the pressure gage, and the indicator lamp indicates that the pump is still operating, the pump should be stopped by placing the switch in the OFF position.

If the pressure begins to drop to a critically low point and the indicator lamp indicates that the pump is not in operation, hold the switch in the spring-loaded MANUAL ON position until the pressure is back to normal.

> **CAUTION**
>
> Do not operate the radar set until radar t-r unit air pressure is above minimum limits.

LIGHTING SYSTEM.

The lighting system is composed of two groups of lights, exterior and interior. These lights operate on both 28-volt alternating and direct current, as well as 115-volt alternating current. The exterior group includes landing lights, taxi lights, formation lights, navigation lights, and code-signalling lights. Interior lighting is accomplished by means of dome, cockpit, and other miscellaneous lights. Receptacles for operating Aldis signal lights are located at the navigator's station, on the pilot's fairing, and at each sighting station.

EXTERIOR LIGHTS.

Landing Lights.

Two retractable landing lights are mounted flush with the fuselage, one on each side of the nose section just above the lower flight deck floor. In airplanes not in group 2 each landing light has a three-position switch which controls extension, illumination, and retraction. In group 2 airplanes each light has a three-position switch which controls extension and retraction. An additional on-off switch energizes the filaments of both lamps.

> **CAUTION**
>
> When operating in extremely cold temperatures, or during icing conditions, the filament control switch should be placed ON for a short time before extending the light. This action will preheat the light assemblies and remove any ice that might interfere with proper extension of the lights.

Taxi Lights (Some Airplanes).

Some airplanes are equipped with two taxi lights located on the jet pods. The lights, located one between the engine housing of each pod, are controlled by a signal switch at the pilot's station.

Taxi Light Switch. The taxi lights are controlled by an ON-OFF switch (31, figure 1-13) located on the bottom right corner of the pilot's instrument panel.

Navigation Lights.

The navigation light system consists of a red light assembly on the left wing tip, a green light assembly on the right wing tip, two yellow and two white lights on the stabilizer close to the fuselage, and two white lights, one on the upper fuselage approximately in line with the wing trailing edge and one on the lower fuselage forward of the wing leading edge. The system is used to indicate the position and direction of motion of the airplane. The wing tip lights and white tail lights operate on a-c power. The yellow tail lights and flasher mechanism operate on d-c power. The wing tip lights and the white and yellow tail lights will burn steadily or can be made to flash alternately through the use of the flasher mechanism. When flashing, one circuit closes for approximately one-half second, then both circuits are open; the other circuit closes for ap-

Section IV
Auxiliary Equipment

T.O. 1B-36D(II)-1

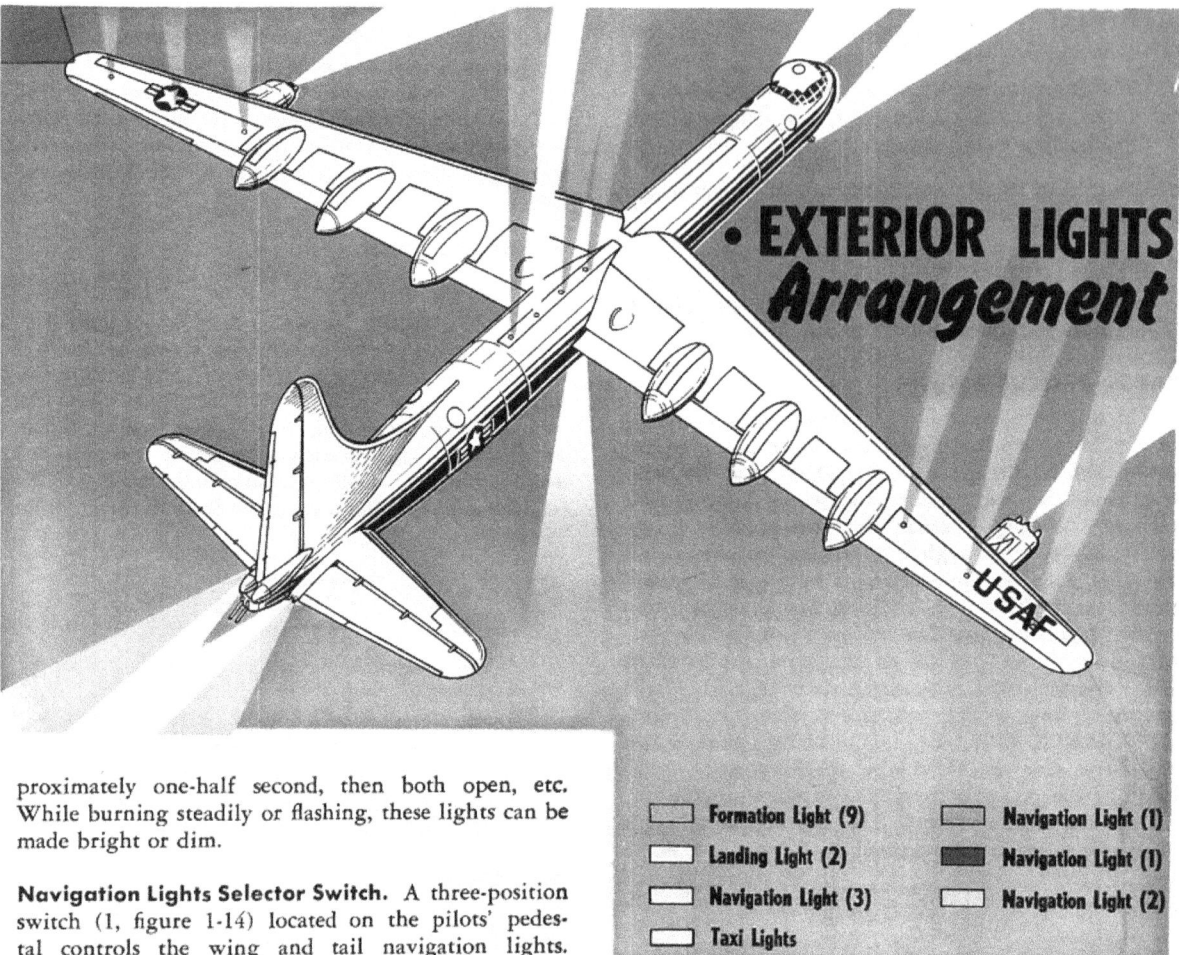

Figure 4-18.

proximately one-half second, then both open, etc. While burning steadily or flashing, these lights can be made bright or dim.

Navigation Lights Selector Switch. A three-position switch (1, figure 1-14) located on the pilots' pedestal controls the wing and tail navigation lights. This switch has positions marked STEADY, OFF, and FLASH. When it is in the STEADY position, the wing tip lights and both the white and yellow lights on the tail will burn continuously. The FLASH position causes the wing tip lights and the white tail lights to flash alternately with the yellow tail lights.

Wing and Tail Navigation Lights Dimming Switch. A two-position switch (8, figure 1-14) on the pilots' pedestal controls the intensity of the wing tip lights and both the white and yellow tail lights. The switch has positions marked BRIGHT and DIM and controls the light intensity accordingly.

Fuselage Navigation Lights Switch. A three-position switch (8, figure 1-14) on the pilots' pedestal controls the action of the two small white lights which are located on the top and bottom of the fuselage. This switch has positions marked BRIGHT, OFF, and DIM, and controls the light intensity accordingly.

Formation Lights.
Nine blue formation light assemblies are installed on the airplane. Three are mounted on the left wing, three on the right wing, and three on the aft part of the upper fuselage. The lights are controlled by a switch (9, figure 1-14) on the pilots' pedestal. The three positions of the switch are OFF, DIM, and BRIGHT.

INTERIOR LIGHTS.

Dome, instrument, control panel, cockpit, table, coaming, and crew station lights are located throughout the forward cabin to provide the crew with adequate illumination. The lights are controlled by built-in dimmer and switch units, panel switches, and rheostats. Mounted on the engineer's circuit breaker panel is one switch-type circuit breaker for control of the nose and main landing gear wheel well lights. On group 2 airplanes the flight deck has three flood lights installed around the navigator's sighting station. The lights illuminate

CREW MEMBERS OXYGEN DURATION-HRS.

CABIN ALT., FT.	GAGE PRESSURE, P.S.I.							BELOW 100
	400	350	300	250	200	150	100	
40,000	10.3 / 10.3	8.8 / 8.8	7.4 / 7.4	5.9 / 5.9	4.4 / 4.4	2.9 / 2.9	1.5 / 1.5	EMERGENCY DESCEND TO ALTITUDE NOT REQUIRING OXYGEN
35,000	10.3 / 10.3	8.8 / 8.8	7.4 / 7.4	5.9 / 5.9	4.4 / 4.4	2.9 / 2.9	1.5 / 1.5	
30,000	7.6 / 7.6	6.5 / 6.5	5.5 / 5.5	4.4 / 4.4	3.3 / 3.3	2.2 / 2.2	1.1 / 1.1	
25,000	6.1 / 7.2	5.3 / 6.2	4.4 / 5.2	3.5 / 4.1	2.6 / 3.1	1.8 / 2.1	0.9 / 1.0	
20,000	4.9 / 8.2	4.2 / 7.0	3.5 / 5.8	2.8 / 4.7	2.1 / 3.5	1.4 / 2.3	0.7 / 1.2	
15,000	3.9 / 10.0	3.3 / 8.5	2.8 / 7.1	2.2 / 5.7	1.7 / 4.2	1.1 / 2.8	0.6 / 1.4	
10,000	3.3 / 13.2	2.8 / 11.3	2.4 / 9.4	1.9 / 7.5	1.4 / 5.7	1.0 / 3.8	0.5 / 1.9	

RED FIGURES INDICATE DILUTER LEVER IN 100% POSITION
BLACK FIGURES INDICATE DILUTER LEVER IN NORMAL POSITION
CYLINDERS — 26 EA. G-1
CREW — 15
WHEN 11 MAN CREW IS USED DURATION INCREASES APPROXIMATELY 25%

Figure 4-19.

the pilots' and the engineer's station. Each light has a three-position switch with RED, WHITE, and a neutral off position. With the white lights on, the blinding effect of lightning is minimized. The red lights are used to preserve night vision.

Lights in the forward turret bay and dome and passage lights in bomb bays No. 1 and 2 are controlled by either of two switches, one on the radio operator's control panel and the other on the bomb bay lights control panel. The aft turret bay and bomb bays No. 3 and 4 dome and passage lights are controlled by either of two switches, one on the bunk equipment panel in the aft cabin and the other on the bomb bay lights control panel. A switch at each wing crawlway entrance controls the wing crawlway lights.

The light in the forward end of the communication tube is controlled by a switch-type circuit breaker on the radio operator's panel. The light in the aft end of tube burns continuously when the push-pull type circuit breaker for the aft cabin dome light switch is closed. The aft cabin dome light is controlled by two switches, one on the left side of the cabin near the communication tube and the other at the entrance hatch. The gunners' cockpit lights are controlled by built-in dimmer and switch units. The switch for the tail cone and tail turret dome lights is a switch-type circuit breaker located above the tail cone entrance hatch.

ALDIS LAMP RECEPTACLES.

Receptacles for operating the Aldis lamps are located at the navigator's station, the pilot's station, and at each sighting station.

LIGHTING SYSTEM EMERGENCY OPERATION.

In the event of failure of all alternators, the only electrical power available will be from the airplane battery. To conserve the strength of the battery it is necessary that all nonessential lights be turned off.

OXYGEN SYSTEM.

The airplane is equipped with a low pressure oxygen system consisting of 24 or 26 type G-1 oxygen cylinders, 5 portable diluter oxygen units, 8 recharger hoses, and oxygen controls at each crew station. The airplane is equipped with D-1 or D-2 automatic pressure-breathing diluter-demand regulators. The oxygen cylinders are on the left side of the bomb bay area; the system is serviced through a single filler valve on the lower left side of the fuselage near the radome. (See figure 1-48.)

Note

The system must be fully charged to 400 psi prior to all flights.

Section IV
Auxiliary Equipment

T.O. 1B-36D(II)-1

Typical OXYGEN PANEL

Figure 4-20.

For combat safety each crew oxygen station is supplied from two distribution lines through automatic check valves. The approximate duration of the oxygen system is given in figure 4-19. Only a pressure-breathing demand oxygen mask will be used above 34,000 feet pressure altitude.

Note

As an airplane ascends to high altitudes where the temperature is normally quite low, the oxygen cylinders become chilled. As the cylinders become colder, the oxygen gage pressure is reduced, sometimes rather rapidly. With a 56°C (100°F) decrease in temperature in the cylinders the gage pressure can be expected to drop 20 per cent. This rapid fall in pressure is occasionally a cause for unnecessary alarm. All the oxygen is still there, and as the airplane descends to warmer altitudes, the pressure will tend to rise again, so that the rate of oxygen usages may appear to be slower than normal. A rapid fall in oxygen pressure while the airplane is in level flight, or while it is descending, is not ordinarily

due to falling temperature. When this happens, leakage or loss of oxygen must be suspected.

D-1 OR D-2 REGULATOR CONTROLS AND INDICATORS.

An automatic pressure-breathing, diluter-demand oxygen regulator (figure 4-20) is at each crew station. Three additional regulators are installed at training stations in the forward cabin. An oxygen flow indicator and a pressure gage are incorporated in the regulator. The function of the regulator is to simulate sea level oxygen pressure conditions in high altitude flight. The regulator accomplishes this by means of an aneroid assembly which progressively delivers a richer oxygen-air mixture to the oxygen mask at correspondingly greater pressures until at high altitude (generally beginning in the vicinity of 34,000 feet) 100 per cent oxygen is being delivered at a pressure varying from 2 to 17 inches of water.

Regulator Diluter Control.

A diluter lever is provided on each oxygen regulator. At NORMAL OXYGEN the lever opens the air inlet valve so that the regulator automatically supplies a proper mixture of air and oxygen to the mask at all altitudes, provided the regulator supply valve lever is ON. The lever at 100% OXYGEN closes the air inlet valve so that 100 per cent oxygen is supplied to the mask for emergency use.

Regulator Supply Valve Lever.

An oxygen supply valve lever is located at the bottom of each regulator panel. The lever, when turned to the ON position, opens the oxygen supply to the regulator. The lever, when turned to the OFF position, cuts off the oxygen supply. A force of approximately 20 inch-pounds should be used in turning the valve.

WARNING

If the supply valve is left ON at an unused station, the oxygen supply will be depleted.

Regulator Emergency Toggle Lever.

The emergency toggle lever provides a means of manually supplying positive pressure to the mask for emergency purposes. Pushing the lever in gives a positive pressure to the mask. This pressure is automatically stopped when the lever is released. This feature of the lever is to be used when testing the fit of the oxygen mask. The lever can also be pushed to either side (right or left). This action locks the lever to give a continuous positive pressure to the mask.

WARNING

Except for testing oxygen mask fit, the emergency toggle lever is not to be used except in an emergency, because the duration of the oxygen supply will be seriously affected.

Section IV
Auxiliary Equipment

Regulator Warning System Switch.

This switch is inoperative because the oxygen system warning signals are not incorporated in this airplane.

Pressure Gage and Flow Indicator.

A combination pressure gage and flow indicator is mounted on the face of each regulator. The pressure gage shows oxygen cylinder pressure and is calibrated from 0 to 500 psi. The range from 400 to 450 psi is marked FULL. The flow indicator consists of a blinker plate which indicates the flow of oxygen by exposing four fluorescent painted segments with each inhalation.

PORTABLE OXYGEN EQUIPMENT.

Five portable oxygen units are provided to furnish the crew with oxygen when entering the unpressurized areas in the airplane while at high altitude and to serve as an emergency system in case of failure of an oxygen panel. Two of these units are in the forward cabin and one is in the aft cabin. The units consist of an A-6 walk-around oxygen cylinder and an A-15 regulator. Eight portable recharger assemblies are in the airplane; four are in the forward cabin, two above the catwalk in the bomb bay, and two in the aft cabin. Any of the eight recharger hoses may be used to fill the portable cylinders.

Note

The A-15 regulator is not a pressure demand regulator and therefore cannot be used above 34,000 feet in an unpressurized cabin. Type A-21 regulators must be used above 34,000 feet up to 45,000 feet.

OPERATIONAL USE OF OXYGEN EQUIPMENT.

Both D-1 and D-2 pressure demand regulators provide adequate protection below approximately 43,000 feet. Protection becomes marginal between 43,000 and 45,000 feet because of the likelihood of mask leakage and the fatigue of breathing against higher pressure settings. Both regulators serve only as emergency devices above 45,000 feet, useful for preserving consciousness long enough to descend to a safe altitude after rapid decompression. As an example, at 50,000 feet no longer than two minutes of consciousness can be anticipated with the D-1 or D-2 regulator.

These limitations of the oxygen equipment impose the following restrictions on crew and aircraft operation.

1. The number of crew members and passengers will not be greater than the number of installed oxygen outlets and walk-around bottles on any flight above 14,000 feet if the aircraft is not pressurized; 20,000 feet if pressurized; or 34,000 feet if walk-around bottles do not have pressure demand regulators. If walk-around bottles are used for a primary source of oxygen, they will be connected to a recharger hose above 35,000 feet.

Note

If passengers who are not qualified air crew members are being carried and walk-around bottles are used as the primary source of oxygen, the altitude will be limited to 30,000 feet.

Preflight Check of Oxygen Equipment.

Each crew member will preflight his oxygen equipment as follows:

1. Regulator and Hose Connections.
 a. Alligator clip (clothing clamp) in proper working condition.
 b. Clamps secure at each end of regulator.
 c. Regulator elbow nut tight.
 d. Connect the attachment strap on the mask male connector to the parachute chest strap by routing the connector strap under the chest strap as close to the center as possible, up behind the chest strap, down in front of the chest strap, and around again; then snap it to the connector.
 e. Connect the mask-to-regulator tubing female disconnect to the mask male connector; listen for the click and look to see that the sealing gasket is only half exposed.
 f. Attach the alligator clip to the end of the mask male connector strap.

2. D-1 or D-2 Regulator Check.
 a. With the regulator supply valve lever OFF, set the diluter lever at NORMAL OXYGEN Cabin air only should be delivered by the regulator. Place the diluter level in the 100% OXYGEN position. Neither cabin air nor oxygen should be delivered by the regulator.
 b. With the oxygen supply lever ON, accomplish the following:
  (1) Check gage for proper pressure (400 to 450 psi or FULL).
  (2) Return diluter lever to NORMAL OXYGEN.
  (3) Move emergency toggle lever to either right or left and check for continuous positive pressure.
  (4) Depress emergency toggle lever and check for greater positive pressure.

Note

With the emergency toggle lever depressed, check the mask for proper fit.

 c. With the regulator supply valve ON, the oxygen mask connected to the regulator, the diluter lever in 100% OXYGEN position, conduct the following check while breathing normally:
  (1) Observe the blinker for proper operation.
  (2) Deflect the emergency toggle lever to the right or left. A positive pressure should be applied to the mask. Return the emergency toggle lever to center position.
  (3) Depress the emergency toggle straight in. A positive pressure should be applied to the mask. Hold your breath to determine whether there is leakage around the mask. Release the emergency toggle lever; positive pressure should cease.

Section IV
Auxiliary Equipment

(4) Return the diluter lever to NORMAL OXYGEN position.

d. Return the oxygen supply lever to OFF, using approximately 20 inch-pounds of torque to insure that the supply valve is completely closed. Then push the emergency toggle lever in momentarily to reset the gage to a zero reading.

Note

If pressure builds up after several minutes, the oxygen supply valve is not fully closed. This condition will cause oxygen to flow from the regulator any time the cabin altitude reaches the altitude at which the regulator begins to meter oxygen.

e. Check the regulator for outward leakage by using the following blow-back test: Remove mask and blow gently into the end of the oxygen regulator hose as during normal exhalation. (Blowing hard may tend to seal a leaky diluter air valve.) Resistance to blowing indicates that the demand diaphragm, the diluter air valve, and the mask-to-regulator tubing are satisfactory; little or no resistance to blowing indicates that they are faulty.

Note

Conduct the blow-back test on all demand regulators twice, once with the diluter valve at the NORMAL OXYGEN position and again at the 100% OXYGEN position.

3. Portable Walk-Around Bottle—Type A-6.

a. Attach recharger hose and fill bottle to at least 400 psi.

b. Detach and listen for leaks in the recharger hose.

c. Check pressure gage. Should be at least 400 psi.

d. Plug mask into regulator and check pull to disconnect. It should be from 10 to 20 pounds.

e. Blow gently into regulator to detect leaks in diaphragm or check valve.

CAUTION

Excessive blowing may rupture diaphragm.

4. Emergency Bail-Out Bottle—Type H-2.

Note

A fully charged H-2 cylinder will last approximately 10 minutes, depending on altitude and temperature.

a. Check pressure gage. Pressure should be 1800 psi.

Note

With a full charge of 1800 psi the oxygen supply will last approximately 10 minutes. Temperature and altitude will vary the duration time.

b. Check adequate fit of all connections.

c. Secure bottle to parachute harness below the D-ring.

Normal Oxygen Procedures.

The following rules will be followed on every altitude flight.

1. Mask will be worn at all times when *cabin* altitude is 10,000 feet and above.

2. *Pressure altitude 10,000 to 28,000 feet and cabin altitude below 10,000 feet.*

Mask and helmet need not be worn. Mask will be plugged into an oxygen regulator or a walk-around bottle and kept accessible near person.

WARNING

When the aircraft is pressurized and the pressure altitude is above 25,000 feet, crew members stationed near blowable structures, such as blisters or large plexiglas panels, will keep their seat belts or safety straps fastened, if provided.

3. *Pressure altitude 28,000 to 35,000 feet and cabin altitude below 10,000 feet.*

At least one crew member in each compartment will remain on oxygen.

The mask will be attached to helmet and plugged into regulator. The helmet will be worn but the mask need not be applied to the face.

Pressure altitude above 35,000 feet and cabin altitude below 10,000 feet.

All crew members will have the mask loosely fitted to face; however, the aircraft commander may, at his discretion, authorize certain crew members to remove their masks. Permission will apply to specific instances *only*.

4. *Pressure altitude above 35,000 feet and cabin altitude above 10,000 feet.*

All crew members will have the mask snugly fitted to face with the oxygen supply lever ON.

5. Oxygen mask and helmet will not be stowed in or near blisters or plexiglas panels.

6. The H-2 bail-out bottle will be attached to the parachute harness just above the accessory ring and connected to the oxygen hose adapter at 28,000 feet. The bottle may be attached either to the left or right side of the harness, depending on crew position.

7. Regulator Settings.

D-1 or D-2 REGULATOR

Cabin Altitude	Regulator Setting
0-10,000 feet	Oxygen Supply Lever OFF
10,000 feet and above	Oxygen Supply Lever ON

Note

The diluter lever will be in the NORMAL OXYGEN position at all times. However, in case of an emergency under 30,000 feet, the 100% OXYGEN position will be used.

Crew Interphone Oxygen Checks. The pilot will initiate a full crew interphone check at frequent intervals as stated below. The check will be made from tail to nose as outlined under the interphone and alarm bell check in "Taxiing," Section II. The check is as follows:

1. Oxygen gage pressure reading in pounds.

2. Position of controls.

3. The compartment commanders will check crew members for unusual behavior symptomatic of hypoxia.

4. Frequency of checks will conform to periods of useful consciousness at various altitudes.

   a. Hourly check by compartments when cabin altitude is under 15,000 feet.

   b. At cabin altitudes of 15,000 to 25,000 feet, check will be made every 15 minutes.

   c. At cabin altitudes above 25,000 feet, compartment checks will be made every 5 minutes and individual checks will be made every 15 minutes.

Oxygen System Emergency Operation.

With symptoms of the onset of hypoxia, or if smoke or fuel fumes should enter the cabin, set the diluter lever of the oxygen regulator to the 100% OXYGEN position. In the event of accidental loss of cabin pressure, set the diluter lever of the regulator to 100% OXYGEN and push the emergency toggle lever to the right or left.

> **CAUTION**
>
> When use of 100% OXYGEN or EMERGENCY becomes necessary, the aircraft commander will be informed of this action. Use of 100% OXYGEN or EMERGENCY will reduce oxygen duration of the airplane. After the emergency is over, set the diluter lever to NORMAL OXYGEN and push the emergency toggle lever to the center position.

If the regulator should become inoperative, disconnect the mask from the airplane oxygen system and connect it to a portable oxygen unit. If an adequately filled portable unit is not available, pull the cord of the H-2 emergency oxygen cylinder.

> **WARNING**
>
> When use of the H-2 emergency oxygen cylinder becomes necessary, the aircraft commander will be informed of this action so that he can immediately descend to an altitude at which oxygen is not required.

OXYGEN DISCIPLINE.

Oxygen discipline is extremely important at high altitude because of the very short period of useful consciousness in the event of an oxygen system malfunction, improperly used oxygen equipment, or an explosive decompression. Training in the altitude chamber should be taken very seriously and practiced religiously during all high altitude flights. In fact the aircraft commander must enforce good oxygen discipline. This discipline should not begin in the air, but on the ground during personal equipment inspection. See to it that every crew member has properly fitted equipment, knows how to use his oxygen equipment, and knows how to handle any emergency situation. Lack of oxygen discipline in a crew could destroy it as surely as an anti-aircraft shell.

Rapid Decompression.

Explosive decompression or sudden loss of cabin pressurization results in an equalization of cabin altitude and airplane altitude within a few seconds time. In aircraft hulls with large cabin volumes, this explosive type of decompression occurs only with the sudden and complete blowout of a large blister or panel. Since time is all-important in preventing hypoxia after explosive decompression, crew members will immediately report hull defects which could possibly cause loss of pressure. If decompression occurs without warning, the following will be accomplished.

1. Notice of the emergency will be immediately transmitted over interphone to provide all crew members time to carry out necessary oxygen procedures.

2. Immediately following this notice, the engineer will announce over interphone the pressure altitude and final cabin altitude in each compartment.

The crew members in the damaged compartment will recognize explosive decompression by the following events: dull booming sound with forceful out-rush of air and usually a formation of fog; forceful expiration of breath with mask chattering back and forth on face; passage of gas and belching; rapid popping of ears or plugging of ears; rasping or screeching in interphone.

Crew members in remote areas of hull may not hear or feel anything except a rapid popping and plugging of ears, which of itself alone should be sufficient warning to crewmen that cabin pressure has been lost. Mechanical effects of the explosive decompression result in considerable suction being exerted toward the blown hull area. Therefore crew members at duty stations near structures which might blow out must keep their seat belt or safety straps fastened when the cabin is pressurized. The communication tube should not be used except in cases of emergency at altitudes above 30,000 feet when cabin pressurization is being used.

Section IV
Auxiliary Equipment

T.O. 1B-36D(II)-1

The extent and severity of physical effects on personnel following explosive decompression depend on the following factors:

1. Rapidity of decompression.

2. Final cabin altitude resulting from decompression.

3. Range of altitude differential or pressure gradient through which cabin decompression has occurred.

4. Duration of time spent without oxygen at resultant altitude.

5. Individual physical condition.

The important physical effects of explosive decompression on personnel are hypoxia and decompression sickness such as bends or chokes (altitude dysbarism). Hypoxia is the most immediate, potentially dangerous, and disabling threat to the air crew. The average useful conscious time is indicated in the following table:

AVERAGE USEFUL CONSCIOUS Time

ALTITUDE	
20,000 Feet	15 Minutes
25,000 Feet	3-4 Minutes
30,000 Feet	1 Minute
35,000 Feet	45 Seconds
40,000 Feet	15-20 Seconds
45,000 Feet	10 Seconds
50,000 Feet	10 Seconds

H1-400-A4

When explosive decompression occurs, perform the following steps as rapidly as possible:

1. If mask is not on face, turn the supply switch on and then apply mask to face.

2. If mask is being worn, turn the lever on before tightening the face straps. The regulator operates automatically when the oxygen supply valve lever is turned ON.

3. Check oxygen hose connections and blinker activity at regulator.

4. All crew members will be accounted for over the interphone as soon as possible, particular attention being given those not at their stations at the time of decompression.

5. If the aircraft is above 40,000 feet and all occupants are not provided with automatic or manual pressure demand oxygen equipment, the aircraft commander will rapidly descend to 40,000 feet and, as soon as the operational situation permits, descend to 34,000 feet or below for additional safety.

6. If the aircraft is above 45,000 feet, the aircraft commander will rapidly descend to 45,000 feet and, as soon as the operational situation permits, descend to 43,000 feet or below for additional safety.

7. All crew members will observe other occupants for symptoms of hypoxia, and if any occupant appears to be in difficulty or has lost consciousness, notify the aircraft commander.

Treatment of Hypoxia Victims.

A crewman evidencing hypoxia symptoms will be assisted by the nearest crew member, if the latter can go to the aid of the victim without detaching himself from his own regulator hose. If this is impossible, he will report intended rescue action over the interphone to the aircraft commander who will approve the action or designate another rescuer if it is essential that the reporting crew member remain at his station. The designated rescuer will act as follows:

1. Connect his mask to a walk-around bottle if one is available, or pull his bail-out bottle valve cable if a walk-around bottle is not available.

2. Turn the hypoxic individual's emergency toggle valve to either side and hold his mask in place forcibly until he regains consciousness and appears rational and able to take care of himself. If the victim's oxygen equipment appears not to be functioning properly and other regulator outlets or walk-around bottles are not available, fasten his mask tightly to his face and pull his bail-out bottle valve cable. Since hypoxia victims may struggle violently and aggressively when regaining consciousness, they must be restrained to prevent dislodging their own or rescuer's masks. If using a walk-around bottle, the rescuer will not allow the pressure to drop below 100 psi without refilling; if using a bail-out bottle, he will not remain disconnected from an oxygen regulator for more than five minutes. An individual should not be disconnected from his walk-around bottle more than one half the average useful conscious time.

3. Whether the victim is immediately revived or not, the rescuer will return to his own station at once, reconnect his oxygen regulator, and report to the aircraft commander the status of the emergency.

4. If the victim has not recovered, the rescuer will return to him and continue revival efforts. If there is doubt that he is breathing, artificial respiration will be employed.

5. If informed that the victim has not recovered, the aircraft commander will determine whether the operational situation will permit immediate descent to an ambient pressure altitude of 15,000 feet or below, at which 100 per cent oxygen and artificial respiration will be adequate to revive the victim.

6. Administration of oxygen and, if necessary, artificial respiration will be continued until the victim has recovered or it is positively determined that he is dead.

Use of Pressure Oxygen Breathing Following Cabin Decompression.

The pressure oxygen system is designed primarily for emergency use and will provide adequate oxygen to the crew during descent of the airplane from an altitude of 50,000 feet down to 35,000 feet or below, where normal diluter-demand oxygen can be used from the regulator. Pressure breathing requires a forceful expiration against an oxygen pressure resistance. At the higher pressures the individual not conditioned to and practiced in pressure breathing will become fatigued, but there is no discomfort or injury inflicted on him as the result of pressure breathing during the time of descent after cabin decompression. Likewise, no damage to the lungs will occur as a result of having the mask on the face and breathing normal or 100 per cent oxygen at the time of descent after cabin decompression or at the time explosive decompression occurs.

Bends, chokes, and creeps; decompression sickness; and altitude dysbarism are synonymous terms and indicate a condition of the body in which nitrogen bubbles are released into the tissue spaces and blood stream as a result of the sudden loss of pressure surrounding the body. This physical effect seldom occurs except after prolonged exposure at cabin altitudes in excess of 35- to 40,000 feet, or after explosive decompression through large pressure differentials to resultant cabin altitudes above 40,000 feet.

The condition is relieved upon descent of the airplane to 30,000 feet or below, or upon repressurization of the cabin. When decompression sickness occurs after decompression, it is seldom disabling and has no permanent after-effects on the body. The incidence and severity of decompression sickness at any given altitude can be markedly reduced by preliminary denitrogenization or by wearing a pressure suit.

Denitrogenization Procedure For Prevention of Decompression Sickness.

Tactical considerations may require that the aircraft complete a specific portion of the mission at an altitude of 40,000 feet without descending to a lower altitude, even though complete pressurization is lost. This requires that the crew receive maximum possible protection against potential decompression sickness. To accomplish this protection the following procedure is outlined:

1. One hour prior to reaching the critical point in the flight the aircraft commander will order all crew members to put on oxygen masks, if not already being worn, and to turn regulator to 100% OXYGEN.

2. Cabin pressure will be maintained at or below 10,000 feet for 30 minutes, during which time the crew will be breathing 100 per cent oxygen.

3. Cabin pressure will then be gradually decreased during the next 30 minutes until a cabin altitude of 30,000 feet is reached. At this point cabin altitude is leveled off and maintained there with crew on 100 per cent oxygen through the critical period of the flight.

4. If cabin pressure is completely lost during the critical period, maximum protection against disabling hypoxia symptoms will be afforded crew members by setting the regulator at 100% OXYGEN.

Use of Walk-Around Bottles.

Walk-around bottles will be used under the following conditions:

1. In an unpressurized aircraft when crew members will be absent from their stations:

   a. Over *ten* minutes between 14,000 and 16,000 feet.

   b. Over *five* minutes between 16,000 and 18,000 feet.

   c. Over *two* minutes between 18,000 and 20,000 feet.

2. In communication tubes in pressurized aircraft at 25,000 feet or above.

3. In a pressurized cabin above 30,000 feet, with mask plugged in to bottle if crew member is not close to regular station. Mask will be worn and plugged in above 35,000 feet unless permission to the contrary has been granted, in which case the crew member not on oxygen will be under the constant observation of one who is.

Precautions in Using Walk-Around Bottles.

1. Keep charged to at least 400 psi when not in use.

2. If recharger hose leaks, keep it attached to a walk-around bottle to conserve oxygen.

3. When using a walk-around bottle, check the pressure gage regularly and recharge when gage reads 100 psi.

AUTOPILOT.

The airplane is equipped with a type E-6 autopilot. This electro-mechanical device automatically positions the control surfaces for level flight, coordinated turns, or flight paths based on information provided by other equipment.

Primary control of the system is accomplished from the autopilot control panel (3, figure 1-14) located on the pilots' pedestal. "Second station" turn control operation can be transferred to the radar observer at the discretion of the aircraft commander.

Calibration controls are also provided for the adjustment of autopilot response through the wide variations in gross weight, cg, air speed, and altitude. These calibration controls are located in the observer's compartment.

PRIMARY CONTROLS.

The primary controls of the autopilot are located on the autopilot control panel (figure 4-21). Individual controls on the autopilot control panel are discussed in the following paragraphs.

Autopilot On-Off Switch.

This switch (6, figure 4-21) controls 115-volt alternating current from the right forward power panel. The autopilot is normally ready for operation three minutes after this switch is placed in the ON position.

Elevator, Rudder, and Aileron Trim Knobs.

These knobs (8, 9, and 2, figure 4-21) are used to apply electrical trim to the autopilot while it is engaged. If the autopilot is ON but not engaged, these knobs will normally oscillate in order to maintain a neutral position with respect to the movement of the control surfaces. Each knob has a push-button-type switch located in its center. These push-button switches can be used to disengage the three axes individually. If an axis is disengaged by one of these switches, the autopilot engage switch must be pressed to re-engage the axis.

Autopilot Engage Switch.

A push-button type switch (4, figure 4-21) is provided to engage the autopilot after the green lights on the autopilot control panel begin to flicker. After the autopilot is engaged, the green lamps will burn steadily. In case of a momentary loss of a-c or d-c power, the autopilot will automatically disengage.

Turn Control Knob.

The turn control knob (3, figure 4-21) is used to establish a coordinated automatic turn in the direction of knob rotation. Maximum bank obtainable is 32 degrees.

Cruise-Bomb Knob.

This knob is not used as a functional control.

Automatic Recovery Switch.

The automatic recovery switch should not be used because airplane response is too violent. This control is covered by a plate on some airplanes.

1. AUTOPILOT RELEASE SWITCH
2. AUTOPILOT ON-OFF SWITCH
3. CRUISE-BOMB KNOB
4. TURN CONTROL KNOB
5. INDICATOR LIGHTS
6. ENGAGE SWITCH
7. ELEVATOR TRIM KNOB
8. AILERON TRIM KNOB
9. RUDDER TRIM KNOB

Figure 4-21.

Autopilot Release Switches.

Both control wheels are equipped with an autopilot release switch (1, figure 4-21). Either switch will release all three control axes simultaneously.

TRANSFER CONTROLS.

The following controls are used during remote or "second station" turn control operation by the radar observer.

N-2 Transfer Switch.

This switch (30, figure 1-13), located on the pilots' instrument panel, is provided to enable the radar observer to utilize the turn control feature of the autopilot. The switch has two positions, RADAR BOMB and PILOT. Normally it is left in the PILOT position and the turn control is operated from the autopilot control panel on the pilots' pedestal. When the switch is placed in the RADAR BOMB position, the autopilot turn control is made available to the radar observer as well as the pilots.

E-2 Turn Control Unit.

The E-2 turn control unit (25, figure 4-39) located at the radar observer's station consists of a turn control knob, a two-position mode selector switch, and an indicator light. When the aircraft commander transfers control to the radar observer, the indicator light will glow. If the mode selector is in MANUAL, the radar observer can maneuver the aircraft with his turn control knob. If the mode selector is in AUTOMATIC, the radar observer can maneuver the aircraft with the tracking handle of the K-( ) system.

CALIBRATION CONTROLS.

All calibration controls are located in the observer's compartment. The directional coupler amplifier assembly is located beneath the radar observer's table. Four calibration control knobs are located under the cover plate of this unit as shown in figure 4-23. The remainder of the calibration controls are located on the main chassis (figure 4-22) above the nose wheel well. Access to the control knobs is gained by removing the covers on the face of the units. Three additional knobs are located on top of the auxiliary calibrator. This unit is mounted in the middle of the chassis as viewed from the top.

Sensitivity Knobs.

The sensitivity knobs establish the minimum signal level for which the amplifier will call for correction.

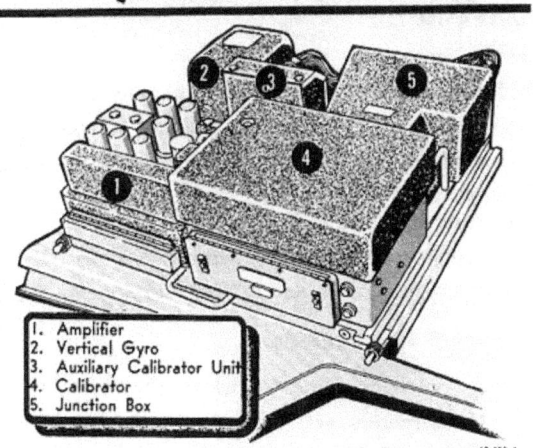

Figure 4-22.

In most cases, input signals come from the reference gyros which detect deviations in the attitude of the aircraft. They may, however, come from the autopilot control panel or from "second station" corrections. Under these conditions the induced signal is "nulled" by the gyros whenever the aircraft reaches the steady state of the maneuver. The sensitivity setting of the amplifier determines the amount the aircraft can deviate from a steady attitude before a corrective maneuver is applied. The range of this adjustment is very small, and it should be carried as high as possible on each axis.

Ratio Knobs.

The settings on these knobs determine the amount of control surface deflection applied for each unit signal that goes into the amplifier or the dynamic response of the aircraft. The range of adjustment on these knobs is great and their settings are quite delicate under most conditions.

Throttling Knobs.

The settings on these knobs determine the speed at which the servos drive and consequently the speed with which the control surfaces move. They are in effect electronic brakes. The higher the setting, the greater the braking action, and the slower the movement of control surfaces.

Automatic Recovery Knobs.

The auto-recovery switch is covered and taken out of the circuit on most of the aircraft. The knobs are still carried at five to maintain bridge balance in the circuit.

E-FS and FS Knobs.

These knobs were used to coordinate formation stick turns. They are still in the circuit. Moving E-FS will change the pitch attitude of the aircraft.

TC Coordination Knob.

This knob is carried at zero. Turns are coordinated with rudder gain in the auxiliary calibrator.

Bomb Coordination Knob.

This knob was used to coordinate turns made from the Norden bombsight. It is still in the circuit but has little or no dynamic effect.

Rate Coordination Knob.

This knob is used to "damp" the action of the rudder. It is the electrical equivalent of a mechanical "dash-

Section IV
Auxiliary Equipment

T.O. 1B-36D(II)-1

1. COMPASS MAXIMUM BANK
2. COMPUTER MAXIMUM BANK
3. PROPORTIONAL RANGE
4. CURVATURE

Figure 4-23. A-11 Directional Coupler Amplifier Assembly

pot." Rudder ratio must be kept high enough to insure flying a good heading. It is a characteristic of most aircraft that rudder ratio must be so high that the aircraft is on the verge of overcorrecting. For this reason the rudder needs "damping."

Up-Elevator Coordination Knob.

This knob is used to control the pitch attitude of the aircraft while it is in a bank.

Rudder Gain Knob.

This knob is used to coordinate all turns. It operates in much the same way as the TC coordination knob does in the unmodified autopilot.

Aileron Roll Rate Knob.

This control acts the same way in the aileron axis as the rate coordination control acts in the rudder axis. It damps the action of the ailerons while the aircraft is rolling in or out of turns. It also helps to keep the ailerons from overcorrecting when in straight and level flight. Its action puts in opposite aileron for any roll.

Rudder Roll Rate Knob.

This control attempts to coordinate the rudder while rolling in and out of turns. While the effect of this control is not too obvious, it aids in smoothing out turns, particularly at higher air speeds.

Compass Maximum Bank Knob.

This control determines the directional stiffness of the system or the amount of corrective bank angle applied per degree of heading error.

Computer Maximum Bank Knob.

This control sets the maximum bank angle the airplane can reach in correcting for a large steering signal from the ground position computer.

Curvature Knob.

The effect of this control is similar to the throttling control on the E-6 amplifier. This knob setting should be carried as high as possible to keep course corrections proportional to the amount of remaining error.

Proportional Range Knob.

This control sets the heading correctional signal required for the airplane to reach the maximum bank angle established by compass maximum bank or computer maximum bank. This could also be considered as the rate of amplifier response to the input signal.

RECOMMENDED CALIBRATION CONTROL SETTINGS.

The control settings shown in figure 4-24 are recommended for satisfactory autopilot performance. All settings, except those which vary with altitude, should remain constant throughout the flight range.

Note

Slight deviations from the settings shown may be necessary for individual airplanes.

OPERATION.

Before Engaging the Autopilot.

1. Attain a safe altitude and manually trim the airplane for straight and level flight. Check with flight instruments.
2. Autopilot on-off switch—OFF.
3. Turn control knob—In detent.
4. Rudder, elevator, and aileron trim knobs—Center.

Engaging the Autopilot.

Note

On airplanes equipped with the type N-1 high latitude compass turn on the compass before turning on the autopilot, so that it can warm up with the autopilot.

RECOMMENDED AUTOPILOT CALIBRATION CONTROL *Settings*

THE SETTINGS ILLUSTRATED ARE FOR 10,000 FT. ALTITUDE

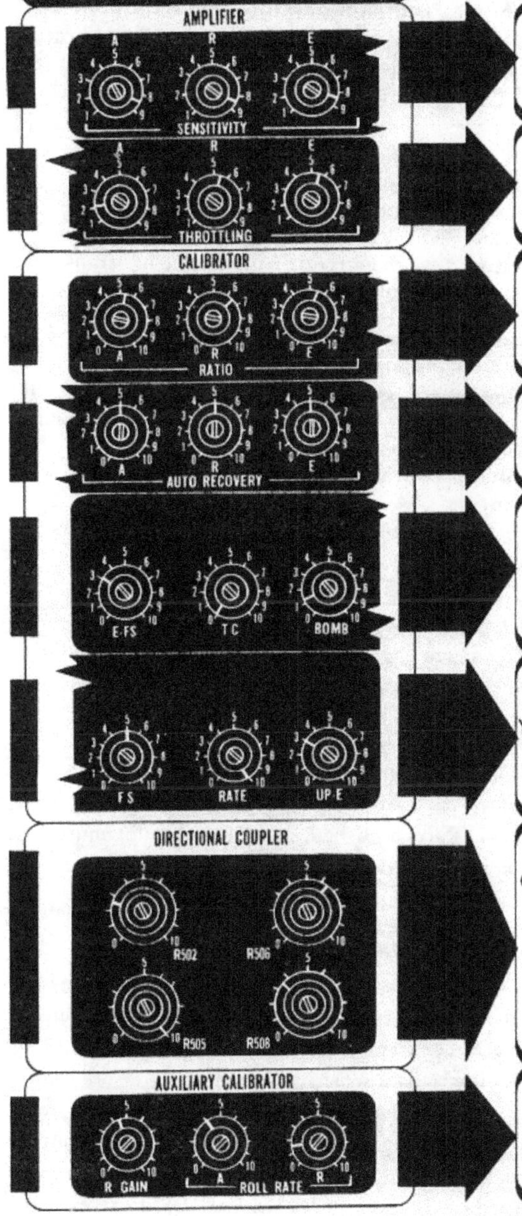

CONTROL	SETTINGS 10,000 FT.	SETTINGS 25,000 FT.	SETTINGS 40,000 FT.
AILERON SENSITIVITY	8 to MAX.	8 to MAX.	8 to MAX.
RUDDER SENSITIVITY	8 to MAX.	8 to MAX.	8 to MAX.
ELEVATOR SENSITIVITY	8 to MAX.	8 to MAX.	8 to MAX.
AILERON THROTTLING	2.0	2.0	2.0
RUDDER THROTTLING	5.5	5.5	5.5
ELEVATOR THROTTLING	5.5	5.5	5.5
AILERON RATIO	5.5	4.0	1.0
RUDDER RATIO	6.5	6.5	6.5
ELEVATOR RATIO	5.5	5.5	5.5
AILERON RECOVERY	5.0	5.0	5.0
RUDDER RECOVERY	5.0	5.0	5.0
ELEVATOR RECOVERY	5.0	5.0	5.0
E. F. S.	3.0	3.0	3.0
TURN COORDINATION	0	0	0
BOMB COORDINATION	1.8	1.8	1.8
F. S. COORDINATION	5.0	5.0	5.0
YAW RATE COORDINATION	10.0	10.0	10.0
UP ELEVATOR COORDINATION	3.0	3.0	3.0
COMPASS MAXIMUM BANK	2.5	2.5	2.5
COMPUTER MAXIMUM BANK	6.5	6.5	6.5
PROPORTIONAL RANGE	3.5	4.0	6.0
CURVATURE	10.0	10.0	10.0
RUDDER GAIN	4.5	3.0	2.0
AILERON ROLL RATE	4.0	4.0	4.0
RUDDER ROLL RATE	1.5	1.5	1.5

61-265-A

Figure 4-24.

1. Place the autopilot on-off switch in the ON position; then wait until the two green indicator lamps begin to flicker before performing step 2 below.

Note

The autopilot will be ready for operation approximately three minutes after it is turned on.

2. Autopilot engage switch—Press firmly.

CAUTION

Do not engage the autopilot while the airplane is turning.

Note

On airplanes equipped with a slaved gyro magnetic compass, clear the annunciator window before engaging the autopilot. Also, do not adjust the PUSH TO SET POINTER knob of the compass while the autopilot is engaged, because it will affect the directional stability of the airplane.

3. After the autopilot is engaged, check the flight instruments. Carefully readjust the autopilot trim knobs on the control panel until the airplane is flying straight and level.

WARNING

Never adjust the manual trim tab on any axis while that axis is engaged.

4. To make coordinated automatic turns, rotate the turn control knob in the desired direction.

Note

If the airplane turns in the opposite direction when the turn control knob is moved out of detent, check manual trim. If it is found to be satisfactory, remove the undesired trim with the autopilot trim knobs.

Disengaging the Autopilot.

1. To temporarily disengage the autopilot, press the release button on either the aircraft commander's or the pilot's control column. This action will release all servo motors simultaneously, but the autopilot will remain on.

2. To disengage the servo motors individually, press the center of the autopilot trim knob for the axis to be disengaged.

3. To stop autopilot operation, place the autopilot on-off switch in the OFF position.

Retrimming.

1. If extensive retrimming of the airplane is required, push the center of the electrical trim knob on the axis to be retrimmed. This will release the servo motor.

2. Trim the surface manually.

3. Re-engage the servo motor by pressing the engage switch.

Operation From Radar Observer's Station.

1. Wait for the indicator light to glow indicating that aircraft commander's transfer switch is in the RADAR BOMB position.

CAUTION

Do not attempt to move mode selector switch to AUTOMATIC until light comes on indicating that the aircraft commander has transferred control.

2. Leave mode selector switch in MANUAL to maneuver aircraft the turn control knob.

3. Move the mode selector switch to AUTOMATIC to maneuver aircraft with the K-( ) tracking handle.

Regaining Control From Radar Observer's Station.

To regain control, the aircraft commander must do one of the following:

1. Move the N-2 transfer switch back to PILOT.
2. Disengage the autopilot.
3. Disengage the aileron axis.
4. Shut the autopilot off.

Note

The N-2 transfer switch will automatically move back to PILOT when either step 2, 3, or 4 is accomplished, and the autopilot must be re-engaged before the N-2 transfer switch can again be placed on RADAR BOMB.

ALTITUDE CONTROL UNIT.

On some airplanes an altitude control unit is provided for use in conjunction with the autopilot in maintaining the aircraft at any desired pressure altitude. The unit is essentially a sensitive barometric pressure sensor that supplies control signals to the autopilot system. When engaged, it provides automatic elevator control for changes in angle of attack resulting from power changes or gross weight variations. The altitude at the time of engagement is the reference altitude. A slip clutch maintains reference altitude even if the control range (approximately ±145 feet) is exceeded. Extreme pressure changes can result in loss of air speed as the unit seeks its reference altitude. The unit is controlled by an On-Off switch (1, figure 4-25) located on the automatic approach and altitude control panel. This panel is mounted on the right side of the pilots' jet control panel. Placing the control switch in the ON position engages the unit.

Note

Before the altitude control unit will enegage, the autopilot elevator axis must be operating (engaged).

The unit can also be used in conjunction with the autopilot to provide altitude control during the localizer phase of the ILAS approach. It allows smooth transition into the glide path phase.

Note

If the altitude control unit is used in conjunction with the automatic approach coupler during the localizer phase of the approach, it will automatically disengage when the approach function of the coupler is placed ON.

AUTOMATIC APPROACH COUPLER UNIT.

Some airplanes are equipped with an automatic approach coupler unit which provides a means of making an automatics ILAS approach. The unit consists of a localizer coupler, a glide path coupler, and two control switches. The coupler unit receives information from the glide path (AN/ARN-5B or AN/ARN-18) and the AN/ARN-14 sets. By modifying this information, the coupler provides signals to the autopilot to furnish directional guidance along the runway heading and vertical guidance down the correct descent angle to the runway.

Controls.

The coupler unit is controlled by two spring-loaded on-off switches which are located on the automatic approach and altitude control panel. This panel is mounted on the right side of the pilots' jet control panel. The switches are spring-loaded in the ON position. When the instrument approach equipment is on and the autopilot is engaged, placing a function switch in the ON position engages its function and the switch is locked in the ON position by a solenoid. Disengaging the autopilot or turning the instrument approach equipment off will disengage the coupler unit and the switch (or switches) will automatically return to OFF.

Localizer Switch. When this switch (2, figure 4-25) is locked in the ON position, the localizer function is engaged. This function supplies signals to the autopilot to hold the aircraft on the beam heading during the localizer and glide slope portions of the landing.

Approach Switch. When this switch (3, figure 4-25) is locked in the ON position, the approach function of the coupler is engaged. This function provides elevation control to center the aircraft on the glide slope beam to give the correct descent angle required to land on the runway.

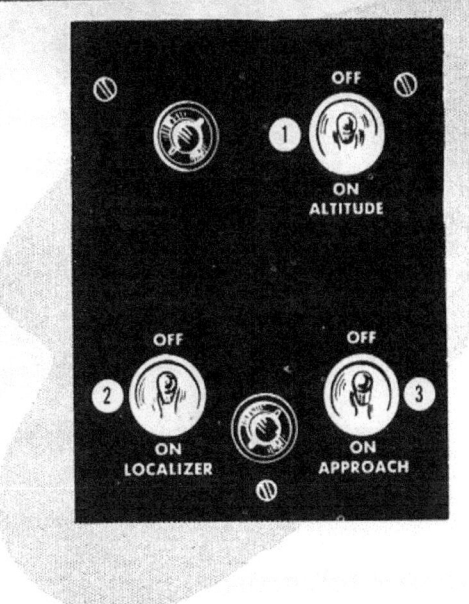

1. Altitude Control Switch
2. Localizer Switch
3. Approach Switch

Figure 4-25.

Operation.

1. Turn the instrument approach equipment on and engage all three axes of the autopilot.

2. When the localizer beam is intersected and the vertical needle of the course indicator leaves its full scale stop, place the localizer switch in the ON position.

Note

The altitude control unit can be used during this phase of the approach.

3. When the center of the glide slope beam is intersected, place the approach switch in the ON position.

4. Maintain normal approach speeds and normal rate of descent.

5. When it is desired to control the aircraft manually, disengage the autopilot.

Note

For automatic approach procedure refer to figure 9-4.

Section IV
Auxiliary Equipment

T.O. 1B-36D(II)-1

Figure 4-26. (Sheet 1)

NAVIGATION EQUIPMENT.

MAGNETIC COMPASS.

A magnetic compass is located directly above the pilots' instrument panel.

SLAVED GYRO MAGNETIC COMPASS SYSTEM (Airplanes not in Group 2).

A J-1 slaved gyro magnetic compass system is incorporated in the airplane. It provides a gyro-stabilized compass which indicates the airplane's magnetic heading without northerly turning error. The gyro is free from drift and tilt, and therefore requires no resetting. The system consists of a master directional indicator (8, figure 1-13) located on the pilot's instrument panel, a flux valve located in the left wing tip, and a repeater indicator located on the navigator's instrument panel. When the compass is slaved (electrically connected) to the flux valve the compass is a directional gyro with a magnetic sense. Operating in this condition, the flux valve senses its position with respect to the earth's magnetic meridian.

Any difference between the indicated heading of the compass and the magnetic heading sensed by the flux valve will be detected by a voltage which will apply a torque to the gyro to align it with the magnetic heading. In the unslaved condition, the compass acts as a directional gyro. A compass slaving switch is located on the navigator's instrument panel and permits the navigator to deslave the compass when the flux valve sends erroneous signals to the gyro. This condition will occur in certain sections of the polar regions where a magnetic compass becomes unreliable.

The slaved gyro magnetic system is connected to the autopilot system and furnishes it with the directional reference signals required to keep the airplane on course during normal autopilot operation.

Slaved Gyro Magnetic Compass Operation.

The slaved gyro magnetic compass system is connected directly to 200-volt alternating current. Therefore, it is on at all times when the airplane power is on. A PUSH TO SET POINTER knob on the master directional indicator is used to quickly synchronize the compass indicator to the heading detected by the flux valve before take-off, or when resetting the indicator after exceeding the operating limits of the gyro.

Note

The gyro is free to operate within 60 degrees of climb or dive (from level flight) and 60 degrees right or left bank.

An annunciator window on the upper right of the master indicator shows whether the gyro is aligned with the heading detected by the flux valve. When

Section IV
Auxiliary Equipment

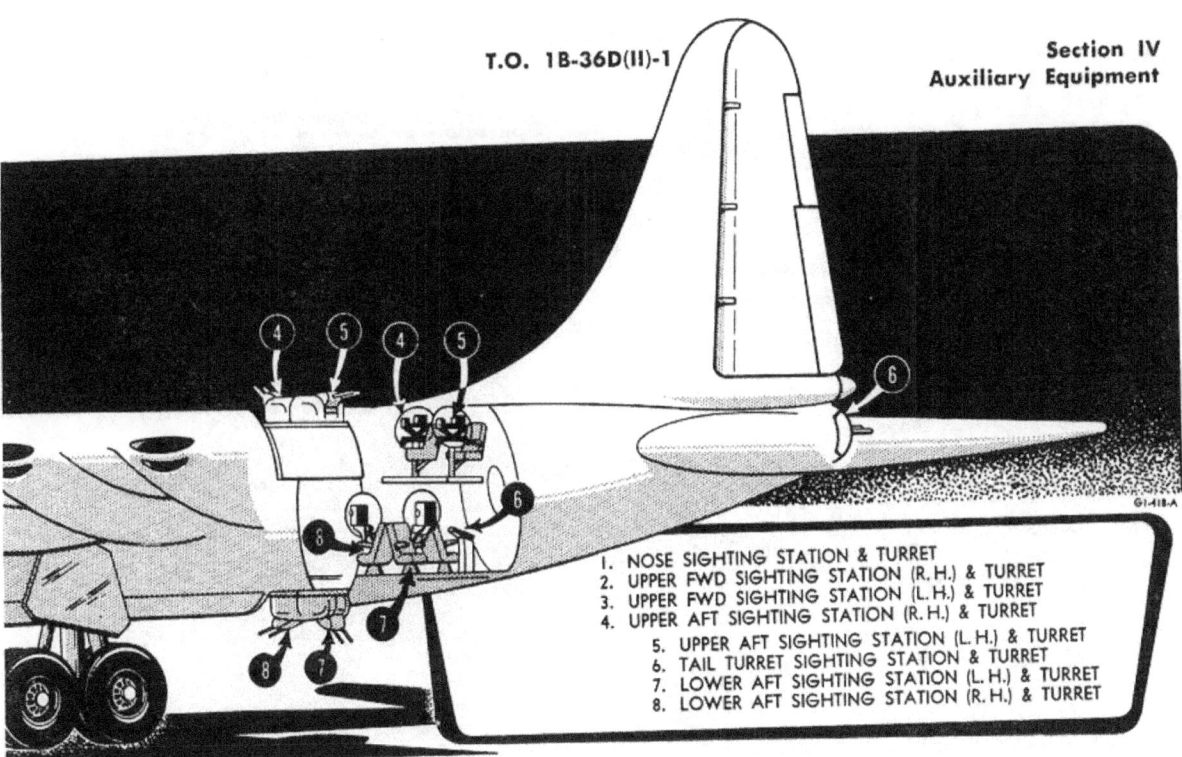

1. NOSE SIGHTING STATION & TURRET
2. UPPER FWD SIGHTING STATION (R.H.) & TURRET
3. UPPER FWD SIGHTING STATION (L.H.) & TURRET
4. UPPER AFT SIGHTING STATION (R.H.) & TURRET
5. UPPER AFT SIGHTING STATION (L.H.) & TURRET
6. TAIL TURRET SIGHTING STATION & TURRET
7. LOWER AFT SIGHTING STATION (L.H.) & TURRET
8. LOWER AFT SIGHTING STATION (R.H.) & TURRET

Figure 4-26. (Sheet 2)

they are aligned, the window is clear of any image. If they are not aligned, the discrepancy is evidenced by the appearance of a dot or cross in the window, depending on the direction of misalignment. During flight it is normal for the dot and cross to appear alternately in the window. If either the dot or cross appear steadily in straight flight (except for a minute or two following a turn) the system is not operating properly.

Note

If it is necessary to adjust the master indicator pointer during flight, make certain that the automatic pilot is off and that the airplane is in a straight and level attitude.

N-1 HIGH LATITUDE COMPASS (Group 2 Airplanes).

The N-1 high latitude compass system is designed to alleviate the problem of polar navigation and to provide a source of directional reference with the degree of accuracy required by a dependent navigational system. It provides two methods of operation: (1) When flying through the high latitudes where the magnetic compass becomes unreliable, the N-1 system operates as a directional gyro that is constantly being corrected for the effects of the earth's rotation by a latitude correction device. (2) On flights in the lower latitudes, the system serves as a gyro-stabilized magnetic compass.

The high latitude compass system includes a master indicator (14, figure 4-13) at the navigator's station, a repeater indicator on the pilots' instrument panel, and a flux valve located in the left wing tip. In addition, the system actuates the rotating compass cards on the radio magnetic indicators at the pilots' and navigator's stations. (Refer to "Radio Receiver AN/ARN-14" of this section.)

When operating as a magnetic compass, the system is "slaved" (electrically connected) to the flux valve. The flux valve senses its position with respect to the earth's magnetic meridian and transmits a heading signal to the master indicator. A synchronizer knob on the master indicator is used to synchronize the indicator quickly with the flux valve when the system is initially put into operation. An annunciator pointer on the master indicator shows in which direction the SYNCHRONIZER knob must be turned to align the indicator with the flux valve. Movement within the small window on the master indicator shows that a misalignment is being corrected. When this movement ceases, the indicator and flux valve are synchronized.

The N-1 high latitude compass system receives electrical power through two on-off switches (19, figure 4-13) which are ganged together on the navigator's instrument panel.

Section IV
Auxiliary Equipment

Operation as a Slaved Magnetic Compass.

1. Turn the N-1 high latitude compass power switch to the ON position.

Note

From 10 to 15 minutes are required for the gyro to reach a synchronous speed and erect.

2. Turn the LATITUDE CORRECTION knob on the master indicator counterclockwise as far as possible.

Note

The small latitude pointer will move to the OFF position, rendering the latitude correction device inoperative and slaving the compass to the flux valve.

Note

During flight, the compass will be temporarily deslaved by a slaving control gyro when the airplane is turning at a rate in excess of approximately 25 degrees per minute.

3. Center the annunciator pointer by using the SYNCHRONIZER knob. Lack of movement in the annunciator window indicates that the flux valve and indicator are synchronized.

CAUTION

Be sure to turn the SYNCHRONIZER knob to the left or right as indicated by the annunciator pointer, since it is possible to center the pointer with the compass 180 degrees off the magnetic heading. A check with the pilots' stand-by compass will verify the accuracy of the adjustment.

The transition to high latitude operation can be made by turning the LATITUDE CORRECTION knob until the latitude pointer indicates the actual latitude. This action deslaves the flux valve and starts the operation of the high latitude drift correction device. Continual movement in the annunciator window indicates that latitude correction is being made. Except for a random wander of 1 degree or less per hour, the indicator will continue to indicate the correct magnetic heading.

CAUTION

The basic magnetic reference will be lost if the synchronizer knob is moved.

Operation as a Directional Gyro.

1. Compass Power Switch—ON.

2. Latitude Correction Knob—Clockwise until pointer indicates latitude of aircraft position.

3. As the airplane changes latitude in flight, reset the latitude pointer to the new latitude.

Note

Setting of the mid-latitude every two degrees is sufficient for proper operation.

4. Engage and rotate the synchronizer knob to the gyro heading reference desired.

Note

Check rotation of the small white dot. The indicator rotates clockwise in northern latitudes and counterclockwise in southern latitudes.

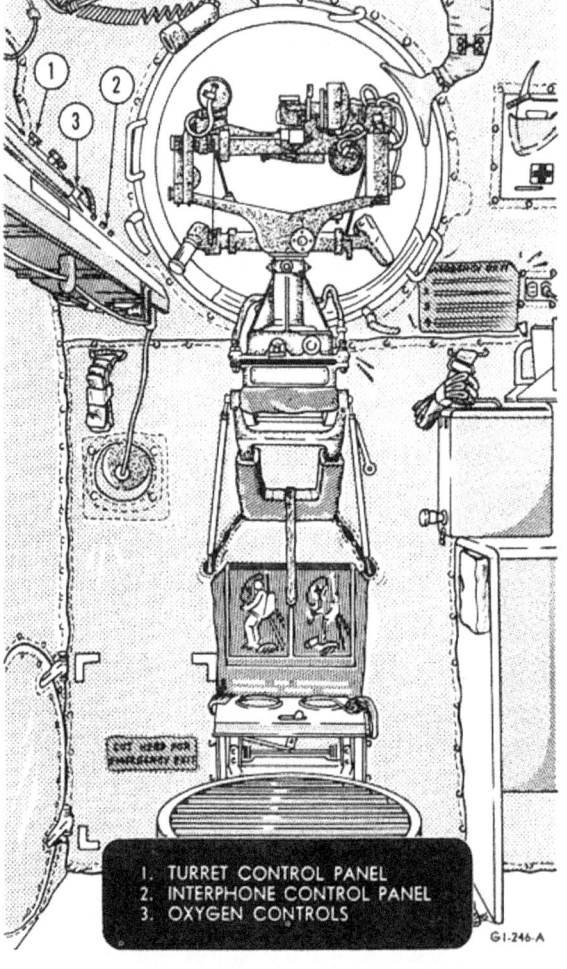

Figure 4-27. Typical Forward Sighting Station

CELESTIAL NAVIGATION PROVISIONS.

Sextant.

Stowage provisions for a periscopic sextant and support have been installed on the left side of the airplane on the floor just aft of the forward wall of the radio operator's compartment. Provisions have been made for the installation of the sextant at the navigator's sighting station.

GUNNERY EQUIPMENT.

The airplane is equipped with eight remote-controlled gun turrets, six of which are retractable. Of the six retractable turrets, two are located on the forward top side of the fuselage, two are on the aft top side, and two are on the aft bottom side. The other two turrets are located at the nose and tail and are nonretractable. Each turret is equipped with two 20-mm cannons. The nose turret has provisions for 400 rounds of ammunition per cannon; the other turrets have provisions for 600 rounds per cannon. The turrets, except the one for the tail, are controlled from corresponding remote sighting stations; the tail turret is operated through radar controls located in the aft cabin. (See figure 4-26.) There is no transfer of turret control between sighting stations. Each sighting station is furnished with a remote gun sight, a turret control panel, and oxygen and interphone controls. The nose sighting station is equipped with a hemisphere-type sight. The forward and upper aft sighting stations are provide with yoke-type gun sights, and the lower aft sighting stations are furnished with pedestal-type sights. The turret control panels are identical for the various stations except the ones for the nose and tail turrets. (See figures 4-30, 33, and 34.)

Note

Gun cameras are provided on all yoke-type gun sights and on B-( ) pedestal-type sights.

NORMAL CONTROLS.

Turret Safety Switch.

This two-position switch is located on each turret junction box. When it is ON, the 28-volt d-c circuit from the thyratron controller to the turret power switch is closed.

Turret Power Switch.

This two-position d-c switch-type circuit breaker on the turret control panel is in series with a turret safety switch in the system junction box; these switches control all d-c power to the turret system.

Turret System Selector Switch.

This four-position switch on the gunners' control panel controls the turret and radar circuits. On the nose turret control panel the switch positions are OFF, WARM UP, and OPERATION. The four positions on the tail turret control panel are OFF, WARM UP, STANDBY, and RADAR. All other turret panels are marked OFF, WARM UP, STANDBY, DOOR OPEN, and OPERATION. All circuits are de-energized when the switch is in the OFF position.

In the WARM UP position the switch supplies 120-volt single-phase a-c power to the gun and feeder heaters, the computer and resolver input unit heaters, and the heaters in the azimuth and elevation gyros.

In the STANDBY position the switch supplies power to the computer, antenna selsyns, the gyro drive selsyns, the thyratron controller, the control indicator, the frequency converter, and stow transformer, turret drive motor fields, and gyros.

In the DOOR OPEN position power is supplied to the turret door motor, thereby opening the turret doors.

Placing the switch in the OPERATION position extends the turret and, when the turret is fully extended, supplies d-c control voltage to the turret control circuits.

The RADAR position supplies d-c power to the tail turret radar control indicator and the antenna drive motors.

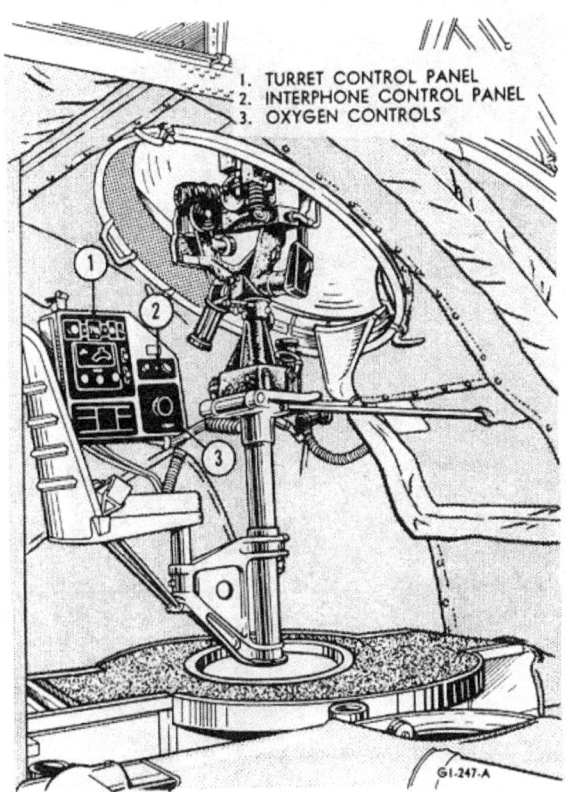

1. TURRET CONTROL PANEL
2. INTERPHONE CONTROL PANEL
3. OXYGEN CONTROLS

Figure 4-28. Typical Upper Aft Sighting Station

Section IV
Auxiliary Equipment

T.O. 1B-36D(II)-1

1. TURRET CONTROL PANEL
2. INTERPHONE CONTROL PANEL
3. OXYGEN CONTROLS

Figure 4-29. Left Lower Aft Sighting Station

A-C and D-C Power (Safe-Fire) Switches.

These switches, ganged together on the control panel, have positions marked SAFE and FIRE. When the A-C POWER switch (the WARM UP switch on some airplanes) is placed in the FIRE position, it allows a-c power to be supplied to the free fire control box circuits. When the D-C POWER switch is placed in the FIRE position, it turns on the gun firing circuit. Placing this switch in SAFE turns off the gun firing circuit.

Note

The gang bar simultaneously places both switches in the SAFE position only.

Gun Camera Switch.

This switch is located on the sighting mechanism, except for the radar-controlled tail turret, where the switch is located on the tail turret control panel. When it is placed in the ON position, the camera operates automatically when the guns are fired.

Altitude-Airspeed Handset Unit.

This unit is located on the control panel. It incorporates three knobs and three dials to be used in setting up data for the computer. The dials consist of true air speed in mph, temperature in degrees centigrade, and altitude in thousands of feet. Proper setting of knobs and dials will furnish the computer with true air speed of the aircraft and air density to aid in properly computing lead prediction and ballistics corrections during turret operation.

Gun Charger Control Switch (Group 2 Airplanes).

A guarded two-position switch, marked HOLD BACK and RELEASE, is located on the lower right corner of the gunner's control panel. When the switch is in the HOLD BACK position, the bolts of both guns of the turret are held back, leaving the breech empty. In the event of a gun jam, placing the switch to HOLD BACK may clear the jam. Placing the switch in RELEASE position allows normal operation of the guns.

Figure 4-30.

Section IV
Auxiliary Equipment

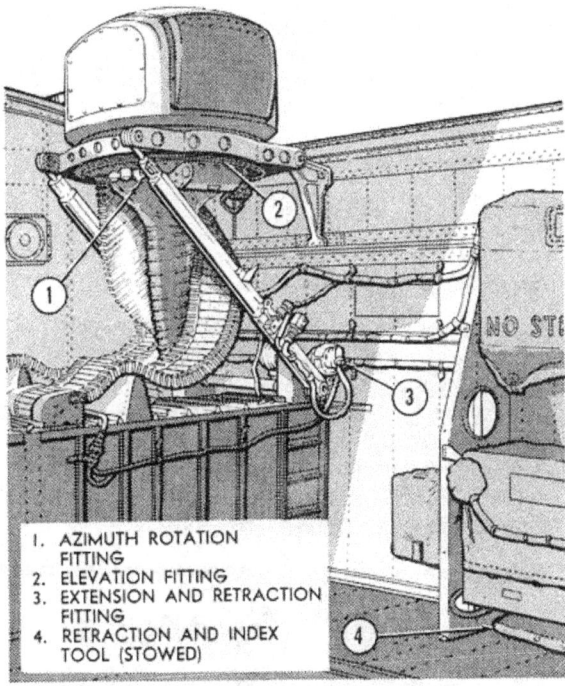

1. AZIMUTH ROTATION FITTING
2. ELEVATION FITTING
3. EXTENSION AND RETRACTION FITTING
4. RETRACTION AND INDEX TOOL (STOWED)

Figure 4-31. Typical Turret

Placing the switch in RELEASE position allows for normal operation of the guns.

Note

For rapid cooling of the guns, place the switch in the HOLD BACK position and turn the turret into the air stream.

Action Switch.
An action switch is located on each sighting mechanism. This switch is located on the left hand control of the hemisphere and the pedestal type sights; it is located on the right hand control of the yoke type sights. The action switch for the tail turret is located on the antenna hand control. Actuating this switch controls the movement of the turret to follow the antenna in manually tracking a target. The nose turret will follow the hemisphere sight reticle when its action switch is depressed. When the switch is released, the turret will automatically return to the position for retracting or stowing.

Computer Switch.
The computer switch is a two-position switch with positions marked IN and OUT. When this switch, located on the gunner's control panel, is in the IN position, ballistics, parallax, and lead prediction are automatically computed and fed into the turret control circuit for corrected gun fire.

Attack Factor Switch.
This two-position switch, marked STRAIGHT LINE and PURSUIT, is located on the gun sight at all sighting stations except the tail gunner's. The tail gunner's attack factor switch is located on the turret control panel. The position in which this switch is placed is determined by the type of approach being made by an attacking aircraft. The STRAIGHT LINE position provides signals to the computer to correct for a straight-line approach. The PURSUIT position provides additional signals to the computer to correct for a pursuit-curve approach.

Heater Power Fuse.
This fuse is located on the control panel. In addition a spare fuse holder is located on the opposite side of the control panel. Insertion or removal of this fuse controls heater power to the gun and feeder heaters when required to do so.

INDICATORS.
Turret-Extended Lamp.
This lamp will glow when the turret is extended and ready for operation.

Turret Door Closed Lamp.
This lamp will glow continuously when the turret is retracted and the doors are closed, provided the uni-switch is not in the OFF or WARM UP position.

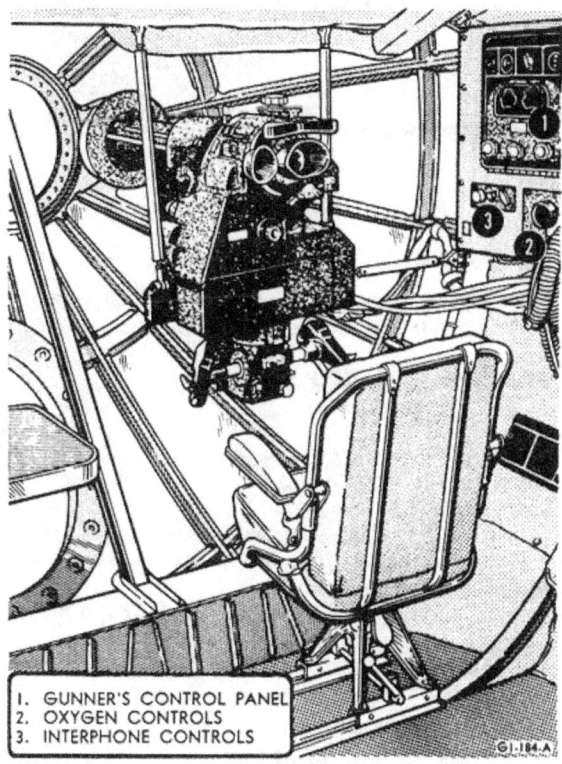

1. GUNNER'S CONTROL PANEL
2. OXYGEN CONTROLS
3. INTERPHONE CONTROLS

Figure 4-32. Nose Sighting Station

Section IV
Auxiliary Equipment

T.O. 1B-36D(II)-1

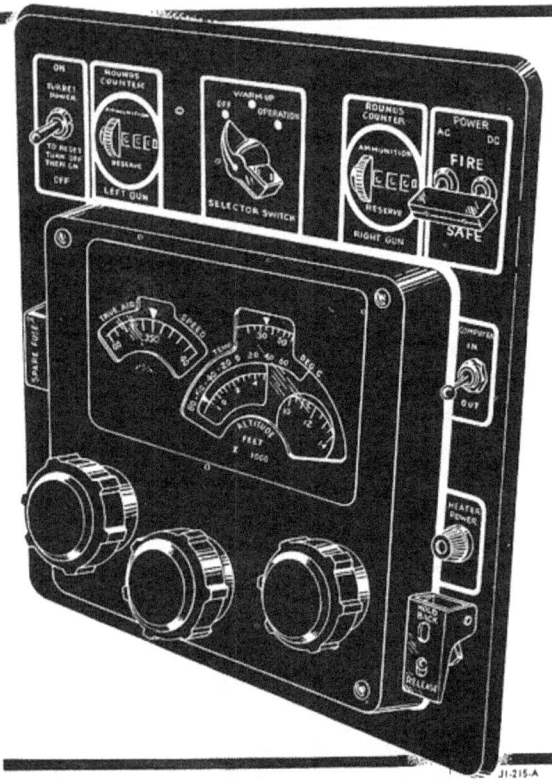

Figure 4-33.

Ammunition Counter Dials.

Two dials on each turret control panel will indicate reserve ammunition for each group in that turret.

EMERGENCY CONTROLS.

Hand Crank.

In case of an emergency the turret can be extended or retracted manually, provided the turret doors are open, by use of a hand crank stowed in the proximity of each turret. The rotor shaft of the turret extend-and-retract motors has a fitting for the crank. The turrets can also be moved in azimuth or elevation manually by applying the hand crank at the fittings provided on the azimuth and elevation drive assemblies. (See figure 4-31.)

RADAR PRESSURIZATION.

A 115-volt, a-c, motor-driven pressure pump located under the upper right sighting platform in the aft cabin provides pressurized air for the radio frequency unit, the modulating unit, and the radio frequency line (wave guide) of the gun laying radar. The system is controlled by a pressure pump switch located at the tail gunner's station. Operation of the system is identical to that of the AN/APQ-31 radar set.

GUNNERY OPERATION.

For operational procedures refer to "Gunnery Amplified Check List," Section VIII.

BOMBING EQUIPMENT.

The airplane incorporates four bomb bays designed to carry varied bomb loads and various sized bombs. Provisions are made for carrying a fuel tank in bomb bay No. 3. The double-folding, gate-action bomb bay doors are hydraulically operated. (See figure 4-37.) Thirty-six removable bomb racks of 15 different types are furnished with each airplane, allowing a number of bomb loading conditions. Design of the bombing

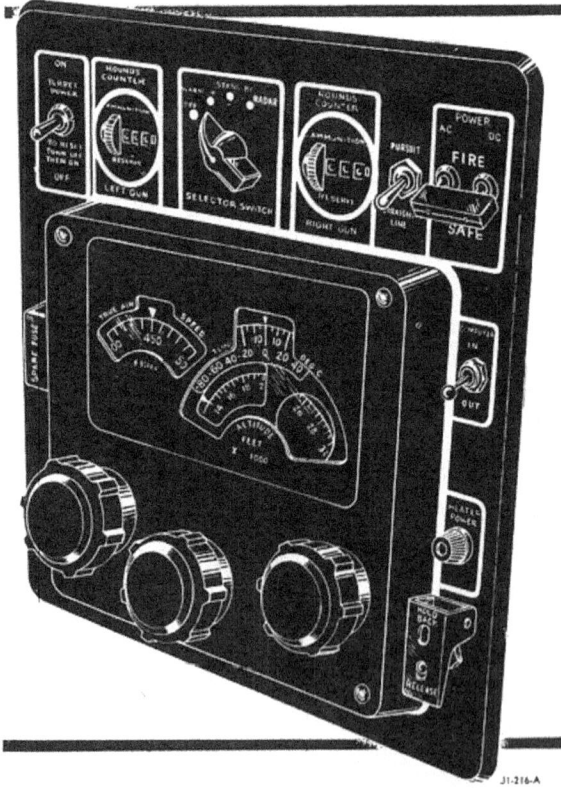

Figure 4-34.

Section IV
Auxiliary Equipment

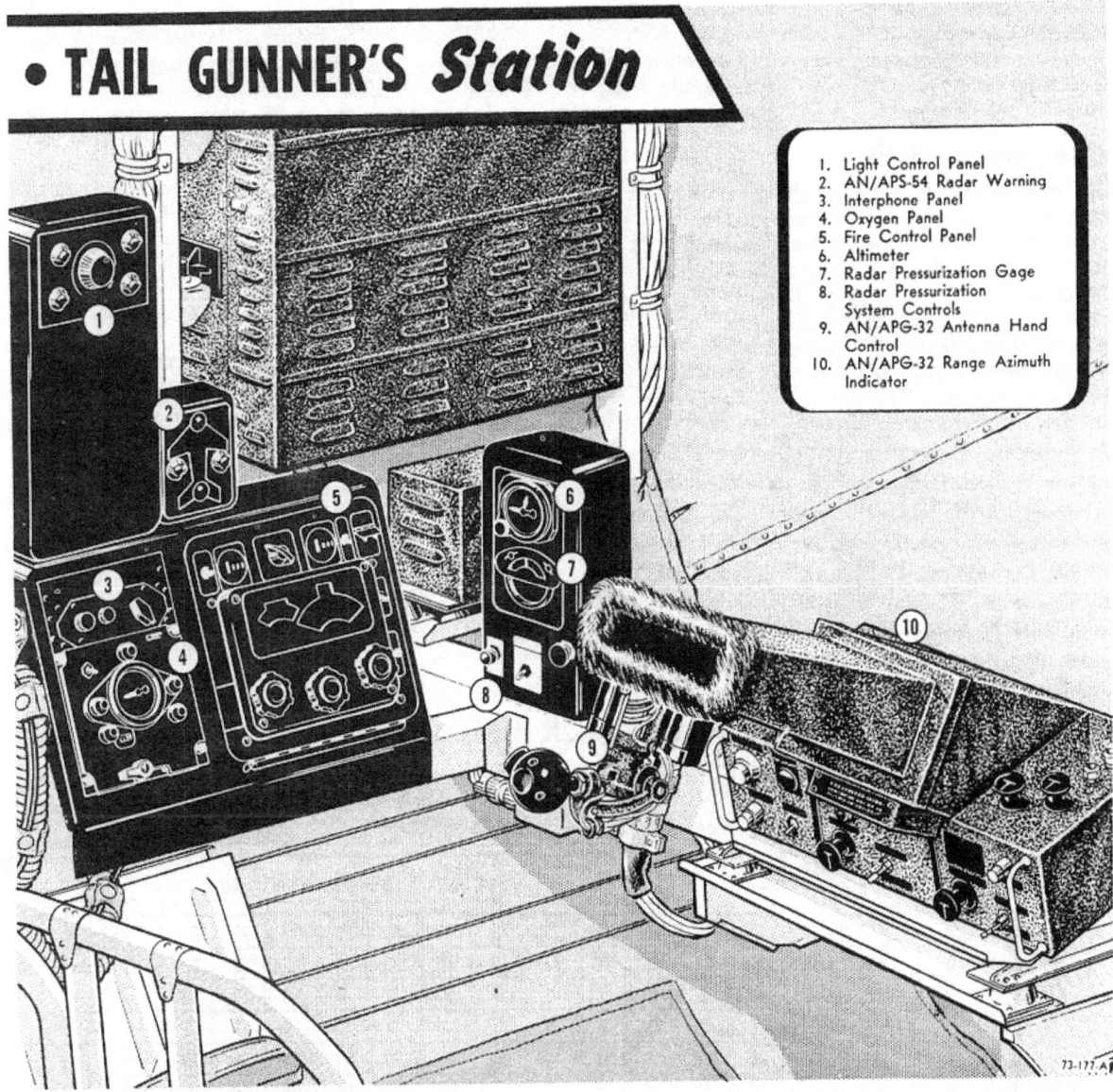

TAIL GUNNER'S Station

1. Light Control Panel
2. AN/APS-54 Radar Warning
3. Interphone Panel
4. Oxygen Panel
5. Fire Control Panel
6. Altimeter
7. Radar Pressurization Gage
8. Radar Pressurization System Controls
9. AN/APG-32 Antenna Hand Control
10. AN/APG-32 Range Azimuth Indicator

Figure 4-35.

equipment is based on 500-, 1000-, 2000-, 4000-, 12,000-, and 22,000-pound bombs. However, 100-, 115-, 125-, 220-, 250-, 325-, and 350-pound bombs can be carried at the 500-pound stations. The forward section, comprising bomb bays No. 1 and No. 2, and the aft section, comprising bomb bays No. 3 and No. 4, are fitted for carrying the various 12,000-, 22,000-, and 43,000-pound bomb loads. The all-electric bomb release system, based on the type A-5 and S-4 bomb rack releases with controls at the radar observer's station (figure 4-42), consists of five individual circuits: a 28-volt d-c nose fuse arming circuit, a 115-volt a-c bomb indicator lamp circuit, a 28-volt d-c circuit for normal release with tail fuse automatically armed, a 28-volt d-c circuit for salvo release with tail fuse automatically safe, and a 28-volt d-c bomb bay door opening circuit. A K-( ) system, consisting of a vertical periscopic bomb sight and the AN/APQ-31 radar-computer equipment, is installed in the airplane. Most of the K-( ) bombing equipment is located in pressurized compartments to facilitate emergency maintenance in flight by the observer. On group 2 airplanes seven inspection windows are provided in the communication tube for checking to see if any bombs have

BOMB RELEASE SEQUENCE.

The tables in figure 4-36 give the general release sequences for dropping bombs from all four bays with all releases installed and cocked. Beginning at the top of the first column, as shown, the sequence passes from rack to rack, firing the lowest release in each rack. When the first layer has been fired in this manner, the rack sequence is repeated again, firing the second release in each rack and so on until all releases have been operated. The sequence is always from rack to rack; two releases on the same rack are never fired in succession, and a rack is not by-passed in the sequence until all releases on that rack have been fired. Although all the releases installed in the airplane are not cocked simultaneously in any normal loading condition, the sequence is given in this manner to cover all conditions. For any particular loading configuration, only the releases to be used will be cocked. In using the tables, whenever an uncocked release is encountered, pass on to the next release in that rack.

hung or jammed in the bomb bay during a bomb drop. An aerial camera is provided in the airplane which can be used for bomb spotting. For additional information regarding the camera, refer to "Photographic Equipment" of this section.

If any of the four bays are not used, the racks in the unused bays will be by-passed in the sequence. For a mixed load, the sequence can be determined by combining information from the two tables.

As an example in using the tables, suppose it is desired to drop fifty-six 500-pound bombs from bays No. 2 and 3 only. In this case stations 2, 4, 8, and 10 in the LH racks and stations 14, 16, 20, and 22 in the RH racks would not be cocked, and the bomb group selector switch for bays No. 1 and 4 would be left open. Then the sequence for the first four layers would be as follows: Bay 2 rt aft 13, 2 lt aft 1, 3 rt fwd 13, 3 lt fwd 1, 2 rt fwd 13, 2 lt fwd 1, 3 rt aft 13, 3 lt aft 1, (end of first layer); 2 center aft 25, 2 lt aft 3, 3 center fwd 25, 3 lt fwd 3, 2 rt fwd 15, 2 lt fwd 3, 3 rt aft 15, 3 lt aft 3, (end of second layer); 2 center aft 26, 2 lt aft 5, 3 center fwd 26, 3 lt fwd 5, 2 rt fwd 17, 2 lt fwd 5, 3 rt aft 17, 3 lt aft 5, (end of third layer); 2 rt aft 15, 3 rt fwd 15, 2 rt fwd 18, 2 lt fwd 6, 3 rt aft 18, 3 lt aft 6, (end of fourth layer). The remainder of the sequence continues in like manner.

Large Bomb Sequence.

With four 12,000-pound bombs loaded, the sequence is forward, aft, forward, aft. For three 22,000-pound bombs, the sequence is forward, aft, aft.

500 AND 1000 POUND BOMB RACK INSTALLATION

BAY	LOC. OF RACK IN BAY	RELEASE STATION NUMBERS													
4	RT. AFT	13	14	15	16	17	18	19	20	21	22	*28	23	*29	24	*30
1	RT. FWD.	13	14	15	16	17	18	19	20	21	22	*28	23	*29	24	*30
4	LT. AFT.	1	2	3	4	5	6	7	8	9	10	11	12			
1	LT. FWD.	1	2	3	4	5	6	7	8	9	10	11	12			
4	RT. FWD.	13	14	15	16	17	18	19	20	21	22	*28	23	*29	24	*30
1	RT. AFT	13	14	15	16	17	18	19	20	21	22	*28	23	*29	24	*30
4	LT. FWD.	1	2	3	4	5	6	7	8	9	10	11	12			
1	LT. AFT	1	2	3	4	5	6	7	8	9	10	11	12			
2	RT. AFT	13	14	*25	*26	15	16	17	*27							
2	LT. AFT	1	2	3	4	5										
3	RT. FWD.	13	14	*25	*26	15	16	17	*27							
3	LT. FWD.	1	2	3	4	5										
2	RT. FWD.	13	14	15	16	17	18	19	20	21	22	*28	23	*29	24	*30
2	LT. FWD.	1	2	3	4	5	6	7	8	9	10	11	12			
3	RT. AFT	13	14	15	16	17	18	19	20	21	22	*28	23	*29	24	*30
3	LT. AFT	1	2	3	4	5	6	7	8	9	10	11	12			END

*RELEASE IN ADJACENT CENTER RACK

Figure 4-36. (Sheet 1) Bomb Sequence Tables

NORMAL CONTROLS.

Master Power Switch.

The master power switch marked ON and OFF, controls the electric power to the nose fuse switch, bomb release switch, and bomb bay door switch.

Bomb Release Selector Switch.

This switch has three positions—K-1, RADIO, and OFF; but the RADIO position is inoperative. When the switch is in the K-1 position, the K-( ) system is effective for bomb release.

Bomb Bay Door Switch.

A spring-loaded switch, marked OPEN and CLOSE and located on the bombing control panel, is provided to control the bomb bay doors. The doors are operated by holding the switch in the desired position until the corresponding indicator lamps light. To prevent damage by buffeting when the bomb bay doors are open, the aft turret doors open and close in conjunction with the bomb bay doors. A bomb bay door switch (32, figure 1-15) is also provided in the pilot's instrument panel.

> **CAUTION**
>
> The turret door interlocking switch, located on bulkhead 8.0 d-c power panel, must be ON during flight for simultaneous operation of the aft turret doors and the bomb bay doors.

Bomb Bay Selector Switches.

Three on-off switches, one each for bomb bays No. 2 and 3 and a single switch for bomb bays No. 1 and 4, are provided to set up the release circuit to the bomb racks when a normal bomb load is being carried. When large bombs are being carried, the No. 2 switch is used for the forward section, which includes bomb bays No. 1 and 2; and the No. 3 switch is used for the aft section, which includes bomb bays No. 3 and 4.

Nose Fuse Switch.

The switch, marked SAFE and ARM is provided for the arming of the nose fuses. All bombs can be armed simultaneously with this switch. When the switch is in the SAFE position during normal release, only the tail fuses will be armed. During salvo the tail fuse will be automatically safe and the nose fuse will either be armed or safe, depending on the position in which the nose fuse switch is placed.

Bomb Station Indicator Lights Switch.

When this switch is placed ON, each indicator light will burn as long as its bomb rack release unit is cocked.

Bomb Station Indicator Light Test Switch.

This switch is provided to test all bomb station indicator lights.

Bomb Interval Control Panel.

A type B-3A intervalometer (13, figure 4-39) is located adjacent to the bombing control panel.

Bomb Release Switch.

A type D-2 switch is provided for releasing the bombs. The switch, stowed above the radar observer's table, is equipped with a long cord so that it can be removed and held in the hand for operational purposes. The bombs are released when the switch is depressed.

Bomb Bay Door Safety Switch.

A two-position, on-off, safety switch is provided at the radar observer's station to prevent injury to personnel by the inadvertent closing of the bomb bay doors during ground checking of the K-( ) system. The

2000 AND 4000 POUND BOMB RACK INSTALLATION

BAY	LOC. OF RACK IN BAY	RELEASE STATION NUMBERS					
4	RIGHT	35	36	37	38	39	40
1	RIGHT	35	36	37	38	39	40
4	LEFT	31	32	33	34		
1	LEFT	31	32	33	34		
2	RIGHT	35	36	37	38	39	40
2	LEFT	31	32	33	34		
3	RIGHT	35	36	37	38	39	40
3	LEFT	31	32	33	34		END

Figure 4-36. (Sheet 2) Bomb Sequence Tables

Section IV
Auxiliary Equipment

T.O. 1B-36D(II)-1

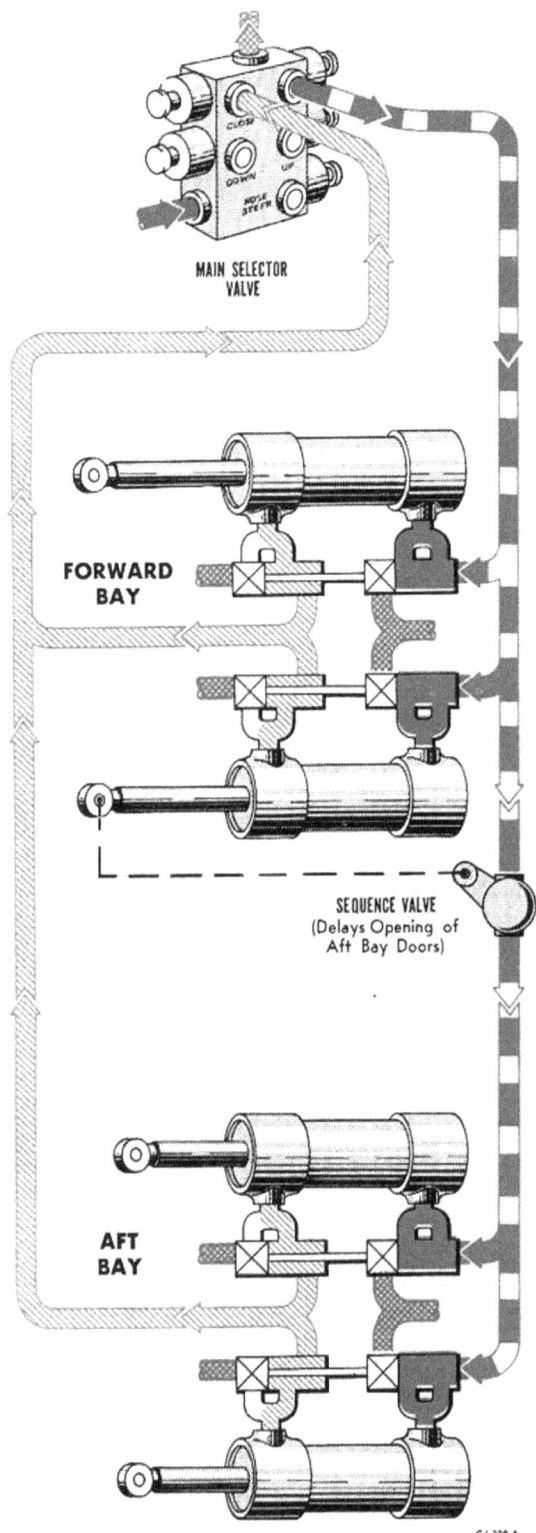

Figure 4-37.

guarded safety position is marked OFF. When the switch is in this position, the K-( ) bombing system will not operate the bomb bay doors. When the switch is ON, operation of the bomb bay doors is automatically controlled by the K-( ) system.

Note

On some airplanes the guarded safety position of the switch is marked DOORS SAFE and the position which permits operation of the bomb doors by the K-( ) system is marked DOORS OPERABLE. On these airplanes the safety switch controls inadvertent opening as well as closing of the doors.

CAUTION

Except during a bombing run, the switch must always be in the guarded OFF position. If left ON and an attempt is made to open the bomb bay doors with the bomb door switch, the doors will go to an intermediate position. If this condition occurs and is not immediately recognized, the hydraulic pumps will burn out as the pump motors will continue to operate even after the bomb bay door switch is released. To correct this condition, place the safety switch in the OFF position.

Note

The above condition is caused by the following electrical configuration. When in the ON position, the bomb bay door safety switch produces a continuous door-closed signal unless broken by the door-closed limit switches. If the bomb bay door switch is actuated, the doors will start to open and will make contact with the closed limit switches. This causes a door-closed and a door-open signal to be sent simultaneously which results in the doors stopping at an intermediate position. In this condition, the pumps will operate continuously.

INDICATORS.

Bomb Bay Door Lamps.

Five bomb bay door lamps, three for OPEN and two for CLOSE, give visual indication of bomb bay door position. The three OPEN lamps are wired through the rack selector switch-type circuit breakers in the bomb bays.

The OPEN lamps glow continuously when the doors are fully open. The CLOSE lamps glow when the doors reach their full-closed position but go out when the bomb bay door switch is released. The light will glow at any time the doors are fully closed and the switch is held in the CLOSE position.

Note

If the CLOSED indicator lamps continue to burn after the bomb bay door switch has been released, check the position of the bomb bay door safety switch at the radar observer's station.

Figure 4-38.

Section IV
Auxiliary Equipment

T.O. 1B-36D(II)-1

RADAR OBSERVER'S *Station*

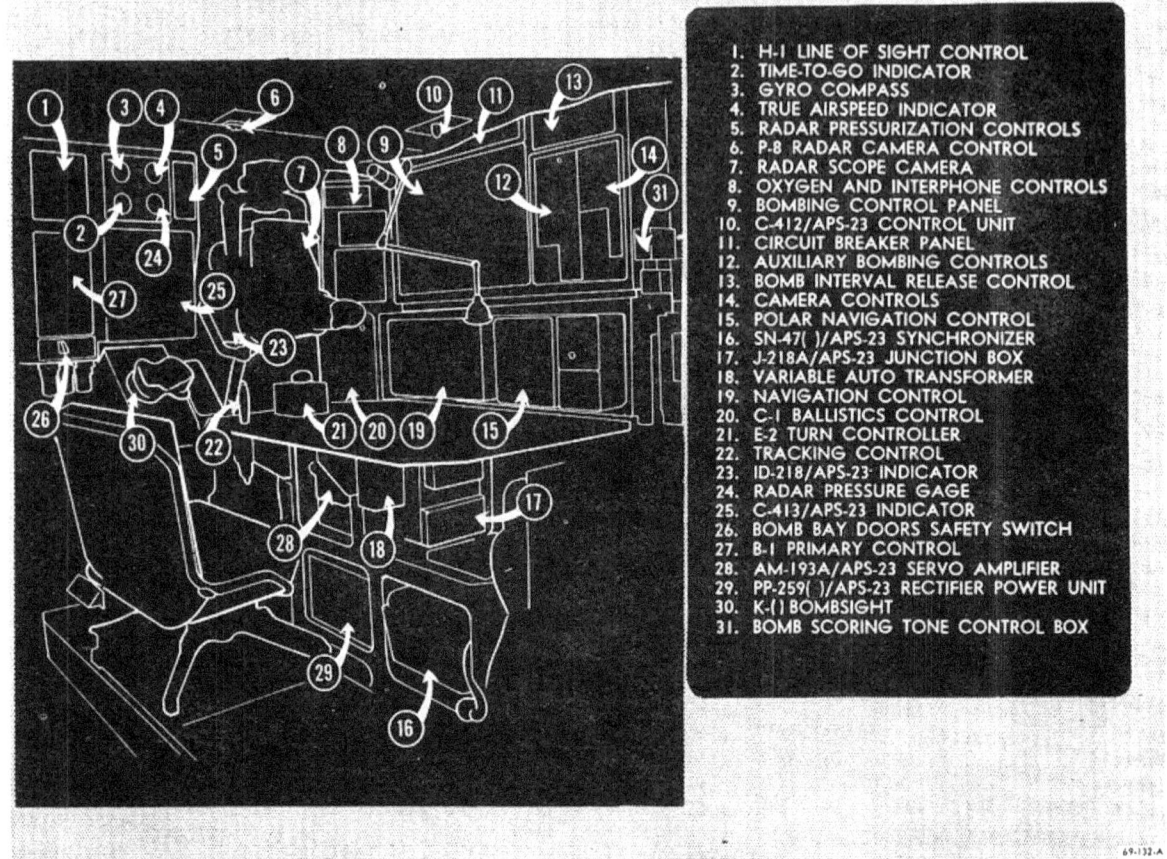

1. H-1 LINE OF SIGHT CONTROL
2. TIME-TO-GO INDICATOR
3. GYRO COMPASS
4. TRUE AIRSPEED INDICATOR
5. RADAR PRESSURIZATION CONTROLS
6. P-8 RADAR CAMERA CONTROL
7. RADAR SCOPE CAMERA
8. OXYGEN AND INTERPHONE CONTROLS
9. BOMBING CONTROL PANEL
10. C-412/APS-23 CONTROL UNIT
11. CIRCUIT BREAKER PANEL
12. AUXILIARY BOMBING CONTROLS
13. BOMB INTERVAL RELEASE CONTROL
14. CAMERA CONTROLS
15. POLAR NAVIGATION CONTROL
16. SN-47( )/APS-23 SYNCHRONIZER
17. J-218A/APS-23 JUNCTION BOX
18. VARIABLE AUTO TRANSFORMER
19. NAVIGATION CONTROL
20. C-1 BALLISTICS CONTROL
21. E-2 TURN CONTROLLER
22. TRACKING CONTROL
23. ID-218/APS-23 INDICATOR
24. RADAR PRESSURE GAGE
25. C-413/APS-23 INDICATOR
26. BOMB BAY DOORS SAFETY SWITCH
27. B-1 PRIMARY CONTROL
28. AM-193A/APS-23 SERVO AMPLIFIER
29. PP-259( )/APS-23 RECTIFIER POWER UNIT
30. K-( ) BOMBSIGHT
31. BOMB SCORING TONE CONTROL BOX

Figure 4-39. (Sheet 1)

Bomb Bay Door Ready Lamp.

On some airplanes a bomb bay door ready lamp is located adjacent to the bomb bay door safety switch and lights when the bomb bay doors can be operated by the K-( ) system.

Nose Fuse Lights.

This light when on, indicates that the bomb nose fuses are armed.

Bomb Station Indicator Lights.

One hundred and thirty-two bomb station indicator lights, one for each station, are located on the bombing control panel. Each light will burn as long as its bomb rack release unit is cocked. Each light will go out as the bomb at its station is released.

Bomb-Size Indicator.

Four bomb-size indicators, one for each bomb bay, can be set manually to show the size of bombs loaded in each bay.

HYDRAULIC FLUID TEMPERATURE CONTROL.

Provisions for maintaining proper hydraulic fluid temperatures for operation of the bomb bay doors are incorporated in the main hydraulic system.

Operation of the system is fully automatic, provided the switch-type circuit breaker (1, figure 1-37) on the engineer's table is in the ON position. In this condition, a circuit is set up to a thermal switch located in the system. The switch then reacts to hydraulic fluid temperatures as follows: When the fluid temperature drops to approximately $-18°C$ ($0°F$), the thermal switch engages. This in turn starts one of the main hydraulic pump motors and energizes the door-close solenoid of the main selector valve. Fluid is then circulated through the system until it reaches a temperature of approximately $38°C$ ($100°F$) at which time

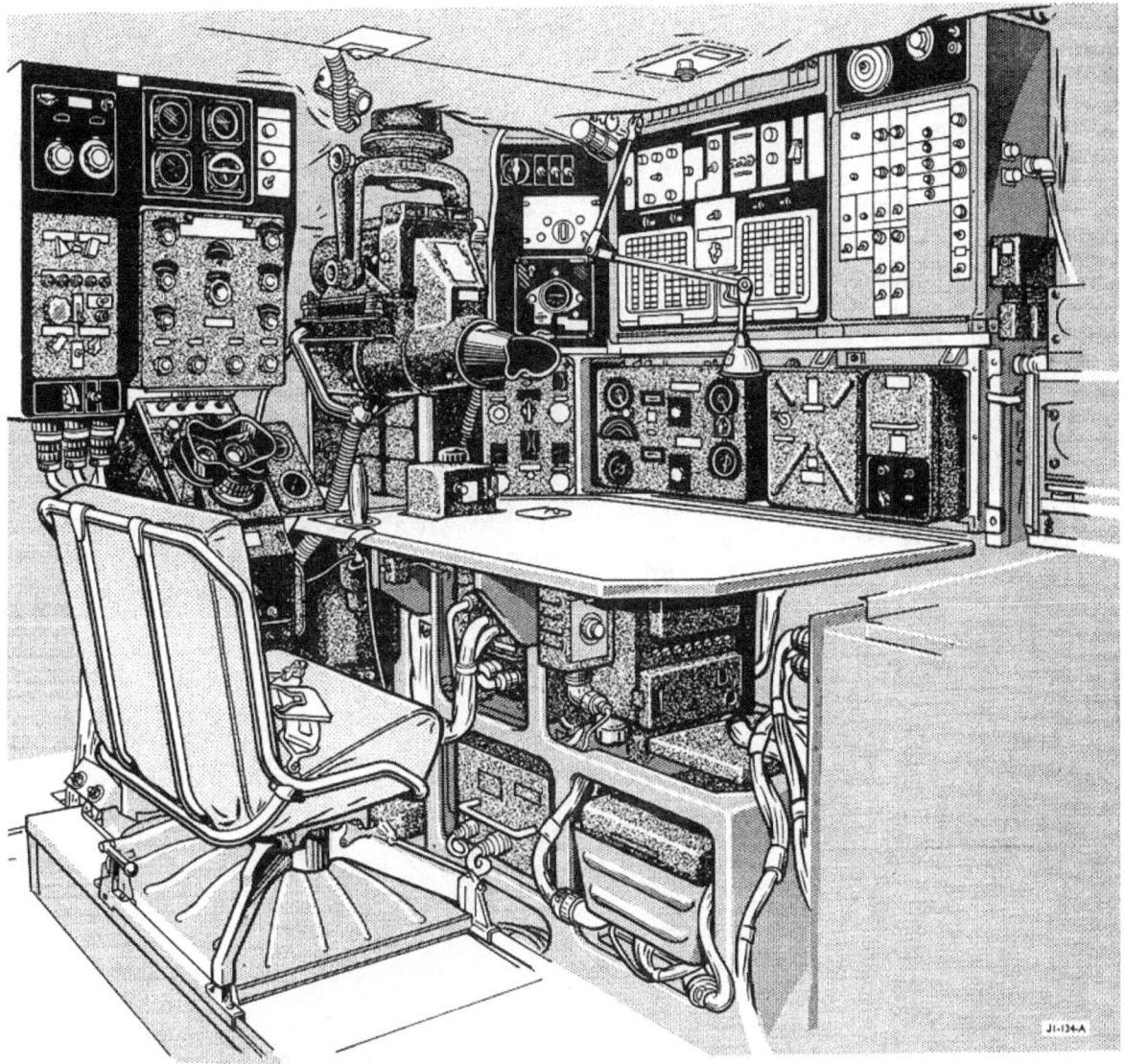

Figure 4-39. (Sheet 2)

the thermal switch opens, the pump stops, and the door-close solenoid is de-energized.

Note

Actuation of a bomb bay door switch will render the hydraulic fluid temperature control inoperative.

EMERGENCY RELEASE CONTROLS.

Bomb Salvo Switches.

Two bomb salvo switches (28, figure 1-14 and figure 4-38) are provided; one each at the pilots' and the radar observer's stations. Each switch has a spring-loaded ON position and OFF position. Holding either switch in the ON position de-energizes the K-system bomb bay door safety circuit, opens the bomb bay doors, and releases the bombs with the tail fuses safe.

Note

If the radar observer's bomb salvo circuit breaker is pulled and the bomb bay doors are closed, the bombs cannot be salvoed by the pilots' salvo switch. If, however, the bomb bay doors are open and the radar observer's circuit breaker is pulled, the bombs can be salvoed by closing the pilot's salvo circuit breaker and holding the pilots' salvo switch in the ON position.

If a bomb bay fuel tank is being carried, it can be salvoed with the bombs, provided the bomb bay tank release selector switch (33, figure 1-15) is in the CAN SALVO position. A lamp, adjacent to each salvo switch, will light when the salvo cycle begins and will go out when the bombs are salvoed and the bomb bay doors are closed.

Note

After salvo, the bomb bay doors must be closed with the bomb bay door switches.

BOMB RELEASE.

The bombs can be released individually, in train, in salvo, by radar, and pneumatically. During bomb release, to maintain airplane trim, the release circuits in bays 1 and 4 are set up so that if bombs are released from either bay, an equivalent is released from the other. Because of this arrangement, when single release is desired, it is necessary to select either bay 2 or 3. For train release any of the four bays can be used.

The bombs can be salvoed from either the pilots' or the radar observer's station. If desired, the bomb bay fuel tank can be salvoed in conjunction with the bombs.

Single Release.

To set up the radar observer's station for single release, proceed as follows:

1. Master Power Switch—ON.
2. Bomb Bay Selector Switch (No. 2 and 3)—ON.
3. Release Transfer Switch (located on the auxiliary bomb control panel)—BOMB RACK RELEASE.
4. Intervalometer Switch—SEL.
5. Nose Fuse Switch—ARM.
6. Bomb Bay Door Switch—OPEN.
7. D-2 Release Switch—Depress to release bombs.

Train Release.

To release the bombs in train, proceed as follows:

1. Master Power Switch—ON.
2. Bomb Bay Selector Switch—ON for desired bays.
3. Release Transfer Switch (located on the auxiliary control panel)—BOMB RACK RELEASES.
4. Intervalometer Switch—TRAIN, and set in desired spacing and number of bombs.
5. Nose Fuse Switch—ARM.
6. Bomb Bay Door Safety Switch—OFF.
7. Bomb Bay Door Switch—OPEN.
8. D-2 Bomb Release Switch—Depress to release bombs.

Salvo Release.

To salvo the bombs, proceed as follows:

1. Pilots' and Radar Observer's Salvo Circuit Breakers—Pushed in.
2. Bomb Bay Tank Release Selector Switch—NO SALVO.
3. Bomb Salvo Switch—Momentarily ON.

Note

Once the salvo circuit is completed, it takes approximately 3 seconds to salvo the bombs. The salvo cycle can be stopped by reactuating either of the salvo switches.

If the two salvo switches are actuated at approximately the same time, the salvo will either not occur or be incomplete; therefore, only one salvo switch must be actuated when it is necessary to salvo bombs.

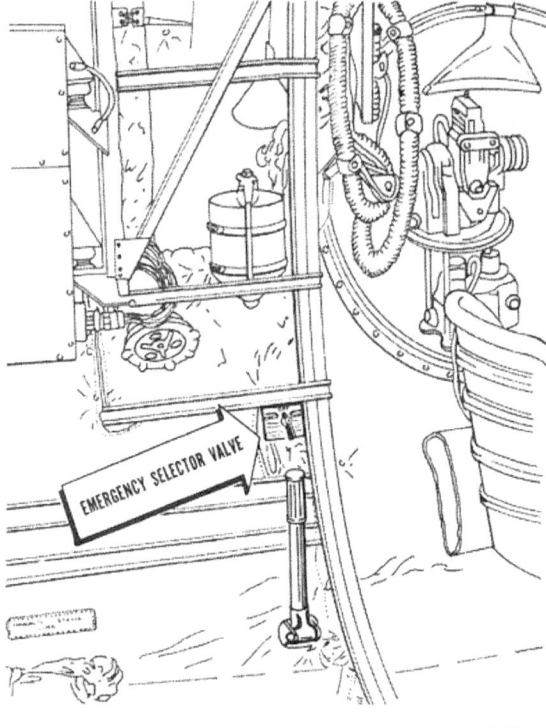

Figure 4-40. Bomb Bay Door Emergency Hydraulic System Controls

4. Bomb Bay Door Switch—CLOSE.

WARNING

The bomb salvo switch-type circuit breakers in the bomb bay must be ON because all electrical impulses to the racks go through these switches.

Note

In the event of electrical power failure the bombs may be salvoed by first pumping the bomb bay doors open manually and then actuating the salvo switch by use of battery power. After salvo has been completed, the bomb bay doors should be pumped closed.

Pneumatic Release.

For information on pneumatic release, refer to "Special Bombing System" of this section.

Radar Release.

For information on radar release of bombs, refer to "Radar Observer," Section VIII. For preflight checks of the system, refer to "K-( ) Bombing System Amplified Preflight Check," Section VIII.

BOMB BAY FUEL TANK SALVO RELEASE.

To salvo the bomb bay fuel tank, proceed as follows:
1. Bomb Bay Fuel Tank Booster Pump Switch—OFF.
2. Bomb Bay Fuel Tank Valve—CLOSE.
3. Pilots' and Radar Observer's Salvo Circuit Breakers—Pushed in.
4. Bomb Bay Fuel Tank Release Selector Switch—CAN SALVO.
5. Bomb Salvo Switch—Momentarily ON.
6. Bomb Bay Door Switch—Close.

WARNING

The bomb salvo switch-type circuit breakers in the bomb bay must be ON because all electrical impulses to the racks go through these switches.

RADAR BOMB SCORING TONE DEVICE.

The radar bomb scoring tone device eliminates the possibility of human error in radar bomb scoring for training crews. The bomb scoring tone control box (31, figure 4-39) has a spring-loaded ON-OFF toggle switch, two connector mounting type sealed relays, and an indicator light. It is located adjacent to the radar observer's auxiliary control panel.

To operate the bomb scoring tone device, proceed as follows: Press the spring-loaded toggle switch to the ON position momentarily. This action starts a 1000-cycle tone from either command set transmitter and lights the tone control box indicator lamp. The tone will remain on until a bomb release signal is received at the tone control box. This signal stops the tone and turns off the indicator lamp. The tone may also be stopped by momentarily pressing the spring-loaded switch to the OFF position.

CAUTION

If the bombs are aboard the aircraft the RBS safety check list under "Radar Observer," Section VIII, will be accomplished prior to the tone check.

K-( ) BOMBING-NAVIGATION SYSTEM.

The K-( ) system functions either optically or by radar to locate and bomb targets. It also records the position of the aircraft in flight. The system incorporates a polar navigation attachment which enables the radar observer to assist the navigator during polar flights. Refer to the radar observer's preflight check list in Section VIII.

UNIVERSAL BOMBING SYSTEM.

The universal bombing system comprises a universal bomb rack, the U-2 pneumatic rack, and associated equipment; an emergency manual release cable system with release handles at the bombardier's station; an arming control manual safe system with control handles on bulkhead 4.0 on the right side of the radio operator's compartment; and the necessary controls at the bombardier's and the pilots' stations. The system can be operated automatically by the radar system or manually by use of the bombardier's D-2 switch. An IFI operator's station equipped with oxygen, interphone, and heater connections is provided at bulkhead 6.0 in the forward bomb bay.

Some airplanes are equipped with two universal systems and some, with four.

Normal Controls.

The controls for the universal bombing system are located at the radar observer's station (12, figure 4-39, and 4-41). A lock pin which is stowed on the side of the release mechanism in the bomb bay provides a means of locking the release manually.

Special Release Switch. The special release switch (3, figure 4-41) receives its power from the POWER-ARM RELEASE circuit breaker. It has two positions, SPECIAL RELEASE and BOMB RACK RELEASES. When placed in the SPECIAL RELEASE position the switch transfers power from the normal bomb racks to the U-2 pneumatic release system.

Revised 18 May 1956

Section IV
Auxiliary Equipment

T.O. 1B-36D(II)-1

SPECIAL BOMB RACK Panel

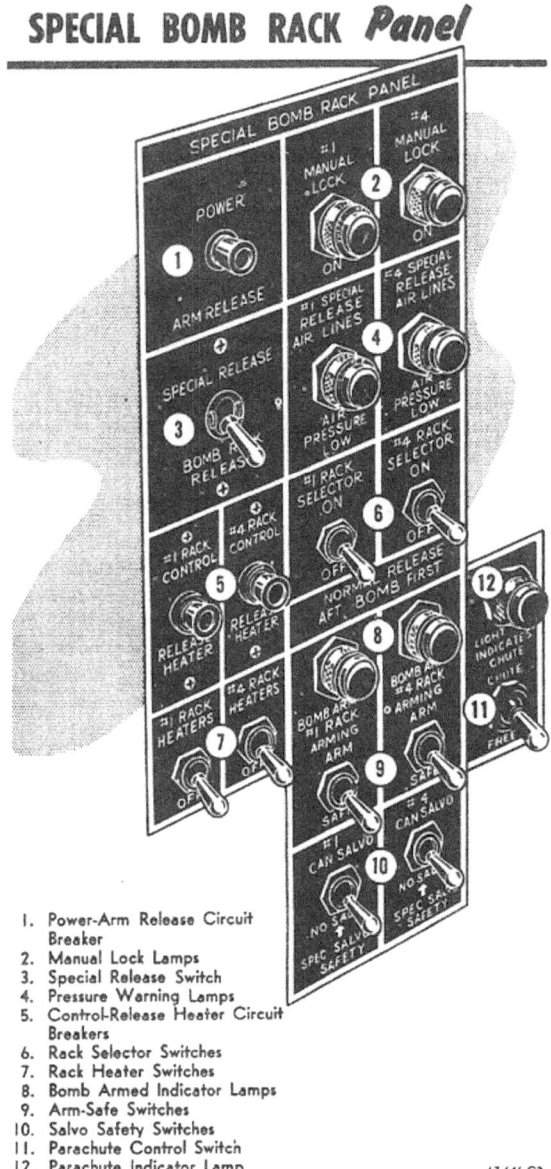

1. Power-Arm Release Circuit Breaker
2. Manual Lock Lamps
3. Special Release Switch
4. Pressure Warning Lamps
5. Control-Release Heater Circuit Breakers
6. Rack Selector Switches
7. Rack Heater Switches
8. Bomb Armed Indicator Lamps
9. Arm-Safe Switches
10. Salvo Safety Switches
11. Parachute Control Switch
12. Parachute Indicator Lamp

Figure 4-41. (Some Airplanes)

Rack Heater Switches. The two-position heater switches, one for No. 1 and one for No. 4 rack (7, figure 4-41) receive 28-volt power through the CONTROL-RELEASE HEATER circuit breakers (5, figure 4-41). When the switches are placed in the HEATER position, they supply power to the U-2 rack and arming control heaters.

Rack Selector Switches. Two ON-OFF rack selector switches (6, figure 4-41), one for No. 1 rack and one for No. 4 rack, provide a means of selecting the racks desired for bombing operation.

Arm-Safe Switches. These spring-loaded three-position ARM-SAFE switches, one for No. 1 and one for No. 4 rack (9, figure 4-41), receive power through the POWER-ARM RELEASE circuit breakers (1, figure 4-41). When the switches are held in the ARM position, they supply power to the arming control solenoids.

Salvo Safety Switches. Two switches marked CAN SALVO and NO SALVO (10, figure 4-41) control salvo operation of the special bombing system. Placing the switches in the CAN SALVO position permits salvo from the U-2 racks by means of the normal salvo system in the airplane.

Indicator Lamps.

Manual Lock Lamps. A MANUAL LOCK ON warning lamp for each U-2 rack is provided on the special bomb rack panel (2, figure 4-41). This push-to-test lamp glows when the manual lock pin is inserted in the respective rack.

Pressure Warning Lamps. A push-to-test low air pressure warning lamp (4, figure 4-41) is provided for each rack. The lamp glows when the pressure in the respective system drops below 625 ($\pm$ 40) psi.

Bomb Armed Indicator Lamps. An indicator lamp (8, figure 4-41) for each ARM-SAFE switch glows when the respective switch is in the ARM position. It is also a push-to-test type lamp.

Emergency Controls.

Emergency controls for the universal bombing system include salvo safety switches on the pilots' instrument panel, the salvo safety switches (10, figure 4-41) on the bombardier's special bomb rack panel, and an emergency release handle located on the floor of the bombardier's station. Placing either of the salvo safety switches in the CAN SALVO position permits salvo from the U-2 rack by means of the normal salvo system in the airplane.

LARGE CARGO SYSTEM.

Provisions are made in bomb bays No. 3 and 4 for carrying a cargo platform on which is mounted an electrically heated U-2 pneumatic release. Normal release of cargo from the platform is accomplished automatically by the K-( ) system controls located on the universal bombing system panel (figure 4-41) or by depressing the D-2 release switch at the bombardier's station. A lock pin which is stowed on the cargo release unit provides a means of locking the release mechanism manually.

Controls for emergency operation of the system are provided at the bombardier's station, on bulkhead 4.0 on the right side of the radio operator's compartment, and in the bomb bay area.

Revised 18 May 1956

Special Bomb Rack Panel

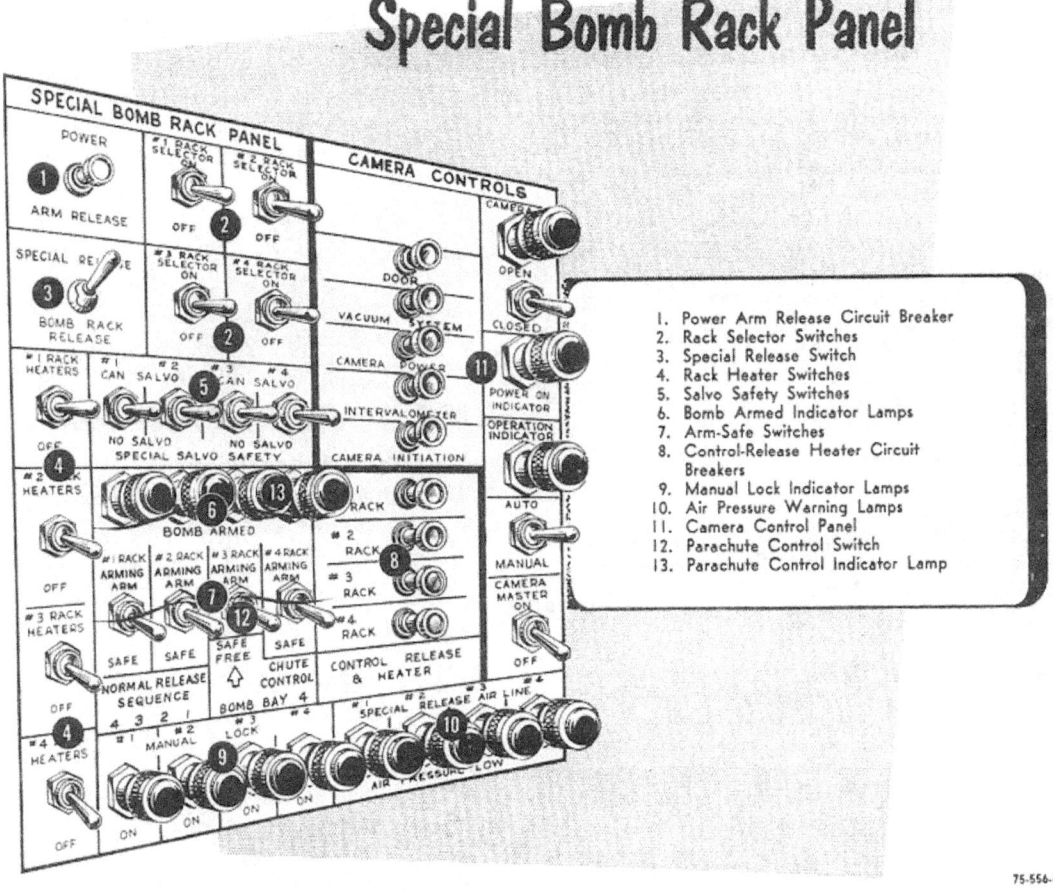

Figure 4-41A. (Some Airplanes)

Normal Controls.
Normal release of the cargo is accomplished by using the controls for rack No. 4. On airplanes with the two-rack special bombing panel a special CHUTE-FREE switch and indicator lamp have been added for control of the cargo parachute. On airplanes with the four-rack panel, the rack No. 3 arming switch and indicator lamp are used for parachute control.

Rack Selector Switch. The on-off rack selector switch (6, figure 4-41) controls power to the arming controls, heaters, and release circuits.

Special Release Switch. The special release switch (3, figure 4-41) marked SPECIAL RELEASE and BOMB RACK RELEASES, receives power from the POWER-ARM RELEASE circuit breaker (1, figure 4-41). When placed in the SPECIAL RELEASE position, the switch disconnects the normal bomb racks from the release circuit and makes release from the cargo racks possible.

Rack Heater Switch. This two-position heater switch (7, figure 4-41) receives power through the CONTROL-RELEASE HEATER circuit breaker (5, figure 4-41). When the switch is placed in the HEATER position, it supplies power to the U-2 release and arming control heaters.

Arming Switch. This spring-loaded three-position switch (9, figure 4-41), marked ARM and SAFE, receives power through the POWER-ARM RELEASE circuit breakers (1, figure 4-41). When the switch is held in the ARM position, it supplies power to the arming control solenoid. When it is held in the SAFE position, it supplies power to the solenoid to make the cargo safe.

Salvo Safety Switches. A salvo safety switch for bomb bay No. 4, marked CAN SALVO and NO SALVO, is located on the pilots' instrument panel (34, figure 1-13) and on the special bomb rack panel (10, figure 4-41). Placing either of these switches in the

Section IV
Auxiliary Equipment

CAN SALVO position permits salvo from the U-2 release by means of the normal salvo system in the airplane. During normal operation the switches are positioned at NO SALVO.

Parachute Control Switch. This two-position switch (11, figure 4-41 and 12, figure 4-41A) receives power from the POWER-ARM RELEASE circuit breaker to control operation of the parachute release arming control. On airplanes with the two-rack special bombing panel the switch is marked CHUTE and FREE. On airplanes with the four-rack panel the switch is marked ARM and SAFE FREE. When the switch is placed in the CHUTE or ARM position, the parachute will open when the cargo is released. When the switch is placed in the FREE or SAFE FREE position, the cargo will fall free when released, with the parachute unopened.

Indicator Lamps.
Manual Lock Lamp. The MANUAL LOCK ON warning lamp (2, figure 4-41) is a press-to-test lamp which glows when the manual lock pin is inserted in the U-2 release unit.

Pressure Warning Lamp. This press-to-test lamp (4, figure 4-41) glows when pressure in the pneumatic release system drops below 625 ($\pm$ 40) psi.

Bomb Armed Indicator Lamp. This press-to-test indicator lamp (8, figure 4-41) lights when the arming control is in the armed position.

Parachute Indicator Lamp. The parachute indicator lamp (12, figure 4-41) lights when the parachute arming control is in the CHUTE or ARM position. It is a press-to-test type lamp.

Emergency Controls.
Manual Release Handle. Two manual release handles for the universal bombing system are located on the floor at the bombardier's station. Manual release of cargo is accomplished by rotating the No. 4 rack handle 90 degrees and pulling out.

Cargo Safe and Free Fall Manual Controls. Two handles for manual operation of the universal bombing system and the cargo system are located on bulkhead No. 4 on the right side of the radio operator's compartment. The left handle, which is marked CARGO SAFE, provides a means of making the cargo safe manually. The right handle, marked NO CHUTE-FREE FALL, positions the cargo parachute release mechanism so that the cargo can be dropped with the parachute unopened. The handles are operated by turning 90 degrees in either direction and pulling out.

Armed-Safe Knob. A knob with positions marked SAFE and ARMED is located on the release mechanism in the bomb bay. When the knob is pulled out, the cargo will be dropped in a safe condition when released. When the knob is depressed so that the ARMED decal shows, the cargo will be dropped in an armed condition when released.

BOMB BAY DOOR EMERGENCY CONTROLS.

Manual Selector Controls.

The hydraulic system main selector valve (figure 3-14) is provided with an OPEN and CLOSE plunger for operation of the bomb bay doors. The plungers are used in conjunction with the hydraulic pump override switch.

Manual Operation of Main Selector Valve.

> **CAUTION**
>
> Do not open the bomb bay doors until the aft turret doors are open.

1. Pilot—Bomb Bay Door Circuit Breaker—Pull out.

2. Radar Observer—Bomb Bay Door Safety Switch —OFF; Bomb Bay Door Circuit Breaker—Pull out.

3. Engineer — Hydraulic Fluid Temperature Control Switch—OFF.

4. Crew Member—Main Selector Valve OPEN or CLOSE Plunger—Hold in until desired action is completed.

5. Engineer—Hydraulic Pump Override Switch— ON.

6. Engineer—Hydraulic Pump Override Switch— OFF, after desired action is complete.

Bomb Bay Door Emergency Hydraulic System.

A fluid supply, a hand pump, and a bomb bay door emergency selector valve (figure 4-40) are the main components of the emergency bomb bay door system. With the selector valve in the OPEN or CLOSE position, operation of the hand pump produces the selected action.

WARNING

When not in use, the emergency selector valve lever must be left in the OFF position. Operation of the normal bomb bay door system with the lever in any position other than OFF will result in flooding the emergency system reservoir and consequent loss of fluid.

Operation of Bomb Bay Door Emergency Hydraulic System. (See figure 4-42.)

CAUTION

Do not open the bomb bay doors until the aft turret doors are open.

1. Pilot—Bomb Bay Door Circuit Breaker—Pull out.
2. Radar Observer's—Bomb Bay Door Safety Switch —OFF; Bomb Bay Door Circuit Breaker—Pulled out.
3. Engineer—Hydraulic Fluid Temperature Control Switch—OFF.
4. Crew Member—Emergency Selector Valve—OPEN or CLOSE as desired.
5. Crew Member—Hand Pump—Operate until the doors are in the desired position.
6. Crew Member—Emergency Selector Valve—OFF.

PHOTOGRAPHIC EQUIPMENT.

Airplanes not in group 2 are equipped with an aerial camera station located just forward of the lower aft

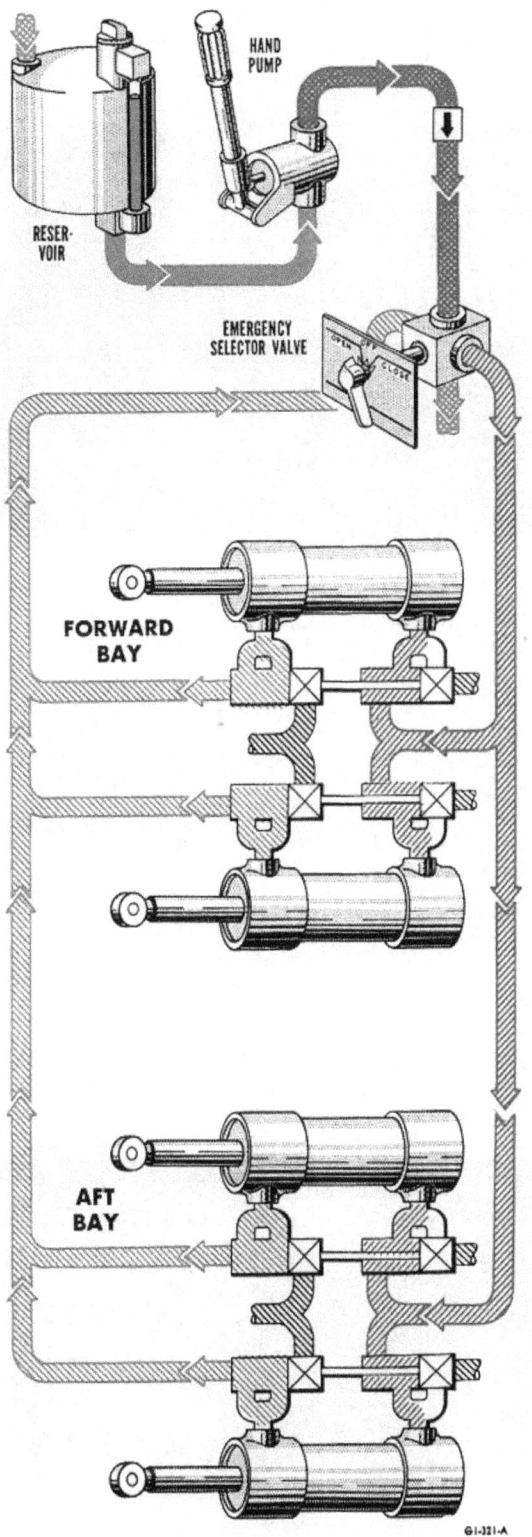

Figure 4-42.

Section IV
Auxiliary Equipment

turret. Any one of the following cameras can be installed at the station for use in either day or night reconnaissance and orientation and for bomb spotting.

TYPE	FOCAL LENGTH -INCHES	USE
K-17	6, 12, or 24	Bomb Spotting & Reconnaissance
K-22	6, 12, or 24	Bomb Spotting & Reconnaissance
K-18	24	Reconnaissance
K-19B	12	Night Photography
K-24	7, 12, or 20	Orientation

Each of these cameras, with the exception of the K-19B, is controlled by an intervalometer located on the radar observer's control panel. The K-19B camera is controlled by a photocell unit located just forward of the camera station. The camera doors are electrically operated and are controlled by either the camera door switch or the bomb bay door switch. A vacuum system is provided to insure proper film position in the camera magazine. Vacuum is supplied by a d-c motor-driven pump which operates automatically when the camera doors are opened.

On group 2 airplanes, the camera station is located below the bunks in the aft cabin. The camera can be operated from either the radar observer's station (figure 4-43) or the camera control box in the aft cabin (figure 4-44).

Any one of the cameras listed below can be installed at this station, depending on the type of photographic coverage desired.

TYPE	FOCAL LENGTH —INCHES	USE
K-22A	6, 12 or 24	Bomb Spotting & Reconnaissance
K-17C	6, 12 or 24	Bomb Spotting & Reconnaissance
K-37	12	Night Photography
K-38	24 or 36	Bomb Spotting

With the exception of the K-37 camera, the cameras can be controlled by the intervalometer at the radar observer's station. They can also be operated by the mode selector switch at the radar observer's station or by the initiation switch in the aft cabin. The K-37 camera is controlled by a photocell unit located adjacent to the camera door. The camera door is controlled by the camera door switches. Also, the door will open when the bomb bay doors open. A vacuum system is provided to insure that the film is flat against the magazine platen. The vacuum system operates automatically when the camera door is open. Vacuum is created either by utilizing the differential between the ambient pressure and the cabin pressure or, if this pressure differential is insufficient, by the action of a pressure switch which will start the operation of a motor-driven vacuum pump. For camera window defrosting, the duct which incorporates the restrictor damper is extended down beneath the aft cabin floor where a fluted vent provides a spray of hot air across the camera window. At this point a smaller duct is routed to the window of the photocell unit for defrosting purposes. The restrictor damper controls the flow of defrosting air to these outlets.

CAMERA CONTROLS.

Camera Master Power Switches.

An on-off camera master power switch is located on the auxiliary bombing control panel. Placing this switch ON supplies electrical power to the control circuits of the camera system. Airplanes in group 2 have an additional master power switch located on the camera control panel in the aft cabin. When ON, this switch supplies power to the entire camera system with the exception of the camera intervalometer.

Intervalometer.

A type B-7 camera intervalometer is located on the radar observer's control panel. The intervalometer controls the automatic operation of the camera and the interval between exposures. Controls of the intervalometer include a single-exposure switch, a start-stop switch, a recycle switch, an exposure counter dial, an interval selector, and a mode selector switch for setting up the electrical circuit for the type of camera operation to be used. The positions of the mode selector switch are NT RECON BOMB SPT, NT ORIEN, DAY ORIEN, DAY RECON, and OFF.

Camera Mode Selector Switch.

A mode selector switch (6, figure 4-43), having an AUTO position and a spring-loaded MANUAL position, is provided on the radar observer's camera control panel. When the switch is in the AUTO position, the operation of the camera is controlled by the intervalometer and camera operation is initiated when the bomb release switch is actuated. When the switch is held in the MANUAL position, camera operation will be initiated and the rate of exposure will be determined by the cycling speed of the camera.

Section IV
Auxiliary Equipment

Airplanes in group 2 have an additional camera door switch located on the camera control box in the aft cabin. This switch is identical in operation to the one provided for the radar observer.

Camera Initiation Switch.

Airplanes in group 2 have a camera initiation switch located on the camera control box in the aft cabin. This on-off switch is spring-loaded in the ON position and is provided for operating the camera from the aft cabin.

INDICATORS.

Camera Operation Indicator Lamp.

A green indicator lamp (5, figure 4-43) is located on the radar observer's camera control panel. When the camera is operating, the lamp will blink at the rate of exposure.

Camera Door Indicator Lamps.

On airplanes not in group 2, two camera door indicator lamps (2, figure 4-43), an amber lamp for OPEN and a red lamp for CLOSED, give a visual indication of the camera door position. These lamps are adjacent to the camera door switch on the radar observer's camera control panel. Group 2 airplanes have a single amber lamp adjacent to the camera door switch. This lamp burns when the camera door is open.

Camera Power-On Indicator Lamps (Group 2 Airplanes).

A camera power-on indicator lamp is located adjacent to each camera master power switch. These white lamps will both light when either camera master power switch is ON.

Camera System Vacuum Gage (Group 2 Airplanes).

A vacuum gage is located on the camera control panel in the aft cabin. The gage indicates the amount of vacuum in inches of mercury.

OPERATION.

Operation of the aerial camera for day reconnaissance is accomplished as follows:

1. Camera master power switch—ON.
2. Camera door switch—OPEN.
3. Check door open indicator lamp on.
4. Intervalometer mode selector switch—DAY RECON.
5. Set desired exposure interval on the intervalometer selector dial.
6. Intervalometer START button—Push.

Note

The warning lamp on the intervalometer will light 2 seconds prior to each exposure.

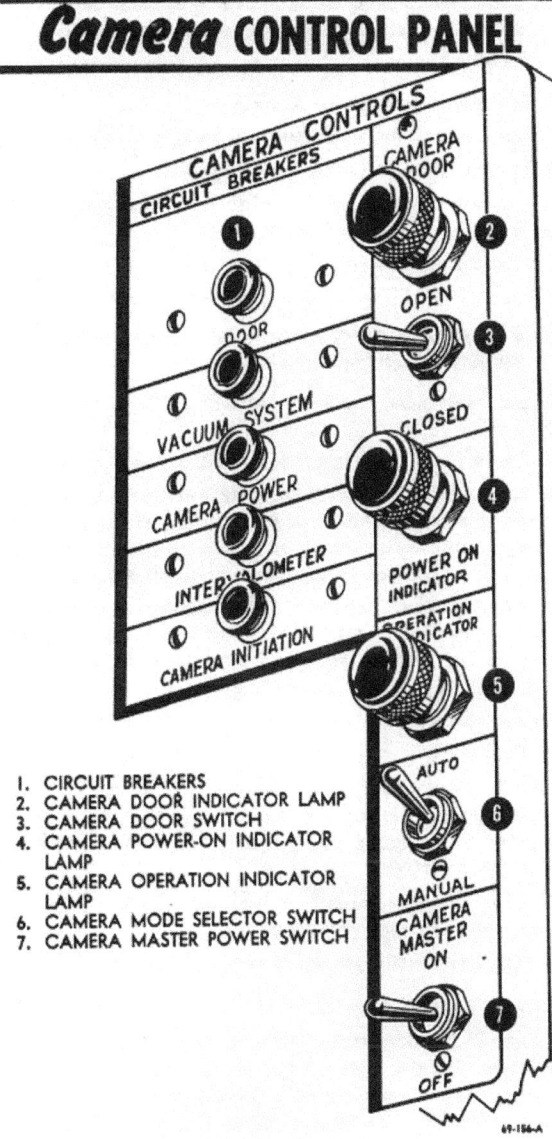

1. CIRCUIT BREAKERS
2. CAMERA DOOR INDICATOR LAMP
3. CAMERA DOOR SWITCH
4. CAMERA POWER-ON INDICATOR LAMP
5. CAMERA OPERATION INDICATOR LAMP
6. CAMERA MODE SELECTOR SWITCH
7. CAMERA MASTER POWER SWITCH

Figure 4-43.

Camera Door Switches.

A three-position switch (3, figure 4-43) is provided on the radar observer's camera panel for operating the camera doors. The switch has a spring-loaded OPEN position, a spring-loaded CLOSE position, and a neutral center position. When the switch is in the neutral position and the camera power switch is on, the camera doors will open when the bomb bay doors open.

Note

The camera doors can be closed only by means of the camera door switch.

Section IV
Auxiliary Equipment

T.O. 1B-36D(II)-1

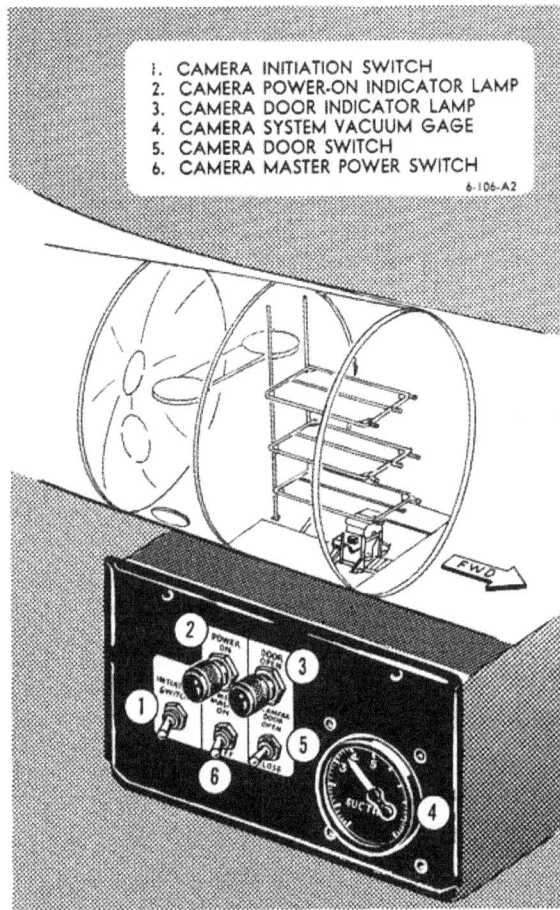

1. CAMERA INITIATION SWITCH
2. CAMERA POWER-ON INDICATOR LAMP
3. CAMERA DOOR INDICATOR LAMP
4. CAMERA SYSTEM VACUUM GAGE
5. CAMERA DOOR SWITCH
6. CAMERA MASTER POWER SWITCH

Figure 4-44. Aft Camera Station (Group 2 Airplanes)

7. Intervalometer STOP button—Push after the desired number of exposures have been made.
8. Camera door switch—CLOSE.
9. Intervalometer mode selector switch—OFF.
10. Camera master power switch—OFF.

For day orientation operation, proceed as follows:

1. Camera master power switch—ON.
2. Camera door switch—OPEN.
3. Check door open indicator lamp on.
4. Intervalometer mode selector switch—DAY ORIEN.
5. Intervalometer selector dial—Set desired length of time for camera operation.
6. Intervalometer START switch—Push.

Note

The camera will operate at its cycling speed for the preset period and then stop. The intervalometer warning lamp will light after the cycle is completed and remain on until the start switch is again actuated. It denotes that the instrument is ready for the next cycle of operation.

7. Camera door switch—CLOSE.
8. Intervalometer mode selector switch—OFF.
9. Camera master power switch—OFF.

To operate the camera for night reconnaissance and bomb spotting, proceed as follows:

1. Camera master power switch—ON.

Note

The camera doors open automatically when the bomb bay doors open.

2. Intervalometer mode selector—NT RECON BOMB SPT.
3. Intervalometer selector dial—Set in bomb fall time.
4. Intervalometer operation is initiated at the instant of bomb release and will actuate the camera at and following bomb strike time. On group 2 airplanes an exposure is also made at the time of bomb release.
5. For night photography, it is necessary only to have the camera master switch ON and the camera doors open, as the camera is tripped automatically when the flash from the bomb strikes the photocell.

Operate the camera from the aft cabin as follows:

1. Camera master power switch—ON.
2. Camera door switch—OPEN.
3. Camera initiation switch—ON. The camera will operate at its cycling speed as long as the switch is held ON.
4. Camera door switch—Hold in CLOSE position upon completion of photography.
5. Camera master power switch—OFF.

RADAR CAMERA.

A type O-15 radar recording camera (7, figure 4-39) is mounted on the radar scope at the radar observer's station. The camera records the luminous images appearing on the radar screen. With each exposure of the scope camera's film a photograph of a clock is made to establish the time of each exposure. The switches for controlling the camera are located on a camera control box (6, figure 4-39) located directly over the radar observer's station.

Radar Camera Controls.

Radar Camera Power Switch. The radar camera power switch is an on-off switch located on the camera control box. Placing the switch in the ON position initiates radar camera operation.

Frequency Selector Switch. The frequency selector switch located on the camera control box has four positions marked EVERY SCAN, EVERY OTHER, 1 EVERY 4 SCANS, and 1 EVERY 12 SCANS. The frequency of camera exposure is obtained by placing the switch in the desired position.

O-15 Camera Preflight.

1. Load the camera magazine in subdued light. Be sure the take-up spool flanges will not bind the film. (Not applicable if the photo lab loads all magazines.) Magazine data card should show:
   a. Date of loading.
   b. Class of film.
   c. Film loader's name.
2. Check the magazine footage dial for sufficient film.
3. Make sure the film emulsion is visible in the slot before attaching the magazine to the camera.
4. Attach the magazine to the camera and check for correct seating. (Hook right side first.)
5. Check the camera diaphragm setting. Usual settings for Class L film are f/4 or f/5.6.
6. Check the inside camera counter against the outside counter and reset if necessary.
7. Wind and synchronize the camera hack watch with the navigator's watch (GCT).
8. Check that the range indicator holes in the data card are not obstructed.
9. Fill out the data card, printing with a soft lead pencil. Do not show security classification.
   a. General area of photography (or photo project number).
   b. True altitude (feet).
   c. Date (GCT).
   d. A/C Type and last 4 digits of serial number.
   e. Type radar.
   f. Last name of radar observer.

Camera Operation.

1. Take 20 frames of blank photos before starting radar photography in order to alleviate any fogging of good photos.
2. Check the rotation of tell-tale indicators on magazine (large red and silver knob is on take-up shaft, small knob is on feed shaft). The check on the take-up spool is the most important, since counter operation and feed shaft rotation can be misleading.
3. Keep camera viewing door closed when photographing, except when viewing the scope, as long as the effectiveness of the bomb run is not impaired.
4. Change data card as GENERAL AREA or FLIGHT ALTITUDE changes.
5. Take five blank exposures at the end of each series of photos (target runs, radar photo lines).
6. Check film footage frequently on long flights.

Camera Postflight.

1. Take 30 exposures at the end of radar scope photography to eliminate the posiblity of fogged photos.
2. Deliver the exposed film to the persons designated to receive it. The Radar Scope Photo Log must be complete and must accompany the film.
3. Make an immediate report to the appropriate radar maintenance or camera maintenance shop if there were camera malfunctions during flight.

MISCELLANEOUS EQUIPMENT.

COMMUNICATION TUBE CART.

The communication tube cart provides transportation through the communication tube which connects the pressurized compartments. Rollers on the cart are mounted on a track laid in the tube. The user lies face-up on the cart and pulls himself along by means of an overhanging rope. The cart is automatically locked in place when it reaches its end of travel. It can be unlocked by pulling the ring on the top surface of the cart. It can be unlocked and brought from the opposite end of the communication tube by turning the handle on the cart return carriage pulley between the tracks. The cart is equipped with brakes for controlling its speed during changes in airplane attitude.

Normal Procedure.

When using the communication tube during flight, the following procedure will be adhered to:

1. Notify the aircraft commander before entering the tube so that no change in aircraft attitude (climb or descent) will be made while the tube is in use.
2. Notify a crew member in the compartment of intended exit so that he can stand by to assist in the event of trouble while traveling through the tube.
3. Travel through the tube will always be made with the feet towards the rear of the aircraft, regardless of the direction of travel. Lie on the cart on your back and use the overhead rope to propel the cart. Rely on stopping the cart with the rope rather than with the hand brake.
4. When using the communication tube while the cabins are pressurized, make sure that the tube doors at both ends are closed with only the small air hole in each door open. This will eliminate the hazard of a crew member being rapidly propelled through the tube in the event of sudden decompression of one of the pressurized compartments.

> **CAUTION**
>
> Keep the communication tube door closed at all times when compartments are pressurized except when crewmen are entering or leaving the tunnel. This is necessary to preclude the possibility of having the door torn out in event of sudden decompression. In addition, because of the possibility of entangling the harness straps in the tunnel cart, do not use the tunnel when wearing a parachute. Extreme care should be exercised in transferring items through the tunnel. Any object striking the tunnel wall can cause weakening or rupture and subsequent decompression. All items transferred through the tunnel shall be pro-

perly secured to the communication tube cart with straps or similar devices prior to transporting them through the tunnel.

ENTRANCE LADDERS.

Two ladders are provided for access to the crew compartments. The forward cabin entrance ladder is permanently attached to the forward bulkhead of the nose wheel well and swings up into the well to its stowed position. The aft cabin entrance ladder stows inside the cabin and provides access to the sighting platform.

PILOTS' NIGHT-FLYING CURTAIN.

When in use, the night-flying curtain is snapped into position between the pilots' and the flight engineer's stations. The curtain is stowed in the pilot's fairing.

SPARE LAMP STOWAGE BOX.

Stowage for spare electric lamp bulbs is provided by a box located aft of the left escape hatch in the forward cabin.

NAVIGATOR'S SEAT.

The navigator's seat rotates approximately 90 degrees right or left and is equipped with a safety belt and control knob lock.

RADAR OBSERVER'S SEAT.

The radar observer's seat is mounted on tracks which permit the seat to be adjusted fore and aft. It rotates sufficiently on its base to allow access to the bombsight and control panel. The seat is equipped with a control knob lock and safety belt.

RADIO OPERATOR'S SEAT.

The radio operator's seat is a free-swivel seat with a fore and aft adjustment, a control knob lock, and a safety belt. On some airplanes the seat is on a fixed base; on others it is on a track which allows movement from side to side.

NOSE GUNNER'S SEAT.

The nose gunner is provided with a bicycle-type seat which is adjustable fore and aft and vertically. The seat is equipped with a padded back rest, a safety belt, and a control lock lever which governs fore-and-aft movement. Vertical movement is controlled by a manual elevation adjustment pin.

FORWARD GUNNERS' SEATS.

The forward sighting stations are not equipped with stationary seats as are the other stations, but are provided with fabric sling-type seats. See figure 4-45. These seats can be rigged into position for scanning and sighting purposes or they may be stowed.

WARNING

The sling-type seats are not to be occupied during take-off and landing; the forward gunners must assume the positions indicated in figure 2-10.

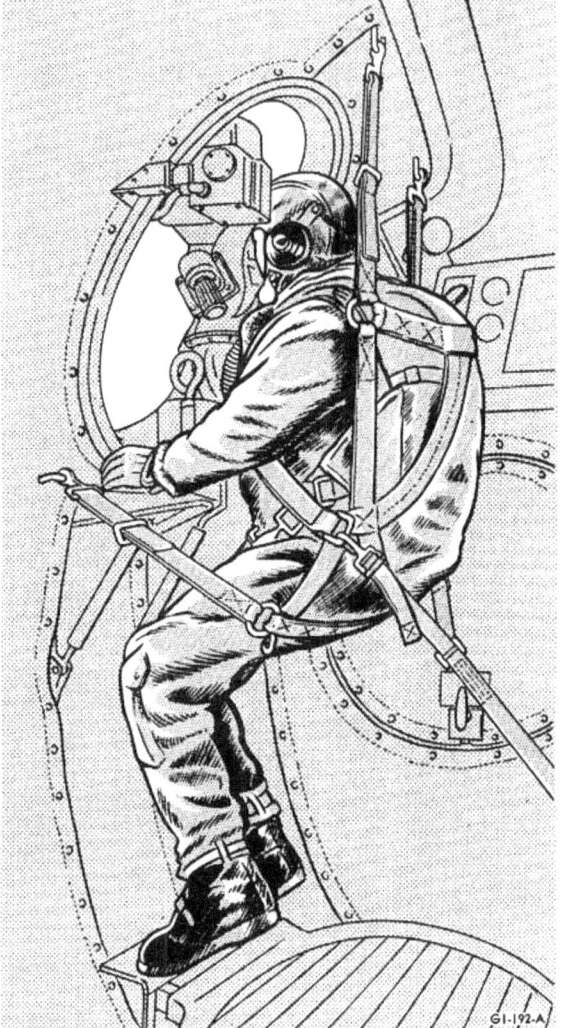

Figure 4-45. Forward Sighting Station Sling-Type Seat

UPPER AFT GUNNERS' SEATS.

Bicycle-type seats similar to those of the nose gunner are provided at these stations. The seats are located on the upper aft gunners' platform and pivot about the base of the sighting support column.

LOWER AFT GUNNERS' SEATS.

The lower aft gunners' seats are designed so they can be used during take-off and landing. For this reason the seats are equipped with inertia reel lock-type shoulder harnesses identical to those provided for the pilots. For further information on this type shoulder harness, refer to "Shoulder Harness Control" in Section I.

WINDSHIELD WIPERS.

The pilots are provided with two windshield wipers. Both wipers are controlled by a single ON-OFF switch

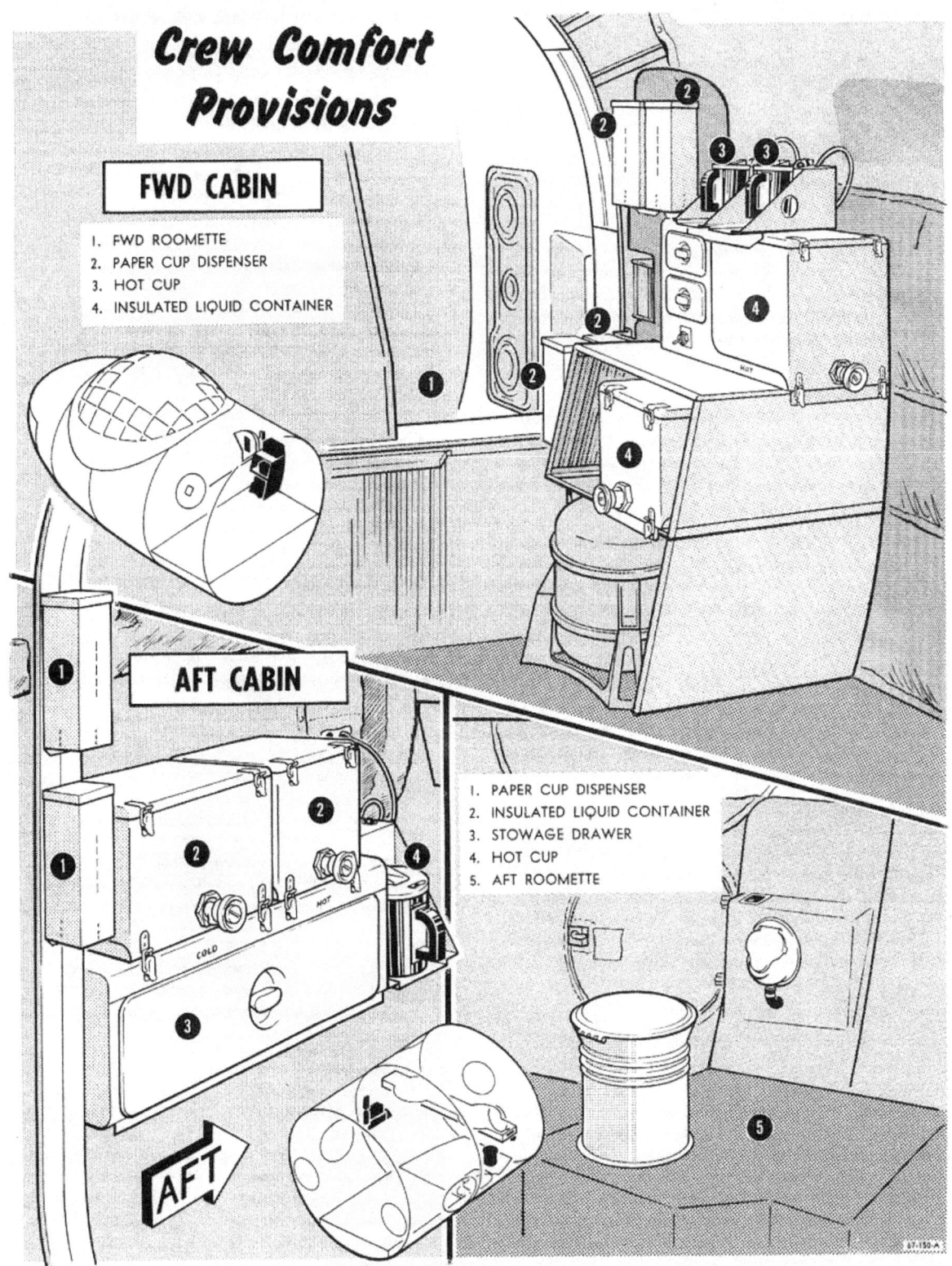

Figure 4-46.

(9, figure 1-13) on the pilots' instrument panel. When the switch is placed in the ON position, 28-volt direct current actuates a relay which completes a 208-volt a-c circuit to the windshield wiper motors.

CREW COMFORT PROVISIONS (GROUP 2 AIRPLANES.)

Bunks.

Six bunks, complete with mattresses, pillows, and blankets, are provided in the aft cabin of the airplane. The bunks are equipped with foot braces, safety harnesses, and safety belts, and are to be used for crew positions during take-off and landing.

Auxiliary Bunks. Provisions are made for the installation of an auxiliary bunk in the forward cabin. When installed it is located aft of the engineer's station in the radio operator's compartment. The bunk has no stowed position but can be readily installed or removed.

Miscellaneous Personal Gear Stowage.

Small hammock-type mesh bags for the stowage of personal gear are located adjacent to each bunk. Small racks are provided on each side of the bunks in the aft cabin for parachute stowage.

Kit Bag Stowage.

Provisions are made to stow parachute bags in the following locations: two in a folding rack on the nose wheel well in the navigator's compartment, and one under the step in the left walkway of the forward cabin.

Hot Cups.

Three hot cups (figure 4-46) are provided for crew use. Two are located adjacent to the liquid containers on the right side of the radio operator's compartment. The other one is located adjacent to the liquid containers on the right side of the aft cabin.

Liquid Containers.

A four-gallon electrically heated liquid container (figure 4-46) is located on the right side of the radio operator's compartment. An insulated drinking water container of the same capacity is mounted adjacent to the heated container. In the aft cabin a four-gallon and a two-gallon insulated drinking water container (figure 4-46) are mounted on the right wall.

Cup Dispensers.

Paper cup dispensers (figure 4-46) are located adjacent to the liquid containers in each compartment.

Frozen Food Oven.

Provisions for an electric oven are located under the scanning platform on the right side of the aft cabin. When installed the oven provides for heating prepared frozen meals or canned rations. The oven is thermostatically controlled and contains six removable shelves, each with detachable heating elements. On some airplanes two push-to-reset buttons above the oven door are used to turn the oven on. On other airplanes an ON-OFF switch for the oven is provided on the utility panel just forward of the aft cabin power panel on the right side of the aft cabin. The thermostatic controls automatically break the circuit.

Operation. To warm frozen foods, proceed as follows:

1. Remove the cellophane wrappers from the packages, but do not remove the metal foil.
2. Place one meal on each shelf.

CAUTION

The oven accommodates six meals; however, if less than six are to be heated, remove the unused shelves from the oven.

3. Place the ON-OFF switch at ON; if installed, and push in both reset buttons.
4. Wait 10 minutes after the pilot light goes out; then remove the meals.

Note

The oven must partially cool before the reset buttons are effective again. If the oven is to be reused immediately, place cold meals on the shelves and leave the door open. If the pilot light comes on when the push-to-reset buttons are pushed, the oven is ready for use.

Canned rations can be heated as follows:

1. Remove shelves 1, 3, and 5 (counting from the top) from the oven.
2. Place 4 to 5 cans on each remaining shelf.
3. Place the ON-OFF switch at ON if installed, and push in the reset buttons.
4. If small cans of food are being heated, remove them when the pilot light goes out. Large cans should be left in the oven a little longer.

CAUTION

Do not push the reset buttons unless cold (room temperature) cans are placed on the shelves.

CAUTION

Always remove the heating elements before cleaning the shelves in water.

Toilet Facilities.

Toilet facilities are provided both in the forward and the aft cabins of the airplane. In the forward cabin the facilities consist of a toilet and a relief tube located forward and to the right of the radio operator's compartment. The relief tube drains into a tank built around the toilet. In the aft cabin the facilities include a toilet and a urinal installed just aft of the entrance hatch. The urinal drains overboard when the button on the floor is depressed.

Section V
OPERATING LIMITATIONS

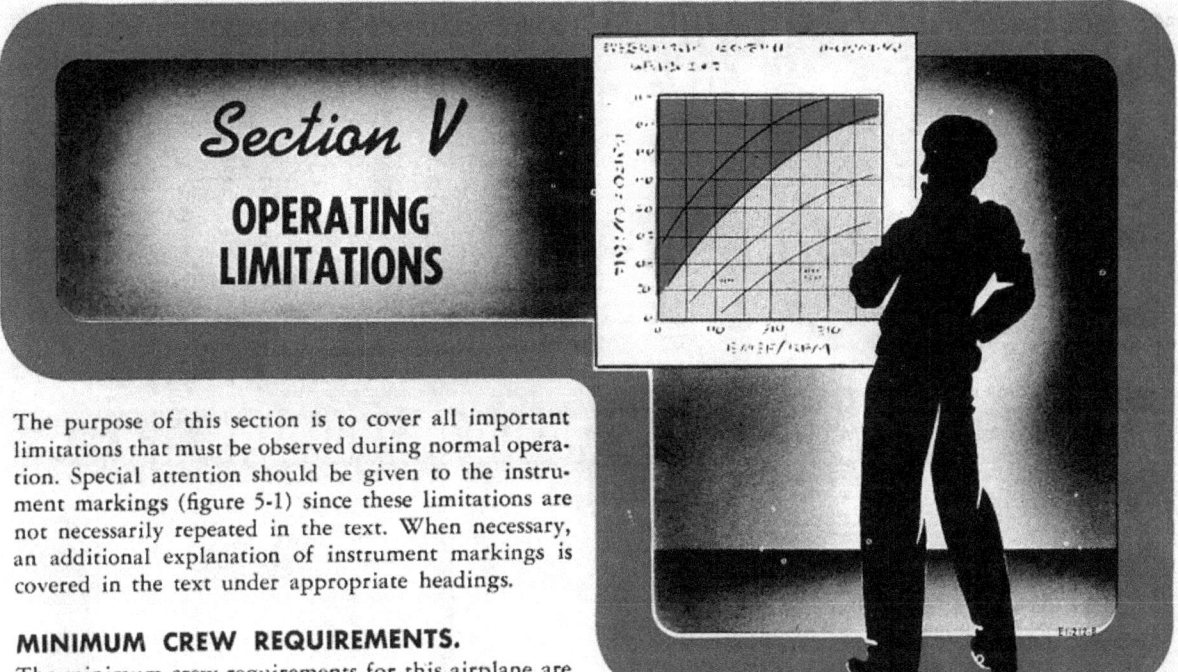

The purpose of this section is to cover all important limitations that must be observed during normal operation. Special attention should be given to the instrument markings (figure 5-1) since these limitations are not necessarily repeated in the text. When necessary, an additional explanation of instrument markings is covered in the text under appropriate headings.

MINIMUM CREW REQUIREMENTS.

The minimum crew requirements for this airplane are the aircraft commander, pilot, two engineers, and two scanners. Additional crew members will be added at the discretion of the wing commander.

INSTRUMENT LIMITATIONS.

The limits marked on the airplane instruments are shown in figures 5-1.

> **Note**
> The limitations marked on the instruments apply to in-flight conditions. They are not intended to indicate ground operating limits.

ENGINE LIMITATIONS.
RECIPROCATING ENGINES.

In addition to the limitations indicated in figure 5-1, the limits discussed in the following paragraphs are imposed on reciprocating engine operation.

Maximum Overspeed.

Maximum overspeed is 3300 rpm. However, if engine speed has reached between 3100 and 3300 rpm the engine must be inspected before the next flight. If the engine speed exceeded 3300 rpm, the engine must be changed. All conditions of overspeeding are to be noted on the Form 781 (Form 1).

Minimum Idle Speed.

Minimum idling speed is 1100 rpm.

> **Note**
> During ground operation of the flaps or jet engine starting, the alternator-equipped engines (2, 3, 4, and 5) must be idled at 1200 rpm.

Engine Limitations with Advanced Spark.

Operation of the reciprocating engines at high cylinder head and carburetor air temperatures with advanced spark will result in detonation and subsequent engine failure. Operation has been found most critical at 160 bmep in the range of 1900 to 2200 rpm. To eliminate the possibility of encountering detonation in the critical range, the following instructions and limits will be strictly adhered to when operating in the advanced spark position.

1. Cylinder head temperature will be maintained at or below 220°C. The desired range for advanced spark operation is 210° to 220°C.

2. Carburetor air temperature will be maintained at or below 20°C. The desired range for advanced spark operation is 15° to 20°C.

Should icing conditions prevail and it is necessary to raise the CAT., while in the critical range (1900 to 2200 rpm) all operation in 30° advanced spark will be discontinued. The CAT. limit in 20° spark advance is 38°C.

Fan Speed Limitations.

Because of structural limitations of the fan, high ratio will not be used below 13,500 feet if the engine speed exceeds 2000 rpm. Between 13,500 and 20,000 feet, the

Figure 5-1. (Sheet 1)

Section V
Operating Limitations

INSTRUMENT MARKINGS

Reciprocating ENGINE INSTRUMENTS

OIL PRESSURE
- 45 Minimum For Speeds Below 2000 RPM
- 50 Minimum For Speeds Of 2000 RPM Or Above
- 55 to 80 Desired Operating Range
- 80 Maximum

FUEL PRESSURE
- 24 Minimum For Flight
- 24 to 26 Normal
- 28 Maximum

TORQUE PRESSURE
- 100 to 203 Manual Lean Permissible
- 203 to 238 Normal Or Rich Required
- 266 Maximum Take-Off (Wet)

CYLINDER HEAD TEMPERATURE
- 150 Minimum Permissible
- 180 to 220 Manual Lean Permissible (With Either Spark Position)
- 220 to 250 Any Power With Rich or Normal Mixture, 20° Spark Above 41,000 Ft. For Powers Above 2025 BHP, Normal or Rich At Any Altitude
- 250 Maximum

Jet ENGINE INSTRUMENTS

TAIL PIPE TEMPERATURE
- 315°C Minimum For Flight
- 315° to 655°C Continuous Operation
- 690°C Maximum For Flight
- 870°C Maximum During Start And Acceleration Only

JET TACHOMETER
- 30 to 96% Continuous Operation
- 100% Maximum For 30 Minutes

JET OIL PRESSURE
- 50 Maximum
- 10-45 Normal Operating Range 85% RPM And Above
- 5 Minimum 75% RPM Pressure Indication Minimum Idle 25% RPM

JET FUEL PRESSURE
- 20 Minimum For Flight
- 20 to 400 Desired Operating Range
- 400 to 500 Permissible At High Speed At Low Altitude With Low Ambient Temperatures
- 500 Maximum

NOTE: LIMITATIONS ARE BASED ON 115/145 GRADE FUEL.

Figure 5-1. (Sheet 2)

Section V
Operating Limitations

T.O. 1B-36D(II)-1

Figure 5-1. (Sheet 3)

high ratio may be used when engine speeds are below 2200 rpm. Either drive may be used above 20,000 feet.

Note

RPM limits are specified for limit CHT or closed air plugs, whichever occurs first. Large increases in cooling air flow obtained by abnormally wide air plug openings will cause fan horsepower to exceed structural limitations of the engine fan drive.

Turbo Overboost Limitations.

If overboost occurs during take-off and the take-off manifold pressure is exceeded by more than 10 inches for a period of 15 seconds, the engine must be changed before the next flight. If the take-off manifold pressure is exceeded by not more than 10 inches for a period of 15 seconds, the engine must be inspected prior to the next flight.

Operating Limits with Alternate Fuel Grade (100/130).

Manual Lean Permissible

Manifold Pressure	25 to 37.5 inches
RPM	1240 to 2230 rpm
Cylinder Head Temperature	150° to 218°C
Carburetor Air Temperature	20°C maximum

Normal Mixture

Manifold Pressure	37.5 to 45.5 inches
RPM	2230 to 2550 rpm
Cylinder Head Temperature	218° to 232°C
Carburetor Air Temperature	38°C maximum

Maximum Allowable

Manifold Pressure	53.5 inches
RPM	2700 rpm
Cylinder Head Temperature	232°C
Carburetor Air Temperature	38°C

CAUTION

When using alternate grade fuel the spark advance setting will not be used.

JET ENGINES.

The limits for jet engine operation which are not shown in figure 5-1 are given in the following paragraphs.

Maximum Overspeed.

Maximum overspeed is 104 per cent rpm. Engine overspeed operation reaching 104 per cent rpm requires that the engine be changed even though over-temperature limits were not encountered.

Minimum Idle Speed.

Minimum idle speed is 25 per cent rpm.

Revised 18 May 1956

JET ENGINE EXHAUST TEMPS VERSUS RPM & OAT.

OAT.	PERCENT RPM	EXHAUST TEMPS.
−18° to 5°C (0° to 40°F)	96-100	680°C (±10)
5° to 27°C (40° to 80°F)	96-100	670°C (±10)
27°C and Above (81°F and Above)	96-100	680°C (±10)

Figure 5-2.

Note

Rapid advancement of the throttle on an engine idling below 25 per cent rpm will probably cause a flame-out. For minimum flight idle speed refer to Appendix 1.

Over-Temperature Operation.

Engine Starts Up to Idle Rpm (Usually Within 2 Minutes). A temperature of 950°C or above for a duration of 2 seconds or more constitutes an overtemperature condition and requires turbine wheel removal and inspection.

All Engine Operation Except Starts. Each of the following constitutes an overtemperature condition:

1. Temperatures of 690°C to 750°C for 40 seconds or more.

2. Temperatures of 750°C to 800°C for 10 seconds or more.

3. Temperatures above 800°C for 2 seconds or more.

Note

The pilot must record the degree and duration of the above overtemperature conditions on DD Form 781 in order that proper maintenance inspection can be accomplished. Failure to record overtemperature conditions could result in turbine failure and possible engine loss.

AIR-SPEED LIMITATIONS.

The maximum continuous indicated speeds and limit dive speeds are shown in figure 5-3. Other limiting air speeds are as follows:

1. The maximum IAS for the following operations is 188 mph because of structural limitations.

a. Landing gear extension and retraction.

CAUTION

To prevent exceeding the structural limitations of the canoe doors, the 188 mph IAS limit will be observed any time the landing gear canoe doors are open or closed and not locked.

Section V
Operating Limitations

T.O. 1B-36D(II)-1

b. Landing light extension.
c. Full aileron deflection.
d. Flap extension.

2. The maximum IAS for bomb bay door operation is 286 mph.

PROPELLER AND FLAP LIMITATIONS.

The operating limits for propellers and flaps are reflected in figure 5-4.

PROHIBITED MANEUVERS.

All acrobatics including spins and stalls are prohibited. The maximum permissible bank while turning is 60 degrees at a gross weight of 357,500 pounds.

ACCELERATION LIMITATIONS.

The diagrams in figure 5-5 show the airplane acceleration limits vs. air speed for altitudes from 10,000 to 45,000 feet for two gross weight conditions. The accelerations as shown represent the limit design factors for the aircraft structure. The airplane must operate within the boundaries of the appropriate curve corresponding to its weight and altitude at all times.

Each of the curves is an envelope of several limiting curves and is the maximum allowable acceleration for any given speed. These limiting curves include maximum wing lift, specified maneuver factors, positive and negative gust factors, buffet boundaries (characterized at low speeds by small buffeting and at high speeds by lift divergence), and the airplane limit diving speeds.

BUFFETING LIMITATIONS.

Figure 5-6 presents the variation of equivalent air speed with gross weight for buffeting at high speed and at stall. The chart can be used to determine the maximum angle of bank limited by buffet when flying at a given altitude, air speed, and gross weight. An example in the use of the curve is included on the chart.

CENTER OF GRAVITY LIMITATIONS.

The forward cg limit varies with gross weight between 17 per cent and 22 per cent MAC. The most aft cg limit it 45 per cent MAC. Refer to T.O. 1-1B-40.

Maximum INDICATED AIR SPEEDS

- Maximum continuous indicated air speeds are based on structural ability to withstand an indicated gust of 50k feet per second velocity.
- Limit dive indicated air speeds are based on flutter and dynamic pressure restrictions. Gusts are not considered; but in general, indicated gusts of 30k feet per second or better can be withstood at these speeds.
- The limit diving indicated air speeds shown in this chart are based on structural limitations of the airframe. Normal diving indicated air speeds must be based on propeller limitations.

WITH JET PODS

ALTITUDE, FEET	MAXIMUM CONTINUOUS INDICATED AIR SPEED — MPH		LIMIT DIVE SPEED — MPH
	370,000 LBS. GROSS WEIGHT	280,000 LBS. G.W. OR LESS	ALL GROSS WEIGHTS
SEA LEVEL	251	267	287
10,000	248	270	291
20,000	242	272	293
27,500	234	276	296
30,000	232	277	282
35,000	229	255	256
40,000	222	227	228
45,000	193	198	199
50,000	167	173	180

WITHOUT JET PODS

ALTITUDE, FEET	MAXIMUM CONTINUOUS INDICATED AIR SPEED — MPH		LIMIT DIVE SPEED — MPH
	357,500 LBS. GROSS WEIGHT	280,000 LBS. G.W. OR LESS	ALL GROSS WEIGHTS
SEA LEVEL	250	250	287
10,000	235	235	280
20,000	221	221	264
25,000	214	214	257
30,000	207	207	249
35,000	200	200	241
40,000	182	182	223
45,000	164	164	199

INTERPOLATE FOR INTERMEDIATE GROSS WEIGHTS

Figure 5-3. Maximum Indicated Air Speeds

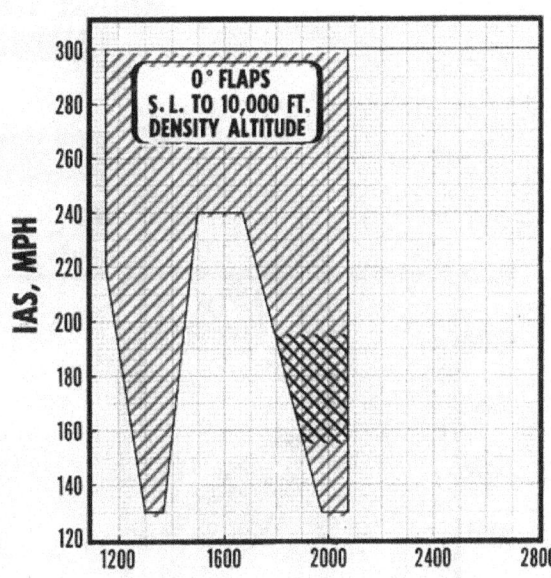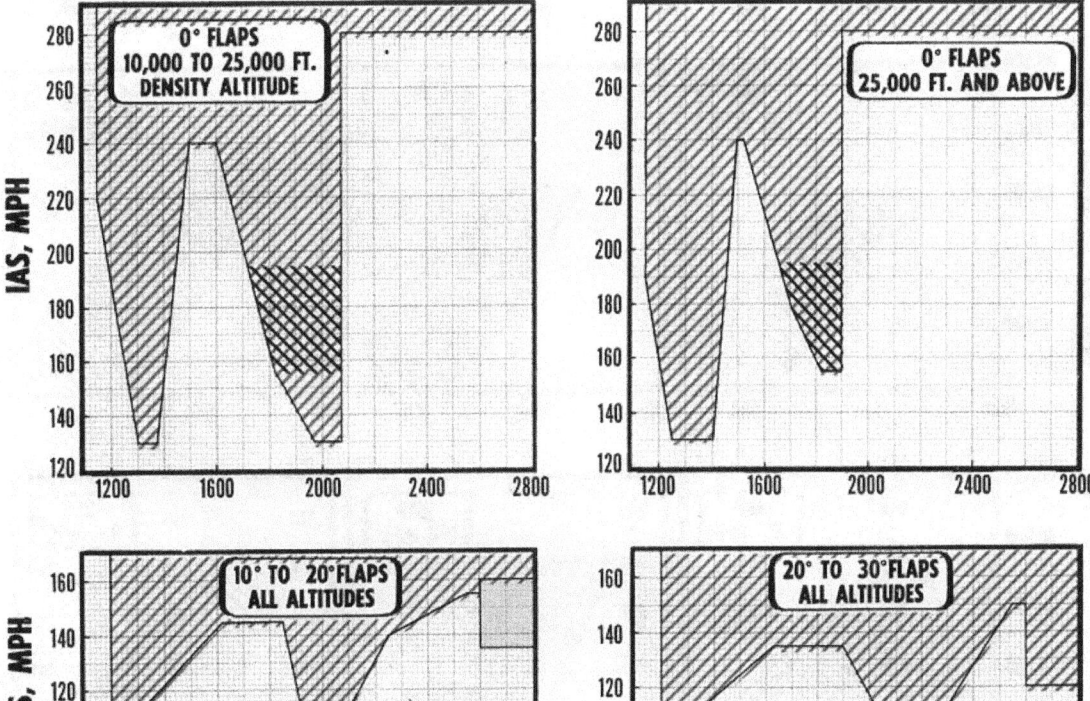

Figure 5-4. (Sheet 1)

Section V
Operating Limitations

T.O. 1B-36D(II)-1

R4360-41 ENGINE
SQUARE TIP PROPELLER LIMITATIONS

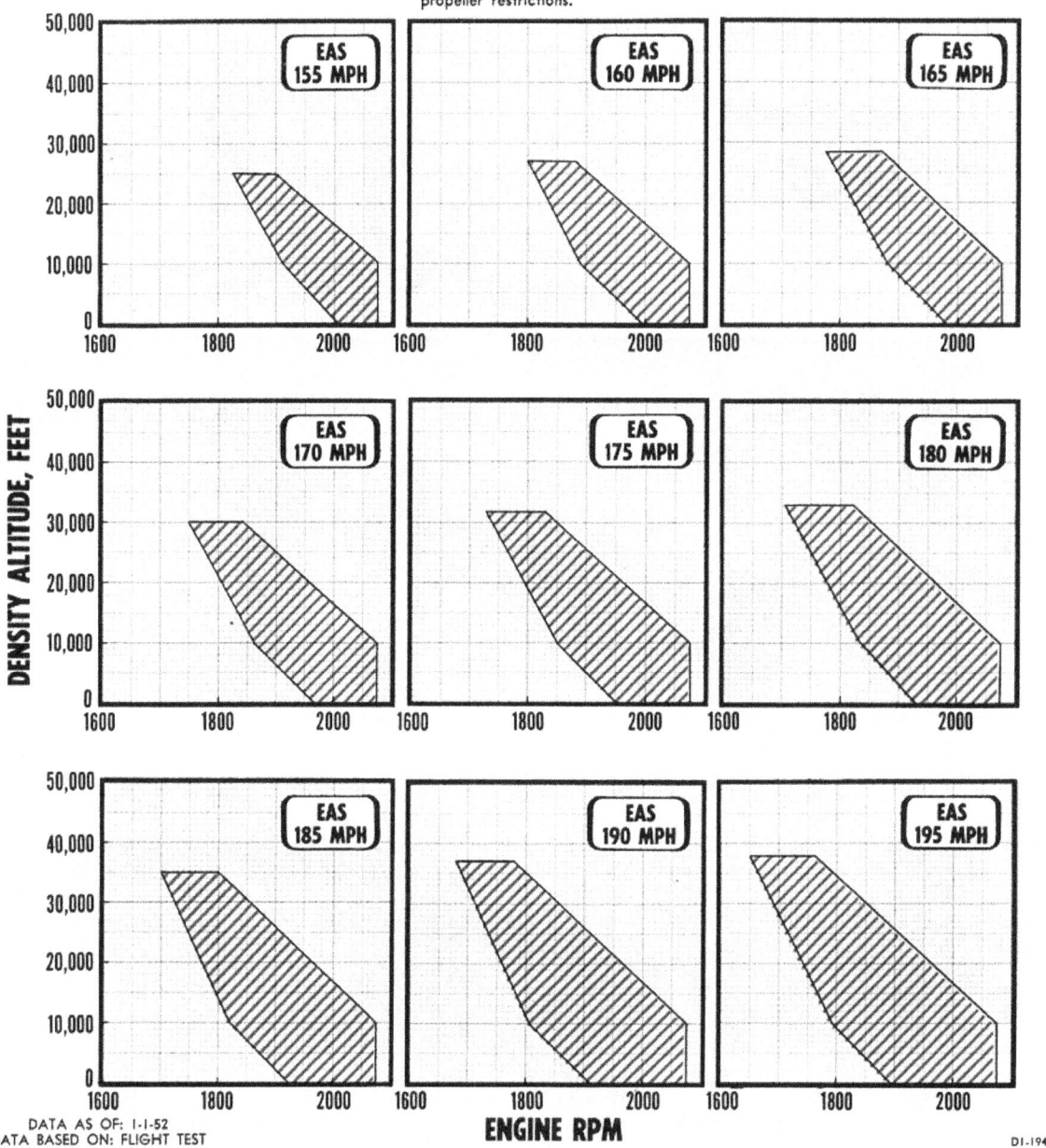

Figure 5-4. (Sheet 2)

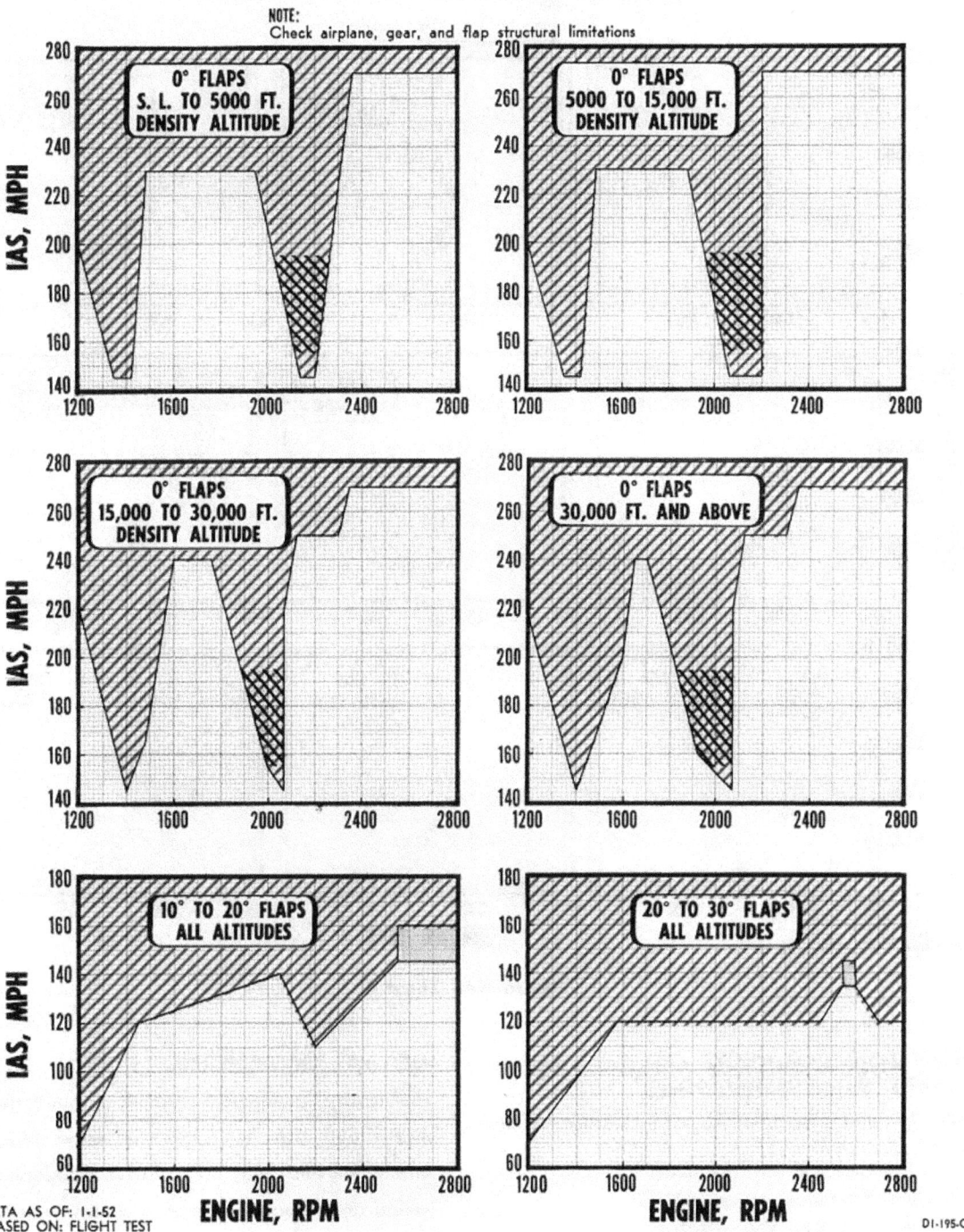

Figure 5-4. (Sheet 3)

Section V
Operating Limitations

T.O. 1B-36D(II)-1

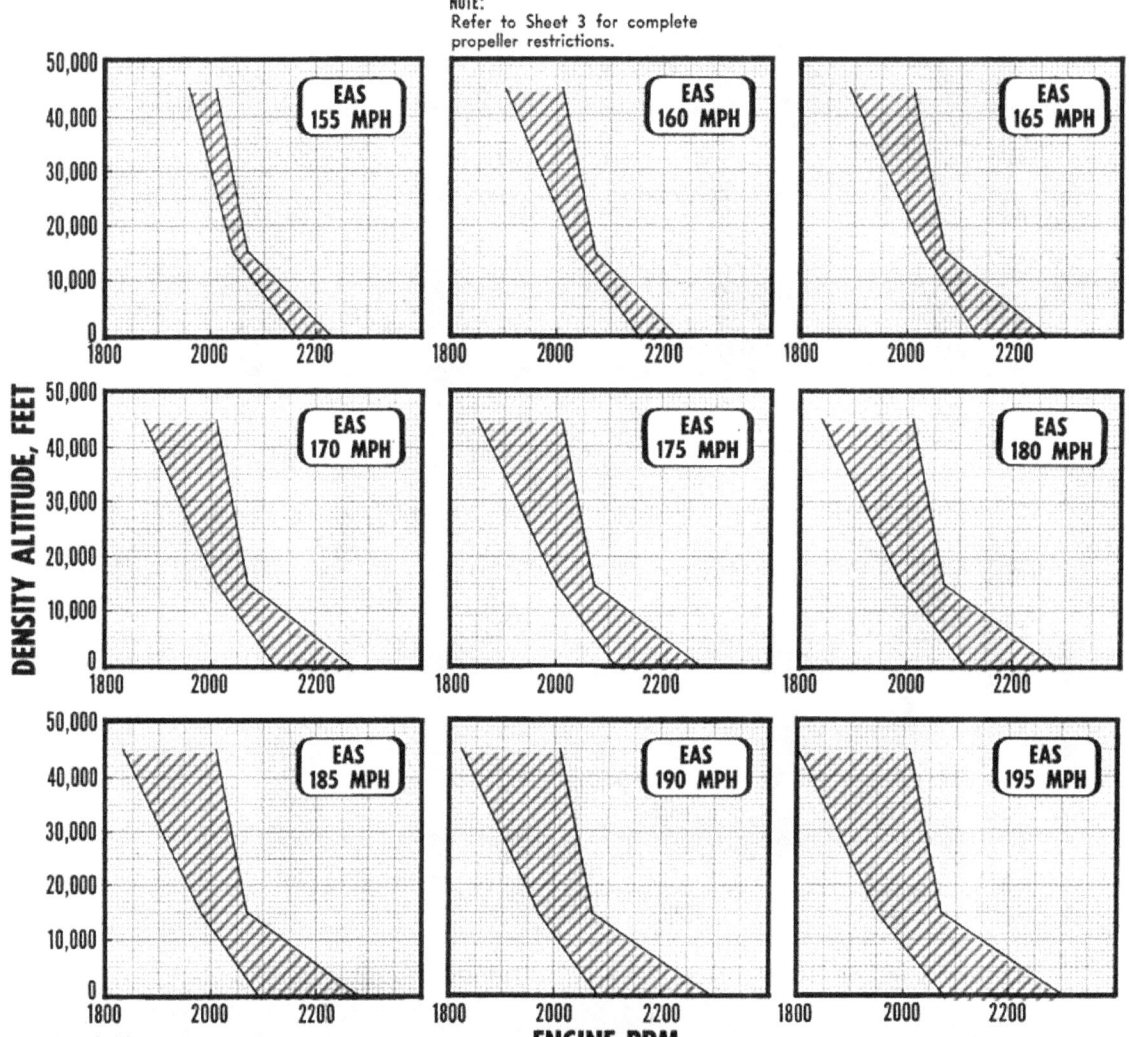

Figure 5-4. (Sheet 4)

HEAT AND ANTI-ICING AIR TEMPERATURE LIMITATIONS.

The maximum allowable heat and anti-icing air temperatures are as follows:
1. Cabin Heat and Tail Anti-Icing Air—215°C.
2. Forward Cabin Duct Air—105°C.
3. Wing Anti-Icing Air—180°C.

The minimum speeds necessary to prevent exceeding these temperatures are given in figure 5-7.

WEIGHT LIMITATIONS.

The airplane is designed to provide optimum performance at high altitudes, an excess of power being available at take-offs and low altitudes. Maximum gross weight for operation is therefore established primarily by structural considerations. These considerations are explained in the following paragraphs.

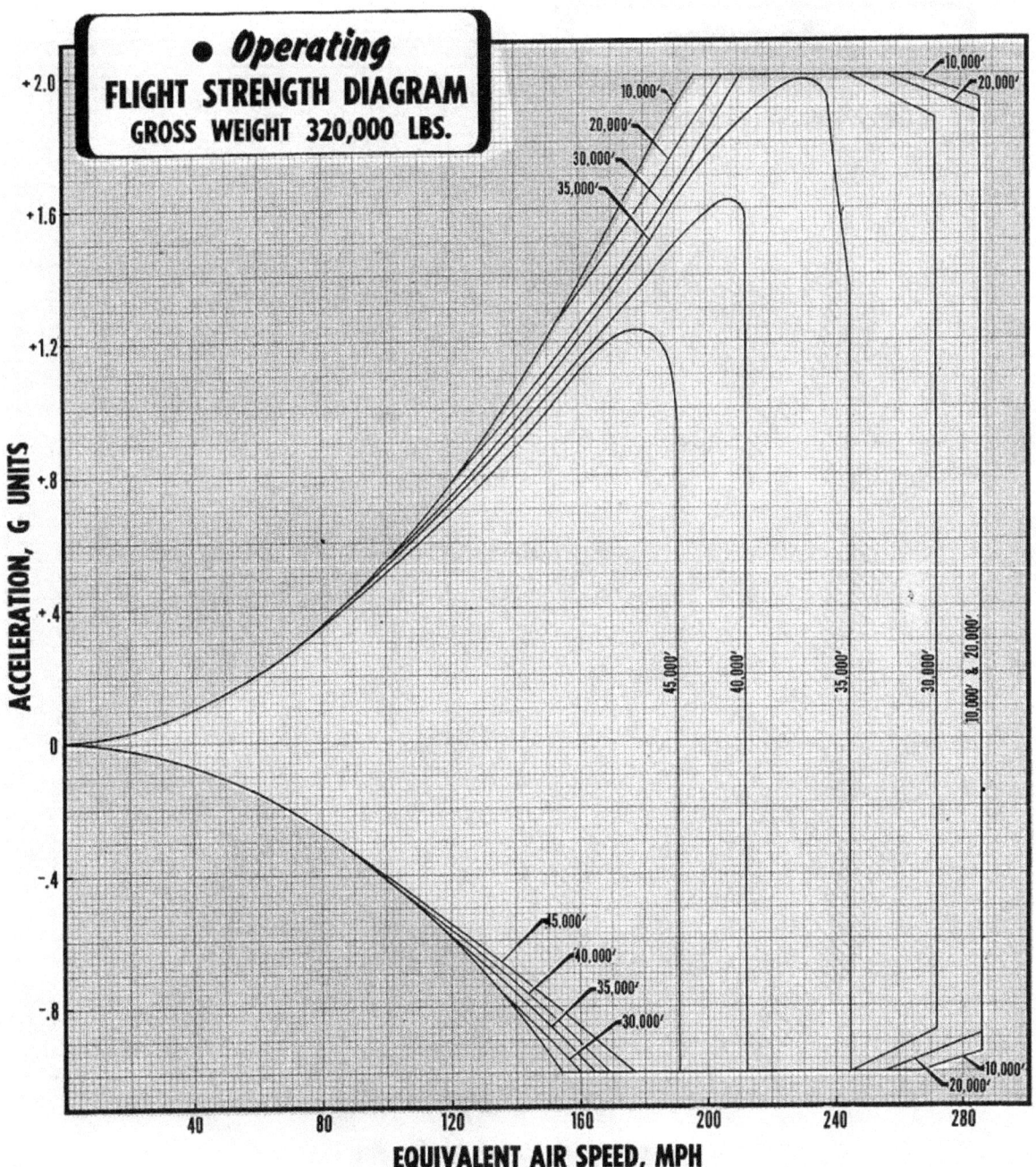

Figure 5-5. (Sheet 1)

LOAD FACTORS.

It is readily understandable that as a structure is loaded to higher weights, its ability to withstand gust shocks or additional maneuver loads becomes increasingly less. The minimum flight factor generally considered acceptable is 2.0. Should a mission involve excessive maneuvering or flight under very turbulent conditions early in the flight, higher factors might be advisable. It should be noted, however, that with the high percentage of expendable load carried by the airplane, the allowable load factor continually increases as the flight progresses.

Section V
Operating Limitations

T.O. 1B-36D(II)-1

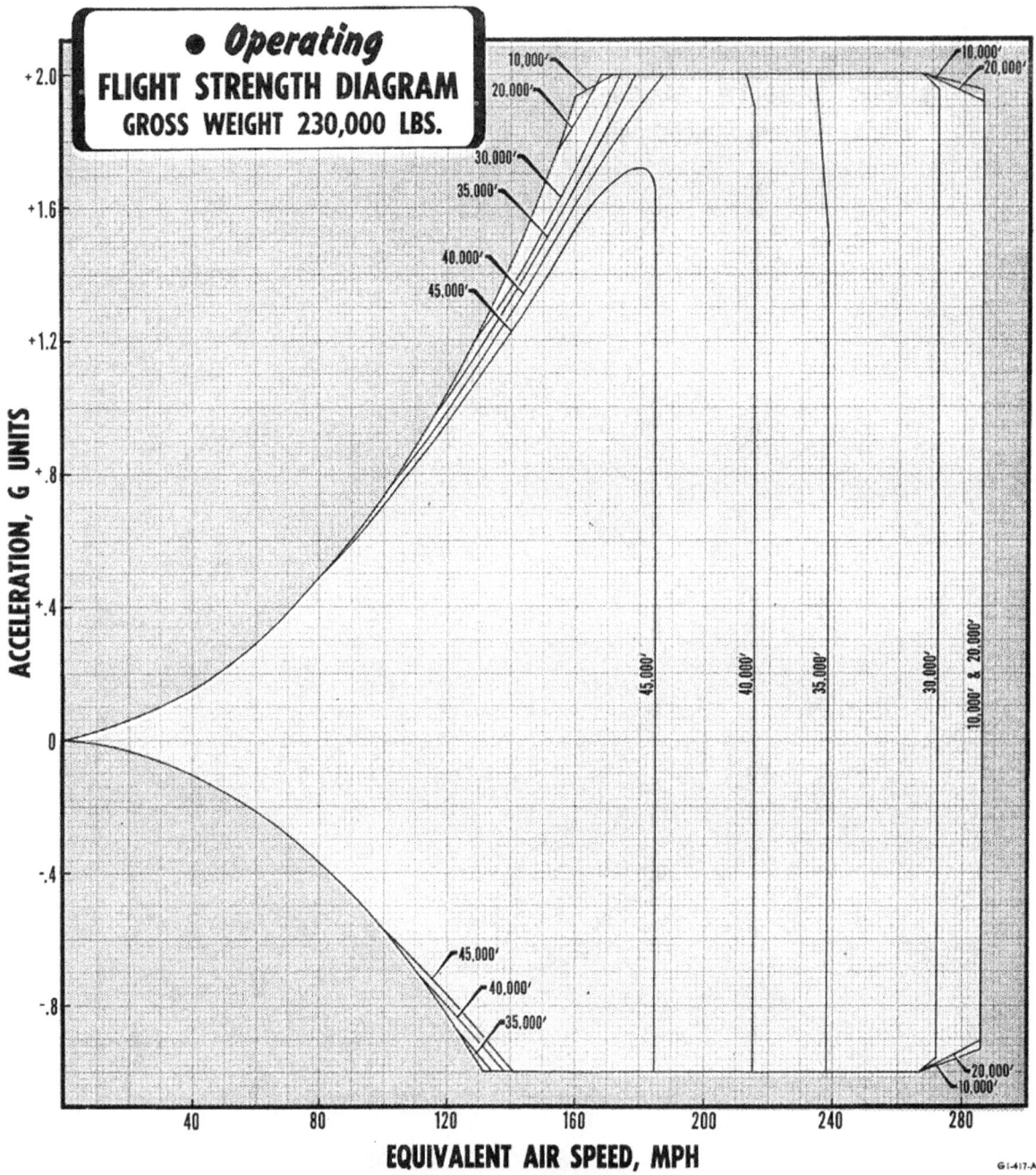

Figure 5-5. (Sheet 2)

DISTRIBUTION OF LOAD.

The maximum load that the airplane can carry is dependent on the way that load is distributed. The weight of an airplane in flight is carried by the wings, and therefore the more load that is carried in the fuselage, the greater will be the bending moment on the wings. This means that the airplane might safely carry 175,000 pounds if 55,000 pounds were carried in the fuselage and 120,000 pounds in the wings. But the same 175,000 pounds would be an unsafe load if 120,000 pounds were carried in the fuselage and 55,000 pounds in the wings.

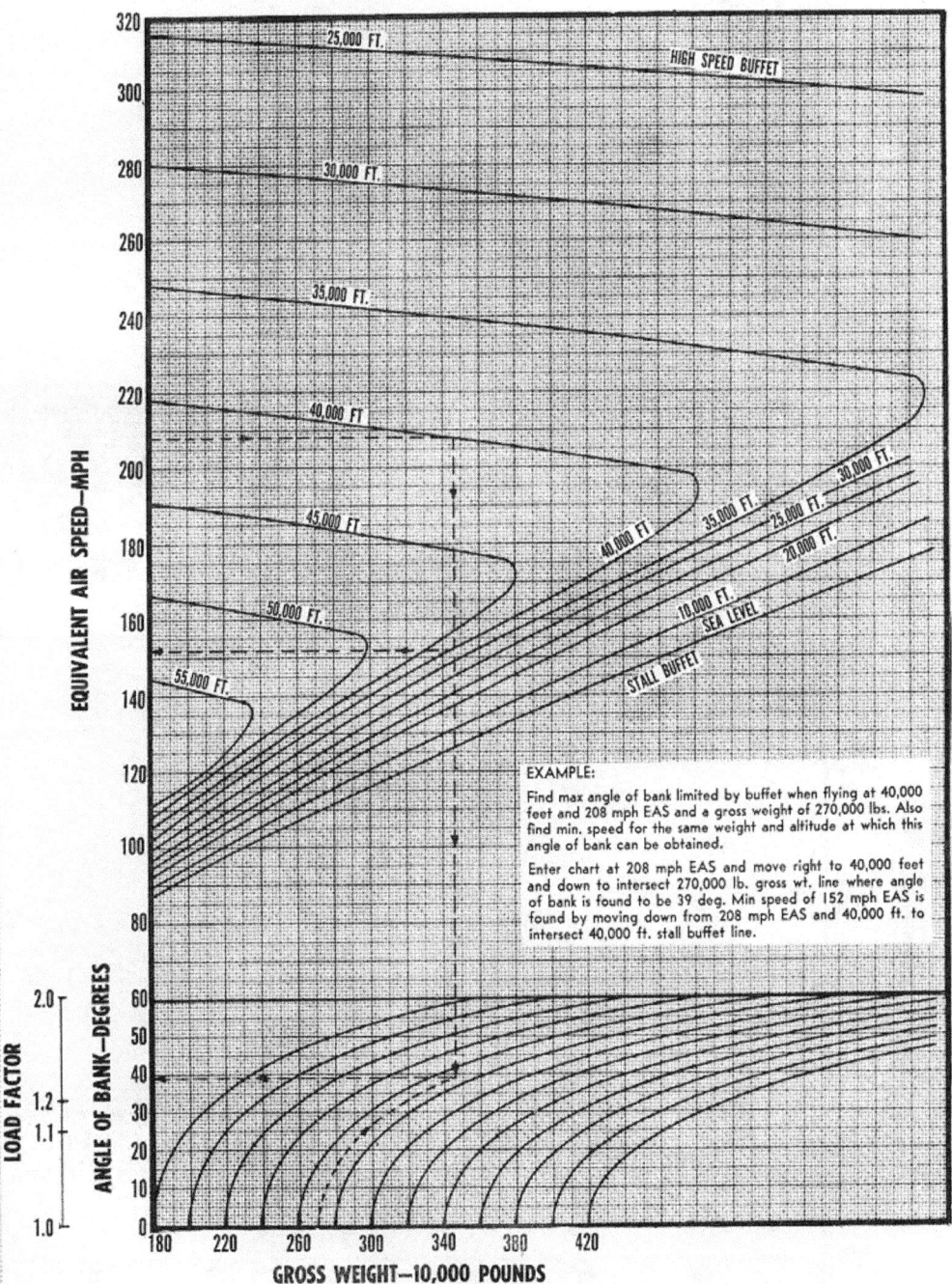

Figure 5-6.

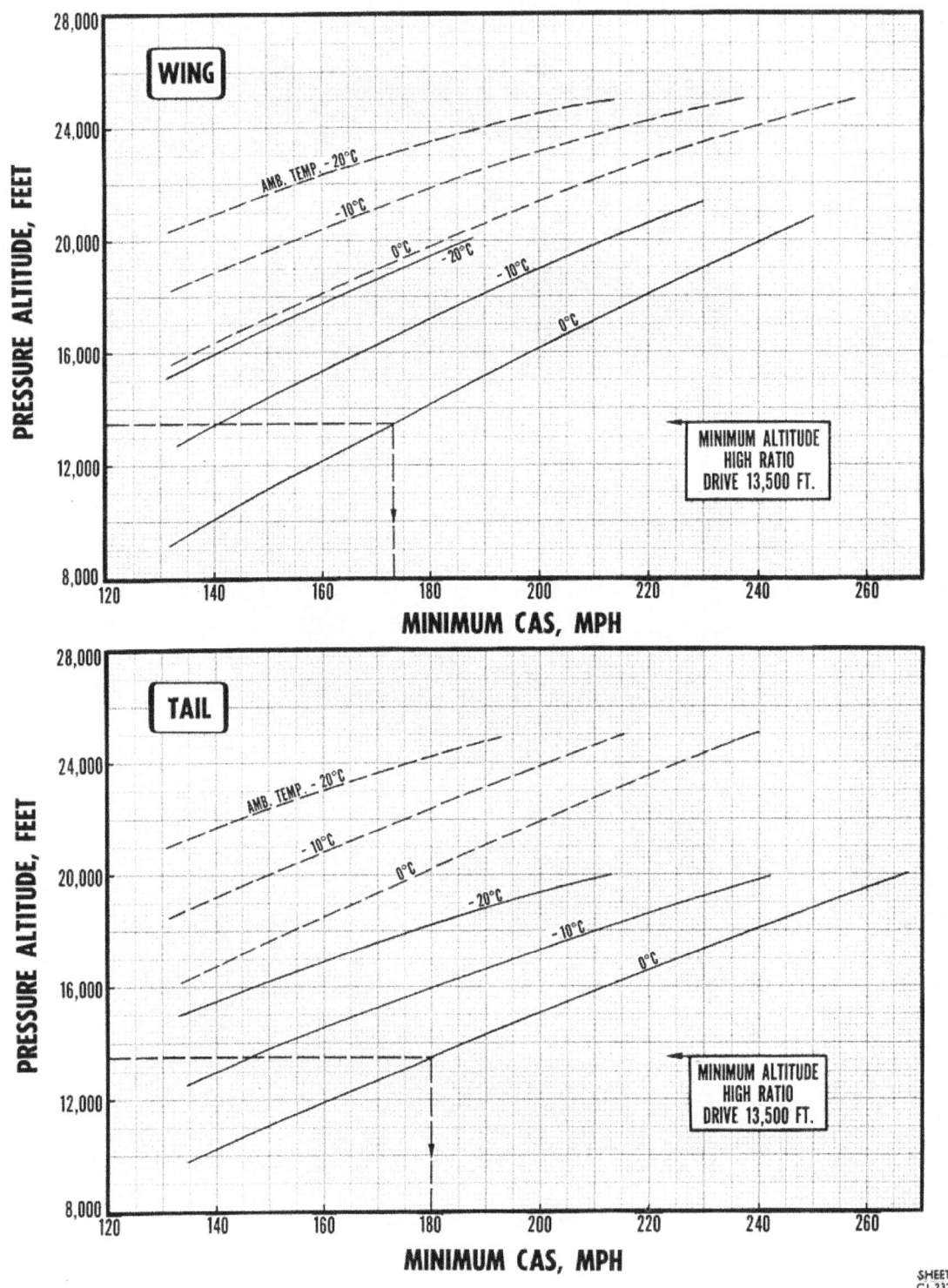

Figure 5-7. (Sheet 1)

HEAT AND ANTI-ICING LIMITATIONS AT 1500 HORSEPOWER

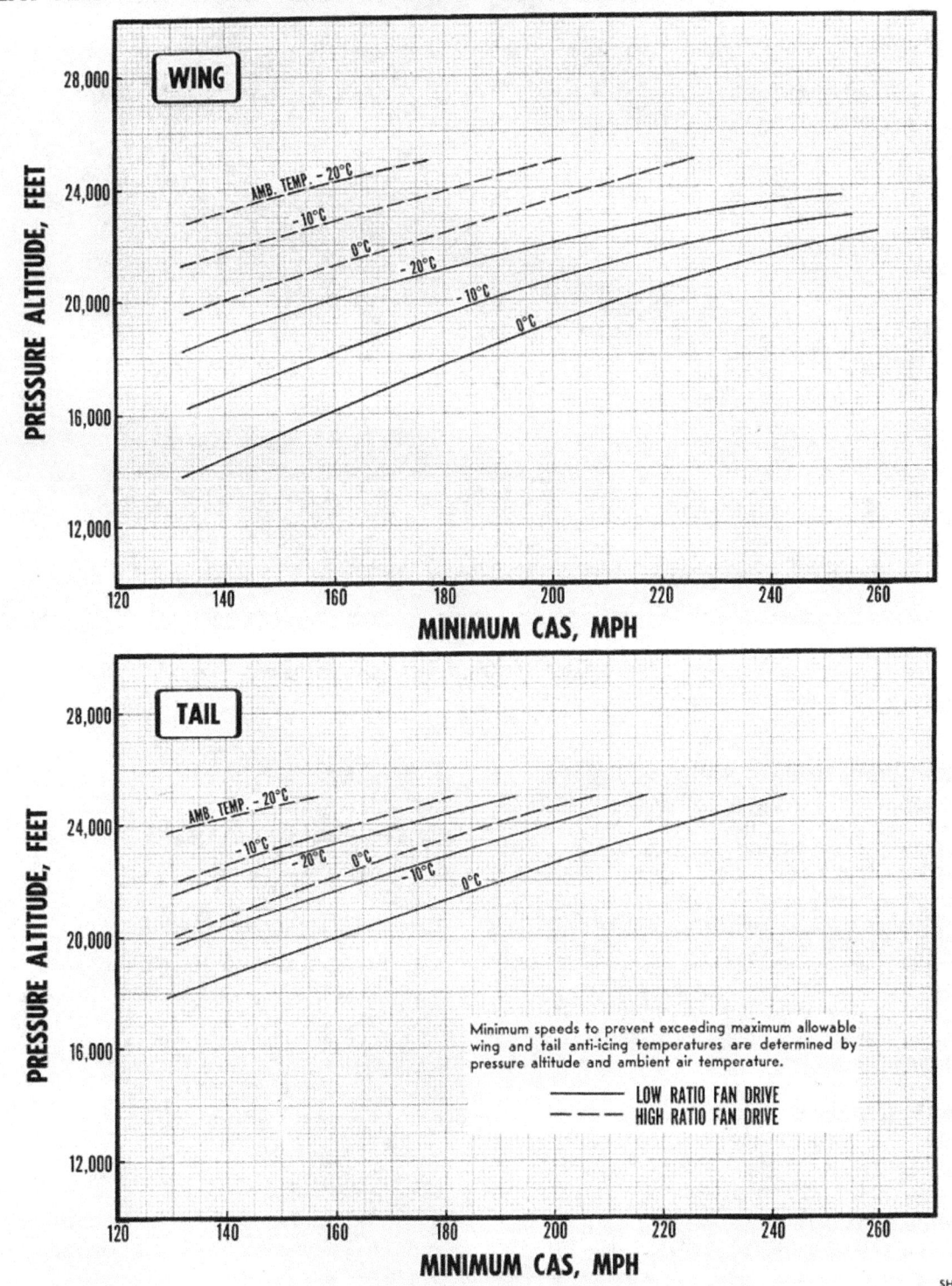

Figure 5-7. (Sheet 2)

Section V
Operating Limitations

T.O. 1B-36D(II)-1

OPERATIONAL WEIGHT LIMITATIONS
WITH PODS

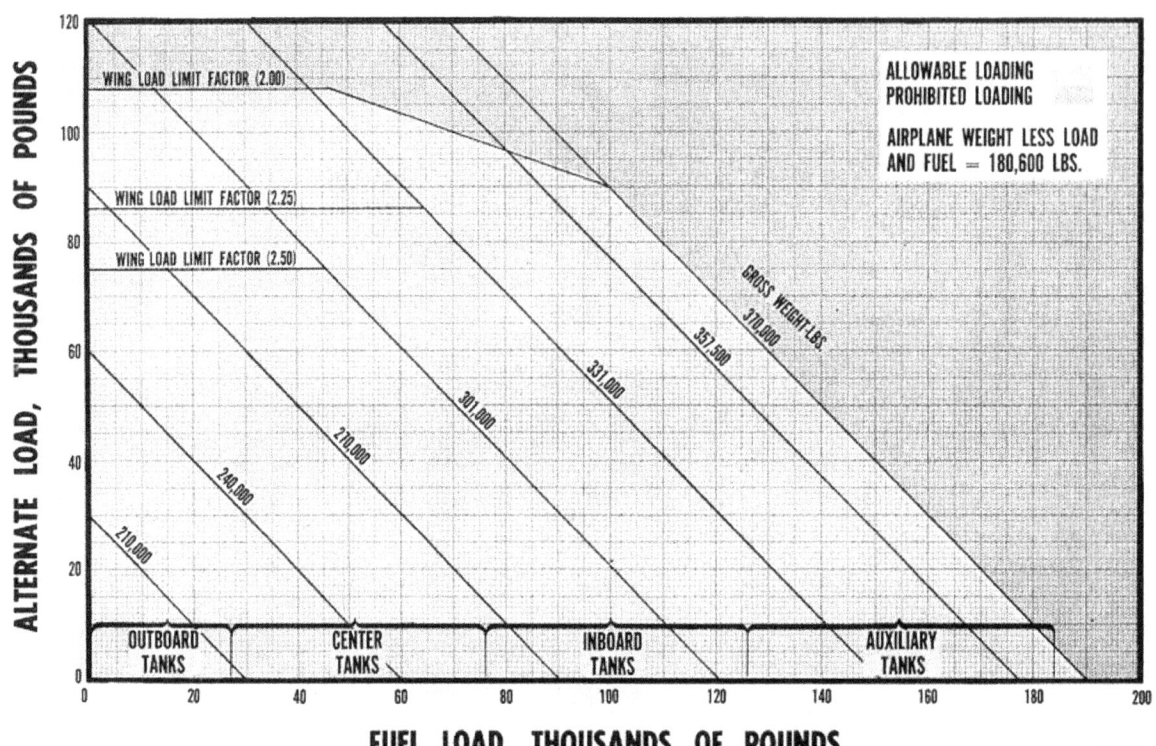

Figure 5-8.

OPERATIONAL WEIGHT LIMITATIONS CHART.

The purpose of the "Operational Weight Limitations Chart" (figure 5-8) is to illustrate the weight carrying capabilities of the airplane in relation to the various criteria that limit safe operation. In this fashion, the flight planner can visualize the type of limitation that is restricting maximum permissible weight and judge for himself, based on the urgency of the mission, as to how near any limitation shall be approached. In other words, the chart serves as a warning of the specific dangers involved in loading the airplane, but leaves the matter of selecting maximum weight in the hands of the flight planner.

Operating Weight.

As shown in the upper right corner of the chart, the data is for B-36D's which weigh 180,600 pounds before any fuel or alternate load is added. The alternate load shown includes only bombs carried in the bomb bay. Alternate load could also include any additional load, such as extra fuel tanks, carried in the fuselage. The weight of the standard crew, oil, ammunition, standard equipment, etc., is included in the 180,600 pounds.

Gross Weight.

The gross weights of the loaded airplane are shown by the lines which slope at a 45-degree angle to the axes of the chart. Note that the zero point of the chart (intersection of the vertical and horizontal axes) represents a gross weight of 180,600 pounds.

Fuel Versus Alternate Load Capacity.

The various wing fuel tank capacities are shown on the chart. In order to provide maximum wing bending relief in flight, fuel should be maintained as far outboard as possible. To accomplish this, when the airplane is fueled the outer tanks should be filled first, then the center, then the inboard, and last the auxiliary wing tanks. In flight the fuel should be used in the reverse order. The load factors shown on this chart are based on this fuel sequencing. At the maximum gross weight of 370,000 pounds, the maximum alternate load is 90,000 pounds provided the cg location is maintained aft of 25 per cent of the mean aerodynamic chord.

The maximum bomb load for the various size bombs are tabulated below:

Size	Quantity	Bomb Wt.-Lbs.	Rack & Equip. Wt.-Lbs.	Total Wt.-Lbs.
500 lbs. (AN-M64A1)	132	68,904	2732	71,636
1000 lbs. (AN-M65A1)	72	71,784	1937	73,721
2000 lbs. (AN-M66-A2)	28	57,736	1552	59,288
4000 lbs. (AN-M56A1)	12	50,412	900	51,312
12,000 lbs. (M-109)	4	50,488	2004	52,492
22,000 lbs. (M-110)	3	69,411	1839	71,250

The design limit factor for the supporting structure of any of the above bomb loads is 2.67.

Wing Flight Load Factors.

Wing flight load factors of 2.00, 2.25 and 2.50 are represented. The 2.00 load factor line represents the minimum normally considered acceptable; the 2.25 and 2.50 load factor lines are included for comparative purposes. A load factor of 2.00 will result in each of the following instances:

1. At a gross weight of 286,600 pounds with no fuel in the wings.

2. At a gross weight of 337,600 pounds with 50,000 pounds of fuel in the wings.

3. At a gross weight of 370,000 pounds with 99,000 pounds of fuel in the wings.

Landing Gear Load Factor.

The landing gear is satisfactory for taxiing and take-off at a gross weight of 370,000 pounds. The maximum allowable gross weight for landing is 357,500 pounds.

Using the Chart.

The chart in figure 5-8 can be used for any B-36D airplane regardless of operating weight provided that the pods are installed and that no external loads are supported by the wing. Any wing loading other than internal fuel, as shown on the chart, would invalidate the wing flight load factor curves. Two examples are given to illustrate the use of the chart.

PROBLEM 1.—Twenty thousand gallons of fuel are required to attack a given target, what is the maximum bomb load that can be carried?

SOLUTION—Having established from Form F that the airplane weighs 180,600 pounds before the fuel and bombs have been added, enter the chart at a fuel weight of 120,000 pounds (20,000 x 6 pounds per gallon). Moving vertically to the line representing a wing limit factor of 2.0, it is determined that a maximum bomb load of 69,000 pounds can be carried. Should it be established from the Form F that the airplane weighs say for example, 185,000 pounds before the fuel and bombs have been added, subtract the difference between 185,000 and 180,600 from the allowable alternate load. That is, a maximum bomb load of 69,000 minus (185,000 minus 180,600) or 64,600 pounds can be carried.

PROBLEM 2.—Determine if a bomb load of 72,000 pounds can be dropped on a target requiring 18,000 gallons of fuel to accomplish the mission.

SOLUTION—Enter the chart at a fuel weight of 108,000 pounds (18,000 x 6 pounds per gallon). Move vertically up the line representing this weight until the line representing an alternate load of 72,000 pounds is reached. The chart indicates that this loading condition is possible since the lines intersect in the green area representing allowable loads.

Section V
Operating Limitations

T.O. 1B-36D(II)-1

Section VI
FLIGHT CHARACTERISTICS

Even though this airplane is the largest tactical type, its pusher design offers some advantages over comparable tractor designs. This is particularly true of flight characteristics and performance.

Uniform weight distribution and servo-tab controls account for the conventional response with normal stick forces. However, more weight is located at correspondingly greater distances from any given control axis. This increased inertia effect reduces the rate of control response. Maneuvers must therefore be planned further ahead.

Along with this maneuver anticipation, you will need increased clearance perception or dimensional awareness. Roll and pitch limits on take-offs and landings are narrowed by the physical dimensions of the airplane.

STALLS.

A study of stall characteristics is primarily a study of those factors which influence the flow of air over the top of the wing. When flow is smooth, lift exists; when flow separates or burbles, lift is largely destroyed.

PROPELLER INDUCED AIRFLOW EFFECT

SHADED WING TIP AREAS OUTSIDE THE PROPELLER ARCS WILL STALL WHEN CRITICAL ANGLE OF ATTACK IS REACHED.

WHEN POWER IS ON, PROPELLER SUCTION DELAYS STALL IN CENTER SECTION BY MAINTAINING SMOOTH AIRFLOW.

Figure 6-1.

Section VI
Flight Characteristics

T.O. 1B-36D(II)-1

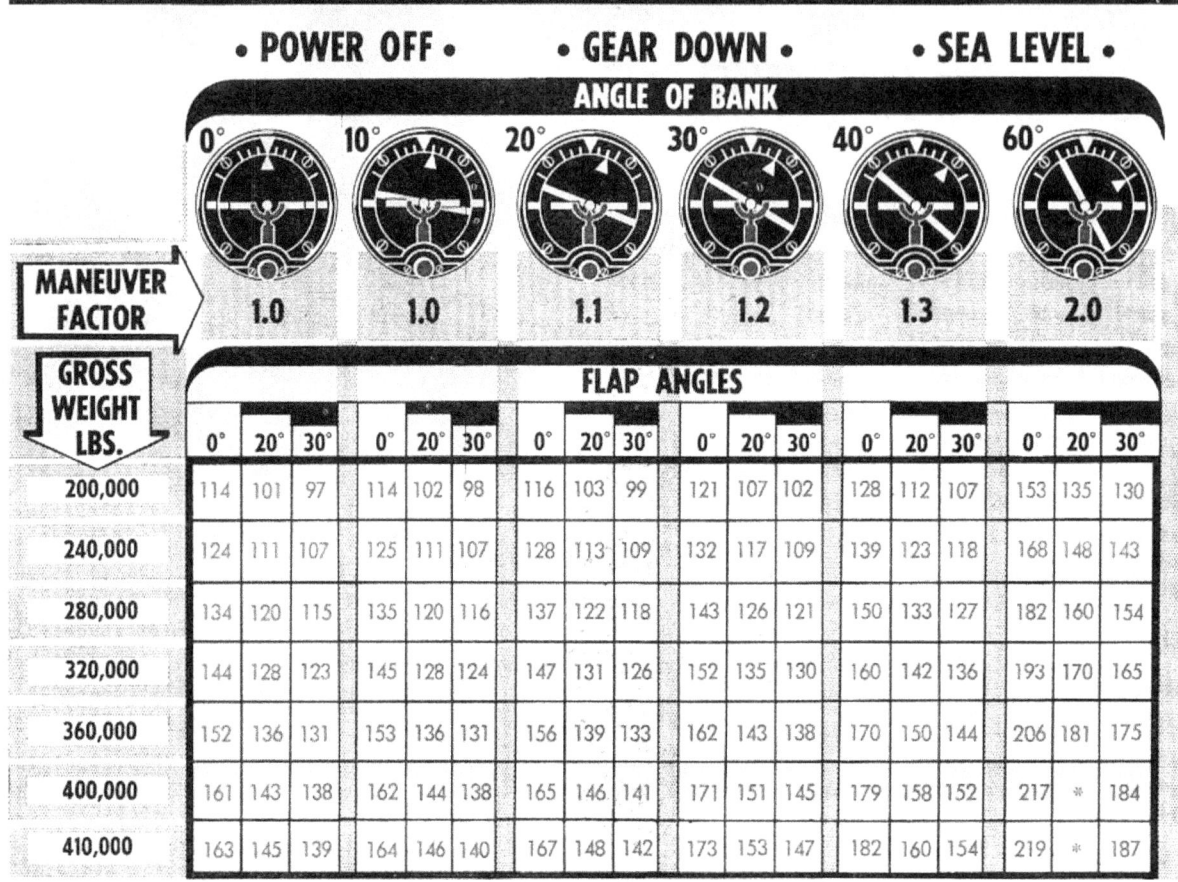

Figure 6-2.

NON-ACCELERATED POWER-OFF STALLS.

Power-off stall characteristics are conventional with unusually distinct warnings. During the entry you will notice tail buffeting, aileron shake, and increased stick resistance. There is a slight tendency to roll as the full stall is approached, but this is controllable.

At full stall, you will notice both roll and pitch down. There is no predominant direction of roll, and with normal recovery technique the amount of roll will be restricted by the inertia effect of the wing.

Recovery is orthodox, and with proper technique you can hold the altitude loss to less than 1500 feet. Flaps may intensify tail buffeting and pitch down, but the position of the landing gear exerts no noticeable effect.

NON-ACCELERATED POWER-ON STALLS.

Full stalls have been accomplished with a power setting of 20 inches M.P. The usual power-off warnings are still present. Tail buffeting is reduced, but aileron shake is more noticeable. In addition, you will notice an unusually high deck angle during the approach. Propeller induced air flow, as shown in figure 6-1, maintains smooth flow over the center section of the wing well beyond the angle at which a stall would normally occur with a tractor type engine installation. This extreme nose-high attitude combined with very low air speed is another stall warning. Since the wing tips extend beyond the propeller air flow effect, separation of flow occurs when the critical angle is reached. This increases the rolling tendency, but roll is controllable

STALLING SPEED Chart

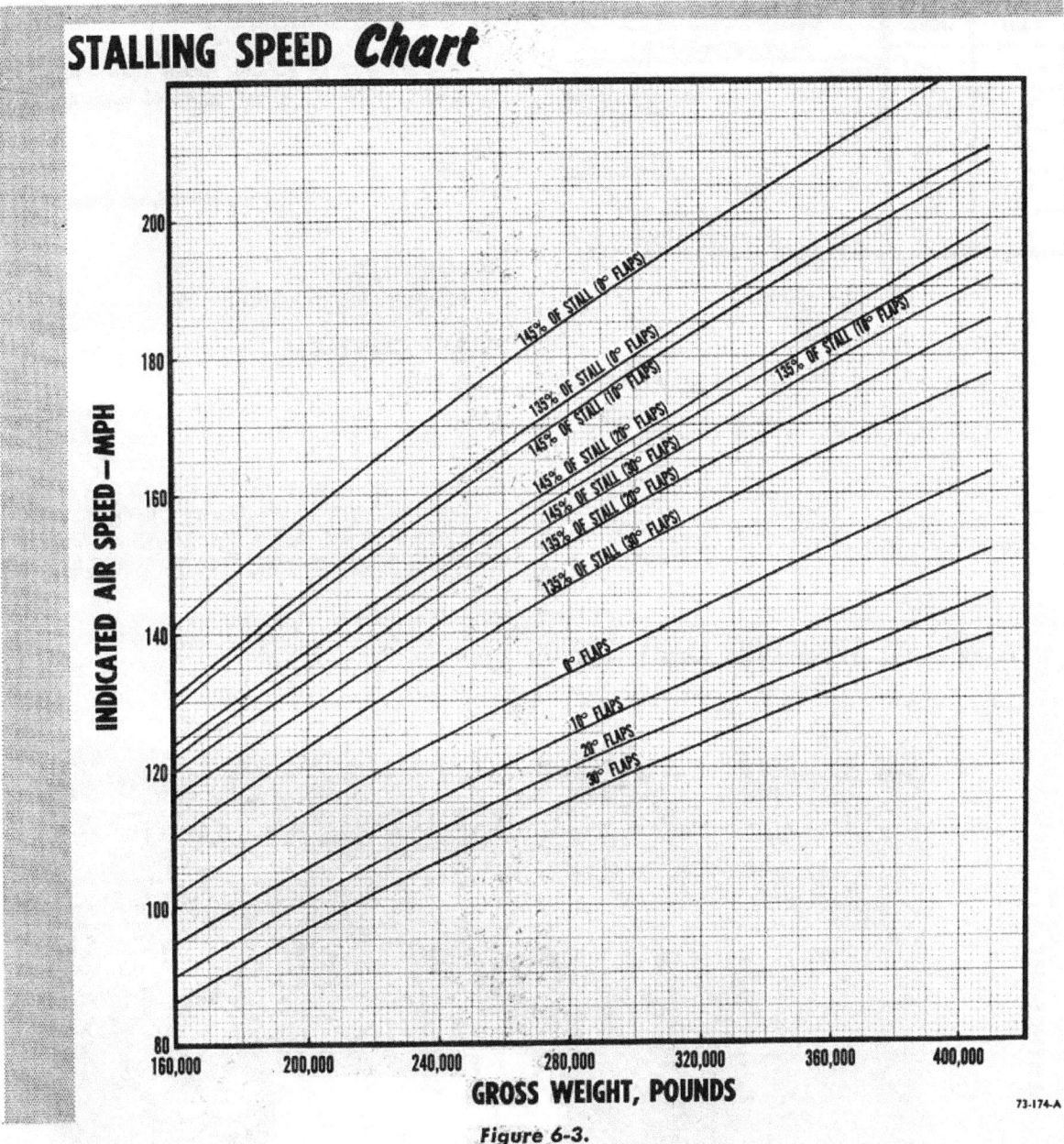

Figure 6-3.

up to complete stall. Conventional recovery technique is effective.

ACCELERATED STALLS.

No accelerated stalls have been accomplished, but entry, stall, and recovery should be normal.

PRACTICE STALLS.

Practice stalls are not permitted.

STALLING SPEEDS.

Calculated stalling speeds for various gross weights, flap settings, and angles of bank are given in figure 6-2. The chart in figure 6-3 presents a quick reference for stalling and approach speeds at different gross weights and flap settings.

Section VI
Flight Characteristics

ANGLE OF BANK	CORRECTION FACTOR
15°	1.016
30°	1.075
45°	1.186
60°	1.410
70°	1.813

CORRECTION FACTOR (ANGLE OF BANK) x STALLING SPEED (LEVEL FLIGHT) = STALLING SPEED (ANGLE OF BANK)

Example:

If the stalling speed in level flight is 114 mph IAS, determine the corrected stalling speed for a 30-degree angle of bank.

From the table find that the correction factor for a 30-degree angle is 1.075. Then substituting in the above formula,

1.075 x 114 = 123 mph IAS,

determine that the corrected stalling speed is 123 mph IAS in this instance.

Figure 6-4.

Note

In figure 6-3, note that curves representing 135 and 145 per cent of stall for 30-, 20-, and 10-degree flaps are not 135 and 145 per cent of the stalling speed curve for the respective flap setting as it might appear. To obtain a per cent of an air speed, apply the percentage to EAS rather than IAS, because compressibility and position errors do not vary with air speed in a straight line.

The relationships of stalling speeds with wings level to stalling speeds at certain angles of bank are given in figure 6-4.

SPINS.

Since spins are absolutely prohibited, no experimental recovery data is available.

ACROBATICS.

All acrobatics are prohibited.

FLIGHT CONTROLS.

TRIM TABS.

Control forces should be trimmed out to maintain normal control response. You should reset the elevator tab just before take-off using 30 per cent MAC as a cg reference point. Allow 1 degree nose-up trim for each 1 per cent cg forward of 30 per cent MAC, or 1 degree nose-down trim for each 1 per cent cg aft of 30 per cent MAC. Actuating either flaps or landing gear will

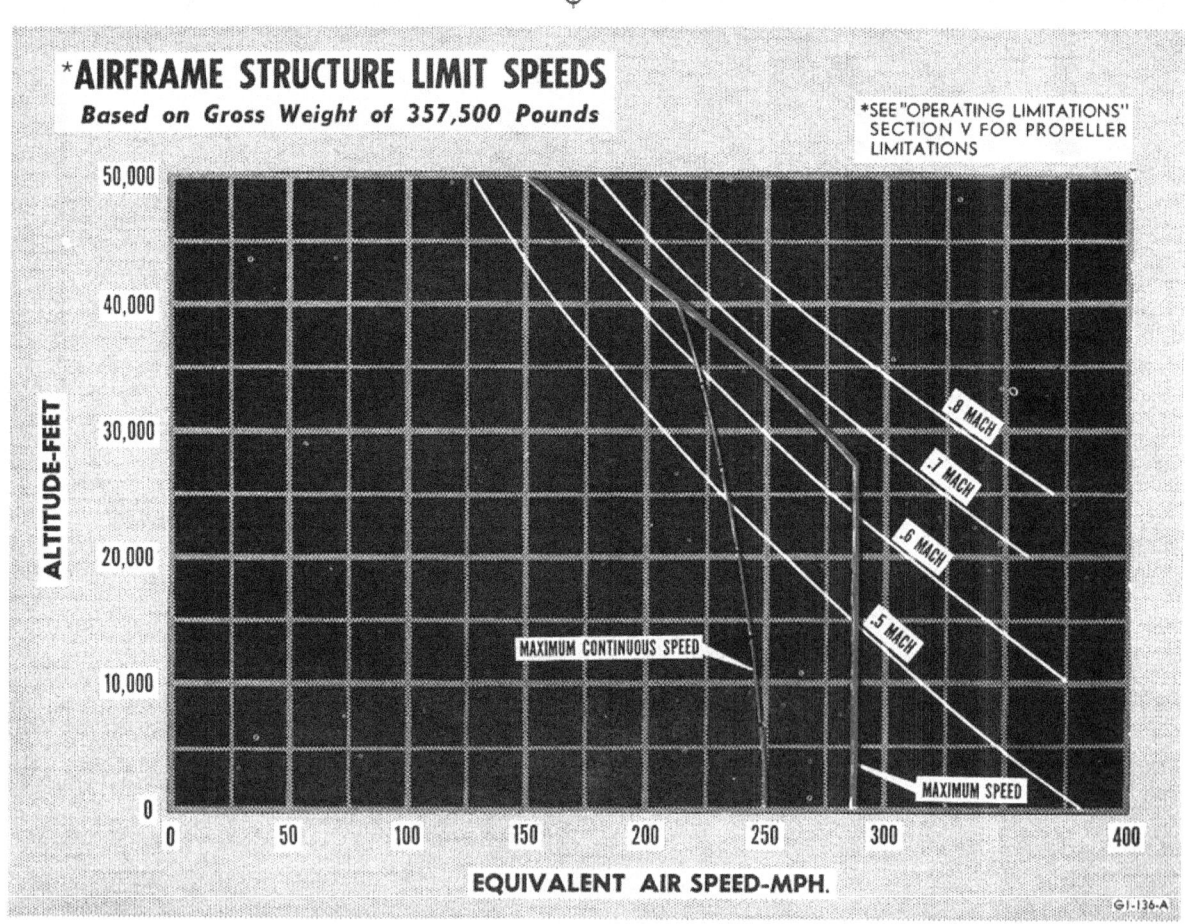

Figure 6-5.

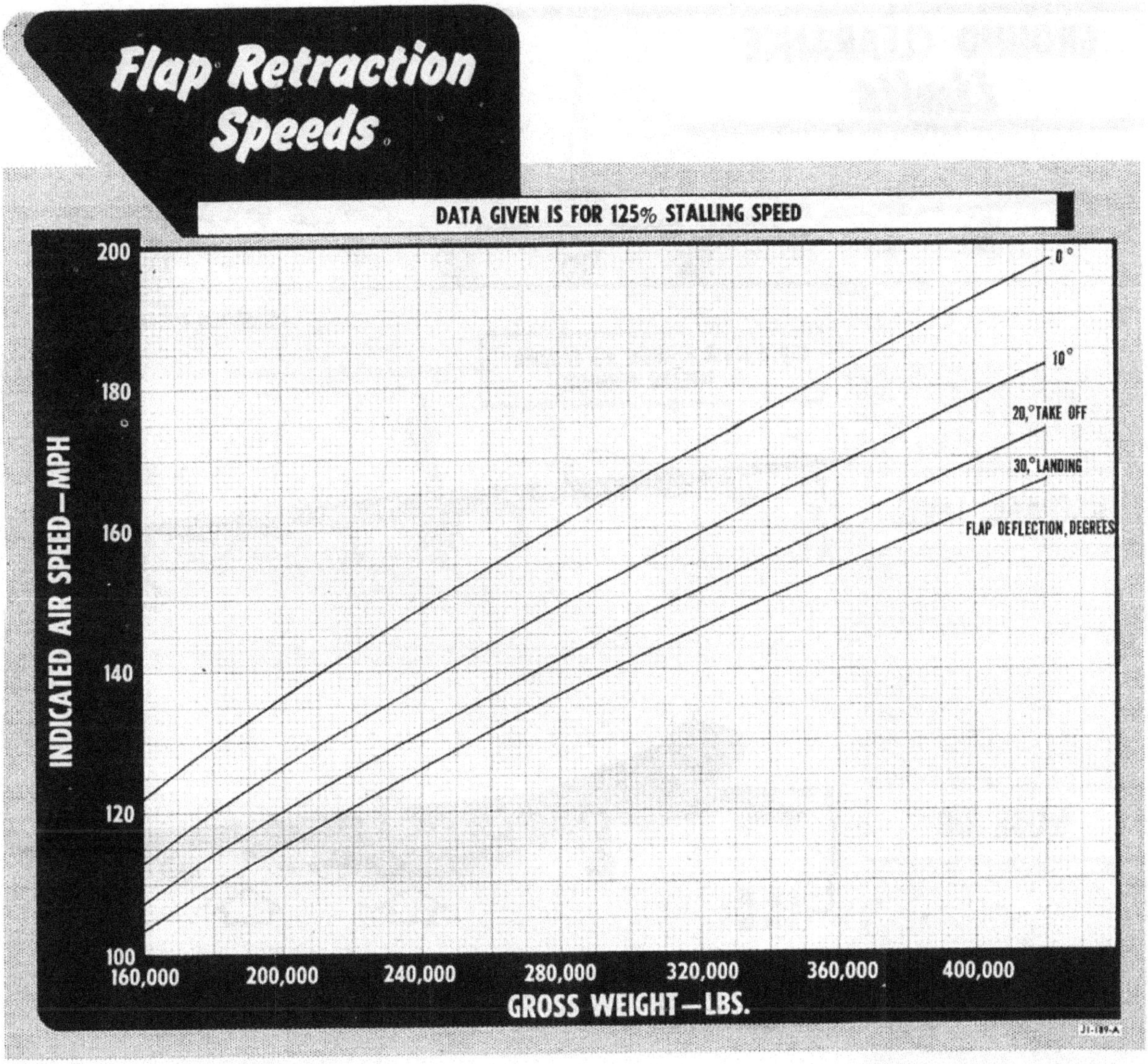

Figure 6-6.

change longitudinal trim. You can minimize the effect of flaps on trim by operating them in increments of 5 degrees, and retrimming the airplane between each operation.

ELEVATORS.

Elevator control is excellent within allowable cg limits. At minimum speed during the take-off run, you will have to apply 50 to 75 pounds of back pressure to establish the proper nose-high take-off attitude. After the "getaway," this pressure can be relaxed, and nose-down trim will be required as the airplane leaves "ground effect."

AILERONS.

Aileron control response equals or exceeds that of the nearest comparable bombardment type. More wheel movement is required at high altitude to obtain the same low altitude effect, but control is still positive.

At low air speed, the control force that ailerons can exert on the airplane is reduced. The resistance or inertia of the wing, however, remains constant. This means that you must allow more time to start and stop lateral movements.

RUDDER.

Rudder control is effective at very low air speeds with gear and flaps down. Under asymmetrical power conditions, air speed must be held above a critical value to maintain rudder effectiveness. These critical control speeds for various power combinations are shown in figure 3-2.

Section VI
Flight Characteristics

GROUND CLEARANCE *Limits*

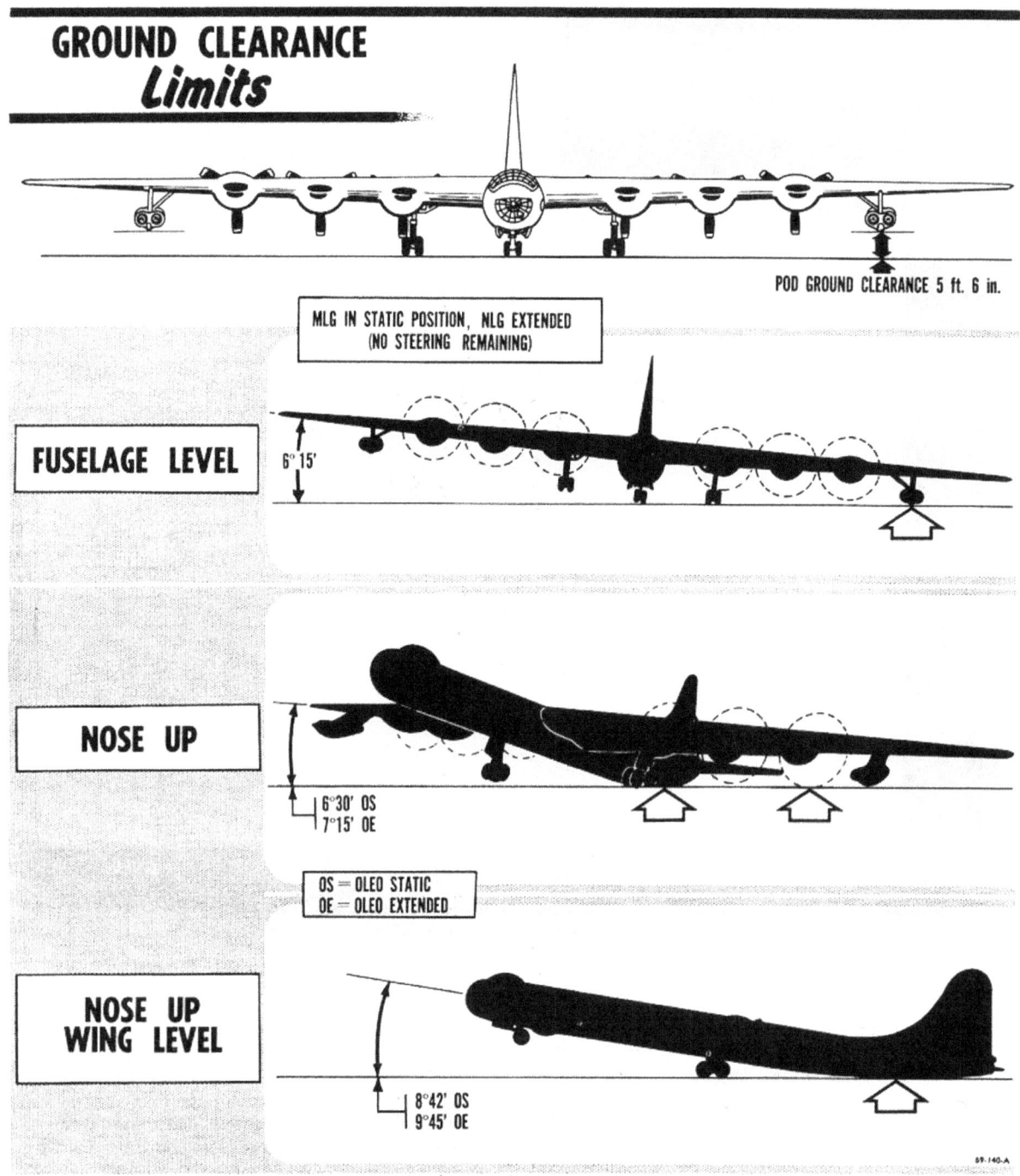

Figure 6-7.

LEVEL FLIGHT CHARACTERISTICS.

The range between slow and high speed flight is unusually large, but the upper air-speed limit is below the Mach number region where compressibility effect begins. Control and stability will be normal for any trimmed condition during slow, cruising, and high speed flight.

Air-speed limits for high speed level flight and high speed descent are shown in figure 6-5. Propeller vibratory stress limits are given in "Operating Limitations," Section IV.

MANEUVERING FLIGHT.

A structural maneuver factor of 2 has been imposed as a limit for full gross weight. This limit restricts banks to 60° or less, and pull-ups to 2 g's or less. As weight decreases, the maneuver factor increases slightly. Refer to figure 6-2 for calculated stalling speeds and induced maneuver factors at various angles of bank.

Stick forces will increase in steep turns and dives, and trim may be required. Response for any trimmed condition, however, will be normal within allowable load, cg, and maneuver limits.

DIVES.

Dives are permissible within the air-speed and propeller limits discussed under high speed level flight. Propeller restrictions can be ignored under stress of military necessity, but limit dive speeds should be observed under all conditions. Undetected flutter could cause structural failure.

Stick forces in dives should be continually trimmed out particularly when inadvertent relaxation would sharply increase the g load.

ASYMMETRICAL POWER CONDITIONS.

Operation with one or more engines inoperative is usually no problem since excess power is available at low altitude. If you are above the control air speed minimum for your power condition, normal turns can be made into the inoperative engines.

AFTER TAKE-OFF.

If you are below critical control air speed after take-off power failure, drop the nose and permit air speed to build up to the required minimum. Consider reducing gross weight if you cannot climb or maintain minimum terrain clearance.

CRUISE.

Power failure during cruising flight should not cause undue concern. Use jet engines to supplement your remaining reciprocating engines if required. Proper flying technique and pilot-engineer coordination will greatly increase the potential range under asymmetrical power conditions.

LANDING.

Partial power landings procedure is discusssed in Section III. The power required to maintain level flight for your landing gross weight with gear and flaps down is shown by tables in the appendix.

FLIGHT WITHOUT JET PODS.

Maximum range missions may require removal of jet pods. However, this does not noticeably change flight characteristics. Take-off and climb performance will be correspondingly reduced by the loss of jet power.

FLAP RETRACTION TECHNIQUE.

When take-off gross weight exceeds 300,000 pounds, you must use proper flap retraction technique to maintain the necessary lift with a safe margin above wingtip stall.

You will recall from the stall discussion that the wing tips extend beyond the influence of propeller induced air flow as shown in figure 6-1. They will stall when their critical angle is reached regardless of power setting. The recommended air speeds for flap retraction are shown graphically in figure 6-6. You should select the ordinate corresponding to your take-off gross weight and record air speeds for each flap setting during the retraction from 20 degrees to 5 degrees. Interpolation will be required for 5-degree increments. After take-off, allow the airplane to accelerate to the air speed recorded for the 20-degree setting; repeat this procedure for each succeeding flap increment until flaps are fully retracted. This technique will carry you through the transition zone with a margin of 25 per cent above stall. If chart air speed exceeds the placard air speed limit for any flap extension, the chart should be given preference. Placard limits on flap extension were imposed by propeller restrictions—not flap structure. Maintaining lift at a safe margin above stall is considered to be more important than briefly extending operation in a propeller vibration zone.

DIMENSIONAL AWARENESS.

As mentioned in the general discussion, this airplane requires that you be more careful of clearances. A picture of clearance danger points with pitch and roll limits is shown in figure 6-7.

Section VII
SYSTEMS OPERATION

RECIPROCATING ENGINES.

THE ENGINEER AND HIS ENGINES.

The engineer of the B-36 is provided with a formidable array of levers and switches to control the output and condition of his engines. Instruments enable him to interpret the results of these manipulations. Because the engines cannot be seen from his station, engine abnormalities are often difficult to diagnose either rapidly or accurately, while in flight. However, with proper interpretation of the instruments coupled with correct and clear information from the aft cabin gunners, fairly effective action can be taken in a minimum of time. Even though the levers and their corresponding instruments are very close together there is a long path between them. The levers and switches by themselves do not produce the instrument reaction. The engine is the necessary link that joins the control to the affected instrument.

The main concern of the engineer is not the portion of the engine to which the control or instrument is attached but rather the power section. It is in the power section that the impact of the power producing temperatures, pressures, and forces is applied and it is there that the results of improper control adjustment or the imposition of unsuitable conditions are felt. Excessive manifold pressure will not blow up the supercharger manifold, but it may blow off a cylinder head. Improper use of the mixture or spark advance controls does not directly harm the carburetor or magnetos, but may cause combustion chamber difficulties.

In spite of this consideration for the power section it appears to be treated with indifference. None of the controls and only one instrument, the cylinder head temperature gage, are connected to this portion of the engine. The control of power section conditions is effected indirectly through other sections. The interpretation of the results of this control is through instruments which indicate the conditions of other sections. *Engine operation is not a matter of memorizing arbitrarily selected numbers. It is knowing what each control ultimately does to the power section and the meaning of the corresponding instrument indications in terms of power section temperatures, pressures, and forces.*

ENGINE RPM.

The adjustment of engine rpm is used to establish engine power output according to the operating requirements such as take-off, climb, or level flight. The engineer must consult operating charts in the appendix to determine the correct rpm for use under the various flight conditions. However, he should be acquainted with the basis for specifying the different rpm settings. Cruise defines the operating limits which apply in sustained level flight when less than normal rated power is used. On the B-36 this must be described in three steps as follows:

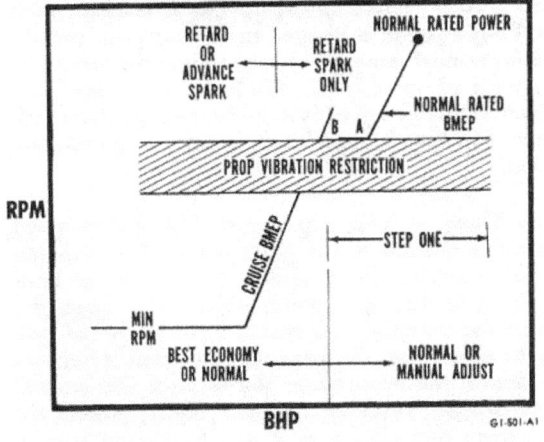

Figure 7-1.

Step One — This step (figure 7-1) considers only powers slightly less than normal rated, such as are used in the early stages of a mission. The maximum permissible bmep for this step is that for normal rated power. As power requirements decrease, the rpm is lowered but the normal rated bmep is maintained. If a propeller restriction is imposed, however, it will be necessary to adjust the power-rpm relationship to avoid the restricted range. In the example shown, when power is reduced to reach the restricted rpm range at point A, further power reduction is accomplished by reduction of torque alone. This continues until point

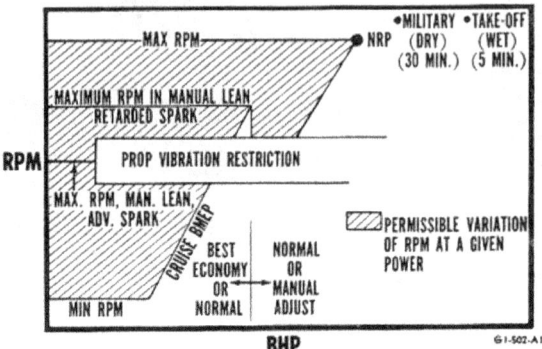

Figure 7-3.

cylinders in order to keep bmep within limits. A minimum rpm is specified to avoid undesirable structural vibration in flight.

Descent.

During a longe range descent, thrust power is reduced so that the airplane will maintain an optimum attitude along the flight path. As the engine output is reduced, the rpm is reduced to lower the true air speed of the propeller blades proportionally. Significant gains in range are realized during long descents by utilizing the minimum practical rpm, provided that bmep limits are not exceeded and cabin pressure can be maintained. A propeller in low rpm produces much less drag than one in higher rpm because it is approaching high blade angle.

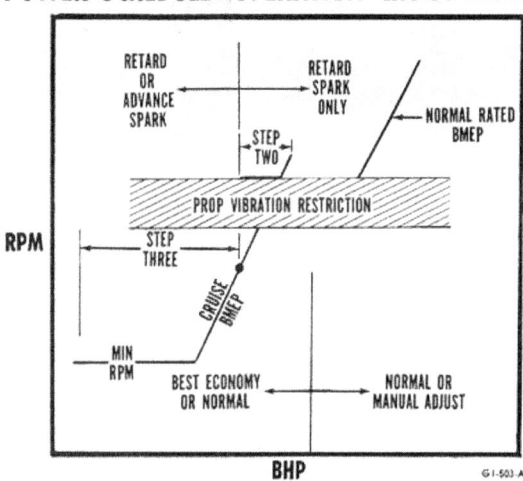

Figure 7-2.

B is reached. The power schedules do not allow operation at normal rated bmep below the propeller vibration restricted range.

Step Two — This step (figure 7-2) is reached when level flight power is lowered to the maximum permitted for manual leaning, but is still above the maximum for using advanced spark. The limits under these conditions can be described as in step one except that maximum bmep and rpm, hence maximum power, are lower.

Step Three — This step (figure 7-2) applies when power is reduced to the point where the spark can be advanced. In this condition the same bmep limit applying to the higher power manual lean range continues but the maximum rpm and power are reduced. In the above cases, the maximum rpm limit is imposed to control the temperature rise through the internal supercharger. However, for time-limited powers the maximum permitted rpm is usually selected because maximum power is the goal. Then it becomes essential to maintain maximum air pumping action of the

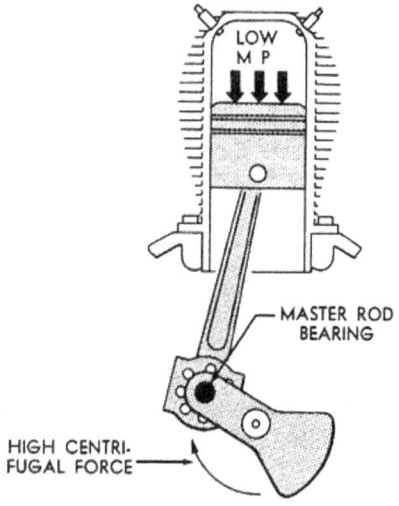

Figure 7-4.

Under these conditions M.P. must be used to furnish gas pressures which reduces the resultant force on the master rod bearing.

It should be noted that gas forces (figure 7-5) at high M.P. and bmep, and not centrifugal force, determine the strength of materials used in cylinder hold-down studs and piston pin.

Ground Operation.

The magnetos are usually checked at field barometric pressure with the propeller in complete low pitch. Combustion flame speed characteristics are used to provide a standard for comparison. The use of this engine speed results in an airflow that causes the carburetor, in NORMAL, to meter approximately "best power" mixture. This minimizes the influence of fuel-air ratio variables. Using one spark plug results in a single flame front requiring a longer time for the completion of the burning process. With the spark in RETARD, this is equivalent to retarding the spark timing about 10 degrees more. The resulting loss of power is indicated by a reduction of rpm and torque pressure (figure 7-6) and is normal reaction. Failure to register such a drop is evidence of improper timing in the advance direction, improper switch action, or other malfunctions.

The lean slow burning mixtures used in flight with advanced spark require earlier ignition by two plugs (figure 7-6) for best combustion. Only one plug firing in each cylinder with the lean cruise mixtures will cause rough operation or backfiring.

RPM variations are also used for ground checks of fan operation. When the fan drive is changed from low to high ratio more power is diverted from the propeller and the engine rpm decreases accordingly. In the air, with constant speed propeller operation, this change is reflected only on the torquemeter reading. The fan ground check is made at the rpm obtained at field barometric manifold pressure because higher rpms would impose excessive fan loads on the fan drive in high ratio.

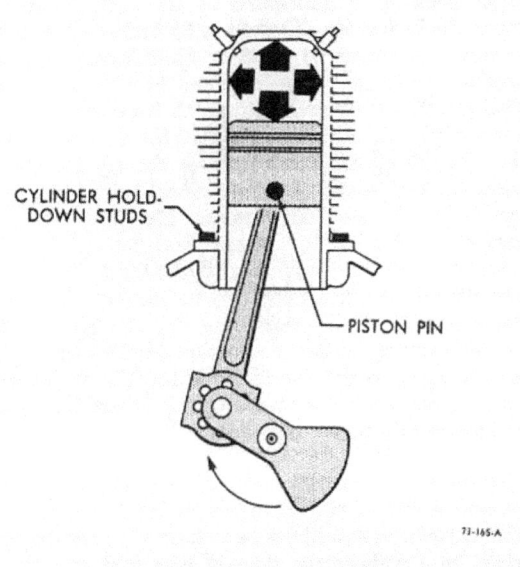

Figure 7-5.

Overspeed.

There are two main forces exerted on the master rod bearings, the resultant of which makes the act of overspeeding critical. The main factor (figure 7-4) is the centrifugal force caused by the inertia of the connecting rod and piston assembly. This force is partially opposed by the cylinder gas pressures, leaving a mean resultant of about 80 per cent of the centrifugal force. Therefore, the resultant must be absorbed by the master rod bearing. The master rod bearing, crankpin, and their lubrication are designed for a 50 per cent overload factor. The centrifugal forces vary as the square of the rpm; therefore, at 120 per cent of normal rated rpm (100 per cent) the centrifugal load is 144 per cent, approaching the critical overload factor of 150 per cent.

EFFECTS OF VARIOUS IGNITION & MIXTURE COMBINATIONS ON TORQUE

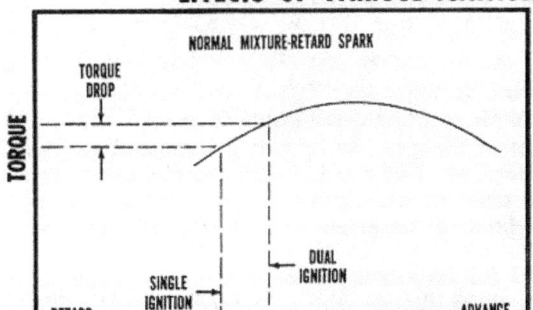 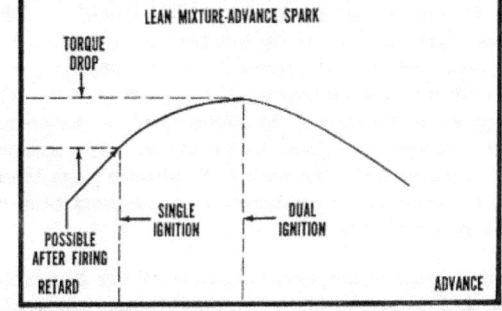

"EFFECTIVE" SPARK ADVANCE DEGREES BEFORE TOP DEAD CENTER

Figure 7-6.

The tachometer is the basic instrument for checking proper position, selection, and functioning of various electrical circuits which control the propellers, master motor speed, the propeller circuit breakers, and the selector and feathering switches. Propeller and control system response is judged by rpm indication. The engine tachometer is also consulted with regard to alternator operation, oil pressure, fuel pressure, oil spewing, and other functions.

MANIFOLD PRESSURE.

For practical purposes manifold pressure is a good tool for engine power setting, and when used with rpm in an unmodified form, a degree of accuracy sufficient for many types of operation is realized. B-36 missions cannot be accomplished with such "rule of thumb" methods, however, and the engineer must have a complete concept of the nature of manifold pressure and the steps that must be taken after rpm and boost adjustment before he can be sure that the engine power output is as specified. Variations in manifold pressure required for take-off power under different atmospheric conditions are the best illustration of the necessary correction of manifold pressure for B-36 operating accuracy.

Test stand calibration of the R4360-41 shows that 3500 bhp is obtained at 2700 rpm and 63 inches manifold pressure when 31 inches Hg exhaust back pressure is imposed, the carburetor air temperature is 38°C, and all other factors are standard, including dry air. However, the engine installation on the B-36 results in an exhaust back pressure greater than 31 inches Hg at take-off power, and more than 63 inches manifold pressure would be needed to obtain 3500 bhp. This increase is required to overcome the additional exhaust pressure.

Dry air is included in the list of "all other factors" but isn't always present for maximum gross weight take-off. The engine produces power in proportion to the amount of dry air consumed and as water vapor displaces dry air its presence constitutes a loss of power producing potential in the charge being pumped into the cylinders. The total pressure of the charge air is the total of the pressures of its component parts (nitrogen, oxygen, water vapor, etc.). Sensing total pressure only, the manifold pressure gage is unable to reject vapor pressure and concentrate only on pressure supplied by air.

Starting with atmospheric pressure, if the barometer reads 29.5 inches Hg and .5 inches Hg vapor pressure is present, the dry air is responsible for 29.0 inches Hg of the barometer reading. By the time the charge has passed through the induction system, the .5 inches of vapor pressure is multiplied by the superchargers to about .98 inches Hg. Therefore, 63 inches of manifold pressure represents 63 —.98 or 62.02 inches of power producing charge—a loss of about 50 bhp per engine. The carburetor cannot distinguish between water vapor and dry air, so it sends in fuel for the water vapor thus furnishing too much fuel for the dry air actually taken in. This results in an additional loss of power for the observed manifold pressure. Humidity often accompanies high outside air temperatures and the combination of the above factors detract from the airplane take-off performance. Humidity corrections outlined in the appendix are for correcting the take-off manifold pressure setting so the air portion of the charge pressure is equal to the maximum allowable charge pressure if bone dry air were used. This correction assures maximum safe power delivery.

The humidity correction factor is used only during take-off since moisture at operating levels is negligible. This correction should not be neglected by the engineer when he calculates the take-off manifold pressure he will use.

The large variations in exhaust back pressure, resulting from the turbosupercharging system, cause discrepancies between the engine manufacturer's calibration and the power obtained in the airplane. The manifold pressure settings specified in the appendix are results of flight testing and with proper corrections of carburetor air temperature variations and humidity to take-off the required accuracy will be obtained.

SUPERCHARGING.

Two conditions of operation govern the procedure of manifold pressure control. If the turbo boost selector (TBS) is at zero, primary regulation is by the throttle and the manifold pressure obtained varies as with more elementary installations. However, because of the drag of the idling superchargers and ducting loss at full throttle and full low pitch, the pressure at the carburetor entrance is only about 26 inches at sea level resulting in a manifold pressure of approximately 46 inches. RPM lower than that for take-off causes reduced internal supercharger compression and accounts for further lowering of the available manifold pressure on the ground. In flight with TBS at zero, variations of indicated air speed influence manifold pressure as the ram pressure changes. As long as performance needs are satisfied, the TBS should be kept at zero due to better fuel economy without the back pressure and increased induction air temperature resulting from turbo use.

With full throttle and constant rpm, the manifold pressure varies directly with carburetor entrance pressure. The job of the turbosupercharger is to keep this pressure constant at a value that permits the internal supercharger to deliver the required manifold pressure for a selected rpm. Setting the TBS directs the pressuretrol to maintain necessary entrance pressure. The pressuretrol proceeds to do this by regulating the waste gate position.

During a climb with normal rated power, with the TBS set and individual turbo-calibration knobs trimmed for the required manifold pressure, the pressuretrol actually works to maintain approximately 27 inches Hg carburetor entrance pressure. If the rpm is reduced with the TBS fixed, the manifold pressure lowers. This occurs because the internal supercharger compression ratio falls with the drop in crankshaft speed, and the pressuretrol is unconcerned with this variation. However, if the indicated air speed were to be lowered, the manifold pressure would be unaffected as the pressuretrol would act on the waste gates and compensate for the reduction of ram pressure.

As the climb progresses at normal rated rpm and the turbosupercharger entrance pressure falls off, the pressuretrol continues to maintain the carburetor entrance pressure demanded by the TBS. The limit is reached when the turbo overspeed control takes over to prevent excessive turbine speed. At this point each supercharger is operating at maximum rpm and engine charge air flow falls off with altitude (figure 7-7) similar to a simple fixed speed supercharger. There is a mild hunting of the turbo overspeed control and the wastegate. This hunting results in a wavering of 2 or 3 inches in manifold pressure. Air speed again exerts a direct influence on the manifold pressure indication.

EFFECTS OF ALTITUDE ON ENGINE OPERATION

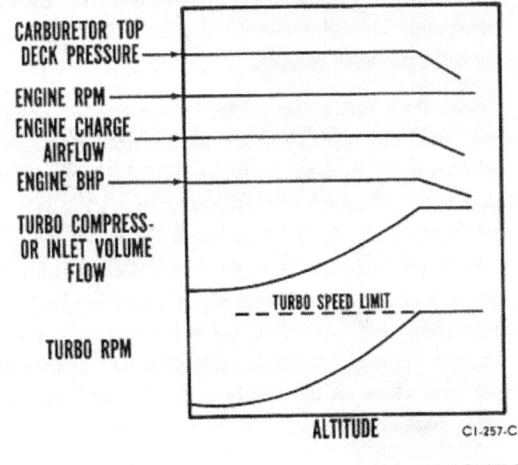

Figure 7-7.

The control sequence is as follows: First, with zero TBS, advance the throttle. Second, when full throttle will not give the needed manifold pressure, advance the TBS as required. Do not obtain manifold pressure with the TBS when the throttle is only partially open except for unusual situations. Damming the induction system (figure 7-8) between the turbos and the manifold by closing or partially closing the throttle, can result in stalling of the turbo-compressors and cause severe cyclic pulsations accompanied by backfiring. Also, using turbos in this manner is inefficient since exhaust back pressure and carburetor air temperature are higher than necessary.

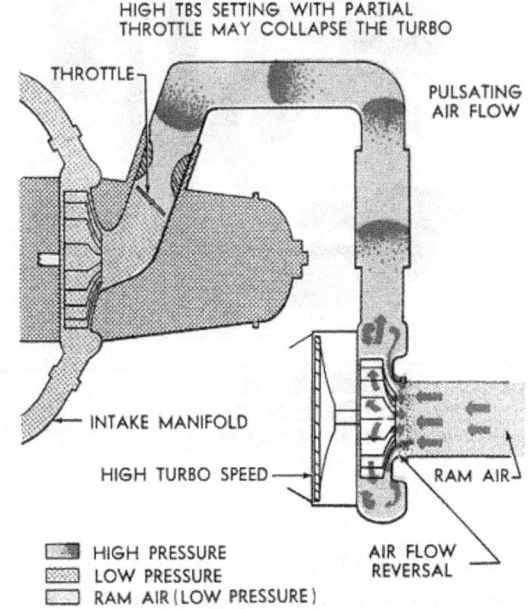

Figure 7-8. Power Collapse with Closed Throttle

Obtaining Maximum Turbo Speed.

It is difficult to operate at a turbo speed near the rpm at which the turbo governors are set to cut in. This is due to the fact that when the turbo rpm reaches the governor setting, the governor will open the waste gate until the turbo rpm is reduced sufficiently to remove the governor's control. At this point the waste gate starts closing and the cycle is repeated, resulting in unstable engine operation. The following procedure is recommended when it is necessary to operate at or near the limiting turbo speed:

1. Shift to manual override.

2. Advance power until the desired engine setting is attained, not to exceed 24,750 turbo rpm.

3. Do not exceed 24,750 rpm on the turbos at any time.

4. Periodically check this reading, particularly with any change in altitude, air speed, or CAT.

TURBO OPERATION

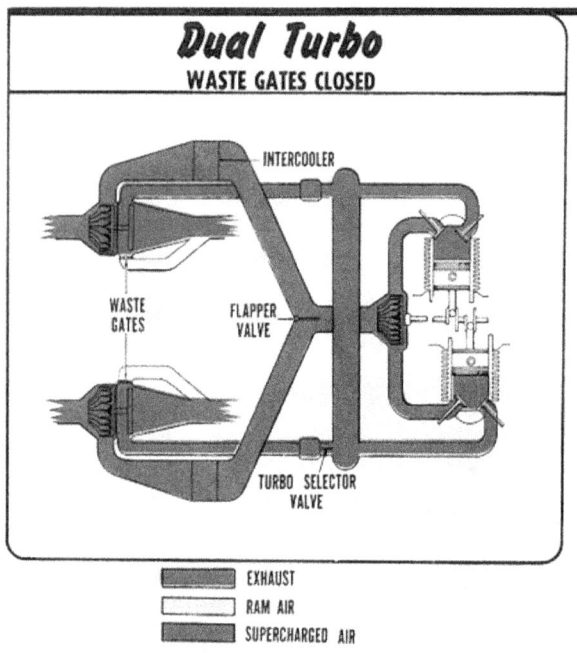
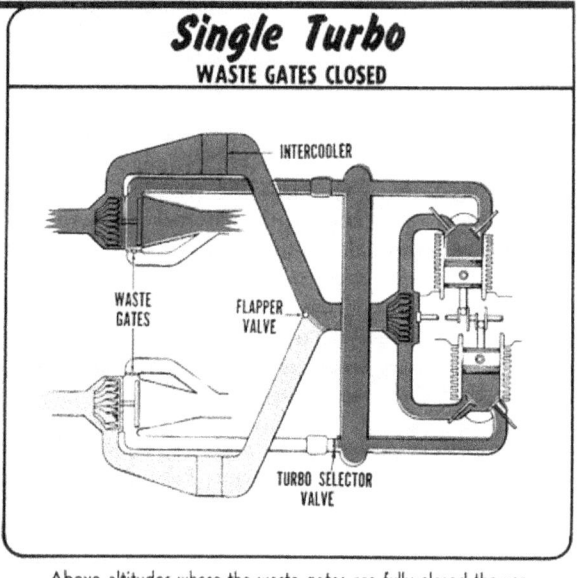

Above altitudes where the waste gates are fully closed the use of single turbo gives an increased air velocity to the engine; however the carburetor air temperature will tend to rise since only one intercooler is effective.

Figure 7-9.

The turbo speed limit of 24,750 rpm is the maximum speed recommended for satisfactory turbo life. Short tests have been conducted at higher speeds to determine what gains in power could be made by exceeding this limit, but the attendant increase of CAT. necessitates further opening the intercooler shutters, thereby increasing drag, reducing air speed, and resulting in no worthwhile increase in performance.

Turbosupercharger Operation.

The use of single turbo in place of dual is necessary if the waste gates close fully. Its use may also be dictated by power collapse or pulsation possibilities at low air flow, low rpm, and high manifold pressure. By using one unit, the quantity of the charge air through the turbosupercharger is increased and stable operation can be maintained. It must be realized that during single turbo operation, there is a difference in the temperature rise from dual operation. Only one intercooler is removing the compression heat; therefore, the carburetor air temperature rises accordingly unless the intercooler shutters are opened. When shifting from dual to single turbo, and when returning from single turbo to dual, the engineer can help the power plant make the change smoothly by following steps favorable to conditions present during the transition.

When shifting from dual to single, one turbo slows down and the other, influenced by the pressuretrol, speeds up to take over the entire pumping load. At first, the unit that is cut out loses speed faster than the active unit speeds up and a momentary drop of 2 to 5 inches manifold pressure results.

If shift does not occur within a reasonable length of time, pull the throttle back sufficiently to allow the turbo to shift. Pulling back the throttle reduces the exhaust gas loading on the selector valve to the left turbo and permits the actuator to break loose the valve gate in the exhaust duct and move it. If the shift is not completed in about one minute, the actuator motor is likely to overheat and burn out. Close observation of the alternator instruments just as switches are thrown often will give clues as to whether circuits and motors are acting properly.

When the shift is from single to dual turbo the selector valve quickly divides the exhaust flow, suddenly denying the active turbo a portion of its energy source, slowing it down. The previously inactive unit speeds up, however, and for a moment the combined output of both is low and a drop in manifold pressure is noticed.

In either case the pressuretrol acts to increase the carburetor deck pressure to that of the TBS setting. There will be a small amount of overshooting, however, before it stabilizes. These momentary changes in air flow should not be allowed to occur with the carburetor mixture leaned to cruising because backfiring can occur. Therefore, the mixture control lever must be in NORMAL before making the shift. Also, the spark advance switch must be in RETARD because early ignition with the faster burning mixture can cause heat to build up in the combustion chamber materials faster than it can be transferred away.

This explains that the spark must be retarded before placing the mixture in NORMAL. However, the spark should not be retarded while operating with a fully leaned cruise mixture because retarded spark with the slow burning fuel-air ratio will cause backfiring. Therefore, the mixture must be partially richened before retarding the spark. This can not be done if the CHT is at its limit, for the increased mixture strength causes an increase of CHT that must be anticipated before starting the shift. Also, when shifting from BOTH to R.H. ONLY a carburetor air temperature rise occurs due to the greater heat rise through the use of single turbo.

Again, this temperature rise should be anticipated and the intercooler shutters must be adjusted accordingly preparatory to shifting to single turbo.

During single turbo operation, icing of the left exhaust tail pipe can occur. Apparently exhaust gases condense and freeze on the tail pipe outlet. There should be no concern on the part of the flight crew relative to any hazard being present from these ice formations. It is possible, however, for enough ice to form, break loose, and strike the fuselage, causing some damage. Icing of this nature can be removed by shifting to dual turbo for a few minutes. However, this decision should be left to the discretion of the aircraft commander since a shift to dual turbo could not be made unless power was advanced with a resultant loss in range.

Shifting Turbos—Dual to Single. It is very desirable to remain in dual turbo as long as power can be maintained. At such time when power can no longer be maintained in dual turbo, proceed as follows:

1. Intercooler shutters—Full open.

WARNING

It is very important to open the intercooler shutters because the CAT. increases very rapidly in single turbo operation. In addition, single turbo selection should never be made in manual lean or advance spark.

2. Air plugs—As required.
3. Work on two symmetrical engines at a time.
4. Spark advance switches—RETARD.

Note

In the event of fully leaned mixture, enrichen the mixture before placing the spark advance switches in RETARD.

5. Mixture control levers—NORMAL.
6. Reduce manifold pressure to 30 inches or below.
7. Shift from dual to single turbo.

Note

Manifold pressure will drop approximately 2 to 5 inches and then will tend to surge upward.

8. After the shift has been completed, increase M.P. to approximately 35 inches while the other turbos are being shifted.

Note

If a shift does not occur within a reasonable length of time, pull throttle back sufficiently to allow the turbo to shift.

9. After all turbos are shifted to single, set desired power.
10. Readjust air plugs and intercooler shutters.

CAUTION

The alertness of the engineer is the only safety factor for maintaining CHT and CAT. below maximum limits.

Shifting Turbos—Single to Dual. The following procedure is for shifting to dual turbo at a constant altitude when additional power is required.

1. Intercooler shutters—As required.
2. Air plugs—As required.
3. Spark advance switches—RETARD.
4. Mixture control levers—NORMAL.
5. Reduce manifold pressure to 35 inches or below.
6. Increase engine speed to at least 2000 rpm.

Note

This is a step toward keeping the power up without exceeding temperature limits during the shifting procedure.

7. Maintain manifold pressure at 35 inches or below.
8. Shift to dual turbo.
9. Intercoolers—Open as required.
10. Retrim engines to power required and readjust air plugs and intercooler shutters.
11. Repeat steps on other engines.

Power Collapse.

Satisfactory operation of the supercharging system requires that a balanced loading of all units be maintained. The pressure rise load of each compressor can be compared to the wing loading of an airplane. Similarly, the charge air velocity through the compressor closely follows the engine rpm and is comparable to the air velocity over a wing. If the load (pressure) is too high for the charge air velocity (rpm), the diffuser and compressor blades stall and power collapse, possibly accompanied by backfiring, takes place. This condition can occur at moderate to high altitudes (figure 7-10) by attempting to maintain a high manifold presure at a low engine rpm. When this is done, the low internal supercharger pressure rise must be made up by driving the turbos faster and the system approaches instability. The turbo pulsation limits are defined in the appendix.

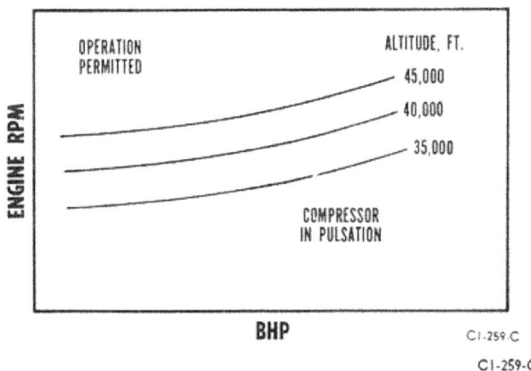

Figure 7-10.

These turbo characteristics cause difficulties during that portion of the flight when the airplane is very light and low power is being established with high bmep. The low engine rpm shifts the manifold pressure load to the turbos and as the rate of air flow diminishes, the velocity through the turbo-compressors is critically slow and blade stalling is approached. When the critical point is reached, stalling occurs and power collapse takes place. There is seldom any instrument warning of this event from the manifold pressure gage, the torquemeter, the tachometer or other instruments, but there is plenty of unmistakable evidence afterward. There is a sudden and complete loss of power. It is so abrupt that the propeller automatic pitch control cannot compensate rapidly enough to maintain engine speed, with the result that rpm drops momentarily and then overshoots the initial setting slightly. When this happens, DON'T CLOSE THE THROTTLE. This would be comparable to pulling back the stick of a stalled airplane.

Placing a dam in the induction system only accentuates the difficulty and will bring on pulsations with attendant backfire.

The solution of this problem is to increase airspeed over the stalled surfaces of the turbosuperchargers, which is comparable to increasing the airspeed of a stalled airplane. The most effective means is to immediately increase the engine rpm which results in an increased velocity through the turbo compressors for the same carburetor deck pressure. In case of a marginally unstable power setting, increasing speed 25 to 50 rpm and lowering the TBS setting slightly to retain the bhp are sufficient to restore harmony by developing balanced loads among the various pumping elements.

Other factors may be adjusted to alleviate the situation and permit maintenance of the established power and bmep. A reduction of charge air temperature permits obtaining the required brake horsepower with less manifold pressure and reduces the pressure loading on the turbos. To accomplish this, lower the carburetor air temperature by opening the intercooler shutters.

Other corrective actions that can be taken from the engineer's station are: reduction of turbo boost, mixture enrichment, use of advanced spark (if within the permissible range), and increase of cabin air flow. Using any one of these steps aids the turbo function, either by increase of air flow and air velocity through the internal supercharger, or by reducing the pressure load on the turbo system.

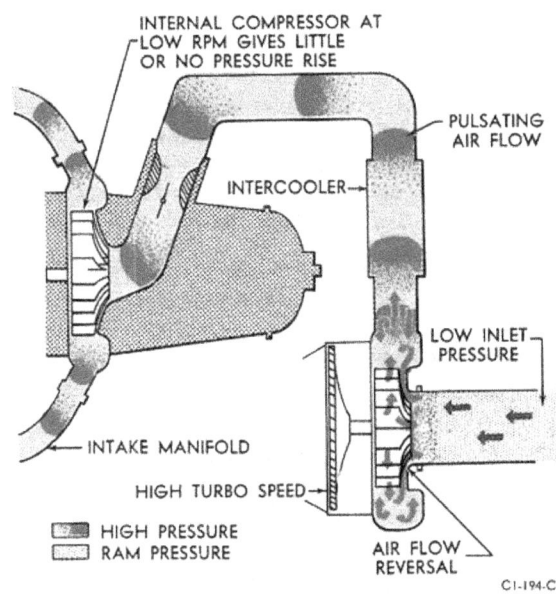

Figure 7-11. Power Collapse

It is apparent from the above considerations that increasing engine speed is the most effective means of recovering from power collapse. If the initial rpm is just marginally unstable, the slight overshooting of rpm after the momentary drop will frequently be enough to unload the turbo and permit self-recovery with no adjustment of controls. An increase of 25 to 50 rpm is then sufficient to prevent recurrence of the trouble.

Seasonal changes in outside air temperature affect the stable rpm-manifold pressure combination by a range of 75 rpm even with the same carburetor air temperature. This is due to the effect on efficiencies of the turbo-compressor and intercooler.

Leakage or restriction in the induction or exhaust systems may contribute to instability. Nicked or damaged turbo or engine compressors are inefficient and cause too high a temperature rise. These conditions reduce the weight of charge air that passes through the system.

Power Collapse Recovery. This procedure is designed to get the power plant into the stable operating range quickly and safely.

> **CAUTION**
>
> Do NOT retard the throttles because this results in an even worse condition of power collapse.

1. Master motor speed control lever—Increase until engine speed increases 25 to 50 rpm.

   Note

   This step will remove all engines from a marginal surge condition.

2. Turbo calibration knob of affected engine—Fully counterclockwise.
3. Spark advance switch of affected engine—RETARD.
4. Mixture control lever of affected engine—NORMAL.
5. Turbo calibration knob of affected engine—Turn clockwise *slowly* to regain power and observe engine rpm.

> **CAUTION**
>
> Don't regain power too rapidly as rpm surges may result.

6. Re-establish proper setting of mixture and spark on affected engine.

CARBURETION.

Carburetor Air Temperature.

Carburetor air temperature is regarded by many as the indication of the possibility of induction system ice formation. It still serves this purpose on the B-36 but also provides other important items of information. As previously shown CAT. must be combined with manifold pressure and rpm to measure air flow. It is also a major factor affecting maintenance of satisfactory operating conditions.

The maximum CAT. is specified to prevent detonation. At engine speeds greater than 1900 rpm with advanced spark, this limit is not ideal but marginal. Occasionally, outside air temperature is 38 degrees plus, and since there is no refrigeration in the induction system, the heat rise through the turbosuperchargers results in a CAT. above the limit. *A reduction of 1 inch manifold pressure for each 5.5°C above 38°C CAT. is then mandatory to insure safety during take-off.* This correction is automatically obtained when the M.P. is corrected for humidity during take-off. As engine speed is reduced from 2700 rpm and the heat rise through the internal superchargers is lowered, the margin increases. When this exists it is possible to consider CAT. with relation to engine efficiency as well as safety.

The power plant is a heat machine and the temperature of component parts or fluids flowing through it affects the combustion process, either directly or indirectly. The temperature level of induction air upon leaving the carburetor not only affects the charge density but also fuel vaporization. When considering rate of air flow at constant manifold pressure, the colder the CAT. the greater the weight packed into the charge air volume. By this measure alone, power should continue to increase as colder air enters, provided other factors are held constant.

However, this increase in power may not be directly proportional to air flow in which case the brake specific fuel consumption will start to increase. This trend (figure 7-12) is below a certain CAT. and is de-

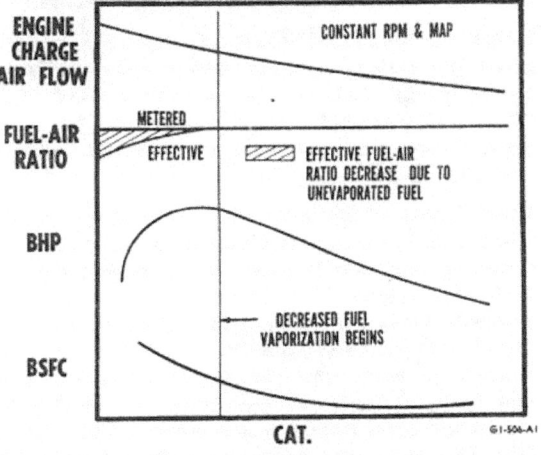

Figure 7-12.

pendent on variables such as rpm, mixture strength, fuel temperature, and the temperature of engine parts which the fuel contacts. Thus, at extremely low temperatures, it is possible for a critical condition to occur which results in power loss and consequently irregular operation.

These phenomena are brought about by failure of the fuel to vaporize in the cold induction air. Obtaining the maximum potential power from a given rate of charge air flow requires complete vaporization of all fuel supplied by the carburetor. Unevaporated fuel, even though finely divided into a spray or mist, does not burn and does not contribute to power. The carburetor does its job by providing fuel according to air flow requirements as previously discussed. It meters, or measures, liquid fuel and is unaware of occurrences downstream. The "measured" fuel-air ratio is based on the proportion of this liquid fuel to air. The "effective" fuel-air ratio is the proportion of vaporized fuel to air and if all the fuel is not vaporized the "effective" fuel-air ratio, which does the work, is lowered.

At high power with a high charge air flow and a rich mixture, this effect can be favorable for a range of temperature reduction as the "effective mixture" is approaching "best power." However, if continued to a frigid extreme, "effective" mixtures leaner than "best power" may result even though the "measured" fuel-air ratio is adequately rich. The unburned fuel often causes "torching" at the exhaust pipe. With cruise powers and lean "measured" mixtures, lack of vaporization results in overly lean "effective" fuel-air ratios and power loss. Because of charge distribution irregularities, some cylinders receive leaner mixture than others and they cease to fire since the mixture supplied to them will not support combustion. The lead in the fuel tends to stay with the unevaporated liquid which hastens its deposit on the combustion chamber surfaces and spark plugs.

Under the conditions described, more power for a given rpm, manifold pressure, and fuel flow is obtained by increasing the CAT. Even though air flow is decreased, the improved combustion resulting from better vaporization gives optimum performance and fuel economy.

Gasoline is a chemical mixture. Some of its components are highly volatile and evaporate easily under any operating condition. But the heavier components must be heated to over 100°C before rapid vaporization is possible. These heavier components finally leave the liquid state from 130° to 150°C. Obviously, air at carburetor air temperature cannot perform this function and large quantities of heat must be added as the charge air flows from the carburetor to the cylinder. The greatest amount comes from the internal supercharger, but its contribution varies with its speed of rotation. At high powers, with high rpm, its heat producing capacity is adequate and excess fuel can be absorbed by the engine without hesitation. As rpm is reduced, the heat rise through the impeller is less and its vaporizing capacity is lowered. At low cruise rpm the small heat rise, combined with low entering air temperature and lean mixture, can cause operating difficulties.

Besides heat from the internal supercharger, further heat exchange occurs through contact with the supercharger housing, intake pipes, and combustion chamber surfaces. The last increment of temperature before combustion is supplied by compression in the cylinder.

Elevated charge temperatures also retard the rate of spark plug fouling. If the heat rise through the internal supercharger is insufficient, control of CAT. effectively assists. A reduction in CAT. is necessary at the highest rpm permitted with advanced spark, since the engine can not tolerate the extra carburetor heat added to the supercharger temperature rise. When the rpm is reduced so that the supercharger rise is sufficiently low, it is permissible to return to the maximum limit.

The simplest application is to use 20°C as the maximum CAT. with manual leaning above 1900 rpm. The low fuel-air ratio lacks the ability to absorb the heat rise of the impeller at the higher rpm. Compensation for this is made by reducing the CAT. In controlling the CAT. by means of the intercooler shutters, set them at minimum opening to obtain maximum limiting temperatures. This reduces the drag of forcing air through the intercoolers and the disturbance of air flow over the wing. However, under maximum range conditions, with high bmep, this may lead to marginal operation, producing power instability. The high CAT. calls for more manifold pressure which, in turn increases the turbine load. A greater turbine load increases the exhaust back pressure which in turn augments the original manifold pressure demand. At the same time, the elevated CAT. and additional back pressure start the CHT in the upward direction.

Besides the primary carburetor air temperature control and the intercooler shutters, three other means of regulation are provided. The preheat system heats induction air by bleeding heated engine cooling air from the engine bay into the intake of the turbo-compressors. This system is used when power and altitude are insufficient to require a heat producing output of the turbosuperchargers. The use of single turbo is accompanied by an increase of CAT. since removal of induction air heat is through one intercooler instead of the usual two.

During icing conditions with low cruise power at low altitude there may not be sufficient heat available from the above means to maintain ice free operation. Under

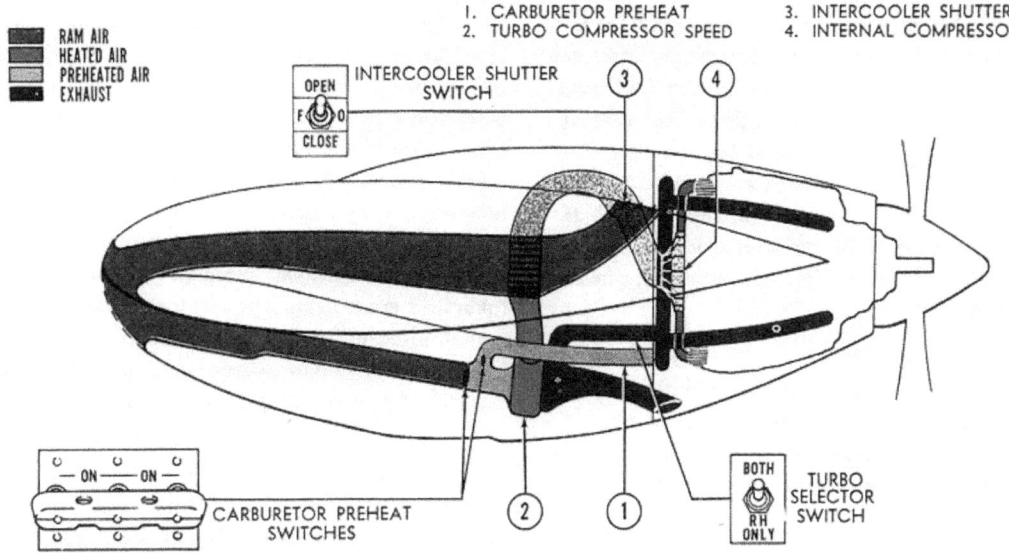

Figure 7-13. Controlling Carburetor Air Temperature

these conditions, another means of quickly raising the CAT. is to advance the TBS to a fairly high setting while controlling manifold pressure with the throttle. This action forces the turbo to higher speed with an increased temperature rise; however, caution should be observed to avoid stalling the turbo compressor and possibly causing unstable engine operation.

In addition to its normal uses, CAT. is useful in checking the induction system condition. Excessive duct leaks on one power plant will cause its turbosuperchargers to increase their speed to maintain the carburetor entrance pressure called for by the TBS. This elevates the CAT. on that engine above the other five, thus giving a positive indication of the trouble.

Backfiring is indicated, momentarily, on the carburetor air temperature gage provided the heat is sufficient to be measured upstream at the carburetor air temperature measuring point. A sustained induction system fire during starting will show a continuous elevation of CAT. During flight, power adjustments approaching instability or power collapse may cause a rise of CAT. As the turbo-compressor becomes less efficient, more of its energy is dissipated in heat, increasing the induction air temperature.

Carburetor air temperature should be noted on the ground before starting and just after shutdown. It is the best indication of fuel temperature in the carburetor body and indicates whether vaporization will be sufficient for the initial firing. Otherwise the mixture may need to be augmented by prime. If an engine is shut down for a short period of time, the residual heat in the carburetor and power plant makes it possible to rely on this heat for vaporizing the fuel in the engine. Then priming is unnecessary. After shutdown, a high CAT. means that fuel trapped in the carburetor will expand producing high internal pressures. This force, if great enough, ruptures diaphragms and damages vent valve seats. The fuel lines and manifold valves should be open when the above conditions exist to allow fuel passage back to the tanks.

Carburetor Impact Icing.

Carburetor icing occurs on the airplane, but is not generally the screen type or throttle body type usually experienced on other aircraft. Some fuel is injected into the induction air at the face of the impeller, the remainder midway between the face and the tips. The charge is immediately subjected to compression heat; therefore, no ice forms due to fuel evaporation. Impact ice can form, however, on the carburetor screens and, in special instances, on the throttles. This is possible when the CAT. is near 0°C and there is high moisture content in the atmosphere. As this ice builds up, it restricts the air flow just as if the throttle were being closed. Any attempt to increase rpm merely aggravates this condition, resulting in an additional loss of power. The expected drop of manifold pressure is accompanied by reduction of torque and fuel flow readings.

This type of icing is prevented by maintaining the CAT. above 5°C. While greater than 0°C is sufficient to keep ice off the screen, there is a slight temperature drop through the throttle body and the extra 5°C takes this into account.

When anticipating icing conditions, the CAT. should be maintained as close to maximum C as possible for the power being used. This is accomplished by closing the intercooler shutters. If this is not adequate, additional carburetor heat is obtained by turning on the carburetor preheat and varying the temperature with intercooler adjustments. If more heat is required, raise CHT if possible and increase the speed of the external superchargers. This is accomplished by retarding the throttle to reduce M.P. approximately 6 inches, and increase the TBS setting to restore the original M.P. If this does not provide sufficient heat, switch to single turbo and repeat the preceding step, providing power conditions permit.

Note

It should be remembered that switching to single turbo reduces the efficiency of the heating and anti-icing systems since one primary heat exchanger is cut out in each nacelle.

If carburetor heat is still insufficient, continue to decrease M.P. in 5-inch decrements and increase TBS to restore M.P. until the desired CAT. is obtained.

It is also possible for ice to form on the throttle and mixture control linkage. This is detected only by attempting to move the controls. In event this type of icing occurs, an altitude should be found where icing conditions do not prevail. Icing conditions are seldom encountered above 25,000 feet; at lower altitudes a change in altitude, either up or down, often removes the airplane from the icing zone.

Carburetor Internal Icing.

The foregoing describes carburetor icing that affects the induction air passages by choking the engine. Another type of icing occurs within the carburetor and restricts the air flow between the A and B chambers, upsetting fuel metering. This flow is restricted by ice forming in the bleeds which connect the passages joining chambers A and B. One of the bleeds is located in the regulator section of the carburetors and the other is located in the automatic mixture control unit of the carburetor. With this type icing the manifold pressure does not decrease since the main air ducts are unaffected but the upset metering causes a fuel flow change. In this case, power, as measured on the torquemeter will rise or fall, depending on the initial fuel-air ratio and the effect of changing fuel-air ratio on power.

This type icing comes in two packages, rich and lean. If fuel flow increases under normal operation, it is probable that atmospheric moisture has found its way to one or both of the bleeds connecting the passages to chamber A and B and frozen. The tendency to freeze is augmented by the temperature reduction that accompanies the drop in pressure of the air flowing between the passages connecting the two chambers. However, the principal cause of freezing of the bleed in the regulator is from cold fuel which flows through nearby chamber D and takes heat from B chamber faster than it is brought in by the small airflow through the bleeds. The principal cause of icing of the bleed in the automatic mixture control unit is low CAT. If both bleeds freeze, the unrelieved A chamber pressure builds up, while that in B chamber decreases, increasing the metering differential to discharge more fuel. In this condition the fuel-air mixture can enrichen 72 per cent more than the normal automatic setting, and if nature takes its course large power losses result. Depending on the mixture setting, and fuel-air ratio, the torque pressure may first increase or decrease. In severe cases, a large loss of torque pressure results, accompanied by torching at the exhaust pipe and, where small leaks occur, in the exhaust system.

Control of the fuel flow by manual leaning when both bleeds are iced is extremely difficult and it may be necessary to approach IDLE CUT-OFF in some cases. Since icing of the bleed in the regulator cannot be readily controlled, the bleed in the automatic mixture control unit, which is located in the carburetor inlet section, must be anti-iced by use of higher CAT. After the bleed is anti-iced the CAT. should be maintained above freezing, preferably between 20°C and the maximum limit, to prevent re-icing of the bleed. Adequate CAT. will not only prevent icing of the bleed, it will also prevent icing of the impact tubes or passages, the entire induction system, and the boost back vent bleed in the automatic mixture control unit. With only the bleed in the regulator iced the mixture can easily be controlled by manual adjustment of the mixture control lever. When a restoration of normal conditions is indicated, a decrease in fuel flow, return the mixture lever to its proper position. The fuel flow must be watched if icing continues during the landing approach, since changing conditions can quickly thaw the bleeds, resulting in extremely lean mixtures.

A leaning process results when moisture collects in the impact tubes and freezes in the passage to the A chamber. (See figure 7-14.) The pressure and temperature drop at the automatic mixture control unit can cause condensation and freezing, thereby blocking air flow to A chamber. This permits its pressure to approach the B chamber pressure. The reduction of pressure difference between A and B chambers is not representative of air flow and causes the carburetor to lessen the fuel supply and "starve" the engine. Again the torque and fuel flow tell the story. In this situation, carburetor preheat is necessary. Enriching the mixture, by using prime together with mixture control adjustment, maintains fuel flow until the heat becomes effective.

Heat application to eliminate icing of the impact tube should be performed in the same order and to the

operating temperature, and the fuel temperature. The rich or bleed type icing is encountered with cold fuel only; in fact, fuel temperatures above 7°C (45°F) thawed out frozen bleeds in laboratory tests.

Other icing effects in the induction system are indicated by unusual turbosupercharger control, peculiar readings of instruments vented to carburetor deck pressure, and undue surging or collapse after shifting to single turbo. Apparently, the carburetor flange and fittings for carburetor deck pressure sampling run cold enough in pusher type installations to cause ice formation over the openings under certain icing conditions even though the CAT. is just above freezing. When the pressuretrol fitting is affected, it is unable to sense changes in carburetor deck pressure and relays signals for small changes in the waste gate setting to increase or decrease M.P. The TBS trim may be approximately set to balance the pressure locked in the sensing line by ice and thus maintain approximate power for several minutes. Eventually, a large loss or gain in M.P. may occur, control of which is regained by playing the trim against the locked pressure. Higher CAT. or warmer atmosphere clears the trouble.

If the fitting that senses carburetor deck pressure for the fuel pump, its pressure gage, the water pump and its pressure gage, becomes iced there are various indications. The degree of indication depends upon the effect of locked pressure on pressure regulating valves, gages, fuel flow, water flow, and whether or not the pressuretrol is iced. Since the fuel pump and gage are balanced to the same ice-locked pressure, the fuel pressure will read the proper value even though the true pressure relative to actual carburetor deck pressure is off. The fuel flow and fuel-air ratio varies under this situation.

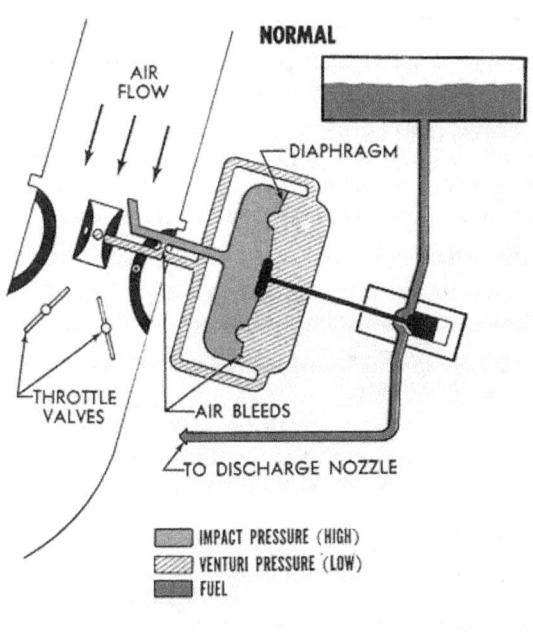
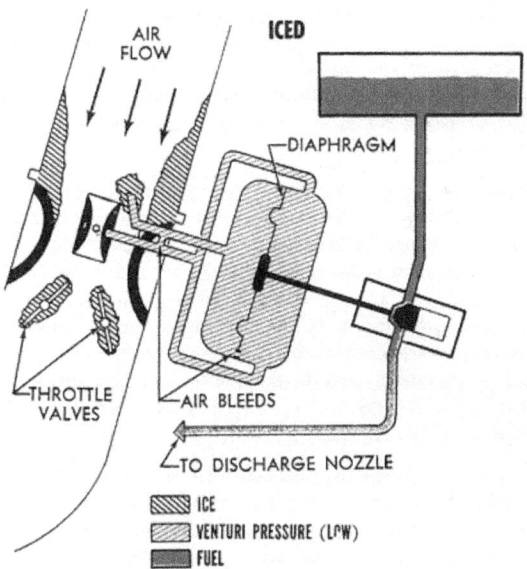

Figure 7-14. Icing of Impact Tube in Carburetor

> **CAUTION**
>
> In the event of water balance line icing, the manifold pressure should not be varied in an attempt to correct water pressure indication.

The intercoolers may partially ice internally when CAT. is below freezing, when air flow is low, and weather is conducive to external icing. When shifting to single turbo there will be an undue surge and power collapse, accompanied by a high CAT. rise before collapse. Returning to a warmer or ice free atmosphere clears the difficulty after a reasonable length of time and single turbo operation becomes normal. It is not known whether operation with high CAT. and a surge-free power will slowly thaw out the partially iced R.H. intercooler and eventually permit full single turbo operation or not. Also, it might be troublesome to resume climb power if the intercoolers were partially iced internally during extended cruise operation with CAT. below freezing.

same degree. However, the cure is more difficult. It is necessary for the metal supporting the carburetor, the automatic mixture control unit, and impact tubes to be warmed sufficiently to melt ice formed internally. Experience shows that manual mixture adjustment gives adequate control until a change of external conditions brings permanent relief. The basic causes for this condition are the affect on the carburetor body temperature of the induction air temperature, the engine cooling air flow temperature, the power plant

Another type of internal icing which may occur is the freezing of water trapped in the fuel side of the regulator. This condition can be prevented by draining the fuel sumps during preflight inspection.

Still another cause of internal icing is the use of fuel which is contaminated with water. Freezing water in contaminated fuel can cause a gradual loss of fuel pressure or high fuel pressure, resulting in loss of reciprocating engine power. Such a condition can be caued by any of the following:

a. Collection and freezing of contaminated fuel in injection and carburetor units.

b. Freezing of water in engine fuel pump pressure regulator cover diaphragm.

c. Condensation in empty or partially empty tanks.

d. Deposits of water collected in natural traps within the fuel tanks and fed into the fuel system during turbulent flight conditions. This condition is particularly true in No. 3 and No. 4 tanks.

e. Freezing of water trapped in the engine fuel transfer pump pressure relief valve diaphragm cover. Abnormally high fuel pressure results from this condition.

The following emergency procedure will be followed in the event a gradual loss of fuel pressure is encountered:

a. Isolate the fuel tanks being used; select and use the remaining tanks.

b. Turn on the booster pumps in the tanks being selected.

c. Start the jet engines as required. Anticipate reciprocating engine power loss.

d. Operate the affected engine or engines on constant prime. Reduce M.P. with the TBS as fuel pressure drops below 26 psi because the mixture will become too lean, resulting in engine backfire or afterfire. Power should stabilize at approximately 2000 rpm, 32 inches M.P., at least 100 psi torque pressure, and from 500 to 700 lb/hr fuel flow. Attempt to maintain maximum CHT and CAT. limits.

Note
If no fuel flow is indicated with the use of the primer, icing has progressed too far and the only alternative is feathering the engine.

e. Begin a gradual descent to a warmer atmosphere. Normally this condition will correct itself around —20°C OAT. if the above procedure is used.

f. When normal fuel pressure is restored, release the primer and return to normal operation.

g. Use fuel from the tanks that were isolated when a lower and warmer altitude is reached.

The following emergency procedure is recommended in the event high fuel pressure is encountered:

a. Retard throttle. If fuel pressure indication follows the throttle, prevent fuel pressure from going overboard and rupturing parts of the fuel injection system by proceeding as follows as quickly as possible.

b. Reduce rpm.

c. Open the tank valves and turn on the booster pumps in the remaining tanks on the affected side.

d. Isolate the affected engine fuel system by use of the manifold valves.

Note
Normally the condition will correct itself when lower and warmer altitudes are reached.

TORQUEMETER.

There are two methods frequently used to estimate reciprocating engine power in airplanes. One utilizes measurement of manifold pressure and engine speed. The other depends on measurement of torque pressure and engine speed. The primary difference between the two is that the manifold pressure method measures, in effect, power put into the engine, while the torque pressure method measures power output of the engine.

Manifold pressure and rpm, at best, are a crude indication of engine power, because they are only a rough measure of charge air flow into the engine. The charge air flow for a particular M.P. and rpm combination varies with CAT., exhaust back pressure, and CHT. Furthermore, power which is developed for a particular charge air flow varies with mixture conditions. Besides the variables within the individual engine, additional variables result from slight differences among engines in valve timing, ignition timing, etc.

Since there is no simple equation relating bhp, M. P., and rpm, this type of schedule must be presented in chart form, such as the power schedule tables or curves found in the appendix. An attempt is made to achieve better accuracy by providing a correction for CAT., and by providing M.P. values for a series of altitudes so the effects of varying back pressure can be approximated. Spark advance and mixture strength are considered with the assumption that definite values of the two factors will be used for each combination of bhp and rpm. However, it is either impossible or impractical to include in charts the other variables mentioned above. Therefore, power schedules leave much to be desired when accurate cruise control is the objective.

The torquemeter provides a direct measurement of the torque transmitted by the crankshaft to the propeller. In most airplanes, practically all torque developed is applied to the propeller, so that engine power may be determined from the following simple equation:

Bhp = constant x torque pressure x rpm.

This equation is independent of the many variables that affect the M.P. method of estimating power.

In this airplane an engine cooling fan is driven by a power take-off in the accessory section of the engine. Under some conditions, the fan absorbs a large amount of power. Fan power is not sensed by the torquemeter, which measures only the part of engine bhp transmitted through the propeller reduction gear. Therefore, the equation for bhp is as follows:

Bhp = propeller shaft hp + fan hp
    = constant x torque pressure x rpm
      + fan hp
(constant for R4360-41 = 0.0043)

Fan power is easily obtained from the cooling fan horsepower curves, so that only torque pressure, rpm, and altitude need be known for the rapid and accurate determination of bhp developed by the engine. To simplify the engineer's work, the above equation was solved for a large number of points along the recommended power schedules, and resultant values of torque pressure were summarized in the appendix. Although torquemeter use is recommended in setting power for accurate cruise control, it must be remembered that the torquemeter senses only the total power output to the propeller shaft, regardless of how the individual cylinders are operating. Thus, if any cylinders are not operating properly due to faulty ignition or other malfunction, the remaining cylinders would have to develop more than their share of power to produce the desired torque. To avoid damage under such conditions, M.P. should be used as a check against torque pressure. The simplest and most useful check is to ascertain that all engines which are set at the same torque, rpm, and fuel flow have manifold pressures within 3 inches of each other but not to exceed 2 inches above the corrected manifold pressure. If any engine requires manifold pressure in excess of the allowable 2 inches required to produce the desired torque, its torque should be reduced until the manifold pressure is within the allowable 3-inch spread.

SPARK SELECTION.

Spark selection is provided on the R4360 engines to obtain the maximum range advantage when using manually leaned mixtures. With retarded spark, cruise power fuel economy improves with decreasing mixture strength to approximately .060 fuel-air ratio. Further manual leaning will not increase fuel economy unless the spark is advanced. With a leaner ratio, flame propagation becomes so slow that combustion energy from the charge is released too late in the power cycle, making the cycle less efficient. When this condition is approached, use of advanced spark improves fuel economy in two ways. First, earlier ignition of the slow-burning mixture results in better timing of the energy release and, consequently, better cycle efficiency. Second, it permits use of leaner mixtures to approximately .055 fuel-air ratio before flame speeds again become too low for efficient operation. Thus, advanced spark provides a 4 to 6 per cent decrease in brake specific fuel consumption for manual lean cruise power operation.

Advancing the spark results in a rise in CHT and increases the cylinder cooling requirements. Because of the additional cooling requirement, it is essential to lean all the way to "best economy" mixture, in order to take full advantage of the cooling effect of lean mixtures. It is desirable to lean through the intermediate mixture range (.067-.070) as rapidly as possible, since the most severe cooling requirements generally occur somewhere between normal and "best economy" mixture strengths. Advanced spark benefits fuel economy most at lean mixtures. Because of the effects on cooling requirements and detonation margin, advanced spark should not be used for operation with normal or rich mixtures.

The engineer must check the spark advance control for proper operation each time it is used. Failure of the actuator to change the spark timing calls for corrective action. Correct operation may be checked by noting the effect on engine power. Advancing the spark normally causes an increase of torque pressure. However, mixture strength may obscure this check on the ground. At 2000 rpm with the mixture in NORMAL, the fuel-air ratio can be near "best power" if the carburetor is set on the rich side. In this case, advancing the spark will show very little torque increase and the operator might conclude that the spark mechanism is stuck in retard. This can be confirmed by switching the ignition to the right or left position which is equivalent to retarding the spark 10 degrees. If the timing is advanced and the mixture is near "best power" little or no change of power will occur. The torque pressure and rpm will remain practically constant because the mixture burns too fast to require advanced spark. If the timing is stuck in retard, the use of single ignition will cause a definite and recognizable power loss. In this event a recheck with the mixture lever in the manual lean range will give a more positive indication whether or not the spark has advanced properly. Lean mixtures on single ignition give large drops in rpm and torque, and sometimes backfire if very lean.

In flight the spark is not advanced until the mixture has its first dose of leaning from normal. In this condition single ignition can cause backfiring. The interpretation of the torque pressure reading is evidence that the timing has changed from retard to advance, or vice versa. With lean mixtures this is quite positive.

The cylinder head temperature rise is a further check that operation is satisfactory, but it is somewhat slow in response. Higher temperatures occur with the use of advanced timing than with retarded, if the mixture strength and other cooling factors are unchanged. While the direction of temperature change shows up in a short time, it takes about 5 minutes for the reading to stabilize after the shift of spark advance.

High spark advance is similar in detonation effect to high carburetor air and cylinder temperatures, high M.P. and high rpm (impeller speed). The combinations of these factors must be taken into consideration when arriving at the limits for the use of advanced spark.

The use of advanced timing may be beneficial if ignition irregularities are present—magneto or plug malfunctioning. If an individual cylinder is operating on one plug, even with the switch in BOTH the effect in that cylinder is the same as though the timing had been retarded 10 degrees. This explains why backfiring can sometimes be eliminated by shifting from RETARD to ADVANCE. With one plug out, the combustion process lasts too long and, in some cases, burning is still going on when the exhaust valve opens. By advancing the spark, timing in the offending cylinder is brought more nearly into line. However, this procedure is used only at powers where advanced spark is permitted. Richer or leaner mixtures may help the situation, depending upon how close the basic carburetor setting is to "best power" at the air flow being used. The use of prime helps the carburetor through a lean range when one or more cylinders are firing on one plug.

If the spark advancing equipment malfunctions, leaving the timing at advance, the engine should not be operated at higher powers than those permitted with advanced spark. In an emergency, when higher power is needed, alleviate the situation by operating that power plant on single magneto rather than dual. This will, in effect, retard the spark.

Procedure For Advancing Spark.

The procedure for advancing spark is included in "Manual Leaning" of this section.

Procedure For Retarding Spark.

The following procedure is used to retard the spark from advanced spark operation.

1. Reduce M.P. approximately 2 inches with the turbo calibration knob.

2. Restore torque pressure by enriching the mixture.

3. Spark advance switch—RETARD and note torque pressure drop. Monitor this procedure with engine analyzer.

4. Gradually enrichen mixture and lower M.P. to maintain the desired torque pressure.

5. Mixture control lever—NORMAL.

MIXTURE CONTROL.

It was shown previously that mixture strength of the charge can be varied and that this variation produces changes in the engine operating condition affecting power, temperature, and spark timing requirements. "Best power" fuel-air ratio (.074-.080 F/A) is desirable when the greatest power from a given charge air flow is required. "Best economy" mixture results in obtaining the given power output with the least fuel flow and is close to .060 with RETARD spark advance and about .055 with ADVANCE. The need for automatic enrichment above "best power" for detonation control was discussed.

The carburetor controls fuel flow by varying two basic factors. First, the fuel control unit, acting as a pressure reducing valve, determines the metering pressure in response to the metering forces. Then the metering unit, in effect, varies the size of the orifice through which the metering pressure forces the fluid. It is a law of hydraulics that the amount of fluid passing through an orifice varies with the pressure drop across the orifice and with the size of the orifice. The internal automatic devices and the mixture control act to determine the effective size of the fuel metering passage. The internal devices—fixed jets and variable power enrichment valve—are not subject to direct external control and by themselves determine the basic shape of the metering curve as the power changes from low cruise to take-off. The mixture control, adjustable from the cockpit, permits a modification of this basic curve by directly changing the size of the effective orifice. The RICH position provides the maximum orifice opening possible for any given air flow. The fuel flow characteristics with this mixture determines the basic shape of the metering curve. If the control lever is fixed in intermediate position a new metering curve is established at leaner fuel-air ratios but with essentially the same shape as with RICH.

Fuel flow variations as a result of mixture control lever movement at fixed rpm and manifold pressure is shown in figure 7-15.

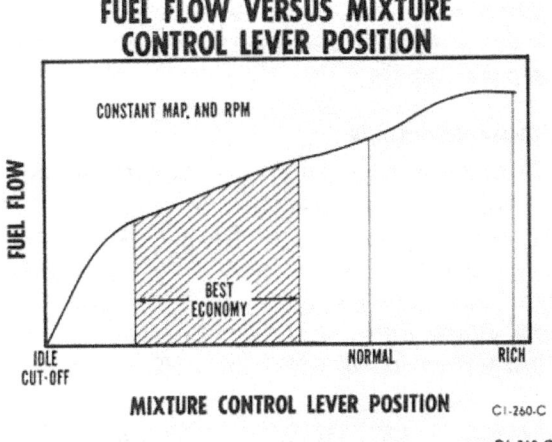

Figure 7-15.

Between 20 and NORMAL a gradual fuel flow increase provides the useful range for manual leaning. A more rapid rise above NORMAL furnishes a comparatively coarse range for manual adjustment. RICH gives the maximum fuel flow for a given air flow and is used most often to assist in cooling the engine under unusually hot conditions. The detented position marked NORMAL is one of an infinite number of fixed positions between IDLE CUT-OFF and RICH. It was selected because metering characteristics accompanying its use provide desirable operation throughout the power range. When operating in NORMAL, the carburetor meters approximately lean "best power" mixture (.078) in the cruising range. The NORMAL setting meets engine requirements, with respect to usual operating temperatures and powers; and its lowest fuel-air ratio (in the cruise power range) accommodates accelerations over a moderate range of cool operating temperatures. The mixture strengths at the high power end are limited by detonation with a suitable safety factor. The basic metering curve with RICH added is shown in figure 7-16. The shape and position of the enriched portion of the curve at the high power end is determined by detonation. The limiting point of detonation at any power is not a fixed value but a variable, determined primarily by the final temperature of the charge as it is compressed and ignited. Adding the detonation limit line to this basic curve reflects the influence of other factors on operating safety. The detonation limits are not sharply defined, but will bounce back and forth even when an engine is tested under controlled conditions in the laboratory.

A 10 to 15 per cent margin seems necessary to be safe. Anything tending to keep the temperature down pushes the detonation limit away from the point of operation and permits higher powers for a given fuel-air ratio. Anything which elevates the charge temperature lowers the detonation limited power. Below about 60 per cent of normal rated power (including fan horsepower) the engine is virtually free of these detonation limits and with reasonable operating temperatures, engine conditioning, and the use of specified fuel, manual leaning can be used.

In the range of power between approximately 60 and 70 per cent normal rated power (including fan hp) manual leaning can be very marginal and the combination of unfavorable factors present must be considered. If the engine is in good condition manual leaning in this range is accomplished satisfactorily and safely, provided the temperature and spark advance limits are observed. If the combustion chambers are allowed to load up with lead and other deposits, the stage is set for detonation and probable preignition unless compensating reductions of carburetor air and cylinder temperature are used.

Mixture strength affects the power available from a given charge air flow, the temperature of the cylinders, and other temperatures. These effects are shown by curves in figure 7-17. The maximum values of torque pressure occur at "best power" fuel-air ratios and fall off as the mixture is enriched or leaned. The fact that loss of power is greater on the lean side explains the need for seemingly large increases of manifold pressure to maintain constant bhp while leaning. For example, during take-off or rated power climb it would be physically possible to lean manually to "best power" mixture. However, the temperature increase shown in the above curve would show its effects on

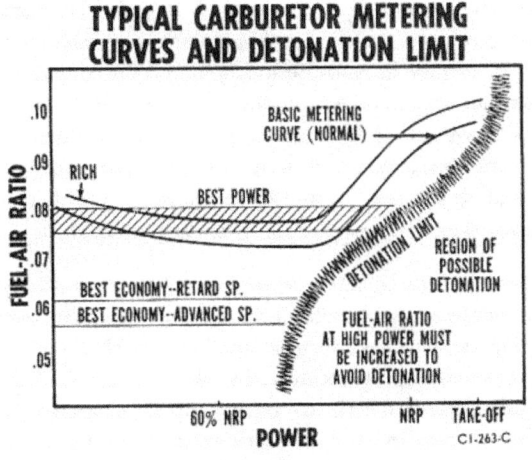

Figure 7-16.

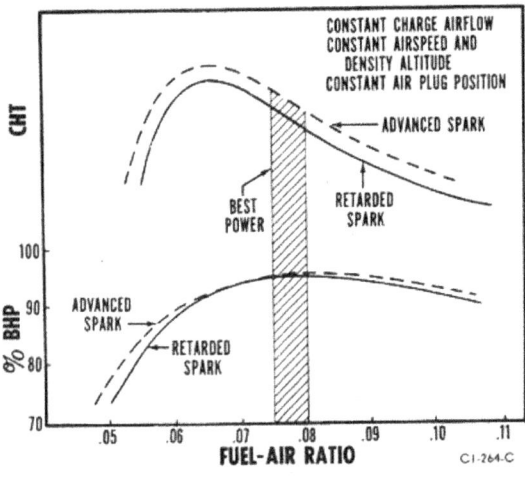

Figure 7-17.

CHT. This would encourage detonation or preignition, backfiring, and burned pistons.

In this situation there would be noticeable loss of power output which could be measured by torque pressure, indicated air speed, rate of climb, and possibly failure to clear obstacles at the end of the runway.

Manual leaning is not only possible and permissible below approximately 75 per cent normal rated power (including fan hp) but is necessary when maximum range is desired. As the fuel-air ratio is reduced below .067, temperatures are reduced (figure 7-17) and cumulative gains are possible by adding the lowered cooling drag to the fuel saving. It is also possible that mixtures leaner than "best economy" are efficient. However, they would be impractical when the mixture distribution to the individual cylinders is such that power becomes unstable. While the bhp per pound cannot be increased, and may even decrease, the miles per pound may be favored by further permissible reduction of the cooling air flow. It is possible, and often desirable, to lean to such an extent with advanced spark that if the timing were retarded the engine would be rough due to poor combustion.

When establishing these super lean mixtures consider the temperature factors. Usually the cruise power setting is made following a rated power climb with all operating temperatures near the maximum. The passage from normal to cruising lean mixtures is safely accomplished if the power plant is well cooled. Do not set up limiting cylinder head and carburetor air temperatures and then lean. First, for a minute or so, hold the temperatures well below the limits to allow piston heads, exhaust valves, spark plugs, and the superchargers to cool. Then adjust the mixture and, finally, establish the operating temperatures.

The idle mixture strength is of great importance. A mixture too lean results in poor acceleration, misfiring with possible plug fouling, and poor flight operation with nearly closed throttle. If the mixture is too rich, extended ground operation causes plug fouling due to carbon.

Manual Adjustment.

Because of manufacturing tolerances of the carburetors, it is possible for fuel flow variations to exist between the six engines, even when they are operating at the same rpm and M.P. (air flow) in NORMAL mixture. (See figure 7-18.) The fuel consumption curves call for a definite fuel flow to each engine when set for climb power or in the high power range. The manipu-

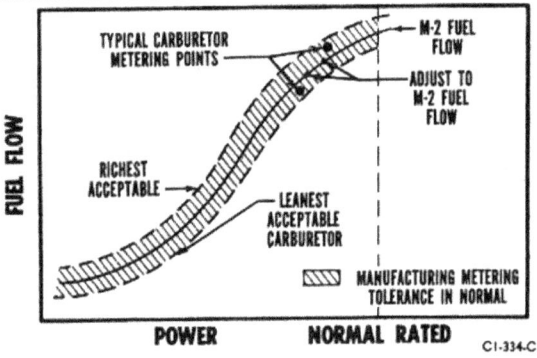

Figure 7-18.

lation of the mixture control lever out of the NORMAL position on either side to attain the proper fuel flow is called manual adjustment.

Manual adjustment is authorized under all flight conditions except take-off, provided the engines are operating properly. Other than insuring that minimum specified fuel flow is provided to each engine, this procedure calls for no unusual attention on the part of the engineer.

Procedure for Manual Adjustment During High Power Operation.

1. Establish power, rpm, and M.P. corrected for CAT. in NORMAL mixture.

2. Manually adjust the fuel flow to the specified

value consistent with the bhp. Refer to "Manual Adjust —20° Spark Advance Fuel Consumption" curve, Appendix 1.

Note

With good conditioned engines the bhp (torque) may be obtained with less corrected M.P. than the power schedule indicates. With poorly conditioned engines, the bhp (torque) may not be obtained even with maximum allowable corrected M.P. and corrected fuel flow. If this condition exists accept the low bhp (torque) and in no case allow the corrected M.P. to exceed 3 inches above the charted value. Also, the spread in M.P. between the six engines must not exceed 3 inches.

Manual Leaning.

The B-36 engine handling practices are conceived primarily to attain long range and to promote engine life compatible with the tactical mission of the airplane. The conventional engine setting practices used on other aircraft will not accomplish these ends. Former limits of bmep, cruise power, and fuel-air ratio arbitrarily set higher than "best economy" result in an operating range considerably below that required. On the B-36, every limit that hinders obtaining maximum miles per pound of fuel is being raised as high as possible as experience progresses. The change from previous practices to B-36 operation has not been without difficulty and, in too many instances, all the apparent differences in engine handling are blamed. It would be more sound to examine each factor separately and see which particular one contributes most to the reduction of engine service life.

The same basic engine, without external supercharging, using lower continuous cruise power and with atmospheric exhaust back pressure, achieves a normal service life with no more difficulty than that involving the maintenance of sufficient overall warmth to insure stable running.

The B-36, with its turbosuperchargers, can sustain high power to higher altitudes than have been flown regularly on service aircraft. This type of operation, requiring the higher sustained powers, results in higher cylinder and carburetor temperatures and more exhaust back pressure than would be encountered at lower levels. These general factors alone are unfavorable to long service life. When the long range cruise techniques are added, a real operating problem is given to the engineer.

Not every factor of combat cruise is unfavorable. The increase of bmep from 150 to 160 for a given power is accompanied by a reduction of the internal supercharger rpm and attendant lower charge-air heat rise which permits a higher bmep detonation limit at the lower rpm. The maximum limit of cruise bmep is often a structural fatigue limit concerned with the loads and deflections on the power transmitting system—rods, crankshaft, reduction gear, and propeller. Low rpm means a less frequent rate of power impulses to these parts and, consequently, is a favorable condition with respect to fatigue failure provided resonant vibration is not encountered. The absolute limit is reached when distress results from a further increase of bmep, even with these favorable low rpms. All previous experience has been at a maximum of 150 bmep but there is no reason to expect that 160 bmep has exceeded a critical value in view of the experience accumulated so far.

The other operating factors are largely unfavorable. The increase of maximum power for use of lean mixture with both retard and advance spark bring the operation much nearer to the detonation limit line and fatigue limits.

With conventional operation, cruising at 1750 maximum bhp and normal mixture still left a good margin of safety commonly called a cushion. This came in handy when substandard ignition, valve operation, or combustion chamber conditions appeared. But with higher power operation and the manual leaning practiced on the B-36, the margin is greatly reduced. When substandard conditions show up, detonation and preignition are more likely.

Other attendant problems can show up with long range cruise. The higher bmep requires that the turbosupercharger assume a greater share of the charge compression load and power collapse can result. Oil spewing, power instability, and ignition difficulties are accentuated by the extreme high altitude of operation. The correction for these malfunctionings can be described with fair accuracy and are covered in other portions of this section.

However, exact steps to avoid detonation and preignition cannot be as accurately described and no "pat" answer can be given for eliminating their occurrence if long range cruise procedures are followed. When the decision is made to leave the comparative safety of the conventional power settings and apply relatively high cruise power with manually leaned mixture, the operation is getting closer to the area where trouble has been known to exist. If detonation and preignition can be avoided, the mission will probably be successful.

The consecutive steps in manual leaning and in returning to a rich mixture must follow a prescribed

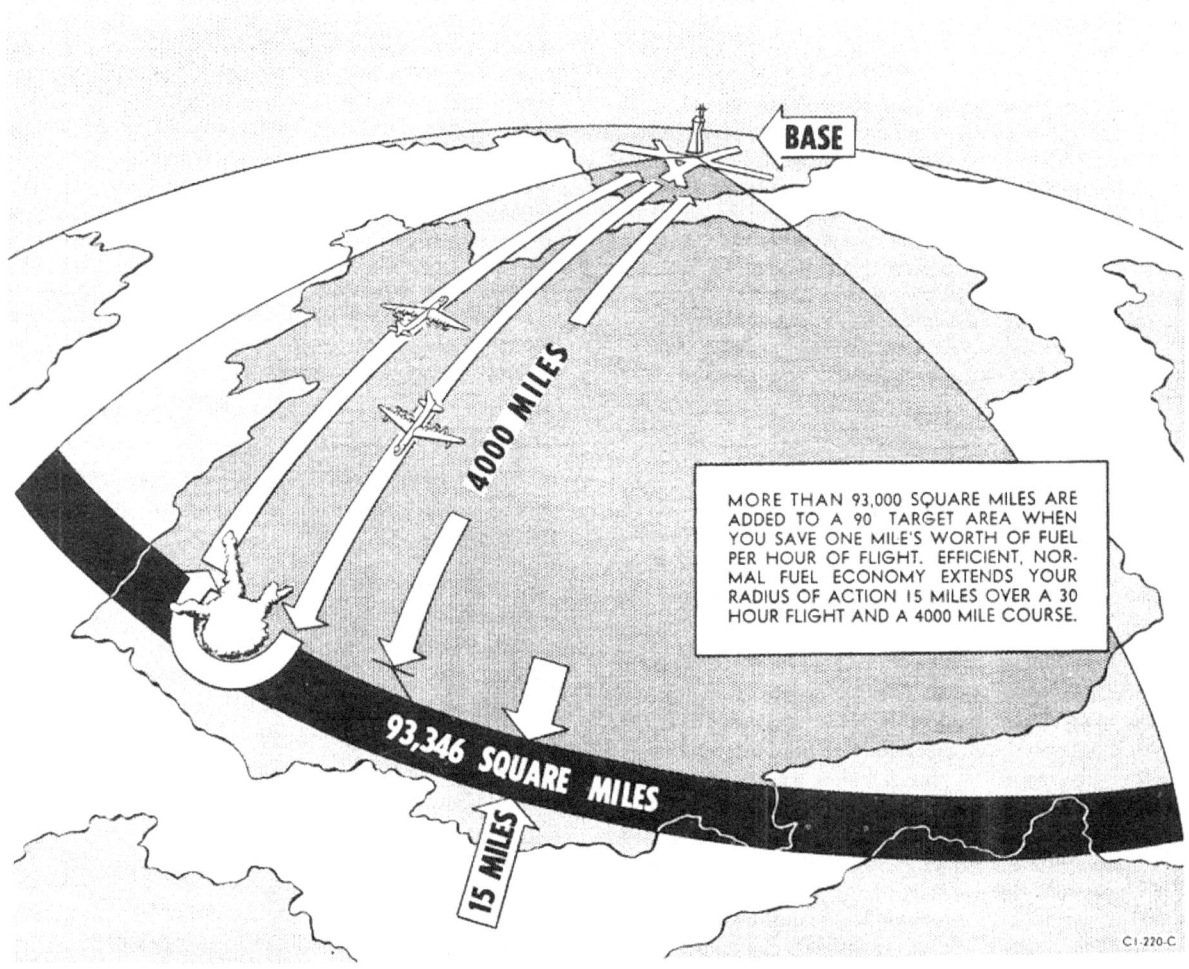

Figure 7-19. Range Extension

procedure which results in approaching the final setting without going into the known danger area at any time. This requires considering the effect of each change on the conditions inside the combustion chamber after the change is made.

The first manual lean power setting may follow an extended climb during which the cylinder heads may have gone to the maximum limit. Immediate leaning with this temperature present is a bad procedure and possible engine damage may result. Some engineers have been pleased to find that the head temperature was reduced by leaning and have used it as the primary means of temperature control at this time. While the indicated temperature came down, there could be no assurance that the other cylinders behaved as well and it can be certain that the temperature of the piston did not lower to the same degree. *Therefore, do not start the manual leaning until the engine is well cooled and do not use mixture for cooling at this time.* Cylinder head temperature is the only direct means of judging the engine temperature and the most successful engineers leave the mixture control alone until the heads are down to 210 to 220°C. The time taken to bring about this cooling also allows the turbosupercharger to drop in temperature even though it has no direct means of advising the engineer.

The detonation limit line is further pushed to the right and out of the way if carburetor air temperature is brought down to 10 degrees or more below the final value.

Manual Leaning—Sea Level to 35,000 Feet. The following procedure is for manual leaning between sea level and 35,000 feet. Manual leaning can be performed at these altitudes with less concern for the immediate effect on CHT and engine condition due to the cooling ability of the more dense air.

CAUTION

Manual leaning in advanced spark is not permitted above 44.8 inches M.P. at 2200 rpm and above 1940 bhp because serious engine damage would probably result. Also, during all manual lean operation the maximum permissible CHT is 220°C. The maximum permissible CAT. in the 1900 to 2200 rpm range is 20°C.

Experience has shown that operation below these limits is essential to avoid detonation and preignition. With advanced spark, the maximum CAT. must be held below 20°C until reduced rpm gives a smaller temperature rise through the internal supercharger. This prevents the final temperature of the charge air from becoming excessive.

Note

It is very important to have the engine instruments calibrated to effect the procedures contained herein. The use of uncalibrated instruments could easily result in establishing dangerous conditions without the engineer being aware of the situation.

After reaching cruise altitude proceed as follows:

1. Spark advance switches—RETARD. The shift from retarded to advanced spark must be delayed until the mixture strength is sufficiently low to permit firing the charge further in advance of top center. Shifting to advanced spark while the mixture is still in the rich, hot burning area can result in immediate detonation possibly followed by preignition and cylinder damage.

2. Air plugs and intercooler shutters—Full open.

3. Insure that CHT and CAT. are below limiting cruise values. By reducing these temperatures to the lowest practicable value the engineer is insuring that the engine is in a condition to receive the lean mixtures with advanced spark.

4. Find "best power" at the desired torque pressure and observe readings. These readings determine relative engine condition and are used as a reference during the manual leaning procedure. Proceed with the following steps on one engine at a time. "Best power" is found by holding torque pressure constant with the turbo calibration knob while at the same time moving the mixture control from NORMAL, either richer or leaner, and noting manifold pressure. "Best power" is the range in fuel flow in which the desired torque pressure is obtained with the least manifold pressure (or for a given M.P. the power is greatest). Those engines requiring the greatest manifold pressure (more than an inch above average or two inches above the lowest) should be watched carefully during the ensuing steps as deficiencies may be present in these units.

5. Move the mixture control lever toward lean until a 25 psi torque drop is obtained. This reduces the mixture strength to a value that is safe to take advanced spark and about as lean as will remain stable in retarded spark.

6. Place the spark advance switch in ADVANCE and note that the torque pressure rises. It is important that the engineer be certain that the spark has advanced. Torque pressure rise is evidence that the change has taken place. Monitoring of each engine by means of the engine analyzer during this operation will provide a further indication that the spark has been advanced.

7. Re-establish desired torque pressure by increasing manifold pressure with the turbo calibration knob.

Note

Normally an increase of approximately $4\ 1/2 \pm 1/2$ inches manifold pressure above best power manifold pressure will produce best economy mixture ratio for constant CAT., torque pressure, and rpm conditions.

8. If the manifold pressure is below the values given in the power schedule of the appendix, continue leaning and re-establish torque with manifold pressure until the charted manifold pressures are obtained (corrected for CAT.). Manifold pressures below the power schedule values are evidence that the mixture has not been leaned sufficiently. If the mixture is still in the range above .061 it is not suitable for advanced spark and further leaning must be accomplished for safe operation.

9. As a further check on the final fuel flow in the event fuel flow meter instrumentation is in doubt, the observed fuel flow at best economy will be slightly above the fuel flow which occurred after reducing torque pressure 25 psi before advancing spark. Every

possible check and cross check should be made throughout this operation to insure that suitable conditions are present. This is also an example of the greater desirability of following relative values rather than absolute values.

10. Once the desired manifold pressure is obtained, check the fuel flow and the fuel-air ratio. If the fuel flow is considerably higher than charted, the engine is in all probability malfunctioning and the fuel-air ratio may be in a dangerous and hot area (over .061). If this is the case reduce fuel flow with the mixture control, thus reducing fuel-air ratio within the desired limits (.055 to .061) and accepting the lower torque obtained.

WARNING

If fuel-air ratio over .061 is required for stable operation, return to 20 degrees spark and adjust mixture to obtain minimum stable operation.

Again the available cross checks are utilized to insure that too much reliance is not placed on any one instrument. The dangers of operating with advanced spark and mixture strengths greater than .061 require this care. If malfunctioning cylinders are encountered it should still be satisfactory to impose the specified manifold pressure on the remaining good cylinders as each of these cylinders is capable of putting out its portion of the indicated horsepower. The torque horsepower should not be maintained at the specified value as this would involve increasing the indicated horsepower in the good cylinders to make up for the deficiency of those that are malfunctioning.

If enrichment to .061 is necessary to obtain stable operation, the manifold pressure must be reduced about 5 per cent from the value used with .056; otherwise the imep of the good cylinders will become excessive and may initiate detonation or preignition.

Note

Any descent other than long range cruise descent must be made in retarded spark, since there is insufficient time to check fuel-air ratio.

12. It must be remembered that the values set forth in the power schedule are most desirable with an engine in proper condition. However, satisfactory operation may be obtained between .055 and .061 fuel-air ratio at slightly lower M.P. values when engine instability is encountered at recommended power schedule values.

13. Subsequent cruise power changes in advanced spark manual lean operation will cause slight changes in fuel-air ratio and a check must be made to insure that the desired values are maintained.

Note

When "best economy" has been obtained, note the position of the mixture control lever with respect to the index markings on the quadrant. This will serve as a reference when manual leaning at higher altitudes.

This note is of particular importance when the power used for reference of the index markings is the same as the anticipated power for operation at higher altitude which will be seen in the procedure for manual leaning above 35,000 feet.

Manual Leaning—35,000 Feet and Above. The problem of manual leaning above 35,000 feet is more critical than the procedure at lower altitudes due to the poor cooling ability of the low density air. As the mixture passes from comparatively rich fuel-air ratios through the chemically best mixture (.067) it becomes very difficult to maintain cylinder head temperatures at a satisfactorily low level. Therefore, the procedure is set up so that this passage is accomplished as rapidly as possible.

Note

Leaning will be accomplished on one engine at a time.

1. Air plugs and intercooler shutters—Full open. A cool engine is even more important at these altitudes than at lower levels.

2. Fan speed switch—HIGH RPM. This further aids cooling.

3. Master motor—2200 rpm. Manual leaning cruise at these altitudes will usually begin at the highest permissible manual lean cruise powers.

4. Spark advance switch—RETARD. The retard position must always be used for any mixtures richer than .061.

5. Mixture control lever—RICH. The advance from NORMAL to RICH further helps in alleviating the tendency for the engine to overheat.

6. Turn turbo calibration knob its full travel counter-clockwise, allowing the CHT and CAT. to drop below limiting cruise values. This still further assists the cooling problem, especially the piston and valves.

7. Fan speed switch—LOW RPM. As the engine is now well cooled, the fan can be operated in the low speed. The engine will shortly receive internal cooling from lean mixtures.

8. Move the mixture control lever toward lean to a predetermined position on the quadrant.

Note

The approximate mixture control lever position should have been noted by the engineer for "best economy" at some lower altitude where manual leaning techniques could be employed under less critical conditions. This procedure has been found necessary to prevvent cylinder overheating.

The evaluation of the engine by noting "best power" mixture has already been performed at lower altitudes. Therefore, time, at the comparatively hot mixture at and near "best power," is saved by dispensing with this part of the procedure. The direct movement of the mixture control to the approximate final position quickly transfers the operation from reliance on external cooling to reliance on internal lean mixture cooling.

9. Spark advance switch—ADVANCE. By now the mixture should be sufficiently lean and the engine still sufficiently cool to accept advanced spark.

10. Increase manifold pressure with turbo calibration knob until desired power schedule value is obtained (corrected for CAT.).

11. Adjust turbo calibration knob until the torque pressure is 5 psi below the desired value.

Note

This value is specified in order to prevent exceeding the bmep on that engine while the other engines are being set.

This procedure permits each engine to stabilize towards its final power and temperature values while settings are being made on the other engines, thus insuring that no engine will exceed its limits during the interval. Reducing the fuel flow quickly across the board to some reasonable value is preferable to letting some engines remain a long time at high flow while a small final gain is being squeezed out of the first ones.

12. Continue the above procedures until all engines have been manually leaned.

13. Make fine adjustments on each engine to obtain the desired setting. If the torque pressure is slightly low or CHT is climbing, adjustment of the manifold pressure is permissible provided it does not exceed the charted value more than 3 inches. If the torque pressure remains low, increase the fuel flow 5 to 15 pounds per hour. If the torque pressure is still low after the above adjustment, accept the torque obtained. If CHT increases beyond limits, reduce M.P. with the turbo calibration knob, enrich the mixture so that the engine will not backfire, and immediately return to retarded spark. Use rich mixture to cool the engines. When the engines are within limits, repeat the above procedure to return to manual leaning.

14. Adjust air plugs and intercooler shutters to desired settings.

Note

Engine stability is improved by operating with lower CAT.

Good engine handling procedures at this time can go far toward gaining the ultimate economy possible. It is generally recognized that it is better to decelerate to cruising air speed rather than allowing the airplane to fall below this air speed in the transition from climb to level flight and then requiring it to accelerate to this stabilized velocity. Many engineers have found it desirable to hold the climb power after leveling off so that the airplane accelerates rapidly to a figure well above the final anticipated value. Some cooling benefits are derived during this period with increasing air speeds. Then power is reduced on all engines to a point which is slightly above the final amount so that while the manual leaning procedure is followed, the necessary power reductions on individual engines do not result in allowing the airplane to decelerate below the recommended air speed.

ENGINE COOLING.

It should be remembered that the R4360 engine is an air-cooled engine and its requirements for cooling air should be met if long life is to be attained. When the cylinder head temperature has stabilized, it is known that equilibrium is being maintained between the heat absorbed by the cylinder head material from combustion and the extraction of this heat by the cooling air flow that is passing through the fin and deflector passages. The rate at which heat is forced into the head from the inside depends upon the amount of heat generated in the combustion chamber to produce indicated horsepower which in turn varies with rpm, manifold pressure, carburetor air temperature, mixture strength, spark advance, and other items affected by the general condition of the engine. The rate at which the heat is removed from the head is dependent upon the weight of the cooling air flow and the temperature difference between the head material and the cooling air. The quantity factor governs the number of air particles participating in the activity. The temperature difference factor is a measure of the heat absorbing capacity of each particle.

These two factors work in opposing directions as the altitude of operation is increased. The decreasing temperature is favorable as it widens the temperature difference of the heat exchange. Unfortunately the decreasing air density, which is unfavorable, reduces the weight of cooling air flow at a rate that overcomes the beneficial temperature factor. If constant power is maintained at high altitude, the cylinder cooling problem becomes increasingly difficult.

The principal factors that control engine cooling are those which regulate the rate of cooling air flow.

Air Speed Versus Cooling.

The air speed indicator reading is a measure of the effects of density and altitude, plus the forward speed of the airplane. Air speed variation generally is only to be used as direct means of cooling control during climbs. At this time a small increase in indicated air speed above that for best rate of climb may materially assist in maintaining satisfactory temperature without appreciable loss of performance. At very low indicated air speeds requiring a high angle of attack, a peculiarity of the aircraft causes a change in the relationship between plug opening and cylinder cooling. In this attitude there is a tendency for the air under the wing to flow around the trailing edge to the upper side. This results in a forward flow through the bottom of the air plug opening which interferes with cooling air flow through a portion of the engine. This may be a limiting factor in attaining a minimum indicated air speed in climb and cruise at high altitude. If cylinder head temperature cannot be controlled by direct means, increased air speed may bring the required relief even though additional power is required.

Engine Fan Operation.

The engine fan is installed to aid in engine cooling. At low air speeds or during ground operation, the fan contributes its greatest share of the cooling load. As air speed increases, the fan becomes increasingly less essential, until at high air speeds, the naturally induced air flow provides most of the cooling air. The fan is driven by the crankshaft through hydraulic couplings. The low speed drive should be used as long as adequate cooling is possible because of the high power requirements of the high speed drive. High speed fan drive should be used only at very high altitudes with normal rated power.

WARNING

The use of high ratio fan operation is restricted because of structural limitations of the fan. (Refer to "Operating Limitations," Section V.)

When engine overheating is experienced, shifting to high fan drive should be accomplished if within structural limitations of the fan. It should be noted that the net loss in thrust caused by shifting from low to high fan is less than indicated by the torque drop because the higher fan power is partially compensated by added jet thrust of the cooling air.

In using the fan speed selection for cylinder head

Figure 7-20. Principal Factors Affecting Engine Cooling

temperature control, the engineer must observe the torque pressure reactions as a check that the fan drive couplings are in satisfactory condition. The shift is performed by changing the flow of oil from the low speed coupling to the high speed coupling. As the low speed coupling drains, the high speed unit is filling and when the process is complete the fan is turning at the higher ratio. For a short interval, during which a quantity of oil still remains in the low speed coupling and the high speed coupling has received a sufficient amount to start transmitting power, the two couplings are bucking each other and more power is being absorbed from the crankshaft than when either coupling is functioning independently. This shows up in a momentary reduction of torque pressure, followed by an increase to a new reading that is below that when the fan was driven at low speed.

This torque oil pressure reaction furnishes a check as to the amount of sludge in the couplings. The maximum drop is 25 psi with a stabilized drop of 10 to 20 psi below the original torque pressure. Upon returning to LOW RPM, the torque should return to the original value.

Air Plug Operation.

The air plug is the remaining direct control over cooling air flow and can be considered as a throttle for the cooling air passage. When the combination of air speed and fan speed results in an excess of air being pumped, over that required to maintain satisfactory temperatures, considerable drag is eliminated by restricting the passage and the weight of air being pumped.

Cooling by Mixture Control.

If, after shifting to high fan drive, additional cooling is required during climb up to 40,000 feet, it can be obtained by increasing air speed or shifting to RICH. If the cylinder head temperatures exceed the limit with

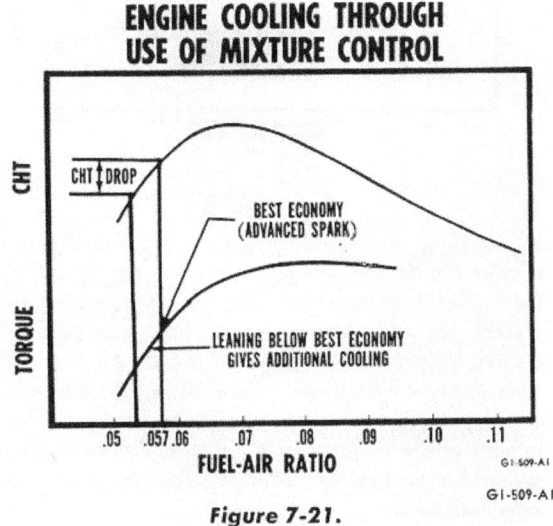

Figure 7-21.

NORMAL mixture and high fan drive in level flight at powers above the limit for manual leaning, shifting to RICH will improve cooling. For powers below this range, the use of RICH mixture provides little improvement, but manual leaning to "best economy" is very effective in reducing temperatures. Over 20°C CHT reductions can be realized by leaning out from NORMAL to "best economy." At the highest manual lean cruise powers, cylinder temperatures will be close to or above the limit in NORMAL mixture. Since normal mixture operation results in cylinder head temperatures higher than the temperature at "best economy," it is advisable to get into the air cooling range of mixtures in one step, rather than several small steps. This is accomplished by leaning out in the first step until the torque drops an amount which requires 4 inches M.P. increase to re-establish torque. A torque drop of 15 psi is generally about right.

To obtain the full benefit of the leaning effect on cylinder head temperature, it is important to lean out all the way to "best economy," because most of the temperature reduction results from the last portion of the mixture control adjustment. Following the initial leaning of 4 inches M.P., a range of 1 or 2 inches M.P. in either direction should be investigated (maintaining constant torque) to establish the minimum fuel flow accurately.

Cylinder Head Temperature.

On airplanes in group 2 the thermocouple for measuring cylinder head temperature is attached to only one of the twenty-eight cylinders. Airplanes in group 2 have thermocouples attached to two of the twenty-eight cylinders of each reciprocating engine. This single temperature connection between the gage and the engine provides a relatively restricted means for "seeing" the over-all heat condition and the resulting effect on combustion and critical parts. The particular cylinder was selected, as the result of ground and flight testing, to be the hottest under most operating conditions.

At low fuel-air ratios and low powers, however, the "hot" cylinder location shifts from the cylinder on which the cylinder head thermocouple is located, to one or more of several other cylinders which may run as much as 20 to 30°C hotter under these conditions than the cylinder with the thermocouple. These results were obtained on engines with ignition and carburetion in good condition. At the same time all limits of temperature, power, and other items were being observed. Therefore, the cylinder head temperature reading is representative of the general engine heat condition rather than evidence of individual cylinder malfunctioning. The chance of finding trouble on any one cylinder is the one out of twenty-eight chances that the difficulty is in the one to which the thermocouple is attached.

Also, the thermocouple is located in the cylinder head at an arbitrarily selected spot which is neither the hottest nor the coldest part of the head. The temperature measured at this point is merely a reference to temperatures at other critical points, especially the piston head, exhaust valve and seat, exhaust valve guide, and spark plug. The relationship between the temperatures at the critical points and the cylinder head temperature demands that limits be established. Experience shows that these limits are necessary, not only to prevent detonation and its destructive results, but also to prevent the formation of sludge and carbon. Failure to observe the CHT limits may also result in lead fouling and spark plug malfunctioning.

In deciding on the cylinder head temperature for operation, a compromise between performance and durability must be made. If the demands for maximum range are foremost, head temperature will be held at the upper limit to reduce the drag of excess cooling air flow. Tactical necessity will dictate this "all-out" operation on occasions. It must be realized that exceeding the limit can lead to difficulty. Since the carburetor air temperature is also held to its limit during maximum cruise, the combination can bring about detonation or preignition if any engine item is in substandard condition.

When tactical demands are not pressing, it is sound judgment to hold more conservative temperatures. Engine operation and life through the years have been best with cylinder head temperaturs 25 to 40°C lower than the maximum limits and there has been no recent change of material which would give the same durability with higher operating temperatures. Operation in this manner serves to keep the engine in a condition permitting sustained "all-out" performance when needed. Habitual use of limiting temperatures reduces the margin of safety and keeps the engine vulnerable to the unknown little things that go wrong or accumulate between inspections, little things that would not be destructive at lower temperatures and powers.

Most of the temperature concern of design, development, and testing has been of the troubles caused by high temperature. Cold temperatures can be equally troublesome with almost the same list of difficulties. Good operation should point to a middle range, where the greatest amount of satisfactory experience has been accumulated.

On the ground, experience has indicated that temperatures lower than 150°C are apt to cause lead fouling troubles. With temperatures above about 220°C, the tendency is toward sludging, rocker box coking, and a hardening of rubber seals and insulation resulting in oil leaks and ignition troubles. For these reasons the cylinder head temperatures on the ground are recommended to be between 200° and 220°C; in emergencies, however, a maximum of 250°C is permissible. For idling conditions the air plug is partially closed; for high power operation the plug is open in order to anticipate the need that will accompany the high power operation. At idling speeds the direction of the wind may offset the ability of the fan to circulate air through the engine and cause some of the cylinders to run excessively hot, even though the one cylinder under observation is within limits.

For take-off it is realized that the power is going to be at the highest value of any time during the operation of the engine. The air speed will be the lowest, at the start, and gradually build up to the speed of the climb after take-off. The usual procedure is to set the air plugs full open, then adjust thereafter to maintain a minimum CHT of 225°C. This procedure will aid in preventing the CHT from exceeding the maximum limits during take-off and initial climb. The required air plug setting to maintain 225°C CHT will vary some with the weight of the airplane as the gross weight affects the acceleration and length of time to attain final speed. The plug setting is also affected by the outside air temperature and can be partially closed for cold weather take-off; however, wide open plugs will usually be required during hot weather.

When the power is reduced from the take-off values to the normal rated power used in climb, there will be a reduction in the fuel-air ratio as delivered by the carburetor. This reduction tends to keep the cylinder head temperatures up and thus requires a fairly wide open setting of the air plug, particularly at low indicated air speed. If the mixture is manually adjusted to something less than the carburetor normal mixture strength, the air plug may have to be opened somewhat to accommodate the CHT rise.

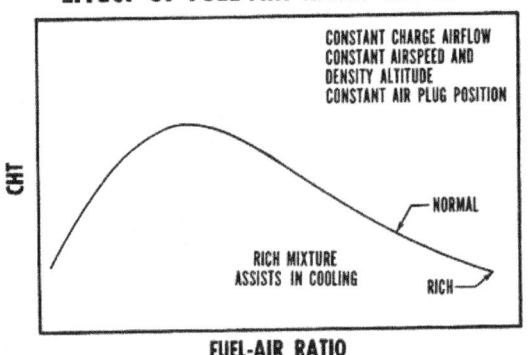

Figure 7-22.

If anything is done during level cruising flight to change the drag of the airplane, such as opening the bomb bay doors, camera doors, or extending the gun turrets, the effect upon the indicated air speed and cooling air should be anticipated and the air plug reset to suit the new condition. If the indicated air speed of the airplane is maintained to carry on the cruise flight control at the weight of the airplane, there will be required an increase in power to offset the drag of the new condition.

It is obvious that increased horsepower will require a readjustment of the air plug. Temperature readings will start to rise very shortly after the increase in horsepower, but it will take three to five minutes for the temperatures to stabilize. This stabilization period is the time in which the air plug must be adjusted to prevent the cylinders from exceeding the limits.

During letdown, with reduced power and the air flow maintained as shown by the indicated air speed, it may not be possible to maintain the cylinder head temperature up to the desired minimum even with the air plugs in a closed position. This should not cause any undue concern unless the engine begins to run rough or backfire. In this case the mixture may be enriched somewhat, if the powers are quite low, in order to approach the .067 fuel-air ratio which is the hottest mixture strength. Also periodic power bursts are helpful in clearing combustion chambers and keeping oil temperature up. Oil temperatures should be maintained above 75°C at all times, if possible, to provide good lubrication.

While preparing for a landing, each time that the drag of the airplane is increased the power requirements are increased, and the cooling must be adjusted to keep the cylinder temperatures within limits. Again, power versus indicated air speed tell of the heat being forced into the cylinder heads and the ability of the air to remove it. The air plug must be opened to enable the engine to use the available air flow provided by the indicated air speed.

During all ground operation, including taxiing, the tendency will be to have the air plug open fairly well. However, it is necessary to adjust the plug opening to keep the cylinder head at a temperature that will not encourage plug fouling. Just prior to shutting down the engine, the cylinder head temperatures should be lowered as much as conveniently possible. Tests of rubber items around the engines, such as the pushrod housing seals and ignition harness installations, show that their temperatures rise considerably after engine shut down as they absorb heat from the cylinders while the cylinders cool. On days when there is no wind to bring cool air into the engine compartment the rubber temperatures can exceed their limiting values five to seven minutes after the engine has been shut down.

The effect on the rubber parts is cumulative. After a number of times of overheating they become hard and brittle. The oil seals lose their resiliency so that they are not able to seal the oil, and leaks ensue. The ignition harness will break down and more than likely cause trouble at altitude. Prolonged running of the engine at cylinder head temperatures below 150°C brings on lead fouling troubles and it does not pay to try to get the cylinder temperatures below 150°C. If the airplane is headed into a stiff breeze, there is less need of getting the cylinder head temperatures down to a low value. Carburetor air temperature after shut down is indicative of the flow of heat from the cylinders to other parts of the engine.

OIL SPEWING.

Oil spewing is a phenomenon connected with high altitude operation of some B-36 aircraft. Such factors as rpm, blowby, scavenge pump efficiency, oil pressure, temperature, viscosity, oil contamination, and crankcase pressure are believed to effect spewing severity, but the exact share each factor contributes to the whole is not agreed upon. Spewing is a limiting factor in that the oil supply may be depleted requiring that the propeller be feathered; also, the oil spewed from the crankcase breather congeals and blows into the props where it is sometimes thrown into the fuselage, causing structural damage.

One of the present "fixes" is a crankcase aneroid valve, which retains crankcase pressure at altitude, and thereby retains scavenge pump efficiency. The aneroids are not completely effective in all cases and are somewhat fail-prone. When they do fail in the closed position, excessive crankcase pressures can result and an excessive number of oil leaks may be encountered. A similar aneroid valve in the oil tank helps retain the oil "head" to the engine. If it fails in the closed position, excessive oil consumption, oil spewing, or oil tank rupture may result.

There is very little the engineer can do about oil spewing except reduce rpm, which is not always feasible. A reduction in altitude, which would constitute a compromise of the mission, may be the last resort.

One type of oil contamination, referred to above, is the presence of "pickling" fluids in the oil. Another type results from the presence of water in the oil.

Water, a product of combustion, condenses out in the cold portions of the oil tank and settles in the sump. When the sump becomes full or sloshes over, the water enters the oil-in line, and is at the temperature of the oil. When the pressure is reduced, by change in altitude or speed of the engine oil pump, there will result a combination of pressure and temperature that causes the water to evaporate and increase its volume. When the water vapor reaches the oil pump, a momentary or extensive drop in oil pressure will result, depending on how long it takes to pump out the vapor and get good oil again. As the oil and water vapors enter the engine oil passages, pressure causes the water vapors to recondense. As the oil and water are released within the engine, the water evaporates again. The resulting expansion increases the pressures in the crankcase and causes or increases oil pressure, breathing, and spewing troubles.

PREVENTION AND ELIMINATION OF SPARK PLUG FOULING.

Spark plug fouling is considered to be undesirable deposits that accumulate on or near the spark plug electrodes and cause misfiring. Fouling may result from carbon, lead, ice, thread lubricant, metal particles, or preservative compounds. The regular ignition system checks will give indications of malfunctions somewhere in the ignition system. Fouling, however, is concerned only with the combustion end of the spark plug and standard checks will not always point directly to the source of trouble. Regular monitoring with the engine analyzer provides a valuable means for determining the operating efficiency of individual spark plugs.

Ground Run-Up.

The tetra-ethyl lead used in the fuel contains certain scavenging agents. These agents unite with the lead and at low cylinder temperatures condense out on the inside of the cylinder. At idling speeds, low cylinder temperatures are especially conducive to lead fouling. However, during ground operation there must be a compromise between high temperatures to prevent fouling, and cold temperatures to prevent overheating of rubber seals, ignition harnesses, and magnetos. Therefore, the CHT must be kept within the established limits by means of air plug adjustment. For the procedures on prevention and elimination of spark plug fouling during ground operation, refer to "Reciprocating Engine Ground Operation," Section II.

Inflight Prevention.

Inflight symptoms and procedures are basically the same as those on the ground except that governing propeller is used rather than fixed pitch; powers are at cruising or climb rather than idling, and very lean mixtures and advance spark may be in use while cruising. The M.P., rpm, and CHT are higher than at idling. The carburetor air temperature varies with weather conditions. These factors are practically all favorable to lead fouling prevention except the very lean mixtures. Periodic changes from rich to lean mixtures

aid inflight prevention. Other mild or severe thermal shocks help. Cylinder heads should not operate during cruise condition for long periods at temperatures lower than 220°C.

Spark Advance. Tests made under laboratory conditions show that the temperature of the spark plug core nose increases about 100°C (180°F) when shifting from retarded to advanced spark (figure 7-23). These tests were made at power settings between cruise and normal rated. It can be seen that use of advanced spark may have considerable effect upon the accumulation of

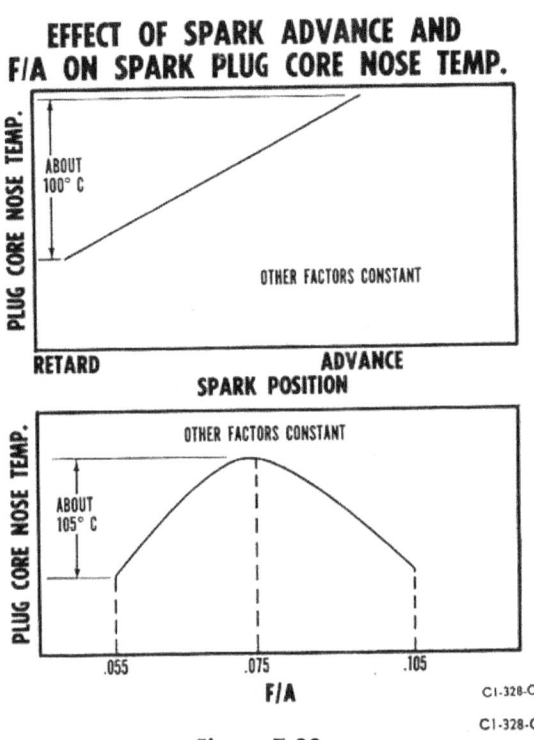

Figure 7-23.

deposits or upon purging of the deposits after they have accumulated. The above example shows only one method of increasing the core nose temperature to prevent fouled spark plugs. The core nose temperature is also affected by many other factors such as: indicated mean effective pressure (imep), exhaust back pressure, fuel-air ratio, CHT, rpm, and CAT.

Fuel-Air Ratio. The study of the effects of fuel-air ratio on spark plug core nose temperatures shows about the *same range of temperature change as for spark advance.* The hottest temperature of the core nose did not come with the mixture strength for hottest gas temperature (0.067) but at 0.075. This apparent discrepancy is associated with the compression effects on the first gases to burn after the flame is farther along and pressures are still increasing. The result is that the first gases to burn, near the spark plug under low pressure, rise to a certain temperature at the time of burning and the temperature increases greatly with further compression. Since the highest power at a given air flow or manifold pressure is found with "best power" mixtures, it may be surmised that the hottest temperature would come with lean "best power" mixtures. The temperatures, found in the test, lowered with fuel-air ratios leaner or richer than 0.075 (figure 7-23). At 0.055 and at 0.105 fuel-air ratios, the temperature of the spark plug core nose was about 105°C (190°F) lower than at 0.075.

Rpm. An occasional increase of rpm may be used beneficially in clearing the combustion chambers. To do this, increase rpm for one or two minutes using cruise M.P., hot mixture strength (0.067 to 0.075), and retarded spark. This purging procedure must be used carefully as operation will be approaching the detonation and preignition limits. The combustion chamber is being subjected to high temperatures, made even higher by the internal supercharger (at moderately high rpm), without the benefit of the rich mixtures ordinarily used with these engine speeds. The high temperatures tend to loosen lead deposits and allow them to be carried out the exhaust.

After this purging, the spark plugs, exhaust valves, and piston heads may have approached dangerous temperatures. It will be beneficial to operate for a minute or so at low rpm and power to allow the heat to dissipate and the temperatures to become lower than cruise power temperatures. When cruise power is resumed the engine temperatures will rise but will take a long time to stabilize completely. If the cruise power is established with internal parts hotter than stabilized values, the temperatures will fall rapidly at first. The remaining degrees take longer, never lowering fully, during which time engine distress may occur. To prevent such trouble, approach limiting temperatures from below rather than above.

Manifold Pressure, BMEP, and Exhaust Back Pressure. These items are discussed together in that they are difficult to separate when an engine is equipped with turbosuperchargers. Laboratory tests show that an indicated mean effective pressure (imep) increase of approximately 60 psi causes the spark plug core nose temperature to rise about 80°C (142°F). This imep change increases the bmep about the same amount because, at a fixed rpm, the change in friction horsepower is small. The same series of tests showed a core nose temperature rise of about 65°C (118°F) when exhaust back pressure is increased from 31 inches Hg to 41 inches Hg. On the aircraft these two effects would

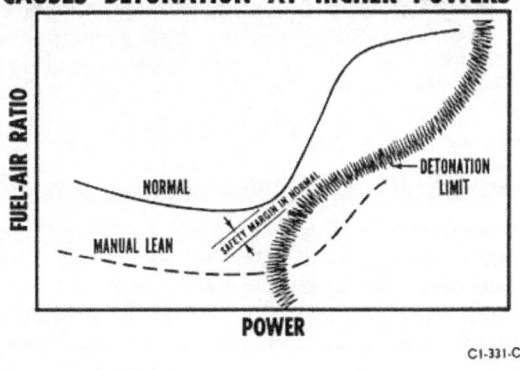

Figure 7-24.

be added together in suitable proportions for dual or single turbo operation and other actual operating conditions.

Cylinder Head Temperature. A cylinder head temperature rise can sometimes be used to aid in clearing fouled plugs. As might be expected, a change in cylinder head temperature produces a change in spark plug core nose temperature practically a degree for a degree. The spark plug core nose in the test for this effect runs about 300°C (710°F) hotter than the cylinder head bayonet thermocouple.

Carburetor Air Temperature. In the single cylinder tests being quoted there was no change in the temperature of the spark plug core nose when inlet air temperature was changed 28°C (50°F). The effect of inlet air temperature on imep and cylinder head temperature was compensated for by changes in manifold pressure and cooling air flow. This was necessary to hold other readings constant. In fact the whole series of tests was run in this manner. These tests show only the effects on the spark plug core nose temperature.

Power Change Rate Effect. Sudden applications of power cause an abrupt change in spark plug insulator temperature with a resultant change in deposit resistance. This change in resistance can cause the plugs to misfire. It is therefore desirable to make major changes in power as gradual as is practical. This causes the plug temperature to rise slowly and gradually rather than in one abrupt change. After extended periods of manual lean operation it would be desirable to extend the change in power over a period of two or three minutes whenever possible. Sudden reductions in power do not create any adverse effects on plug fouling.

High Power Before Landing. Some operators have derived benefit from use of normal rated power for a minute or two, five or ten minutes before entering the landing pattern. This gives a purging effect after descent and, if ineffectual, a chance to size up the engines so that discrepancies can be reported and cleared up. To determine engine condition at high power it is recommended that a survey of all engines through ignition analysis be made after descent and prior to landing. In-flight checks of this nature are useful in reducing the running time on the ground after flight.

CONTROL OF DETONATION AND PREIGNITION.

Detonation limits almost all phases of B-36 engine operation. Its sustained occurrence in moderate form causes inefficient combustion and deterioration of combustion chamber parts. Short intervals of severe detonation cause in-flight failure necessitating shutdown.

When the mixture control is in NORMAL, detonation protection (figure 7-24) is provided by the "built-in" carburetor settings if other limits are observed. When mixture is leaned from NORMAL, the "built-in" margin is eliminated and the maintenance of detonation-free operation requires the greatest judgment of the engineer. He must rely on experience, either his own or someone else's. Remember, it is not the engine that detonates, but the charge air mixture and this is basically a condition brought about by temperature.

At high power all the high temperature factors are unfavorable. The high rpm means the fast turning internal supercharger is giving its highest heat rise. The large amount of charge air being consumed produces high quantities of heat. Therefore the greatest mixture enrichment is required with maximum engine output. As power *and rpm* are reduced, the temperature factors become more favorable and it is possible to reduce mixture strength with safety. Eventually, power and rpm reduction reach a point below which it is possible to use "best power" fuel-air ratio without detonation. Finally, at still lower power and rpm, "best economy" fuel-air ratio is entirely safe. The carburetor was originally set for normal mixture use during all operation above 70 per cent normal rated (including fan) horsepower. The fan power is included to relate mixture strength to indicated horsepower, which describes the actual situation inside the cylinder. However, the B-36 range requirements are important enough to use manual adjustment up to normal rated power to compensate for differences in carburetor; however, care must be exercised in making these adjustments because of the possibility of erroneous instrument readings.

During manual leaning, engine operation is approaching the area of possible detonation. However, the lower fuel-air ratio is only one of the factors that make this procedure so marginal. To determine the effect of the many variables on the detonation limit, it is necessary to run the engine on a test stand. This must be done so that one factor can be checked while all others are held constant.

For instance, the test engine may be run with all known variables, except M.P., held constant. Readings taken at various increments of M.P. show that for most of the way horsepower and CHT increase in a straight line relationship with increasing M.P. (See figure 7-25). The situation changes, however, if the M.P. is pushed far enough, the power line sags and the cylinder temperature line begins an upward swing. In a change from straight lines to curves, points A and A' are definite indications that detonation is present. By the time it progresses to a degree of evidence, it is mildly destructive. The operational interest is to the left of A and A' where detonation is present but not noticable. To find these incipient stage limits, special analyzers are necessary that detect the slightest traces by the vibration effect on cylinder structure. This instrumentation indicates the immediate limit of safe operation to be left of B-B'.

Additional information is obtained in the same manner with different fuel-air ratios. Another series is run at different rpm using the previous series of constant fuel-air ratios. This is continued until every conceivable combination of rpm, fuel-air ratio, cylinder head temperature, carburetor air temperature, spark advance, and fuel grade has been tested. In addition to operating variables, design factors such as compression ratio, valve timing, cam profile, combustion chamber configuration, and spark plug type can be "cranked in." Also, conditions not within operation control such as humidity and exhaust back pressure are held constant or accounted for by accepted corrections.

The result of the study is data plotted in an orderly manner. Distinguishing the variations of rpm from the rest of the data shows the effect of engine speed on the detonation limit to power (figure 7-26). Rpm exerts influence principally through its relation to the internal supercharger temperature rise. With high rpm, the charge entering the cylinder is hottest and most likely to detonate. As engine speed reduces, the charge cools and is less likely to kindle ahead of the normal flame

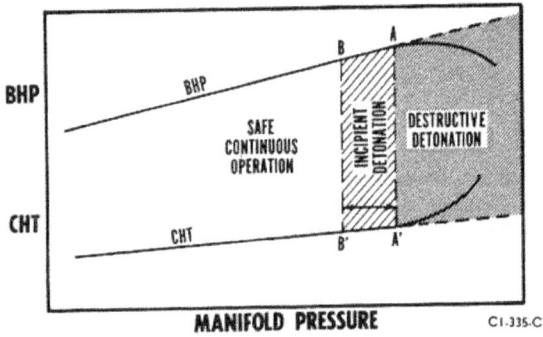

Figure 7-25.

EFFECTS OF OPERATING VARIABLES ON DETONATION LIMITS

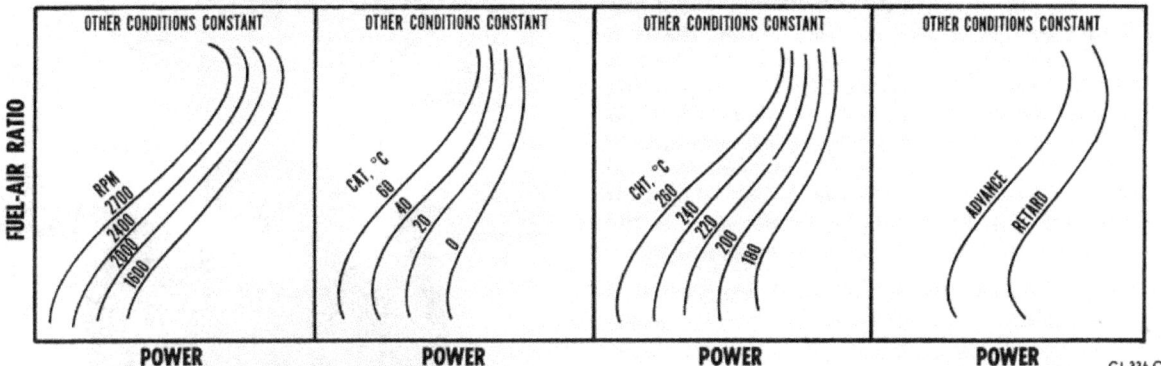

Figure 7-26.

front. Do not confuse this with data based on unsupercharged engines, where heat does not rise ahead of the normal flame front and the main detonation influence of rpm has a favorable turbulence effect as rpm increases. This occurs in supercharged engines but is outweighed by the heat rise factor.

Carburetor air temperature influence (figure 7-26) is similar to that of rpm because of its effect on the temperature of the unburned charge before and during combustion.

The cylinder head temperature (figure 7-26) also influences the heat condition of the charge.

Spark advance, another variable subject to the engineer's control, also has a definite effect on the detonation limit as shown in figure 7-26.

Humidity or water vapor in the atmosphere has a strong effect upon detonation, possibly because the water molecules disassociate into hydrogen and oxygen atoms as the temperature rises during combustion. Tests show that there is a greater tendency toward detonation with dry air than with humid air. Lubricating oil has a very low octane or performance number and severely lowers the rating of a fuel when mixed with it, as it might if an oil tank leaks into the fuel tank. Leaking impeller shaft oil seal rings are not likely to give this type of trouble because of the reversal of flow past the seals between low manifold pressure, when oil is drawn into the induction system, and high manifold pressure, when charge air leaks into the crankcase.

Backfiring.

The most frequent causes of backfiring are the use of excessively lean mixtures, which burn too slowly, and failure of the ignition system to provide a satisfactory spark. The two main classes of ignition malfunctions are energy losses in the system external to the cylinder and plug fouling from lead or other materials. The former results in insufficient voltage across plug electrodes and the latter in a short circuit instead of a spark. The external system performance depends on magneto pressurization and ventilation, clean connection throughout the system, and good insulation.

Mild backfiring due to lead fouling may be encountered during sustained flight at lean mixture settings. If it occurs, increase power *slowly*, keeping just within the range of mild backfiring until the backfiring ceases.

> **CAUTION**
>
> Sudden acceleration of power must be avoided as it may produce severe backfiring.

If operating with retarded spark and backfiring persists, it is sometimes stopped by shifting to spark advance, reducing power if necessary.

TRIM OF ENGINES VERSUS TRIM OF AIRCRAFT CONTROL.

When, for any reason, the power of one or more engines is low, or the propeller is feathered, some consideration must be given to the effects on the aircraft trim and miles per pound of fuel. Except for wing or fuselage warpage, the rudder and aileron trims will be in neutral positions when the engines are all evenly balanced on power, and the aircraft loads and drag items are balanced. If an outboard engine is low on power or its cooling drag is high compared to the other engines there is a yawing effect (a torque), the opposite good engine tending to turn the airplane toward the side with low power. An equal and opposing torque must be generated by the rudder which is offset at first by the pilot pushing on the rudder pedal, then he transfers this load to the trim tab by an appropriate setting of the trim tab control. The offset rudder generates some drag that slows the aircraft or requires a little more power from all the engines to maintain speed. The offset rudder causes the aircraft to crab very slightly to follow the desired track, causing the air to flow over the wing with a cross component. The cross component works on the dihedral of the wing, setting up a slight rolling tendency that the pilot holds off for a little while with the wheel and soon transfers to the aileron trim tabs. The asymmetrical ailerons cause additional drag, slowing the airplane further and requiring additional rudder trim at the slower speed to trim the airplane, or additional power to maintain speed.

Under circumstances of this nature, it may be well to consider balancing up the engines by reducing power on the opposite outboard good engine, approximately equal to an outboard engine, about two-thirds of the loss in power of a center engine, and about one-third of the loss of an inboard engine. The proportionate reductions are due to the distances of the respective engines from the airplane center line. The total power required is attained by increasing the rpm of all engines to divide the loss of power of one engine among the others. Variations of this scheme can be applied by dividing the unequal power among two or three engines. It does not pay to shut down one good engine to balance another that is shut down. Here engine trim must be compromised with control trim. If the control trims get cockeyed, it is well to check engine trim.

The engineer and the pilot must cooperate closely at all times to obtain best range results. Precision piloting can be nullified by inaccurate power plant handling and it is equally true that top quality engineering can be cancelled by indifferent airplane handling. Five to ten miles an hour indicated air speed can be lost by sloppy airwork which can use up all the fuel that a good engineer can save.

ENGINE ANALYZER.

The engine analyzer, when installed as an air-borne unit, provides a means of accurately and quickly evaluating the ignition system while in flight or during ground operation. On some airplanes, through use of a vibration pickup mounted on individual cylinders, complete engine analysis is possible through interpretation of the various vibrations (figure 7-27) caused by valve closings and other cylinder vibrations.

Through regular use of ignition analysis, it is possible to determine the firing characteristics of all spark plugs and detect the various degrees of malfunctions in the rest of the ignition system. Weak and mistimed magnetos, open, shorted, or disconnected ignition leads, arcing or out of synchronization breaker points, as well

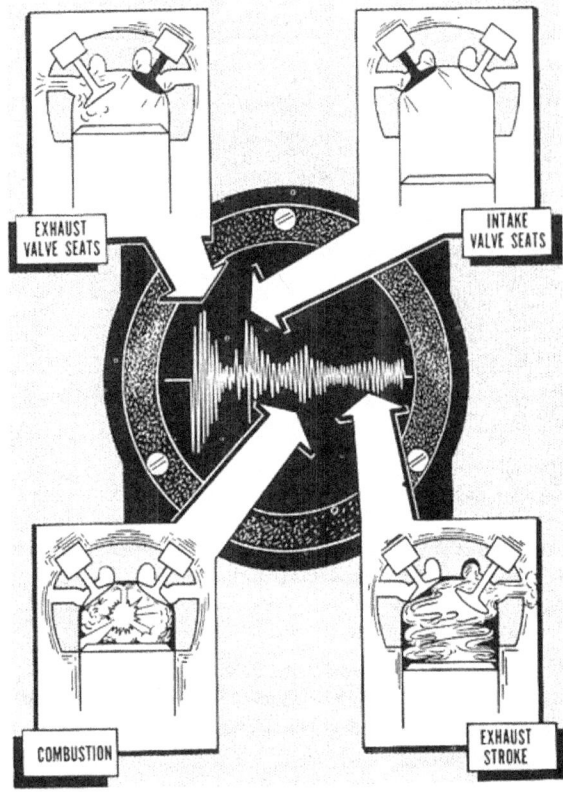

Figure 7-27. Normal Cylinder Vibration Pattern (Some Airplanes)

as various distributor malfunctions can all be detected (figure 7-29). As combustion within the cylinder has a definite effect on the characteristics of the ignition pattern, intake manifold failures and valve malfunctions may often be detected. Individual defective spark plugs or other defective ignition units can, in this manner, be detected and replaced prior to severe malfunctioning of the engine. Considerable time and replacement part saving is thereby accomplished by replacing only those components of the ignition system known to be causing trouble. Also, in the case of malfunctioning engines due to causes other than ignition, it is possible to establish the serviceability of the ignition system and look further for possible carburetion or valve system malfunction.

Ignition analysis is particularly valuable in determining those components of the ignition system breaking down only at altitude. Very often engine malfunction is experienced at altitude operation, but returns to normal when trouble shooting procedures are applied on the ground. Through application of ignition analysis at altitude such items as weak condensers, ignition harness failures, and misfiring spark plugs may be detected.

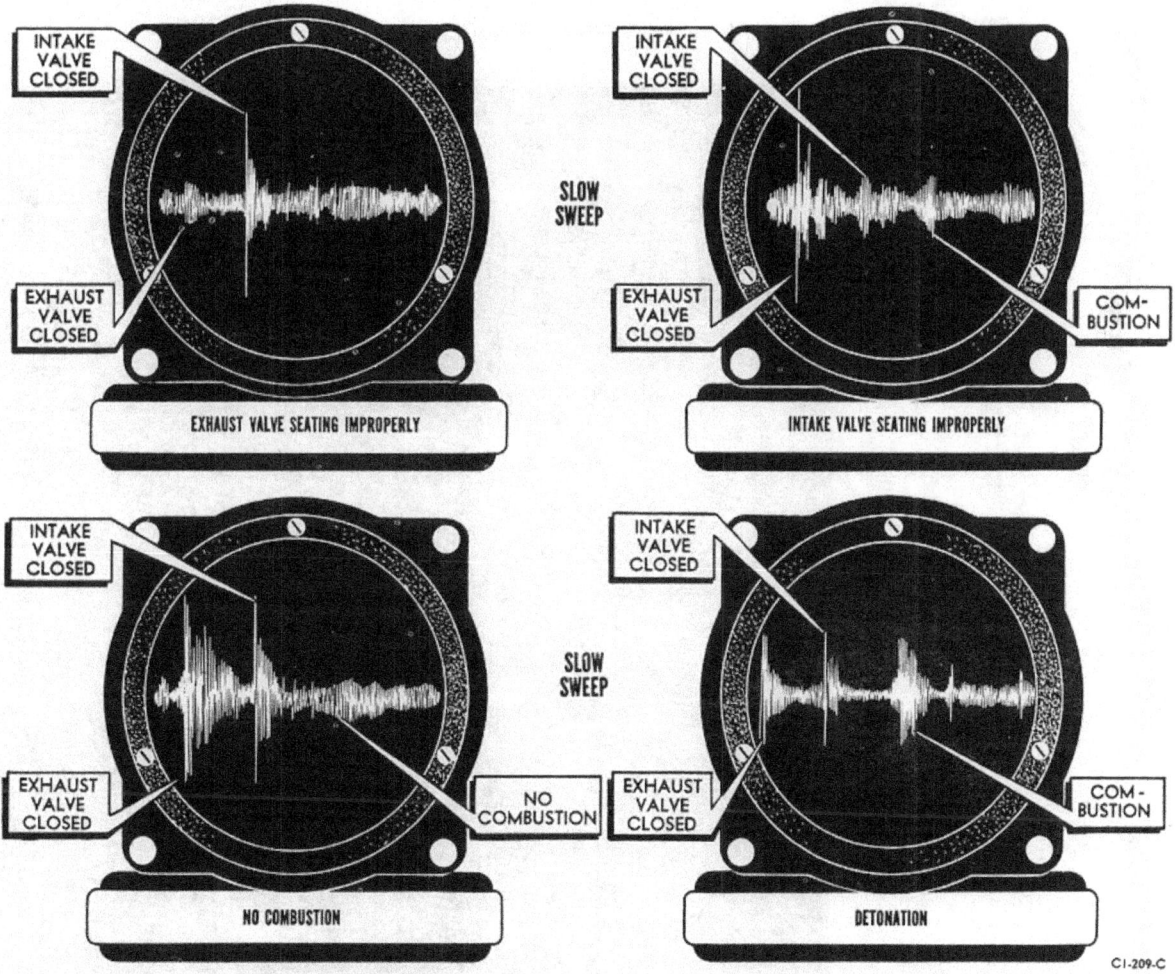

Figure 7-28. Abnormal Cylinder Vibration Patterns (Some Airplanes)

When regularly applied in flight, the engine analyzer has been particularly valuable in detecting lead fouling of spark plugs in their early stages. The application of prime in purging procedures is far more effective when applied prior to complete shorting of the spark plug. In addition it is possible to determine the effect the application of prime has had, and whether additional applications are required to complete the desired procedure.

The engine analyzer should be employed whenever a magneto check is made in judging ignition system performance. It must be remembered that "no excessive drop-off" on either the left or right circuits is not necessarily an indication of "no trouble," since the system being checked might have equal dead components in both halves of the system and selecting either half of the dual ignition system will make no difference in output. In performing ground checks of suspected engines, magneto checks at higher power settings are not advisable. The engine analyzer can be safely utilized in detecting those spark plugs whose operation is satisfactory at normal magneto check engine powers but cut out at higher power.

It should be realized that the engine analyzer does not replace the present methods of trouble shooting or malfunction correction, but rather is a valuable aid or tool in supplementing these checks. The secret of successful analyzer utilization is that of a competent operator who can accurately interpret the patterns and who will use good, sound, logical reasoning in arriving at his decision for corrective action.

Cylinder Vibration Analysis (Some Airplanes).

Vibration analysis on all cylinders should be made not only during the ground check, but also following each power change and before descent from altitude. Use a slow sweep to ascertain that all valves are functioning

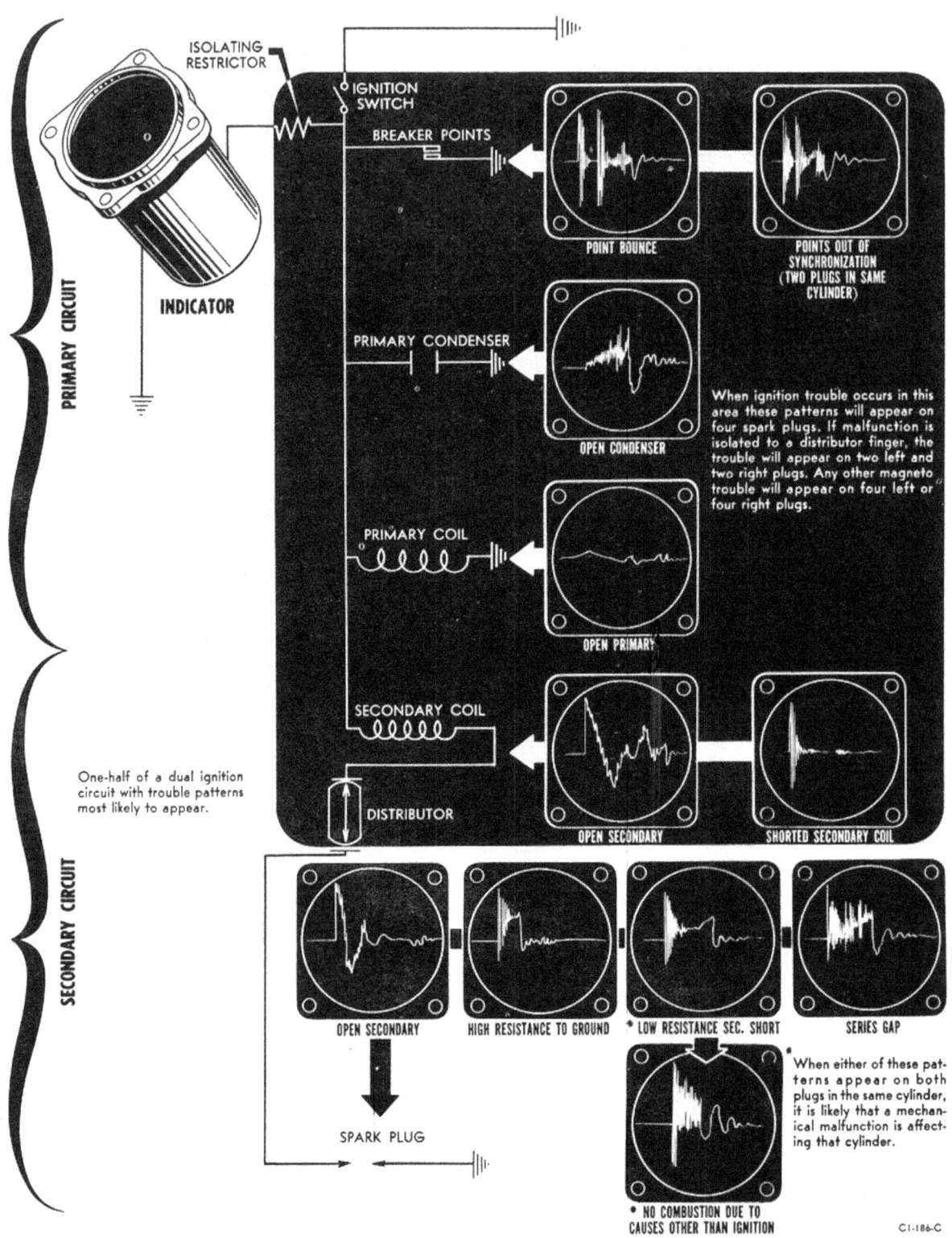

Figure 7-29. Typical Patterns of Ignition Malfunctions

properly and that combustion is within the normal limits (not exceeding the exhaust valve closing event in amplitude) and that no mechanical malfunction is evident. Use vibration analysis at all other times as considered necessary, based on engine instrument indications and other engine checks.

To operate the engine analyzer for vibration analysis, proceed as follows:

1. Engine analyzer power switch ON.

Note

Allow approximately one minute for the power supply-amplifier and the indicator tube to warm up.

2. Condition selector switch knob—Pull out to obtain vibration patterns.

3. Condition selector switch—Set index line within the sector containing the number of the engine to be checked.

4. Pickup selector switch—Align the index line with the number of the cylinder to be checked.

5. Cycle switch—Place cycle switch dial with the designation E.C. (exhaust closing) approximately aligned for cylinder D1.

Note

Cycle switch setting must always correspond to the cylinder selected by the pickup selector or the reading will be inaccurate.

6. Indicator—Complete vibration pattern for cylinder D1.

7. Check all the remaining cylinders by selecting with the pickup selector switch and repositioning the cycle switch.

8. Repeat the above steps to check the other engines by repositioning the condition selector switch to the other engine sectors.

9. For an expanded pattern of any portion of the vibration pattern, push in the knob on the cycle switch for fast sweep, and index the cycle switch dial to the desired portion of the engine cycle to be inspected.

Ignition System Analysis.

For ignition analysis the engine analyzer is operated as follows:

1. Engine analyzer power switch—ON.

Note

Allow approximately one minute for the power supply-amplifier and the indicator tube to warm up.

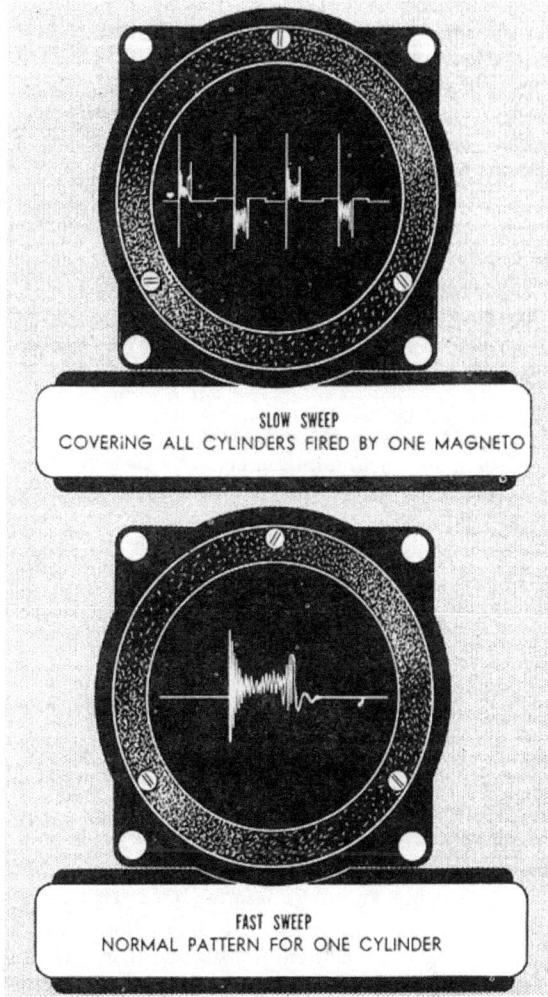

Figure 7-30. Normal Ignition Pattern

2. Condition selector switch knob—Push in to obtain ignition patterns.

3. Condition selector switch—Place index line on L, R, or B within the sector for the engine to be checked. Indexing the dial to L, R, or B determines whether the pattern will be for the left, right, or for both magnetos of the particular row of cylinders to be checked.

4. Cycle switch—Align the IGN index line with the number of the cylinder to be shown first in the series of patterns for one magneto.

5. Cycle switch knob—Pull out to obtain a slow sweep covering the ignition patterns for all of the cylinders fired by the magneto. The cylinder selected by the cycle switch will appear to the left on the indicator followed by the other three in the order of firing of that magneto.

6. If all four patterns are abnormal during the slow sweep, the malfunction is associated with that portion

of the magneto circuit that is common to all four ignition circuits. This would indicate magneto or distributor difficulty.

7. If a partial quantity of the series are abnormal, position the cycle switch to bring one of the abnormal patterns to the left side of the screen.

8. Cycle switch knob—Push in for a more thorough examination of the expanded pattern of any abnormal cylinder.

9. Repeat the above steps for left and right sides of all magnetos. It is suggested that at slack work periods all ignition patterns be investigated on the fast sweep for malfunctions that may not be observed on the slow sweep.

Magneto Synchronization Check.

The magneto synchronization check is made to determine that both magnetos simultaneously fire the two plugs in the cylinder. The magneto points are timed to row D, therefore, should be checked on row D. For this check proceed as follows:

1. Engine analyzer power switch—ON.

   Note

   Allow approximately one minute for the power supply-amplifier and the indicator tube to warm up.

2. Condition selector switch knob—Push in to obtain ignition patterns.

3. Condition selector switch—Index line on B under the engine number to be checked.

4. Cycle switch knob—Push in for fast sweep.

5. Cycle switch—Align the IGN index line with D1. This superimposes the ignition patterns of the left and right magnetos. If the magnetos are synchronized the patterns coincide and appear as one; otherwise, they overlap and the one appearing to the left is advanced with regard to the other. By measuring the distance on the scope between the points of breaker point opening and allowing 1/32-inch to equal 1 degree of crankshaft travel, the amount of synchronization error may be determined.

6. Repeat the above procedure for all magnetos on each engine.

Two methods are available for determining which magneto, right or left, is out of synchronization. The first is as follows:

1. Engine analyzer power switch—ON.

   Note

   Allow approximately one minute for the power supply-amplifier and the indicator tube to warm up.

2. Condition selector switch knob—Push in.

3. Condition selector switch—Set to R under the engine number to be checked.

4. Measure the exact distance between the start of the horizontal trace at the left edge of the indicator screen and the point at which the breaker points open.

5. Condition selector switch—Set to L.

6. Repeat the measurement.

7. The pattern with the shorter horizontal trace is advanced with respect to the other.

8. Compare the length of the traces to that obtained when the synchronizing generator was installed to determine which magneto is advanced or retarded with respect to the crankshaft position.

The second method is as follows:

1. Engine analyzer power switch—ON.

   Note

   Allow approximately one minute for the power supply-amplifier and the indicator tube to warm up.

2. Push in the knob on condition selector switch to obtain ignition patterns.

3. Set the condition selector switch to L. If activity of small magnitude is observed ahead of the breaker point opening, that activity is caused by the right magneto because of inductive pickup, indicating that the right magneto is opening early.

4. Switch the condition selector switch to R and this should eliminate the activity.

Perform the synchronization check for each magneto on the engine and repeat on the remaining engines.

Rpm Synchronization Analysis.

In comparing engine rpm of the different engines, engine number one is used as a reference and the other engine speeds are compared to its speed. This check should be made at any time that engine rpm synchronization system malfunction is suspected. To make this check proceed as follows:

1. Engine analyzer power switch—ON.

   Note

   Allow approximately one minute for the power supply-amplifier and the indicator tube to warm up.

2. Cycle switch—Any position with knob in for fast sweep.

3. Condition selector switch knob—In to obtain ignition patterns.

4. Condition selector switch—Align the index line in the SYN sector with the number of the engine to be compared to engine number one.

5. Indicator—The ignition pattern will be stationary on the screen if the engines are synchronized, and moving if they are not synchronized. A progressive horizontal shift to the right indicates that the selected engine is under speed with respect to engine number one; a shift to the left indicates that the selected engine is over speed with respect to number one.

6. Condition selector switch—Index to each of the remaining SYN positions.

PROPELLERS.

If an engine is operating at less than master motor rpm and the propeller pitch changing system is actuated to move the blades from positive to reverse pitch or from reverse to positive pitch, the blades will stop before entering the normal operating range of either positive or reverse pitch. This stoppage is due to the necessary tolerance within the propeller limit switch system which prevents energizing two pitch changing systems simultaneously. If at this time the throttle is advanced past the point at which it is necessary to bring the engine up to master motor rpm and the master motor is set below 2700 rpm, the engine speed will exceed the rpm set on the master motor because of the low propeller blade angle. This excessive rpm condition will last for only a short time until the constant speed feature of the propeller system increases the propeller blade angles to give the desired rpm; however, this excess rpm condition reduces propeller efficiency and should be avoided. To eliminate overspeeding above master motor rpm (below 2700 rpm), a decrease rpm signal must be sent to the propeller pitch changing mechanism before the throttle is advanced. The decrease rpm signal is sent by reducing master motor rpm two or three hundred rpm below the rpm indicated on the engine tachometer.

This signal causes the pitch changing mechanism to increase the propeller blade angles, moving them into the normal operating range. The master motor can then be set to the desired rpm and the throttle can be advanced without engine overspeeding.

The manual pitch change system can also be utilized to transmit the increase blade angle signal to the pitch changes mechanism. Transmission of the signals can be accomplished by moving the propeller selector switch to the DEC RPM position and holding it there until a two or three hundred engine rpm drop occurs. The selector switch can then be moved to the AUTOMATIC OPERATION position and the throttle advanced without an overspeed condition occurring.

Propeller limitation charts in Section V must be observed closely. The limitations are based on propeller vibrations, which can be of such a nature that they will weaken the propeller shaft. The vibrations result from combinations of rpm, density altitude, and EAS. The vibratory forces are caused by power impulses imposed as each cylinder fires; by the aerodynamic disturbances created as a blade or blades pass through a region of turbulent air behind the wing or adjacent to the fuselage; and by other causes such as misfiring cylinders, malfunctioning vibration dampers, and extended flaps. By avoiding these vibration limitations areas you will prevent undue strain and fatigue of the metallic components of which your aircraft is constructed.

It must be understood that operation of the propeller in a restricted range will shorten its life and that the vibration stresses mentioned are present in the blades, hub, and shaft, even though no vibration of the aircraft is noticeable to the crew. However, if emergencies dictate that the propeller be operated in a restricted range for a limited period of time, there should be no hesitancy and no cause for alarm. Except in emergencies affecting safety of flight or during very brief periods of time required to go through a restricted region to reach a higher or lower rpm, propellers shall not be operated in a restricted range. An accurate log should be kept of all operation within a restricted range and will include length of time, horsepower, altitude, EAS and rpm.

FEATHERING.

On this airplane the engine nacelles are not parallel with the fuselage center line in the horizontal plane. The nacelles are "toed in" at the propeller end, resulting in the propellers on one wing having a slightly different relative wind than those on the other wing. This condition may lead to propellers on engines No. 1, 2, and 3 windmilling in a direction opposite to normal operation when they are feathered. This rotation can be stopped by utilizing the manual pitch changing system to make a slight blade angle change. Refer to "Reciprocating Engine Shutdown," in Section III.

REVERSE PITCH.

The jet engines should be inoperative during reverse pitch to avoid the necessity of counteracting their forward thrust and to prevent debris lifted from the ground by the propellers being drawn into the jet intakes.

JET ENGINES.

The primary purpose of the jet engines is to provide additional power for take-off, climb, and operation in the target vicinity. High altitude cruise at high gross weights also requires operation of the jets. When performing high gross weight landings, the jets should be operated in accordance with the instructions given in "Partial Power Landing," Section III, to provide additional power in the event a go-around is necessary. Requirements of the jets at various configurations and powers may be determined from the charts in Appendix I.

The jets are ground operated by the flight crew for only a short time, normally being started after the airplane is aligned with the runway just prior to take-off.

Section VII
Systems Operation

T.O. 1B-36D(II)-1

WINDMILLING.

Windmilling of the jets in flight with the air plug doors open causes an increased drag; consequently, the doors should be closed when the engines are not operating. Some air leakage through the doors is provided intentionally so that the engine will rotate to circulate oil and to prevent freezing of the rotors at low temperatures. If the jets will not windmill at sufficient rpm to circulate oil and to prevent freezing of the rotors with the doors closed, the air plug doors should be opened enough to maintain sufficient windmilling rpm.

FUEL SYSTEM.

FUEL DENSITY VARIATION.

Because of the wide range of climatic conditions under which this airplane operates, it is not feasible to assume that the fuel weight per gallon is always the same. With full wing tanks, it is possible to have an error of 4500 pounds if the actual density is 15/100 of a pound per gallon different from an assumed weight. To prevent such errors, the weight of the fuel can be more closely computed by using the following procedure.

Fuel Weighing Procedure.

1. Establish the weight of a U.S. standard gallon of Specification 115/145 fuel at 60°F by contacting the inspector at the fuel supply depot or by using the hydrometer method. (This should be done each week.)

2. Obtain the temperature (by use of a thermometer) and the dip stick or liquidometer volume of fuel in the tanks.

3. Enter the chart of figure 7-31 at the fuel temperature and get the temperature correction factor.

4. Correct the observed volume to U.S. standard gallons at 60°F.

5. Multiply the total U.S. standard gallons by the standard gallon weight.

NORMAL CRUISE.

During normal cruise, use all fuel in the bomb bay tank first, auxiliary wing tanks second, inboard tanks third, center tanks fourth, and outboard tanks last. This is necessary to maintain the wing bending moments at a minimum. (Refer to "Distribution of Load," Section V.)

Note

Whenever both the jet and the reciprocating engines are being used, it is essential that fuel be supplied from two tanks in each wing.

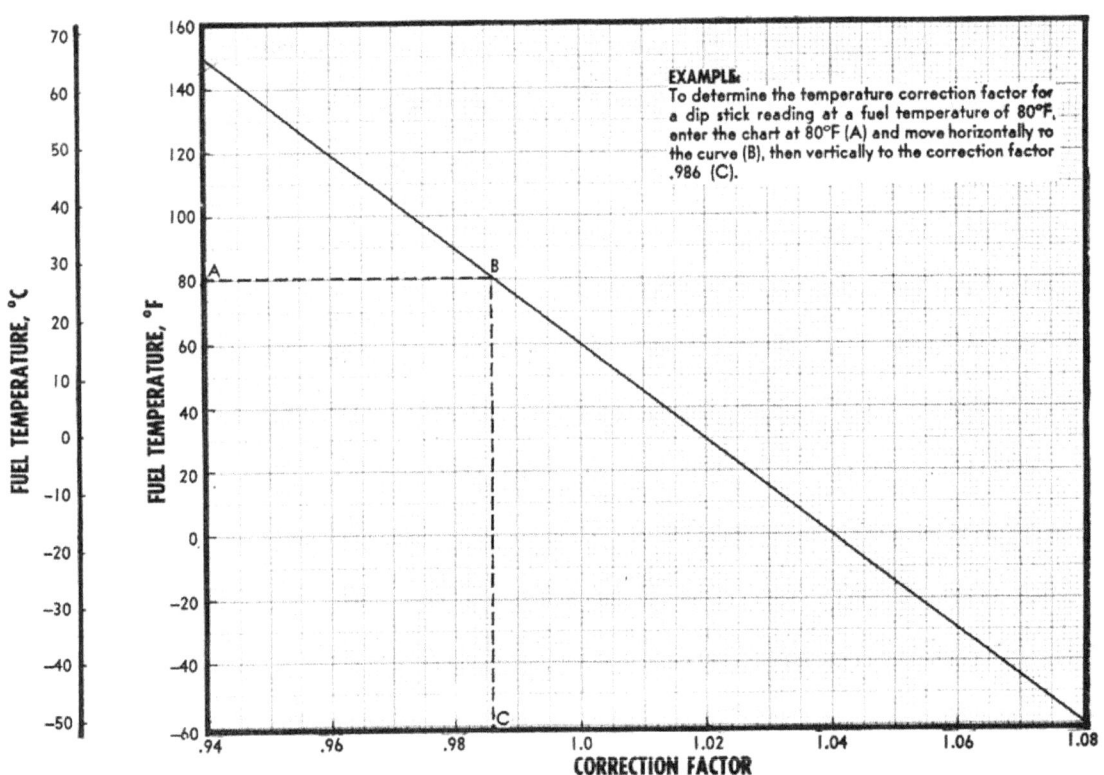

Figure 7-31.

Because residual fuel of the empty tank will collect at the booster pump, it is usually advantageous to open the tank valve and turn on the booster pump approximately one hour after the tank was originally turned off. The booster pump should be allowed to operate five minutes to assure complete drainage of the tank.

Note

It is not recommended that any fuel tank valve be closed after take-off until the related tank has been emptied. This eliminates the possibility of fuel being trapped in a tank by a fuel valve malfunction in the CLOSE position at an altitude that would make manual operation of the valve difficult. If the valve malfunctions when in the OPEN position, fuel flow reversal due to a faulty check valve and fuel usage from the tank can be controlled by the booster pump.

ELECTRICAL SYSTEM.

TRANSFORMER-RECTIFIER UNIT.

The transformer-rectifier unit is used to convert a-c power to d-c power. Each unit consists of a transformer, a rectifier, and a cooling fan. The transformer reduces the normal a-c voltage and the rectifier converts the alternating current into direct current. The rectifier is a stack of selenium-coated plates through which the alternating current must pass. Metallic selenium on the rectifier plates permits the alternating current to pass through the plates in one direction only; hence, the alternating current becomes "direct" current. The fan is used to cool the rectifier stack. The d-c output of a t-r unit is automatically maintained as the load of the t-r units demand, but the input of 3-phase a-c is the controlling factor.

THE ALTERNATOR.

The alternator converts mechanical energy into electrical energy. The alternator consists of a stator assembly within which a rotor assembly is driven by the constant speed drive unit. Windings around the four sets of field poles on the rotor are energized by an exciter generator when the engine is operating and the exciter control relay is closed. When the alternator field poles are energized, magnetic fields are created and the alternating current is produced in the stator coils. The stator assembly consists of three sets of coils, one for each of the alternating current phases. When

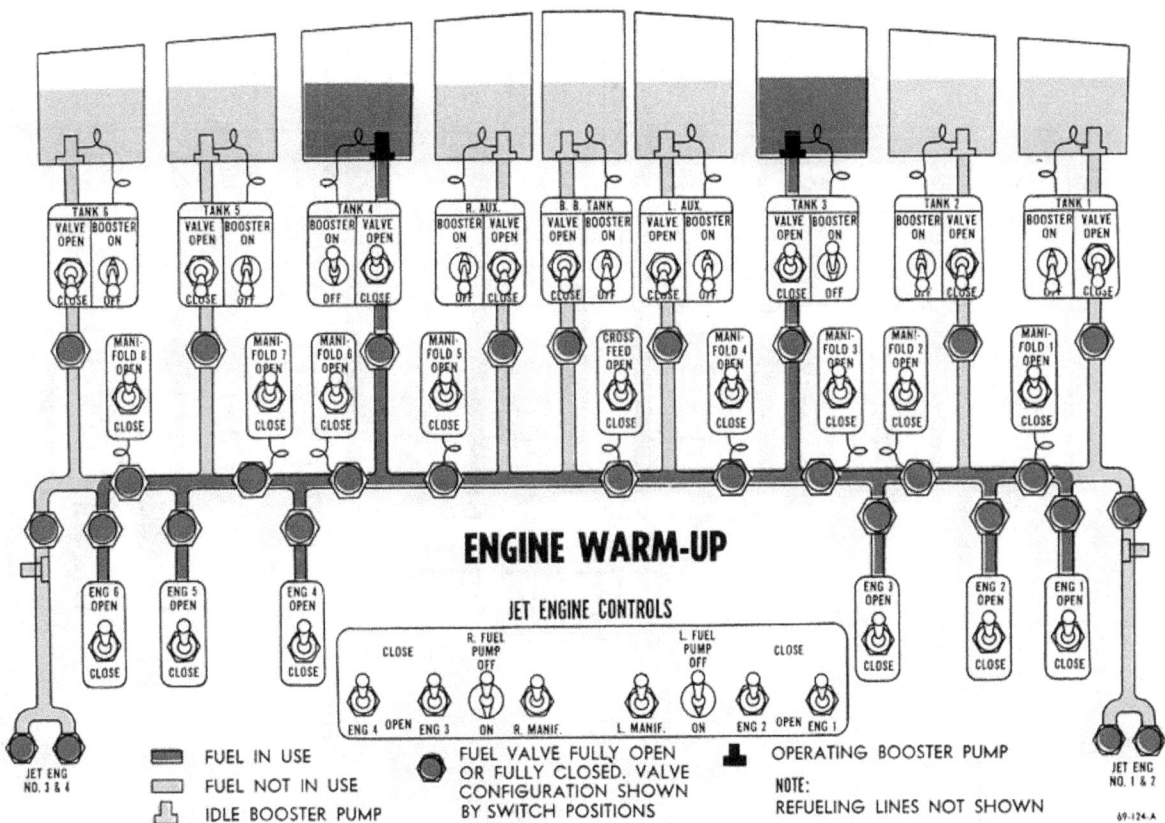

Figure 7-32. (Sheet 1) Fuel Management

the rotating field poles are energized, the coils in the stator will supply three-phase alternating current at a frequency determined by the speed of rotation and at a voltage fixed by the strength of the alternator magnetic field.

Exciter Generator.

The exciter generator which supplies voltage to the alternator field poles is integral with the alternator. The exciter is a self-excited, shunt-wound, direct-current generator. A carbon stack voltage regulator is connected in series with the shunt circuit. Because the generator is self-excited and shunt-wound, it energizes its own magnetic field through the shunt circuit. The exciter armature is on the same shaft as the alternator rotor and current is directed from one to the other by means of slip rings.

When the exciter armature rotates at a constant speed, its electrical output depends on the amount of resistance in the shunt field circuit. This resistance is controlled directly by the voltage regulator and indirectly by means of the voltage control knob. The amount of exciter output to the alternator controls the alternator output voltage. Since the carbon stack controls the exciter shunt field strength and the exciter output, it regulates the voltage of the alternator.

Constant-Speed Drive Unit.

The constant-speed drive unit drives the alternator at a constant speed with the mechanical input it receives from the reciprocating engine. The unit consists of a variable angle wobble plate, a fixed angle wobble plate, and a cylinder block assembly which contains motor pistons at one end and pump pistons at the other. The cylinder block assembly is rotated between the wobble plates by gears on an input shaft which is attached to the universal connection from the engine. The pump pistons rotate against the variable angle wobble plate and pump hydraulic fluid to the motor pistons, which turn the fixed angle wobble plate. When rotated, the fixed angle wobble plate turns the output shaft, which is connected to the alternator.

The speed of the output shaft is equal to the input shaft speed plus the speed change caused by the action of the motor pistons on the fixed angle wobble plate. The cylinder block assembly is connected to the fixed angle wobble plate so that the motor pistons can either increase or decrease the speed of the output shaft with respect to the input shaft. The increase or decrease in output shaft speed depends on the direction of oil flow from the pump pistons to the motor pistons, and the amount of speed change depends on the rate of oil

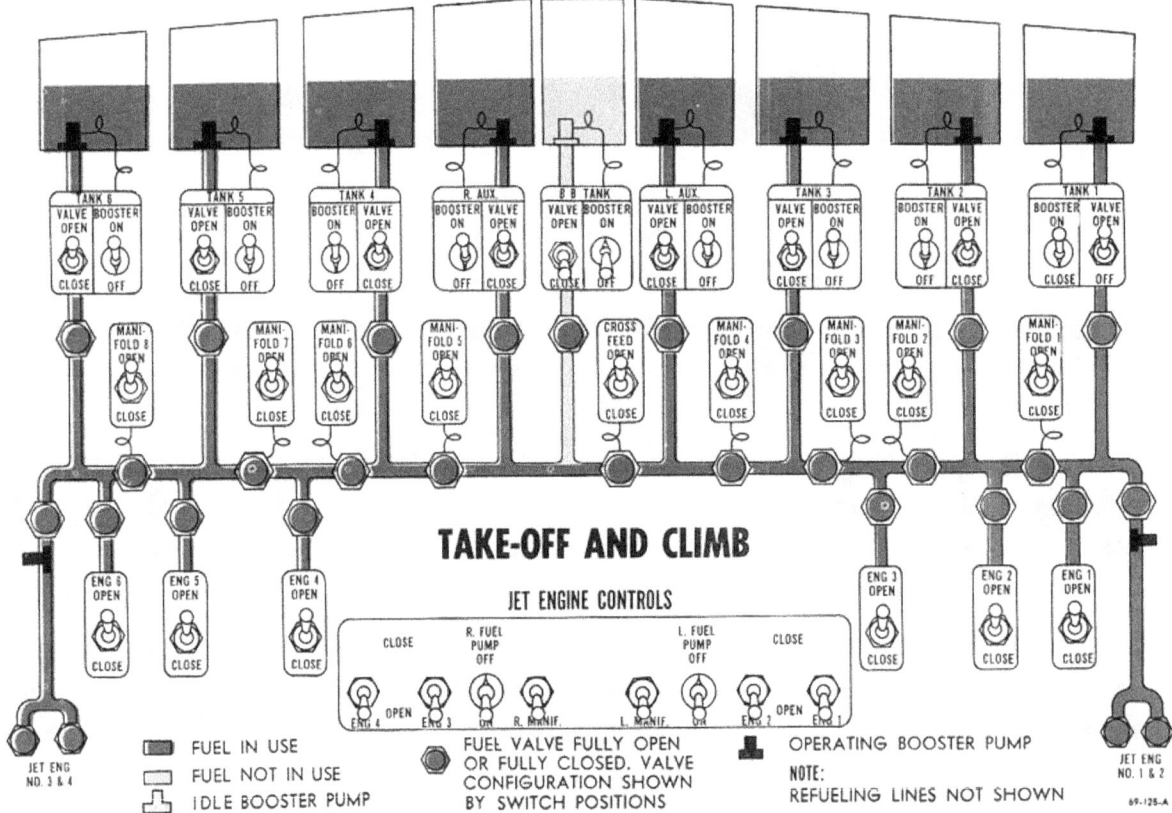

Figure 7-32. (Sheet 2) Fuel Management

flow. The displacement of the pump pistons and the direction of oil flow are controlled by the position of the variable angle wobble plate. The position of the variable angle wobble plate thus controls the increase or decrease in the output shaft speed of the constant-speed drive unit. A constant output speed is maintained by controlling the position of the variable angle wobble plate.

CONTROLLING THE A-C SYSTEM.

The a-c system is controlled by regulating the output of the alternators. There are three types of alternator controls: frequency controls, voltage controls, and load division controls. In addition, protective devices are provided to protect the alternator from overloads, short circuits, and overspeeding. The frequency controls regulate the action of the constant-speed drive unit, and the voltage controls regulate the strength of the alternator magnetic field. The load division controls affect these other controls to assure equal real and reactive load division among the alternators. Both real and reactive loads must be equally shared by the paralleled alternators to prevent either mechanical overload or excessive current drain through the windings of any one alternator. The reactive load does not impose a mechanical load, but is a part of the current drain through the alternator windings.

Frequency Controls.

The alternator frequency controls consist of a tachometer generator on the output shaft of the constant-speed drive unit, a rectifier in the governor junction box, the engineer's frequency control knob, a spring-biased governor pilot valve and solenoid assembly, and a servo unit which positions the variable angle wobble plate on the constant-speed drive unit. A frequency adjustment rheostat in the governor junction box adjusts the frequency control limits.

The tachometer generator produces 3-phase alternating current which is directly proportional to the speed of the drive unit output shaft. This current is rectified and applied to the control coil in the governor solenoid assembly. The engineer's frequency control knob regulates the amount of resistance in the circuit between the rectifier and the control coil. The magnetic pull of the control coil acts against the spring bias and positions the pilot valve in the assembly. When the output speed of the drive unit is correct, the tachometer generator current is sufficient to center the pilot valve, preventing a flow of oil to the control piston in the servo unit. However, any change in the output speed affects the tachometer voltage, causing the control coil to reposition the pilot valve. Depending on the posi-

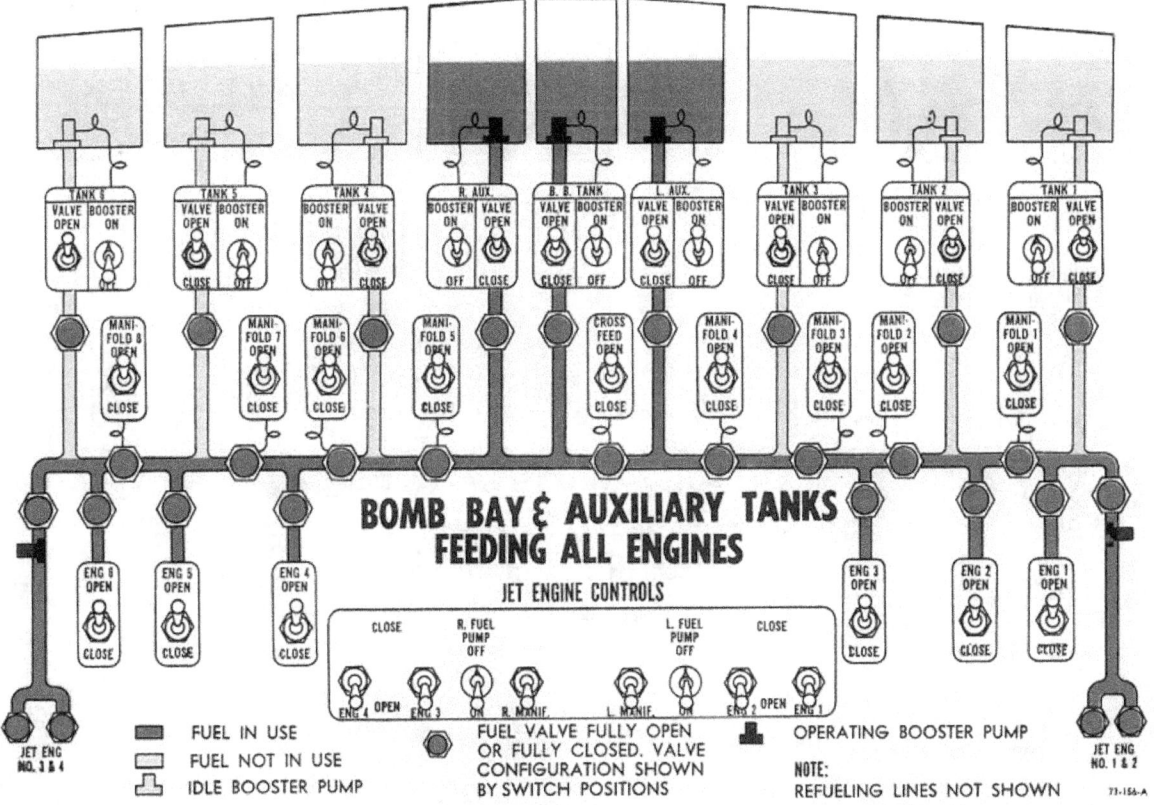

Figure 7-32. (Sheet 3) Fuel Management

Section VII
Systems Operation

tion of the pilot valve, oil will flow to either side of the control piston in the servo unit, which is attached to the variable angle wobble plate on the constant-speed drive unit. The flow of oil will change the position of the control piston and cause the wobble plate to move in the direction which will restore the original speed required for the drive unit. The flow of oil ceases when the output speed is corrected and the tachometer current in the control coil repositions the pilot valve. The frequency controls are automatic and should not require manual adjustment except for temperature changes which affect the frequency.

Note

The frequency will drop with a decrease in ambient temperature or a considerable increase in load. By the same token, frequency will increase as the temperature of the alternator conductors increases as in the case of an alternator being initially placed on the line, or a rise in the ambient temperature.

Note

On some airplanes, an alternator constant-speed drive temperature compensator has been installed to eliminate large frequency drops caused by the change in ambient temperature.

Voltage Controls.

The alternator voltage is adjusted by the engineer's voltage control knob and automatically controlled by the voltage regulator unit. The voltage regulator unit consists of two line transformers, a rectifier, a regulator coil, and a carbon stack resistor. A voltage adjusting rheostat adjusts the voltage control limits. Compensating resistors are also provided for temperature changes and a damping transformer is provided to reduce hunting or prolonged oscillation of voltage changes. A mutual reactor located in the voltage regulator senses unbalanced reactive loads between alternators.

Three-phase voltage from the alternator is rectified, and the d-c current flows through the regulator coil in direct proportion to the alternator voltage except as modified by the mutual reactors. The carbon stack is composed of a number of carbon discs kept under compression by a spring. Current in the regulator coil creates a magnetic force which opposes the spring force and tends to decrease the compression on the stack when the current flow is increased. When the stack compression decreases, its electrical resistance increases. The carbon stack is in series with the exciter shunt field circuit and when the stack resistance increases,

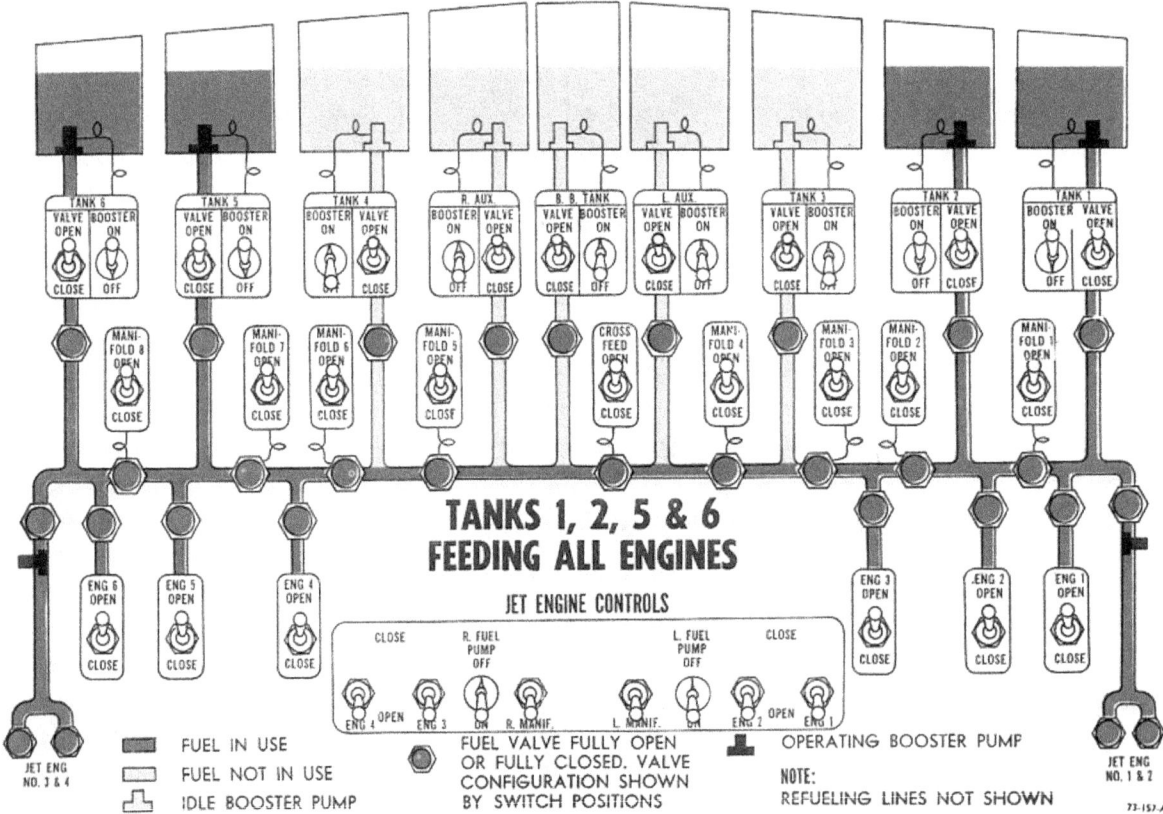

Figure 7-32. (Sheet 4) Fuel Management

the strength of the exciter shunt field decreases, causing reduced alternator voltage output. Since the current in the regulator coil directly influences the alternator voltage, any change in alternator voltage affects the carbon stack resistance which acts to restore the voltage to its previous level.

Real Load Division.

The ability of an alternator to assume real load in kilowatts depends on the mechanical torque applied to it by the constant-speed drive unit. After the alternators have been paralleled, they normally will not change their frequency output. However, the torque applied to each alternator may be changed by its drive unit. The torque may be increased by causing the drive unit to attempt to speed up the alternator. This can be done with the engineer's frequency control knob or by the load equalization circuit. When the drive unit attempts to speed up, the alternator rotor will not revolve faster, because it is electrically locked in parallel; but the added torque from the drive will permit it to assume more real load.

Automatic division of the real load is accomplished by a load equalization circuit after the engineer's controls have been set. Basically the circuit consists of four droop coils, one in each governor solenoid assembly. Each droop coil has the same effect as the control coil on the pilot valve and the action of the constant-speed drive unit. When the alternators are unequally sharing real load, each droop coil receives rectified current from load measuring transformers in each governor junction box. A droop control rheostat in each governor junction box adjusts the sensitivity of each droop coil.

The four droop coils are parallel-connected in a circuit so that when the alternators are equally sharing real load, no current flows through the droop coils. When an alternator assumes unequal load, current flows through the droop coils in proportion to the unbalance in load division. This unbalance in current results in the pilot valves being repositioned to cause the overloaded alternators to reduce torque and the others to increase torque until the load is equally divided again. The action of the droop circuit ceases when the load is equally divided.

Reactive Load Division.

The ability of an alternator to assume reactive load in kilovars depends on its magnetic field strength. After the alternators have been paralleled, they normally will not change their voltage output. However, the output of the exciter to the alternator field may be changed with the engineer's voltage control knob or by the reactive load division circuit. When the exciter output is increased to a paralleled alternator, it increases the ability of that alternator to assume more reactive load.

The reactive load division circuit consists of the mutual reactor in each voltage regulator and a current transformer for each mutual reactor. The transformers supply the reactors with current when the alternators are unequally sharing reactive load. The four mutual reactors are in series. Therefore, when the alternators are sharing equal reactive load, only an insignificant amount of current passes through the mutual reactors and the regulator coils in the voltage regulators are not affected. However, when the alternators assume unequal reactive loads, current proportional to the unequal load on each alternator flows through its mutual reactor. The effect on the regulator coils is the same as if the alternators were producing different voltages. The regulator coils change the resistances in the carbon stacks so that the overloaded alternators will receive less excitation and the others more excitation until the loads are equally divided again. The action of the reactive load division circuit ceases when the reactive loads are equally shared.

Load Variations.

A load variation of 4 kw or less on an alternator in a paralleled a-c system is not abnormal and does not require any action. If the variation is in excess of 4 kw, however, close all bus tie-breakers and remove the alternator with the largest load variation from the line. This action should alleviate the excessive load condition. If it does not, return the alternator to the line and remove each of the other alternators one at a time until the one causing the load variation is located. Flash the field of this alternator and return it to the line. If the load variation persists, remove the bad alternator from the line and operate the good alternators. If it later becomes necessary to return the defective alternator to the line, connect it to an isolated bus and operate the other alternators on the remaining buses, making certain that the load limitations are not exceeded.

ALTERNATOR PROTECTIVE DEVICES.

Exciter Ceiling Relay.

An exciter ceiling relay protects the alternator from overloads. It consists of a thermal switch connected to the alternator breaker and the exciter control relay. When the alternator is overloaded, the thermal switch closes and completes a 28-volt d-c circuit to open the alternator breaker and de-excite the alternator.

Differential Protection Relay.

A differential protection relay protects the alternator from short circuits in the alternator windings. It consists of a transformer installed around the power and ground return leads for each phase and a switch connected to the alternator breaker and the exciter control relay. When the power and ground return leads have unequal current passing through them, the transformers are energized by the difference in current and close the switch, completing a 28-volt circuit to open the alternator breaker and de-excite the alternator.

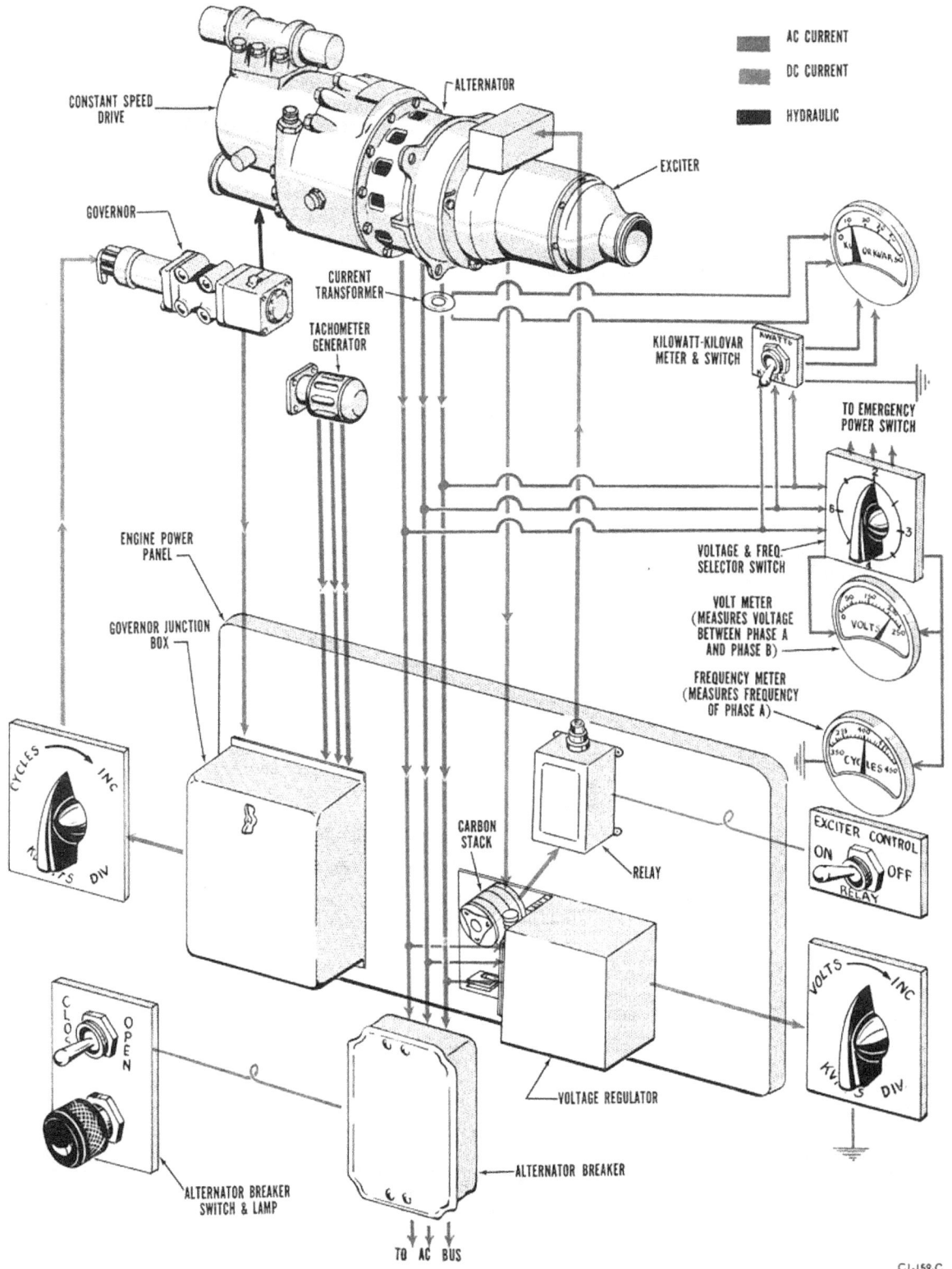

Figure 7-33. Alternating-Current Control Schematic

KVA DETERMINATION

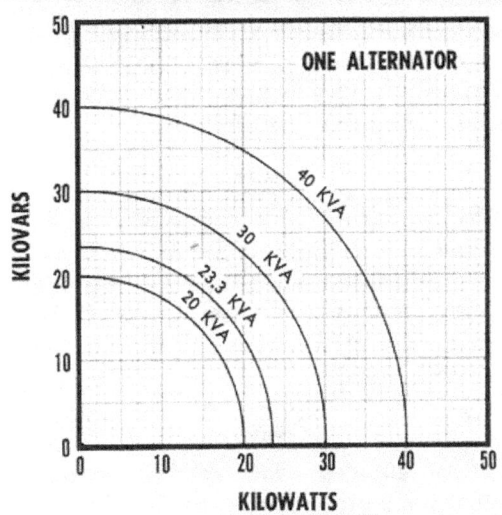

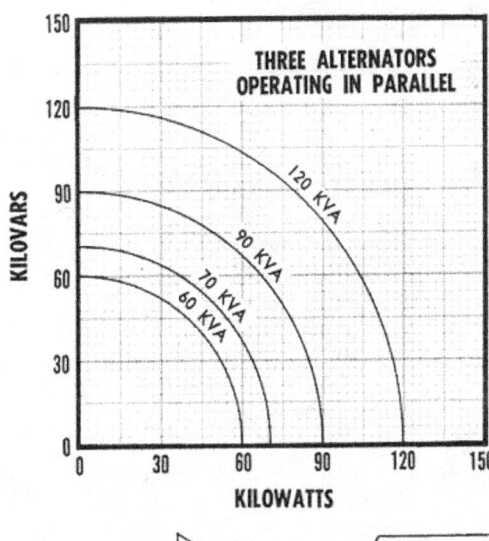

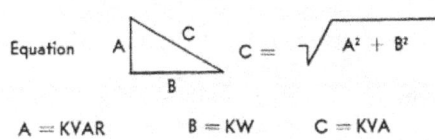

A = KVAR B = KW C = KVA

Figure 7-34.

Alternator Overspeed Control.

A constant-speed drive overspeed control protects the alternator from excessive speeding. It consists of a centrifugal switch in the tachometer generator and a coil in the governor pilot valve and solenoid assembly. When the output shaft speed is excessive, the centrifugal switch closes and completes a 28-volt d-c circuit to the coil in the governor solenoid. The energized coil pulls the pilot valve to an extreme position which causes the drive unit to go into full underdrive and reduce the output speed to a minimum. When the drive unit is locked in underdrive, the alternator frequency closely follows engine rpm.

NORMAL OPERATING PROCEDURES.

Four Good Alternators.

When four good alternators are available, three alternators will be operated in parallel with all bus tie-breakers closed. The remaining alternator will be excited and on stand by, provided the maximum load does not exceed 70 KVA (approximately 23 KVA's per alternator). (See figure 7-34.) If the electrical load exceeds 23 KVA per alternator, operate all four alternators in parallel.

Three Good Alternators.

If only three good alternators are available, operate the alternators in parallel with all bus tie-breakers closed. It is desirable to reduce all alternator loads to a maximum of 23 KVA per alternator, if practicable, by removing nonessential loads.

Note

If three or more good alternators are available, use standard manual leaning procedure for 30-degree spark advance, best economy operation, if maximum range is desired. If less than three good alternators are available but maximum range engine performance is imperative for safe return of the aircraft, continue to use standard manual leaning procedure for 30-degree spark advance, best economy operation.

Two Good Alternators.

If only two good alternators are available, operate them in parallel with all bus tie-breakers closed. It is desirable to reduce all electrical loads to a maximum of 23 KVA per alternator, if practicable, by removing nonessential electrical loads.

Less Than Three Good Alternators (Range Unimportant).

If range is unimportant and less than three good alternators are available, set up required power with 20-degree spark advance, normal mixture and dual turbo.

Electrical Loads.

The following is a list of significant electrical loads which can be removed at the discretion of the crew, depending on tactical requirements.

AC Electrical Loads	Approximate Average KW
Cabin Heaters	34
Turrets	22
Jet Anti-Icing	10
Cabin Air Booster Fan	9 (high speed)

Section VII
Systems Operation

AC Electrical Loads	Approximate Average KW
Oil Vent Line Heaters	1.5
Hydraulic Pump Temperature Cycling	11
K-( ) Equipment	13 (intermittent max)
Oven, Hot Cups	5
Jet-Oil Tank Heaters	2

DC Electrical Loads	Approximate Average Amps
Tail Radar	15
Chaff Dispensers	30
RCM Equipment	14.4
Radio Equipment	74 (maximum)
Special Bombing Equipment	102 (maximum)
K-( ) Equipment	41
Autopilot	15

CHART FOR ELECTRICAL SYSTEM TROUBLE SHOOTING.

Directions for using the trouble shooting chart: The "Parallel Condition" column indicates the initial abnormal condition which would be noted while a malfunctioning alternator is operating in parallel with other alternators. After the breaker of the affected alternator is opened, the no-load operation should be observed and compared with the conditions shown in the "Isolated Condition" column. Directly opposite the isolated condition is shown the trouble-shooting procedure which should be followed.

Note

The malfunctioning alternator may be determined by splitting the bus four ways. Isolate the affected alternator by opening its alternator breaker. If necessary, the bus tie breakers may be closed after the affected alternator is isolated.

Note

When operating under reduced electrical power, the cabin heaters should be turned off to conserve power.

PARALLEL CONDITION	ISOLATED CONDITION	PROCEDURE
Frequency oscillations (Isolate alternator with largest variation in KVAR or KWATT load.)	Voltage oscillation ($\pm$ 10 volts)	1. Polarity of exciter field may be reversed—Flash the field. If the field is not flashed, leave unexcited.
	Frequency oscillations.	1. Rotate frequency control knob rapidly back and forth to free sticky governor. Isolate alternator if fault cannot be corrected.
No KWATT or KVAR indications.	No frequency — No voltage — One or both synchronization lights out.	1. Alternator failure is indicated. 2. Be sure alternator breaker is opened. 3. Check AC INST fuses at engine power panel.
Alternator will not stay on line.	All readings normal when alternator breaker is opened and alternator re-excited.	1. De-excite alternator. 2. May be caused by the protective devices. In emergency, disconnect cannon plugs from exciter ceiling relay and differential protection relay at engine power panel.
Negative KVAR and KWATT load. (Alternator motoring)	Erratic or no frequency or voltage.	1. Slipping clutch or broken drive shaft—Open alternator breaker. 2. In emergency, replace carbon stack with stack from non-operative unit.
	Low frequency—Low voltage—Alternator frequency varies with engine speed.	1. Unit is in underdrive—Isolate alternator and manually reset. 2. If underdrive condition persists, use alternator at 2700 rpm engine speed.
No d-c power to alternator control panel. No KVAR or KWATT indication on one alternator, but power is apparently being supplied by the alternator.	No frequency, voltage low or zero, synchronization lights dim or out.	1. Reset bus tie control circuit breaker on engineer's table. 1. Check AC INST fuses at engine power panel. 2. Remove alternator from line and use only in emergency on isolated bus.

ELECTRICAL SYSTEM TROUBLE SHOOTING (Cont'd)

PARALLEL CONDITION	ISOLATED CONDITION	PROCEDURE
Low or negative KVAR load.	Low voltage with little or no control.	1. Check A C I N S T fuses at engine power panel. 2. Check adjustment of voltage regulator rheostat at the engine power panel. 3. Remove either wire from terminal D-9 at the engine distribution panel and adjust voltage regulator rheostat at engine power panel. 4. In emergency only, replace carbon stack with stack from a non-operative unit (excitation must be off to remove stack).
Low KWATT load—Some control. KVAR's normal.	Frequency low—Some control.	1. Readjust frequency control rheostat on governor control junction box at the alternator control panel.
	No frequency, low voltage.	1. Check A C I N S T fuses at engine power panel.
High KVAR load—No control.	High voltage—No control.	1. Check AC PWR EQUIP. fuse at engine power panel. 2. Replace carbon stack when excitation is OFF. 3. De-excite alternator.
High KVAR load — or KVAR division wandering over wide range.	Frequency and voltage readings normal.	1. Isolate alternator and split bus.
High KWATT load—or KW division wanders over wide range.	Abnormal frequency control.	1. Readjust frequency rheostat in the governor control junction box at engine power panel. 2. May be sticky governor—Rotate frequency control knob rapidly back and forth to free.
	Normal control.	1. Isolate alternator and split bus if trouble persists.
Complete loss of power.		See "Emergency Electrical Operation" of Section III.

EMERGENCY OPERATION OF ELECTRICAL EQUIPMENT.

When a unit fails to operate because of a faulty electrical circuit, power can be applied to the unit by the use of wire jumpers. It is suggested that two jumpers be prepared for this purpose. One jumper should be made of heavy wire capable of carrying the largest 3-phase power load which may be encountered; the other jumper can be made of relatively thin wire for use on low current circuits. Each jumper should incorporate a switch. The three-phase jumper should incorporate a three-pole switch. These switches are important for the following reasons:

a. When the jumper is connected from the unit to the power line, the circuit will remain open until the switch is closed. This eliminates the possibility of dangerous sparking.

b. If the limit switch of a unit is inoperative, the circuit will be kept open until the second crew member is prepared to observe movement of the unit.

c. If the circuit carries three-phase power, the three gang switch will permit all phases to be connected simultaneously.

CAUTION

Application of three-phase power to a motor when all three phases aren't connected may cause motor damage.

Connect the jumper to the unit first, and then to the power line with insulated metal clips having a maximum of contact surface and a minimum of exposed outer surface.

WARNING

Because dangerous voltages will be encountered in various parts of the airplane, always open the circuit breakers or remove the fuses which will de-energize the circuit before attaching a jumper.

The procedures given in the following table are to be used when a unit fails to operate because of a faulty electrical circuit.

UNIT	TERMINAL LOCATION	OPERATION	
		TO CLOSE VALVE	TO OPEN VALVE
Aft Cabin Pressure Shutoff Valve	Just forward of aft cabin	1. Apply 115-volt AC to pigtail B.	1. Apply 115-volt AC to pigtail A.
		TO CLOSE BREAKER	TO OPEN BREAKER
Alternator Breaker	On aft side of Alternator Control Panel 2, 3, 4, or 5.	1. Open bus tie breakers to isolate alternator: Then momentarily apply 28-volt DC to terminal A6 (28-volt DC power available at terminals B2 and B3).	1. Momentarily apply 28-volt DC to terminal A8 (28-volt DC available at terminals B2 and B3).
		TO CLOSE RELAY	TO OPEN RELAY
Alternator Exciter Control Relay	On aft side of Alternator Control Panel 2, 3, 4, or 5.	1. Apply 28-volt DC to terminal B11 (28-volt DC available at terminals B2 and B3).	1. Apply 28-volt DC to terminal B10 (28-volt DC available at terminals B2 and B3).
		TO CLOSE DOORS	TO OPEN DOORS
Bomb Bay Doors	Landing Gear Control Relay Panel	1. Apply 28-volt DC to terminal B2 of hydraulic fluid temperature control relay. Also apply 28-volt DC to terminal X1 and ground terminal X2 of the No. 1 hydraulic pump relay.	1. Apply 28-volt DC to terminal C1 on the bomb bay door open relay. Also apply 28-volt DC to terminal X1 and X2 of the No. 1 hydraulic pump relay.
		2. If the main selector valve fails to operate, depress the CLOSE plunger on the valve. If pump No. 1 fails to operate, No. 2 may still be operative; however, if No. 2 pump is also inoperative, apply 28-volt DC to terminal X1 and ground X2 of No. 2 pump relay.	2. If the main selector valve fails to operate, depress the OPEN plunger on the valve. If pump No. 1 fails to operate, No. 2 may still be operative; however, if No. 2 pump is also inoperative, apply 28-volt DC to terminal X1 and ground X2 of No. 2 pump relay.

EMERGENCY OPERATION OF ELECTRICAL EQUIPMENT (Cont'd)

UNIT	TERMINAL LOCATION	OPERATION	
		TO CLOSE BREAKER	TO OPEN BREAKER
Bus Tie Breaker 2-3 3-4 4-5 5-2	Bhd. 7.2 terminal strips	Apply 28-volt DC to terminal: C-18 on L.H. Strip C-15 on L.H. Strip C-18 on R.H. Strip C-15 on R.H. Strip (28-volt DC available at Bhd. 8.0 DC Power Panel.)	Apply 28-volt DC to terminal: C-19 on L.H. Strip C-16 on L.H. Strip C-19 on R.H. Strip C-16 on R.H. Strip (28-volt DC available at Bhd. 8.0 DC Power Panel.)
		TO CLOSE VALVE	TO OPEN VALVE
Cabin Pressure Wing Shutoff Valve	Overhead in bomb bay No. 3	1. Apply 115-volt AC to pigtail B.	1. Apply 115-volt AC to pigtail A.
		TO CLOSE AIR PLUG	TO OPEN AIR PLUG
Engine Air Plug	At Engine Distribution Panels	1. Apply 28-volt DC to terminal A9 of engine distribution panel. 2. If motor fails to operate, connect jumpers between the following air plug motor relay terminals: T1 to L1; T2 to L3; T3 to L2.	1. Apply 28-volt DC to terminal A10 of engine distribution panel. 2. If motor fails to operate, connect jumpers between the following air plug motor relay terminals: T1 to L1; T2 to L2; T3 to L3.
		FOR LOW RPM	FOR HIGH RPM
Engine Fan	At Engine Distribution Panels	1. Apply 115-volt AC to terminal A1. NOTE: Circuit breaker on engineer's panel must be open.	1. Apply 115-volt AC to terminal A2. NOTE: Circuit breaker on engineer's panel must be open.
		TO CLOSE DOOR	TO OPEN DOOR
Engine Oil Flight Cooling Door	At Engine Distribution Panels	1. Apply 115-volt AC to terminal N5. NOTE: Fuse must be removed from engine power panel.	1. Apply 115-volt AC to terminal N4. NOTE: Fuse must be removed from engine power panel.
		TO CLOSE DOOR	TO OPEN DOOR
Engine Oil Ground Cooling Door	At Engine Distribution Panels	1. Apply 115-volt AC to terminal N7. NOTE: Fuse must be removed from engine power panel.	1. Apply 115-volt AC to terminal N6. NOTE: Fuse must be removed from engine power panel.
		TO RETRACT	TO EXTEND
Flaps (Inboard)	At L.H. Wing-Fuselage Splice (L.H. Flap) or R.H. Wing-Fuselage Splice (R.H. Flap) At Flap Control Relay Panel	1. Apply 28-volt DC to terminals A1 and A4. 2. If motor still fails to operate, check fuses, and if blown, replace. Apply 28-volt dc to motor reversing relay terminal X1 and speed relay terminal X1. Ground speed relay terminal X2.	1. Apply 28-volt DC to terminals A2 and A4. 2. If motor still fails to operate, check fuses, and if blown, replace. Apply 28-volt dc to motor reversing relay terminals Y2 and speed relay terminal X1. Ground speed relay terminal Y1.

Section VII
Systems Operation

EMERGENCY OPERATION OF ELECTRICAL EQUIPMENT (Cont'd)

UNIT	TERMINAL LOCATION	OPERATION	
		TO RETRACT	TO EXTEND
Flaps (Center)	At L.H. Wing-Fuselage Splice (L.H. Flap) or R.H. Wing-Fuselage Splice (R.H. Flap)	1. Apply 28-volt DC on terminals A5 and A8.	1. Apply 28-volt DC on terminals A6 and A8.
	At Flap Control Relay Panel	2. If motor still fails to operate, check fuses, and if blown, replace. Apply 28-volt DC to motor reversing relay terminal X1 and speed control relay terminal X1. Ground speed relay terminal X2.	2. If motor still fails to operate, check fuses and if blown, replace. Apply 28-volt DC to motor reversing relay terminal Y2 and speed relay terminal X1. Ground speed relay terminal Y1.
		3. If fuses not blown, or fuses continue to blow and motor fails to operate, connect jumpers between the following terminals: T1 on reversing relay to L13 on speed relay, T2 to L11, T3 to L12.	3. If fuses not blown, or continue to blow and motor does not operate, connect jumpers between the following terminals: T1 on reversing relay to L13 on speed relay, T2 to L12, T3 to L11.
		4. If the motor does not run, remove the jumpers and connect them as follows: T1 on reversing relay to L3 on speed relay, T2 to L1, T3 to L2.	4. If the motor does not run, remove the jumpers and connect them as follows: T1 on reversing relay to L3 on speed relay, T2 to L2, T3 to L1.
Flaps (Outboard)	At L.H. Wing-Fuselage Splice (L.H. Flap)	1. Apply 28-volt DC to terminals A10 and A12.	1. Apply 28-volt DC to terminals A9 and A12.
	At R.H. Wing-Fuselage Splice (R.H. Flap)	2. Apply 28-volt DC to terminals A9 and A12.	2. Apply 28-volt DC to terminals A10 and A12.
	At Speed Control and Motor Reversing Relay	3. If motor still fails to operate, check fuses, and if blown, replace. Apply 28-volt DC to motor reversing relay terminal X1 and speed control relay terminal X1. Ground speed relay terminal X2.	3. If motor still fails to operate, check fuses, and if blown, replace. Apply 28-volt DC to motor reversing relay terminal Y2 and speed control relay terminal X1. Ground speed relay terminal Y1.

EMERGENCY OPERATION OF ELECTRICAL EQUIPMENT (Cont'd)

UNIT	TERMINAL LOCATION	OPERATION	
		TO RETRACT	TO EXTEND
		4. If fuses not blown, or fuses continue to blow and motor fails to operate, connect jumpers between the following terminals: T1 on reversing relay on L13 on speed relay, T2 to L11, T3 to L12.	4. If fuses not blown, or continue to blow and motor does not operate, connect jumpers between the following terminals: T1 on reversing relay to L13 on speed relay, T2 to L12, T3 to L11.
		5. If the motor does not run, remove jumpers and connect them as follows: T1 on reversing relay to L3 on speed relay, T2 to L1, T3 to L2.	5. If the motor does not run, remove jumpers and connect as follows: T1 on reversing relay to L3 on speed relay, T2 to L2, T3 to L1.
Fuel Booster Pump	At Engine Distribution Panels	TO OPERATE 1. Apply 28-volt DC to pump relay terminal X1. Ground terminal X2. 2. If pump fails to operate, add jumpers between the following relay terminals: L1 to T1; L2 to T2; L3 to T3.	
Hydraulic Pump	At Landing Gear Control Panel	TO OPERATE 1. Apply 28-volt DC to pump motor relay terminal XI. Ground terminal X2. 2. If pump fails to operate, apply 28-volt DC to No. 2 pump relay terminal X1 and ground terminal X2.	
Intercooler Controls	At Engine Distribution Panels	TO OPEN SHUTTERS 1. Apply 115-volt AC to terminal B12 for LH shutter and C12 for RH shutter.	TO CLOSE SHUTTERS 1. Apply 115-volt AC to terminal B13 for LH shutter and C9 for RH shutter.
Landing Gear	At Landing Gear Control Panel	TO RETRACT 1. Apply 28-volt DC to terminal X2 of retract relay and ground terminal X1. Also, apply 28-volt DC to terminal X1 and ground terminal X2 of the No. 1 hydraulic pump relay.	TO EXTEND 1. Apply 28-volt DC to terminal X2 of the extend relay and ground terminal XI. Also apply 28-volt DC to terminal X2 of the No. 1 hydraulic pump relay.

Section VII
Systems Operation

T.O. 1B-36D(II)-1

EMERGENCY OPERATION OF ELECTRICAL EQUIPMENT (Cont'd)

UNIT	TERMINAL LOCATION	OPERATION		
		TO RETRACT	TO EXTEND	
		2. If the main selector valve fails to operate, depress the UP plunger on the valve. If No. 1 pump fails to operate, No. 2 may still be operative; however, if No. 2 is also inoperative, apply 28-volt DC to terminal X1 and ground X2 of No. 2 pump relay.	2. If the main selector valve fails to operate, depress the DOWN plunger on the valve. If No. 1 pump fails to operate, No. 2 may still be operative; however, if No. 2 is inoperative also, apply 28-volt DC to terminal X1 and ground X2 of No. 2 pump relay.	
		TO EXTEND	TO ILLUMINATE	
Landing Light	Landing Light Pressure Disconnect	Apply 28-volt DC to pin B of landing light pressure disconnect.	Apply 28-volt AC to pin C of landing light pressure disconnect.	
		TO CLOSE DUMP VALVE	TO OPEN DUMP VALVE	
Nacelle Dump Valves	At RH Fuselage Wing Splice (Cabin Heat and Tail Anti-Icing Only)	1. Apply 115-volt AC to terminals A16 and A18.	1. Apply 115-volt AC to terminals C12 and C9.	
	At Engine Distribution Panels 3 and 4	2. If motor fails to operate, apply 115-volt AC to terminal M16. NOTE: Circuit breakers on engineer's table must be open.	2. If motor fails to operate, apply 115-volt AC to terminal M15. NOTE: Circuit breakers on engineer's table must be open.	
		TO INCREASE RPM	TO DECREASE RPM	TO FEATHER
Propeller	At Engine Distribution Panels	1. Apply 28-volt DC to terminal A3.	1. Apply 28-volt DC to terminal A4.	1. Apply 28-volt DC to terminal B7.
		TO ADVANCE	TO RETARD	
Spark Advance	At Engine Distribution Panels	1. Apply 115-volt AC to terminal A13. NOTE: Circuit breakers on engineer's panel must be open.	1. Apply 115-volt AC to terminal A14. NOTE: Circuit breakers on engineer's panel must be open.	
		FOR SINGLE TURBO	FOR DUAL TURBO	
Turbo Selector Valve	At Engine Distribution Panels	1. Apply 115-volt AC to terminal B5. NOTE: Circuit breaker on engineer's panel must be open.	1. Apply 115-volt AC to terminal B6. NOTE: Circuit breaker on engineer's panel must be open.	
		TO CLOSE VALVE	TO OPEN VALVE	
Wing Anti-Icing Controls	At Engine Distribution Panels 1, 2, 5, and 6	1. Apply 28-volt DC to terminal X1 of anti-icing dump valve relay. Ground terminal X2.	1. Apply 28-volt DC to terminal X1 of anti-icing dump valve relay. Ground terminal X2.	
		2. If motor fails to operate, apply 115-volt AC to terminal M16. NOTE: Fuses must be removed from power panel.	2. If motor fails to operate, apply 115-volt AC to terminal M15. NOTE: Fuses must be removed from power panel.	

ENGINE INSTRUMENT TROUBLE SHOOTING (Group 2 Airplanes).

These procedures should be used when it is determined that any of the following equipment is malfunctioning:

Torque meter indicating system
Manifold pressure indicating system
Fuel flow indicating system
Fuel pressure indicating system
Oil pressure indicating system
Water pressure indicating system

A power failure to the above-named instruments will be indicated when the indicator arms do not vibrate and remain motionless when a change in power setting is accomplished.

1. If all of the previously mentioned instruments for one engine cease operation, check the corresponding ENGINE SELSYN INSTRUMENTS FUSE at the instrument fuse panel.

2. If the torquemeter, fuel flow indicator, or the manifold pressure gage for one engine ceases operation, check the corresponding instrument amplifier by replacing it with the spare amplifier.

Note

The engine instrument amplifiers are located in a rack adjacent to the instrument fuse panel.

3. If all of the previously listed instruments for all engines cease operation, place the ALTERNATE-NORMAL switch on the instrument fuse panel in the ALTERNATE position. If the instruments resume operation, the normal transformer is inoperative.

a. If some, but not all, of the instruments resume operation, check the fuses in the instrument fuse panel.

b. If all of the instruments remain inoperative, check the INST PWR-NORMAL and INST PWR-ALT fuses in the engineer's fuse panel. If these fuses are blown and continue to blow when replaced, the power transformers in the instrument fuse panel may be shorted. When this occurs or when power is not obtained after a fuse is replaced without it being blown, both the normal and alternate transformers are probably inoperative. In such an emergency, power can be restored to the related instruments by jumping 28-volt ac to the instrument fuse panel as follows:

(1) Remove the INST PWR-NORMAL and INST PWR-ALT fuses.

(2) Detach the instrument fuse panel to gain access to the alternate-normal switch terminals.

(3) Remove the transformer leads, and connect a 14-gauge jumper wire to the terminals on either side of the switch.

(4) Connect the jumper wire to a clip in the 28-volt a-c power panel. Insert a 20-amp fuse to complete the circuit.

CAUTION

Do not use the landing lights while this power is jumped from the 28-volt a-c power panel; otherwise the lighting transformer will burn out.

Note

Any lighting transformer in the lighting system may be used for 28-volt ac when all of the lighting requirements are removed.

(5) If the alternate-normal switch is inoperative in both positions, connect 26 or 28-volt a-c power from any source to terminals 1, 3, 5, 7, 9 and 11 of the "B" terminal strip in the instrument fuse panel. This procedure should be used only in an emergency which justifies the risk of wiring burnouts, since wiring will not be properly fused with this circuit. Shorted wiring, faulty indicators, or bad transmitters will be indicated by pointers which are motionless, or oscillate or rotate rapidly. If changing amplifiers and replacing fuses do not remedy the malfunction, use other instruments to judge engine operation.

Cylinder Head Temperature Instruments.

A power failure to the cylinder head temperature instruments is indicated when the indicator arm does not vibrate and remains motionless when a change in air plug opening is accomplished or a change in cooling requirements occurs.

1. If the CHT indicator ceases operation for one engine, check the CYLINDER HEAD TEMPERATURE AMPLIFIER fuse for that engine at the instrument fuse panel.

2. If the CHT indicator remains inoperative, check the corresponding CHT amplifier by replacing it with the spare amplifier.

3. If the CHT indicators for all engines cease operation, check the CYL HD TEMP IND fuse at the engineer's fuse panel.

4. If some but not all CHT indicators resume operation, check the fuses and amplifiers at the instrument fuse panel.

5. If the power line from the engineer's fuse panel is broken, 115-volt ac may be jumped to the instrument fuse panel for emergency operation of all the CHT indicators. To jump 115-volt ac, proceed as follows:

a. Remove the CYL HD TEMP IND fuse.

b. Detach the instrument fuse panel to gain access to terminal strip "A."

Section VII
Systems Operation

c. Disconnect the lead from terminal 7 and connect 115-volt ac to the terminal from any source such as the right forward cabin power panel.

Note

Do not use the original fuse clip in the engineer's panel because the power may be shorted and will blow the fuses when the circuit is completed.

A short circuit in the wiring of the CHT indicator will probably cause the indicator pointer to read extremely low. Change the setting of the CHT selector switch to check for a short.

1. If new setting results in a reasonable reading, a short exists between the temperature bulb and the selector switch.

2. If the low reading remains unchanged, amplifier or indicator failure or wiring fault is indicated.

An open circuit will cause the indicator arm to rotate rapidly. Change the setting of the CHT selector switch to check for an open circuit.

1. If rotation stops when switch is changed, an open circuit exists between the bulb and the selector switch.

2. If the rotation continues, an amplifier or indicator is faulty or the return ground connections or selector switch circuits are open.

LANDING GEAR SYSTEM.

LANDING GEAR RETRACTION.

When the landing gear control switch is moved to the RETRACT position and the airplane is airborne, both main system hydraulic pumps are energized and the main selector valve is actuated to direct hydraulic fluid, under pressure, into the gear-up lines. The pressure is routed to the door directional valve from where it is routed to the sequence shutoff valve which is open when the main gear is locked in the up or down position. At the same time, pressure is routed to and stops at the up sequence valve which is closed. Pressure is also routed to the up end of the nose gear actuating cylinder to retract the nose gear. After passing through the door directional valve and the sequence shutoff valve, the flow divides with part of it going to the door unlatching cylinder and the remainder to the up side of the door actuating cylinder. The fluid going to the up side of the door actuating cylinder preloads the actuator in the up position. This preloading is necessary to prevent airloads from pulling the door open suddenly and cavitating the actuating cylinder when the door latches are released. Preloading also permits easier opening of the door latches. When the fluid

passes through the door unlatching cylinder, opening the latches, it enters the down side of the door actuating cylinder to extend the door to the full down position.

As the door becomes fully extended, the mechanical linkage between the door actuating cylinder and the sequence valves opens the up sequence valve and the down sequence valve. When the up sequence valve is opened, fluid is routed to the main gear unlatching cylinder and through the cushion valve. The unlatching cylinder unlatches the main gear and breaks the side brace. The fluid which passes through the cushion valve is routed to the main gear actuating cylinder and the gear begins retraction. While the gear is retracting, the mechanical linkage between the actuating cylinder and the door directional valve positions the directional valve actuating cylinder. However, the door cannot close because the sequence shutoff valve is closed preventing the flow of return fluid from the down port of the door actuator. When the gear is full up the side brace falls into place and automatically locks. As the main gear latch falls into place, the sequence shutoff valve is actuated to the open position. The opening of this valve allows return fluid to escape from the down side of the door actuator. This permits fluid to enter the up side of the actuator, raising the door. As the door rises, fluid is forced from the down port of the door actuator through the door unlatching cylinder. This holds the door latches open until the door is completely closed, at which time the flow through the unlatching cylinder ceases and the door latches fall into place, locking the door in the up position. As the latches fall into place, the door limit switches are actuated, shutting off the hydraulic pumps.

LANDING GEAR EXTENSION.

When the landing gear control switch is moved to the EXTEND position, the No. 1 hydraulic pump is energized and the main selector valve is actuated to direct hydraulic fluid under pressure into the gear-down lines. The pressure is routed to the door directional valves from where it is routed to the sequence shutoff valve. At the same time, pressure is routed to and stops at the down sequence valve, which is closed, and to the nose gear actuating cylinder to extend the nose gear. After passing through the door directional valve and the sequence shutoff valve, the flow divides with part of it going to the door unlatching cylinder and the remainder to the upside of the door actuating cylinder. From the door unlatching cylinder the flow enters the down side of the door actuating cylinder. This divided flow combines action to unlock and actu-

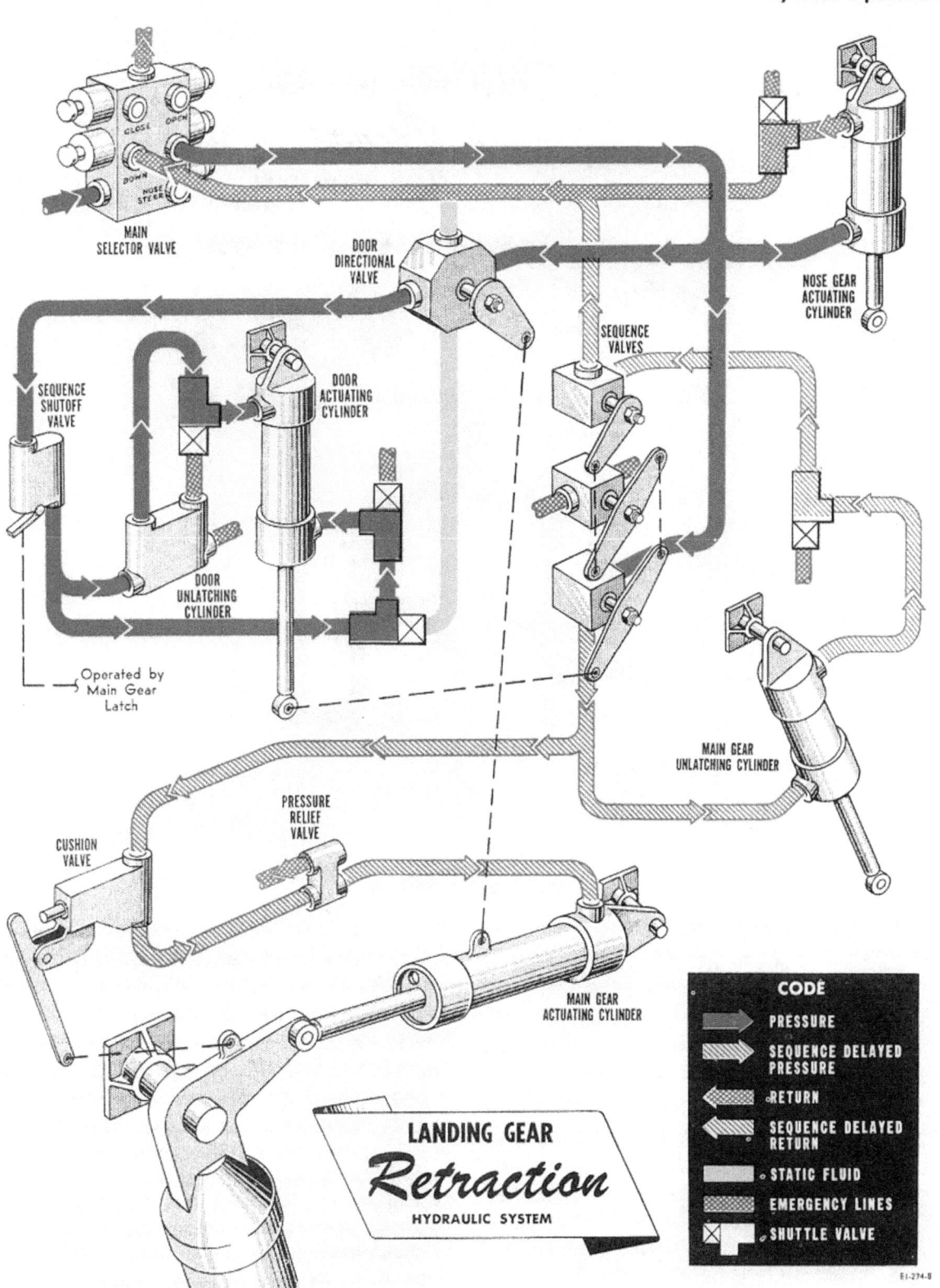

Figure 7-35. (Sheet 1)

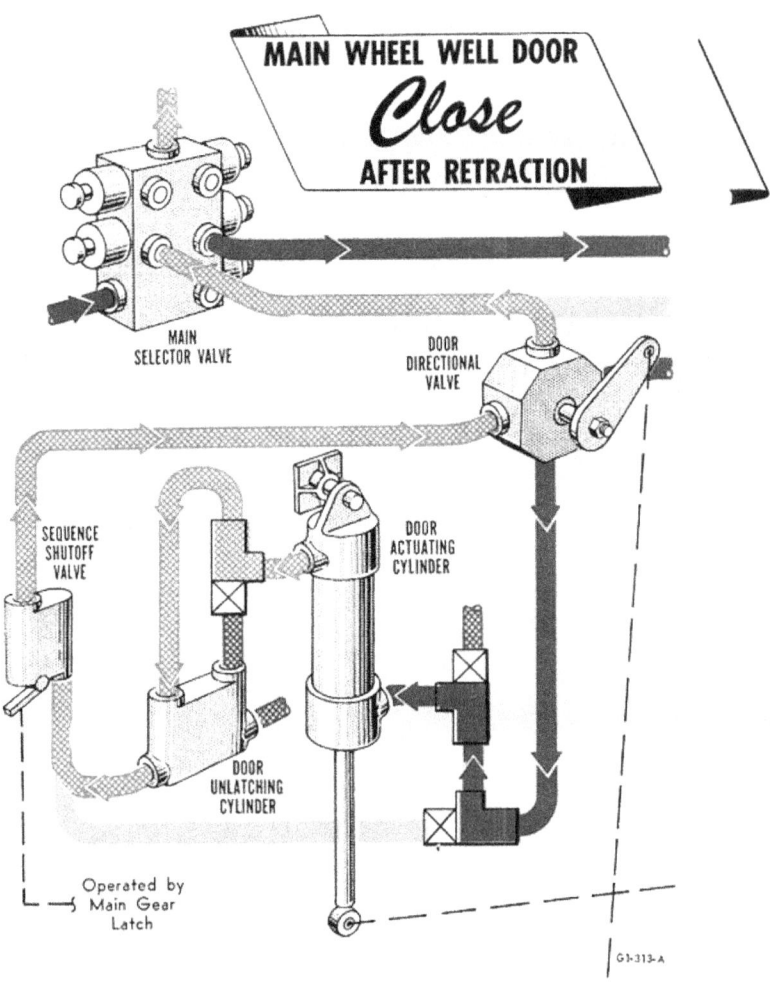

Figure 7-35. (Sheet 2)

ate the main gear door to the down position in the same manner as in gear retraction. As the door becomes fully extended, the mechanical linkage between the door actuating cylinder and the sequence valves opens the up sequence valve and the down sequence valve. When the down sequence valve is opened, fluid is routed to the top of the main gear unlatching cylinder and to a port in the cushion valve for preloading the main gear actuating cylinder and raising the gear slightly. The pressure at the top of the unlatching cylinder unlocks the gear and breaks the side brace, allowing the gear to fall of its own weight. The preloading reduces the initial shock of the fall and a restrictor built into the main gear actuating cylinder controls the speed of extension. After the first 10 degrees of extension the passage in the cushion valve, used to preload the actuator, is closed and the passage to the gear up line is open. This allows the fluid to return from the actuating cylinder to the reservoir through the cushion valve, the up sequence valve, and the up port of the mail selector valve. When the gear is fully extended the side brace straightens and the pressure in the unlatching cylinder allows the gear to lock in the down position. While the gear is extending, the mechanical linkage between the actuating cylinder and the door directional valve positions the directional valve to direct fluid to the door actuating cylinder, raising and locking the doors in the up position as in the gear retraction sequence. The hydraulic pump is shut off when the door latches fall into place, actuating the door limit switches.

T.O. 1B-36D(II)-1

Section VII
Systems Operation

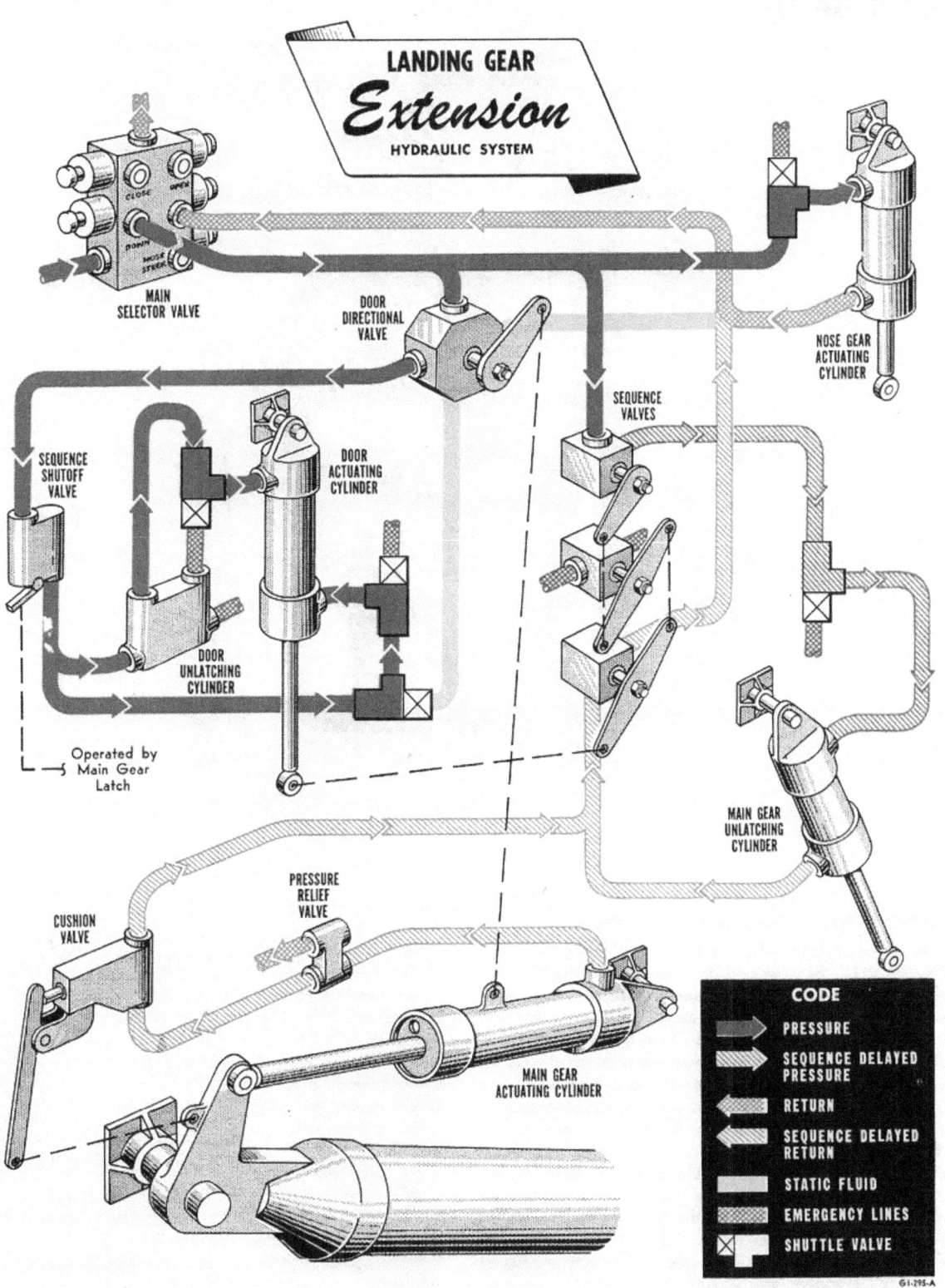

Figure 7-36. (Sheet 1)

365

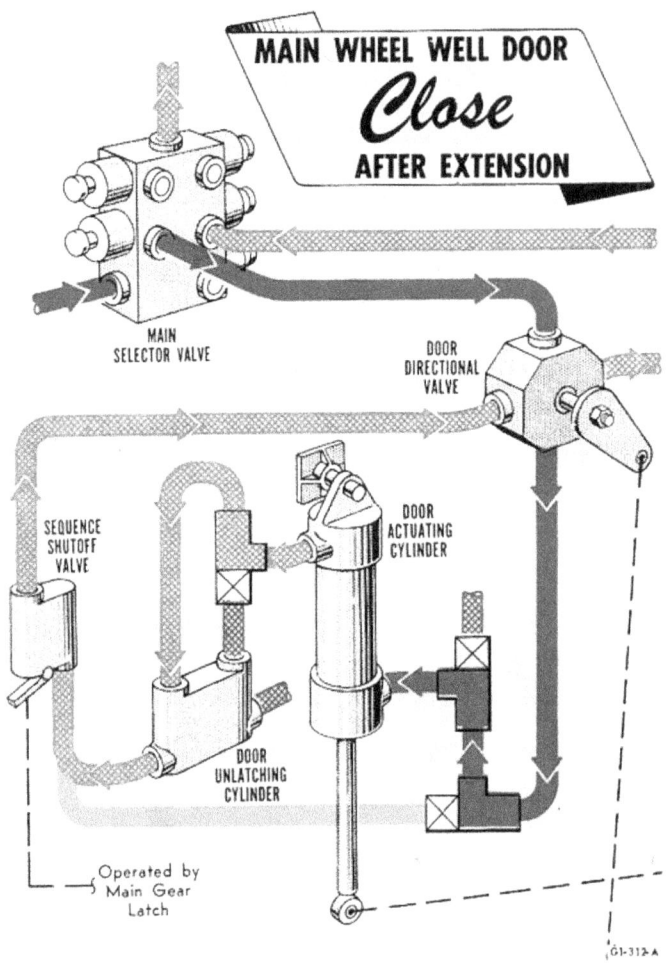

Figure 7-36. (Sheet 2)

LANDING GEAR EMERGENCY EXTENSION.

When the emergency selector valve is placed in the EXTEND LG position and the hand pump is operated, hydraulic fluid under pressure is directed into the emergency gear down line. The pressure is routed to the up side of the door actuating cylinder, to the door unlatching cylinder, and to the nose gear actuating cylinder to extend the nose gear. At the same time, pressure is routed to and stops at the emergency down sequence valve, which is closed. Pressure to the up side of the door actuating cylinder preloads the cylinder in the up position to prevent rapid opening of the door. This also permits easier opening of the door latches. When the fluid passes through the door unlatching cylinder, opening the latches, it enters the down side of the door actuating cylinder to extend the door to the full down position. As the door becomes fully extended, the mechanical linkage between the door actuating cylinder and the sequence valves opens the up sequence valve and the emergency down sequence valve. When the emergency down sequence valve is opened, fluid is routed to the top of the main gear unlatching cylinder and to a port in the cushion valve for preloading the main gear actuating cylinder. The pressure at the top of the unlatching cylinder unlocks the gear and breaks the side brace, allowing the gear to fall of its own weight. The preloading reduces the initial shock of the fall and a restrictor built into the main gear actuating cylinder controls the speed of extension. After the first 10 degrees of extension the passage in the cushion valve, used to preload the actuator, is closed. This allows fluid to return from the actuating cylinder to the main system reservoir through the cushion valve, the up sequence valve, and the up port of the main selector valve. When the gear is fully extended, the side brace straightens and the pressure in the unlatching cylinder allows the gear to lock in the down position. After an emergency hydraulic extension, the main gear doors will remain open.

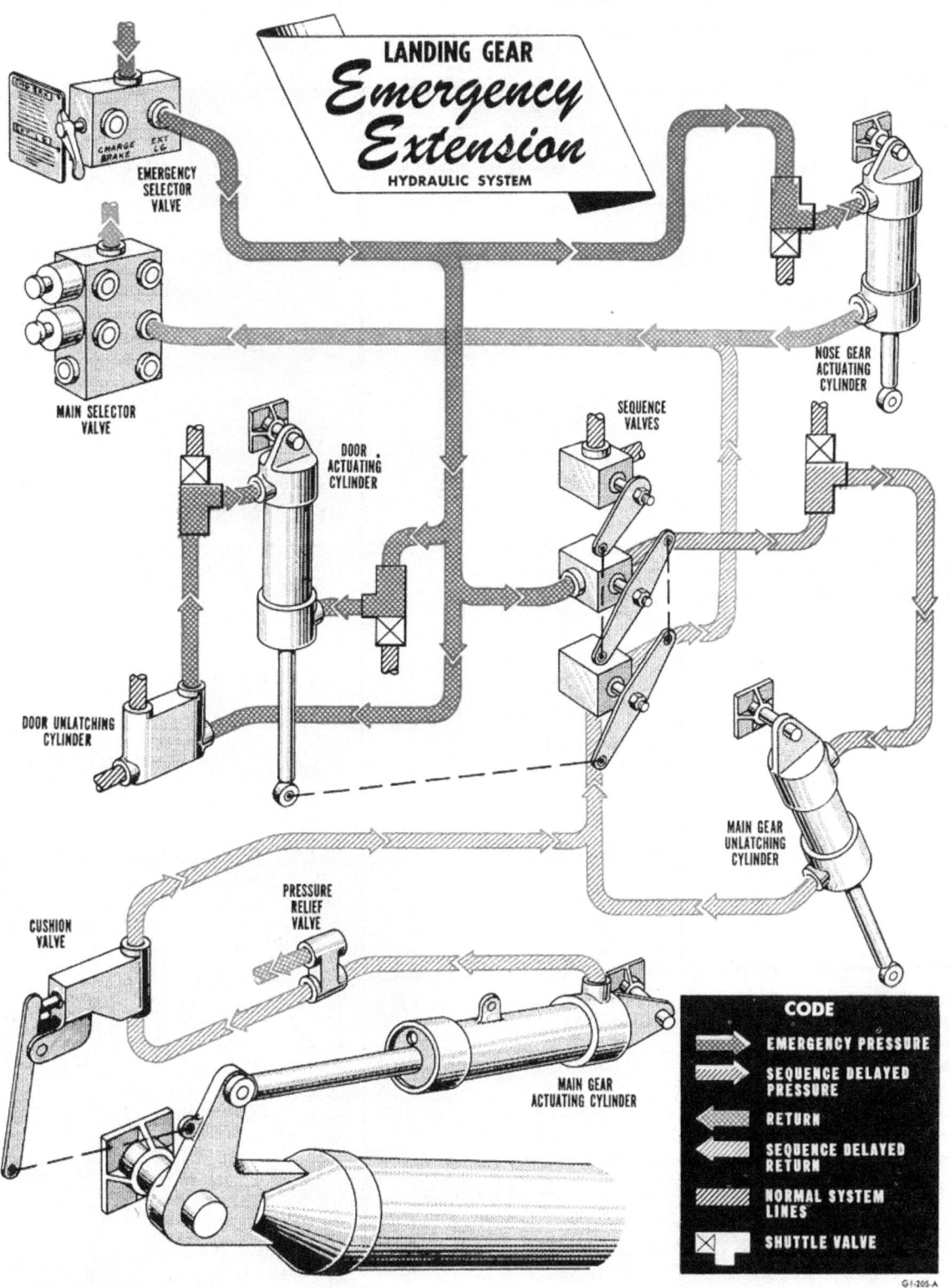

Figure 7-37.

LANDING GEAR SYSTEM TROUBLE SHOOTING.

Listed below are troubles which may be encountered and remedied in flight.

Trouble	Probable Cause	Remedy
All gears fail to retract.	Hydraulic system malfunction.	Refer to "Emergency Landing Gear Operation," Section III.
	Failure of d-c control power.	Check all d-c fuses. Check output to pilot's circuit breaker panel.
	Selector valve not operating.	Check fuses in d-c control system; operate selector valve manually.
	Low fluid supply.	Fill main reservoir to proper level.
	Safety switch malfunction.	Refer to "Emergency Landing Gear Operation," Section III.
Nose gear retracts, canoe doors open, but neither main gear moves.	Main gear latch link rods disconnected.	Connect latch link rods.
	Low fluid supply.	Add fluid to main reservoir.
	Relief valve malfunction.	Retract doors then extend for a short distance. Repeat 2 or 3 times then retract gear.
	Side brace too tight.	Remove two one-quarter inch bolts from nut on side brace. Loosen nut until side brace clearance is not less than .030 inch or not more than .100 inch. Retract gear and replace bolts in nut.
Canoe doors open, nose gear retracts, pressure falls from approximately 2800 to 500 psi and neither main gear moves.	Relief valve cracks open and by-passes fluid.	Reset relief valve by moving landing gear switch to neutral and allowing pressure to fall to zero. Then place switch in RETRACT. If relief valve does not reset enter the bomb bay and tap on relief valve located beneath main hydraulic reservoir.
Left main gear does not retract.	Latch link rod disconnected.	Connect latch link rod.
	Relief valve malfunction.	Extend gear and make several attempts to retract. If gear does not retract enter wing crawlway and tap on relief valve. Repeat retraction attempt.

LANDING GEAR SYSTEM TROUBLE SHOOTING (Cont'd)

Trouble	Probable Cause	Remedy
Nose gear retracts, canoe doors open but main gears do not move (pressure remains at 2800 to 2900 psi).	Main selector valve malfunction.	Move landing gear switch to OFF, to EXTEND, and then to RETRACT.
Nose gear retracts, canoe doors open, both main gears retract half-way and stop. Pressure remains at 2700 to 2900 psi.	Low fluid supply.	With landing gear switch OFF add fluid to main reservoir.
A canoe door does not close after a retraction sequence.	Restrictor in shuttle valve on door actuating jack is jammed.	Loosen nut on restrictor valve and let fluid escape. When the door is up and locked remove the restrictor, clean.
Both canoe doors open 6 to 8 inches and stop during retraction. None of the gears move and gage pressure is approximately 2800 psi.	Emergency selector valve in GEAR RETRACT position.	Place landing gear switch in EXTEND and allow doors to lock closed. Place emergency selector valve in CHARGE BRAKE and then place landing gear switch in RETRACT.
A canoe door starts to close before the gear is fully retracted.	Sequence shutoff valve malfunction.	Place landing gear switch in EXTEND with gunners observing door action. Retract gear one third up and then extend. Repeat 3 or 4 times and then retract. **CAUTION** Let pump cool 2 minutes out of every 10.
Canoe door does not open, gear cannot extend.	Jammed restrictor valve on gear door actuator causing hydraulic lock.	Drain fluid from actuator by loosening nut on "T" fitting on lower end of actuator and push in on plunger protruding from nut.
Main gear and doors operate normally, nose gear extends 10 20 degrees and stops.	Jammed restrictor valve causing hydraulic lock.	Place landing gear switch in neutral, place emergency selector valve in GEAR EXTEND and pump gear down with emergency hand pump. Or loosen line from forward side of nose gear relief valve and allow fluid to escape.
Main gear and doors retract normally, pressure 2800 psi but nose gear will not lock into place. When pressure is relieved nose gear falls freely down.	Striker plate too tight.	Enter radar dome, remove inspection plate and use emergency latching hook or screw driver to push latch into place. **CAUTION** Turn all radar off and leave the landing gear control switch in RETRACT.

Section VII
Systems Operation

LANDING GEAR SYSTEM TROUBLE SHOOTING (Cont'd)

Trouble	Probable Cause	Remedy
Emergency hydraulic reservoir overflows with landing gear switch in RETRACT.	Shuttle valve malfunctions.	Reposition shuttle valves by moving landing gear switch to EXTEND then to RETRACT.
	Bomb bay door switch in OPEN or CLOSE position.	Return bomb bay door switch to neutral position.
No pressure indication.	Pumps not operating.	Check fuses in d-c control system and a-c power to pump.
	Low fluid supply.	Fill main reservoir to proper fluid level.
Main gear retracts; nose gear does not.	Emergency release pin pulled.	Replace pin. Refer to "Emergency Retraction of Nose Landing Gear," Section III.
Pumps do not stop at end of cycle.	One or more limit switches not actuating.	Pull circuit breakers.
	Faulty relay.	Remove pump fuses to prevent overheating.
All gears fail to extend.	Hydraulic system malfunction.	Refer to "Emergency Landing Gear Operation," Section III.
	Failure of d-c control power.	Check fuses in d-c control system and a-c power to pump.
Retraction exceeds time limits.	One pump inoperative.	Check a-c fuses in pump power circuit. Check fuses in a-c power to pumps.
Hydraulic fluid lost during gear operation.	Leaky connections.	Tighten connections, disconnect reservoir pressure line and refill reservoir.
Main gear door fails to retract and lock.	Air speed too high.	Reduce air speed.

NOSE WHEEL STEERING SYSTEM TROUBLE SHOOTING.

Listed below are troubles that may be encountered and remedied in flight.

Trouble	Probable Cause	Remedy
No pressure indication.	Blown fuse.	Check all nose steering fuses. Check circuit breaker on pilot's panel.
	Broken gage line.	Check gage line connections.
No pump action.	Blown fuse.	Check all nose steering fuses. Check circuit breaker on pilot's panel.
No actuation.	Selector valve malfunction.	Manually position selector valve.
	Relief valve stuck in open position.	Lightly tap relief valve.
	Nose gear extension too high.	Bleed nose strut.

BOMB BAY DOOR SYSTEM TROUBLE SHOOTING.

In the event of improper bomb bay door operation the emergency system should be employed as directed in "Bomb Bay Door Emergency Hydraulic System," Section IV. However, listed below are troubles that may be encountered and remedied in flight.

Trouble	Probable Cause	Remedy
Doors do not open, pumps operating.	Hydraulic malfunction.	Refer to "Bomb Bay Door Emergency Hydraulic System," Section IV.
	Solenoid on selector valve not operating.	Depress plunger on selector valve.
Doors do not open, no pump operation.	Control circuit malfunction.	Check circuit breakers and 28-volt d-c fuses.
	Pump power failure.	Check a-c fuses to pump.
Doors open, then close part way.	Door-open pump limit switches out of adjustment.	Hold bomb bay door switch in OPEN position until doors lock open.
Lamp does not light, bomb bay doors open.	Rack selector circuit breaker open.	Close circuit breaker at d-c power panel.
Door operation exceeds time limits.	One pump inoperative.	Check fuses in a-c power to pumps.
Door opens part way and pumps continue to operate.	Bomb bay door switch actuated when bomb bay door safety switch is ON.	Place bomb bay door safety switch OFF.
Doors open part way and fluid pressure ruptures emergency reservoir in aft cabin.	Emergency selector valve at reservoir is not in OFF position.	Place valve in OFF position. Check fluid level in reservoir.

WING AND TAIL ANTI-ICING.

Wing and tail anti-icing is accomplished by passing heated air through the leading edges of the wing and tail surfaces. The heat for this air is obtained from the engine exhaust gases as it flows through the primary heat exchangers. (See figure 4-6.) As the temperature and rate of flow of the anti-icing air depend on such engine operating conditions as the use of dual or single turbo, high or low turbo boost, and high or low engine fan drive, the effectiveness of the anti-icing system is directly influenced by engine operation. Therefore, it may be necessary, in some instances, to operate "off schedule" of the engine power configurations given in Appendix 1 to obtain adequate anti-icing throughout the wide range of icing conditions which may be encountered. Information in the following paragraph describes methods in which the effectiveness of the anti-icing system can be increased by operating the engines "off schedule." For a description of the anti-icing system, refer to "Heat and Anti-Icing System," Section IV.

OFF SCHEDULE OPERATION.

Dual turbo operation increases the anti-icing system air flow over that obtained in single turbo. Closed waste gate limitations with dual turbo require operation at higher rpm with a resulting lower bmep and higher fuel flow than single turbo in the low power range. The charts in figure 7-38 show power plant operating limits from sea level to 30,000 feet with dual turbo throughout the operating range. Additional anti-icing air flow can be obtained by operating the engine fan at high rpm when only low rpm is required for cooling. As shown in figure 5-7, high fan drive is required to prevent the anti-icing air temperature from exceeding the limits at altitudes approaching 25,000 feet.

Above 25,000 feet, if icing is encountered, modulating the dump valve by means of the anti-icing switches is required in addition to high fan drive to prevent the anti-icing air temperature from exceeding the limits. This is accomplished by jiggling the anti-icing switches

Section VII
Systems Operation

Wing and Tail ANTI-ICING
DUAL TURBO POWER SCHEDULE

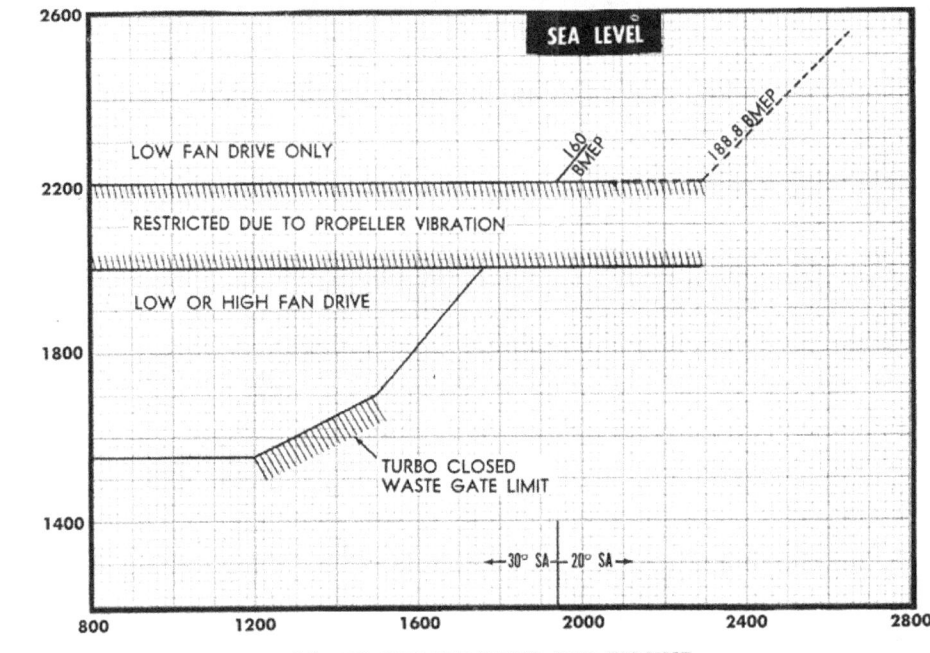

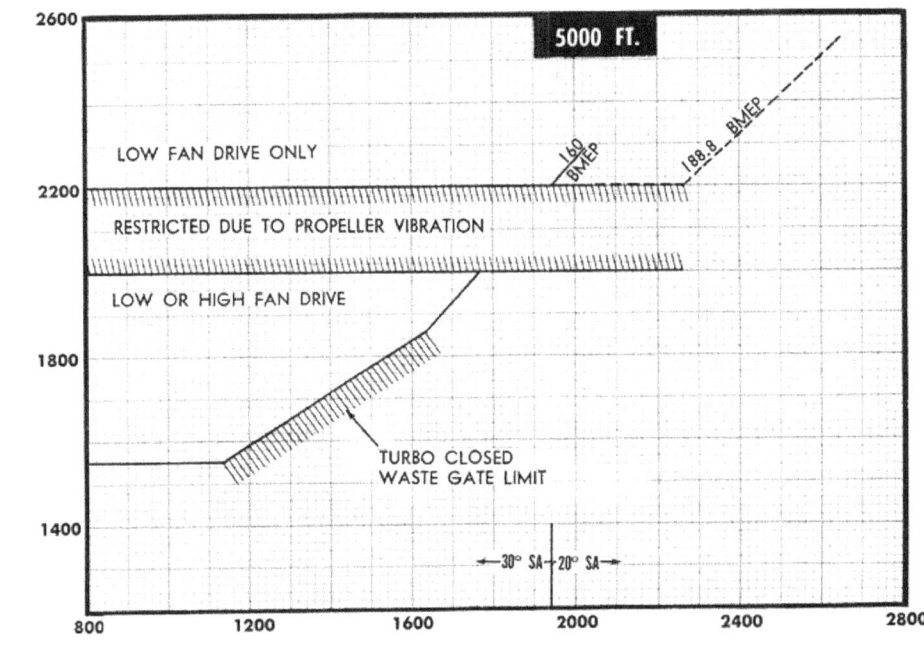

Figure 7-38. (Sheet 1)

Wing and Tail ANTI-ICING
DUAL TURBO POWER SCHEDULE

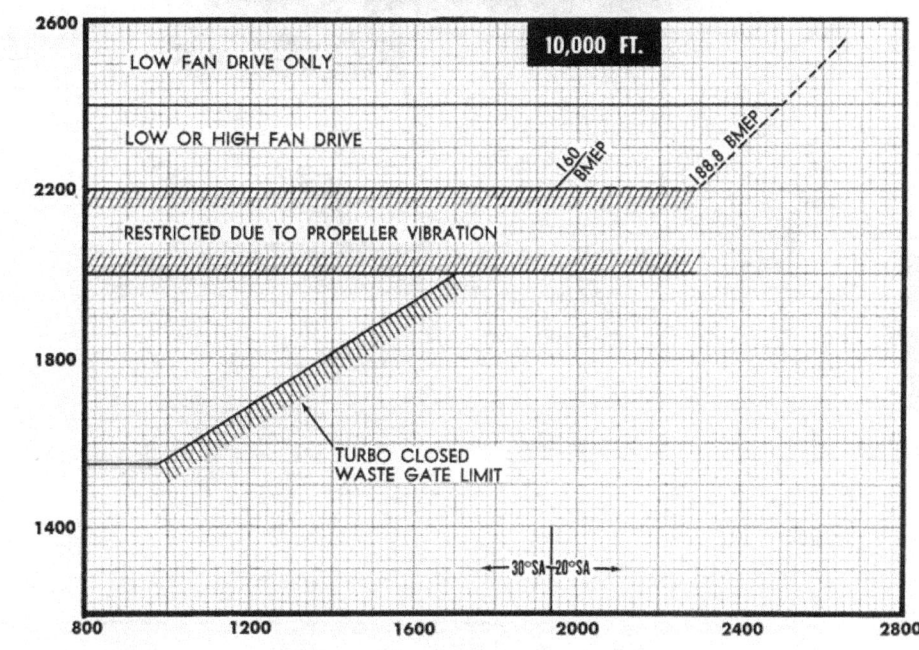

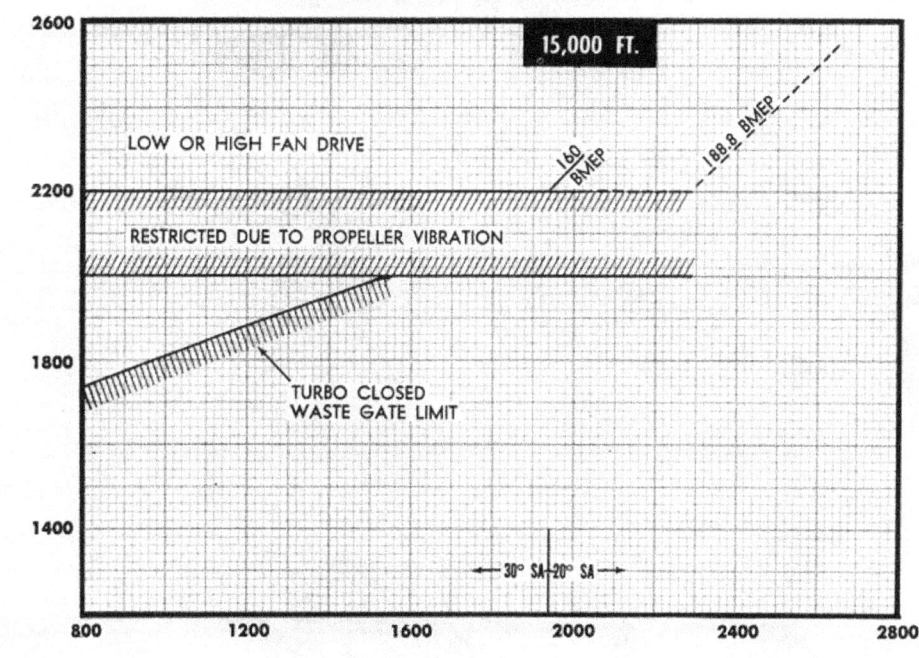

Figure 7-38. (Sheet 2)

Section VII
Systems Operation

T.O. 1B-36D(II)-1

Wing and Tail ANTI-ICING
DUAL TURBO POWER SCHEDULE

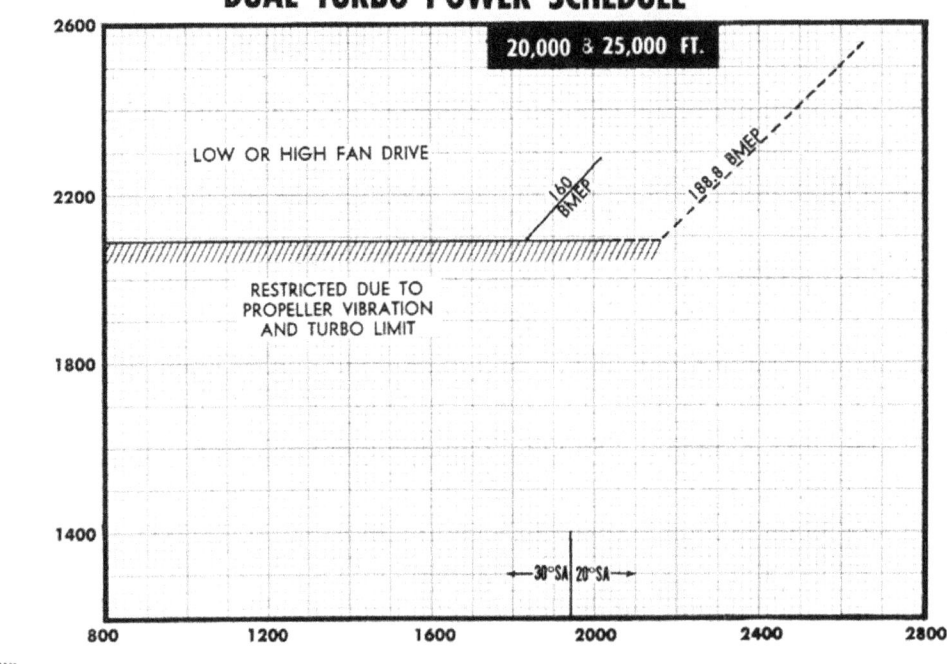

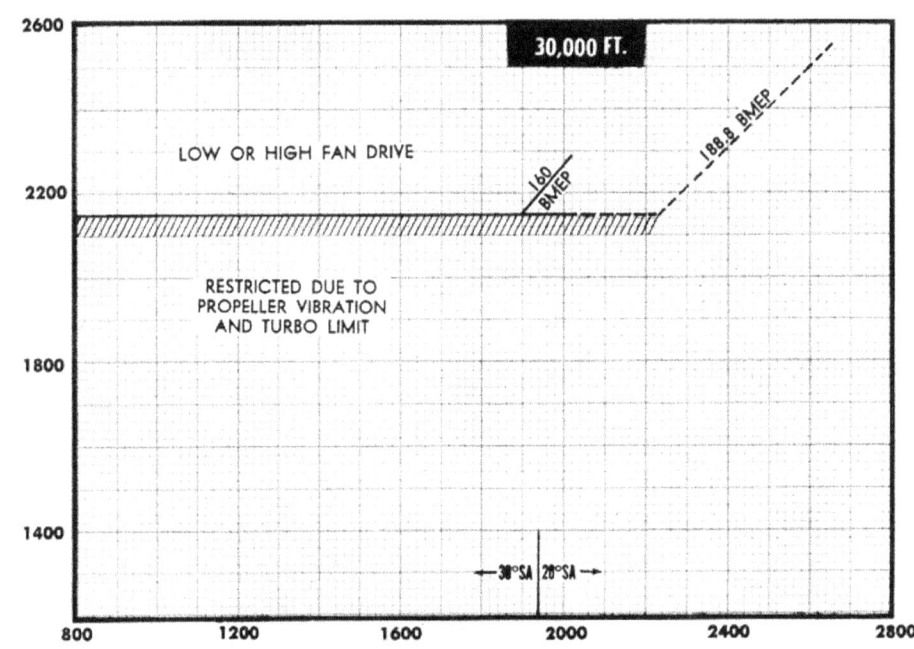

Figure 7-38. (Sheet 3)

from the full ON position toward OFF until the air temperatures are within limits. This reduces the effectiveness of the system, but icing encountered above 25,000 feet is normally light. The use of high fan drive may result in over-cooling the engine. If the CHT cannot be maintained above 170°C when the mixture setting is in manual lean, an increase in CHT may be obtained by first returning to the 20-degree spark advance position and then increasing the fuel-air ratio slightly.

This, however, will increase fuel consumption somewhat. If the CHT still remains appreciably lower than 170°C, it will be necessary to revert to low fan drive. If the carburetor preheat system is in use and the use of high fan drive reduces the CAT. below 0°C with closed intercooler shutters, an indication of carburetor icing will dictate reverting to low fan drive.

SPECIFIC OPERATING INSTRUCTIONS.

The wing and tail anti-icing systems must be placed in operation as soon as ice formation is observed on either the wing or tail surfaces. Icing conditions can be detected by observing other airplane surfaces for ice formation or by observation of water droplets or ice on the outside of the pilots' enclosure windows when the ambient air temperature is 0°C (32°F) or below. At night, frequent checks of the wing and tail surfaces should be made for indications of ice formation. When operation of the anti-icing systems is required, an attempt should be made to hold the flight path and brake horsepower constant, changing other operating conditions if necessary. As the severity of icing conditions will vary over a wide range, the necessary steps to obtain adequate anti-icing will also vary. The following procedure indicates steps to be taken progressively to obtain satisfactory anti-icing. When this procedure is used, the propeller and engine normal operating limitations given in Section V and the dual turbo waste gate limits shown in figure 7-38 must be observed.

1. Wing anti-icing and cabin heat and tail anti-icing control switches—ON.

Note

To insure full closure of the dump valves, begin this operation with the valves in the full open position and then hold the switches in the ON position for a minimum of 25 seconds. This will prevent the actuators from "torquing out" before the valves have completely closed.

2. If operating in single turbo, increase engine rpm above the dual turbo closed waste gate limit shown in figure 7-38.

Note

To maintain and approximately constant thrust horsepower, decrease torque pressure 7 psi for each 100 rpm increase in engine speed. If applicable, retard the spark and increase the mixture setting to NORMAL before performing the above step.

3. Engine supercharger switches—BOTH.

4. Cabin temperature control switch—As required but not to exceed 105°C duct temperature for the enclosure defrosting air.

5. All fan speed control switches—HIGH RPM.

CAUTION

To prevent exceeding the structural limitations of the fan, refer to "Fan Speed Limitations," Section V.

6. Increase engine rpm.

7. If icing of the tail becomes critical, the temperature of the tail anti-icing air can be increased by jiggling the cabin temperature control switch toward the DECREASE position.

8. Change altitude to reduce the severity of the icing conditions.

Note

During all operation do not allow the wing anti-icing temperature to exceed 180°C or the tail anti-icing temperature to exceed 215°C.

Ice Runback and Afterfreezing.

Since the anti-icing system extends to only 12 per cent of the wing chord, in particularly severe conditions, formation of ice aft of the front spar may occur due to "runback" and "after freezing." De-icing of this portion of the wing can be accomplished only by changing altitude until an ambient temperature above 0°C (32°F) is reached.

AUTOPILOT SYSTEM.

A fundamental autopilot design assumption is that the airplane to be controlled is rigid. This assumption applies to small airplanes with negligible error. Large airplanes, however, must either be more flexible or must sacrifice useful load for additional weight of structure.

CHARACTERISTIC RESPONSE CURVE.

The characteristic E-6 response curve is shown in figure 7-39. Note that servo correction signals at any given time are proportional to the remaining error. Normal

Section VII
Systems Operation

T.O. 1B-36D(II)-1

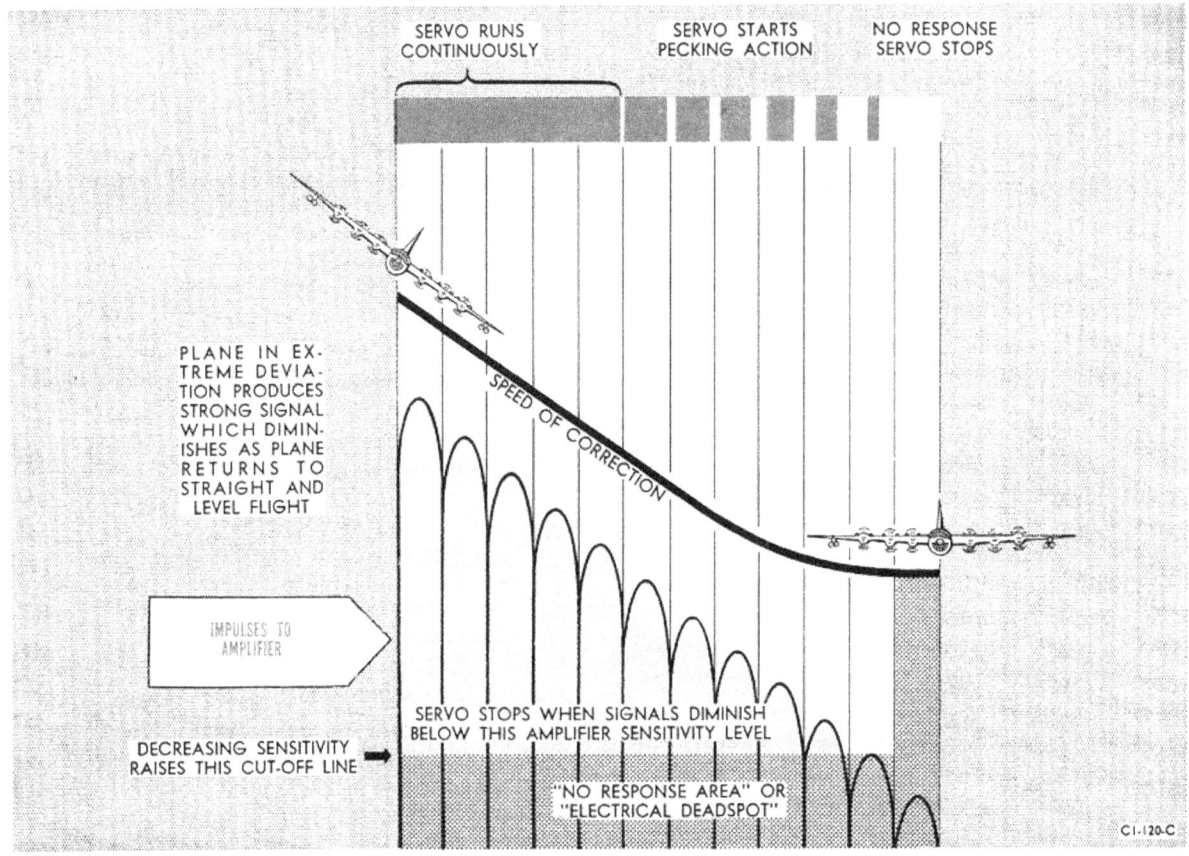

Figure 7-39. Autopilot Response Curve

corrections should be smooth with no overshoot or undershoot. The shaded electrical deadspot area is a graphical representation of the effect of the sensitivity controls.

FAMILIARIZATION WITH CALIBRATION CONTROLS.

Before you attempt to set the autopilot calibration controls for optimum performance, study the effect of each control by operating it through its range of adjustment while all other settings are constant. Use the basic settings tabulated in "Autopilot," Section IV for the initial calibration control configuration. Turn on the autopilot, trim the airplane, and engage autopilot. Go down to the chassis and manipulate each of the following controls:

Sensitivity.

Turn all three sensitivity knobs down near zero and notice that the aircraft becomes sluggish but still flies a good heading straight and level. Turn them all up to 10 and notice that the controls become a little jittery but the aircraft itself is not affected and still flies straight and level. Turn them back to zero again and notice that you can still make a normal maximum bank turn with the turn control knob. Carry sensitivity as high as possible—further adjustment here is somewhat futile.

Ratio.

Turn all three ratio knobs to zero and notice that the aircraft gets "sloppy" in all three axes. Notice the altimeter and compass. The aircraft will hold neither altitude nor heading. Try a maximum bank turn with the turn control knob. Notice how long it takes to get into the bank and establish any degree of co-ordination. Set the knobs back to the basic setting and increase them (one axis at a time) toward 10. In aileron, notice that a wing tip "hunt" occurs near a knob setting of 7.5 to 8. In rudder (use caution) notice that the tail begins to "hunt" and shake near a knob setting of 8. In elevator, notice that the aircraft begins to "porpoise" near 8.5 to 9. At these increased settings the aircraft is overcorrecting for small gyro displacements, therefore overshooting gyro null points. The aircraft reacts this way because too much control movement is being used to correct for these small displacements. Once this overshoot is started, it easily becomes divergent. Ratio settings are the most important ones on the autopilot. They should be your first adjustment in correcting for an abnormal flight condition.

Throttling.

Turn aileron ratio up just to the point where a wing tip "hunt" appears. Then turn aileron throttling to zero and notice that the "hunt" increases in frequency and amplitude. Now turn aileron throttling up to 10 and notice that the "hunt" has practically disappeared or at least has been reduced to a very low frequency and amplitude. Try the same procedure with the elevator axis. Be very careful if you try it with the rudder —this is one of the best ways to develop a divergent tail shake (empennage oscillating about yaw axis with increasing amplitude). Throttling is second only to ratio in importance. These knobs are particularly handy in getting rid of bumps, shakes, and shudders during high speed turns.

Automatic Recovery.

The automatic recovery switch is obstructed on most airplanes, but the knobs on the calibrator are still active. Moving them with the autopilot engaged will change the attitude of the aircraft—leave them alone. These knobs may have been set from their basic settings to reduce the "hash level" in the autopilot.

E-FS and FS.

These knobs were used to co-ordinate formation stick turns. They are still in the circuit but they should not be changed. Moving E-FS will change the pitch attitude of the aircraft.

TC Co-Ordination.

Leave this knob at zero. Turns are co-ordinated with the rudder gain knob on the auxiliary calibrator.

Bomb Co-Ordination.

This knob has little or no dynamic effect on any axis. Set it at 1.8.

Rate Co-Ordination.

Turn this knob to zero and notice that the tail begins to "hunt." Make a small turn and notice that the aircraft "fish-tails" (mild oscillating about yaw axis) around the turn. Place this knob at 10 and leave it there. This circuit still does not provide enough damping for this aircraft.

Up-Elevator Co-Ordination.

Go into a 20-degree bank turn and turn this knob up to 6. Notice that the aircraft is climbing in the turn. Reduce the setting to zero. Notice that the aircraft is diving in the turn. Adjust this knob so that altitude is held constant during turns in both directions. This knob may require frequent adjustment on long flights. It should be readjusted every time a large change in manual elevator trim is required. A compromise setting may be required to equalize performance in right and left turns. This is caused by the exceedingly long length of elevator rigging in the aircraft.

Rudder Gain.

Set this knob at 10, and notice that the aircraft makes a skidding turn. Set it at zero and notice that the aircraft makes a slipping turn. Adjust for a co-ordinated turn and leave it alone, except for altitude corrections.

Aileron Roll Rate.

Turn this knob to zero and go into a turn. Notice that the aircraft is on the verge of a wing tip "hunt." It will probably overshoot the roll-in and roll-out of the turn and wind up with a wing tip "hunt." Turn the knob up to 10 and notice how sluggish the response is during the roll-in and roll-out of a turn. This knob is very sensitive—adjust it to the point just below which the aircraft begins to "hunt" and overshoot in turns.

Rudder Roll Rate.

First try the zero setting and then go into a 20-degree bank turn. Notice that the aircraft tends to have a rudder "bump" (transient instability about the yaw axis) when rolling in and out of the turn. Now turn the knob up to 10 and notice that the aircraft actually "skids" when rolling in and out of the turn. This circuit puts in bottom rudder for any roll. The amount depends on the knob setting. Adjust for the type roll-in and roll-out turns that you prefer. Once set, this knob rarely needs readjustment.

Compass Maximum Bank.

Note
Of the four knobs on the directional coupler amplifier, this is the only one of interest to the pilot. The other three knobs concern the operation of the autopilot in "second station."

Turn this knob (figure 4-23) to zero and displace the slaved gyro magnetic compass (with the caging knob) 10 degrees and hold it there. Notice that the aircraft takes up a 12.5 degree bank (1.25 degrees per degree of heading displacement). Recover, turn the knob to 10, and repeat the procedure. Notice that the aircraft

Section VII
Systems Operation

T.O. 1B-36D(II)-1

takes up a 26.5 degree bank (2.65 degrees bank per degree of heading displacement). In turbulence or at low air speeds (150 IAS), reduction to zero is recommended. Normally, however, 2.5 is the optimum setting.

On airplanes with the N-1 compass system, turn the compass maximum bank knob to zero, displace the directional gyro about 2 degrees in the shock mount, and hold it there. (Notice that the airplane takes up a 2.5-degree bank (1.25 degrees per degree of heading displacement.) Recover, turn the knob to 10, and repeat the procedure. Notice that the airplane takes up a 6.0-degree bank (3.00 degrees bank per degree of heading displacement). In turbulence or at low air speeds (150 IAS), reduction to zero is recommended. Normally, however, 2.5 is the optimum setting.

IN-FLIGHT ADJUSTMENT OF AUTOPILOT.

Now that you are familiar with the individual calibration controls, you must learn to refine the basic settings for top performance under all conditions. All adjustments herein pertain to *minor* variations from the recommended nominal settings given in section IV. No attempt should be made to adjust the autopilot without using the nominal settings as a starting point. The following procedure is recommended for in-flight adjustment.

1. Upon reaching a safe altitude, turn the autopilot ON.

2. Trim the aircraft very delicately for "hands off" straight and level flight.

Note

Do this very meticulously because you are setting up the attitude the autopilot will interpret from the reference gyros and maintain electronically.

3. When the green lights begin to flicker, engage the autopilot. In the event that one of the electrical trim knobs is oscillating when the engage switch is pressed, the autopilot will be out of "electrical trim" and the knob will have to be adjusted. If one knob is moving rapidly, hold it at its point of least resistance while you press the engage switch. Another method involves the use of the calibration unit. Turn throttling on the oscillating axis up to 10. If the knob still oscillates, reduce sensitivity on the same axis until oscillation stops. Engage autopilot and set calibration knobs back to their normal settings.

4. Crack the turn control knob out of its detent—first one direction, then the other. If the aircraft banks momentarily in the wrong direction then goes into the correct turn, the autopilot needs trimming. Repeat the check in the other direction before making any adjustments. Find out which surface is the biggest offender. Use only the autopilot trim knobs.

  a. Lift up the wing that is dropping in the wrong direction.

  b. Try the turn control again. If the bank in the wrong direction persists, the ailerons are not out of trim. Trim the wing tip back where it was.

  c. Trim in a reasonable amount of bottom rudder for a turn in the desired direction. Try the turn control knob again. Most of the maladjusted trim should be gone. Both surfaces could have been out of adjustment.

  d. If the condition persists, disengage the autopilot, retrim manually, and repeat this procedure.

You should now be set up for a good straight and level flight.

5. Try a few 20-degree bank turns and see if the aircraft holds altitude in both directions. If not, adjust the UP-E co-ordination knob toward 10 for "nose up" and toward zero for "nose down."

6. Check the needle and ball for co-ordination and adjust the rudder gain knob for slip or skid.

7. Check the roll-in and roll-out. If the aircraft "bumps" or "hunts" (transient instability in the yaw axis), turn the rudder throttling up and rudder ratio down.

CAUTION

Do not use ratio unless necessary. Turn rudder throttling up before turning the rudder roll rate up. Then turn the rudder ratio down if necessary. Use these knobs in the above order and use only as much as required to eliminate the oscillation.

8. Check the recovery of the aircraft when in the "second station" automatic recovery.

Note

Establish optimum performance with the autopilot control panel before attempting to adjust "second station" automatic flight controls.

  a. Displace the pilot's data indicator to obtain the maximum bank angle; then go into "second station" automatic.

Note

The K( ) system configuration must be in BOMB and SYNC before placing the E-2 switch in AUTOMATIC.

  b. Observe the PDI for undershoot or overshoot of the zero point when the aircraft automatically centers it.

  c. If the aircraft undershoots, correct by increasing proportional range.

  d. If the aircraft overshoots, correct by decreasing proportional range.

MALFUNCTION AND CORRECTIONS.

If the autopilot appears to be maladjusted and abnormal flight response appears, there are two questions you should ask yourself.

    a. What has changed?

    b. What would I be doing to the controls to make the aircraft fly like this?

Divergent Rudder Shake.

If the aircraft shakes violently in the yaw axis with increasing amplitude either in turns or straight and level, use the following procedure:

1. Disengage autopilot and go into a sharp bank turn. Level out when shake disappears.
2. Set rudder ratio at 4 or below.
3. Set rudder throttling at 10.
4. Set compass maximum bank at 0.
5. If rudder shake is only in "second station" automatic operation, request radar-bombardier to reduce directional stiffness (proportional range).
6. Re-engage autopilot and try it again.

Rudder Hunt.

If the aircraft oscillates constantly at a regular frequency in the yaw axis either in turns or in straight and level flight, use the following procedure:

1. Reduce rudder ratio.
2. Set rate co-ordination up to 10.

Sluggish Rudder.

If the aircraft is sluggish in yaw and will not hold heading, use the following corrective measures:

1. Increase rudder ratio.
2. Set rate co-ordination at 10.
3. Increase directional stiffness (compass maximum bank or, if in second station, proportional range).

Nose Hunt in Turns.

If the aircraft oscillates in the yaw axis in turns or appears to make turns in steps, use the following corrective measures:

1. Increase rudder throttling.
2. Set rate co-ordination to 10.
3. Decrease rudder ratio.
4. For modified autopilot, decrease rudder roll rate.

Wing Tip Hunt.

If the aircraft oscillates constantly at small but regular frequency in the roll axis and has no noticeable yaw, use the following procedure:

1. Reduce aileron ratio.
2. Increase aileron throttling.
3. Increase aileron roll rate.

Loose rigging is very capable of causing a wing tip "hunt," but it is usually accompanied by a yaw "hunt."

The combination produces a "dutch roll" (wing tip describing an ellipse). Loose rigging should be spotted by the general feel of the controls at the higher altitudes. If loose rigging is suspected the following procedure will confirm your suspicion and alleviate the problem to some extent.

1. Rudder ratio at 1 or 2.
2. Rudder throttling at 10.
3. Increase aileron ratio until the "hunt" stops.
4. Write up "Loose Rigging" in the Form 1.
5. If just one wing or the cross rigging is loose, adjustment will not help.

Sluggish Roll Axis.

(Do not confuse this condition with wing tip "hunt.") If the aircraft is "sloppy" in heading, occassionally drops a wing, and "wallows" erratically in straight and level flight, use the following procedures:

1. Increase aileron ratio.
2. Increase directional stiffness (compass maximum bank toward 10).

Aircraft Dips Wing in Opposite Direction when Starting Turn.

If the aircraft dodges in the wrong direction before going into a turn, the following corrective action should be used:

1. Go through electrical trim procedure discussed under "In-Flight Adjustment of Autopilot," of this section.
2. If this does not help, the vertical flight gyro is faulty.

Note

If this condition occurs in both directions, the equipment is faulty or the rigging is exceptionally bad.

Aircraft Overshoots Roll Out Of Turn Made With Turn Control Knob.

If the aircraft has a slight roll overshoot followed by a slow yaw overshoot recovery, try the following remedy:

1. Move the turn control back in to detent very slowly.
2. Turn aileron ratio down.
3. Turn aileron throttling up.
4. Turn aileron roll rate toward 10.

PDI Goes off Center During Bomb Run.

If the pilot's data indicator (PDI) goes off center when control is transferred into "second station" automatic and stays off for the entire run, the aircraft-bombing computer-autopilot combination may be out of trim. If the PDI jumps off center quickly when control is transferred, the trim of the aircraft may not be aligned with the PDI. For corrective action:

1. Center the PDI with the autopilot rudder trim knob.

2. Use the aileron trim knob to keep the wings level and the elevator trim knob to control the pitch attitude.

Note

Do not use the turn control to center the PDI.

If the PDI drifts slowly off center, and the above corrective measures do not keep it centered, the PDI synchro, the bombing computer-autopilot syncro, or both, may be misaligned. If a misalignment is indicated, write it up for ground maintenance.

Green Lights Will Not Come On.

If the green lights fail to come on, try the following procedures:

1. Check that all circuit breakers are in. There are two on the autopilot calibrator chassis, and one on the copilot panel.

2. See if the trim knobs are effective. Turn the knobs both ways and see if they drive back. If one is inoperative, turn it by hand until the green lights come on; then engage the autopilot. If it seems too erratic in one axis, pull out the tubes located in the amplifier on the main autopilot chassis for that axis, and drive the trim knobs by hand until the lights come on.

3. If one of the tubes is burned out, there are some spares in the spare turbo amplifier. The TE-5 is interchangeable with the 1274.

4. Work the autopilot release switches on the control wheels a few times. If the green lights remain out when the autopilot tubes are lighted and the trim knobs are responding properly, it is a good indication that the autopilot release switches are open. If the switches cannot be closed, they can be by-passed with a jumper to engage the autopilot. Momentarily short terminals 1 and 2 on the "Autopilot Terminal Strip" to see if the lights come on. If the lamps light, place a jumper between the terminals, engage the autopilot, and use it as normal.

WARNING

The release switches are now by-passed and cannot be used for disengaging. To disengage the autopilot, place the autopilot power switch in the OFF position or disengage each axis individually from the pedestal.

Elevator Trim Knob Malfunction.

If the first few trim knob adjustments do nothing and the last one produces a violent change, the following procedures will apply:

1. Increase elevator ratio until a "hunt" appears.

2. Remove the "hunt" with elevator throttling.

3. Shake the control column when you put in a correction.

Autopilot Becomes Sluggish.

If the aircraft "wallows" after 10 to 15 hours, the following corrective procedure should be used. The aircraft is much lighter now and is probably overcorrecting rather than "wallowing."

1. Reduce ratio in the oscillating axis.

2. Reduce directional stiffness.

Aircraft Precesses.

If the aircraft precesses, it is probably caused by the slaved gyro magnetic compass or the N-1 high latitude compass.

1. Make sure the navigator has the slave switch IN or the power switch on.

2. Have the compasses checked.

Section VIII
CREW DUTIES

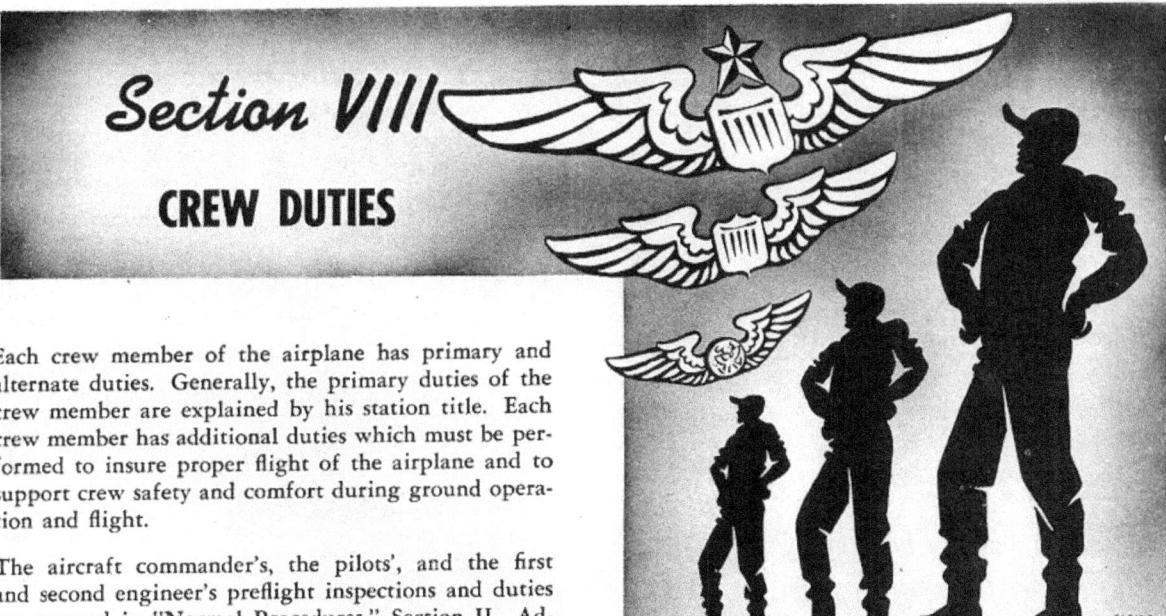

Each crew member of the airplane has primary and alternate duties. Generally, the primary duties of the crew member are explained by his station title. Each crew member has additional duties which must be performed to insure proper flight of the airplane and to support crew safety and comfort during ground operation and flight.

The aircraft commander's, the pilots', and the first and second engineer's preflight inspections and duties are covered in "Normal Procedures," Section II. Additional duties and responsibilities of other crew members, including the aircraft commander, are assigned in the following text. It is your individual responsibility to be familiar with each item of equipment and to be able to inspect it thoroughly for any irregularities. Don't let this inspection become so routine that you check it off as completed without doing a thorough job. Remember, it is not just your life at stake but also the lives of your fellow crew members.

AIRCRAFT COMMANDER.

The aircraft commander is responsible for the issuance of instructions governing all phases of flight operation. His duties and preflight inspection are given in "Normal Procedures," Section II. His responsibilities with regard to formal crew briefing are discussed in the following paragraphs.

RESPONSIBILITIES.

A formal crew briefing should be conducted by the aircraft commander as soon as possible after detailed mission planning. The first item that the aircraft commander should cover in his crew briefing is a recapitulation of the mission plan to insure that all crew members are completely familiar with the requirements to be accomplished. In case of doubt in any crew member's mind, the aircraft commander should completely review that phase of the mission. He should discuss personal equipment to be carried and assign additional duties such as compartment commanders, and the drawing of extra parachutes, water jugs, and lunches to the various crew members. Before dismissing the crew, he should again check to make certain that each member is aware of the schedule for reporting to the aircraft, of station time, and of take-off time. If the aircraft commander has paid close attention to the pre-mission planning and has conducted his briefing well, one of the most difficult phases of flying a mission will have been accomplished successfully.

Personal Equipment Requirements.

Personal equipment plays such an important part in the safety and comfort of the crew during a flight that the aircraft commander must never assume that all crew members are adequately equipped. It is his responsibility to make certain prior to flight that each crew member knows what equipment he must carry. He will perform a formal crew inspection before boarding the aircraft. Personal equipment used in the B-36 is similar to that used in several other aircraft. In the briefing that you will attend prior to flight, either the operations officer or the aircraft commander will specify the equipment needed on the specific flight for which you have been briefed.

Common sense will tell you that if you are scheduled for any altitude work you will need heavy clothing, oxygen equipment, and bail-out bottles plus your normal gear. Keep the cabin heat at a minimum when flying over cold regions so that your crew may wear their heavy clothing with comfort. In this manner, if an emergency occurs, the crew will be properly clothed for survival. Oxygen masks will be carried on all flights by all crew members regardless of altitudes to be flown. The following additional minimum clothing and equipment will be carried by each crew member on all flights above 28,000 feet:

1. Oxygen mask, pressure demand (type A-13, A-13A, or A-15) with adapter for use with H-2 emergency

Section VIII
Crew Duties

cylinder (bail-out bottle). Demand oxygen mask, type A-14, may be substituted when foregoing types are not available, but only for flights up to 34,000 feet. No attempt will be made to use the type A-14 as a pressure breathing mask.

2. Emergency oxygen cylinder, type H-2, attached to parachute.

3. Helmet, flying, intermediate, type A-11, standard.

4. Goggles, type B-8, for eye and face protection in case of a high altitude bail-out.

5. Jacket, flying, winter, type B-11, standard, or M-1.

6. Trousers, flying, winter, type A-10, standard.

7. Gloves, flying, winter, type A-9A, or gloves, flying, intermediate, type A-11A, insert glove, rayon.

8. Shoes, flying, intermediate, type A-6A.

For overwater flights the following minimum personal equipment will be carried in addition to the above:

1. Mae West for each crew member.
2. Gibson Girl radio.
3. One-man life raft for each crew member.
4. One 20-man life raft for crew.
5. Anti-exposure suit for each crew member.
6. Applicable survival kits.

Time Schedules.

It is very important that all crew members know crew inspection time, when to complete their preflights, final crew briefing, etc. The aircraft commander, assisted by the pilot and copilot, should see that all crew members meet these schedules; nothing makes a crew more slovenly than stragglers. Insist on promptness!

RADAR OBSERVER.

The radar observer operates the radar set and the K-( ) bombing system. Following is an abbreviated check list for this position, an abbreviated check list for the K-( ) system, and a preflight check list for the Special Bombing System.

Note

All pertinent information, checks, and cross-checks will be made over interphone.

This aircraft has snap action bomb bay doors.

PREFLIGHT

1. Mission Planning
   a. Preflight Time .... RADAR SHOP NOTIFIED
   b. Mission Orders .... CHECKED
   c. Target Data .... CHECKED
   d. Blank Forms .... CHECKED
   e. Target Study .... COMPLETED
   f. Ultrasonic Requirements .... IF APPLICABLE
   g. Flight Plan and Weather .. CHECKED WITH NAVIGATOR
   h. Form 781 (Form I) and Maintenance Log .. CHECKED

2. Preflight (Arrival at Aircraft)
   a. Periscope Sight Cover .... REMOVED
   b. Bomb Door Ground Locks .... INSTALLED
   c. Bomb Door Limit Switches .... INSPECTED
   d. Racks and Bombs .... CHECKED
   e. K-38 Camera .... MANUALLY OPERATE
   f. IFI Station Bomb
      Bay #4 .... OXYGEN REGULATOR CHECKED
   g. Circuit Breakers Bulkhead 8.0 .... ON
   h. Circuit Breakers Bulkhead 7.0 .... ON
   i. Circuit Breakers Bulkhead 6.0 .... ON
   j. IFI Station Bomb
      Bay #1 .... OXYGEN REGULATOR CHECKED
   k. Equipment in Radome .... CHECKED
   l. K-System Gyro Fuses in Left Fwd Power Panel . CHECKED
   m. Spare Amplifier and Tube Kit .... CHECKED
   n. Radar External Power Switch (If Applicable) ... ON
   o. Constant Speed Motor Switch .... ON
   p. AM-193 .... STAB
   q. Computer Amplifier Rack and Fuses .... CHECKED
   r. K-System Component Cabling .... CHECKED
   s. Stab Amplifier Rack and Fuses .... CHECKED
   t. Directional Amplifier (Coupler) .... CHECKED
   u. Radar Junction Box and Fuses .... CHECKED

3. Preflight (Station)
   a. Bomb Door Safety Switch .... OFF
   b. Bomb Bay Selector Switch .... OFF
   c. Intervalometer .... TRAIN AND ZERO
   d. Bomb Panel Circuit Breakers .... OFF
   e. Special Bomb Panel Circuit Breakers .... OFF
   f. Camera Circuit Breakers .... OFF
   g. Tone Switch .... OFF
   h. Bomb Master Switch .... OFF
   i. Special Bomb Panel Rack Release ..... AS DESIRED
   j. Bomb Arming Switch .... OFF
   k. Salvo Switch & Light .... SAFETIED AND OFF
   l. O-15 Camera Switch .... OFF
   m. Pressure Pump Switch .... ON
   n. Preheat and Cooling Switch .... AS DESIRED
   o. Normal & Private Interphone .... CHECKED
   p. Oxygen .... CHECKED
   q. Table and Instrument Lights .... CHECKED
   r. Preflight Radar in Accordance With SOP
   s. Preflight O-15 and K-38 Camera
   t. Turn Radar Off

4. Duties at Station Time
   a. Personal Equipment .... STOWED
   b. Survival and Combat Equipment .... STOWED
   c. Safety Belt .... CHECKED

5. Pre-Taxi Duties
   a. Aircraft Power .... CHECKED WITH F/E
   b. Function Switch .... STAB
   c. Fwd Entrance Ladder .... STOWED
   d. Ground Cord & Nose Wheel Down Lock ..... STOWED
   e. Forward Entrance Hatch .... CLOSED
   f. All Circuit Breakers & Switches ..... AS BRIEFED
   g. Camera Doors .... CLOSED
   h. APS-23 Power Switch ..... STAND BY AFTER JET START, IF DESIRED

INFLIGHT

1. Turn On and Operate K-System
2. Pre-Bombing Check (Actual Drop)
   a. Ballistic Data .... CHECKED
   b. Bomb Panel Circuit Breakers .... ON
   c. Special Bombing Panel Circuit Breakers . AS BRIEFED
   d. Master Switch .... ON
   e. Bomb Arming Switch .... AS BRIEFED
   f. Bomb Station Indicator Light Switch .... ON
   g. Special Normal Rack Switch .... AS BRIEFED
   h. Vertical Camera Circuit Breakers .... ON

Section VIII
Crew Duties

    i. Intervalometer . . . . AS BRIEFED
    j. E-6 Autopilot Ratio . . . . SET FOR AUTOMATIC RUN AT BOMBING ALTITUDE
    k. Bomb Bay Selector Switches . . . . ON JUST PRIOR TO RELEASE AND OFF IMMEDIATELY AFTER DOORS CLOSE
    l. Special Bombing Rack Selector Switches ON JUST PRIOR TO RELEASE AND OFF IMMEDIATELY AFTER DOORS CLOSE
    m. Bomb Bay Door Safety Switch . . . . . ON JUST PRIOR TO RELEASE AND OFF IMMEDIATELY AFTER DOORS CLOSE

3. Pre-Bombing Check (RBS)
    a. Ballistic Data . . . . CHECKED
    b. Bomb Bay Doors . . . . CLOSED & CIRCUIT BREAKER OUT
    c. Bomb Bay Tank Safety Switch . . . . NO SALVO
    d. Bomb Bay Selector Switches . . . . OFF
    e. Salvo Circuit Breakers . . . . PULLED
    f. Pilot's & Bombardier's Salvo Switches . . . . OFF
    g. Notify A/C that RBS Safety Check List is Complete
    h. All other Bomb Panel Circuit Breakers . . . . ON
    i. Master Switch . . . . ON
    j. Vertical Camera Intervalometer . . . . ON
    k. Vertical Camera Door . . . . OPEN
    l. Intervalometer . . . . AS DESIRED
    m. Vertical Camera Intervalometer . . . . AS BRIEFED
    n. Tone . . . . CHECKED WITH RBS

4. RBS and Camera Safety Check List
    a. Bomb Bay Doors . . . . CLOSED
    b. All Salvo Switches . . . . OFF
    c. Tank Salvo Switches . . . . NO SALVO POSITION
    d. Bomb Bay Selector Switches . . . . OFF
    e. Special Release-Bomb Rack Release Switch in Special Release Position
    f. Bomb Bay Safety Switch . . . . OFF

5. Bomb Run Check List
    a. Prior to Pre-IP
       (1) Perform Safety Check List . . . . COMPLETED
       (2) TAS Computed and Checked . . . . COMPLETED
       (3) Precomputed Ballistics . . . . SET
       (4) Offset Information Set & Checked . . . . . COMPLETED
       (5) Simulated Bomb Run . . . . COMPLETED
    b. Prior to IP
       (1) Altitude Measurement . . . . COMPLETED
       (2) Adjusted Bombing Altitude & Ballistics . . . . . SET
       (3) Label Camera Data Plate . . . . CHECKED
       (4) True Heading Checked With Navigator . . . . CHECKED
       (5) Set Up D-2 Nav Unit & Complete Bomb Run On IP . . . . COMPLETED
    c. Bomb Run
       (1) Proper Positioning of Switches for Bomb Run . . . . CHECKED
       (2) Call A/C 30 N.M. From Target . . . . COMPLETED
       (3) Complete Bomb Run . . . . COMPLETED
       (4) After Bombs Away Call Necessary Information to Pilot . . . . COMPLETED

PRIOR TO LANDING

1. Pre-Landing Duties
    a. Monitor GCA or Instrument Let-Down Until Cleared by A/C
    b. Turn Off APS-23
    c. Sighting Angle Dial . . . . 45°
    d. Bombing Mode Switch . . . . LOS
    e. Function Switch . . . . STAB

POSTFLIGHT

1. Complete the Following:
    a. Function Switch . . . . . . OFF WHEN AIRCRAFT IS PARKED
    b. Station . . . . POLICED
    c. K-System Maintenance Form . . . . COMPLETED
    d. All Malfunctions . . . . . NOTED ON AIRCRAFT FORM 781 (FORM 1)
    e. All Logs and Forms . . . . FILLED OUT

K-( ) System Preflight Check.

The following list is an abbreviated preflight check list for the K-( ) system. For a comprehensive preflight of this equipment refer to the observer's manual.

1. Preliminary Inspection:
    a. External and safety check—Complete.
    b. Bomb bay and radome check—Complete.
    c. Forward cabin—Check.

2. Preoperational Check Control Knob Setting Check:
    a. Control unit—Checked.
    b. Indicator—Checked.
    c. Variac—Checked.
    d. Primary control—Checked.
    e. Line of sight—Checked.
    f. Ballistics control—Checked.
    g. Navigation control—Checked.
    h. Polar navigation unit—Checked.
    i. Periscope—Checked.

3. Turn-On:
    a. One to five minute check—Completed.
    b. Auxiliary equipment check—Completed.
    c. Radar voltage check—Completed.

4. Radar Operation Check—Completed.

5. Computer Operation:
    a. Polar navigation control check—Completed.
    b. Computer voltage and TAS—Completed.
    c. Optics, LOS, and forward sighting check—Completed.
    d. Optics tracking and memory point check—Completed.
    e. PPI tracking, memory point, and 0-15 camera check—Completed.
    f. RAI tracking, memory point, and Y-3 camera check—Completed.
    g. Tracking control, fix dials, and offset sector check—Completed.
    h. Offset sighting check—Completed.
    i. Radar altitude and emergency bombing check—Completed.
    j. Navigation unit and pressure check—Completed.
    k. APS-23—Off.

6. Ballistics and Bomb Release Check:
    a. Tone check—Completed.
    b. Ballistics and bomb release check—Completed.
    c. Vertical camera check—Completed.
    d. Release angle and bomb rack check—Completed.
    e. Autopilot second station check—Completed.
    f. Bombing problem check—Completed.

7. Function Switch and K-3 Preheat—Off.

8. Bomb Bay and Camera Doors—Closed.

9. Bombing Switches and Circuit Breakers—Off.

10. Periscope Dome Cover—Replaced.

11. Form 781 (Form 1) and Radar Maintenance Form—Completed.

Section VIII
Crew Duties

K-( ) System Day-of-Flight Check.
Abbreviated Day-of-Flight Check List.

1. Preoperational Check—Completed.
2. Turn-On and Voltage Check—Completed.
3. Radar Operation Check—Completed.
4. Computer Operation Check—Completed.
5. Ballistics, Bomb Release, and Vertical Camera Check—Completed.
6. Bomb Rack Check—Completed (optional).
7. Bombing Problem Check—Completed (optional).
8. Turn-Off—Completed.

Expanded Day-of-Flight Check List.

1. Preoperational Check:
   a. APS-23 Switches OFF or properly positioned.
   b. Computer switches OFF or properly positioned.
2. Turn-On and Voltage Check:
   a. One to five minute check:
      (1) Stabilization power supply voltage check (STAB position).
      (2) Initial radar voltage check.
      (3) Heading and mag var check.
      (4) Auxiliary equipment check. (Pressure pump, RT unit and modulator blowers, spare amplifiers, and desiccant.)
   b. Radar voltage check.
3. Radar Operation Check:
   a. Check for picture, range marks, etc.
4. Computer Operation Check:
   a. Turn function switch to NAV and check voltages and TAS.
   b. Optics, LOS, and forward sighting checks.
   c. Lat-Long counter drive check.
   d. Offset sighting check.
   e. Radar altitude check. (Set on 5000 feet.)
   f. Pressure check (optional).
   g. Memory point and optical tracking check. (Set ramp in counters; turn constant speed motor on.)
   h. PPI, memory point, and 0-15 camera check.
   i. RAI and Y-3 camera check.
   j. Radar tracking control check:
      (1) NAV and PPI position; check fix dial and cross hair movement.
      (2) NAV and OB position; check cross hair movement.
      (3) TRACK and PPI position; check sector orientation and fix dial movement.
   k. Nav unit check.
      (1) Check the LAT and LONG counters read ramp coordinates.
      (2) Set in mag var.
      (3) Set in first metro wind.
5. Ballistics, Bomb Release, and Vertical Camera Checks:
   a. Tone check (VHF on other than tower frequency).
   b. Ballistics control check.
   c. Bomb release check.
   d. Vertical camera check.
   e. Bomb rack check (optional).
   f. Bombing problem (optional).
   g. Turn off the APS-23 and computer.

K-( ) System Altitude Determination.
Primary Method.

1. Power Switch—SCAN FAST.
2. Function Switch—TRACK.
3. Radar Altitude Switch—ON.
4. Receiver Gain and Tilt-Adjust for sharp first ground return.
5. B-Scope Focus and Intensity-Adjust for well defined cross hairs and target.
6. Altitude Control—Bring first ground return down to range mark.
7. Radar Altitude Switch—OFF.

Secondary Method (PPI only).

1. Aircraft in level flight over reasonably flat terrain of known elevation.
2. Adjust for good scope presentation.
3. Range Control—Shortest usable range (must be greater than altitude).
4. Cross Hairs-Range Marks Switch—CROSS HAIRS.
5. Master Function Switch—NAV.
6. Power Switch—SCAN OFF.
7. Altitude Switch—ON.
8. Antenna Tilt—Down for best definition of first ground return.
9. Receiver Gain—Adjust to give first ground return appearance of faint range mark.
10. Altitude Control Knob—Depress and turn until range marks and first ground return merge and bloom.
11. Altitude Switch—OFF.

Elevation of Terrain Unknown.

1. Adjust Radar for Normal Presentation.
2. Master Function Switch—TRACK.
3. PPI-OB switch—OB.
4. Cross Hairs-Range Marks Switch—CROSS HAIRS.

Note

Aiming point must be positively indentified in both the optics and B-scope.

5. Tracking Control—Place B-scope cross hairs on selected point.
6. Altitude Control—Place optics cross hairs on same selected point.
7. Read Altitude.

K-( ) System Wind Determination Check.

1. Check Radar Altitude.
2. Master Function Switch—TRACK.
3. Cross Hairs-Range Marks Switch—CROSS HAIRS.
4. Place optics or B-scope cross hairs on target with tracking handle.
5. Memory Point-Displacement Switch—MEMORY POINT.

CAUTION

Cross hairs *must* be on a recoverable target at this instant.

Note
Minimum 15-seconds delay.

6. Return cross hairs to target with tracking handle. (Do not slew.)

Note
Maximum memory point operation 5 minutes.

7. Memory Point-Displacement Switch—DISPLACEMENT.
8. Read wind components from navigation unit dials.

Navigation Departure and Fixing.

1. Measure altitude.
2. Check variation.
3. Place cross hairs on departure point or reference point and make wind run. Leave function switch in TRACK.
4. With cross hairs synchronized on departure point, or reference point, hold Plane's Position-Reference Point switch in REFERENCE POINT.
5. Using latitude and longitude set knobs, set departure point or reference point coordinates and release Plane's Position-Reference Point switch.
6. Function Switch—NAV.
7. Take fixes at regular intervals to correct Plane's Position Counter.

Beacon Navigation.

1. Master Function Switch—NAV.
2. Cross Hairs—Range Marks Switch—RANGE MARKS.
3. Power Switch—SCAN FAST.
4. Variac—FULL CCW.
5. Tuning Function Control—BEA AFC.
6. Range Control Knob—Desired range.
7. Variac Control—Clockwise until signal is received.

Note
If AFC does not operate properly, use manual tuning.

8. Take range and bearing fix on center of leading signal and subtract 1 n. m.

Preflight Check of Universal Bombing System.

The following check of the special bombing system should be performed 24 to 48 hours prior to loading:

Note
This preflight check is for airplanes equipped with universal bomb racks in bomb bays 1 and 4. On airplanes having universal racks in all 4 bomb bays, 2 and 3 will be checked in the same manner as 1 and 4.

1. Check that the armament section has installed a new drier cartridge.
2. Check Form 781 (Form 1).
3. Bomb bay doors open; ground locks installed.
4. Push to test all applicable lights.
5. Low Pressure Warning Light—Off.
6. Function Switch—STAB.
7. All Circuit Breakers on Bulkhead No. 6 and No. 8—Off.
8. U-2 Release Hooks—Latched.
9. Manual Locks—Installed (Lock lights on).
10. Door Safety Switch—OFF.
11. Bomb Panel Master Switch—ON.
12. Intervalometer—ON and SELECT.
13. Radar Observer Circuit Breaker Panel—BOMB RELEASE, INTER-HEATER and table light on; all others off.
14. Special Bomb Rack Panel:
  a. Power-Arm Release Circuit Breaker—On.
  b. Special-Bomb Rack Release—BOMB RACK RELEASE.
  c. Rack Control and Heater Circuit Breakers—On.
  d. Heater Switches—HEATER.
  e. No. 1 Rack Selector Switch—ON.
  f. No. 4 Rack Selector Switch—OFF.
  g. No. 1 and No. 4 Arming Switches—Momentarily SAFE.
  h. No. 1 and No. 4 Salvo Safety Switches—NO SALVO.
15. Pull Manual Release Handles—Neither rack should release.
16. Manual Lock Removed—Light Out.
17. Manual Release Handles Pulled—Rack should release.
18. Relatch No. 1 and No. 4 Hooks, Press D-2 Switch—Neither rack should release.
19. Special Bomb Rack Switch—SPECIAL RELEASE.
20. Depress D-2 Switch—No. 1 rack should release.
21. Relatch No. 1 Hook; No. 1 Rack Selector Switch—OFF; No. 4 Rack Selector Switch—ON.
22. Depress D-2 Switch—No. 4 rack should release.
23. Relatch No. 4 Hook.
24. Bomb Bay Doors—Locks removed, doors cleared.
25. Bomb Door Circuit Breakers—In, doors closed.
26. Depress D-2 Switch—Neither rack will release.
27. Bomb Door and Bomb Release Circuit Breakers—Off.

Section VIII
Crew Duties

28. Master Switch—OFF.
29. Pull Manual Release Handle—Neither rack should release.
30. Rack Selector Switch—ON for rack desired; other switch OFF.
31. Bomb Bay Doors—Cleared.
32. Bomb Door Safety Switch—ON (Prior to release).
33. Release through K System—Doors should open and then close after rack releases.
34. Function Switch, Bomb Door Safety Switch, and Rack Selector Switch—OFF.
35. Relatch Hook; Check Air Pressure.
36. Bulkhead No. 6 BOMB SALVO NO. 1—ON; Pneumatic Rack Junction Box Circuit Breakers—On.

Note

If pressure is above 1200 psi, the compressor circuit breaker should be turned off.

37. Bulkhead No. 8 BOMB SALVO NO. 4—ON; Pneumatic Rack Junction Box Circuit Breakers—On.
38. Arming Switches—ON (One at a time, lights on, arming shafts go to ARMED position).
39. Pull Arming Shafts—Lights go out.
40. Arming Switch—ARM.
41. Manual Safe—Pull; arming shafts should go to SAFE position; lights should go out.
42. Arming Switch—ARM; lights on (Safe light out).
43. Arming Control Heaters—Checked.
44. Heater Switch—OFF; circuit breaker pulled.
45. Camera Master Switch—Circuit breaker in.
46. Radar Observer's Circuit Breaker Panel—Bomb impulse switch ON; all others OFF.
47. Pilot's Salvo Safety Switch No. 4—CAN SALVO.
48. Pilot's Salvo Safety Switch No. 1—NO SALVO.
49. No. 2 and No. 3 bomb bay contents checked impossible to salvo.
50. Bomb Doors—Cleared.
51. Pilot's Bomb Salvo Circuit Breakers—In.
52. Salvo Switch ON—No salvo should occur.
53. Radar Observer's Salvo Circuit Breaker—In.
54. Pilot's Salvo Switch—Actuate; after light has been on three seconds, rack should release. Deactivate Salvo Circuit.
55. Repeat steps 47 through 54—No. 1 rack should release (pilot's salvo safety switch No. 1 CAN SALVO).
56. Relatch both hooks.
57. Camera doors should be open; camera should have actuated on salvo.
58. Camera Circuit Breakers—Off.
59. Pilot's Salvo Safety Switch—NO SALVO; circuit breaker pulled.
60. Special Bomb Rack Panel Salvo Safety Switches—NO SALVO.
61. Actuate Radar Observer's SALVO Switch—No salvo should occur.
62. Special Bomb Rack Panel Salvo Safety Switches—CAN SALVO.
63. Actuate Radar Observer's SALVO Switch—Both racks should release. Deactivate Salvo Circuit.
64. Bomb Bay Door Ground Locks—Installed.
65. Bulkhead No. 6 and No. 8 Circuit Breakers—Off.
66. Record discrepancies in Form 781 (Form 1).

Switch Positions For Universal Bomb Release.
1. Manual Lock—Removed.
2. Bulkhead No. 6 and No. 8 Circuit Breakers—ON.
3. Master Power Switch—ON.
4. Bomb Door Circuit Breakers—In.
5. Bomb Release Circuit Breakers—In.
6. Inter-Heater Circuit Breakers—In.
7. Intervalometer—SELECT.
8. Special Bomb Panel Circuit Breakers—In.
    a. Special Release Switch—SPECIAL RELEASE.
    b. Rack Heater Switch—HEATER.
    c. Radar Observer's and Pilot's Salvo Safety Switches—NO SALVO.
    d. Rack Selector Switch—As desired.

NAVIGATOR.

The navigator operates the installed navigational equipment. Following is an abbreviated check list for this position:

PREFLIGHT

1. Mission Planning
    a. Mission Requirements ... UNDERSTOOD
    b. Weather ... CHECKED
    c. No Wind Flight Plan ... COMPLETED
    d. Maps and Charts ... CHECKED AND ANNOTATED
    e. Target Study ... COMPLETED
    f. Navigation Kit and Aux Equipment ... CHECKED
2. Preflight (Day Preceding Flight)
    a. Form 781 (Form 1) ... CHECKED
    b. Circuit Breakers (As Desired) ... IN
    c. Oxygen Equipment and Pressure ... CHECKED
    d. Interphone (Normal and Private) ... CHECKED
    e. Lights (Table, Dome and Fluorescent) ... CHECKED
    f. Compass, Altimeter, and Air Speed Calibration Cards (When Applicable) ... CHECKED
    g. Compasses ... CHECKED
    h. Loran ... CHECKED
    i. Standby Gyro ... CHECKED
    j. Radio Compass ... CHECKED
    k. Accessible T-R Unit (When Applicable) ... CHECK WIRING, SECURITY, FOREIGN MATERIAL AND FAN OPERATION
    l. Aircraft Clocks (When Applicable) ... CHECKED
    m. Pilot's Magnetic Compass ... CHECKED
    n. Astro Position Interphone ... CHECKED
    o. Astro Position Oxygen Equipment ... CHECKED
    p. Astro Panel (Applicable Aircraft) ... CHECKED
    q. Periscopic Sextant Mount Alignment ... CHECKED
    r. Periscopic Sextant ... CHECKED AND STOWED
    s. Loran Antenna ... CHECKED
    t. Static Ports (Open and Clean) ... CHECKED
3. Preflight Station (Day of Mission)
    a. Form 781 (Form 1) ... CHECKED
    b. Equipment (Personal and Navigational) ... STOWED
    c. Circuit Breakers (As Required) ... IN
    d. Oxygen Equipment and Pressure ... CHECKED
    e. Oxygen Report (To Radio Operator) ... COMPLETE
    f. Interphone (Normal and Private) ... CHECKED

Section VIII
Crew Duties

    g. Lights (Table, Dome & Fluorescent) .... CHECKED
    h. Safety Belts .... CHECKED
    i. Compasses (See N-1 Compass Preflight) ...... CHECKED
    j. Loran .... CHECKED
    k. Altimeter Setting 29.92" .... COMPLETED
    l. Standby Gyro (Caged & Off) .... CHECKED
    m. Aircraft Clocks (If Applicable) .... CHECKED
    n. Astro Position Interphone .... CHECKED
    o. Astro Position Oxygen Equipment .... CHECKED
    p. Astro Position Panel (Applicable Aircraft) ... CHECKED
    q. Periscopic Sextant Mount .... CHECKED
    r. Periscopic Sextant .... CHECKED & STOWED
    s. Time Hack (Obtained at Navigator's
       Convenience) .... OBTAINED
    t. Static Ports (Open and Clean) .... CHECKED
4. Crew Inspection .... COMPLETED

INFLIGHT

1. Initial Heading .... TO A/C
2. Navigational Methods As Described In SAC Manuals
3. RCT Information to Crew (When Applicable)

BOMB RUN CHECK

1. Prior to Pre-IP
    a. Direct Aircraft to Pre-IP .... AS BRIEFED
    b. Compute TAS .... CHECKED WITH VO AND FE
    c. At Pre-IP Direct Aircraft to IP .... AS BRIEFED
2. Prior to IP
    a. Check True Heading .... CHECKED
    b. Using VO Latest Wind, Compute Mag Heading
       From IP to Target, Notify Pilot .... COMPLETED
3. Bomb Run
    a. At Bombs Away Record Time and True
       Heading .... COMPLETE
    b. Compute Bombs Away Wind and Inform VO COMPLETED

POSTFLIGHT

1. Turn Off All Switches and Equipment .... COMPLETE
2. Police Station .... COMPLETE
3. Record All Nav. Write-Ups in Form 781 (Form I) COMPLETE
4. Turn In All Maps, Charts, Logs and
   Forms Required .... COMPLETE

OBSERVER.

The Observer assists the Radar Observer and Navigator when required. Following is the abbreviated check list for this position.

PREFLIGHT

1. Mission Planning
    a. Mission Orders .... CHECKED
    b. Mission Folder & Observer's Kit .... COMPLETE
    c. Target Study .... COMPLETE
    d. Flight Plan and Weather .... CHECKED
2. Preflight (Arrival at Aircraft)
    a. Nose Turret Access Door .... SECURE
    b. Personal Equipment .... CHECKED & STOWED
    c. Parachute Static Line .... CHECKED
    d. Cabin First Aid Kit .... CHECKED
    e. Cabin Heater .... OFF
    f. Spare Bulb Box .... FILLED
    g. Portable Oxygen Bottle .... FILLED
    h. Oxygen Pressure .... CHECKED
    i. Normal & Private Interphone .... CHECKED
    j. Dome Lights .... CHECKED
    k. Spare Sextant .... CHECKED & STOWED
    l. 28 V DC and Right Forward Power Panels ... CHECKED
    m. Assist Navigator & Radar Operator .... AS REQUIRED

INFLIGHT

1. After Take-Off
    a. Assist Navigator & Radar Observer .... AS REQUIRED

2. Prepare for Landing
    a. Auxiliary & Misc Equipment .... SECURED

POSTFLIGHT

1. Nose Turret Sighting Station
    a. Oxygen Panel .... OFF
    b. Malfunctions .... REPORTED IN FORM 781 (FORM I)

BOMB RUN CHECK

1. Prior to Pre-IP
    a. O-15 Camera Checked For Proper Operation COMPLETED
    b. Offset Data .... CHECKED
    c. Safety Check List .... CHECKED
2. Prior to IP
    a. Max-Range From IP O-15 Camera ... 1 EVERY 12 SCANS
    b. Altitude Measurement & Adjustment .... CHECKED
    c. Cross Check Computations & Ballistic
       Data Settings .... COMPLETED
    d. Read True Heading In Heading Unit As
       Nav Obtains True Heading Check .... COMPLETED
3. Bomb Run
    a. Cross Check Following Switches For Actual Drop:
       (1) Bombing & Camera Panel Circuit Breakers ...... IN
       (2) Auxiliary Panel Circuit Breakers .... IN
       (3) Bomb Master Switch .... ON
       (4) Bomb Station Indicator Light Switch .... ON
       (5) Bomb Arming Switch .... AS BRIEFED
       (6) Intervalometer .... AS DESIRED
       (7) Camera Intervalometer .... AS BRIEFED
       (8) Special Rel Bomb Rack Release Switch .. AS DESIRED
       (9) Bomb Bay Door Safety Switch .... ON
       (10) Bomb Bay Special Rack Selector Switch .... ON JUST
           PRIOR TO RELEASE AND OFF
           IMMEDIATELY AFTER RELEASE
    b. Cross Check Following Switches for RBS Run
       (1) Intervalometer .... AS DESIRED
       (2) Bomb Bay Selector Switch .... OFF
       (3) Bomb Bay Door Safety Switch .... OFF
       (4) Bomb Bay Doors .... CLOSED, CB PULLED
       (5) Salvo Circuit Breakers .... PULLED
       (6) Camera Circuit Breakers .... ON
       (7) RBS Tone & Intervalometer Heater
          Circuit Breakers .... IN
       (8) All Other Bomb Panel Circuit Breakers .. PULLED
       (9) Master Switch .... ON
       (10) K-38 Camera Doors .... OPEN
       (11) Camera Intervalometer .... AS BRIEFED
    c. O-15 Camera on At 30 Mile Call ...... 1 EVERY 2 SCANS
    d. Inform VO Position of Offset Switch .... COMPLETED
    e. Function Switch Bomb Position .... CHECKED
    f. N-2 Transfer Switch (Autopilot) .... RADAR BOMB
    g. E-2 Turn Control (Autopilot) .... AUTOMATIC
    h. Inform VO When ECO Light On .... CHECKED
    i. Inform VO When Memory Point Light On .... CHECKED
    j. Inform Pilot When 15 N.M. From Target ...... CHECKED
    k. Tone "On" 20 Seconds To Go .... COMPLETED
    l. Tone "Off" at "Bombs Away" .... COMPLETED
    m. Maintain Camera Log & Record Necessary
       Flight Information .... COMPLETED
    n. When 30 N.M. Past Target .... 1 EVERY 12 SCANS
    o. Camera Off .... AS BRIEFED

FIRST RADIO-ECM OPERATOR.

The first radio-ECM operator operates the high frequency communications equipment, the defensive ECM equipment and the IFF. The following is a check list for this position.

Although these duties are primarily the responsibility of the first radio-ECM operator, he may delegate any of these duties to the radio-ECM operator as required.

VISUAL PREFLIGHT

1. Exterior of Aircraft
    a. Location and Type of ECM Antenna .... CHECKED

Section VIII
Crew Duties

    b. Liaison, Compass, ILS, Loran, Marker Beacon, VHF, UHF, IFF and ARN-14 Antennas, Insulators and Mounts .... CHECKED
    c. Static Dischargers .... CHECKED
2. Form 781 (Form 1) and "G" File .... CHECKED
    a. Coaxial Cable Connections to IFF on "J" Station Antennas on Top of Battery Access Panel .... CHECKED

PREFLIGHT OPERATIONAL EQUIPMENT CHECK

1. Hydraulic Selector Valve .... CHARGE BRAKES
2. Hydraulic Tank Level (and Spare Fluid) .... CHECKED
3. Compartment and Tunnel Lights .... CHECKED
4. All Plugs, Cables and Connections .... CHECKED
5. All Fuses, Spare Fuses and Circuit Breakers .... CHECKED
6. Spare Bulbs .... CHECKED
7. All Defensive ECM Equipment Installed .... CHECKED
8. All Interphone Equipment and Stations in Radio Compartment, Nose Compartment, and Flight Deck Including Speakers, Amplifiers and/or Channel 3 and 4 Power Supplies, if Applicable (AN/AIC-10); Emergency D-C Power Supply Relay Fuse (Engineers' Fuse Panel), and Operation of D-C Power Supply with AC Off .... CHECKED
9. AN/ARC-8 or ARC-21X and Antenna Connections .... CHECKED
10. IFF (Including Detonator Circuit, Fuses and Counter Readings) .... CHECKED
11. AN/ARC-3 and ARC-27 (All Channels) .... CHECKED
12. AN/ARN-5A or AN/ARN-18 (If Applicable) .... CHECKED
13. RC-103A (If Applicable) .... CHECKED
14. AN/ARN-14 (If Applicable) .... CHECKED
15. BC-453 (If Applicable) .... CHECKED
16. AN/ARN-6 or ARN-7 (Both Stations) .... CHECKED
17. AN/ARN-12 .... CHECKED
18. Radio Operator's T-R Unit .... CHECKED
19. C-1 Amplifier (If Installed in Forward Compartment) .... CHECKED

CREW INSPECTION

1. As Outlined in Section II, Normal Procedure .... COMPLIED
2. All Required Personal Equipment .... CHECKED
3. Radio-ECM Operator's Kit, Including Coding and Identification System .... CHECKED
4. Tool Kit and VHF Crystals Necessary for Flight .... CHECKED

PREFLIGHT (DAY OF FLIGHT)

1. Operational Check (Radio Operators' Compartment)
    a. Load Aircraft and Stow Equipment .... CHECKED
    b. All Required Circuit Breakers .... IN
    c. Check Normal and Private Interphone Using Oxygen Mask and Helmet, Verifying Side-tone .... CHECKED
    d. Oxygen Station (and Mask) .... CHECKED
    e. Mixer Amplifier, all Switches .... CHECKED
    f. ECM Defensive Equipment .... CHECKED
    g. AN/ARC-3 Crystals .... INSTALLED
    h. AN/ARC-27, Channelization .... CHECKED
    i. Hydraulic Selector Valve .... CHARGE BRAKES
    j. Compartment and Tunnel Lights .... CHECKED
    k. Communication Tube Cart .... CHECKED
    l. Cabin Pressure Regulator .... ON
    m. Cabin Pressure Relief Valve .... CLOSED
    n. Cabin Pressure Air Manual Shutoff Valve .... OPEN
    o. Nose Latching Hook .... STOWED
    p. Cabin Heater .... CHECKED
    q. IFF .... CHECKED
2. Operational Check (Flight Deck)
    a. Circuit Breakers on Pilot's Panel .... IN
    b. VHF, all Channels .... CHECKED
    c. UHF, all Channels .... CHECKED
    d. Liaison .... CHECKED
    e. Radio Compass .... CHECKED
    f. ILS (AN/ARN-5B and RC-103B, or AN/ARN-18 and RC-103B or AN/ARN-14 and AN/ARN-5B, Whichever is Installed) .... CHECKED
    g. Mixer Amplifier Switches (Left and Right Seat) .... CHECKED
    h. Range Filters (Pilot and Copilot) .... CHECKED
    i. Marker Beacon Lamp .... CHECKED
    j. Engineers' Interphone Circuit Breakers and Wing Crawlway Interphone Lamp .... CHECKED IN & OFF
    k. RBS Tone Switch and Automatic Tone .... CHECKED WITH OBSERVERS
3. Operational Check (Nose Compartment)
    a. Radio Compass .... CHECKED
    b. Circuit Breakers and Fuses .... IN

FINAL CREW BRIEFING

1. As Outlined in Section II, Normal Procedures .... CHECKED
2. A/C Informed of Discrepancies .... CHECKED

STATIONS (START ENGINES)

1. On Private Interphone .... STANDBY
2. Liaison Set Tuned to Tower Frequency .... CHECKED
3. Alarm Bell, Oxygen, Interphone .... REPORTED

TAXI

1. Interphone Compartment Report (Normal) .... READY
2. Observers at Both Upper Forward Escape Hatches with Aldis Lamps (Night) .... CHECKED
3. Nose Compartment Clear, Hatches Closed and all Personnel in Take-off Position .... REPORTED

TAKE-OFF

1. Safety Belt .... FASTENED
2. Parachutes .... ON
3. Nose Gear and Doors .... REPORTED UP

CRUISE

1. Mission .... AS BRIEFED
2. Parachute and Oxygen Equipment as Regulation Requires .... COMPLIED

LANDING

1. On Normal Interphone .... STANDBY
2. Emergency Hydraulic Selector Valve .... CHARGE BRAKES
3. Nose Gear Down and Locked After Engineer Reports "Pressure Relieved" .... REPORTED
4. Nose Strut (As Required) .... BLED
5. Liaison Set Tuned to Tower Frequency .... CHECKED
6. Nose Compartment Clear and Personnel in Landing Position .... REPORTED
7. Parachute .... ON

TAXI

1. Observers at Both Upper Forward Escape Hatches with Aldis Lamp (Night) .... CHECKED

POSTFLIGHT

1. All Equipment .... OFF
2. Radio-ECM Logs and ECM Forms .... COMPLETED & SIGNED
3. Form 781 (Form 1) .... COMPLETED
4. Relief Containers .... EMPTIED
5. Radio Compartment .... CLEANED

UPPER AFT GUNNER (LEFT).

This is the senior gunner of the crew. He is responsible to the aircraft commander for acceptance preflight of gunnery equipment and all other gunnery activities of the crew. This gunner accomplishes the following duties:

Note

For amplification of the gunnery check list and emergency procedures, refer to "Gunnery Amplified Check List," following this abbreviated check list.

PREFLIGHT

1. GUNNERY EQUIPMENT PREFLIGHT AND LOADING

NOTE

THE FOLLOWING PROCEDURE MUST BE ACCOMPLISHED BY A TWO-MAN TEAM UTILIZING INTERPHONE.

Check turret status.
Check external turret bay door tracks.

a. VISUAL INSPECTION

AT SIGHTING STATION

(1) All switches OFF or SAFE, heater power fuse removed.
(2) Check sighting station.
(3) Selector switch to STANDBY.
(4) Selector switch DOOR OPEN and OPERATION in coordination with man in turret bay.
(5) All switches OFF or SAFE.
　　(a) Turret power switch OFF first.

ON WAY TO TURRET BAY

Check turret bay door motor, cables and pulleys.
Check door-open limit switch.
Check fuses in a-c turret power panel.

AT TURRET BAY

(1) Turret safety switch SAFE.
(2) Turret bay clear, check stow marks.
(3) Turret safety switch ON, check thyratron blower.
(4) Must stand by turret safety switch until turret is fully extended.
(5) Turret safety switch SAFE.
(6) Remove gun enclosure and access panels.
(7) Remove feeder and check that gun is cleared of round in chamber.
(8) Remove breechblocks, inspect guns, chargers and feeder winders. Re-install breechblocks.
(9) Inspect feeders, link chutes.
(10) Install feeders, feeder winder and operating lever connected.
(11) Selsyns.
(12) Limit switches, actuator and mechanical stops (turret).
(13) All AN connectors, motors, units and cables on turret.
(14) Brakes locked.
(15) All other AN connectors, motors, units and cables in turret bay.
(16) Boosters, ammo cans and ammo feed chutes.
(17) Limit switches (torque tube).
(18) Remove thyratron cover and check fuses and tubes.

NOTE

PROCEED TO THE TURRET BAY AND VISUALLY PREFLIGHT INDIVIDUAL TURRET.

b. OPERATIONAL

AT SIGHTING STATION

(1) Turret power switch OFF.
(2) Selector switch WARM UP and heater fuse IN.
　　(a) After heater check, remove fuse.
(3) Selector switch OPERATION.
　　(a) Turret power switch ON.
(4) 28.5V DC check.
(5) Check sight for operation.

AT TURRET BAY

(1) Turret safety switch SAFE.
(2) Check heaters.
(3) Turret safety switch ON.
(4) 28.5V DC check.
(5) Stand clear, observe equipment operation and notify gunner at sight steps (7) through (18).

Section VIII
Crew Duties

AT SIGHTING STATION (Cont'd.)

    (6) Gun camera switch ON, gun camera operation.
    (7) 1 and 31 speed operation.
    (8) Safe-fire switches FIRE.
    (9) Gun charger, boosters and feeders winder operation.
    (10) Limit switches backout and stowing circuits.
    (11) OOSFI.
    (12) Contour follower.
    (13) Fire interrupter.
    (14) Firing Circuit check after charger disconnected.
    (15) Safe-fire switches safety wired SAFE.
    (16) Computer.
        (a) Computer switch OUT after check.
    (17) Boresight check.
    (18) All switches OFF or SAFE.
        (a) Turret power switch OFF first.
  c. LOADING
    (1) Inspect ammo.
    (2) Load ammo.
    (3) Link and case ejection chutes installed.
    (4) Spent case containers closed.
    (5) Arm feeders.
    (6) Final turret checks.
    (7) Replace gun enclosure and access panels.
    (8) Set round counters.
    (9) Selector switch OPERATION, retract turret and close turret bay door.
    (10) All switches OFF or SAFE.
    (11) Place warning sign on control panel.
    (12) Proper entry Form 781 (Form 1) and Form F.

2. CREW INSPECTION
  a. Spare Parachute and Bail-Out Bottle . . . . . CHECKED
  b. Battle Splints and Blood Plasma . . . . AS REQUIRED
  c. Turret Retraction Tool . . . . CHECKED

3. COMBAT STATION
  a. Oxygen and Interphone . . . . CHECKED
  b. Personal Equipment . . . . STOWED
  c. Trouble Light . . . . CHECKED
  d. Sight and Control Panel Switches . . . . OFF
  e. Sight Stowed and Locked . . . . CHECKED
  f. Blister For Proper Installation, Cracks and Cleanliness . . . . CHECKED
  g. Safety Belt . . . . CHECKED
  h. Aldis Lamp For Operation . . . . CHECKED

4. CREW DUTIES
  a. Emergency Escape Rope . . . . CHECKED
  b. Aft Cabin Heat and Pressurization Ducting for Security and Condition . . . . CHECKED
  c. Aft Cabin TR Unit . . . . . . SECURITY OF MOUNT AND BLOWER ACTION
  d. Aft Cabin Pressure Regulator . . . . . SAFETY WIRED IN OPEN POSITION
  e. Oxygen Regulators on Bunks . . . . CHECKED
  f. Visual Inspection UAL Turret and Turret Bay Door . . . . CHECKED
  g. Turret Safety Switch . . . . ON
  h. Check on Removal of Rudder Locks . . . . . AS REQUIRED
  i. Final Crew Brieng . REPORT DISCREPANCIES IN FORM 781 (FORM 1) PART II AND TO A/C

5. PRIOR TO TAKE-OFF
  a. Blister Defroster (Replace After Take-Off) . . . . REMOVED
  b. Sight In Down Position (Up Position After Take-Off) . . . . LOCKED
  c. Safety Belt . . . . FASTENED

INFLIGHT

1. GUNNERY EQUIPMENT OPERATION AND AERIAL FIRING
  a. Safe-Fire Switches . . . . SAFE
  b. Heater Power—ON and OFF . . . . AS REQUIRED
  c. Turret Power Switch . . . . ON
  d. Selector Switch in Sequence . . . . OPERATION
  e. Round Counters . . . . SET
  f. Target Size Knob . . . . SET
  g. Handset Unit . . . . SET
  h. Gun Camera . . . . CHECKED
  i. Computer . . . . IN
  j. Attack Factor Switch . . . . SET AS REQUIRED
  k. Reticle . . . . SET
  l. Sight and Turret Operation . . . . CHECKED

AT TURRET BAY (Cont'd.)

    (7) Thyratron tubes firing.

    (9) Check hold-back and manual charge.

    (14) Disconnect chargers at guns; check firing circuit.
    (15) Reconnect chargers.

    (18) Turret safety switch SAFE.

    (9) Turret safety switch ON, must stand by turret safety switch until turret is fully retracted.

AT SIGHTING STATION (Cont'd)

   m. Safe-Fire Switches .... FIRE

CAUTION

SAFE-FIRE A-C WARMUP SWITCH REQUIRES 3 MINUTE WARMUP PERIOD PRIOR TO FIRING. THIS APPLIES EVERY TIME SWITCH IS TURNED ON. NOT APPLICABLE TO SYSTEMS UTILIZING FREE-FIRE BOX.

   n. Burst Control .... AS REQUIRED
2. GUNNERY PORTION OF MISSION COMPLETED
   a. Safe-Fire Switches .... SAFETY WIRED SAFE
   b. Heater Power Fuse .... REMOVED
   c. Guns Cooled .... 20 MINUTES
   d. Turret Stowed and Retracted .... COMPLETED
   e. All Switches .... OFF
3. PREPARE FOR LANDING
   a. Blister Defroster (Replace After Landing) .... REMOVED
   b. Sight In Down Position (Up Position After Landing) .... LOCKED
   c. Auxiliary and Miscellaneous Equipment .... SECURED
   d. Safety Belt .... FASTENED

POSTFLIGHT

1. AFTER LANDING
   a. Sighting Station and Area .... CLEANED
   b. Interphone Cords .... STOWED
   c. Oxygen Panel Settings & Oxygen Hose .... SECURED
   d. Guns and Gunnery Equipment Secured .. TURRET SAFETY SW-SAFE AND WARNING SIGNS POSTED
   e. Malfunctions .... REPORTED
   f. Gunnery Forms and Reports .... COMPLETED

GUNNERY AMPLIFIED CHECK LISTS.

Blister Station Check List.

1. Turret Status.

   a. Check turret status. Senior gunner will check on status of all turrets and gunnery equipment. Check with maintenance personnel, Form 781 (Form 1), and other appropriate forms before commencing preflight. Other gunners will check with senior gunner on status of turret and gunnery equipment.

Note

Notify the aircraft crew chief of any discrepancies encountered during preflight of gunnery equipment, so that he will enter them in Form 781 (Form 1) and submit a work order to clear discrepancies.

   b. External turret bay door tracks. The tracks are on the exterior of the fuselage. Check for and remove any obstructions. Check for dents or bent areas in each track which might cause a binding action of the door rollers. A dry clean condition of the tracks is desired.

   c. Check turret bay door motor, connections, drums, cables and pulleys. Check for security of mounting. Visually check that cables are not fouled or frayed. Manually check that tension is present on cables. Check door open limit switch. Actuate the plunger manually and note that spring tension is sufficient to reposition the plunger when released. Check for security of mounting and damage.

Section VIII
Crew Duties

Note

Because of location and the possibility of damaging the fragile metal of the tunnel, only visual inspection of the left forward and lower aft door motor, connections, drums, cables and door open limit switches can be made.

 d. Check fuses in the a-c turret power panel. Check that 10 and 50 amp fuses are installed. Check that adequate spares are available.

2. Visual Inspection.

 a. At Sighting Station.

  (1) All switches OFF and SAFE.

   (a) Selector switch OFF.

   (b) Turret power switch OFF.

   (c) Safe-fire switches SAFE.

   (d) Heater power fuse REMOVED. Check for continuity.

   (e) Computer switch OUT.

   (f) Charger switch RELEASE.

   (g) Gun Camera Switch OFF.

  (2) Check sighting station.

   (a) Check proper feel of sight controls in azimuth and elevation. (If not correct, adjust friction adjustment for desired tension.)

   (b) Clean sight optical surfaces by wiping the surface with a soft cloth or lens tissue.

   (c) Check sight filters for cleanliness.

   (d) Check mounting and AN connectors for security.

   (e) Check sight locking handle for freedom.

   (f) Check sight selsyns and selsyn caps for tightness and selsyn contactor plug for proper installation and security.

   (g) Check gun camera for security of mounting and AN connectors for tightness. Open magazine access cover. Move magazine latch and note that spline gear protrudes.

   (h) Check that peep sight arrangement is workable.

   (i) Check stow pins for proper locking operation.

  (3) Selector switch STANDBY. Turret power switch ON.

Note

After approximately 100 (±30) seconds delay, the door closed lamp comes ON, indicating turret bay doors are closed and d-c power is available for operation.

CAUTION

If thyratron blower does not operate, turn selector switch OFF.

  (4) Selector switch DOOR OPEN and OPERATION in coordination with man in turret bay.

 b. In Turret Bay.

  (1) Turret Safety switch SAFE.

  (2) Turret bay clear. Check stow marks. To insure that drive motor brakes are engaged, check to see that stow marks are lined up and manually attempt to move the guns. The brakes must be locked prior to extending turret.

  (3) Turret safety switch ON. Check thyratron blower. Check by holding hand in front of blower opening to see whether blower is operating.

CAUTION

Do not let fingers come in contact with rotary fan.

  (4) The man in turret bay must stand by the tur-

AT SIGHTING STATION (Cont'd)

(a) Turn selector switch to DOOR OPEN. DOOR CLOSED lamp should go OUT. The door should open until the door limit switch is actuated, de-energizing the door motor.

(b) Turn selector switch to OPERATION. The turret should extend until the turret extended limit switch is actuated, de-energizing the retract motor. The turret extended lamp should come on.

(5) All switches OFF or SAFE.

CAUTION

The turret power switch will be turned OFF first before any switches at the panel are turned OFF.

IN TURRET BAY (Cont'd)

ret safety switch until turret is fully extended and watch for malfunctions.

Note

The RED light on the face of the junction box will be on when the turret safety switch is SAFE.

CAUTION

In case of any malfunction turn turret safety switch OFF and notify gunner at sight. Check that the retract arms are fully engaged; any looseness of the arms will cause extreme vibration when guns are fired.

(5) Turret safety switch SAFE.

(6) Remove gun enclosure and access panels

(a) Check turret dome and gun enclosures for cracks, dents, fasteners, clearance, and security.

(b) Place gun enclosure and dome assembly panels in a safe place where they will not be damaged.

(7) Remove feeder and check that gun is cleared of round in the chamber. Inspect that chamber is *cleared*. If there is a round in the chamber, use the following procedure: Remove the driving spring, unlock the breechblock with unlocking tool, and extract the round.

(8) Remove breechblocks, inspect guns, chargers and feeder winders.

(a) After gun has been CLEARED, remove rear buffer assembly and breechblock group. Check gun tube for obstructions.

(b) Check guns for the following: Receiver and tube clean and excess oil removed. Receiver interior for burrs, deformations, and general condition. Presence of charging lug (Rhode-Lewis or Johnson Farebox Chargers).

Round sensing switch and plunger for proper spring tension. Breechblock contact properly installed and safety wired. Disassemble the breechblock and inspect for broken, loose or worn parts; burrs and deformation insulation worn or missing; all parts wiped dry and reassembled; reinstall the breechblock in the receiver. Replace the rear buffer and driving spring assemblies.

Check for security of mount and attachment, scribe marks aligned on the magazine slide and receiver, magazine slide anchor secured, and anchor nuts tight. Insure firing leads move freely for gun recoil (no clamps).

Check for presence of cotter keys, lock washers, and safety wire.

(c) Check gun chargers for the following: Security of mount and attachment. Charging stud is installed. Charging stud retainer is in place (GE charger only). Charger switch is in NEUTRAL position.

Section VIII
Crew Duties

T.O. 1B-36D(II)-1

IN TURRET BAY (Cont'd)

(d) Check feeder winders for the following: Security of mount and attachment and the locking device for proper operation.

(e) Check cables for good condition and connectors for security on guns, chargers, and feeder winders.

(9) Inspect feeders and link chutes. Check for the following:

(a) Links or ammo in the feeder.

(b) Feeder mouth for burrs and deformation.

(c) Operating lever locks in down position.

(d) Feeder for excess oil or grease.

(e) Feeder cover or adapter is of proper series.

(f) Link deflector and link chute for obstruction or damage.

(g) Link chute is installed with wide side away from the feeder.

(h) Cartridge guides, control pawl and holding dog for freedom of movement.

(i) Star wheels and link strippers for damage.

(j) Connectors for damage.

(k) Presence of cotter keys and safety wire.

(10) Install feeders, feeder winder, and connect operating lever.

(a) Install the feeder and make sure the magazine latch locks it to the gun.

(b) Connect the operating lever to the bracket on the gun and lock it.

(c) Connect the feeder winder to the feeder and lock it.

(d) Connect feeder and gun heater leads.

(11) Selsyns (turret) check for the following:

(a) Selsyns and selsyn caps for tightness.

(b) Contactor plugs for proper installation and security.

(c) Selsyns covers for proper installation.

(12) Limit switches, actuators, and mechanical stops.

(a) Check advance contour limit and elevation and azimuth limit switches for security of mount, damage, and proper spring tension when actuated manually.

(b) Check actuators and mechanical limit stops for proper installation.

(13) All AN connectors, motors, units, cables on turret. Check the following:

(a) All turret electrical cables for good condition and connectors for security.

(b) Drive motors are properly mounted.

(c) Drive motor brush holders for security of mount.

(d) Contour follower assembly for damage and proper installation.

(e) Fire interrupter flexible drive cable and azimuth gear drive for proper installation and damage.

394

AT SIGHTING STATION (Cont'd)

IN TURRET BAY (Cont'd)

(f) Inner and outer rings for cracks, broken gear teeth, or foreign matter.

(14) Turret Movement (MANUAL). Disengage the drive motor brakes and check that turret moves smoothly and freely in azimuth and elevation.

(15) Brakes locked. Check that drive motor brakes are locked. Lever should be in VERTICAL position.

(16) All other AN connectors, motors, units, and cables in turret bay.

(a) Check computer and resolver input unit. Check dials for damage, electrical cables for good condition, and connectors for security.

(b) System junction box, frequency converter, and fire control box. Check electrical cables in good condition and connectors for security.

(c) Check security of mount and condition of shock mounts where applicable on all units. Check for presence of external ground strap secured.

(17) Boosters, ammo cans, and ammo feed chutes.

(a) Check boosters for the following: AN connectors secured and boosters rotating properly.

Note

On lower turrets, the booster motors have been removed, check that rollers free wheel.

(b) Check ammo cans for cleanliness, damaged areas, and dry condition.

(c) Check ammo feed chutes for proper mount, bent or damaged links, configuration, and cleanliness.

(18) Limit switches (torque tube). Remove housing on the torque tube and check turret retracted A & B switches, turret extended and stow power hold on switches for security of mount, damage, and proper spring tension when actuated manually.

(19) Remove thyratron cover and check fuses and tubes.

(a) Check electrical cables for good condition and connectors for security.

(b) Check all fuses for proper installation and continuity.

(c) Check power thyratron tubes for proper installation and that tube plates are not damaged.

3. Operational Check.

Note

Check that personnel and stands are cleared of turrets before operating. Be sure that turret is cleared of ammunition and that power is available. *Do not load guns* until the operational check has been completed and units do not require maintenance.

a. At Sighting Station
 (1) Turret power switch OFF.
 (2) Selector switch WARM UP and heater fuse IN.

b. In Turret Bay.
 (1) Turret safety switch SAFE.
 (2) Check heaters.

Section VIII
Crew Duties

AT SIGHTING STATION (Cont'd)

(a) Heater power fuse IN.
(b) Allow gun and feeder heaters to warm up.

> **CAUTION**
>
> Heaters should be left on just long enough to check operation.

(c) When operation of heaters has been checked, remove fuse.
(3) Selector switch OPERATION.
(a) Selector switch directly to OPERATION position.
(b) Turret power switch ON.
(4) 28.5-volt d-c Check.

> **CAUTION**
>
> While man in turret bay is checking 28.5-volt d-c output at turret junction box *do not* close action switch or move selector switch at panel.

(5) Check sight for operation.
(a) Check sight lamp rheostat for operation and check sight reticle brilliance.
(b) Check that both filaments on reticle lamp are operative by moving double filament switch.
(c) Check that range handle turns free and smooth and range numerals cover complete range smoothly.
(d) Check that target size numerals cover complete range.
(e) Check computer lamp ON.
(f) Parallax error of sight. Line up on a target which can be easily seen and covered by center dot. Acceptable requirement is that center dot should not move completely off the target when eye is moved vertically and horizontally across viewing aperture of optic head.

Note

Target must not be less than one mile away.

(6) Gun camera operation.

Note

Before starting operation, check to see that shutter speed knob is set at index for desired frames per second. *Do not* change speed when camera is running.

(a) Camera switch ON.
(b) Close action switch; depress triggers.
(c) Check shutter operation.
(d) Check to see that spline gear rotates.
(e) Release triggers. Check over-run control and trigger indicator operate.
(f) Insert camera aligning indicator in the camera and observe that reticle is centered on the reference marks.

IN TURRET BAY (Cont'd)

(a) Check to see that heaters become warm.
(b) Notify gunner at sight when heaters have been checked.

(3) Turret safety switch ON.

Note

On lower turrets install aft panel to prevent turret main power cable from being damaged.

(4) 28.5-volt d-c Check. Check line 143 at turret junction box for 28.5-volt d-c output. If necessary adjust R-43 in thyratron controller to get desired voltage.

> **CAUTION**
>
> Use extreme caution to avoid shorting out other wires in turret junction box.

(5) Stand clear, observe equipment operation and notify gunner at sight steps. (6) thru (17).

AT SIGHTING STATION (Cont'd)

 (g) Camera switch OFF.

(7) 1 and 31 speed operation.
 (a) 31 speed selsyn check. Move sight slowly and smoothly in azimuth and then elevation. See that turret follows sight.
 (b) 1 speed selsyn check. Slew sight rapidly out of alignment with turret in azimuth and then elevation. See that turret rapidly comes into alignment.

(8) Safe-fire switches to FIRE.

(9) Gun charger, boosters and feeder winder operation.
 (a) At control panel, place charger to HOLDBACK position; charger should charge and hold the breechblock to the rear position. Place charger switch to RELEASE position. Charger should release breechblock.
 (b) Close action switch and press triggers.

(10) Limit switches backout and stowing circuit.
 (a) Close action switch and move sight until turret goes into a limit. Depress trigger; boosters, chargers and feeder winders should not operate.
 (b) Move sight in the opposite direction, keeping triggers depressed. Turret should backout smoothly off the limits. Boosters, chargers and feeder winders should operate.
 (c) Check all limits in elevation and azimuth.
 (d) Release action switch; turret should automatically stow.

(11) OOSFI circuit.
 (a) Move sight about 90 degrees out of correspondence with turret.
 (b) Simultaneously depress action and trigger switches.
 (c) Check that boosters, chargers and feeder winders do not operate until turret is within 3 degrees of alignment with sight.
 (d) Repeat steps (a) thru (c) in elevation.

(12) Contour follower. With action switch closed, move the turret along and against the contour follower, forward and aft. Depress triggers.

(13) Fire interrupter. Depress triggers and move line of bore through the jet pods, wings, propeller arcs, vertical, and horizontal stabilizers.

(14) Firing circuit check after charger disconnected.

IN TURRET BAY (Cont'd)

(7) Thyratron tubes firing. While turret is being operated, check to see that all elevation, azimuth, and d-c power thyratron tubes are firing properly. No excessive over-heating and no cross firing should occur. Check for a bluish purplish color while firing; no firing above the plate or at base of tube should occur. A pinkish-orange or whitish color indicates a bad tube which should be replaced.

Note

If tubes are *not* operating properly, notify gunner at sight to turn system OFF.

(9) Check holdback and manual charge.
 (a) Place charger switch to CHARGE position; the charger should automatically charge and release breechblock. Place charger switch to HOLDBACK position; the charger should charge and hold the breechblock to the rear position. Place switch to NEUTRAL position; the charger should release breechblock.
 (b) Check that chargers operate and feeder winders rotate in proper direction.

(10) Check that boosters, chargers, and feeder winders do not operate on any limit.

(12) Observe that the guns do not come in contact with any part of fuselage and clear the blisters and the green house. The firing circuit should be open; boosters, chargers, and feeder winders should not operate while on contour. See that turret backs out of contour properly.

(13) Fire interrupter. Check that boosters, chargers, and feeder winders do not operate when guns are pointed at jet pods, wings, propeller arcs, vertical and horizontal stabilizers.

(14) Disconnect chargers at guns.

Note

When disconnecting or reconnecting gun

Section VIII
Crew Duties

AT SIGHTING STATION (Cont'd)

(a) Close action switch; point guns to an unrestricted firing area.

> **CAUTION**
>
> Do not release action switch any time during this check.

(b) Depress triggers and have assistant check that gun fires; check both guns.

> **WARNING**
>
> While checking firing circuit, insure that when triggers are released, the firing circuit is OUT. If there is an indication that the firing circuit is still functioning after the triggers are released, get it repaired *immediately* and do not load the guns until it has been repaired.

(15) Safe-fire switches safety wired in SAFE position before continuing with other checks.

(16) Computer check.

(a) Range check. Computer switch IN; action switch closed. Turn range handle from 300-yard range to 1500-yard range. Place hand on gyroscopes to check for operation.

(b) Check resolver input unit dials by moving sight in elevation and azimuth.

(c) Set altitude *minimum* and air speed *maximum* at handset unit and range *maximum* (1500 yards) at sight.

(d) Lead check. Close action switch and track steadily for some distance. Stop sight abruptly and observe the movement of the turret. The turret should stop when the sight is stopped and then creep in the opposite direction.

(e) Windage check. Close action switch, move sight broadside, place computer switch to OUT. Guns should swing slightly to the rear; place computer switch to IN. The windage correction should come back IN and move the guns slightly forward.

(f) Gravity check. With action switch closed, move the sight aft and slightly above horizontal where windage correction is minimum. Turn computer switch OUT, guns should move down. Turn computer switch IN; guns should move up.

(g) Set attack factor switch to PURSUIT position and then STRAIGHT LINE position. There will be slight movement of the guns.

(h) Turn computer switch OUT.

> **CAUTION**
>
> Do not turn selector switch to off position when action switch is actuated since it may

IN TURRET BAY (Cont'd)

charger cables be sure that turret safety switch is in OFF position.

(a) Secure gun charger cables to prevent damage to them while making this check.

> **CAUTION**
>
> Be sure that breechblock is in battery position before inserting magic wand. Use caution in placing any part of the body in front of gun muzzles.

(b) Insert firing circuit tester in tube of gun and push it against firing pin. (This will prevent firing pin from ground out on firing pin port.)

(15) Reconnect chargers.

(16) Computer check.

(a) Check that the range and ballistics dials follow the range movements at the sight.

(b) Check that resolver input unit dials follow sight movements in azimuth and elevation.

(d) Check azimuth and elevation correction dials for movements during lead check.

AT SIGHTING STATION (Cont'd)

cause a computer malfunction or damage contour follower.

(17) Boresight check.

(a) Tape or otherwise close action switch, and aim the sight at a distant object, 1000 feet for each foot of parallax.

(b) Have observer check that guns are pointed at same object as the sight.

(18) All switches OFF or SAFE.

Note

Turret power switch will be turned off *first* before any switches at panel are turned off. This procedure will prevent accidental retraction of turret.

(a) Selector switch OFF.

IN TURRET BAY (Cont'd)

(17) Boresight check. Check that guns are pointed at same object as the sight by use of boresighting tool.

(18) Turret safety switch SAFE.

(a) Replace thyratron cover.

Loading Ammunition and Arming Guns.

1. External turret safety switch OFF.
2. Inspect ammunition.
   a. Check rounds and links for cleanliness, corrosion, scratches, loose primers, loose projectiles, bent or major dented cases; inspect links for broken stripping ears or bent areas.
   b. Check linkage set at 2-9/32 ($\pm$ 1/16) inches.
   c. Check that the belt is flexible and all rounds are held securely in position.
3. Load ammunition.
   a. Disconnect the ammunition feed chutes from the booster assembly.
   b. Remove the ammunition can covers.
   c. Place the proper link end of the belt in the can first.

Note

Make sure a round is in the double link end of the belt or a single link is bent or secured in a manner to prevent the link from catching on the ammunition feed chute. This depends on the type of belt used.

Note

Ammunition cans will be loaded as shown by decals on the cans.

   d. Lay the ammunition in the can as evenly as possible.

Note

Never fill the ammunition cans so full that the can cover must be forced in place. The ammunition will be jammed.

   e. When the cans are filled, thread the belt through the booster and replace the ammunition can cover; reconnect the ammunition chute.

4. Link and case ejection chutes installed (uppers only).
5. Spent case containers closed (uppers only).
6. Arm feeders.
   a. Before loading the feeder mechanism, check that the operating lever is inserted in the operating lever bracket, and that the magazine latch is locking the feeder to the gun.
   b. Place the proper link end of the belt into the feed mechanism. Place the rounds over the star wheel so that the link stripping ears are riding over the link strippers.
   c. Wind the feeder mechanism until the clutch slips. Three links should be stripped in the process of winding the feeder mechanism.

Note

If the double link is fed into the feeder, only two links will be stripped.

7. Final turret checks. Make the final check of the drive motor brakes engaged, operating levers engaged and driving spring retainers locked. Firing and charging leads connected. Feeder winders should be locked.
8. Replace gun enclosures and access panels.
9. Set round counters. Set at number of rounds loaded per gun.
10. Retractable Turrets.

WARNING

Do not make ground operational check of turrets after guns have been armed.

   a. Retract turrets and close doors.

Section VIII
Crew Duties

b. Have a gunner stand by on a turret safety switch in turret bay until turret is fully retracted and doors are closed.

Note

Watch ammunition chutes for binding action during retraction.

11. All switches OFF and SAFE (retractable turrets). External turret safety switch ON (nose and tail).

12. Place warning signs on control panels, and forward and aft hatches. WARNING: HOT GUNS

13. Proper entry Form 781 (Form 1) and Form F. The senior gunner will insure that the total number of rounds loaded on the aircraft are entered on Form 781 (Form 1). The senior gunner will advise the flight engineer of the ammunition load so that it will be entered on Form F.

Do not load the guns HOT.

Note

In the event the mission is postponed for more than 48 hours after completion of turret system preflight, the guns will be unloaded and ammunition withdrawn to the ammunition cans. The turrets will be extended, the firing circuits will be checked, and the ammunition will be reloaded into the guns within 24 hours of the rescheduled take-off time.

In Flight Gunnery Operating Procedures.

Prior to Take-Off. Check that all switches on the control panel are at OFF, SAFE, RELEASE, and OUT and that gun camera switches on the sights are OFF. The nose sight switches for the sight dome heater and desiccator will be OFF.

Gunnery Equipment Operation and Aerial Firing.
Turrets may be extended for cold soak period prior to reaching firing range. Do not operate the turret or turn the firing switches ON until directed by the aircraft commander after the airplane is on the firing range. On training missions where the turret is not loaded with ammunition, practice turret operation, search and fire area techniques, and target reporting.

1. The nose gunner will turn the selector switch to WARM-UP position and the desiccator and dome heater switch to the ON position as soon as practical after take-off. These switches will remain on throughout the flight. (B-type system's selector switch must be placed in OPERATION position for desiccator operation.) The tail gunner will turn the external-normal switch to NORMAL and the pressure system to AUTOMATIC as soon as practical after take-off.

2. Switching procedure. Before entering a zone in which turret use is anticipated, the senior gunner will request permission from the aircraft commander prior to energizing the RCT systems. The systems will be turned ON as ordered by the senior gunner and all gunners will confirm by interphone. Before reaching the firing range establish the following conditions:
   a. Safe-fire switches—SAFE.
   b. Heater power.

   (1) Turn on guns and feeder heaters no longer than 30 minutes prior to firing. Leave heaters on during firing.

   (2) If condition exists where firing of guns is delayed, operate gun and feeder heaters in cycles of no longer than 30 minutes OFF and 30 minutes ON until firing is resumed. When firing is resumed, turn on heaters immediately and leave on during firing.

   (3) Turn heaters off when gunnery portion of missions is completed.

Note

Allow blister systems to warm up a minimum of 30 minutes on STANDBY prior to operating turrets.

   c. Turret power switch to ON.
   d. Round counters set at number of rounds loaded.
   e. Target size knob set to the wingspan of type fighter expected.
   f. Handset unit. Adjusted in accordance with information received from the navigator. For C systems these settings will be true air speed, corrected outside air temperature, and pressure altitude.

Note

Some handset units require true air speed in KNOTS and others in MPH. Be sure to check handset unit for required type air speed before requesting air speed from navigator.

For B systems these settings will be equivalent air speed, corrected outside air temperature and pressure altitude.

Note

If there is a change of ± 5 MPH or KNOTS, ± 500 feet of altitude or ± 5 degrees of temperature deviation from the setting on the handset unit, a new setting must be established.

   g. Gun camera. Put magazine in camera and turn camera switch ON. Set camera settings as required. Check that film in magazine turns properly.
   h. Computer switch IN as required.
   i. Attack factor switch set as required. Normally this position is PURSUIT.
   j. Reticle set at slightly less than 1500 yards.
   k. Check sight and turret operation.

> **CAUTION**
>
> Just prior to commencing firing, check the one speed selsyn control and make sure sight and turret are in alignment. Loss of one speed selsyn control means loss of OOSFI. This could be very dangerous and cause self-inflicted damage to a formation.

3. The following steps apply to the tail gunner only.
   a. Selector switch to STANDBY.

> **CAUTION**
>
> Allow four minutes for necessary warm-up time delay before turning selector switch to RADAR.

   b. Selector switch to RADAR.
   c. Indicator unit, radar set, antenna, and turret operation checked.
   d. Safe-fire switch to FIRE. Only when permission has been granted by aircraft commander and aircraft is over firing range.

> **CAUTION**
>
> Whether in combat or in training the following will be accomplished prior to firing. The safe-fire a-c warm-up switch requires a 3-minute warm-up period prior to firing. This applies every time the switch is turned on. (Not applicable to systems utilizing free fire box.)

Cooling Guns and Burst Control. Conservation of equipment and other conditions require that restrictions be placed on missions conducted for training.
1. Aim guns away from own aircraft and other friendly aircraft.
2. Fire in 2- to 3-second bursts with a cooling period of 45 to 60 seconds between bursts.

Note

The purpose of the firing burst and cooling in paragraph 2 above is to conserve the life of gun tubes during training flights.

3. Aim guns to a clear area while cooling between bursts.

> **WARNING**
>
> Never allow guns to point to exposed parts of the aircraft at any time.

4. Aim guns to a clear area when ordered to cease firing or when gun firing has been completed.
   a. Turret power switch OFF.
   b. Safe-fire switch SAFE.
5. Safety precautions to avoid self-inflicted damage by runaway guns.
   a. Aim guns away from own aircraft and other friendly aircraft.
   b. Set safe-fire switch to SAFE and gun charger switch to HOLDBACK.
   c. If above procedure does not stop runaway gun, let it fire and keep the other gun ready for action.

> **CAUTION**
>
> Do not release action switch or turn turret power switch off during this condition.

Gunnery Portion of Mission Completed.
1. Safe-fire switch SAFE.
2. Cool guns 20 minutes prior to stowing.
3. Turret moved to stow position and stowed.
4. All switches OFF or SAFE.

Note

Place pressure system in NEUTRAL prior to landing.

Prepare for Landing. Turn dome heater OFF just prior to leaving the nose section to go to your landing position.

After Landing Procedures.

Prior to Leaving Station. Desiccator switch turned to OFF.

Before Leaving Aircraft.
1. Gun clearance procedure.
   a. Check that gunnery control panel switches are OFF and turret safety switch is SAFE.
   b. Place red flag with white lettered words HOT GUNS on control panel selector switches.
   c. Place a larger red flag with white lettered words HOT GUNS at the forward and aft hatches.
   d. Clearance of live ammunition from the guns will be accomplished by an armament analysis team only.
2. Report RCT discrepancies. Any discrepancies of equipment will be reported to the senior gunner who will enter them in Form 781 (Form 1). Other discrepancies will be reported to the engineer.
3. Gunnery report forms. The senior gunner will fill out the gunnery report forms and collect all camera film. Return the film to the camera section.
4. Tail radar inflight report. The tail gunner will insure that the report is properly filled out and turned in to appropriate personnel.

Combat Operations.

The principles outlined below must be followed under combat conditions.

Section VIII
Crew Duties

T.O. 1B-36D(II)-1

Approaching the Combat Area. Enroute to the target, gunnery equipment will be tested and guns fired at low altitude only. You will be briefed or the aircraft commander will direct when to accomplish this operation. The senior gunner will direct the switching procedure and retractable turrets will be extended under his direction. Under his direction the guns will be positioned in an unrestricted area and test fired a short burst. So far as possible, any malfunctions indicated will be corrected. After the operation is completed, turrets will be retracted and switches will be turned OFF or SAFE.

Reaching the Combat Area. When enemy fighters appear, the following conditions should prevail:

1. Sight unlocked.
2. Gunners hand set preset in accordance with information received from the navigator. For C systems these settings will be true air speed, corrected outside air temperature, and pressure altitude. For B systems these settings will be equivalent air speed, corrected outside air temperature, and pressure altitude.

Note

In combat, this information should be checked every 10 minutes.

3. Turret in the extended stow position.
4. System energized.
5. Gun and feeder heaters warm; heater fuse IN as far as possible. The cycle of heater use (IN for 30 minutes and OUT for 30 minutes) will be followed. The fuse should be left in during firing.
6. Target size knob set to the wingspan of the type of fighter expected.
7. Reticle set at slightly less than 1500 yards.
8. Computer switch IN.
9. Attack factor switch set at PURSUIT.
10. Magazine in camera and camera switches on.

How to Fire.

1. When you sight an enemy, recheck the target size knob, and close the action switch.
2. When the enemy aircraft's wing tips just touch the edge of the reticle previously set to reflect a range a little short of 1500 yards, start framing the target. If your aircraft is rolling, yawing, or in evasive action, continue to track smoothly with the center reticle dot on target. Precise ranging is mandatory for accurate fire. The computer will make necessary corrections.

Note

Your computer prediction errors will be directly proportional to your errors in ranging.

3. Use burst control. Fire in bursts of 2 to 3 seconds. Between bursts recheck your aiming point. Adherence to a mandatory cooling period between bursts is not required.

4. The normal position of the attack factor switch is PURSUIT. The attack factor switch will be placed in STRAIGHT LINE position when the following situations are recognized.

   a. An enemy fighter attacking you is not flying a pursuit curve.

   b. An enemy aircraft is attacking another ship in your formation (support fire).

How to Fire From Radar Tail Position. This position is the most important single defensive position of the aircraft and must be manned at all times. This must be done even at the cost of abandoning a visual sighting station. Whenever an attack develops from this sector, opening fire must be performed at the maximum range of just short of 1500 yards. Firing will be in bursts of 2 to 3 seconds. A mandatory cooling period between bursts is not required. Efficient operation of the gun laying radar system requires emphasis on the following:

1. The operator must remain in search until the last possible moment. Then he must switch to hand control and lock on the target in such a manner that he can and will open fire at maximum range.

   a. The operator must be adept at interpreting the scope presentation. He must recognize the time when a fighter abandons the attack or the fighter has been hit.

   b. As soon as this condition happens the operator must switch to search and be ready to immediately lock on any other target that may have appeared.

Cooling Guns. During lulls in firing, sufficient control of the guns and turret must be maintained to insure that they always point at an unrestricted area (in formation). Keep guns in designated cooling position a minimum of 20 minutes prior to stowing and retracting turrets.

After the Mission. After landing, guns must be cleared of ammunition. This requirement does not necessarily mean gunners will clear the guns of ammunition. Duration of flight and locally established policies will determine responsible personnel.

Emergency Procedures.

Turret Stowing and Retraction. In the event a turret will not stow or retract electrically proceed as follows:

1. Place all switches OFF or SAFE.
2. Proceed to turret bay with turret hand crank.

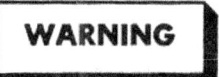

Before proceeding to turret bay, contact the pilot or radar observer to make sure all bomb bay door switches and circuit breakers are off.

Section VIII
Crew Duties

· EMERGENCY SIGHTING ·

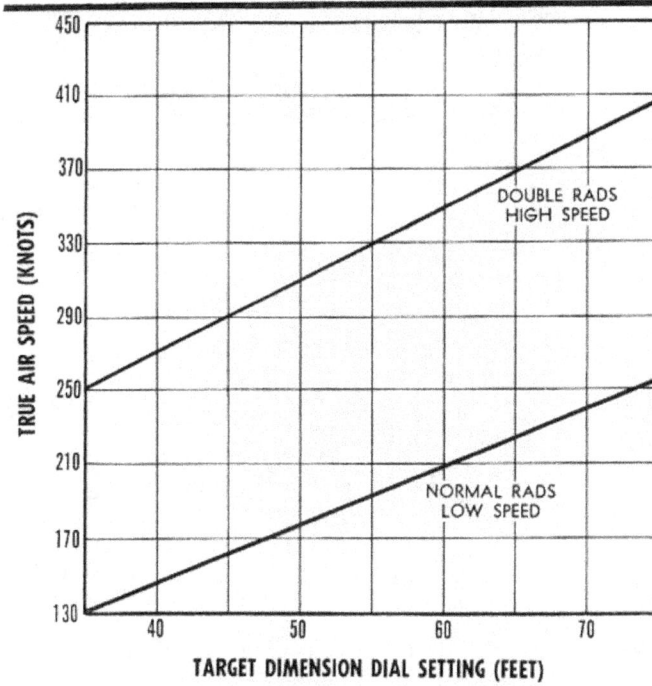

FIGHTER ANGLE OFF	DEFLECTION IN RADS
0°	0
11¼°	½
22½°	1
45°	2
90°	2½

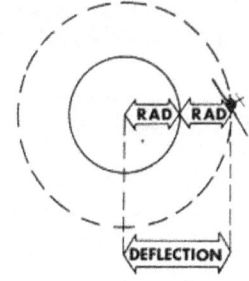

NOTES:
1. Set Minimum Range (Maximum Reticle)
2. Set T.D. Dial Versus True Air Speed
3. Take Specified Deflection Between Attacking Fighter And Your Tail — Always

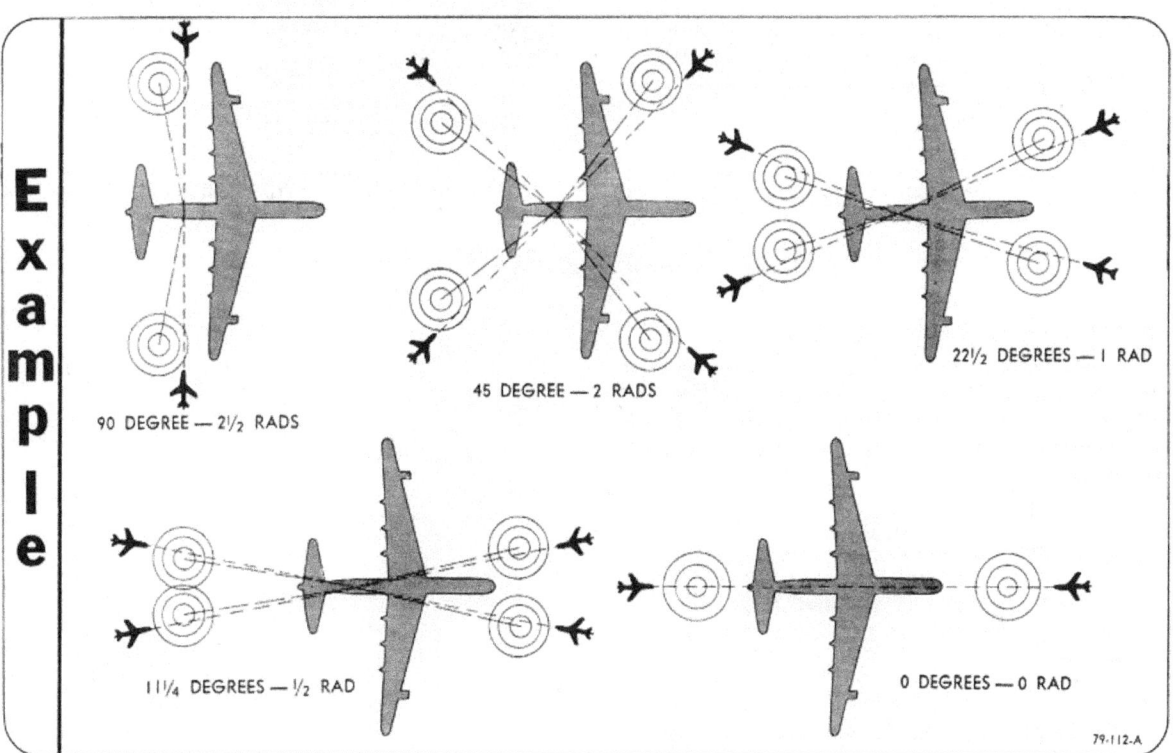

Figure 8-1.

3. Insert hand crank into rotor shaft of elevation drive motor, rotate until elevation stow marks are aligned.

4. Repeat the procedure in step 3 for azimuth.

5. Insert hand crank into rotor shaft of the retract motor and rotate until turret is properly retracted.

6. Close turret bay doors.

WARNING

Never attempt to stow turret while inflight by disengaging drive motor brakes.

Emergency Sighting Methods. In case of computer failure during operation, the gun sight can be used as an accurate ring sight. Since the size of the ring is adjustable by moving the target dimension dial, you can use it to lay off accurate deflections, which will take into account your exact true air speed.

1. If your computer fails, proceed as follows:

   a. Turn computer switch OFF.

   b. Obtain true air speed from navigator, then set your target dimension dial according to the table in figure 8-1.

   c. Turn range wheel or grip until the reticle circle is full size (minimum range).

   d. Use the sight like an ordinary optical sight and apply the standard rules of position firing, with one exception for a fighter attacking at 90 degrees, allow 2 1/2 rads deflection instead of 3. At 45 degrees, use 2 rads, at 22 1/2 degrees use 1 rad, and at 11 1/4 degrees use 1/2 rad.

   e. If your bomber is moving along steadily and not taking evasive action, use standard rule of laying off deflection between the fighter and your tail along the fighter's line of apparent motion.

   f. If your bomber is taking evasive action, lay off the deflection along an imaginary line between the fighter and the point on the horizon toward which your tail is pointing.

   g. Start firing at the opening range recommended for position firing in your theater. Normally this range is 1000 yards.

   h. On the breakaway of an attack, if the fighter seems to hang motionless in the air, hit him by using this system:

   (1) Upper forward gunners: Aim one-half wing span toward the nose of the bomber.

   (2) All other stations: Aim point blank.

2. Reticle bulb failure. If both filaments of your reticle bulb burn out and you have no spare, you must rely on the emergency ring and post sight. This sight is mounted on the optic head where it can be easily pulled into position. The sight is too small to be used as a ring sight to lay off deflections in rads, but it can be used as a reference point to show where your guns are pointing. Common sense will have to be used by the gunner in laying off deflections with this sight. If reticle bulb is burned out, but the computer is working:

   a. Line bead of the post in the center of the ring.

   b. Turn range handle to reach your maximum and minimum limits back and forth and set at approximate medium range.

Note

Do not move range handle after you have set it at medium range.

   c. Line up the bead of the post on the nose of the fighter.

UPPER AFT GUNNER (RIGHT).

This crew member is the aircraft electrician-gunner. He will be available for each gunnery preflight. His inflight duties include electrical maintenance and trouble shooting. This crew member accomplishes the following duties:

Note

In the event a copilot is not assigned to the crew, this gunner will be assigned to the left forward position and a turret system mechanic gunner will be assigned to man this station.

Note

For amplification of the gunnery check list and emergency procedures, refer to "Gunnery Amplified Check List, Upper Aft Gunner (Left)," of this section.

PREFLIGHT

1. GUNNERY EQUIPMENT PREFLIGHT AND LOADING

NOTE

THE FOLLOWING PROCEDURE MUST BE ACCOMPLISHED BY A TWO MAN TEAM UTILIZING INTERPHONE.

Check turret status.
Check external turret bay door tracks.

a. VISUAL INSPECTION

AT SIGHTING STATION

(1) All switches OFF or SAFE, heater power fuse removed.
(2) Check sighting station.
(3) Selector switch to STANDBY.
(4) Selector switch DOOR OPEN and OPERATION in coordination with man in turret bay.
(5) All switches OFF or SAFE.
   (a) Turret power switch OFF first.

ON WAY TO TURRET BAY

Check turret bay door motor, cables and pulleys.
Check door-open limit switch.
Check fuses in a-c turret power panel.

AT TURRET BAY

(1) Turret safety switch SAFE.
(2) Turret bay clear, check stow marks.
(3) Turret safety switch ON. Check thyratron blower.
(4) Must stand by turret safety switch until turret is fully extended.
(5) Turret safety switch SAFE.

(6) Remove gun enclosure and access panels.
(7) Remove feeder and check that gun is cleared of round in chamber.
(8) Remove breechblocks, inspect guns, chargers and feeder winders. Re-install breechblocks.
(9) Inspect feeders, link chutes.
(10) Install feeders, feeder winder and operating lever connected.
(11) Selsyns.
(12) Limit switches, actuator and mechanical stops (turret).
(13) All AN connectors, motors, units and cables on turret.
(14) Brakes locked.
(15) All other AN connectors, motors, units and cables in turret bay.
(16) Boosters, ammo cans and ammo feed chutes.
(17) Limit switches (torque tube).
(18) Remove thyratron cover and check fuses and tubes.

NOTE

PROCEED TO THE TURRET BAY AND VISUALLY PREFLIGHT INDIVIDUAL TURRET.

b. OPERATIONAL

AT SIGHTING STATION

(1) Turret power switch OFF.
(2) Selector switch WARM UP and heater fuse IN.
   (a) After heater check, remove fuse.
(3) Selector switch OPERATION.
   (a) Turret power switch ON.
(4) 28.5V DC check.
(5) Check sight for operation.
(6) Gun camera switch ON, gun camera operation.
(7) 1 and 31 speed operation.
(8) Safe-fire switches FIRE.
(9) Gun charger, boosters and feeder winder operation.
(10) Limit switches backout and stowing circuits.
(11) OOSFI.
(12) Contour follower.
(13) Fire interrupter.
(14) Firing circuit check after charger disconnected.
(15) Safe-fire switches safety wired SAFE.
(16) Computer.
   (a) Computer switch OUT after check.
(17) Boresight check.
(18) All switches OFF or SAFE.
   (a) Turret power switch OFF first.

c. LOADING

(1) Inspect ammo.
(2) Load ammo.
(3) Link and case ejection chutes installed.
(4) Spent case containers closed.
(5) Arm feeders.
(6) Final turret checks.

AT TURRET BAY

(1) Turret safety switch SAFE.
(2) Check heaters.

(3) Turret safety switch ON.

(4) 28.5V DC check.
(5) Stand clear, observe equipment operation and notify gunner at sight steps (7) through (18).

(7) Thyratron tubes firing.

(9) Check hold-back and manual charge.

(14) Disconnect chargers at guns; check firing circuit.
(15) Reconnect chargers.

(18) Turret safety switch SAFE.

Section VIII
Crew Duties

AT SIGHTING STATION (Cont'd)

    (7) Replace gun enclosure and access panels.

    (8) Set round counters.

    (9) Selector switch OPERATION, retract turret and close turret bay door.

    (10) All switches OFF or SAFE.

    (11) Place warning sign on control panel.

AT TURRET BAY (Cont'd)

    (9) Turret Safety Switch ON, must stand by turret safety switch until turret is fully retracted.

2. CREW INSPECTION
   - a. Spare Oxygen Equipment .... AS REQUIRED
   - b. First Aid Kits (Aft Cabin) .... CHECKED
3. COMBAT STATION
   - a. Oxygen and Interphone .... CHECKED
   - b. Personal Equipment .... STOWED
   - c. Trouble Light .... CHECKED
   - d. Sight and Control Panel Switches .... OFF
   - e. Sight Stowed and Locked .... CHECKED
   - f. Blister for Proper Installation, Cracks and Cleanliness .... CHECKED
   - g. Safety Belt .... CHECKED
   - h. Aldis Lamp For Operation .... CHECKED
4. CREW DUTIES
   - a. Emergency Escape Rope .... CHECKED
   - b. Left Aft Cabin Power Panel FUSES, CIRCUIT BREAKERS, 3 PHASE LIGHTS—SECURED
   - c. Aft Cabin Dome Lights .... CHECKED
   - d. Aft Auxiliary Cabin Heaters (Two) .... CHECKED
   - e. Tail Cone Lights .... CHECKED
   - f. Galley and Oven Switches OFF .... CHECKED
   - g. Right Aft Cabin Power Panel .... FUSES, CIRCUIT BREAKERS, 3 PHASE LIGHTS—SECURED
   - h. Aft Turret Bays and Bomb Bay Dome Lights .... CHECKED
   - i. Right and Left Aft Turret Power Panel FUSES, CIRCUIT BREAKERS, 3 PHASE LIGHTS—SECURED
   - j. Visual Inspection UAR Turret .... CHECKED
   - k. Turret Safety Switch .... ON
   - l. Final Crew Briefing .... REPORT DISCREPANCIES IN FORM 781 (FORM 1) AND TO A/C
5. PRIOR TO TAKE-OFF
   - a. Blister Defroster (Replace After Take-Off) .... REMOVED
   - b. Sight In Down Position (Up Position After Take-Off) .... LOCKED
   - c. Safety Belt .... FASTENED

INFLIGHT

1. GUNNERY EQUIPMENT OPERATION AND AERIAL FIRING
   - a. Safe-Fire Switches .... SAFE
   - b. Heater Power—ON and OFF .... AS REQUIRED
   - c. Turret Power Switch .... ON
   - d. Uniswitch In Sequence .... OPERATION
   - e. Round Counters .... SET
   - f. Target Size Knob .... SET
   - g. Handset Unit .... SET
   - h. Gun Camera .... CHECKED
   - i. Computer .... IN
   - j. Attack Factor Switch .... SET AS REQUIRED
   - k. Reticle .... SET
   - l. Sight and Turret Operation .... CHECKED
   - m. Safe-Fire Switches .... FIRE

CAUTION

SAFE-FIRE A-C WARMUP SWITCH REQUIRES 3 MINUTE WARMUP PERIOD PRIOR TO FIRING. THIS APPLIES EVERY TIME SWITCH IS TURNED ON. NOT APPLICABLE TO SYSTEMS UTILIZING FREE-FIRE BOX.

    n. Burst Control .... AS REQUIRED
2. GUNNERY PORTION OF MISSION COMPLETED
   - a. Safe-Fire Switches .... SAFETY WIRED SAFE
   - b. Heater Power Switch .... REMOVED
   - c. Guns Cooled .... 20 MINUTES
   - d. Turret Stowed and Retracted .... COMPLETED
   - e. All Switches .... OFF

3. PREPARE FOR LANDING
   a. Blister Defroster (Replace After Landing)... REMOVED
   b. Sight In Down Position (Up Position
      After Landing) .... LOCKED
   c. Auxiliary and Miscellaneous Equipment .... SECURED
   d. Safety Belt .... FASTENED

POSTFLIGHT

1. AFTER LANDING
   a. Sighting Station and Area .... CLEANED
   b. Interphone Cords .... STOWED
   c. Oxygen Panel Settings and Oxygen Hose ...... SECURED
   d. Guns and Gunnery Equipment Secured ... TURRET SAFETY
                          SW-SAFE AND WARNING SIGNS POSTED
   e. Malfunctions .... REPORTED

LOWER AFT GUNNER (LEFT).

This gunner is responsible for preflight and use of gunnery equipment. This gunner accomplishes the following duties:

PREFLIGHT

1. GUNNERY EQUIPMENT PREFLIGHT AND LOADING

   #### NOTE

   THE FOLLOWING PROCEDURE MUST BE ACCOMPLISHED BY A TWO-MAN TEAM UTILIZING INTERPHONE.

   #### NOTE

   FOR AMPLIFICATION OF THE GUNNERY CHECK LIST AND EMERGENCY PROCEDURES, REFER TO "GUNNERY AMPLIFIED CHECK LIST, UPPER AFT GUNNER (LEFT)," OF THIS SECTION.

   Check turret status.
   Check external turret bay door tracks.
   a. VISUAL INSPECTION

   #### AT SIGHTING STATION

   (1) All switches OFF or SAFE, heater power fuse removed.
   (2) Check sighting station.
   (3) Selector switch to STANDBY.
   (4) Selector switch DOOR OPEN and OPERATION in coordination with man in turret bay.
   (5) All switches OFF or SAFE.
       (a) Turret power switch OFF first.

   #### ON WAY TO TURRET BAY

   Check turret bay door motor, cables and pulleys.
   Check door-open limit switch.
   Check fuses in a-c turret power panel.

   #### AT TURRET BAY

   (1) Turret safety switch SAFE.
   (2) Turret bay clear, check stow marks.
   (3) Turret safety switch ON. Check thyratron blower.
   (4) Must stand by turret safety switch until turret is fully extended.
   (5) Turret safety switch SAFE.
   (6) Remove gun enclosure and access panels.
   (7) Remove feeder and check that gun is cleared of round in chamber.
   (8) Remove breechblocks, inspect guns, chargers and feeder winders. Re-install breechblocks.
   (9) Inspect feeders, link chutes.
   (10) Install feeders, feeder winder and operating lever connected.
   (11) Selsyns.
   (12) Limit switches, actuator and mechanical stops (turret).
   (13) All AN connectors, motors, units and cables on turret.
   (14) Brakes locked.
   (15) All other AN connectors, motors, units and cables in turret bay.
   (16) Boosters, ammo cans and ammo feed chutes.
   (17) Limit switches (torque tube).
   (18) Remove thyratron cover and check fuses and tubes.

Section VIII
Crew Duties

T.O. 1B-36D(II)-1

NOTE

PROCEED TO THE TURRET BAY AND VISUALLY PRE-FLIGHT INDIVIDUAL TURRET.

   b. OPERATIONAL

AT SIGHTING STATION

(1) Turret power switch OFF.
(2) Selector switch WARM UP and heater fuse IN.
   (a) After heater check, remove fuse.
(3) Selector switch OPERATION.
   (a) Turret power switch ON.
(4) 28.5V DC check.
(5) Check sight for operation.
(6) Gun camera switch ON, gun camera operation.
(7) 1 and 31 speed operation.
(8) Safe-fire switches FIRE.
(9) Gun charger, boosters and feeder winder operation.
(10) Limit switches backout and stowing circuits.
(11) OOSFI.
(12) Contour follower.
(13) Fire interrupter.
(14) Firing circuit check after charger disconnected.
(15) Safe-fire switches SAFETY WIRED SAFE.
(16) Computer.
   (a) Computer switch OUT after check.
(17) Boresight check.
(18) All switches OFF or SAFE.
   (a) Turret power switch OFF first.

   c. LOADING

(1) Inspect ammo.
(2) Load ammo.
(3) Arm feeders.
(4) Final turret checks.
(5) Replace gun enclosure and access panels.
(6) Set round counters.
(7) Selector switch OPERATION, retract turret and close turret bay door.
(8) All switches OFF or SAFE.
(9) Place warning sign on control panel.

AT TURRET BAY

(1) Turret safety switch SAFE.
(2) Check heaters.

(3) Turret safety switch ON.

(4) 28.5V DC check.
(5) Stand clear, observe equipment operation and notify gunner at sight steps (7) through (18).

(7) Thyratron tubes firing.

(9) Check hold-back and manual charge.

(14) Disconnect chargers at guns; check firing circuit.
(15) Reconnect chargers.

(18) Turret safety switch SAFE.

(7) Turret safety switch ON, must stand by turret safety switch until turret is fully retracted.

2. CREW INSPECTION
   a. Heated and Insulated Liquid Containers
     (Aft Cabin) .... FILLED
   b. Mattresses, Pillows and Blankets (Aft Cabin) AS REQUIRED

3. COMBAT STATION
   a. Oxygen and Interphone .... CHECKED
   b. Personal Equipment .... STOWED
   c. Trouble Light .... CHECKED
   d. Sight and Control Panel Switches .... OFF
   e. Sight Stowed and Locked .... CHECKED
   f. Blister for Proper Installation, Cracks
     and Cleanliness .... CHECKED
   g. Safety Straps and Belt (Seat and Floor
     Attachments) .... CHECKED
   h. Aldis Lamp for Operation .... CHECKED

4. CREW DUTIES
   a. Emergency Escape Rope .... CHECKED
   b. Walk-Around Bottle .... FILLED
   c. Parachute Static Line .... CHECKED
   d. Emergency Hydraulic Reservoir (Oil Level
     and Lever Off) .... CHECKED
   e. Fire Extinguishers .... CHECKED
   f. Tunnel Door .... PROPER FIT AND FLANGE VALVE OPEN
   g. Tunnel Cart (Trial Run) .... CHECKED FOR PROPER
                                           OPERATION
   h. Visual Inspection of LAL Turret .... CHECKED
   i. Turret Safety Switch .... ON
   j. Final Crew Briefing .... REPORT DISCREPANCIES IN
                       FORM 781 (FORM 1) AND TO A/C
   k. Left Gear Safety Lock .... REMOVED

5. PRIOR TO TAKE-OFF
   a. Blister Defroster (Replace After Take-Off) .... REMOVED
   b. Safety Belt and Shoulder Harness .... FASTENED

Section VIII
Crew Duties

AT SIGHTING STATION (Cont'd)

INFLIGHT

1. AFTER TAKE-OFF
   a. Flap and Landing Gear Report............AS REQUIRED
   b. Engine and Intercooler Report............AS REQUIRED

2. GUNNERY EQUIPMENT OPERATION AND AERIAL FIRING
   a. Safe-Fire Switches................................SAFE
   b. Heater Power—ON and OFF.........AS REQUIRED
   c. Turret Power Switch..................................ON
   d. Selector Switch in Sequence............OPERATION
   e. Round Counters......................................SET
   f. Target Size Knob....................................SET
   g. Handset Unit...SET
   h. Gun Camera.....................................CHECKED
   i. Computer...IN
   j. Attack Factor Switch................SET AS REQUIRED
   k. Reticle..SET
   l. Sight and Turret Operation...............CHECKED
   m. Safe-Fire Switches................................FIRE

CAUTION

SAFE-FIRE A-C WARMUP SWITCH REQUIRES 3 MINUTE WARMUP PERIOD PRIOR TO FIRING. THIS APPLIES EVERY TIME SWITCH IS TURNED ON. NOT APPLICABLE TO SYSTEMS UTILIZING FREE-FIRE BOX.

   n. Burst Control...........................AS REQUIRED

3. GUNNERY PORTION OF MISSION COMPLETED
   a. Safe-Fire Switches............SAFETY WIRED SAFE
   b. Heater Power Fuse..........................REMOVED
   c. Guns Cooled...........................20 MINUTES
   d. Turret Stowed and Retracted...........COMPLETED
   e. All Switches..OFF

4. PREPARE FOR LANDING
   a. Blister Defroster (Replace After Landing)....REMOVED
   b. Safety Belt and Shoulder Harness..........FASTENED
   c. Landing Gear and Flap Report............AS REQUIRED
   d. Engine and Intercooler Report............AS REQUIRED

POSTFLIGHT

1. AFTER LANDING
   a. Sighting Station............................CLEANED
   b. Interphone Cords............................STOWED
   c. Guns and Gunnery Equipment Secured TURRET SAFETY SW-SAFE WARNING SIGNS POSTED
   d. Malfunctions..............................REPORTED
   e. Left Gear Safety Lock.....................REPLACED

LOWER AFT GUNNER (RIGHT).

This gunner is responsible for preflight and use of gunnery equipment. This gunner accomplishes the following duties:

PREFLIGHT

1. GUNNERY EQUIPMENT PREFLIGHT AND LOADING

NOTE

THE FOLLOWING PROCEDURE MUST BE ACCOMPLISHED BY A TWO-MAN TEAM UTILIZING INTERPHONE.

NOTE

FOR AMPLIFICATION OF THE GUNNERY CHECK LIST AND EMERGENCY PROCEDURES, REFER TO "GUNNERY AMPLIFIED CHECK LIST, UPPER AFT GUNNER (LEFT)," OF THIS SECTION.

Check turret sratus.
Check external turret bay door tracks.

   a. VISUAL INSPECTION

ON WAY TO TURRET BAY

Check turret bay door motor, cables and pulleys.
Check door—open limit switch.
Check fuses in a-c turret power panel.

Section VIII
Crew Duties

AT SIGHTING STATION
(1) All switches OFF or SAFE, heater power fuse removed.
(2) Check sighting station.
(3) Selector switch to STANDBY.
(4) Selector switch DOOR OPEN and OPERATION in coordination with man in turret bay.
(5) All switches OFF or SAFE.
   (a) Turret power switch OFF first.

AT TURRET BAY
(1) Turret safety switch SAFE.
(2) Turret bay clear, check stow marks.
(3) Turret safety switch ON. Check thyratron blower.
(4) Must stand by turret safety switch until turret is fully extended.
(5) Turret safety switch SAFE.
(6) Remove gun enclosure and access panels.
(7) Remove feeder and check that gun is cleared of round in chamber.
(8) Remove breechblocks, inspect guns, chargers and feeder winders. Re-install breechblocks.
(9) Inspect feeders, link chutes.
(10) Install feeders, feeder winder and operating lever connected.
(11) Selsyns.
(12) Limit switches, actuator and mechanical stops (turret).
(13) All AN connectors, motors, units and cables on turret.
(14) Brakes locked.
(15) All other AN connectors, motors, units and cables in turret bay.
(16) Boosters, ammo cans and ammo feed chutes.
(17) Limit switches (torque tube).
(18) Remove thyratron cover and check fuses and tubes.

NOTE

PROCEED TO THE TURRET BAY AND VISUALLY PREFLIGHT INDIVIDUAL TURRET.

  b. OPERATIONAL

AT SIGHTING STATION
(1) Turret power switch OFF.
(2) Selector switch WARM UP and heater fuse IN.
   (a) After heater check, remove fuse.
(3) Selector switch OPERATION.
   (a) Turret power switch ON.
(4) 28.5V DC check.
(5) Check sight for operation.
(6) Gun camera switch ON, gun camera operation.
(7) 1 and 31 speed operation.
(8) Safe-fire switches FIRE.
(9) Gun charger, boosters and feeder winder operation.
(10) Limit switches backout and stowing circuits.
(11) OOSFI.
(12) Contour follower.
(13) Fire interrupter.
(14) Firing circuit check after charger disconnected.
(15) Safe-fire switches SAFETY WIRED SAFE.
(16) Computer.
   (a) Computer switch OUT after check.
(17) Boresight check.
(18) All switches OFF or SAFE.
   (a) Turret power switch OFF first.

  c. LOADING
(1) Inspect ammo.
(2) Load ammo.
(3) Arm feeders.
(4) Final turret checks.
(5) Replace gun enclosure and access panels.
(6) Set round counters.
(7) Selector switch OPERATION, retract turret and close turret bay door.
(8) All switches OFF or SAFE.
(9) Place warning sign on control panel.

AT TURRET BAY
(1) Turret safety switch SAFE.
(2) Check heaters.
(3) Turret safety switch ON.
(4) 28.5V DC check.
(5) Stand clear, observe equipment operation and notify gunner at sight steps (7) through (18).
(7) Thyratron tubes firing.
(9) Check hold-back and manual charge.

(14) Disconnect chargers at guns, check firing circuit.
(15) Reconnect chargers.

(18) Turret safety switch SAFE.

(7) Turret safety switch ON, must stand by turret safety switch until turret is fully retracted.

2. CREW INSPECTION
  a. Heated and Insulated Liquid Containers
    (Assist LAL Gunner) .... FILLED
  b. Mattresses, Pillows and Blankets
    (Assist LAL Gunner) .... AS REQUIRED

3. COMBAT STATION
  a. Oxygen and Interphone .... CHECKED
  b. Personal Equipment .... STOWED
  c. Trouble Light .... CHECKED
  d. Sight and Control Panel Switches .... OFF
  e. Sight Stowed and Locked .... CHECKED

Section VIII
Crew Duties

AT SIGHTING STATION (Cont'd)

    f. Blister for Proper Installation, Cracks and Cleanliness .... CHECKED
    g. Safety Straps and Belt (Seat and Floor Attachments) .... CHECKED
    h. Aldis Lamp for Operation .... CHECKED

4. CREW DUTIES
    a. Emergency Escape Rope .... CHECKED
    b. Cabin Pressure Manual Shut-Off Valve .... SAFETY WIRED OPEN
    c. Vacuum Relief Valve Strap .... CHECKED
    d. Walk-Around Bottle (right) if Installed .... FILLED
    e. Hand Axe .... CHECKED
    f. Bomb Bay Entrance Door for Proper Fit .... CHECKED
    g. Visual Inspection LAR Turret and Turret Bay Door .... CHECKED
    h. Turret Safety Switch .... ON
    i. Final Crew Briefing .... REPORT DISCREPANCIES FORM 781 (FORM 1) PART II AND TO A/C
    j. Right Gear Safety Lock .... REMOVED

5. PRIOR TO TAKE-OFF
    a. Blister Defroster (Replace After Take-Off) .... REMOVED
    b. Safety Belt and Shoulder Harness .... FASTENED

INFLIGHT

1. AFTER TAKE-OFF
    a. Flap and Landing Gear Report .... AS REQUIRED
    b. Engine and Intercooler Report .... AS REQUIRED

2. GUNNERY EQUIPMENT OPERATION AND AERIAL FIRING
    a. Safe-Fire Switches .... SAFE
    b. Heater Power—ON and OFF .... AS REQUIRED
    c. Turret Power Switch .... ON
    d. Selector Switch in Sequence .... OPERATION
    e. Round Counters .... SET
    f. Target Size Knob .... SET
    g. Handset Unit .... SET
    h. Gun Camera .... CHECKED
    i. Computer .... IN
    j. Attack Factor Switch .... SET AS REQUIRED
    k. Reticle .... SET
    l. Sight and Turret Operation .... CHECKED
    m. Safe-Fire Switches .... FIRE

CAUTION

SAFE-FIRE A-C WARMUP SWITCH REQUIRES 3 MINUTE WARMUP PERIOD PRIOR TO FIRING. THIS APPLIES EVERY TIME SWITCH IS TURNED ON. NOT APPLICABLE TO SYSTEMS UTILIZING FREE-FIRE BOX.

    n. Burst Control .... AS REQUIRED

3. GUNNERY PORTION OF MISSION COMPLETED
    a. Safe-Fire Switches .... SAFETY WIRED SAFE
    b. Heater Power Fuse .... REMOVED
    c. Guns Cooled .... 20 MINUTES
    d. Turret Stowed and Retracted .... COMPLETED
    e. All Switches .... OFF

4. PREPARE FOR LANDING
    a. Blister Defroster (Replace After Landing) .... REMOVED
    b. Safety Belt and Shoulder Harness .... FASTENED
    c. Landing Gear and Flap Report .... AS REQUIRED
    d. Engine and Intercooler Report .... AS REQUIRED

POSTFLIGHT

1. AFTER LANDING
    a. Sighting Station .... CLEANED
    b. Interphone Cords .... STOWED
    c. Guns and Gunnery Equipment Secured .... TURRET SAFETY SW-SAFE AND WARNING SIGNS POSTED
    d. Malfunctions .... REPORTED
    e. Right Gear Safety Lock .... REPLACED

AT TURRET BAY (Cont'd)

Section VIII
Crew Duties

T.O. 1B-36D(II)-1

TAIL GUNNER.

This gunner is responsible for preflight and use of gunlaying radar equipment. This gunner accomplishes the following duties:

NOTE

FOR AMPLIFICATION OF THE GUNNERY CHECK LIST, REFER TO "GUNNERY AMPLIFIED CHECK LIST, UPPER AFT GUNNER (LEFT)," OF THIS SECTION.

PREFLIGHT—AN/APG-32( )

1. GUNNERY EQUIPMENT PREFLIGHT AND LOADING
   a. VISUAL INSPECTION.
      (1) Check turret status.
      (2) All switches OFF or SAFE. Heater Power Fuse removed.
      (3) Spare bulbs.
      (4) Check desiccant.
      (5) Fuses and circuit breakers (indicator, aft power panel).
      (6) All units in pressurized compartment.
      (7) Remove thyratron and radar central covers, check thyratron fuses and tubes.
      (8) External turret safety switch OFF.
      (9) Remove enclosure assembly.
      (10) All radar units in unpressurized compartment.
      (11) Boosters and ammo cans.
      (12) Remove feeder and check that gun is cleared of round in chamber.
      (13) Remove breechblocks, inspect guns and chargers. Reinstall breechblocks.
      (14) Inspect feeders and link chutes.
      (15) Install feeders and operating levers connected.
      (16) Brass and ammo chutes.
      (17) Limit switches, actuators and mechanical stops.
      (18) Selsyns and drive motors.
      (19) Complete brass chute inspection (OUTSIDE).
      (20) Inspect and engage feeder winders.
      (21) Complete gun and turret inspection (OUTSIDE).
      (22) Turret movement (MANUAL).
      (23) Brakes locked.
   b. OPERATIONAL.
      (1) Turret clear for operation.
      (2) Selector switch WARM UP, heater fuse IN, check heaters.
         (a) After heater check, remove fuse.
         (b) External turret safety switch ON.
      (3) Wave guide shutter action.
      (4) Selector switch STANDBY and check thyratron and all radar blowers.
      (5) Thyratron controller timed out.
      (6) Radar central timed out.
      (7) 28.5V DC check.
      (8) Selector switch RADAR.
      (9) Scope presentation.
      (10) Indicator unit controls.
      (11) 1 and 31 speed operation. Check thyratron tubes firing.
      (12) Check wave guide and RF head for RF leakage.
      (13) Safe-fire switches FIRE.
      (14) Gun charger booster and feeder winder operation.
      (15) Antenna and turret limit switches, backout and stowing circuits.
      (16) OOSFI.
      (17) Pressure system check. Dump pressure after check.
      (18) Disconnect chargers at guns.
      (19) Firing circuit check.
      (20) Reconnect chargers and safe-fire switches SAFE (safety wired).
      (21) Computer check.
      (22) All switches OFF or SAFE.
      (23) Replace thyratron and radar central cover.
      (24) External-normal switch to EXTERNAL.
   c. LOADING AMMUNITION AND ARMING GUNS.
      (1) External turret safety switch OFF.
      (2) Inspect ammunition.
      (3) Load ammunition.
      (4) Arm feeders.
      (5) Final turret checks.
      (6) Replace gun enclosures and access panels.
      (7) Set round counters.
      (8) External turret safety switch ON.
      (9) Place warning signs on control panels, forward and aft hatches.
      (10) Proper entry in Form 781 (Form 1) and Form F.

2. CREW INSPECTION
   a. Hot Cups .... CHECKED
   b. Toilet Paper .... CHECKED
   c. Paper Cups .... CHECKED

3. COMBAT STATIONN
   a. Oxygen and Interphone .... CHECKED
   b. Personal Equipment .... STOWED
   c. Trouble Light .... CHECKED
   d. Indicator Unit, Radar Set and Control Panel Switches .... OFF
   e. Aft Cabin Altimeter (If Installed) ..... SET AT 29.92 INCHES HG
   f. Safety Belt .... SECURED

4. CREW DUTIES
   a. Aft Cabin Entrance Door for Proper Fit ..... CHECKED
   b. Emergency Escape Rope (Under Catwalk) ... CHECKED
   c. Galley Equipment for Cleanliness and Security. CHECKED
   d. Roomette for Water and Paper Towels ..... CHECKED
   e. Oxygen Regulator in Roomette .... CHECKED
   f. Tail Cone Entrance Door Proper Fit .... CHECKED
   g. Visual Inspection of Tail Turret .... CHECKED
   h. External Turret Safety Switch .... ON
   i. Turret Safety Switch .... ON
   j. Final Crew Briefing .... REPORT DISCREPANCIES IN FORM 781 (FORM 1) AND TO A/C
   k. Nose Gear Safety Lock .... REMOVED

CAUTION

CHECK LATCH ROD AND EMERGENCY RELEASE PIN FOR PROPER INSTALLATION ON NOSE GEAR.

5. PRIOR TO TAKE-OFF
   a. Ladder .... REMOVED & STOWED
   b. Aft Cabin Entrance Door .... CLOSED
   c. Safety Belt .... FASTENED

INFLIGHT

1. GUNNERY EQUIPMENT OPERATION AND AERIAL FIRING
   a. Safe-Fire Switches .... SAFE
   b. External/Normal Switch .... NORMAL
   c. Pressure System .... AUTOMATIC
   d. Heater Power .... ON & OFF AS REQUIRED
   e. Turret Power Switch .... ON
   f. Round Counters .... SET
   g. Handset Unit .... SET
   h. Computer .... IN
   i. Attack Factor Switch .... SET AS REQUIRED
   j. Selector Switch .... STANDBY

CAUTION

ALLOW FOUR MINUTES FOR NECESSARY WARM UP TIME DELAY BEFORE TURNING SELECTOR SWITCH TO RADAR POSITION.

   k. Selector Switch .... RADAR
   l. Indicator Unit, Radar Set, Antenna and Turret Operation .... CHECKED
   m. Safe-Fire Switches .... FIRE

CAUTION

SAFE-FIRE A-C WARM-UP SWITCH REQUIRES 3 MINUTE WARM-UP PERIOD PRIOR TO FIRING. THIS APPLIES EVERY TIME SWITCH IS TURNED ON. NOT APPLICABLE TO SYSTEMS UTILIZING FREE FIRE BOX.

   n. Burst Control .... AS REQUIRED

2. GUNNERY PORTION OF MISSION COMPLETED
   a. Safe-Fire Switches .... SAFETY WIRED SAFE
   b. Heater Power Fuse .... REMOVED
   c. Guns Cooled .... 20 MINUTES
   d. Turret Stowed .... COMPLETED
   e. All Switches .... OFF
   f. Handset Altitude Knob (B System Only). MAX ALTITUDE
   g. Pressure System .... OFF

3. PREPARE FOR LANDING
   a. Auxiliary and Miscellaneous Equipment ...... SECURED
   b. Safety Belt .... FASTENED

POSTFLIGHT

1. AFTER LANDING
   a. Sighting Station and Area .... CLEANED
   b. Interphone Cords .... SECURED
   c. Oxygen Panel Settings and Oxygen Hose ..... SECURED
   d. Indicator Unit Cover .... REPLACED
   e. Guns and Gunnery Equipment Secured .. TURRET SAFETY
      SW-SAFE AND WARNING SIGNS POSTED
   f. Nose Gear Safety Lock .... REPLACED
   g. Malfunctions .... REPORTED FORM 781 (FORM 1)
   h. Radar Report .... COMPLETED

Tail Gunner's AN/APG-32( ) Equipment Amplified Check List.

Visual Inspection.

1. Check with senior gunner on status of turret and gunnery equipment before commencing preflight.

2. All switches OFF or SAFE and heater fuse REMOVED.
   a. Turret power switch OFF.
   b. Selector switch OFF.
   c. Safe-fire switches SAFE.
   d. All indicator controls fully CCW.
   e. Heater power fuse REMOVED. Check for continuity.
   f. External-normal switch NORMAL.
   g. Turret safety switch SAFE.
   h. Pressure system switch OFF.
   i. Computer switch OUT.
   j. Charger switch RELEASE.

3. Spare bulbs. Check spare bulbs on indicator.

4. Check desiccant. Check desiccant blue down to change line.

5. Fuses and circuit breakers.
   a. Check indicator circuit breakers IN.
   b. Right aft cabin power panel circuit breaker IN.
   c. Check fuses in right aft cabin power panel for proper rating and spares.
     (1) RCT 3 fuses—40 amps.
     (2) Pressure pump fuse—10 amps.
     (3) Tail radar fuse—one 10 amp, one 20 amp.

6. All units in pressurized compartment. Check electrical cables for damage and connectors for tightness. Check units for proper installation, damage and loose or missing parts.
   a. Antenna hand control.
   b. Range, azimuth indicator.
   c. Voltage regulator.
   d. Pressure pump system connections.
   e. Computer, resolver input unit, and gyro drive unit.
   f. System junction box and fire control box.
   g. Control panel.
   h. Thyratron controller.

7. Remove thyratron and radar central covers.
   a. Thyratron.
     (1) Check all fuses for proper installation and continuity.
     (2) Check power thyratron tubes for proper installation and that tube plates are not damaged.
   b. Radar central.
     (1) Check all electrical cables for damage and connectors for tightness.
     (2) Check that all sub-units are tight and all tube shields are in place.
     (3) Check CAL-NORMAL switch to NORMAL.
     (4) Check antenna control switch (S901) to ON.
     (5) AFC-MANUAL switch to AFC.
     (6) SCAN-CONTROL switch (S-902) for clockwise position.

8. External turret safety switch OFF.

> **CAUTION**
>
> This switch must always be placed to the OFF position when personnel are on or at the turret. The only exceptions to this rule are indicated on the check list (OPERATIONAL).

9. Remove gun enclosure assembly.
   a. Check for dents, fasteners, clearance, and security.
   b. Place the enclosure in a safe place where it will not be damaged.

10. All radar units in unpressurized compartment.
   a. All cable connections at bulkhead 12 for damage.

> **CAUTION**
>
> At bulkhead 12, be careful not to step on cables near tail cone entrance door. These are coaxial, IFF, etc., cables which are very delicate.

   b. Check pressure system lines for damage in tail cone.
   c. Check wiring along fuselage to tail unit.
   d. Radar modulator and RF head.
     (1) Check electrical cables for damage, connectors for tightness, and units for bonding straps.
     (2) Inspect hat, ring, and clamp for damage.
     (3) Check for paint peeling on units.
     (4) Check blowers for freedom of rotation.
   e. Wave guide assembly.
     (1) Check that caps on bi-directional coupler are tight.
     (2) Check rubber on flexible wave guide for damage.

f. Check that antenna screen door is closed and S-1709 is in the ON position.

11. Boosters and ammo cans.
    a. Check for proper rotation.
    b. Check ammunition cans for cleanliness, dry condition, and damage.

12. Remove the feeder and check that the gun is cleared of the round in the chamber. If there is a round in the chamber, use the following procedure: Remove the driving spring; unlock the breechblock with the unlocking tool; and extract the round.

13. Remove breechblocks and inspect guns and chargers.
    a. After the gun has been cleared, remove the rear buffer assembly and breechblock group. Check gun tube for obstructions.
    b. Check guns for the following:
        (1) Receiver and tube clean and excess oil removed.
            (a) Receiver interior for burrs, deformation, and general condition.
            (b) Presence of lug on carrier slide (Rhode-Lewis or Johnson Farebox Chargers).
        (2) Round sensing switch and plunger for proper spring tension.
        (3) Breechblock contact properly installed and safety wired.
        (4) Disassemble the breechblock and inspect for the following:
            (a) Broken, loose, or worn parts.
            (b) Burrs and deformation.
            (c) Insulation worn or missing.
            (d) All parts wiped dry and re-assembled.
            (e) Re-install the breechblock in the receiver. Replace the rear buffer and driving spring assemblies.
        (5) Security of mount and attachment.
        (6) Scribe marks are aligned on the magazine slide and receiver.
        (7) Magazine slide anchor secured and anchor nuts tight.
        (8) Firing leads moving freely for gun recoil (no clamps).
        (9) Presence of cotter keys, lock washers, and safety wire.
    c. Check gun chargers for the following:
        (1) Security of mount and attachment.
        (2) Charging stud installed and charging stud retainer in place (GE charger only).
        (3) Charger switch in NEUTRAL position.
    d. Check cables and AN connectors on guns and chargers for good condition.

14. Inspect feeders and link chutes. Check for the following:
    a. Links or ammo in the feeder.
    b. Feeder mouth for burrs and deformation.
    c. Operating lever locks in down position.
    d. Feeder for excess oil or grease.
    e. Feeder cover or adapter of proper series.
    f. Link deflectors and link chutes for obstruction or damage.
    g. Link chute installed with wide side away from the feeder.
    h. Cartridge guides, control pawl, and holding dog for freedom of movement.
    i. Star wheels and link strippers for damage.
    j. Connectors for damage.
    k. Presence of cotter keys and safety wire.

15. Feeders installed and operating levers connected.
    a. Install the feeder and make sure that the magazine latch locks it to the gun.
    b. Connect the operating lever to the bracket on the gun and lock it.

16. Brass and ammo feed chutes.
    a. Check the ammo chutes for proper mount, bent or damaged links, proper configuration, and cleanliness.
    b. Check brass chutes for obstruction, damaged areas, and security of mount; check that sliding deflectors are secured; check deflector springs.

17. Limit switches, actuators, and mechanical stops. Check azimuth and elevation limit switches for security of mount, damage, and proper spring operation when actuated manually. Check actuators and mechanical stops for proper installation.

18. Selsyns and drive motors.
    a. Check selsyns and selsyn caps for tightness, contactor plugs for proper installation and security, and selsyn covers for proper installation.
    b. Check drive motors. Check brush holders for security of mount, electrical cables for damage, and connectors for tightness. Check security of mount.

19. Complete brass chute inspection (Outside). See paragraph 16 to complete the remainder of brass chute inspection which could not be accomplished from inside of aircraft.

20. Inspect and engage feeder winders. Inspect for the following:
    a. Damaged electrical cables and tightness of connectors.
    b. Security of mount and attachment.
    c. Free wheeling.
    d. Proper operation of locking device.

21. Complete gun and turret inspection (Outside). See paragraph 13 to complete gun inspection which could not be accomplished from inside the aircraft.

22. Turret Movement (Manual). Disengage turret drive motor brakes and check that turret moves smoothly and freely in azimuth and elevation.

23. Brakes locked; re-engage drive motor brakes.

Operational Check.

1. Turret clear for operation. Check that personnel and stands are cleared of turrets before operating. Be sure that turret is cleared of ammunition and that power is available. *Do not load guns* until operational check has been completed and units do not require maintenance.

2. Selector switch WARMUP, heater fuse IN; check heaters. When the feeder and gun heater become warm, remove the heater fuse.

> **CAUTION**
>
> Heaters should be left on just long enough to check operation.

External turret safety switch ON; turret power and turret safety switches ON.

3. Wave guide shutter action. Check operation of the wave guide shutter by switching from WARMUP to STANDBY to WARMUP. Have an observer check for clicking action of wave guide shutter at the transmission line.

> **CAUTION**
>
> Always make sure the wave guide shutter is operational before checking pressure.

4. Selector switch STANDBY. Check thyratron and all radar blowers.
   a. Check the thyratron blower for operation.
   b. Check radar central, RF head, and modulator external blowers for operation. Check internal blower by placing hand on unit.

> **CAUTION**
>
> If thyratron or any radar blowers are not operating, turn system OFF. Do not let fingers come in contact with rotary fans.

5. Thyratron timed out. After 100 ($\pm$30) seconds, check to see whether thyratron controller times out.

6. Radar central timed out. After 3 minutes and 45 ($\pm$10) seconds, check that radar central times out. Observe that the AFC XTAL current oscillates, indicating that the radar central has timed out.

7. 28.5-volt d-c check. Check line 143 at turret junction box for 28.5-volt d-c output; if necessary, adjust R-43 in thyratron controller to get desired voltage.

> **CAUTION**
>
> Use extreme caution to avoid shorting out other wires in turret junction box. While assistant is checking 28.5-volt d-c output at turret junction box do not close action switch.

Note

If turret junction box does not have a test jack for checking d-c voltage, use the external turret safety switch as a checking point. Voltage should read 28.5-volt dc. If no external turret safety switch is installed on the aircraft, then check test jack J-66 at the thyratron controller for 31.5-volt d-c voltage reading.

8. Selector Switch RADAR. Adjust intensity.

> **CAUTION**
>
> An intense spot may burn the screen of the cathode ray tube.

9. Scope Presentation.
   a. Check the search pattern by observing the azimuth motion of sweep and elevation UP and DOWN lights.
   b. Check jizzle width is 30 degrees.
   c. Check azimuth deflection amplitude.
   d. Check range sweep amplitude.
   e. Check vertical and horizontal centering.
   f. Check for normal ground presentation.
   g. Check that the alarm lamp is lit when the sweep passes over a target or ground return.

Note

If many targets are present, the ALARM lamp may be lit continuously.

10. Indicator unit controls.

Note

Two man team is needed for the following checks.

a. Check L.O.—MANUAL control. Tune manually for best targets. Maximum current and best targets should occur together, and current should be approximately .7 to .9 ma. Switch to L.O. Targets and current should be approximately the same as in MANUAL. AFC light should then be OUT.

b. Check operation of range search limit control.
   (1) Turn IF gain fully clockwise.
   (2) Turn range search limit fully clockwise.
   (3) Depress action switch. The jizzle width should now be approximately 7 degrees and the range gate should now sweep from zero to 8000 yards repeatedly.
   (4) Turn range search limit fully counterclockwise, but do not actuate the switch. The range gate should now sweep from zero to 2000 yards repeatedly.
   (5) Turn range search limit fully counterclockwise, actuating the switch. The Range Gate should now disappear.

c. IF gain, alarm, AGC and lock on check.
   (1) Turn IF gain control counterclockwise until targets begin to appear. Alarm light will light as targets appear.

(2) Check that the range gate locks on weak targets.

(3) Turn IF gain fully CCW, actuating the switch. Lock on strong target; observe weak targets disappear. Lock on distant target; observe that guns do not spiral or hunt.

d. Check range IN—OUT switch for proper operation.

e. Depress the search button. Check that the turret returns to stow position and the antenna goes into automatic search.

f. Check operation of long range-short range switch.

11. 1 and 31 speed operation and thyratron tubes firing.

a. Press action switch.

b. Thirty-one speed check. Slowly move hand control; the antenna, indicator sweep, and turret should follow the hand control smoothly. Check both directions, in azimuth and elevation.

c. One speed check. Slew hand control; turret should follow rapidly. Check both directions in azimuth and elevation.

d. While turret is being operated, check to see that all azimuth, elevation and d-c power thyratron tubes are firing properly. No excessive overheating and no cross-firing should occur. Check for a bluish purple color while firing. No firing should occur above the plate or at the base of the tube.

Note

A pinkish orange or whitish color indicates a bad tube which should be replaced.

12. Check wave guide and RF head for RF leakage.

13. Safe-fire switches FIRE.

14. Gun charger, booster, and feeder winder operation.

a. At the turret, place charger switch to HOLD-BACK position; charger should charge and hold the breechblock to the rear position. Place switch to NEUTRAL position; the charger should release breechblock. Place the charger switch to CHARGE position; the charger should automatically charge and release breechblock.

b. At control panel, place charger switch to HOLD-BACK position. Charger should charge and hold breechblock to the rear position. Place charger switch to RELEASE position. Charger should release breechblock.

c. Press firing button. Chargers and boosters should operate and feeder winders should rotate in proper direction.

15. Antenna and turret limit switches; backout and stowing circuits.

a. Press the action switch and move the antenna and turret into a limit. The turret should stop and then the antenna. Press the firing button; the boosters, chargers, and feeder winders should not operate. Check that the turret does not drift at extreme antenna position.

b. Move hand control in the opposite direction, keeping the firing button actuated. Antenna and turret should move off the limits smoothly; boosters and chargers should operate. Release the firing button and action switch; the turret should stow and the antenna should go into automatic search.

c. Repeat this procedure right and left in azimuth, up and down in elevation.

Note

Elevation turret limits may not always be actuated by use of hand control movement because of positioning of antenna limits.

16. OOSFI.

a. Depress action switch; move guns into azimuth limit.

b. Slew the guns toward opposite azimuth limit and depress firing button. Do not go into the limit.

c. Chargers and boosters should not operate until guns are within 3 degrees of alignment with antenna.

d. Repeat the above for elevation.

17. Pressure System Check.

a. Place system in SEARCH.

b. Press manual switch ON and build pressure up to 40 as indicated by tail radar pressure gage.

c. Check for leakage by observing the pressure gage. The gage reading should not drop lower than 39 within a period of 15 minutes.

d. While pressure is built up to 40, check for ballooning of flexible wave guide.

e. If leakage is within tolerance, push the DRAIN pressure button and drain pressure until gage again reads 30.

Note

The pressure will increase slightly due to heating of units, this increase in pressure will vary in different geographical locations.

18. Disconnect chargers at guns.

CAUTION

When disconnecting or reconnecting gun charger cables be sure that turret safety switch or external turret safety switch is in OFF position.

19. Firing Circuit Check.

a. Close action switch; point guns to an unrestricted area.

> **CAUTION**
>
> Be sure that breechblock is in battery position before inserting magic wand. Use extreme caution in placing any part of the body in front of gun muzzles.

> **CAUTION**
>
> Do not release action switch at any time during this check.

b. Have an assistant insert firing circuit tester in tube of gun and push it against firing pin. (This will prevent firing pin from grounding out on the firing pin port.)

c. Depress firing button and have assistant check that gun fires. Check other gun by same method.

> **WARNING**
>
> While checking firing circuit insure that when triggers are released the firing circuit is *out*. If there is an indication that the firing circuit is still functioning after the firing button is released, get it repaired *immediately* and *do not load* the guns until it has bee repaired.

d. After firing circuit check, release action switch and put system in SEARCH.

20. Reconnect chargers; safe-fire switches SAFE and safety wired in SAFE position before continuing with other checks.

21. Computer Check.

a. Range check.

(1) Computer switch IN and attack factor switch PURSUIT.

(2) Set range beyond 1000 yards. Jog RANGE IN-OUT switch downward until range gate locks on the 1000-yard marker. The computer range dial should read 1000 (± 20) yards.

(3) LOCK on the 500-yard marker. Computer range dial should read 500 (± 10) yards.

(4) With the attack factor switch in STRAIGHT-LINE position, the readings for 500-yard marker should read 477 (± 10) yards. 1000-yard marker should read 982 (± 20) yards.

(5) Check ballistic dial changes with range movement.

b. Set altitude MINIMUM, air speed MAXIMUM at handset unit and lock range 1000-yard marker.

(1) Lead check. Close action switch and track steadily for some distance. Stop the hand control abruptly and observe the movement of the turret. The turret should stop when the hand control is stopped and then creep in the opposite direction. Check both directions in azimuth and elevation.

(2) Windage check. Close action switch. Move antenna as close to broadside as possible without getting turret on a limit. Place computer switch to OUT. Guns should swing slightly to the rear, place computer switch to IN. The windage correction should come back IN and move the guns slightly forward.

(3) Gravity check. Move the antenna and turret straight aft and zero degrees elevation. Move computer switch to OUT; guns should move down slightly. When the computer switch is moved IN, the guns should jump up slightly.

c. Check that resolver input unit dials correspond to movements of antenna.

d. Check that elevation and azimuth correction dials follow antenna movement.

e. Computer switch OUT.

f. CAL-NORMAL switch to NORMAL.

> **CAUTION**
>
> Do not turn selector switch to off position when action switch is actuated, as it may cause a computer malfunction.

22. All switches OFF or SAFE.

a. Turn intensity control fully counterclockwise.

b. Turret power switch OFF.

c. Selector switch OFF.

d. Turn external turret safety switch OFF.

23. Replace thyratron and radar central covers.

24. External-normal switch to EXTERNAL.

Section VIII
Crew Duties

T.O. 1B-36D(II)-1

SECOND RADIO-ECM OPERATOR (RIGHT FORWARD GUNNER).

The second radio-ECM operator is also the right forward gunner. He assists the first radio-ECM operator and, in addition, will assist in the preflight of gunnery equipment. The following are his duties:

NOTE

FOR AMPLIFICATION OF THE GUNNERY CHECK LIST AND EMERGENCY PROCEDURES, REFER TO "GUNNERY AMPLIFIED CHECK LIST, UPPER AFT GUNNER (LEFT)," OF THIS SECTION.

VISUAL PREFLIGHT

1. Form 781 (Form 1) .... CHECKED

PREFLIGHT OPERATIONAL EQUIPMENT CHECK

1. Walk-Around Bottles and Filler Hose .... CHECKED
2. All Interphone Equipment and Stations in Bomb Bay, Aft Compartment, and Tail, Including Speakers, Amplifiers and/or Channel 1 and 2 Power Supplies (AN/AIC-10) (If Applicable) .... CHECKED
3. Radome (Applicable ECM Balun Units and IFF Inertia Switch) .... CHECKED
4. All Fuses and/or Circuit Breakers in Aft Compartment and Tail .... CHECKED
5. AN/ARN-6, Cables, Plugs, for Security (If Applicable) .... CHECKED
6. AM-203/ARA-19, Cables, Plugs, for Security, (If Applicable) .... CHECKED
7. ID-251/ARN, Cables, Plugs, for Security, Heading Checked with Gyros on, Against Pilot's Magnetic Compass or N-1, with Magnetic Heading Set in (If Applicable) .... CHECKED
8. DY-66 ( )/ARN-14, Cables, Plugs, for Security (If Applicable) .... CHECKED
9. RT-178/ARC-27, Cables, Plugs, for Security (If Applicable) .... CHECKED
10. R-252 ( )/ARN-14, Cables, Plugs, for Security (If Applicable) .... CHECKED
11. AN/ARC-21, Cables, Plugs, for Security (If Applicable) .... CHECKED
12. Chaff dispensers Checked and Loaded ...... AS REQUIRED

GUNNERY PREFLIGHT

1. GUNNERY EQUIPMENT PREFLIGHT AND LOADING

NOTE

THE FOLLOWING PROCEDURE MUST BE ACCOMPLISHED BY A TWO-MAN TEAM UTILIZING INTERPHONE.

Check turret status.
Check external turret bay door tracks.
a. VISUAL INSPECTION

AT SIGHTING STATION

(1) All switches OFF or SAFE, heater power fuse removed.
(2) Check sighting station.
(3) Selector switch to STANDBY.
(4) Selector switch DOOR OPEN and OPERATION in coordination with man in turret bay.
(5) All switches OFF or SAFE.
　(a) Turret power switch OFF first.

ON WAY TO TURRET BAY

Check turret bay door motor, cables and pulleys.
Check door-open limit switch.
Check fuses in a-c turret power panel.

AT TURRET BAY

(1) Turret safety switch SAFE.
(2) Turret bay clear, check stow marks.
(3) Turret safety switch ON. Check thyratron blower.
(4) Must stand by turret safety switch until turret is fully extended.
(5) Turret safety switch SAFE.

(6) Remove gun enclosure and access panels.
(7) Remove feeder and check that gun is cleared of round in chamber.

AT SIGHTING STATION (Cont'd)

AT TURRET BAY (Cont'd)

(8) Remove breechblocks, inspect guns, chargers and feeder winders. Re-install breechblocks.
(9) Inspect feeders, link chutes.
(10) Install feeders, feeder winder and operating lever connected.
(11) Selsyns.
(12) Limit switches, actuator and mechanical stops (turret).
(13) All AN connectors, motors, units and cables on turret.
(14) Brakes locked.
(15) All other AN connectors, motors, units and cables in turret bay.
(16) Boosters, ammo cans and ammo feed chutes.
(17) Limit switches (torque tube).
(18) Remove thyratron cover and check fuses and tubes.

NOTE

PROCEED TO THE TURRET BAY AND VISUALLY PREFLIGHT INDIVIDUAL TURRET.

b. OPERATIONAL

AT SIGHTING STATION

(1) Turret power switch OFF.
(2) Selector switch WARM UP and heater fuse IN.
   (a) After heater check, remove fuse.
(3) Selector switch OPERATION.
   (a) Turret power switch ON.
(4) 28.5V DC check.
(5) Check sight for operation.
(6) Gun camera switch ON, gun camera operation.
(7) 1 and 31 speed operation.
(8) Safe-fire switches FIRE.
(9) Gun charger, boosters and feeder winder operation.
(10) Limit switches backout and stowing circuits.
(11) OOSFI.
(12) Contour follower.
(13) Fire interrupter.
(14) Firing circuit check after charger disconnected.
(15) Safe-fire switches SAFETY WIRED SAFE.
(16) Computer.
   (a) Computer switch OUT after check.
(17) Boresight check.
(18) All switches OFF or SAFE.
   (a) Turret power switch OFF first.

c. LOADING

(1) Inspect ammo.
(2) Load ammo.
(3) Link and case ejection chutes installed.
(4) Spent case containers closed.
(5) Arm feeders.
(6) Final turret checks.
(7) Replace gun enclosure and access panels.
(8) Set round counters.
(9) Selector switch OPERATION, retract turret and close turret bay door.
(10) All switches OFF or SAFE.
(11) Place warning sign on control panel.

AT TURRET BAY

(1) Turret safety switch SAFE.
(2) Check heaters.

(3) Turret safety switch ON.

(4) 28.5V DC check.
(5) Stand clear, observe equipment operation and notify gunner at sight steps (7) through (18).

(7) Thyratron tubes firing.

(9) Check hold-back and manual charge.

(14) Disconnect chargers at guns, check firing circuit.
(15) Reconnect chargers.

(18) Turret safety switch SAFE.

(9) Turret safety switch ON, must stand by turret safety switch until turret is fully retracted.

CREW INSPECTION

1. As Outlined In Section II, Normal Procedures....CHECKED
2. All Required Personal Equipment................CHECKED

PREFLIGHT (DAY OF FLIGHT)

1. Sight and Control Panel Switches .... OFF
2. Sight Stowed and Locked........................CHECKED
3. Defroster Nozzle Removed......................CHECKED
4. Blister For Proper Installation, Cracks and Cleanliness ....CHECKED
5. Trouble Light..................................CHECKED
6. Safety Straps and Sling-Type Seat..............CHECKED
7. Aldis Lamp For Operation......................CHECKED
8. Night Flying Curtain............................CHECKED
9. Visual Inspection of Turret and Turret Bay Doors..CHECKED

Section VIII
Crew Duties

AT SIGHTING STATION (Cont'd)

10. Turret Safety Switch .... ON
11. All Loose Equipment in R/O Compartment, Radome and Right Catwalk .... SECURED
12. Check Private and Normal Interphone Using Oxygen Mask and Helmet, Verifying Side-Tone (If Applicable) .... CHECKED
13. Walk-Around Bottles and Filler Hose .... CHECKED
14. Oxygen Mask and Oxygen Station .... CHECKED
15. Facility Charts (VOR and LF/MF), Supplementary Flight Information Book, Pilots ILS, East-West Handbooks (Foreign as required) corrected to date ... CHECKED
16. Fire Axe, First Aid Kits, and Fire Extinguishers ... CHECKED
17. Gibson Girl and URC-4 (If Applicable) .... STOWED
18. Spare Parachute and Oxygen Equipment .... STOWED
19. Hot and Cold Liquid Containers and 2 Hot Cups. STOWED

FINAL CREW BRIEFING

1. According to Section II, Normal Procedures ..... CHECKED
2. A/C Informed of Discrepancies .... CHECKED

STATIONS (START ENGINES)

1. At Emergency Hydraulic Pump, on Interphone if Possible (Private) .... STANDBY

TAXI

1. At Emergency Hydraulic pump, on Normal Interphone .... STANDBY

TAKE-OFF

1. In Take-Off Position .... READY
2. Parachute .... ON

CRUISE

1. Sight Locked In Up Position .... CHECKED
2. Defroster Nozzle Replaced .... CHECKED
3. GUNNERY OPERATION AND AERIAL FIRING
   a. Safe-Fire Switches .... SAFE
   b. Heater Power .... ON-OFF AS REQUIRED
   c. Turret Power Switch .... ON
   d. Selector Switch in Sequence .... OPERATION
   e. Rounds Counter .... SET
   f. Target Size Knob .... SET
   g. Handset Unit .... SET
   h. Gun Camera .... CHECKED
   i. Computer .... IN
   j. Attack Factor Switch .... AS REQUIRED
   k. Reticle .... SET
   l. Sight and Turret Operation .... AS REQUIRED
   m. Safe-Fire Switches .... FIRE

CAUTION

SAFE-FIRE A-C WARMUP SWITCH REQUIRES 3 MINUTE WARMUP PERIOD PRIOR TO FIRING. THIS APPLIES EVERY TIME SWITCH IS TURNED ON. NOT APPLICABLE TO SYSTEMS UTILIZING FREE-FIRE BOX.

   n. Burst Control .... AS REQUIRED
4. GUNNERY PORTION OF MISSION COMPLETED:
   a. Safe-Fire Switches .... SAFETY WIRED SAFE
   b. Heater Power Fuse .... REMOVED
   c. Guns Cooled .... 20 MINUTES
   d. Turret Stowed and Retracted .... COMPLETED
   e. All Switches .... OFF
5. Parachute and Oxygen Equipment As Regulations Require .... COMPLIED

AT SIGHTING STATION (Cont'd)

LANDING
1. Defroster Nozzle Removed ....CHECKED
2. Sight Stowed In Down Position and Locked........CHECKED
3. In Landing Position, Parachute On................READY

TAXI
1. At Emergency Hydraulic Pump, on Interphone
   if Possible ....STANDBY

POSTFLIGHT
1. Sighting Station................................CLEANED
2. Interphone Cords...............................SECURED
3. Turret Safety Switch SAFE and Warning Signals Posted
4. Oxygen Station ....SECURED
5. Compartment ....CLEANED
6. Malfunctions Reported to First Radio-ECM
   Operator ....CHECK

LEFT FORWARD GUNNER.

This is the copilot of the crew. In addition to his other duties, he will assist in the preflight of gunnery equipment. Inflight duties include gunnery equipment operation. He accomplishes the following duties:

Note

In the event a copilot is not assigned to the crew, this station will be manned by the aircraft electrician gunner.

NOTE

FOR AMPLIFICATION OF THE GUNNERY CHECK LIST AND EMERGENCY PROCEDURES, REFER TO "GUNNERY AMPLIFIED CHECK LIST, UPPER AFT GUNNER (LEFT)," OF THIS SECTION.

PREFLIGHT
1. GUNNERY EQUIPMENT PREFLIGHT AND LOADING

NOTE

THE FOLLOWING PROCEDURE MUST BE ACCOMPLISHED BY A TWO-MAN TEAM UTILIZING INTERPHONE.

Check turret status.
Check external turret bay door tracks.

a. VISUAL INSPECTION

AT SIGHTING STATION

(1) All switches OFF or SAFE, heater power fuse removed.
(2) Check sighting station.
(3) Selector switch to STANDBY.
(4) Selector switch DOOR OPEN and OPERATION in coordination with man in turret bay.
(5) All switches OFF or SAFE.
   (a) Turret power switch OFF first.

ON WAY TO TURRET BAY

Check turret bay door motor, cables and pulleys.
Check door-open limit switch.
Check fuses in a-c turret power panel.

AT TURRET BAY

(1) Turret safety switch SAFE.
(2) Turret bay clear, check stow marks.
(3) Turret safety switch ON. Check thyratron blower.
(4) Must stand by turret safety switch until turret is fully extended.
(5) Turret safety switch SAFE.
(6) Remove gun enclosure and access panels.
(7) Remove feeder and check that gun is cleared of round in chamber.
(8) Remove breechblocks, inspect guns, chargers and feeder winders. Re-install breechblocks.
(9) Inspect feeders, link chutes.
(10) Install feeders, feeder winder and operating lever connected.
(11) Selsyns.

Section VIII
Crew Duties

AT SIGHTING STATION (Cont'd)

NOTE

PROCEED TO THE TURRET BAY AND VISUALLY PRE-FLIGHT INDIVIDUAL TURRET.

b. OPERATIONAL

AT SIGHTING STATION
(1) Turret power switch OFF.
(2) Selector switch WARM UP and heater fuse IN.
   (a) After heater check, remove fuse.
(3) Selector switch OPERATION.
   (a) Turret power switch ON.
(4) 28.5V DC check.
(5) Check sight for operation.
(6) Gun camera switch ON, gun camera operation.
(7) 1 and 31 speed operation.
(8) Safe-fire switches FIRE.
(9) Gun charger, boosters and feeder winder operation.
(10) Limit switches backout and stowing circuits.
(11) OOSFI.
(12) Contour follower.
(13) Fire interrupter.
(14) Firing circuit check after charger disconnected.
(15) Safe-fire switches safety wired SAFE.

(16) Computer.
   (a) Computer switch OUT after check.
(17) Boresight check.
(18) All switches OFF or SAFE.
   (a) Turret power switch OFF first.

c. LOADING
(1) Inspect ammo.
(2) Load ammo.
(3) Link and case ejection chutes installed.
(4) Spent case containers closed.
(5) Arm feeders.
(6) Final turret checks.
(7) Replace gun enclosure and access panels.
(8) Set round counters.
(9) Selector switch OPERATION, retract turret and close turret bay door.
(10) All switches OFF or SAFE.
(11) Place warning sign on control panel.

2. CREW INSPECTION
   a. Extra duties completed .... AS REQUIRED

3. COMBAT STATION
   a. Oxygen and Interphone .... CHECKED
   b. Personal Equipment .... STOWED
   c. Trouble Light .... CHECKED
   d. Sight and Control Panel Switches .... OFF
   e. Sight Stowed and Locked .... CHECKED
   f. Blister for Proper Installation, Cracks and Cleanliness .... CHECKED
   g. Safety Straps and Sling-Type Seat .... CHECKED
   h. Aldis Lamp for Operation .... CHECKED
   i. Night Flying Curtain .... STOWED

4. CREW DUTIES
   a. Visual Inspection of Turret and Turret Bay Door .. CHECKED
   b. Turret Safety Switch .... ON
   c. Extra Duties .... AS REQUIRED
   d. Escape Ropes .... STOWED

5. PRIOR TO TAKE-OFF
   a. Blister Defroster (Replace After Take-Off) .... REMOVED
   b. Sight In Down Position (Up Position After Take-Off) .... LOCKED

AT TURRET BAY (Cont'd)
(12) Limit switches, actuator and mechanical stops (turret).
(13) All AN connectors, motors, units and cables on turret.
(14) Brakes locked.
(15) All other AN connectors, motors, units and cables in turret bay.
(16) Boosters, ammo cans and ammo feed chutes.
(17) Limit switches (torque tube).
(18) Remove thyratron cover and check fuses and tubes.

AT TURRET BAY
(1) Turret safety switch SAFE.
(2) Check heaters.

(3) Turret safety switch ON.

(4) 28.5V DC check.
(5) Stand clear, observe equipment operation and notify gunner at sight steps (7) through (18).
(7) Thyratron tubes firing.

(9) Check hold-back and manual charge.

(14) Disconnect chargers at guns; check firing circuit.
(15) Reconnect chargers.

(18) Turret safety switch SAFE.

(9) Turret safety switch ON, must stand by turret safety switch until turret is fully retracted.

INFLIGHT

1. GUNNERY EQUIPMENT OPERATION AND AERIAL FIRING
    a. Safe-Fire Switches .... SAFE
    b. Heater Power .... ON-OFF AS REQUIRED
    c. Turret Power Switch .... ON
    d. Selector Switch in Sequence .... OPERATION
    e. Round Counters .... SET
    f. Target Size Knob .... SET
    g. Handset Unit .... SET
    h. Gun Camera .... CHECKED
    i. Computer .... IN
    j. Attack Factor Switch .... SET AS REQUIRED
    k. Reticle .... SET
    l. Sight and Turret Operation .... AS REQUIRED
    m. Safe-Fire Switches .... FIRE

CAUTION

SAFE-FIRE A-C WARMUP SWITCH REQUIRES 3 MINUTE WARMUP PERIOD PRIOR TO FIRING. THIS APPLIES EVERY TIME SWITCH IS TURNED ON. NOT APPLICABLE TO SYSTEMS UTILIZING FREE-FIRE BOX.

    n. Burst Control .... AS REQUIRED
2. GUNNERY PORTION OF MISSION COMPLETED
    a. Safe-Fire Switches .... SAFETY WIRED SAFE
    b. Heater Power Fuse .... REMOVED
    c. Guns Cooled .... 20 MINUTES
    d. Turret Stowed and Retracted .... COMPLETED
    e. All Switches .... OFF
3. PREPARE FOR LANDING
    a. Blister Defroster (Replace After Landing) ..... REMOVED
    b. Sight In Down Position (Up Position After Landing) .... LOCKED
    c. Auxiliary and Miscellaneous Equipment ...... SECURED
    d. Safety Belt .... FASTENED

POSTFLIGHT

1. AFTER LANDING
    a. Sighting Station and Area .... CLEANED
    b. Interphone Cords .... STOWED
    c. Oxygen Panel Settings and Oxygen Hose ..... SECURED
    d. Guns and Gunnery Equipment Secured .. TURRET SAFETY SW-SAFE AND WARNING SIGNS POSTED
    e. Malfunctions .... REPORTED

NOSE GUNNER.

This is the third observer of the crew. In addition to his other duties, he will assist in preflight of gunnery equipment. Inflight duties include gunnery equipment operation. He accomplishes the following duties:

NOTE

FOR AMPLIFICATION OF THE GUNNERY CHECK LIST AND EMERGENCY PROCEDURES, REFER TO "GUNNERY AMPLIFIED CHECK LIST, UPPER AFT GUNNER (LEFT)," OF THIS SECTION.

PREFLIGHT

1. GUNNERY EQUIPMENT PREFLIGHT AND LOADING
    a. VISUAL INSPECTION
        (1) Check turret status.
        (2) All switches OFF or SAFE. Heater power fuse removed.
        (3) Check sighting station.
        (4) Check desiccant.
        (5) Link and brass compartment.
        (6) Check fuses in right forward cabin power panel (RCT and desiccator).
        (7) All units in pressurized compartment and radar antenna well.
        (8) Remove thyratron cover and check fuses and tubes.
        (9) External turret safety switch OFF.
        (10) Remove gun enclosure and dome assembly panels.
        (11) Remove feeder and check that gun is cleared of round in the chamber.
        (12) Remove breechblocks, inspect guns, chargers and feeder winders. Re-install breechblocks.
        (13) Inspect feeders, link chutes.
        (14) Install feeders, feeder winder and operating lever connected.
        (15) Motors, units, cables, AN connectors.
        (16) Turret movement (MANUAL).
        (17) Brakes locked.
        (18) Selsyns
        (19) Limit switches, actuators and mechanical stops.
        (20) Rollers, ammo cans and ammo feed chutes.
        (21) Dome cover removed and sight dome cleaned.
    b. OPERATIONAL
        (1) Selector switch WARMUP, dome heater switch ON, and heater fuse IN, check heaters.
            (a) After heater check, remove fuse, dome heater switch OFF.
            (b) External turret safety switch ON.
            (c) Turret power and turret safety switches ON.

Section VIII
Crew Duties

(2) Selector switch OPERATION, check thyratron blower—thyratron timed out.
(3) 28.5V DC check.
(4) Check sight for operation.
(5) Check desiccator for operation.
(6) Check wiper for operation.
(7) Gun camera switch ON, gun camera operation.
(8) 1 and 31 speed operation and thyratron tubes firing.
(9) Safe-fire switches FIRE.
(10) Check gun chargers and feeder winder operation.
(11) Limit switches, back-out and stowing circuits.
(12) OOSFI circuit.
(13) Disconnect chargers at guns.
(14) Firing circuit check.
(15) Reconnect chargers and safe-fire switches SAFETY WIRED SAFE.
(16) Computer.
  (a) Computer switch OUT after check.
(17) Boresight check.
(18) All switches OFF or SAFE.
(19) Thyratron cover replaced.

c. LOADING
(1) Inspect ammo.
(2) External turret safety switch OFF and dome cover replaced.
(3) Load ammo.
(4) Arm feeders.
(5) Final turret checks.
(6) Replace gun enclosure and dome assembly panels.
(7) External turret safety switch ON.
(8) Place warning sign on control panel.
(9) Set round counters.

2. CREW INSPECTION
3. COMBAT STATION
   a. Oxygen and interphone............................CHECKED
   b. Personal equipment...............................STOWED
   c. Trouble light.....................................CHECKED
   d. Sight and control panel switches......OFF AND SAFE
   e. Sight stowed and locked..........................CHECKED
   f. Safety belt......................................CHECKED
   g. Nose turret access door.........................SECURED
4. CREW DUTIES
   a. Turret safety switch..................................ON
   b. External turret safety switch.........................ON
   c. Visual inspection of nose turret.................CHECKED
   d. Dome sight cover..................................REMOVED

INFLIGHT

1. AFTER TAKE-OFF
   a. Dome heater and desiccator............................ON
2. GUNNERY EQUIPMENT OPERATION AND AERIAL FIRING
   a. Safe-fire switches..................................SAFE
   b. Heater Power...................ON—OFF AS REQUIRED
   c. Turret Power Switch...................................ON
   d. Selector Switch in Sequence..................OPERATION
   e. Round counters..SET
   f. Handset unit..SET
   g. Target size knob......................................SET
   h. Gun camera.......................................CHECKED
   i. Computer..IN
   j. Attack factor switch......................SET AS REQUIRED
   k. Reticle...SET
   l. Sight and Turret Operation......................CHECKED
   m. Safe-Fire Switches...................................FIRE

CAUTION

SAFE-FIRE A-C WARMUP SWITCH REQUIRES 3 MINUTE WARMUP PERIOD PRIOR TO FIRING. THIS APPLIES EVERY TIME SWITCH IS TURNED ON. NOT APPLICABLE TO SYSTEMS UTLIZING FREE-FIRE BOX.

   n. Burst Control...............................AS REQUIRED
3. GUNNERY PORTION OF MISSION COMPLETED
   a. Safe-Fire Switches...................SAFETY WIRED SAFE
   b. Heater Power Fuse..............................REMOVED
   c. Guns Cooled...................................20 MINUTES
   d. Turret Stowed..................................COMPLETED
   e. All Switches..OFF

4. PREPARE FOR LANDING
   a. Auxiliary and miscellaneous equipment..........SECURED
   b. Dome heater..OFF

POSTFLIGHT

1. AFTER LANDING
   a. Desiccator and Control Panel Switches.............OFF
   b. Sighting station and area.....................CLEANED
   c. Sight Dome Cover..............................REPLACED
   d. Interphone cord................................STOWED
   e. Oxygen panel settings and oxygen hose.........SECURED
   f. Guns and gunnery equipment secured....TURRET SAFETY SWITCH—SAFE AND WARNING SIGNS POSTED
   g. Malfunctions..................................REPORTED

AMPLIFIED CHECK LISTS.

Nose Station Amplified Check List.

Visual Inspection.

1. Check turret status. Check with senior gunner on status of turret and gunnery equipment before commencing preflight.

2. All switches OFF or SAFE; heater power fuse REMOVED.

   a. Selector switch OFF.

   b. Turret power switch OFF.

   c. Safe-fire switches SAFE.

   d. Charger switch RELEASE.

   e. Heater power fuse REMOVED. Check for continuity.

   f. Computer switch OUT.

   g. Dome heater switch OFF.

   h. Desiccator switch OFF.

   i. Turret safety switch SAFE.

3. Check sighting station.

   a. Check proper feel of sight controls in azimuth and elevation. (If not correct, adjust friction adjustment for desired tension.)

   b. Clean sight optical surfaces by wiping surface with a soft cloth or lens tissue.

   c. Check mounting and AN connectors for security and presence of safety wire.

   d. Check sight selsyns and selsyn caps for tightness and selsyn contactor plug for proper installation and security.

   e. Check gun camera for security of mount and AN connectors for tightness. Open magazine access cover. Move magazine latch and note that spline gear protrudes.

   f. Check that spare bulbs are installed.

   g. Check stow pins for proper locking operation.

4. Check desiccant.

   a. Check crystals in static desiccators; they must be blue.

   b. Check crystals in external desiccators; they must be blue down to the change line.

   c. Check that air tube connections are tight and air tubes are in good condition.

5. Link and brass compartment.

a. Check that all expended cases and links are removed.

b. Check that compartment is clean and dry.

c. Check that link and case wiper assembly parts are securely mounted.

6. Check fuses in the right forward cabin power panel.

a. Check RCT fuses for proper rating (40 amps).

b. Check desiccator fuses for proper rating (10 amps).

c. Check that spare fuses are available.

7. Check all units in pressurized compartment and radar antenna well.

a. Check computer and resolver input unit. Check dials for damage. Check electrical cables for good condition and connectors for security.

b. Check frequency converter, gyro drive unit, system junction box, fire control box. Check electrical cables for good condition and connectors for security.

Note

The frequency converter, resolver input, and gyro drive units are located in the radar antenna well.

8. Remove thyratron cover. Check fuses and tubes.

a. Check all electrical cables for good condition and connectors for security.

b. Check all fuses for proper installation and continuity.

c. Check power thyratron tubes for proper installation and check that tube plates are not damaged.

Note

This procedure may not be practical on some aircraft because of location of equipment.

9. External turret safety switch OFF. This switch is located on the right hand side of the fuselage at the nose of the aircraft.

CAUTION

This switch must always be placed to the OFF position when personnel are on or at the turret. The only exceptions to this rule are indicated on the check list (OPERATIONAL).

10. Remove gun enclosure and dome assembly panels.

a. Check turret dome and gun enclosures for cracks, dents, fasteners, clearance, and security.

b. Place gun enclosure and dome assembly panels in a safe place where they will not be damaged.

11. Remove feeder and check that gun is cleared of round in the chamber. Inspect that chamber is *cleared*.

If there is a round in the chamber, use the following procedure: Remove the driving spring, unlock the breechblock with an unlocking tool, and extract the round.

12. Remove breechblocks, inspect guns, chargers, and feeder winders.

a. After gun has been *cleared*, remove rear buffer assembly and breechblock group. Check gun tube for obstructions.

b. Check guns for the following:

(1) Receiver and tube clean and excess oil removed.

(a) Receiver interior for burrs, deformations, and general condition.

(b) Presence of charging lug on carrier slide (Rhodes-Lewis or Johnson Farebox Chargers).

(2) Round sensing switch and plunger for proper spring tension.

(3) Breechblock contact properly installed and safety wired.

(4) Disassemble breechblock and inspect for the following:

(a) Broken, loose, or worn parts.

(b) Burrs and deformation.

(c) Insulation worn or missing.

(d) All parts wiped dry and reassembled.

(e) Reinstall breechblock in receiver. Replace rear buffer and driving spring assemblies.

(5) Security of mount and attachment.

(6) Scribe marks aligned on magazine slide and receiver.

(7) Magazine slide anchor secured and anchor nuts tight.

(8) Insure that firing leads move freely for gun recoil (no clamps).

(9) Presence of cotter keys, lock washers, and safety wire.

c. Check gun chargers for the following:

(1) Security of mount and attachment

(2) Charging stud installed. Charging stud retainer in place (GE charger only).

(3) Charger switch in NEUTRAL position.

d. Check feeder winders for the following:

(1) Security of mount and attachment.

(2) Locking device for proper operation.

e. Check electrical cables for good condition and connectors for security on guns, chargers, and feeder winders.

13. Inspect feeders and link chutes. Check for the following:

a. Links or ammo in the feeder.

b. Feeder mouth for burrs and deformation.

c. Operating lever locks in down position.

Section VIII
Crew Duties

d. Feeder for excess oil or grease.

e. Cover or adapter of proper series.

f. Link deflector and link chute for obstruction or damage.

g. Link chute installed with wide side away from the feeder.

h. Cartridge guides, control pawl, and holding dog for freedom of movement.

i. Star wheels and link strippers for damage.

j. Connectors for damage.

k. Presence of cotter keys and safety wire.

14. Install the feeders and feeder winder; connect operating lever.

a. Install the feeder and make sure the magazine latch locks it to the gun.

b. Connect the operating lever to the bracket on the gun and lock it.

c. Connect the feeder winder to the feeder and lock it.

d. Connect feeder and gun heater leads.

15. Motors, units, cables, AN connectors. Check the following:

a. Turret electrical cables for good condition and connectors for security.

b. Drive motors for proper mounting.

c. Drive motor brush holders for security of mount.

16. Turret movement (MANUAL). Disengage the drive motor brakes and check that turret moves smoothly and freely in azimuth and elevation.

17. Brakes locked. Double check that drive motor brakes are locked. Levers should be in VERTICAL position.

18. Selsyns. Check for the following:

a. Selsyn and selsyn caps for tightness.

b. Contactor plugs for proper installation and security.

c. Selsyn covers for proper installation.

19. Limit switches, actuators, and mechanical stops.

a. Check elevation and azimuth limit switches for security of mount, damage, and proper spring tension when actuated manually.

b. Check actuators and mechanical limit stops for proper installation.

20. Rollers, ammo cans, and ammo feed chutes.

a. Check that rollers free wheel.

b. Check the ammo cans for cleanliness, damage areas, and dry condition.

c. Check ammo feed chutes for proper mount, bent or damaged links, configuration, and cleanliness.

d. Install ammo feed chutes on feeder mechanism.

21. Dome cover removed and sight dome cleaned. To clean exposed surface of dome, remove all dust and use alcohol, benzol, ether, or a neutral soap and water solution.

Operational Check.

Note

Check that personnel and stands are clear of turrets before operating. Be sure that turret is cleared of ammunition and that power is available. *Do not load guns* until operational check has been completed and units do not require maintenance.

1. Selector switch WARM UP and heater fuse IN.

a. Heater fuse IN and dome heater switch ON.

b. Allow gun, dome, and feeder heaters to warm up.

CAUTION

Heaters should be left on just long enough to check operation.

c. External turret safety switch ON.

d. When operation of heaters has been checked, remove fuse and turn dome heater switch OFF.

2. Selector switch OPERATION; check thyratron blower-thyratron timed out.

a. Turret power and turret safety switches ON.

b. Check thyratron blower. Check by holding hand in front of blower to see whether blower is operating.

CAUTION

Do not let fingers come in contact with rotary fan.

CAUTION

If thyratron blower does not operate, turn selector switch OFF.

Note

After approximately 100 ($\pm$30) seconds delay, d-c power is available for operation.

3. 28.5-volt d-c Check. Check line 143 at CBS1 on control panel for 28.5-volt d-c output. If necessary, adjust R-43 in thyratron controller to get desired voltage.

CAUTION

Use extreme caution to avoid shorting out other wires in control panel.

4. Check sight for operation.

a. Check sight lamp rheostat for operation and check sight reticle brilliance.

b. Check that both filaments on recticle lamp are operative by moving double filament switch.

c. Check centering of ranging ring and recticle dot.

d. Check that range is fixed at 900 yards.

e. Check that target size numerals cover complete range.

f. Check computer OUT lamp. Lamp should be on (small red light below range numerals).

g. Check that filter knob introduces into line of sight a clear or polaroid filter.

h. Check that density knob increases or decreases density of polaroid filter.

i. Check that eyepiece can be adjusted between scale limits of minus 2 and plus 1 diopters.

j. Parallax error sight. Line up on a target which can be easily seen and covered by center dot. Acceptable requirement is that center dot should not move completely off the target when eye is moved vertically and horizontally across viewing aperture of optic head.

Note

Target must not be less than one mile away.

5. Check desiccator for operation.

a. Turn desiccator switch ON. Desiccator pump and motor should operate.

b. Check for free smooth operation of pump.

c. Check that there is no binding of action or smoke.

Note

Leave desiccator switch ON until completion of operational check.

6. Check wiper for operation. Close action switch and check that the link and case wiper assembly move back and forth.

7. Gun camera switch ON. Gun camera operation.

Note

Before starting operation, check to see that shutter speed knob is set at index for desired frames per second. *Do not* change speed when camera is running.

a. Close action switch and depress triggers.

b. Check that shutter operates.

c. Check that spline gear rotates.

d. Release triggers. Check that the overrun control and trigger indicator operate.

e. Release action switch and turn camera switch OFF.

f. Insert camera aligning indicator in the camera and observe that reticle is centered on reference marks.

8. One and 31-speed operation and thyratron tubes firing.

a. Thirty-one speed selsyn check. Move sight optics slowly and smoothly in azimuth and then elevation. See that turret follows sight.

b. One speed selsyn check. Slew sight optics rapidly out of alignment with turret in azimuth and then elevation. See that turret rapidly comes into alignment.

c. While turret is being operated, check to see that all elevation, azimuth and d-c power thyratron tubes are firing properly. No excessive overheating and no crossfiring should occur. Watch for a bluish purple color while firing. No firing above the plate or at base of tube should occur. If tubes are not operating properly, turn the system off.

Note

A pinkish-orange or whitish color indicates a bad tube which should be replaced. It may not be practical to perform step c on some aircraft due to the location of equipment.

9. Safe-fire switches—FIRE.

10. Gun charger and feeder winder operation.

a. At the turret, place charger switch to HOLDBACK position; charger should charge and hold the breechblock in the rear position. Place switch to NEUTRAL position; the charger should release breechblock. Place the charger switch to CHARGE position; the charger should automatically charge and release breechblock.

b. At the control panel, place charger switch to HOLDBACK position; charger should charge and hold breechblock in the rear position. Place charger switch to RELEASE; charger should release breechblock.

c. Depress triggers. Check that chargers operate and feeder winders rotate in proper direction.

11. Limit switches, backout and stowing circuits.

a. Close action switch and move sight optics until turret goes into a limit. Depress triggers; chargers and feeder winders should not operate.

b. Move sight optics in opposite direction, keeping trigger depressed. Turret should backout smoothly off the limits; chargers and feeder winders should operate.

c. Check all limits in elevation and azimuth.

d. Release action switch. Guns should automatically stow.

12. OOSFI Circuit.

a. Move sight optics about 25 degrees in azimuth from guns stowed position.

b. Simultaneously depress action and trigger switches.

c. Check that chargers and feeder winders do not operate until turret is within 3 degrees of alignment with sight optics.

d. Repeat steps a through c in elevation.

13. Disconnect chargers at guns. Secure gun charger cables to prevent damage to them while making this firing circuit check.

**Section VIII
Crew Duties**

> **CAUTION**
>
> When disconnecting or reconnecting gun charger cables, be sure that turret safety switch or external turret safety switch is in OFF position.

14. Firing Circuit Check.

   a. Close action switch; point guns to an unrestricted firing area.

> **CAUTION**
>
> Do not release action switch any time during this check. Be sure that breechblock is in battery position before inserting magic wand. Use caution in placing any part of the body in front of gun muzzles.

   b. Have an assistant insert firing circuit tester in tube of gun and push it against firing pin. (This will prevent firing pin from grounding out on the firing pin port.)

   c. Depress triggers and have assistant check that gun fires. Check other gun by same method.

> **WARNING**
>
> While checking firing circuit, insure that when triggers are released that the firing circuit is OUT. If there is an indication that the firing circuit is still functioning after the triggers are released, get it repaired *immediately* and *do not load* the guns until it has been repaired.

15. Reconnect chargers and place safe-fire switches in SAFE.

   a. Insure that charger connectors are properly connected.

   b. Safe-fire switches safety wired in SAFE position before continuing with other checks.

16. Computer Check.

   a. Range check.

   (1) Attack factor switch PURSUIT, computer switch IN, action switch closed.

   (2) Check that range dial reads approximately 900 yards.

   b. Check that resolver input unit dials follow sight movements in azimuth and elevation.

   c. Set altitude *minimum*, air speed *maximum* at handset unit.

   d. Lead check.

   (1) Close action switch and track steadily for some distance. Stop sight optics abruptly and observe the movement of the turret. The turret should stop when the sight optics are stopped and then creep in the opposite direction.

   (2) Check azimuth and elevation correction dials on the computer for movements during this check.

> **Note**
>
> Azimuth and elevation correction dial check may not be practical on some aircraft because of location of equipment.

   e. Windage check. Close action switch; move sight optics as close to broadside as possible without getting turret on a limit. Place computer switch to OUT; guns should swing slightly to the rear. Place a computer switch to IN; the windage correction should come back IN and move the guns slightly forward.

   f. Gravity check. With action switch closed, stow sight optics forward in zero degrees elevation. Turn computer switch OUT, guns should move down. Turn computer switch IN, guns should move up.

   g. Set attack factor switch to PURSUIT position and then STRAIGHT-LINE position. There will be a slight movement of the guns.

   h. Computer switch OUT.

> **CAUTION**
>
> Do not turn selector switch to off position when action switch is actuated as it may cause a computer malfunction.

17. Boresight check.

   a. Tape or otherwise secure the action switch in closed position while making this check.

   b. Aim the sight at a distant object (at least 1000 feet away for each foot of parallax).

   c. Insert boresighting tool in guns.

   d. Have assistant check that guns are pointing at the same object as the sight.

18. All switches OFF or SAFE.

   a. Turret power switch OFF.

   b. Selector switch OFF.

   c. Turret safety switch SAFE.

   d. Desiccator switch OFF.

19. Thyratron cover replaced.

BOMB TEAM CHECK LIST.

This check list should be used for all bombing runs. Prior to the start of any RBS attack, the initial radio contact and altitude assignment should be received as soon as possible prior to the Pre-IP.

PRIOR TO PRE-IP

PILOTS

1. Receive ETA to Pre-IP.
2. Bomb Run Safety Check Completed (RBS attacks).
3. All engine and oxygen checks, etc., will be completed before reaching Pre-IP.

4. Receive IAS.

5. Instrument Cross Check.
6. The Aircraft Commander and FE will stabilize the desired IAS and the Radar Observer will cross check his TAS indicator and reset if variance is evident.
7. Practice bomb run on Pre-IP.
   a. Autopilot second station automatic check.
   b. Check PDI and time to go for proper operation.
8. Complete practice run, checking tone and/or release.
9. Receive magnetic heading and ETA to IP.
10. Stabilize altitude at bombing altitude in preparation for measurement by the Radar Observer if not previously accomplished.

ENGINEERS

1. FE will compute TAS to be maintained on the bomb run.
2. FE will advise the Navigator who will cross check computations for accuracy.
3. Upon agreement between the FE and Navigator as to accuracy of TAS, the FE will advise the Radar Observer of TAS and the Aircraft Commander of the desired indicated air speed.
4. Instrument Cross Check.
5. Stabilize IAS with the Aircraft Commander.

6. Maintain bomb run air speed.

PRIOR TO IP

PILOTS

1. Tone check with RBS. (RBS)
2. Receive magnetic heading, drift, G-S and ETA to target.
3. Receive call over IP and Bomb Safety Check completed.
4. Advise crew over IP.
5. Advise Navigator and Radar Observer when on target heading.

ENGINEERS

PRIOR TO TARGET

PILOTS

1. Receive distance from target reports. Co-ordinate radio calls with Pilot.
2. When requested by Radar Observer to switch to second station, check PDI BOMB POSITION LIGHT "ON" and turn N-2 Transfer Switch to RADAR BOMB position.
3. Receive Radar Observer report, target city identified, and heading correction, if required.
4. Advise the Radar Observer if the autopilot is not correcting in accordance with PDI indications.
5. Aircraft Commander calls time-to-go at following times: "(1) Start movement of TG; (2) 120 sec; (3) 90 sec, 60 sec, 45 sec, 30 sec, 15 sec."

NOTE

NOTIFY RADAR OBSERVER TO TURN TONE TO ON AT 30 SEC TO GO. (RBS ATTACKS)

6. Radar Observer reports target area identified and synchronized.

ENGINEERS

1. Maintain IAS.

Section VIII
Crew Duties

T.O. 1B-36D(II)-1

BOMB RUN CHECK LIST (ACTUAL).

PRIOR TO PRE-IP

RADAR OBSERVER

1. Bomb bay doors closed, circuit breakers pulled.
2. Bomb bay selector switches OFF.
3. Special bomb release switch in SPECIAL.
*5. Call Pilot—Bomb bay tank safety switch in NO SALVO.
*6. Pilot and VO salvo switch OFF.
*7. Salvo circuit breaker pulled.
*8. Call Pilot "Safety Check Complete."
9. All other bomb panel circuit breakers ON.
10. Bomb intervalometer SELECT and 6 bombs or more.
11. Master power switch ON.
12. Vertical camera power switch and circuit breaker—As desired.
13. Vertical camera intervalometer as desired.
14. Set in offset information.
15. Set in precomputed ballistics.
*16. Pilot, Engineer, and Observer's instrument cross check.
17. Assist Navigator in control times.
*18. Cross check TAS with Aircraft Commander and reset if variance is noted.
*19. Make practice bomb run on Pre-IP checking following:
　a. Autopilot second station automatic check.
　b. Wind determination.
　c. Offset capability.
　d. Navigation unit counters and Mag Var.
20. Refine wind if desired and inform Nav.
21. Complete practice run, checking release.
*22. Measure altitude (if not previously accomplished) and coordinate with Aircraft Commander.

NAVIGATOR

*1. Notify Aircraft Commander of ETA to Pre-IP.
2. Direct aircraft to Pre-IP.
3. Hack O-15 camera watch and complete O-15 data plate.

*4. Observer's instrument cross check.

*5. Compute bomb run TAS.

*6. Obtain wind from VO, and compute magnetic heading and ETA to IP, notify Aircraft Commander.

OBSERVER

1. Recheck following:
　(a) Bomb bay doors closed, circuit breakers pulled.
2. Bomb bay selector switches OFF.
3. Special bomb release switch in SPECIAL.
4. Bomb bay door safety switch safetied OFF.
5. All other bomb panel circuit breakers ON.

6. Check bomb intervalometer SELECT and 6 bombs or more.
7. Check master power switch ON.
8. Check camera panel and intervalometer settings.
*9. Pilot, Engineer, and Observer's instrument cross check.

10. Recheck and install O-15 data plate.
11. O-15 camera operational check—40 frames.
12. Check offset information.
13. Check setting of precomputed ballistics.

14. Give altitude measurement reading to VO.

PRIOR TO IP

RADAR OBSERVER

1. Altitude measured and adjusted.
2. Compute and adjust ballistic data.
3. Check heading repeater.
4. Visually recheck all switches and circuit breakers.
5. Make wind run on IP and give to Navigator.
6. Reset navigation control unit.
7. Call pilot, "Over IP-Bomb run check Complete."

NAVIGATOR

1. Compute data for TH check.
2. Check heading unit.
*3. Obtain wind from VO and compute magnetic heading, drift, GS, and ETA to target relay to VO and Aircraft Commander.

OBSERVER

1. Check computed against measured altitude.
2. Check adjusted altitude setting.
3. Check ballistic computations and settings.
4. Obtain TH check.
5. Visually recheck all switches and circuit breakers.
6. Open vertical camera doors.
7. Turn on O-15 camera at IP if applicable.

* Co-ordination Items

Section VIII
Crew Duties

PRIOR TO TARGET

RADAR OBSERVER

1. Bomb panel circuit ON.
2. Special bomb panel circuit breakers as briefed.
3. Bomb arming switch as briefed.
4. Bomb station indicator lights ON.
*5. Request Radar Bomb position from Aircraft Commander.
6. Special-normal rack switch briefed.
7. Intervalometers—as briefed.
8. Bomb bay door safety switch safety wire broken.
9. Bomb bay selector switches ON just prior to release.
10. Special bombing rack selector switches ON just prior to release.
11. Bomb bay door safety switch ON just prior to release.
*12. Report to Aircraft Commander "Target area identified" and initial heading correction if required.
*13. Report to Aircraft Commander "Target identified and synchronized."

*14. Make "Bombs away" call.
15. Bomb bay door safety switch OFF immediately after doors close.
16. Special bomb rack selector switch OFF.
17. Bomb bay selector switches OFF.
18. Complete bombing data.

NOTE
PRIOR TO DEPARTING BOMB RANGE, PERFORM BOMB SAFETY CHECK LIST.

NAVIGATOR

1. Assist VO in target identification.

2. Records "Bombs away" time, TH, and TAS.
3. Assist VO with bombing data.

OBSERVER

1. Check bomb panel circuit breakers ON.
2. Check special bomb panel circuit breakers.
3. Check bomb arming switch.
4. Check bomb station indicator lights.
5. Check special-normal rack switch.
6. Check intervalometers.
7. Check bomb bay door safety switch safety wire broken.
8. Check function switch to BOMB.
9. Check N-2 transfer switch.
10. Check bomb bay selector switches ON just prior to release.
11. Check special bomb rack selector.
12. Keep VO informed of ECO, memory point, and offset conditions.
13. Inform VO "TG DRIVING."
14. Turn on Y-3 at 120 seconds, if applicable.
15. Check TG when called by Aircraft Commander.
16. Check with VO for bomb bay door safety switch ON.
17. Inform VO "Bombs away."
18. Check operation of vertical camera.
19. Check bomb bay door safety switch OFF.
20. Check special bomb rack selector switch OFF.
21. Check bomb bay selector switches OFF.
22. Assist VO with bombing data.

NOTE
PRIOR TO DEPARTING BOMB RANGE, CHECK BOMB SAFETY CHECK LIST COMPLETE.

BOMB RUN CHECK LIST (RBS)

PRIOR TO PRE-IP

RADAR OBSERVER

1. Bomb bay doors closed; circuit breakers pulled.
2. Bomb bay selector switches OFF.
3. Special bomb release switch in SPECIAL.
4. Bomb bay door safety switch.
*5. Call Pilot, "Bomb bay tank safety switch in NO SALVO."
*6. Pilot and VO salvo switch OFF.
*7. Salvo circuit breaker PULLED.
*8. Call Pilot, "Safety check complete."
9. All other bomb panel circuit breakers ON.
10. Bomb intervalometer SELECT and 6 bombs or more.
11. Master power switch ON.
12. Vertical camera power switch and circuit breaker, as desired.

NAVIGATOR

1. Notify Aircraft Commander of ETA to Pre-IP.
2. Direct aircraft to Pre-IP.
3. Hack O-15 camera watch and complete O-15 data plate.

OBSERVER

1. Recheck following:
   a. Bomb bay doors closed; circuit breakers pulled.
2. Bomb bay selector switch OFF.
3. Special bomb release switch in SPECIAL.
4. Bomb bay door safety switch safetied OFF.
5. All other bomb panel circuit breakers ON.

6. Check bomb intervalometer SELECT and 6 bombs or more.

* Co-ordination Items

Section VIII
Crew Duties

T.O. 1B-36D(II)-1

13. Vertical camera intervalometer, as desired.
14. Set in offset information.
15. Set in pre-computed ballistics.
*16. Pilot, Engineer, and Observer instrument cross check.
17. Assist Navigator in control time.
*18. Cross check TAS and reset if variance is evident.
*19. Make practice bomb run on Pre-IP, checking following:
  a. Autopilot second station automatic check
  b. Wind determination
  c. Offset capability
  d. Navigation unit counters and Mag Var.
20. Refine wind if desired and inform Navigator.
21. Complete practice run, checking tone and release.
*22. Measure altitude (if not previously accomplished): co-ordinate with Aircraft Commander.

*4. Pilot, Engineer, and Observer instrument cross check.

5. Compute bomb run TAS.

*6. Obtain wind from VO and compute magnetic heading and ETA to IP; notify Aircraft Commander.

7. Check master power switch ON.
8. Check camera panel and intervalometer.
*9. Pilot, Engineer, and Observer instrument cross check.

10. Recheck and install O-15 data plate.
11. O-15 camera operational check—40 frames.
12. Check offset information.
13. Check setting of pre-computed ballistics.

14. Give altitude measurement reading to VO.

PRIOR TO PRE-IP

RADAR OBSERVER

1. Altitude measured and adjusted.
2. Compute and adjust ballistic data.
3. Check heading repeater.
4. Visually recheck all switches and circuit breakers.
5. Tone check with RBS.
6. Make wind run on IP and give to Navigator.
7. Reset Navigation control unit.
*8. Call Pilot, "Over IP-bomb run check complete."

NAVIGATOR

1. Compute data for TH check.
2. Check heading unit.
*3. Obtain wind from VO and compute magnetic heading, drift, GS, and ETA to target; relay to VO and Aircraft Commander.

OBSERVER

1. Check computed against measured altitude.
2. Check adjusted altitude setting.
3. Check ballistic computations and settings.
4. Obtain TH check.
5. Visually recheck all switches and circuit breakers.
6. Open vertical camera doors.
7. Turn on O-15 camera at IP.

PRIOR TO TARGET

RADAR OBSERVER

1. Complete bomb run as briefed.
*2. Request Radar Bomb position from Aircraft Commander.
*3. Reports to Aircraft Commander, "Target city identifed" and initial heading correction, if required.
*4. Report to Aircraft Commander "Target identified and synchronized."

5. Make "Bombs away" call.

6. Call wind components to Navigator.

NAVIGATOR

*1. Give RBS directed position reports to Pilot.

2. Record "Bombs away" time and release TH (Check N-1 against VO TH indicator)

3. Call Pilot, giving RBS information (TH, wind, TAS).

OBSERVER

1. Check function switch to BOMB.
2. Check N-2 transfer switch.
3. Keep VO informed of ECO, memory point, U offset conditions.
4. Inform VO "TG driving."
5. Turn on Y-3 at 120 seconds if applicable.
6. Check TG when called by Aircraft Commander.
7. At 20 seconds to go—Check with VO for tone ON.
8. Assure tone break and inform VO "Bombs away."
9. Record O-15 exposure number at release.
10. Check operation of vertical camera.
11. Call TH to Navigator.
12. Turn off cameras as briefed.

* Co-ordination Items

Section IX
All Weather Operation

This section contains discussions and specific procedures pertaining to operation of the airplane at night, under instrument conditions, in thunderstorms, in cold weather, in hot weather, and in the desert. The normal operating instructions of Section II are repeated only when the unity of this section requires duplication. Operation of the various systems and equipment is discussed in Section VII.

Night Flying Procedures

Night flying and instrument flying are identical in many points of technique. Take-off, climb, and landing will require instrument reference when visual orientation becomes uncertain. Since most missions involve night flying, the following items should be checked prior to each flight.

1. Taxi lights.
2. Landing lights.
3. Position lights.
4. Formation lights.
5. Wing crawlway lights.
6. Instrument panel lights.
7. Flight deck flood lights.
8. Aldis lamps (1 in forward compartment—2 for aft gunners).
9. Spare bulbs.
10. Flashlights.
11. Night-flying curtains.
12. Flight instrument switches—ON.
13. Flight indicators and instruments operating.
14. VHF, UHF, low frequency, ILAS, radio compass, and VOR.
15. N-1 compass uncaged and erecting (group 2 airplanes).

NIGHT TAKE-OFF.

1. Keep cockpit lights dim to protect night vision.
2. Use night-flying curtain to permit engineer to illuminate his panel.
3. Check flight instruments during taxi turns.
4. Be particularly alert for taxi strip obstructions. Use Aldis lamp or dispatch wing walkers to check clearances with flashlights.
5. Line up with runway; have nose wheel straight.
6. Landing lights extended and ON.
7. Set gyro to zero or to 5-degree mark nearest runway heading.
8. Perform usual checks.
9. During the ground run, the aircraft commander should maintain visual contact, and the pilot should watch instruments.
10. After the "getaway," aircraft commander should go on instruments, and pilot should maintain visual contact to prevent airplane from settling back onto the runway.

NIGHT CLIMB.

1. Use nose down trim after leaving ground effect if climb becomes too steep.

2. Retract flaps in the usual 5-degree increments, re-trimming between retractions.

Note

Flap retraction technique for take-off gross weight in excess of 300,000 pounds is discussed in Section VI, "Flight Characteristics."

3. Landing lights retracted and OFF.
4. Maintain take-off power until airplane is "clean" and altitude is between 500 and 1000 feet above the terrain.
5. Maintain optimum climb speed.

NIGHT LANDING.

1. Make normal checks. Gunners should use Aldis lamps for visual inspections.
2. Use landing lights for last part of final approach.
3. Use caution in judging height over the end of the runway.

Instrument Flying Procedures

The instrument flight characteristics of this airplane are conventional. Operation of flaps and landing gear do not cause pitch changes that would be dangerous at any stage of instrument flight.

Duplicate flight instrumentation is provided along with all standard electronic aids to instrument navigation and approach. The limiting factor will usually be availability of ground facilities. You will have to consult applicable radio and navigational charts for specific local equipment and procedures.

BEFORE STARTING ENGINES.

Prior to starting the engines and with the portable power cart operating, check the following:
1. Windshield wiper operation and blade contact.
2. Pitot heater operation.
3. Navigation lights.
4. Flight instrument switches—ON.
5. Flight indicators operating and instruments erecting.
6. Cockpit lights and flashlights.
7. VHF, UHF, low frequency, ILAS, radio compass, and VOR.
8. N-1 high latitude compass uncaged and operating (group 2 airplanes).
9. Slaved gyro magnetic compass uncaged and operating (airplanes not in group 2).
10. Position cockpit heat and anti-icing valves for maximum windshield defrost.
11. Place pilots' ventilating fans ON to aid windshield defrost.

AFTER STARTING ENGINES.

Check the anti-icing equipment for proper operation and then turn OFF after starting the engines.

DURING TAXI.

During taxi, check:
1. Landing lights.
2. Turn needles.
3. Gyros and compass (for proper swing and operation).

BEFORE TAKE-OFF.

Check the following items before take-off:
1. Radio receivers tuned to proper stations.
2. Altimeter and gyros set.
3. Pitot heater ON (if icing conditions exist).

Flight instruments require a maximum of 15 minutes for warm-up.

TAKE-OFF.

The aircraft should be flown off the ground as during a visual take-off; however, instrument take-off should not be attempted unless there is sufficient visibility to aid in steering the aircraft during the initial take-off roll.

In aircraft equipped with J-8 attitude indicator, because of the high angle of pitch on take-off, the horizon bar will ride near the bottom of the indicator, and only limited pitch and roll information will be displayed. Therefore, during the instrument take-off, the air-speed indicator will have to be used to provide additional pitch information. Since the aircraft accelerates rapidly after becoming air-borne, use caution to prevent exceeding the maximum flap speed.

The following instrument take-off procedure is recommended:
1. Visually align the aircraft on the center line of the runway with nose wheel straight.
2. Use normal elevator tab and flap settings.
3. Set miniature aircraft reference on attitude indicator as desired.
4. Set gyro to zero or to 5-degree mark nearest runway heading.
5. Position cockpit heat and anti-icing valves for maximum flow to pilots' enclosure in the event icing conditions are encountered on take-off.
6. Advance power and make normal VFR take-off.
7. Retract landing gear after becoming definitely airborne.

8. Retract flaps in accordance with the procedure in Section VI, if your take-off gross weight exceeds 300,000 pounds.

9. Apply nose-down trim as required between flap retractions.

10. Establish climb configuration.

11. Anti-icing equipment ON (if required).

INSTRUMENT CLIMB.

1. Maintain optimum climb speed.

INSTRUMENT CRUISING FLIGHT.

Extended operation on instruments can usually be avoided by cruising at high altitude. As you increase your flight level, the number of cloud types that can exist is substantially reduced. While you are cruising on instruments, the following points are significant:

| CAUTION |

At no time should the aircraft be permitted to enter an unusual attitude which might result in exceeding the critical Mach number and entering the buffet or compressibility range.

1. Trim airplane "hands off" before engaging autopilot.

2. Repeat "hands off" trimming operation every half hour to compensate for cg changes.

3. Avoid extreme turbulence if possible.

4. If you cannot avoid turbulence, disengage autopilot and fly "attitude" rather than "altitude."

5. Cross check all instruments and electronic aids.

SPEED RANGE.

The rapidity with which you must scan all flight instruments varies with the speed of flight. While this airplane has very wide speed range for a bomber, normal operating speeds are not high enough to make instrument flight more difficult. Ordinarily, the speeds established by cruise control requirements will be the desirable instrument speeds.

RADIO AND NAVIGATION EQUIPMENT

The dependability of electronic aids to instrument flight and navigation is closely related to the influence of the various types of static. Man-made static, precipitation static, and dust static can be controlled or suppressed. Crash static from active storm areas, however, cannot be controlled. This accounts for the increased dependence on very high frequencies which are comparatively immune to this type of interference. Electrical disturbances will affect equipment with frequencies below 75 mc within a radius of several thousand miles. Therefore, under severe instrument conditions, VHF equipment will offer greater dependability.

TABLE OF ELECTRONIC Aids

Low to High Frequency	Very High Frequency or Above
Liaison Radio	Instrument Approach Indicator
Radio Range Receiver	Command Sets
Radio Compass	Marker Beacon Receiver
Loran Set	Radar Equipment

AIR-BORNE RADAR.

This equipment permits visual or contact flight precision under instrument conditions. The amount and accuracy of information obtained through radar scope interpretation depend largely on the skill of the operator. Distinctive terrain features can be used for navigation regardless of prevailing visibility. Relative bearings and distances can be read directly from the scopes; relative altitudes can be determined by comparing flight altitude with map elevation lines or color codes. When the radar system is used for navigation, radar-observed drift corrections can be coupled directly from the radar ground position computer to the autopilot. Grid navigation in latitudes above the 70th parallel can also be accomplished with certain parts of the radar system. A great circle path between the high latitude entry and exit points can be followed by reference to a free gyro rather than magnetic field of the earth in the polar regions.

At low altitude, the strong ground echo and the greater apparent speed of the airplane relative to the ground make accurate scope interpretation almost impossible. For this reason, instrument low approaches accomplished exclusively by air-borne radar are not recommended.

Turbulence does not provide a discontinuity that would show up on the radar scope. Thunderstorm research, however, shows that rain and turbulence are related. Consequently, you can pick the smoothest path through a thunderstorm area by avoiding strong rain echoes. This path should be selected before entering the storm area. Heavy local rain will temporarily block the radar scope with strong echoes.

Absolute altitude can be read from the radar scope with a degree of accuracy that depends on the terrain. When the ground is smooth, accuracy is best; when the ground is rough or hilly, the scope shows altitude above an "average" ground level. The radial distance on the scope to the first ground echo is the altitude index.

Section IX
All Weather Operation

Typical RADIO RANGE PROCEDURE

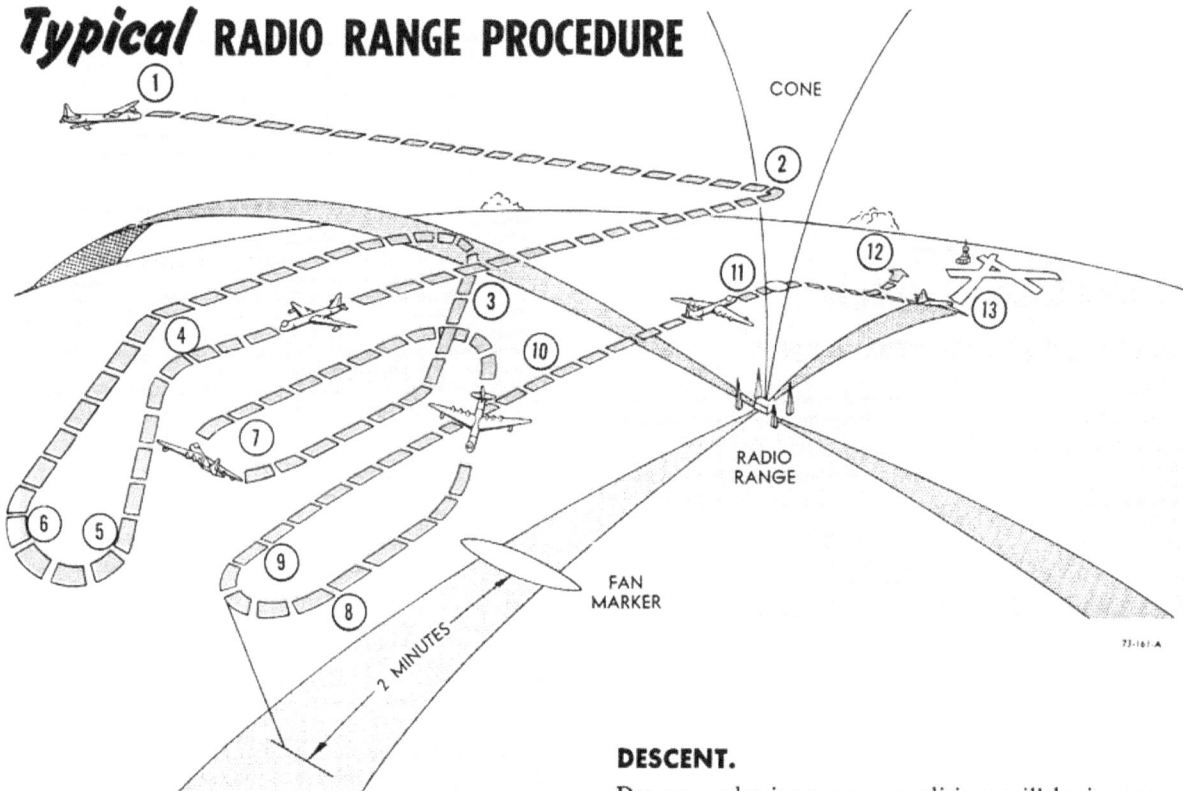

Range procedures will remain fundamental until new techniques are developed. More precision is offered by GCA and ILAS for low approaches, but preliminary orientation and holding on the radio range are usually required.

1. Obtain approach clearance upon entering control area.
2. Hold as directed–Monitor all conversations.
3. Report leaving each assigned altitude promptly.
4. Note outbound drift correction.
5. Standard turn procedure.
6. Cross check needle frequently during last 90° of turn toward inboard heading–adjust turn to give "on course" indication when turn is complete.
7. Report reaching and leaving each assigned holding fix.
8. Time your holding pattern to put you over the holding fix at expected approach time.
9. Complete check list prior to this point except:
    a. Flaps–extended 10°.
    b. IAS–150 or 135% stall–whichever is greater.
10. Extend flaps 20°–stabilize IAS at final approach speed.
11. Establish proper rate of let down by reducing MP (on 6 engines) 1" for each 100 ft./min. rate of descent desired.
12. If you are not contact at specified minimum, use "missed approach" procedure.
13. Flaps–extend 30° on final approach to the runway after reaching visual flight conditions.
14. Report "below" all clouds as soon as possible.

Figure 9-1.

DESCENT.

Descent under instrument conditions will be in accordance with normal procedures discussed in Section II unless atmospheric conditions dictate changes in power settings. Rapid drops in CHT should be avoided, and prolonged operation with CHT below 170°C can cause lead fouling and poor acceleration. If icing conditions exist, it will be necessary to change power settings to provide sufficient heat for carburetor, wing, and tail de-icing.

HOLDING.

Endurance ordinarily is not critical. If you are required to hold while waiting for airways or approach clearance, use maximum endurance power settings for your gross weight and altitude. A typical holding procedure is shown in figure 9-1 in conjunction with the radio range procedure.

INSTRUMENT APPROACHES.

Equipment is provided for the reception of radio range, ILAS, and GCA signals. ILAS and omnidirectional range signals are interpreted by visual indicators. Approaches based on any combination of equipment are recommended for additional safety. See figures 9-1, 9-2, 9-3, and 9-4 for instrument approach procedures.

Some aircraft are equipped with an automatic approach system which provides a means of making an automatic ILAS approach. For information concerning the description and operation of this equipment, see "Automatic Approach Coupler Unit," Section IV.

Typical GCA PROCEDURE

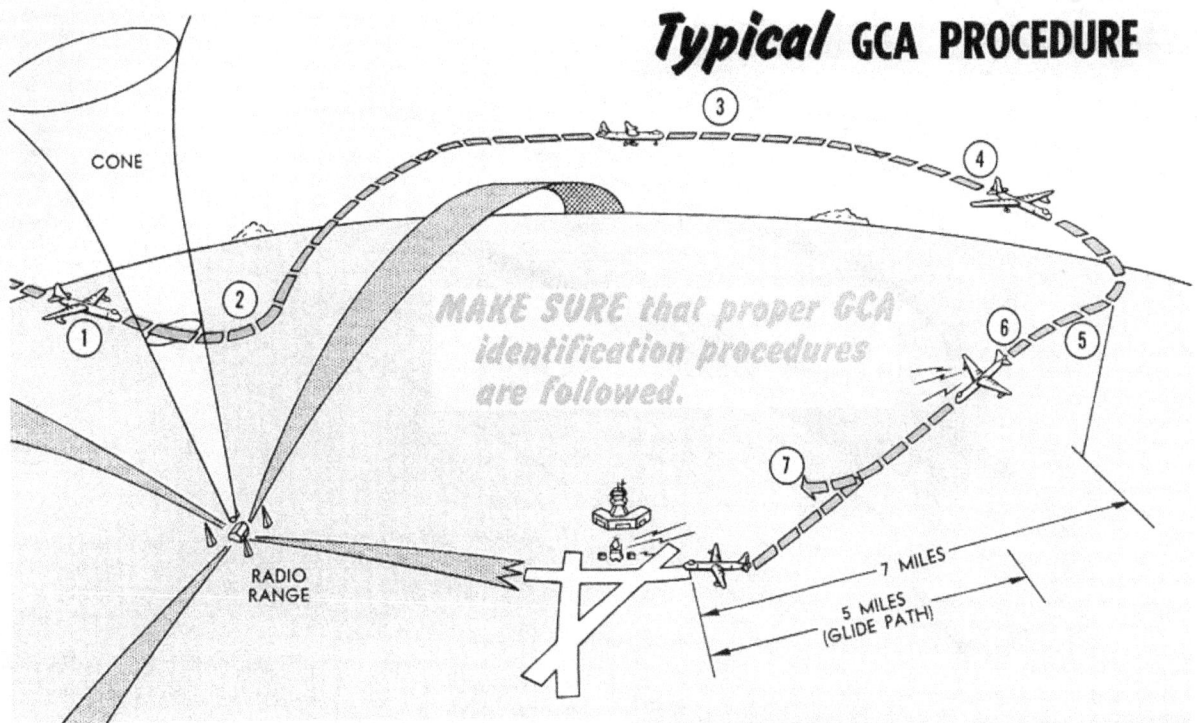

MAKE SURE that proper GCA identification procedures are followed.

The following points of technique will apply to all instrument approaches:

1. Consult applicable radio and navigational charts for specific local procedure.
2. Limit flaps to 20 degrees until landing is assured.
3. Pilot should double check aircraft commander's procedure.
4. Pilot should check for runway or high intensity approach light as aircraft commander reaches final stage of approach.

CAUTION

Do not change from your approach system until you are in the clear. Partial visibility can introduce serious errors in depth perception.

ICE, SNOW, AND RAIN.

Proper technique is essential when flying in ice, snow, or rain. The various types of icing are probably the greatest hazard, but rain and snow can impair forward visibility to the extent that instrument technique will be required. If propeller icing is experienced, intermittent rapid increases in rpm should be made in an effort to rid the propeller of ice.

ICE.

The following configuration will provide maximum heat for wing, windshield, and tail de-icing.
1. Dual turbo.
2. High rpm.
3. High engine fan speed.

This system is usually referred to as GCA. The instrument publications should be consulted for procedure in obtaining a GCA channel. Low frequencies are usually available if VHF equipment is inoperative.

1. Turn as directed by GCA. Report leaving cone.

2. Descend as directed to GCA traffic altitude.

3. Complete check list prior to this point except:
    a. Flaps – extend 10°.
    b. IAS – 150 or 135% stalling speed, whichever is greater.

4. Extend flaps 20° – stabilize IAS at 150 mph or 135% stall, whichever is greater – descend as directed to final approach altitude.

5. Level off at final approach altitude, stabilize IAS at final approach speed.

6. When you intercept glide path, reduce power on 6 engines approximately 1" MP for each 100 ft/min rate of descent required. After air speed and descent rate stabilize, adjust power as required.

7. Flaps – extend 30° on final approach to the runway after reaching visual flight conditions.

Figure 9-2.

Section IX
All Weather Operation

T.O. 1B-36D(II)-1

Typical ILAS PROCEDURE

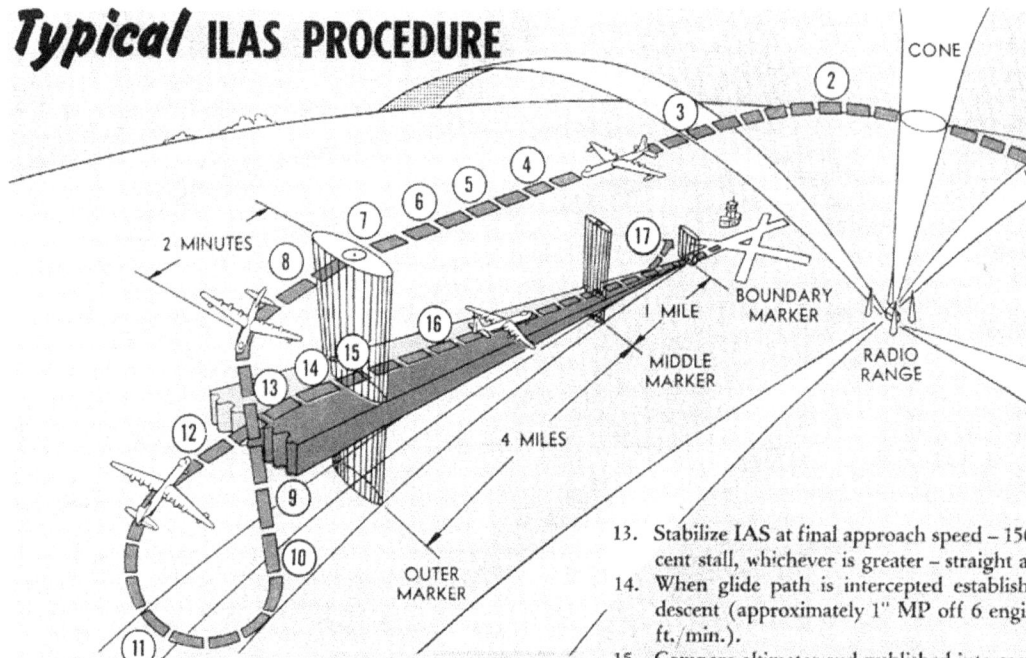

ILAS is the standard designation for this low approach system. Procedures and minimums are also defined in applicable radio and navigational charts. When both ILAS and GCA facilities are available, an ILAS with GCA monitor is desirable from the standpoint of safety. If signal strength is too low to give accurate needle deflections, red warning flags appear in the indicator.

1. After clearance has been received, descend to initial approach altitude.
2. Perform final landing check; set propellers, extend gear, and set flaps to 20°.
3. Use low frequency homing facility to aid interception of localizer beam outbound at an angle of less than 30°.
4. Bring ILAS cross pointer into normal sequence of crosscheck (outbound deflections are reversed).
5. If interception is made close to localizer, turn to corrected published heading (use metro winds or drift calculated during holding procedure) until localizer needle settles to a steady indication.
6. Center the localizer needle (outbound).
7. Course should be established within 1 or 2 degrees. (Degrees of bank should not exceed degrees of correction indicated).
8. Note outbound drift correction.
9. Complete check list prior to this point except:
    a. Flaps – extend to 30°
    b. IAS – 150 or 135% stall – whichever is greater.
10. Standard turn procedure.
11. Cross check needle frequently during last 90° of turn toward inbound heading – adjust turn to give "on course" indication when turn is complete.
12. Descend to final approach altitude.
13. Stabilize IAS at final approach speed – 150 IAS or 135 per cent stall, whichever is greater – straight and level flight.
14. When glide path is intercepted establish proper rate of descent (approximately 1" MP off 6 engines for each 100 ft./min.).
15. Compare altimeter and published intersection altitude – allowable error is 50 feet. If error is excessive and ground is not visible, go around.
16. Increase speed of cross check and make smooth coordinated corrections as soon as pointers deviate – avoid over controlling.
17. Flaps–extend 30° on final approach to the runway after reaching visual flight conditions.

4. Low air speeds.
5. Maintain maximum allowable CHT and CAT.
6. Maintain maximum allowable anti-icing temperature.

When the anti-icing system is operated correctly during a severe icing condition and flow-back freezing is encountered, the anti-icing system has failed and every effort should be made to leave the icing area.

The anti-icing system should be turned on before entering icing conditions. In severe icing conditions, flow-back freezing may be encountered, and this will result in a loss of air speed. Under these conditions, ice may also form along the bomb bay doors. Periodic opening and closing of the doors will break up this accretion. If windshield is icing or frosting, accomplish the following:

1. Position valves for maximum heat in forward compartment. (Refer to "Heat and Anti-Ice Systems," Section IV.)
2. Direct air flow to pilots' enclosure, and position pilots' air circulating fans for windshield defrosting.
3. Turn on booster fan to increase flow of air in pressure duct.

During flight in heavy icing conditions, especially in freezing precipitation and thunderstorms, icing of the induction system may be encountered. (Refer to "Carburetion," Section VII.)

Figure 9-3.

Automatic APPROACH PROCEDURE

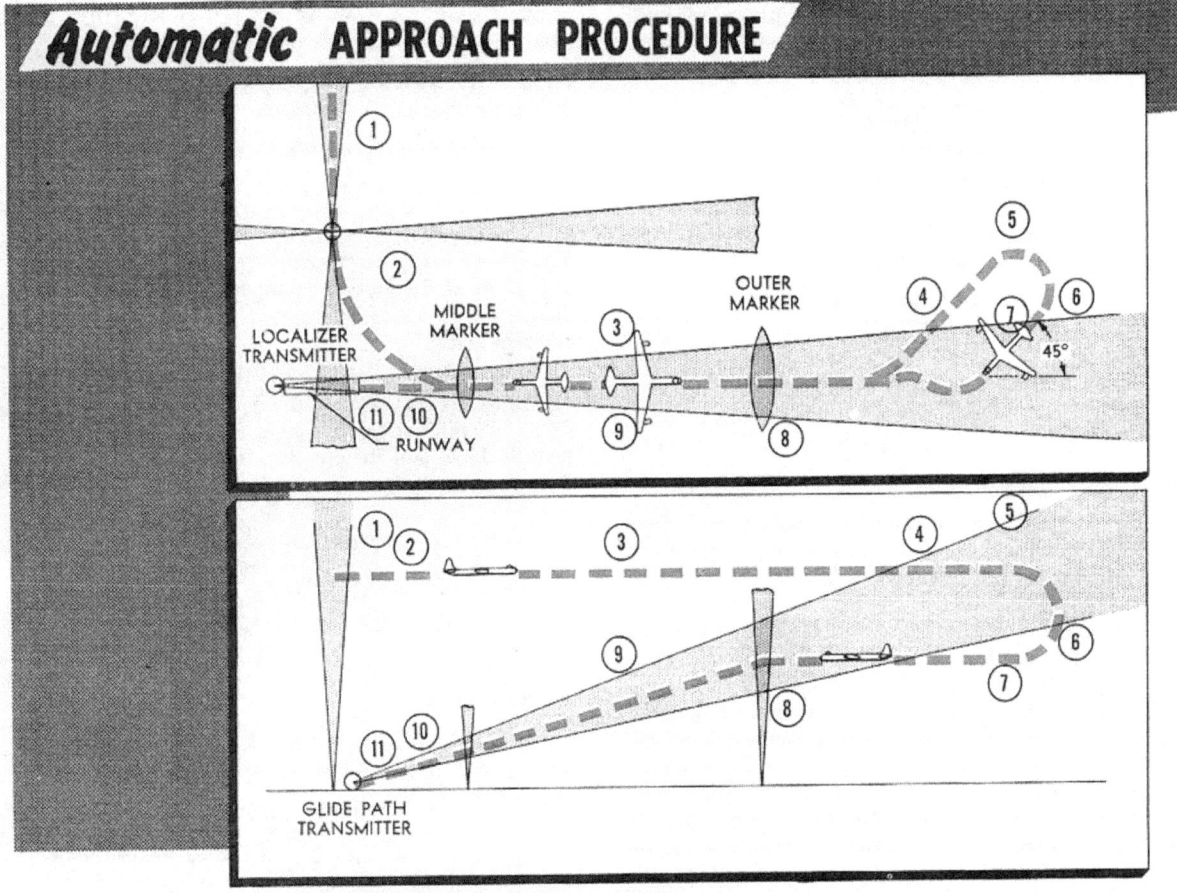

The procedure for making an automatic approach is essentially the same as the ILAS procedure described in figure 9-3. Since the autopilot controls the flight attitude of the aircraft during the automatic portion of this procedure, its three axes must be engaged before this portion of the approach pattern is reached. The approach pattern is devised to allow the aircraft to approach the beam at a sufficient angle and a sufficient distance from the station to have the aircraft lined up on the localizer beam before the outer marker is passed. The altitude, which is automatically maintained if the altitude control unit is engaged, should be approximately 1500 feet if possible. This altitude permits interception of the localizer well below the glide path and allows sufficient time for the aircraft to align itself on the localizer course before the glide path is intercepted.

1. After clearance has been received, descend to initial approach altitude.
2. Perform final landing check—set propellers, extend gear, and set flaps to 20 degrees.
3. Use normal ILAS procedure in flying the outbound leg.
4. Use standard turn procedure.
5. Descend to final approach altitude and turn the altitude control switch on.
6. Approach the beam at approximately 45 degrees.
7. As soon as the localizer needle leaves its stop, place the localizer switch in the ON position.
8. When the glide path needle reaches its approximate center position, place the approach switch in the ON position.
9. Use throttles to maintain normal approach speeds.
10. After reaching visual flight conditions, disengage the autopilot and extend flaps to 30 degrees.
11. Complete the landing manually.

Figure 9-4.

Emergency Use of Carburetor Preheat.

Induction system icing can occur at carburetor air temperatures below $+15°C$. In event it becomes necessary to add additional heat to maintain the CAT. above $+15°C$ throughout a descent to touch-down, the following procedure will apply. Use single turbo and a high turbo setting with part throttle down to the traffic pattern altitude, with carburetor preheat off. At traffic pattern altitude, with the carburetor preheat circuit breakers pulled, place the carburetor preheat switch to the ON position. Advance the throttle on one engine at a time to 37 inches M.P. and shift to dual turbo. As the shift occurs, push the carburetor preheat

Section IX
All Weather Operation

circuit breaker in for that engine. This procedure will maintain adequate CAT. during and after shifting from single to dual turbo.

> **CAUTION**
>
> In icing conditions, it is imperative to maintain the CAT. well above the icing range during the transition of the turbo shift. Repeat these steps for the other five engines.

> **CAUTION**
>
> If the landing is rejected, turn the carburetor preheat switch OFF as go-around power is applied.

Jet Engine Icing.

The jet engines can be seriously affected by icing. Ice forms on the fixed inlet screens and compressor inlet guide vanes and restricts the flow of inlet air. The reduced air flow causes a loss in thrust and a richer fuel-air mixture. As thrust decreases the rpm decreases and as the fuel-air mixture becomes richer the tail pipe temperature increases. In an attempt to maintain rpm the automatic fuel control routes a greater amount of fuel to the combustion chambers which further increases the tail pipe temperature. Once the ice begins to restrict the air flow and the tail pipe temperature starts to rise it may be only a matter of seconds until turbine failure occurs if corrective action is not taken. Critical ice build-up on inlet screens can occur in less than one minute; if the inlet screens are not installed, critical ice build-up on the inlet guide vanes can occur in four minutes or less.

Icing of external surfaces cannot be regarded as an indication of jet engine icing because the engines can ice to a serious extent before external icing is evident. When flying at relatively low airspeed and with a high power setting, as in a climb, the intake air is sucked, instead of rammed into the compressor inlet. This suction causes a decrease in air temperature, and air at ambient temperature above freezing may be reduced to sub-freezing temperatures as it enters the compressor inlet. Free moisture in this air may become super cooled and cause engine icing while no external icing is evident. The maximum temperature drop which can occur is approximately 5°C (9°F). This maximum drop occurs at high rpm on the ground. The drop will become less as rpm decreases or as air speed increases.

The initial indication of engine icing is an increase in tail pipe temperature and usually this is the only indication before complete engine failure. Since icing and failure can occur very rapidly the tail pipe temperature indicator must be watched closely when possible icing conditions are present.

Icing Prevention. To prevent jet engine icing the following should be observed:

1. Avoid atmospheric icing conditions whenever feasible.

2. If possible, avoid take-offs with jet engines operating when temperature is between —10°C (14°F) and 5°C (41°F) if fog is present or the dew point is within 4°C (7°F) of the ambient temperature. These are conditions under which jet engine icing can occur without external icing.

3. If the ambient temperature is in the range of 0°C (32°F) to 5°C (41°F) and the dew point is within 4°C (7°F) of ambient temperature, the jet engines should be shut down and the air plug doors closed.

> **Note**
>
> The above procedure should be used only to avoid icing when the temperature and dew point are conducive to the formation of ice caused by a drop in air temperature as it is sucked into the jet engine air intake. Do not follow this procedure if icing conditions already exist.

4. If icing conditions are encountered at freezing atmospheric temperatures, immediate action should be taken as follows:

> **Note**
>
> The rate of engine icing for a given atmospheric icing intensity with outside air temperature below freezing is relatively constant at the speeds this airplane flies. Ram pressure heating of air at high speeds does not offset the icing conditions.

a. If practical, change altitude rapidly by climb or descent in layer clouds or vary course as appropriate to avoid cloud formations.

b. If the jets are operating, shut them down.

> **CAUTION**
>
> It is permissible to use the jet engines while encountering ice if threatened with loss of aircraft due to shutting down of jet engines. A continuous surveillance of jet tail pipe temperature and such power reduction of the jet engines as may be required to hold these temperatures within the allowable limit is necessary to prevent the possibility of major damage to the aircraft. The rise in tail pipe temperature due to ice blockage can be very rapid and the consequence of not shutting down the jets is turbine buckets erupting through the jet pod nacelle.

c. Close the air plug doors.

d. Apply pod preheat, depending upon requirement for wing anti-icing.

Note

Do not apply heat to air plug doors.

Starting Engine After Leaving Icing Conditions.

To start engines after leaving icing conditions proceed as follows:

1. Apply pod preheat if not already on.

2. Determine whether rotor is free as follows (without cracking throttle):

a. Crack air plug doors.

Note

Tap tachometers for early rpm indication.

b. If rotor does not turn, open air plug doors fully.

CAUTION

Do not attempt to open doors with ice visible on jet pod lips and doors. If ice is visible and ambient temperature is below 5°C (41°F) do not apply heat to the air plug doors. This temperature restriction is necessary to prevent ice melted at the air plugs refreezing in the compressor section and stopping engine rotation causing possible damage to the engine.

c. If rotor does not turn with doors fully open, apply starter for a maximum of 5 seconds.

CAUTION

Starter will burn out if operated over 5 seconds or if reapplied over three times in rapid succession with rotor locked.

d. With air plug doors fully open and with the correct windmilling rpm, attempt a normal air start.

CAUTION

The pilot should be alert for excessive tail pipe temperatures due to intake air blockage or any indication that pieces of ice have damaged the compressor.

SNOW.

Impaired forward visibility is the main problem when flying in a snowstorm. Windshield wipers and maximum windshield defrost will improve forward visibility under this condition. Side visibility will not be greatly reduced. Optimum anti-ice configuration should be maintained.

RAIN.

Forward visibility in rain is also a serious problem. Side visibility will not be seriously impaired, but final approaches in heavy rain will be rather difficult. Proper windshield wiper blade contact will reduce the hazard considerably.

TURBULENT AIR AND THUNDERSTORM FLYING.

Flight through a thunderstorm should be avoided. However, since circumstances may force you to fly into a zone of severe turbulence, you should be familiar with the piloting techniques recommended for these conditions. Power setting and pitch attitude are the keys to proper piloting technique when flying in turbulent air. The power setting and pitch attitude required for the proper penetration air speed are established before entering the storm. This power setting and pitch attitude, if maintained throughout the storm, will result in a constant air speed, regardless of any false readings of the air-speed indicator. Specific instructions for preparing to enter a storm and flying in it are given in the following paragraphs.

CAUTION

On entering thunderstorms and areas of excessive precipitation close surveillance of alternators must be maintained because it is possible for the d-c exciter generator commutator to collect enough moisture that it will drown out completely. The volts and cycles will go to maximum negative readings and the alternator will not automatically come off the line. Re-excitation is possible and normal power can be restored after the airplane has emerged from the precipitation area and the d-c exciter generator has had time to dry.

APPROACHING THE STORM.

It is imperative that you prepare the airplane prior to entering a zone of turbulent air. If the storm cannot be seen, its proximity can be detected by radio crash static and strong rain echoes picked up by the airborne radar. Prepare the airplane as follows:

1. Disengage the autopilot.

2. Maintain sufficient CHT and CAT. to preclude the possibility of engine or carburetor icing.

3. Mixture controls—NORMAL.

4. Pitot heater switches—ON.

5. Carburetor preheat—As required.

6. Throttle—Adjust as necessary. A safe comfortable penetration speed in severe turbulence is 60 knots above stall for the weight and configuration being flown.

7. Check gyroscopic instruments for proper settings.

8. Safety belts—Tightened. (Check with crew members.)

9. Turn off radio equipment rendered useless by static.

10. At night, turn on the white flight deck flood lights to minimize the blinding effect of lightning.

WARNING

Do not lower the landing gear or the flaps as they merely decrease the aerodynamic efficiency of the airplane.

IN THE STORM.

1. Maintain power setting and pitch attitude (established before entering the storm) throughout the storm. Hold these constant and your air speed will be constant—regardless of what the air-speed indicator reads.

2. Devote all of your attention to flying the airplane.

3. Expect turbulence, precipitation, and lightning, but do not allow them to cause you undue concern.

4. Maintain attitude. Concentrate principally on holding a level attitude by reference to the artificial horizon.

5. Do not "chase" the air-speed indicator, since doing so will result in extreme airplane attitudes. If a sudden gust should be encountered while the airplane is in a nose-high atitude, a stall might easily result. A heavy rain may partially block the pitot tube pressure head, causing the reading on the air-speed indicator to decrease by as much as 70 mph.

6. Use as little elevator control as possible to maintain your atitude in order to minimize the stresses imposed on the airplane.

7. The altimeter is unreliable in thunderstorm flying because of differential barometric pressures within the turbulent area. A gain or loss of several thousand feet may be expected. Make allowances for this error in determining minimum safe altitude.

Note
Normally, the least turbulent area in a thunderstorm will be at an altitude of 6000 feet above the terrain. Altitudes between 10,000 feet and 20,000 feet are usually the most turbulent.

Cold Weather Procedures

The following procedures are written as a supplement to the instructions in Section II, "Normal Procedures," and should be complied with when cold weather conditions are encountered. The success of the next day's operation depends greatly on advanced planning and the preparations made during engine shutdown and postflight procedures. Because of their importance, these procedures will be treated first and at the same time a logical sequence of events will be maintained. Because of the mission of the B-36, which is long range, it would be normal for a flight to start in a warm climate and end in a cold climate. *Therefore, cold weather procedures start with engine shutdown and postflight procedures.*

ADVANCED PLANNING.

Proper advanced planning can mean success or failure of an entire cold weather operation. When planning, bear one thing in mind—"an ounce of prevention is worth a pound of cure."

1. The first part to consider is proper ground heating equipment. Each crew compartment should be heated, as well as the reciprocating engines and jet pods. Make sure there are the proper number of heaters, heater ducts, and electrical power plants for each aircraft. (Sixteen heaters per aircraft desired.)

2. Make sure there are ample fueling facilities for the power plants and heaters.

3. If night work is anticipated, have ample supply of stand lights and drop lights.

4. All engineers and crew chiefs should be properly briefed on oil dilution during engine shutdown and engine starting in cold weather. This will be explained later in this section.

5. Snow and ice removal equipment should accompany each aircraft.

6. Two B-2 stands and two B-1 stands per aircraft are a minimum to be able to maintain an aircraft. More stands should be used if available. All stand steps and platforms should be coated with sheets of No. 3 grit sand paper. This is to prevent slipping when feet are wet.

7. Safety straps and ropes should be used while walking on slick wings.

8. A fuel tank repair crew should be set up to take care of existing leaks.

9. Aircraft servicing equipment should be checked and sumps drained before use.

10. A kit of cold weather handling equipment should be made up for each aircraft. This section relates the proper handling of this equipment.

POST FLIGHT PROCEDURES.

STOPPING RECIPROCATING ENGINES.

1. Air Plug Switches—OPEN.
2. Master Motor Speed Control Lever—Full DECREASE.
3. Propeller Selector Switches—FIXED PITCH.
4. Alternator Controls—Positioned.
5. Dilute engine for anticipated temperature.
6. During the last minute of the dilution period specified in figure 9-5, in order to clean spark plugs, operate engines at 1600 to 1700 rpm and manually adjust to best power, provided oil temperature does not exceed 50°C and the cylinder head temperature is limited to a maximum of 150°C. This clearing procedure will be abandoned if oil temperature reaches 50°C or cylinder head temperature rises above 150°C; however, the dilution period will be completed.
7. Close throttle.

Note

Never open throttles after shutdown.

8. Open air plugs to prevent post shutdown increase of engine temperature, which is conducive to subsequent condensation within cylinders.
9. Very slowly move the mixture control to IDLE CUT-OFF, thus allowing the chambers to be completely scavenged of moisture and carbon.
10. Fuel Tank Valve Switches—CLOSE.
11. Engine Fuel, Cross-Feed, and Manifold Valve Switches—OPEN.

Note

Allowing these valves to remain open will prevent fuel expansion damage to the main manifold line.

12. Ignition Switches—OFF, after propellers have stopped.
13. Intercooler Shutter Switches—CLOSE, until intercooler shutters are fully closed.
14. Static Propeller Feather Check—Completed.
15. Engine Analyzer Power Switch—OFF.
16. Battery Switch—OFF.

OIL DILUTION.

To accomplish satisfactory starting of engines in cold weather, it is imperative that each engine oil system be diluted in accordance with the following procedure:
1. Stop engines, check oil level, and service if necessary. Allow engines to cool until oil temperatures are 10°C to 50°C. While waiting for oil temperature to reduce to that required for dilution, service oil tanks and drain condensate from the oil tank sumps, oil cooler drains, and Y-drains. Experience has shown that in order to prevent accumulation of ice in the tank oil-out line, oil tank sumps must be drained from 10 to 45 minutes after shutdown.

Note

The sumps should not be drained after dilution. Draining the sumps after dilution would permit undiluted oil to enter the tank hopper and sump.

2. Restart the engines and idle at 1200 rpm.
3. Hold the oil dilution switches ON as long as required for proper oil dilution. The per cent dilution required will vary according to the lowest expected OAT. The dilution time required will vary according to whether diluent remains in the system from a previous dilution. If the engines have been operated for less than one hour following a full dilution it will be necessary to accomplish only a partial dilution when the engines are shut down to replace the diluent which has boiled off. Experience has shown that boil-off is influenced by CHT, oil temperature, bhp, and other factors and for this reason an exact determination for redilution following short engine runs is not practical. The two tables shown in figure 9-5 will give the required dilution at various OAT's and an approximation of the diluent remaining after certain periods of engine run.

The operation of the dilution system is indicated by a fuel pressure drop to approximately 20 psi. If this pressure drop is not obtained, investigate the cause. Pay particular attention to dilution solenoids which may be stuck, dilution lines which may be plugged, and restrictor fittings which may be reversed.

CAUTION

Do not allow the engine oil pressure to fall below 15 psi during dilution. If necessary, stop the engine until oil temperature drops to 10° to 50°C. If the oil temperature rises above 60°C during dilution, the engine must be shut down until the oil temperature drops sufficiently to allow completion of dilution on the next attempt.

4. Release the dilution switch at 500 rpm as the engine is being shut down and check for an increase in fuel pressure. This is important because only diluted oil must be circulated through the engine oil system.
5. Insure that the oil dilution valves are fully closed by performing the following check:

   a. With fuel booster pumps ON, note fuel pressure and fuel flow indications.

   b. Hold the oil dilution switch ON long enough to note fuel pressure drop and fuel flow increase.

   c. Oil dilution switch OFF and observe fuel pressure rise to original value and fuel flow drop to

Section IX
All Weather Operation

T.O. 1B-36D(II)-1

OIL DILUTION Tables

Table I

EXPECTED OUTSIDE AIR TEMPERATURE	PERCENT DILUTION REQUIRED	DILUTION TIME REQUIRED (MINUTES)
4°C (40°F)	0	0
4°C (40°F) to −4°C (25°F)	10	2
−4°C (25°F) to −12°C (10°F)	15	3
−12°C (−10°F) to −21°C (−5°F)	20	4
−21°C (−5°F) to −29°C (−20°F)	25	6
−29°C (−20°F) to −37°C (−35°F)	30	8
−37°C (−35°F) to −53°C (−65°F)	35*	12

*MAXIMUM AVAILABLE

Table II

ENGINE RUN TIME (MINUTES)	PERCENT DILUENT REMAINING			ENGINE CONDITION
	35% DILUTION	25% DILUTION	15% DILUTION	
0	35	25	15	IDLE
1	32.5	23	14	IDLE
3	25	20	12	IDLE
5	19	18	10	IDLE
10	16	15	8	IDLE
15	15	11	7	MAG. CHECK
20	11	8	6	MAG. CHECK
25	9	6	5	OTHER CHECKS
30	7	5	5	OTHER CHECKS
35	6	5	4	OTHER CHECKS
40	5	4	3	OTHER CHECKS
45	4	3	3	OTHER CHECKS

For a full dilution use Table I. For a partial dilution obtain the percent diluent remaining from Table II and apply this value and the total percent dilution required to Table I to obtain the dilution times for these percentages. The difference in the time required, as indicated by Table I, will be the dilution time required to obtain the desired final dilution.

Example: If the expected OAT. is −29°C (−20°F) the dilution required will be 25 percent, as indicated on Table I. Then say the engine had been run at idle for 10 minutes and shut down. The diluent remaining would be 15 percent as indicated in the "Diluent Remaining, 25 Percent Dilution" column in Table II. Table I indicates that 6 minutes is required for 25 percent dilution and 3 minutes is required for 15 percent dilution. Therefore 3 minutes (6 minutes minus 3 minutes) is the dilution time required to replace the diluent lost during the previous engine operation.

NOTE

The required dilution for −53°C (−65°F), which is 40 percent, cannot be obtained on this aircraft but satisfactory operation can be obtained with the maximum dilution now obtainable, which is 35 to 37 percent.

Figure 9-5.

original value. If either fails to return to the original value, the dilution valve did not close. In either case, corrective action must be taken.

Note

Under no circumstances will the oil dilution valves be used as a means of relieving trapped pressure in the fuel lines.

AFTER ENGINE SHUTDOWN.

After engine shutdown, the following procedure should be followed:

1. Drain fuel tank and booster pump drains before moisture freezes. If fuel tanks are kept filled, condensation in fuel lines and drains will be minimized.

2. Inspect turbo oil system vents and drains. Drain condensation.

3. Approximately 30 minutes after stopping engines, turn each propeller through 10 blades by energizing the starter continuously.

4. Install air intake ducts, engine, turret, nose compartment, blister, pilots' enclosure, and pitot mast covers. Install tape over static ports.

5. If wings are dry and no wind condition prevails, wing and elevator covers may be used. Wing covers should not be used if wings are wet because of the possibility of freezing the covers to the wings. If wing covers are available but surfaces are wet, coat surfaces with defrosting fluid and install covers. If wing covers are not available, section covers should be made locally.

6. Position the propeller blades so that two blades are down and one is up. Cover the tip of the blade that is up to prevent ice and snow from entering the anti-icing air exit opening.

7. Drain the overflow and filler lines for the roomette waste tanks. Drain all liquid containers.

POWER PLANT SERVICING.

The following is a list of oils that must be used in the engines and auxiliary power units during cold weather operations.

SERVICE INFORMATION Table

1. **Reciprocating Engines** • Specification MIL-L-6082, grade 1100 lubricating oil.

2. **Jet Engines and Turbosuperchargers** • Specification MIL-L-6081 grade 1010 or 1005 above −20°F, grade 1005 below −20°F.

3. **Propellers**
   Hub • MIL-O-6086 Grade M.
   Power Section • MIL-L-7870

4. **Engine Instruments** • Service the oil pressure lines of engine instruments with hydraulic oil, Specification MIL-O-5606 in accordance with instructions contained in T.O. 05-70-6.

5. **Water Injection** • 60 percent methyl alcohol and 40 percent distilled water, thoroughly mixed.

SNOW AND ICE REMOVAL.

The removal of ice and snow can present quite a problem if preparations have not been made prior to its arrival. The following is a list of do's and don'ts and the equipment needed in the combating and removal of ice and snow.

1. It is necessary that all frost, snow, and ice be removed from the wings, tail surfaces, and propellers prior to flight. Even a slight amount of frost will disturb air flow over the air foil and reduce lift. Loose snow can be removed with a long-handled broom. Melted and refrozen snow is extremely difficult to remove.

WARNING

To insure free movement of control surfaces and wing flaps, the hinge points and the areas between fixed and movable surfaces must be cleared of ice and snow.

2. Removal of frost and any light coating of ice may be accomplished by the use of defrosting fluid in accordance with Specification No. 3609. If snow or freezing rain is anticipated, the wing and control surfaces should be coated with defrosting fluid prior to arrival. Surfaces coated with deicing fluid should be inspected every 4 hours and resprayed if necessary.

CAUTION

a. Due to the rapid evaporation characteristic of defrosting fluid, contact with the skin at low temperatures may cause serious frost bite.

b. Do not use picks, knives, or other sharp pointed objects to break ice as damage to the aircraft structure will result.

c. Use extreme caution when walking on surfaces after application of defrosting fluid.

d. The fluid should not be sprayed on engine surfaces or into engine air ducts leading to the carburetor or oil coolers.

e. After use of defrosting fluid, inspect surface hinge areas and remove deposits of slush; use heat if necessary.

f. Do not use defrosting fluid on sighting blisters or any other panes used for gun sighting.

g. During visual preflight, rotate the jet engines with the starter to assure freedom of movement. If ice is present, apply heat as soon as possible.

PREHEAT OF ENGINES AND AIRCRAFT.

1. Check the Y-drains and oil tank sumps for oil flow. If oil does not flow, apply external heat to Y-drain.

CAUTION

Do not drain more than one half pint in order to prevent undiluted oil from entering the oil line.

2. Oil screens should be checked before each flight during the early part of the cold weather period to remove engine sludge which has been washed down by oil dilution. After the first five or six oil dilutions, oil screens will be checked according to existing regulations.

3. Check turbo oil system drains for free flow and the turbo oil tank vents for freedom from frozen condensate. Insert a heavy wire in the vent line to check the first right angle bend in the line for freedom from ice.

4. Check all fuel, water, and oil tank vent lines and crankcase breathers for freedom from frozen condensate. (See figure 9-6.)

5. Apply external heat to the oil tank vent line aneroid valve for 30 minutes prior to starting. It has been found that during ground operation under cold weather conditions, ice forms in the aneroid valve, blocking the oil tank vent line. This results in excessive pressures being built up in the tank which will cause structural damage to the oil tank.

Section IX
All Weather Operation

> **CAUTION**
>
> After engine start, observe the oil tank vents for fifteen minutes for signs of escaping vapors which indicate that the aneroid valve is thawed and the line is open. If vapors are not observed, shut down the engine immediately and apply more heat to the aneroid valve.

It appears that the most critical period of operation is immediately after starting—probably the valve is warmed later by hot gases from the engine being pumped back to the tank by the scavenge pumps.

6. Always preheat the engines any time oil dilution was not accomplished and OAT. is less than 0°C (32°F) or any time engines were diluted and OAT. is less than —9°C (16°F). Preheat as follows:

a. Connect two heater ducts to the air intake cover at the leading edge of the wings.

b. Install the engine cover (if not previously installed).

c. Connect one heater duct at the oil Y-drain access cover if temperature is below —40°C (—40°F).

d. Heat until cylinder head temperature indicates at least 0°C; oil will flow from the Y-drain and propellers can be pulled through. Always leave the air plug and intercooler shutters closed for all preheating.

7. Warm the oil supply by plugging in the external power source to the heating receptacle on the wing lower surface near each oil tank. The heaters heat the oil tank hopper and tank oil-out line. Use of heat is necessary when the OAT. is below the pour point of the oil which will vary from —7° to —18°C (+20° to 0°F).

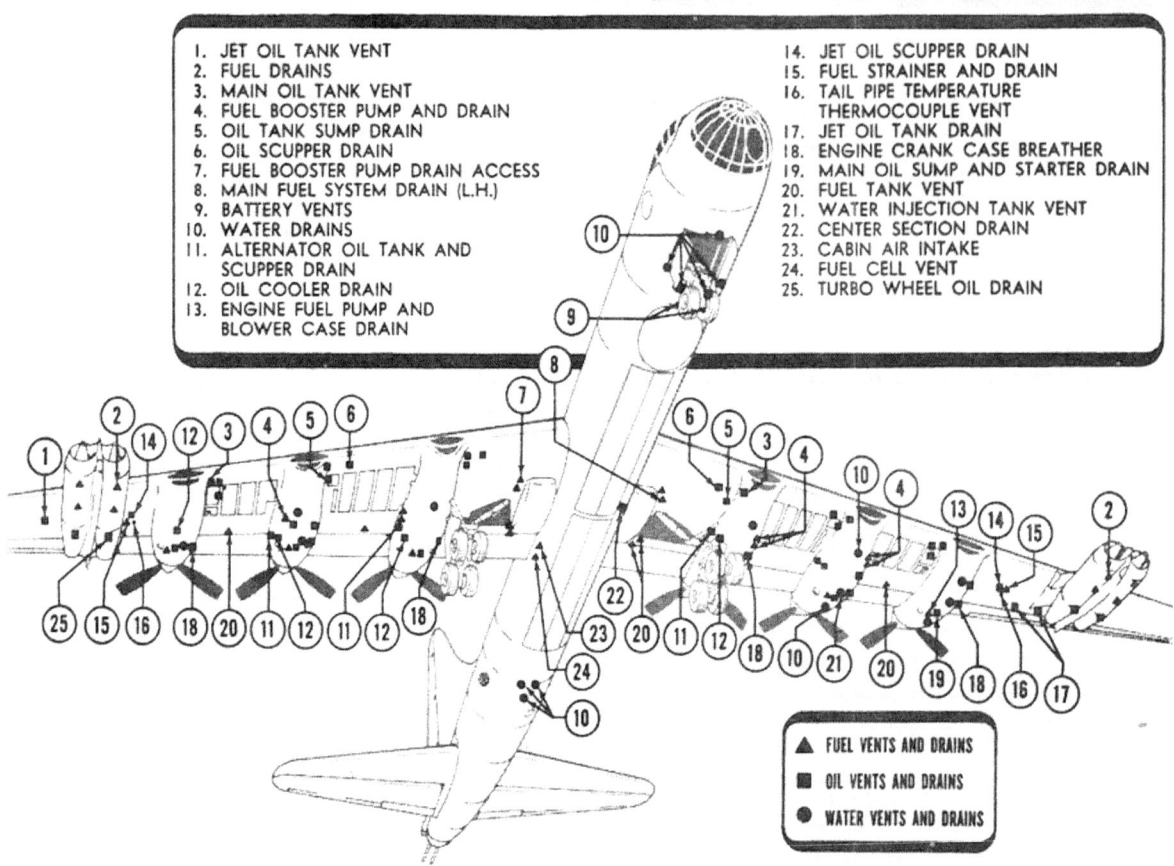

Figure 9-6.

GROUND Heating

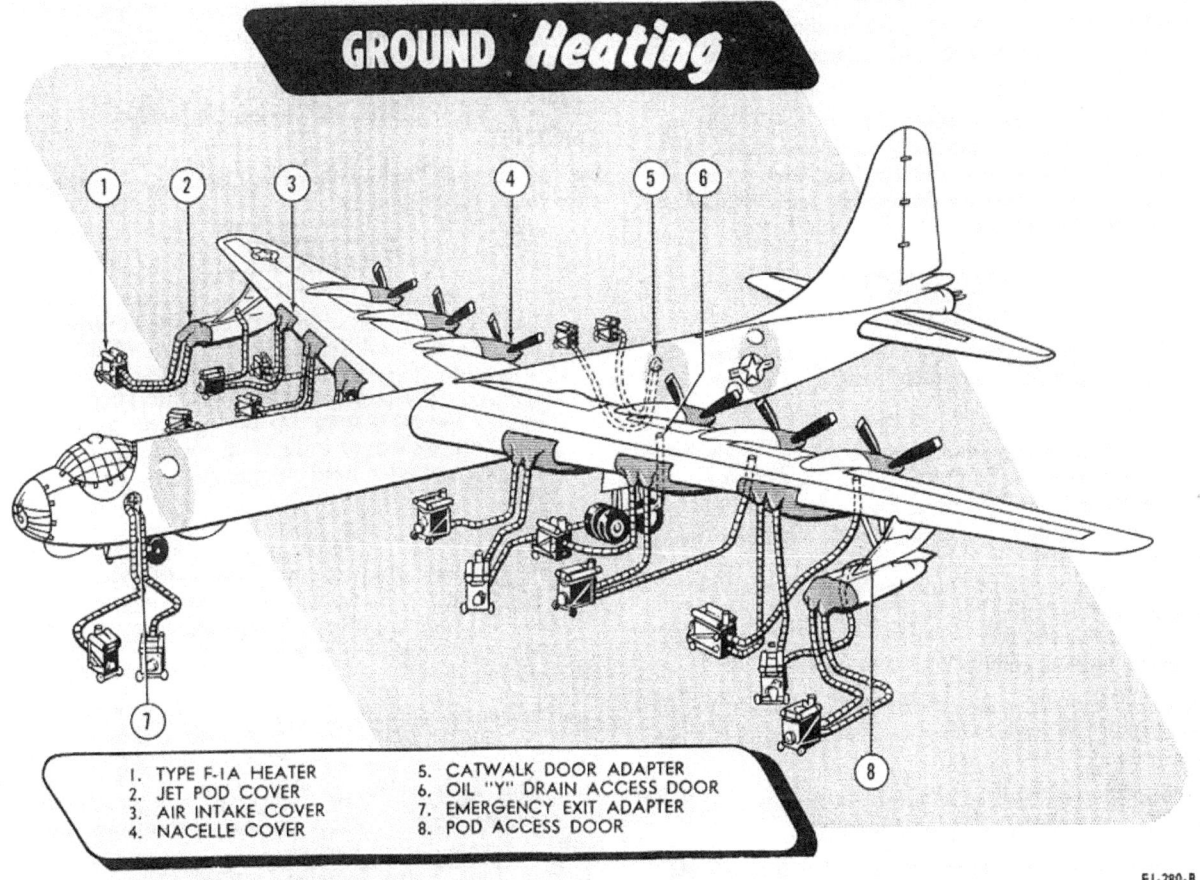

1. TYPE F-1A HEATER
2. JET POD COVER
3. AIR INTAKE COVER
4. NACELLE COVER
5. CATWALK DOOR ADAPTER
6. OIL "Y" DRAIN ACCESS DOOR
7. EMERGENCY EXIT ADAPTER
8. POD ACCESS DOOR

Figure 9-7.

OIL HEATING TIME Requirements

Outside Air Temperature	Time
−7°C (+20°F) to −23°C (−10°F)	10 minutes
−23°C (−10°F) to −29°C (−20°F)	20 minutes
−29°C (−20°F) to −34°C (−30°F)	30 minutes
−34°C (−30°F) to −40°C (−40°F)	40 minutes

The heaters must be completely covered with oil before using them to prevent coking of the oil and overheating of the heating elements. Therefore, do not operate the heaters if the oil level is below 145 gallons.

Note

To check for proper heater operation, see that the power consumption is 45 to 50 amperes for each heater installation; otherwise, because of their locations, it will be impossible to tell whether or not the heaters are functioning.

CAUTION

The hopper heaters heat only the oil in the hopper and tank oil-out line. The warm return oil from the engine will melt oil in the tank and if a serious oil leak develops the melting rate may not be of sufficient speed to replenish the oil in the hopper. This would result in an insufficient oil flow to the engine. Watch oil pressures closely since the oil level liquidometer may be in congealed oil and may not show a change in oil level.

8. Turn on oil tank vent electric heaters 30 minutes prior to engine start. Operation of the heaters should be checked by inserting finger in the vent outlet 20 minutes after turning switch ON.

9. If low or no oil pressure is indicated after engine start, heat the oil-in line from the tank bulkhead to the oil shutoff valve. An effective method of heating the line is to cover the line with a piece of canvas and direct hot air under it.

10. Preheat the crew compartments to heat flight instruments, radios, dynamotors, rectifiers, radar, and other equipment within the airplane, and to retard the formation of frost on transparent areas when the crew enters the airplane.

> **CAUTION**
>
> Do not operate electrical cabin heaters unless two or more alternators are paralleled on the line.

11. To reduce engine power failure during flight due to fuel starvation when OAT. is low enough to cause ice crystals to form in the fuel system, the main strainers, carburetor and master control D chamber inlet screens, and all fuel system moisture drains should be drained prior to flight. This is especially true when single-point refueling is used, since experience has shown that moisture is more likely to be found after refueling by this method.

12. Check the fuel system for leaks and check all fuel drains for free flow. Apply heat where necessary to obtain flow.

13. Install warm battery or heat cold battery if it has not been removed after preceding flight.

14. Check the tires and shock struts for proper inflation.

> **CAUTION**
>
> Checking and servicing of tires and shock struts may result in valve leakage. Usually this can be corrected by applying external heat.

If the aircraft has been parked more than 48 hours in temperatures of —40°C (—40°F) or below, the tires must be heated and rotated. Heat should be left on the tires for at least 15 minutes after rotation to eliminate the flat spot.

15. Remove the covers of the engines, wing, tail, guns, pilots' enclosure, nose compartment, blisters, and pitot masts. Also remove tape from static ports.

16. Remove ice, snow, and frost from the fuselage, wings, and horizontal stabilizer. Inspect gun turret door tracks and remove ice and snow. Snow can be removed by brushing with brooms, use of portable heaters and alcohol, or by vibrating a rope across the wing surface. Ice must be removed carefully to prevent scratching or marring the wing surfaces.

17. Remove ice, frost, snow, and dirt from the landing gear shock struts, actuating cylinders, wheels, and brakes. After shock struts and actuating cylinders are clean, wipe with a hydraulic-fluid-soaked cloth.

BEFORE STARTING RECIPROCATING ENGINES.

Use the normal "Before Starting Check List," except omit items 14, 17, and 18.

> **CAUTION**
>
> In the event the air plugs were inadvertently left open, do not attempt to close them until the engines are started and sufficient heat from the engine has warmed the air plug actuator and jackscrews. Do not open the air plugs, intercoolers, or inflight oil cooler doors until the cylinder head temperature reaches 170°C.

Note

Normal starts can be made when the cylinder head temperature reaches 0°C. No damage can result from prolonged heating, whereas considerable difficulties may result from insufficient heat.

STARTING RECIPROCATING ENGINES.

The engineer will start the engines as follows:

1. Engine Analyzer Power Switch—ON. This allows the analyzer time to warm up for monitoring the ignition system during starting.

2. Fuel Tank Valve Switches—OPEN. Use a minimum of two tanks containing fuel.

3. Booster Pumps of Tanks Being Used—ON. To provide positive fuel pressure (10 to 14 psi) to engine-driven fuel pump and fuel under pressure to primer. The primer is effectively inoperative without pressure.

4. Voltage and Frequency Selector Switch—No. 4 position. See that bus voltage provided by external power source is within limits by moving the selector switch to the bus position. Then move it to the No. 4 position. This will allow you to observe voltage and frequency of engine being started.

5. Throttle Levers—As Required. If it becomes necessary to restart a relatively "hot" engine, a more open throttle setting may be required.

6. Inform ground observer, "Ready to start engines, clear No. 4."

7. Engine No. 4 Starter Switch—ON. Energize starter continuously for nine blades. Maintain contact with the observer for reports of propeller movement. This procedure is followed to minimize the possibility of damage in the event of a liquid (hydraulic) lock.

Note

Nine blades are necessary to provide an adequate liquid lock check.

Section IX
All Weather Operation

8. No. 4 Engine Ignition Switch—BOTH after nine blades of propeller rotation.
9. Prime as required.
10. No. 4 Mixture Control Lever—NORMAL.

> **CAUTION**
>
> Maximum continuous cranking time is *one minute*; then allow the starter to cool a minimum of *three minutes*.

11. Report, "Alternator normal, oil and fuel pressure normal."

> **CAUTION**
>
> If oil pressure does not register 25 psi within 30 seconds, the engine will be shut down and the cause investigated.

Note

Minimum oil pressure at ground idle speed after oil has reached operating temperature is 25 psi.

Adjust voltage to 208 volts and check frequency for normal indication to allow control circuits to stabilize. Move the voltage and frequency selector switch to the number of the next alternator-equipped engine to be started.

Note

The frequency will increase with the temperature of the control circuit resistor.

Do not move the frequency control knob beyond the mechanical stop during ground operation. If the mechanical limit is exceeded overspeeding may occur.

> **CAUTION**
>
> a. If excitation of the alternator is not immediately apparent, the field will be flashed. If flashing the field fails to excite the alternator, shut down the engine. With no meter indication, malfunctions which might cause alternator damage would not be evident.
>
> b. Alternators must be excited and properly governed before advancing the throttles above 1400 rpm. This is necessary so that the alternators can be checked when the engines are run up. If the frequency of any alternator increases with an increase in engine rpm and cannot be adjusted, then the affected engine must be shut down and the constant-speed drive unit checked. Otherwise an overspeed condition may be reached, causing the units to disintegrate and causing a serious fire.

12. Repeat steps 4 through 11 for starting engines 5, 6, 3, 2, and 1. Since No. 1 and No. 6 engines are not alternator-equipped, references to alternators in the starting procedure should be disregarded.

Note

If the engine stops running with the mixture control in NORMAL, the lever should be returned to the IDLE CUT-OFF position. After the starter has been allowed to cool, the starting procedure may be repeated.

1. Possible starting troubles and the proper corrective action are shown in the table below.
2. If the oil pressure is too high after starting, or if it fluctuates and drops back with an increase of engine rpm, do not exceed idle rpm until the oil temperature

Trouble	Probable Cause	Corrective Action
Failure to start	Frosted spark plugs	Additional preheat
Low fuel pressure	Faulty oil dilution valve	Check for stuck valve
Low oil pressure	Congealed oil in lines	Apply heat to lines
	Faulty instrument pressure for lack of fluid in lines or congealed oil	Check instrument Check instrument system and bleed lines with hydraulic fluid
High oil pressure which falls off or fluctuates when rpm is increased	Heavy viscous oil	Additional preheat to tank and lines if pressure is below limits
Props not controllable	Stuck solenoids	Apply heat
Oil leakage from turbos into shroud	Turbo oil tank vent obstructed with ice	Clear vent
	Faulty anti leak valve	Replace valve

449

reaches minimum allowable. Erratic or high oil pressures may be caused by the high viscosity of the oil due either to applications of insufficient preheat or to insufficient dilution after the last flight.

> **CAUTION**
>
> If fuel pressure is lower than normal, check for a stuck oil dilution valve.

3. If no indication of oil pressure is obtained within 50 seconds after starting, shut down. After approximately 5 minutes, make a restart and run an additional 50-second period. If pressure is still not obtained, shut down and check for oil flow at Y-drain. If no flow is obtained at the Y-drain apply heat in this area for 30 minutes. If flow is satisfactory from Y-drain, apply heat to oil lines between tank and oil shutoff valve for 30 minutes. The primary and most common causes for lack of oil pressure indications are:

   a. Congealed oil in the engine oil-in line, usually near the tank.

   b. Failure of oil pressure gage to indicate properly because of congealed oil in the pressure lines or transmitter.

> **Note**
>
> To minimize this type of trouble, purge the pressure lines with hydraulic fluid after every fifth start.

4. If oil pressure drops after a few minutes of ground operation, shut down the engine and check the following:

   a. Y-drain for congealed oil or ice.
   b. Blown lines or oil coolers.
   c. Failure of pressure gage.
   d. Oil strainers for foreign materials which might indicate that engine failure is the cause of low oil pressure.
   e. Insufficient hopper heat.

> **Note**
>
> Oil dilution may be used to reduce viscosity of the oil if time does not permit normal engine warm-up or if the oil pressure is too high for a prolonged period.

> **CAUTION**
>
> Dilute oil with care because engine failure can result from over-dilution.

ENGINE WARM-UP.

After engine start with air plug and intercooler shutters closed, if the OAT. is −18°C (0°F) or below or if 170°C CHT cannot be obtained, the following engine warm-up procedure should be used:

1. Idle the engines at 1000-1200 rpm with carburetor preheat ON until oil-in temperature reaches minimum limits.

2. With the propeller master motor set at 2700 rpm, increase engine rpm to 1550 rpm.

3. After power has stabilized, reset master motor to 1550 rpm and increase M.P. to 30 inches.

4. When oil-in temperature reaches 60°C or above, increase rpm to 2000 and maintain 30 inches M.P.

> **Note**
>
> While waiting for the engines to warm up, make all field barometric pressure checks except high fan and magneto check.

5. When oil-in temperature reaches 70°C, turn carburetor preheat OFF and make high power checks.

> **CAUTION**
>
> Do not go above 2200 rpm until oil-in temperature reaches 70°C or above.

6. Attempt to maintain CHT from 210° to 225°C during all ground operation. This may require keeping the air plugs fully closed.

> **Note**
>
> It would require from 45 minutes to one hour of engine operation at normal temperatures to evaporate all the fuel in the diluted oil. Even though high oil inlet temperatures of 70°C (158°F) and above would shorten the period, this procedure is not recommended. Normal warm-up procedure will evaporate sufficient fuel to assure normal scavenging.

7. After several days layover, during which time the engine has been started and diluted several times, it is advisable to ground run the engine for at least 30 minutes at normal cylinder head and oil inlet temperatures prior to take-off. It is also recommended that the oil level be checked; it may have fallen considerably due to evaporation of gasoline. The ground run will tend to eliminate any excess dilution which might otherwise cause oil discharge through the breathers or loss in oil pressure during high power take-off or operation.

DURING ENGINE WARM-UP.

1. Ignition Switch Check—Idle rpm.
2. Engine-Driven Fuel Pumps—Check.
3. Heat and Anti-Icing Check—Completed.

> **Note**
>
> To prevent overheating of the tail structure do not allow the temperature of the tail anti-icing air to exceed 105°C (221°F) during ground operations. Use the cabin heat and tail anti-icing control switches to reduce the temperatures of the tail anti-icing air.

4. Alternator Checks—Completed.
5. Engine Oil-In Temperature—Minimum 70°C.

6. Check all instruments for proper operation.

7. To prevent the flight instruments from cooling and to aid in windshield defrosting, operate the cabin heating system as follows:

   a. Increase the manifold pressure on the inboard engines until a good cabin heat air flow is obtained. If the air thus supplied is insufficiently warm for defrosting, turn on the tail anti-icing system and place the cabin booster fan switch in the LOW RPM position to raise the temperature of the cabin heating air at the secondary heat exchanger.

   b. Increase cabin temperature and aid defrosting by utilizing the auxiliary cabin heaters.

> **CAUTION**
>
> To avoid overloading the a-c system because of the high power requirements of the auxiliary cabin heaters, do not operate these heaters unless two or more alternators are on the line.

8. Check windshield wiper operation.

9. Operate the wing flaps and bomb bay doors through at least one cycle.

ENGINE RUN-UP.

> **CAUTION**
>
> After engine start, observe the oil tank vents for 15 minutes for signs of escaping vapors which indicate that the aneroid valve is thawed and the line is open. If vapors are not observed, shut down the engine immediately and apply more heat to the aneroid valve.

Use normal engine run-up procedures as outlined in Section II.

STARTING JET ENGINES.

Use the normal starting procedure.

Note

A slightly longer cranking period will probably be required to bring the jets up to starting rpm than is required in warmer weather.

TAXIING AND PARKING.

1. Avoid use of brakes as much as possible during last part of taxiing and parking. This prevents the brakes from getting hot and then freezing. If brakes are frozen heat can be used, but the aircraft should be moved as soon as brakes are thawed to prevent re-freezing.

> **CAUTION**
>
> Under certain snow and ice conditions the use of differential power and braking may result in a skipping or lateral skidding action of the nose wheel. This skipping action can best be overcome by stopping the airplane, changing the nose wheel angle, and resuming taxiing. Light braking may be erratic and lack proper brake "feel"; therefore, control ground speed with one pair of propellers in reverse. Use propeller reversing with caution as the resulting snow cloud may blind the pilot. Reversing the outboard propellers will reduce this possibility.

2. Wheel covers should be installed when the airplane is parked and snow and ice are present.

BEFORE TAKE-OFF.

1. Keep CHT as high as possible within allowable limits using the air plugs to control temperatures.

> **CAUTION**
>
> Flight indicators are not very reliable at temperatures below −43°C (−45°F). For this reason cabin heating is very necessary during warm-up and take-off, and all flight instruments must be cross checked.

2. Frequent exercising of the brakes during power stabilization and prior to take-off may prevent brakes from freezing.

> **CAUTION**
>
> Brakes will not hold the aircraft during high power runs on ice and snow.

TAKE-OFF.

> **WARNING**
>
> Ice on the horizontal stabilizer can seriously reduce the effectiveness of the elevators to the extent that take-off attitude cannot be attained.

1. Turn on pitot heaters and the wing and tail anti-icing systems if precipitation is encountered or if icing conditions are anticipated at the beginning of the take-off roll. Icing conditions may exist where there is visible moisture in the air at outside air temperatures of 7°C (45°F) and below. Most severe icing conditions usually occur in the range from 0°C (32°F) to −15°C (5°F) OAT.

2. If oil dilution was used on previous engine shutdown, take-off can be made as soon as oil pressure is normal, engine operation is smooth, and CHT is up to 180°C. Precaution must be taken to insure that the oil pressure is normal. Oil pressure below normal may be due to over-diluted oil. Cold oil properly diluted has the same viscosity as warm undiluted oil and therefore the same ability to circulate and properly

Section IX
All Weather Operation

lubricate the engines. The term "over-dilution" has been used to indicate any amount of dilution which causes the engine scavenging system to break down and discharge diluted oil through the engine breather.

3. In order to avoid overtaxing the engine on take-off or to avoid standing short on take-off horsepower available, it is essential to make the proper humidity and CAT. correction to manifold pressure. These corrections modify the value of M.P. necessary to develop the torque corresponding to 3500 bhp. This is especially true in cold weather operation where it is quite easy to take more than 3500 bhp out of the engine if normal M.P. is used.

CAUTION

Do not pull more than 3500 bhp torque. Also, do not exceed the corrected M.P. while trying to attain 3500 bhp, since an engine malfunction may exist.

4. Under certain cold weather conditions water injection may cause drowning of cylinders and loss of power due to improper vaporization of the water mixture. Since limiting operating temperatures (CAT., CHT, water temperature, etc.) have not been established, *it is urgent that a test on at least one engine be performed prior to take-off to determine whether operation at wet take-off power is satisfactory.* This test period should be of at least one minute duration. The results of this check will determine whether water injection should be used for take-off. Loss of torque and rough running are indications of improper engine operation with water injection.

Note

Do not exceed 3250 bhp unless water injection is used.

5. It is advisable to maintain CAT. above freezing, if possible to do so without exceeding the maximum CAT. limit. The desired temperature range is from +20° to +35°C to avoid carburetor icing as well as to aid in vaporizing the fuel and water.

Note

The CHT measured on D-5 cylinders should be at least 225°C also to aid in vaporizing the fuel and water.

It is recognized that use of the carburetor preheat system may result in excessive CAT. at take-off power if used at ambient temperatures in excess of −12°C (10°F). At ambient temperatures higher than this the preheat system is not needed due to adequate temperature rise from turbo compression. It is suggested that under these conditions, CAT. be controlled by intercooler shutters.

For ambient temperatures of −12°C (10°F) or less, use of the preheat system should be attempted. The exact upper limit of outside air temperature at which preheat should be used has not definitely been established, but tests have been proposed to evaluate the preheat system at or near the previously defined upper limit of OAT. at which carburetor preheat could be used.

Although the CAT. may be within limits with carburetor preheat ON at the beginning of the take-off run, the application of full power may cause the CAT. to increase rapidly and exceed the safe range resulting in loss of manifold pressure and power. In view of this, *any aircraft operating in cold weather with an OAT. of −12°C (10°F) or lower should make a preliminary preheat evaluation by performing a simulated take-off and trying the system on one engine.*

To do this the intercooler shutters should be OPEN, the CHT should be at the low limit, and the preheat system should be operated with the circuit breaker at the start of the take-off roll. *The results of this test will determine whether it is safe to use preheat on all six engines for take-off.*

If CAT. is maintained in the range specified, the worst icing that could be encountered would be in the small mixture control bleed at the bottom of the regulator resulting in an enrichment that can be easily controlled with the mixture control lever. *If CAT. is not kept above freezing there is danger of icing the entire induction system and metering elements of the carburetor. Icing of the impact tubes and/or passages can result in dangerous leaning which cannot be controlled. Icing of the split mixture control bleed in the boost hanger will result in a very high enrichment that is difficult to control with the mixture control lever.*

Note

The engineer should watch the carburetor air temperature indicator and be ready to reduce CAT. by opening the intercooler shutters or by turning off the carburetor preheat system.

6. Turn off all auxiliary cabin heaters until after the landing gear and flaps are up.

7. Instruct the gunners to watch for locked wheels during take-off. Don't be alarmed if the brakes should lock temporarily while on snow and ice, because you will be able to retain control of the airplane. Ordinarily, the brakes will not hold the airplane on ice and snow above normal rated power.

8. If discharge through the oil breather is noted at take-off, reduce rpm as quickly as practicable and operate engines at moderate powers for 10 to 15 minutes

before increasing rpm. Oil discharge should cease soon after the reduction in rpm. When most of the diluted oil has been expelled as indicated by normal oil pressure and temperature, normal engine operation can be resumed. If the oil discharge does not cease after reducing rpm, land and investigate the cause. Should the persistent discharge of oil be caused by high dilution of oil throughout the tank, drain the oil from the tank and refill with undiluted oil.

DURING FLIGHT.

For *all* operation, maintain the recommended range of CAT. to (1) aid in fuel vaporization, (2) reduce tendency to lead-foul spark plugs, and (3) improve fuel economy to extend range.

APPROACH.

1. Follow the normal procedure except use carburetor preheat as required and, if possible, employ a long, low approach to aid in keeping cylinder heads above critically low temperatures of 170°C and the oil temperature above 75°C.

2. Apply carburetor preheat as required during the entire landing operation. If a sudden acceleration is necessary, heat will be available for fuel vaporization regardless of how low cylinder head temperatures have dropped. However, should full power be required for a take-off or a go-around, keep carburetor air temperature below maximum allowable limit and be ready to reduce or shut off carburetor preheat. (See "Emergency Use of Carburetor Preheat" of this section.)

3. The air plugs should be closed during prolonged glides or approaches.

4. Temperature inversions are common in winter in arctic regions. Thus, the air may be from 15° to 30°C (27° to 54°F) colder on the ground than at altitude. Therefore, care must be taken to avoid rapid cooling when letting down. Extend the landing gear and use partial flaps to reduce air speed. Also, regulate the intercooler shutters to eliminate excessive engine cooling. Maintain cylinder head temperatures above 170°C minimum.

LANDING.

When landing on slick or icy runways and traction is poor, nose wheel steering may have little effect on directional control of the airplane, even though it is operating properly. When landing on a dry runway spotted with ice, it is possible to skid the nose gear on the ice and damage it by a full deflection. Directional control should be maintained with the throttles until the airplane is almost completely stopped. Practice this procedure on dry runways so as to become accustomed to the reverse action of the throttles when the propellers are in reverse thrust position. When landing in loose snow, exercise caution during reverse thrust application to prevent obscuring the runway with flying snow particles. Obscuring the runway with flying snow is especially possible below 50 mph.

The following precautions should also be observed:

1. Use the brakes with caution when landing on snow or ice.

2. When reversing propellers, apply only enough power to decelerate airplane without obstructing vision by blowing snow.

3. Toward the end of the landing roll turn off the wing, empennage, and propeller anti-icing.

4. Approach the end of the runway very slowly to prevent skidding when turn is started.

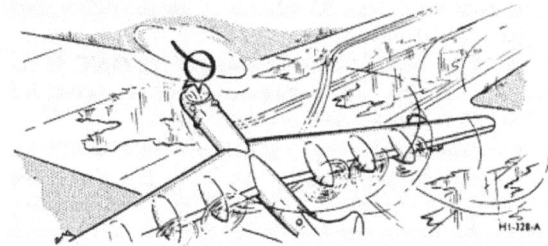

KITS AND LOOSE EQUIPMENT.

The following is a list of kits and their components needed for smooth operation during arctic conditions:

1. Snow and Ice Removal Kit for Each Aircraft.

   a. Two brooms.

   b. Two squeegees with 6-inch handles.

   c. Two safety harnesses with 150 feet of rope for each harness. (For walking on slick wings.)

   d. 150 yards of cheese cloth.

   e. Wing and elevator covers if available.

   f. Two barrels of deicing fluid, Specification No. 3609.

2. Engine and Aircraft Duct Cover Kit.

   a. Six air intake covers.

   b. Six engine covers.

   c. Six propeller tip covers.

   d. Two main landing gear strut covers.

   e. Eight main gear tire covers and two nose wheel tire covers.

   f. Six oil-in line covers. (These will have to be locally manufactured.)

   g. Electrical harnesses for oil tank hopper heaters.

   h. Four jet engine covers.

3. Miscellaneous Equipment.

   a. One rubber hose, one and one-half inches by 10 feet (for servicing auxiliary power units and heaters from bomb bay manifold stopcock).

   b. One large funnel, 6 inches by 1 inch.

   c. One five-gallon bucket.

   d. Three drop lights with 100-foot cord for each.

   e. One complete copy of cold weather operating instructions.

Section IX
All Weather Operation

CHECK LIST—COLD WEATHER.

PRE-HEATING.

1. Engine—Supply external heat through engine tunnel until D-5 cylinder reaches at least 0°C. Remove just before engine start.

2. Hopper Sump and Line—Use electrical heat one minute for each 1°F below 0°F, prior to engine start. Cut circuit just prior to engine start.

3. Oil Tank Vent Line—Use electrical heat at least 30 minutes prior to engine start and continue heat after start.

4. Flight Deck Instruments—Supply external heat to flight deck for at least 30 minutes prior to engine start to warm instruments.

5. Oil Tank Vent Aneroid Valve—If the OAT. is below 0°C (32°F), apply external heat to valve for at least 30 minutes prior to engine start.

6. Oil Line—If the OAT. is below —40°C (—40°F), (1) supply external heat to the oil-in line from the shutoff valve to the oil tank. The most effective method for doing this is to cover the line with canvas and direct hot air under it for at least 30 minutes. (2) Supply external heat through the Y-drain access for at least 30 minutes. Leave heat on until oil pressure is satisfactory on starting.

Note

It is assumed that the oil was properly diluted prior to cold soak; if not, a longer period will be required.

BEFORE STARTING ENGINES.

1. Check turbo oil system drains for free flow and turbo oil tank vents for frozen condensate.

2. Check all fuel, water, oil tank, and crankcase breather vents for frozen condensate.

3. Check all fuel and oil line hose clamps for tightness.

OIL PRESSURES.

1. If oil pressure does not reach 25 psi in 50 seconds after engine start, shut down engine and proceed as follows:

  a. Reinstall the engine tunnel heat ducts to continue engine preheat.

  b. Check for oil flow at the Y-drain. If no flow is obtained apply heat in this area. If flow is satisfactory from the Y-drain apply heat to the oil lines between tank and oil shutoff valve. Apply the heat as recommended under "Preheat of Engines and Aircraft," step 6 thru 9 of this section.

  c. Supply hopper sump and line heat for at least an additional 30 minutes.

  d. Continue heat to flight deck.

  e. Purge the oil pressure indicating line with hydraulic oil, Specification MIL-O-5606, per instruction in T.O. 5P2-1-1 even if it has been previously purged.

  f. Supply external heat directly to oil pressure transmitter for at least 20 minutes.

  g. Check oil shutoff valve manually to make certain it is open.

  h. Prevent oil tank pressurization by method recommended under "Preheating," step 5.

2. Repeat engine starting procedure outlined under starting engines. If oil pressure does not reach 25 psi in 50 seconds on this second attempt, shut down and check for bad instrument or transmitter, or for obstruction in the oil-in line.

Hot Weather Procedures

BEFORE ENTERING AIRPLANE.

1. Cool the crew compartments by the use of type A-1 portable coolers. The 15-foot refrigerant lines can be routed into the cabins through the entrance hatches.

2. Check all fabric surfaces and control surface hinge points for freedom from fungus. If fungus is evident, remove it from all surfaces, except the fabric surfaces, with a stiff brush or compressed air. Use a clean soft cloth for the fabric surfaces.

3. Inspect the oleo struts and tires for cleanliness and proper inflation.

4. Inspect all limit switches for moisture.

5. Remove the engine and air duct covers and other protective covers.

ON ENTERING AIRPLANE.

1. Operate all movable surfaces.

2. If necessary, warm electrical instruments with an external source of heat until all moisture is eliminated.

3. Inspect gun turret bays for excess moisture and remove by the application of heat.

4. Start the cabin ventilating fans as soon as the external power supply is connected.

5. Check the wing and fuselage drainage and ventilating holes.

STARTING RECIPROCATING ENGINES.

Use the normal starting procedure, except a more open throttle may be required.

1. Operate the engine-driven fans only in low ratio.

2. Do not overprime the engines.
3. Do not exceed cylinder head temperature limits.

DURING ENGINE RUN-UP.

Use normal run-up procedures as outlined in Section II. During hot weather operation carburetor air temperatures in excess of 38°C will occur. Carburetor air temperatures as high as 60°C may be experienced when ambient air temperatures are 27°C and higher. However, this should have no detrimental effect on the engine. A combination of extremely high carburetor air temperatures and high cylinder head temperatures will possibly cause engine detonation.

STARTING JET ENGINES.

Use the normal starting procedure.

TAKE-OFF AND LANDING.

Extremely warm weather necessitates a longer take-off and landing run, and increases the sinking speed of the airplane. Maximum cylinder head temperatures for take-off must be kept within limits. If high carburetor air temperatures are being encountered during ground run-up, use the following procedure:

1. Engineer—Make the propeller reverse safety check immediately after completion of the final engine check.

Note

The aircraft will be taxied into take-off position WITHOUT the use of propeller reversing.

2. Pilot—Set full take-off power on jet engines.
3. Engineer—Set "no boost" power on reciprocating engines. Report to aircraft commander, "Power is set."
4. Aircraft Commander—Release brakes.
5. Engineer—Advance TBS to full take-off power (corrected for humidity), water injection on.
6. Engineer—Report to aircraft commander prior to nose-up speed, "Power stabilized, propeller governing."

STOPPING ENGINES.

Stop the engines as soon as possible. Use normal procedure.

Desert Procedures

BEFORE ENTERING AIRPLANE.

1. Cool the crew compartments by the use of two type A-1 portable coolers.
2. Make sure the carburetor air filters are installed and connected.
3. Check the operation of the filter doors.
4. Operate all movable surfaces.
5. Use a cloth moistened with hydraulic fluid to wipe the nose and both main gear shock struts and exposed portions of actuating cylinders free of dust and sand.
6. Check tires and shock struts for proper inflation.
7. Remove ground cooling ducts, engine and airplane covers.

ON ENTERING AIRPLANE.

1. Start the cabin ventilating fans as soon as the external power supply is connected.
2. Clean the instrument panels with a lint-free cloth to remove any dust or sand.
3. Operate all instruments that can be checked without engine operation by using an external source of power.

STARTING RECIPROCATING ENGINES.

Use the normal starting procedure, except a more open throttle may be required.
1. Operate engine-driven fans in low ratio only.
2. Do not overprime the engines.

ENGINE WARM-UP.

1. Conduct ground operation in a minimum amount of time.

CAUTION

Do not operate the engine-driven fans in high ratio during ground operation or take-off.

2. Do not exceed cylinder head and carburetor air temperature limits.

STARTING JET ENGINES.

Use the normal starting procedure.

TAKE-OFF AND LANDING.

See "Take-off and Landing" under "Hot Weather Procedures" of this section.

STOPPING ENGINES.

1. Park the airplane into the wind.
2. Stop the engines a soon as possible.

Section IX
All Weather Operation

T.O. 1B-36D(II)-1

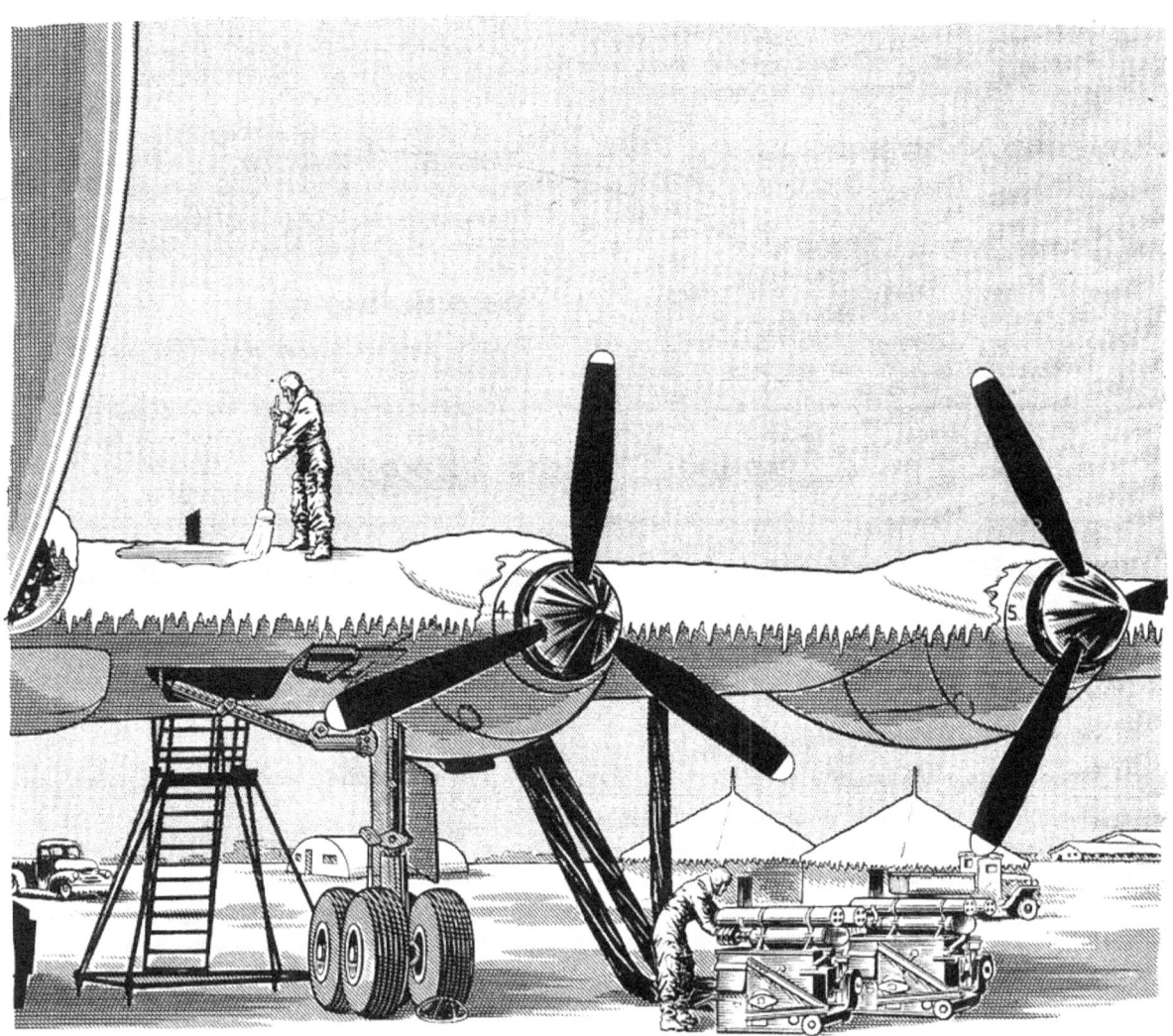

	Page
Autopilot (Continued)	
Turn Control Knob	252
Up-Elevator Co-ordination	377
Up-Elevator Co-ordination Knob	254
*Autopilot Control Panel	252
*Autopilot Main Chasis	253
*Autopilot Response Curve	376
Auxiliary Bunks	282
*Auxiliary Cabin Heater	228
Auxiliary Cabin Heaters	229
Auxiliary Equipment	85
Axes, Hand	82

B

	Page
Backfiring	339
Bail-Out	
Free Fall	201
General	198
High Altitude	200
Overwater	201
Polar	201
*Bail-Out Routes and Exits	199
Balance Knob, Master Temperature Indicator	77
Base Leg	167
Battery Receptacles, Master Temperature Indicator	77
Battery Switch	41
Battle Splint Kits	82
BC-453-B Radio Range Receiver	239
Beacon Navigation	385
Before	
Approach—Crash Landing	192
Approach—Ditching	195
Climb or High Power Operation	156
Entering Airplane—Desert Procedures	455
Entering Airplane—Hot Weather Procedures	454
Landing	164
Leaving Aircraft	173
Starting Engines	95, 434
Starting Engines—Cold Weather Check List	454
Starting Reciprocating Engines, Cold Weather Procedures	448
Take-Off	148, 434
Take-Off—Cold Weather Procedures	451
BMEP—Spark Plug Fouling	337
Boarding Aircraft	133
*Bomb Bay Door Emergency Controls	272
*Bomb Bay Door Emergency Hydraulic System Schematic	275
*Bomb Bay Door Normal Hydraulic System Schematic	268
Bomb Bay Door System	
Emergency Controls	274B
Emergency Hydraulic System	66, 275

	Page
Lamps	269
Ready Lamp	270
Safety Switch	267
Switch	267
Trouble Shooting	371
Bomb Bay Fuel Tank Release Controls	34A
Bomb Bay Fuel Tank Salvo Release	273
Bomb Bay Fuel Tank Release Selector Switch	34
*Bomb Sequence Tables	266
Bomb Team Check List	429
Bombardier—Gunner Selector Valve —Defrosting System	223
*Bombing Control Panel	269
Bombing System	
Bomb Bay Selector Switches	267
Bomb Co-ordination Knob, Autopilot	253
Bombing-Navigation System, K-( )	273
Bomb Interval Control Panel	267
Bomb-Size Indicator	270
Bomb Station Indicator Lights	270
Bomb Station Indicator Lights Switch	267
Controls, Normal	267
Coordination	377
Emergency Release	272
Emergency Release Controls	271
Equipment	264
Indicators	269
Nose Fuse Switch	267
Pneumatic Release	273
Radar Release	273
Radar Scoring Devise	273
Release Selector Switch	267
Release Sequence	266
Release Switch	267
Salvo Release	272
Salvo Switches	271
Single Release of Bombs	272
Train Release	272
Universal	273
Booster Fan, Cabin Air	221
Booster Pump Switches, Fuel	32
*Brake Emergency Hydraulic Controls	211
*Brake System	74
Brake System	
Controls	75
Emergency Hydraulic System	66
Emergency Pressure	217
General	73
Indicators	75
Parking Brake Lever	75
Parking Brake Switch	75
Pressure Gage	75
Pump Pressure Override Switch	75
Pump Switch	75
Use in Emergency Stopping	217
Warning Lamp, Low Pressure	75

*Denotes Illustration

Alphabetical Index

	Page
Briefing, Final Crew	145
Briefing, Formal	133
Buffeting Limitations	288
Bunks	282
Bunks, Auxiliary	282
Burst Control, Gunnery	401
Bus Controls, Alternator	40
Bus Indicators, Alternator	40

C

	Page
Cabin	
Air Booster Fan	221
Altimeters	221
Heat Switches	219
Heaters, Auxiliary	229
Heater Control, Auxiliary	229
Heater Power Switch	229
Heating	222
Heating Air Temperature Warning Lamps	220
Heating Controls	222
Heating System, Operation of	223
Pressure Control, Emergency	228
Pressure Control, Normal	221
Pressure Indicators	221
Pressure Shutoff Valve Switches	221
Pressurization	220
Temperature Control Switch	219
Temperature Control Valve Indicator Lamp	220
Ventilation	229
*Cabin Pressure vs. Atmospheric Pressure	220
*Calculated Stalling Speeds	302
Calibration Controls, Autopilot	253
Calibration Controls, Familiarization with	376
Calibration Controls Settings, Autopilot	254
Call Circuit	234
Camera	
Camera Door Indicator Lamps	277
Camera Door Switches	277
Controls	276
Controls, Radar	278
Indicators	277
Initiation Switch	277
Intervalometer	276
Master Power Switches	276
Mode Selector Switch	276
O-15 Operation	279
Operation	277
Operation Indicator Lamps	277
Power-On Indicator Lamps	277
Radar	278
Vacuum Gage	277
Carburetor	
Air Filter Switch	4
Air Temperature	317

	Page
Air Temperature Control	3
Air Temperature—Spark Plug Fouling	337
Carburetion	317
Emergency Use of Preheat	439
Impact Icing	319
Internal Icing	320
Manual Adjustment	326
Preheat Switches	4
Cargo System, Large	**274**
Cart, Communication Tube	279
Celestial Navigation Provisions	261
Center of Gravity Limitations	288
Characteristic Response Curves, Autopilot	375
Check Switch, Master Temperature Indicator	77
Checks	
Bomb Run	430
Bomb Team	429
Cold Weather Check List	454
Crew Interphone Oxygen	249
Engineer's Standard Check List	93
Gunnery Amplified List	391, 424
K-( ) System Preflight	383
Magneto Synchronization	344
Pilots' Standard Check List	91
Preflight Operational Equipment	89
Preflight Oxygen Equipment	247
Preflight Universal Bombing System	**385**
Circuit Breakers, A-C Equipment	47
Circuit Breaker, Alternator Field Flashing	38
Circuit Breakers and Fuses	44
Circulating Fans, Pilots' Air	228
Climb	
Before	156
Control	597
Emergency Curves	582
Initial	153
Instrument	435
Night	433
To High Altitude	160
Cold Weather Check List	454
Cold Weather Procedures	442
Combat Interphone System	232
Command Radio AN/ARC-3	238
Command Radio AN/ARC-27	239
Command Radio Equipment	238
*Communication and Associated Electronic Equipment	233
Communication Equipment	232
Communication Tube Cart	279
Compass	
Magnetic	258
Maximum Bank, Autopilot	377
Maximum Bank Knob, Autopilot	254
N-1 High Latitude	259
Radio AN/ARN-7( )	240
Slaved Gyro Magnetic	258
Compensating Rheostat Knob, Master Temperature Indicator	77

*Denotes Illustration

	Page
Computer Maximum Bank Knob, Autopilot	254
Computer Switch, Gunnery	263
Condition Selector Switch, Engine Analyzer	79
Constant-Speed Drive Unit	348
Constant-Speed Drive Underdrive Releasing	204
Contact, Crash Landing	193
Contact, Ditching	198
Control Columns	67
*Control Surface Deflections	67
Control Surface Locks	67
Controls	
Air Intake, Jet Engine	24
Alternator	36
Alternator Overspeed	353
Altitude Unit	256
Anti-Icing	219, 222
Anti-Icing, Jet Pod	231
Automatic Approach Coupler	257
Autopilot, Primary	252
Auxiliary Cabin Heater	229
Bomb Bay Door Emergency	274B
Bomb Bay Tank Release	34A
Bombing, Normal	267
Brake System	75
Bus, Alternator	40
Cabin Heating	222
Cabin Pressure	221
Calibration, Familiarization with	376
Camera	276
Carburetor Air Temperature	3
D-1 or D-2 Oxygen Regulator	246
Defrosting	222
Detonation	338
Emergency Bomb Release	271
Emergency Cabin Pressure	221
Emergency Fuel	34
Emergency Gunnery	264
Emergency Power	63
Engine Analyzer	79
Flap Emergency	69
Flap Normal	68
Flight	66, 304
Frequency, Alternator	349
Fuel Regulator, Jet Engine	20
Fuel System	32
Gunnery, Normal	261
Heating	219
Heating, Jet Pod	231
Hydraulic Fluid Temperature	270
Landing Gear Normal	69
Landing Gear System Manual Selector	71
Main Gear Manual Extension	71
Mixture	3, 324
Nose Landing Gear Manual Extension	72
Nose Wheel Steering	72

	Page
Oil System, Jet Engine	30
Oil System, Reciprocating Engine	16
Oxygen Regulator	246
Preignition	338
Pressure Refueling	34
Pressure Regulator, Cabin	222
Propeller Feather	15
Propeller, Normal	13
Propeller Pitch	14
Radar Camera	278
Regulator Diluter, Oxygen	246
Shoulder Harness	84
Surface	67
Throttle—Reciprocating Engines	2
Transfer, Autopilot	252
Turbo	4
Turbo Boost	181
Universal Bombing	273
Voltage, Alternator	350
Controlled Crash Landing	191
*Controlling Carburetor Air Temperature	319
Conversion Factors	361
Cooling	
Air Speed vs	331
By Mixture Control	333
Fan Horsepower, R4360-41	520
Guns	401
Oil, Reciprocating Engine	17
Reciprocating Engine	10, 331
Copilot's Ditching Responsibilities	198
Corrections, Autopilot	379
Coupler Unit, Automatic Approach	257
Coupler Unit Controls	257
Crash Landings	
Approach	193
Before Approach	192
Contact	193
Controlled	191
General	190
On Take-Off	190
*Crash Landing Exits and Entrances	193
Crew	
Briefing, Final	145
Comfort Provisions	282
Flight	1
Inspection	133
Interphone Oxygen Checks	249
Minimum Requirements	283
Safety at Altitude	160
*Crew Comfort Provisions in Forward Cabin	281
Crew Duties	
Aircraft Commander	136, 381
Anti-Icing	223
Copilot	140
Ditching Responsibilities	195
First Engineer	141

*Denotes Illustration

Alphabetical Index

	Page
Crew Duties (Continued)	
First Radio Operator	387
General	381
Gunner, Left Forward	421
Gunner, Left Lower Aft	407
Gunner, Left Upper Aft	389
Gunner, Nose	423
Gunner, Right Forward	418
Gunner, Right Lower Aft	409
Gunner, Right Upper Aft	404
Gunner, Tail	412
Heating	223
Navigator	386
Observer	387
Pilot's	137
Pressurization	223
Radar Observer	382
Second Radio ECM Operator	418
Second Engineer	144
*Crew Inspection	134
*Crew Positions for Take-Off and Landing	147
Critical Equipment A-C Power Distribution	206
Cross-Feed Valve Switch, Fuel System	32
Cross-Wind Landings	170
Cruise	
Cruise No. 1	156
Cruise No. 4	161
General	307
High Altitude	160
Instrument Cruising Flight	435
Normal	346
Cruise-Bomb Knob, Autopilot	252
Cup Dispensers	282
Cups, Hot	282
Curtain, Pilots' Night-Flying	280
Curvature Knob, Autopilot	254
Curves, Characteristic Response	375
Curves, Emergency Climb	582
Cycle Selector Switch, Engine Analyzer	79
Cylinder Head Temperature	
General	333
Indicators	77
Instruments	361
Spark Plug Fouling	337

D

	Page
Dampers, Restrictor Heating	223
Day-of-Flight Check, Radar Observer's K-( ) System	384
Decelerations, Jet Engine	128
Decompression, Rapid	249
Decompression Sickness, Denitrogenization Procedure for Prevention of	251
Decompression, Use of Pressure Oxygen Breathing Following Cabin	251

	Page
Definitions, Air-Speed	460
Defrosting System	
Controls	222
General	222
Normal Operation	224
Nozzles	223
Denitrogenization Procedure for Prevention of Decompression Sickness	251
Density Altitude Chart	460
Density Chart	461
Depressurization, Emergency	228
Depressurization, Nose Gear Strut	162
Descent	
Control	744
Emergency	188
From High Altitude	161
General	161, 310, 436
Normal	161
Rapid	161
Desert Procedures	455
Design Gross Weight	1
Detailed Mission Planning	133
Detonation, Controls	338
*Diagnosing Smoke and Fire	184
Differential Protection Relay, Alternator	351
Dimensional Awareness	307
Dimension, Airplane	1
*Direct-Current Power Distribution	39
Direct-Current System	
Equipment Fuses and Critical Breakers	54
Feeder Fuses	46
General	40
Power Switches, Safe Fire	262
*Directional Coupler Amplifier Assembly	254
Discharge Selector Switch, Fire Extinguisher	80A
Disengaging Autopilot	256
Distribution of A-C Power to Critical Equipment	206
Distribution of Load	294
Ditching	
Approach	198
Before Approach	195
Contact	198
Crew Responsibilities	195
General	194
Overwater Flight	195
*Ditching Positions and Exits	194
Ditching Responsibilities	
Aft Gunners	198
Aircraft Commander's	195
Copilot's	198
First Engineer's	196
First Radio ECM Operator's	197
Navigator's	196
Observer's	198
Pilot's	196

*Denotes Illustration

	Page
Ditching Responsibilities (Continued)	
Radar Observer's	198
Second Engineer's	197
Second Radio Operator's	197
Tail Gunner's	197
Dives	307
Door Release Handle, Main Gear	71
Drag Factors	160
*Dual Turbo Operaton	314
Duct Air Temperature Gage	219
Dump Valves, Pressurization	221, 222
During	
Engine Run-Up, Hot Weather	455
Engine Shutdown (Reciprocating)	131
Engine Warm-Up	109, 147
Engine Warm-Up—	
Cold Weather Procedures	450
Flight—Cold Weather Procedures	453
Taxi	434
Duties, Crew	381

E

	Page
E-2 Turn Control Units, Autopilot	253
*ECM General Arrangement	235
E-FS and FS Knobs, Autopilot	253, 377
*Effects of Altitude on Engine Operation	313
*Effects of Various Ignition and Mixture Combinations on Torque	311
Electrical System	
Alternating-Current	34
Chart for Trouble Shooting	354
Direct-Current	40
Emergency Operation	203, 355
Emergency System	63
Excessive Loads	202
External Power Source	36
Fire	188
General	34, 202, 347
Loads	353
Obtaining Emergency Power	204
Trouble Shooting	354
Electronic Equipment	232
Elevator	
General	305
Trim Knob Malfunction	380
Trim Knobs, Autopilot	252
Trim Tab Contorl Wheels	67
Trim Tab Indicators	67
Elimination of Smoke	188
Elimination of Spark Plug Fouling	336
Emergency	
Anti-Icing System Operation	228
Bomb Bay Door Controls	274B
Bomb Bay Door Hydraulic System	66, 275
Bomb Release	272

	Page
Bomb Release Controls	271
Brake Hydraulic System	66
Brake Pressure	217
Cabin Pressure Control	228
Carburetor Preheat, Use of	439
Circuit Selector Switch	63
Controls	274
Climb Curves	582
Depressurization	228
Descent	188
Electrical Power, Obtaining	204
Electrical Power Operation	203
Electrical System	63
Electrical System Operation	355
Entrance, Crash Landing	194
Equipment	80
Escape Ropes (Some Airplanes)	82
Flap Control	69
Flap Switches	69
Flight Procedures in Event of Complete A-C Power Failure	205
Fuel Controls	34
Gunnery Controls	264
Hydraulic Extension of Landing Gear	210
Hydraulic Selector Valve Control	66
Ignition Switch	12
Interphone Operation	234
Landing Fields	189
Landing Gear Extension	366
Landing Gear Hydraulic System	66
Landing Gear Operation	208
Lighting System Operation	245
Oxygen System Operation	249
Pitch Setting Before Landing	183
Power Control	63
Pressure Controls	221
Stopping	217
Throttle Control Override Switches, Jet Engine	22
*Emergency Electrical Power Distribution	62
*Emergency Flap Controls	208
*Emergency Retraction of Nose Landing Gear	215
Enclosure Anti-Icing	222, 227
Engage Switch (Autopilot)	252
Engaging Autopilot	254
Engine Analyzer	
Condition Selector Switch	79
Controls	79
Cycle Selector Switch	79
Cylinder Vibration Analysis	79
General	79, 340
Ignition Analysis	79
Indicators	80
Pickup Selector Switch	79
Power Switch	80
Engine Power Schedules, R4360-41	479
Engineer	
Ditching Responsibilities	196, 197

*Denotes Illustration

Alphabetical Index

	Page
Engineer (Continued)	
Engines, Responsibility of	309
Fuse Panel, Alternate Source of A-C Power to	63, 203
Standard Check List	93
Visual Preflight Inspection	140
*Engineer's A-C Power Control Panel	37
*Engineer's Auxiliary Control Panel	28
*Engineer's Auxiliary Instrument Panel	24, 25
*Engineer's Hydraulic Control Panel	65
*Engineer's Main Control Panel	26
*Engineer's Main Instrument Panel	22, 23
*Engineers' Preflight Inspection Routes	142
*Engineer's Propeller Control Panel	14
*Engineer's Seat	84
*Engineer's Station	21
*Engineer's Table	26, 27
Engines (See Jet Engines or Reciprocating Engines)	
Before Starting	95, 434
Before Take-Off	148
Cooling, Reciprocating	10, 331
Cooling Fan Horsepower, R4360-41	520
Engine-Driven Fuel Pump Failure	201
Failure	175
Failure During Take-Off	180
Fan Operation, Reciprocating	332
Fire In Flight	186
Fuel Flow	536
Instrument Trouble Shooting	361
Jet	18
Limitations	283
Reciprocating	2
Run-Up	115, 147
Run-Up, Postflight	171
Shutdown, Oil Dilution after	178
Starter Limitations, Jet Engine	128
Starter Switches	13, 28
Torquemeter Pressure	523
Valve Switches, Fuel System	32
Warm-Up—Desert Procedures	456
Entering the Airplane	
Before—Desert Procedure	455
Before—Hot Weather Procedures	454
Desert Procedures	455
Hot Weather Procedures	454
Entrance, Crash Landing Emergency	194
Entrance Ladders	280
Escape Ropes, Emergency	82
Excessive Electrical Loads	202
Exciter Ceiling Relay, Alternator	351
Exciter Control Relay Switch	38
Exciter Generator	348
*Exhaust and Anti-Icing Air Flow	11
Exhaust Back Pressure—Spark Plug Foulnig	337
Extension, Landing Gear	362

	Page
Extension, Landing Gear Emergency	366
Extension of Landing Gear, Emergency Hydraulic	210
Extension Control, Main Landing Gear Manual	71
Exterior Lights	243
*Exterior Lights Arrangement	244
*External Drain and Vent Locations	446
External Power Source	36
External Power Supply Switch	36

F

	Page
Factors, Drag	160
Factors, Load	293
Failure	
Engine	175
Engine-Driven Fuel Pump	201
Engine Failure During Take-Off	180
Jet Engines Fail to Start	128
Propeller	183
Familiarization with Calibration Controls	376
Fans	
Cabin Booster	221
Cabin Heater Fan Control Switch	229
Engine Operation	332
Pilots' Air Circulating	228
Speed Switches	11
Feather Controls, Propeller	15
Feathering Propellers	345
Field Flashing, Alternator	205
Field Flashing Circuit Breaker, Alternator	38
Final Approach	167
Final Crew Briefing	145
Fires	
Detection Switches, Jet Engines	82
Detector System, Jet Engines	82
Detector System, Reciprocating Engines	80A
Electrical	188
Engine Fires on Ground	186
Extinguisher System, Reciprocating Engine	80
Extinguishers, Hand	82
Fuselage	187
General	186
Inflight Fire Fighting Procedures	186, 187
Warning Lamps, Reciprocating Engine	80A, 180
Wing	187
First Aid Kits	82
First Engineer's Ditching Responsibilities	196
First Radio ECM Operator's Ditching Responsibilities	197
First Radio ECM Operator's Duties	387
*Flap Limitations	289
*Flap Retraction Speeds	305
Flaps	
Controls, Emergency	69
Controls, Normal	68

*Denotes Illustration

	Page
Flaps (Continued)	
Emergency Switches	69
Limitations	288
Master Selector Switches	69
Position Indicator	68
Retraction Technique	307
Switch	68
System	68, 208
System Indicators	68
Warning Horn	69
Flight	
Characteristics	161
Characteristics with Partial Power	175
Control System	66
Controls	304
Crew	1
During—Cold Weather Procedures	453
Emergency Procedures in Event of Complete A-C Power Failure	205
Instrument Cruising	435
Instrument Switches	77
Level Flight Characteristics	306
Load Factors, Wing	299
Maneuvering	307
Overwater, Preparation for Ditching	195
Procedures, Instrument	434
Rules to be Enforced on Each	146
Without Jet Pods	307
*Flight Control Lock Operation	68
*Flight Control Lock Switch	67
Flying Procedures, Night	433
Forced Landings	190
Formal Briefing	133
Formation Lights	244
*Forward Cabin Arrangement	5
Forward Cabin Dump Valve	221
*Forward Cabin Heating and Defrosting Controls	224
*Forward Cabin Manual Pressure Controls	222
Forward Gunner's Seat	280
*Forward Sighting Station Sling-Type Seat	280
*Forward Sighting Station, Typical	260
Free Fall—Bail-Out	201
Frequency Control Knob	38
Frequency Controls, Alternator	349
Frequency Selector Switch	38
Frequency Selector Switch, Radar Camera	278
Frozen Food Oven	282
Fuel-Air Ratio Determination	525
Fuel-Air Ratio—Spark Plug Fouling	336
Fuel vs Alternate Load Capacity	298
Density Variation	346
*Fuel Management	347
Fuel System	
Booster Pump Switches	32
Controls	32
Controls, Emergency	34

	Page
Cross-Feed Valve Switch	32
Engine Valve Switches	32
Flow	536
Flow Indicators	33
Fuel Valves, Manual Operaton of	201
General	32, 201, 346
Indicator Lamps Dim-Bright Knob	33
Indicators	33
Manifold Valve Switches	32
Pressure Gages	33
Pump Failure, Engine-Driven	201
Quantity Gages	34
Regulator Controls, Jet Engine	20
Tank Valve Switches	32
Valve Indicator Lamps	34
Weighing Procedure	346
*Fuel System Schematic	30
*Fuel Tank Capacities	33
*Fuel Temperature Correction Chart	346
*Fuse and Circuit Breaker Panel Locaitons	42
Fuses	
A-C Equipment	47
A-C System Feeder	44
D-C System Feeder	46
General	44
Heater Power, Gunnery	263
Fuselage Fire	187
Fuselage Navigation Lights Switch	244

G

	Page
*GCA Procedure	437
Gages	
Brake System Pressure	75
Camera System Vacuum	277
Duct Air Temperature	219
Fuel Pressure	33
Fuel Quantity	34
Hydraulic Pressure	66
Oil Pressure, Jet Engines	30
Oil Pressure, Reciprocating Engine	16
Oil Quantity, Reciprocating Enignes	17
Oil Temperature, Reciprocating Engine	16
Oxygen Pressure	247
Tail Anti-Icing Air Temperature	220
Water Pressure	10
Wing Anti-Icing Air Temperature	220
Galvanometer Pointer, Master Temperature Indicator	77
*General Arrangement Diagram	4
General Mission Planning	88
Go-Around	170
Gross Weight	298
Gross Weight and Altitude vs Air Speed	161
Gross Weight, Design	1
*Ground Clearance Limits	306

	Page
*Ground Heating	447
Ground Operation Reciprocating Engine	109, 311
Ground Refueling Safety Switch	**34**
Ground Run-Up—Spark Plug Fouling	336
Gunnery	
A-C Power Switches	262
Action Switch	263
Ammunition Counter Dials	264
Amplified Check List	391
Attack Factor Switch	263
Burst Control	401
Computer Switch	263
Controls, Emergency	264
Controls, Normal	261
Cooling Guns	401
D-C Power Switches	262
Emergency Procedures	402
Equipment	261
Gun Camera Switch	262
Gun Charging Switch	262
Hand Crank	264
Heater Power Fuse	263
Indicators	263
Inflight Operation	399
Loading Ammunition	399
Operation	264
Radar Pressurization	264

H

	Page
Hand Axes	82
Hand Crank, Gunnery Emergency	264
Hand Fire Extinguishers	82
*Heat and Anti-Icing Limitations at 1500 Horsepower	297
*Heat and Anti-Icing Limitations at Normal Rated Power	296
Heat and Anti-Ice Selector Valve	222
Heaters	
Auxiliary Cabin	229
Cabin Heater Power Switch	229
Jet Engine Oil	232
Oil	232
Oil Tank Hopper	232
Oil Tank Vent Line	232
Pitot Tube	232
Power Fuse, Gunnery	263
Heating System	
Air Temperature Limitations	292
Cabin	222
Controls	219
Crew Responsibilities	223
General	219
Indicators	219
Jet Pod	230
Normal Operation	224

	Page
Operation of Cabin Heating System	223
Outlets	223
*Heating System Schematic	226
Heavy Gross Weight Landings	169
High Altitude Bail-Out	200
High Altitude, Climb to	160
High Altitude Cruise	160
High Altitude, Descent from	161
High Latitude Compass, N-1	259
High Latitude Compass Operation	260
High Power Before Landing—Spark Plug Fouling	337
High Power Operations, Before Climb	156
Holding, Instrument	436
Horn, Flap Warning	69
Horn, Landing Gear	70
Horsepower, Engine Cooling Fan	520
Horsepower, Jet Engine Thrust	531
Hot Cups	282
Hot Starts, Jet Engine	128
Hot Weather Procedures	454
How to Make a Good Preflight	134
Hydraulic System	
Bomb Bay Door Emergency	66, 275
Brake Emergency	66
Emergency Selector Valve Control	66
Fluid Temperature Control	270
Fluid Temperature Switch	66
General	65
Landing Gear Emergency	66
Landing Gear Emergency Extension	210
Main	65
Pressure Gage	66
Pump Override Switch	66
*Hydraulic Power Supply Schematic	64
Hypoxia Victims, Treatment of	250

I

	Page
*ILAS Procedure	438
Icing	
Carburetor Impact Tube	319
Carburetor Internal	320
General	437
Jet Engine	440
Prevention	440
Removal of Ice	445
*Icing of Impact Tube in Carburetor	321
Identification Set AN/APX-6	241
Ignition System	
Analysis	79, 343
Jet Engine	28
Reciprocating Engine	11
Start Switches, Jet Engine	28
Switches	12

*Denotes Illustration

	Page
Indicator Lamps	
Bomb Station	270
Cabin Temperature Control Valve	220
Camera Door	277
Camera Operation	277
Camera Power-On	277
Fuel Dim-Bright Knob	33
Fuel Valve	34
Landing Gear	70
Pressure Refueling Valve	34
Propeller Normal Pitch	15
Universal Bombing	273
Indicators	
Aileron Trim	67
Air-Speed	76
Alternator	36
Anti-Icing	219
Attitude Gyro	77
Bomb Size	270
Bombing	269
Brake System	75
Bus, Alternator	40
Camera	277
Control Lock	68
Cylinder Head Temperature	77
Elevator Trim Tab	67
Engine Analyzer	80
Flap Position	68
Flap System	68
Fuel	33
Fuel Flow	33
Gunnery	263
Heating System	219
Master Temperature	76, 220
Nose Wheel Steering	72
Oil System, Jet Engine	30
Oil System, Reciprocating Engine	16
Oxygen Flow	247
Oxygen Regulator	246
Pressurization	221
Propeller	13
Rudder Trim Tab	67
Tail Pipe Temperature	78
Torquemeter	76
Inflight Fire Fighting Procedures	186
Ignition Switch, Camera	277
Initial Climb	153
Inspection	
Aircraft Visual Preflight	134
Crew	133
Engineer's Preflight	140, 454
Instrument	
Approach Equipment	240
Approaches	436
Climb	435

	Page
Cruising Flight	435
Errors	467
Flight Procedure	434
Limitations	283
Trouble Shooting	361
*Instrument Markings	284
Instruments	
Cylinder Head Temperature	361
Flight Switches	77
General	75
Jet Engine	78
Intercooler Shutter Switches	3
Interior Lights	244
Interphone System	
Call Circuit	234
Combat	232
Emergency Operation	234
General	232
Mixed Signals and Command	237
Private Channel	232
Radio Operator's Control Panel	238
Wing Control Switch	234
Intervalometer, Camera	276

J

	Page
*Jet Engine Control Panel	29
*Jet Engine Danger Areas	127
*Jet Engine Requirements	182
Jet Engines	
Accelerations	128
Air Intake Control	24
Air Plug Anti-Icing	230
Air Plug Switches	25
Anti-Icing	230
Anti-Icing Controls	231
Before Take-Off	148
Cautions to Observe	127
Decelerations	128
Emergency Throttle Control Override Switches	22
Failure to Start	128
Fire Detection Switches	82
Fire Detector System	82
Fire in Flight	187
Fire on Ground	186
Fire Warning Lamps	82
Fuel Flow	536
Fuel Regulator Controls	20
Fuel System	32
General	18, 345
Heating System	230
Hot Starts	128
Icing	440
Ignition System	28
Instruments	78

*Denotes Illustration

Alphabetical Index

	Page
Jet Engines (Continued)	
Limitations	287
Minimum Throttle Burst RPM	529
Nose Cone Anti-Icing	230
Oil Heater Switch	232
Oil Heaters	232
Oil System	29
Pod Anti-Icing and Heating Controls	231
Pod Anti-Icing System	230
Pod Heating System	230
Preheating	230
Preheating Controls	230
Simultaneous Starts	159
Starter Limitations	128
Starting	127, 147
Starting (Air)	156
Starting—Cold Weather Procedures	451
Starting—Desert Procedures	456
Starting—Hot Weather Procedures	455
Starting Procedure	128
Starting System	28
Stopping (Air)	154
Stopping (Ground)	130
Strut Anti-Icing	230
Tachometers	78
Tail Pipe Temperature	530
Throttle Control Levers	20
Throttle Control Selector Switches	20
Throttle Sensitivity	127
Thrust Horsepower	531
Windmilling	346

K

K-( ) Bombing-Navigation System	273
K-( ) System Altitude Determination	384
K-( ) System Day of Flight Check	384
K-( ) System Preflight Check	383
K-( ) Wind Determination Check	385
Kilowatt-Kilovar Selector Switches	38
Kit Bag Stowage	282
Kits, Battle Splints and Blood Plasma	82
Kits—Cold Weather Equipment	453
Kits, First Aid	82
Knives	82
*KVA Determination	353

L

Ladders, Entrance	280
Lamp Receptacles, Aldis	245
Lamps	
Air Maximum Temperature Warning	220
Bomb Bay Door	269
Bomb Bay Door Ready	270
Brake Low Pressure Warning	75
Cabin Temperature Control Valve Indicator	220

	Page
Camera Door Indicator	277
Camera Operation Indicator	277
Camera Power-On Indicator	277
Fire Warning	80A, 82
Fuel Valve Indicator	34
Landing Gear Indicator	70
Phase Sequence	36
Pressure Refueling Valve Indicator	34
Propeller Normal Pitch Indicator	15
Propeller Reverse Warning	15
Special Bombing System Indicator	274
Synchronizer	40
Turret Door Closed	263
Turret-Extended	263
Landings	
Before	164
Cold Weather	453
Controlled Crash	191
Crash	190
Cross-Wind	170
Desert	456
Distance	749
Emergency Pitch Setting Before	183
Fields, Alternate	189
Fields, Emergency	189
Fields, Primary	189
Forced	190
General	168
Heavy Gross Weight	169
Hot Weather	455
Lights	243
Minimum Run	169
Night	434
Normal	162
Partial Power	182
Landing Gear	
Control Switch	69
Emergency Extension	366
Emergency Hydraulic Extension	210
Emergency Hydraulic System	66
Emergency Operation	208
Extension	362
General	69, 362
Indicator Lamps	70
Latch Link Pin	72
Latch Release Lever	72
Load Factor	299
Main Gear Door Release Handle	71
Main Gear Manual Extension Control	71
Manual Hoist	72
Manual Selector Controls	71
Normal Controls	69
Nose Gear, Emergency Retraction	215
Nose Gear, Manual Extension of	216
Nose Gear Release Handle	72
Nose Landing Gear Emergency Latch Hook	72

*Denotes Illustration

Alphabetical Index

	Page
Landing Gear (Continued)	
Nose Landing Gear Manual Extension Controls	72
Nose Wheel Steering System	72
Retraction	362
Trouble Shooting	368
Warning Horn	70
*Landing Gear Emergency Extension Schematic	367
*Landing Gear Emergency Hydraulic Controls	211
*Landing Gear Extension Schematic	365
*Landing Gear Position Indications	71
*Landing Gear Retraction Schematic	363
Large Bomb Sequence	266
Large Cargo System	**274**
Latch Link Pin, Landing Gear	72
Latch Release Lever, Landing Gear	72
Leaning, Manual	327
Leaving Aircraft, Before	173
Left Forward Gunner's Duties	421
*Left Lower Aft Sighting Station	262
*Left Main A-C Power Panel	145
Level Flight Characteristics	306
Liaison Radio Set AN/ARC-8	239
Life Rafts	82
Lights	
Bomb Station Indicator	270
Emergency Operation	245
Exterior	243
Formation	244
General	243
Interior	244
Landing	243
Navigation	243
Nose Fuse, Bombing	270
Taxi	243
Limitations	
Acceleration	288
Air-Speed	287
Anti-Icing Air Temperature	292
Buffeting	288
Center of Gravity	288
Flaps	288
Heating Air Temperature	292
Instrument	283
Jet Engine	287
Jet Engine Starter	128
Operational Weight Limitations Chart	298
Propeller	288
Reciprocating Engine	383
Weight	292
Liquid Containers	282
Load	
Distribution of	294
Electrical	353
Factors	293
Fuel vs Alternate Load Capacity	298
Landing Gear Load Factor	299

	Page
Reactive Load Division	351
Real Load Division	351
Variations, Alternator	351
Wing Flight Load Factors	299
Localizer Switch, Approach Coupler	257
*Location of Transformer-Rectifier Units	40
Locks, Control Surface	67
Long Range Operation at Constant Altitude	670
Long Range Operation at Optimum Altitude	737
Loose Equipment—Cold Weather Equipment	453
Loren Set AN/APN-9( )	241
Low Pressure Warning Lamp, Brake	75
Lower Aft Gunners' Duties	407, 409
Lower Aft Gunners' Seats	280

M

	Page
*Main Differences Table	2
*Main Hydraulic Selector Valve Controls	209
Main Hydraulic Selector Valve—Manual Operation	209, 274
Main Hydraulic System	65
Main Indicator Pointer, Master Temperature Indicator	77
*Main Landing Gear Arrangements	70
*Main Landing Gear Lock Indicator Flag	210
Main Landing Gear Manual Extension Control	71
*Main Wheel Door Closing Schematic	364
Magnetic Compass	258
Magneto Synchronization Check	344
Malfunction, Elevator Trim Knob	380
Malfunctions, Autopilot	379
Maneuvering Flight	307
Maneuvers, Prohibited	288
Manifold Pressure	312
Manifold Pressure, Take-off	477
Manifold Pressure—Spark Plug Fouling	337
Manifold Valve Switches, Fuel System	32
Manual	
Extension Control, Main Landing Gear	71
Hoist, Landing Gear	72
Leaning	327
Mixture Control Manual Adjustment	326
Operation of Main Selector Valve	209
Pressurization Shutoff Valves	221
Selector Controls—Hydraulic Main Selector Valve	71, 274
*Manual Extension of Main Landing Gear	212
*Manual Extension of Nose Landing Gear	216
*Manual Operation of Fuel and Oil Valves	202
Marker Beacon Set AN/ARN-12	241
Master Motor Control Lever, Propeller	13
Master Power Switch—Bombing	267
Master Power Switch, Camera	276
Master Tachometers	14
Master Temperature Indicator Balance Knob	77

*Denotes Illustration

Alphabetical Index

T.O. 1B-36D(II)-1

	Page
Master Temperature Indicator (Continued)	
Battery Receptacles	77
Check Switch	77
Compensating Rheostat Knob	77
Galvanometer Pointer	77
General	76, 220
Main Indicator Pointer	77
Selector Switch	76
Slide Wire Rheostat Knob	77
Switch	77
*Maximum Indicated Air Speeds	288
Maximum Crew Requirements	283
*Minimum IAS for Zero Yaw	179
Minimum Nose-Up Air Speed	573
Minimum-Run Landings	169
Minimum Throttle Burst Rpm, J47-19	529
*Minimum Turning Radius	124
*Miscellaneous Emergency Equipment	192
Miscellanous Equipment	279
Miscellaneous Personal Gear Stowage	282
Mission Examples	762
Mission Planning, Detailed	133
Mission Planning, General	88
Mixed Signals and Command, Interphone	237
Mixed Signals and Liaison, Interphone	238
Mixture Control	
Cooling by	333
General	3, 324
Levers	3
Manual Adjustment	326
Manual Adjustment During Power Operation	326
Override Switches	3
Selector Switches	3
Motoring, Alternator	205

N

	Page
N-1 High Latitude Compass	259
N-2 Transfer Switch, Autopilot	252
Navigation	
Beacon	385
Departure and Fixing	385
Equipment	258, 435
Light Dimming Switch	244
Lights	243
Lights Selector Switch	244
Provisions, Celestial	261
Navigator's Ditching Responsibilities	196
Navigator's Duties	386
*Navigator's Instrument Panel	232
Navigator's Seat	280
*Navigator's Station	237
Night	
Climb	433

	Page
Flying Procedures	433
Landing	434
Night-Flying Curtain, Pilots'	280
Take-Off	433
Non-Accelerated Power-Off Stalls	302
Non-Accelerated Power-On Stalls	302
Normal Cruise	346
Normal Controls, Bombing	267
Normal Controls, Gunnery	261
Normal Controls, Main Landing Gear	69
Normal Controls, Pressurization	221
Normal Controls, Wing Flap	68
*Normal Cylinder Vibration Patterns	340
Normal Descent	161
*Normal Ignition Pattern	343
Normal Landing	162
Normal Operation of Cabin Heating and Defrosting	224
Normal Propeller Controls and Indicators	13
Nose	
Cone Anti-Icing	230
De-Ice Control Switch	232
Fuse Lights	270
Fuse Switch, Bombing	267
Hunt in Turns	379
*Nose Gear Strut Pressure Release Valve	72
*Nose Gunner's Control Panel	264
Nose Gunner's Duties	423
Nose Landing Gear	
Emergency Retraction	215
Manual Extension of	216
Manual Extension Controls	72
Release Handle	72
Strut Depressurization	162
Strut Pressure Release Valve	73
*Nose Landing Gear Strut Load and Depressurization	162
*Nose Sighting Station	263
Nose-Up Air Speed, Minimum	573
Nose Wheel Steering	
Controls	72
Indicator	72
Switch	72
System	72
Trouble Shooting	370
*Nose Wheel Steering Hydraulic System	73
Nozzles, Defrosting	223

O

	Page
O-15 Camera Preflight	279
Observer's Ditching Responsibilities	198
Observer's Duties	387
Obtaining Maximum Turbo Speed	313
Obtaining Cabin Ventilation in Flight	229
Obtaining Cabin Ventilation on Ground	229
*Oil Dilution Tables	444

*Denotes Illustration

	Page
Oil System	
Controls, Jet Engine	30
Controls, Reciprocating Engine	16
Cooling, Reciprocating Engine	17
Dilution After Engine Shutdown	178
Dilution, Cold Weather Procedures	443
Dilution Switches, Reciprocating Engine	16
Door Mode Selector Switches, Oil Cooler (Some Airplanes)	17
Door Override Switches, Oil Cooler (Some Airplanes)	18
General	201
Heaters	232
Indicators, Jet Engine	30
Indicators, Reciprocating Engine	16
Jet Engine	29
Pressure Gages, Jet Engine	30
Pressure Gages, Reciprocating Engine	16
Quantity Gages, Reciprocating Engine	17
Reciprocating Engine	16
Shutoff Valve Switches, Jet Engine	30
Shutoff Valve Switches, Reciprocating Engine	16
Spewing	181, 335
Tank Hopper Heaters	232
Tank Vent Line Heaters	232
Temperature Gages, Reciprocating Engines	16
Valves, Manual Operation of	201
*Oil Tank Capacities	16
*Operating Flight Strength Diagram	293
Operating Weight	298
Operation	
Aerial Camera	277
Air Plug	333
Anti-Icing System	223
Approach Coupler Unit	257
Autopilot	254
Bomb Bay Door Emergency Hydraulic System	275
Cabin Heating System	223
Cabin Pressurization	228
Defrosting System Normal	224
Electrical System Emergency	355
Emergency Electrical Power	203
Emergency Interphone	234
Emergency Landing Gear	208
Emergency Oxygen System	249
Engine Fan	332
Frozen Food Oven	282
Gunnery	264
Heating System Normal	224
Identification Set AN/APX-6	241
Landing Gear Emergency	208
Lighting System Emergency	245
Main Hydraulic Selector Valve, Manual Operation	274B
Main Selector Valve, Manual Operation	209

	Page
Manual Operation of Fuel and Oil Valves	201
Pressurization System	223
Reciprocating Engine Ground	109, 311
Slaved Gyro Magnetic Compass	358
Turbosupercharger	314
Operational Equipment Check, Preflight	89
Operational Use of Oxygen Equipment	247
*Operational Weight Limitations	298
Operational Weight Limitations Chart	298
Outlets, Heating	223
Outside Air Thermometers	76
Oven, Frozen Food	282
Overheating Anti-Icing System	228
Override Switches	
Brake Pump Pressure	75
Emergency Throttle Control, Jet Engine	22
Hydraulic Pump	66
Mixture Control	3
Oil Cooler Door (Some Airplanes)	18
Turbo	6
Overspeed	311
Overwater Bail-Out	201
Overwater Flight, Preparation for Ditching	195
Oxygen	
Checks, Crew Interphone	249
Discipline	249
Emergency Operation	249
Equipment, Operational Use	247
Equipment, Portable	247
Equipment, Preflight Check	247
Flow Indicator	247
General	245
Pressure Gage	247
Procedure, Normal	248
Regulator Controls and Indicators	246
Walk-Around Bottles, Precautions in Using	251
Walk-Around Bottles, Use of	251
*Oxygen Consumption Table	245

P

	Page
Panels	
Bomb Interval Control	267
Radio Operator's Interphone Control	238
Transformer-Rectifier Test Unit	41
Parachute Static Lines	82
Parking Brake Lever	75
Parking Brake Switch	75
Parking—Cold Weather Procedures	451
Partial Power, Flight Characteristics with	175
Partial Power Landing	182
Partial Power Take-Off	181
Pattern, Traffic	163
Performance Determination for Alternate External Configurations	756
*Permissible Rpm Variation	310
Personal Equipment Requirements	381

*Denotes Illustration

Alphabetical Index

	Page
Phase Sequence Lamp Test Switch	36
Phase Sequence Lamps	36
Photographic Equipment	275
Pilot-Bombardier Selector Valve—	
Defrosting System	223
Pilots' Air Circulating Fans	228
Pilots' Command Radio Selector Switch	238
Pilot's Ditching Responsibilities	196
*Pilots' Instrument Panel	19
*Pilots' Interphone Panel	234
*Pilots' Jet Control Panel	31
Pilots' Night-Flying Curtain	280
*Pilots' Pedestal	19, 20, 22
*Pilots' Radio Controls	240
*Pilots' Seats	84
Pilots' Seats	84
Pilots' Standard Check List	91
*Pilot's Station	15
Pitch Change System, Propeller	13
Pitot Static System	76
Pitot Tube Heaters	232
Planning Advanced—	
Cold Weather Procedures	442
Planning, Detailed Mission	133
Planning, General Mission	88
Pneumatic Release of Bombs	273
Polar Bail-Out	201
Portable Oxygen Equipment	247
Postflight Engine Run-Up	171
Postflight Procedures—Cold Weather	443
Power	
Alternate Source of A-C	203
Asymmetrical Power Conditions	307
Emergency Control	63
Emergency Electrical	203
External Source	35
External Supply Switch	36
Obtaining Emergency Electrical	204
Power Change Rate Effect—	
Spark Plug Fouling	337
Power Collapse	316
Power Collapse Recovery	317
Power Plant Servicing—	
Cold Weather Procedures	444
Power Schedules, R4360-41	479
Switch, Engine Analyzer	80
*Power Collapse	316
*Power Collapse with Closed Throttle	313
*Power Schedule—Operation Cruise BMEP	310
*Power Schedule—Operation at Normal	
Rated BMEP	309
Practice Stalls	303
Preflight Check of K-( ) System	383
Preflight Check of Oxygen Equipment	247
Preflight Check of Universal Bombing System	385
Preflight Inspection, Aircraft Visual	134
Preflight Inspection, Engineers'	140, 454

	Page
Preflight Operational Equipment Check	89
Preheat	
Cold Weather Check List	454
Controls, Jet Pod	231
Engine and Aircraft	445
Jet Pod	230
Switches, Carburetor	4
Preignition, Controls	338
Preparation for Overwater Flight	195
Pressure Gages	
Brake	75
Fuel	33
Hydraulic	66
Oil, Jet Engine	30
Oil, Reciprocating Engine	16
Oxygen	247
Water	10
Pressure Refueling Controls	34
Pressure Refueling Valve Indicator Lamps	34
Pressure Refueling Valve Switches	34
Pressurization System	
Crew Responsibilities	223
Emergency Pressure Controls	221
General	220
Indicators	221
Manual Shutoff Valves	221
Normal Controls	221
Operation	223
Pressure Regulator Control	222
Pressure Relief Valves	222
Radar	243, 264
*Pressurization System Schematic	226
Prevention of Spark Plug Fouling	336
Primary Controls, Autopilot	252
Primary Landing Fields	189
Priming System	13
*Principal Factors Affecting Engine Cooling	332
Private Interphone Channel	232
Procedures	
Cold Weather	442
Fuel Weighing	346
Hot Weather	454
Inflight Fire Fighting	186
Instrument Flight	434
Jet Engine Starting	128
Manual Adjustment of Mixture Control	
During Power Operation	326
Manual Leaning	327
Night Flying	433
Oxygen, Normal	248
Postflight—Cold Weather	443
Spark, Advancing	324
Spark, Retarding	324
Stopping Reciprocating Engines	130
Prohibited Maneuvers	288
*Propeller Induced Air Flow	301
*Propeller Limitations	289

*Denotes Illustration

Alphabetical Index

	Page
Propellers	
Controls, Normal	13
Emergency Pitch Setting Before Landing	183
Emergency Stopping, Use of Propellers in	217
Failure	183
Feather Controls	15
Feathering	345
General	13, 345
Indicators, Normal	13
Limitations	288
Master Motor Control Lever	13
Master Tachometers	14
Normal Pitch Indicator Lamps	15
Pitch Change System	13
Reverse Pitch	345
Reverse Pitch Controls and Indicators	14
Reverse Pitch Switch	14
Reverse Warning Lamps	15
Reverse Selector Switches	14
Runaway	183
Selector Switches	13
Tel-Lamps	14
Unfeathering During Flight	179
Proportional Range Knob, Autopilot	254
Protective Devices, Alternator	351
Provisions, Celestial Navigation	261

R

	Page
Radar	
AN/APQ-31 Set	243
Air-Borne	435
Bomb Scoring Tone Device	273
Camera	278
Camera Controls	278
Identification Set AN/APX-6	242
O-15 Camera Preflight	279
Pressurization	243
Pressurization, Gunnery	264
Release of Bombs	273
*Radar Observer's Camera Controls	277
Radar Observer's Crew Duties	382
Radar Observer's Day-of-Flight K( ) System Check	384
Radar Observer's Ditching Responsibilities	198
Radar Observer's Preflight K( ) System Check	384
Radar Observer's Seat	280
*Radar Observer's Station	270
Radio	
AN/ARC-3 Command Set	238
AN/ARC-27 Command Set	239
AN/ARC-8 Liaison Set	239
AN/ARN-7( ) Compass	240
AN/ARN-14 Receiver	241
AN/CRC-7 Set (Walkie-Talkie)	240
BC-453-B Range Receiver	239
Command Equipment	238
Equipment	435

	Page
Pilots' Command Selector Switch	238
*Radio Operator's ARC-27 Control Unit	239
*Radio Operator's Interphone Panel	238
Radio Operator's Seat	280
*Radio Operator's Station	230
*Radio Range Procedure	436
Rain	437
*Range Extension	328
Range Receiver BC-453-B, Radio	239
Range, Speed	435
Rapid Decompression	249
Rapid Descent	161
Rate Co-ordination, Autopilot	377
Rate Co-ordination Knob, Autopilot	253
Ratio, Autopilot	376
Ratio Knobs, Autopilot	253
RC-193A Marker Beacon	241
Reactive Load Division, Alternator	351
Real Load Division, Alternator	351
*Reciprocating Engine Air Plug Indications	12
*Reciprocating Engine Fire Extinguisher System Schematic	81
*Reciprocating Engine Nacelle General Arrangement	8
*Reciprocating Engine Oil Cooling	18
*Reciprocating Engine Oil System Schematic	17
Reciprocating Engines	
Alternate Power Schedule	543
Analyzer	340
Before Starting	95, 434, 448
Carburetion	317
Carburetor Air Temperature Control	3
Cooling System	10, 331
Descent	310
During Engine Shutdown	131
During Engine Warm-Up	109
During Warm-Up	147
Fire Detector System	80A
Fire Extinguisher System	80
Fire in Flight	186
Fire on Ground	186
Fire Warning Lamps	80A
Fuel Flow	525
Fuel Flow Indicators	33
General	2, 309
Ground Operation	109, 311
Ignition System	11
Limitations	283
Manifold Pressure	312
Manifold Switches	32
Mixture Controls	3, 324
Oil Dilution After Engine Shutdown	178
Oil System	16
Overspeed	311
Overspeeding (Runaway Propellers)	183
Postflight Run-Up	171
Power Collapse	316

*Denotes Illustration

Alphabetical Index

	Page
Reciprocating Engines (Continued)	
Power Collapse Recovery	317
Power Schedules	479
Priming System	13
Propeller System	13
RPM	309
Run-Up	115, 147
Selector Switches—Fire Extinguishing System	80 A
Shifting Turbos	315
Shutdown in Flight	176
Starting	106, 147
Starting Before—Cold Weather Check List	454
Starting Engines—Cold Weather Check List	454
Starting—Cold Weather Procedures	448
Starting—Desert Procedures	455
Starting—Hot Weather Procedures	455
Starting System	13
Stopping	130, 172
Stopping, Cold Weather Procedures	443
Supercharging	312
Throttle Controls	2
Torquemeter	322
Turbo System	4
Turbosupercharger Operation	314
Valve Switches, Fuel System	32
Warm-Up—Cold Weather Procedure	450
Water Injection System	7
*Recommended Autopilot Calibration Control Settings	254
Refueling Controls, Pressure	34
Refueling Safety Switch, Ground	34
Refueling Valve Indicator Lamps, Pressure	34
Refueling Valve Switches, Pressure	34
Regulator Controls, Fuel	20
Regulator Controls and Indicators, Oxygen	246
Regulator Diluter Control, Oxygen	246
Regulator Emergency Toggle Lever, Oxygen	246
Regulator Supply Valve Lever, Oxygen	246
Regulator Warning System Switch, Oxygen	247
Release, Emergency Bomb	272
Release Sequence, Bomb	266
Release Switches, Autopilot	252
Release Switches, Special Bomb	273
Releasing the Constant-Speed Drive From Underdrive	204
Response Curves, Characteristic	375
Restoring Normal Electric Power	203
Restrictor Dampers—Defrosting System	223
Retraction, Landing Gear	362
Retrimming Autopilot	256
Reverse Pitch, Propeller	345
Reverse Pitch Switch, Propeller	14
RPM	
Engine	309
Spark Plug Fouling, Effect on	337
Synchronization Analysis	344
Ropes, Emergency Escape (Some Airplanes)	82

	Page
Rudder	
Gain, Autopilot	377
Gain Knob, Autopilot	254
General	305
Hunt	379
Pedals	67
Roll Rate Autopilot	377
Roll Rate Knob, Autopilot	254
Trim Knobs, Autopilot	252
Trim Tab Control Knob	67
Trim Tab Indicator	67
Rules to be Enforced on Each Flight	146
Run-Up	
Ground (Spark Plug Fouling)	336
Postflight Engine	171
Reciprocating Engine	115, 147, 451
Runaway Propeller	183

S

	Page
Safe Approach Weight	748
Safe-Fire Switches (A-C and D-C Power)	262
Safety at Altitude, Crew	160
Safety Belts	146
Salvo Release, Bomb Bay Fuel Tank	273
Salvo Release of Bombs	272
Salvo Switches, Bomb	271
Seats	
Engineer's	84
Forward Gunner's	280
Lower Aft Gunners'	280
Navigator	280
Nose Gunner's	280
Pilots'	84
Radar Observer's	280
Radio Operator's	280
Upper Aft Gunner's	280
Second Engineer's Ditching Responsibilities	197
Second Radio ECM Operator's Ditching Responsibilities	197
Selector Switches	
Bomb Bay	267
Bomb Bay Tank Release	34 A
Bomb Release	267
Camera Mode	276
Circuit, Emergency	63
Discharge, Fire Extinguisher	80A
Engine Analyzer Condition	79
Engine Analyzer Cycle	79
Engine Analyzer Pickup	79
Flap Master	69
Frequency	38
Kilowatt-Kilovar	38
Master Temperature Indicator	76
Mixture Control	3
Navigation Lights	244

*Denotes Illustration

	Page
Selector Switches (Continued)	
Oil Cooler Door Mode (Some Airplanes)	17
Pilots' Command Radio	238
Propeller	13
Propeller Reverse	14
Radar Camera Frequency	278
Reciprocating Engine Fire Extinguisher	80A
Throttle Control, Jet Engine	20
Transformer-Rectifier Test Unit	41
Turret System	261
Voltage	38
Sensitivity, Autopilot	376
Sensitivity Knobs, Autopilot	253
Sensitivity, Throttle	127
*Service Diagram	83
Servicing, Power Plant—Cold Weather Procedures	444
Sextant	261
Shifting Turbos	315
Shoulder Harness Control	84
Shutdown, After Engine—Cold Weather Procedures	444
Shutdown in Flight, Reciprocating Engine	176
Simultaneous Starts, Jet Engines	159
Single Release of Bombs	272
*Single Turbo Operation	314
Slaved Gyro Magnetic Compass Operation	258
Slaved Gyro Magnetic Compass System	258
Slide Wire Rheostat Knob, Master Temperature Indicator	77
Sluggish Roll Axis	379
Sluggish Rudder	379
Smoke Elimination	188
Snow	437
Snow Removal	445
Spare Lamp Stowage Box	280
Spark	
Advance, Spark Plug Fouling	336
Advance Switches	13
Advancing	324
Retarding	324
Selection	323
Spark Plug Fouling	
BMEP	337
Carburetor Air Temperature	337
Cylinder Head Temperature	337
Exhaust Back Pressure	337
Fuel-Air Ratio	336
Ground Run-Up	336
High Power Before Landing	337
In-Flight Prevention	336
Manifold Pressure	337
Power Change Rate Effect	337
Prevention and Elimination of	336
RPM	337
Spark Advance	336

	Page
*Special Bomb Rack Panel	274
Specific Humidity Determination	477
Specific Range Curves	579
Speed Range	435
Speeds, Stalling	304
Spewing, Oil	181, 335
Spins	304
Stalls	301
*Stalling Speed Chart	303
*Stalling Speed Correction Table	304
Stalling Speeds	304
Standard Altitude Table	461
Starter Limitations, Jet Engine	128
Starting	
After Leaving Icing Conditions	441
Engines, After	434
Engines, Before	95, 434
Engines, Before—Cold Weather	448
Engines—Cold Weather	448
Jet Engines	127, 147
Jet Engines—Cold Weather Procedures	451
Jet Engines—Desert Procedures	456
Jet Engines—Hot Weather Procedures	455
Reciprocating Engines	106, 147
Reciprocating Engines—Cold Weather Procedures	448
Reciprocating Engines—Desert Procedures	455
Reciprocating Engines—Hot Weather Procedures	455
System, Jet Engine	28
System, Reciprocating Engines	13
Starts Hot, Jet Engine	128
Starts, Simultaneous Jet Engine	159
Station Time	146
Steering Switch	72
Steering System, Nose Wheel	72
Steering Wheel, Nose	72
Stopping	
Emergency	217
Engines, Cold Weather Procedures	443
Engines—Desert Procedures	456
Engines—Hot Weather Procedures	455
Jet Engines (Air)	154
Jet Engines (Ground)	130
Reciprocating Engines	130, 172
Storm, Approaching the	441
Storm, In the	442
Stowage, Miscellaneous Personal Gear	282
Stowage, Kit Bag	282
Strut Depressurization, Nose Gear	162
Supercharger Switches	4
Supercharging	312
Surface Controls	67
Surface Control Locks	67
Survival Suits	82

*Denotes Illustration

Alphabetical Index

T.O. 1B-36D(II)-1

	Page
Switches	
Action, Gunnery	263
Aft Cabin Pressure	221
Aileron Trim Tab	67
Air Plug, Jet Engine	25
Air Plug, Reciprocating Engine	11
Alternator Breaker	38
Alternator Breaker Hold-In	38
Approach Coupler	257
Approach Coupler Localizer	257
Attack Factor, Gunnery	263
Autopilot Automatic Recovery	252
Autopilot Engage	252
Autopilot On-Off	252
Autopilot Release	252
Battery	41
Bomb Bay Door	267
Bomb Bay Door Safety	267
Bomb Bay Selector	267
Bomb Bay Tank Release Selector	34 A
Bomb Release	267
Bomb Release Selector	267
Bomb Salvo	271
Bomb Station Indicator Light Test	267
Bomb Station Indicator Lights	267
Booster Pump, Fuel System	32
Brake Pump	75
Brake Pump Pressure Override	75
Cabin Air Booster Fan Control	221
Cabin Heat	219
Cabin Heater Control	229
Cabin Heater Power	229
Cabin Pressure Shutoff Valve	221
Cabin Temperature Control	219
Camera Door	277
Camera Initiation	277
Camera Master Power	277
Camera Mode Selector	276
Carburetor Air Filter	4
Carburetor Preheat	4
Check, Master Temperature Indicator	77
Circuit, Emergency Selector	63
Computer, Gunnery	263
Condition Selector, Engine Analyzer	79
Control Lock	68
Cross-Feed Valve, Fuel System	32
Cycle Selector, Engine Analyzer	79
Discharge Selector, Fire Extinguisher	80A
Emergency Flap	69
Emergency Throttle Control Override, Jet Engines	22
Engine Primer	13
Engine Valve, Fuel System	32
Exciter Control Relay	38
External Power Supply	36
Fan Control, Auxiliary Cabin Heater	229
Fan Speed	11

	Page
Flap	68
Flap Master Selector	69
Flight Instrument	77
Frequency Selector	38
Fuel Tank Valve	32
Fuselage Navigation Lights	244
Ground Refueling Safety	**34**
Gun Camera	262
Gun Charging	262
Hydraulic Fluid Temperature	66
Hydraulic Pump Override	66
Ignition	12
Ignition Start, Jet Engine	28
Intercooler Shutter	3
Jet Engine Fire Detection	82
Jet Engine Oil Heater	232
Jet Engine Pod Preheat Control	231
Kilowatt-Kilovar Selector	38
Landing Gear	69
Manifold Valve, Fuel System	32
Master Power-Bombing	267
Master Temperature Indicator	77
Master Temperature Indicator Selector	76
Mixture Control Override	3
Mixture Control Selector	3
N-2 Transfer, Autopilot	252
Navigation Light Dimming	244
Navigation Lights Selector	244
Navigator's Directional Gyro Control	77
Nose De-Ice Control	231
Nose Fuse, Bombing	267
Oil Cooler Door Mode Selector (Some Airplanes)	17
Oil Cooler Door Override (Some Airplanes)	18
Oil Dilution, Reciprocating Engine	16
Oil Shutoff Valve, Jet Engine	30
Oil Shutoff Valve, Reciprocating Engine	16
Parking Brake	75
Phase Sequence Lamp Test	36
Pickup Selector, Engine Analyzer	79
Pilots' Command Radio Selector	238
Power Switch, Engine Analyzer	80
Pressure Refueling Valve	34
Propeller Reverse Pitch	14
Propeller Reverse Selector	14
Propeller Selector	13
Reciprocating Engine Fire Extinguisher Selector	80A
Radar Camera Frequency Selector	278
Radar Camera Power	278
Regulator Warning System Switch	247
Safe-Fire (A-C and D-C Power)	262
Spark Advance	13
Starter, Reciprocating Engine	13
Starter, Jet Engine	28
Steering	72
Supercharger	4
Tail Anti-Icing	219

*Denotes Illustration

	Page
Switches (Continued)	
Taxi Lights	243
Throttle Control Selector, Jet Engine	20
Transformer-Rectifier Test Unit Selector	41
Turbo Change-Over	6
Turbo Override	6
Turbo Vernier	7
Turret Power	261
Turret Safety	261
Turret System Selector	261
Universal Bomb Arm-Safe	274
Universal Bomb Rack Heater	274
Universal Bomb Rack Selector	274
Universal Bomb Release	273
Universal Bomb Salvo Safety	274
Voltage Selector	38
Water Injection	8
Wing Anti-Icing	219
Wing Interphone Control	234
Symbols and Abbreviations	460
Synchronization Analysis, RPM	344
Synchronization Check, Magneto	344
Synchronization Lamps, Alternator	40

T

	Page
Tachometers, Jet Engine	78
Tachometers, Master	14
Tachometers, Turbo	7
Tail Anti-Icing Switches	219
Tail Anti-Icing	371
Tail Anti-Icing Air Temperature Gages	220
Tail Gunner's AN/APG-32( ) Check List	413
*Tail Gunner's Control Panel	264
Tail Gunner's Ditching Responsibilities	197
*Tail Gunner's Duties	412
*Tail Gunner's Station	265
Tail Pipe Temperature	530
Tail Pipe Temperature Indicators	78
Take-Off	
Aborting	180
After	152, 307
Before	148, 434
Before—Cold Weather Procedures	451
Cold Weather Procedures	451
Crash Landing on Take-Off	190
Correction for Runway Slope	564
Desert Procedures	456
Distance	555
Engine Failure During	180
General	150
Hot Weather Procedures	455
Instrument Flight Procedures	434
Manifold Pressure	477
Night	433
Partial Power	181
Refusal Speed and Accelerate-Stop Distance	576

	Page
Velocity	565
Take-Off and Landing Data Card	761
Tank Release Controls, Bomb Bay	34
Tank Release Selector Switch, Bomb Bay	34
Tank Valve Switches, Fuel System	32
Taxi, During	434
Taxi Lights	243
Taxiing	115, 123, 171
Taxiing—Cold Weather Procedures	451
TC Co-ordination, Autopilot	377
TC Co-ordination Knob, Autopilot	253
Tel-Lamps, Propeller	14
Temperature, Carburetor Air	317, 337
Temperature Control, Carburetor Air	3
Temperature Control, Hydraulic Fluid	270
Temperature Control Switch, Cabin	219
Temperature Conversion Chart	461
Temperature, Cylinder Head	333, 337
Temperature Indicator, Cylinder Head	77
Temperature Indicator Master	76
Taxiing, Instrument Flight	434
Temperature Limitations, Heat and Anti-Icing	292
Temperature, Tail Pipe	530
Thermometers, Outside Air	76
Throttles	
Control Levers, Jet Engine	20
Control Selector Switches, Jet Engine	20
Controls, Reciprocating Engine	2
Sensitivity	128
Throttling, Autopilot	377
Throttling Knobs, Autopilot	253
Thunderstorm Flying	441
Time Schedule	382
Time, Station	146
Toilet Facilities	282
Torquemeter	322
Torquemeter Indicators	76
Torquemeter Pressure	523
*Traffic Pattern	163
Train Release of Bombs	272
Transfer Controls, Autopilot	252
Transformer-Rectifier	
General	347
Test Unit Ammeter	63
Test Unit Panel	41
Test Unit Selector Switch	41
Test Unit Voltmeter	63
*Transformer-Rectifier Test Unit	41
Treatment of Hypoxia Victims	250
Trim of Engines vs Trim of Aircraft Control	339
Trim Tabs	304
Trouble Shooting	
Bomb Bay Door	371
Chart for Electrical System	354

*Denotes Illustration

Alphabetical Index

	Page
Electrical System	354
Engine Instrument	361
Landing Gear	368
Nose Wheel Steering	370
*Turbo Compressor Pulsation Limits	316
Turbosupercharger System	
Boost Control	181
Boost Selector	5
Change-Over Switches	6
Controls	4
General	4
Obtaining Maximum Speed	313
Operation	314
Override Switches	6
Shifting Turbos	315
Tachometers	7
Vernier Switch	7
Turbulent Air Flying	441
Turn Control Knob, Autopilot	252
*Turret and Sighting Station Locations	258
Turrets	
Power Switch	261
Safety Switch	261
Selector Switch	261
Turret Door Closed Lamp	263
Turret-Extended Lamps	263
*Typical Gunner's Control Panel	262
*Typical Oxygen Panel	246
*Typical Patterns of Ignition Malfunction	342
*Typical Time Schedule	88
*Typical Turret	263

U

	Page
Unfeathering Propellers During Flight	179
Universal Bombing System	
Arm-Safe Switches	274
Armed Indicator Lamps	274
Controls	273
Indicator Lamps	274
Rack Heater Switches	274
Rack Selector Switches	274
Release Switch	273
Manual Lock Lamps	274
Preflight Check	385
Pressure Warning Lamps	274
Salvo Safety Switch	274
Switch Positions	386
Up-Elevator Co-ordination, Autopilot	377
Up-Elevator Co-ordination Knob, Autopilot	254
Upper Aft Gunner's Duties	389, 404
Upper Aft Gunners' Seats	280
*Upper Aft Sighting Station	261

V

	Page
Vacuum Relief Valves	222
Valves	
Bombardier-Gunner Selector Valve—Defrosting System	223
Dump	222
Forward Cabin Dump	221
Heat and Anti-Ice Selector	222
Nose Strut Pressure Release	73
Pilot-Bombardier Selector—Defrosting System	223
Pressure Relief	223
Pressurization Manual Shutoff	221
Vacuum Relief	222
Variations, Alternator Load	351
Velocity in Take-Off Ground Run	565
Ventilation Equipment	228
Ventilation in Flight, Cabin	229
Ventilation on Ground, Cabin	229
Voltage Control Knob	38
Voltage Controls, Alternator	350
Voltage Selector Switch, Alternator	38
Voltmeter, Transformer-Rectifier Test Unit	63

W

	Page
Walk-Around Bottles, Precautions in Using	251
Walk-Around Bottles, Use of	251
Walkie-Talkie	240
Warm-Up	
During Engine	109, 147
During Engine—Cold Weather Procedures	450
Engine—Desert Procedures	456
Reciprocating Engine—Cold Weather Procedures	450
Warning Horn, Flap	69
Warning Horn, Landing Gear	70
Warning Lamps	
Anti-Icing Air Temperature	220
Brake System Low Pressure	75
Cabin Heating Air Temperature	220
Fire	80A, 82
Propeller Reverse	15
Water	
Injection Switches	8
Injection System	7
Pressure Gages	10
Weight	
Design Gross	1
Gross	298
Limitations	292
Operating	298
Operational Limitations Chart	298

*Denotes Illustration

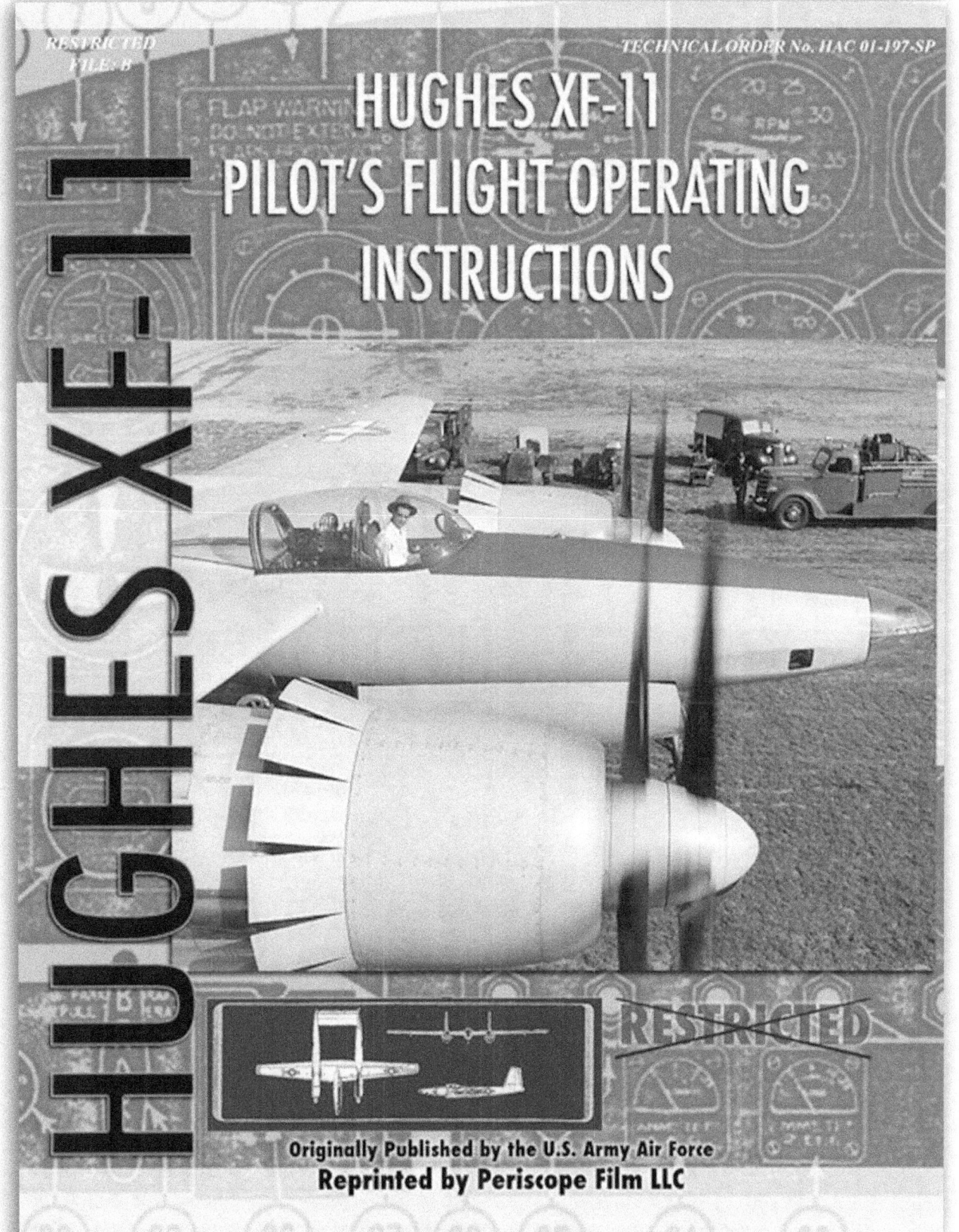

NOW AVAILABLE!

SPRUCE GOOSE
HUGHES FLYING BOAT MANUAL

RESTRICTED

Originally Published by the War Department
Reprinted by Periscope Film LLC

NOW AVAILABLE!

EPIC BATTLES OF WWII

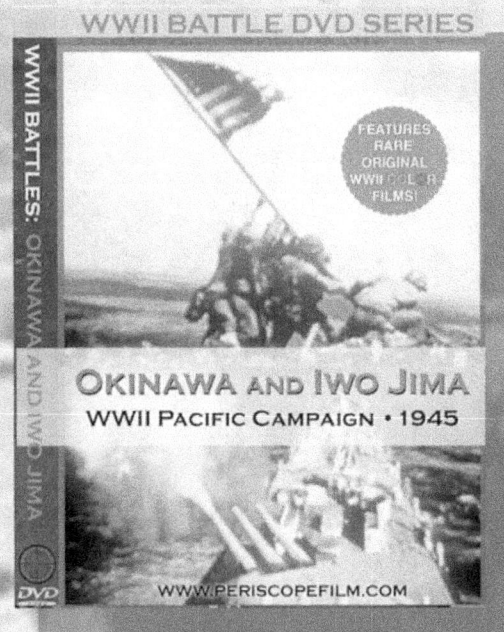

NOW AVAILABLE ON DVD!

Aircraft At War DVD Series

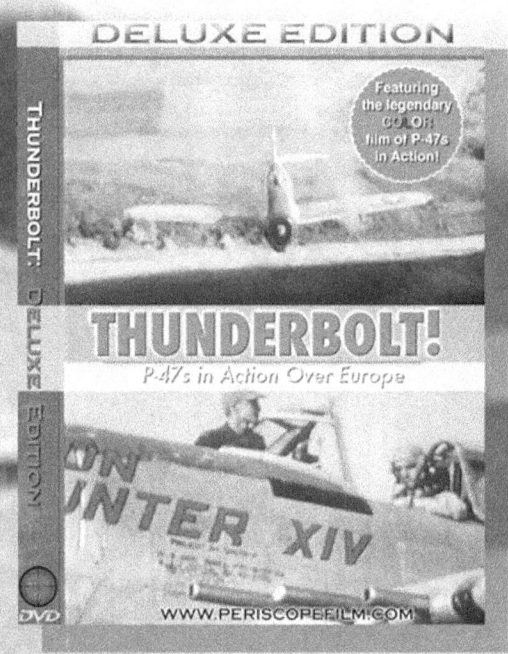
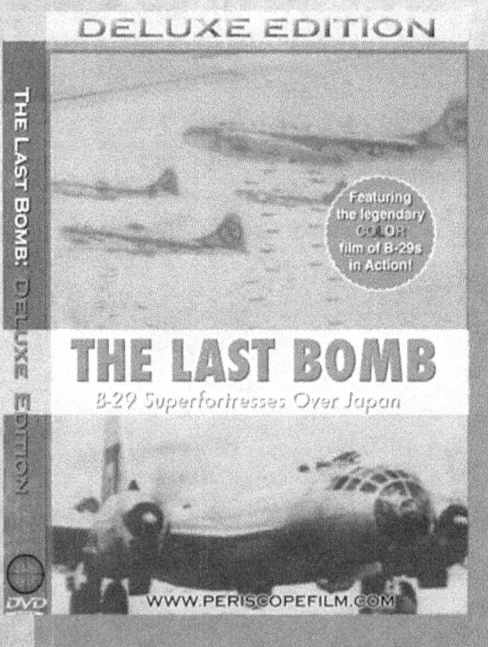
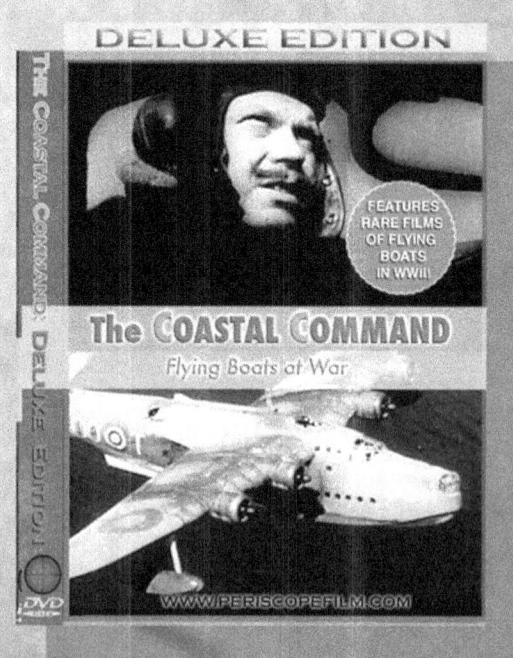

Now Available!

WARSHIPS DVD SERIES

AIRCRAFT CARRIER MISHAPS
SAFETY AND TRAINING FILMS

PeriscopeFilm.com

Now Available on DVD!

SPRUCE GOOSE

HUGHES FLYING BOAT MANUAL

~~RESTRICTED~~

Originally Published by the War Department
Reprinted by Periscope Film LLC

NOW AVAILABLE!

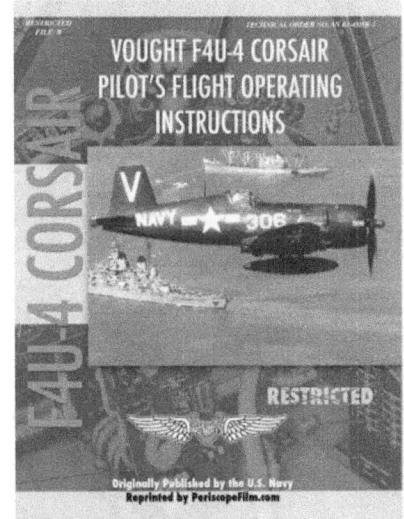
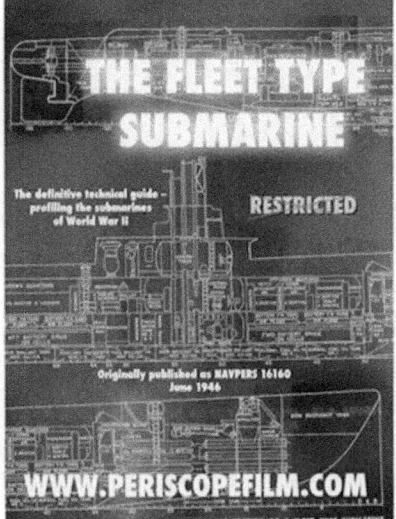

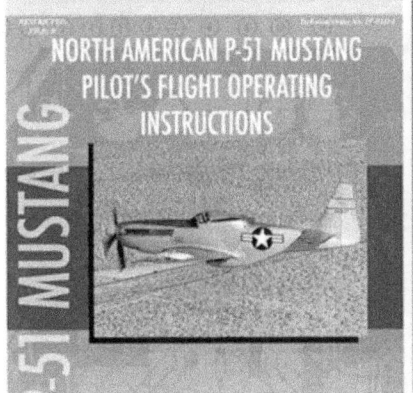

ALSO NOW AVAILABLE
FROM PERISCOPEFILM.COM

©2010 Periscope Film LLC
All Rights Reserved
ISBN #978-1-935327-87-5   1-935327-87-9

www.ingramcontent.com/pod-product-compliance
Lightning Source LLC
Chambersburg PA
CBHW081754300426
44116CB00014B/2116